http://eatdrink.timeout.com

Co

C000171767

EDITION **22**

Unbiased reviews
The reviews in this guide are based on the experiences of *Time Out* restaurant reviewers. Restaurants, bars and cafés are visited anonymously, and *Time Out* pays the bill. No payment of any kind has secured or influenced a review.

The Restaurants

Eating on a Budget

On the Town

Parties & Shops

Maps & Indexes

About the Guide

RESTAURANTS BY AREA
After restaurants have been divided by cuisine, they are then listed under the area and district of London in which they are situated.

The main area headings in the order they appear in the guide are:
Central: the area bounded by Marylebone Road in the north, the Thames in the south, Edgware Road in the west and Whitechapel in the east.
West: Bayswater to Holland Park, Shepherd's Bush, Acton and so on.

South West: South Kensington, Chelsea, Fulham and over the river to Putney and Wimbledon. **South:** Waterloo, Battersea, Clapham, Brixton, Tooting etc. **South East:** Lewisham, Greenwich, Deptford, Woolwich etc. **East:** from Shoreditch out to Epping. **North East:** Hackney, Stoke Newington and so on. **North:** Camden Town, Archway and northwards. **North West:** Hampstead, Maida Vale, West Hampstead, Kilburn, Willesden etc. **Outer London:** restaurants are listed by borough then by county.

Thus you'll find The Ivy under Central, then under Covent Garden followed by the postcode, WC2. If you don't know or can't remember what part of town a restaurant is in, just check the alphabetical index (starting on p415) to find the page number. In the main body of the guide, and in the indexes, the restaurants are listed in alphabetical order (ignoring the articles 'the', 'a' in English; 'le', 'la', 'les' in French, and so on). Thus, you'll find La Galette (in the French section) under G not L.

THE STAR SYSTEM
The star system means you can identify top performers at a glance. A red star ★ next to a restaurant means that it is, of its type, very good indeed. A green star ★ is to help identify London's more budget-conscious eateries. The cut-off point for qualifying for a green star is an average of £15 (for a three-course meal or its equivalent, not including drinks or service).

NEW ENTRIES
Last year we introduced a [NEW] symbol, to make it obvious which restaurants are new to the guide. In some cases these are brand-new establishments; in other cases we've reviewed a different branch from the last edition, or an existing restaurant for the first time.

AWARD NOMINEES
We've also highlighted the restaurants that were winners or runners-up in *Time Out*'s Eating & Drinking Awards 2004. For more info on the awards, *see p20*.

OPENING HOURS
We've given times of last orders rather than closing times (except in cafés and bars). Restaurants stay open for at least half an hour after last orders, often longer. The times given were correct when we went to press, but hours and days of opening alter frequently. It's always best to book a table by phone and, while doing so, check the opening hours and times of service in advance.

TRANSPORT
Where an underground or rail station is mentioned, it is within a ten-minute walk of the restaurant, unless otherwise implied by the listing (for example: Finsbury Park tube/rail then W7 bus). Where no tube or rail transport is convenient, we've listed the closest and most convenient bus routes. Stations on the Docklands Light Railway have been given a DLR suffix, for example: Crossharbour DLR.

South

Waterloo SE1

★ ★ Sadique [NEW]
2004 WINNER BEST NEW RESTAURANT
11 Bastard Yard, SE1 1GE (7123 4567/ www.sillyridiculous.com). Waterloo tube/rail.
Lunch served noon-3pm, **dinner served** 5.30-11.30pm Mon-Sat. **Main courses** £10.95-£19.75. **Set meal** (noon-3pm, 5.30-7pm, 10-11.30pm Mon-Sat) £15 2 courses, £19 3 courses. **Minimum** £9. **Service** 12.5%. **Cover** £1. **Credit** AmEx, DC, JCB, MC, V.
The original, and still the best, purveyor of *cuisine de la cruauté,* Sadique continues to court the headlines with its unique culinary style. Described by the restaurant's founder, Rufus Bludgeonly-Brawn, as 'not for the carrot-nibbling veggies of this world,' Sadique's menu offers such rarities as freshly squeezed squid ink or live-boiled terrapin with a 'moving spaghetti' sauce. We began with a dish of succulent hand-rammed foie gras, followed by the 'slowly, slowly catchy monkey curry' (only for parties of five or more). Staff cut a dash in their slaughterhouse chic of rubber aprons and white wellington boots, although we did find that the tiled acoustics of the dining room can make conversation near to impossible. Oh, and one last thing: don't miss the chance to send the goldfish in the transparent toilet cisterns through their 'spin cycle'. It's hilarious.
Babies and children admitted; high chairs. Booking advisable. Disabled: toilet. No-smoking tables. Tables outdoors (10, terrace). **Map 11 N8**.

PRICES
We have listed the cheapest and most expensive main courses available in each restaurant. In the case of many oriental restaurants, prices may seem lower, but remember that you often need to order more than one main course to have a full meal. We have also given the price of set meals (if applicable), and specified when they are available and how many courses are offered (for example: **Set lunch** £10 2 courses. **Set dinner** £15 2 courses, £19 3 courses).

MINIMUM CHARGE
Minimum charges are given in the listings, together (where applicable) with the hours when they are in operation. These may be during a busy period or after midnight, for example. Even if we haven't stated a minimum charge, assume that you are expected to have at least a main course. If you want less than that, ask if it's OK. In coffee bars, cafés and brasseries it usually doesn't matter how little you spend.

SERVICE CHARGE
Often the restaurateur adds a percentage to the bill as a service charge. Where this happens we have given that percentage in the listings. Otherwise, tipping is at the customer's discretion. If you are dissatisfied with the level of service provided, you don't have to pay a service charge, even if it is listed on the bill.

COVER CHARGE
This fixed charge may be imposed by the restaurateur to cover the cost of table linen, rolls and butter, crudités and similar extras. Where it is charged, we specify the amount (for example: **Cover** £1).

CREDIT CARDS
The following abbreviations are used: AmEx (American Express); DC (Diners Club); JCB (Japanese credit card); MC (MasterCard); and V (Visa).

RESTAURANT REVIEWS VIA YOUR MOBILE

Available on all UK mobile phone networks. For more information, visit **eatdrink. timeout.com**.

UNBIASED REVIEWS

The reviews in this guide are based on the experiences of *Time Out* restaurant reviewers. Restaurants, pubs, bars and cafés are visited anonymously, and *Time Out* pays the bill. No payment or PR invitation of any kind has secured or influenced a review.

ADVERTISERS

We would like to stress that advertisers have no control over editorial content. No restaurant, bar, café or shop has been included because its owner has advertised in the guide: an advertiser may receive a bad review or no review at all.

TIME OUT EATING & DRINKING WEBSITE

This guide (plus other *Time Out* guides) is also available online at http://eatdrink.timeout.com. For details, *see p18*.

SERVICES

Babies and children We've tried to reflect the degree of welcome extended to babies and children in restaurants. If you find no mention of either, take it that the restaurant is unsuitable (perhaps because it's a late-night dine and dance place) or that the management is unenthusiastic about kids. 'Babies and children admitted' implies a degree of reluctance on the part of the restaurateur to admit babies and/or children, or a lack of facilities for them, and we've duly recorded any qualifications to admission (children over 6 years admitted early evening, and so on). If kids are welcome, we've said so: 'Babies and children welcome'. We've also pinpointed the restaurants that cater for kids (children's menu, high chairs, toys, crayons etc).
Booking advisable/essential are self-explanatory. We also state if a restaurant does not accept bookings.
Disabled: toilet means the restaurant has a specially adapted toilet on the premises, which implies that disabled customers (and wheelchairs) can get into the restaurant. However, we cannot guarantee this, and no matter how good the arrangements appear, we recommend phoning in advance to check feasibility.
Dress rules Many restaurateurs dislike customers turning up shirtless and/or in shorts in summer, but few impose rules. A jacket and tie are demanded only by the more formal establishments, but restaurateurs generally prefer customers to wear 'smart' dress. Where there are rules we state them. 'Dress: smart casual' means that you can wear jeans, but they'd better be clean.
No smoking 'No-smoking tables' means that the restaurant has made some attempt to separate smokers and non-smokers; 'No smoking' means it's banned.
Facilities for parties Almost all restaurateurs will push a couple of tables together for a party. We've listed restaurants with separate rooms, floors, even banqueting suites for parties. Book in advance and check if there is a charge. *See also the new **Parties** section, starting on p331.*
Tables outdoors We've tried to be specific about how many tables are available and whether they're out on the pavement or in a back garden. If you want to sit outside, say so when you book, although many restaurants refuse to take bookings for outdoor tables and – irritatingly – allocate them on a first come, first served basis.
Takeaway service We've listed restaurants that run a regular takeaway service. If you can only take food out at certain times, we've said so; otherwise the service is available throughout the restaurant's opening hours. We also mention if there's a **Delivery service.**
Vegetarian menu Most restaurants claim to have a vegetarian dish on the menu. We've tried to highlight those that have made a concerted effort to attract and cater for vegetarian diners.
Map reference All restaurants that appear on our street maps (starting on p360) are given a reference to the map and grid square on which they can be found.

Published by

Time Out Guides Limited
Universal House
251 Tottenham Court Road
London W1T 7AB
Tel +44 (0)20 7813 3000
Fax +44 (0)20 7813 6001
email guides@timeout.com
www.timeout.com

Editorial

Editor Cath Phillips
Consultant Editor Guy Dimond
Deputy Editor Phil Harriss
Copy Editor Peter Watts
Researchers Jill Emeny, Cathy Limb
Proofreader John Pym

Editorial/Managing Director
Peter Fiennes
Series Editor Sarah Guy
Deputy Series Editor Cath Phillips
Business Manager Gareth Garner
Editorial Co-ordinator Anna Norman
Accountants Sarah Bostock, Abdus Sadique

Design

Art Director Mandy Martin
Deputy Art Director Scott Moore
Senior Designer Tracey Ridgewell
Designer Oliver Knight
Junior Designer Chrissy Mouncey
Digital Imaging Dan Conway
Ad Make-up Charlotte Blythe

Picture Desk

Picture Editor Jael Marshner
Deputy Picture Editor Tracey Kerrigan

Picture Researcher Ivy Lahon
Picture Desk Assistant/Librarian
Karin Andreasson

Advertising

Sales Director/Sponsorship
Mark Phillips
Sales Manager Alison Gray
Advertisement Sales Tammy Green, Matthew Salandy, Jason Trotman
Advertising Assistant Lucy Butler
Copy Controller Amy Nelson

Marketing

Marketing Director, Guides
Mandy Martinez
US Publicity & Marketing Associate
Rosella Albanese

Production

Guides Production Director
Mark Lamond
Production Controller Samantha Furniss

Time Out Group

Chairman Tony Elliott
Managing Director Mike Hardwick
Group Financial Director
Richard Waterlow
Group Commercial Director Lesley Gill
Group General Manager
Nichola Coulthard
Group Art Director John Oakey
Online Managing Director David Pepper
Group Production Director Steve Proctor
Group IT Director Simon Chappell
Group Circulation Director
Jim Heinemann

Sections in this guide were written by
African & Caribbean Fiona McAuslan, Nana Ocran; The Americas (North American) Christi Daugherty; (Latin American) Christi Daugherty, Claire Fogg, Cordelia Griffiths, Chris Moss; British Simon Le Quesne, Roopa Gulati; Chinese Hugh Baker, Ian Fenn, Fuchsia Dunlop, Rachel Harris, Phil Harriss; East European Ingrid Emsden, Viv Groskop, Janet Zmroczek; Fish Lily Dunn, Cath Phillips, Janice Fuscoe; French Ismay Atkins, Tom Coveney, Jonathan Cox, Simon Cropper, Kevin Ebbutt, John Ghazvinian, Sarah Guy, Elaine Hallgarten, Ruth Jarvis, Sam Le Quesne, Cath Phillips, Nick Rider, Ethel Rimmer, Caroline Taverne, Simon Tillotson, Peter Watts, Natalie Whittle; Gastropubs Simon Coppock, Kevin Ebbutt, Claire Fogg, Sarah Guy, Andrew Humphreys, Sam Le Quesne, Patrick Marmion, Lesley McCave, Cath Phillips, Peter Watts, Natalie Whittle; Global Susan Low; Greek Marc Dubin; Hotels & Haute Cuisine Helen Barnard; Indian Guy Dimond, Jim Driver, Roopa Gulati, Phil Harriss, Sejal Sukhadwala; International Ismay Atkins, Claire Fogg, Sue Webster; Italian Jenni Muir; Japanese Simon Cropper, Terry Durack, Tobias Hill, Kei Kikuchi, Susan Low; Jewish Judy Jackson; Korean Susan Low; Malaysian, Indonesian & Singaporean Jenny Linford; Mediterranean Nick Rider, Ethel Rimmer; Middle Eastern Andrew Humphreys, Jenny Linford, Ros Sales; Modern European Ismay Atkins, Jonathan Cox, Guy Dimond, Will Fulford-Jones, Janice Fuscoe, John Ghazvinian, Sarah Guy, Ruth Jarvis, Sam Le Quesne, Susan Low, Patrick Marmion, Lesley McCave, Cath Phillips, Nick Rider, Ethel Rimmer, Ros Sales, Sejal Sukhadwala, Caroline Taverne, Simon Tillotson; North African Andrew Humphreys, Ros Sales, Janet Zmroczek; Oriental Jonathan Cox, Claire Fogg, John Ghazvinian, Cordelia Griffiths, Pendle Harte, Anna Norman; Portuguese Terry Durack; Spanish Ismay Atkins, Claire Fogg, John Ghazvinian, Laura Mannering, Lesley McCave, Chris Moss, Nick Rider, Ethel Rimmer; Thai Sejal Sukhadwala; Turkish Ken Olende; Vegetarian Cathy Limb, Sejal Sukhadwala; Vietnamese Fuchsia Dunlop, Sarah Guy, Tim Luard; Budget Tom Lamont; Fish & Chips Jim Driver; Pizza & Pasta Eleanor Dryden, Will Fulford-Jones, Cordelia Griffiths, Cathy Limb, Chris Moss, Anna Norman; Brasseries Ismay Atkins, Tom Coveney, Jonathan Cox, Patrick Marmion, Anna Norman, Nick Rider, Ethel Rimmer, Caroline Taverne; Cafés Eleanor Dryden, Will Fulford-Jones, Roopa Gulati, Pendle Harte; Bars Peterjon Cresswell, Andrew Humphreys; Pubs Jim Driver; Wine Bars Phil Harriss; Eating & Entertainment Cathy Limb; Parties Amy Lee-Jones; Food Shops Jenny Linford; Courses Jenny Linford; Drink Shops Jenny Linford.

Additional reviews written by Simon Coppock, Guy Dimond, Eleanor Dryden, Kevin Ebbutt, Jill Emeny, Peter Fiennes, Claire Fogg, Will Fulford-Jones, Kevin Gould, Sarah Guy, Elaine Hallgarten, Pendle Harte, Phil Harriss, Ronnie Haydon, Tom Lamont, Sharon Lougher, Chris Moss, Anna Norman, Ken Olende, Ros Sales, Mirelle Saranz, Veronica Simpson, Sejal Sukhadwala, Peter Watts, Natalie Whittle, Yolanda Zappaterra. Thanks to Shane Armstrong, Yuko Aso, Mike Harrison, Debbie Lougher.

Subject Index Jacqueline Brind.

Cover credits Photography by Rob Greig. Fork from a selection by IITTALA at Skandium, 86 Marylebone High Street, London, W1U 4QS (020 7935 2077/www.skandium.com).
Openers credits Photography by Ed Marshall. Spoon, cocktail shaker, and salt and pepper mills from a selection at the Conran Shop (020 7589 7401/www.conran.com). Pasta ladle and corkscrew from a selection at Divertimenti (020 7935 0689/www.divertimenti.co.uk).
Photography by pages 8, 9, 10, 11, 12, 21, 44, 52, 53, 152, 198, 265, 326, 331, 335, 339, 343, 344, 345, 346, 348, 349, 350, 351, 352 Heloise Bergman; pages 13, 21, 39, 40, 41, 48, 56, 58, 75, 78, 82, 95, 96, 97, 112, 133, 136, 137, 146, 149, 157, 158, 159, 164, 177, 183, 187, 211, 217, 218, 221, 244, 251, 273, 294, 300, 308, 317, 319 Tricia de Courcy Ling; pages 18, 31, 34, 68, 69, 77, 86, 115, 118, 123, 127, 140, 141, 145, 201, 211, 224, 225, 243, 299 Alys Tomlinson; pages 21, 25, 43, 91, 92, 100, 101, 109, 188, 196, 233, 277, 310, 311 Thomas Skovsende; pages 37, 65, 105, 168, 180, 259, 260, 274, 278 Michael Franke; pages 50, 51, 129, 193, 235, 262 Maja Uphoff; pages 63, 88, 163, 205, 227, 239, 255, 263, 324 Britta Jaschinski; pages 99, 171, 202, 206, 247, 293, 304 Ming Tang-Evans; page 106 Ulrike Leyens; pages 212, 213 Rogan MacDonald; pages 307, 318, 321 Ingrid Rasmussen; page 329 Matt Carr.

Maps by JS Graphics – john@jsgraphics.co.uk. Maps 1-18 & 24 are based on material supplied by Alan Collinson and Julie Snook through Copyright Exchange.

Colour reprographics by Icon, Crowne House, 56-58 Southwark Street, London SE1 1UN.

Printed and bound by Cooper Clegg Ltd, Shannon Way, Tewkesbury, Glos GL20 8HB.
While every effort and care has been made to ensure the accuracy of the information contained in this publication, the publisher cannot accept responsibility for any errors it may contain.

Where to...

DO BRUNCH

Brunch is offered Sat and Sun, unless stated otherwise. *See also* **Cafés** and **Brasseries**.

Ashbells The Americas p35
The Avenue (Sun)
  Modern European p210
Bank Aldwych
  Modern European p207
Bluebird
  Modern European p216
Butlers Wharf Chop House
  British p48
Canyon The Americas p36
Christopher's
  The Americas p30
Cru Restaurant, Bar & Deli
  Modern European p221
The Fifth Floor (Sun)
  Modern European p209
1492 The Americas p40
Joe Allen The Americas p30
Notting Grill British p47
Niksons (Sun)
  Modern European p218
Penk's International p150
PJ's Grill (daily)
  The Americas p30
Ransome's Dock (Sun)
  Modern European p218
Rapscallion
  International p147
Sequel
  International p148
Terminus Bar & Grill
  Modern European p206
Wapping Food
  Modern European p221

HAVE SUNDAY LUNCH

See also **Gastropubs**.

The Abingdon
  International p145
The Belvedere French p83
Blue Elephant Thai p251

Bush Bar & Grill
  Modern European p216
Butlers Wharf Chop House
  British p48
The Glasshouse
  Modern European p222
Hakkasan Chinese p56
Medcalf British p42
Monsieur Max French p89
Putney Bridge
  Hotels & Haute Cuisine p115
Rosmarino Italian p167
Sonny's
  Modern European p216

EAT LATE

Balans Brasseries p294
Bar Italia Cafés p302
Brick Lane Beigel Bake
  Jewish p181
Café Bohème
  Brasseries p294
Le Caprice
  Modern European p211
Circus Modern European p212
Costa Dorada
  Eating & Entertainment p329
Erenler Turkish p264
Hard Rock Café
  The Americas p31
Istanbul Iskembecisi
  Turkish p260
The Ivy
  Modern European p207
Lahore Karahi Indian p128
Mangal II Turkish p261
Le Mercury Budget p278
Ryo Japanese p176
Sariyer Balik Turkish p263
Le Shop Budget p276
Sömine Turkish p262
Smollensky's on the Strand
  The Americas p33
Tinseltown
  Eating & Entertainment p330
Vingt-Quatre
  Eating & Entertainment p330

EAT ALONE

ASK Pizza & Pasta p284
Busaba Eathai Thai p246
Café Delancey
  Brasseries p297
Camden Arts Centre Café
  Cafés p305
Fine Burger Co Budget p279
Food for Thought
  Vegetarian p267
Gourmet Burger Kitchen
  Budget p277
Hamburger Union
  Budget p276
Ikkyu Japanese p172
Itsu Oriental p231
K-10 Japanese p169
Le Shop Budget p276
Little Bay Budget p288
Masala Zone Indian p121
Pepper Tree Thai p251
Pizza Express
  Pizza & Pasta p284
Ryo Japanese p176
Star Café Budget p279
Sweetings Fish p71
Tate Modern Café: Level 2
  Brasseries p296
Wagamama Oriental p233
World Food Café
  Vegetarian p267

TAKE A DATE

Almeida French p88
Andrew Edmunds
  Modern European p212
Aurora
  Modern European p204
L'Aventure French p89
Back to Basics Fish p71
Café des Amis Wine Bar
  Wine Bars p321
Café du Marché French p76
Le Caprice
  Modern European p213
Chez Bruce French p85
Club Gascon French p78

pure nastro

Where to... continued

Fino Spanish p237
J Sheekey Fish p73
Julie's Wine Bars p323
Kettners Pizza & Pasta p285
Lightship Ten
   International p148
Lindsay House British p45
Mango Room
   African & Caribbean p29
Momo North African p223
Moro Spanish p237
Odette's
   Modern European p221
Orrery Modern European p209
La Poule au Pot French p76
Potemkin East European p69
Quo Vadis Italian p158
The Real Greek
   Souvlaki & Bar Greek p107
The River Café Italian p160
Shumi Italian p158
Sugar Hut Thai p251
Les Trois Garçons French p86
La Trompette French p83
La Trouvaille French p82
Villandry
   Modern European p209
Zetter Italian p152

TAKE THE KIDS

See also **Cafés, Brasseries, Fish & Chips, Pizza & Pasta.**

Benihana Japanese p175
Blue Elephant Thai p251
Blue Kangaroo
   Brasseries p295
Boiled Egg & Soldiers
   Cafés p303
Bush Garden Café Cafés p303
Café Pacifico
   The Americas p39
The Depot Brasseries p295
Dexter's Grill
   The Americas p35
fish! Fish p74
Frizzante@City Farm

   Cafés p304
La Galette French p79
Giraffe Brasseries p298
Marine Ices Budget p278
Nando's Portuguese p235
Le Petit Prince French p88
Pavilion Tea House
   Cafés p306
Planet Hollywood
   The Americas p32
Rainforest Café
   Eating & Entertainment p330
Smollensky's on the Strand
   The Americas p33
Tootsies The Americas p34
The Victoria
   Gastropubs p95
Wagamama Oriental p233

SPOT A CELEB

Bar Italia Cafés p302
Bibendum
   Modern European p217
Le Caprice
   Modern European p211
Le Gavroche
   Hotels & Haute Cuisine p113
Gordon Ramsay
   Hotels & Haute Cuisine p116
Joe Allen The Americas p30
J Sheekey Fish p73
The Ivy
   Modern European p207
Locanda Locatelli
   Italian p156
Mr Chow Chinese p56
Nobu Japanese p175
The River Café Italian p160
San Lorenzo Italian p155
Shepherd's British p47
Sketch: The Lecture Room
   Hotels & Haute Cuisine p113
The Wolseley
   Modern European p210
Zilli Fish Fish p73
Zuma Japanese p173

FIND THE UNFAMILIAR

See also **Global**.

Ali Baba Middle Eastern p198
Archipelago
   International p143
Armadillo The Americas p40
Café Sol y Luna
   The Americas p41
Esarn Kheaw Thai p249
Fish Hoek Fish p73
Fook Sing Chinese p52
Lee Fook Chinese p62
MVH International p145
Nahm Thai p246
Providores & Tapa Room
   International p144
St John British p42

LOVE THE LOOK

Asia de Cuba
   International p144
Baltic East European p68
Benares Indian p118
Cinnamon Club Indian p125
Crazy Bear Oriental p229
Criterion French p81
E Pellicci Budget p280
Hakkasan Chinese p56
Inc Bar & Restaurant
   Modern European p219
Loungelover Bars p314
MVH International p145
Sketch: The Lecture Room
   Hotels & Haute Cuisine p113
Smersh Bars p314
Sumosan Japanese p175
Trailer Happiness Bars p311
Les Trois Garçons French p86
Wapping Food
   Modern European p221
Wheeler's Fish p73
Wódka East European p67
Yauatcha Chinese p57
Zuma Japanese p173

CAFÉ MET

Latte al Cioccolato

Streets ahead

We've introduced a new section to the guide this year, covering London's best food and drink shops. To celebrate, **Guy Dimond** explores two of the capital's best foodie neighbourhoods.

Illustrations by **Takako Okuma**

'What are the latest trends?' It's something that all food writers are regularly asked by both their editors and acquaintances. The temptation might be to say 'topless Korean barbecue restaurants' or other made-up nonsense. Many column inches are taken up in speculation about trends that never take off, or never really began.

Truthfully, in a city the size of London, trends are slow to develop and difficult to identify beyond the broadest macro-economic observations: that we spend more on eating out, but also more on ready meals, than ever before. That the rich eat well, and that the poor don't. That the diseases of western affluence (obesity, heart disease) now affect the poorest sectors of London society much more than they do the richest sectors.

Yet the more affluent of us spend a growing amount of our rising incomes on shop-bought food (even though the percentage is still among the lowest in Europe). Not simply because we are eating more, but because better-off people can afford to be more discerning. One look at the huge growth in sales of organic produce reveals the huge number of people willing to pay more for what they perceive as better-quality produce.

Discerning food shopping is not just about buying Kenyan organic peas from the supermarket. While supermarkets can be applauded for giving almost everyone access to high-quality, inexpensive food, they have undoubtedly created dreary shopping environments; have made business tough for small producers and retailers; and have an unhealthy grip on the production, pricing and distribution of food in the UK. Books such as *Not On The Label: What Really Goes Into The Food On Your Plate* by Felicity Lawrence, and *Shopped: The Shocking Truth About British Supermarkets* by Joanna Blythman have increased awareness of the harm done to once-diverse high streets by supermarket giants, but a war of words alone can't hope to resist the domination of the big five stores.

Which brings us back to trends. If there has been one major trend among food-lovers in the past couple of years, it's the shift from moaning about supermarkets and the loss of neighbourhood shops to actually doing something about it. More and more food-lovers are shopping at local street markets instead of lamenting their decline. Farmers' markets are springing up so fast in every neighbourhood in the capital that it's hard to keep track. Borough Food Market – the jewel in the crown among London's food markets, but, incredibly, barely a few years old – now has more visitors than Madame Tussaud's.

In addition, there has also been a rise in the number of quality food shops with a significant diversity of stock, from 'ethnic' stores to high-class delis and specialists. So many places are opening these days that a new one appears almost every week in the Food & Drink pages of *Time Out* magazine. Some of these shops appear in areas historically associated with a specific national or regional cuisine. This is usually down to immigrants settling in an area and then setting up shops to cater for their culinary needs. But in other areas the reasons for a boom in food shops are more complex. Below, we look at two London neighbourhoods that have both seen a vast transformation in their food shops, but for very different reasons.

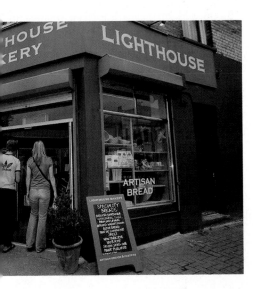

Marylebone Village

Marylebone has always been an expensive neighbourhood: it's adjacent to Mayfair and about as centrally located as you'll find. Yet the glut of fine food shops is a recent phenomenon. It started, unusually, with the pro-active involvement of a landlord, in what was almost a social and retail experiment. The Howard de Walden Estate (owned by three sisters who collectively make the *Sunday Times* rich list) owns much of this once-dowdy area, specifically Marylebone High Street and the surrounding 92 acres. Most of the area is residential, and part of the Estate's promise to its high-rent residents is to provide a high level of services. Thus a string of quality shops and eateries has been encouraged to settle along Marylebone High Street with the offer of favourable rents and even help with fitting out the sites. The Estate's website, www.marylebonevillage.com, provides a detailed directory of the area's shops and services.

'Desirable' shops were approached by Andrew Ashenden and Simon Baynham, two directors of the Estate, and invited to open a branch of their business in the Marylebone manor. One of the big turning points was when Patricia Michelson of La Fromagerie, a much-lauded cheese shop in Highbury, was invited to open a second branch in Marylebone. 'They were very helpful in meeting my needs,' she says, 'but just as importantly they listened and understood that I wanted to be sure they would keep the big chains out and encourage like-minded small independents. I opened La Fromagerie in Moxon Street in November 2002. Less than a year later, with my encouragement, Howard de Walden also allowed a Sunday farmers' market to open in a car park in Moxon Street, and the transformation of the area is incredible. Two years ago it was dead on a Sunday, but now it's buzzing.'

Newest to the area is Chantal Coady, owner of Rococo Chocolates, which has been based in the King's Road for 21 years. 'I was approached by Simon with the encouragement of Patricia Michelson. I had no plans for a second branch, but they make a very convincing case. It's good to have a landlord you can have a relationship with, who has a face. They are very hands-on, and very interested in the regeneration of the neighbourhood.'

This regeneration is something recognised and much appreciated by the people who shop there regularly, such as food writer Nigel Slater, who goes there three times a week. 'People often tell me that London is made up of "villages". I suspect those who think that have never actually lived in one. But Marylebone really does have that village feeling, with

Eat the world

London's 'ethnic' enclaves are a joy for food-lovers to explore. Here are some of the best districts for gastronomic adventures. The prime neighbourhoods for food from the Indian subcontinent – **Tooting** (*see p352*), **Southall** (*see p351*) and the **Ealing Road, Wembley** (*see p349*) – are covered under Food Shops. These are great places to pick up unusual seafood (flying fish, parrot fish) and exotic fruits such as breadfruit. *See p349* and the **African & Caribbean** section, starting on p24.

Brixton
African and Caribbean food and culture are centred around Brixton's covered markets. These are great places to pick up unusual seafood (flying fish, parrot fish) and exotic fruits such as breadfruit. *See p349* and the **African & Caribbean** section, starting on p24.

Chinatown
The block enclosed by Lisle Street, Gerrard Street, Wardour Street and Newport Court doesn't only hold an abundance of Cantonese restaurants, it's also a key district for Far Eastern food shops – selling everything from live carp to dried fungus, with major sidelines in Japanese and South-east Asian comestibles. *See p349* and the **Chinese** section, starting on p49.

Edgware Road
The stretch from Marble Arch to the Marylebone flyover is more Middle Eastern than Beirut. The dominant style is Lebanese – with various meze, pastries and sheesha up for grabs – but there are also some Iranian shops and restaurants, and almost every other Arab or Middle Eastern nationality represented. See the **Middle Eastern** section, starting on p197.

Golborne Road
Ladbroke Grove's Little Morocco; see the **North African** section, starting on p223. The road is also home to a small Portuguese enclave; see the **Portuguese** section, starting on p234.

Golders Green
A wealth of Jewish bakeries and delis, kosher and not, reside in NW11. See the **Jewish** section, starting on p181.

Green Lanes
The Harringay stretch of this long road has attracted Greek-Cypriot, Turkish and an increasing number of Kurdish food shops. Turkish enterprises are also much in evidence at the Newington Green end of Green Lanes. *See p350* and the **Turkish** section, starting on p257.

New Malden
Home to Korean cafés and restaurants aplenty, plus a couple of good but small Korean grocers. See the **Korean** section, starting on p185.

Stockwell
London's Little Lisbon. Explore the area around the South Lambeth Road and the Stockwell Road for Portuguese bars, restaurants, bakeries and delis. See the **Portuguese** section, starting on p234.

small, independent shops where they know you by name; an independent bookseller, butcher and cheesemonger; a proper market day (Sunday) and very few of the global names. Even the big supermarket there is a Waitrose: to my mind, the most acceptable of the "big five"', says Slater.

The best way to explore the area is by starting at the Bond Street tube end and walking down Marylebone Lane (more interesting than the more obvious James Street). On the right you'll pass the **Union Café**, sausage specialist **Biggles**, and **Le Cordon Bleu**, the venerable cookery school established in London in 1933. Further up, on the left, is the fabulous art deco interior of the **Golden Hind** fish and chip shop. Turning right into Marylebone High Street proper, you'll be heading north, into the heart of the 'village'. Pâtisseries, coffee shops and fine food retailers come at you thick and fast. But before you head north, take a little diversion into George Street, across the road. **No.6** is a smart delicatessen-café with a daily changing menu of wholesome dishes to eat in or take away. Don't get too distracted, though: there are plenty more delights to come.

Although part of a hugely successful French chain, Paul is a great place to stock up on breads and other baked goods, such as fruit tarts. The dark but elegant little café always seems to have a few seats spare and is a good place to meet up with friends. **Patisserie Valerie at Sagne** is much more old-school, but is decent alternative, just a few doors away and with a genuinely ancient interior. Between the two is the **Providores & Tapa Room**, a ground-floor brasserie and first-floor restaurant run by New Zealanders. Peter Gordon and Anna Hansen have created a great range of brunchy snacks and global tapas, from grilled chorizo or salted edamame to more complex dishes such as beetroot, sorrel and parmesan risotto.

Keep heading north to a solitary market stall selling flowers, and you'll find Moxon Street and **La Fromagerie**. It's worth a good exploration. There's a humidity- and temperature-controlled cheese room, accessible via a heavy sliding door, stocked with more than 100 varieties of prime-condition French cheeses (both the well-known and the very obscure). There are also great breads, tip-top charcuterie, lots of prepared dishes to take away, and myriad tempting victuals. The eating area is perpetually busy, with a shared large table that people crowd around.

Almost next door is butcher **Ginger Pig**. Carcasses hang in a corner of the premises, and meat is cut to order. Also of note is a display cabinet stocked with excellent filled pies, faggots, sausage rolls and other prepared meat products. New to Moxon Street is **Total Organics**; just opening as we went to press, this is a branch of the excellent fruit and veg stall at Borough Market.

One of the biggest attractions in the neighbourhood is **Marylebone Farmers' Market**, motivation to get out of bed on a Sunday morning since July 2003 (it's only open 10am-2pm). The market is held in the Cramer Street car park, just off Moxon Street; you'll always find great things to sample, including Chegworth Valley fruit juices, and baked goods from several of London's top bakeries.

Back on Marylebone High Street, continue north for a healthy diversity of shops – from a place that fixes steam irons to a shop selling expensive accoutrements for New Age dabblers. The newest food shop of interest is undoubtedly **Rococo**. Chantal Coady creates wittily modelled chocolates using best-quality ingredients, then packages them in highly distinctive wrapping (she designs it herself). Nearby

are new-wave vegetarian diner **Eat & Two Veg** and a fine fishmonger, **Blagden's**. A hop, skip and a jump to the north is **Orrery Epicerie** – an adjunct to Terence Conran's **Orrery** restaurant – which sells a small but desirable selection of deli victuals with customary Conran aplomb.

Should this food-lovers' haven leave you wanting to replenish your *batterie de cuisine* and hone your cooking skills, help is at hand. **Divertimenti** is arguably the best cookware and tableware shop in London; its new expanded premises on Marylebone High Street now have room for a ground-floor café and a basement demonstration kitchen. The cookery classes tend to be one-offs or short courses, but are perfect for inspiration, especially if you're not sure what to do with the vast array of top-quality foodstuffs acquired around the neighbourhood.

Marylebone Village map key

1. Orrery (7616 8000; see p209) and **Orrery Epicerie** (7616 8036); both 55 Marylebone High Street, W1M 3AE (www.orrery.co.uk).
2. Eat & Two Veg 50 Marylebone High Street, W1U 5HN (7258 8599/www.eat andtwoveg.com); see p267.
3. Blagden's 65 Paddington Street, W1U 4JA (7935 8321); see p353.
4. Divertimenti 33-34 Marylebone High Street, W1U 4PT (7935 0689/www.divertimenti. co.uk); see p355.
5. La Fromagerie 2-4 Moxon Street, W1U 4EW (7935 0341/ www.lafromagerie.co.uk); see p299 and p347.
6. Total Organics 6 Moxon Street, W1U 4ER (7935 8626).
7. Ginger Pig 8-10 Moxon Street, W1U 4EW (7935 7788); see p353.

8. Marylebone Farmers' Market Cramer Street car park, W1U 4EA (7704 9659); see p347.
9. Pâtisserie Valerie at Sagne 105 Marylebone High Street, W1U 4RS (7935 6240/ www.patisserie-valerie.co.uk); see p301.
10. The Providores & Tapa Room 109 Marylebone High Street, W1U 4RX (7935 6175/www.the providores.co.uk); see p144.

11. Paul 115 Marylebone High Street, W1U 4BS (7224 5615); see p299.
12. No.6 6 George Street, W1U 3QX (7935 1910); see p293.
13. Golden Hind 73 Marylebone Lane, W1U 2PN (7486 3644); see p281.
14. Union Café 96 Marylebone Lane, W1U 2QA (7486 4860).
15. Biggles 66 Marylebone Lane, W1U 2NU (7224 5937).

Northcote Road

The story of the renaissance of Northcote Road in Battersea is very different from that of Marylebone Village, not least because its gentrification is so recent. Clapham Junction railway station – now the country's busiest – was built in 1863, and the Victorian terraced houses around it sprang up in the 1870s and 1880s. Street traders followed, and by 1910 Northcote Road was the main street market for the area. But by the 1980s the market appeared to be in decline, with a growing number of stalls selling tat and few of the neighbouring shops worth a special journey; even Clapham Junction's once-grand department store, Arding & Hobbs, was in dire need of resuscitation. But the 1990s saw house prices soar in this part of Battersea, and gentrification of the neighbourhood has, of course, affected Northcote Road.

Now the market stalls are once again selling high-quality fresh produce – better fruit and veg than you'll find in most supermarkets, and for a fraction of the price. There is also an excellent, well-priced bakery stall (three enormous croissants for £1.60) and even one selling a dozen types of olives from wooden barrels.

The street market itself is enough to draw crowds, but the biggest changes have occurred in the area's shops (although some do predate last decade's gentrification). **Northcote Fisheries** has been selling wet fish since 1992, and now supplements North Sea and Atlantic fish with brightly coloured Caribbean parrot fish and snapper, as well as pavement boxes of breadfruit, yam and other Caribbean veg.

If starting here – the Clapham Junction end of Northcote Road – you might be struck by the huge number of wine merchants. Besides the chains (Nicolas, Oddbins, Phillips Newman) there are numerous small, high-quality wineries. The best of them is the exemplary, if terribly named, **Philglas & Swiggot**: it has a great wine selection and no clichéd 'brands' such as Blossom Hill and Jacob's Creek.

The meat in Northcote Road's sandwich comes at **Gourmet Burger Kitchen**, the best place for a quick lunch (if you're lucky you might get an outside table by the market stalls, or just inside the french windows, right by the thick of the action). It is run by New Zealanders, and service is as friendly as pie; burger quality, from fillings to buns, is beyond reproach too. For a lazier meal, there's Italian stalwart **Osteria Antica Bologna** on the other side of the road.

Next door to GBK is **Kelly's Organics**, noticeable from its impressive display of appealing foodstuffs: a far cry from the pill-popping 'health food' shops once associated with the quest for healthier produce. Prices at Kelly's may be high, but so is quality. In a small lean-to alongside Kelly's, from Thursday to Saturday, you'll find an outlet of **Cope's Seafood Company**, a great place to buy fresh hake, halibut, turbot and a raft of other seafood, from scallops to clams to live lobsters.

Think you've discovered food shopping nirvana already? Wait until you spot **Hamish Johnston** in the adjacent corner shop. This cheese specialist is one of the best in London, with impeccably kept cheeses – mostly British, Irish, French – and an appealing array of accoutrements, including several types of oatcake.

Although the best food shopping mostly takes place on the west side of Northcote Road, look across the street for an old-timer, **Salumeria Napoli**, which sells top-quality salami and other Italian produce. Also on the east side is a handsome corner building that houses one of the oldest and

best butchers in London – **A Dove & Son**. Dove's is that rare thing, a butcher where quality comes first, and where customers can get their meat trimmed just the way they want it: aged beef, tender lamb, game, and fowl. Not a shrink-wrapped plastic pack in sight.

Before being lured into **La Cuisinière**, the stylish cookware and tableware shop next to Dove's, cross back over the street for one of the highlights of Northcote Road: **Lighthouse Bakery**. Set up by master baker Elizabeth Weisberg and her partner Rachel Duffield, Lighthouse is proud to use no chemical additives or artificial enhancers in its artisan breads and pastries. The variety is imaginative too: English spelt and Gloucester rye breads (plus a few European styles) alongside novelties such as seasonal cakes and biscuits.

The busy section of both the market and the food shops appears to peter out after Lighthouse, but it's worth an extra five minutes' walk – beyond the creditable butcher **Hennessy's**, which sells organic meats – to find Italian deli **I Sapori**. Michelin-starred chef Stefano Cavallini became tired of running a hotel restaurant (at the Halkin) three years ago, and instead set up this Italian deli at the 'wrong end' of Northcote Road. He has defied expectations not just by staying in business with little passing trade, but also without dumbing down the produce he sells. His stock is resolutely top-class stuff: fresh pastas, Italian cheeses, oils, salamis, and salads – all from a chilled display cabinet – as well as a fine selection of bottled and pickled Italian goods. Some people shop there just for the ice-cream (Albagold, made in Acton).

Also at the southern end of Northcote road is another good wine merchant, the **Grape Shop**, and reliable and popular Modern European bar-restaurant **Niksons**.

As Felicity Lawrence, local resident and author of *Not On The Label*, puts it: 'I used to schlep over to Borough Market and then realised how much I was missing practically on my doorstep. We go there at least once a week. It's an incredibly social experience – you always end up meeting friends and neighbours, but we have also got to know the shopkeepers. I love the way the market has supported the local shops and enabled specialist places – like the sports shop and the bookshop where the owners are real experts and can give advice – to survive.'

Guy Dimond is the Food & Drink Editor of
***Time Out* magazine in London**

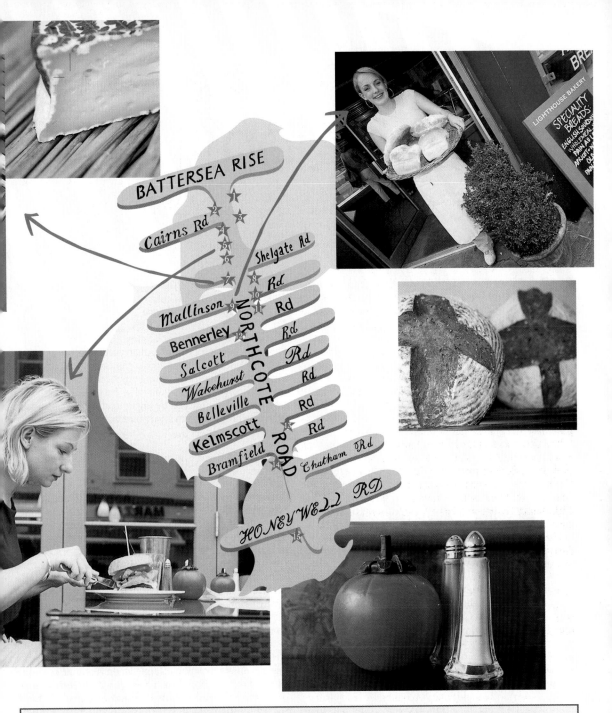

Northcote Road map key

1. Northcote Fisheries
14 Northcote Road,
SW11 1NX (7978 4428).
2. Philglas & Swiggot
21 Northcote Road,
SW11 1NG (7924 4494/
www.philglas-swiggot.co.uk);
see p357.
3. Osteria Antica Bologna
23 Northcote Road,
SW11 1NG (7978 4771/
www.osteria.co.uk); see p164.
4. Phillips Newman
28 Northcote Road,

SW11 1NZ (7924 7374).
5. Gourmet Burger Kitchen
44 Northcote Road,
SW11 1NZ (7228 3309/
www.gbkinfo.co.uk);
see p277.
6. Kelly's Organics
46 Northcote Road, SW11
1NZ (7207 3967); see p352.
7. Hamish Johnston
48 Northcote Road, SW11
1PA (7738 0741); see p347.
8. Salumeria Napoli
69 Northcote Road,

SW11 1NP (7228 2445).
9. Lighthouse Bakery
64 Northcote Road,
SW11 6QL (7228 4537/
www.lighthousebakery.co.uk);
see p347.
10. A Dove & Son
71 Northcote Road,
SW11 6PJ (7223 5191/
www.doves.co.uk); see p353.
11. La Cuisinière
81-83 Northcote Road,
SW11 6PJ (7223 4487);
branch at 91 Northcote

Road (7223 4409).
12. Hennessy Butchers
80 Northcote Road,
SW11 6QN (7228 0894).
13. The Grape Shop
135 Northcote Road,
SW11 6PX (7924 3638).
**14. I Sapori di Stefano
Cavallini** 146 Northcote
Road, SW11 6RD (7228
2017); see p351.
15. Niksons 172-174
Northcote Road, SW11 6RE
(7228 2285); see p218.

Grape expectations

You'd like to know more about wine.
But where to start? **Sejal Sukhadwala** explains the options.

Illustrations by **Takako Okuma**

We've all been here before: it's the end of a long, tough week at work. The restaurant has had rave reviews, and you were lucky to get a table. You've been looking forward to spending a relaxed evening in fine company. The dining room, bedecked with flowers and candles, looks beautiful, and there is the anticipation of exquisite food hanging in the air. Suddenly, a snooty sommelier appears out of nowhere and asks whether sir (it's always 'sir', never 'madam', who may well be paying the bill) would like to order the wine. 'A bottle of house red/white, please,' is all you can muster in response. The sommelier sneers knowingly and skulks away. Memo to self: must learn more about wine, so can order confidently in restaurants.

There is no shortage of courses and events designed to boost your knowledge, confidence and enjoyment of the pleasures of the grape. But where do you start? The first step is to distinguish between a tutored tasting, a wine event and a wine course. Sure, you will learn something on all three, but there are degrees of learning, and your choice must depend on whether you want to seriously grasp the topic, or simply enjoy a fun night out.

Tutored tastings are one-off events, usually held in the evening. Often they are led by well-known wine writers or TV personalities, and held at famous or glamorous venues, such as Lord's Cricket Ground or the Whitehall Banqueting Hall. It's usually the attractiveness of the venue or the star power of the personality that is the real draw. Such tastings are ideal if you're after a lighthearted social evening, want to meet fellow wine enthusiasts, or cannot make a regular commitment to attend a full-length course.

Wine bars and wine merchants also hold tastings – but their primary aim is to sell wine. They're perfect if you want to build up a wine collection as they give you a chance to sample the product before you buy. Many wine merchants and supermarkets have wine clubs that will deliver specially chosen wines at certain times of the year to help

you broaden your repertoire. Wine-related events include quizzes, competitions and wine dinners: multi-course meals with different wines to match each course. Their purpose is social rather than academic.

For true oenophiles, although the occasional dabble in wine tasting is fine, booking on a reputable course is the best option. Courses typically involve between five and 30 sessions, and are tutored by highly qualified, independent experts, whose main aim is to communicate their knowledge and love of wine.

Tutored tastings & wine events

Among the wine bars and wine merchants, **Corney & Barrow** (see p357) offers informal tastings to members at its west London wine shop. **Bibendum Wine** (see p358) runs tutored tastings on topics ranging from blue-chip Bordeaux to cask sample tastings (a chance to try a new vintage for the first time). **Lay & Wheeler** (see p358) has a programme of tastings in London and Essex, led by wine authorities such as Jancis Robinson. And the **Balls Brothers** chain (see p357) organises tutored and blind tastings, competitions and quizzes.

If you're interested in trying wines from a specific country, it's worth contacting embassies and language and cultural institutes. For example, tastings at the **French Institute** (7073 1375/www.institut-francais.org.uk) include special sessions on the meaning of appellation d'origine contrôlée (AOC), and on pairing French cheeses with French wines.

The **International Wine & Food Society** (see p355) is a useful source of reference books, and members with specialist wine knowledge. It organises vineyard trips for members and occasional tastings, and distributes monographs on wine-related topics. Other clubs include **Red Epicurus** (www.redepicurus.com), a gastronomic society that holds wine tastings open to everyone, and the award-winning **Wine Society** (01438 741177/www.thewine society.com), which sells specially selected wines to members and arranges tastings and other events.

In addition, wine museum **Vinopolis** (see p355) hosts numerous wine tastings and dinners throughout the year, while the **Cutting Edge Food & Wine School** (01580 881281/www.cuttingedgefoodandwineschool.co.uk), based in rural East Sussex, offers weekend wine tutorials by one of the UK's top sommeliers, Henri Chapon. And England's

From food at the bar to a Michelin Star.

largest vineyard, the wonderful **Denbies Wine Estate** near Boxhill in Surrey (01306 876616/www. denbies vineyard.co.uk) runs tours around the estate and tutored tastings of English wines. Among London restaurants, the **Bank** group (7379 5088/www.bankrestaurants. com) holds food and wine pairing evenings hosted by ex-sommelier Peter Lowe, and Harvey Nichols' the **Fifth Floor** (*see p209*) has 'flights of wine' dinners arranged by head sommelier Robert Giorgione, during which meals are accompanied by five taster glasses of themed wines (eg 'red' or 'New World').

Wine courses

OK, so your new relationship with wine is coming along nicely, but you're way past the first flush of flirtation. Now you want to get serious. You're ready to commit. You want to get to know wine better.

Attending a couple of wine tastings is a good way to check whether or not a fully-fledged wine course is right for you. However, if you simply do a series of isolated tastings, you'll end up spending a lot of money, and won't gain much insight or sense of perspective. On p355, we've rounded up some of the best-known wine courses in London. Of these, Michael Schuster's critically acclaimed **WineWise** is a good introduction if you've ever been baffled by pompous know-it-alls who describe wine as having the aroma of 'honeysuckle, leather and nectarine jam, with a smidgen of autumnal bonfires crossed with the whiff of Cuban cigars'. The course places a strong emphasis on learning to taste wines and describe them accurately.

Connoisseur, and the prestigious **Leiths School of Food & Wine**, offer sessions on pairing food with wine, whereas **Tim Atkin's Wine 'Uncorked' Series** cautiously looks at the dos and don'ts of food and wine matching. If you want to learn about fine wines, major auction houses such as **Christie's** and **Sotheby's** are a good bet, and if you want optional assessment and a certificate, try the **Wine Education Service** (WES, 8423 6338/www.wine-education-service.co.uk), which runs a wide range of courses all over London. It is not to be confused with the **Wine & Spirit Education Trust** (WSET), an educational charity that offers prestigious, internationally recognised qualifications, primarily aimed at people working in the wine hospitality or retail industry.

Obtaining a qualification isn't necessary – unless, of course, you wish to work in the industry. The top qualification is Master of Wine (MW). Before you embark on a course, it's worth checking whether your tutors are MW, or at least have a WSET or other recognised qualification. Other than obvious factors such as dates, venue, class size and cost, when picking a course you should also check what the price covers. Most courses provide tasting glasses, spittoons, water and water biscuits, booklets and handouts. But does it also include food (which may be important if you're attending a class straight after work)? Are trips to vineyards included? Are there any visiting lecturers, such as wine producers? If it's a weekend course, do you have to pay extra for accommodation?

Most beginner's courses are themed on either grape variety or major wine-producing regions; the choice you make is purely personal, depending on whether you want to learn more about, say, chardonnay or Californian wines. If you book on a course with a regional focus, make sure it covers the specific country you want to learn about; many such courses are specifically about French regional wines. It's a good idea to compare different programmes before booking. Whatever you choose, all courses aimed at novices have a relaxed, easy-going atmosphere, and are invariably fun and sociable – as you would expect from a group of people after a few glasses of wine.

However, you're still unsure whether doing a wine course is for you. You have a nagging feeling that it could be full of geeky anoraks and pretentious wine snobs. If that's what's keeping you from taking the plunge, consider this: if you've bought this guide, it's because you love good food and want to know where to find it. Well, wine courses teach you how to really taste – and to differentiate between taste and flavour, and texture and body. They enable you to use all your senses and become more aware and discriminating. They help sharpen your taste buds and develop your palate. So in learning how to taste wine, you will also learn how to taste food.

Resources

BOOKS & CD-ROMS
● **Oz Clarke's Encyclopedia of Wine** (Little Brown).
● **Oz Clarke's Wine Guide** CD-Rom (Dorling Kindersley).
● **Wine** by Hugh Johnson (Mitchell Beazley).
● **The Oxford Companion to Wine** edited by Jancis Robinson (OUP).
● **Essential Winetasting** by Michael Schuster (Mitchell Beazley).
● **Wine with Food** by Joanna Simon (Mitchell Beazley).

WEBSITES
● **www.wineontheweb. co.uk** and **www.wine-pages.com** both have up-to-date news, features, reviews and events.
● **www.brizard.co.uk** and **www.waitersfriend.co.uk** both sell gifts, gadgets and accessories for the wine enthusiast, including tasting games and Le Nez du Vin – a wine education tool that uses bottled aromas.
● **www.winesite.co.uk** is 'the voice of the wine and spirit trade', and features UK and international news and events.
● **www.decanter.com** is the official website of *Decanter* magazine.

WINE HOLIDAYS
● **Arblaster & Clarke Wine Tours** 01730 893344/www.arblaster andclarke.com.
● **Wessex Wine Tours** 01752 846880/www.winetours.com.
● **Wine Club Tours** 01730 895353.
● **Winetrails** 01306 712111/www.winetrails.co.uk.

Hello!

As the guide went to press, scores of new restaurant openings were planned. Dates are approximate, as are many other details.

SEPTEMBER 2004

Babes 'n' Burgers
275 Portobello Road, W11 (7727 4163).
Terrible name, but the burgers should be good – it's about serving fresh food fast, not, heaven forbid, fast food.

The Gun
27 Coldharbour, E14 (7515 5222).
Restored gastropub on the banks of the Thames, from the people behind the White Swan.

Island Restaurant & Bar
Lancaster Terrace, W2 (7551 6070).
Modern European cookery from an ex-Sonny's chef on a prime site by Hyde Park.

Refuel
Soho Hotel, 4 Richmond Mews, W1 (7559 3000).
The Soho Hotel is the latest Firmdale Hotel, this time in Soho. Expect high prices, but good service and atmosphere.

Sea Cow
57 Clapham High Street, SW4 (7622 1537).
Second branch of the excellent East Dulwich fish and chip place.

OCTOBER

Amaya
Halkin Arcade, 19 Motcomb Street, SW1 (7823 1166).
Another smart Indian from the Chutney Mary people. This one will be half bar, half grill. The speciality, though, will be biriani.

Homage
Waldorf Hilton, Aldwych, WC2 (7759 4080).
A European-style 'grand café', created as part of the Waldorf's refurbishment. The main room (not open to the public for several years) will seat 100, plus there will be a 60-seat bar and 40-seat pâtisserie.

The Grocer
21 Warwick Street, W1 (7437 7776).
The site that was the Sugar Club still has the same owners, but is being converted into a food store and brasserie.

Jason's
Jason's Wharf, opposite 60 Blomfield Road, W9 (7286 6752).
Reopening in early October under new management – Christian Sandefeldt, previously of Aquarium restaurant.

Paternoster Chop House
Warwick Court, Paternoster Square, EC4 (7029 9400).
Yet another Conran bar and restaurant in the City, this time serving hearty British food.

NOVEMBER

Albannach
66 Trafalgar Square, WC2.
Modern Scottish bar-restaurant.

Bluebird Club & Dining Rooms
350 King's Road, entrance in Beaufort Street, SW3 (7559 1000).
The private members' Bluebird Club is having another revamp, under Tom Conran (Terence's son). The upstairs Dining Rooms will be open to the public, serving British food.

Harlem
469 Brixton Road, SW9.
The much-delayed Brixton branch of the W11 'soul diner', with a bar, diner and private members' club.

Running Horse
50 Davies Street, W1 (7493 1275).
Tom Etridge gastropub to open after a facelift.

DECEMBER

W'Sens
12 Waterloo Place, SW1.
The Pourcel brothers, who run a Michelin three-star restaurant in Montpelier, are opening a three-floor venue serving Asian-tinged French dishes.

2005

Maze
London Marriott Hotel, 10-13 Duke Street, W1 (7493 1232).
Gordon Ramsay Holdings has lured Jason Atherton back from Verre in Dubai for this new hotel restaurant, opening 'January'.

Nobu Too
15 Berkeley Street, W1.
This new branch of Nobu is due to open in 'summer 2005'.

Pengelley's
164 Sloane Street, SW1.
Ian Pengelley, chef behind E&O, is opening his own place where Monte's used to be.

Roast
The Floral Hall, Borough Market, Stoney Street, SE1.
Iqbal Wahhab (of the Cinnamon Club) is behind this British restaurant in a glass-walled building above Borough Market.

Goodbye!

We say a tearful farewell to all the venues that have changed hands or turned in their lunch pail since the last edition.

Anda
The first miss for restaurant hit-machine Alan Yau; it waved the white flag after a year.

Bern'e
Old-school Bethnal Green greasy spoon, recently greased.

Café Arabica
Middle-Eastern hangout in W10; the same outfit still run a stall at Borough Market.

Cafeteria
Unimaginatively named diner in Ladbroke Grove, now out with the dregs.

Chintamani
High-end Turkish restaurant, gone the way of the Ottoman Empire.

Dakota
Modern American in Notting Hill, now out of the saddle.

The English Garden
Returned to the potting shed. Site now replanted with **Rasoi Vineet Bhatia** (*see p126*).

Fiction
Vegetarian in Crouch End: it has gone (and that's a fact).

Fleur
An unexpected closure for Gordon Ramsay; Fleur is pushing up the daisies.

The Gate, NW3
Belsize Park branch of Hammersmith vegetarian, swung shut for good.

Gaudí
One of London's top Spanish restaurants, now retired for the long siesta.

Jason's
A change of ownership and a revamp for this canalside restaurant, but reopening soon with a Modern European menu.

Jimmy's
Salt beef bar in Edgware, hugely popular and mourned by many. Under same ownership, it is now Greek restaurant Taverna Taverna.

Khew
Basement oriental on fashion-conscious South Molton Street – now so last year.

Lan Na Thai
Waterside Thai venue in Battersea: a brief incarnation.

Mezzo
Conran's gastrodrome was never popular with the critics; it's now being transformed into a Cuban joint, Floridita (*see p36*).

192
Popular bar-restaurant of the 1980s and '90s, didn't last through the Noughties.

Pharmacy
A living artwork by Damien Hirst, it became a bitter pill.

Polish White Eagle Club
Balham's Eagle has landed, falling prey to refurbishment.

Poons
Chinatown café that specialised in wind-dried meats: gone with the wind.

Prospect Grill
Reborn as **Hamburger Union** (*see p276*), still run by the same people.

River Walk
It occupied the troubled location at the base of the Oxo Tower, but has now gone for a long stroll.

Samphire
Modern European in Tufnell Park, washed away with the turning tide.

Soulard
Adieu to Dalston's trad French bistro.

Stepping Stone
Battersea stalwart, now French restaurant the **Food Room** (*see p83*).

The Sugar Club
The Kiwi owners that brought Pacific Rim food to London are transforming it into a delicatessen and brasserie, the Grocer (*see left*).

Table Café
No longer inhabiting Habitat.

Tartuf
The Alsatian tartes flambées were a breath of fresh air, but Tartuf has breathed its last.

During the year-long lifetime of this guide, restaurants will inevitably change name, change hands or close. We therefore recommend giving the venue a ring before you set out – especially if your visit involves a long trip.

Cooking the book

The *Time Out Eating & Drinking Guide* is compiled every year by journalists who have a passion for food, and for finding the best places to eat and drink. Many of them also have extraordinary expertise in specialist areas; a few are trained chefs, but most are just enthusiasts. For example, the principal compiler of the Chinese section is an internationally recognised authority on regional Chinese cooking (and a Mandarin speaker to boot). Two of the authors of the Indian chapter are recognised experts in north Indian and Indian vegetarian cookery (they are also, respectively, Hindi and Gujarati speakers). The editor of the Japanese chapter is a Japanese speaker with extensive knowledge of Japanese food.

The restaurants, gastropubs and cafés included in the guide are the best of their type. For the weekly *Time Out* magazine alone, our reviewers visit around 200 new places every year. The better discoveries are then included in this guide. On top of that, reviewers check other new openings, as well as all the restaurants included in the previous edition of the guide. We then eliminate the also-rans to create the list of London's best eateries that this guide represents.

Although our reviewers are often experts in their field, they are in one sense no different from other members of the public: they always visit restaurants anonymously. This is why the reviews in this guidebook are more likely to match your own experience than reviews you might read elsewhere. Recognised critics receive preferential treatment, so it is much harder to trust their judgment. They get better treatment from the staff and more attention from the kitchen, which invariably colours their impressions of a restaurant. However, when *Time Out* reviews restaurants for either the annual *Time Out Eating & Drinking Guide* or the Food & Drink pages of the magazine, we make every possible effort to do so anonymously. There is no hob-

nobbing with PRs, no freebies and no launch parties. We feel our readers have a right to know what eating at that restaurant might be like for them, as opposed to what it's like for a recognised critic or industry expert. The result is reviews that you might recognise as being consistent with your own experiences.

Last year we introduced a **NEW** symbol into the guide. As you might expect, this indicates places that are new to this edition. This doesn't always mean they're brand-new restaurants – in some cases, we've found an existing restaurant that is good enough to include, or visited a different branch from the one reviewed last time, or reintroduced a previously dropped entry – though many have opened since the 2004 edition.

Glenfiddich Trophy 2004

The Glenfiddich Awards (founded and sponsored by the whisky company) are food and drink journalism's answer to the Oscars. The 2004 Awards saw Guy Dimond, *Time Out* London magazine's Food & Drink editor, not only scoop the award for Best Restaurant Critic, but also win the top prize overall – the Glenfiddich Trophy, in recognition of his current work on the weekly magazine, but also for past work in compiling this annual restaurant guide.

In the words of one of the judges, the Trophy is awarded to 'the best of the best – the award winner who is deemed to have made an outstanding contribution to our understanding of food and drink. In Dimond's case, the judging panel recognised the depth, quality and consistent integrity of his reporting on eating and drinking in London. His reviews and commentaries are unpretentious, crisp, unfailingly fair, and written with the needs of consumers in mind. He was the unanimous choice for the Trophy.'

Previous winners of the Glenfiddich Trophy include Rick Stein, Derek Cooper, Jancis Robinson, Nigel Slater, Hugh Fearnley-Whittingstall and Elizabeth David.

eatdrink.timeout.com

In addition to our print publications, *Time Out* also has an online service dedicated to providing impartial reviews and information on more than 3,000 of the best restaurants, bars and budget eateries in London and the UK.

The website is regularly updated from this guide, plus our bestselling *Cheap Eats in London*, *London Pubs & Bars* and *Eating & Drinking in Great Britain & Ireland*, all annual publications – as well as with weekly news and reviews about all the latest openings from our weekly *Time Out* London magazine.

The site offers invaluable information compiled by *Time Out*'s stable of anonymous reviewers. It's as user-friendly as the guides, with an easy search function. All reviews are listed for those establishments that appear in more than one guide. Subscribers (who pay an annual fee) can send in their own restaurant recommendations and reviews, and there's an online booking facility. A mobile phone version is also available on all UK networks.

For more information, and to enjoy a 14-day free trial, visit **eatdrink.timeout.com**.

Eating & Drinking

AWARDS 2004

Rounding up the capital's most impressive new bars, gastropubs and restaurants, *Time Out* honoured the very best in ten categories in its 15th annual awards.

H ere at *Time Out* we're proud of our reputation for championing the best of London's eating and drinking places. Not just those with the grandest credentials, either, but the little places too, the ones you're not likely to read about anywhere else, that are, in their own field, exceptional. This is the ethos behind our broad coverage of London's gastronomic delights – from weekly reviews in *Time Out* London magazine to our numerous guides. And this is why our annual Eating & Drinking Awards take in not only London's restaurant élite, but also representatives from neighbourhood restaurants, gastropubs and bargain eateries as recommended by *Time Out* readers and selected by *Time Out* judges.

With a fresh crop of new reviews appearing each week in *Time Out* magazine (and rounded up each year in this guide), the list of potential candidates can seem dauntingly long, so when the time comes for us to assess and hand out the awards for the year's most impressive new openings, we turn to our readers for help.

HOW THE AWARDS WORK

The first stage begins in the spring of each year. In the weekly magazine, we ask you to nominate your favourite bars, pubs and restaurants in several categories. These categories, which vary each year, reflect the diverse needs and tastes of London's diners and drinkers. In 2004 they covered: the best new restaurant and the best drinking dens; the top spot to take the family; where to eat the city's best vegetarian; the pick of the local restaurants; top-of-the-range gastropubs; the slickest design; the best bargain eats; and the finest Chinese food in town.

Once the mailbags are nice and full, we embark on stage two. This involves drawing up a series of shortlists based on your recommendations and the views of our independent (and strictly anonymous) reviewers. Since our reviewers visit every establishment as normal paying punters (we never accept PR invitations or freebies of any kind), a consensus of opinion soon emerges. The results of this year's awards are listed on the right.

AND THE WINNERS ARE...

BEST BAR
Winner
Milk & Honey *See p310.*
Runners-up
Dusk *See p311.*
Loungelover *See p314.*
Salt Whisky Bar *See p307.*
Tom & Dick's *See p311.*

BEST PUB
Winner
The Sultan *See p317.*
Runners-up
The Elgin *See p317.*
Lamb *See p315.*
Salisbury Hotel *See p319.*
Wenlock Arms *See p319.*

BEST LOCAL RESTAURANT
Winner
Medcalf (British) *See p42.*
Runners-up
Balham Kitchen & Bar (Brasseries) *See p295.*
Brula (Modern European) *See p222.*
1492 (Latin American) *See p40.*
Sea Cow (Fish & Chips) *See p283.*

BEST GASTROPUB
Winner
Coach & Horses *See p90.*
Runners-up
Anchor & Hope *See p97.*
The Easton *See p90.*
The Hartley *See p97.*
The Wells *See p102.*

BEST FAMILY RESTAURANT
Winner
Frizzante@City Farm (Budget) *See p304.*
Runners-up
Blue Kangaroo (Brasseries) *See p295.*
Bush Garden Café (Cafés) *See p303.*
fish! (Fish) *See p74.*
Wagamama (Oriental) *See p233.*

BEST CHINESE RESTAURANT
Winner
Hakkasan *See p56.*
Runners-up
Lee Fook *See p62.*
Mandarin Kitchen *See p59.*
Mr Chow *See p56.*
Royal China (Docklands) *See p60.*

BEST CHEAP EATS
Winner
The Vincent Rooms (Brasseries) *See p294.*
Runners-up
African Kitchen Gallery (African & Caribbean) *See p24.*
Cocum (Indian) *See p126.*
Kimchee (Korean) *See p187.*
Story Deli (Pizza & Pasta) *See p289.*

BEST VEGETARIAN MEAL
Winner
Manna (Vegetarian) *See p270.*
Runners-up
East@West (Oriental) *See p229.*
Eat & Two Veg (Vegetarian) *See p267.*
Morgan M (French) *See p88.*
Sagar (Indian) *See p125.*

BEST DESIGN
Winner
Loungelover (Bars) *See p314.*
Runners-up
Benares (Indian) *See p118.*
Inc Bar & Restaurant (Modern European) *See p219.*
Trailer Happiness (Bars) *See p311.*
Yauatcha (Chinese) *See p57 & p302.*

BEST NEW RESTAURANT
Winner
The Wolseley (Modern European) *See p210.*
Runners-up
Fino (Spanish) *See p237.*
Le Petit Max (French) *See p85.*
Plateau (French) *See p86.*
Tom Aikens (Hotels & Haute Cuisine) *See p116.*

Hakkasan

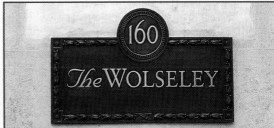

160 The WOLSELEY

Sultan

This year's judges: Jessica Cargill-Thompson, Laura Lee Davies, Jim Driver, Fuchsia Dunlop, Sarah Guy, Phil Harriss, Ronnie Hayden, Andrew Humphreys, Sam Le Quesne, Cath Phillips.

Have your cake!

Time Out's online eating and drinking guide provides easy, instant access to over 3,000 restaurant, bar and café reviews, taken from our acclaimed 'Eating & Drinking', 'Cheap Eats', 'Pubs & Bars' and 'Eating & Drinking in Great Britain & Ireland' guides.

PLUS

Constant updates with features and new reviews from *Time Out* London, as well as a restaurant-booking service and weekly critics' choice.

TIMEOUT.COM/EATING

The Restaurants

African & Caribbean

'African & Caribbean' is a useful catch-all title for restaurants in this section, although a rather misleading one: there are as many differences as similarities between the various cuisines represented here.

London's Caribbean restaurant scene has long been dominated by **Cottons** in Chalk Farm, and the nearby **Mango Room** in Camden, both at the top end of the island eating experience. However, **Freshh** – a relatively new kid on the block just down the road from Cottons – is modestly holding its own with a broad selection of Caribbean staples and international fare. Ealing is also doing pretty well with popular party venue **BB's**, which now has some local competition in the form of the Euro-Carib menu at **Tyme**.

When it comes to African restaurants, there seems to have been a surge of Ethiopian and Eritrean choices across the city. **Lalibela** and **Addis** probably lead the way, although there's quite a plethora of decent venues, including **Asmara**, **Merkato** and guide newcomers **Demera**, **Senke** and **Tobia**. For a taste of West Africa, it's still long-established **Calabash** at the edge of Covent Garden's piazza that is the biggest draw, with dishes from Senegal, Togo, Liberia and elsewhere, although bijou gems such as the **Gap** restaurant and jazz bar in Stoke Newington, and **Angie's** in Westbourne Park are doing their bit for the Nigerian kitchen.

AFRICAN

Central

Covent Garden WC2

★ Calabash

The Africa Centre, 38 King Street, WC2E 8JR (7836 1976). Covent Garden, Embankment or Leicester Square tube/Charing Cross tube/rail.
Bar **Open** 5.30-11pm Mon-Sat.
Restaurant **Lunch served** 12.30-2.30pm Mon-Fri. **Dinner served** 6-10.30pm Mon-Sat. **Main courses** £6.95-£8.10. **Service** 10%. **Credit** MC, V.
There's a sort of faded glory to this subterranean restaurant inside the Africa Centre, with its slightly shabby red carpet, miscellaneous pictures and banks of small wooden tables topped with African-printed cloths. The fact that Calabash has been holding its own for the best part of 40 years stands as testament to its popularity with tourists, local workers and visiting band members from Africa and the African diaspora. Dishes represent the Ivory Coast, Senegal, Nigeria and the Sudan, and are pretty reasonably priced, with main courses for under a tenner. Although the menu seems to have stayed the same for at least the past decade, this is still a good venue if you're after some African fare in the centre of town. Service is humble to the point of being subdued, but that's not to say that it isn't efficient. Spinach and peanut stew with rice was smooth, richly flavoured and very moreish. Saffron-seasoned couscous with lamb and vegetables wasn't bad; containing a large chump of meat, it was the slightly overcooked carrots and green beans that were disappointing. To drink, there are African beers and wines.

Babies and children welcome. Booking advisable; essential weekends. Separate rooms (in Africa Centre) for hire, seat 80 and 100. Takeaway service. **Map 18 L7**.

Euston NW1

★ African Kitchen Gallery `NEW`

2004 RUNNER-UP BEST CHEAP EATS
102 Drummond Street, NW1 2HN (7383 0918). Euston Square tube/Euston tube/rail. **Meals served** 6-11pm Mon; noon-10.30pm Tue-Sun. **Main courses** £5.50-£6.50. **Corkage** £1. **Credit** AmEx, MC, V.
The venue is tiny – just space for half a dozen tables by the glass display counter – but the flavours are big and prices low at this café-cum-art gallery. Run by a Spanish and West African duo, the Gallery offers a mix of African and Caribbean cooking, much of it reheated in microwaves, visible in the minuscule kitchen at the back. Microwaving is fine for the egusi stews (featuring ingredients such as tender steak, or fresh spinach, combined with a sauce of ground melon seeds, tangy to the point of acidity). And even the chicken savannah, crunchy with fresh ginger, and spicy with cinnamon bark, was OK. But the mixed starters had deep-fried plantain as their centrepiece, and this was leathery. A pity, as the rest of the dish (juicy meat dumplings, tuna fish cakes) was enjoyable, as were the bottles of zesty palm juice drink, the rice and peas, and the dense, moist banana flan. Service is solicitous, and the premises (full of African art for sale) diverting.
Babies and children admitted. Booking advisable. No-smoking tables. Table outdoors (1, pavement). Takeaway service. Vegetarian menu. Vegan dishes. **Map 3 J3**.

King's Cross N1

★ Addis

42 Caledonian Road, N1 9DT (7278 0679). King's Cross tube/rail/73 bus. **Meals served** noon-midnight Mon-Fri. **Main courses** £5.95-£8.50. **Credit** MC, V.
This well-designed restaurant features sunset-coloured walls, Ethiopian artefacts and an area for traditional-style eating from mesabs (handwoven dome-topped tables). It's a popular venue for clusters of East African men, who converge at lunchtime to chat, smoke or sip traditional coffee. It's also quite a good catch-all for tourists, being just a few minutes from King's Cross station. There's a lot to choose from on the menu, with almost 30 main meal options including chicken stews and minced beef dishes, but only one fish dish: samak muhamar, deep-fried snapper cooked in spiced batter, with fresh salad. It wasn't bad, although the fish can be boney. The meat offerings are sturdier, such as tibs fer fer: cubes of lean lamb fried in onions and served with enjera. Vegetarian options are more imaginative, with fuul musalah, an East African dish of crushed fave beans topped with feta cheese and falafal and sautéed in sesame oil, sounding particularly appealing.
Babies and children welcome. Book weekends. No-smoking tables. Takeaway service. **Map 4 L2**.

★ Merkato Restaurant

196 Caledonian Road, N1 0SL (7713 8952). King's Cross tube/rail. **Meals served** noon-midnight daily. **Main courses** £5-£10.
Set lunch £12 3 courses. **Set dinner** £20 4 dishes (minimum 2). **Credit** MC, V.
Merkato (which once occupied larger premises on the other side of the Caledonian Road) is a homely café and restaurant, complete with pavement seating enclosed by a neat white picket fence. With no room for the former crafts centre or a platform for musicians, this smaller, less traditionally styled – and possibly more manageable – venue is laid-back and comfortable. It's obviously popular with local Ethiopians, including, on our visit, two tables of stylish young girls who greeted the owners warmly before selecting a platter of dishes laid out on a large bed of enjera. The traditional menu is broad, with lunchtime specials such as a generous portion of rice with mixed and spiced vegetables for under a fiver. Gomen – spinach cooked in butter and mild spices – with enjera was a tasty and filling option, with the owner helpfully warning of the potency of an accompanying dish of powdered dried red pepper. Chicken, beef and fish dishes are served as wots (stews), with plenty of herbs and spices. The food isn't ideal if you're feeling weight-conscious as there's a strong bias towards ghee or butter in most meals, but if you're after sustenance, Merkato is a good choice.
Babies and children welcome; high chairs. Booking advisable Fri, Sat. Tables outdoors (4, pavement). Takeaway service. **Map 4 M1**.

West

Notting Hill W11

Mandola

139-141 Westbourne Grove, W11 2RS (7229 4734/www.mandolacafe.com). Notting Hill Gate tube/23, 27, 31 bus. **Meals served** noon-11.30pm Mon-Sat. **Lunch served** 1-4.30pm, **dinner served** 6.30-11pm Sun. **Main courses** £6.50-£10.50. **Set meal** £17 2 courses, £20 3 courses. **Service** 10%. **Credit** MC, V.
A Westbourne Grove fave, this café and restaurant is the place for sumptuous Sudanese cuisine and friendly service. No alcohol is served, but there's a BYO policy (and off-licence next door). The menu offers a gorgeous selection of traditionally spiced and flavoured dishes that can all be comfortably mixed and matched. Salads include mish, a strained and spiced yoghurt, which partners well with main meals such as salmak magli – spicy, fried fillets of tilapia with rice and mixed vegetables. Salads, usually served with warm pitta bread, are generally a good option. Try salata daqua (onions and cabbage in a peanut sauce) or salata Aswad (aubergine salad cooked in lime juice, spiced oil and peanuts). The vegetarian selection includes adas, an excellent lentil stew with caramelised garlic. For afters, mango ice-cream contains fresh chunks of fruit, and Sudanese spiced coffee comes sizzling with clove and cinnamon flavours. Things get pretty lively in the evenings, particularly at weekends, when it's a good idea to book a table in the well-designed restaurant area. The space is decorated with various crafts and artefacts – some of which are for sale.
Babies and children admitted. Booking advisable weekends. Separate room for hire, seats 25. Takeaway service. **Map 7 A6**.

Shepherd's Bush W12

Demera `NEW`

129 Askew Road, W12 9AU (8762 0234). Goldhawk Road tube. **Meals served** noon-11.30pm daily. **Main courses** £6-£12. **No credit cards.**
This two-room restaurant is a cosy haven for Ethiopian-style dining in Shepherd's Bush. At the front of the restaurant is a bar furnished with an assortment of leather or fur-lined stools, divans and mesabs (traditional hourglass-shaped wicker tables with domed covers), while the back room holds small linen-topped tables. Staff are exceptionally friendly, with smiles all round for any newcomers to East African cuisine. They're also swift with advice and explanations of the menu, which covers a wide range of lamb, beef, chicken and vegetarian fare, plus fried or stewed fish and prawn dishes. We enjoyed fish dulet, a lovely concoction of chopped cod with chilli and herbs, and chicken doro wot, a hot peppered stew with hard-boiled egg. Ye-tsom beya'aynetu – a platter of eight vegetarian dishes including

The Restaurants

chickpeas in herbs and spices, spinach and cottage cheese, creamed sweetcorn, spiced mushrooms – was excellent. Served on a huge platter of enjera, the meal was a finger-lickin' delight.
Babies and children admitted. Booking advisable. Takeaway service. **Map 20 A2.**

Westbourne Park W9

Angie's

381 Harrow Road, W9 3NA (8962 8761/ www.angies-restaurant.co.uk). Westbourne Park tube. **Meals served** noon-11pm Mon-Sat; 1-10pm Sun. **Main courses** £12-£25. **Service** 10%. **Credit** MC, V.
Family-run Angie's is a smart affair, with banks of tables covered in pristine white tablecloths, and red velvet-cushioned chairs with gold-painted legs. Service comes from burgundy-waistcoated and white-shirted staff. Weekday lunchtimes feature a half-price offer on rice dishes, which means a bumper portion of jollof rice with spicy, tomato-cooked fried tilapia for £6. Other cut-price options include 'mama-put-meal' (white rice with vegetable stew), fried rice meal with green peas and crab sticks or a tailored choice with beef, chicken, assorted meat or fish. Other Nigerian staples include soups such as efo-riro (spinach and herbs) or egusi (melon seed mixed with spinach, bitter leaf and dried fish). More elaborate dishes also feature as Angie's is big on group bookings, parties and weddings. Choose from grilled whole fish, whole guinea fowl or the super lobster special (£50) – a grand crustacean prepared with olive oil, potato and spicy mixed vegetables – which needs a day's notice and deposit. At quieter times, much of the atmosphere is provided by soft medleys of African gospel.
Babies and children welcome. Booking advisable. Disabled: toilet. No-smoking tables. Takeaway service; delivery service. **Map 1 A4.**

South

Brixton SW9

★ Asmara

386 Coldharbour Lane, SW9 8LF (7737 4144/ www.asmararestaurant.co.uk). Brixton tube/rail. **Dinner served** 5.30pm-midnight daily. **Main courses** £4-£7.50. **Set meals** £25 (vegetarian) 6 courses, £27 (non-vegetarian) 7 courses. **Credit** MC, V.
Asmara offers warm Eritrean hospitality, often from traditionally dressed staff who do a good job of making you feel at home. Starters are split between vegetable-based options such as lentils, and spicy vegetable soups or Italian dishes. Meat dishes include stews such as derho kulwa (fried chicken cubes in spicy stew), minchit-abish (hot or mild minced beef stew) and kulwa (steak tartar with spiced butter). Vegetarian and vegan options feature green lentils; finely ground chickpeas with olive oil; and spinach with ricotta. A popular choice is the mixed array of vegetarian dishes, which provides a little bit of everything; a nice addition to this is ketcha fitfit – own-made bread marinated with butter and yoghurt. Main courses can also be eaten with rice in hot tomato sauce, couscous or kinche – cracked wheat flavoured with butter and yoghurt. Don't miss the coffee ceremony, which will undoubtedly take place at some point. A waitress entices each table with a tray of freshly roasted Ethiopian coffee beans, before serving a fresh brew from an earthenware jebena jug, with a bowl of fresh popcorn.
Babies and children welcome; high chairs. Booking advisable. Separate room for hire, seats 40. Takeaway service. Vegan dishes. **Map 22 E2.**

North

Finsbury Park N4

★ Senke [NEW]

1B-1C Rock Street, N4 2DN (7359 7687). Finsbury Park tube/rail. **Meals served** noon-midnight daily. **Main courses** £5-£7.50. **Credit** MC, V.

The entrance hall to this pleasant Ethiopian bar/restaurant has a community noticeboard with writing in the distinctive Amharic script, and most of its clientele are Ethiopian. Despite some language difficulties with the waitress, it was a friendly and welcoming spot. You can sit at tables covered in deep red cloths, or in another room with traditional Ethiopian furniture. Meals are served on a bed of enjera on a tray (rather than the traditional basket). All dishes are emptied on to this and more enjera is supplied to eat with. The food is very filling, and so it's probably best to avoid dishes that have further enjera flakes mixed in with them. We ordered awaze tibs (spicy lamb fried in hot sauce) and doro alicha wot (chicken with a boiled egg, with garlic and ginger), with a vegetable selection (ye-tsom beya'aynetu) to drink, try tej honey wine, and finish with cardamom spiced tea.
Babies and children admitted. Booking advisable weekends. Takeaway service.

African Kitchen Gallery

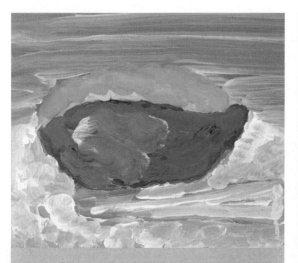

MANGO ROOM

Traditional & Modern

Caribbean Cuisine

10 -12 KENTISH TOWN RD

CAMDEN TOWN

LONDON NW1 8NH

TEL: 020 7482 5065

FAX: 020 7482 2429

EMAIL: info@mangoroom.co.uk

www.mangoroom.co.uk

Kentish Town NW5

★ ★ Lalibela
137 Fortress Road, NW5 2HR (7284 0600).
Tufnell Park tube/Kentish Town tube/rail/
134 bus. **Dinner served** 6pm-midnight daily.
Main courses £6.95-£8.50. **Credit** AmEx, DC,
JCB, MC, V.
Lalibela's lush decor manages to entice a variety
of diners for well-spiced platters of Ethiopian food.
There are two eating areas: one on the ground floor,
which extends into the art gallery, so diners sit
surrounded by paintings, prints, photographs and
what looks like a wooden altar. Upstairs is another
space, also packed with East African crafts and
artworks, where we sat at a window seat, almost
at eye level with the buses passing along Fortress
Road. The menu offers around 40 dishes – meat,
seafood (prawns and cod) and vegetarian – mostly
cooked in combinations of tomato and peppers.
Enjera, the traditional bitter pancake-style bread,
is available, but we went for the lighter option of
plain rice and herb- and butter-seasoned mashed
potato. Tofu wot – marinated beancurd cooked in
tomato, herbs and garlic – was very good, and
surprisingly filling. Shiro alicha (mushroom wot)
was claimed to be blended with peas, shallots and
mild spices; although tasty, it was pretty much just
mushrooms and a well-seasoned sauce. Boiled and
seasoned cabbage and carrots were a nice addition,
as was a yoghurt and cucumber salad.
Babies and children welcome; high chairs. Booking
advisable. Takeaway service. Vegetarian menu.
Vegan dishes. **Map 26 B3.**

★ ★ Queen of Sheba NEW
12 Fortress Road, NW5 2EU (7284 3947).
Kentish Town tube/rail. **Meals served** 1-11.30pm
Mon-Sat; 1-10.30pm Sun. **Main courses** £5-
£10.50. **Set lunch** £7.50 2 dishes. **Credit** MC, V.
What was once the Eritrean Red Sea restaurant is
now the Ethiopian Queen of Sheba. It's a modestly
sized venue with brown-hued decor that includes
banks of heavy wooden tables, sculpted bamboo
window shades and Coptic lettering etched on the
glass. Ethiopia is known for having the spiciest
dishes in Africa, and the Queen of Sheba doesn't
disappoint. Beef, lamb and chicken feature heavily,
but no fish. There's also a decent selection of pulse-
heavy vegetarian options, from roasted chickpeas
to spicy red lentils in hot pepper sauce. For
starters, we tried a Sheba salad of lettuce,
tomatoes and onions, and excellent engouday tibs:
sautéed mushrooms with wild spice and softly
fried onions. Mains are deceptively filling. Gomen
(beautifully warm spinach sautéed with onion,
garlic and jalapeños) and awaze tibs (diced lamb
cooked in tomato and chilli) were presented in
earthenware bowls, almost like an African version
of tapas. This is a good place for easy dining, with
traditional music merging into mainstream jazz,
although it's the consistently potent aromas of
incense and roasted Ethiopian coffee beans that
provides a serene sense of being elsewhere.
Babies and children welcome; high chairs.
Tables outdoors (2, patio). Takeaway service.
Map 26 B4.

North West

West Hampstead NW3

★ Tobia NEW
First Floor, Ethiopian Community Centre, 2A
Lithos Road, NW3 6EF (7431 4213). Finchley
Road tube. **Meals served** noon-midnight Tue-
Sun. **Main courses** £4.85-£9.50. **Credit** AmEx,
DC, MC, V.
Located inside the decade-old Ethiopian
Community Centre, Tobia (the ancient name for
Ethiopia) is plain but spacious. Unlike most
Ethiopian restaurants, which offer Italian-
influenced, tomato-based Eritrean dishes, the
menu is exclusively Ethiopian. We started with
own-made tej: amber-coloured wine fermented
with gesho hops, honey and ginger – an acquired
taste. Tender leg of lamb marinated in clarified
butter and baked in banana leaves (a rare, ancient
dish traditionally slow-cooked over charcoals)

came with cracked wheat and assorted chilli and
spice-based condiments. Vegetarians fare well (the
Coptic Christian diet is vegan for nearly two-thirds
of the year) with spicy wots made from lentils, split
peas, spinach and roasted crushed chickpeas,
served with enjera – and only vegetarian dishes are
served on Wednesday and Friday. The traditional
coffee ceremony, central to Ethiopian culture and
steeped in superstition and social and religious
significance, comes complete with burning
frankincense and dense, spiced bread. Tobia is not
for the uninitiated as it makes no concessions to
western tastes. However, if you're already a fan of
Ethiopian cuisine, there's much to enjoy in chef-
proprietor Sophie Sirak-Kebede's honest, homely
cooking and warm hospitality.
Babies and children welcome. Booking advisable
weekends. No-smoking tables. Takeaway service.
Vegetarian menu (Wed, Fri). Vegan dishes.
Map 28 A3.

CARIBBEAN

West

Bayswater W2

★ Mr Jerk
19 Westbourne Grove, W2 4UA (7221 4678).
Bayswater or Queensway tube. **Meals served**
11am-10.45pm Mon-Sat; noon-10pm Sun.
Main courses £5-£7.50. **Service** 10%.
Credit AmEx, DC, MC, V.
The Westbourne Grove branch of Mr Jerk is more
communal than its slightly older Wardour Street
sibling. Wooden tables are neatly set with bottles
of hot pepper sauce, ketchup, mayo and wine lists,
and there's a sense of laid-back ease in the neat
elongated space with mint green walls and
features that include Afro-centric paintings, a
much-admired rastaman wall sculpture and an
MTV-tuned plasma screen. It's a welcoming spot,
with upbeat service and a full menu for brunch,
lunch and dinner. Appetisers, meat, chicken,
seafood or vegetable dishes all benefit from jerked,
steamed or curried treatment, with halal meat used
(with certificates to prove it). Prices are reasonable
and portions large. Mains include curried mutton,
peppered steak, steamed snapper and jerk chicken,
all served with salad and seasoned rice or rice and
peas. Rotis are a good bet, with an excellent prawn
option bumped up with large diced potatoes in a
rich curry sauce. There's a takeway service too,
and the fresh juices go down a storm in summer.
Babies and children welcome; high chairs.
No-smoking tables. Takeaway service. **Map 7 B6.**
For branch see index.

Ealing W13

BB's
3 Chignell Place, off Uxbridge Road, W13 0TJ
(8840 8322/www.bbscrabback.co.uk). Ealing
Broadway tube/rail/West Ealing rail. **Lunch**
served 11.30am-2.30pm Mon-Fri. **Dinner**
served 6.30-11.30pm Mon-Fri; 6.30pm-12.30am
Sat. **Main courses** £9.50-£12.95. **Service** 12.5%
for parties of 6 or more. **Credit** MC, V.
There's something quite endearing about naming
particular dishes after your offspring, which is just
what Grenadian chef and owner of BB's, Brian
Benjamin, has done. 'Twins Benjamin' is a lovely
combination of red mullet and sea bream on a bed
of sweet potato, okra and mixed peppers. Also
good is 'scampi Ashley' with mushrooms cooked in
saffron with white wine, and 'king prawns Seretse'
in butter with lobster sauce. Dishes (mainly fish)
are accompanied by plain rice or rice and peas,
served in scooped-out coconut shells – a nice touch.
Also recommended are parrot fish calypso with
lime and pepper sauce, and BB's Crabback (the full
name for this decade-old restaurant) – a gorgeous
concoction of crabmeat baked with cream, white
wine and cheese. Located at the end of a
nondescript alleyway, BBs is a quirky spot, and
tends to be very popular with wedding and

birthday parties (so it's wise to book at weekends).
Celebrants often leave their compliments to the chef
by way of scrawled messages on the graffiti-
covered walls.
Babies and children welcome; high chairs. Booking
essential Thur-Sat. Disabled: toilet. No-smoking
tables. Tables outdoors (4, pavement). Vegan dishes.

Tyme NEW
133 Uxbridge Road, W13 9AU (8840 7222/
www.tyme.co.uk). Ealing Broadway tube/rail/
West Ealing rail. **Lunch served** noon-3pm
Thur, Fri. **Dinner served** 6-11pm Tue-Thur;
6pm-midnight Fri, Sat; 6-10pm Sun. **Main**
courses £13.75. **Set lunch** £10 2 courses.
Set dinner £20 3 courses. **Service** 10%.
Credit AmEx, DC, MC, V.
First-time restaurateurs Trevor and Lynn
Campbell opened Tyme in summer 2003 – and
they're doing well. Heritage cooking is the order of
the day, with a menu that skilfully reflects the
kitchens of Jamaica, Grenada and Europe.
Enticing combinations come in the way of starters
such as duck and fig terrine with toasted guava
cornbread; warm feta with aubergine and chickpea
salad; and marinated prawn skewers with mango
salsa. The mains have more of a Caribbean slant
such as fillet of red snapper with spinach, lentils
and sweet potato sauce. Other island-influenced
options are curried coconut prawns with sweet
potato, and curried goat or jerk chicken breast with
plantain; chicken breast fillets drizzled with chilli
chocolate sauce give a congenial nod to Mexico.
Tyme calls itself a 'piano restaurant bar', which is
appropriate enough as the modestly sized grand
piano by the bar is often occupied by jazz, soul or
classical musicians on weekend nights.
Babies and children welcome; high chairs. Booking
advisable; essential Fri, Sat. Entertainment: jazz
8pm Fri-Sun. No smoking.

South

Brixton SW2, SW9

★ Bamboula
12 Acre Lane, SW2 5SG (7737 6633). Brixton
tube/rail. **Meals served** 11am-11pm Mon-Fri;
noon-11pm Sat; 3-11pm Sun. **Main courses** £6.90-
£8.50. **Service** (after 5pm) 10%. **Credit** MC, V.
Though the celebrated Sunday buffet is no more,
Bamboula still does a brisk trade. Even midweek,
the tables were packed at this bijou little place.
Sunshine-yellow walls, rampant greenery, wicker
chairs and a bamboo bar all aim at recreating a
beach hut atmosphere (complete with a smattering
of ants escaping the plant pots), but execution is
restrained enough to avoid being tacky. Snacks
include jerk chicken sandwiches made from
hardough bread, patties and plantain. The main
menu features standard Caribbean favourites
served in generous portions. Oxtail in a rich sauce
with butterbeans was tender, with the meat falling
off the bone, while the ackee and saltfish was
among the best we've had. Side orders were equally
accomplished: vegetables in coconut sauce were
surprisingly piquant and the festival was filling,
though the rice and peas could have done with a
touch more thyme. Home-made drinks such as
Guinness punch and a syrupy sorrel are worth
sampling. Deserts include rum and raisin ice-
cream and tropical fruit crumble, though you'll
need hollow legs to do them justice.
Babies and children admitted. Booking advisable
Fri, Sat. Takeaway service. **Map 22 D2.**

Brixtonian Havana Club
11 Beehive Place, SW9 7QR (7924 9262/
www.brixtonian.co.uk). Brixton tube/rail. **Open**
5.30pm-midnight Mon-Wed, Sun; 5.30pm-2am
Thur-Sat. **Dinner served** 7-11pm daily. **Main**
courses £15. **Set meal** (Sun) £35 buffet incl
unlimited champagne. **Credit** MC, V.
Meals at this colourful barn of a restaurant tend
to be served only 'towards the weekend', according
to the owner, so bookings are a must. In fact, the
Brixtonian is far more geared to rum and cocktail
drinkers – over 300 different rums are said to be on
offer, although we decided not to count them – with
free club nights of South African and Caribbean

Menu

African

Aloco: fried plantain with a hot tomato sauce.

Ayeb or **iab**: cottage cheese and yoghurt.

Berbere: an Ethiopian seasoning of paprika, chilli, cinnamon and other spices.

Cassava, **manioc** or **yuca**: a family of coarse roots that are boiled and pounded to make bread and various other farinaceous dishes. There are bitter and sweet varieties (note that the bitter variety is poisonous until cooked).

Egusi: ground melon seeds, added to stews and soups as a thickening agent.

Enjera, **enjerra** or **injera**: a spongy, flannel-like bread from Ethiopia and Eritrea, which doubles as an eating implement and is served with meat, vegetable or fish dishes.

Froi: fish and shrimp in an aubergine stew.

Fufu: a stiff pudding of maize or cassava (qv) flour, or pounded yam (qv).

Gari: a solid, heavy pudding made from ground fermented cassava (qv), served with thick soups.

Ground rice: a kind of stiff rice pudding served to accompany soup.

Jollof rice: a kind of hot, spicy risotto, with tomatoes, onions and (usually) chicken.

Kelewele or **do-do**: fried plantain.

Kenkey: a starchy pudding that's prepared by pounding dried maize and water into a paste, then steaming inside plantain leaves. Usually eaten with meat, fish or vegetable stews.

Moi-moi or **moin-moin**: steamed beancake, served with meat or fish.

Ogbono: a large seed similar to egusi (qv). Although it doesn't thicken as much, it is used in much the same way.

Pepper soup: a light, peppery soup made with either fish or meat.

Shito: a dark red-hot pepper paste from Ghana, made from dried shrimps blended with onions and tomatoes.

Suya: a spicy Nigerian meat kebab.

Tuo or **tuwo**: a stiff rice pudding, sometimes served as rice balls to accompany soup.

Ugali: a Swahili word for bread made from cornmeal and water.

Ugba: Nigerian soy beans; also called oil beans.

Waakye: a dish of rice and black-eyed beans mixed with meat or chicken in gravy.

Waatse: rice and black-eyed beans cooked together.

Wot: a thick, dark sauce made from slowly cooked onions, garlic, butter and spices – an essential component in the aromatic stews of East Africa. **Doro wot**, a stew containing chicken and hard-boiled eggs, is a particularly common dish.

Caribbean

Ackee: a red-skinned fruit with yellow flesh that looks and tastes like scrambled eggs when cooked;

traditionally served in a Jamaican dish of salt cod, onion and peppers.

Bammy: pancake-shaped, deep-fried cassava bread, commonly served with fried fish.

Breadfruit: introduced from West Africa in 1792 by Captain Bligh, this football-sized fruit has sweet, creamy flesh that's a cross between sweet potato and chestnut. Eaten as a vegetable.

Bush tea: a herbal tea attributed with anti-toxin or medicinal properties. It can be made from anything from cerese (a Jamaican vine plant) to mint or fennel.

Callaloo: the spinach-like leaves of either taro or malanga, often used as a base for a thick soup flavoured with pork or crabmeat.

Channa: chickpeas.

Coo-coo: a polenta-like cake of cornmeal and okra.

Cow foot: a stew made from the foot of the cow, which is boiled with vegetables. The cartilage gives the stew a gummy or gelatinous texture.

Curried (or **curry**) **goat**: more usually lamb in London; the meat is marinated and slow-cooked until tender.

Dasheen: a root vegetable with a texture similar to yam (qv).

Escoveitched (or **escovitch**) **fish**: fish fried or grilled and then pickled in a tangy sauce with onions, sweet peppers and vinegar.

Festival: deep-fried, slightly sweet dumpling often served with fried fish.

Foo-foo: a Barbadian dish of pounded plantains, seasoned, rolled into balls, and served hot.

Jerk: chicken or pork marinated in chilli and hot spices, then slowly roasted or barbecued.

Peas or **beans**: black-eyed beans, black beans, green peas and red kidney beans (the names are pretty much interchangeable).

Pepperpot: traditionally a stew of meat and cassereep, a juice obtained from cassava; in London it's more likely to be a meat or vegetable stew with cassava.

Phoulorie: a Trinidadian snack of fried doughballs often eaten with a sweet tamarind sauce.

Plantain or **plantin**: a savoury variety of banana that is cooked and used in much the same way as potato.

Rice and peas: rice cooked with kidney or gungo beans, pepper seasoning and coconut milk.

Roti: the Indian flatbread, usually filled with curried fish, meat or vegetables.

Saltfish: salt cod, classically combined with ackee or callaloo (qv).

Sorrel: not the European herb but a type of hibiscus with a sour-sweet flavour. Used to flavour a traditional Christmas drink.

Soursop: a dark green, slightly spiny fruit; the pulp, blended with milk and sugar, is a refreshing drink.

Sweet potato: most varieties of this tuberous root have a sweetish taste, although some are drier than others.

Yam: a large tuber, with a yellow or white flesh and slightly nutty flavour.

sounds, such as the fortnightly Sharp. However, the traditional Caribbean cuisine is excellent (and worth the rather erratic service), with the menu changing each month to focus on a different Caribbean island. Cuba was represented on our visit, with starters featuring vegetable and mango soup and rabbit terrine, while satisfyingly filling mains included vegetable casserole in coconut sauce and cornmeal with spicy crab. Both came with rice and black peas and a bumper portion of chunky, perfectly fried plantain. Music can be a tad loud, but you can always burn off your meal on the heaving dancefloor.
Booking essential. Dress: smart. Entertainment: jazz 9pm Wed; DJs 9.30pm Thur-Sat; opera recital monthly (call for details). **Map 22 E1**.

★ Jacaranda Garden

11-13 Brixton Station Road, SW9 8PA (7274 8383). Brixton tube/rail. **Meals served** noon-5pm Mon; noon-6pm Tue-Fri; noon-7pm Sat. **Main courses** £4.50-£6.95. **No credit cards**. Though not exclusively a Caribbean café-cum-restaurant, Jacaranda does a mean escovitch fish with jollof rice, and jerk chicken with rice and peas, as well as Caribbean seafood gumbo. Other delights include salads, pasta and warm focaccio with fillings that include melted cheese. It's a one-woman, one-waitress show, and is hugely popular with SW9 locals, who chat loudly in the ground-floor café as dishes materialise from the kitchen. Many a gathering also takes place in the sunny upstairs restaurant that looks out over the railway section of Brixton market. Jacaranda has long won over this particular corner of south-west London, and is also well loved for its gorgeous slabs of carrot or chocolate cake, coffees, hot chocolate and overall sense of ease.
Babies and children welcome. No-smoking tables. Separate room for hire, seats 40. Tables outdoors (5, pavement). Takeaway service. **Map 22 E1**.

Streatham SW16

Trini's

13 High Parade, Streatham High Road, SW16 1EX (8696 9669). Streatham Hill rail/57, 118, 133, 159 bus. **Meals served** noon-10.30pm Tue-Sat; 2-10.30pm Sun. **Main courses** £7-£10. **No credit cards**.
A large restaurant on a pedestrianised section of Streatham High Road, Trini's seems to do its best business towards and on the weekend. The food is good and prices are reasonably low, but there's a tendency for things to be 'off the menu', which can make eating here a bit touch and go. Shrimp curry with plain rice and plantain was very good, and came with a generous dollop of crisp, freshly made coleslaw. Saltfish with rice and peas also went down well, as did some home-made sorrel juice; the owner generously topped up our glasses from the end of a freshly made batch. Macaroni pie, phoulorie with tamarind dipping sauce and roti pancakes with fish, meat or pumpkin filings are good bets too. If you like entertainment with your meal, jazz sessions and steel pans on Sundays were being promoted on our visit.
Babies and children welcome; high chairs. Book weekends. Entertainment: jazz 2-6pm Sun. No smoking. Restaurant available for hire. Takeaway service.

South East
Herne Hill SE24

Brockwells

77-79 Norwood Road, SE24 9AA (8671 6868). Herne Hill rail/3, 68, 196 bus. **Open** 5pm-midnight Mon; 5pm-2am Tue, Thur; 5pm-1am Wed; 5pm-3am Fri, Sat; 1pm-2am Sun. **Dinner served** 5-10pm Mon-Sat. **Meals served** 2-10pm Sun. **Main courses** £8.50-£10.95. **Set buffet** (Sun) £4.95-£9.95. **Service** 10%. **Credit** JCB, MC, V.
At one time, this bar/restaurant on the edge of Brockwell Park worked best as a drinking venue with the occasional club night (classic soul, reggae), but the restaurant side of things has definitely picked up. On weekday and Saturday

evenings you can enjoy Caribbean cuisine with a few global concessions. Oxtail soup, ackee and saltfish with seasoned rice, jerk chicken, curried goat, battered prawns in sweet chilli sauce, chicken nuggets or drumsticks with fries – all are on the menu. We rolled up on a Sunday afternoon for the all-you-can-eat buffet. Dishes were brought in from the kitchen rather than laid out on a table, with apologies for the limited vegetarian options. Still, multiple orders of brown stew fish, mixed cabbage, carrot and okra, rice and peas, fries and fried plantain were not to be sniffed at. Service was excellent; the genuinely friendly and attentive staff made a concerted effort to ensure all customers, including some excitable children, were well catered for. Decor – soft black leather sofas, bleached wood, chrome fittings – looks a tad dated. *Babies and children welcome until 9.30pm; children's portions. Booking advisable. Dress: smart casual; no caps or trainers. Entertainment: DJs 9pm Tue, Fri-Sun; DJs/open mic 7pm Wed, Thur.* **Map 23 A5**.

East

Shoreditch E2

★ Anda de Bridge

42-44 Kingsland Road, E2 8DA (7739 3863/ www.andadebridge.com). Old Street tube/rail/ 26, 48, 55, 67, 149, 242, 243 bus. *Bar* **Open** 4pm-midnight Mon-Wed, Sat; 11am-midnight Thur, Fri; 4-11.30pm Sun. *Restaurant* **Lunch served** 11am-3pm, **dinner served** 6-11.30pm daily. **Main courses** £5-£10. *Both* **Credit** AmEx, DC, MC, V.
Anda de Bridge wins points for its unpretentious decor (exposed brickwork, low-level hessian seating and lovely stone bar), cracking tunes (reggae, ska and dub, with decent DJs at the weekend) and easy-going atmosphere. With less traffic than some of its Shoreditch neighbours, this bar-cum-restaurant is a highly likeable spot for impromptu eats. A simple Caribbean menu covers all the usual bases with jerk meat and fish, ackee and saltfish, and brown stew chicken. Starters offer a dash of Spanish (manchego cheese served with quince) as well as more traditional dishes such as succulent fried plantain. All portions are generous, with the fresh fish particularly good. Tender red snapper in delicately seasoned coconut salsa was excellent. Jerk chicken was less successful, however – merely char-grilled chicken pieces with a pot of barbecue sauce on the side. There was similar variance in the side dishes, with top-notch rice and peas winning hands down over a flabby, boiled (rather than fried) bammy. Much was redeemed by friendly staff and a fine choice of drinks; among the highlights are Carib lager and a wealth of dark and silky rums, including some rare Jamaican imports.
Babies and children admitted. Disabled: toilet. Entertainment: DJs 8pm Thur-Sat. Separate room for hire, seats 60. Takeaway service. **Map 6 R3**.

North

Camden Town & Chalk Farm NW1

★ Cottons

55 Chalk Farm Road, NW1 8AN (7485 8388/ www.cottons-restaurant.co.uk). Chalk Farm tube. **Dinner served** 5pm-midnight Mon-Thur; 5pm-1am Fri. **Meals served** noon-1am Sat; noon-midnight Sun. **Main courses** £9.95-£14.50. **Set meal** £17.50 2 courses, £21 3 courses. **Service** 12.5%. **Credit** MC, V.
Cottons was heaving on a Saturday night. Squeezing past the resident DJ and the scrum of drinkers in the bar, we took a seat in the largest of the three dining areas, where staff supplied us with some great Mojitos. The ever-evolving menu now includes weekend two-course lunch specials and members-only dining on Wednesday nights. Impressive starters include smoked marlin with braised leeks and passion fruit dressing, and an 'Island meze' of creole prawns, aubergines, saltfish fritters and roti. Fish, meat and vegetable main

courses are all substantial, from jerk blue swimmer crab with dumplings to whole sea bass with samphire, or marinated duck, and chump of lamb. Carnivorous options include mixed jerk meat grill – pork ribs, chicken pieces, lamb and sausage, served with rice and peas. Metagee is a popular vegetarian dish, a gratin of sweet potatoes, yam, green banana, okra and pumpkin all ladled with a creamy coconut sauce; a generous plateful of grilled, garlicky bread slices and plantain was a fine addition. You might struggle for room, but if you're able, the crème brûlée or flaming rum cake are fine way to conclude your meal.
Babies and children welcome. Book weekends. No-smoking tables. Separate rooms for hire, seating 20 and 35. Tables outdoors (2, pavement). **Map 27 B1**.

Freshh Caribbean Restaurant & Bar NEW

48 Chalk Farm Road, NW1 8AJ (7916 8935/ www.freshh.co.uk). Chalk Farm tube. **Meals served** noon-10.30pm daily. **Main courses** £10.50-£15. **Credit** MC, V.
Deceptively small from the outside, Freshh opens into a multi-level venue with a subterranean lounge room, a pastel-green bar on the ground floor, and an upper restaurant with stairs leading to an open roof terrace. Business can be a tad slow, with quiet lunchtimes and uncrowded evenings, but this is a restaurant that takes its food seriously. A well-thought out menu includes Caribbean staples such as jerk chicken, escovitch fish and curried goat, plus fresh tortilla wraps, filled ciabatta rolls and Thai fish cakes. To drink there are freshly made juices (carrot, pineapple) and Guinness punch. A lively sweet potato korma was an excellent vegetarian choice, with a spicy sauce blended to smooth perfection. Also good was the mixed fish stir-fry: juicy portions of fresh prawns, crab claws, tender kingfish and snapper in a ginger and lemon sauce. Families will be happy with the 'Kids Time' menu, offering mini pizzas, fish fingers, baked beans, ice-cream and soft drinks. Worth a visit.
Babies and children welcome; children's menu; high chairs. Booking advisable. Entertainment: DJ 8pm Fri, Sat. No-smoking tables. Separate rooms for hire, seating 14 and 45. Tables outdoors (9, roof garden). Takeaway service. **Map 27 B1**.

★ Mango Room

10 Kentish Town Road, NW1 8NH (7482 5065/ www.mangoroom.co.uk). Camden Town tube. **Lunch served** noon-3pm Tue-Sat. **Dinner served** 6pm-midnight Mon-Sat. **Meals served** noon-11pm Sun. **Main courses** £9.50-£12.50. **Service** 10%; 12.5% for parties of 5 or more. **Credit** MC, V.
Split into two rooms with raw brickwork, comfortably worn wooden floors, and large, abstract Keith Haringesque pictures, Mango Room subtly fuses the Caribbean with international influences. Options have stayed pretty much the same over the past few years, with dishes such as ackee and avocado or curried goat sitting nicely with lamb steak, or mussels in coconut sauce. A good choice was tender kingfish with mango sauce, rice and peas, and fried plantain. Salmon fillet with rice was also fine, although the fish was slightly dry until our benevolent waiter fetched some coconut and peanut sauce from the kitchen. The specials on our visit were all fish dishes, among them grilled snapper, whole sea bass and king prawns with basmati rice. We finished with an exquisite warm sticky toffee pudding, and beautifully sculpted fresh mango. Apart from our affable waiter, service from the rest of the staff went from nervous to po-faced.
Babies and children welcome; high chairs. Booking advisable weekends. No smoking tables. Separate room for hire, seats 30. Takeaway service. **Map 27 D2**.

Stroud Green N4

Hannah's

96 Stroud Green Road, N4 3EN (7263 4004). Finsbury Park tube/rail. **Meals served** 11am-11.30pm Mon-Sat; 1-11pm Sun. **Main courses** £6.40-£10.95. **No credit cards**.

One of two affiliated Caribbean restaurants located on Stroud Green Road (the other is Hummingbird – *see below*), Hannah's wins points for its suitably unhurried and pleasantly laid-back atmosphere as well as its extensive Indo-Caribbean menu that reflects its Trinidadian ownership. The menu is ample. For starters, our appetite was whetted by phoulorie drizzled with a sour-sweet mango sauce. Crab and callaloo soup was tasty, but slightly marred by splinters of crab shell. Vegetarians are well catered for, with the likes of vegetable or potato and chickpea curry, and aloo pie. Caribbean favourites such as curried goat, chicken, duck or beef, and jerk chicken, are also well executed, but the real winner is the seafood – there's even lobster on offer. Our tender white fish in spicy sauce was a successful marriage of tomato, scotch bonnet pepper and butter: tasty but mild enough not to overwhelm. Rice and gungo peas were perfectly done, as was the plantain. Leave room for puddings – it would be a crime to miss the rich rum cake steeped in rum and served with warm Tia Maria sauce.
Babies and children welcome; high chairs. Booking advisable. No-smoking tables. Takeaway service.

Hummingbird

84 Stroud Green Road, N4 3EN (7263 9690). Finsbury Park tube/rail. **Meals served** noon-midnight Mon-Sat; 1-11pm Sun. **Main courses** £6.50-£19.95. **Credit** MC, V.
A Trinidadian favourite on Stroud Green Road (and affiliated with the nearby Hannah's – *see above*), Hummingbird does well with north London locals who drop by for takeaway patties or generously sized meat, fish or vegetable rotis from the front counter. Dining inside the cream-coloured venue brings an impressively long menu. Typical starters are spiced shrimp with peppers, lime and ginger; sweet potato cheese bake; and a range of soups (crab and callaloo, creamy spinach and pepper). Cou cou fish stew or red fish fillets in a rich tomato stew with cornmeal, coconut and okra polenta are tasty choices, and well-spiced stewed or curried dishes of chicken, goat, lamb or vegetables come with liberal portions of plantain, yam, rice and peas or seasoned salad – much of the food can be fairly filling. Extravagance comes in the form of whole lobster cooked in white wine sauce, or huge king prawns coated in honey and served with white rum and lime pepper sauce. Tempting desserts include chocolate rum cake and coconut turnover.
Babies and children welcome; high chairs. Book weekends. Tables outdoors (2, pavement). Takeaway service. Vegetarian menu.

North West

Kilburn NW6

★ Planet Caribbean

11 Malvern Road, NW6 5PS (7372 4980). Kilburn Park tube/Queen's Park tube/rail. **Meals served** 8.30am-midnight Mon-Fri; 10am-midnight Sat; noon-midnight Sun. **Main courses** £5-£7.50. **No credit cards**.
While you're unlikely to cross town to dine at Planet Caribbean, it's a good drop-in option if you're in the area, offering a reasonable range of standard Caribbean meals. Essentially a takeaway, the interior is a little prosaic, with a scattering of chairs and tables with well-worn plastic covers. However, what it lacks in atmosphere it makes up in hospitality. Staff are friendly as well as accommodating: although many of the menu choices were unavailable, they were happy to knock up what we wanted while we waited. For starters, saltfish fritters were light, fluffy and very tasty, though the dry doughy dumpling was disappointing. Mains included a goat roti served with a mixed salad – ample, but a little overcooked – and a succulent ackee and saltfish. Or choose jerk chicken, peppered steak and red bean stew. There weren't any desserts, although fruit cake is sometimes available. A useful pit stop.
Babies and children welcome; high chairs. No-smoking tables. Tables outdoors (2, pavement). Takeaway service; delivery service.

The Americas

NORTH AMERICAN

If there is a theme among London's US-themed restaurants, it's burgers and ribs; virtually all the restaurants listed in this section offer one or both. While this is as reflective of modern American cooking as steak and kidney pie is of modern British cuisine, it's also thoroughly understandable: good burgers are worth hunting down, and quality ribs are just as rare in this town. For the best burgers, head to Westbourne Grove for **Lucky 7** and newcomer **Harlem**, or to Oxford Street for the excellent **Eagle Bar Diner** (the recent crop of gourmet fast-food burger bars are covered in the **Budget** section). For the best ribs, visit **Bodean's** in Soho or Spitalfields Market's funky **Arkansas Café**. **Christopher's** and **Canyon** offer the best modern American cuisine, while for outstanding modern Southern cooking there's **Ashbells**, which we consider one of London's best, and most unusual, restaurants in any category.

Central

City E1

★ Arkansas Café

Unit 12, Old Spitalfields Market, E1 6AA (7377 6999). Liverpool Street tube/rail. **Lunch served** noon-2.30pm Mon-Fri; noon-4pm Sun. **Dinner served** by arrangement. **Main courses** £5-£14.50. **Service** 10% for parties of 5 or more. **Credit** MC, V.

This wonderfully eccentric restaurant hovering on the edge of Spitalfields Market is justifiably popular. Its Arkansan owner, Bubba, presides over the barbecue pit, greeting customers with a wave of his spatula while he cooks huge piles of tender beef brisket, pork ribs, perfect duck and juicy chicken. Customers sit on a mishmash of church pews and garden chairs. Highlights include smoky roast beef marinated in a tangy-sweet sauce, and excellent side dishes of fresh baked beans, coleslaw, purple cabbage and cold new potatoes in a tart vinegar dressing – all at thoroughly reasonable prices. Service is efficient and polite, although you may have to wait if you arrive at peak times on a Sunday. A new feature is that you have to pay when you order – presumably an indication that some customers have done a runner into the market crowd. More fool them, as they probably missed out on the tooth-achingly sweet desserts of pecan pie and banana cake.
Babies and children admitted. Booking advisable; bookings not accepted Sun. No-smoking tables. Separate room for parties, seats 50. Tables outdoors (Sun only, 30, terrace inside market). Takeaway service. **Map 12 R5.**

Covent Garden WC2

Belushi's

9 Russell Street, WC2B 5HZ (7240 3411/ www.belushis.com). Covent Garden tube. **Meals served** 11am-midnight Mon-Sat; noon-10.30pm Sun. **Main courses** £4.95-£8.95. **Credit** MC, V.

There appears to have been a coup at this Chicago-themed hamburger joint, as it has gone all Aussie in the past year. Australian surfing posters now cover pictures of the Red Hot Chili Peppers, an Oz flag hangs in front of the kitchen door, and the US slackers who used to hangout here have been replaced by Antipodean windsurfers on their gap year. The same is true of the menu, where oniony Chicago burgers now jostle for space next to the 'Aussie Works' version. Not that we're prejudiced or anything, but standards seem to have slipped a little too. Our onion rings weren't fully cooked, with gooey raw mush around the slices. Butterfly king prawns resembled the frozen kind; if these were fresh, Cleveland is near Melbourne. Even the Chicago burger was not as flavourful as we remember it. On the plus side, the Elwood chicken sandwich – chicken breast with avocado on ciabatta (named after the non-Belushi Blues Brother) – was much better than the burger. But service, which has always been a bit grumpy, was full-on surly. Hey, if they don't want your business, people, take it elsewhere.
Babies and children admitted. No smoking (restaurant). Separate room for parties, seats 50. Tables outdoors (2, pavement). **Map 18 L6L.**
For branches see index.

★ Christopher's

18 Wellington Street, WC2E 7DD (7240 4222/ www.christophersgrill.com). Covent Garden tube. Bar **Open/food served** noon-11pm Mon-Sat. *Restaurant* **Brunch served** 11.30am-3pm Sat, Sun. **Lunch served** noon-3pm Mon-Fri. **Dinner served** 5-11pm Mon-Sat. **Main courses** £12-£28. **Set meal** (5-7pm, 9.30-11pm Mon-Sat) £12.75 2 courses, £16.75 3 courses. *Both* **Service** 12.5%. **Credit** AmEx, DC, MC, V.

Christopher's remains one of London's best restaurants for modern American cuisine. The decor of the first-floor restaurant is cool and contemporary, with cream and chocolate tones, and the ground-floor bar is excellent for cocktails, either before or after dinner. Over the years the once-stilted service has loosened up and is now downright cheerful. The menu changes seasonally. A starter of Chesapeake Bay crab salad in chilled tomato and herb bisque made a perfect summer dish, with smoky flavours and lots of fresh crab. Maryland crab cake was similarly packed with meat, light and ungreasy. For mains, spicy blackened salmon came atop fresh spring greens – very rich, very tasty – though the monterey mash didn't work for us as we kept trying to avoid the thick cheese topping. Blackened ribeye arrived cooked just as requested and, at 10oz, was a generous size. A side order of green vegetables was very green indeed, with broccoli, mangetout and peas all but glowing in the dish; all perfectly crisp, but a touch bland. The lemon tart with mascarpone ice-cream was so fabulous we'd make a return visit just for this.
Babies and children welcome; children's menu; high chairs. Booking advisable (especially lunch). Dress: smart casual. Separate room for parties, seats 40. **Map 18 L7.**

Joe Allen

13 Exeter Street, WC2E 7DT (7836 0651). Covent Garden tube. **Brunch served** 11.30am-4pm Sat, Sun. **Meals served** noon-12.45am Mon-Fri; 11.30am-12.45am Sat; 11.30am-11.15pm Sun. **Main courses** £8.50-£15. **Set brunch** £17.50 2 courses, £19.50 3 courses incl drink. **Set meal** (noon-3pm Mon-Fri, 5-6.45pm Mon-Sat) £14 2 courses, £16 3 courses incl coffee. **Credit** AmEx, MC, V.

It's all very theatrical in this brick basement restaurant – or, at least, theatrical circa the 1970s and 1980s, if the posters on the walls are anything to go by. The menu is stuck in a time-warp too, with dishes such as chopped chicken livers. But all is forgiven by the regulars, most of whom are West End theatre cast and crew, because this is their traditional hangout. There was a time, actors maintain, when the food that was served here was great; some of it still is, but best stick to the basics and avoid the more ambitious mains. A starter of crab salad with avocado dressing was a bit bland, though tasty enough and with lots of meat. The lunch-only salt beef sandwich on rye with sauerkraut and thin fries was very good indeed, juicy and well flavoured, but for £9 it should have been. Indeed, as on past visits, we found Joe Allen an expensive place for what it offers (£15 for an unspectacular fillet steak with fries, for example), the service uninterested and the whole experience something of a chore.
Booking advisable. Entertainment: pianist 9pm-1am Mon-Sat; jazz trio 8-11pm Sun. No-smoking tables. **Map 18 L7.**

PJ's Grill

30 Wellington Street, WC2E 7BD (7240 7529/www.pjsgrill.net). Covent Garden tube. **Brunch served** noon-4pm daily. **Meals served** noon-1am Mon-Sat; noon-4pm Sun. **Main courses** £8.95-£13.95. **Set meal** (5-7.30pm Mon-Sat) £9.95 2 courses. **Service** 12.5%. **Credit** AmEx, DC, JCB, MC, V.

There's a theatrical ambience to this long, narrow West End restaurant. The walls are plastered with old film posters and the tables are surrounded by little brass plaques with the names of regulars, many of whom have acted or crewed at the numerous nearby theatres. There's a big pre- and post-theatre rush. The menu focuses on French-American bistro classics, with daily specials providing variety; don't expect much in the way of surprises. Cold asparagus with parmesan made a plentiful and light starter, while crispy duck in pancake was an effective creation, the meat moist and rich. A special of venison with dauphinoise parsnips was tender (no mean feat with game) and the sauce excellent, while ribeye steak with seared foie gras was a nicely cooked, high-quality cut of meat, though mangetout was an unimaginative accompaniment. Chips were copious and crisp. Puddings are similarly traditional (lemon tart, chocolate cake, pavlova) but well done – and sometimes doing something simple well is more admirable than trying something unusual and doing it badly.
Babies and children welcome; children's menu; high chairs. Booking advisable. Entertainment: jazz pianist 10.30pm-1am Wed-Sat. Tables outdoors (5, pavement). **Map 18 L6.**
For branch see index.

TGI Friday's

6 Bedford Street, WC2E 9HZ (7379 0585/ www.tgifridays.co.uk). Covent Garden tube/ Charing Cross tube/rail. Bar **Open** noon-11pm Mon-Fri; 11am-11pm Sat; noon-10.30pm Sun. *Restaurant* **Meals served** noon-11.30pm Mon-Fri; 11am-11.30pm Sat; noon-11pm Sun. **Main courses** £4.75-£16.75. *Both* **Credit** AmEx, MC, V.

We could go on and on about this place: the waiters are adults and should be allowed to dress accordingly; the music is jarring; and so is the damned bell that is rung whenever the bartender gets a tip. But whatever we say, you'll either love TGIF or hate it. Food prices are on the high side, but portions are generous and the kids are kept happy. For a starter, we chose from the Jack Daniels menu (cross-marketing, anyone?). The Three for All (potato skins, chicken wings and fried cheese with three dips) was big, filling and tasty. A main course of baby back ribs was huge too, the ribs hanging over the edge of the plate, accompanied by masses of onion rings. A baked potato stuffed with sour cream, cheese, chives and bacon was perfect, and a house salad was fine and fresh; the two together served as a satisfying and fairly priced main. Desserts – large ice-cream confections – are a speciality, but we were too full to try them and, to be honest, too eager to leave.
Babies and children welcome; children's menu (dinner); high chairs; toys. Disabled: toilet. No-smoking tables. Takeaway service. **Map 18 L7.**
For branches see index.

Leicester Square W1

Planet Hollywood

Trocadero, 13 Coventry Street, W1D 7DH (7287 1000/www.planethollywood.com). Piccadilly Circus tube. **Meals served** 11.30am-1am Mon-Sat; 11.30-12.30am Sun. **Main courses** £9.95-£19.95. **Service** 12.5%. **Credit** AmEx, DC, MC, V.
What a long way this place has come. And we don't mean that in a good way. Whereas once upon a time you'd almost expect to wait ages for a table, now you're straight in and seated before you know it. Best to come with a family – at least that way you might get a booth, rather than a cheap-looking wooden table. Service was similarly shaky. The long menu features the requisite burgers, pastas, steaks and salads. Hell, there's even a 'Marco Pierre White Specialities' section (he's a shareholder). Nachos comprised ten flat discs with a generous amount of melted cheese and chicken. A huge burger tasted like production-line fare, while rôtisserie chicken came with a sickly sauce (our fault for picking forestière, aka mushroom, from the choice of seven). Fries, though, were hot and fresh. Desserts, previously a forte, seemed to have gone downhill; chocolate chip brownies with ice-cream and sauce were nothing special. As if proof were needed that standards have fallen mightily, one of the loos in the ladies had no seat.
Babies and children welcome; children's menu; high chairs; nappy-changing facilities. Booking advisable (not Sat). Disabled: toilet. No-smoking tables. Separate room for parties, seats 80. **Map 17 K7**.

Marylebone W1

Black & Blue

90-92 Wigmore Street, W1V 3RD (7486 1912/ www.blackandblue.biz). Bond Street tube. **Meals served** noon-11pm Mon-Thur, Sun; noon-11.30pm Fri, Sat. **Main courses** £8-£25. **Service** 12.5%. **Credit** MV, V.
The newest outlet in this worthwhile and ever-expanding steakhouse chain looks much like others. Big torches burn out front, while, inside, neutral colours lead the way. Seating is in sleek leather booths and at a long central table. Music is kept to an acceptable level. Staff are remarkably friendly, particularly given how demanding some of the customers were on our visit. Best of all, the food is of a reliably high quality. Artichoke and spinach dip (a starter) arrived hot, cheesy and marvellously unhealthy, with plenty of tortilla chips for dipping. Steaks are the raison d'être here, so that's what we tried. Mains of ribeye and sirloin steak were both perfectly cooked to order: tender inside, smoky and crisp on the outside. Each came with a decent mixed green salad that wasn't a mere afterthought, and fine, if unspectacular, chips. The house red is fair value at £4 a glass. If you can persevere after such a hearty meal, the lemon tart with butterscotch sauce and ice-cream makes a refreshing coda.
Babies and children admitted. Bookings not accepted. No-smoking tables. Tables outdoors (2, pavement). **Map 9 G6**.
For branches see index.

Mayfair W1

Hard Rock Café

150 Old Park Lane, W1K 1QZ (7629 0382/ www.hardrock.com). Hyde Park Corner tube. **Meals served** 11.30am-midnight Mon-Thur, Sun; 11.30am-1am Fri, Sat. **Main courses** £7.25-£13.95. **Minimum** main course when busy. **Service** 12.5% on bills over £30. **Credit** AmEx, MC, V.
We've never figured out why so many people visit Hard Rock Café restaurants around the world. The London branch may be the most popular on the globe, as queues seem to form the minute it opens and fade away only after closing time. Inside, the (not that hard) rock blasts too loudly (we say again), the pretty waitresses are impatient but polite, and it's all impersonally friendly. The Hard Rock nachos were of generous size, cheesy and good. The Hard Rock burger (on reflection, it's quite an unfortunate name) was less so on all counts: relatively small, a bit dry and somehow flavourless. Better, surprisingly, are the salads; there are five types served with a variety of dressings, all big enough for a family of three (we exaggerate only slightly). Take the Cobb Salad, which has rows of grilled chicken, avocado, bacon, cheese, tomato, egg and red onion arranged on top of salad leaves like stripes on a flag. Finishing it was never an option. We didn't try the barbecue, though it's another house special of some fame. So the food is perfectly acceptable – but we'd never queue an hour for it.
Babies and children welcome; children's menu; high chairs; toys. Bookings accepted only for parties of 10 or more. No-smoking tables. Tables outdoors (10, pavement). Takeaway service. **Map 9 H8**.

Oxford Street W1

★ Eagle Bar Diner

3-5 Rathbone Place, W1T 1HJ (7637 1418/ www.eaglebardiner.com). Tottenham Court Road tube. **Open** noon-11pm Mon-Wed; noon-midnight Thur, Fri; 11am-1am Sat; 11am-6pm Sun. **Meals served** noon-11pm Mon-Wed; noon-11.30pm Thur, Fri; 11am-midnight Sat; 11am-6pm Sun. **Main courses** £4-£8.75. **Credit** MC, V.
This trendy, cool, reliably good restaurant is an oasis off the hellish hustle of Oxford Street. The look is posh diner – leather banquettes at arty angles, high-backed green booths and a slick bar at the front – and the menu is much the same. It's heavy on the hamburgers, but these are not run of the mill. The grilled tuna burger was gorgeous (juicy and cooked to perfection) as was the 8oz beefburger with danish blue cheese. Both were served with attention to detail: the rolls were fresh, the salad crisp, the fries (fat or skinny versions)

Harlem. See p33.

MUSIC LIVES HERE

Hard Rock CAFE

Hard Rock CAFE

LONDON

150 OLD PARK LANE

NEAREST UNDERGROUND: GREEN PARK / HYDE PARK CORNER

TELEPHONE: 0207 514 1700

LONDON SALES@HARDROCK.COM

salty. The only downside was the coleslaw, which had too much mayonnaise, was too warm and, we suspect, hadn't been crisp for some time before it arrived at the table. But we got over it when our peanut butter and banana milk shake arrived. Who knew you could buy heaven in a glass for just over three quid? The alcoholic drinks are great too, including decent cocktails (such as American-themed Eagle Favourites and eight Martinis) and little-seen Brooklyn Lager. This diner also does a good line in breakfasts for those who like to start the day with pancakes and eggs.
Babies and children welcome (until 8pm Thur-Sat). Disabled: toilet, ramp. Entertainment: DJs from 8pm Thur-Sat. Takeaway service. **Map 17 K6**.

Piccadilly W1

Cheers
72 Regent Street, W1R 6EL (7494 3322/www. cheersbarlondon.com). Piccadilly Circus tube.
Bar **Open** noon-3am Mon-Sat; noon-12.30am Sun.
Restaurant **Meals served** noon-10pm daily.
Main courses £6.95-£12.90. **Minimum** £7.
Set meal (noon-6pm Mon-Fri) £2.95 1 course.
Service 12.5% for parties of 6 or more.
Both **Credit** AmEx, MC, V.
What to say, huh? This large theme restaurant has many minus points: it's named after the 1980s TV comedy, some of the dishes are named after characters on that show, there's a *Cheers* souvenir shop by the front door…This is all wrong on so many levels – and yet things actually aren't as bad as they could be. The service is usually good and the food is reasonable for the money. The clam chowder seems to get thicker every year, but the flavour is excellent and there's a whole ocean of clams in there. Both our starters (barbecue ribs, and beer-batter onion rings) were huge and delicious. The rings were quite greasy, but better than most in London. The cheeseburgers are huge and worth the price (£7.65), but our peperone pizza was mediocre: soggy, with a disappointing crust. Despite such shortcomings, this is the best of the US-theme chains.
Babies and children welcome (until 6pm in restaurant); children's menu; crayons; high chairs. Disabled: toilet. Dress: smart casual. No-smoking tables. **Map 17 J7**.

Soho W1

★ Bodean's
10 Poland Street, W1F 8PZ (7287 7575/ www.bodeansbbq.com). Oxford Circus or Piccadilly Circus tube.
Deli **Open** noon-11pm Mon-Sat; noon-10.30pm Sun.
Restaurant **Lunch served** noon-3pm, **dinner served** 6-11pm Mon-Fri. **Meals served** noon-11pm Sat; noon-10.30pm Sun. **Main courses** £6-£12. **Set meals** (minimum 8) £15.95 2 courses, £18.95 3 courses. **Service** 12.5%.
Both **Credit** AmEx, MC, V.
From the rich, sweet smell leaking out to the street, to the pig-shaped doorknob, this place is all about roasted meat. Vegetarians, beware. Everyone else: embrace your inner carnivore and plunge in, because Bodean's is the best barbecue venue in London. The downstairs restaurant is certainly popular – booking is necessary even midweek, although you can eat in the upstairs diner area – but the new Clapham branch (opened May 2004) may relieve some pressure. Waiters are friendly to the point of giddiness, though we had to remind them to bring a couple of dishes (excellent barbecue baked beans in molasses-tinged tomato sauce, and perfect baked potato) and they still delivered the coleslaw we'd politely pointed out we hated. But what matters is the carcass on the plate. A full rack of baby back ribs threatened to take up half the table with its juicy, marinated goodness, while a more reasonable half-slab of pork ribs (ample for most people) was cooked to perfection. We've never had poorly cooked meat here; it's never dried out, never overdone, never underdone. Prices are fair. Chase it down with a bottle of Samuel Adams beer or a Lynchburg Lemonade with a kick of Jack Daniels. Now, that's what we call supper.

Babies and children welcome: children's area; high chairs. Booking advisable (restaurant). No smoking (noon-5pm Sat, Sun). Restaurant & deli available for hire. Tables outdoors (4, pavement). Takeaway service; delivery service (over £75 only). **Map 17 J6**.
For branch see index.

★ Ed's Easy Diner
12 Moor Street, W1V 5LH (7434 4439). Leicester Square or Tottenham Court Road tube.
Meals served 11.30am-midnight Mon-Thur, Sun; 11.30am-1am Fri, Sat. **Main courses** £4.40-£5.50. **Minimum** (6pm-midnight Fri-Sun) £4.45.
Service 12.5%. **Credit** AmEx, MC, V.
This souped-up 1950s-style diner is well known to many Londoners, who have discovered that its inexpensive, freshly made burgers are just the thing when they're in the mood for something a step up from standard fast food. On a recent visit we tried to experience the other side of Ed's – to seek its gourmet soul, if you will – by sampling the 'atomic' onion rings (rings served with an array of dips including chilli con carne, cheese, sour cream, guacamole and salsa). Not an improvement: the sauces weren't that impressive, and such fine onion rings are much better naked. The hamburgers are perennially good: made-to-order, greasy in just the right way, with the cheese of your choice and all the usual fixings. The shakes and malts are also excellent; the butterscotch malt is a dessert in itself. We're happy to say that nothing changes at Ed's: the food is still enjoyable, the jukebox music is still cloying enough to make you worry about other people's tastes, and the attitude is still determinedly festive.
Babies and children welcome; children's menu; crayons. No smoking. Tables outdoors (4, pavement). Takeaway service; delivery service. **Map 17 K6**.
For branches see index.

Strand WC2

Smollensky's on the Strand
105 Strand, WC2R 0AA (7497 2101/www. smollenskys.co.uk). Covent Garden, Embankment or Temple tube/Charing Cross tube/rail.
Bar **Open** noon-11pm Mon-Wed; noon-12.30am Thur-Sat; noon-10.30pm Sun.
Restaurant **Meals served** noon-midnight Mon-Wed; noon-12.30am Thur-Sat. **Main courses** £8.50-£22.95. **Set meal** noon-7pm, after 10.30pm Mon-Fri) £10 2 courses, £12 3 courses.
Service 12.5%.
Both **Credit** AmEx, DC, MC, V.
Every year we come to Smollensky's with a cynical attitude – it's too touristy, too heavily advertised – and every year we have another excellent meal. Our most recent visit was no exception. Starters were good: vegetable wun tuns were perfectly crisp on the outside, juicy and flavourful inside, while mushroom tart (big enough to serve as a main course) provided delicate, smoky mushrooms in a creamy sauce, all cradled in flaky pastry. Steak is the main attraction when it comes to mains, with such options as sirloin with béarnaise sauce and ribeye with peppercorn sauce. Each was large, tender and cooked precisely as requested. Sides of creamed spinach and french fries were well seasoned and fresh. Once again we have to give this place credit: good food, reasonable prices and a pleasant atmosphere.
Babies and children welcome; children's menu, booster seats; entertainment (noon-4pm Sat, Sun); high chairs; toys. Booking advisable. Entertainment: pianist 7.30-10.30pm Mon-Sat; DJ 10pm-12.30am Fri, Sat; jazz 8-10.30pm Sun (£6 cover). No-smoking tables. **Map 18 L7**.
For branches see index.

Victoria SW1

Harvard Bar & Grill `NEW`
101 Buckingham Palace Road, SW1W 0SJ (7868 6249). Victoria tube/rail. **Lunch served** noon-3pm Mon-Fri. **Dinner served** 5.30-11pm Mon-Sat. **Main courses** £11.50-£22.
Set lunch £12.50 2 courses, £15 3 courses.
Set dinner £15 2 courses, £17.50 3 courses.
Credit AmEx, DC, MC, V.

This new restaurant has retained many of the fittings of the Christopher's branch it replaced: the cool iron chandeliers and the fabulous towering posters of US skyscrapers, as well as the same bar, with its low sofas and blue backlighting. The menu is similar too, emphasising, as Christopher's did, steaks and lobster. Grilled squid salad with a delicate sesame dressing was a satisfying size, tender and delightfully flavoured. Shrimp bisque was enormous, rich and deliciously decadent. For mains, we went where we were led; well-cooked, medium-sized grilled lobster arrived juicy and drizzled with butter. Baked duck marinated in maple syrup was divine, the meat moist and the syrup giving it just the right level of sweetness. Sides of mashed potatoes and garlic green beans were good too. Desserts range from cheesecake to ice-cream; pear and chocolate tart was more cake-like than we'd imagined, but lovely. The appealing wine list has some moderately priced options. Service is efficient if a little abrupt. A fine choice for a slightly posh evening out with the parents.
Babies and children welcome; high chairs. Disabled: toilet. **Map 15 H10**.

West

Bayswater W2

★ Harlem `NEW`
78 Westbourne Grove, W2 5RT (7985 0900/ www.harlemsoulfood.com). Bayswater or Notting Hill Gate tube. **Open** 10.30am-2am Mon-Sat; 10.30am-midnight Sun. **Meals served** 10.30am-midnight daily. **Service** 12.5%. **Credit** AmEx, DC, MC, V.
When this trendy, wood-panelled restaurant/bar opened in early 2004, it was barraged with bad notices. Its soul food was soulless, reviewers declared, its portions large but stodgy. Harlem was all attitude. We wonder if we went to the same place, because on our visit the food was excellent. Moreover, the room is attractive, with banquette and table seating, plenty of polished wood and nice touches everywhere. Service, from hip young things, was cool but friendly enough. The menu offers 'home cooking'-style Southern favourites. For starters, fried corncakes were tiny and chewy, filled with sweetcorn and topped with avocado sauce and sour cream, while a big portion of lightly battered squid was drizzled with a tangy dressing. To follow: an enormous and perfectly cooked hamburger with a mound of excellent fries; and a thick 10oz sirloin, grilled precisely to order, topped with onion rings and resting on wilted spinach. The steak was so good we willed ourselves to finish it, but the portion was just too large. Still, we felt obliged to try the white chocolate cheesecake with fresh berries. Heavenly. A couple of Brooklyn beers – and what more do you need? A new branch opens in Brixton in autumn 2004.
Babies and children welcome. Booking advisable. Entertainment: DJ 9pm Mon-Sat. Restaurant. **Map 7 B6**.
For branch see index.

Chiswick W4

Coyote Café
2 Fauconberg Road, W4 3JY (8742 8545/ www.coyotecafe.co.uk). Chiswick Park tube/ Gunnersbury tube/rail. **Meals served** 5-10.30pm Mon-Fri; 10am-11pm Sat; 10am-10.30pm Sun.
Main courses £5-£15. **Service** 12.5% for parties of 6 or more. **Credit** AmEx, MC, V.
This is one of those restaurants that we'll forgive many things. For a start, it's a gourmet restaurant in a pub, and that pub can get quite rowdy. But we forgive them. Our table was squeezed in by the door to the toilets, where there shouldn't be a table at all. We forgive that too. Forgiveness is not in our nature, so why are we being so generous? Because the ribeye steak in mole sauce with crispy thin fries and tobacco onions is so astonishingly good. It's our favourite steak among all London's North American restaurants – tender, a good size and surrounded by a smoky, bitter mole sauce. Other likeable options include baked chipotle chicken: succulent chicken breast wrapped in thin slices of

Ashbells

ham and stuffed with mild chillies, then roasted. Specials, which used to include such exotica as zebra steaks, now comprise more ordinary fare; we hope the taming down doesn't go too far since Coyote Café's excellent Southwestern menu is unique in the capital.
Babies and children welcome; children's menu; high chairs. Book dinner. Disabled: toilet. Tables outdoors (7, pavement).

Holland Park W11

Tootsies Grill

120 Holland Park Avenue, W11 4UA (7229 8567/www.tootsiesrestaurants.co.uk). Holland Park tube. **Meals served** 11am-11pm Mon-Thur; 11am-11.30pm Fri; 9am-11.30pm Sat, Sun. **Main courses** £5.95-£11.95. **Service** 12.5%. **Credit** AmEx, MC, V.

This growing chain (11 outlets in London at the last count) is a handy option: the menu is affordable, the food is good if basic, and it's very child-friendly. At this branch, big windows look out over leafy Holland Park Avenue, and old posters portray both British and American themes. We visited on a busy Sunday afternoon, but staff coped well. For starters, grilled prawns arrived with shells and heads still in place. This made for some messy peeling, but the end result was worth it as the shellfish were big, fresh and plump. Grilled chicken breast sandwich with avocado was delightful and would have been a nod to healthy living were it not for the hefty slice of melting brie plonked on top and the pile of good chips on the side. Hamburgers take centre stage on the menu, and with every reason: they're thick and juicy, cooked to order, with every imaginable variation

available. Tootsies' milkshakes are also fabulous (the butterscotch is recommended unreservedly), and desserts are all serious ice-cream concoctions.
Babies and children welcome; children's menu; crayons; high chairs. No-smoking tables. Tables outdoors (3, pavement). Takeaway service.
Map 19 B5.
For branches see index.

Kensington W8

Sticky Fingers

1A Phillimore Gardens, W8 7QG (7938 5338/ www.stickyfingers.co.uk). High Street Kensington tube.
Bar **Open** noon-8pm Mon-Sat.
Restaurant **Meals served** noon-11pm Mon-Sat; noon-10.30pm Sun. **Main courses** £9.25-£17.95.
Both **Credit** AmEx, DC, MC, V.

You eat to the beat at Sticky Fingers, where an impressive rock 'n' roll pedigree (courtesy of co-owner Bill Wyman, formerly of the Rolling Stones) lures punters who might otherwise baulk at the prices or avoid its unsurprising menu. There's a background throb of golden oldies, and items from Mr Wyman's souvenir collection hang upon every wall. Weekday lunchtimes see well-preserved west London mums playing with their chop salads, while their rubicund tots feast on burgers, pasta and chocolate milk shakes from the children's menu; evenings attract a rowdier champagne-and-fajita crowd. Having complained about the service, attitude and underwhelming food in the past, we were cheered by a friendly waitress and the prompt arrival of lunch. Neither did a big bowl of lip-smacking onion soup disappoint, although £7.25 seemed steep for another starter of crispy duck with pancakes. A steak sandwich, covered with caramelised onions and mushroom slivers, came tumbling out of a huge wodge of ciabatta. Other happy discoveries included light battered onion rings, a fine species of chip, and a warm, dense but not too sugary brownie for pudding, whose grainy vanilla ice-cream companion sweetened it very pleasantly.
Babies and children welcome; children's menu; entertainment (face-painting 1.30-3.30pm Sat, Sun); high chairs. Booking advisable. Separate area available for hire, seats 50. Takeaway service. Map 7 A9.

Ladbroke Grove W11

★ Ashbells

29 All Saints Road, W11 1HE (7221 8585/ www.ashbells.co.uk). Ladbroke Grove or Westbourne Park tube. **Lunch served** noon-3pm Mon-Fri. **Brunch served** noon-4pm Sat, Sun. **Dinner served** 6.30-11.30pm Mon-Sat. **Main courses** £10-£17.50. **Set lunch** (Mon-Fri) £8.95 2 courses, (Sat, Sun) £12.95 1 course and glass of Buck's Fizz. **Service** 12.5%. **Credit** AmEx, DC, MC, V.
This tiny restaurant run by Ashbell McElveen, the former US television chef, has introduced London to the best of upscale Deep South cuisine. A batik of Josephine Baker overlooks the pleasantly decorated room, where diners sit on comfortable banquettes, surrounded by plush cushions. The kitchen turns out glorious British versions of Southern favourites, such as corn pudding, collard greens and pulled pork. Start with a delicious watermelon Martini, then try the light and fluffy crab cake starter: two plump, crisp cakes bursting with fresh crab meat. Or sample the sweet smoked salmon with cool cucumber and mint hash – light and refreshing. For mains, the pork ribs are the chef's own version, in a thick, spicy tomato-barbecue sauce; the meat fell off the bone, and came with chewy fried grits (similar to polenta) and collard-style greens. Pulled barbecue pork arrived surrounded by soupy grits; their mild flavour, combined with the powerfully spiced meat, was exhilarating. Puddings can be heavy (fruit cobblers, warm banana pudding), but the poundcake (resembling a dense sponge cake) with berries was refreshing. It would be nice to have ice-cream on the menu though.
Babies and children admitted. Booking advisable. Dress: smart. No-smoking floor. Restaurant available for hire. Separate room for parties, seats 20. Tables outdoors (2, pavement). Map 19 B2.

Westbourne Park W2

★ Lucky 7

127 Westbourne Park Road, W2 5QL (7727 6771). Royal Oak or Westbourne Park tube. **Meals served** 7am-11pm Mon-Sat; 9am-10.30pm Sun. **Main courses** £4.25-£7.95. **No credit cards.**
The worst thing about this Tom Conran stylised take on the US diner is its size: it's tiny, just a handful of big booths that you will likely be called on to share with strangers. The best thing about Lucky 7 is the food. The menu is short and sweet, consisting of a few hamburgers (many of them fish or vegetarian), sides, salads and ice-cream. All of it is done quite well – burgers are big and juicy, cooked to order; fries are skinny and crisp; onion

rings are fat and good, but with a tendency to become greasy too quickly; shakes and sundaes are calorific and addictive. We ordered a cheeseburger with all the toppings, fries and a chocolate shake. While the fries turned up far too early, it was all so satisfying that we could not bring ourselves to complain about the generally ethereal service. Also, the waiters were cooler than us. Creative options include a crab-meat burger, bean burger and burgers with toppings like salsa and avocado. Our advice: don't come here if you don't like burgers, or if you're afraid of strangers.
Babies and children admitted; high chairs. Bookings not accepted. Takeaway service. Map 7 A5.

South West

Chelsea SW3

Big Easy

332-334 King's Road, SW3 5UR (7352 4071/ www.bigeasy.uk.com). Sloane Square tube then 11, 19, 22 bus. **Bar Open** noon-11pm Mon-Fri; 11am-11pm Sat; 11am-10.30pm Sun. **Main courses** £7.95-£14.95. *Restaurant* **Meals served** noon-11.30pm Mon-Thur; noon-12.20am Fri; 11am-12.20am Sat; 11am-11.20pm Sun. **Main courses** £8.95-£22.50. **Set lunch** (noon-5pm Mon-Fri) £7.95 2 courses. **Service** 12.5%.
Both **Credit** AmEx, MC, V.
This is the most American of London's US-style restaurants, with a rustic decor typified by metal Tabasco signs, and a gone fishin' attitude. The mood was as raucous as ever, with a two-piece band playing Lynyrd Skynyrd and Crowded House hits, the mostly American clientele happy and a little tipsy, and everything appropriately down-home and very Southern. A startlingly spicy starter of voodoo chicken wings was cooled down by a blue cheese dip, but the clam chowder (although creamy and thick) could have used more clams and potatoes. A half portion of roasted lobster was delightful and filling, while the ribeye steak was simply massive (14oz) and cooked as ordered. Sides of french fries and garlic spinach were fine too, but at £3.10 a bottle the beer seemed a bit pricey. Service is admirably friendly, though our peppercorn sauce was forgotten somewhere amid the hustle and the bustle. An excellent spot for a night out with friends, but you wouldn't want to come here to propose.
Babies and children welcome; children's menu; crayons; high chairs; nappy-changing facilities. Entertainment: music from 8.30pm daily. No-smoking service. Tables outdoors (5, pavement). Takeaway service. Map 14 D12.

Wimbledon SW19

★ Jo Shmo's

33 High Street, Wimbledon, SW19 5BY (8879 3845/www.joshmos.com). Wimbledon tube/rail then 93 bus. **Meals served** noon-11pm Mon-Sat; noon-10.30pm Sun. **Main courses** £5.95-£14.50. **Credit** AmEx, MC, V.
This modern diner (set up by the firm behind the ASK pizza chain) serves fast food the way it ought to be. The decor is pleasing: all dark wood and bare lights, with stark, interesting black and white photographs. Service is quick and relentlessly efficient. The menu leans in a similar direction to Tootsies (*see p34*), with burgers leading the way, followed by other basic faves such as ribs, grills and pasta. A starter of chicken wings arrived hot and juicy, with an appetising sauce. Burgers come in endless variations, but we stuck to the cheeseburger – and very good it was too: big, succulent and hearty. A bountiful portion of crunchy onion strings was addictive. Salads are excellent too; they take several forms, providing a healthy alternative to the otherwise meaty menu. This is another US-style restaurant climbing aboard the milk shake trend, but we have no problem with the return of such comfort food; the vanilla shake makes a sweet alternative to bottled beer. Prices are fair and families are looked after, with plenty of options for smaller folk.

Babies and children welcome; children's menu; high chairs. Disabled: toilet. No-smoking tables. Tables outdoors (pavement).
For branch see index.

South

Wandsworth SW17, SW18

Dexter's Grill & Bar

20 Bellevue Road, SW17 7EB (8767 1858). Wandsworth Common rail. **Meals served** *Summer* 11am-11pm Mon-Fri; 10am-11pm Sat; 10am-10.30pm Sun. *Winter* noon-11pm Mon-Fri; 11am-11pm Sat; 11am-10.30pm Sun. **Main courses** £7-£15. **Service** 12.5%. **Credit** AmEx, MC, V.
Owned by the same company as Tootsies (*see p34*), this family restaurant is a useful spot. With exposed brick walls, large windows and friendly staff, it's a very welcoming place. The menu puts an emphasis on gourmet sandwiches, hamburgers and fresh salads. A starter of butterfly prawns arrived fresh and steaming hot, with a sweet Thai sauce. For mains, we went for the build-your-own salad, creating an oriental affair with chicken satay and peanut sauce, which was filling and fresh. Even better was a large juicy hamburger, served with lots of crisp chips. For puddings, your best bet is to try one of the house speciality ice-cream dishes; portions are big enough to satisfy three. Don't overlook the smoothies and shakes either.
Babies and children welcome; children's menu; crayons; high chairs; toys. Booking advisable weekends. No-smoking tables. Separate rooms for parties, seats 25 and 40. Tables outdoors (9, patio). Takeaway service.

Outback Steakhouse

Dolphin House, Riverside West, Smugglers Way, SW18 1EG (8877 1599/www.outbackpom.com). Wandsworth Town rail. **Meals served** 5-11pm Mon-Fri; 4-11pm Sat; noon-9pm Sun. **Main courses** £6.99-£17.99. **Credit** AmEx, JCB, MC, V.
Enormous in the States, the Outback chain's theme is simple if cynical: Australia as seen from 10,000 miles away, by people who have never been there. However, the food is reliably good, staff are remarkably nice and it's very family friendly. Portions are enormous, so passed on the Too Right French Onion Soup and went instead for the Grilled Shrimp on the Barbie (get the picture?). Embarrassing though the dish was to order, the result was pleasing: plenty of fat prawns, nicely seasoned and served with a tangy sauce. For mains, prime rib is a popular option, available in 16oz, 12oz or 8oz portions. The latter was more than ample, thick cut, tender and excellently grilled, and served with fresh steamed vegetables. There are also lots of grilled steaks, ribs and fish to choose from, and a 'Joey's Menu' for kids. If you can deal with the copyrighted faux-Aussie attitude, there's nothing really wrong with this place.
Babies and children welcome; crayons; high chairs; toys. Disabled: toilet. No-smoking tables. Takeaway service.
For branches see index.

East

South Woodford E18

Yellow Book Californian Café

190 George Lane, E18 1AY (8989 3999/ www.theyellowbook.co.uk). South Woodford tube. **Lunch served** noon-2.30pm Mon-Fri. **Dinner served** 6.30-10pm Mon; 6.30-11pm Tue-Fri. **Meals served** noon-11pm Sat; noon-10pm Sun. **Main courses** £6.50-£13.95. **Credit** MC, V.
We've had good and bad experiences here over the years, but think we've cracked it: go in the summer, sit in the garden. The interior is noisy and can get too hot, but the garden is charming, with wooden tables arranged around trees, and hanging flower baskets. The menu wanders across the multicultural state of California. Fried goat's cheese with peppercorn salsa was light and delicious; better still was squid stuffed with prawns and spices, then grilled and served with a sweet chilli sauce. For mains, salmon kabayaki

featured slim, marinated slices of fish, tender and juicy, on a plate of sizzling vegetables, served with a separate bowl of noodles tossed with soy sauce; it managed to be both filling and light at the same time. Rump of lamb was a beautifully cooked, good-sized portion served on a huge pile of minted mash potatoes. There are plenty of puds – some modern, some as trad as knickerbocker glory. Service was more attentive than on previous visits. *Babies and children welcome (Mon-Thur, Sun only); high chairs. Bookings not accepted weekends. No-smoking tables. Tables outdoors (8, patio). Takeaway service (pizza, non-busy periods).*

North
Islington N1

Santa Fe
75 Upper Street, N1 0NU (7288 2288/ www.santafe.co.uk). Angel tube.
Bar **Open** 5-11pm Mon-Fri; noon-11pm Sat; noon-10.30pm Sun.
Restaurant **Meals served** 5-11pm Mon-Fri; noon-11pm Sat; noon-10pm Sun. **Main courses** £8.25-£17.95.
Both **Credit** AmEx, JCB, MC, V.
This Southwestern restaurant has undergone changes in the past year, most of them good (a new menu, improved cooking) and some not so good (loud music and a bar atmosphere spreading into the dining area). A guacamole and salsa starter came with excellent tortilla chips – although not enough to use up all the tangy, mayonnaise-like guacamole and good salsa. Prawns and corncakes featured perfectly grilled prawns with tiny, blini-like corncakes and more salsa. To follow, rack of ribs was a generous portion of juicy, well-seasoned meat, accompanied by excellent fries. Regrettably, the grande chilli con queso was not as impressive. It was really just chilli con carne with attitude; the flavour was nice, but it was too dry and came with tiny hard squares of halloumi cheese (monterey jack or even cheddar would have been better). Puddings tend to be quite heavy (cheesecake, apple cobbler and the like), but there are also fresh sorbets and ice-creams to soothe the palate. *Babies and children welcome; children's menu; high chairs; nappy-changing facilities; toys. Disabled: toilet. No-smoking tables. Separate room for parties, seats 50.* **Map 5 O2.**

Outer London
Richmond, Surrey

Canyon
The Towpath, Richmond Riverside, Richmond, Surrey TW10 6UJ (8948 2944). Richmond tube/rail. **Brunch served** 11am-3.30pm Sat, Sun. **Lunch served** 11am-3.30pm Mon-Fri. **Dinner served** 6-10.30pm daily. **Main courses** £11-£19. **Service** 12.5%. **Credit** AmEx, MC, V.
An evening at this breezy riverside restaurant is always a pleasure. With striking views of the Thames and an extensive outdoor terrace, Canyon is the perfect location for dramatic summer sunsets. It's pleasant in winter too, when you can sit snugly inside the glass walls. On the downside, the menu is short, which means we often end up ordering dishes we don't want: on our most recent visit, cod in a herb crust with cold potato salad and shrimps. The cod was flaky and delicately flavoured, but we'd have preferred fries to salad – and we counted exactly three tiny shrimps. Fillet of beef was a nice thick cut, but wasn't cooked as requested (we asked for medium-rare, and it arrived very rare indeed; yet even so it tasted burnt). Accompanying 'cottage mash' (flavoured mince atop mashed potatoes) was interesting, but made the dish far too heavy; vegetables would have been better. Desserts were the saving grace: a refreshing lemon tart (though the caramelised sugar on top was unnecessary), and a soothing chocolate pot. Service was faultless and the view is lovely, but it's time for a new direction in the kitchen. *Babies and children welcome; children's menu; high chairs. Booking advisable. Disabled: toilet. No-smoking tables. Tables outdoors (12, courtyard; 16, terrace).*

LATIN AMERICAN

Undoubtedly, London's ethnic diversity is the main reason for its exciting food scene. Yet though the city has a sizeable population from Central and South America, little inspiration seems to be evident in its Latin American restaurants. When dining out on the food of their homeland, the capital's Colombians and Ecuadoreans appear to limit their diet to basic stews, poultry and chips, and heavy sweets in lacklustre cantinas. Brazilians and Argentinians tend to steer clear of the expensive restaurants that fly their respective culinary flags.

The problem is due partly to the rather dull, clichéd dishes of maize-based Incaic imports and barbecued meat offered here. London's Latin American restaurants show little willingness to explore the assorted exotic meats, fish and seafood – guinea pig, llama, deer, spider crab, for instance – and large range of herbs and spices to be found across Latin America. Service and atmosphere is generally in a poor state too, as if the tired attitudes of the chefs has overflowed into the front of house.

It is some compensation this year that dashing pan-continental **1492** has opened in Fulham, and that little **Armadillo** in Hackney continues to turn out creative cross-border fusion with panache. However, across the capital, Latin American dining needs a Cuban-style revolution to shake it out of its torpor. Which is exactly what's in the offing with Terence Conran's latest venture, **Floridita** (100 Wardour Street, W1F 0TN; 7314 4000). Taking over the cavernous space that was Mezzo, this grand Cuban restaurant and bar, modelled on the famous Havana joint of the same name (patronised by the likes of Hemingway in its '50s heyday), promises a flamboyant mix of music, cocktails, cigars and Latin American food, with seating for up to 300. Opening is planned for October 2004.

Argentinian
Central
Holborn WC2

The Gaucho Grill
125-126 Chancery Lane, WC2A 1PU (7242 7727/www.thegauchogrill.co.uk). Chancery Lane tube. **Meals served** noon-11pm Mon-Fri. **Main courses** £9-£20. **Service** 10% for parties of 6 or more. **Credit** AmEx, DC, JCB, MC, V.
Cowhide stools and racks of Mendozan plonk may allude to the Argentine countryside, but this Gaucho Grill is a refined steakhouse for City slickers. At the Chancery Lane outlet there are usually more people sipping cocktails on the ground floor than dining upstairs. Staff have to (and do) put in a major effort to make this a welcoming restaurant. The veal sweetbreads, fillet steak and empanadas are all tasty, and the meat is evidently top-grade, Argentinian export-quality prime. Chorizo was lean but short on spice, though the accompanying rye bread was good. Far more serious was the fact that just about everything was served cold: a fault that needs correcting urgently. The don pedro (ice-cream and whisky) dessert was luscious if runny, and pancakes were lovely. Staff are knowledgeable about the lengthy wine list, which yielded a fine Norton malbec. Since our visit, much of the Gaucho Grill menu has been revamped (by US chef Douglas Rodriguez) to provide lighter dishes and more for vegetarians; hopefully this will give the place a boost. *Booking advisable. Disabled: toilet. Restaurant available for hire. Takeaway service.* **Map 11 N6.**
For branches see index.

Earl's Court SW10

El Gaucho
88 Ifield Road, SW10 9AD (7823 3333). Earl's Court or West Brompton tube/14 bus. **Dinner served** 6.30-11pm Mon-Sat. **Main courses** £12.90-£17.90. **Credit** MC, V.
The long trek across the Audi-dotted pampas of SW10 towards El Gaucho deserves to be rewarded with a hearty meal of meat and trimmings. As it turned out, the steaks were more than satisfactory – and as thick as anything a real gaucho would cut into – but that other Argentine staple, the milanesa (veal cutlet), was sub-standard: oily, stringy, and far too big for one person. Side orders of a fried empanada, a massive (almost rude) chorizo and a provoleta (barbecued provolone) were better, but none seemed to have enough of the requisite flavourings (parsley and red peppers, especially). Steaks are served *a caballo* ('on horseback', meaning with eggs on top): a truly great combo on this grade of meat. For dessert, dulce de leche pancake was stodgy but yummy, doused in a creamy milk jelly. Drinks include a good range of Argentinian and Chilean wine, Quilmes beer, and yerba maté tea to drink in or take home. El Gaucho has a gentle buzz. The gaucho balls hanging from the ceiling and the Argentinian iconography (Carlos Monzón boxing, Evita waving, Che saluting, Maradona doing something with his hand too) are understated and smart. *Children welcome. Booking advisable Fri, Sat. Takeaway service.* **Map 13 C12.**
For branches see index.

Battersea SW11

La Pampa Grill
60 Battersea Rise, SW11 1EG (7924 4774). Clapham Junction rail. **Dinner served** 6pm-midnight Mon-Sat; 6-11pm Sun. **Main courses** £7.95-£15.50. **Service** 10% for parties of 7 or more. **Credit** MC, V.
'All our meat is from Argentina,' brags the menu. This is, of course, highly important – but is not enough to justify ignoring everything else a restaurant should provide. Colombian-owned, Portuguese-run, La Pampa Grill steakhouse needs a gaucho to get things going, both inside and outside the kitchen. Salads were dreary; the chimmichurri was a thin, tasteless version of the original Argentinian sauce, and the wrong colour

entirely; and even the sirloin (wherever it came from) was not a brilliant piece of meat. On the upside, the fillet steak was a fine hunk of tender joy, and the Trapiche oak-casked red provided the perfect accompaniment. There is, however, no attempt to pull in other dishes from central Argentina: whether stews and pies, or simple suckling pig and kid. A dessert of basic pancakes in dulce de leche (milk pudding) was passable. Service was sloppy and slow, devoid of chatter. Frankly, at the prices charged to eat this kind of elite meat, we expect more of a restaurant.
Babies and children welcome. Booking advisable; essential Sat. Separate area for parties, seats 25. **Map 21 C4.**
For branch see index.

Brazilian

Central

Oxford Street W1

★ Brasil by Kilo NEW
17 Oxford Street, W1D 2DJ (7287 7161). Tottenham Court Road tube. **Meals served** noon-9pm daily. **Main courses** 99p per 100g. **No credit cards.**
This unpretentious Brazilian café is tucked into the ugly – and horrendously busy – Oxford Street/ Tottenham Court Road junction. Load up your plate from a dozen hot dishes and cold salads, then get the plate weighed; you pay 99p per 100g. It's an uncomplicated system, with fewer strings than a dental-floss bikini – and it's hard to spend more than a fiver. The best Brazilian dishes are simple, home-style fare, such as frango ensopado, cuts of chicken sautéed with spices including annato, a powdered seed that stains the eventual stew a yellowish-orange colour. Other hot dishes from the daily changing menu might include, abobora refogada (pumpkin fried with garlic), feijoada (pork and black bean stew) or pernil assado (roast pork). The cold buffet is less inspiring. A cooler cabinet holds pudim caramel and other Portuguese-style baked puddings. Don't miss the fruit juices, made from frozen fruit purées imported from Brazil. Try cupuaca, which smells like fermenting melon, or umbu, which has a slightly sour/astringent taste and an aroma that resembles a mix between under-ripe strawberry and lemon.
Babies and children welcome; high chairs. No smoking. Separate room for parties, seats 40. Takeaway service. **Map 17 K6.**

West

Westbourne Grove W2

Rodizio Rico
111 Westbourne Grove, W2 4UW (7792 4035). Bayswater tube. **Lunch served** noon-4.30pm Sat. **Dinner served** 6-11.30pm Mon-Sat. **Meals served** 12.30-10.30pm Sun. **Set buffet** £11.90 vegetarian, £18 barbecue. **Service** 10%. **Credit** MC, V.
Modelled on the urban churrascarias (busy, ranch-like steakhouses) found throughout Brazil, Rodizio Rico is centred on the meat that is served up on a sword and taken from table to table. There's a smallish self-service salad selection to prepare the ground, some rice, farofa (fried cassava flour), fried plantain and beans, but the only reason for paying the all-you-can-eat rate is the meat. After some fair sausages, fatty but tasty pork on the rib, and a nice little chicken heart, came the beef. Cheaper cuts at first, but bide your time and eventually the prize of small, lean and tender sirloin with edges heavily salted and charred arrives; it can't fail to delight. Brahma beer is probably the best booze option on the poor drinks list, but the guaraná soft drink is worth trying if you want an energising tipple. Pancakes and ice-cream for afters were more than enough – and you have to pay extra for them. One warning: if you want to control how much salt you have, make sure you advise the waiters, as the normal dose here is designed to replace the lost minerals of a sweating samba dancer.
Babies and children welcome; high chairs. Booking advisable; essential dinner. Separate room for parties, seats 55. Tables outdoors (6, pavement). **Map 7 B6.**

North

Archway N19

Sabor do Brasil
36 Highgate Hill, N19 5LS (7263 9066). Archway tube. **Lunch served** by appointment Tue-Sun. **Dinner served** 7-11pm Tue-Sun. **Closed** Aug. **Main courses** £4-£12.50. **Set buffet** £12.50. **Cover** £1.50 Wed. **Service** 10%. **No credit cards.**
Some are drawn to this out-of-the-way canteen by its laid-back, low-profile family atmosphere. The service, it's true, can't be faulted, as all diners are warmly welcomed, whether for the first or umpteenth time. But energy and enterprise are lacking, and the cooking is in need of an overhaul. Traditional rice, bean and veg dishes, elementary fish dishes and platters of mushrooms, broccoli, beans and pasta may well appeal to those who want Brazilian without the dancing and the high cost of barbecue restaurants – but they don't provide even the most basic thrill to your taste buds. Cod moqueca and goat stew were tasty enough, but neither had the kick or substance of the originals (a moqueca in Bahia or Búzios can be a near-religious experience). If you're familiar with Bahian and other Brazilian cuisines, have a chat with the maître d' and you might be able to get a shrimp and coconut vatapá or some other challenging creation out of chef Alberina's kitchen. Otherwise, you'll probably be disappointed if hoping to sample the varied dishes of this massive nation. Lots of charm and affability – little in the way of heat and spice.
Babies and children welcome; high chair. Booking advisable; essential Wed, Fri, Sat. Entertainment: band 8-11pm Wed (phone for details). Separate room for parties, seats 35. **Map 26 B1.**

Colombian

South

Brixton SW9

La Mazorca
384 Brixton Road, SW9 7AW (7274 1919/ www.lamazorca.co.uk). Brixton tube/rail. **Meals served** noon-11pm daily. **Main courses** £6.75-£11.20. **Set lunch** (Mon-Fri) £5.25 2 courses. **Credit** AmEx, MC, V.
Maize, yucca, rice and roast chicken are the staples of the Colombian diet, whatever the social class. Expanding midriffs are only kept in check by hill walking in steaming jungles and endless salsa sessions. Transplant this stodge feast to a coldish evening in Brixton, however, and there's little tropical buzz about the experience. The soups and fish stews are fair peasant food, but clumsily seasoned. Best was probably a plate of chips and steak – not quite Argentinian in girth, but lean, well grilled and salted to perfection. Stews came piled high with unrecognisable seafood and vegetable ingredients, the individual properties of which were levelled by doses of black and red pepper, cumin (perhaps) and draughts of boring stock. However, the atmosphere is warm, thanks to the throb of salsas and merengues and the frantic chatter of the Ecuadorean and Colombian extended families. Staff are rushed off their feet on Friday and Saturday evenings. One thing is clear: food comes a distant second after socialising. A glass of aguardiente assailed and then anaesthetised the taste buds, leaving no memory of the meal at all.
Babies and children welcome; children's menu; high chairs. Booking advisable weekends. Entertainment: guitar music 7pm Sat, Sun. Takeaway service. **Map 22 E1.**

Sabor do Brasil

Cuban

South

Waterloo SE1

Cubana
48 Lower Marsh, SE1 7RG (7928 8778/ www.cubana.co.uk). Waterloo tube/rail.
Bar **Open** noon-midnight Mon, Tue; noon-1am Wed-Fri; 6pm-1am Sat.
Restaurant **Lunch served** noon-3pm Mon-Fri. **Dinner served** 5-11pm Mon-Fri; 6-11pm Sat. **Main courses** £6.45-£10.45. **Set lunch** £5.95 2 courses, £7.95 3 courses.
Both **Credit** AmEx, DC, JCB, MC, V.
The big corner site looks promising from the outside, but it's a disjointed affair within, split uneasily over three cramped floors, with a machine gun hanging by the dining area nicely illustrating what passes muster as decoration. It's tasteless – and the same can be said of the limited culinary repertoire. Empanadillas were greasy; Creole-style prawns mediocre and the accompanying black beans and rice dry. As for the char-grilled steak strip salad, the well-done meat had been hacked into a handful of wodges, with one particularly fatty piece left prominently on the plate. To add insult, a glass was dirty and the dishes still wet from washing. Service came with a grimace; the truculent waitress seemed to be modelling herself on Kelly Osbourne. Several big parties were unduly jolly, but they'd been drinking rather than eating.
Babies and children welcome. Booking advisable. Music (salsa 11pm-1am Wed-Sat). Tables outdoors (4, pavement). **Map 11 N9.**

North

Islington N1

Cuba Libre
72 Upper Street, N1 0NY (7354 9998). Angel tube. **Meals served** 11am-11pm daily. **Main courses** £9.95-£11.95. **Service** 12.5%. **Credit** JCB, MC, V.

Tag-teamers Fidel and Che are gesticulating wildly, there's a tiny broken window above the doorway, and if you look closely you'll spy some parrots perched on the balcony. OK, so all these things are only papier-mâché mannequins or faded frescos, but you get the gist – Cuba Libre is about conjuring up the rough and tumble of a bustling bodega, and what with cocktail promos, a functional tapas menu and hearty specials, most punters end up revelling in the heavenly Havana tackiness. Boozing is the undeniable priority here, with aspiring writers seeking inspiration at the bottom of a Hemingway Special (rum, grapefruit juice, maraschino and lime), but bottled beers Cuban Tinima and Mexican Negra Modelo sit better alongside the traditional main courses. Bacalao aporreado con yuca is the full Cuban experience, as the spiced cod fish cakes arrive with cassava mash and ubiquitous moros y cristianos (black beans and rice), while ropa vieja a la cubana, another golden oldie, might translate as 'old rags' but is in fact an absolute mountain of tender shredded beef. Indeed, wven the most ravenous revolutionary might not have room for arroz con leche (rice pudding), but a zesty café cubano nicely rounds off the themed fun.
Babies and children welcome (until 6pm). Booking advisable. Tables outdoor (8, pavement). **Map 5 O2**.

Mexican & Tex-Mex

Central

Covent Garden WC2

Café Pacifico
5 Langley Street, WC2 8JA (7379 7728/ www.cafepacifico-laperla.com). Covent Garden tube. **Meals served** noon-11.45pm Mon-Sat; noon-10.45pm Sun. **Main courses** £7.95-£15.95. **Set lunch** £10 1 course & Margherita or 2 Mexican beers. **Service** 12.5%. **Credit** AmEx, MC, V.
This relentlessly Latin-themed restaurant is big and raucous, but the food is reliably authentic Tex-Mex, and the service is friendly even when the room is so packed that you can't hear yourself think. It's also an absolute favourite with US expats, so it must be doing something right. A combo starter included fried prawn balls (too bready), rich fried cheese (excellent), onion rings (adequate) and crisp chicken taquitos – fried, chicken-filled corn tortillas (very good). For mains, taquiza was an enormous sizzling plate of grilled steak, chicken and gammon with spices, peppers and cactus. It was tasty if strangely sweet, and came with lots of sauces and flour tortillas. Degustacion del pacifico featured small portions of several dishes including a chicken enchilada, a flat beef taco and a folded cheese quesadilla, plus helpings of beans, rice and salsa that almost overflowed the plate. No complaints then: apart from the soggy and tough quesadilla. Prices are high – £13.95 for beef fajitas for one, £25.95 for two; £2 for a small bowl of tortilla chips and salsa – but we'll keep going back for the hectic atmosphere and the good food.
Babies and children welcome; children's menu; high chairs. Bookings not accepted Fri, Sat. **Map 18 L6**.

La Perla
28 Maiden Lane, WC2E 7JS (7240 7400/ www.cafepacifico-laperla.com). Covent Garden tube/Charing Cross tube/rail. **Meals served** noon-11.45pm Mon-Sat; 4-10.30pm Sun. **Main courses** £7.25-£13.50. **Credit** AmEx, MC, V.
This small, pleasant restaurant (plenty of polished wood and big windows looking out on to Charlotte Street) is the antidote to most of the over-themed 'Let's pretend we're in Cancun!' Mexican restaurants in London. In fact, its relationship with Mexico seems to be somewhat precarious (tostadas with feta cheese?). The menu is short and very basic; the main focus seems to be on the excellent Margaritas and Mexican beer. Still, the atmosphere is warm and that's what everybody's here for. The

chicken burrito plate was sizeable: a flour tortilla stuffed with chicken, cheese and all the fixings, served with generous supplies of refried beans and rice – all as it should be. Green vegetable enchilada was a flour tortilla filled with well-spiced vegetables and baked. It was fine, but would have been better with the more traditional corn tortilla. Service was consistently friendly and prompt.
Babies and children admitted. Booking advisable. **Map 18 L7**.

Piccadilly W1

Destino NEW
25 Swallow Street, W1B 4QR (7437 9895). Piccadilly Circus tube.
Bar **Open** noon-3am Mon-Sat.
Restaurant **Open** 5pm-midnight Mon-Sat; 5pm-10pm Sun. **Main courses** £10-£21. **Service** 12.5%.
Both **Credit** AmEx, DC, MC, V.
Formerly a rather cheesy theme restaurant called Down Mexico Way, this space (owned by the people behind the Gaucho Grill – *see p36*) has been transformed. It's gone upscale, with heavy tables, tiled walls, dim lighting and thick candelabra. The ground floor holds a trendy bar, the first floor an elegant restaurant and the second floor a nightclub. While the bar and club can be noisy and packed, the restaurant is lowkey. It also eschews the usual Tex-Mex trappings of cheese and heavy sauces piled on top of cheap cuts of meat; this was the lightest, most flavoursome Mexican food we've had this side of Texas. A starter of ceviche resembled a tangy cold stew, thick with prawns, molluscs and white fish. Steamed chicken tacos – mildly spiced chicken wrapped in tortillas – were perfect. Steak fajitas employed a good cut of meat (it was the first time we'd been asked how we wanted our fajita meat cooked), served with freshly made flour tortillas. Prices are reasonable; the atmosphere is excellent.
Babies and children admitted (restaurant only); high chair. Booking advisable. Music (DJs 6pm Mon-Sat). Separate room for parties, seats 14. **Map 17 J7**.

Trafalgar Square SW1

Texas Embassy Cantina
1 Cockspur Street, SW1Y 5DL (7925 0077/ www.texasembassy.com). Charing Cross tube/rail. **Meals served** noon-11pm Mon-Wed; noon-midnight Thur-Sat; noon-10.30pm Sun. **Main courses** £7.50-£16.95. **Service** 12.5% for parties of 6 or more. **Credit** AmEx, DC, MC, V.
The ground floor of this vast, two-storey restaurant was packed at lunchtime, but British accents were few and far between. Locals probably keep away because of the location at the edge of touristy Trafalgar Square, and the prices, which are a bit steep. It's probably not the food, which is imperfect but quite good, or the atmosphere, which is cheerily, authentically Texan: from the licence plates nailed to the wall, to the country music on the stereo. A starter of bean and cheese nachos was a good size, though cost £8.99. Best of all, it arrived piping hot, the cheese nicely stringy and the jalapeño peppers crisp. Pork deshebrada – two roasted pork tacos, with rice and beans – was a nice idea that didn't really work. The honey-roasted pork was too rich and strongly flavoured, and didn't mix well with the taco shells. Worse, it dripped grease on to the plate. Luckily, another main of barbecue ribs and chicken flautas (spiced chicken wrapped in tortillas and deep-fried) was delicious. A cooling dessert of cappuccino ice-cream may not have been particularly Tex-Mex, but was highly enjoyable nonetheless.
Babies and children welcome; children's menu; crayons; high chairs. Booking advisable. Disabled: toilet. Separate room for parties, seats 120. Tables outdoors (8, pavement). **Map 17 K7**.

South

Clapham SW4

Café Sol
56 Clapham High Street, SW4 7UL (7498 9319/www.cafesol.net). Clapham Common or Clapham North tube. **Meals served** noon-

Destino

midnight Mon-Thur, Sun; noon-2am Fri, Sat. **Main courses** £5.95-£9.95. **Service** 10% for parties of 6 or more. **Credit** AmEx, DC, MC, V.
This is a by-the-books Tex-Mex theme restaurant. The decor – all sunny colours and Mexican village scenes – is your first hint that no culinary surprises await. Sure enough, the food is the usual cheese-heavy fare (even the rice gets a sprinkling of cheese); there's the requisite complimentary small bowl of tortilla chips and salsa; and Corona beer is the regulation thirst-quencher. Once you understand this, though, there's no reason not to have a good time, as the mood is nice and cheery and the food is nice and reliable. The enchilada combo consisted of three enchiladas (beef, chicken, vegetables) served with rice and beans. Another main course of chicken fajitas arrived sizzling, with a big plate of accompaniments and four warm flour tortillas. For dessert, fragrant coconut ice-cream tasted like a holiday. The waitresses couldn't have been nicer, the music was at an acceptable level and the location on Clapham High Street is handy for most forms of transport.
Babies and children welcome; high chairs. Book dinner Fri, Sat. Tables outdoors (6, pavement). Takeaway service. **Map 22 B1**.

Pan-American

South West
Fulham SW6

★ **1492** NEW
2004 RUNNER-UP BEST LOCAL RESTAURANT
404 North End Road, SW6 1LU (7381 3810/ www.1492restaurant.com). Fulham Broadway tube. **Brunch served** 11am-3pm Sat, Sun. **Lunch served** 12.30-3pm Mon-Fri. **Dinner served** 6pm-midnight daily. **Main courses** £8.50-£17. **Service** 12.5%. **Credit** AmEx, MC, V.
Named after the year Columbus 'discovered' America, 1492 specialises in pan-Latin American food, offering dishes that hail from Mexico to the Caribbean. And they're the real thing: no tacky Tex-Mex or ponchos here. Burnt sienna paintwork, exposed brickwork, dark wood and colourful paintings provide a casual setting, and the South American staff are utterly charming – possibly the friendliest in London. Starters include two kinds of ceviche; the Mexican version, served atop a tortilla with guacamole, was tasty enough, but not as good as the tangy Peruvian. Many dishes have a touch of sweetness, from the creamily smooth Venezuelan black bean soup, via the tiger prawn and banana curry, to the Brazilian moqueca (a fabulous Bahian stew of white fish cooked with garlic, onions, tomatoes, red pepper, chilli and coconut milk, served with vatapá, a fluffy – and distinctly weird-tasting – dried shrimp purée). Steak (from Argentina and Uruguay) and chicken dishes (from Puerto Rico, Guatamala and Mexico) also appear on the menu. Decent cocktails are worth a go at £4.95 each (£3.50 for non-alcoholic, £6.80 for champagne cocktails). By the time we left, the place was packed – and deservedly so.
Babies and children welcome: children's menu; high chairs. Booking advisable. No smoking. Separate room for parties, seats 30. **Map 13 A13**.

South East
London Bridge & Borough SE1

★ **El Vergel**
8 Lant Street, SE1 1QR (7357 0057/www.elver gel.co.uk). Borough tube. **Meals served** 8.30am-3pm Mon-Fri. **Main courses** £3.80-£5.50. **No credit cards**.
Tucked down a side street behind Borough Market, El Vergel is a deservedly popular hole-in-the-wall café. Queues often snake down the road. Opening hours are limited to weekday breakfast and lunchtimes, but as well as standard sandwich bar

fare, you'll find several classic South American dishes. Menus are chalked on blackboards fixed to the funky, graffiti-covered walls. Place your order at the counter and then fight for one of the few tables inside or, if the sun is shining, grab a chair outside on the pavement. Steak sandwiches (churrascos), the house speciality, come with cheese or avocado and tomato salsa on fresh flatbread rolls. They're perfect: the steak is thin, tender and marinated in garlic, and the piquant salsa gives just the right kick. Empanadas filled with meat or spinach are tasty too, generously stuffed with olives and a bite of chilli. There's also a pleasing variety of sandwiches, plus chunky wedges of Spanish tortilla and full English breakfasts with a salsa and chorizo twist.
Babies and children welcome. No smoking. Tables outdoors (10, pavement). Takeaway service. Vegetarian menu. **Map 11 P9**.

North East
Hackney E8

★ **Armadillo**
41 Broadway Market, E8 4PH (7249 3633/ www.armadillorestaurant.co.uk). Bethnal Green tube then 106, 253 bus/26, 48, 55 bus. **Meals served** 6.30-10.30pm daily. **Main courses** £9.50-£16.50. **Service** 12.5% for parties of 5 or more. **Credit** AmEx, DC, JCB, MC, V.
Blond wood tables and assorted artefacts in recesses on the walls combine with soft Latin beats on the stereo to create an indisputably stylish but

satisfyingly laid-back atmosphere at this small place, the winner of the *Time Out* Best Local Restaurant award in 2003. The São Paulo-born chef, Rogerio David, has put together an eclectic and regularly changing menu, plundering a wide selection of ingredients and dishes from right across Latin America. We started with a mixed relish of feta, radishes, olives, yellow beetroot and jicama (aka Mexican potato, an unusual tuber with a crunchy texture and a slightly sweet, nutty flavour). Cheese and spring onion pasteizinhos followed: a kind of maize ravioli, with a delicious tomato vinaigrette to set it off. The maté tea-smoked quail, chorizo and sweet corn humitas were too dry, though. Main courses were simply thrilling. Argentinian fillet steak with churrasco and sautéed taro root was tender and came bursting with flavour, while fried sea bass with okra ratatouille was perfectly cooked and absolutely delicious. Service was relaxed but attentive, making the whole evening a pleasure. A highly recommended neighbourhood restaurant.
Babies and children welcome. Booking advisable; essential Fri, Sat. Separate room for parties, seats 30. Tables outdoors (4, garden; 1, balcony).

North
Islington N1

Sabor NEW
108 Essex Road, N1 8LX (7226 5551/ www.sabor.co.uk). Angel tube/Essex Road rail/bus 19, 38, 73. **Lunch served** noon-2.30pm, **dinner**

1492

served 6-10.30pm Mon-Sat. **Main courses** £7.50-£14.50. **Set lunch** £10 2 courses, £12.50 3 courses. **Credit** MC, V.

A sleekly modern interior, an interesting Latin American menu, and good-looking, friendly staff: what more could you want from a nuevo Latino restaurant? Quite a few things. Some peace, for a start: all those attractive hard surfaces make this one very loud dining room, especially when it fills with the most chatty of Islington's chattering classes. Second: a spanking good rendition of the food. We like the idea of rounding up great dishes from myriad sources such as Peru, Brazil, Colombia, Argentina and Chile, but only if the results are a success. Ceviche consisted of chewy monkfish swimming in citrus juices; we were unimpressed and left most of it uneaten. Another let-down was the swordfish escabeche: swordfish steak smothered in a strange, thick coating that resembled barbecue sauce. Other dishes also had good presentation, but disappointing flavour. Causa (a Peruvian dish of mashed potato layered with pieces of fish and vegetables) tasted bland. Empanaditas were tiny and pretty, yet not the genuine article either. However, two of our orders were moreish and perfectly prepared: quinoa salad; and Caipirinha, the Brazilian cachaça (rum-like) cocktail. Despite some dud or downright dull dishes, Sabor is a friendly and attractive place, and it's open all day as a café. It's certainly worth popping in for a drink, but keep your expectations low when it comes to ordering food.
Babies and children welcome; booster seats. Booking advisable. **Map 5 P1.**

Peruvian

South East

London Bridge & Borough SE1

Tito's

4-6 London Bridge Street, SE1 9SG (7407 7787). London Bridge tube/rail. **Lunch served** noon-3pm Mon-Fri. **Dinner served** 6-11pm Wed-Fri. **Meals served** noon-11pm Sat, Sun. **Main courses** £7.90-£13.50. **Set lunch** £7.90 3 courses. **Credit** AmEx, MC, V.

Entering Tito's is like walking into a backpacker restaurant in Peru. Located above a sandwich bar next to the hellish hustle of London Bridge station, it's decorated with touristy artefacts and a large mural of Machu Picchu. Cane tables are covered in white cloths, but can't hide the fact that the restaurant is slightly scruffy. The menu offers Peruvian classics, including seafood dishes and specialities like marinated heart. The number of Latin Americans dining here is testament to its authenticity. Chicken tamal – a cornflour patty wrapped in a banana leaf – was tasty and huge. Fish ceviche, equally large, provided a good kick of chilli and coriander. Main courses were excellent: lomo saltado (sautéed strips of steak and potatoes) was fresh and tasty, with lots of tomatoes and fried onions, while tender seco de cerdo (pork) came in a lovely coriander sauce, with

delicious refried beans. Peruvian food is not gourmet cuisine, and Tito's doesn't pretend to be anything that it isn't. If you're looking for a genuine taste of the Andes, and simple, well-cooked fare, it's a great spot.
Babies and children welcome; high chairs. Booking advisable Fri-Sun. Takeaway service. Vegetarian menu. **Map 12 Q8.**

Tower Bridge SE1

Fina Estampa

150 Tooley Street, SE1 2TU (7403 1342). London Bridge tube/rail. **Bar Open** noon-10pm Mon-Fri; 6-10pm Sat. *Restaurant* **Meals served** noon-10.30pm Mon-Fri, 6-10.30pm Sat. **Main courses** £7.95-£14.95. **Service** 10%. **Credit** AmEx, DC, MC, V.

Located just five minutes away from London Bridge station, Fina Estampa is an oasis of Peruvian charm with very welcoming staff. Enjoy a pre-dinner Pisco Sour (Peruvian brandy mixed with lime juice, sugar and egg white: Peru's signature drink) on one of the inviting leather sofas in the bar area, which boasts an excellent view that looks out over Tower Bridge. The restaurant at the back is small and intimate, with floor-length white tablecloths and Peruvian artefacts on the walls. Having enjoyed this place in the past, we were surprised that starters of ceviche (raw white fish marinated in lemon, onions and coriander) and papa a la huancaina (potatoes in a cheesy sauce) proved to be disappointing. The ceviche was overwhelmingly fishy, with little marinade to help it down. The potatoes were bland – and expensive at £5.95. Thankfully, main courses were a big improvement, bursting with flavour and varied textures. Beautifully cooked seco of chicken came with a light coriander sauce and delicious, thick stewed beans; lomo saltado consisted of strips of glazed beef stir-fried with chunky chips, red onions and tomatoes. There's a small but well-chosen Latin American wine list. Well worth a visit.
Babies and children admitted. Booking advisable; essential dinner Sat. Dress: smart casual. Takeaway service. **Map 12 Q8.**

Venezuelan

Central

Fitzrovia NW1

Café Sol y Luna NEW

103 Hampstead Road, NW1 3EL (7387 4064). Warren Street tube/Euston tube/rail. **Dinner served** 5-11pm Mon-Sat. **Main courses** £8-£13. **Tapas** £3-£4.50. **Service** 10% for parties of 4 or more. **Credit** MC, V.

As London's only Venezuelan restaurant, Sol y Luna might expect to be a hot destination. It's not, which seems doubly unfair given the friendly service and excellent food on offer. Sure, the plastic plantain plants might not be to everyone's taste, but the high-ceilinged ground-floor bar-restaurant is invitingly airy, with tropical hues adding vibrancy. More importantly, the food – a mixture of Caribbean and South American, with all the sweet notes such a combination suggests – is tasty, and pitched a notch above the homespun fare familiar to those who've experienced London's Latin American restaurant scene. The traditional cachapitas de jojoto starter offered three hot corn pancakes topped with melted mozzarella. To follow, asado negro a la antañona, a 19th-century colonial recipe, consisted of thick slices of beef, roasted with sugar cane to produce a dark, caramel glaze. It was good, but chalupas a la venezolana (corn pie filled with shredded chicken) won out, due to being given a decent counterpoint (in the shape of capers and olives) to take the edge off the sweetness. Desserts are limited, but, in all, Sol y Luna is worth trying. It's just a shame more diners haven't cottoned on.
Booking advisable. Separate room for parties, seats 30. **Map 3 J3.**

British

The past year has seen yet another interesting crop of new British restaurants springing up in the capital, from the excellently informal **Medcalf** to the suited sobriety of Gary Rhodes's new venture **Rhodes Twenty Four**, sited (guess where?) 24 floors above the City. You'll find inventive cooking, cutting-edge design and a bucolic setting at **Inn The Park**, plus great steaks, perfect roasts and quality chops everywhere from Fulham to Farringdon, not to mention the flashing tureens and Jeevesian swish of the hotel dining rooms. Trendy or traditional, it's all here – the only hard part is choosing where to go.

Central

City E1, EC2

Rhodes Twenty Four NEW
24th Floor, Tower 42, Old Broad Street, EC2N 1HQ (7877 7703/www.rhodes24.co.uk). Bank tube/Liverpool Street tube/rail. **Lunch served** noon-2.15pm, **dinner served** 6-8.30pm Mon-Fri. **Main courses** £11.60-£22.50. **Service** 12.5%. **Credit** AmEx, DC, MC, V.
Never mind location, 'windows, windows, windows' is the magic formula for success at this new venture from the spiky-haired chef. A wall of floor-to-ceiling glass eclipses the 24th-floor dining room's bland, beige interior with what must be some of the finest views in town. Norman Foster's Gherkin looms large in the foreground, with the rest of the Square Mile arranged like a miniature Toy Town at its feet. The menu is all about grass-roots British grub, with a roster of traditional recipes ingeniously updated. Macaroni cheese, for instance, is laced with truffles and served with chestnut mushrooms, watercress and rocket salad; pan-fried skate wing is elegantly partnered with langoustines, soft leeks and ham. And, of course, there's always the trademark jam roly-poly pudding. High points of a recent visit included a delicious own-made piccalilli served with a starter of warm smoked eel and English leaves, and a deeply satisfying main of mutton and onion suet pudding; less impressive was the sickly 'jaffa cake pudding'. You may have to look hard to find many cheap wines on the list, but the staff will be happy to assist you in your quest.
Babies and children admitted. Booking essential, 2-4 weeks in advance. Disabled: toilet. Dress: smart casual. **Map 12 Q6.**

St John Bread & Wine
94-96 Commercial Street, E1 6LZ (7247 8724/ www.stjohnbreadandwine.com). Aldgate East tube/Liverpool Street tube/rail. **Meals served** 8am-10.30pm Mon-Sat; 8am-10pm Sun. **Main courses** £11-£15. **Service** 12.5% for parties of 6 or more. **Credit** AmEx, MC, V.
The brasserie version of London's most idiosyncratic British restaurant, Bread & Wine is an endearingly miniaturised version of the original St John (*see below*): the Scrappy-Doo to Smithfield's Scooby. You'll find the same slaughterhouse aesthetic – white-painted bricks, plain wooden furniture, steel pipes – except here it's a little cosier. The menu's more relaxed too: not quite as blood-soaked as the original, which prides itself on using every part of the pig except the squeal. Instead, several dishes are available throughout the day: porridge and prunes for breakfast, say, or seed cake and a glass of Madeira for elevenses. Both lunch and dinner offerings range between gap-filling snacks (potted pork, smoked sprats with

horseradish) and full-blown main courses such as salt veal and carrots, or roast guinea fowl with chicory and watercress. A blackboard lists daily specials; on our last visit, Old Spot chop with own-made pickle was so good we ordered a second helping. Naturally, there's also fantastic bread (you can glimpse some impressive dough-kneading apparatus in the open kitchen). The wine list is an interesting selection of regional French bottles; both the house white and red are worth a punt.
Babies and children welcome: high chairs. Booking advisable. Takeaway service. **Map 12 S5.**

Clerkenwell & Farringdon EC1

★ Medcalf NEW
2004 WINNER BEST LOCAL RESTAURANT
40 Exmouth Market, EC1R 4QE (7833 3533). Angel tube/Farringdon tube/rail/38 bus. **Open** 10am-11pm Mon-Fri; 7-11pm Sat; noon-10.30pm Sun. **Food served** 10am-8.45pm Mon-Thur; 10am-7.45pm Fri; noon-5pm Sun. **Main courses** £8.50-£12. **Credit** MC, V.
This former butcher's shop pitches itself perfectly for the locale: by day it's a diner, offering breakfast and lunch to local workers; from mid-afternoon to mid-evening there's a bar menu; by night it's a drinking den, with DJs playing on Friday and Saturday nights. The wines are well chosen, the beer selection great (Erdinger weissbier on draught) and the staff charming, but it's the food that's the real winner. The short menu has first-class ingredients (mainly seasonal, often organic) treated simply so their quality shines through. Lunch starters included oysters; an excellent warm salad of artichokes, asparagus and rocket; and crab meat mixed with mascarpone, a fat dollop served on toast, with bright purple orach leaves. The pièce de résistance was the accompanying, fantastically intense tomato broth, served in a shot glass. For mains, seared Rossmore scallops (the biggest we've seen) came with broad bean and mint purée, bacon and roasted vine tomatoes – again, the individual flavours clear and bright. Don't miss the chunky chips, served with (bliss!) gravy, and finish with a classic pud (pavlova, vanilla ice-cream with hot chocolate sauce). Throw in an engaging rough and ready look, and Medcalf appeals on all counts.
Babies and children welcome (before 7pm). Bar available for hire. Disabled: toilet. Entertainment: DJs 7pm Fri, Sat. Tables outdoors (4, garden). **Map 5 N4.**

Quality Chop House
92-94 Farringdon Road, EC1R 3EA (7837 5093). Farringdon tube/rail. **Lunch served** noon-3pm Mon-Fri; noon-4pm Sun. **Dinner served** 6-11.30pm Mon-Sat; 7-11.30pm Sun. **Main courses** £6.95-£16.25. **Set lunch** (Mon-Fri) £9.95 2 courses. **Credit** AmEx, MC, V.
As its name suggests, the QCH is an updated, upgraded version of the working man's canteen. The cloth-cap aesthetic remains in such details as the black and white flooring, glass panels and the wooden booths of the twin dining rooms, but the proliferation of City suits at lunch leaves no doubt as to the more ambitious remit of the kitchen. A starter of tomato, roquefort and gruyère tart with mixed leaves made a tasty beginning, while an enormous salmon fish cake with spinach and sorrel sauce was a suitably impressive sequel. Other choices might include a simple but delicious main course of four lamb chops with chips and grilled tomatoes, or an unashamedly old-school serving of prawn cocktail spooned on to half an

avocado. Desserts are similarly unreconstructed – crème caramels, cheesecakes, sticky toffee puds and the like. There are decent wines by the glass, which, if combined with the £9.95 two-course lunch menu, can make for an exceedingly good-value meal. The friendly, competent waiters take the restaurant's watchwords of quality and civility (printed at the top of the menu) very seriously.
Babies and children welcome. Booking advisable. No-smoking tables. **Map 5 N4.**

★ St John
26 St John Street, EC1M 4AY (7251 0848/ 4998/www.stjohnrestaurant.com). Farringdon tube/rail.
Bar **Open/food served** 11am-11pm Mon-Fri; 6-11pm Sat. **Main courses** £3-£15.
Restaurant **Lunch served** noon-3pm Mon-Fri. **Dinner served** 6-11pm Mon-Sat. **Main courses** £13-£19. **Service** 12.5% for parties of 6 or more. **Credit** AmEx, DC, JCB, MC, V.
Its whitewashed walls, steel kitchen counters and telltale signs of a previous incarnation as a smoke house have won St John favour with carnivores in City suits. The daily menu doesn't bother with dish descriptions, but the professional and friendly service team is happy to offer all the explanations you might want. A pan-fried bacon chop, although tender, was let down by a mound of cloyingly sweet prune chutney. If pig's nose and tail, and deep-fried calf's brain are not for you, perhaps you'll be enticed by the few seasonal vegetarian choices that sing out from among the roast meats and braises. Our purple sprouting broccoli salad starter was appealingly crisp, and made memorable by a lovely vinaigrette dressings. Puds are to die for. We loved our wedge of treacle tart with its lemon-and-syrup-drenched breadcrumb filling. Fans of full-on meaty flavours, and fabulous nursery puddings, this spot is for you.
Babies and children welcome; high chair. Booking essential. Disabled: toilet. No cigars or pipes (restaurant). Separate room for parties, seats 18. **Map 5 O5.**

★ Top Floor at Smiths
Smiths of Smithfield, 67-77 Charterhouse Street, EC1M 6HJ (7251 7950/www.smithsof smithfield.co.uk). Farringdon tube/rail. **Lunch served** noon-3pm Mon-Fri; noon-3.45pm Sun. **Dinner served** 6.30-10.45pm Mon-Sat; 6.30-10.30pm Sun. **Main courses** £19-£28. **Set lunch** (Sun) £25 3 courses. **Service** 12.5%. **Credit** AmEx, DC, MC, V.
The icing on a three-tiered confection of bar, brasserie and high-end restaurant, Top Floor is a light, sophisticated dining room with splendidly Dickensian views of Farringdon's domes and rooftops. The main axis of the menu is a choice of fine meats from such distinguished suppliers as Islay Butchers and Chesterton Farm, which is unsurprising given the restaurant's location opposite Smithfield Market, but there are many non-carnivorous (and equally delicious) options. Our meal began with a beautifully judged starter of tender squid with roast chilli dressing; an omelette of tiger prawns, ginger and Thai basil was similarly impressive. There are plenty of choices for mains – ranging from loin of venison to roast halibut – but Top Floor's beef is renowned, and not to order it would seem a shame. The longhorn sirloin, for instance, is aged for 25 days; to take your first mouthful of that tender, juicy flesh with its braid of scorched, succulent fat is to know that good things do indeed come to those who wait. Puddings are as rich as the clientele looks, and the wine list is varied. If you're here in summer, bag a table on the charming terrace.
Babies and children welcome; high chairs. Booking advisable. Disabled: lift, toilet. Tables outdoors (8, terrace). **Map 11 O5.**

Covent Garden WC2

Rules
35 Maiden Lane, WC2E 7LB (7836 5314/ www.rules.co.uk). Covent Garden tube. **Meals served** noon-11.30pm Mon-Sat; noon-10.30pm Sun. **Main courses** £15.95-£19.95. **Credit** AmEx, DC, JCB, MC, V.

Loved by American tourists, tweedy out-of-towners and wealthy Londoners, Rules dines out on its claim to be London's oldest surviving restaurant. It certainly looks the part – you may find yourself eating under the scrutiny of a stuffed stag's head or a lordly buffer in a gilt frame – and if you're at all rich or famous, you can expect several staff members to drop by your red velvet banquette and politely enquire if everything's OK. The chances are that you'll answer in the affirmative: the cooking at Rules is nothing if not dependably good. Still fresh in our memory from a recent meal is a tasty starter of stilton and walnut tart with pear and apple chutney, while the smoked haddock fish cakes were among the best we've had (large petals of haddock on a vivid bed of buttered spinach). Puddings offer the reliable delights of classic sponges, tarts, mousses and the like. The wine list is especially strong on Rhône and Burgundy. As you'll see from the menu, the restaurant also has its own estate in the High Pennines, much to the wide-eyed delight of some of its Dubya-style customers.
Babies and children admitted; high chairs. Booking essential. Dress: smart casual. No smoking. Separate rooms for parties (phone 7379 0258), seating 12, 16, 18 and 24. **Map 18 L7.**

Fitzrovia W1

Stanleys
6 Little Portland Street, W1W 7JE (7462 0099/ www.stanleyslondon.com). Oxford Circus tube. **Meals served** noon-11pm Mon-Sat. **Main courses** £8.50-£10.95. **Service** 12.5% for parties of 6 or more. **Credit** AmEx, DC, MC, V.
To walk into Stanleys is to enter the gastro-heaven of the thirtysomething lad. On the menu: sausages and mash – but really nice bangers, mind. Behind the bar: beer, served in jugs. Serving the beer: waitresses, pretty ones mostly. To sit on: blokey leather banquettes. And so on. Basically, it's the set of the 'If Carlsberg made restaurants' ad that never got aired, and guess what? It works. In fact, it works a treat. Why wouldn't it? The grub is

fantastic: starters include the usual brasserie faves (maybe fish cakes, tapas or soup – cream of courgette and mint being a typical example), while main courses are dominated by a line-up of imaginative sausages. Italian pork and smoked pancetta sausage, for instance, comes with cannellini beans; turkey sausage comes with cranberry gravy; and the spicy lamb and pork version is paired with a pineapple salsa. Naturally, there are alternatives (everything from tuna steaks and chicken breasts to simple burgers), but that's not why the crowds flock here. They come for quality meat, stuffed in a tube, with a jug of Staropramen on the side. Who can blame them?
Babies and children welcome; high chairs. Book weekends. Disabled: toilet. No-smoking tables. **Map 9 J5.**

Knightsbridge SW1

Rib Room & Oyster Bar
Carlton Tower, 2 Cadogan Place, SW1X 9PY (7858 7053/www.carltontower.com). Knightsbridge tube. **Lunch served** 12.30-2.45pm daily. **Dinner served** 7-10.45pm Mon-Sat; 7-10.15pm Sun. **Main courses** £20-£35. **Set lunch** (Mon-Fri) £22 2 courses, £27 3 courses; (Sun) £38 3 courses. **Service** 12.5%. **Credit** AmEx, DC, MC, V.
It may have something to do with its location in a swanky Knightsbridge hotel, but the Rib Room tends to leave you with the feeling that you could have spent your money to greater effect elsewhere. It's a nice enough space (an elegant, breezy dining room with a long open kitchen) and the service is pleasant (albeit of the 'top up your glass every few seconds' school), but the food is a different matter. Starters are mostly the wrong side of a tenner, despite being a pretty ordinary selection of prawn cocktails, caesar salads, smoked salmon and the like. Some of the mains top the £30 mark. We opted for the set menu (with very limited choice) and found that our beef with all the trimmings had been replaced by a solitary, very ordinary steak, which required us to shell out for extra side orders

of spuds and an anaemic, carvery-style cauliflower cheese. Still, imaginative puddings like pear, ginger and honey crumble with pear sorbet earn their £7 price tags. The Oyster Bar seemed to be doing a brisk trade on the day we visited, whereas the Rib Room was left to us and a handful of business lunchers.
Babies and children admitted: high chairs. Booking advisable. Disabled: toilet. Dress: smart casual; no shorts; no trainers. Entertainment: pianist 7-10pm Mon-Sat. Separate room for parties, seats 10-18. **Map 14 F9.**

Mayfair W1

★ Dorchester Grill Room
The Dorchester, 53 Park Lane, W1A 2HJ (7317 6336/www.dorchesterhotel.com). Hyde Park Corner tube. **Breakfast served** 7-11am Mon-Sat; 7.30-11am Sun. **Lunch served** 12.30-2.30pm daily. **Dinner served** 6-11pm Mon-Sat; 7-10.30pm Sun. **Main courses** £21-£30. **Set lunch** (Mon-Sat) £22 2 courses incl coffee; £25.50 3 courses incl coffee; (Sun) £32.50 3 courses. **Set dinner** £39.50 3 courses incl coffee. **Credit** AmEx, DC, JCB, MC, V.
Resolutely old school and grand enough to induce a reverential hush among even the most boisterous diners, the Grill Room, with its splendid tapestries and ornate banquettes, makes a fabulous setting for what is invariably a fine feed. First comes the trolley of own-made breads to test your self-discipline, then a little something from the chef in the form of a dainty amuse-bouche (a shot glass of soup, say, or a tiny tartlet). From then on, each course is ferried to the table coyly hidden beneath flashing silver cloches, while sombre waiters congratulate you on your choices and the sommelier guides you with shamanic aplomb through his wine list. Highlights from a recent meal were a garden-fresh cream of artichoke soup, a delicate main course of royal bream on a bed of mussels and lobster, and the signature dish of ribeye of beef with peerless yorkshire pudding. The dessert trolley – two storeys of wobbly jellies, creamy gateaux and fresh fruit – is impossible to

Rhodes Twenty Four

Medcalf. See p42.

resist. Cheeses are well kept and also worth saving room for. One last tip: take your coffee in the lobby (possibly the grandest in town).
Babies and children welcome; high chairs. Booking advisable; essential weekends 1 week in advance. Disabled: toilet. Dress: smart casual. Vegetarian menu. **Map 9 G7**.

The Guinea Grill
30 Bruton Place, W1J 6NL (7499 1210/ www.youngs.co.uk). Bond Street or Green Park tube.
Pub **Open** 11am-11pm Mon-Fri; 6.30-11pm Sat. **Food served** noon-2.30pm Mon-Fri. **Bar snacks** £6.50-£6.95.
Restaurant **Lunch served** 12.30-2.30pm Mon-Fri. **Dinner served** 6.30-11pm Mon-Sat. **Main courses** £11.50-£27. **Cover** £1.50. **Service** 12.5%. **Credit** AmEx, DC, JCB, MC, V.
If pies have a spiritual home, this must surely be it. So adept are the Guinea Grill's chefs at plonking pastry lids on well-flavoured fillings that they have been crowned not once, not twice but three times 'National Steak & Kidney Pie Champions'. An impressive feat, but the best was yet to come. In 2000, the Mayfair pie-makers hit an all-time high

as they found themselves clearing space in the trophy cabinet for the Steak Pie of the Century Award. And having once again broken the crust of a steak and mushroom offering, we can add ours to the list of congratulations – plenty of meat, feather-light pastry, rich gravy: the works. You'll also find various fish dishes (roast monkfish wrapped in cured ham was the tasty opposite number to our pie), plus lamb shank, pork belly and steaks. Among the starters, Cornish crab soup with a nippy rouille is always a good bet. Desserts are appealing too (though pie-eaters will find they won't have room for anything too ambitious), and this being a Young's pub, you can get a decent pint as well as a fair choice of wines.
Booking essential (restaurant). No cigar/pipes area. No piped music or jukebox. Separate room for parties, seats 20. **Map 9 H7**.

Piccadilly W1

Fortnum & Mason
181 Piccadilly, W1A 1ER (7734 8040/ www.fortnumandmason.co.uk). Green Park or Piccadilly Circus tube.

Fountain (ext 2492) **Breakfast served** 8.30-11.30am, **meals served** 11.30am-7.45pm Mon-Sat. **Main courses** £9-£24.
St James's (ext 2241) **Morning coffee served** 10am-noon, **lunch served** noon-2pm, **afternoon tea served** 3-5.30pm Tue-Sat. **Set lunch** £20 2 courses, £23 3 courses.
Both **Service** 12.5%. **Credit** AmEx, DC, JCB, MC, V.
There are two restaurants in this department store so beloved of those in search of presents for grannies, dignified mothers, maiden aunts and other members of the headscarf sisterhood. We avoided the more formal St James's Restaurant and ate instead at the Fountain, which looks as if it has been furnished by someone who enjoys sitting in conservatories, doing jigsaw puzzles, dabbling in watercolours and so on. And very nice it was too. From the all-day menu, the classic calf's liver, bacon, mash and onion gravy combo was a winning version with a rich, sticky pool of sauce. Blackened salmon with mash, garlic spinach and spicy tomato sauce was a nicely tamed version of a Cajun classic. Desserts are homely and wholly satisfying: blackberry and

pear crumble with clotted cream seemed to bring with it the smell of a country kitchen and the drone of bees in a rose garden; sundaes such as Knickerbocker Glory and Dusty Road provide grandparents with a final chance to crank up the little 'uns' sugar levels one notch further before handing them back to Mum and Dad.
Babies and children welcome; high chairs. Booking advisable. Dress: smart casual; no shorts. No-smoking tables (Fountain only). Separate room for parties, seats 32. **Map 17 J7**.

Soho W1

Atlantic Bar & Grill

20 Glasshouse Street, W1B 5DJ (7734 4888/ www.atlanticbarandgrill.com). Piccadilly Circus tube.
Bar **Open** noon-3am Mon-Sat.
Restaurant **Lunch served** noon-3pm Mon-Fri. **Dinner served** 6-11.30pm Mon-Sat. **Main courses** £11.50-£18.50. **Set dinner** (6-7pm Mon-Fri) £14.50 2 courses, £16.50 3 courses. **Service** 12.5%.
Both **Credit** AmEx, DC, MC, V.
Ten years ago, when Brad was pushing past Keanu to get to the front of the queue here, the velvet rope routine undoubtedly had its place. But now that all seems a little bit silly. Having given your name to the clipboard-clutcher (and been eyeballed by the doormen), you make your way downstairs to find the place is half empty. Sure, the Atlantic still looks the part (the dining room is grand, red and chandelier-ed), but the A-list boys have disappeared – so why hasn't the attitude? That question aside, the Atlantic remains a rather nice place for a meal. The food, for one thing, is pretty much always on the money. A starter of Atlantic chowder of langoustine, mussels, clams, sea bass and pancetta was a delicious meal in itself (and worth its hefty price tag of £12.50), while a main course of grilled Buccleuch sirloin with watercress, own-made fries and béarnaise was a tender lump of beautifully marbled meat. This left no room for desserts, but a double espresso was clearly a product of very high-quality coffee. So, great food, charming service and a fab wine list, just a shame about the circus at the door.
Babies and children welcome. Booking advisable. Dress: smart casual; no trainers. Entertainment: DJ 10pm Fri, Sat. Separate room for parties, seats 70. **Map 17 J7**.

★ Lindsay House

21 Romilly Street, W1V 5AF (7439 0450/ www.lindsayhouse.co.uk). Leicester Square tube. **Lunch served** noon-2.30pm Mon-Fri. **Dinner served** 6-11pm Mon-Sat. **Main courses** (lunch) £18-£22. **Set meal** (6-6.45pm Mon-Sat) £24 2 courses, £29.50 3 courses. **Set dinner** £48 3 courses. **Credit** AmEx, DC, MC, V.
To be buzzed into this elegant restaurant (and there is a buzzer; it deters the riff-raff, you see) is to be given a passport to a world where cured foie gras is rolled in spiced gingerbread, where butter-poached haddock comes with parsnip cream, and where ordinary cheeses are usurped by the likes of stinking bishop with brioche. Such high-quality ingredients are carefully sourced, often from Irish producers and often by the chef himself (Richard Corrigan is known for his hands-on approach). Once the produce reaches the kitchen it is given a thorough and imaginative seeing-to. Creamed risotto of marinated ceps, for instance, was the highlight of a recent visit. Of the two dining rooms, the ground-floor space is more intimate, but they both share a pared-down aesthetic (bare floorboards, muted colour scheme). Staff strike the right balance between being pleased to see you and being happy to leave you alone; the wine list achieves a similar harmony between quality and price. One last thing: do your bit to keep gluttony on Soho's roster of deadly sins and try the £59 tasting menu. You won't regret it.
Babies and children admitted. Booking advisable. Dress: smart casual. Separate rooms for parties, seating 8, 14 and 20. Vegetarian menu. **Map 17 K6**.

St James's SW1

Wiltons

55 Jermyn Street, SW1Y 6LX (7629 9955/ www.wiltons.co.uk). Green Park or Piccadilly Circus tube. **Lunch served** 12.30-2.30pm, **dinner served** 6.30-10.30pm Mon-Fri. **Main courses** £16-£50. **Credit** AmEx, DC, MC, V.
Where to begin? Let's try this for starters: if you take your jacket off in the dining room at Wiltons, someone will come and tell you to put it back on. 'So what?' you might say, 'It's a formal restaurant; some people like that.' Fair enough. But what about this: a starter of smoked wild salmon costs £17; main-course grilled dover sole costs £28. Or this: grilled turbot for 40 quid. It's not just that these are high prices – after all, you won't find many restaurants with Wiltons' postcode serving bargain-basement nosh – but what you get for your moolah is pretty ordinary grub. Still, that's not the point, is it? In reality, the kind of people who come to sit (jackets on) in this clubby dining room consider it worthwhile because they can order dishes like dover sole 'Silver Jubilee' (cooked the way Her Maj likes it) and they can look around and see other people who are doing the same kind of thing. In a nutshell then: expensive fish restaurant seeks rich clients for jacket-wearing, eating food the Queen apparently likes, and maybe more.
Babies and children admitted. Booking advisable; essential Mon-Thur. Disabled: toilet. Dress: jacket; no jeans or trainers. Separate room for parties, seats 18. **Map 17 J7**.

Inn The Park `NEW`

St James's Park, SW1A 2BJ (7451 9999/ www.innthepark.co.uk). Green Park or Piccadilly Circus tube. **Breakfast served** 8am-11am Mon-Fri; 9-11am Sat, Sun. **Lunch served** noon-3pm Mon-Fri; noon-4pm Sat, Sun. **Dinner served** 6-10.30pm daily. **Main courses** £8.50-£17.50. **Credit** AmEx, MC, V.
This striking new venture in St James's Park has a true roll-call of British talent. Food comes courtesy of restaurateur Oliver Peyton; the striking wooden building, partly covered by a turf roof, with a sweeping glass front and veranda, is by architect Michael Hopkins; while the chic, if sauna-like interior is by Tom Dixon (of Habitat fame). There's an all-day café menu – breakfast, self-service snacks, afternoon tea – but for lunch and dinner the place becomes a full-blown restaurant serving produce-led, seasonal British dishes. We liked the Bury black pudding, served as a starter with beetroot, poached egg and watercress salad. Pollock deep-fried in beer batter was perfect, served with fresh pea mash. Neal's Yard cheeses, and a traditional prawn cocktail were also hits. Other dishes disappointed. Mixed fish grill amounted to a few small, scrap-like pieces, while chocolate truffle cake tasted little better than mass-produced versions. And if the kitchen goes to the trouble of sourcing rare-breed pork, you'd hope it would be cooked properly; ours was overdone. To be fair, the Inn had only just opened when we visited, and should have no doubt settled down.
Babies and children welcome; high chairs, toys. Booking advisable. Disabled: toilet. No smoking (indoors). Tables outdoors (20, terrace). Takeaway service. Vegan dishes. **Map 10 K8**.

Strand WC2

The Savoy Grill

The Savoy, Strand, WC2R 0EU (7420 2065/ www.gordonramsay.com). Covent Garden or Embankment tube/Charing Cross tube/rail. **Lunch served** noon-2.45pm Mon-Fri; noon-3pm Sat, Sun. **Dinner served** 5.45-11pm Mon-Sat; 6-10.30pm Sun. **Set meal** (lunch, 5.45-6.45pm Mon-Sat) £30 3 courses. **Set dinner** £50 3 courses, £60 tasting menu (7-11pm Mon-Sat). **Credit** AmEx, MC, V.
Where the fat cats come to ensure they don't get any slimmer, the Savoy Grill is still favoured by the old guard despite Marcus Wareing's rejuvenation of its menu. At lunch, the work of Savile Row tailors is amply displayed, while the futures of

Harley Street cardiologists are steadily secured. The dining room has lost none of its subdued glamour over the years (somewhere amid the buzz of conversation, big deals are surely being made). The sense of occasion is heightened by staff who know how to make themselves available without being present at every mouthful. Pre-prandial amuse-bouches are thoughtfully explained, as is the menu proper and the wine list. Highlights of our meal were a wonderfully rich starter of rillette of Scottish salmon with avocado purée, frisée salad and chives, and a brace of delicious mains (steamed fillet of sea bass with parma ham tortellini; marinated leg of rabbit with herb gnocchi). Warm rice pudding with poached pear and dark chocolate sorbet seemed like a weak finish, but in the context of any other meal would probably have been outstanding. A definite winner, then.
Babies and children welcome; high chairs. Booking essential. Disabled: toilet. Dress: jacket; no denim or trainers. Vegetarian menu. Vegan dishes. **Map 18 L7**.

Simpson's-in-the-Strand

100 Strand, WC2R 0EW (7836 9112/ www.simpsons-in-the-strand.com). Embankment tube/Charing Cross tube/rail. **Breakfast served** 7.15-10.30am Mon-Fri. **Lunch served** 12.15-2.30pm Mon-Sat; noon-3pm Sun. **Dinner served** 5.30-10.45pm Mon-Sat; (Grand Divan) 6-8.30pm Sun. **Main courses** £19.50-£23.50. **Set breakfast** £15.50-£17.50. **Set meal** £15.50 2 courses, £18.75 3 courses. **Service** 12.5%. **Credit** AmEx, DC, JCB, MC, V.
Tailor-made for starched-collar dining, the expansive Grand Divan is a formidable hall with high ceilings, dark wood panelling and crisp white table linen. It is popular with wealthy tourists, and a haunt of wine-swilling power brokers on gravy-train expense accounts. Simpson's has panache even if the cooking does occasionally dip to boarding-school standards. Service is always professional, remaining friendly and efficient even when the restaurant gets busy. Best bets are the great hunks of roast beef, carved at the table from the gleaming trolley. Our generous helping, juicy and tender, was top-notch, but let down by overcooked vegetables and lacklustre gravy. Pumpkin soup was thick, creamy, and comforting, yet with only the barest hint of enticing spice. Good old-fashioned treacle pudding won us over; the soft sponge, crowned with sticky syrup and surrounded by a moat of own-made custard, was – like the restaurant – endearingly nostalgic.
Babies and children welcome. Booking advisable. Disabled: toilet. Dress: smart casual. Separate rooms for parties, seating 50 and 120. **Map 18 L7**.

Victoria SW1

Boisdale

13 Eccleston Street, SW1W 9LX (7730 6922/ www.boisdale.co.uk). Victoria tube/rail.
Bar **Open** noon-1am Mon-Fri; 7pm-1am Sat. **Snacks** £6-£14. **Admission** £10 (£3.95 if already on premises) after 10pm Mon-Sat.
Restaurant **Lunch served** noon-2.30pm Mon-Fri. **Dinner served** 7-11pm Mon-Sat. **Main courses** £15-£27. **Set lunch** £14 2 courses. **Set meal** £17.45 2 courses. **Service** 12.5%.
Both **Credit** AmEx, DC, MC, V.
This restaurant may well have tartan-upholstered chairs, and waitresses in kilts; it may even have Macsween haggis on the menu, but somehow it manages to avoid any suggestion of tackiness. Sure, Boisdale wears its Scottishness on its sporran, but the place also has other strings to its bow – such as regular jazz performances, or an intimate bar just made for enjoying that final little dram before the long journey home. But the menu is an undoubted draw too, featuring an impressive roster of ingredients sourced directly from Scotland. A starter of marinated Orkney herring, for instance, is served with an earthy roast beetroot and leaf salad, while salad of hot-smoked wild Rannoch Moor venison is wonderfully rich in its tarragon and truffle dressing. Mains are centred on a decent choice of superb Aberdeen Angus steaks,

but also stretch to more eclectic dishes such as slow-roasted pork belly with puy lentils, caramelised apples and cider sauce. Puddings are sinful (baked banana cheesecake with rum and butterscotch sauce), and the collection of cigars and whiskies is an epicure's dream.
Babies and children admitted. Function rooms. Entertainment: jazz 10pm-midnight Mon-Sat. Tables outdoors (4, conservatory). **Map 15 H10. For branch see index.**

The Goring Hotel
Beeston Place, Grosvenor Gardens, SW1W 0JW (7396 9000/www.goringhotel.co.uk). Victoria tube/rail.
Bar Open 24hrs daily.
Restaurant Breakfast served 7-10am Mon-Sat; 7.30-10.30am Sun. **Lunch served** 12.30-2.30pm Mon-Fri, Sun. **Dinner served** 6-10pm daily. **Set lunch** £26 2 courses, £29.50 3 courses; (Sun) £24 2 courses. **Set dinner** £34 2 courses, £40 3 courses. **Service** 12.5%. **Credit** AmEx, DC, MC, V.
Football managers of the 'man marking' school of tactics could learn a thing or two from the waiters at this stately hotel dining room, where guests are treated with an attentiveness that is nothing short of extreme. What's more, the setting is one of rather stifling traditionalism – albeit with a certain note of grandeur (chandeliers illuminate the hotel-like fabrics). But it's the cooking that counts, and, (perhaps somewhat surprisingly) the menu here comes up trumps with a range of simple but deftly rendered classics. Best end of lamb, for instance, arrives in a brioche crust, nicely pink and tender, while fillet of haddock is served with a perfectly poached egg and a nip of horseradish sauce. Among the starters, dressed Cornish crab and smoked Somerset eel are typical dishes; the care that has been taken to source ingredients is evident in every mouthful. Desserts come on a trolley and the wines are chosen from a substantial list, which certainly doesn't lack opportunities for those who are keen to part with their cash.
Babies and children welcome (lounge area). Disabled: toilet. No-smoking tables. No piped music or jukebox. **Map 15 H10.**

Westminster SW1

Shepherd's
Marsham Court, Marsham Street, SW1P 4LA (7834 9552/www.langansrestaurants.co.uk). Pimlico or Westminster tube. **Lunch served** 12.30-2.45pm, **dinner served** 6.30-11pm Mon-Fri. **Main courses** £19.50. **Set meal** £26 2 courses incl coffee, £29 3 courses incl coffee. **Service** 12.5%. **Credit** AmEx, DC, JCB, MC, V.
While we wouldn't dare make jokes about tax payers' money, it's safe to say that a great many politicos make Shepherd's their restaurant of

---

Best of British

For steaks
Dorchester Grill Room (*see p43*), **Notting Grill** (*see above*), **Popeseye Steak House** (*see above*), **Top Floor at Smiths** (*see p42*).

For taking an old biddy
The Goring Hotel (*see above*), **Rules** (*see p42*), **Wiltons** (*see p45*).

For impressing a young hottie
Atlantic Bar & Grill (*see p45*), **Lindsay House** (*see p45*), **Medcalf** (*see p42*).

For doing deals
Butlers Wharf Chop House (*see p48*), **Rhodes Twenty Four** (*see p42*), **Shepherd's** (*see above*), **Top Floor at Smiths** (*see p42*).

For pies and sausages
The Guinea Grill (*see p44*), **Stanleys** (*see p43*).

---

choice when taking time out from the corridors of power across the road. The space itself is nice enough (the kind of sober, clubby dining room you might expect, with one or two private rooms that are often in full swing at lunchtime), and the food is also no great surprise given that one of the faces on the menu is that of the late Mr Langan. Brasserie faves come to the fore, as in a pleasantly creamy starter of stilton and onion tart (although the house caesar salad was a little too fishy for our taste). Mains run to pies, fish cakes and cumberland sausages, with the odd maize-fed chicken breast thrown in for good measure. We greatly enjoyed a pink and juicy marinated lamb steak during a recent meal, and have had pleasurable experiences with the roast trolley in the past. Puddings are a more sophisticated version of what they were at school (but we'd never dream of saying the same about the clientele).
Babies and children welcome. Booking advisable. No-smoking tables. Separate room for parties, seats 32. **Map 16 K10.**

West

Holland Park W11

★ Notting Grill
123A Clarendon Road, W11 4JG (7229 1500/ www.awtonline.co.uk). Holland Park tube.
Bar Open 6.30-11pm Mon-Thur; 6.30pm-midnight Fri, Sat; noon-10.30pm Sun.
Restaurant **Brunch served** noon-4pm Sat, Sun. **Dinner served** 6.30-10.30pm Mon-Thur; 6.30-11.30pm Fri, Sat; 4-10pm Sun. **Main courses** £12-£25. **Service** 12.5%.
Both **Credit** AmEx, JCB, MC, V.
Cosy and inviting, Notting Grill feels like a smart neighbourhood pub with a spacious dining area, open kitchen and brick-fronted bar. Celebrity chef Antony Worrall Thompson can usually be seen fronting kitchen affairs two nights a week. The restaurant's claim to culinary fame lies in its sizzling steaks and grills, tastefully supported by a generous and varied wine list. Regulars here are likely to be wealthy and to have expensive tastes. A timbale of white crab meat made a refreshing, clean-tasting starter, the juicy crab flakes working well with dollops of mango-studded sweet chilli chutney. Our gold star, however, went to the steak au poivre – a meltingly soft fillet crusted with sharp but not pungent peppercorns, surrounded by a sublime, brandy-laced cream sauce. Salt marsh lamb chops were impressive too: dark-glazed on the outside; pink, sweet-tasting flesh within. Only a pudding of banoffi pie fell short of expectations, with its lacklustre caramel sauce filling. Despite the occasional gripe, we found few faults with the food, and the service is smooth, well informed and friendly.
Babies and children welcome; high chairs. Booking advisable. No-smoking tables. Separate room for parties, seats 80. Tables outdoors (6, terrace; closes 10pm). **Map 19 A4. For branch (Kew Grill) see index.**

Kensington W8

Maggie Jones's
6 Old Court Place, Kensington Church Street, W8 4PL (7937 6462). High Street Kensington tube. **Lunch served** 12.30-2.30pm daily. **Dinner served** 6.30-11pm Mon-Sat; 6.30-10.30pm Sun. **Main courses** £5.20-£8.95 lunch, £7-£19.50 dinner. **Set lunch** £15.50 3 courses. **Cover** £1 (dinner). **Service** 12.5%. **Credit** AmEx, DC, JCB, MC, V.
Eccentric but loveable, Maggie Jones's is crammed with wicker baskets, bunches of dried flowers, and an assortment of farming tools. Flickering candles, chunky wooden tables and an occasional church pew add to the quirky nature of this sprawling venue. Staff are a cheerful bunch, gently directing customers looking for privacy to the relative calm of the alcoves. These are sited a fair distance away from the boisterous office groups and families with excitable young children. Cooking isn't adventurous or memorable, but it is hearty. Fisherman's pie was satisfying in a homely way,

---

without being stodgy: flaky chunks of perfectly cooked white fish, cloaked in creamy white sauce, came topped with dollops of silky-smooth mashed potato. Puddings aren't much to write home about. Crème brûlée was more in line with milky baked custard instead of a calorie-laden treat. At least you'll find rustic charm here, even if the cooking isn't to everyone's taste.
Babies and children welcome; high chairs. Booking advisable. Disabled: toilet. **Map 7 B8.**

Olympia W14

Popeseye Steak House
108 Blythe Road , W14 0HD (7610 4578). Olympia tube/rail. **Dinner served** 7-10.30pm Mon-Sat. **Main courses** £9.95-£45.50. **Service** 12.5%. **No credit cards.**
If you don't like steak, you may as well stop reading now; this place is definitely not for you. But if sinking your teeth into a fine cut of quality cow is your idea of a good time, welcome to paradise. That's not to suggest that Popeseye is a swanky joint; in fact, it's something of a curiosity. The dark floorboards and white walls seem to belong in a Soho bistro, while the sight of the proprietor merrily cooking away in a corner of the small dining room conjures up a kind of holiday feel, a bit like being in a Greek taverna. The menu is wonderfully direct in its approach, offering nothing more than various weights and cuts of steak, all of which are served with the mandatory chips and the option of a heavily dressed green salad. The prices might look a bit hefty, but you'll know where the money was spent as soon as you take your first mouthful. Clove-spiked apple crumble is typical of the tasty desserts, while the inexpensive house red makes for a fine accompanying slurp.
Babies and children admitted. Booking advisable. **For branch see index.**

South West

Chelsea SW3

Foxtrot Oscar
79 Royal Hospital Road, SW3 4HN (7352 7179). Sloane Square tube/11, 239 bus. **Lunch served** 12.30-2.30pm Mon-Fri; 12.30-3.30pm Sat; 12.30-4pm Sun. **Dinner served** 7-11pm Mon-Sat. **Main courses** £7.95-£13.50. **Service** 12.5%. **Credit** MC, V.
Despite paper napkins on the tables, football on the telly and cheeseburgers on the menu, this spot is actually a jolly smart Chelsea restaurant. The wooden floor, exposed brick walls and well-stocked cocktail bar provide an elegant setting for backslapping bonhomie among the suited regulars. Paintings (on loan from an art gallery) hang on the walls, providing food for thought while the well-heeled customers dip their french fries into ketchup. Cooking is tame. A decent mediterranean salad, with olive-oil-anointed courgettes and peppers, made a fresh and flavoursome start to supper. Our main course wasn't such a hit; chicken breast filled with mozzarella, pesto and tomatoes lacked bite and seemed like a 1970s-style British take on Italian cooking. Top marks to the chocolate pecan pie, though, for its super-squishy chocolate sponge and retro swirl of whipped cream on the side. Given the pricey location, Foxtrot Oscar is great value for money. Service is spot on too.
Babies and children welcome; high chairs. Booking advisable. Separate room for parties, seats 30. **Map 14 F12.**

Fulham SW10

Sophie's Steakhouse & Bar
311-313 Fulham Road, SW10 9QH (7352 0088/www.sophiessteakhouse.com). South Kensington tube. **Meals served** noon-11.45pm Mon-Fri; 11am-11.45pm Sat; 11am-10.45pm Sun. **Main courses** £6.95-£16.50. **Set meal** (noon-6pm Mon-Fri) £9.95 2 courses. **Service** 12.5% for parties of 5 or more. **Credit** AmEx, MC, V.

Inn The Park. See p45.

There are two reasons for visiting this thriving steakhouse. The first, and happily the most common, is to try the excellent brasserie food and enjoy some efficient service from the friendly staff. The second seems only to apply to a species of pure-bred Sloane indigenous to the area; it involves showing off your newest pink shirt while talking loud, offensive drivel to similarly attired acquaintances. Noisy neighbours notwithstanding, this brick, banquettes and bare boards diner can generate a fun buzz, especially at weekends when it always appears to be full. The food is superb. The chicken in a caesar salad had the mouth-watering whiff of the charcoal grill; another starter of Cornish crab salad with basil, coriander and mayonnaise was a delicate assembly job of clean, fresh flavours. A few specials are chalked up on the board, but a perennial favourite of ours is the house fillet steak, which comes with chips and a heavenly sauce of the chef's own devising; it is best consumed with one of the expertly dressed green salads. Puds are good too. Wines are available just as freely by the glass as by the bottle. *Babies and children welcome; children's menu; high chairs. Disabled: toilet. Tables outdoors (10, pavement).* **Map 14 D12.**

South

Battersea SW11

Jack's Place

12 York Road, SW11 3QA (7228 8519). Clapham Junction rail. **Lunch served** (Sept-Easter) noon-3pm Sun. **Dinner served** 6-11pm Tue-Sat. **Main courses** £10.50-£18.50. **Set lunch** (Sun Sept-Easter) £17.50 3 courses. **Service** 10%. **Credit** MC, V.
If you're at all hazy about the definition of the phrase 'proper geezer', one glance at the septuagenarian Jack, erstwhile fairground boxer-turned-restaurateur, should be enough to set you straight. Clad in apron, braces and shirtsleeves, he chats amiably with diners while maintaining a sparky banter with his staff (who are, of course, all members of his family). The place itself is like a family album come to life – dozens of framed

photos compete for space with all manner of memorabilia (check out the hat collection by the door). Best of all is the menu, whose list of prawn cocktails, melon and parma ham, and numerous cuts and styles of steak reads like a Best Of… 1970s Dining. And very good it is too – dressed crab was wonderfully fresh, and a main course of steak chasseur was perfectly cooked and smothered in a rich, tasty sauce. Portions are huge and prices are kind to the wallet (the wine list, in particular, is great value, if limited). Jack's Place is an example of the kind of good-quality working-class catering that seems so prevalent in other countries and so frequently lacking in our own. *Babies and children admitted. Booking essential lunch; advisable dinner. Vegetarian menu.* **Map 21 B2.**

South East

East Dulwich SE22

Franklins

157 Lordship Lane, SE22 8HX (8299 9598). East Dulwich rail. **Open** noon-11pm Mon-Wed; noon-midnight Thur-Sat; noon-10.30pm Sun. **Main courses** £11-£15. **Set lunch** (noon-5pm Mon-Fri) £9 2 courses, £12 3 courses. **Credit** AmEx, MC, V.
Having snatched the crown from Le Chardon further down Lordship Lane, Franklins now seems to be the restaurant of choice among the discerning punters of East Dulwich. Its modern take on British food is by now a familiar one, but the daily menu here is more imaginative than most and the kitchen proves to be consistently capable of delivering the goods. Our latest meal got off to a flying start with a deliciously meaty hors d'oeuvre of soused mackerel, potato and bacon. A main course of succulent baked ham with garlicky dauphinoise did nothing to lower the standards. Also impressive was a second main of lamb leg served with creamed spinach; ditto, seasonal side orders of buttery sprout tops and firm, earthy charlotte spuds. To finish, chocolate tart and mint sorbet was like the After Eight mothership. The setting is also nicely in tune with the laid-back but

elegant esprit of the place. Everything from the bright, open-plan dining room to the wood-panelled bar area that adjoins it conspires to put you at your ease. Staff are charming, with the odd grumpy exception. *Babies and children welcome; high chairs. Disabled: toilet. Separate room for parties, seats 30. Booking advisable weekends. Tables outdoors (3, pavement).* **Map 23 C4.**

Tower Bridge SE1

Butlers Wharf Chop House

Butlers Wharf Building, 36E Shad Thames, SE1 2YE (7403 3403/www.conran.com). London Bridge tube/rail/Tower Gateway DLR/ 47, 78, 142, 188 bus. *Bar* **Open** noon-3pm, 6-11pm Mon-Sat; noon-4pm Sun. **Brunch served** noon-4pm Sat, Sun. **Set brunch** (Sat, Sun) £13.95 2 courses, £16.95 3 courses. **Set meal** (noon-3pm, 6-11pm Mon-Fri; 6-11pm Sat) £9 2 courses, £11 3 courses. *Restaurant* **Lunch served** noon-3pm daily. **Dinner served** 6-11pm Mon-Sat. **Main courses** £12.50-£17. **Set lunch** £19.75 2 courses, £23.75 3 courses. *Both* **Service** 12.5%. **Credit** AmEx, DC, JCB, MC, V.
While it's quite apparent that Sir Tel is the éminence grise behind this riverside restaurant, the Chop House has a touch more individuality than some of the other more uniform stops on the Conran express. From the idiosyncratic meat cleaver emblem to the sunny decor and picture-postcard views of Tower Bridge, this whole operation comes across as bright and lively – both qualities that are reflected in the attitude of the eager, helpful staff. A recent starter of warm leek and wensleydale tart with tomato and shallots was a simple but effective combination of flavours and textures. Nevertheless, it was the main course of steak and kidney pudding that stole the show: one of the best versions we've tasted. Desserts appear on the menu alongside their ideal partner of sticky wine, but we enjoyed our trifle well enough on its own. One last thing: don't be surprised to find yourself within earshot of a rowdy office party, particularly towards the end of the week. *Booking advisable. Dress: smart casual. Tables outdoors (12, terrace). Vegan dishes.* **Map 12 R8.**

East

Shoreditch EC2

Rivington Bar & Grill

28-30 Rivington Street, EC2A 3DZ (7729 7053). Liverpool Street or Old Street tube/rail. *Bar* **Open/food served** noon-midnight Mon-Sat; noon-11pm Sun. *Restaurant* **Brunch served** noon-4.30pm Sun. **Lunch served** noon-3pm Mon-Fri. **Dinner served** 6-11pm daily. **Main courses** £8.50-£18.50. **Service** 12.5%. **Credit** AmEx, DC, MC, V.
As you'd expect from one of the trendiest corners of an already achingly trendy part of town, the Rivington is a pretty cool operation – and it knows it. The walls are white (except for the occasional, tasteful nude portrait); the venetian blinds are dark; the light fittings sport hip little shades. In summer, the blinds are open, allowing light to flood into the room (not to mention views of the odd Nathan Barley type en route to the Bricklayer's Arms, just a short micro-scoot down the street). A short list of snacks offers some tasty, reasonably priced gap-fillers such as suckling pig bap with bramley apple sauce, but the real action is to be found on the main menu. Wonderful soups like smoked haddock and potato or cider and onion appear alongside beefier starters of pressed ox tongue with pickled beets, or ham hock with dandelion salad. Roast free-range chicken with baked garlic and parsley sauce is typical of the more grown-up mains, while own-made fish fingers are a delicious take on a nursery favourite. Desserts might be treacle tart or bread and butter pud; wines are varied and affordable. *Booking advisable. Takeaway service (deli). Vegetarian menu.* **Map 6 R4.**

Chinese

The growing Chinese population of London is slowly transforming the range of Chinese food available in the capital. *Time Out*'s informal investigations have found young Chinese workers and students from all over China hanging out in Chinatown. We've run into chefs from Hunan, Fujian and the north-eastern provinces who have come over on work permits; students from Taiwan, Guangdong and even the Chinese community in Burma. Some live in London, others work in restaurants in the counties and come to town occasionally to stock up on ingredients for Chinese cooking.

Over the past year, *Time Out* magazine has run features on the cheap, trendy cafés that have proved a big hit with young east Asians and other Londoners; and on restaurants specialising in Fujianese and north-eastern dishes that were previously unknown in the capital (our favourite regional treats include the Fujianese oyster cakes and sweet potato balls at **Fook Sing** – *see p52*). It's all a refreshing change from the Cantonese mainstream. There's also a new Chinese bakery, the **Wonderful Patisserie** (45 Gerrard Street, W1D 5QQ; 7734 77629) where you can pick up mooncakes, preserved duck eggs encased in pastry and squidgy glutinous rice balls. The range of ingredients available in the supermarkets is expanding all the time.

We've also come across various fascinating food-making skills on display in Chinatown and beyond. In the windows of the **Jen Café** (4-8 Newport Place, WC2H 7JP) and the **Li Kou Fu** restaurant (3-4 Macclesfield Street, W1V 7LB), you can watch staff wrap jiao zi, the delicious boiled dumplings of Beijing and northern China. Stop for a few moments outside the **Feng Shui Inn** (*see p51*) and marvel at the sugar craftsman stretching pale toffee into improbably fine and flossy strands of 'dragon beard candy' (long xu tang). And if you're splashing out on a romantic dinner at **Mr Chow** (*see p56*) – one of the restaurants shortlisted for this year's Best Chinese Restaurant category of the *Time Out* Eating & Drinking Awards – make sure you are there for the dazzling nightly display of noodle-pulling by one of the chefs. It's great to see the new wave of Chinese immigrants and visiting workers bringing their talents into play. We just hope that Cantonese restaurants allow their Hunanese junior chefs to whet our appetites with some of the vibrant, spicy flavours of that region before too long.

Of course, Chinatown restaurant menus continue to be dominated by the usual Anglo-Cantonese fare: spring rolls, sweet-and-sour pork, chicken in black bean sauce and the like. This is the fault of customers as much as chefs and restaurant managers. As the manager of **Imperial China** (*see p53*), Simon Tang, explains: 'When we relaunched the restaurant in 2003, we tried offering a few more unusual dishes, but people seemed to prefer the more conventional Chinese restaurant food. We can still cook off-menu if people request it.'

Outside Chinatown there have been some interesting developments. Dim sum, the

Cantonese snacks traditionally served during the daytime with a pot of tea, are now being offered day and evening with beer or cocktails at newcomer **Drunken Monkey** (*see p61*), a loud, exuberant bar in Shoreditch – and pretty good they are too. Alan Yau, the discreet entrepreneur behind **Hakkasan** (*see p56*), opened his new venture, **Yauatcha** (*see 57*), to a fever of publicity in spring 2004. Yauatcha also serves dim sum all day and evening, and the standard of food is as high as that of Michelin-starred Hakkasan, even if the decor isn't quite as thrilling. What is most pioneering about Yauatcha, though, is the beautiful tea room, where you can sample dozens of different teas, an unprecedented range in London, and feast on Eurasian pâtisserie.

So things are looking good, but it's still noticeable that the best places for authentic Chinese food are off the touristy Chinatown beat. The restaurants shortlisted for the Best Chinese Restaurant category of the 2004 *Time Out* awards, and the eventual winner – Hakkasan – are all in other parts of London. And there's one fly in the ointment: a clampdown on illegal Chinese workers in restaurant kitchens that, according to a report in the *Guardian*, is having a disastrous effect on the catering industry. We hope this won't stymie the exciting diversification of London's Chinese food scene.

A FEW TIPS

Set menus in Chinese restaurants tend to pander to outdated western stereotypes of Chinese food, featuring only clichéd dishes such as sweet-and-sour pork, and egg-fried rice. Our advice – apart from in a handful of restaurants such as **Memories of China** (*see below*) and the Dorchester hotel's **Oriental** (*see p57*) – is to avoid them at all costs. Order instead from the main menu and, if possible, the seasonal specials list. London restaurants with really enticing chef's specials (translated into English) include **Mr Kong** (*see p53*), **Four Seasons** (*see p58*) and **Phoenix Palace** (*see p57*). The main menus at **Yming** (*see p57*), **Mr Chow** and the four **Royal Chinas** (*see p57, p59, p60 and p62*) are inspiring in themselves, and if you really want a walk on the wild side, put yourself in the hands of Mr Peng at **Hunan** (*see below*) or give chef Ringo Lo at **Lee Fook** (*see p62*) a few days' notice for a special banquet.

The art of ordering a Chinese meal lies in assembling a variety of dishes, differing from one another in terms of their main ingredients, cooking methods and flavours. Starters are easy: just order as you please and remember there is life beyond the usual deep-fried snacks (a cold meat platter or steamed seafood can make a delicious beginning to the meal). For main courses, aim to order one dish for every person in your party, and then one or two extra, and share everything.

Choose a variety of main ingredients so things don't get repetitive. Then try to balance dry, deep-fried dishes, with slow hot-pots and crisp stir-fries; rich roast duck with fresh vegetables; gentle tastes with spicy flavours.

Ask your waiter about seasonal greens: you may find the restaurant has pak choi, gai lan (chinese broccoli), pea shoots, water spinach and other marvellous Chinese treats. Most Chinese people fill up on plain steamed rice, which is a good foil to the flavours of the other food and much more comfortable than that old takeaway staple, egg-fried rice. Desserts are not one of the fortes of Chinese cuisine, and you rarely find much beyond the old clichés of red-bean paste pancakes and toffee bananas (we admire the strategy of Mr Chow, which imports French pastries from a nearby pâtisserie). Better, in most cases, to order an extra savoury dish and stop at a café afterwards if you want something sweet.

A new scheme offers patrons of Chinatown restaurants and supermarkets a 50 per cent discount on parking in the Chinatown Square car park: a great boon for those stocking up on heavy Chinese groceries (the minimum full price for parking is a hefty £9 for two hours). Look out for the notices in windows of participating businesses, and make sure your till receipt is stamped on the way out.

Central

Belgravia SW1

★ Hunan

51 Pimlico Road, SW1W 8NE (7730 5712).
Sloane Square tube. **Lunch served** 12.30-
2.30pm, **dinner served** 6-11pm Mon-Sat.
Set meal £31-£150 per person (minimum 2).
Service 12.5%. **Credit** AmEx, DC, MC, V.

We got a table by booking three days ahead and gave notice we wanted the chef's recommended meal. Our enquiry about the number of courses produced the reply: '12 or 14, maybe 15 or 16: how hungry are you?' There were 16, not counting the 'picking dishes' up front, nor the elegant red bean pancake dessert. This is Hunan cuisine, so many dishes were hottish, but none fiercely so. Clear soup with minced pork and ginger, served in a bamboo tube, was excellent. Chicken appeared twice: once minced with green chillies (to be eaten wrapped in lettuce leaf), and once smoked in a hot sweet sauce. The waiter told us a third dish was chicken legs, but the bones were so small and the delicious meat so tender that we reckoned it was 'field chicken' (tin gai), the Chinese for frog. We also tried cuttlefish balls that exploded with flavour when the crisp covering was broached; ethereally delicate tempura-style french beans; prawns with salt and chillies; perfect black-cooked pork belly with preserved vegetable; spinach balls in sesame seed coating; beancurd in a star anise sauce – and more. No dish was less than good and most were excellent. Not cheap, but worth it.
Booking essential. No-smoking tables. Separate room for hire, seats 10-15. Vegetarian menu.
Map 15 G11.

★ Ken Lo's Memories of China

65-69 Ebury Street, SW1W 0NZ (7730 7734).
Victoria tube/rail. **Lunch served** noon-2.30pm
Mon-Sat. **Dinner served** 7-11pm Mon-Sat;
7-10.30pm Sun. **Main courses** £4.50-£27.
Set lunch £18.50-£21.50 per person
(minimum 2). **Set dinner** £30-£48 per person
(minimum 2). **Cover** £1.20. **Service** 12.5%.
Credit AmEx, DC, MC, V.

This upmarket restaurant caters to a smart, cosmopolitan clientele who were enthusiastically sampling champagnes from the impressive wine list when we visited. The decor is muted but stylish, with fresh hyacinths on the tables, and there are some pleasant private rooms. Service is attentive and congenial. Unusually for a restaurant catering mainly to tourists, Memories offers authentic, high-quality pan-regional cuisine. We began with three-spiced deep-fried squid: large, succulent chunks on a bed of crisp salty seaweed, with a little heat provided by red chillies. Sliced fish pepper pot soup was lovely, with pickled

Sheng's Tea House

greens floating in a delicate milky broth. Sichuan crispy aromatic duck (always a favourite), accompanied by pancakes and plum sauce, was faultless. The à la carte is rather compact, but the restaurant offers several well-chosen set meals, some tailored to large parties. The Imperial Banquet, which includes shark's fin soup, looks especially tempting. Quality teas are offered too, including the famed Dragon Well green tea. Unlike last year, this time we were untroubled by cigarette smoke. On a Saturday evening the restaurant was well populated but far from busy, and we enjoyed a leisurely and very pleasant meal.
Babies and children welcome. Booking advisable. Separate room for hire, seats 26. Takeaway service. **Map 15 H10.**
For branch see index.

Bloomsbury WC1

★ Sheng's Tea House
68 Millman Street, WC1N 3EF (7405 3697). Russell Square tube/68 bus. **Lunch served** noon-3pm Mon-Fri. **Dinner served** 6-10.30pm Mon-Fri. **Main courses** £6.50-£7.95. **Credit** AmEx, MC, V.
Sheng's is small and somewhat off the beaten track, but is much patronised by the office workers of Gray's Inn Road and the postgraduate residents of nearby Goodenough College. It has a limited menu of northern, southern and South-east Asian dishes, with soup noodles predominating. For starters, squid with chilli and salt (disappointing on last year's visit) was excellent in flavour, consistency and freshness. Bang bang chicken (fingers of white meat and cucumber with a thick sauce of peanut and sesame) was good of its kind, though rather too sweet. For main courses, noodles with beef and chilli lacked incisiveness, being neither spicy nor flavourful; it came swimming in a watery, salty, curryish, coriander-enhanced soup. By contrast, fried oak-smoked noodles with prawns and black beans was very good indeed. Qingdao beer comes in bottles, and there's a varied choice of other drinks. On our visit, desserts were few and simple, and not all were available. Service was unobtrusive and friendly.
Babies and children admitted. Booking advisable. Disabled: toilet. No smoking. Tables outdoors (4, pavement). Vegetarian menu. **Map 4 M4.**

Chinatown W1, WC2

★ Café de HK
47-49 Charing Cross Road, WC2H 0AN (7534 9898). Leicester Square or Piccadilly Circus tube. **Meals served** noon-11pm daily. **Main courses** £4.50-£12. **Credit** AmEx, MC, V.
Bright and fun, this two-floor café (ground-floor canteen counter for takeaways, plus mezzanine dining space) attracts Chinese teenagers who sit by the large windows to view Charing Cross Road's street life and listen to pop music. Hard wooden benches mean they don't linger long. The menu too is geared to quick pit-stops; it's a huge list embracing meal-in-one rice and noodle plates, 'bubble teas' (sweet iced teas with glutinous globes of sweet-potato starch that you suck through large straws like a pea-shooter in reverse), bizarre Eurasian snacks (luncheon pork and fried egg sandwich), and a melange of multinational meals, from borscht to spaghetti bolognese. Chinese soup of the day was comforting pork stock containing the odd green leaf and boiled carrot. Next, cuttlefish, spare rib, chicken wing and salted egg was a small portion of each roast meat on lukewarm, chewy rice with half a fridge-cold salty egg still in its shell. We added further salinity to the meal with braised lettuce in a pungently cheesy hot beancurd sauce. Not haute cuisine, then, but a good laugh.
Babies and children welcome. Bookings not accepted. No-smoking tables. Takeaway service. Vegetarian menu. **Map 17 K6.**

★ Café TPT
21 Wardour Street, W1D 6PN (7734 7980). Leicester Square or Piccadilly Circus tube. **Meals served** noon-midnight Mon-Sat; noon-11.30pm Sun. **Main courses** £6.50-£24. **Set meal** £9.50, £11 2 courses. **Service** 10%. **Credit** MC, V.
Opened in 2003, Café TPT is notable for its handsome wooden tables and stools that belie the modesty of the plainly decorated white minimalist little interior. The menu too is replete with modest dishes: the type of stir-fries found throughout Chinatown and beyond. Most interesting are the small batch of specials (steamed chicken with red medlar berry and red dates, for instance), the odd Malaysian dish (penang laksa), the Malaysian-influenced desserts (red bean ice water glass jelly) – and the forbidden fruits of the Chinese menu. Why, given that Café TPT is a new operation, and given the fluency in English of the clued-up staff, should the most enticing food be listed in Chinese only (both on a laminated card and on pink paper strips stuck to the walls)? We munched through a welter of mediocre meat (honey-roast pork), and a vast plateful of malayan ho fun (fresh from the wok, but an inelegant assembly dusted with curry powder) with only the vibrant fresh choi sum in oyster sauce to console us. Our Chinese neighbours, meanwhile, tucked into all manner of appetising-looking meal-in-one rice plates and appeared much happier.
Babies and children welcome; high chair. Takeaway service. **Map 17 K6.**

★ Canton
11 Newport Place, WC2H 7JR (7437 6220). Leicester Square or Piccadilly Circus tube. **Meals served** noon-11.30pm Mon, Sun; noon-midnight Tue-Thur; noon-12.30am Fri, Sat. **Main courses** £5.20-£9. **Set meal** £10 2 courses. **Credit** AmEx, JCB, MC, V.
Little natural light manages to negotiate the window display of roast ducks – flaunting their shiny brown breasts – and permeate this low-priced Chinatown stalwart. No matter. The interior is notable only for its lack of room and, apart from the single round banqueting table at the back, tables must often be shared. Never mind. Staff act out their lives before their customers: arguing, laughing, spilling wine. Bear with it. The food at Canton is tremendous value and completely outshines its environs: from crisp baby crab with chilli and salt, and an extremely appetising crab meat and beancurd broth, to ultra-fresh gai lan (chinese broccoli: a waiter popped out to buy it), succulent roast duck (served hot, off the bone), and a wonderful belly pork and preserved vegetable hot-pot. Even the meal-in-one Singapore-style ho fun noodles was a cut above the norm, featuring fresh pasta, plump prawns and crunchy shards of peppers in a curry powder-tinged stir-fry. Only some lacklustre sliced scallops and vegetables on rice and the basic house white wine failed to inspire. The cost of this feast for two (including service): £48.50.
Babies and children admitted. Separate room for hire, seats 22. Takeaway service. **Map 17 K6.**

Chinese regional cookery

Chinese cuisine is conventionally divided into four major schools: the fresh Cantonese cooking of the south; the sweeter, oilier food of Shanghai and the east; the strong spicy cuisine of western China (especially Sichuan and Hunan provinces); and northern cookery, which is typified by a reliance on breads and noodles, and by famous dishes such as mongolian hot-pot and peking duck, rather than by any dominant flavouring style. Beyond these four great culinary regions, many provinces, not to mention cities and towns, have their own special dishes.

London's restaurant scene is dominated by the Cantonese, many of whom originated in Hong Kong. Cantonese tastes have inevitably influenced the development of British Chinese cooking (Cantonese people don't, for example, much like spicy food, and they tend to tone down the flavours of the Sichuanese dishes on their menus).

A few restaurants in London do venture off the beaten track. For some of the spicy flavours of western China, try idiosyncratic **Hunan** (*see p49*) in Belgravia, which has dishes you can't find anywhere else in London. Chinatown's **Ecapital** (*see p51*) is the only place where we've found Shanghainese specialities such as 'lion's head' meatballs and 'vegetarian goose'.

North China (*see p58*) in Acton offers a delicious cold meat platter and a fine peking duck (served in three courses, including not only the familiar duck skin with pancakes, but also a duck-and-vegetable stir-fry and a final duck soup). **Mr Chow** (*see p56*) in Knightsbridge presents in spectacular fashion the hand-pulled pasta that is ubiquitous among the Muslims of northern China; just watch as a chef comes out of the kitchen to whack a ball of dough into a delicate skein of noodles.

For Fujianese specialities, check out **Rong Cheng** (*see p57*) and **Fook Sing** (*see p52*).

★ Chuen Cheng Ku

17 Wardour Street, W1D 6PJ (7437 1398).
Leicester Square or Piccadilly Circus tube.
Meals served 11am-11.45pm Mon-Sat;
11am-11.15pm Sun. **Dim sum served** 11am-
10.30pm daily. **Main courses** £6.80-£9.50.
Dim sum £1.95. **Set meal** £8.80 2 courses,
£12 3 courses. **Service** 10%. **Credit** AmEx,
DC, JCB, MC, V.
In a breaking of ranks and a breaking of tradition
(caused perhaps by the opening of Yauatcha – *see
p57*), Chuen Cheng Ku has started serving dim
sum in the evenings as well as at lunch. This is
one of central London's biggest restaurants
(stretching from Wardour to Rupert Street, on
three storeys) and though Chinese Londoners –
and some others – pack the place at midday,
dinners have been sparsely attended, despite a
vast full menu encompassing the likes of stewed
eel with garlic in hot-pot. It's worth coming just
for the surroundings: red carpets, stackable old
chairs, antediluvian grey wallpaper, elaborate
chandeliers. Stainless-steel trolleys full of snacks
jostle for position from 11am; it's best to arrive
soon after, as the dumplings start looking tired by
noon. Point to what you fancy, after consulting the
laminated picture list. We advise centring a meal
around a dish cooked at table, perhaps tender baby
squid with crisp beansprouts and coriander leaves.
Then stodginess, as you might find in reheated
(and too sweet) pork puffs or forlorn-looking
refried cheung fun, is alleviated. We enjoyed
desserts: a stiff mango pudding and moreish
sesame seed buns with a sweet eggy filling. Long
may the trolleys trundle.
*Babies and children welcome; high chairs. Booking
advisable. No-smoking tables. Separate rooms for
hire, seat 40, 60, 100 and 180. Takeaway service.
Vegetarian menu.* **Map 17 K7.**

★ Crispy Duck NEW

27 Wardour Street, W1V 6PR (7287 6578).
Leicester Square or Piccadilly Circus tube.
Meals served 10am-4am daily. **Main courses**
£5-£18. **Set meal** £10.50 2 courses; £11.50-
£12.50 3 courses (minimum 2). **Service** 10%.
Credit AmEx, MC, V.
Spread over several floors, Crispy Duck is
nonetheless quite cramped; get a seat on the
ground floor if you can, where a large mirror helps
to make the room feel a bit bigger and more
comfortable. Handwritten Chinese menus adorn
the walls. Crispy Duck has one of the most
extensive choices of food of all the Chinatown
cafés, but it's the cheap one-dish meals (rather than
the duck, crispy or otherwise) that draw the
Chinatown locals who fill the restaurant daily.
Most of these meals are prepared by a chef
ensconced in the restaurant's ground-floor window,
surrounded by hanging duck and pork. Our fried
noodle with mixed roast meat arrived generously
topped with large chunks of chinese leaf and huge
slices of crispy pork and char siu. The sauce was
thick and gloopy, reminiscent of a comforting
street-hawker dish. Fish and pig's intestine congee
arrived perfectly cooked. The newer branch in
Gerrard Street offers the same menu, but without
the one-dish meals that have made the original's
name (though these can probably be rustled up if
you know what you want). Service at both
restaurants varies widely, from helpful and
attentive to rude and disobliging.
*Babies and children welcome. Separate room for
hire, seats 20. Takeaway service. Vegetarian
menu.* **Map 17 K7.**
For branch see index.

Dragon Inn NEW

12 Gerrard Street, W1D 5PR (7494 0870).
Leicester Square or Piccadilly Circus tube.
Meals served 11am-3am daily. **Main courses**
£4-£18. **Dim sum** £1.90-£3.20. **Set meal** £9.50
2 courses; dim sum £9.90 per person (minimum
2). **Service** 10%. **Credit** AmEx, DC, JCB, MC, V.
Tucked behind a very modest shopfront, this
friendly restaurant does a nice line in dim sum,
which, unusually, it continues serving into the
small hours of the night. Cheung fun was suitably
soft and slithery, while chive and prawn dumplings

with translucent wrappers and fresh, juicy fillings
were delicious. Char siu pork puff pastries were
nice and light, and richly stuffed, and sautéed slabs
of turnip paste studded with shrimp and pork
were fragrant and tasty (if a little greasy). The
main menu offers some interesting Cantonese
specials. We tried stewed turbot with bitter melon
in black bean sauce, and enjoyed the fresh green
bite of the melon and the well-seasoned sauce,
although the fish seemed to have been fried in
advance and was lacking in crispness. Staff are
friendly, and Dragon Inn is popular with Chinese
diners. The downside is poor ventilation, which
gives the dining room a distinctive 'Chinese
restaurant' smell.
*Babies and children welcome; high chairs.
Separate rooms for hire, seat 35 and 60.
Takeaway service. Vegetarian menu.* **Map 17 K6.**

ECapital

8 Gerrard Street, W1D 5PJ (7434 3838).
Leicester Square or Piccadilly Circus tube.
Meals served noon-11.30pm Mon-Thur;
noon-midnight Fri, Sat; noon-10.30pm Sun.
Main courses £8.50-£22. **Minimum** £9
(dinner). **Set meal** £8.50-£32 per person
(minimum 2). **Service** 12.5%. **Credit** AmEx,
DC, JCB, MC, V.
ECapital is the only place in London to specialise
in the food of Shanghai and eastern China. A
separate section of the menu offers notable
Shanghainese dishes such as braised yellow eel,
and 'lion's head' meatballs, and a card on the table
listing specials included the Hangzhou delicacy of
prawns stir-fried with Dragon Well tea leaves – a
dish we've never previously encountered in the UK.
With all this to choose from, we abandoned the rest
of the menu and went for a regional feast. All the
dishes were refreshingly different, though of
variable quality. Best was the assorted cold starters,
which included morsels of sweet marinated fish,
delicate 'drunken chicken', a pressed terrine of pig's
ear (which had a beautiful appearance and
intriguing texture), and 'vegetarian goose' made
from many-layered beancurd. The pork 'in the
poet's style' (aka dong po pork, named after the
famous poet Su Dongpo) was gorgeous, braised to
tender submission in a rich, dark gravy. Steamed
fillet of monkfish came with an unusual topping of
crunchy yellow bean paste: interesting, but very
salty. This isn't the best Chinese food in London,
but we recommend it for a taste of the East.
*Babies and children welcome; high chair.
Booking advisable weekends. Separate room for
hire, seats 50. Takeaway service. Vegetarian
menu.* **Map 17 K6.**

Feng Shui Inn

*6 Gerrard Street, W1D 5PG (7734 6778/
www.fengshuiinn.co.uk). Leicester Square or
Piccadilly Circus tube.* **Meals served** noon-
11.30pm daily. **Main courses** £6.80-£24.80.
Set meal £12.80-£26.80 (minimum 2). **Service**
10%. **Credit** MC, V.
This relative newcomer to the Chinatown block (it
opened in 2003) has a pleasant ambience, inspired,
so the menu says, by the travellers' inns of pre-
communist China. It is a warren of small spaces,
decked out with old-fashioned wooden tables and
chairs, offerings of fruit on an elaborate shrine to
the god of wealth, and hanging clusters of
imitation red and gold firecrackers. The place
seems popular with young Chinese as well as
westerners. There's the standard range of Anglo-
Chinese dishes, plus a number of more interesting
Cantonese specialities. Steamed chicken in 'special
superior stock' was delightful, the tender flesh
lying on a bed of snaking greens in a rich and
refreshing broth. The classic pei pa beancurd
(globes of mashed tofu deep-fried and served in a
rich gravy-like sauce) was a little greasy, but still
delicious. A clay hot-pot of eel and roast belly pork
was as robustly tasty as you'd expect. The good
food, affable staff and unusual decor all
contributed to an enjoyable evening.
*Babies and children welcome; high chairs. Book
weekends. Entertainment: karaoke (call for
details). Separate rooms for hire, seating 12,
20 and 40. Takeaway service. Vegetarian menu.*
Map 17 K7.

Fook Sing. See p52.

★ Fook Sing

25-26 Newport Court, WC2H 7JS (7287 0188).
Leicester Square or Piccadilly Circus tube.
Meals served 11am-10.30pm daily. **Main
courses** £3.90-£4.30. **Set lunch** £4 1 course
incl soft drink. **No credit cards**.
The newest wave of Chinese local cuisines to reach
London comes from the coastal province of Fujian,
across the strait from Taiwan. A large section of
Fook Sing's menu is devoted to Fujianese dishes,
with ingredients such as whelk, tripe, eel, frog,
mussels, pig's liver and 'beef miscellany' (ngau
jaap: an amalgam of the parts that don't often
figure on menus). Otherwise, the limited offerings
fall under a few commonly available headings such
as fried dishes, soups (including congee, aka rice
porridge) and noodles, with seafood and soup
noodles predominating. Servings are generous and
most customers order just one bowl, rather than
the usual communal dishes. Take time to study the
menu (there's at least one copy in English) and
experiment. We liked the 'seafood wok-bin', a clear
soup made from scallop, prawns, squid, oyster, fish
balls and mussels with mushrooms, spring onion,
ginger and rice noodles. If they haven't sold out (as
they invariably do by mid-afternoon), try the
speciality 'oyster cakes': crisp, fried, samosa-type
wraps containing beansprouts, mushrooms, pak
choi and, of course, oysters. This tiny café is very
clean and extraordinarily cheap.
Babies and children welcome. Takeaway service.
Vegetarian menu. **Map 17 K6**.

Golden Dragon

28-29 Gerrard Street, W1D 6JW (7734 2763).
Leicester Square or Piccadilly Circus tube.
Meals served noon-11.30pm Mon-Thur;
noon-midnight Fri, Sat; 11am-11pm Sun. **Dim
sum served** noon-5pm Mon-Sat;
11am-5pm Sun. **Main courses** £6.50-£25.
Dim sum £1.80-£3.90. **Set meal** £12.50-£35
per person (minimum 2). **Service** 10%.
Credit AmEx, DC, MC, V.

An open dining room, garish decor, pink
tablecloths, toothpicks on the table, bustling staff
constantly patrolling, service just short of brusque
– a meal at Golden Dragon is highly evocative of
eating in Hong Kong. Portions are generous. We
started with freshly sliced '100-year-old eggs' (pei-
dan) with pickled ginger, then a plate of golden
roast pork belly: tasty and crisp. The third dish,
mapo doufu, hadn't the required chilli-heat or the
tongue-numbing power of sichuan pepper; the
small cubes of beancurd floundered in a
flavourless sauce. Dark green gai lan was fresh and
plentifully dressed with pounded garlic; it was
undercooked – certainly a better fault than
overcooking – but the full succulence of the
vegetable is not brought out by such light-
handedness. A final dish of stewed eel with garlic
was served bubbling in an earthenware pot over a
small flame. It smelled and tasted delicious, but
there was very little eel, the bulk of the pot being
taken up with chunks of indifferent beancurd,
small offcuts of char siu pork, and mushroom
pieces in a heavy sauce. The bill was slapped on
the table the moment we finished.
Babies and children admitted; high chairs.
Booking advisable. Separate rooms for hire, seat
20 and 40. Takeaway service. Vegetarian menu.
Map 17 K7.

Golden Dynasty

14 Lisle Street, WC2H 7BE (7734 8580).
Leicester Square or Piccadilly Circus tube. **Meals
served** noon-11.30pm Mon-Fri; 11am-11.30pm
Sat; 10am-10.30pm Sun. **Main courses** £5-£6.
Set meal £11.50-£18 per person (minimum 2).
Service 10%. **Credit** AmEx, JCB, MC, V.
Golden Dynasty's smart modern interior of bright
green walls and contemporary Chinese prints has
a light, airy feel. The main menu isn't as extensive
as many you'd find in Chinatown, but cooking
standards are generally high. Sweet and sour
crispy fish boasted generous chunks of cod
drizzled with a rich, tasty sauce. The black bean

sauce accompanying our tofu stuffed with minced
prawn was delightfully understated. A chef's
special of stuffed scallops with roast duck
disappointed, but only because it failed to meet our
expectations; the dish simply consisted of slices of
scallop overlaid with slices of duck. Dim sum is
also available during the day; the menu offers the
usual snacks plus a few imaginative specials. The
latter can be hit or miss. Stir-fried turnip paste with
shredded carrot and cabbage was something of a
mishmash, but steamed stuffed beancurd with
fantail prawn was a tasty work of art resembling
a fish, complete with wolfberries for eyes.
Customers during our recent trips were mostly
Chinese. Staff were pleasant and on the ball, but
failed to tell us about the choice of teas available.
Babies and children welcome; high chairs.
Separate room for hire, seats 30. Takeaway
service. Vegetarian menu. **Map 17 K7**.

Harbour City

46 Gerrard Street, W1V 7LP (7287 1526/
7439 7859). Leicester Square or Piccadilly Circus
tube. **Meals served** noon-11.30pm Mon-Thur;
noon-midnight Fri, Sat; 11am-10.30pm Sun.
Dim sum served noon-5pm Mon-Sat; 11am-
5pm Sun. **Main courses** £5.50-£20. **Dim sum**
£1.90-£5.50. **Set meal** £13.50-£15.50 per person
(minimum 2); £15.50-£16 per person (minimum
4); £16.50-£21.50 per person (minimum 6).
Service 10%. **Credit** AmEx, JCB, MC, V.
One of the Chinatown restaurants with a high
proportion of Chinese customers (we know it's a
cliché, but it really is a good sign), Harbour City
offers some quite interesting cooking. Regrettably,
many of the rarer dishes – steamed eggs with
beancurd, eel with garlic and pork, and duck with
fermented beancurd among them – are on the
Chinese-language menu (how we wish it was
translated). We tried the dim sum on our most
recent visit. A special of taro spring rolls was
superb: sweet, sumptuous taro paste encased in
perfectly crisp pastry. Steamed crab and coriander

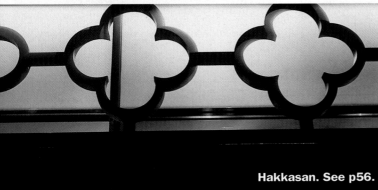

Hakkasan. See p56.

★ Imperial China
White Bear Yard, 25A Lisle Street, WC2H 7BA (7734 3388/www.imperial-china.co.uk). Leicester Square or Piccadilly Circus tube. **Meals served** noon-11.30pm Mon-Sat; 11.30am-10.30pm Sun. **Dim sum served** noon-6pm Mon-Fri; noon-5pm Sat, Sun. **Main courses** £6-£24. **Dim sum** £2.20-£3.50. **Minimum** £10. **Set meal** £14.95-£30 per person (minimum 2). **Service** 12.5%. **Credit** AmEx, JCB, MC, V.

A year on, the revamped ex-China City is still elegant. We were shown an impoverished dim sum list in English, and were disconcerted to find the Chinese menu little fuller. Not a good beginning, yet we were delighted to be served some of the tastiest delicacies to be had in London. Pride of place goes to the fried taro paste croquettes (yu kok), a common item, but here with the most ethereal crisp taro embracing a fragrant semi-liquid filling of pork, mushroom and green onion. Steamed pork buns (char siu bao), another staple, were generously packed with sweet pork; cuttlefish cakes with coriander were fresh and nicely chewy; and the fried turnip cake provided a solid foundation for the other flavours. More unusual were the curry chicken pies: crumbly pastries with a minced filling reminiscent of Pan Yan pickle, which used to spice up lacklustre English food. 'Steamed beef and pineapple dumplings in butterfly' looked exciting, and tasted almost as good. The rice flour wrappers to the steamed cheung fun were exemplary in their thinness and translucence. We finished with a plate of fresh fruit and a bill of well under £30 for two.
Babies and children welcome; high chairs. Booking advisable. Disabled: toilet. Entertainment: pianist 7.30-10.30pm Mon-Sat. No-smoking tables. Separate rooms for hire, seat 14 and 70. Tables outdoors (4, courtyard). Vegetarian menu. **Map 17 K7**.

Joy King Lau
3 Leicester Street, WC2H 7BL (7437 1132/1133). Leicester Square or Piccadilly Circus tube. **Meals served** noon-11.30pm Mon-Sat; 11am-10.30pm Sun. **Dim sum served** noon-4.45pm Mon-Sat; 11am-4.45pm Sun. **Main courses** £6.50-£20. **Dim sum** £1.90-£2.90. **Set meal** £9.80-£35 per person (minimum 2). **Service** 10%. **Credit** AmEx, DC, MC, V.

This Chinatown stalwart has been a popular dim sum haunt for years, but our most recent daytime visit was disappointing. Both har gau (prawn dumpling) and siu mai (pork dumpling) seemed mass-produced, while cheung fun were thick and a little doughy. The spring roll wrappers were overcooked and tasted of oil. Turnip paste worked better; it had a thick, firm consistency and flavoursome diced meat. Glutinous rice in lotus leaf was also tightly packed and well flavoured. An evening visit was better, when we sampled the traditional Cantonese food for which the restaurant is famed. Fish maw with crabmeat soup featured loads of maw and crab in a good stock. Mangetout pea shoots were perfectly stir-fried with garlic. The star, however, was braised duck with assorted meat: half a duck presented within a circle of pak choi and doused with a rich star anise sauce containing king prawn, pig skin, squid and chinese mushrooms. Service was efficient rather than attentive; the bill came without our asking. On the ground floor, green and pink panels are backlit with Chinese characters; upstairs, the decor is a little plainer.
Babies and children welcome; high chairs. Booking advisable Fri, Sat; essential Sun. Separate area for hire, seats 12-30. Takeaway service. Vegetarian menu. **Map 17 K7**.

Mr Kong
21 Lisle Street, WC2H 7BA (7437 7341/9679). Leicester Square or Piccadilly Circus tube. **Meals served** noon-2.45am Mon-Sat; noon-1.45am Sun. **Main courses** £5.90-£26. **Minimum** £7 after 5pm. **Set meal** £10 per person (minimum 2); £22 per person (minimum 4). **Credit** AmEx, DC, JCB, MC, V.

There's a raft of enticing dishes to be savoured here: proper Chinese food, intricately prepared. Yet there are drawbacks too. Top among these is the

---

dumplings with frilly, cockscomb tops were lovely (though filled with crabstick rather than crab), and vegetarian spinach dumplings infused with the tastes of fried garlic and sesame oil were also enjoyable. Rice congee was flavoured more by spring onion than the few rather chewy strands of dried scallop, but it was soft and comforting, and went very well with the deep-fried dough sticks served on a separate dish. Following a thorough refurbishment, decor is now bright and tasteful. Service was adequate but unremarkable.
Babies and children welcome; high chairs. Booking advisable; essential Fri-Sun. Separate room for hire, seats 60-70. Takeaway service. Vegetarian menu. **Map 17 K7**.

★ Hing Loon
25 Lisle Street, WC2H 7BA (7437 3602/7287 0419). Leicester Square or Piccadilly Circus tube. **Meals served** noon-11.30pm Mon-Thur; noon-midnight Fri, Sat; noon-11pm Sun. **Main courses** £3.70-£7.80. **Set lunch** £4.50 2 courses. **Set dinner** £5.80, £7.50, £9.50 per person (minimum 2). **Credit** AmEx, JCB, MC, V.

At lunch, this tiny nook attracts diners who pop in for one of the many cheap meal-in-one rice and noodle dishes. By night, though, all manner of folk stop by – from besuited ex-colonials to slinky young Chinese – making a happy hubbub. All are shoe-horned into the minuscule ground-floor room where they can look at the owner's collection of banknotes displayed on the wall. The roomier first-floor space only seems to be used as a last resort. Staff are brisk and friendly, increasingly so if 'proper' Chinese food is ordered from the vast menu. Scrutinise the chef's specials list at the front for the pick of the crop. Lamb with beancurd skin in hot-pot is a warming stew from northern China, the meat tender and on the bone. Scallop cakes with seasonal vegetables arrive crisp and springy, straight from the pan, the scallop morsels forming a layer over minced prawns. We also savoured the strong cheesy flavours of stir-fried spinach with

preserved hot beancurd and chilli. House wine is pretty basic, but it only costs £6.95, helping to make a meal here a bargain.
Babies and children welcome. Takeaway service. Vegetarian menu. **Map 17 K7**.

Hong Kong
6-7 Lisle Street, WC2H 7BG (7287 0352). Leicester Square or Piccadilly Circus tube. **Meals served** noon-11.30pm Mon-Thur; noon-midnight Fri, Sat; 11am-11pm Sun. **Dim sum served** noon-5pm daily. **Main courses** £6-£9. **Dim sum** £2-£3.50. **Set meal** £11-£30 per person (minimum 2). **Service** 10%. **Credit** AmEx, JCB, MC, V.

For some years now, this light, L-shaped, low-key little restaurant has been getting on with serving dim sum to a mainly Chinese clientele. On our most recent visit, we were pleasantly surprised by both the scope and quality of the lunchtime menu (which includes pictures of all the dumplings). There's a Japanese slant to some dishes, including the cigar-like crispy seafood rolls, wrapped in seaweed; and the sweet, succulent baby octopus Japanese-style (served cold with pickles and sprinkled with sesame seeds). We can also enthuse about the pan-fried chive dumplings in a wispy-light eggy batter, and the shark's fin dumpling in soup (a mighty ravioli full of meat and vegetable morsels, plus a generous helping of transparent, resilient strands of shark's fin – a flavour-free 'texture food') in delicate stock. We weren't so enamoured with the rather stodgy desserts (black glutinous rice balls with a sweet eggy filling, and rice balls with black sesame seeds), but the preceding delicacies and the congenial service left us happy. The full menu is less alluring (unless you can decipher the Chinese menu), but does include some classic Cantonese dishes such as baked salted chicken.
Babies and children welcome; high chairs. Booking advisable. Separate room for hire, seats 60. Takeaway service. Vegetarian menu. **Map 17 K7**.

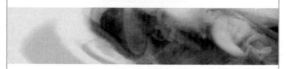

dining area. The ground floor is cramped, with little table space for elaborate feasting, but worse – far worse – is the basement, where a bland white room isn't enhanced by the pervading smell of toilet freshener. The staff ushered a newly arrived (posh) couple upstairs, when seats became free, leaving us to fester underground. The menu is long and confusing, with the best dishes listed under 'manager's recommendations', 'special vegetarian dishes' (a notable selection), and 'miscellaneous dishes'. Steamed razor clam with glass noodles and garlic was interesting, though the shellfish was overcooked. In contrast, a main course of stewed beef flank needed another ten minutes in the pot for complete tenderness. And though kon chin baby squid with chilli were cooked to crisp, yielding perfection, they came in a one-paced sweet sauce. Steamed beancurd and egg white topped with diced mixed vegetables was a delicately flavoured egg-custard concoction scattered with asparagus and carrots, but – partly because we know Kong's can do better – we left despondent.
Babies and children welcome; high chairs. Booking advisable. Separate room for hire, seats 30. Takeaway service. Vegetarian menu. **Map 17 K7**.

New Diamond
23 Lisle Street, WC2H 7BA (7437 2517/ 7221). Leicester Square or Piccadilly Circus tube. **Meals served** noon-3am daily. **Main courses** £5.80-£22. **Minimum** £10 after 5pm. **Set meal** £10.50-£20 per person (minimum 2). **Credit** AmEx, DC, MC, V.
We've previously enjoyed New Diamond's signature dish of fried crispy spring pigeon, so maybe the kitchen was having an off-night on our latest visit: the skin wasn't very crisp and the flesh was overcooked. A shame: the meal started well with a generous bowl of clam and pork with beancurd soup; the stock was well made and the addition of kai choi (mustard cabbage) to the soup provided a definite crunch. Tong choi (water spinach) Malaysian-style was prepared with finesse, but the same could not be said for the prawn-stuffed 'three treasures' of aubergine, pepper and beancurd; the aubergine tasted strongly of oil. Most disappointing was the chef's special of stuffed fillet steak rolls in black pepper sauce: the steak rolls were tough and covered with an unpleasant sheen; we couldn't taste the pepper in the black pepper sauce; and the mismatched stuffing of enoki mushrooms was stringy and tough. Perhaps unsurprisingly, most diners were non-Chinese. Service was brusque yet fairly attentive; our tea cups were regularly replenished. A fairly recent refurbishment and the use of large, well-spaced tables provide a light and airy feel.
Babies and children welcome; high chairs. Booking advisable. Takeaway service. Vegetarian menu. **Map 17 K7**.

New Mayflower
68-70 Shaftesbury Avenue, W1B 6LY (7734 9207). Leicester Square or Piccadilly Circus tube. **Meals served** 5pm-4am daily. **Main courses** £6.50-£45. **Minimum** £8. **Set dinner** £12-£22 per person (minimum 2). **Service** 10%. **Credit** AmEx, MC, V.
There is a crispness to both the clean, unfussy decor and the service at New Mayflower that speaks of efficient management. Waiting staff are attentive, knowledgeable and friendly, whether dealing with Chinese or western customers, and there's a relaxed patter of content conversation everywhere – the effect is comfortable enjoyment. A little bowl of complimentary sweet pickled vegetables allowed us to hone our chopstick technique while we waited for the tasty starter of crispy duck and pancakes. Fancying strong flavours, we ordered off-menu a fried cake of minced salted fish and pork, nicely blended with water chestnut for scrunch-feel. On the waiter's recommendation we chose as our vegetable course ung choi (water spinach) redolent of chillies and fermented beancurd, and in-your-face basic. The subtleties of a mixed squid and scallop dish might have been lost in such company, but thanks to freshness and well-timed cooking, they held their own and brought the meal into balance. Plain

boiled rice was the other toner-down of flavour, though the generous portions of all dishes meant that we had to go easy on the starch. After all this, the bill was very reasonable.
Babies and children welcome; high chairs. Booking essential. Separate room for hire, seats 30. Takeaway service. **Map 17 K7**.

New World
1 Gerrard Place, W1D 5PA (7734 0396). Leicester Square or Piccadilly Circus tube. **Meals served** 11am-11.45pm Mon-Sat; 11am-11pm Sun. **Dim sum served** 11am-6pm daily. **Main courses** £4.90-£10.50. **Dim sum** £2-£5. **Set meal** £9.50-£50 per person (minimum 2). **Minimum** £5 evening. **Credit** AmEx, DC, MC, V.
You'll be asked to wait in line if you visit three-storey New World after noon on a Sunday. Despite its tremendous size, the restaurant's elaborately decorated dining rooms will be packed full of mostly Chinese diners enthusiastically selecting dim sum from heated trolleys pushed by waitresses. On our last visit, Chinese dough stick cheung fun demonstrated not all food works best this way, being soggy and inedible, rather than crisp with a light wrapper. Prawn cheung fun fared better. Suckling pig from the barbecue trolley was truly scrumptious. A card on our table announced the arrival of a new chef from Hong Kong and a number of specialities cooked to order. Of these, shiitake mushroom topped with mashed squid, broccoli and half a quail's egg was pleasant enough. The translucent wrapper of a chicken and vegetable dumpling was too thick, but the spicy filling was tasty. Fried noodle with shredded fillet steak and pickled vegetable tasted much better than it looked; the sauce was tinted red, but the beef was succulent and the pickled vegetable sweet and crunchy. Service was brisk but friendly. Pu-erh tea with its earthy taste proved a welcome change from omnipresent jasmine. Best to go for the spectacle, not the food.
Babies and children welcome; high chairs. Bookings not accepted lunch Sun. No-smoking tables. Separate rooms for hire, seat 5-200. Takeaway service. **Map 17 K7**.

★ Poons
4 Leicester Street, WC2H 7BL (7437 1528). Leicester Square or Piccadilly Circus tube. **Meals served** noon-11.30pm daily. **Main courses** £4.60-£6.30. **Set meal** £15-£17 3 courses. **Service** 10%. **Credit** AmEx, MC, V.
After 35 years of trading, the original Poons caff of Lisle Street closed in summer 2004. But around the corner on Leicester Street, this more seemly, less cramped venue – run by another branch of the Poon dynasty – continues serving the family's renowned specialities. The menu is vast and appealing, ranging from a relatively modest lunchtime dim sum list to full-menu specials such as a crisp, intensely savoury roast squab. Wind-dried meats, with a mouth-watering savoury-sweet tang, shouldn't be missed; order a mixed plateful (duck and various sliced sausages) for only £4.60. We can also vouch for the belly pork and preserved vegetable casserole (one of many hot-pots); the scrumptious cold starter of shredded chicken and jellyfish in spicy peanut sauce (served with strips of cucumber); and another Poons' special, the voluptuous dessert of deep-fried milk encased in nanometrically thin batter. Drawbacks were the slightly wizened quails' eggs sautéed with mixed veg, the rather stodgy deep-fried oysters, and the basic house white. Furnishings on both floors are bright in an elegant yet faintly clinical way. Service is inoffensive, if a bit slow. This branch of Poons featured in the very first *Time Out Eating & Drinking* guide; long may it continue.
Babies and children welcome; high chairs. Booking advisable weekends. No-smoking tables. Separate room for parties, seats 20. Takeaway service. Vegetarian menu. **Map 17 K7**.

Royal Dragon
30 Gerrard Street, W1D 6JS (7734 0935). Leicester Square or Piccadilly Circus tube. **Meals served** noon-3am Mon-Sat; 11am-3am Sun. **Dim sum served** noon-5pm Mon-Sat; 11am-5pm Sun. **Main courses** £6.30-£9.

Best Chinese

For a treat
Feel like a Hollywood film star at **Mr Chow** (see p56), and a kung fu film star at **Hakkasan** (see p56).

For mould-breaking Chinese food
Tear up the menus and try the chef's selection at **Hunan** (see p49) or a bespoke banquet (by prior arrangement) at **Lee Fook** (see p62).

For delectable dim sum
You can't beat **Hakkasan** (see p56) and **Yauatcha** (see p57); next in line are the **Royal Chinas** (see p57, p59, p60 and p62), **Imperial China** (see p53), **Yi-Ban** (see p60) and **Phoenix Palace** (see p57).

For a taste of the regions
Try Shanghainese fare at **ECapital** (see p51), a taste of Fujian at **Rong Cheng** (see p57) and **Fook Sing** (see p52), and spicy western food at **Hunan** (see p49) and **North China** (see p58).

For inspiring specials
Check out the supplementary menus at **Mr Kong** (see p53), **Four Seasons** (see p58), **Phoenix Palace** (see p57), and the **Royal Chinas** (see p57, p59, p60 and p62).

For vegetarians
Buddhist 'meats' are on the dim sum menu at **Golden Palace** (see p62).

Dim sum £1.80-£4.90. **Set meal** £11-£18.50 per person (minimum 2). **Service** 10%. **Credit** AmEx, MC, V.
Last year we commented that the service here could be a 'bit rude', but this was certainly not the case on our latest visit. When two bottles of our chosen wine turned out to be sub-standard, the response could not have been more courteous or accommodating. Another improvement is that tedious muzak has given way to easy-listening Canto-pop. The menu, like the restaurant, is not huge, yet is adequate. Food was good, if not brilliant. Steamed scallops made a fresh, sweet appetiser, but came with a lacklustre sauce. Eel with black beans was on the bland side and perhaps slightly undercooked, resulting in a springy texture; and our green dish of gai lan (chinese broccoli) would have been sent back for a little more cooking had it not been redeemed by being so very fresh. Mui-choi kau-yuk was excellent: earthenware-cooked pork with preserved vegetables – a generous portion of properly fat-streaked, melt-in-the-mouth meat sitting on a bed of chopped vegetables in savoury-sweet juices.
Babies and children welcome; high chairs. Separate rooms for hire, seat 15 and 30. Takeaway service. Vegetarian menu. **Map 17 K7**.

SoChina NEW
38 Gerrard Street, W1D 5PB (7287 1313/ www.sochina.co.uk). Leicester Square or Piccadilly Circus tube. **Meals served** noon-11.30pm, **dim sum served** noon-6pm daily. **Main courses** £6-£9.50. **Dim sum** £2-£3.50. **Set meal** £10-£35 per person (minimum 2). **Service** 12.5%. **Credit** AmEx, DC, JCB, MC, V.
The name has changed, but the interior and even the matchbooks remain unchanged since this prime Gerrard Street site was called Aaura. Smiling greeters on the street, a flash interior (three airy, bright floors – including a mezzanine – with grey tiled flooring, a blond wood bar, big mirrors, plus two mighty dragons picked out in fairy lights on the wall) and a diverting menu also demand attention. Pity about the slushy Hong Kong pop music, though. The dim sum list has photos of all

Yauatcha

60-odd dishes. Here you'll find most of the regulars, but also unusual regional dishes: deep-fried bread roll, Peking-style, is a doughy offering served with condensed milk; shanghai spring onions pastry resembled a faintly stodgy apple turnover but had a delectable filling. Cooking aims at the heights, yet doesn't always get there. So though the slithery-fresh monk's-style vegetarian cheung fun (filled with mushrooms and crunchy slices of baby sweetcorn) was sublime, the sweet sesame dumplings were too thickly clad and had a gritty sugary coating. The full menu too has enticements, besides the many stir-fries: hot-pot with pork knuckle, Shanghai-style, for instance. Service on our visit was over-abundant, if well meaning.

Babies and children welcome; high chairs. Disabled: toilet. Separate room for hire, seats 40. Takeaway service. Vegetarian menu. **Map 17 K7**.

Fitzrovia W1

★ Hakkasan

2004 WINNER BEST CHINESE RESTAURANT

8 Hanway Place, W1T 1HD (7907 1888). Tottenham Court Road tube. Bar **Open** noon-12.30am Mon-Wed; noon-1.30am Thur-Sat; noon-midnight Sun. *Restaurant* **Lunch served** noon-3.15pm Mon-Fri; noon-4.30pm Sat, Sun. **Dinner served** 6-11.30pm Mon-Wed, Sun; 6pm-12.30am Thur-Sat. **Main courses** £11.50-£40. **Dim sum** £3.50-£16. *Both* **Service** 13%. **Credit** AmEx, MC, V.

Few London restaurants can beat the thrill of descending the green slate staircase into Hakkasan. Incense smoke and outlandish flowers greet you as you enter a subtly lit space of dark latticed screens that evokes the old houses of pre-revolutionary China. Started by the innovative Alan Yau, Hakkasan breaks the Chinatown mould by offering fine, pricey Chinese food in a venue that satisfies both western and oriental tastes. The dim sum is unrivalled in London. Come at lunchtime for crisp triangular pastries stuffed with venison; translucent, emerald green dumplings filled with prawn and fragrant chinese chives; and light-as-a-feather deep-fried snacks (stick to tea and it'll cost around £25 a head). Evening dining is a more mixed experience. Booking a table is ludicrously difficult. The cooking can be superb, but on a recent visit main courses weren't as startling as we remembered. 'Tong Fong' soft-shelled crabs, deep-fried and tossed with garlic and curry leaves, were superbly light but under-salted, and the garlicky salsa lacked pzazz. A stir-fry of asparagus, lily bulb and lotus stem with black pepper was tasty but not as fine as we've known it. One nice surprise was the richly flavoured sanbei chicken. Dessert was perfection itself: a tall dome of baked alaska stuffed with praline ice-cream and mandarin sorbet. There's a fine wine list and enticing cocktails, and service was helpful and well-informed. Come here for a really special occasion.

Booking advisable; essential dinner. Disabled: toilet. Dress: smart casual. Entertainment: DJ 9pm daily. Restaurant available for hire. Separate area for hire, seats 65. **Map 17 K5**.

Knightsbridge SW1

★ Mr Chow

2004 RUNNER-UP BEST CHINESE RESTAURANT

151 Knightsbridge, SW1X 7PA (7589 7347). Knightsbridge tube. **Lunch served** 12.30-3pm, **dinner served** 7pm-midnight daily. **Main courses** £12.50-£34. **Set lunch** £17 2 courses, £21 3 courses. **Service** 12.5%. **Credit** AmEx, DC, JCB, MC, V.

Fabulously expensive and fabulously glamorous in a slightly lived-in way, Mr Chow has changed little over the years. There are smoked mirrors, silver walnut-whip lampshades and high-quality linen; a short, sexy menu and a fashionable clientele. You don't expect such a chic restaurant to know its stuff when it comes to Chinese food, but Mr Chow does – think of it as a grandfather of Hakkasan (*see above*). Yes, there's sweet-and-sour pork, and red food dye is used, but you'll also find some brilliant, authentic Chinese dishes.

The Mr Chow noodles were a delicious rendition of a classic northern snack rarely found in London: lovely, springy hand-pulled pasta served with minced pork in a sweet, beany sauce. Drunken fish (slippery pieces of sole in a sweet, fragrant sauce) was superb, and the red-cooked pork knuckle sublimely tender (though excessively red). Less interesting were the squab in lettuce and the beijing chicken with walnuts. The highlight of an evening here is the live noodle-making demo: a chef teasing dough into spaghetti-thin pasta in a series of crazy looping movements. Service is slick and European in style.

Babies and children admitted. Booking advisable lunch; essential dinner. Separate room for hire, seats 75. Takeaway service. **Map 8 F9**.

Marylebone W1, NW1

Phoenix Palace

3-5 Glentworth Street, NW1 5PG (7486 3515). Baker Street tube. **Meals served** noon-11.30pm Mon-Sat; 11am-10.30pm Sun. **Main courses** £6.50-£25. **Set meal** £14 2 courses, £24 3 courses. **Service** 12.5%. **Credit** AmEx, JCB, MC, V.

Without doubt, Phoenix Palace's menu is among the most exciting in Chinese London – both its dim sum list and the lengthy full menu. The latter includes such banqueting centrepieces as baked lobster, and steamed dover sole with tangerine peel, as well as seasonal specials such as mixed funghi on tofu. We flitted in for lunchtime snacks: past the shiny bar area and into the capacious, windowless dining space at the rear (big round tables lending some class, though the place still resembles a hotel lounge). No dim sum menu was given to us: the first mistake in service that was confused and distant throughout. Several of the dishes are rare, if not new to London. Some are bizarre: peppered ostrich fillet on pulled noodles, or mini sausage rolls (which tasted as if they contained tinned frankfurters). Others were sublime: prawn and duck tientsin pasta soup exhibited a wealth of tongue-caressing textures; pork in yam croquettes melted in the mouth. Yet chicken in soya pastry roll (actually beancurd skin) had been overcooked, leaving the baby sweetcorn too soft. A pleasing multinational mix of diners (including plenty of Chinese) eats here. The Palace has the potential to be one of the best, but its act needs tightening.

Booking advisable. Takeaway service; delivery service. **Map 2 F4**.

Royal China

24-26 Baker Street, W1U 7AB (7487 4688/ www.royalchinagroup.co.uk). Baker Street tube. **Meals served** noon-11pm Mon-Thur; noon-11.30pm Fri, Sat; 11am-10pm Sun. **Dim sum served** noon-5pm daily. **Main courses** £7-£30. **Dim sum** £2.20-£4.50. **Set meal** £28-£38 per person (minimum 2). **Service** 12.5%. **Credit** AmEx, MC, V.

It pains us to write anything negative about the much-loved Royal China chain, which has been serving some of the best dim sum in London for years, but this branch looks in need of a revamp and a management shake-up. True, we arrived midweek at the end of the lunch shift, but we don't expect such a poor level of service and messy toilets in a restaurant of this calibre. Happily, the kitchen remains on good form. High points of our dim sum included luscious steamed scallop dumplings, with generous chunks of scallop and crunchy morsels of courgette. The steamed duck dumplings from the daily specials menu (well worth inspecting) were an unusual idea, but the execution was superb: slivers of duck combined with prawn and vegetable to create a rich but not overpowering mouthful, contained in a translucent pale green parcel. Also delicious was the glutinous rice in lotus leaves, the fresh scent of the leaves infusing the rice; it was packed with tasty chunks of chinese sausage and silky oyster mushrooms. Sesame paper prawns were also excellent, loaded with crisp toasted sesame seeds, the prawns moist and tender inside a light pastry wrapper.

Babies and children welcome; high chairs. Booking essential. Separate room for hire, seats 15. Takeaway service. Vegetarian menu. **Map 9 G5**.

Mayfair W1

★ Kai

65 South Audley Street, W1K 2QU (7493 8988/ www.kaimayfair.co.uk). Bond Street or Marble Arch tube. **Lunch served** noon-2.30pm Mon-Fri; 12.30-3pm Sat, Sun. **Dinner served** 6.30-11pm Mon-Sat; 6.30-10.30pm Sun. **Main courses** £11-£39. **Set lunch** £23 2 courses. **Service** 3.5%. **Credit** AmEx, DC, JCB, MC, V.

Kai's menu isn't huge, but it contains some fancifully named and wildly expensive dishes that must be there to tempt those with more money than sense. We've tried stag's penis soup in Hong Kong (hey, who hasn't?) and know that its prowess-enhancing properties are illusory, so we were not seduced by Kai's £32-a-shot version, exotically entitled 'celestial thunder'. Moving on swiftly, most dishes on the menu are choice and very well executed. Chew yim calamares made a good starter: tender squid crisply fried with just the right quantity of garlic, chilli and spiced salt. Then came melt-in-the-mouth Alaskan snowfish (black-skinned cod), fried to a fine crispness on the outside, but not one second overcooked and entirely devoid of grease. The claypot chinese bacon with garlic cloves was dark, dryish, slightly sweet and strongly flavoured with large purple-red leathery dried chillies – delicious. Sichuan-style stir-fried spicy aubergine was also sweetish and strongly flavoured, but didn't seem to unbalance the meal. Excellent wine, delicate desserts, complimentary chocolates artfully presented and unobtrusively attentive service completed a very pleasant experience.

Babies and children welcome; high chairs. Booking advisable. Dress: smart casual. Separate rooms for hire, seat 6 and 12. **Map 9 G7**.

Oriental

The Dorchester, 55 Park Lane, W1A 2HJ (7317 6328/www.dorchesterhotel.com). Green Park or Hyde Park Corner tube. **Lunch served** noon-2.30pm Mon-Fri. **Dinner served** 7-11pm Mon-Sat. **Main courses** £17.50-£29. **Set lunch** £17-£22 3 courses. **Set dinner** £48-£95. **Credit** AmEx, DC, JCB, MC, V.

Last year we protested about the Oriental's clientele and their mobile phones. This year was the same: much of our visit to the Dorchester hotel's luxurious Chinese restaurant was disturbed by a nearby diner using his mobile as a speakerphone; staff failed to intervene. The food was patchier than usual. We couldn't fault our selection from the new dim sum menu (including shanghai dumplings and shark's fin dumplings with coriander), competitively priced at £3 each. A key characteristic was coarse fillings that had clearly been handmade with a great deal of notable finesse. Attention to detail was also evident in the flawlessly prepared deep-fried mashed taro dumplings, the outside crust resembling an almost hairy surface. Mains weren't as good. Head chef Kenneth Poon's signature dish of braised brisket of beef with chinese turnip and carrot lacked depth. Gai lan with garlic had been somewhat overcooked. Pan-fried egg noodles with shredded pork and sichuan preserved vegetables was a bland hotchpotch. Service was attentive and the surroundings are lush and exquisite, but next time we may opt for one of the private dining rooms decked out in Chinese, Indian or Thai styles – just to get away from those mobiles.

Booking advisable dinner. Disabled: toilet. Dress: smart casual; no jeans or trainers. Separate rooms for hire, seat 6, 10 and 16. Vegetarian menu. **Map 9 G7**.

Piccadilly W1

★ Rong Cheng NEW

72 Shaftesbury Avenue, W1D 6NA (7287 8078). Leicester Square or Piccadilly Circus tube. **Meals served** noon-11pm daily. **Main courses** £4.50-£11.80. **Set meal** £9.50 3 courses (minimum 2). **Credit** JCB, MC, V.

Rong Cheng is an unusual restaurant with two chefs specialising in different regional cuisines.

One cooks everyday dishes from Fujian in south-eastern China; the other food from the Dong Bei – the north-eastern provinces bordering the easternmost part of Russia and Korea. These two strands of cooking attract Chinese customers from both regions, who sit and natter in their different dialects. And the restaurant also offers a standard Anglo-Canto menu for people who don't want to try something new. On our last visit we went Fujianese, and enjoyed clams in the shell with a sauce of red fermented beancurd, a soup of springy white fish balls filled with minced pork, and a plate of delicious snaking yellow noodles scattered with seafood. A gently peppered soup of seafood, beancurd and wispy egg white was pretty good too. This isn't posh food by any means, but it's tasty and refreshingly different. Staff are laid-back and friendly, and the restaurant is spick and span, though simply decorated.

Takeaway service. **Map 17 K7**.

Soho W1

★ Yauatcha NEW

2004 RUNNER-UP BEST DESIGN
15 Broadwick Street, W1F 0DE (7494 8888). Oxford Circus tube. *Tea house* **Tea/snacks served** 9am-11pm Mon-Sat; 9am-10.30pm Sun. **Set tea** £19 per person. *Restaurant* **Meals served** noon-11pm Mon-Sat; noon-10pm Sun. **Dim sum served** noon-11pm Mon-Fri; 11am-midnight Sat; 11am-10.30pm Sun. **Main courses** £3.50-£12. **Dim sum** £3-£14.50. *Both* **Service** 12.5%. **Credit** AmEx, MC, V.

Costing £4.2 million, deeply chic Yauatcha is the latest venture from restaurateur Alan Yau, the man behind Wagamama (*see p233*), Busaba Eathai (*see p246*) and Hakkasan (*see p56*). It occupies the basement and ground floors of Richard Rogers' new Ingeni building. In the basement, cool grey tables and chairs lie under a dark ceiling that twinkles with star-like bulbs. A tropical fish tank extends the whole length of the bar. This is a casual venue aimed at grazing dim sum eaters and sippers of tea; unusually, dim sum is served from 10am until late (note that you there's a 90-minute table turnaround). Tea is one of the highlights. Look out for dark, smoky Yunnanese tea, and huang jin gui from Fujian province, a magnificently sweet and fragrant oolong. The dim sum menu resembles Hakkasan's, and is just as tempting. Slithery cheung fun was stuffed with spankingly fresh prawns and gai lan (chinese broccoli), while pork and spring onion cakes had crisp, melt-in-the-mouth pastry. Steamed mooli cake with dried shrimp turned out to be a delicious porridgy goo, enlivened by coriander. Chiu chow dumplings, filled with minced pork and peanuts, were well-crafted but a little bland. The short dessert list included a delectable sichuan pepper panna cotta, accompanied unnecessarily with cocoa sorbet and a fruit coulis. Service can be a bit disordered. More thrilling than the dim sum zone is the exquisite tea room upstairs (*see p302*), home to some of the most shatteringly beautiful pâtisserie in London.

Babies and children welcome. Booking essential. Disabled: toilet. No smoking. Takeaway service. **Map 17 J6**.

Yming

35-36 Greek Street, W1D 5DL (7734 2721/ www.yming.com). Leicester Square, Piccadilly Circus or Tottenham Court Road tube. **Meals served** noon-11.45pm Mon-Sat. **Main courses** £5-£10. **Set lunch** (noon-6pm) £10 3 courses. **Set meal** £15-£20 per person (minimum 2). **Service** 10%. **Credit** AmEx, DC, JCB, MC, V.

Avoiding the usual run of Cantonese dishes, Yming likes to be different – yet, despite our waiter's claims, it doesn't serve only northern Chinese food. We started with steamed pork dumplings: savoury and accompanied by a simple but nicely judged sauce of tender ginger needles in vinegar. The chicken dish that followed was also simple: strips of white breast meat fried with bitter-hot red pepper slices. Our next choice, daringly made to catch the menu's adventurous

Rong Cheng. See p57.

spirit, was neither simple nor good: a concoction of shelled prawn balls in a sauce studded with mango pieces; it was nauseatingly sweet and an insult to the prawns. Any Cantonese restaurant worth its salt will offer half a dozen or more fresh vegetables, but Yming's menu was very short in this department: only pak choi or 'four season beans' were available. We chose the latter and were agreeably surprised by the authentic dry-fried dark green beans in finely chopped red chilli and black fermented soybeans. Yming occupies a corner site, with wrap-around windows that make for a comfortable, bright lunch venue. Service was friendly and competent.
Babies and children admitted. Book weekends. No-smoking tables. Separate rooms for hire, seating 10 and 18. Takeaway service.
Map 17 K6.

West

Acton W3

★ North China
305 Uxbridge Road, W3 9QU (8992 9183/ www.northchina.co.uk). Acton Town tube/ 207 bus. **Lunch served** noon-2.30pm, **dinner served** 6-11pm daily. **Main courses** £5-£8.80. **Set meal** £14-£18 per person 3 courses (minimum 2). **Credit** AmEx, DC, MC, V.
On a Monday night this smart, intimate restaurant was packed with locals tucking into the stir-fries that make up the bulk of the menu. Having given

the required 24-hours' notice, we went for the peking duck in three courses, and a few other dishes that stood out. First, the pan-grilled handmade dumplings, which easily surpassed the mass-produced equivalents served elsewhere. The mixed cold meat selection was great too, doused in a potent garlic sauce on a bed of shredded vegetables. Sliced fillet of sole in wine sauce melted in the mouth, just as the menu promised. Our duck spectacular began with wrapping gloriously golden, crisp duck skin into handmade pancakes, along with cucumber, spring onion and hoi sin sauce. Next, we folded large chunks of duck and vegetables into lettuce leaves. No sauce: it wasn't needed. The final course was a deliciously rich milky soup made from the bones, ginger and little else: tremendous. For dessert, we asked about North China's legendary red bean paste pancake served with strawberry coulis, a stroke of genius by the chef. 'Only the Chinese know about the red bean paste pancake,' said our friendly waitress. Not any more.
Babies and children welcome; high chairs. Booking advisable; essential dinner Fri, Sat. Separate room for hire, seats 36. Takeaway service; delivery service. Vegetarian menu.

Bayswater W2

Four Seasons
84 Queensway, W2 3RL (7229 4320). Bayswater or Queensway tube. **Meals served** noon-11.15pm Mon-Sat; noon-10.45pm Sun. **Main courses**

£5.50-£25. **Set meal** £12.50 2 courses; £14.50-£17.50 per person (minimum 2). **Service** 12.5%. **Credit** AmEx, MC, V.
There's infuriatingly good food to be found at Four Seasons. Infuriating because, with all the trials and tribulations of an evening here, a meal can too often be a pretty dismal affair. We had to queue for 20 minutes for our pre-booked table. Once we were seated, the staff's main objective, it seemed, was to get us out again as quickly as they could. They chivvied us to order quickly, which given the capacious menu, is not easy. Look to the 'chef's recommendations' at the back for the pearls. Start with soup of the day (comforting pork broth with lotus seeds, perhaps). Next, don't miss the cantonese duck: an astonishingly luscious creature. Fish cake with seasonal vegetables, and meltingly delicious minced pork and aubergine hot-pot were faultless. Only deep-fried squid (mistranslated on the menu as 'dried squid', which doesn't sound quite so appetising) was prosaic, though tender. Chinese locals cram into the thin room, barely noticing the basic furnishings of cream-painted brick, mirrors and plastic plants. Tourists eat here too, though they're likely to be treated as ignorant: fit only for set meals. We had to holler for chopsticks. That such mayhem occurs on a Tuesday (albeit in July) shows Four Seasons' popularity – but next time we'll order takeaway duck, and duck out.
Babies and children welcome. Takeaway service. Vegetarian menu.
Map 7 C6.

Magic Wok

100 Queensway, W2 3RR (7792 9767).
Bayswater or Queensway tube. **Meals served**
noon-11pm daily. **Main courses** £5-£12.50.
Set meal £11.20-£24 per person (minimum 2).
Service 12.5%. **Credit** AmEx, MC, V.
The fantastic six whole pages of chef's specials
promised delights, yet on our latest visit Magic
Wok failed to shine. This is a busy restaurant, but,
tellingly, there wasn't a single Chinese diner, unlike
at the culinary superior Four Seasons (*see p58*) just
up the road. Deep-fried crispy soft-shell baby crab
with garlic and spicy chilli was the best part of our
meal, the crab shell soft enough to be consumed
whole; it made an excellent appetiser accompanied
by plenty of cold beer. After this, however, things
went downhill fast. Deep-fried chilli prawns in
crispy parcels were greasy and unaccountably
flavoured with curry sauce. Steamed chicken with
dried lily and black fungus in lotus leaves sounded
wonderful, but the texture of the meat was
spongy and off-putting. A special of steamed
turbot with winter vegetables and mung bean
threads was better, though not generous with the
fish. And monks vegetable rolls wrapped in
beancurd (another special) were almost entirely
tasteless. Not the most exciting of meals. Then
again, most customers were ordering sweet-and-
sour pork, which perhaps explains why, on our
visit, the chef was not inspired to fulfil the
promise of the menu.
Babies and children admitted. Book dinner.
Separate room for hire, seats 40. Takeaway
service. **Map 7 C6.**

★ Mandarin Kitchen

2004 RUNNER-UP BEST CHINESE
RESTAURANT
14-16 Queensway, W2 3RX (7727 9012).
Bayswater or Queensway tube. **Meals served**
noon-11.30pm daily. **Main courses** £5.90-£25.
Set meal £10.90 per person (minimum 2).
Credit AmEx, DC, JCB, MC, V.
The British HQ of the lobster trade, this place
claims to serve 50 to 100 of them every night:
steamed, dry-fried with spices and garlic, slathered
in black bean sauce, or even as Japanese sashimi.
We took ours with lashings of fragrant ginger and
spring onion, on a bed of noodles; it was
gorgeously fresh and juicy (though the noodles
don't rival those at Royal China). Six dainty oysters
steamed in their rugged shells with a scattering of
salted olive leaves were excellent, and stewed pork
with preserved vegetables was a fine version of a
rustic Chinese dish, the meat braised to melting
tenderness, its flavours sharpened by the dark
mustard greens. A cold platter of chaozhou duck
with a garlicky dip was a little disappointing, and
stir-fried pea leaves weren't fresh enough.
Generally, the Mandarin is a reliable bet for
spankingly fresh seafood, and a magnet for
discerning east Asians. Service tends to be good
these days. Don't expect to be thrilled by the decor,
which is steadfastly 1970s with its undulating,
textured ceiling and smoked-glass mirrors; the
street frontage is so nondescript you'd walk
straight past if you didn't know better.
Babies and children welcome; high chair. Book
dinner. Takeaway service. **Map 7 C7.**

★ Royal China

13 Queensway, W2 4QJ (7221 2535/
www.royalchinagroup.co.uk). Bayswater or
Queensway tube. **Meals served** noon-11pm
Mon-Thur; noon-11.30pm Fri, Sat; 11am-10pm
Sun. **Dim sum served** noon-5pm daily.
Main courses £6-£29. **Dim sum** £1.90-£2.70.
Set meal £28-£36 per person (minimum 2).
Service 12.5%. **Credit** AmEx, MC, V.
The original branch of the glittering chain of
black-lacquered restaurants has long been famed
for its dim sum, but this year we sampled a meal
from the full menu. To get the best from this is
tricky – but memorably rewarding. For a start, just
skim-read the main à la carte (the only one that's
displayed outside). The best cooking is to be found
on the separate pamphlet of chef's specials. From
this, winter melon soup with dried scallops had
various textural treats (lotus seeds, soft melon, a

plump prawn) in delicate stock, while shredded
chicken tossed with green bean pasta (one of
several alluring cold dishes) contained strips of
crunchy carrot and cucumber, and resilient jelly
fish in a sesame oil dressing – marvellous. Main
courses maintained the standard with crispy
chicken stuffed with glutinous rice (two elongated
breasts encased in batter with a thin layer of
flavourful rice); minced pork and dried scallop hot-
pot with Japanese beancurd (savour the luxurious
beancurd: like barely cooked egg white); and sugar
snaps with root vegetables and preserved olives
(the olives adding pungency and appealing
gumminess). Desserts too are fabulous, and service
(from gold-jacketed waitresses) is solicitous.
Babies and children welcome; high chairs. Book
Fri, Sat; bookings not accepted lunch Sat, Sun.
Separate room for hire, seats 40. Takeaway
service. **Map 7 C7.**

South West
Earl's Court SW5

Mr Wing

242-244 Old Brompton Road, SW5 0DE (7370
4450/www.mrwing.com). Earl's Court tube.
Meals served 12.30pm-midnight daily.
Main courses £6.95-£26.95. **Set meal**
£32.95 per person (minimum 2) 3 courses.
Cover £2. **Credit** AmEx, DC, JCB, MC, V.
Mr Wing's menu is less extensive than most, yet
harbours several Thai-inspired dishes. We steered
clear of these, starting with a competently
executed but pricey wun tun soup. Barely had we
finished when our steamed scallops arrived,
overpowered by salty black bean sauce. Curiously,
one scallop arrived bereft of its accompanying
bean thread noodles. This apparent lack of
attention proved a sign of things to come. The
'emperor' combination of battered fish and minced
prawn would normally be a good match, but
spring onion sauce made the dish extremely soggy.
An impressive-sounding saké clay pot of chicken,
lily buds, red dates and wood-ear mushrooms was
similarly unappetising; the dates were sweet and
the lily flower crunchy, but the chicken was
overcooked. Hand-pulled noodles with chinese,
straw and wood-ear mushrooms were overwhelmed
by garlic. The sounds of running water from the
entrance waterfall, jazz music and a loud tea kettle
provided the backdrop to our meal. Although our
waitress was pleasant and attentive, she could do
little to rescue us from this disappointing meal.
Subdued lighting, a dark-wood dining room and
an unjustified cover charge added to our gloom.
Babies and children welcome. Booking advisable
lunch; essential dinner. Entertainment: jazz
musicians 8.15-11.45pm Fri, Sat. Separate
rooms for hire, seat 15-90. Takeaway service.
Map 13 B11.

Putney SW15

Royal China

3 Chelverton Road, SW15 1RN (8788 0907).
East Putney tube/Putney rail/14, 37, 74 bus.
Lunch served noon-3.30pm Mon-Sat;
noon-4pm Sun. **Dinner served** 6.30-11pm
Mon-Sat; 6.30-10.30pm Sun. **Dim sum served**
noon-3.30pm daily. **Main courses** £5.50-£40.
Dim sum £1.80-£5. **Set meal** £23-£35
per person (minimum 2). **Service** 12.5%.
Credit AmEx, DC.
Once, but no longer part of the Royal China chain,
this restaurant still sports the distinguishing black
lacquer and gold interior. It's also one of the few
south London venues to offer dim sum. Service is
friendly and helpful. We opened with a 'thousand
year old' egg and pickled ginger, and had intended
a scallop and asparagus dish to follow, but the
waitress volunteered that the scallops were frozen
and that for fresh ones we should have the steamed
scallops in shell. We didn't regret being persuaded;
the succulent molluscs were huge, served with
glass noodles and the usual sauce of chilli,
coriander and soy. Crisp-roast chicken was
overcooked by Cantonese standards and the
prawn-paste stuffing did little for it, but it looked

appetising and was indeed quite tasty. We also
accepted a recommendation to try the gai lan
(chinese broccoli) served in a dark brown sauce
with a covering of sliced oyster mushrooms; it
made a change, but the delicious green vegetable
wasn't enhanced by the bland sauce, and the price
seemed high. Desserts were excellent: a very tasty
mango pudding and London's best pan-fried red
bean pancake (dau-sa woh-beng).
Babies and children welcome. Booking advisable;
bookings not accepted lunch Sun. Takeaway
service; delivery service (within 3.5-mile radius).

South Kensington SW3

Good Earth

233 Brompton Road, SW3 2EP (7584 3658).
South Kensington tube. **Meals served** noon-
11pm Mon-Sat; 12.30-10.45pm Sun. **Main**
courses £7-£12. **Set lunch** £9.95 2 courses.
Set dinner £25 2 courses, £35 3 courses.
Service 12.5%. **Credit** AmEx, MC, V.
This smart Knightsbridge restaurant delivers a
pleasant and low-key dining experience. The menu
offers a range of South-east Asian dishes plus a
fairly limited batch of more standard Chinese food.
Malaysian chicken salad was a fresh and zingy
starter, alongside a dish of plump, tasty, soft-shell
crabs. Soups included Thai-style tom yum and an
excellent vegetarian wun tun, the dumplings
freshly made with crunchy water chestnuts.
Unusually for Chinese restaurants, vegetarians are
fairly well catered for. For mains, we dipped into
Malaysia again with sambal monkfish: well-
textured chunks in a fairly dry hot and sour sauce.
A dish of stir-fried tofu with mangetout was
unusually sweet, yet nicely done. Although many
of the dishes are given Sichuan-style names, the
cuisine here is anything but traditional. There is
strong Japanese influence in both the presentation,
which is very attractive, and the cooking, which
tends towards clean and understated flavours.
Babies and children welcome. Booking advisable.
Takeaway service; delivery service (within 3-mile
radius). Vegetarian menu. **Map 14 E10.**
For branches see index.

South
Waterloo SE1

Four Regions

County Hall, Riverside Building, Westminster
Bridge Road, SE1 7PB (7928 0988/
www.fourregions.co.uk). Westminster tube/
Waterloo tube/ rail. **Lunch served** noon-3pm
daily. **Dinner served** 6-11.30pm Mon-Sat;
6-11pm Sun. **Main courses** £7-£12. **Set meal**
£25-£38 per person (minimum 2). **Credit** AmEx,
DC, JCB, MC, V.
There's no finer London location for a restaurant
than the old County Hall. If you're lucky enough
to get a window seat, you'll have breathtaking
views. So captivating was the sight, we almost
forgot why we were here. The bang bang chicken
starter brought us down to earth with a bump; its
sesame and peanut sauce was overly sweet,
containing undissolved granules of sugar. Chicken
with asparagus soup was better, comprising good-
quality stock and fresh asparagus. Tropical crispy
duck was overdone and somewhat tough as a
result; its orange sauce had little flavour, the
promised Grand Marnier seemingly absent. We
expected the double-cooked pork belly hot-pot to
have been braised in its accompanying sauce, but
instead the sauce seemed to have been poured on
top prior to service. Consequently, the distinctive
star anise flavour was absent. Given our lack of
success with dishes thus far, we expected little
from our final selection of bamboo pith and green
vegetable. We were surprised. This delectable dish
offered a delightful crunch and starred in an
otherwise lacklustre meal. Waiters were cheerful
and attentive, but busy; the warm, wood-panelled
room was heaving with tourists when we left.
Babies and children welcome; high chairs. Booking
essential. Restaurant available for hire. Separate
room for hire, seats 160. Takeaway service.
Vegetarian menu. **Map 10 M9.**
For branch see index.

Dim sum

The Cantonese term 'dim sum' means something like 'touch the heart'. It is used to refer to the vast array of dumplings and other titbits that southern Chinese people like to eat with their tea for breakfast or at lunchtime. It's an eating ritual simply known as 'yum cha', or 'drinking tea'. Many of London's Chinese restaurants have a lunchtime dim sum menu, and at weekends you'll find them packed with Cantonese families. A dim sum feast is one of London's most extraordinary gastronomic bargains: how else can you lunch lavishly in one of the capital's premier restaurants for as little as £15 a head?

Dim sum are served as a series of tiny dishes, each bearing perhaps two or three dumplings or a small helping of steamed spare ribs or seafood – think of it as a Chinese version of tapas, served with tea. You can order according to appetite or curiosity: a couple of more moderate eaters might be satisfied with half a dozen dishes, while *Time Out*'s

greedy reviewers always end up with a table laden with little snacks. Some people like to fill up with a plateful of stir-fried noodles, others to complement the meal with some delicious stir-fried greens from the main menu.

But however wildly you order, if you stick to the dim sum menu and avoid more expensive specials that waiting staff may wave under your nose, the modesty of the bill is sure to come as a pleasant surprise. The low price of individual dishes (most cost between £1.80 and £3) makes eating dim sum the perfect opportunity to try more unusual delicacies – chicken's feet, anyone?

Two London restaurants serve dim sum Hong Kong-style, from circulating trollies: the cheerful **New World** (*see p55*) and the rather-less-cheerful **Chuen Cheng Ku** (*see p51*). Some of the snacks are wheeled out from the kitchen after being cooked; others gently steam as they go or are finished on the trolley to order. The

trolley system has the great advantage that you see exactly what's on offer, but if you go at a quiet lunchtime some of the food may be a little jaded by the time it reaches your table. Other places offer the snacks à la carte, so everything should be freshly cooked.

Dim sum lunches at the weekend tend to be boisterous occasions, so they are great for children (though remember that adventurous toddlers and hot dumpling trolleys are not a happy combination). Strict vegetarians are likely to be very limited in their menu choices, as most snacks contain either meat or seafood (honourable exceptions include **Golden Palace** in Harrow – *see p62* – which has a generous selection of vegetarian snacks).

HOW TO EAT DIM SUM
The first thing to remember is that most restaurants cease serving dim sum at four or five in the afternoon, when the rice-based evening menus

take over. However, led by **Yauatcha** (*see p57*), a few pioneers, including **Chuen Cheng Ku** (*see p51*), **Dragon Inn** (*see p51*) and **Drunken Monkey** (*see p61*), are starting to serve the snacks at night. More often, though, when restaurants list so-called dim sum on the evening menus, they are just referring to a few lonely dumplings offered as starters, not to the whole yum cha ritual described above. Dim sum specialists always list the snacks on separate, smaller menus, which are roughly divided into steamed dumplings, deep-fried dumplings, sweet dishes and so on. Try to order a selection of different types of food, with plenty of light steamed dumplings to counterbalance the heavier deep-fried items. If you are lunching with a large group, make sure you order multiples of everything, as most portions consist of about three dumplings.

Tea is the traditional accompaniment to the feast. Some restaurants offer a

South East

Greenwich SE10

Peninsula
Holiday Inn Express, Bugsby's Way, SE10 0GD (8858 2028). North Greenwich tube. **Meals served** noon-11pm Mon-Fri; 11am-11pm Sat, Sun. **Dim sum served** noon-5pm Mon-Fri; 11am-5pm Sat, Sun. **Main courses** £5.90-£9. **Dim sum** £1.90-£3.20. **Set meal** £14-£18 per person (minimum 2). **Service** 10%. **Credit** AmEx, MC, V.

Don't be put off by the fact that Peninsula occupies the entire ground floor of a new hotel standing in wasteland within sight of the infamous Dome. It serves seriously authentic Cantonese food from a menu as extensive as anything in Chinatown. At 7pm just one table was occupied, but by 7.30pm the place was humming, and more than half the customers were Chinese. Out of curiosity we tried the oysters and roast pork with garlic, which arrived still bubbling in its clay cooking pot: it looked good, but we decided the ingredients were no better suited to each other than they sounded. Baked squid with salt and (chilli-) pepper was a bit soggy, quite chewy and sparsely salted. Much better was spinach with fermented beancurd (fu-yu boh-choi), which was full of heady pungent flavour. It was off-menu, and we tested the kitchen further by asking for bitter melon and beef; this was superb, the thick fermented black soybean sauce holding together the slippery bitterness of the melon and the sweet juiciness of the meat. Portions were generous and the bill moderate. Well worth the trip to Greenwich (and parking is easy).
Babies and children welcome; high chairs; nappy-changing facilities. Booking not accepted before 5pm. Disabled: toilet. Separate rooms for parties, seating 40 and 100. Takeaway service.

East

Docklands E14, E16

★ Royal China
2004 RUNNER-UP BEST CHINESE RESTAURANT
30 Westferry Circus, E14 8RR (7719 0888). Canary Wharf tube/DLR/Westferry DLR. **Meals served** noon-11pm Mon-Thur; noon-11.30pm Fri, Sat; 11am-10pm Sun. **Dim sum served** noon-5pm daily. **Main courses** £7-£40. **Dim sum** £2.20-£4.50. **Set meal** £28-£36 per person (minimum 2). **Service** 12.5%. **Credit** AmEx, DC, JCB, MC, V.

Forget the Bayswater branch, with its stressful weekend queueing, and head instead to this jewel in the Royal China crown. On a warm spring evening, we sipped champagne cocktails on the outside terrace, watching the sun set over the glittering sweep of the Thames. The menu here is one of the best and most authentic Cantonese selections in town; the specials list (translated) offers more unusual dishes (suckling pig for £150, anyone?). The dishes we tried were a successful lot. Whole king prawns were deep-fried and encrusted with a delicious paste of salted duck egg yolk; slithery razor clams came stir-fried with crisp celery in a rich shrimpy sauce. Green beans tossed in a succulent relish of minced pork and dark olives were also good, but the highlight of the meal was unquestionably the garlicky hot-pot of eel and bitter melon. Dim sum are excellent too. Customers are thoroughly international, with a high proportion of Chinese. Service, though occasionally hectic, is much better than at the Bayswater branch. The place is done up in typical Royal China style, with plenty of gilding and lacquer. Merits a visit thanks to the food, but what really makes this place special is the glorious riverside location.

Babies and children welcome; high chairs. Booking advisable; essential lunch Mon-Fri. Disabled: toilet. Separate room for parties, seats 30. Tables outdoors (20, terrace). Takeaway service; delivery service.

Yi-Ban NEW
London Regatta Centre, Dockside Road, E16 2QT (7473 6699/www.yi-ban.co.uk). Royal Albert DLR. **Meals served** noon-11pm Mon-Sat; 11am-11pm Sun. **Dim sum served** noon-5pm Mon-Sat; 11am-5pm Sun. **Main courses** £6-£25. **Dim sum** £2-£2.50. **Set meal** £19 3 courses. **Service** 10%. **Credit** AmEx, MC, V.

Located in post-industrial E16, Yi-Ban's first-floor dining room offers great views of the Royal Albert Dock and London City Airport. Spacious and airy, with large windows and a wooden floor, it's an extremely elegant venue. At night multicoloured lights bathe the inner walls of translucent white material, introducing a more modern feel. The main menu contains the expected Cantonese favourites, plus a few interesting additions, but the best dishes were on the Chinese-language menu. Our first waiter refused to translate, but the second advised us well. The house soup featured pork and lotus root; it had tremendous depth of flavour, having been cooked all day. We'd also recommend the stuffed prawn salt and pepper pigs' intestines – a delightful change from the beancurd equivalent – and the mouth-watering aubergine, chicken and salted fish hot-pot (omitted from the main menu selection). Generous and perfectly executed mixed-meat fried noodles completed the meal. Daytime dim sum here compares well with that of many other restaurants, including nearby Royal China (*see above*) – and we've rarely had to queue. Service can be variable, though. Drinks include a respectable wine list plus a selection of teas.
Babies and children welcome; high chairs. Disabled: toilet. Takeaway service. Vegetarian menu.

selection of different teas, although they may not tell you this unless you ask. Musty bo lay (pu'er in Mandarin Chinese) or fragrant 'Iron Buddha' (tie guanyin) are delicious alternatives to the jasmine blossom that is normally served by default to non-Chinese guests. Waiters should keep your teapots filled (at no extra cost) throughout the meal: just leave the teapot lid tilted at an angle or upside down to signal that you want a top-up.

London's best dim sum are found at siblings **Hakkasan** (*see p56*) and **Yauatcha** (*see p57*), which offer a sublime selection of dumplings in glamorous settings, and the impeccable **Royal China** restaurants in Bayswater (*see p59*), Baker Street (*see p57*), Docklands (*see below*) and St John's Wood (*see p62*). The dim sum at **Phoenix Palace** (*see p57*) and **Imperial China** (*see p53*) are also impressive, and **Royal Dragon** (*see p55*) scores on food if not on atmosphere. There's also friendly

Shanghai in Dalston, **Yi-Ban** in Docklands (for both, *see below*), **Royal China** in Putney (*see p59*), **Local Friends** in Golders Green and **Golden Palace** in Harrow (for both, *see p62*).

The following is a guide to the basic canon of dim sum served in London (spelling may vary depending on the transliteration used):

Char siu bao: fluffy steamed bun stuffed with barbecued pork in a sweet-savoury sauce.
Char siu puff pastry or **roast pork puff**: triangular puff-pastry snack, filled with barbecued pork, scattered with sesame seeds and baked in an oven.
Cheung fun: slithery sheets of steamed rice pasta wrapped around fresh prawns, barbecued pork or deep-fried dough sticks and splashed with a sweet soy-based sauce. At its best, it is meltingly delicious, although some non-Chinese dislike the texture.
Chiu chow fun gwor: soft steamed dumpling with a

wheat-starch wrapper, filled with pork, vegetables and peanuts. Chiu chow is a regional Chinese cooking style that is popular in Hong Kong.
Chive dumpling: steamed prawn meat and Chinese chives in a translucent wrapper.
Har gau: steamed minced prawn dumpling with a translucent wheat-starch wrapper.
Nor mai gai or **steamed glutinous rice in lotus leaf**: lotus-leaf parcel enclosing moist sticky rice with pork, mushrooms, salty duck egg yolks and other bits and pieces, infused with the herby fragrance of the leaf.
Paper-wrapped prawns: tissue-thin rice paper enclosing plump prawn meat, sometimes scattered with sesame seeds, deep-fried.
Sago cream with yam: cool, sweet soup of coconut milk with sago pearls and morsels of taro.
Scallop dumpling: delicate steamed dumpling filled with scallop (sometimes with prawn) and vegetables.

Shark's fin dumpling: small steamed dumpling with a wheaten wrapper pinched into a frilly cockscomb shape on top; it is filled with minced prawn and pork, and, if you're lucky, tiny fronds of shark's fin.
Siu loon bao: Shanghai-style round dumpling with a whirled pattern on top and a juicy minced pork filling.
Siu mai: a little gathered dumpling with an open top, a wheatflour wrapper and a minced pork filling; traditionally it is topped with a little crab coral, but minced carrot and other substitutes are common.
Taro croquette or **yam croquette**: egg-shaped, deep-fried dumpling with a frizzy, melt-in-your mouth outer layer made of mashed taro, with a savoury minced pork filling.
Turnip paste: heavy slab of creamy paste made from glutinous rice flour and white oriental radishes, studded with fragments of wind-dried pork, sausage and dried shrimps and fried to a golden brown on either side.

The Restaurants

Shoreditch E1

Drunken Monkey NEW
222 Shoreditch High Street, E1 6PJ (7392 9606/www.thedrunkenmonkey.info). Liverpool Street tube/rail/35, 47, 242, 344 bus. **Meals served** noon-11.30pm Mon-Fri; 6pm-midnight Sat; noon-11.30pm Sun. **Dim sum served** noon-11.30pm Mon-Fri; 6-11.30pm Sat; noon-10.30pm Sun. **Main courses** £4.50-£6.50. **Dim sum** £2.50-£4.50. **Service** 10%. **Credit** AmEx, MC, V.
If you want Chinese food in the pub, you'll be delighted by Drunken Monkey. Owners Heath Ball and Stephen Chan serve dim sum, but have ditched the daytime only custom and the traditional serving of tea. Instead, dumplings and simple meals are offered alongside cocktails, wines and beers. Chinese red lanterns shed a rosy light over a long bar and repro Chinese antique tables, conjuring up a decadent scene of old China, or of trendy bars in today's Beijing and Shanghai. A thumping soundtrack adds to the atmosphere. The restaurant serves one-dish meals of barbecued pork or roast duck with rice, noodle soups and even peking duck, but most appealing are the dumplings and snacks. Most dishes we tasted were authentic and surprisingly good. Juicy prawns came in feather-light rice paper; deep-fried strips of squid were fabulous with their deep kiss of garlic and chilli. Some steamed dumplings had a tendency towards sogginess, but the siu mai were exemplary and the lotus leaf rice fragrant and delicious. A stir-fry of chinese broccoli was perfectly seasoned if somewhat overdone. The drinks list plays with the oriental theme, using Asian flavours such as lychee juice and saké.
Babies and children welcome. Entertainment: DJs 9pm Tue-Sun. Separate room for parties, seats 30. Takeaway service. **Map 6 R4.**

North East
Dalston E8

★ Shanghai
41 Kingsland High Street, E8 2JS (7254 2878). Dalston Kingsland rail/67, 76, 149 bus. **Meals served** noon-11pm, **dim sum** served noon-5pm daily. **Main courses** £5.20-£7.20. **Dim sum** £2.90-£3.90. **Set meal** £12.90-£14.90 per person (minimum 2). **Credit** MC, V.
This hugely popular Dalston restaurant occupies the premises of an old eel and pie shop, and a few eel-inspired decorations remain. Food varies from mediocre to delightful. Hot-and-sour soup was heavy and harshly vinegared, but steamed monkfish was a delicate assembly of pale fish flesh and shiitake mushrooms with lashings of fragrant garlic. Malaysian-style spinach was juicy, with intense shrimp-paste seasoning and flashes of scarlet chilli. The dim sum tends to be good. The atmosphere is laid-back, staff are always friendly, and it's a favourite venue for hilarious, uninhibited karaoke evenings in the private rooms at the back – but bear in mind that the set menus served at such parties are not the best the kitchen can offer.
Babies and children welcome; high chairs. Booking advisable. Disabled: toilet. Separate rooms for parties, both seating 45. Takeaway service. Vegetarian menu. **Map 25 B5.**

North
Camden Town & Chalk Farm NW1

★ The New Culture Revolution
43 Parkway, NW1 7PN (7267 2700). Camden Town tube. **Lunch served** noon-11pm daily. **Main courses** £4.60-£10. **Set meal** £5.50. **Service** (over £20) 10%. **Credit** AmEx, JCB, MC, V.

This cheerful, family-friendly noodle bar is fine for a quick carbohydrate fix. It's simply and tastefully furnished with Chinese modern art; classical music plays; and the young waiters are charming. The menu and presentation is simplicity itself. This worked well for some dishes, less well for others. Grilled prawns with green chilli and garlic were fresh and enjoyable. Other offerings were distinctly lacking in finesse. A salad of soggy chunks of lotus root over chilly iceberg lettuce in soy sauce dressing is one fusion experiment we'll not be revisiting. Sichuan chilli beef lao mein noodles was a big, solid, bland bowl of comfort food, without a hint of chilli and too much green pepper. A new South-east Asian strand to the menu, including laksa and curries, promises a few more concessions to taste buds – but the distinctly moreish guo tei pan-fried dumplings are still the best reason to visit. They come with a range of fillings including fish: hardly traditional, but very tasty.
Babies and children welcome; high chairs. Booking advisable; essential weekends. No-smoking tables. Separate room for parties, seats 20. Takeaway service. **Map 27 C2.**

Swiss Cottage NW3

★ Green Cottage
9 New College Parade, Finchley Road, NW3 5EP (7722 5305/7892). Finchley Road or Swiss Cottage tube. **Meals served** noon-11.15pm daily. **Main courses** £5.80-£17. **Set meal** £12.50-£25 per person (minimum 2). **Service** 10%. **Credit** (over £10) AmEx, MC, V.
Food at Green Cottage is a more than an adequate distraction from the restaurant's dreary ground-floor dining room, where a dark brown ceiling casts a gloomy shadow. The off-menu soup of the day had proved too popular with other diners, so instead we opted for pickled cabbage, pork and beancurd soup. The cabbage was sweet and

crunchy and the broth came packed with ginger, but not enough to balance the chef's exuberant addition of soy sauce. Next, we tried a selection of barbecued meat – the dish that draws Chinese people here from across London. The roast duck was fatty, just as the Chinese like it; the taste was incredible. The pork (both crispy roast and char siu) was excellent too. Roasted chicken in red beancurd sauce was moist and the skin crisp. Its sauce, served as a dip, was deliciously tart, with an unusually deep flavour that we've been craving ever since. Seafood chow mein finished our meal, but only because the restaurant's popular dessert of chilled sago with melon had sold out. Service was polite and attentive. Next time, we'll go earlier in the evening and sample the impressive selection of Buddhist vegetable dishes too.
Babies and children welcome. Booking advisable; essential dinner. Restaurant available for hire. Takeaway service. Vegetarian menu.
Map 28 B4.

Map 28 B4.

North West
Belsize Park NW3

Weng Wah House
240 Haverstock Hill, NW3 2AE (7794 5123/ www.wengwahgroup.com). Belsize Park tube/ 168, 268, C11 bus. **Lunch served** 12.30-2.45pm, **dinner served** 6-11.30pm Mon-Fri. **Meals served** 12.30pm-midnight Sat; 12.30-11.15pm Sun. **Main courses** £5.30-£9.90. **Set lunch** £4.95 2 courses. **Set meal** £12.50-£18.50 per person (minimum 2). **Service** 10%. **Credit** JCB, MC, V.
Most of our fellow diners at Weng Wah House were non-Chinese. The ground-floor dining room is bright and modern, with large, well-spaced tables. On previous visits we've enjoyed the mapo doufu (diced beancurd and dried chillies mixed with minced pork) and spinach in fermented beancurd and chilli. This time we tried the dim sum. A chef's special of mussels encased in a thin batter was way too peppery. Steamed ostrich sticky parcel (a variation on mixed meat dumpling) had an overwhelming smoky flavour that tasted artificial. Stir-fried turnip paste in XO sauce was much better, the cubes of turnip paste working well alongside the sauce, beansprouts and strips of pork. Cuttlefish cakes with coriander were moist, tasty and perfectly deep-fried. Conversely, pan-grilled vegetable beancurd rolls had absorbed too much oil, affecting the flavour. Going off menu, we enjoyed crispy fried noodles with seafood; the portion was small but delicately seasoned. Service was friendly yet disorganised (we only discovered almond cuttlefish balls had sold out after we'd twice queried their whereabouts). As we contemplated a rather mixed meal, the ceiling started to vibrate. The karaoke had begun upstairs.
Babies and children welcome; high chairs. Booking advisable dinner. Separate room for parties, seats 70-80. Takeaway service. Vegetarian menu. Map 28 C4.
For branches (Hainanese Buffet, Weng Wah Buffet) see index.

Golders Green NW11

Local Friends
28 North End Road, NW11 7PT (8455 9258). Golders Green tube. **Meals served** noon-11pm, **dim sum served** noon-10pm daily. **Main courses** £5.50-£7. **Dim sum** £2.10-£4.50. **Set meal** £11-£19 per person (minimum 2). **Service** 10%. **Credit** AmEx, JCB, MC, V.
A small restaurant with a large menu that seeks to cover the full range, from sweet-and-sour to gourmet. Dim sum, unusually, are served right up to 10pm. This may be a strategy for survival in an area spoilt for restaurant choice, but there's a price to be paid in quality of cuisine. A starter of stuffed crab claws rewarded us with dry meat and burned tongues, a tribute of sorts to the speed with which the food came to the table. Prawn balls with ginger and onions were short on prawns and shorter on ginger. Crisp-skinned chicken (ja ji gai) was

overcooked and low on flavour. Iceberg lettuce with oyster sauce was pleasantly reminiscent of noodle-shop offerings in Hong Kong, but again fractionally overcooked, so it had lost too much crispness. 'Three stuffed treasures' (yeung saam bo) of aubergines, beancurd and peppers in a black bean and ginger sauce on a sizzling plate was the tastiest dish of the meal. This wasn't a bad experience – complimentary warm salted peanuts on arrival and orange segments at the end, a friendly welcome from the staff and thoughtful attention to our comfort while eating – but the food wasn't memorable.
Babies and children welcome. Booking advisable weekends. Separate room for parties, seats 45. Takeaway service. Vegetarian menu.

St John's Wood NW8

★ Royal China
68 Queen's Grove, NW8 6ER (7586 4280). St John's Wood tube. **Meals served** noon-11pm Mon-Sat; 11am-10pm Sun. **Dim sum served** noon-4.45pm Mon-Sat; 11am-4.45pm Sun. **Main courses** £6-£50. **Dim sum** £2.20-£3.50. **Set lunch** (noon-5pm Mon-Fri) £11 3 courses. **Set dinner** £28-£36 per person (minimum 2) 4 courses. **Service** 12.5%. **Credit** AmEx, DC, MC, V.
This is one of the smallest branches in the Royal China group and can get very busy. Arriving without a reservation early one evening, we were asked to finish our meal in 90 minutes. We took little notice of the gilded surroundings, and went straight to the menu. Soup of the day started the meal well, with pork, watercress, carrot and chinese date in a hearty, flavoursome broth. An intermediate course of steamed fresh scallops was pricey, but the shellfish were large, impeccably cooked and delicious, accompanied by a soy sauce-based dip. Fragrant yam duck was moist, delicate and rich; a dip of bright red sweet and sour sauce complemented the dish well, being equally deep in flavour. Chicken with beancurd and salted fish hot-pot was among the best we've tasted, with large chunks of tofu soaking up the gorgeous flavour of the fish. We also enjoyed a generous portion of crispy fried noodles with sliced beef in black bean sauce before tucking into an incredibly refreshing dessert of sago cream with yam flavour. Service can be haphazard and occasionally dreadful, but this time everything was spot on. Good job too. We left seconds before our time was up.
Babies and children welcome; high chairs. Book dinner Mon-Fri; bookings not accepted Sat, lunch Sun. Separate rooms for parties, seating 14 and 21. Takeaway service. Map 28 A5.

Outer London
Harrow, Middlesex

★ Golden Palace
146-150 Station Road, Harrow, Middx HA1 2RH (8863 2333). Harrow-on-the-Hill tube/rail. **Meals served** noon-11.30pm Mon-Sat; 11am-10.30pm Sun. **Dim sum served** noon-5pm Mon-Sat; 11am-5pm Sun. **Main courses** £5.20-£7.50. **Dim sum** £2.20-£3.20. **Set meal** £18-£24.50 per person (minimum 2). **Service** 10%. **Credit** AmEx, DC, MC, V.
For years now, Chinese from all over have beaten a path to Golden Palace, and it's easy to see why. The varied menu of skilfully prepared dim sum surpasses that of many a Chinatown eatery. The main menu offers a wide-ranging selection of Cantonese classics, and the restaurant also excels at vegetarian 'mock' duck and other wheat gluten-based snacks. Charcoal vegetarian roast pork was particularly enjoyable, boasting an interesting taste and texture that we hadn't experienced before. Our remaining selection of dim sum was superb too: light and generously filled oven-baked roast pork pastries; perfectly cooked deep-fried 'doughnut' cheung fun; and packed-to-the-rafters scallop cheung fun. If we're really picky, we weren't keen on the fried chicken and cheese

dumpling, which was perfectly deep-fried but tasted of little. The ravishingly moist Thai-style cuttlefish cake made up for it. So did the freshly made taro cake, which had exactly the right taste and texture. The two dining rooms are spacious and light, with large tables surrounded by showy displays of fruit and flowers. Service was prompt and attentive.
Babies and children welcome: high chairs. Booking advisable dinner. Disabled: toilet. Separate rooms for parties, seating 60 and 100. Takeaway service. Vegetarian menu.

Ilford, Essex

Mandarin Palace
559-561 Cranbrook Road, Gants Hill, Ilford, Essex IG2 6JZ (8550 7661). Gants Hill tube. **Lunch/dim sum served** noon-4pm, **dinner served** 6.30-11.30pm daily. **Main courses** £2.50-£22. **Dim sum** £2-£3.80. **Set dinner** £22.90 4 courses. **Service** 10%. **Credit** AmEx, DC, MC, V.
The existence of Mandarin Palace on the edge of the Gants Hill roundabout attests to the Chinese theory that you can find the best food in the most unlikely places. The restaurant's main menu reflects its 20-year history of catering to westerners, but we've been impressed over several visits by the recently introduced dim sum list, the standard of which rivals London's best. There's a no-MSG policy too. First out of the kitchen was fried squid paste: the three golden patties were generous in size, lightly deep-fried and wonderfully tender. Tasty har gau (prawn dumplings) featured whole prawns and a delicate wrapper; they had clearly been handmade with a great deal of skill. Char siu puff pastry had a light crust and was packed with sweet-tasting pork. Another highlight was cheung fun stuffed with scallop. Beancurd roll, with its filling of chinese mushrooms, chicken and thin threads of vegetable, hit the spot too. Complementary slices of watermelon brought our feast to an end. The staff cheerfully continued to serve their way round the quirky interior, which is packed full of ornaments, birdcages, lanterns, Chinese paintings and silk screens. Mandarin Palace is a real find.
Babies and children welcome; high chairs. No-smoking tables. Separate area for parties, seats 30. Takeaway service; delivery service (within 2-mile radius). Vegetarian menu.
For branch see index.

Surbiton, Surrey

★ Lee Fook
2004 RUNNER-UP BEST CHINESE RESTAURANT
76 The Broadway, Tolworth, Surbiton, Surrey KT6 7HR (8399 9793). Tolworth rail/265, 281, 406, K1, K2 bus. **Lunch served** noon-2.30pm, **dinner served** 5.30-11pm daily. **Main courses** £4-£10.50. **Set dinner** £16-£20 3 courses. **Service** 10%. **Credit** MC, V.
Chef Ringo Lo puts his passion for cooking into the creation of special menus on request. Give him a few days' notice and he'll rustle up a fabulous feast to the required budget. Expect to see dishes you've never encountered before, prepared with unusual flair. On our last visit, the stir-fried eel was a magnificent entwining of bamboo shoot, red pepper, celery, coriander and various mushrooms, with succulent strips of eel, served with melt-in-the-mouth wisps of fried pastry. A steamed lobster with rice wine, ginger and wolfberries was beautiful, but a little earthy in taste. The pièce de résistance was a platter of boned quails, stuffed with minced prawn and dark wind-dried sausage, lightly fried and draped in a delicate egg white sauce: stunning. Lo has a profound understanding of the arts of flavour and texture; those seriously interested in Chinese food should hasten to his door. Aside from the food, there's little to draw anyone out from central London; this is a modest restaurant, though clean and comfortable.
Babies and children welcome; high chairs. Booking advisable. No-smoking tables. Takeaway service; delivery service.

**Drunken Monkey.
See p61.**

East European

Thankfully, in recent years many of the more mediocre eastern European restaurants that gave the cuisine a bad name have closed; only the truly competitive have survived. Eastern European restaurants now tend to fall into three categories. There are the home-from-home granny's kitchens, packed with expats talking in their native language (**Daquise, Polanka, Erebuni** and **Tbilisi** are among the best). Then there are the vodka specialists, which sometimes offer great food on the side; the rather brilliant **Na Zdrowie** has cornered the market here, although **Tsar's Bar** still has the most imaginative vodka list in town (a shame about the high prices, and that food is an afterthought). And finally there are the more upmarket pretenders (**Potemkin, Baltic**), which provide fabulous authentic regional food to such a high standard that they can rival top restaurants of any cuisine.

The more eclectic, expensive venues equal anything you would find nowadays in Moscow, Prague or Warsaw. By contrast, their homespun cousins offer food of a type you might be served in someone's home. It's comforting to know how easy it is to find real khachapuri (Georgian cheese flatbread), the perfect buttery Russian mushroom julienne and the stodgiest pierogi imaginable, right here in London.

At time of writing the future of two stalwarts of the east European scene was uncertain. The **Czech Restaurant** in Hampstead (currently at 74 West End Lane, NW6 2LX, 7372 5251) is likely to move premises, while the **Polish White Eagle Club** in Balham (211 Balham High Road, SW17 7BQ, 8672 1723), one of our favourite home-cooking haunts, was about to be taken over and refurbished. It's not clear whether it will remain a Polish restaurant.

ARMENIAN

South West
South Kensington SW7

★ Jakob's
20 Gloucester Road, SW7 4RB (7581 9292).
Gloucester Road tube. **Meals served** 8am-10pm Mon-Sat; 8am-5pm Sun. **Main courses** £6.50-£11. **Credit** AmEx, MC, V.
Jakob's looks like a friendly, local Italian deli. It is actually a friendly, local Armenian deli with a vast choice of unexpectedly good and authentic dishes. To be unfair to Armenian food, which warrants a far more extravagant description, it is something of a mix between Italian, Greek, Turkish and Iranian cuisine. Vegetarian lasagne and spinach filo pie were both perfect, but it's the huge salad selection that makes a visit here so worthwhile: first-rate tabouleh, blistered red peppers in a spicy vinaigrette, carrot with cumin and coriander – all very simple and very fresh. There are also splendid desserts; poppy-seed cake, chocolate cake and cheesecake come highly recommended. An ideal lunchtime haunt, the conservatory at the back is light and airy if rather cramped. Service is swift but slightly confused (choose your food from the

deli, but order drinks from a waiter). Good wines and excellent soft drinks (fresh fruit juices, own-made lemonade) are a bonus.
Babies and children welcome; high chairs.
Booking advisable. No-smoking tables. Table outside (1, pavement). Takeaway service; delivery service. **Map 7 C9.**

GEORGIAN

North East
Hackney E8

Little Georgia
2 Broadway Market, E8 4QJ (7249 9070).
London Fields rail/26, 48, 55, 106, 236 bus.
Café **Open** 9am-6pm Mon; 9am-7pm Tue-Sat; 10am-7pm Sun. **Main courses** £4-£6.
Restaurant **Dinner served** 7-10pm Tue-Thur, Sun; 7-10.30pm Fri, Sat. **Main courses** £10-£14.
Both **Credit** JCB, MC, V.
We'd heard reports of changes at Little Georgia – it's now a (very popular) café with a mixed menu in the daytime – but the Georgian food is still delivering in the evenings. Efficient and friendly service from an overworked waitress, and an enjoyable buzz added to the success of the meal. It's a spacious, airy spot, with neutral decor and mellow, occasionally Georgian music. Georgian mezze for two was vast; as a starter it would have fed four. The non-vegetarian version features aubergines stuffed with spicy lamb, slices of chicken kiev (very retro), and far more successful spicy beetroot and carrot salads with grated walnuts, stuffed peppers and a choice of cheese bread (khachapuri) or bean bread (lobiani). Thank goodness we were sharing just one main, baje (fried poussin – not much meat on this one – in a walnut sauce, with rice). Everything was a bit rich, but that's a matter of taste. Our only real disappointment was that no Georgian wines are on the list, though a South African sauvignon blanc was fine. On our next visit, we'll starve ourselves for a few days in advance.
Babies and children welcome (daytime). Booking advisable Fri, Sat. Tables outdoors (3, pavement).

North
Holloway N7

★ Tbilisi
91 Holloway Road, N7 8LT (7607 2536).
Highbury & Islington tube/rail. **Dinner served** 6.30-11pm daily. **Main courses** £6.25-£8.45.
Credit AmEx, MC, V.
The cooking and general vibe at Tbilisi were more impressive than on previous visits. The decor is fairly plain – dark wooden chairs and tables, paintings of Georgian scenes, and a few knick-knacks – but the relaxed atmosphere and friendly service are key in helping diners forget the busy road outside. Starters come in sets, named after regions of Georgia. Kaheti featured excellent, fresh carrot and beetroot salads with that most characteristic of Georgian ingredients, spicy walnut sauce, and everyone's favourite, khachapuri (soft yeasty bread stuffed with cheese). Beetroot soup was vividly flavoured and full of tasty vegetables. Main courses of spring chicken tabaka (flattened fried chicken in a choice of plum or walnut sauce) and chanakhi (lamb and aubergine stew in a rich tomato sauce) were equally good.

Despite all the nuts, spices and cheese, everything was prepared with a pleasingly light touch. The wine list has several good options; glasses of the Georgian house red and white (Tamada) slipped down nicely. A great, fairly priced place for something a bit different: Tbilisi deserves success.
Babies and children welcome. Booking advisable Fri, Sat. Restaurant available for hire. Separate room for parties, seats 40.

HUNGARIAN

Central
Soho W1

Gay Hussar
2 Greek Street, W1D 4NB (7437 0973).
Tottenham Court Road tube. **Lunch served** 12.15-2.30pm, **dinner served** 5.30-10.45pm Mon-Sat. **Main courses** £9.50-£16.50. **Set lunch** £16.50 2 courses, £18.50 3 courses.
Service 12.5%. **Credit** AmEx, DC, JCB, MC, V.
This place easily lives up to its legendary political reputation. Stuffed full of Westminster caricatures and guffawing diners, the Gay Hussar is worth visiting for the atmosphere alone, which sparkles any night of the week. The menu is also deservedly famous, consisting of dish after dish of unpronounceable Hungarian classics. Herring fillet was superb: fresh and own-made. Fish dumplings were (quite rightly) heavy, creamy and moreish. We ordered two different pancakes for main course and relished both: chicken pancakes came in a spicy paprika sauce; goulash pancakes were caked in meaty splendour (not to be recommended for hot weather). Desserts also shine; both the cloyingly sweet walnut pancakes, and the poppy-seed strudel (a little easier to manage) were delicious. There are plenty of well-priced fine wines, and the obligatory bottle of Bull's Blood was full-flavoured. With good old-fashioned service and Hungarian mamma's food, the Hussar remains a classic.
Babies and children welcome. Book dinner.
Separate rooms for parties, seating 12 and 20.
Map 17 K6.

POLISH

Central
Holborn WC1

★ Na Zdrowie The Polish Bar
11 Little Turnstile, WC1V 7DX (7831 9679).
Holborn tube. **Open** 12.30-11pm Mon-Fri; 6-11pm Sat. **Meals served** 12.30-10pm Mon-Fri; 6-10pm Sat. **Main courses** £4.60-£6.50.
Credit MC, V.
We visited while a renovation was in progress, but this did nothing to detract from our enjoyment of Na Zdrowie. Smallish, with yellow walls, stylised silver Polish eagles and a mix of low and high tables, it has a kind of cosy-meets-industrial vibe. The showpiece is undoubtedly the bar, with row upon row of enticingly gleaming bottles, including a good selection of Polish beers. The vodka menu is very impressive, featuring more than 60 varieties sensibly arranged and lovingly described. There's a choice of ten clear vodkas; more exotic offerings include orzechowa (walnut), kminkowy (caraway seed) and palikotowka (intriguingly described as 'smoking cat'). Yet food isn't just an afterthought. Although we'd been warned the kitchen wasn't fully operational due to the works, fresh and very tasty dishes were swiftly delivered: a salad of tender, almost melting herring with beetroot, and superb grilled smoky kielbasa sausage with dill-studded mash. Other staples such as placki ziemniaczane (potato pancakes), bigos, barszcz and herring are on the menu, with cheesecake and szarlotka (apple cake) for dessert. Perfect for

after-work drinks – we could hardly drag ourselves away – Na Zdrowie is a real winner.
Bookings not accepted. Tables outdoors (3, pavement). Takeaway service. Vegetarian menu. **Map 18 L5**.

Mayfair W1

L'Autre
*5B Shepherd Street, W1J 7HP (7499 4680).
Green Park tube.* **Lunch served** noon-2pm Mon-Fri. **Dinner served** 5.30-10.30pm daily. **Main courses** £7.50-£12.40. **Service** 12.5%.
Credit AmEx, MC, V.

You either get L'Autre or you don't. Cramped, with shabby olde worlde decor and cracked table mats, it's reminiscent of places that cater to pensioners' coach parties on the Isle of Wight. But on a weekday evening there was no shortage of diners: an eclectic bunch, some of whom were speaking fondly of previous visits. The menu features a bizarre combination of Polish and Mexican dishes, complemented by an international wine list and good Polish beer (Zywiec). Barszcz was properly intense, while a plate of Polish charcuterie featured smoky ham and good garlicky sausage. The mains were less successful.

Smoked trout blinis were two very ordinary pancakes stuffed with hot, overpowering smoked fish and white cheese, so heavy that even one was a bit of a trial. Smoked trout fillets in mustard sauce also disappointed: a gloopy white sauce with little trace of mustard, on a bed of over-puréed mash with spinach. Tired iceberg salad did little to relieve the stodge. Altogether the meal was rather hard work (and we certainly had no room for puddings), though frozen vodkas rounded things off pleasantly.
Booking weekends. Tables outdoors (3, pavement). **Map 9 H8**.

Tbilisi

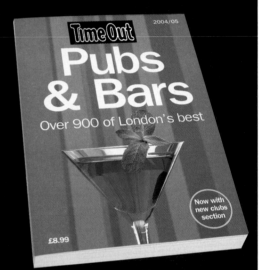

West

Bayswater W2

Antony's

54 Porchester Road, W2 6ET (7243 8743/
www.antonysrestaurant.com). Royal Oak tube.
Dinner served 6-11pm Mon-Sat. **Main courses**
£7.50-£13.80. **Cover** 70p. **Credit** MC, V.
Antony's has a beguilingly timeless, relaxing
atmosphere. We received a warm welcome from the
charming Polish hostess; locals are greeted with
an embrace. It's that kind of place: all the warmth
of granny's kitchen but with smart, starched
tablecloths, subtle lighting and music, and
professional, smooth service. The food continues
the theme, offering many good Polish standards,
prepared with a light touch. There are some
international diversions too, such as king prawns
flambéed in vodka. Starters were excellent:
peppery and richly beetrooty barszcz, and salmon
tartare infused with dill and lemon and attractively
presented with frizzled leeks and pools of zingy
lemon dressing. Mains didn't disappoint, and
portions are very generous. That most ubiquitous
of Polish dishes, kotlet schabowy, was a tender
pork escalope in breadcrumbs that well-nigh
covered the plate; zrazy featured equally tender
slices of beef with a good stuffing in tasty, meaty
gravy. Sautéed potato, tomatoey cabbage and
coarsely grated beetroot made excellent
accompaniments. For pudding, try nalesniki
pancakes filled with lemony sweet cheese, paired
with a glass of strong sweet wisniowka (cherry
vodka). One of Royal Oak's best kept secrets.
*Babies and children welcome; high chairs. Booking
advisable weekends. Restaurant and bar available
for hire. Separate room for parties, seats 30-40.
Vegetarian menu.* **Map 7 C5.**

Ealing W5

★ Café Grove

65 The Grove, W5 5LL (8810 0364). Ealing
Broadway tube/rail. **Meals served** 11am-11pm
Mon-Sat; 11am-10.30pm Sun. **Main courses**
£5-£7.50. **Credit** MC, V.
This funky little neighbourhood café really is a
gem. Popular with local Poles, Café Grove offers an
enjoyable deli-style brunch menu as well as
authentic Polish treats. There's art on the walls and
artistry in the food. The fluffy melt-in-the-mouth
concoction that here is called cheesecake is the
closest thing to cake heaven we've tasted. Savoury
dishes are mostly delectable too. Our red borscht
and zurek were spicy, flecked with herbs, and had
a richness of flavour that would give any other
cuisine a good run for its money. To call them
beetroot soup and fermented soup, respectively, is
almost an insult. Slightly less spectacular was the
beef stroganoff that came with the blinis. It was a
bit glutinous and shy of flavour. However, golabki
(spicy meat and rice parcels wrapped in cabbage
leaves), served with a rich, creamy tomato sauce,
did not disappoint. Café Grove has a pleasant
informal atmosphere, friendly, prompt service and
low prices. We waddled home rather envying the
residents of W5.
*Babies and children admitted. Book Sat, Sun.
Separate room for parties, seats 30. Tables
outside (2, pavement). Takeaway service.
Vegan dishes.*

Hammersmith W6

★ Lowiczanka Polish
Cultural Centre

238-246 King Street, W6 0RF (8741 3225).
Ravenscourt Park tube.
Coffee shop **Open** 9.30am-9pm daily.
Bar/restaurant **Lunch served** 12.30-3pm daily.
Dinner served 6.30-11pm Mon-Thur, Sun; 7pm-
midnight Fri, Sat. **Main courses** £6.90-£12.70.
Set lunch £7.50 3 courses. **Credit** AmEx, JCB,
MC, V.
Don't be put off by the rather forbidding concrete
exterior. Tucked away on the first floor of a
thriving cultural centre, Lowiczanka offers
authentic Polish staples at sensible prices. Plenty

of Poles eat here – always a good sign. The interior
is classy without being stuffy, with several well-
spaced tables and a large front window
overlooking a balcony. Quiet on weekday evenings,
the place livens up at weekends when a dance band
appears. The menu is vast, with sauerkraut heavily
featured; it's good for ravenous meat-eaters, less so
for vegetarians. Starters were of wild boar pâté and
herring dressed daintily in sour cream were
flawless. Mains are hearty. Bigos (classic hunter's
stew of sausage with sauerkraut and fresh cabbage)
was a perfect marriage of well-developed flavours
and contrasting textures, the tender, honey-sweet
shreds of cabbage perfectly partnering slices of
juicy sausage. Also recommended are the
comforting doughy parcels of pierogi. Meringue
nest with forest fruits makes an ideal light finale.
All our choices were consistently well executed and
faithful to tradition.
*Babies and children welcome; high chairs. Book
lunch Sat, Sun. Disabled: toilet. Entertainment:
gypsy band 8pm-midnight Fri-Sun. No-smoking
tables. Separate rooms for parties, seating 60 and
200. Tables outdoors (5, patio). Takeaway service
(coffee shop). Vegetarian menu. Vegan dishes.*
Map 20 A1.

★ Polanka

258 King Street, W6 0SP (8741 8268).
Ravenscourt Park tube. **Meals served** noon-
10pm Mon-Sat; noon-8pm Sun. **Main courses**
£4-£7.50. **Unlicensed. Corkage** £1 wine;
£5 spirits. **Credit** AmEx, MC, V.
A few minutes away from Lowiczanka (see above),
Polanka offers a less formal setting in which to
sample a wide variety of Polish dishes at wallet-
friendly prices. The modest café-cum-restaurant is
at the back of a well-stocked deli. It is decorated
with rustic paraphernalia: dried flower wreaths, a
picket fence and a spinning wheel. Radio 1 plays
innocuously in the background. You really get a
taste of the old country here, with unfussy yet
lovingly prepared food. In keeping with tradition,
each dish is a meal in itself. Some items are rarely
found in London, such as pork loin in beer batter:
a naughty, fattening, comforting and ab-fab
creation. Starters were also first-rate, especially
succulent herring with finely chopped onion and
moist, tender, tangy gherkin. Pancakes of grated
potato were fried to golden perfection. The meal
ended with a less than wonderful pancake with
blueberry jam; a better choice might have been the
poppy-seed or apple cake, both of which can be
bought at the deli.
*Babies and children welcome; high chairs. Booking
advisable. No-smoking tables. Separate rooms for
parties, seating 8 and 36. Takeaway service.*
Map 20 A1.

Kensington W8

Wódka

12 St Alban's Grove, W8 5PN (7937 6513/
www.wodka.co.uk). Gloucester Road tube. **Lunch
served** 12.30-2.30pm Mon-Fri. **Dinner served**
7-11.15pm daily. **Main courses** £10.90-£14.50.
Set lunch £11.50 2 courses, £14.50 3 courses.
Credit AmEx, MC, V.
Minimalist, modern and cool, Wódka always
attracts a young office crowd. This is the slightly
more restrained, laid-back sister restaurant to
Baltic (see p69). Great cocktails, an extensive wine
list and an excellent menu of dishes from all over
central and eastern Europe are among the
attractions. To start, herring fillet with potato and
dill salad was a let-down, as the herring resembled
supermarket rollmops; we had expected the real
thing at Wódka. Moldavian aubergine and peppers
with minted yoghurt and cucumber salad was far
better: awash with herbs, and positively singing
with freshness. To follow, a wonderfully authentic
roast pork belly with horseradish coleslaw had just
the right horseradish kick (a Russian essential).
Another main course, chicken kiev, was excellent:
aromatic and buttery. The desserts are gorgeous
too. Naslesniki (Polish crêpes filled with sweet
cheese, nuts and raisins) is a creamy dream, while
white chocolate cheesecake is simply heavenly.
Service is efficient, but could be more congenial.

Wódka remains a great spot for a girls' lunch, a
romantic but simple diner à deux or a rather
upmarket work-night out.
*Babies and children admitted. Booking advisable.
Separate room for parties, seats 32. Tables
outdoors (2, pavement).* **Map 7 C9.**

Shepherd's Bush W12

★ Patio

5 Goldhawk Road, W12 8QQ (8743 5194).
Goldhawk Road tube. **Lunch served** noon-
3pm Mon-Fri. **Dinner served** 6-11.30pm daily.
Main courses £7.50-£9. **Set meal** £14.95
3 courses incl vodka shot. **Credit** AmEx, DC,
JCB, MC, V.
Patio was packed even early on a Sunday evening:
a sure sign that this cosy, friendly local knows
what it is up to. Step through the doors and you're
transported into a typical, slightly grand Polish fin
de siècle room, reminiscent of Cracow or Warsaw.
Lush rugs, fresh flowers, huge gilt mirrors and a
piano add to the atmosphere. Most diners opt for
the extremely good-value three-course Polish menu
(£14.95 including a vodka), though steaks are
available à la carte. This is Polish home-style
cooking: fresh ingredients, lovingly prepared. Red
barszcz (white is also offered) was vibrant and
peppery; placki were a touch soggy, but tasty.
Mains of cod in dill sauce and beef gulasz with
roasted buckwheat (kasha) came with six different
vegetables and surowki (grated raw vegetable
salads) including notable beetroot, red cabbage and
crispy roast potatoes. Complimentary coconut cake
and melon precede desserts, which might include
a good substantial cheesecake, cheese pancakes or
fresh fruit. The friendly Polish owner presides over
all, keeping everything running smoothly yet
never too busy for a chat.
*Book dinner Fri, Sat. No-smoking tables. Separate
area for parties, seats 45. Takeaway service.*
Map 20 C2.

South West

South Kensington SW7

Daquise

20 Thurloe Street, SW7 2LP (7589 6117). South
Kensington tube. **Meals served** 11.30am-11pm
daily. **Main courses** £5.50-£12.50. **Set lunch**
(noon-3pm Mon-Fri) £7.50 2 courses incl glass
of wine & coffee. **Credit** MC, V.
A charming olde worlde diner with brown leather
booths and wooden panelling, Daquise is
unpretentious but entirely indulgent. Softly
spoken, motherly Polish staff attend to your every
whim. Plates piled high with carbohydrates are
rushed out of the kitchen with alarming speed.
The menu is truly authentic. Starters are all
uncomplicated and good: Ukrainian barszcz was
juicy with beetroot and thick with cream; fresh
herrings were served with a luxurious, plumped-
up sour cream. Main courses are stodgy, wintry
fare. The Polish vegetarian platter was enjoyable,
if impossible to finish: potato pierogi, mushroom
golabki and potato pancake with apple sauce – the
perfect comfort food. Blinis with salmon were
unashamedly simple: fluffy buckwheat confections
with top-class salmon and lashings of sour cream.
The cakes and pancakes are beyond compare too.
You sense that someone in the kitchen is not only
Polish but really cares about the food.
*Babies and children welcome. Booking advisable.
No-smoking tables. Separate room for parties,
seats 25.* **Map 14 E10.**

Ognisko

55 Exhibition Road, Prince's Gate, SW7
2PN (7589 4635/www.ognisko.com). South
Kensington tube.
Bar **Open** noon-11pm daily. **Bar snacks**
£1.40-£5.20.
Restaurant **Lunch served** 12.30-3pm, **dinner
served** 6.30-11pm daily. **Main courses** £9-£14.
Set meal £11 3 courses.
Both **Credit** AmEx, DC, MC, V.
This is a romantic place in the old-fashioned sense:
it has the feel of a gentlemen's club, with candles,
peach tablecloths, a room hung with huge

The Restaurants

portraits, and a roaring fire. The menu is a decent mix of traditional Polish and a few attempts at modern classics. It's best to stick to the more authentic dishes. The blini starter portion, however, disappointed: one soggy, large buckwheat pancake smothered in sour cream and top-notch smoked salmon. Aubergine roulade with feta cheese and red pepper sauce was better: fresh and tangy. Next, fillet of beef with caramelised shallots and rösti potatoes was OK; the meat was perfect but it came with a far-too-sweet sauce. Linguini with prawns in chilli sauce suffered from the same problem: too much sugar. Yet the desserts – chocolate-topped orange cheesecake, Polish-style, and Grand Marnier crème brûlée – were sublime. Service is brusque but efficient. We were pleased by the high standard of the wine list, which includes an excellent half bottle of Pouilly-Fumé.

Babies and children welcome; children's portions; high chair. Booking advisable. Dress: smart casual. Separate room for parties, seats 150. Tables outdoors (10, terrace). **Map 14 D9.**

South

Clapham SW4

Café Wanda

153 Clapham High Street, SW4 7SS (7738 8760). Clapham Common tube. **Meals served** noon-11pm Mon-Fri; 11am-11pm Sat; 11am-7pm Sun. **Main courses** £4.95-£13.95. **Credit** AmEx, MC, V.

Wanda maintains a pleasant, relaxed vibe that many eateries in the neighbourhood lack. At the entrance there's a cake display to drool over; English and Italian café fare is also offered. But head for the restaurant proper at the back, where fine traditional Polish food is served. It's an ideal setting for either an intimate meal or a larger gathering. On a Saturday night, we were soothed by a guitar duo playing superb but unobtrusive gypsy jazz. To drink, there's a fair choice of (pricey) vodkas, but the list of unusual cocktails is more enticing. The menu features less than a dozen Polish specialities – all generous one-dish meals – and predictably little for vegetarians. Blinis were good: hefty, satisfying buckwheat pancakes, perfectly complemented by fillings such as smoked salmon and sour cream. A main course of klopsy (meatballs) with rice was a bit of a disappointment; it lacked flavour and was slightly underdone, as was pierogi with mushrooms and sauerkraut. However, the accompanying salad was fresh, finely shredded and crunchy. Things perked up for pudding, with a delectable raspberry mousse that put a good, though not special, cheesecake in the shade. Service throughout was timely and efficient.

Babies and children welcome. Booking advisable weekends. Entertainment: pianist 8.30-11pm Sat (phone for details). Tables outdoors (3, pavement). Takeaway service. **Map 22 B2.**

Waterloo SE1

★ Baltic

74 Blackfriars Road, SE1 8HA (7928 1111/ www.balticrestaurant.co.uk). Southwark tube. *Bar* **Open/snacks served** noon-11pm daily. *Restaurant* **Lunch served** noon-3pm Mon-Fri. **Dinner served** 6-11.15pm Mon-Sat. **Meals served** noon-10.30pm Sun. **Main courses** £9.50-£14. **Set meal** (noon-3pm, 6-7pm) £11.50 2 courses, £13.50 3 courses. **Service** 12.5%. *Both* **Credit** AmEx, MC, V.

Baltic was back on its usual excellent form on our last visit. The spacious interior, complete with 'wall of amber' bar and amber sculptures, makes a great setting for the modern, varied menu and beautiful, efficient waiting staff. The food is a rare thing for an eastern European restaurant: adventurous as well as authentic. There are touches of Latvian, Lithuanian, Georgian and Armenian cuisine, as well as Russian and Polish staples. A starter of roast beetroot with spices, carrot crisps and sour cream was a gamble that paid off: meltingly good. Moldavian salad of

Erebuni

aubergines and peppers was equally well executed. The main-course mixed blini plate is wonderful: aubergine caviar, keta caviar, smoked salmon and trout, and herrings – all served with fresh toppings (sour cream, onion, eggs). Extra blinis were offered too. Roast cod served with a kasza (buckwheat) risotto was superb: a great idea beautifully done with a modern twist, which exemplifies Baltic's philosophy. The wine list is notable, the cocktails even better. Baltic is still London's best and most innovative east European restaurant.

Babies and children welcome; high chair. Booking advisable dinner. Disabled: toilet. Entertainment: jazz 7-10pm Mon, Sun. Separate room for parties, seats 30. Tables outdoors (5, courtyard). **Map 11 O8.**

North

Hampstead NW3

Zamoyski Restaurant & Vodka Bar

85 Fleet Road, NW3 2QY (7794 4792). Hampstead Heath rail/24 bus. **Lunch served** by appointment. **Dinner served** 6.30-11pm Mon; 5.30-11pm Tue-Sun. **Main courses** £7.95-£11.95. **Service** 10% for parties of 6 or more. **Credit** AmEx, MC, V.

This patch of affluent north London isn't short on restaurants, but even midweek we found Zamoyski busy with an older, typically Hampstead crowd.

salad and rough mashed potato. Desserts tempted (apple cake, cheesecake, sweet cheese or cherry pancakes), but we only had room for delectable fruit vodkas; apricot, pomegranate and raspberry are recommended. There are also many clear vodkas, along with Polish and Czech beers and an international wine list. A local that gets it just right.
Babies and children welcome. Booking advisable weekends. Entertainment: Russian music 8.30-11pm Sat. No-smoking tables. Separate room for parties, seats 40. Takeaway service. Vegetarian menu. **Map 28 C3**.

RUSSIAN

Central

Clerkenwell & Farringdon EC1

★ Potemkin

144 Clerkenwell Road, EC1R 5DP (7278 6661/ www.potemkin.co.uk). Farringdon tube/rail.
Bar **Open** noon-11pm Mon-Fri; 6pm-midnight Sat. **Meals served** noon-10.30pm Mon-Fri; 6-10.30pm Sat.
Restaurant **Lunch served** noon-3pm Mon-Fri. **Dinner served** 6-10.30pm Mon-Fri; 6-10.30pm Sat. **Main courses** £9.50-£16. **Set lunch** £5.99 1 course; £10 2 courses. **Set dinner** £20 3 courses incl vodka & breads. **Service** 12.5%.
Both **Credit** AmEx, DC, JCB, MC, V.
Potemkin is small but well rounded, with a mirrored restaurant in the basement and a bustling vodka cocktail bar upstairs. The place is run by a stylish Russian woman, and its menu is clever and authentic. Russian specialities are lovingly prepared, and presented ever so slightly tongue-in-cheek. All the old favourites are present, including selyodka pod shuboy ('herring under a fur coat', meaning covered in beetroot), and pelmeni (dumplings) in vinegar or sour cream. The caviar zakuski could be better: great caviar, too few blinis. Kamchatka crab salad was very fresh and packed full of crab. Kuritza zapechonnaya (breast of chicken) was delicious, oozing with garlic and herbs. Baked quail with a berry sauce was juicy, moist and tender. Most amazing of all are the desserts: a sumptuous chocolate truffle cake, and addictive blinchik stvorogom (pancake with cream cheese). Potemkin also provides fantastic service, a young atmosphere and a superb drinks list – fabulous cocktails, a vast choice of vodka shots and great wines at good prices. We drank Georgian wine (well worth £16 a bottle).
Booking advisable. Dress: smart casual. No-smoking area. **Map 5 N4**.

Marylebone W1

Tsar's Bar

Langham Hotel, 1C Portland Place, W1V 1JA (7636 1000/www.langhamhotels.com). Oxford Circus tube.
Bar **Open** noon-midnight Mon-Fri; 5pm-midnight Sat. **Meals served** noon-11pm Mon-Fri; 5-11pm Sat.
Restaurant **Lunch served** noon-2.30pm Mon-Sat; 12.30-3pm Sun. **Dinner served** 6-10.30pm daily. **Main courses** £7.50-£14.50.
Both **Credit** AmEx, DC, JCB, MC, V.
Although this hotel bar boasts one of the longest and most impressive vodka lists in London, the combination of high-priced food, fawning waiters and a rather corporate feel means it is strictly for special occasions only. Even then, order carefully. The zakuski menu is quite good if you choose the right things: tiny lamb shashlik came sizzling on a doll-size barbecue; mushroom blinis were melt-in-the-mouth; potato cakes were pleasingly filling. The pirozhki were tough, though, and the blinis served with sevruga caviar were just awful: penny-sized, wafer-thin pastry cut-outs to carry a couple of eggs. There were some potato blinis to make up for this, but they were dry and lacking in flavour. A real shame, as the caviar was excellent and the

accompaniments perfect (chopped egg, onion, chives, sour cream on a silver platter). The pricey drinks list features a sparkling Russian wine: the lovely Sovetskoye champagne, which is not easy to come by in London.
Booking advisable weekends. Disabled: toilet (hotel). Entertainment: music 6-9.30pm Wed-Fri. No-smoking. Separate room for parties, seats 60. **Map 9 H5**.

St James's W1

The Caviar House

161 Piccadilly, W1V 9DF (7409 0445/ www.caviar-house.com). Green Park or Piccadilly Circus tube. **Meals served** noon-10pm Mon-Sat. **Main courses** £13-£32 (caviar from £45). **Service** 12.5%. **Credit** AmEx, DC, JCB, MC, V.
If it's serious caviar and a sense of occasion you're after, then the Caviar House does a fine job, but beware the damage to your bank balance. Style-wise the place is a bit of a dated mish-mash – peachy walls with a few Russian artefacts, squashy brown circular banquettes and super-crisp linen tablecloths. We had fun observing how the waitresses (formal but friendly) dealt with our fellow diners: businessmen with money to burn, glam families and elderly Mayfair worthies. The Tsar's Palette (at £49 the cheapest caviar starter) was more than enough for two: excellent farmed Italian caviar (in an exquisite dish decorated with sturgeon motifs) and smoked salmon. Other caviars start at around £66 a portion. Ours was served with appropriate ceremony on a marble slab with carved wooden knives and little dishes of salmon tartare, oil, rock salt and a basket of dark breads. Mains of sautéed turbot and spicy char-grilled prawns, and a bourride of lobster and scallops in a slightly too creamy saffron sauce were also enjoyable. Drinks don't come cheap either; we stuck to a glass each of good house champagne and a vodka for pud, but still had little change from £150 for two.
Babies and children admitted. Booking advisable for parties of four or more. Dress: smart casual. **Map 17 J7**.

West

Acton W3

Rasputin

265 High Street, W3 9BY (8993 5802). Acton Town tube/70, 72, 207, 266 bus. **Meals served** noon-midnight daily. **Main courses** £7.50-£14.95. **Cover** £1. **Service** 10%. **Credit** MC, V.
This year Rasputin succeeded in delivering more culinary artistry than during previous visits. The menu still contains an ambitious range of meat dishes, at slightly high prices given the location. Time-honoured staples such as chicken kiev and beef stroganoff are listed alongside venison, wild boar shashlik and Muscovite fish platter. The Russian offerings (such as a perfectly executed Rasputin steak with pepper and cream sauce) are a better bet than the Polish dishes. A flavoursome russian salad featured a medley of chopped vegetables, egg and mayonnaise, studded with fragments of sausage that lent the dish a delicious subtle smokiness; it was way ahead of a mundane pierogi. The restaurant wasn't busy on a Saturday night and Rasputin's sombre portrait, which takes pride of place on the back wall, could have been overwhelming. However, our spirits were lifted by complimentary vodkas and by members of the local judo club who invited us to dance with them and make merry. What's more, the ever-friendly and knowledgeable proprietress gave us a welcome that made us forget about the rather unappealing location. An entertaining spot.
Babies and children welcome. Booking advisable dinner. Separate room for parties, seats 40.

Bayswater W2

Erebuni

London Guards Hotel, 36-37 Lancaster Gate, W2 3NA (7402 6067/www.erebuni.ltd.uk). Lancaster Gate tube. **Dinner served** 5pm-1am

Decor is reminiscent of the building's pub origins – dark wooden furniture, and exposed brickwork. A lone waitress managed to be friendly and efficient, though somewhat overworked. 'Polish mezze', including soup, savoury and dessert dishes, is extremely good value at £9.95 a person, but we opted for the à la carte. Good pierogi, gently fried, were stuffed with wild mushrooms, pork and cheese. Losos ukrainski was a torte of beetroot, smoked salmon, smoked trout and dill; it didn't quite live up to its promise, the flavours somehow not sharp enough. Next, both veal cutlet in breadcrumbs, and koulebiaka with a dill sauce were generous and well executed, served with excellent vegetables: beetroot, red cabbage, carrot

Mon-Sat. **Main courses** £6.50-£18.50. **Set dinner** (Mon-Thur) £15 2 courses. **Service** 10%. **Credit** MC, V.

One of London's best-kept secrets, Erebuni serves Russian, Armenian and Georgian specialities. All are freshly cooked by a Ukrainian chef. The emphasis here is on the homemade and the homespun. The decor is quite bizarre: fairy lights and checkered tablecloths in a basement bar in this backstreet hotel. You can usually hear Russian and central Asian voices here – generally a good sign for authentic food. The khachapuri (Georgian cheese flatbread) is gorgeous and moreish; at Erebuni the puff pastry variant is served, oozing with butter and melted cheese. Mushroom julienne was gloriously reminiscent of the Russian real thing: mushrooms finely chopped and baked in butter, cheese and sour cream. A main course of 'plov', or pilaf, with chunks of tender lamb was delicious and aromatic. Chicken tabaka (a dish of Georgian spatchcocked chicken) was also lovingly prepared. Staff will lavish you with complimentary vodka if they're having a quiet night, and there's always a fine array of (ever-changing) Russian and Ukrainian beers. Service is erratic but friendly.

Babies and children welcome. Booking advisable. Entertainment: musicians 7pm Fri, Sat; karaoke Mon-Sat. Restaurant available for hire. Takeaway service. **Map 8 D6**.

Menu

Dishes followed by (Cz) indicate a Czech dish; (G) Georgian; (H) Hungarian; (P) Polish; (R) Russian; (Uk) Ukrainian. Others have no particular affiliation.

Bigos (P): hunter's stew made with sauerkraut, various meats and sausage, mushrooms and juniper.
Blini: yeast-leavened pancake made from buckwheat flour, traditionally served smothered in butter and sour cream; **blinchiki** are mini blinis.
Borscht: classic beetroot soup. There are many varieties: Ukrainian borscht is thick with vegetables; the Polish version (**barszcz**) is clear. There are also white and green types. Often garnished with sour cream, boiled egg or little dumplings.
Caviar: fish roe. Most highly prized is that of the sturgeon (**beluga**, **oscietra** and **sevruga**, in descending order of expense), though **keta** or salmon caviar is underrated.
Chlodnik (P): cold beetroot soup, shocking pink, served with sour cream.
Coulebiac (R): see koulebiaka below.
Galabki, golabki or **golubtsy:** cabbage parcels, usually stuffed with rice or kasha (qv) and sometimes meat.
Golonka (P): pork knuckle, often cooked in beer.
Goulash or **gulasz (H):** rich beef soup.
Kasha or **kasza:** buckwheat, delicious plain roasted, light and fluffy with a nutty flavour.
Kaszanka (P): blood sausage made with buckwheat.
Khachapuri (G): flatbread; sometimes called Georgian pizza.
Knedliky (Cz): bread dumplings.
Kolduny (P): small meat-filled dumplings (scaled-down pierogi, qv) often served in beetroot soup.

Kotlet schabowy (P): breaded pork chops.
Koulebiaka or **kulebiak (R):** layered salmon or sturgeon pie with eggs, dill, rice and mushrooms.
Krupnik (P): barley soup, and the name of a honey vodka (because of the golden colour of barley).
Latke: grated potato pancakes, fried.
Makowiec or **makietki (P):** poppy-seed cake.
Mizeria (P): cucumber salad; very thinly sliced and dressed with sour cream.
Nalesniki (P): cream cheese pancakes.
Paczki (P): doughnuts, often filled with plum jam.
Pelmeni (R): Siberian-style ravioli dumplings.
Pierogi (P): ravioli-style dumplings. Typical fillings are sauerkraut and mushroom, curd cheese or fruit (cherries, apples).
Pirogi (large) or **pirozhki** (small) **(R):** filled pies made with yeasty dough.
Placki (P): potato pancakes.
Shashlik: Caucasian spit-roasted meat (usually lamb).
Shchi (R): soup made from sauerkraut.
Stroganoff (R): beef slices, served in a rich sour cream and mushroom sauce.
Surowka (P): salad made of raw shredded vegetables.
Ushka or **uszka:** small ear-shaped dumplings served in soup.
Vareniki (Uk): Ukrainian version of pierogi (qv).
Zakuski (R) or **zakaski (P):** starters, traditionally covering a whole table. The many dishes can include pickles, marinated vegetables and fish, herring, smoked eel, aspic, mushrooms, radishes with butter, salads and caviar.
Zrazy (P): beef rolls stuffed with bacon, pickled cucumber and mustard.
Zurek (P): sour rye soup.

South West

Earl's Court SW10

Nikita's

65 Ifield Road, SW10 9AU (7352 6326/ www.nikitasrestaurant.com). Earl's Court tube. **Dinner served** 7-11.30pm Mon-Sat. **Main courses** £9.50-£14.95. **Set meals** £22.50-£36.50 4 courses incl coffee. **Cover** £1.50. **Service** 12.5%. **Credit** AmEx, JCB, MC, V.

Arriving at Nikita's to find a raucous Polish wedding in full-swing – not mentioned when we called to book – we were ushered downstairs into an airless cave-like room. This was pleasantly decorated in dark red with comfortable cushioned banquettes, with just enough room for a weighty wooden table. Without comment, a heavy velvet curtain was pulled across the entrance. Claustrophobia set in as the merry sounds of the wedding, accordionist and all, boomed on outside. Things didn't get off to a good start. A stroppy waitress argued at length that the wisniowka (thick, sweet, cherry vodka) brought instead of the jarzebiak (light, straw-coloured, dry, rowanberry vodka) we ordered, was indeed the latter. Waits for food and drink were interminable. A smoked fish platter (salmon, halibut, keta caviar and sturgeon), not cheap at £25 for two, was OK, but the scone-like blinis were excessively heavy and greasy.

Mains were mediocre: beef shashlik was dull, served just with rice; loin of pork stuffed with apple was tender and tasty enough. Standards of food and service should be much higher at these prices.
Booking advisable; essential Thur-Sat. Dress: smart casual. Entertainment: gypsy music 8.30-11.30pm Fri, Sat. Separate rooms for parties, seating 6, 15 and 45. Vegan dishes. Vegetarian menu. **Map 13 C12**.

North

Camden Town & Chalk Farm NW1

Trojka

101 Regent's Park Road, NW1 8UR (7483 3765/www.troykarestaurant.co.uk). Chalk Farm tube. **Meals served** 9am-10.30pm daily. **Main courses** £6-£35. **Set lunch** (noon-4pm) £6.95 2 courses. **Corkage** £3 wine. **Credit** AmEx, MC, V.

This local haunt is a credit to chi-chi Primrose Hill. With its cosy decor, shelves of matrioshka dolls and 1920s Russian art, Trojka is romantic and bohemian. As long as you don't expect anything too fancy (service is hit and miss), you'll enjoy yourself. The newly expanded menu is excellent, with a mix of Russian, Polish and Hungarian dishes – although the main theme is Russian and it's done well. Starters of russian salad (an authentic potato and vegetable mix) and blinis with marinated herring were unfussy and simple. Coulebiac came as an individual puff pastry salmon pie nestled in a rich tomato sauce: heavy and hearty. Kotlety pozharskiye ('cutlets' or, rather, patties of veal and chicken) were lightly spiced and just right. A Hungarian chocolate torte and rich baked cheesecake were both enjoyable, if nothing special. Good Ukrainian beer, some passable wines, not-bad coffee and a breakfast/brunch menu all help make Trojka a fine all-rounder as well as decent value for money.
Babies and children welcome; high chairs. Book dinner Fri, Sat. Entertainment: Russian folk music 8-10.30pm Fri, Sat (£1 cover). No-smoking tables. Tables outdoors (3, pavement). Takeaway service. **Map 27 A1**.

Islington N1

★ Luba's Place

164 Essex Road, N1 8LY (7704 2775). Angel tube/Essex Road rail/38, 56, 73, 341, 476 bus. **Meals served** 6-11pm Tue-Thur; 6pm-midnight Fri, Sat. **Main courses** £4.99-£10. **Set meal** £4.95 2 courses. **Service** 10%. **Credit** MC, V.

Luba's was once something of a party zone, but Saturday night found only us and another couple dining. All was shabby, with tatty menus and faded hand-written notices in the windows. Dingy orange walls, amateurish oil paintings, lace-curtain tablecloths and a bizarre music mix encompassing 'Maggie May' and Mozart helped produce the authentic air of a restaurant in small-town Russia during the Communist era. Gloom descended, despite the charming if amateurish service. Food quality was haphazard: blini (an ordinary pancake) stuffed with dry grated apple, herring and raw onion was positively unpleasant, whereas 'herring in a fur coat' (russian salad with herring, heavy on beetroot and smothered in thick sour cream) was quite tasty. To follow, chicken shashlik was deliciously tender, yet came with old, badly reheated rice and tasteless aged vegetable salads. The latter also appeared with the placki: decent potato pancakes, crunchy and chewy at the same time, but let down by dry, over-fried mushrooms with sour cream in lieu of the promised mushroom sauce. Nevertheless, Luba's styles itself 'the vodka restaurant' and its choice of 68 varieties (including Ukrainian, Latvian and Lithuanian bottles seldom found in London) is undoubtedly the highlight of the place. Only for serious drinkers.
Babies and children admitted. Book weekends. Entertainment: Russian folk music 8pm Fri, Sat. Takeaway service. **Map 5 P1**.

Fish

London has a good collection of places to eat some excellent fish and seafood, ranging from the old-fashioned and traditional (lunchtime-only **Sweetings** is a particular fave) to the ultra-smart (plenty of options in the City, Mayfair and St James's) to the chain restaurants and more budget affairs. Special mention should go to celebrity hangout **J Sheekey**, City joint **Fishmarket** and Chiswick neighbours **Fish Hoek** and **FishWorks**.

Central

City EC2, EC3, EC4

Chamberlain's

23-25 Leadenhall Market, EC3V 1LR (7648 8690/www.chamberlains.org). Bank tube/ Liverpool Street tube/rail.
Bar **Open** noon-11pm Mon-Fri.
Restaurant **Meals served** noon-9pm Mon-Fri. **Main courses** £16-£27. **Set dinner** (5-9pm) £16.95 3 courses.
Both **Credit** AmEx, DC, MC, V.
This smart City restaurant has a lovely location in picturesque Leadenhall Market, just around the corner from the Lloyd's building – hence the preponderance of besuited expense-accounters. Hence, also, the prices: at lunch, most starters top £10 and a main of fish and chips with mushy peas comes in at a daunting £19.95. There are three spaces: a basement bar, a casual, light-filled ground-floor restaurant (with summer seating 'outside' in the covered market) and a posher first-floor room, with leather chairs and a frosted glass wave feature that's topped, rather oddly, with red and blue water bottles. A shame that the pretty fish-patterned plates adorning each table are only for show (food arrives on plain crockery). The fish – fresh from the market – is good quality, and the cooking has its flourishes. Lobster bisque was a suitably rich starter, while sautéed scallops with butterfly tiger prawns yielded plump, tasty specimens that went well with a pile of squid-ink pasta and a delicately flavoured vanilla sauce. On the downside, service was slightly scatty, and the wine list offers a meagre choice by the glass. Puds are predictable – crème brûlée, apple tart, summer pudding – but acceptable.
Booking advisable lunch. Children admitted. Disabled: toilet. No-smoking tables. Separate room for hire, seats 60 (dinner and Sat, Sun only). Tables outdoors (18, pavement). **Map 12 Q7**.

★ Fishmarket

Great Eastern Hotel, Bishopsgate, EC2M 7QN (7618 7200/www.fish-market.co.uk). Liverpool Street tube/rail. **Lunch served** noon-2.30pm, **dinner served** 6-10.30pm Mon-Fri. **Main courses** £10-£26. **Service** 12.5%. **Credit** AmEx, DC, MC, V.
A Friday lunch at Fishmarket witnesses the consumption of a lot of oysters and tall glasses of champagne. We sat in the buzzy bar this year – a casual change to the more formal dining room. The food is reliably good. Delicious rock oysters were reasonably priced at £8 for six. A starter of finely shredded pickled crab with seaweed and cucumber came with a lovely light soy and mirin dressing. Main courses were equally impressive: roast bream with aubergine caviar and tomato salsa was rich and flavourful, while turbot with spring vegetables – baby asparagus, peas and mushrooms – and fennel cream was a lighter choice. Alternatively, there are some spectacular crustacea dishes, such as langoustine, lobster and Cornish crab. Service

was extremely professional; we only had an hour spare to eat and both courses were brought promptly. Fishmarket is a lovely place for lunch.
Babies and children welcome; high chairs. Booking advisable; essential lunch. Disabled: toilet. **Map 12 R6**.

Sweetings

39 Queen Victoria Street, EC4N 4SA (7248 3062). Cannon Street tube/rail/Bank tube/ DLR. **Lunch served** 11.30am-3pm Mon-Fri. **Main courses** £10.50-£24.50. **Credit** AmEx, JCB, MC, V.
About as preserved as a jar of pickled fish, Sweetings has been serving City folk traditional dishes for more than 100 years. Everything about this place is old school, from the mahogany-topped counters and the efficient staff, to the suited and booted gents eating unfussy fare accompanied by buttered sliced bread and silver tankards of ale. The menu is quintessentially English: potted shrimps, fried whitebait, scampi and chips, fish pie and, wait for it... spotted dick, bread and butter pudding, and baked jam roll. Although there is no sign of salad, you will find the odd 'foreign' dish in the form of moules marinière and Mediterranean prawns. Mains consist of dover sole, halibut, turbot, salmon, sea bass and so on, grilled, poached or fried, with sides of potatoes, peas or creamy spinach. Swordfish with lemon butter was succulent and silky, and the fish and chips was a huge slab of nicely battered haddock. There's a very good range of wine and vintage ports to splash out on, plus a sandwich counter offering the likes of fresh crab.
Babies and children admitted. Bookings not accepted. Dress: smart casual. Restaurant available for hire, seats 30 (dinner only). Takeaway service. **Map 11 P6**.

Clerkenwell & Farringdon EC1

Rudland & Stubbs

35-37 Greenhill Rents, Cowcross Street, EC1M 6BM (7253 0148). Farringdon tube/rail. **Meals served** noon-10.45pm Mon-Fri. **Main courses** £10.50-£22. **Service** 12.5%. **Credit** AmEx, DC, MC, V.
R&S has a calm, civilised, breezy feel, particularly in summer when the front of the restaurant opens out to let in the muted sounds of the quiet Farringdon side street on which it is located. The interior is simple and clean, the original tiled columns and dark-wood bar still intact from its days as a sausage factory, with trad jazz playing quietly from an old-style radio. The menu is traditional with a twist: crab caesar salad with parmesan toast was an elegantly flavoured dish, while smoked salmon with apple and chilli was fresh and gingery. A dish of mussels with white wine and celery was tasty, but the star of the show was butterfish; it was succulent and appropriately buttery, and nicely complemented by a pea-flavoured summer vegetable broth. The best time to appreciate Rudland & Stubbs's light dishes and fresh and airy atmosphere is at lunchtime, when City folk fill the tables.
Booking advisable lunch. Children admitted. Tables outdoors (3, pavement). **Map 5 O5**.

Covent Garden WC2

Zilli 2

8-18 Wild Street, WC2B 5TA (7240 0011/ www.zillialdo.com). Covent Garden tube. **Lunch served** 12.30-3pm, **dinner served** 5.30-11.30pm

Mon-Sat. **Main courses** £9-£20. **Set meal** £16.90 2 courses, £19.90 3 courses. **Service** 12.5%. **Credit** AmEx, DC, MC, V.
Zilli 2 is definitely the poorer cousin to Zilli Fish (*see p73*). It shares a similar interior, with wave-shaped booths, a fish tank bar and comfortable seating, but it all feels rather contrived and overdone. Added to which, the menu is not nearly as interesting, but prices are just as high: a meal for two and a bottle of wine set us back more than £100. The meal started and ended on a good note: seared tuna sushi was beautifully presented and very tasty, though the accompanying wasabi lacked bite and consistency, while a dessert of panna cotta was dreamy. It was the main courses that let the evening down: the lettuce in the swordfish caesar salad was slimy, and although the fish itself was light and fluffy, there wasn't enough to the dish to warrant £18.50. Similarly, with fish skewers, the fish itself – prawn, tuna and swordfish – was okay, but the sauce – leek and saffron – was so buttery that it was unpalatable, more like something you'd expect to project from your mouth than put into it. Service was distracted – nothing like the professionalism of Zilli Fish. Perhaps it was just a bad night, but these restaurants, although similar in some ways, certainly don't share the same standards.
Babies and children welcome; children's portions, high chairs, entertainment (Sun lunch). Booking advisable. Disabled: toilet. No-smoking tables. Restaurant available for hire. Separate room for hire, seats 70. Tables outdoors (5, pavement). **Map 18 L6**.

Fitzrovia W1

★ Back to Basics

21A Foley Street, W1W 6DS (7436 2181/ www.backtobasics.uk.com). Goodge Street or Oxford Circus tube. **Lunch served** noon-3pm, **dinner served** 6-10.30pm Mon-Sat. **Main courses** £12.75-£15.95. **Service** 12.5%. **Credit** AmEx, DC, MC, V.
Back to Basics must be the perfect restaurant for fish lovers. Everything is dedicated to the piscine world, from the bright fish T-shirts worn by staff, through the fishy mosaic on the walls, to the innovative and colourful dishes. If you like interesting combinations and robust flavours, choosing from the massive selection chalked up on the blackboard menu will not be an easy task. Cornish skate with crispy bacon and mushy pea salsa? Fillet of mahi mahi, with mussels, clams, chilli and garlic? Mackerel with sun-dried tomatoes and halloumi on a bed of lentils? The skate was finished, so we opted for the mackerel, as well as a wonderfully abundant bowl of mussels and hot and spicy crab claws as starters. Portions are large and inexpensive, and the food is almost always as good as it sounds. The restaurant itself is charming, small and intimate, occupying a corner site in an attractive, quiet, almost Parisian part of Fitzrovia, with multicoloured globe lights and windows all around. In summer, the outside tables are crammed. Perfect.
Babies and children admitted. Booking essential. Tables outdoors (17, pavement). Takeaway service. **Map 3 J5**.

Leicester Square W1, WC2

Livebait Café Fish

36-40 Rupert Street, W1D 6DW (7287 8989/ www.santeonline.co.uk/cafefish). Leicester Square or Piccadilly Circus tube.
Bar **Open** noon-11pm Mon-Sat; 2-9pm Sun.
Canteen **Meals served** noon-11pm Mon-Sat; 2-9pm Sun. **Main courses** £7.95-£14.50. **Set meal** £10 2 courses.
Both **Service** 12.5%. **Credit** AmEx, DC, MC, V.
As the name suggests, this is the more relaxed arm of Livebait (*see p74*). Its central London location can make it a busy affair – people shuffle in and out in time to catch the next film or theatre performance – and the menu is thus considerably briefer, to make the choosing process quicker and easier. On past visits, the speediness of it all was

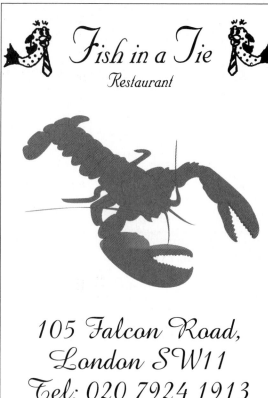

a greater selling point than the cooking, but this year the food was also thoroughly impressive. The restaurant was comfortably busy on a Friday lunchtime, and the acoustics are excellent, pushing sounds away and allowing us to enjoy our meal without distraction. We skipped starters – a selection of shellfish and the usual suspects (smoked salmon with capers, fish cakes) and headed straight for grilled salmon – a lovely piece of fish, cooked beautifully – and monkfish crepenettes – a tail of monkfish twirled around mushroom and bacon and wrapped in sausage skin. Served on a bed of spinach and rösti potatoes, this was a tasty, hearty dish. Side orders of new potatoes, and rocket and parmesan salad were both very good, the servings big enough to share. *Babies and children admitted; children's menu; high chairs. Booking advisable. Disabled: toilet. No-smoking tables.* **Map 17 K7.**

Manzi's
1-2 Leicester Street, WC2H 7BL (7734 0224/ www.manzis.co.uk). Leicester Square tube. **Lunch served** noon-3.45pm, **dinner served** 5-11.15pm Mon-Sat. **Main courses** £9.95-£50. **Service** 12.5%. **Credit** AmEx, DC, MC, V.
Even though Manzi's has been a London staple for more than 70 years, it feels as Italian as its name. And although time has seen many changes here, the decor hasn't moved much past the 1970s – it's kitschly ornate, with checked tablecloths and painted girls dancing across the ceiling. There aren't many places like this any more, probably not even in Italy. The huge menu lists about every fish and shellfish you could hope for in various unfussy guises – lobster thermidor, tiger prawns provençal, calamari, fish and chips – and servings are large and wholesome, often generously laden with potatoes. Poached skate with black butter and capers was enjoyable: a huge piece of fleshy fish served with a side order of perfectly al dente vegetables. A special of sea trout with rocket pesto was delicious, but swamped by the accompanying potato salad. Mediterranean prawns were firm and tasty, and served with unnecessarily generous splodges of mayonnaise and marie rose sauce. Prices are about average for the centre of town, but it's wise to visit only when very hungry. *Babies and children admitted. Booking advisable. Dress: smart casual. Separate room for hire, seats 45.* **Map 17 K7.**

★ J Sheekey
28-32 St Martin's Court, WC2N 4AL (7240 2565/www.caprice-holdings.co.uk). Leicester Square tube. **Lunch served** noon-3pm Mon-Sat; noon-3.30pm Sun. **Dinner served** 5.30pm-midnight Mon-Sat; 6pm-midnight Sun. **Main courses** £10.75-£29.75. **Set lunch** (Sat, Sun) £14.75 2 courses, £18.50 3 courses. **Cover** £2. **Credit** AmEx, DC, MC, V.
J Sheekey shares many wonderful things with its sister restaurant, The Ivy – elegant and discreet design, simple but sublime food, plus a more upmarket class of celebrity. In the past, we've always found it easy to make a booking – but not any more it seems. A phone call at the beginning of May couldn't get us the table we wanted until August. Is this due to a surge in popularity or just more tables kept back for the rich and famous as is the well-documented policy at The Ivy? Either way, this remains one of our favourite fish restaurants. Dressed crab was wonderfully fresh, served with grated egg and parsley. Excellent main courses include delicately flavoured sea trout with steamed clams and samphire, and a more robust lemon sole belle meunière with soft roes, shrimps and brown butter. Desserts were excellent: a raspberry trifle was rich and extremely fruity. Although it's easy to spend a lot of money at Sheekey's (watch those side dishes), it is also easy to keep the bill down. The average main course is under £20, which makes it more reasonable than some of the restaurants in this chapter – great value for money with such superior cooking. Treat yourself to a bargain set lunch at the weekend. *Babies and children welcome; high chairs; colouring books. Booking essential. Vegetarian menu.* **Map 18 K7.**

Mayfair W1

Scott's
20 Mount Street, W1K 2HE (7629 5248). Bond Street or Green Park tube. *Bar* **Open/meals served** noon-11pm Mon-Fri; 5pm-11pm Sat. **Snacks** £8-£23. *Restaurant* **Lunch served** noon-3pm Mon-Fri. **Dinner served** 6-11pm Mon-Sat. **Main courses** £15-£32. *Both* **Service** 12.5%. **Credit** AmEx, DC, JCB, MC, V.
There are many good things about dining at London's oldest fish restaurant: it's large, with comfortable chairs and well-spaced tables, but, most importantly, the food is consistently good. The menu has many old faves – scallops and bacon, or Scott's fish pie – with dishes cooked and presented beautifully. Potted shrimps were delicately spiced and soft enough to spread on toast; haddock fish cake was pungent, served on a bed of spinach and a pool of electric green parsley sauce; fish and chips was made up of two pieces of fish, so light they were like croissants, and thick wedge-like potatoes. More unusual dishes included a subtle, light offering of crayfish with avocado and chive salad, or red mullet with red pepper sauce and samphire. However, there are also some blips. Staff are a little ambivalent, some don't speak much English and the maître d' didn't even know (or care) whether head chef Michael McEnearny used to cook at Pharmacy (he did). And as for the decor... think *Dynasty* on an acid trip: a mishmash of expensive-looking paintings, shell-shaped lights and a pastel-painted wall that resembles a mermaid's grotto. All the good taste is obviously saved for the kitchen. Sadly, the future looks shaky for this venerable institution; at time of writing, Scott's closure appeared imminent. It may yet be saved, but do phone before you visit. *Babies and children admitted; high chairs. Booking advisable. Dress: smart casual. Separate room for hire, seats 22. Tables outdoors (7, pavement).* **Map 9 G7.**

Soho W1

Zilli Fish
36-40 Brewer Street, W1F 9TA (7734 8649/ www.zillialdo.com). Piccadilly Circus tube. **Meals served** noon-11.30pm Mon-Sat. **Main courses** £8.70-£28. **Credit** AmEx, DC, MC, V.
Dining at Zilli Fish is always enjoyable, not specifically for the food, which is hit and miss and expensive, but for the warm Italian atmosphere. Much like a big and welcoming family, staff are always friendly and Zilli himself can often be seen dining, socialising, cooking and even serving. There are a lot of pasta dishes, such as handmade spaghetti chitarra, with cherry tomatoes and spicy prawns, and spaghettini with whole fresh lobster (for a whacking £25), while fish dishes tend to be of the hearty variety – jumbo scallops, Mediterranean jumbo prawns oriental-style, or deep-fried squid with white radish and sweet chilli sauce. Zilli likes it rich and portions are big: a generous helping of mussels came in a garlicky tomato sauce, which was tasty if a little oily; monkfish stew was not so generous on the fish, but had plenty of potatoes; and a beautiful big sea bass was perfectly cooked and infused with lashing of rosemary. The richest hit came in the form of crème brûlée – thick and sticky on the top, pure indulgence in the middle. *Babies and children welcome. Booking advisable. Tables outdoors (3, patio).* **Map 17 J7.** **For branch see index.**

St James's SW1

Green's
36 Duke Street, SW1Y 6DF (7930 4566/ www.greens.org.uk). Green Park or Piccadilly Circus tube. **Lunch served** *Sept-Apr* 11.30am-3pm Mon-Sat; noon-3pm Sun. *May-Aug* 11.30am-3pm Mon-Sat. **Dinner served** *Sept-Apr* 5.30-11pm Mon-Sat; 5.30-9pm Sun. *May-Aug* 5.30-11pm Mon-Sat. **Main courses** £11-£40. **Cover** £2. **Credit** AmEx, DC, MC, V.

This English institution has just celebrated its 20th anniversary, and things were buzzing on our recent visit, even if the majority of diners were American and Japanese. Despite the slight stuffiness of the interior, members of staff are always friendly, down to earth and attentive. There is also no sense of the meal being rushed due to multiple bookings; we were able to spend three hours over dinner. The menu is traditional; typical dishes are smoked salmon and scrambled egg or smoked haddock with a soft poached egg and mashed potato. A few meat dishes are also thrown in, such as steak or bangers and mash. A starter of smoked trout mousse was a little over-bready, but accompanied by a delicious french bean and red onion salad. Smoked fish platter was also good, made up of eel, trout, tuna and salmon. Poached dorset plaice was subtly flavoured but rich, with its lobster cream sauce, while seared fillet of sea bream was a much lighter dish, served with roasted peppers, shallots and tapenade cream. A dessert of coffee and ginger mousse provided the perfect finishing touch to a very good meal. *Babies and children welcome. Booking essential. Dress: smart casual, no jeans or trainers. Separate room for hire, seats 36.* **Map 17 J7.**

Wheeler's
12A Duke of York Street, SW1Y 6LB (7930 2460). Piccadilly Circus tube. **Lunch served** noon-2.30pm Mon-Fri. **Dinner served** 5.30-11pm Mon-Sat. **Main courses** £12.50-£30. **Service** 12.5%. **Credit** AmEx, DC, MC, V.
We are pleased to hear that changes are afoot at Wheeler's because a recent visit left us feeling it was stuck in a time-warp. New management comes in the form of Matthew Brown, ex-chef of the Belvedere, who intends to spark up the menu to attract a younger crowd. It certainly needs it. Wheeler's has sold itself as a beautifully preserved slice of tradition, but when the menu displays six variations of dover sole and a Saturday evening is so quiet you can hear a pin drop, such tradition starts to feel a little tired. The setting is stunning: a sweeping oak staircase joining four narrow dining rooms. Green fabric walls, silver cutlery and stark linen – all this Brown intends to change very little. There are certainly skilled hands in the kitchen: omelette Arnold Bennett was cheesy and creamy, and served in a copper pan; salmon tartare of diced salmon with chives was light and fresh, crowned with a perfectly cooked quail's egg and caviar; and haddock on a bed of welsh rarebit and spinach with cream sauce was as rich and tasty as it sounds. Food this good, with a little more atmosphere and verve, could be a winning formula. *Babies and children admitted. Booking advisable dinner. No-smoking tables.* **Map 17 J7.**

West

Chiswick W4

★ Fish Hoek
8 Elliott Road, W4 1PE (8742 0766). Turnham Green tube. **Lunch served** noon-2.30pm Tue-Sun. **Dinner served** 6-10.30pm daily. **Main courses** £9.75-£30. **Set lunch** £11.50 2 courses, £16.50 3 courses. **Service** 12.5% for parties of 6 or more. **Credit** MC, V.
This lovely restaurant specialises in South African fish dishes. Named after a seaside suburb of Cape Town, it's a small, bright space decorated with sepia-tinged fishing photos (many are family pictures of Pete Gottgens, the owner). It can get uncomfortably crammed, especially on Friday and Saturday nights when there are two fixed sittings at the rather inconvenient times of 7 and 9.30pm. Such considerations soon fade, though, thanks to a buoyant atmosphere, knowledgeable service from South African staff, and great cooking. The menu offers a veritable ocean of choice, with around 30 fish and 12 shellfish dishes, most of them available in half or full portions rather than as starters and mains. South African species to look out for include snoek, stumpnose and kabeljou, but there are also exotica from the Indian Ocean and Caribbean, plus domestic fish (herring, salmon, plaice). The shellfish comes mainly from

Mozambique, and the wine list – predominantly whites – is exclusively South African. All our dishes – including snoek pâté with apricot and red onion chutney, char-grilled kingfish with chive mash, black pepper and strawberry salsa, and stumpnose with butternut mash and vine tomatoes – were excellent and attractively presented. Puds, such as banana and chocolate spring rolls with ice-cream, are equally inventive. A delightful one-off.
Babies and children admitted. Booking advisable. Disabled: entrance ramp. No-smoking tables.

★ FishWorks
6 Turnham Green Terrace, W4 1QP (8994 0086/www.fishworks.co.uk). Turnham Green tube. **Lunch served** noon-3pm Tue-Sat; noon-5pm Sun. **Dinner served** 6-10.30pm Tue-Sat. **Main courses** £12.90-£20. **Credit** AmEx, MC, V.
Busy Turnham Green Terrace is the setting for the first London branch of this mini chain (there are also outlets in Bristol, Bath, Christchurch and another opens at 89 Marylebone High Street at the end of 2004). At the front is the fishmonger; beyond that is the two-level restaurant, a bright, modern space with colourful maritime paintings, blond wood furniture and a perky, friendly vibe. An attractive back garden is covered by a big blue canopy. Choose from 'classic' dishes such as River Fowey estuary mussels or smoked salmon (many available in starter or main course sizes), shellfish galore (from oysters, crab and humble winkles all the way up to fruits de mer with native lobster for £70), plus daily specials. Expect fresh, quality ingredients, cooked without fuss or frills. The best dish was a fantastic fisherman's stew, served in its copper cooking pan. Crammed with big chunks of fish, clams and langoustines, in a stock of tomatoes and onions, and flavoured with thyme and garlic, it was a lip-smacking treat. Flaky roast cod with sage and tomatoes was also excellent. Extras included chewy crusty bread and marvellous mash, though braised fennel was too tough to be enjoyable. Staff were affable, if slightly ditzy on our visit. Enjoyed your meal? Then enrol at the cookery school (alternate Mondays) or buy the recipe book.
Babies and children welcome; children's menu and portions; high chairs. Booking advisable; essential weekends. Disabled: access. No smoking. Tables outdoors (5, pavement; 2, terrace).
For branch see index.

South West
Earl's Court SW5

Lou Pescadou
241 Old Brompton Road, SW5 9HP (7370 1057). Earl's Court tube. **Lunch served** noon-3pm daily. **Dinner served** 7pm-midnight Mon-Fri; 6.30pm-midnight Sat, Sun. **Main courses** £7.90-£14. **Set lunch** (Mon-Fri) £10.90 3 courses. **Set meal** (lunch, 6.30-8pm Sat, Sun) £14.50 3 courses. **Cover** £1.50. **Service** 15%. **Credit** AmEx, DC, MC, V.
A visit to this Earl's Court destination promises fine fish, and something extra. The intimate space, furnished with wooden tables and chairs, heavy linen and 'fish' crockery, appears to be dominated by the eccentric maître d' – tall, slightly manic, and reminiscent of a French Basil Fawlty – his gregariousness adding to the restaurant's charm. Respectable house wine (from a predominantly French list) is served in charming ceramic jugs. The food does not disappoint either. After a tasty deep-fried prawn wrap with dipping sauce, the white crab starter was impressive, in size, freshness and quality. Mains included a lovely slab of tuna on a bed of sautéed peppers, courgettes and onion, while red mullet was beautifully presented and tasted great. Only the desserts failed to reach a high standard. Lemon crème brûlée was overcooked and under-lemony, while three little pots of 'coffee, chocolate and vanilla' lacked strong flavour and texture. But this is a fun place, filled with regulars, and service is prompt and friendly. Another quirk is the downstairs bar (empty on our visit), with rugby shirts, photographs and other memorabilia plastered all over the walls.

Babies and children welcome; children's menu (£5.50); high chairs. Booking advisable. Separate room for hire, seats 40. Tables outdoors (8, terrace). Takeaway service. **Map 13 B11**.
For branch (The Stratford) see index.

South Kensington SW3
Bibendum Oyster Bar
Michelin House, 81 Fulham Road, SW3 6RD (7589 1480/www.bibendum.co.uk). South Kensington tube. **Meals served** noon-10.30pm Mon-Sat; noon-10pm Sun. **Main courses** £10-£31. **Service** 12.5%. **Credit** AmEx, DC, MC, V.
Located in the entrance to the Michelin building, this is an ideal spot from which to appreciate that structure's quirky tiling and high echoey ceilings. On a warm summer's day, it's a welcome breezy retreat, although it can be a little eerie when all the shoppers have gone home. But this place is very much geared to lunchtime diners: the menu doesn't have the usual starters and mains, but instead a selection of native and rock oysters, crustacea, caviar and a handful of lunch-sized/side order dishes, which could be something as simple as egg mayonnaise and potted shrimps. Rare tuna with tomatoes and tapenade comprised two huge slabs of succulent meat, beautifully pink and textured, but a less successful dish of grilled squid with oriental salad would have satisfied only the smallest appetite. Compensation came in the form of a dessert of lemon posset (lemon-fresh and thick like clotted cream), wonderful, big side salads and copious helpings of crispy bread and unsalted butter. One of the nicest and most accessible choices in the area for lunch.
Babies and children welcome; high chairs. Bookings not accepted. Disabled: lift; ramp. Dress: smart casual. Tables outdoors (5, pavement). **Map 14 E10**.

Poissonnerie de l'Avenue
82 Sloane Avenue, SW3 3DZ (7589 2457). South Kensington tube. **Lunch served** noon-3pm, **dinner served** 7-11.30pm Mon-Sat. **Main courses** £12.50-£27. **Set lunch** £16 2 courses, £24 3 courses. **Cover** £1.50. **Service** 15%. **Credit** AmEx, DC, JCB, MC, V.
A smart address makes this Kensington French restaurant a pricey affair, but diners get a lot for their money (and we don't just mean the lobster-motif carpet and the gilt-framed seafaring paintings). Staff are charming, efficient and prompt. The menu reads like a novel, with plenty of enticing specials. Portions are huge to overwhelming. Not wanting a buttery/cream overload, we opted for the 'cleaner' dishes: carpaccio of tuna was tender to melting, and given punch by roasted pimento peppers and rocket. Mackerel tartare was a mound of lightly flavoured fish with capers, dill and slices of brown toast. An enormous, tasty slab of john dory from the specials list was nicely complemented by a bed of roasted fennel; equally good, and just as large, was wild salmon steak. Our only complaint was that the john dory was undercooked to the extent that the flesh still clung to the bone. Prices are not extortionate, but the bill can mount up when you add on side dishes (a side salad of a few pieces of lettuce and cubes of tomatoes was not worth the £3 price tag) – but what do you expect when you're dining out in Brompton Cross?
Booking advisable dinner. Children admitted (babies admitted lunch only). Dress: smart casual. Separate room for hire, seats 20. Tables outdoors (6, pavement). **Map 14 E10**.

South
Kennington SE11

The Lobster Pot
3 Kennington Lane, SE11 4RG (7582 5556/ www.lobsterpotrestaurant.co.uk). Kennington tube/ Elephant & Castle tube/rail. **Lunch served** noon-2.30pm, **dinner served** 7-10.45pm Tue-Sat. **Main courses** £14.50-£19.50. **Minimum** (8-10pm) £23. **Set lunch** £11.50 2 courses, £14.50 3 courses. **Set meal** £21.50 3 courses, £39.50 8 courses. **Service** 12.5%. **Credit** AmEx, DC, JCB, MC, V.

After numerous visits over the years to this South London treasure, we realise that a truly successful meal here is dependent on whether Hervé is in the kitchen. The gimmicky interior, decked out like the inside of a boat with portholes behind which fish swim about, is always charming, but the food is definitely better when the moustached, Breton T-shirt-wearing owner is manning the pots – as he was on our most recent visit. We enjoyed starters of perfectly cooked scallops served on a skewer of rosemary, and langoustines with own-made mayonnaise. Main courses were equally good: a restaurant favourite (apparently he's been serving it for 12 years) of king prawns in a buttery garlic- and parsley-infused sauce, and poached skate wing, which was meaty and tasty. The vegetable accompaniments are French-minimal – a few mini new potatoes, al dente courgettes and baby carrots. The Lobster Pot always seems to be full, mainly with loyal locals sucking on lobster with bibs around their necks – and we can see why it's so popular: there's a great sense of French humour to the place, mainly thanks to the unique interior and the gangly waiters who look like they've just stepped out of *Amélie*.
Babies and children admitted; high chairs. Booking advisable. Dress: smart casual. Separate rooms for hire, seat 20 and 28. **Map 24 O11**.

Waterloo SE1
Livebait
41-45 The Cut, SE1 8LF (7928 7211/ www.santeonline.co.uk/livebait). Southwark tube/ Waterloo tube/rail. **Meals served** noon-11pm Mon-Sat; 12.30-9pm Sun. **Main courses** £9.75-£29. **Set meal** (2.30-7pm) £14.50 2 courses, £18.50 3 courses. **Service** 12.5%. **Credit** AmEx, DC, JCB, MC, V.
Livebait is great for a pre- or post-event meal, particularly at this branch close to the Old and New Vics and the South Bank. It serves its purpose well – clean, functional interior (classic fishmonger tiling), simple, unfussy menu and friendly, efficient staff. In addition, the food is often surprisingly good, although not as good as when Theodore Kyriakou was the chef-proprietor. We enjoyed tender squid in lovely succulent batter, but a special of sardines was a little greasy. Salmon and cod fish cake with sorrel sauce was hearty and generous on the fish front (though too large for a small appetite), while pan-seared tuna was perfectly adequate. Popular with local suits, there's a lot of braying and smoking over white wine, prawns and langoustines, all of which is made more noticeable by the hard tiled walls and bright white lighting. A purveyor of reasonable fish dishes at reasonable prices, but not much more, Livebait may need to pull its socks up if it wants to continue competing successfully with the growing number of Livebait lookalikes.
Babies and children admitted; high chairs. Booking advisable. Disabled: toilet. No-smoking tables. **Map 11 N8**.
For branches see index.

South East
London Bridge SE1

fish!
2004 RUNNER-UP BEST FAMILY RESTAURANT
Cathedral Street, SE1 9AL (7407 3803/www.fish diner.co.uk). London Bridge tube/rail. **Meals served** 11.30am-11pm Mon-Fri; noon-11pm Sat; noon-10.30pm Sun. **Main courses** £8.95-£17.95. **Service** 12.5%. **Credit** AmEx, MC, V.
Gourmands who routinely shop for top-notch groceries in neighbouring Borough Market may not flinch at the prices here, but when you're feeding a family, fish! can hardly be called an economy option. The standard of the food, however, seems much improved since the downsizing of the chain under the Loco aegis. The food is enjoyable – even the grilled chicken, chips and ice-cream on the children's menu (£6.95) was excellent, the chicken a moist piece of breast with a crispy char-grilled skin. On the main menu, the fish available each day is highlighted; you can

FishWorks

The last time we visited Winkles it had only just opened, and we were impressed by its easy slide into the fish restaurant pool. A year down the line, things are still looking good – not brilliant, but good. It's a brave move to open a specialist restaurant in an area dominated by council estates and takeaways, but, judging by the turnout, Winkles has managed to keep the locals happy with its uncomplicated dishes, bright decor and friendly staff. The star dish was scallops, served in their shells with a smoky soy sauce, beansprouts and spring onions, but we paid for it – £9.50 for a starter in the East End? Most other dishes were more reasonably priced. Fish and chips weighed in at £8.50: tender cod in a perfect dark and crispy batter, with minty mushy peas and golden chips. However, a special of sweet Thai mussel soup wasn't so impressive: it had no discernable Thai flavour to it, and tasted decidedly artificial. Sangria was on special offer (at £2.50 a glass), and was a tasty if odd accompaniment to fish. Service was an improvement on last year.
Babies and children admitted; children's portions; high chairs. Booking advisable weekends. Disabled: toilet. No-smoking tables. Tables outdoors (3, pavement). Takeaway service.

South Woodford E18

Ark Fish Restaurant NEW
142 Hermon Hill, E18 1QH (8989 5345). South Woodford tube. **Lunch served** noon-2.15pm Tue-Sat. **Dinner served** 5.30-9.45pm Tue-Thur; 5.30-10.15pm Fri; 5.30-10.30pm Sat. **Meals served** noon-8.45pm Sun. **Main courses** £8.50-£22. **Service** 10% for parties of 6 or more. **Credit** MC, V.
Fans of fish 'n' chips will be familiar with Faulkner's (*see p283*), a popular fish and chip restaurant in Dalston. Now the owners have opened Ark further east in sunny South Woodford. A bigger, better and more ambitious venture, it has a bright, modern, open-plan set-up, half smoking, half no-smoking. No bookings are taken, so there's a fast turnaround, and plenty of staff to cater to this. When busy there's about a 40-minute wait for a table, but the pleasant bar area offers a chance to muse the down-to-earth menu. We had to try the fish and chips, of course: a large piece of haddock in a thin nutty batter, with hand-cut chips and deliciously minty peas. Sea bass with tapenade was not such a success – the fish was delicious, but the accompanying curried potatoes were clumsy. A dish of scallops with garlic and salad was better, and Mediterranean prawns with garlic butter were perfectly cooked. A dessert of bakewell tart was fine but for the custard, which tasted as if it had started life as powder. The wine list majors on reasonably priced Italian whites.
Babies and children welcome; children's menu; high chairs. Bookings not accepted. No-smoking tables.

North
Finsbury Park N4

Chez Liline
101 Stroud Green Road, N4 3PX (7263 6550). Finsbury Park tube/rail. **Lunch served** 12.30-2pm Tue-Sat. **Dinner served** 6.30-10.30pm Tue-Sun. **Main courses** £10.95-£17.75. **Set meal** £12.75 2 courses. **Credit** AmEx, MC, V.
On a recent visit to this charming Mauritian restaurant we were very pleased to see it had been refurbished. We were also pleased that there were more staff and that the place was almost full. In addition, the food was much improved. Yes, things are looking up for Chez Liline. In the past, signature dishes have tended to focus on unusual fish with robust, spicy sauces, but this visit showed influences taken from more corners of the globe. Tartare and seared tuna with wasabi and soy sauce was a big departure in its elegant presentation and fine subtle flavour, while Thai green curry with tiger prawns was a refined example of a South-east Asian staple. More true to Chez Liline's reputation was grouper with blackbean sauce and chilli: good fleshy fish and a

order it grilled or steamed, with a sauce of either salsa, herb and garlic butter or hollandaise. Halibut was a firm, flavoursome fillet, easy on the palate, hard on the wallet. Filling and lemony salmon fish cakes with spinach were wholly delicious, and cod, chips and mushy peas are highly recommended. Eating here on a busy bank holiday was a mistake, however, as flustered staff can be a tad fish-like memory-wise – puddings were a long time coming. Apologies all round and lovely ice-cream and apple crumble soothed the situation.
Babies and children welcome; children's menu; crayons; high chairs. Booking advisable. Disabled: toilet. Tables outdoors (30, pavement). Map 11 P8.

Tower Bridge E1

Aquarium
Ivory House, St Katharine-by-the-Tower, E1W 1AT (7480 6116/www.theaquarium.co.uk). Tower Hill tube/Tower Gateway DLR. **Brunch served** (summer only) noon-4pm Sun. **Lunch served** noon-3pm Mon-Fri. **Dinner served** *Summer* 6-10pm Mon-Sat. *Winter* 6-10pm Tue-Sat. **Main courses** £14-£24. **Service** 12.5%. **Credit** AmEx, DC, MC, V.
As we were reminded several times, it's all change at Aquarium: new owners (from Lightship Ten; *see p148*), management, head chef and menu. After glutinous mushroom sushi amuse-gueules, we tucked into beautiful, jewel-like seared carpaccio of blue fin tuna and a tart fine of scallops, tiger

prawns and pork belly that was almost as impressive. The list of fresh seafood yielded half a hefty brown devon crab, happily unadorned but for toast and tools, but the red mullet papillote struggled for balance with its tapenade and semi-sun-dried tomatoes. Warm dark chocolate fondant was perfect for dessert, quite outpacing its honeycomb ice-cream and a nose ahead of a decent apple tart. Our waitress was unable to answer some basic questions and misdescribed one of the dessert wines: but it was her first day. The outdoor terrace, which bellies out into one of the quieter of St Katharine's many docks, is cheerfully intimate, particularly when the tabletop tealights come out at night. On Sunday afternoons jazz bands play: outside on the terrace in summer, inside in winter.
Babies and children welcome; high chairs. Booking advisable. Dress: smart casual. Entertainment: jazz 1pm Sun (summer). Restaurant available for hire. Separate room for hire, seats 60. Tables outdoors (14, terrace). Map 12 S8.

East
Bethnal Green E2

Winkles
238 Roman Road, E2 0RY (8880 7450/ www.winklesseafood.com). Mile End tube/Bethnal Green tube/rail. **Meals served** noon-10.30pm Tue-Sat; noon-9pm Sun. **Main courses** £7-£22. **Service** 12.5%. **Credit** AmEx, MC, V.

hearty sauce. For dessert, crème brûlée was rich and creamy, just as it should be. Our only gripe was that, despite the increase in staff numbers, service was very slow – but an unprompted apology from the owner put this small hiccup in the shadow of an overall successful meal.
Babies and children admitted. Booking advisable. Restaurant available for hire.

Islington EC1

The Fish Shop
360-362 St John Street, EC1V 4NR (7837 1199/ www.thefishshop.net). Angel tube/19, 38, 341 bus. **Brunch served** noon-5.30pm Sun. **Lunch served** noon-3pm, **dinner served** 5.30-10.30pm Tue-Sat. **Main courses** £10.95-£24.50. **Set meal** (noon-3pm, 5.30-7pm Tue-Sat) £13.50 2 courses, £17 3 courses. **Service** 12.5%.
Credit AmEx, DC, MC, V.
This smart, bright restaurant is run by the owners of the former Upper Street Fish Shop, a much-loved, and considerably more casual, type of eaterie. We're still not completely convinced by the move upmarket. The space is certainly attractive, with big windows and mirrors to reflect the light, but the food was disappointing. The menu is quite basic, covering fish and chips (cod, haddock, plaice or skate, in batter, or egg and matzo meal), shellfish and the likes of smoked haddock chowder or halibut steak. Starters included good smoked herring on new potatoes with a mustard dressing, and hot haddock smoky – a creamy, cheese-baked dish. But mains were bland. A plate of fish and chips were not as good as those served in the original Fish Shop, and salad niçoise was insipid. Perhaps we just chose the wrong dishes, because the diners beside us appeared to be enjoying their fish pie. Prices are decent for a fish restaurant – and they also stock a range of fine wines and ports, plus a selection of decent cocktails alongside the usual bottle beers – but we suggest that this one forks out for some better supplies. Nice restaurant, but unfortunately the fish just doesn't come up to scratch.
Babies and children welcome; children's portions. Booking advisable dinner Fri, Sat. Disabled: toilet. Tables outdoors (10, terrace). **Map 5 O3.**

Outer London
Barnet, Hertfordshire

Loch Fyne Restaurant
12 Hadley Highstone, Barnet, Herts EN5 4PU (8449 3674/www.loch-fyne.com). High Barnet tube/Hadley Wood rail. **Meals served** 9am-10pm Mon-Fri; 10am-10.30pm Sat; 10am-9.30pm Sun. **Main courses** £7.95-£15.95. **Set lunch** £9.95 2 courses incl side dish. **Service** 10% for parties of 6 or more. **Credit** AmEx, MC, V.
No credit cards.
Like its sister branches, the Barnet outpost of Loch Fyne is an airy, light-filled room, with chunky wooden furniture, specials displayed on a large blackboard, a wonderful piscine display of the ocean's finest, and a menu that may not be as wild as the salmon but is always reliable. Experience suggests that the simplest dishes work best. Oysters and shellfish are a speciality (farmed by sister company Loch Fyne Oysters), but we enjoyed an incredibly fresh fillet of smoked organic salmon, sashimi-style, with wasabi and soy sauce. Bass was a beautifully cooked piece of fish, although the small portion of artichoke and olive garnish added little. Fillet of wild dorade was better, accompanied by impeccably seared scallops and braised fennel. Desserts were unexciting, of the banoffee pie or sorbet school, though a selection of Scottish and Irish cheese with oatcakes might have been interesting if we'd had enough room. The wine list naturally covers plenty of whites, with many decent bottles coming in at under £12. The chain also has branches in central London, including Covent Garden and Chalk Farm.
Babies and children welcome; children's menu; high chairs. Booking advisable. No-smoking tables. Tables outdoors (7, terrace). Vegetarian menu.
For branches see index.

French

London's *grand amour* for French cuisine continues. The number of high-quality Gallic restaurants in the capital grows yearly, from homely Parisian-style bistros to some of the city's most glamorous dining destinations. Two runners-up for the Best New Restaurant gong in *Time Out's* Eating & Drinking Awards 2004 appear in this section – Max Renzland's Wandsworth bistro **Le Petit Max**; and Conran's new Docklands venture, **Plateau** – as well a runner-up for the Best Vegetarian Meal award, in the shape of **Morgan M** in Islington.
Other noteworthy newcomers include **Le Cercle** in Belgravia (sibling of funky Club Gascon), **Rosemary Lane** in the City, and – agreeably – a number of restaurants outside city-centre postcodes, including **Chez Kristof** in Hammersmith, **Bistrotheque** in Bethnal Green and the **Food Room** in Battersea (offspring of the acclaimed **French Table** in Surbiton). All evidence that Londoners love a good restaurant on their doorstep – which is why it's sad to bid farewell this year to much-loved stalwart **Soulard**, in Hackney, which closed in 2004 after 21 years in business.
For other French restaurants, see **Hotels & Haute Cuisine** (starting on p110). Bon appetit!

Central
Belgravia SW1

Le Cercle NEW
1 Wilbraham Place, SW1X 9AE (7901 9999). Sloane Square tube.
Bar **Open** noon-midnight Tue-Sat.
Restaurant **Lunch served** noon-3.30pm, **afternoon tea served** 3-5.30pm, **dinner served** 5.30-11pm Tue-Sat. **Tapas** £3-£15. **Service** 12.5%. **Credit** AmEx, JCB, MC, V.
Some French restaurateurs try a different approach to the norm. Foremost among them are Vincent Labeyrie and Pascal Aussignac, who founded Club Gascon (*see p78*). Le Cercle is their new venture. How is Chelsea going to take to this funky basement? Staff wear leather aprons. The bar is leather-fronted. Our seats were leather. There's even a bar overlooking the dining area, with brown leather chaise longues. We hid behind long net curtains, a clever touch that gives this high-ceilinged basement even more of a nightclub feel. The menu lists dishes in snack-sized portions, not tied to one French region; glasses of wine are suggested as matches. First was stuffed and braised artichoke, followed by a delicate, immaculately dressed green salad. Both were impeccable, as you might hope when paying nearly £5 per nibble. Next came snails: little garlicky ones cooked in their own frail shells. Tender baby squid arrived with asparagus and mangetout, a winning combination. Black pudding was correctly dark and bloody; grilled andouillette was a good version of the chitterling sausage, but the fetid aroma is challenging. In contrast, veal sweetbreads didn't linger long on the plate. Service is sweet.
Babies and children welcome. Bookings not accepted after 8pm. Disabled: toilet. No-smoking tables. **Map 15 G10.**

La Poule au Pot
231 Ebury Street, SW1W 8UT (7730 7763). Sloane Square tube. **Lunch served** 12.30-2.30pm Mon-Sat; 12.30-3.30pm Sun. **Dinner served** 6.45-11pm Mon-Sat; 6.45-10pm Sun.

Main courses £12-£20. **Set lunch** £15.50 2 courses, £17.50 3 courses. **Service** 12.5%. **Credit** AmEx, DC, MC, V.
Fully booked on a regular basis, Belgravia's own traditional corner bistro combines simple French food with a convivial Gallic atmosphere to good effect. The restaurant is a warren of candlelit corners with abrupt yet friendly waiters darting between tables of swooning couples and well-heeled parties. Some of the menu's more complex dishes sometimes disappoint, but if you stick to well-tried favourites (such as escargots or coq au vin) it's hard to go wrong. A starter of asparagus was a springtime treat of thick green stalks served with the lightest of hollandaise sauces; venison pâté du chef was rich and gamey, if a little too chunky. Râble de lapin à l'ail (a mouth-watering main course of rabbit saddle oozing juicy stock and laden with roasted garlic and shallots) came with a bubbling pot of buttery potato gratin. We'd hoped that the cassoulet d'oie – a steaming goose stew packed with thick slices of salami and butter beans – would be more herby and fragrant, but it was warming and flavoursome nonetheless. One dark rich chocolate mousse and an excellent bottle of Crozes-Hermitage later, we re-emerged into the London night rosy-cheeked and replenished with joie de vivre.
Babies and children welcome; high chairs. Booking essential. Separate room for parties, seats 16. Tables outdoors (15, terrace). **Map 15 G11.**

Roussillon
16 St Barnabas Street, SW1W 8PE (7730 5550/ www.roussillon.co.uk). Sloane Square tube. **Lunch served** noon-2.30pm Wed-Fri. **Dinner served** 6.30-10.30pm Mon-Sat. **Set lunch** £23 2 courses, £30 3 courses. **Set dinner** £45 3 courses. **Set meal** £65 7 courses. **Service** 12.5%. **Credit** AmEx, MC, V.
The lights glinting through the bay window give Roussillon an inviting Dickensian feel. Once inside, though, you almost do a double-take. How does somewhere serving such wonderful, indulgent food manage to maintain such a restrained, puritanical atmosphere? Our fellow diners seemed cowed into quietness, when they should have been purring with pleasure. To start, amuse-bouches – small dishes of smoked eel with chickpea beignets and swiss chard roulade – were irrepressible. Lobster soup arrived with a small mousse sitting in the middle of a wide white bowl; this was lovingly filled with the soup from a copper pan by a reverential waitress. The fresh pea risotto was little short of tremendous; a confit of milk-fed Pyrennean lamb was glorious. Another waitress returned with advice on how to eat the caramelised lemon financier (don't go near the orange marmalade on the edge of the plate unless there's pudding on your spoon: it was to be eaten on its own). There's a fixed price for three dishes, not courses, so you can have any combination (three of the same dish, three puddings – anything goes). It's almost as if the restaurant is trying to have fun.
Babies and children admitted. Booking advisable. Dress: smart casual. No-smoking tables. Restaurant available for hire. Separate room for parties, seats 28. Vegetarian menu. **Map 15 G11.**

City E1, EC2, EC3, EC4

Le Coq d'Argent
No.1 Poultry, EC2R 8EJ (7395 5000/ www.conran.com). Bank tube/DLR.
Bar & grill **Lunch served** 11.30am-3pm Mon-Fri. **Main courses** £12-£17.

Restaurant **Breakfast served** 7.30-10am, **lunch served** 11.30am-3pm Mon-Fri. **Brunch served** noon-3pm Sun. **Dinner served** 6-10pm Mon-Fri; 6.30-10pm Sat. **Main courses** £15-£20. **Set brunch** (Sun) £22.50 2 courses, £25 3 courses. **Set lunch** (Mon-Fri) £24 2 courses, £28.50 3 courses.
Both **Service** 12.5%. **Credit** AmEx, DC, JCB, MC, V.
This City-centre Conran joint occupies a prime spot atop No.1 Poultry, a postmodern juggernaut of a building, with a circular roof garden-cum-bar (and adjoining lawn) offering fine skyline views. Lunch – as you'd expect – is when it's operating at full throttle, with all the tables occupied, the place abuzz and the shoe-shine guy standing sentry outside the roof-top lifts. This year we ate in the bar and grill, which offers a pared-down version of the restaurant menu. A very hit-and-miss meal ensued. Baked haddock with ratatouille, although charmingly served in a copper pan, was one of the dullest dishes we've ever eaten; the ratatouille tasted as though it had come out of a tin. Accompanying frites were no better than any burger chain could manage. And suddenly not having any blinis (though advertised on the menu) and substituting them with toast without checking that this was acceptable seemed amateurish. However, rock oysters were superb, as was the cheese plate. Beef stew was also up to scratch. Staff were very pleasant, but hesitant. The location, views and roof-top garden mean that Coq d'Argent won't be short of custom, but on the evidence of this meal, customers are being sold short.
Babies and children admitted; high chairs. Booking advisable. Disabled: lift; toilet. Entertainment: jazz 12.30-4pm Sun. Restaurant available for hire. Tables outdoors (13, restaurant terrace; 25, bar terrace). **Map 11 P6.**

1 Lombard Street

1 Lombard Street, EC3V 9AA (7929 6611/ www.1lombardstreet.com). Bank tube/DLR.
Bar **Open** 11am-11pm Mon-Fri. **Food served** 11.30am-10.30pm Mon-Fri.
Brasserie **Breakfast served** 7.30-11am, **meals served** 11.30am-10.30pm Mon-Fri. **Main courses** £12.50-£27.50. **Set dinner** (6-10.30pm) £19.50 5 courses.
Restaurant **Lunch served** noon-3pm, **dinner served** 6-10pm Mon-Fri. **Main courses** £27.50-£29.50. **Set lunch** £34 2 courses, £36 3 courses. **Set dinner** £36 6 courses.
All **Service** 12.5%. **Credit** AmEx, DC, JCB, MC, V.
City slickers flock to this splendid location at the very heart of the Square Mile. The large, domed and whitewashed brasserie (a Grade II-listed former banking hall) is filled with a cacophony of bankers and lawyers taking advantage of the relative bargain offered by the set lunch menu. So loud is the din, in fact, that staff have difficulty concentrating and tried several times to deliver the wrong order to our table. The food's a mixed bag and prices are undeniably steep. A simple lunch of warm mushroom salad with green beans and celeriac, a salmon fish cake with chips on the side, and lemon meringue tart to follow will set you back £37 without water, wine or coffee. Venture into the exclusive 'fine dining' restaurant at the back and the bill will rise even further. Here, London restaurant veteran Herbert Berger's menu might yield a gratin of crayfish with artichokes and spinach purée and a liquorice and dill velouté (£17), followed by splendid roast lamb fillet with parsnip and black truffles, crispy potato and quince galette and caramelised foie gras (£29.50), from a menu that courts exotic flavours but stays firmly in the classical mould.
Babies and children admitted. Booking advisable lunch. Disabled: lift; toilet. Restaurant available for hire. Separate room for parties, seats 40. **Map 12 Q6.**

★ Rosemary Lane NEW

61 Royal Mint Street, E1 8LG (7481 2602/ www.rosemarylane.btinternet.co.uk). Tower Hill tube/Fenchurch Street rail/Tower Gateway DLR. **Lunch served** noon-2.30pm Mon-Fri. **Dinner served** 5.30-10pm Mon-Sat. **Main**

courses £13-£18. **Set meal** £14 2 courses, £17 3 courses. **Service** 12%. **Credit** AmEx, MC, V.
It's hard to imagine a more unprepossessing location so close to the City – on a bleak stretch of road opposite the elevated DLR. Once you're inside this converted pub, though, seated at a smartly laid table, the mood changes dramatically. The decor is muted (taupe drapes and banquettes, dark wood panelling) apart from splashes of colour from a few paintings; the atmosphere is low key (although not stifling) – what matters is the food. Menus change every six weeks, and are serious stuff: French cuisine with a touch of California. Every dish we tried worked a treat. The simplest was a vibrantly beautiful, flavour-packed spring pea soup with white truffle oil and croûtons (from the prix-fixe, an absolute steal for the quality). Equally successful were more involved mains such as pan-fried red mullet with arugula nage, oyster mushroom and leek fricassée, herb salad and little cresses; and seared diver scallops with preserved gold beetroot, girolles and pea shoots, and chive beurre blanc. The rabbit, duck and mushroom pâtés (a starter) deserve mention too, as do the crab and salmon eggs amuse-bouche and the pineapple sorbet palate cleanser. A tiny restaurant run with passion.

Babies and children welcome. Booking advisable lunch. Dress: smart casual. Restaurant available for hire. **Map 12 S7.**

Clerkenwell & Farringdon EC1

★ Café du Marché

22 Charterhouse Square, Charterhouse Mews, EC1M 6AH (7608 1609). Barbican tube/ Farringdon tube/rail. **Lunch served** noon-2.30pm Mon-Fri. **Dinner served** 6-10pm Mon-Sat. **Set meal** £27.95 3 courses. **Service** 15%. **Credit** MC, V.
You get to this accomplished, welcoming, rustic-accented brasserie through a narrow alleyway that provides a very promising olfactory prelude. The savoury scents curl along it from dining rooms on ground and first floors, both similarly furnished (rickety wicker chairs, white table linen aplenty); we mounted the brick-walled corkscrew staircase to the bare-boarded, barn-beamed Grenier, a spacious and airy room with a large bar at one end and big windows at the other. Food is copious and, while resting on French foundations, folds in styles and ingredients from other corners of the world. The main courses of our three-part £27.95 lunch

Patterson's. See p81.

Le Petit Max. See p85.

menu included chunky, char-grilled magret de canard in cranberry jus (tasty, if a tad tough, and as French as you please); starters included melon with chorizo, and vitello tonnato; and desserts included parfait au 'summer pudding'. The main courses came with a large side dish of delicious, golden matchstick frites and a heavy wooden bowl of green salad. The highlight? One of the simplest dishes, a starter of tomato salad with mozzarella: oil and balsamic dressing perfectly judged, ingredients first rate and – magic touch – sprinkled with grains of coarse salt. The place is popular, so book ahead.

Babies and children admitted. Booking advisable. Disabled: toilet. Entertainment: jazz duo 8-11pm Thur. Separate rooms for parties, seating 30 and 70. Tables outside (4, pavement). **Map 5 O5.**

★ **Club Gascon**

57 West Smithfield, EC1A 9DS (7796 0600). Barbican tube/Farringdon tube/rail. **Lunch served** noon-2pm Mon-Fri. **Dinner served** 7-10pm Mon-Thur; 7-10.30pm Fri, Sat. **Main courses** £5.30-£29. **Tapas** £6-£16.50. **Set meal** £38 5 courses. **Service** 12.5%. **Credit** AmEx, MC, V.

Renowned as a foie gras specialist, Club Gascon is, as you might assume, a plush, pricey venue frequented by holders of gold Coutts cards. But it is no bastion of conservatism. Food, from conception to presentation, is witty, challenging and imaginative. So is the environment: lots of incongruous shapes and materials assembled into clubby, natural warmth. Both are beguiling, as are the black-clad but distinctly non-uniform staff. The menu is divided into five sections that will bewilder newcomers. Following advice, we each ordered one 'Route du Sel', one foie gras, one fish or meat dish and one vegetable assemblage. It sounds a lot – and it was. If the idea here is tapas, the kitchen needs to learn about the 'small' part. But overeating was

no hardship. A frothed olive emulsion amuse-gueule preceded deep-flavoured jugged mushrooms and ham, and a Gascon pie (duck mousse with a mushroom filling) that elicited an actual frisson of pleasure. The foie gras, cooked with a lemon reduction and pertly served with lemon sorbet in two giant spoons, and in a pâté with maple syrup and a pancake, was similarly awesome. Other courses were similarly awesome, bar a cappuccino of lobster and black pudding with asparagus that should perhaps have stayed on the drawing board. The whole was artfully accompanied by a succession of wines by the glass chosen by our waiter. A blowout, but one that we won't forget.

Babies and children admitted. Booking essential. Restaurant available for hire. **Map 11 O5.**

Covent Garden WC2

Chez Gérard at the Opera Terrace

45 East Terrace, The Market, The Piazza, WC2E 8RF (7379 0666/www.santeonline.co.uk). Covent Garden tube. *Brasserie* **Meals served** 11am-5pm daily. **Set meal** £8 2 courses. *Restaurant* **Lunch served** noon-3pm Mon-Sat; noon-3.30pm Sun. **Dinner served** 5.30-11.30pm Mon-Sat; 5.30-10.30pm Sun. **Main courses** £10-£15. **Set meal** (5.30-7pm) £13.25 2 courses, £16.75 3 courses. **Cover** £1.50. *Both* **Service** 12.5%. **Credit** AmEx, DC, JCB, MC, V.

Chez Gérard commands a sizeable rooftop chunk of Covent Garden piazza, with ringside views of the general madness below. In summer, the sun-shaded, palm-fronded terrace is not a bad place to be, provided you can get a seat – if not, you'll be stuck to a camel-leather banquette in the airless greenhouse of a restaurant behind. Either way, the food isn't brilliant. The menu contains dozens of

French dishes, from garlic-butter snails to red mullet soup, but the house speciality of steak (in myriad cuts) and chips (in giant bowls) takes centre stage. Most people seemed to chomp away happily, although a steak tartare came with almost negligible garnishes of crushed cornichons, onions and capers – not enough to mix in with the meat and make it tangy. Yet this was better than the starter of bland melted camembert d'Isigny, flanked by an assortment of ageing crudités that amounted to two lettuce leaves, one radish and… that was nearly it. A glass of pinot noir, served lukewarm, showed more sloppiness. Fellow diners are a mix of family tourist outings, the odd businessman and, on our visit, two ladies dining in exchange for coupons from the *Radio Times*.

Babies and children welcome; high chair. Booking essential. Restaurant available for hire. Tables outdoors (20, terrace). **Map 18 L6.** **For branches see index.**

Incognico

117 Shaftesbury Avenue, WC2H 8AD (7836 8866/www.incognico.com). Leicester Square or Tottenham Court Road tube. **Lunch served** noon-3pm, **dinner served** 5.30pm-midnight Mon-Sat. **Main courses** £11.50-£25. **Set meal** (noon-3pm, 5.30-7pm) £12.50 3 courses. **Service** 12.5%. **Credit** AmEx, DC, MC, V.

A popular choice among businessmen and wealthy tourists, Incognico is a modern brasserie that gives its clients what they want. The dark wooden dining room oozes austere grandeur; the staff are formal and efficient; the wine cellar is well stocked; and the foie gras-laden menu is appetising without being challenging. Starters such as artichoke stuffed with foie gras and mushroom duxelle, and escalope of foie gras with orange, hint at extravagance and culinary sophistication, but when both came drizzled in an identikit Madeira sauce we felt a little disappointed. Still more

Madeira sauce was heaped over goujons of calf's liver, yet failed to hide the meat's lack of tenderness. Baby dover sole was firm, fleshy and slunk off the bone, but was let down by another unimaginative sauce – a plain pot of tartare that wouldn't have been out of place in a high-street chip shop. A zesty slice of lemon tart aside, this was an unspectacular meal that didn't justify a bill that topped £100 for two (with a bottle of house red). If you're still curious (Incognico was founded by Nico Ladenis, now retired), then pop in at lunch for the £12.50 set menu.
Babies and children welcome; high chairs. Booking essential. Dress: smart casual. Restaurant available for hire. **Map 17 K6**.

Mon Plaisir

21 Monmouth Street, WC2H 9DD (7836 7243/ www.monplaisir.co.uk). Covent Garden or Leicester Square tube. **Lunch served** noon-2.15pm Mon-Fri. **Dinner served** 5.45-11.15pm Mon-Sat. **Main courses** £13.95-£22. **Set lunch** £12.95 2 courses, £15.95 3 courses. **Set meal** (5.45-7pm) £13.95 2 courses, £15.95 3 courses incl glass of wine and coffee. **Service** 12.5%. **Credit** AmEx, MC, V.
What do you expect? A name that sounds like a snippet of Gauloise-edged pillow talk; a blue enamel number plaque and a huge tricolore out front; four dining areas dripping with francophile finery, Josephine Baker posters, nicotine-dragged ceilings and Byrrh bottles: of course, it's often packed. How many diners are return visitors, though, is open to speculation. For staff seem to have learned their trade from Alphonse Agaçant's classic 1932 catering manual, *Rien à foutre* (released in an expurgated English edition under the title *Food with a Bad Mood*). OK, there's no such book – but the prevailing ill-temper here is all too close to the popular image of French 'service', and the *plaisir* tends to go out of a meal when staff are so plainly not enjoying each other's – or the customers' – company (as when one gave another a not-so-sotto voce roasting for serving a drink in the wrong glass). That said, the food is tolerably good – our snails starter was much as you'd expect, the succulent poitrine de canard with red berry sauce was precisely cooked, though the carré d'agneau was tougher – and the menu is all French classics in the onion soup/steak tartare/clafoutis category. Nothing here is cheap, though.
Booking advisable. Children welcome. Separate room for parties, seats 28. **Map 18 L6**.

Fitzrovia W1

Elena's L'Étoile

30 Charlotte Street, W1T 2NG (7636 7189). Goodge Street or Tottenham Court Road tube. **Lunch served** noon-2.30pm Mon-Fri. **Dinner served** 6-10.45pm Mon-Sat. **Main courses** £14.95-£19.85. **Service** 12.5%. **Credit** AmEx, DC, JCB, MC, V.
Elena's L'Étoile has the kind of genuine character that can only be earned with many years of service. There's a world of difference between the other, increasingly slick eateries of Charlotte Street and this gem, which transports you back in time to Parisian bistros of old, with its browning walls, velvet-backed chairs and creaky floorboards. The menu majors on conservative French (and occasional Italian) classics. A starter of potato pancake with salmon, cream and chives was delicately flavoured, while mains yielded a crispy lemon sole with saffron mash and a fine rib-eye steak with cep sauce and creamed spinach, all assisted by an excellent £23 Morgon. For dessert, a selection of sorbets were slightly watery. We like Elena's, and we really want to love it; it's just that prices are high for what is good – but not always memorable – cuisine. But if you're crying out for an alternative to sleek, pine-filled eateries with mechanical service, it hits the nail on the head. On our last visit, eightysomething Elena Salvoni herself was nowhere to be seen, but we were assured that she still oversees procedures during the week. Photos of London luvvies cover the walls, confirming Elena's place within the hearts of London's showbiz darlings.

Babies and children welcome. Booking advisable; essential lunch. Separate rooms for parties, seating 14, 16 and 30. **Map 9 J5**.

Knightsbridge SW1, SW3

Brasserie St Quentin

243 Brompton Road, SW3 2EP (7589 8005/ www.brasseriestquentin.co.uk). Knightsbridge or South Kensington tube/14, 74 bus. **Lunch served** noon-3pm daily. **Dinner served** 6-10.30pm Mon-Thur; 5.30-10.30pm Fri, Sat; 5.30-10pm Sun. **Main courses** £9.50-£23.50. **Set meal** (noon-7.30pm) £14.50 2 courses, £16.50 3 courses. **Service** 12.5%. **Credit** AmEx, DC, JCB, MC, V.
The St Quentin is a place of quality cooking, good-pedigree diners and genial, chaotic waiters. There's a slightly stagey feel to the decor, with its reds, blacks and mirrors, but this doesn't detract from the generally relaxed and unassuming atmosphere. The menu is full of good, robust brasserie stuff, while the wine list is an event; those intimidated by the choice can always play safe with the delicious house merlot. A starter of chicken and wild mushroom sausages with a lentil gravy was slightly salty, but rich with carefully blended tastes – much better than a feuilleté of escargots, with the tiny snails nearly drowned in cream and garlic, although the pastry crust was a crisp, golden mop for the flavours. The time lag between starters and mains ('Ze chef has burnt ze chicken and is remaking it,' our waiter told us cheerfully) was long enough for us to start questioning value for money here, but gorgeously tender grilled (not burnt) chicken, and fresh wild sea bass with love-it-or-hate-it chervil, produced happiness. To finish, chocolat fondant and crème brûlée were decent, if not show-stopping.
Babies and children welcome; high chair. Booking advisable. Dress: smart casual. Separate room for parties, seats 20. **Map 14 E10**.

Drones

1 Pont Street, SW1X 9EJ (7235 9555). Knightsbridge or Sloane Square tube. **Lunch served** noon-2.30pm Mon-Fri; noon-3.30pm Sun. **Dinner served** 6-11pm Mon-Sat. **Main courses** £9.50-£22. **Set lunch** (Mon-Fri) £14.95 2 courses, £17.95 3 courses; (Sun) £19.50 3 courses. **Service** 12.5%. **Credit** AmEx, DC, MC, V.
To savour the full feeling of retro glamour at this Marco Pierre White venture, go in the evening, when the 1930s club-style decor comes off better. The walls are covered with black and white photographs of showbiz legends, lighting is low and the place buzzes. During the day, grandes dames meeting their grandchildren, local ladies who lunch and a few business couples seem to make up the clientele. The menu matches the timeless concept, listing an alluring selection of brasserie classics divided into hors d'oeuvres, salads, pastas, fish, roasts and grills, and so on. Prices vary widely, but never stray into the downright unreasonable given the quality of ingredients and cooking involved, though vegetables cost extra. British favourites (potted shrimps; dressed crab served with melba toast; dover sole; grilled calf's liver with bacon and fried onions) keep company with Mediterranean interlopers (gazpacho perhaps, or grilled tuna with aubergines, tomato and basil) – and there's a Drones burger with club sauce for the truly conservative diner. Prices on the mostly French wine list are steep, but a broad range is offered by the glass.
Babies and children admitted. Booking essential. Restaurant available for hire. Separate room for parties, seats 45. **Map 15 G10**.

★ Racine

239 Brompton Road, SW3 2EP (7584 4477). Knightsbridge or South Kensington tube/ 14, 74 bus. **Lunch served** noon-3pm Mon-Fri; noon-3.30pm Sat, Sun. **Dinner served** 6-10.30pm Mon-Sat; 6-10pm Sun. **Main courses** £9.50-£18.75. **Set meal** (lunch, 6-7.30pm) £15.50 2 courses, £17.50 3 courses. **Service** 14.5%. **Credit** AmEx, JCB, MC, V.

Very chic, very Knightsbridge and possibly a little hard-edged, Racine is the essence of a Parisian brasserie transported to London. Winner of the Best New Restaurant category in *Time Out*'s 2003 Eating & Drinking Awards, it continues to garner rave reviews and plays to a packed house. Draw aside the theatrical heavy drape that shields the door and step into a room lined with mirrors and deep-green banquettes, filled with enthusiastic diners. Staff negotiate the melee with impersonal efficiency. Chef Henry Harris's French bourgeois food has rustic leanings which show up in simple starters like tomatoes baked with basil and crème fraîche on toasted brioche, but the classics play a leading role. There are salty slices of bayonne ham offset by creamy celeriac remoulade; baked asparagus when in season; langoustines sliced in half and grilled (slightly too much) with lashings of garlic, butter and parsley; cod served with a spicy crab butter sauce; and, of course, steak with plenty of excellent frites. Finish with a perfect petit pot au chocolat. A good choice for a Paris-meets-London night out.
Babies and children admitted; high chair. Booking advisable. Dress: smart casual. No-smoking tables. **Map 14 E10**.

Marylebone W1

★ La Galette

56 Paddington Street, W1U 4HY (7935 1554/ www.lagalette.com). Baker Street tube. **Meals served** 9.30am-11pm Mon-Fri; 10am-11pm Sat, Sun. **Main courses** £5.60-£8.95. **Set lunch** (noon-5pm Mon-Fri) £6.95 2 courses. **Service** 10% for parties of 6 or more. **Credit** AmEx, MC, V.
The galette is the savoury, buckwheat sibling of the crêpe – a hearty Breton staple, and the Parisian equivalent to the post-pub kebab. At this restaurant it gets very near to being glamorous, cooked with a feather-light touch and served in a setting that owes more to Scandinavia (lovely warm lamps and classy pale woods) than it does to *vieille* France (red velvet curtains and a few rows of banquettes). There are olives, salads, pâtés and the like for starters, but skip all that to achieve the savoury-sweet double bill comfortably. Thin, judiciously crisp and not too buttery, the galettes here are a delight: the paysanne with lardons (small bacon cubes), cream and onions was miraculously light, while the wild mushrooms in the forestière had a lovely, earthy meatiness. Our sweet crêpes were made with a slightly flakier batter, but are still worth it for high-quality toppings such as delicious, dark melted chocolate. The galette's drinking partner, cider, is extremely well represented, with choices from Normandy and Brittany, all served in delicate ceramic bowls.
Babies and children welcome; high chairs. Bookings not accepted for under 6 people. Disabled: ramp. No smoking. Restaurant available for hire. Tables outdoors (2, terrace). Takeaway service. **Map 3 G5**.

Garangers

114-115 Crawford Street, W1H 2JQ (7935 8447/www.garangers.com). Baker Street tube. **Lunch served** noon-2.15pm Mon-Fri. **Dinner served** 7-10.15pm Mon-Sat. **Main courses** £9.80-£16.90. **Set lunch** £12.90 2 courses. **Credit** AmEx, MC, V.
Franck Garanger's little shopfront restaurant in the Marylebone hinterland is likeable and just a little strange. Both the food, and in particular the enthusiastic service, are draws. But the prices, half-baked decor and location (a little too far off the beaten track) let the side down. The menu is divided up into sections entitled 'novice', 'intermediary' 'professional' and 'expert', but don't let this put you off: the Mediterranean-influenced cooking is innovative and mostly pretty good. Dishes come artfully arranged on dramatic crockery. A 'novice' Mediterranean tart was served warm, filled with tomato, peppers, courgette and aubergine, and spiced up with some balsamic onion compote. Spicy Andalusian gazpacho came in a glass bowl, with a dash of aged Jerez vinegar and tapenade croûtons on the side. Less of a hit,

Take Time Out with perrier at home

Caribbean Perrier

- 20 cl of Perrier
- 10 cl of freshly squeezed orange juice
- a splash of passion fruit juice

Take a tall glass. Mix chilled Perrier and the freshly squeezed orange juice. Then add the splash of passion fruit juice.

Scandinavian Perrier

- 15 cl of Perrier
- 2 teaspoonfuls of brown sugar
- 6-8 fresh basil leaves
- 4 cl of vodka
- 1/2 freshly squeezed lemon

Crush the sugar and basil in a tall glass. Add the freshly squeezed lemon juice. Then pour in the vodka and top up with Perrier. Stir well.

Mauritian Perrier

- 10 cl of Perrier
- 4 wedges of fresh cut lime
- 2 teaspoonfuls of brown sugar
- 4 cl of white rum

Crush lime wedges and sugar in the bottom of a glass. Pour in rum, then top up with Perrier.

SOURCE
perrier
BOTTLED AT SOURCE
VERGÈZE, FRANCE

however, were some Moroccan-spiced lamb patties, flavoured with apricots and cumin and served with creamy polenta – disappointingly sweet and dry. Though it's probably not quite the thing to mention them here, the toilets 'with unusual piped sounds' are an experience in themselves.

Babies and children admitted. No-smoking tables. Restaurant available for hire. Separate bar for parties, capacity 100. **Map 2 F5.**

Mayfair W1

Deca

23 Conduit Street, W1S 2XS (7493 7070/ www.decarestaurant.com). Oxford Circus tube. **Lunch served** noon-3pm, **dinner served** 5.30-11pm Mon-Fri. **Main courses** £12.50-£25. **Set meal** (lunch, 5.30-7pm) £12.50 3 courses. **Service** 12.5%. **Credit** AmEx, DC, MC, V.

A neat, expensive-looking conversion of a smart townhouse, Deca has an air of all-round poshness. This strikes you at first as unappetising, an impression cemented by the staid, moneyed clientele and the lavish use of wealth-indicators like foie gras on the menu (we counted ourselves lucky it wasn't served for pudding). That aside, the food is fairly conservative modern French with few surprises. And it's good, with nary a bum note. Smoked salmon was delicately lemon-fragrant (though we thought the word 'wild' might have been added to the menu description considering the £12.50 cost); truffle risotto was quite exquisite; and calf's liver with bacon and onions arrived perfectly turned out. But for all that, we didn't feel that the prices were justified: good food alone does not a top-class restaurant make. Service and surroundings were pleasant enough, but the bottom line is that Deca is a little dull, and when your bill easily crests £100 for two you want either the food or the atmosphere to sparkle.

Babies and children admitted. Booking essential. Disabled: toilet. Separate room for parties, seats 16. **Map 9 H/J6.**

★ Embassy

29 Old Burlington Street, W1S 3AN (7851 0956/www.embassylondon.com). Green Park or Piccadilly Circus tube. **Lunch served** noon-3pm Tue-Fri. **Dinner served** 6-11.30pm Tue-Sat. **Main courses** £14.50-£25. **Set meal** (lunch, 6-8pm) £16.95 2 courses, £19.95 3 courses. **Service** 12.5%; 15% for parties of 10 or more. **Credit** AmEx, MC, V.

When we visited Embassy, chef Gary Hollihead was preparing to lose his famous flowing locks for charity in aid of Great Ormond Street Hospital. We hope this won't have a Samson-like effect and diminish his considerable prowess in the kitchen. Hollihead produces exquisite dishes in jewelled colours, with flavours perfectly balanced and ingredients just so. The only disappointment comes in the gold leaf and white leather corporate surroundings – which possibly go down well with the Mayfair business clientele who are typical. Prices are steep too. But compensation comes in the form of an extremely good-value set lunch, which enables you to sample slivers of seared tuna with peppery wasabi dressing and sweet peppers. Follow this with pan-fried salmon with dill hollandaise and creamy champ mash, and finish with a petite moulded tiramisu crisscrossed with espresso sauce. At £19.95 for three courses this is a bargain indeed. Going à la carte yielded some pure steamed scallops served in a clear broth, offset by rich, flavour-packed beef rossini with foie gras, spinach and truffle oil. The excellent wine list offers a small yet well-balanced selection by the glass but few bargains.

Babies and children admitted. Booking advisable. Dress: smart casual. Restaurant available for hire. Tables outdoors (6, terrace). **Map 9 J7.**

Mirabelle

56 Curzon Street, W1Y 8DN (7499 4636). Green Park tube. **Lunch served** noon-2.30pm Mon-Sat; noon-3pm Sun. **Dinner served** 6-11pm daily. **Main courses** £14.50-£25. **Set lunch** (Mon-Sat) £16.50 2 courses, £19.50 3 courses; (Sun) £19.50 3 courses. **Service** 12.5%. **Credit** AmEx, MC, V.

With its Mayfair address, Marco Pierre White at the helm and what has to be one of the largest mirrorballs in London, Mirabelle is every inch the glamorous restaurant. The inevitable business lunches and dinners can be a turn-off, but, in general, this isn't a starchy place, and the atmosphere is usually buoyant. The culinary events – and each dish here really is an event, courtesy of head chef Phil Cooper – commenced with lightly seared melt-in-the-mouth scallops atop a tarte tatin of sweet, caramelised endive, and an extraordinary ham omelette, with a gorgeous creamy texture. Mains continued in this perfect vein. A venison dish was richly flavoursome, set off by the currants on top, but it was the lobster that stole the show: beautifully seasoned, generously portioned and served with a fantastic creamy potato purée. A slightly stale slice of raisin bread served with our cheeseboard was, on complaint, whipped away and promptly replaced, accompanied by two glasses of vintage port on the house. We have come to expect impeccably suave but rarely stuffy service here, alongside classic French cuisine of the highest order. In short, Mirabelle is reliable splurging territory.

Babies and children welcome; high chairs. Booking advisable. Dress: smart casual. Entertainment: pianist dinner Fri, Sat, lunch Sun. Restaurant available for hire. Separate rooms for parties, seating 33 and 48. **Map 9 H7.**

Patterson's NEW

4 Mill Street, W1S 2AX (7499 1308/ www.pattersonsrestaurant.com). Bond Street or Oxford Circus tube. **Lunch served** noon-3pm Mon-Fri. **Dinner served** 6-11 Mon-Sat. **Main courses** £17-£20. **Set lunch** £15 2 courses, £20 3 courses. **Service** 12.5%. **Credit** AmEx, MC, V.

A newcomer to the Mayfair restaurant scene this year, Patterson's seems to have settled comfortably into its elegant stride and proves a welcome foil to some of its more glitzy neighbours. The restaurant is family-run and it's the warmth and skill of the staff, good atmosphere and simple, contemporary surroundings that win you over as much as the careful classical French cooking from chef Raymond Patterson. The place is buzzier at lunchtimes, the attraction being a short, daily changing menu that might offer crêpes with crab and a pea velouté, followed by courgette flowers filled with ratatouille and served with asparagus purée, then a perfect pear tatin to finish – all at a very reasonable price. In the evening, diners get down to the serious business of sampling an assiette of five foie gras preparations, or perhaps some sweetly roasted scallops offset by a warm mushroom salad. A main course of veal came simply braised and served with pavé potatoes and buttery, baby spring vegetables. Desserts depart slightly from the classical French form; rhubarb with sablé and rhubarb ripple sorbet, and lemon-glazed blueberry cheesecake perhaps recall Patterson's days as chef at the Garrick Club.

Babies and children welcome; high chairs. Booking advisable. No-smoking tables. Separate room for parties, seats 30. Vegetarian menu. **Map 9 H/J6.**

La Rascasse at Café Grand Prix

50A Berkeley Street, W1J 8HA (7629 0808/ www.cafegrandprix.com). Green Park tube. *Pit brasserie* **Meals served** 10am-11pm Mon-Fri. **Main courses** £6-£10. *La Rascasse restaurant* **Lunch served** noon-3pm Mon-Fri. **Dinner served** 6-11pm Mon-Sat. **Main courses** £13.50-£21.50. **Service** 12.5%. *Both* **Credit** AmEx, MC, V.

You have to feel sorry for anyone doing the cooking at La Rascasse. Even Lancastrian prodigy Chris Haworth's inventive and ambitious menu can't hope to compete with the absurdity of the surroundings. And we don't just mean the Formula One theme or the garish wall paintings of Cliff Richard and Elton John, for sale at £6,000 each. Between the colossal marbled columns, purple backlighting and full-length drapery, London's largest restaurant resembles a vast hangar waiting

for an episode of *Footballers' Wives* to walk through it. Perhaps surprisingly, some of the food here isn't half bad. A starter of asparagus with vodka beetroot, cured salmon and crème fraîche was brilliantly executed and stylishly presented. A main course of red snapper with lemongrass and chilli sauce was rich and fragrant, if a little lifeless, while lamb cutlets with a provençal tian and smoked aubergine was a resounding success. Desserts, however, were a disappointment. Apple tart with cinnamon ice-cream just came and went, and bitter chocolate tart with pistachio ice-cream tasted strange. The last straw was when the dessert menu arrived with the words 'les fruits de mer' written inexplicably on the cover. Gentlemen, start your engines.

Babies and children welcome; high chairs. Booking advisable (no booking for brasserie). Disabled: lift; ramp; toilet. Restaurant available for hire. Separate room for parties, seats 30. **Map 9 H7.**

Piccadilly W1

Criterion

224 Piccadilly, W1J 9HP (7930 0488). Piccadilly Circus tube. **Lunch served** noon-2.30pm, **dinner served** 5.30-11pm Mon-Sat. **Main courses** £10.50-£22.50. **Set meal** (noon-2.30pm, 5.30-7pm) £14.95 2 courses, £17.95 3 courses. **Service** 12.5%. **Credit** AmEx, DC, JCB, MC, V.

The huge gilded neo-Byzantine hall, bang on Piccadilly Circus, that Criterion fortuitously occupies is quite arresting for first-time visitors, with a gold-leaf ceiling mosaic and lavish features. The menu is something of an entente cordiale between French classics – onion soup, snails, and no less than nine types of steak – and Brit entries, such as cumberland sausage and mash, roast chicken, and fried haddock and chips. All our chosen dishes were well executed (as well they should be at these prices), but a starter of quails' eggs maintenon with hollandaise sauce, with its warm, rich texture, was a particular high point. Slow-roast duck with apple sauce hit the spot, while rib-eye au poivre was, as our waiter warned, intensely pepperly but incredibly tender. From a tempting dessert menu, a rich panna cotta with champagne-poached strawberries was a fine conclusion to the evening. Still, Criterion could do more to match its grand setting: the service was a little wooden and the toilets weren't up to scratch for a pricey restaurant. The clientele on this occasion was a lively mix of pre-theatre diners, tourists, businessmen and after-work groups, with the dress code spanning T-shirts and jeans to smart dinner garb.

Babies and children welcome; high chairs. Booking advisable. Dress: smart casual. Restaurant available for hire. **Map 17 K7.**

St James's SW1

Brasserie Roux

8 Pall Mall, SW1Y 5NG (7968 2900). Piccadilly Circus tube. **Lunch served** noon-3pm Mon-Fri; 12.30-3pm Sat, Sun. **Dinner served** 5.30-11.30pm Mon-Sat; 5.30-10.30pm Sun. **Main courses** £6.50-£21.50. **Service** 12.5%. **Credit** AmEx, DC, JCB, MC, V.

Occupying a handsome, lofty-ceilinged corner space within the Sofitel hotel, Brasserie Roux is a cool, airy, relaxing spot in which to enjoy some classic Gallic bistro dishes – albeit at West End rather than Rive Gauche prices. The decor features pale yellow tones and possibly the world's largest lampshades, while the menu revolves around the sort of hearty cuisine that provides a glow in cool weather, but which seemed overly heavy for the baking summer's day of our most recent visit. Nevertheless, we couldn't resist the retro challenge of a monster vol-au-vent stuffed with chicken, sweetbreads and mushrooms, followed by the onglet cut of beef (rarely found on this side of the Channel) with a piquant béarnaise and crisp fries. Sea bass with sautéed potatoes and red wine jus was also perfectly acceptable, just not terribly thrilling – as could also be said of the eggy pecan

pie that followed. There's nothing actively wrong with Brasserie Roux, it's just that, for this sort of outlay, you'd hope for something more memorable. *Babies and children welcome; children's menu; high chairs. Booking essential. Disabled: toilet (in adjoining Sofitel St James hotel). Dress: smart casual. No-smoking tables.* **Map 17 K7**.

Soho W1

★ L'Escargot Marco Pierre White

48 Greek Street, W1D 4EF (7437 2679). Leicester Square or Tottenham Court Road tube. Ground-floor restaurant **Lunch served** noon-2.15pm Mon-Fri. **Dinner served** 6-11.30pm Mon-Fri; 5.30-11.30pm Sat. **Main courses** £12.95-£14.95. **Set meal** (lunch, 6-7pm Mon-Fri) £14.95 2 courses, £17.95 3 courses. **Service** 12.5%.
Picasso Room **Lunch served** 12.15-2pm Tue-Fri. **Dinner served** 7-11pm Tue-Sat. **Closed** Aug. **Set lunch** £19.95 2 courses, £25.50 3 courses. **Set meal** £42 3 courses. **Service** 15%.
Both **Credit** AmEx, DC, JCB, MC, V.
A faintly snooty woman on the reception desk, pristine-suited maîtres d', swarms of classically garbed waiters, a clientele that's largely suits and the elderly: this Soho institution (moniker given visual expression in mosaic snails here and there) is formal, expensive and, praise be, worth very nearly every penny. (Formal? Not, at least, in the ground-floor gents, decorated with a large framed portrait of Cindy Crawford, naked but for a few artfully arranged pearls.) We dined in the street-level art deco über-brasserie, all high ceiling, bevelled mirrors, crisp menu folders and still crisper tablecloths and napkins, and looser-collared than the stately first-floor Picasso Room (which closes for August). A tarte tatin of caramelised onion topped with goat's cheese was faultless; nine snails, each set in a small tee of mousseline, were succulent and flavourful; Blenheim Estate lamb slices on herb risotto were tender, although calf's liver was a tad overcooked. A very decent bottle of 2002 Brouilly cost £25.50, chosen from a cellar that boasts 500 wines. Minor niggles included the over-attentive topping up of wine glasses, the slightly livid lighting and unappealing accoustics in the back room.
Babies and children admitted to ground-floor restaurant. Booking essential weekends. Dress: smart casual. Separate rooms for parties, seating 24 and 60. **Map 17 K6**.

La Trouvaille

12A Newburgh Street, W1F 7RR (7287 8488/ www.latrouvaille.co.uk). Oxford Circus tube. **Lunch served** noon-3pm Mon-Sat; noon-3.30pm Sun. **Dinner served** 6-11pm Mon-Sat. **Set lunch** £16.95 2 courses, £19.75 3 courses. **Set dinner** £24.50 2 courses, £29.50 3 courses. **Service** 12.5%. **Credit** AmEx, DC, JCB, MC, V.
If you're after a quirkily romantic dinner, La Trouvaille will do the trick. Its setting on one of Soho's more characterful backstreets is appealing (and tranquil – even when the nearby pub is overspilling with Friday-night drinkers), as is the decor: dark yellow walls, flamboyant mirrors, idiosyncratic cutlery, soft-focus lighting. And the young French waiters (all male) are the personification of Gallic charm. And then there's the food: fanciful French concoctions that certainly win points for inventiveness and flair. Sometimes the flavours are just too subtle: a starter of meltingly soft marinated sardines with a pile of crunchy white radish curls came with a very pleasant jus, but the promised liquorice and oyster flavours were undetectable. And sometimes they're too strong: tender, pan-fried octopus with fennel and marjoram – a kind of warmish salad with a shot glass of tomatoey harrissa on the side – was overpowered by the marjoram. The best dish was perfectly cooked Herdwick mutton fillet with grilled courgettes, garlic, and lavender sauce – complete with a flagpole sprig of lavender. For dessert, marinated pears came with black truffle honey and intriguing-sounding but plain-tasting tobacco ice-cream. Ingredients are impeccable, the

Plateau. See p86.

wine list a treat; even if the cooking doesn't always scale the heights you might hope, you're in for a memorable meal. A find indeed.
Babies and children welcome. Booking advisable. Separate room for parties, seats 20. Tables outdoors (3, pavement). **Map 17 J6**.
For branch (Brasserie La Trouvaille) see index.

Strand WC2

The Admiralty
Somerset House, Strand, WC2R 1LA (7845 4646/ www.somerset-house.org.uk). Temple tube. **Lunch served** noon-2.30pm daily. **Dinner served** 6-10.30pm Mon-Sat. **Main courses** £16.50-£22.50. **Service** 12.5%. **Credit** AmEx, DC, JCB, MC, V.
The Admiralty has a problem with its lovely location. Hidden within the old Navy Office in the wing of Somerset House overlooking the Thames, the restaurant gets nil passing trade and, although it maintains a strong reputation for quality cuisine (despite changing hands and losing a head chef this year), its gracious high-ceilinged dining rooms are often sparsely populated. Prices are high (£18-£19 for mains), but not outrageous for French regional food that's rarely less than excellent. We relished a deeply satisfying but not overly rich crispy confit leg of lamb with nuggets of foie gras and 'champ' potato, and an unusual hot-smoked salmon on a celeriac and apple remoulade (the fish was cooked on the outside, raw within). Mains were also class acts: breast of corn-fed chicken with cabbage, bacon, onions and a buttery almond morel cream was superior comfort food; pan-fried fillet of brill with boulangère potato and smoked bacon jus starred a sea-sweet piece of fish. Desserts were good, if not exceptional; the elements in the iced prune parfait with hazelnut and sultana biscotti and dark chocolate mousse were fine, but didn't do anything for each other. Minus marks, though, for bringing the bill before requested, and leaving the credit card slip open.
Babies and children welcome; high chairs. Booking advisable. Disabled: toilet. Dress: smart casual. No-smoking tables. Restaurant available for hire. Separate room for parties, seats 30. **Map 10 M7**.

West

Chiswick W4

La Trompette
5-7 Devonshire Road, W4 2EU (8747 1836). Turnham Green tube. **Lunch served** noon-2.30pm Mon-Sat; 12.30-3pm Sun. **Dinner served** 6.30-10.45pm Mon-Sat; 7-10.30pm Sun. **Set lunch** £21.50 3 courses; (Sun) £25 3 courses. **Set dinner** £32.50 3 courses, £42.50 4 courses. **Service** 12.5%. **Credit** AmEx, JCB, MC, V.
The room looked vibrant on our visit – tan leather ceiling, mushroom-coloured, bamboo-textured walls – and was filled with a wide range of enthusiastic diners, from first dates to old friends to families with young children. It's quite an achievement for a local to be so attractive to so many, and a mark of the expertise of La Trompette's owners, who also run Chez Bruce (*see p85*) and the Glasshouse. The meal started underwhelmingly, with dried-out bread (though it varied in style). Starters were better and substantial – monkfish and plaice came wrapped in a sheet of pasta with crab broth; translucent layers of sliced smoked pork loin arrived with tiny carrots and crisp toasted orange morsels of mimolette cheese. There was a slight dip in the wow factor for the main courses: chicken, slowly cooked in vin jaune with mushrooms and truffles, was tender but not as fragrant as the ingredients suggested; a fillet of turbot with pasta-wrapped crab was good yet not startling. Desserts more than compensated. Strawberry salad arrived, theatrically, in a tall Martini glass, topped with frothy pink mousse (all it lacked was a sparkler), while the Valrhona chocolate puddings included an exquisite mini-soufflé.
Babies and children welcome; high chairs. Booking advisable. Disabled: toilet. Tables outdoors (7, terrace).

Le Vacherin NEW
76-77 South Parade, W4 5LF (8742 2121/ www.levacherin.co.uk). Chiswick Park tube/rail. **Lunch served** noon-3pm Tue-Sat; noon-5pm Sun. **Dinner served** 6-10.30pm Mon-Thur, Sun; 6-11pm Fri, Sat. **Main courses** £9.50-£14. **Set lunch** £11.95 2 courses, £14.95 3 courses. **Service** 12.5%. **Credit** JCB, MC, V.
Gallic-style screens in the nondescript window offer one of the few clues that this place, plonked in a parade of shops, is in fact a French restaurant. Inside, Parisian prints, heavy droplet chandeliers and paper tablecloths all aspire to create a bistro vibe, but it's too stiff to be convincing. Not that the well-heeled Chiswick locals seem to mind. Choosing from owner-chef Malcolm John's daily specials, we were impressed with our first course: a winning combination of poached pears in red wine, contrasting with tangy crumbled roquefort, astringent rocket leaves and crisp rashers of warm streaky bacon. Griddle-fried scallops served with black pudding and saucy morel mushrooms didn't make the grade, however. A sloppy appearance on the plate was further let down by bitter-tasting wine in the sauce and less-than-juicy scallops. The seductively dark, full-bodied black pudding, was spot on, though. For dessert, delicious îles flottantes came drizzled with buttery caramel sauce and was our star dish. What seals the French flavour isn't so much the cooking, although that's good in parts, but the smooth professionalism of the all-French service team.
Babies and children welcome; high chairs. Booking advisable. No smoking. Separate room for parties, seats 25.

Hammersmith W6

★ Chez Kristof NEW
111 Hammersmith Grove, W6 0NQ (8741 1177). Goldhawk Road tube/Hammersmith tube/rail. **Deli Open** 8am-8pm daily.
Restaurant **Lunch served** noon-3pm, **dinner served** 6-11.15pm Mon-Fri. **Meals served** noon-11.15pm Sat, Sun. **Main courses** £9-£18. **Service** 12.5%. **Credit** AmEx, JCB, MC, V.
This new venture (opened summer 2004) occupies the same spot as ill-fated French restaurant Maquis. But if anyone can make an unlucky site good, owner Jan Woroniecki – proprietor of East European restaurants Wódka (*see p67*) and the wonderful Baltic (*see p68*) – can. The space is elegant and modern, with huge French windows opening on to the street, good lighting, a Baltic-like chandelier and low-key music. More crucially, the cooking is the real deal, more French than 'La Marseillaise'. For starters: 'jellied pig's head and veal trotters', served with the traditional accompaniment of sauce gribiche. Dense and intensely flavoured, it was as good as you'll find anywhere in France. Next, grand aioli, a provençal dish of a generous fillet of poached cod served over boiled potato, fennel bulb and boiled egg, topped with a big dollop of aioli: simple perfection. We visited in the first week; when the menu and service were still a bit shaky – roast pigeon with puy lentils contained so much bacon that it dominated the flavour of the dish – but practice should make perfect. Woroniecki is a drinks connoisseur, and this is reflected in a hugely impressive cocktail list, a collection of first-rate spirits, and a mostly French wine list that includes a few reds for trying chilled.
Babies and children welcome; children's menu; high chairs; films. Booking advisable. Disabled: toilet. Dress: smart casual. No-smoking tables. Separate room for parties, seats 50. Tables outdoors (24, terrace). Takeaway service. **Map 20 B3**.

Holland Park W8

★ The Belvedere
Off Abbotsbury Road, in Holland Park, W8 6LU (7602 1238). Holland Park tube. **Lunch served** noon-2.30pm Mon-Sat; noon-3pm Sun. **Dinner served** 6-11pm Mon-Sat. **Main courses** £12.75-£18. **Set lunch** £14.95 2 courses, £17.95 3 courses; (Sun) £19.50 3 courses. **Service** 12.5%. **Credit** AmEx, MC, V.

There's a touch of magic about this Marco Pierre White restaurant on the edge of Holland Park, which seems to spirit you away from London to somewhere timeless and relaxed. The setting helps: the silence of the street, intimate tables among the aspidistras, the mirrored walls reflecting a high ceiling hung with frosted glass lamps and silvered balls. Service was efficient and friendly, and food was outstanding. Celery velouté, a creamy soup, came laced with chervil and garlic and had a soft boiled egg under the surface, the yolk ready to burst. Warmed oysters in their shells with chanterelles, brown butter and potato purée were excellent and visually stunning. Aberdeen Angus daube in redcurrant sauce was tender yet robustly flavoured, with green olives and red peppers. Braised pig's trotter (an MPW signature) was rich without being cloying, its soft sticky skin stuffed with veal shin in mousse-like puréed pork. Vanilla ice-cream with armagnac and fat prunes had plenty of each, while superbly frothy pistachio soufflé had a ball of chocolate ice-cream dropped on top. Given the quality, a meal is great value – just watch the wine list, which offers plenty of choice but few bargains.
Babies and children welcome; high chairs. Booking essential. Restaurant available for hire. Separate room for parties, seats 20. Tables outdoors (5, terrace).

South West

Battersea SW8, SW11

Le Bouchon Bordelais NEW
5-9 Battersea Rise, SW11 1HG (7738 0307/ www.lebouchon.co.uk). Clapham Junction rail/ 35, 37 bus. **Bar Open** 10am-11pm Mon-Sat; 10am-10.30pm Sun. *Restaurant* **Meals served** noon-11pm Mon-Sat; noon-10.30pm Sun. **Main courses** £9.50-£35. **Service** 12.5%. *Both* **Credit** AmEx, MC, V.
Le Bouchon isn't new, but the injection of culinary expertise by Michel Roux, chef-patron at Le Gavroche (*see p113*), is. The mustard wall panels framed by glossy wood, francophilery in neat frames and tidy tricolore bunting are all too soigné to be powerfully reminiscent of meals in Gaul. The food, of course, has come a long way – though the performance we witnessed was shaky. One starter, pan-fried foie gras on braised savoy cabbage drizzled with port sauce, was intensity and delight; the other, melon gazpacho containing a quenelle of basil and mint and a scrunch of parma ham was a less persuasive statement, though refreshing. Filet de beouf turned out to be a small mountain of beef, cooked to within a whisker of the Platonic ideal of steak, partnered by light, flaxen frites – and, sadly, a limp embarrassment of a side salad and a banal pepper sauce. The pavé de cabillaud (cod) atop squid ink risotto was more consistent, and our £28 bottle of 2001 Gigondas was excellent. The real rub here, though, is the service. The all-French waiters were faultlessly genial; yet one table by the door was completely forgotten, and although we turned up early in the evening when things were still quiet, we waited an age between starter and mains.
Babies and children welcome; children's menu; crèche; high chairs. No-smoking tables. Separate room for parties, seats 28. Tables outdoors (8, terrace). **Map 21 C5**.

★ The Food Room NEW
123 Queenstown Road, SW8 3RH (7622 0555). Battersea Park or Queenstown Road rail/137, 156 bus. **Lunch served** noon-2.30pm Sun. **Dinner served** 7-10.30pm Mon-Thur; 7-11pm Fri, Sat. **Main courses** £10.50-£15.50. **Set lunch** £13.50 2 courses, £16.50 3 courses. **Service** 12.5%. **Credit** MC, V.
Opened in summer 2004, the Food Room is the new sibling of Surbiton's popular the French Table (*see p89*). Its very name tells you it doesn't belong to the *ancien régime*. The jolly-hockey-sticks waitresses are fabulously welcoming, yet professionally restrained; they can explain what a 'piperade' is without chuckling. The dining room

Best for Michelin stars

Every January, the *Michelin Guide* (aka Le Guide Rouge) makes its pick of London's haute-cuisine (predominantly French-based) restaurants. Stars are valid for one year only. Are they places for stuffing yourself or for stuffed shirts? Decide at the following, all awarded stars in 2004.

Three stars

Hotels & Haute Cuisine
Gordon Ramsay.

Two stars

Hotels & Haute Cuisine
The Capital; Le Gavroche; Pied à Terre; The Square.

One star

British
Lindsay House; Savoy Grill.
Chinese
Hakkasan.
French
Chez Bruce; Club Gascon; L'Escargot Marco Pierre White; Mirabelle; 1 Lombard Street; Roussillon.
Hotels & Haute Cuisine
Angela Hartnett at the Connaught; Aubergine; Foliage; Gordon Ramsay at Claridge's; The Greenhouse; L'Oranger; Pétrus; Putney Bridge; Tom Aikens.
Indian
Tamarind; Zaika.
Italian
Locanda Locatelli; The River Café; Zafferano.
Japanese
Nobu.
Modern European
McClements; Orrery.
Thai
Nahm.

is unfussy, trim and smart. There's no muzak, no gimmicks; the only showing-off is done on the plate. A 'garlic cappuccino' wasn't overpoweringly flavoured, merely there to give a piquancy (and some froth) to a starter of juicy pan-fried frogs' legs. Another starter of rabbit confit, served with cep oil, wild mushrooms and parmesan shavings was also subtly aromatic; every forkful deserved to be lingered over. The dishes in this haute-inspired style of modern French food comprise many small elements, artfully arranged – to give diversity of colour, form and texture. Every flavour and aroma in the main courses worked together. Best end of lamb was beautifully pink and tender, making a good foil to the offal intensity of pan-fried sweetbreads; sage leaves, a lamb reduction and aubergine relish rounded out the dish. Any Italian would be proud of the risotto, served with lightly smoked grey mullet, baby artichokes and asparagus. Ingredient quality and freshness shone, from the own-made breads to a pudding of shortbread (light, buttery) served with fresh strawberries, mousseline and strawberry ice-cream. The Food Room is everything that's great about French food, without the fuss.
Babies and children admitted. Booking advisable. Dress: smart casual. No-smoking tables.

Le Petit Max NEW

2004 RUNNER-UP BEST NEW RESTAURANT
14 Chatfield Road, SW11 3SE (7223 0999). Clapham Junction rail. **Lunch served** noon-2pm daily. **Dinner served** 7-10pm Mon-Sat. **Main courses** £9.50-£20. **Set lunch** £14.50 2 courses. **Set meal** £18.50 3 courses. **Service** 12.5%. **Credit** DC, MC, V.

Set in a fairly unappealing riverside development (but without compensatory views), Le Petit Max has to work hard to overcome the location. Inside, the warm welcome, cosy red furnishings and low-key comfortableness of the place take over. The menu is a heart-warming read: bayonne ham with cornichons, Norfolk asparagus with hollandaise, rillettes of pork and duck with remoulade and Poilâne bread, and – star starter – Cantabrian anchovies with butter, shallots and more of the very edible Poilâne. Mains stick to the same reassuring formula. There's plenty of fish, much of it Cornish (dover sole meunière with pommes vapeur, fritto misto, grilled tronçon of Cornish turbot with deep-fried courgettes), but witch sole with frites was rather tired (although the frites were magnificent). It was the meat dishes that shone; if confit belly of pork and smoked morteau sausage with mustard sauce is on the menu, order it. Finish with a classic pudding such as pot au chocolat with vanilla ice-cream, or a splendid baba savarin au rhum with red fruits and Chantilly. Service is headed by chef-patron Max Renzland; he has to compensate for some rather ditzy waitresses. An honest-to-goodness French bistro in SW11.
Babies and children welcome; high chairs. Booking advisable (weekends). Disabled: toilet. Table outdoors (1, pavement). **Map 21 A3**.

Chelsea SW3

Le Colombier

145 Dovehouse Street, SW3 6LB (7351 1155). South Kensington tube/14 bus. **Lunch served** noon-3pm Mon-Sat; noon-3.30pm Sun. **Dinner served** 6.30-10.30pm Mon-Sat; 6.30-10pm Sun. **Main courses** £12-£19. **Set meal** £14.50 2 courses (lunch Mon-Sat), £16.50 2 courses (6.30-7.30pm Sun). **Service** 12.5%. **Credit** AmEx, JCB, MC, V.

With its corner setting and, in summer, a choice between the cosy interior and the glazed pavement area, Le Colombier meets the needs of its specific market well. Old moneyed couples love the place, with its white linen tablecloths and crystal decanters so cumbersome you need staff to help pour your wine. The food, like the customers, tends towards the rich and occasionally eccentric: a crisp chicory and roquefort salad with walnuts had a dressing of oil with cream, not vinegar; a garlicky snail and mushroom fricassée on toasted brioche had more than enough thick cream. That said, the ingredients used throughout were faultless, and their flavours, where appropriate, intense. Toulouse sausage was dense and porky, with savoury puy lentils; the fillet steak (cooked slightly less than requested) was extremely tender and its béarnaise sauce nicely sharp but eggy. The (creamy) parfait with prunes and armagnac needed more of both latter ingredients, though a crème brûlée was so wide and shallow it was virtually all delicious caramel. Le Colombier's French waiting staff are courteous and efficient. In all, this is a convivial, safe and comforting place, an indulgent refuge for Chelsea's wealthier diners.
Babies and children welcome; high chair. Booking advisable; essential dinner, lunch Sun. Dress: smart casual. Separate room for parties, seats 30. Tables outdoors (13, terrace). **Map 14 D11**.

Putney SW15

L'Auberge

22 Upper Richmond Road, SW15 2RX (8874 3593/www.ardillys.com). East Putney tube. **Dinner served** 7-10pm Tue-Sat. **Main courses** £11.95-£14.50. **Set dinner** £16 3 courses. **Service** 12.5%. **Credit** MC, V.

Cutting to the chase, the puddings at L'Auberge are excellent; even the most savoury-toothed might be tempted to start, continue and end the meal with them. We began more conservatively, with a highly successful pheasant and ground hazelnut terrine, which included layers of apricot, damson and fig and came with redcurrant jelly. Grilled goat's cheese was tangy and fresh – at its peak – and toasted hazelnuts went well alongside. By now we

had begun to notice how good the service was; our waitress knew the wine list inside out (all of it looked good value). Explaining that our choice of wine had run out, she suggested a better alternative. The room has been decorated and seems more French this year, shaking off the previous trattoria feel. A main course of wild boar daube was properly gamey, while a daube of beef (from the £16 set menu) was tasty but not as tender as it could have been. To the puddings, though… crème brûlée with pistachio and honey was, without question, the best we had tasted; tarte tatin was perfection too, with soft sweet pastry and thick, melting apple. It's a shame we were the only customers on the Tuesday evening we visited.
Babies and children welcome. Booking advisable for large parties. Restaurant available for hire.

South

Clapham SW4

Gastro

67 Venn Street, SW4 0BD (7627 0222). Clapham Common tube/Clapham High Street rail. **Breakfast served** 8am-3pm, **meals served** noon-midnight daily. **Main courses** £10.45-£16.50. **Service** 12.5%. **No credit cards.**

An established, perennially popular and defiantly French venue, Gastro is sited opposite Clapham's Picture House. French memorabilia abounds; iced oysters tempt from the bar; and staff address you in their home language. There's a proper dining room around from the bar, but otherwise you take your chances from a fairly cramped selection of tables for seating. During the day, Claphamites, tempted away from the flakier establishments close by, flock here for café au lait, croissants (which you can enjoy on benches outside on sunnier days) or even a French fry-up (don't even think about asking for ketchup). You'll find all the classics on the menu – from moules marinière to steak frites – and some daily specials. A shared plate of charcuterie is perfect to get the juices flowing, particularly when accompanied by one of the many fine wines; try the fantastically robust Côtes du Rhône. Fish dishes are nearly always done well (the monkfish didn't disappoint on our most recent visit), and lamb with a ginger crust and root vegetables drew sighs of delight. Try the delicious fromage blanc to round off a meal. Long live the entente cordiale.
Babies and children welcome. Booking advisable. Disabled: toilet. No-smoking tables. Restaurant available for hire. Separate room for parties, seats 22. Tables outdoors (4, pavement). **Map 22 A2**.

Wandsworth SW17

★ Chez Bruce

2 Bellevue Road, SW17 7EG (8672 0114/ www.chezbruce.co.uk). Wandsworth Common rail. **Lunch served** noon-2pm Mon-Fri; 12.30-2.30pm Sat; noon-3pm Sun. **Dinner served** 6.30-10.30pm Mon-Sat, 7-10pm Sun. **Set lunch** £23.50 3 courses (Mon-Fri), £25 3 courses (Sat), £29.50 3 courses (Sun). **Set dinner** £32.50 3 courses. **Service** 12.5%. **Credit** AmEx, DC, JCB, MC, V.

Bruce Poole's scintillating restaurant is approaching its tenth anniversary, but remains Wandsworth's top venue. It's not stuffy, partly because diners (lunching ladies, City boys, Piers Morgan in his pomp) give the impression they've just dropped into their local caff – and yet are excited to be here. The space is compact (a dozen tables downstairs, a few more up some rickety stairs in the less sought-after first floor), but breezy bow windows looking on to the Common and a preponderance of white (walls, linen, aproned staff) keep it feeling fresh. Bruce changes his menu regularly, but dishes are robust and with strong French or Mediterranean influences. Starters could be vitello tonnato (exquisitely thin slices of veal, salad leaves, a pert tuna and anchovy dressing), foie gras and chicken liver parfait on toasted brioche, or a velvety, chilled pea soup with goat's cheese. Mains are heartier. Of eight choices on our visit, there was a confit and fillet of pork with chorizo and bean salad; fillet of beef with persillade of shin and an intense bourguignon sauce; a hunk of neatly roasted cod with olive oil mash. Puddings (including a ludicrously chocolatey pudding with praline sauce) are generally excellent, but we recommend the cheeseboard (£5.50 supplement). The wine list is justly acclaimed. Service is French-flavoured, but nonetheless friendly.

Babies and children admitted (lunch). Booking essential. Dress: smart casual. No smoking. Separate room for parties, seats 16 (lunch Mon-Sat; dinner Mon-Thur, Sun).

Waterloo SE1

County Hall Restaurant

County Hall, SE1 7PB (7902 8000). Embankment or Westminster tube/Charing Cross or Waterloo tube/rail. **Breakfast served** 6.30-11am Mon-Fri; 7-11am Sat, Sun. **Lunch served** 12.30-3pm, **afternoon tea served** 2.30-5.30pm, **dinner served** 5.30-10.30pm daily. **Main courses** £15-£22. **Set meal** £23.50 2 courses, £26.50 3 courses. **Credit** AmEx, DC, MC, V.

It wasn't the restaurant's fault we had to walk three-quarters of the way around the County Hall perimeter before discovering its entrance (through the Marriott Hotel on Westminster Bridge Road). But staff were to blame for our 30-minute wait in the bar before we were seated at our pre-booked table without apology; that three of the items we tried to order weren't on the menu; that the house red came in at a whopping £19; and that we were handed the wrong (even more expensive) bill at the end of the meal. All this was a real shame considering that the food – served in a long, wood-panelled and unexceptional room with views of the river – was largely very good. Starters of creamed butternut squash soup and roulade of Loch Fyne salmon and lobster were unexciting, but the slow-cooked English pork was delicious, and tournedos of beef rossini with truffle sauce was faultless. Which is all well and good, but at this level and at these prices, every part of the dining experience should be blemish-free. As we said last year: County Hall seriously needs to pull its socks up.

Babies and children welcome; children's menu; high chairs. Booking advisable. Disabled: toilet. Entertainment: pianist or guitarist 6.30-10.30pm Thur, Fri. No-smoking tables. Takeaway breakfast. Map 10 M9.

RSJ

33 Coin Street, SE1 9NR (7928 4554/ www.rsj.uk.com). Waterloo tube/rail. **Lunch served** noon-2pm Mon-Fri. **Dinner served** 5.30-11pm Mon-Sat. **Main courses** £11-£17. **Set meal** £15.95 2 courses, £17.95 3 courses. **Service** 12.5%. **Credit** AmEx, DC, MC, V.

Within a utilitarian dining room lurks one of London dining's best-kept secrets, the RSJ wine list: a multi-paged ode to the French grape. It's this prodigious choice that has discerning drinkers flocking to a fine restaurant that's unassuming in appearance, unpretentious of menu and highly unlikely to leave you wanting more. The food is classic French with a British twist, and the two- or three-course set menu is smart value. Smoked haddock risotto with crisp pancetta and a soft poached egg set a standard that warm tart of new-season English asparagus and crème fraîche with a mint and lemon pistou couldn't quite match. To follow, boiled then baked ham with cider and spices, served with buttery swede and Jersey royals, quince jelly and orange sauce, was excellent. And if the char-grilled ribeye (with buttered spinach and swede, potato and pear rösti topped with port salut cheese and béarnaise sauce) was cooked a smidgen too long, it didn't spoil a lovely cut of meat. Too bloated for dessert, we took another look at the exceptional wine list; the restaurant runs a wine club for those wanting to find out more. A gem.

Babies and children admitted. Booking advisable. Separate room for parties, seats 25. Map 11 N8.

Bethnal Green E2

Bistrotheque NEW

23-27 Wadeson Street, E2 9DR (8983 7900/ www.bistrotheque.com). Bethnal Green tube/ Cambridge Heath rail/8 bus. **Bar Open** 5.30-11pm Mon-Sat; 5.30-10.30pm Sun. *Restaurant* **Lunch served** noon-4pm Sun. **Dinner served** 6.30-10.30pm Mon-Sat; 6.30-10pm Sun. **Main courses** £8-£25. **Service** 12.5%. **Credit** AmEx, MC, V.

Once you've found the building, finding the restaurant might also be a challenge; grey walls and a solitary flight of stairs mark the entrance. Follow the distant voices and you're soon greeted by a vista of tables bearing tea-lights. Set over two floors of an old clothing factory, this quietly groovy bistro boasts two dining rooms, a bar (the Napoleon), the Playroom ('Coming soon – tranny lipsynching'), and an 'entertainment space'. Daily specials underpin the main menu, with retro dishes such as coq au vin and steak tartare sitting alongside more modern combinations: scallops, black pudding, mash and chilli jam, say. We opted for onion soup gratinée, a dense, dark, rich broth; and artichoke vinaigrette, which we consumed with enthusiasm, although the dressing lacked pep. Next, cod and chips (two light, fluffy pieces of cod in slightly overcooked batter, with thick-cut chips) slipped down a treat, and was given a refreshing lift by a delicious cold pea and mint purée. Desserts were faultless: an intense, compellingly moreish chocolate pot with hazelnut toffee had serious depth; the light, delicate flavours of the crème brûlée hit all the right spots. We left charmed by the experience.

Babies and children welcome; high chairs. Booking advisable. Disabled: toilet. Entertainment: cabaret 9pm Wed; pianist and singer 8.30pm Fri. Separate room for parties, seats 50.

Brick Lane E1

★ Les Trois Garçons

1 Club Row, E1 6JX (7613 1924/www.lestrois garcons.com). Liverpool Street tube/rail/8, 388 bus. **Dinner served** 7-10pm Mon-Wed; 7-10.30pm Thur-Sat. **Main courses** £12.50-£22. **Set dinner** (Mon-Wed) £20 2 courses, £24 3 courses. **Service** 12.5%. **Credit** AmEx, DC, JCB, MC, V.

The decor here is of the kind that makes you wonder whether someone has spiked your drink: a grinning stuffed crocodile wears a crown, while a similarly defunct tiger sports a tiara; antique handbags hang by threads from the ceiling; jewelled drapes sparkle in the light of Murano chandeliers. It's a little piece of restaurant theatre, and the kitchen tries to ensure that the show goes on. Among the starring roles are starters such as sautéed tiger prawns with crushed herbs, delicate Jersey royals (that queen of potatoes) and garlic- and coconut-spiked tomato sauce. Main-course oven-roasted chicken wrapped in bayonne ham was beautifully tender and came with celeriac mash and a light dijon mustard sauce. An excellent cheeseboard usually waylays us when it comes to the final course, but desserts such as chocolate soufflé with poached strawberry and kiwi provide distracting alternatives. Prices are not low, but if you choose well from the excellent wine list, you can probably get away with a two-figure bill for two. And by the way, there's more 'Changing Rooms' on mescaline' in the restaurant's cocktail bar just around the corner.

Booking advisable. Restaurant available for hire. Separate room for parties, seats 10. Map 6 S4.

Docklands E14

★ Plateau NEW

2004 RUNNER-UP BEST NEW RESTAURANT

Canada Place, Canada Square, Canary Wharf, E14 5ER (7715 7100/www.conran.com). Canary Wharf tube/DLR. **Bar & Grill Meals served** noon-11pm Mon-Sat; noon-4pm Sun. **Main courses** £9.75-£32.

Restaurant **Lunch served** noon-3pm Mon-Fri, Sun. **Dinner served** 6-10.30pm Mon-Sat. **Main courses** £14.50-£27. *Both* **Service** 12.5%. **Credit** AmEx, DC, MC, V.

The brave new world that is Canary Wharf is mirrored in the faintly futuristic interior of Sir Terence Conran's Plateau. The place is filled with light – there's a long glass wall – and there are several distinct spaces: a bar area, the grill room, the restaurant and a wonderfully unexpected covered terrace, decorated with cacti, olive trees and lavender. Design touches include classics from the 1950s (Eero Saarinen tulip chairs; David Mellor cutlery). The fourth-floor location gives views over Canada Square and, less glamorously, Billingsgate Market. As the name suggests, the Grill menu lists grills and rotisserie dishes, plus crustacea; in the restaurant there's more variety (although the likes of rotisserie salmon with blood orange beurre blanc and runner beans are still a possibility). Starters of ribbons of raw tuna with avocado and a soy-based dressing, and butternut squash and mascarpone ravioli were intensely flavoured and set a very high standard. Mains – vegetable nage with barley and pureed broccoli, and spiced monkfish à la plancha with mushroom broth – easily matched them. There are tempting desserts (chocolate fondant with fromage blanc sorbet, say) and a substantial wine list; what's more, staff are friendly and on-the-ball. E14 finally has somewhere really special.

Babies and children welcome; high chairs. Booking advisable. Disabled: toilet. Dress: smart casual. Separate room for parties, seats 24. Tables outdoors (2, pavement). Vegetarian menu.

Shoreditch EC2

South

128 Curtain Road, EC2A 3AQ (7729 4452). Old Street tube/rail. **Lunch served** noon-3pm, **dinner served** 6-10.30pm Mon-Sat. **Main courses** £9.50-£14. **Set lunch** £12.95 3 courses. **Service** 12.5%. **Credit** JCB, MC, V.

Shoreditch now being merely hip, rather than achingly so, a broader mix of restaurants and bars thrives. South is conspicuous by being entirely and enjoyably attitude-free: a pleasant, beige, many-windowed ground-floor space conceived, like the menu and service, to be just, well, nice. We were greeted by an attractive bread board and a confident wine recommendation (a Picpoul de Pinet 2003), then handed a short, appealing menu of uncomplicated classics. A puy lentil and bacon salad was a surprisingly light and crispy confection. The brown shrimps weren't as pleasing – just copious – though we liked the acerbically garlicky aïoli. Goat's cheese soufflé was less puffy than expected, but good (if rich), and the accompanying mesclun was a quality leaf mix. Sea bream arrived expertly turned out on its bed of marinated, grilled aubergine, tomatoes and peppers. A respectable clafoutis and free-refill coffees finished off an enjoyable evening, stage-managed by a waiter whose friendly, intuitive and unimposing service was a pleasure to experience.

Babies and children welcome. Booking advisable. Disabled: toilet. No-smoking tables. Restaurant available for hire. Map 6 R4.

Crouch End N8

Bistro Aix

54 Topsfield Parade, Tottenham Lane, N8 8PT (8340 6346/www.bistroaix.co.uk). Finsbury Park tube/rail then W7 bus/91 bus. **Lunch served** noon-3pm, **dinner served** 6.30-11pm Tue-Sun. **Main courses** £11.50-£15. **Set lunch** £11.50 2 courses. **Set meal** (Sun) £13.50 2 courses, £16.50 3 courses. **Service** 12.5%. **Credit** AmEx, MC, V.

Bistro Aix set high standards in its first year, with an inventive, light approach to French food, skilled cooking, charming staff, and a comfortably buzzy atmosphere. The narrow space is decorated in mellow colours, and at the back there are more tables in an attractive conservatory. The wine list is sizeable, but pricey. On our latest visit the sure

Les Trois Garçons

Morgan M

The Restaurants

touch was harder to find. Service seemed uncoordinated, nervous, anonymous and slow, if well meaning. Of our food, the starters came closest to matching previous experiences. A salade gourmande featured richly flavoured smoked duck breast and confit of duck, together with an enjoyable mix of walnuts, fennel and leaves; in seared scallops with bacon, spring greens and lime butter, the excellent seafood and the other components tended to cancel each other out. Mains were far less inspiring. Steak frites served several ways is a menu fixture; steak with a shallot and red onion relish was a decent piece of meat, with an over-sweet sauce. Most disappointing was roast sea bass with citrus and olive oil compote, grilled avocado, spinach and pine nuts: the fish was dry, the sauce overpowering, the whole thing sloppily done. We hope Aix soon regains its stride.
Babies and children welcome. Booking essential weekends. Restaurant available for hire. Tables outside (11, conservatory).

Les Associés

172 Park Road, N8 8JT (8348 8944). Finsbury Park tube/rail then W7 bus. **Lunch served** noon-3pm Sun. **Dinner served** 7.30-10pm Tue-Sat. **Main courses** £11.20-£16. **Set dinner** (Tue-Fri) £12.50 2 courses, £14.50 3 courses. **Credit** DC, MC, V.
Tucked into a residential street, Les Associés is a little niche of French tradition, complete with pretty summer terrace, cosy bourgeois decor and background *chanson* tracks. Service by the owners, the 'Associés' (another of whom is the very able chef), and their staff is charming, slightly idiosyncratic and unmistakeably Gallic. Rather than follow fashions, the restaurant presents classic French cooking very well, with imagination and attention to details – like all the enjoyable French extras, such as great bread, a decent cheese course, and the candied orange rinds served with coffee. The regularly changing menus are supplemented by daily specials, which are worth trying. In pan-fried scallops with red peppers and Noilly sauce, the sauce was deliciously smooth and delicate; warm asparagus with hollandaise was an equally enjoyable mix

(with a high butter content). For mains, panache of fish with tomatoes and fine garlic featured excellent sea bass and monkfish, while leg of rabbit came au civet, in a wonderfully punchy, classic red-wine sauce. Standard ingredients are invariably made less ordinary by skilful presentation and fine accompaniments. The wine range is relatively small, but presented with knowledge. One leaves feeling nicely pampered.
Babies and children welcome. Booking advisable. No-smoking tables. Restaurant available for hire. Tables outdoors (5, garden).

Holloway N7

Morgan M NEW

2004 RUNNER-UP BEST VEGETARIAN MEAL
489 Liverpool Road, N7 8NS (7609 3560). Highbury & Islington tube/rail. **Lunch served** noon-2.30pm Wed-Fri, Sun. **Dinner served** 7-10.30pm Tue-Sat. **Set lunch** £19.50 2 courses, £23.50 3 courses. **Set dinner** £30 3 courses. **Service** 12.5%. **Credit** DC, MC, V.
Chef/patron Morgan Meunier, who was previously at the Admiralty (*see p83*), opened Morgan M in late summer 2003. His cooking style has remained much the same, so, as before, there's a 'garden' menu as well as the à la carte. Almost unheard of in a French restaurant, this consists of six courses (seven with cheese) that will delight any vegetarian – the best of which was chilled gazpacho with aubergine caviar croûton and tomato and olive oil sorbet. The odd dish was a little bland (young vegetables braised and à la grecque, for example), but such an accusation can be levelled at the main menu too. On the whole, though, flavours come through loud and clear in dishes such as fillet of sea bass steamed with pastis, razor clams, asparagus and grilled fennel, served with saffron cream; or a pudding of raspberry soufflé with strawberry coulis, rhubarb and Jurançon ice-cream. There's a wine list and a level of service to match. Neither staff nor venue are stuffy, although the latter lacks buzz. Booking is essential. A word of warning: the chef tours the restaurant at the end of the evening, so be ready with your thoughts on the meal.

Babies and children welcome. Booking essential. Dress: smart casual. No smoking. Separate room for parties, seats 12. Vegetarian menu.

Hornsey N8

Le Bistro

36 High Street, N8 7NX (8340 2116). Turnpike Lane tube/Hornsey rail/41, W3 bus. **Lunch served** 12.30-3.30pm Sun. **Dinner served** 7-11pm Mon-Sat; 7-10pm Sun. **Set meal** £10.50, £18.50 2 courses; £12.95, £22 3 courses. **Service** 10%. **Credit** MC, V.
There has been a bistro on this site for more than 20 years, which could explain why Le Bistro seems to have lost some of its je ne sais quoi. When under-populated, the place looks as much like a railway waiting room as a French restaurant. We started well enough (except for the rubbery egg on the bacon and potato salad), with a good goat's cheese salad and a fish soup that tasted as if it had come from a jar yet was perfectly acceptable. Main courses of grilled sea bass (albeit with an insipid anchoïade) and rack of lamb both passed muster. A soggy tarte au citron arrived without the stated kumquat, but with a convoluted explanation for its absence. Our chosen wine, from the all-French list, was unavailable, so we were generously offered a slightly more expensive bottle for the same price – but then had to argue the toss when the bill came. Service was pleasant, though when we politely asked the ebullient manager for the original bill as we left, his charm deserted him. 'Poor value' has to be the verdict on this relic of better days.
Babies and children welcome; high chairs. Booking advisable. Tables outdoors (15, garden).

Islington N1

★ Almeida

30 Almeida Street, N1 1AD (7354 4777/ www.conran.com). Angel tube/Highbury & Islington tube/rail. **Lunch served** noon-2.30pm Mon-Fri; noon-3pm Sat, Sun. **Dinner served** 5.30-10.45pm Mon-Sat; 5.30-9.30pm Sun. **Main courses** £12-£19. **Set meal** (lunch, 5.30-7pm daily; 10-10.45pm Mon-Sat) £14.50 2 courses; £17.50 3 courses. **Service** 12.5%. **Credit** AmEx, DC, MC, V.
What is it with Conran restaurants? The mega joints tend to be hit-and-miss affairs, with plenty of swagger on the design front, but something lacking in the kitchen, but the smaller operations – such as this low-key sleek spot opposite the Almeida theatre – are models of sophisticated dining on all fronts. Calming green and gold tones, soft lighting and a well thought-out layout ensure a relaxed ambience, while the regional French cooking offers plenty to delight and impress. Classic dishes abound (escargots, frogs' legs, steak tartare, coquille st jacques, steak au poivre) and, not surprisingly, meat eaters fare best, though there's also crustacea (lobster, first-class oysters) and a handful of fish dishes, including a simple but exquisite grilled halibut with hollandaise sauce. Trolley dollies will be delighted with the charcuterie and tarts trolleys, while tempting desserts include the likes of strawberry soufflé, pot au chocolat, and cheese (great value at £5.50). The predominantly French wine list yielded a good Languedoc rosé for £22, and offers masses of choice by the glass and half-bottle. The menu du jour is limited, but nicely priced. Other bonuses include impeccable service from French staff, and a sexy, purple and red bar offering tapas (oysters, serrano ham, anchovies) and good cocktails.
Babies and children welcome; high chairs. Booking advisable. Disabled: toilet. No-smoking tables. Restaurant available for hire. Separate room for parties, seats 20. Tables outdoors (5, pavement). Map 5 O1.

Kentish Town NW5

★ Le Petit Prince

5 Holmes Road, NW5 3AA (7267 3789). Kentish Town tube/rail. **Lunch served** 12.30-2.30pm Tue-Fri. **Dinner served** 6.30-11pm Tue-Sat. **Main courses** £5.90-£11.50. **Service** 10%. **Credit** MC, V.

London needs more places like Le Petit Prince. From a little shopfront behind Somerfield, the pride of Kentish Town continues to serve good, honest, French country cooking with a North African twist – and not a hint of pretension. A collection of *Little Prince* books from around the world hangs from the walls. The gregarious French proprietors bend over backwards to make diners feel at home. Food is of the bistro rather than blue-ribbon variety, but impossible not to love. A starter of Burgundy escargots in parsley butter, rich and characterful, left us drooling. Salad of smoked duck and pine nuts arrived generously apportioned, with tender, gutsy slices of meat. Despite the solid range of French staples, such as roquefort salad or coq au vin, it's hard to resist going for the speciality: Moroccan-style couscous cooked with your choice of chicken, lamb, beef or merguez sausage, and served with a bottomless trough of rich mixed vegetable broth. This is serious comfort food, so filling we nearly passed on dessert, which would have been a mistake. Blackcurrant and lime 'ice cake' left us in awe of the abilities of the pint-sized kitchen in the back of the room.
Babies and children welcome. Book weekends. Restaurant available for hire. Takeaway service. Vegetarian menu. **Map 26 B5.**

Palmers Green N13

Café Anjou
394 Green Lanes, N13 5PD (8886 7267/ www.cafeanjou.co.uk). Wood Green tube then 329 bus/Palmers Green rail. **Lunch served** noon-2.30pm, **dinner served** 6.30-10.30pm Tue-Sun. **Main courses** £8.45-£10.95. **Set lunch** (noon-2pm Tue-Sat) £7.45 1 course incl coffee and beverage. **Set meal** (Tue-Fri, lunch Sat) £12.95 2 courses, £14.45 3 courses. **Service** 10% for parties of 7 or more. **Credit** AmEx, MC, V.
It's hard to get excited about a place that's as resolutely suburban in its appeal as Café Anjou. However, if you can look past the tinny 1980s soundtrack and the tired-looking patrons, there's a lot to like about this local boîte. The proprietors have clearly made serving fresh, inventive French food a priority, and it shows. A starter of artichoke with a duxelle of minced mushrooms was superbly executed, while chicken livers cooked in port with grated beets and pine nuts had a mild and pleasing spiciness to them. Mains were a mixed bag: monkfish provençale with tomatoes and olives just sort of sat there, waiting to be eaten, while a brochette of lamb done 'à la marocaine' (with aubergine relish and yoghurt), despite being a glorified kebab, was as tender and flavourful as any we've tried. To finish, a dessert of bread and butter pudding with Baileys was probably always going to be a bad idea, yet a rich, intense little pot au chocolat with orange Curaçao turned out to be about three spoonfuls of pure luxury. Worth the proverbial trip? Probably not, but certainly one thing to love about Palmers Green.
Babies and children welcome; children's menu (Sun); high chairs. Booking essential dinner Fri, Sat. Restaurant available for hire.

North West

St John's Wood NW8

L'Aventure
3 Blenheim Terrace, NW8 0EH (7624 6232). St John's Wood tube/139, 189 bus. **Lunch served** 12.30-2.15pm Mon-Fri. **Dinner served** 7.30-10.30pm Mon-Sat. **Set lunch** £18.50 3 courses incl coffee. **Set dinner** £31.50 3 courses. **Service** 12.5%. **Credit** AmEx, MC, V.
St John's Wood at lunchtime can be tricky for parking – which may explain the empty tables in this pretty, very French restaurant. The conservatory proved a pleasant setting for what was a mainly successful meal both in quality and cost. Three courses for £18.50 is a bargain par excellence (prices almost double in the evening for the same menu of classic French cuisine). Presentation is flawless, and taste is the order of the day with such starters as vegetable tart (containing the ingredients of ratatouille, grilled);

saucissons de volaille aux pistaches was good, as was a beautiful salad of artichokes. To follow, oven-roasted lamb, of fine quality, was perfectly cooked. The supreme of chicken arrived without its mango risotto (a nod to modernity); this eventually appeared as barley not rice, a delicious alternative. An anticipated carpaccio of orange with passion fruit wasn't available, but a melange of sorbets was first class. The main disappointment was a grainy, too dense crème brûlée. Liquids (both water and wine) are costly. Service, while adequately polite, had a certain laziness about it: quite unnecessary when we were the only customers. Inevitably the evenings are more atmospheric: c'est la vie.
Babies and children welcome. Booking advisable dinner. Tables outdoors (6, terrace). **Map 1 C2.**

Outer London
Hampton Hill, Middlesex

★ Monsieur Max
133 High Street, Hampton Hill, Middx TW12 1NJ (8979 5546/www.monsieurmax.co.uk). Richmond tube then R68, R70 bus/Fulwell rail. **Lunch served** noon-2.30pm Mon-Fri, Sun. **Dinner served** 7-9.30pm daily. **Set lunch** (Mon-Fri) £20-£30 2 courses; (Mon-Fri, Sun) £25-£35 3 courses. **Set dinner** £37.50 3 courses. **Corkage** £8.50 half-bottle, £14.50 bottle, £25 magnum. **Service** 12.5%. **Credit** AmEx, DC, MC, V.
This is an astonishing achievement for a restaurant in an outer London location. Inside, every inch is crammed with the distressed bric-a-brac of 1950s provincial France: mismatched cutlery, odd chairs, old Michelin guides. The various dining areas take on a different character every few metres, from light and airy to red, plush and seductive. Staff are friendly, French and efficient; the food is exceptional in quality and complexity. Perhaps chef Alex Bentley feels he needs to provide all the trimmings to draw customers from farther afield. As if the black truffle and parmesan risotto wasn't enough, it had an egg on top, cooked in red wine then fried in breadcrumbs and served so the yolk was warm and still runny: fantastic. The detailed menu only lists some of the many ingredients: sea bass was said to have four accompaniments, but came with more (sardine and foie gras in a spring roll case, parsnips and saffron, asparagus, seaweed, hollandaise…), while lamb rump came with at least eight. All were delicious, if potentially overwhelming. A real treat was the rhubarb crumble soufflé: floatingly light, the top broken so the rhubarb sauce could trickle down inside. Somewhere very special.
Children over 8 years admitted. Booking essential. Restaurant available for hire.

Richmond, Surrey

Chez Lindsay
11 Hill Rise, Richmond, Surrey TW10 6UQ (8948 7473). Richmond tube/rail.
Crêperie **Meals served** 11am-11pm Mon-Sat; noon-10pm Sun. **Main courses** £4.25-£8.95. **Set lunch** (noon-3pm Mon-Sat) £6.50 2 courses.
Restaurant **Lunch served** noon-3pm Mon-Sat; noon-4pm Sun. **Dinner served** 6-10.45pm Mon-Sat; 5.30-10pm Sun. **Main courses** £10.75-£15.75. **Set meal** £15.75 3 courses incl sparkling cider.
Both **Credit** MC, V.
Chez Lindsay's poky yellow dining room is where refined Breton cooking is served to Richmond's discerning bourgeoisie, south-west London's blue-rinse brigade and foodie Francophiles. Alongside crêpes and galettes, the menu offers an abundance of fish and seafood dishes, as well as meaty classics such as andouillette (chitterling sausage). Huîtres chaudes au cidre was a decadent starter – a plate of six warm oysters that came bursting with a sumptuous cream and cider sauce and stuffed with chopped onion and spinach. Crêpe St Jacques was a fine and crispy crêpe filled with leeks and topped with queen scallops, served with salad. One of the daily specials, a main course millefeuille d'asperges

et crabes, was a revelation: three thin layers of puff pastry sandwiching a rich mixture of fresh crab meat and crunchy green asparagus. Struggling to find room for dessert, we decided to share a crème brûlée; it was as light and creamy as we'd hoped. With most of the clientele practising their pidgin French on the good-humoured waiters, and chef-owner Lindsay Wotton flitting between tables, Chez Lindsay is a comforting suburban appropriation of regional France.
Babies and children welcome; high chairs. Booking advisable. No cigars or pipes. Separate room for parties, seats 40.

Surbiton, Surrey

★ The French Table
85 Maple Road, Surbiton, Surrey KT6 4AW (8399 2365). Surbiton rail. **Lunch served** noon-2.30pm Wed-Fri, Sun. **Dinner served** 7-10.30pm Tue-Sat. **Main courses** £10.80-£15.80. **Set lunch** (Wed-Fri) £12.50 2 courses, £15.50 3 courses; (Sun) £16.50 3 courses. **Service** 12.5%. **Credit** MC, V.
Since the French Table opened in 2001, Sarah (front-of-house) and Eric (chef) Guignard have built a solid local following. On past visits we've always liked the place, while having certain reservations. Our most recent meal, however, was outstanding: evidence that the kitchen has really hit its stride. The conception and execution of dishes is reaching new highs with the likes of a delicate, refreshingly light salad of crab with julienne of vegetables, subtly flavoured with curry; and an exceptional cannelloni of spinach and almonds with pan-fried frogs' legs and garlic cappuccino. The spirit of carefully restrained playfulness extends to the main courses: we rhapsodised over the sweet-sharp contrasts of the caramelised pork belly with celeriac purée, green tomato chutney, tomato panisse and port reduction; and the multi-flavour/texture explosion of barbary duck with spinach, rillette croustillant and parsnip ice-cream. Add in service that remains as exemplary as ever (a baby was accommodated without a murmur) and you have what is now undoubtedly one of the top dining destinations south of the river. New sister venture the Food Room (*see p83*) in Battersea is continuing the good work.
Babies and children welcome; children's portions (Sun set meal £7.50); high chairs. Booking advisable; essential weekends. No-smoking tables.

Twickenham, Middlesex

★ Ma Cuisine
6 Whitton Road, Twickenham, Middx TW1 1BJ (8607 9849). Twickenham rail. **Lunch served** noon-2.30pm Mon-Sat. **Dinner served** 6.30-10.30pm Mon-Thur; 6.30-11pm Fri, Sat. **Main courses** £9-£13.95. **Set lunch** £12 3 courses. **Service** 10%. **Credit** JCB, MC, V.
This bistro is the feisty little brother of the acclaimed McClements two doors along and, in its way, is at least as successful. Sure, the decor in the tapering dining room makes no great promises – plastic tablecloths with a red and white check, cheap pine panelling – but the food is much better than you could hope for, at prices that (when compared to those of central London) you may scarcely believe. No wonder the place is usually full. For £4.95, the salade niçoise included two freshly grilled slices of moist tuna and perfectly crisp green beans; for £5 came two thick rounds of creamy foie gras with a sharp mango salsa. The tender rabbit that followed was excellent, with its rich blanquette sauce flavoured with tarragon. Lamb tagine, however, was wet and slightly greasy; containing rosemary and carrot, it seemed more like Irish stew (enviously, we noticed the next table getting a much better version). Puddings (£3.95) were cheerful: though slightly stodgy, crêpes suzette had a hint of orange and lots of caramel; lemon tart had a nice tang. Could Ma Cuisine be any friendlier, more relaxed or better value? Bluntly: no.
Babies and children welcome. Booking advisable; essential weekends. Separate room for parties, seats 25. Tables outdoors (4, terrace).
For branch see index.

Gastropubs

Not so long ago London pub meals were pretty awful affairs – sandwiches with curling crusts, pork pies as hard as crabshells and a hot cabinet where leathery sausages would irradiate for days on end. In 1975 fewer than ten per cent of the capital's pubs served hot food. Now the figure is more than 90 per cent, even if much of it is pre-cooked and reheated in the infernal microwave.

In these heady days it seems that the birth of the gastropub was inevitable, with the **Eagle** in Farringdon usually cited as the first. Opened in 1991, it was a catalyst for a new approach to pub cuisine – and, indeed, to dining out in general. Who knows how long it was before the first queasy coupling of the words 'gastro' and 'pub' (the term appeared in this guide for the first time in 1997), but, gawd, hasn't it caught on? Barely a week goes by without some dodgy old pub reopening with an open kitchen where the darts alley used to be. Other standard ingredients are stripped wooden flooring, mismatched schoolroom furniture and bed-headed young staff. Menus (which are often scrawled up on a chalkboard) typically have a Mediterranean slant with something seared, something char-grilled and lots of balsamic, polenta and rocket. Islington and west London are the natural home of these enterprises, but they're rapidly becoming a city-wide phenomenon, even sprouting in such unlikely surroundings as Bow.

This year, in particular, has seen an explosion of gastropubs on the scene; notable newcomers include three runners-up in the Best Gastropub category of the *Time Out* Eating & Drinking Awards 2004 – the **Anchor & Hope** in Waterloo, the **Easton** in Farringdon and the **Hartley** in Bermondsey – and the winner – the **Coach & Horses**, also in Farringdon.

A growing trend we've noticed sees the gastropub going upmarket. There's been a move away from the all-in-one boozing/eating space furnished with battered tables and chairs to the provision of a separate, ultra-smart dining room, offering food of a quality (and price) on a par with many of London's 'proper' restaurants. Examples include the **Wells** in Hampstead (another runner-up for Best Gastropub 2004), and new arrivals the **White Swan Pub & Dining Room** in the City and the **Ebury** in Pimlico.

Central
City EC4

White Swan Pub & Dining Room NEW
108 Fetter Lane, EC4A 1ES (7242 9696). Chancery Lane or Holborn tube.
Bar **Open** 11am-11pm Mon-Fri. **Main courses** £8.50-£14.
Restaurant **Set lunch** £20 2 courses, £25 3 courses. **Set dinner** £24 2 courses, £28 3 courses. **Service** 12.5%.
Both **Lunch served** noon-3pm, **dinner served** 6-10pm Mon-Fri. **Credit** AmEx, MC, V.
The modern but pubby-looking ground floor and mezzanine space at this refurbished city haunt doesn't prepare you for the elegant dining room on the first floor. Here a small room is transformed by mirrors, a few deco touches, lots of white and much natural light into a very desirable, unstuffy place to eat. There's a lot of crossover between the two menus: a succulent, punchily flavoured grilled tuna with confit tuna and green bean salad with citrus dressing appeared on both, as did summer salad (an excellent, very English dish), plus the daily special of truffle and mozzarella arancini. Escabeche of salmon trout with orange and saffron followed by fillet of bream with chorizo, basil and crème fraîche (another winning combo) could also have been eaten swiftly downstairs – but it would have been a real shame not to linger in the tranquil dining room. Save the pub for quick lunches, when what you fancy is welsh rarebit for £3.50 or beef burger with tomato salsa and guacamole for £8.95. The place is full at lunch, but not much eating seems to happen in the evenings, particularly in the pub, which reverts to its previous incarnation as a stand-up drinking den, albeit with a far superior drinks list.
Booking essential (restaurant). Restaurant available for hire, seats 40 (Sat, Sun only). **Map 11 N5.**

Clerkenwell & Farringdon EC1, WC1

★ Coach & Horses NEW
2004 WINNER BEST GASTROPUB
26-28 Ray Street, EC1R 3DJ (7278 8990/ www.thecoachandhorses.com). Farringdon tube/rail. **Open** 11am-11pm Mon-Fri; 6-11pm Sat; noon-3pm Sun. **Lunch served** noon-3pm Mon-Fri, Sun. **Dinner served** 7-10pm Mon; 6-10pm Tue-Sat. **Main courses** £9.95-£13.95. **Credit** MC, V.
Like the pumpkin and mice that are depicted in its logo, the Coach & Horses has been the object of an impressive feat of conjuring: where the traditional boozer once stood is a stylish, sophisticated gastropub. Its pub identity has been preserved in wonderfully traditional touches such as the etched glass and wood panelling that are dotted around, while discreetly modern light fittings and blond wood furniture provide a contemporary gloss. But the real highlight is the kitchen. Typical starters would be a perfectly cooked globe artichoke or a gorgeously simple combination of squid, chorizo, garlic and parsley. A choice of around five mains includes the likes of poached organic salmon with fennel, sorrel and cucumber, or beautifully tender rabbit with judion beans, piquillo peppers and oregano. A recent stand-out pudding of chocolate brownie, malt ice-cream and a shot glass of milkshake was a sweet dream come true. The wine list is great (and well annotated), and service is never less than charming. There are a few outside tables too, perfect for languid summer afternoons. *Babies and children welcome; high chairs. Tables outdoors (8, garden).* **Map 5 N4.**

Eagle
159 Farringdon Road, EC1R 3AL (7837 1353). Farringdon tube/rail/19, 38, 63, 341 bus. **Open** noon-11pm Mon-Sat; noon-5pm Sun. **Lunch served** 12.30-3pm Mon-Fri; 12.30-3.30pm Sat, Sun. **Dinner served** 6.30-10.30pm Mon-Sat. **Main courses** £5-£15. **Credit** MC, V.
Claimed by many as the original gastropub, this tiny, one-room, stripped-and-stranded affair next to the *Guardian*'s offices is constantly packed, as much with drinkers as with diners. With not a great deal in the way of starters or desserts on the blackboard menu, this is still very much a pub that serves food rather than a restaurant with the added bonus of a bar, as many gastropubs seem to have become. Most customers come here to have something to drink, pause for a bite to eat, and then stay on to drink some more. Food – prepared in an open kitchen that segues into the bar – remains excellent. It's hearty: steak and sausages or fish, often paired with accompaniments that avoid the predictable – lentils come with the bangers, for example; shredded cabbage with the steak. Beers are from Charles Wells, and are lovely. The Eagle remains an excellent venue for superior soaking-up of decent booze and company.
Babies and children admitted. Bookings not accepted. Tables outdoors (4, pavement). **Map 5 N4.**

★ Easton NEW
2004 RUNNER-UP BEST GASTROPUB
22 Easton Street, WC1X 0DS (7278 7608/ www.theeaston.co.uk). Farringdon tube/rail/19, 38 bus. **Open** noon-11pm Mon-Thur; noon-1am Fri, Sat; noon-10.30pm Sun. **Lunch served** noon-3pm, 1-4pm Sun. **Dinner served** 6-10pm Mon-Sat; 6-9pm Sun. **Credit** MC, V.
There's a real neighbourhood feel to the Easton – a kind of sunny, 'I'm OK, you're OK' vibe – which is particularly impressive given its slightly tucked-away location. Part of the reason for its popularity undoubtedly resides in the look of the place (wonderful retro wallpaper, a convivial U-shaped bar) and in the friendliness of the staff, but what really distinguishes it from the competition is the food. The choice may not be vast (the day's dishes are on the blackboard), but what they do, they do well. Main-course roast lamb chump on couscous salad with mint yoghurt and harissa was a highlight of a recent meal – clear, uncomplicated flavours shining through in every mouthful – while char-grilled ribeye with roast squash, herb butter and rocket was another simple but deeply satisfying dish. Chocolate panettone bread and butter pudding was a discreetly inventive finale. The selection of wines is good (making this a nice place to come just for a drink), and the cappuccinos are among the best in town.
Babies and children admitted (daytime only). Entertainment: DJs occasional Fri, Sat. Tables outdoors (5, pavement). **Map 5 N5.**

Peasant
240 St John Street, EC1V 4PH (7336 7726/ www.thepeasant.co.uk). Angel tube/Farringdon tube/rail/19, 38 bus. **Open** noon-11pm daily. **Lunch served** noon-4pm Mon-Fri. **Dinner served** 6-11pm Sat. **Main courses** £9-£15. **Set lunch** £12.50 2 courses, £14.75 3 courses. **Service** 12.5%. **Credit** AmEx, MC, V.
Ambition – or could that be pretension? – is what marks out the Peasant from its numerous gastropub siblings. In a thin room above the bar (there's a separate menu for downstairs pub-dwellers) at the Angel end of St John Street, this sparsely furnished dining area holds unexpected marvels. Grilled kangaroo salad with green beans, coriander, crispy shallots and den miso dressing? Crocodile and crab cakes on kohlrabi, spring onion and chilli salad with tomatillo jam? There's the hardy perennial of goat's cheese salad if all this seems a bit adventurous (or non-vegetarian) but, hey, why not live a little? Main courses are less exotic but no less interesting: roast lamb chump with spinach and leek flan on a brunoise of watercress and carrot was rather tasty; roast brill with sautéed black beans, chorizo and avocado with piquillo pepper relish was an intriguing delight. Desserts are fattening – dark chocolate and wattleseed truffle with coffee cream, short bread and chocolate wafer – but you've already come this far, so why stop now? Bad news: decadence comes at a price, and you'll emerge well fed but feeling a little short-changed. Can't fault the effort, though.
Babies and children welcome; high chairs. Booking advisable. Tables outdoors (4, garden terrace; 5, pavement). **Map 5 O4.**

Sutton Arms
6 Carthusian Street, EC1M 6EB (7253 0723). Barbican tube/rail.
Bar **Open** noon-11pm Mon-Fri; 7-11pm Sat. **Main courses** £5.75-£8.50.
Restaurant **Main courses** £13-£17. **Set lunch** £14.95 2 courses.

Both **Lunch served** noon-2.30pm, **dinner served** 6-9.30pm Mon-Fri. **Credit** AmEx, MC, V. The Sutton Arms was a finalist for *Time Out*'s Best Gastropub award in 2003; not long after that, chef Rosie Sykes moved on (in December 2003) and the kitchen is now being run by someone else. While the standard of ingredients and cooking is still pretty good, our meal didn't blow any socks off. The ground-floor bar has a pleasantly uncluttered ambience, good beer and a fine jukebox, but dinner is served up the stairs in a small and slender room on the first floor. Smooth chicken liver pâté was unremarkable,

but a special of cream of asparagus soup was superb; enter a restaurant in May and you won't be able to move for asparagus, but this serving stood out. Sautéed sirloin with cream and brandy peppercorn on wensleydale mash with crispy leeks didn't quite live up its billing, while rare roasted best end of lamb was beautifully tender, but the accompanying leek and potato cake was a bit dull. The closing croissant bread and butter pudding with marmalade glaze left us on a high. Good service and decent wines add to the appeal.
Restaurant available for hire. **Map 5 O5**.

Holborn WC1

Perseverance

63 Lamb's Conduit Street, WC1N 3NB (7405 8278). Holborn or Russell Square tube. **Open** 12.30-11pm Mon-Sat; 12.30-10.30pm Sun. **Lunch served** 12.30-3pm Mon-Fri, 12.30-4pm Sun. **Dinner served** 7-10pm Mon-Sat. **Main courses** £8-£14. **Service** 12.5%. **Credit** AmEx, DC, MC, V.
Dramatically different from the boisterous, be-flocked pub below, the discreet first-floor restaurant is an intimate little space. Its mode of

Coach & Horses

Easton. See p90.

decoration – chandelier, maroon curtains and walls of burnished gold – belies the fact that it belongs to the comfortable and laid-back school, rather than the formal and rigid one. Our waitress didn't raise an eyebrow when two extra diners joined our table, throwing the ordering out of synch; she even suggested we move to a different table to better accommodate ourselves. The menu is a short and none-too-ambitious roster of European standards. We followed a vegetable terrine starter (tasty enough, though far from extraordinary) with mains of duck with lentils, featuring gorgeously smoky pulses and moist duck with crisp, salty-sweet skin, plus sea bass with spinach – a good juicy fillet on fresh, barely cooked spinach, served with an OK though dispensable tomatoey sauce on the side. Ribeye steak (with foie gras) was similarly juicy and successful. Uncomplicated food, cooked with care and served with friendly patience, made for a very pleasant evening. Oh, and the wine list featured quite a few good bottles for under £20.
Babies and children admitted (lunch only).
Booking advisable. Tables outdoors (6, pavement).
Map 4 M4.

Marylebone NW1

Queen's Head & Artichoke

30-32 Albany Street, NW1 4EA (7916 6206/ www.theartichoke.net). Great Portland Street or Regent's Park tube. **Open** *11am-11pm Mon-Sat; noon-10.30pm Sun.* **Lunch served** *12.30-3pm,* **dinner served** *6.30-10.15pm Mon-Sat.* **Meals served** *12.30-10pm Sun.* **Main courses** £8.50-£12.50. **Service** 12.5%. **Credit** AmEx, MC, V.
This spruced-up Victorian boozer retains enough of the old features to feel like a proper pub, while bare floorboards, huge frosted windows and stripped wooden tables create an airy feel suited to dining. The decor is plain, with the colourful wall-mounted masks round the back regrettably hidden from view. The extensive and varied tapas

menu is popular with the young professionals who patronise the joint; we chose from the main menu, which seems to change regularly. A selection of artisan breads with olive oil and balsamic got the meal off to a good start. Mains were good, but didn't quite live up to their mouth-watering descriptions: dorade was well cooked with a strong flavour, but the leek, courgette and pea risotto on which it came was bland and overcooked, with little trace of leek. Grilled Black Mountain ribeye with thyme jus lacked a certain something, but the gratin dauphinois accompaniment was good. A mixed berry pavlova with whipped cream rounded off the meal nicely. Although not especially memorable, dishes are well priced, and the down-to-earth staff are suitably efficient.
Babies and children admitted. Booking advisable. Separate room for parties, seats 45. Tables outdoors (6, pavement; 4, courtyard). **Map 3 H4**.

Pimlico SW1

Ebury NEW

11 Pimlico Road, SW1W 8NA (7730 6784/ www.theebury.co.uk). Sloane Square tube/ Victoria tube/rail/11, 211 bus.
Bar **Open** *noon-11pm Mon-Sat; noon-10.30pm Sun.*
Brasserie **Lunch served** *noon-4pm,* **dinner served** *6-10.30pm daily.* **Main courses** £9.95-£18.
Restaurant **Dinner served** *6-10.30pm Mon-Sat.* **Set dinner** £25 2 courses, £29.50 3 courses.
All **Credit** AmEx, MC, V.
More gastrobar than gastropub, the smart-looking Ebury is owned by Tom Etridge, who also runs Modern European newcomer the Farm. Sleek, well-dressed punters lounge around the low-slung communal tables and leather banquettes next to the massive, 1960s-style windows or perch on stools as bartenders jiggle cocktail shakers or dispense choices from the interesting wine list (beer is not a strong point). A shortish brasserie-style menu is served in the ground-floor bar;

upstairs is a formal dining room, with table linen, gorgeous chandeliers and more ambitious prix-fixe fare (three courses for £29.50). We ate downstairs, where there's also a seafood bar. Typical dishes include steak, toulouse sausages, fish and chips, and mussels: fine plump specimens in a delicious herby broth. Pasta with an over-rich mushroom and tarragon sauce would easily have fed two (it, and a few other dishes, are available in two sizes). For afters, try hot chocolate pudding or cheeses from La Fromagerie. Prices are reasonable for this part of town; the house white, a perfectly acceptable Jacques Veritier, was only £12.50.
Babies and children welcome. Disabled: toilet. Separate room for hire, seats 60. **Map 15 G11**.

Soho W1

Endurance

90 Berwick Street, W1F 0QB (7437 2944). Tottenham Court Road or Oxford Circus tube. **Open** *noon-11pm Mon-Sat; 12.30-10.30pm Sun.* **Lunch served** *12.30-4pm Mon-Sat; 1-4.30pm Sun.* **Main courses** £6-£12. **Service** 12.5%. **Credit** MC, V.
Despite the name, the Endurance isn't afraid of change. A few years ago it was the Berwick Street boozer that hipsters avoided at all costs. Nowadays, night-time sees the studiedly scruffy interior filled with fashionable folk, crammed cheek-by-jowl, smoking hard and listening to one of the choicest jukeboxes around. Lunchtime is a different story again; the shabby wooden tables are covered by pristine white tableclothes, wine glasses replace pints of lager and you can actually see the floor. Only the customers' trendy haircuts remain the same. Soho's solo gastropub is a good 'un, the menu ever-changing, unspectacular but always well balanced between meat, fish and veggie. After a goat's cheese starter, served with a delicious warmed crostini, pork belly with apple mash was lovely, while pea and asparagus risotto

was market-fresh (as it should be, with the market only five yards away). Being a pub, the beer's good, but a short, sharp wine list does the job and with enough bottles under your belt you can get a head start on the evening rush when the Jamie Oliver-alikes hit the bar.
Booking advisable. Tables outdoors (8, garden). Games (darts). Map 17 J6.

West

Chiswick W4

Bollo
13-15 Bollo Lane, W4 5LR (8994 6037/www.the bollo.co.uk). Chiswick Park tube. **Open** noon-11pm Mon-Sat; noon-10.30pm Sun. **Lunch served** noon-3pm Mon-Fri; 12.30-3.30pm Sat, Sun. **Dinner served** 7-10pm daily. **Main courses** £9-£13. **Service** 10%. **Credit** AmEx, MC, V.
This large corner pub is a handsome affair with its green-tiled exterior and picture windows. De rigueur knackered furniture occupies the drinking area; there's also a dedicated dining room, part of the same overall space, but distinctive by virtue of its carpet, leather chairs and smarter tables. During the day, light pours in through a grand central skylight. The menu makes for plain reading but fine dining. Asparagus, leek and potato soup was tasty, as was tender (cold) octopus with a tomato, potato and green bean salad, the octopus pieces cleverly held together in a flat sheet by the lightest of jellies. For mains, courgette and ricotta ravioli – huge stuffed roundels – arrived with an alarmingly bright yellow saffron butter sauce, while two hefty, triangular chunks of tuna came with roast potatoes, and chilli and sun-dried tomato relish. The unusual shape meant the outside was well charred while the inside remained raw: lovely. There's a reasonable wine list and a couple of ales. Friendly staff add to the vibe; a shame that the place was half empty on our visit.
Babies and children welcome (until 7pm); high chairs. Booking advisable weekends. Tables outdoors (12, pavement).

Pilot
56 Wellesley Road, W4 4BZ (8994 0828). Gunnersbury tube/rail. **Open** noon-11pm Mon-Sat; noon-10.30pm Sun. **Lunch served** noon-3pm Mon-Fri; 12.30-3.30pm Sat, Sun. **Dinner served** 6.30-10pm Mon-Sat; 6.30-9pm Sun. **Main courses** £7-£11.50. **Credit** AmEx, MC, V.
Deep in leafy Chiswick, the Pilot looks the part with its battered furniture, stripped floorboards and decent selection of drinks (including bottled St Peter's ales). The air of slight shabbiness is not unappealing and the backyard is pleasant, but the adjoining rear extension is low-ceilinged and noisy. Dishes are ambitious-sounding, but not always successful; the cooking is definitely more home than haute. For starters, smoked haddock, prawn and salmon fish cakes came with a mango salsa that featured agreeable chunks of fleshy fruit, while a mixed platter (for two) of roast peppers, tabbouleh, houmous, parma ham, goat's cheese and pitta was excellent. Not so the leek tart (far too much cheese, not enough leek, accompanied by oversalted rocket). Portions are gargantuan, and ingredients mount up with alarming abandon: how about pumpkin, aubergine and wilted spinach, with fennel, pepper and tomato ragoût and artichoke pancake (really a glorified ratatouille) or baked crab with chilli and corn, coconut sticky rice and black bean salsa served on a lotus leaf? Puds – sticky toffee pudding (actually cake with toffee sauce) – are hearty, and the staff are affable.
Babies and children admitted (until 7pm). Booking advisable. Disabled: toilet. Separate room for parties, seats 25. Tables outdoors (12, garden).

Ealing W5

Ealing Park Tavern
222 South Ealing Road, W5 4RL (8758 1879). South Ealing tube. **Bar Open** 5-11pm Mon; 11am-11pm Tue-Sat; noon-10.30pm Sun. **Tapas served** 5-10.30pm Mon-Sat; 5-9pm Sun. **Tapas** £2.50-£4.50.

Restaurant **Lunch served** noon-3pm Tue-Sat; noon-4pm Sun. **Dinner served** 6-10.30pm Mon-Sat; 6-9.30pm Sun. **Main courses** £8-£13. **Service** 12.5% for parties of 5 or more. *Both* **Credit** AmEx, MC, V.
One half of this humungous corner pub is dedicated to drinkers; the rest – a bright, airy space next to the open kitchen, a smaller, darker room for smokers, and, best of all, a large, attractive garden with umbrellas and huge stone tables – is for diners. The shortish but daily changing menu is scrawled on a blackboard above the kitchen, which involves a bit of toing and froing while deciding what to order. Starters on our visit included a first-rate crab cake with samphire (a nice seasonal touch) and bisque, the powerful flavours working very well together. Tasty grilled prawns came with that gastropub staple, rocket, and a somewhat insipid lime and chilli mayonnaise – and the inclusion of the heads was a bit annoying, making the portion seem larger than it really was. Main courses offered the likes of veal T-bone, roast sirloin with a hat-sized yorkshire pud (going down a storm with fellow diners), and a hefty chunk of perfectly cooked cod atop delicious tomato mash that instead of being merely tomato-flavoured, was studded with actual cherry tomatoes. There's some good beers and a nicely priced wine list, with a commendable 18 choices by the glass. Staff were a friendly and attentive bunch.
Babies and children welcome; high chairs. Booking advisable. Tables outdoors (25, garden).

Hammersmith W6

Stonemason's Arms
54 Cambridge Grove, W6 0LA (8748 1397). Hammersmith tube. **Open** noon-11pm Mon-Sat; noon-10.30pm Sun. **Lunch served** noon-3pm Mon-Fri; 12.30-3.30pm Sat, Sun. **Dinner served** 6.30-10pm Mon-Sat; 6.30-9.30pm Sun. **Main courses** £7.75-£12.75. **Service** 10% for parties of 7 or more. **Credit** AmEx, MC, V.
The Stonemason's Arms shares owners with the Pilot (*see above*), as well as a similar look (cream walls, maroon wainscoting) and vibe (young, noisy – partly because of the low ceiling – and slightly shambolic). The food is on a par too: hearty home cooking with no pretensions. And it obviously suits its clientele well: the place was packed on a midweek evening. A starter of batatas [sic] bravas was really just fat chips in a spicy tomato and onion sauce, topped by melted cheese and a big dollop of sour cream: not exactly authentic, but perfectly palatable. Grilled halloumi came with smoked leeks and a good, smoky babaganoush, but the deep-fried piquillo peppers stuffed with goat's cheese were cloyingly rich. The sole vegetarian main, butternut squash and mushroom risotto 'cake', was a messy but tasty splodge;

Best Views

Skyline
Eat with your head in the clouds at **Rhodes Twenty Four** (British), feel like a high-flier on the roof at **Le Coq d'Argent** (French) or relish the vista from **Windows** (Hotels & Haute Cuisine) at the Park Lane Hilton. Shiny skyscrapers loom next to **Plateau** (French) in Docklands.

River
Stunning South Bank waterscapes at **Four Regions** (Chinese), **People's Palace** (Modern European) and the **Oxo Tower Restaurant, Bar & Brasserie** (Modern European). Further east, check out the **Blueprint Café** (Modern European), **Butlers Wharf Chop House** (British) and **Le Pont de la Tour** (Modern European).

---

meat-eaters fare best, with such stalwarts as cumberland sausages, roast lamb and rump of beef. Puds include the likes of sticky toffee pudding with ice-cream, and tiramisu. There's Leffe and Hoegaarden on draught, plus a couple of real ales (both off on our visit). The Grand Union in Westbourne Grove (45 Woodfield Road, W9 2BA; 7286 1886) is part of the same group.
Babies and children welcome (until 7pm). Booking advisable. Separate room for hire, seats 25. Tables outdoors (4, pavement). Map 20 B4.

Kensal NW10

★ William IV
786 Harrow Road, NW18 1TF (8969 5944/ www.william-iv.co.uk). Kensal Green tube. **Open** noon-11pm Mon-Wed; noon-midnight Thur-Sat; noon-10.30pm Sun. **Lunch served** noon-3pm Mon-Fri; 12.30-4pm Sat; noon-4.30pm Sun. **Dinner served** 6-10.30pm Mon-Wed; 6-11pm Thur, Fri; 7-11pm Sat; 6.30-9.30pm Sun. **Main courses** £7.90-£16. **Set lunch** (Mon-Fri) £8 1 course incl glass of wine; (Sun) £14 2 courses, £17 3 courses. **Service** 10% for parties of 5 or more. **Credit** AmEx, DC, MC, V.
It's worth enduring the long drag of Harrow Road to reach this culinary oasis. The new look of this grand old pub retains that essential pub warmth. Adjoining the popular bar, the restaurant is compact without feeling crowded and opens on one side to a pretty garden. Wooden floors and panelling and touches of stained glass create a clean, unfussy environment in which to savour a small but adventurous menu. Starters may include Spanish charcuterie with marinated green chillies and toast or a flawless marinated cauliflower, red onion and goat's cheese salad. Mains included a gorgeous medley of slow-roast belly of pork with mussels, chorizo and arothino beans, and roast fillet of cod complemented by chickpea, red onion and coriander salad. The adventurousness of the menu was perfectly matched by an informative and enticing wine list. Top marks to the staff who did their utmost to minimise delays. A most satisfying dining experience and jolly good value.
Babies and children welcome; high chairs. Booking essential. Entertainment: DJ 9pm Thur-Sat. Separate room for hire, seats 100. Restaurant. Tables outdoors (15, garden).

Ladbroke Grove W10

Golborne Grove [NEW]
36 Golborne Road, W10 5PR (8960 6260/ www.groverestaurants.co.uk). Westbourne Park tube. **Open** noon-11pm Mon-Thur; noon-11.30pm Fri, Sat; noon-10.30pm Sun. **Lunch served** noon-3.45pm Mon-Sat; noon-3.30pm Sun. **Dinner served** 6.30-10.15pm Mon-Thur; 6.30-10.45pm Fri, Sat; 6.30-9.45pm Sun. **Main courses** £8.50-£15. **Service** 12.5%. **Credit** AmEx, DC, MC, V.
Between Golborne Road's souk-like 'little Morocco' and the concrete behemoth of Trellick Tower squats the gastropub formerly known as Golborne House. It's now under new management, but you'd struggle to tell the difference from the previous regime. The food is just as good, the atmosphere just as laid-back and the drinks list every bit as choice. The earthy decor behind big plate windows is terracotta- and wood-based. You'll struggle to detect a theme in the solid cooking – unless there's a term that marries starters such as roasted red peppers stuffed with cream cheese stilton on the one hand, and pan-seared king scallops, pesto mash and grilled chorizo on the other. Mains include pumpkin ravioli swimming in spicy tomato sauce, next to organic salmon with saffron risotto.
Babies and children admitted. Booking advisable. Separate room for hire, seats 40. Tables outdoors (6, pavement). Map 19 B1.

North Pole
13-15 North Pole Road, W10 6QH (8964 9384/www.massivepub.com). Latimer Road or White City tube. **Bar Open** noon-11pm Mon-Sat; noon-10.30pm Sun. **Main courses** £6.50-£14. *Restaurant* **Main courses** £8.50-£14. **Service** 10%.

Both **Lunch served** noon-3pm Mon-Thur; noon-4pm Fri-Sun. **Dinner served** 6-9.30pm daily. **Credit** AmEx, DC, MC, V.
Still good for chilling, the North Pole's gastronomic credentials have slipped a little. And waiting 40 minutes for food from a pretty simple menu on a quiet Thursday lunchtime isn't the best introduction. But rest assured, the cooking is still fine if limited. It's even occasionally adventurous: tossing lavender in with roast chicken breast, and making something surprisingly tasty of a three-mushroom, rocket and potato salad. But there's not much depth here. Nachos, burgers, steaks and mussels felt like lowest-common-denominator cuisine and an acknowledgement that the days of courting a more sophisticated palate are gone. There is also a cover charge for eating in the restaurant area, which is all but indistinguishable from the rest of the bar. Real ale is well kept and the conservative wine list is satisfactory. All in all, it remains a good bet for young apprentices at the BBC and middle-aged, leather-faced ravers fondly recalling their salad days in Ibiza from leather couches set on bare-board floors.
Babies and children admitted (restaurant). Booking advisable lunch. Restaurant available for hire. Tables outdoors (6, pavement).

Olympia W14

Cumberland Arms

29 North End Road, W14 8SZ (7371 6806). West Kensington tube/Kensington (Olympia) tube/rail. **Open** noon-11pm Mon-Sat; noon-10.30pm Sun. **Lunch served** 12.30-3pm Mon-Sat; 12.30-3.30pm Sun. **Dinner served** 7-10.30pm Mon-Sat; 7-10pm Sun. **Main courses** £7-£13. **Credit** MC, V.
Floral magnificence abounds at the Cumberland Arms, at least in summer when you can hardly see the place thanks to the overflowing window boxes and hanging baskets. Drinkers and diners mingle at the ramshackle assortment of tables in the spacious, wood-panelled interior or in the open yard along one side. In fact, lots of people weren't eating the night we visited – more fool them, because there's some tasty, Mediterranean-slanted dishes on offer. Bright pink beetroot soup with cumin and yoghurt (served cold or hot) was a refreshing starter; other choices include a mixed antipasti plate, and parma ham and mushroom risotto. Mains are feisty and robust – witness tuscan sausages with cannellini beans and tomato chill jam, or moroccan beef tagine with dates, coriander and roast garlic mash. Dishes may lack finesse, but flavours are good. Whole sea bass – nicely priced at £12.50 – came with couscous salad and a dollop of yoghurt mixed with cucumber and mint. The sultanas and apricot chunks added to the couscous weren't exactly subtle – but it worked, and the fish was lovely. Afters are an afterthought: just two choices. Genial staff added to the laid-back, unpretentious vibe. A good wine list and some well-kept ales too.
Babies and children admitted. Tables outdoors (10, pavement).

Havelock Tavern

57 Masbro Road, W14 0LS (7603 5374/ www.thehavelocktavern.co.uk). Shepherd's Bush tube/Kensington (Olympia) tube/rail. **Open** 11am-11pm Mon-Sat; noon-10.30pm Sun. **Lunch served** 12.30-2.30pm Mon-Sat; 12.30-3pm Sun. **Dinner served** 7-10pm Mon-Sat; 7-9.30pm Sun. **Main courses** £8.50-£12.50. **No credit cards.**
This blue-tiled corner pub obviously fills a niche in the increasingly gentrified residential area between Shepherd's Bush and Olympia; it was heaving on a Tuesday night. The quietest area is the narrow passage en route to the small backyard; the main room, with its capacious windows, large bar and crowded wooden tables, is a cacophonous spot best suited to boozy nights with mates rather than romantic encounters. The menu offers around a dozen dishes, half of which are helpfully available in small or large portions. The food's not bad: juicy warm mackerel came with crunchy sliced fennel and a tangy lemony dressing, while beetroot, chard and roast garlic tortelloni was pleasant, if lacking in thrills. Char-grilled squid

(tender but oddly gritty) went well with avocado salsa – but contained no hint of the advertised cos lettuce or roast tomatoes; instead all three dishes relied on that gastropub standby, a copious pile of rocket. To finish: an average gooseberry fool, and a (hardish) brown sugar meringue piled with raspberries and strawberries. The wine list (from £10 a bottle) covers all the usual bases, and staff are amiable. Note: pay when ordering; only cash or cheques are accepted.
Babies and children welcome; high chairs. Bookings not accepted. Disabled: ramp. Tables outdoors (6, garden; 2, pavement). **Map 20 C3**.

Shepherd's Bush W6

★ Anglesea Arms

35 Wingate Road, W6 0UR (8749 1291). Goldhawk Road or Ravenscourt Park tube. **Open** 11am-11pm Mon-Sat; noon-10.30pm Sun. **Lunch served** 12.30-2.45pm Mon-Sat; 12.30-3.30pm Sun. **Dinner served** 7-10.15pm Mon-Sat; 7-10.15pm Sun. **Main courses** £10.95-£16.95. **Set lunch** (Mon-Fri) £9.95 2 courses, £12.95 3 courses. **Credit** MC, V.
This perennially popular place has the appeal of a well-worn but much-loved sweater. Drinkers stick to the low-lit front part of the pub, while the no-smoking back area next to the open kitchen is reserved for diners (though you can eat anywhere you can find a free table – not always easy, especially as you can't book). The few pavement tables are chocka on summer evenings. Everything on the menu – chalked up on a large blackboard – sounds enticing. Ingredients are first-rate, from the warm and moreish own-made bread to the super-fresh Irish and French oysters, and there's definitely an accomplished hand at work in the kitchen. Sautéed wild mushrooms with broad beans, baby leeks and a poached egg on top was a simple but classy starter, zinging with freshness, while a main of turbot worked a treat with mustardy crushed potatoes and crisp green beans. Summery puds included profiteroles with chocolate mousse, and goat's curd cheesecake with strawberries. The wine list is fairly priced (house bottles at £10.95) and offers plenty of drinkable options by the glass. We've heard complaints about slow service, but staff were perky and accommodating on a busy Sunday night.
Babies and children welcome; high chairs. Bookings not accepted. No-smoking area. Tables outdoors (5, pavement). **Map 20 A3**.

Westbourne Park W2

★ Cow Dining Room

89 Westbourne Park Road, W2 5QH (7221 0021). Royal Oak or Westbourne Park tube. **Bar Open** noon-11pm Mon-Sat; noon-10.30pm Sun. **Lunch served** noon-4pm daily. **Dinner served** 6-11pm Mon-Sat; 6-10pm Sun. **Main courses** £10-£14. *Restaurant* **Brunch served** noon-2.30pm Sat. **Lunch served** 12.30-3.30pm Sun. **Dinner served** 7-11pm Mon-Sat; 7-10.30pm Sun. **Main courses** £13-£18. *Both* **Service** 12.5%. **Credit** MC, V.
The clocks seem to have been set back to the 1950s upstairs at the airy, lace-curtained upstairs room that makes up the Cow Dining Room – and not because they're nostalgic for rationing or dusty furnishings. Rather, this is a classy reinvention of the old-fashioned standards of British cuisine. Building on the fishy menu that is served downstairs in the pub, the menu opens up with a fusillade of oysters, then it's into a choice of starters that show a touch of daring. Try the new season's garlic soup or squid, chorizo and piquillo peppers – you won't find them done better on the Costa Brava. Orecchiette pasta with broad beans, peas and artichokes sounded plain but proved divine, while, among the mains proper, skate wing was a soft, fresh, sensual delight, and the tiny whole roast chicken was a gorgeous treat, with sautéed potatoes, tender broad beans and a fine jus. Some of the best-kept beers in London are available from the bar below and the wine list is a model of taste and fiscal discretion. As for service, 12.5% seemed almost too little.

Babies and children admitted (lunch only, restaurant). Bookings not accepted (bar); essential (restaurant). Restaurant available for hire, seats 32. **Map 1 A5**.

Oak

137 Westbourne Park Road, W2 5QL (7221 3599). Royal Oak or Westbourne Park tube. **Open** 6.30-midnight Mon; noon-midnight Tue-Sat; noon-11pm Sun. **Lunch served** noon- 3pm Tue-Fri. **Meals served** noon-10.30pm Sat; noon-10pm Sun. **Main courses** £10-£14. **Service** 12.5%. **Credit** AmEx, DC, MC, V.
The Oak is Notting Hill's upmarket Pizza Hut, where upmarket means pricey. On an average day there are a dozen pizzas available, with prices ranging from a sensible £7.50 for a margherita to £12.50 for an amalfi – mozzarella, spiced salami, capers, anchovies, oregano and chilli. Baked in a wood-fired oven, the pizzas are constructed from good ingredients – but if you're not in the mood for baked dough, do not despair. Good alternatives include seared tuna or a very fine tagliata (grilled, sliced sirloin steak served on a bed of rocket with a prodigious quantity of parmesan shavings). Starters range from bruschetta to a variety of crudités. Desserts are a little kinder on the wallet, and a good wine list adds a rosy tint to the cheeks of the many dating couples dotted around the room. No booking is allowed, but staff are very accommodating and when you get a bill for £63 covering two courses for two, three glasses of wine and one bottle of mineral water, you can see why the place is so popular.
Babies and children admitted (until 6.30pm). Bookings not accepted. Tables outdoors (3, pavement). **Map 7 A5**.

Westbourne

101 Westbourne Park Villas, W2 5ED (7221 1332/www.thewestbourne.com). Royal Oak or Westbourne Park tube. **Open** 5-11pm Mon; noon-11pm Tue-Sat; noon-10.30pm Sun. **Lunch served** 12.30-3pm Tue-Fri; 12.30-3.30pm Sat, Sun. **Dinner served** 7-10pm Mon-Sat; 7-9.30pm Sun. **Main courses** £9-£13. **Credit** AmEx, MC, V.
The Westbourne and the Cow (*see above*) used to lead the pack, but now many other venues are catching up. On a Friday lunchtime the sun-drenched south-facing terrace filled up quickly; in the evening it often bursts its banks allowing the sea of socialites to spill on to the street. Expect a standard gastropub menu of soups, salads and pasta dishes. Try a huge hunk of tuna steak on a bed of lettuce, croutons and garlic dressing or lamb chops with couscous. The cooking is fair, but it used to be very good, and if you have to wait half an hour after you've paid until you receive your food, you're liable to expect wonders. Staff are also too busy to bring drinks to your table, so you'll have to queue at the bar while your food goes cold. And yet, with its junk-shop chic and trendy vibe, the Westbourne remains one of the key venues in the area. Very Notting Hill.
Babies and children admitted. Bookings not accepted Fri-Sun evenings. Tables outdoors (14, terrace). **Map 7 B5**.

Chelsea SW3

★ Lots Road Pub & Dining Room

114 Lots Road, SW10 0RJ (7352 6645). Fulham Broadway tube then 11 bus/Sloane Square tube then 11, 19, 22 bus. **Open** 11am-11pm Mon-Sat; noon-10.30pm Sun. **Meals served** noon-10pm Mon-Thur, Sun; noon-10.30pm Fri, Sat. **Main courses** £8-£13. **Credit** MC, V.
There are lots of reasons to make it down to this little pocket of Chelsea, and if all gastropubs were like Lots Road, the world would be a happier place. A sunny chrome-fitted bar, beautifully finished oak floors, colourful abstract paintings and good quality food at reasonable prices add up to a chic and cheerful atmosphere. Starters range from avocado, halloumi, parma ham and pear salad to crab and broad bean omelette. Mains feature standards such as house burgers or sausage and

mash, as well as lamb rump with pak choi, red onion and rice salad – adventurous without being reckless. Roast sirloin with seasonal veg maintained a heartily Anglo-Saxon presence. Desserts are halfway between boarding school (bread and butter pudding) and the US (lime pie). The well-kept real ales and wine list is arguably this eaterie's finest feature; the commendable by-the-glass wine range offers impressive variety. All of which makes the Sunday offer (on our visit) of main course and dessert for £12.50 after 6pm irresistible wherever you are in London.
Babies and children admitted. Disabled: toilet. No smoking (restaurant). Restaurant available for hire, seats 45. Takeaway service. **Map 13 13C.**

Fulham SW6

Atlas

16 Seagrave Road, SW6 1RX (7385 9129/ www.theatlaspub.co.uk). West Brompton tube/rail. **Open** noon-11pm Mon-Sat; noon-10.30pm Sun. **Lunch served** 12.30-3pm daily. **Dinner served** 7-10.30pm Mon-Sat; 7-10pm Sun. **Main courses** £8-£12. **Credit** MC, V.
Part of the same stable as Olympia's Cumberland Arms (*see p94*), this smallish pub near the back of the elephantine Earl's Court exhibition centre exudes an air of shabby bonhomie. A youngish crowd lounge at battered wooden tables, while original Victorian panelling, tumbling window boxes and genial staff create a cosy vibe. The Mediterranean-slanted food is very similar to what's on offer at the Cumberland. Typical dishes include turkish lamb meatballs, grilled swordfish, and plump, peppery tuscan sausages; the latter came with lovely, rosemary-scented puy lentils and a mousse of parsnip, dijon mustard and honey (nicer than it sounds). A risotto of artichoke hearts

and dolcelatte was creamy, but over-oily. Portions are more than generous, and most people don't bother with starters or desserts, though Donald's white chocolate and almond cake is worth a punt. To drink, there are some good ales (London Pride, Deuchars' Caledonian IPA, Imp from Battersea's Haggard's Brewery) and a well-priced wine list with plenty by the glass. In fine weather, take advantage of the courtyard at the side.
Babies and children admitted (until 7pm). Bookings not accepted. Separate room for hire, seats 40. Tables outdoors (9, garden). **Map 13 12B.**

Sheen SW14

★ Victoria

10 West Temple Sheen, SW14 7RT (8876 4238/ www.thevictoria.net). Mortlake rail. **Open** 8am-11pm Mon-Sat; 8am-10.30pm Sun. **Breakfast served** 8-9.30am Mon-Fri; 8-10am Sat, Sun. **Lunch served** noon-2.30pm Mon-Fri; noon-3pm Sat; noon-4pm Sun. **Dinner served** 7-10pm Mon-Sat; 7-9pm Sun. **Main courses** £9.95-£16.95. **Service** 12.5%. **Credit** AmEx, MC, V.
A remote backstreet of residential East Sheen is the surprising location for this charming restaurant with small hotel attached (or is it the other way around?). It's not really a gastropub; there is a bar, but it's small and basically an adjunct of the restaurant. And the cooking is definitely a notch above (in quality and pricing) what you'll find in many gastropubs. For starters, chorizo provided a spicy, meaty kick to garlic and saffron soup, while imam bayildi was an excellent rendition – moist, tangy and fully flavoured. Mains impressed too: bright beetroot risotto was a creamy delight with chunks of crunchy beetroot (though it was hard to discern the promised

horseradish and chives). Pan-fried halibut was cooked just right (even if the crust was too salty), accompanied by pea purée and a rich beurre blanc. Whatever you do, don't miss dessert: we swooned over a scrumptious summer pudding, while raspberry ripple ice-cream was crammed with fruit. The young waitresses were charm personified, and the comprehensive drinks list yielded a ruby-rich Stellenbosch red. An assured hand has been at work on the look too, with smart white walls, well-spaced tables and a spacious, bright conservatory. Kids will enjoy the timber play area on the back patio.
Babies and children welcome; books; children's menu; high chairs; play area (garden). Booking essential weekends. Restaurant available for hire. Separate area for hire, seats 34. Tables outdoors (10, garden).

Southfields SW18

★ Earl Spencer

260-262 Merton Road, SW18 5JL (8870 9244/ www.theearlofspencer.co.uk). Southfields tube. **Open** 11am-11pm Mon-Sat; noon-10.30pm Sun. **Lunch served** 12.30-2.30pm Mon-Sat; 12.30-3pm Sun. **Dinner served** 7-10pm Mon-Sat; 7-9.30pm Sun. **Main courses** £7.50-£12.50. **Credit** AmEx, MC, V.
This grand Edwardian drinking palace had an interior makeover last year (the outside was being done when we visited) and has already scooped awards (including as a runner-up in *Time Out's* 2003 Best Gastropub category) for its fine, mainly British, fare. The menu changes daily and orders are taken (no booking tables) at the large U-shaped bar. There's freshly baked bread on the counter, an array of own-made pickles, and a choice of cask-conditioned ales, affordable wines or seasonal

Garrison. See p97.

specials such as elderflower or lemon barley and ginger soda to imbibe. With complimentary bread and show-stopping starters such as pork, chickpea and chorizo terrine (with a delicious rhubarb and apricot chutney), it's easy to fill up quickly. Our deep-fried ricotta, squash, spinach and parmesan dumplings, while a touch dry, were still wolfed down. Chef Mark Robinson – formerly of Pont de la Tour and the Earl's sibling, the Havelock Tavern (*see p94*) – then excelled with a melt-in-your-mouth lamb and mint risotto. Char-grilled rare tuna, with a generous helping of cherry tomatoes, was perfect – and didn't require the large dollop of garlic mayonnaise that came with it. Desserts such as boozy chocolate and pecan ice-cream, and melon and tamarillo sorbets had to wait for another day. Oh, to be one of those lucky people who live close enough to Southfields for this to be a local.
Babies and children admitted; high chairs. Bookings not accepted. Separate room for hire, seats 70. Tables outdoors (10, patio).

Wandsworth SW18

Alma

499 Old York Road, SW18 1TF (8870 2537/ www.thealma.co.uk). Wandsworth Town rail. **Open** 11am-11pm Mon-Sat; noon-10.30pm Sun. **Lunch served** noon-4pm daily. **Dinner served** 6-10.30pm Mon-Sat; 6-9.30pm Sun. **Main courses** £9-£13. **Service** 10% for parties of 10 or more. **Credit** AmEx, MC, V.
The inviting green glazed tiles of the Alma are the first things you see as you leave the train station and its central bar can get very full with pink-shirted, rugby-loving Wandsworthians on their way home from the City – posters for a charity dinner with Brian Moore adorned the walls. The dining room, with its airy, farmhouse kitchen feel, offers a pleasant retreat, although the wobbly pine tables need some attention (the carpenter died earlier in 2004, apparently). The all-day menu is changed every couple of months and the meat is supplied from owners Charles and Linda Gotto's Dorking farm (currently on an organic conversion scheme). Our starter of buffalo mozzarella, broad bean, mint and rocket salad (with surprise red onions) was fresh and generously portioned. And it was the same story for a lovely, massive helping of chicken and leek open pie with crispy pancetta and rosemary mash and smoked haddock, polenta and parsnip rösti, sautéed spinach and poached egg. Even on a quiet night the kitchen had hit the spot. Smiley, friendly waitressing and a shared white chocolate and Baileys bread pudding meant we left with a Ready Brek glow. Wine starts at £10.40. Mainly a place for locals, but worth dropping by if you're in the area and need to fill up. The owners also run the Ship (*see p97*).
Babies and children admitted; high chairs. Booking advisable. Disabled: toilet. Separate room for parties, seats 70. **Map 21 A4.**

Freemasons NEW

2 Wandsworth Common Northside, SW18 2SS (7326 8580). Clapham Junction rail. **Open** noon-11pm Mon-Sat; noon-10.30pm Sun. **Lunch served** noon-3pm Mon-Fri; 12.30-3.30pm Sat; 12.30-4pm Sun. **Dinner served** 6.30-10pm Mon-Sat; 6.30-9.30pm Sun. **Main courses** £8-£11.50. **Credit** AmEx, MC, V.
Gastropubs are a fine thing when they turn an unlucky location into the focal point of a slightly dull neighbourhood. Which is exactly what's happened on this corner site between Wandsworth Common and Clapham Junction, which has been everything from a Café Med to a Livebait. In previous lives it was spookily quiet; now you need to book in advance. Clearly the beer, boards and open-kitchen formula is just what the area needed. The Freemasons' kitchen produces the kind of nosh that suits casual pub eating. A few dish descriptions sounded a little odd though: why Brazilian crab cakes? Had they been fully waxed? They tasted good though, carefully presented with salmon roe and sweet chilli sauce. Main courses might include pan-fried venison fillet served with potato rösti, slow-roasted tomatoes and red wine jus, or a risotto with sweet potato, piquillo pepper,

Hartley

The Restaurants

spinach and mascarpone. The best dish was a pud of warm tarte tatin good enough to make us want to return soon. To drink, there's fine Timothy Taylor Landlord beer, or a surprisingly decent global wine selection with a dozen by the glass. *Babies and children welcome; high chairs. Tables outdoors (8, patio).* **Map 21 B4**.

Ship

41 Jew's Row, SW18 1TB (8870 9667). Wandsworth Town rail. **Open** 11am-11pm Mon-Sat; noon-10.30pm Sun. **Meals served** noon-10.30pm Mon-Sat; noon-10pm Sun. **Credit** AmEx, DC, MC, V.

Tucked away behind industrial land, the Ship – owned by the people behind the Alma (*see p96*) – is not an easy place to find or get to, but is worth the effort for a quintessentially English experience of warm beer and meat by the Thames. On summer weekends you can eat riverside from the barbecue or dine alfresco in the sunken garden and terrace. The daily changing menu features produce from the Suffolk Cross lambs, Middle White Pigs, Short Horn cows and Black Rock Hens – 'all specially chosen for their succulence' – that owners Charles and Linda Gotto keep on their Home Farm. Seasonal fare of good, local provenance: let's have more of it. We sampled the gazpacho and some fresh English asparagus that was served with an (unnecessary) fried Home Farm egg. Our lamb steak was a bit rubbery and not the greatest cut of meat – maybe excused by the fact it was the Monday night of a sunny bank holiday weekend. While our huge ribeye steak was done correctly, the chips it came with were highly seasoned; tasty enough, but only misleadingly listed as 'hand cut' on the menu. A chocolate chiller thriller – a mix of Mars and other firm confectionery favourites – scored a big hit with us and other diners. The service can get a bit sketchy, particularly when it's busy, but was fine on the night. *Babies and children admitted (before 7pm). Separate room for hire, seats 15. Tables outdoors (30, riverside garden).* **Map 21 A4**.

South

Waterloo SE1

★ Anchor & Hope NEW

2004 RUNNER-UP BEST GASTROPUB

36 The Cut, SE1 8LP (7928 9898). Southwark tube or Waterloo tube/rail. **Open** 5-11pm Mon; 11am-11pm Tue-Sat. **Lunch served** noon-2.30pm Tue-Sat. **Dinner served** 6-10.30pm Mon-Sat. **Main courses** £10.80-£14. **Credit** MC, V.

Things really seem to be kicking off on the Cut: first Kevin Spacey takes the Old Vic under his wing, then one of London's best gastropubs opens its doors just a few yards up the road. And aptly enough, there's a certain sense of theatre to the Anchor & Hope's menu, which can stretch to such unusual combinations as snail, preserved rabbit and watercress salad (delicious, by the way). The space itself is a low-key arrangement of relaxed bar area and slightly more formal dining room, elegantly partitioned by a curtain. As for the menu, you can expect wonderfully delicate starters like greens and mozzarella on toast or heartier mains such as perfectly pink lamb neck with green tomatoes. Rice pudding and rhubarb pot would be a typical finale. So, no complaints, then? Not quite: for some reason, you can't book a table here, which left us (and others) waiting longer than we'd have liked. Still, a decent range of sherries and inventive bar snacks (bruschetta, lamb chops and the like) helped the time pass quickly. *Babies and children welcome. Bookings not accepted. Tables outdoors (4, pavement).* **Map 11 N9**.

South East

Bermondsey SE1

Garrison

99-101 Bermondsey Street, SE1 3XB (7089 9355/ www.thegarrison.co.uk). London Bridge tube/rail. **Open** noon-11pm Mon-Sat; noon-10.30pm Sun.

Lunch served noon-3.30pm Mon-Fri; 12.30-4pm Sat, Sun. **Dinner served** 6-10pm Mon-Sat; 6-9.30pm Sun. **Main courses** £6.90-£14. **Service** 12.5%. **Credit** AmEx, MC, V.

Full of sunlight, pleasant breezes and an assortment of tiny Formica tables and bright, blond wood furniture, the Garrison feels more like a trendy beachside snack shack than a pub. It's very much an after-work chatting space, and music is kept low so that couples, friends in twos and larger gangs can drink and debate at volume. It is also very popular, so booking is advised. Food is classic 'new pub', with soups, seafood, salads and other such elementary teasers to start, and mains tending towards the healthy likes of sea bass, cod fillet (served with crab mash) and a rather dry haddock and prawn pie. There is a (smallish) duck dish and lamb shank if you want something less wholesome. Beer was on the warm side, and a sampling of the wines on offer by the glass suggested the bottles are occasionally very good, but uneven – a Chablis was more boring than the fizzy water. Desserts include a crispy crème brûlée, and decent ice-cream. Service from two different waiters was fast, friendly and accommodating. The Garrison hasn't quite put food at the centre of its plans yet, but the ingredients are there for it to become a top gastropub. *Babies and children admitted (lunch Sat, Sun only). Booking advisable. Disabled: toilet. Separate room for hire, seats 40.* **Map 12 Q9**.

★ Hartley NEW

2004 RUNNER-UP BEST GASTROPUB

64 Tower Bridge Road, SE1 4TR (7394 7023/ www.thehartley.com). Borough tube/Elephant & Castle tube/rail then 1 or 188 bus. **Open** noon-11.30pm Mon-Fri; 11am-11pm Sat; noon-10.30pm Sun. **Lunch served** noon-3pm Mon-Fri; 11am-5pm Sat. **Dinner served** 6-10pm Mon-Sat. **Meals served** 11am-6pm Sun. **Main courses** £7.50-£13.50. **Credit** MC, V.

In an odd part of town where, until relatively recently, eating in the pub would have meant taking peanuts with your pint, the Hartley comes as a welcome shot in the arm. For one thing, it's easy on the eye (claret-coloured walls, exposed brick, floorboards, fun black and white prints dotted around) but, more importantly, it has an inventive menu that manages not to lapse into pretentiousness. A specials board touts interesting combinations (pork belly with frogs' legs, chorizo, parsley and garlic springs to mind), while the menu proper offers half a dozen choices in each course. Organic meat from Ginger Pig farms shines through in dishes such as terrine of foie gras, chicken and ham knuckle or main-course roast suckling pig with new season garlic (the highlight of our most recent visit). Otherwise, the house 'salmon and smoked salmon' fish cakes are some of the best we've tasted. Puddings are simple but devastatingly delicious; wines are good and affordable. Staff are polite, knowledgeable and justifiably proud of their product. *Babies and children welcome (before 6pm). Entertainment: jazz 8pm alternate Tue.*

Dulwich SE22

Palmerston NEW

91 Lordship Lane, SE22 8EP (8693 1629). East Dulwich rail. **Open** noon-11pm Mon-Sat; noon-10.30pm Sun. **Lunch served** noon-2.30pm Tue-Sat; noon-5pm Sun. **Dinner served** 7-10pm Mon-Sat. **Main courses** £9-£14. **Credit** MC, V.

The Palmerston, when it was just a bog-standard pub, was strictly an old blokes and cheap beer kind of joint. A fresh lick of paint and the recent appearance of a menu in the window signalled change, as did the sweetbreads listed on the menu. Three weeks after opening, it was already heaving with young East Dulwich professionals who clearly appreciate chef Jamie Younger's enthusiasm for seasonal British produce (or was it the wallet- and palate-friendly wine list?). Lamb sweetbreads were succulent and perfectly complemented by peas, mint and slivers of crispy bacon. A roast rump of Welsh lamb with garlic and rosemary was every bit as good. An adjacent

table of four declared the steak superb and the haddock and sweetcorn soup 'a perfect balance of flavours'. Roast fillet of wild sea bass was flavoursome, partnered with crème fraîche and a relish of tomato, broad bean and tarragon. Cheeses were superb and winsomely paired with fig chutney – much better than the bland desserts. Well-cooked, well-sourced food with a menu that changes daily. The old blokes are now pining into their pints up the road at the Forresters.
Babies and children welcome; high chairs. Booking advisable weekends. No-smoking rooms. Tables outdoors (5, pavement). **Map 23 C4**.

East
Bow E3

Morgan NEW
43 Morgan Street, E3 5AA (8980 6389/ www.geronimo-inns.co.uk). Mile End tube.
Open noon-11pm Mon-Sat; noon-10.30pm Sun.
Lunch served noon-3pm Mon-Sat; noon-4pm Sun. **Dinner served** 7-10pm Mon-Sat. **Main courses** £10.95-£15.50. **Credit** MC. V.
Given the handsome location in an unusually well-scrubbed bit of Bow, it's no surprise that the refit of the Morgan Arms has produced classic comfort in the familiar gastropub mode – plump leather sofas, Sunday-supplement fireplace decorations, plus some funky touches like the plastic fluorescent discs in the windows. The somewhat Sloaney clientele is a warm mix of drinkers and diners (half the pub is reserved for the latter) and, despite being kept busy, staff are chatty and helpful. It's a shame, then, that the food doesn't live up to an exciting menu. The selection of nibbles (chilli peppers stuffed with feta, olives, roasted garlic) was a muted success, largely thanks to superb bread, but lamb kebab starters were chewy and their pea and mint houmous a disappointment, while the main-course calf's liver lacked the proper creamy texture. It can't help that the 'very elegant open kitchen' (according to the website) seemed barely big enough for the three chefs to stand abreast. The high-walled paved garden is a definite bonus in warmer weather. All in all? Not yet the treat it promised to be.
Disabled: toilet. Tables outdoors (11, garden; 4, pavement).

Hackney E8

Cat & Mutton NEW
76 Broadway Market, E8 4QJ (7254 5599). London Fields rail/Bethnal Green tube then 106, 253 bus/26, 48, 55 bus. **Open** 6-11pm Mon; noon-11pm Tue-Sat; noon-10.30pm Sun.
Lunch served noon-3pm Tue-Sat; noon-5.30pm Sun. **Dinner served** 6-10pm Mon-Sat. **Set dinner** (Mon) £12.50 2 courses, £15 3 courses. **Credit** AmEx, MC, V.
The Cat & Mutton was previously a hard-faced Hackney boozer whose epitaph came in the unedifying form of a yellow police sandwich board outside the door reporting an assault. Out with the old local, in with the new: never was the tipping point of gentrification so starkly illustrated as it is here. The new Cat & Mutton is a handsome space, tactfully converted (plenty of wood, school chairs, exposed brickwork and massive plate-glass windows). Add to this big-taste, robust cooking and it's no surprise that the genial crowd of regulars seem only too happy to make this a home from home. Sunday lunch is a big draw (despite pretty hefty prices), while at other times you can expect starters such as sweet potato and cherry tomato confit salad or a simple soup of the day (perfect for dunking some of the excellent own-made bread). Mains range from barnsley chop to roast trout with herb couscous, while puddings are nicely rendered versions of gastropub staples (vanilla bean ice-cream with Illy 'liquor', for example). The only downside is the service, which was routinely (and unapologetically) forgetful during both our visits.
Babies and children admitted; high chairs. Booking advisable. Entertainment: DJs 5.30-10.30pm Sun. Tables outdoors (6, pavement).

Shoreditch EC2
Fox Dining Room
28 Paul Street, EC2A 4LB (7729 5708). Old Street tube/rail. **Open** noon-11pm Mon-Fri. **Lunch served** 12.30-3pm, **dinner served** 6.30-10pm Mon-Fri. **Main courses** £10.25. **Set meal** £15 2 courses, £19.75 3 courses. **Credit** MC, V.
Above the type of careworn old-school boozer you can't help but admire in the middle of fashion-forward Hoxton lies the Fox Dining Room. But while the name might sound highfalutin, really this is just an ordinary second bar, given over to anyone caring for a short daily menu enriched by seasonal produce. From the dark-wood pub tables to the steady approach to service, everything feels acceptable – never giving undue cause for praise or consternation – and that includes the food. To start, the heavy prospect of lentil and lemon soup was lifted by a light zestiness, and skate benefited from a cucumber and caperberry counterpoint. Main dishes proved pleasant enough: asparagus tart with hollandaise had long spears of the vegetable balanced between two free-floating tiles of puff pastry, while sea bass came with a thicket of moreish purple sprouting broccoli. Some unadventurous puds included a rhubarb and almond option so scant on fruit that it resembled bakewell tart. Fair overall, but lacking the gastro flair that would encourage destination dining.
Babies and children admitted. Booking advisable. Restaurant available for hire, seats 36. Tables outdoors (6, terrace). **Map 6 Q4**.

Victoria Park E3
Crown
223 Grove Road, E3 5SN (8981 9998/ www.singhboulton.co.uk). Mile End tube/277 bus. **Open** 5-11pm Mon; noon-11pm Tue-Fri; 10.30am-11pm Sat; 10.30am-10.30pm Sun. **Breakfast served** 10.30am-12.15pm Sat, Sun. **Lunch served** noon-4pm Tue-Fri; 12.30-4pm Sat, Sun. **Dinner served** 6.30-10.30pm Mon-Sat; 6.30-10pm Sun. **Main courses** £8-£14.50. **Set lunch** (Tue-Fri) £6.50 1 course incl drink. **Credit** MC, V.
One of London's few fully organic gastropubs, this venture from the Singhboulton team – also at the Duke of Cambridge; *see p100* – is an airy boozer that has kept its easy-going charm. But while impeccably sourced dishes and organic beverages (some spirits, a handful of lagers and an extensive wine list) can do little wrong in the eyes of virtuous foodies, the service is woefully inadequate. Greeted by staff with the kind of troubling haircuts that demand quarantining in Hoxton Square, we were invited to have gin and tonic. Subsequently, we learned they'd run out of tonic. The upstairs dining area is adjacent to a function room, so a stream of party-goers pushed past, sometimes leaning on our table, sometimes just hailing each other loudly and trading air-kisses. On occasion, the restaurant closes due to group bookings and, judging by our experience, that would seem the less disruptive option. Our food tasted consistently good: the simplicity of starters such as babaganoush and chicken liver pâté, and mains of chilli con carne and whole baked trout allowed the quality of the ingredients to sing. Pear crumble and rhubarb cheesecake sounded appetising, but slack service meant we didn't hang around to find out.
Babies and children welcome; high chairs. Booking advisable weekend. Disabled: toilet. No smoking (restaurant). Restaurant available for hire. Separate rooms for hire, seat 20 and 30. Tables outdoors (8, terrace; 5, balcony).

North
Archway N19

★ St John's
91 Junction Road, N19 5QU (7272 1587). Archway tube. **Open** 5-11pm Mon; noon-11pm Tue-Sat; noon-10.30pm Sun. **Lunch served** noon-3.30pm Tue-Fri; noon-4pm Sat, Sun. **Dinner served** 6.30-11pm Mon-Sat; 6.30-10.30pm Sun. **Main courses** £9-£14. **Service** 12.5% for parties of 6 or more. **Credit** AmEx, MC, V.
Welcome to your new favourite place to eat. A pub. In Archway. Who'd have thought it? The front room houses the usual mismatched chairs and tables, and distressed leather sofas, arranged around a sweeping bar of waxed wood. The dining room is church-hall big, painted murky green and maroon, with a high golden ceiling and the oddest assemblage of slightly freakish portraits. However, the mood stays light thanks to full tables (bookings are a must) and chatty but efficient staff. Food is terrific. The blackboard menu features presumably whatever was fresh at market that day – lots of red meat, some fish, but, on a recent visit, only one dish for vegetarians. Fresh loaves are stacked at the serving counter and sliced for newly arrived diners. Squid was scored with a crosshatch pattern, rolled and presented with a little bouquet of tentacles sticking out of the middle. A breast of duck was garnished with a roast pear. The squid ink risotto that accompanied a slab of seared tuna was slightly crunchy and not at all soggy (plus there's the fun of seeing your dining partner with lips dyed like Marilyn Manson's). Desserts include the sticky toffee pudding of your dreams. The crowd is pleasingly varied in age, dress and attitude, the one common denominator being that all know a good thing when they taste it.
Babies and children welcome; booster seats. Booking essential. Tables outdoors (7, patio). **Map 26 B1**.

Camden Town & Chalk Farm NW1
Engineer
65 Gloucester Avenue, NW1 8JH (7722 0950/ www.the-engineer.com). Chalk Farm tube/31, 168 bus. **Open** 9am-11pm Mon-Sat; 9am-10.30pm Sun. **Breakfast served** 9-11.30am Mon-Fri; 9am-noon Sat, Sun. **Lunch served** noon-3pm Mon-Fri; 12.30-3.30pm Sat, Sun. **Dinner served** 7-11pm Mon-Sat; 7-10pm Sun. **Main courses** £10.50-£16.50. **Service** 12.5%. **Credit** MC, V.
Drinkers get short shrift at the Engineer. They have to squeeze into one L-shaped half of the ground floor, while diners get the other half, plus an extension, plus the upstairs dining room. Despite all this dedication, what you get on your plate can be a bit hit or miss. While we liked the soup of the day (a clever mix of coriander, carrot and coconut, in which all three flavours were distinct), and the failure with the crispy whitebait was our fault for ordering adventurously only to realise a couple of mouthfuls later that we didn't like these fishy takes on pork scratchings, the main courses were genuinely disappointing. Jerk baby chicken was bright and flavoursome with red peppers, pineapple, parsley and rice stained purple by kidney beans, but it was also unsophisticated – like something that's served on a paper plate at Notting Hill Carnival. Cornish dressed crab was lacking in meat and far too cold. If we were to visit again – and it's a lovely space with plenty of snug corners and pleasant staff – we'd stick to the seared tuna or roast rack of lamb, confining any flair to the wine list, which is very good indeed.
Babies and children welcome; high chairs. Disabled: toilet. Booking advisable. Separate rooms for hire, seat 20 and 32. Tables outdoors (15, garden). **Map 27 B2**.

★ Lansdowne
90 Gloucester Avenue, NW1 8HX (7483 0409). Chalk Farm tube/31, 168 bus.
Bar **Open** 6-11pm Mon; noon-11pm Tue-Sat; noon-10.30pm Sun. **Lunch served** 12.30-3pm Tue-Sat; 12.30-4pm Sun. **Dinner served** 7-10pm Mon-Sat; 7-9.30pm Sun.
Restaurant **Lunch served** 1-4pm Sun. **Dinner served** 7-10pm Tue-Sat. **Service** 12.5%.
Both **Main courses** £8.50-£15.50. **Credit** MC, V.
Pull up at the Lansdowne in anything less than an MG or another sporty little number, and you're liable to be struck by the sudden onset of a crippling inferiority complex. This is a pub for the pretty people – as in pretty rich and pretty smug about it. Which isn't to take anything away from the place itself, a good-looking, open-plan boozer that exudes good cheer (and good health, courtesy

Cat & Mutton

of organic drinks including Clausthaler lager, bottled Breton cider, Burrow Hill cider and Woodforde's Wherry Bitter). You can eat in the bar area or plump for the upstairs restaurant – a simple, high-ceilinged room with a sober but sexy black and red colour scheme, a smoky jazz soundtrack and a sweet Lithuanian waitress. The food is largely superb. Dishes are vaguely Mediterranean and range from the trad (gazpacho) to the ambitious (crab and pea ravioli). Standouts were the mustardy beignets that accompanied a seared slab of ribeye, and the unusual mix of pappardelle with chicken livers. The only disappointment were the desserts; on a previous visit, we melted over a gingerstem panna cotta, but this time a summer fruit pavlova was oversized and rock-hard. Pavlovan hiccup aside, the Lansdowne remains in the top percentile of gastropubs, which is why booking is essential, particularly at weekends.
Babies and children welcome (restaurant; before 7pm bar). Booking advisable weekends. Disabled: toilet. Restaurant available for hire. Tables outdoors (8, pavement). **Map 27 B2**.

Queens
49 Regent's Park Road, NW1 8XD (7586 0408/ www.geronimo-inns.co.uk). Chalk Farm tube/ 31, 168, 274 bus. **Open** 11am-11pm Mon-Sat; noon-10.30pm Sun. **Lunch served** noon-3pm Mon-Sat; 12.30-4pm Sun. **Dinner served** 7-10pm Mon-Sat; 7-9pm Sun. **Main courses** £7.95-£14.95. **Credit** MC, V.
Let's face it, if you've got a lovely old corner pub practically on the grassy verge of Primrose Hill, you're not going to serve Fray Bentos pies and Smash (although given the strength of the location, you could probably get away with it), but, to its credit, the Queens has also managed not to succumb to the clichés of the identikit gastropub. It may have some of the ingredients (the snugs of the ground-floor bar, the briskly modern decor in the upstairs dining room, a smattering of tapenade and parmesan shavings among its dishes), but this is a place with heart (and history) and what it does, it does well and with an endearing lack of pretension. Starters include the likes of sesame and soy beef salad with crispy noodles, and soup of the day (for a very reasonable £3.95). Char-grilled rump of lamb with sweet potato wedges, spinach and feta parcel is a typically tasty main course. More adventurous dishes might include seared duck breast with wonderful Jersey royals partnered with chorizo. If you have the stamina, try a pudding too; and why not dip into some of the wines available by the glass. Service is never less than excellent.
Babies and children admitted. Booking advisable; essential Sun. Tables outdoors (3, balcony; 3, pavement). **Map 27 A2**.

Islington N1, N7

Barnsbury
209-211 Liverpool Road, N1 1LX (7607 5519/ www.thebarnsbury.co.uk). Angel tube/Highbury & Islington tube/rail. **Open** noon-11pm Mon-Sat; noon-10.30pm Sun. **Lunch served** noon-3pm Mon-Fri; noon-4pm Sat, Sun. **Dinner served** 6.30-10pm Mon-Sat; 6.30-9.30pm Sun. **Main courses** £8.50-£14. **Service** 12.5%. **Credit** AmEx, MC, V.
It may be hard up against dark and down-at-heel Liverpool Road, but with millionaires' rows just a skip away, the Barnsbury is hardly slumming it. Not a me-too gastropub, it calls itself a 'freehouse and dining room', and is refreshingly modest. Chandeliers cleverly fashioned out of wine glasses light the horseshoe bar, which acts as an easy-going concierge to the front and rear dining areas – the former far more cosy with its (albeit fake) fire and constant chatter; wood floors, of course, reach to all corners. The menu is democratic, split between stalwarts such as french onion soup and more adventurous numbers such as smoked chicken with pepper and orange relish. A salad of warm chorizo was lovely: the fulsome taste of the chorizo bitten back deliciously by al dente butter beans and bittersweet cherry tomatoes. Another

starter, a prawn and crayfish cocktail, was decent but unexceptional and, in keeping with the generally disappointing accompaniments (sadly, even the chips), its side of pumpernickel bread was rather dry. The hearty path seems the best to take: a main of char-grilled ribeye steak was judiciously rare and covered with an earthy wild mushroom sauce. The puddings are nothing to dream about, but when knocked back with a bottle of the rich St Gilles house red, only the most spoilt Islingtonian would think to complain.

Babies and children welcome; high chairs. Booking advisable. Disabled: toilet. Restaurant available for hire, seats 80. Tables outdoors (4, pavement; 6, garden). **Map 5 N1**.

Centuria

100 St Paul's Road, N1 2QP (7704 2345). Highbury & Islington tube/rail/30, 277 bus. **Open** 5-11pm Mon-Fri; noon-11pm Sat; noon-10.30pm Sun. **Dinner served** 6-11pm Mon-Fri. **Meals served** 12.30-11pm Sat; 12.30-10.30pm Sun. **Main courses** £6.95-£12.50. **Credit** MC, V.
Just on the border of hinterland Islington, Centuria harvests a healthy weekend crop of young local families and twentysomething couples. But if you live outside, or even inside, the food-crammed N1 postcode, this is not food worth leaving a Sunday bed for. Choice is not the problem – the long menu (which stays the same for about two months) skips from Mediterranean to gastropub to seafood, and is boosted by a sizeable blackboard specials menu. The cooking, however, is lacklustre. Cod with a yoghurt 'crust' and stir-fried vegetables was soggy and textureless; lamb tagine with prunes and sweet onion was unremittingly tough and eventually taken off our bill. The chefs, in full open-kitchen view, even look a bit bored – regularly provoking the grill into high flames and smoke. Disappointing given the light, tasty starters of prawn tempura and grilled veg and halloumi cheese, and a shame since the restaurant itself, which is annexed to an airy, relaxed pub room, is a pleasant space. Service, too, is good-natured.
Children admitted; high chairs. Booking advisable. Restaurant available for hire, seats 75. Tables outdoors (6, pavement). **Map 25 A5**.

★ Drapers Arms

44 Barnsbury Street, N1 1ER (7619 0348/ www.thedrapersarms.co.uk). Highbury & Islington tube/rail. **Open** noon-11pm Mon-Sat; noon-10.30pm Sun. **Lunch served** noon-3pm daily. **Dinner served** 7-10pm Mon-Sat. **Main courses** £9-£15. **Service** 12.5%. **Credit** AmEx, MC, V.
Considering quite how swanky some of the housing is around these parts, the Drapers Arms has done a fine job of remaining boho in feel. The ground-floor bar is nice and airy, lots of light shines in, and there's outdoor space at the back. Food can be eaten on this level, or in the more elegant first-floor dining room. Drinks run from pints to a short but decent list of wines. The menu can get pretty ambitious (baked aubergine risotto cake with pimentos and fried halloumi), but offers comfort food too (own-made beef burger with guacamole, bacon and blue cheese), plus a few brunch items on Sunday (full cooked breakfasts, including a veggie version). The quality is high: a starter of fried goat's cheese with almonds, lamb's lettuce and orange was a delicate treat; gazpacho with crostini of white anchovies was more robustly flavoured, but also lip-smackingly good. To follow, a generous portion of caesar salad with chilli tiger prawns, and deep-fried plaice, pea purée and chips with crème fraîche tartare sauce maintained the high, with only the slightly dried-out chips spoiling the party. Finish with the likes of sticky toffee pudding and you'll be more than set up for the day.
Babies and children welcome; high chairs. Booking advisable. Tables outdoors (20, garden). **Map 5 N1**.

Duchess of Kent NEW

441 Liverpool Road, N7 8PR (7609 7104/ www.geronimo-inns.co.uk). Highbury & Islington tube/rail. **Open** noon-11pm Mon-Sat; noon-10.30pm Sun. **Lunch served** noon-3pm Mon-Fri;

Wells. See p102.

noon-4pm Sat. **Dinner served** 7-10pm Mon-Sat. **Meals served** noon-8pm Sun. **Main courses** £7.95-£14.95. **Set lunch** £5.95 1 course and drink. **Credit** MC, V.
Geronimo! we thought, as soon as we walked in. And we were right: this is the latest gastropub from the highly acclaimed Geronimo Inns, a growing little pub chain. Geronimo places all look different, but they share a distinctive well-furnished look. Not all serve great food, but this one does. Everything on the menu sounded mouthwatering: a cool starter of watermelon, feta cheese and pumpkin seed salad was ideal on the summer's day we visited. Tender and delicately fried squid was equally modern Mediterranean, nicely paired with a lime and coriander mayonnaise. Main courses include a rib-eye steak with fat chips and a béarnaise sauce, cooked beautifully rare, and the portion so generous we couldn't finish it. Roast skate wing was a lighter dish, served with lemon and caper butter and new potatoes. Puds include banana brûlée and chocolate tart. This Duchess has made an impressive transition from common boozer to gastropub gentry.
Babies and children admitted. Booking advisable dinner. Disabled: toilet. Tables outdoors (10, pavement).

Duke of Cambridge

30 St Peter's Street, N1 8JT (7359 3066/ www.singhboulton.co.uk). Angel tube. **Open** noon-11pm Mon-Sat; noon-10.30pm Sun. **Lunch**

served 12.30-3pm Mon-Fri; 12.30-3.30pm Sat, Sun. **Dinner served** 6.30-10.30pm Mon-Sat; 6.30-10pm Sun. **Main courses** £9.50-£15. **Service** 12.5% for parties of 5 or more. **Credit** MC, V.
This organic pub and restaurant is perennially popular. It's easy to see the attraction; even in the main open-plan pub area there's an easy-going ambience. A shame then that the food lets the side down. There's no questioning the owners' integrity – the commitment to organic ingredients is so strong that they apologise for not being able to get hold of organic whiskies. But it can seem as if the ingredients are thrown together, as if the quality speaks for itself. Courgette, spinach and mint soup, and smoked mackerel terrine with pickle, relish and butter beans were helped by their simplicity. Ribeye with chorizo and potato stew, watercress and herb butter was, it must be said, weird. The steak was excellent, but the stew was a mush of nothingness. A lamb burger with braised lentils, green beans, semi-dried tomatoes and olive salsa and tapenade met with a more approval – again, the excellent meat standing out – but was, again, rather bizarre. Desserts were better: a gooey chocolate brownie with chocolate sauce and crème fraîche was spot-on. Drinks are a forte, but staff seem to get more brusque and less efficient the busier the place gets. The pub is owned by the same company that runs the Crown (see p98).
Babies and children welcome; high chairs. Booking advisable. No smoking. Restaurant available for hire, seats 35. Tables outdoors (6, courtyard; 4, pavement). **Map 5 O2**.

House

63-69 Canonbury Road, N1 2DG (7704 7410/ www.inthehouse.biz). Highbury & Islington tube/rail. **Open** 5-11pm Mon; noon-11pm Tue-Sat; noon-10.30pm Sun. **Lunch served** noon-2.30pm Tue-Sun. **Dinner served** 6-10.30pm Mon-Fri; 6.30-10.30pm Sat, Sun. **Main courses** £12.95-£45. **Service** 12.5%. **Credit** MC, V.

The House won the best gastropub award at the *Time Out* Eating & Drinking Awards in 2003. It's got a lot going for it, not least chic decor and a lively atmosphere. Service doesn't always hit the spot, though – we were given a frosty welcome, and a couple of waiters were a bit offhand. Starters were good – crispy duck salad with watercress, beanshoots and oriental dressing. The duck was meaty, yet crisp on the outside; the sauce tangy but sweet. Mains continued the good work. Deep-fried lemon sole in chilli ciabatta breadcrumbs was much lighter than it sounded. Corn-fed chicken with mashed potatoes, baby leeks and chillied hazelnuts also hit the spot, the meat juicy, the mash creamy. The only bum note came from disappointing desserts. Warm gingerbread with clotted cream was comforting, but the big chunks of ginger weren't to our liking. Banana tatin with coconut ice-cream was worse – the pastry bogged down by dry, mushy fruit. An interesting wine list adds a final upbeat note.
Babies and children welcome. Bookings not accepted. Disabled: toilet. No-smoking tables. Tables outdoors (6, garden).

Northgate

113 Southgate Road, N1 3JS (7359 7392). Angel tube/Essex Road rail/38, 73 bus. **Open** 5-11pm Mon-Fri; noon-11pm Sat; noon-10.30pm Sun. **Lunch served** noon-4pm Sat, Sun. **Dinner served** 6.30-10.30pm Mon-Sat; 6.30-9.30pm Sun. **Main courses** £9-£13.50. **Set lunch** (Sun) £12.50 2 courses. **Credit** MC, V.

With its mint green walls, brass fittings and mini chandeliers, the Northgate's dimly lit back dining room certainly has an appealing and arresting ambience. Dishes tend to be refreshingly straightforward and prices reasonable given the decent portion sizes. However, our most recent meal here was a bit of a hit and miss affair: high points at either end, with disappointment coming in between. We kicked off with a huge bowl of spiced lentil and coriander soup with yoghurt – excellent, thick, earthy. Barbecue baby back ribs could have made a main course, and though it wasn't the meatiest of cuts the tangy tomatoey sauce shone through. Mains were a let-down in comparison. Char-grilled ribeye steak was good quality, with requisite charcoal taste, but the accompanying chips were merely so-so and the beans on the crunchy side of al dente. Confit of duck leg with braised butter beans, pancetta and cabbage was an unsuccessful, flavourless mishmash. But the meal ended on a real high in the form of a melt-in-the-mouth raspberry and mascarpone crème brûlée, and a moist, rich, flourless chocolate cake with fresh strawberries.

Staff are friendly and the welcoming main pub area serves a couple of well-kept real ales, so we'll be back for another whirl.
Babies and children admitted (restaurant). Booking advisable. Tables outdoors (10, patio). **Map 6 Q1.**

Social

33 Linton Street, Arlington Square, N1 7DU (7354 5809/www.thesocial.com). Angel tube. **Open** 5-11pm Mon-Fri; noon-11pm Sat; noon-10.30pm Sun. **Dinner served** 5-10.30pm Mon-Fri. **Meals served** 12.30-10.30pm Sat; 12.30-9.30pm Sun. **Main courses** £7-£13.50. **Credit** AmEx, MC, V.

Set on the corner of leafy Arlington Square, the Social stays true to its boozer roots, with an old pub sign (Hanbury Arms) outside and a panelled interior, leather sofas and fireplace inside. From the brief menu, mixed smoked fish comprised of layers of decent salmon and haddock, with nicely dressed leaves (the latter popped up repeatedly). Chicken liver pâté was smooth yet substantial, the fruity chutney adding some oomph. A burger was a bargain at £7, and a veritable bundle of taste, with fantastic chips on the side. Lemon chicken with crushed new potatoes and mushrooms came as an amorphous mass rather than separate ingredients – not bad in itself, but pretty boring to chomp through. Again, ingredients were top-notch, the mushrooms juicy, the chicken nicely char-grilled. The lone waitress was a bit offhand, but on the right side of casual. The shortish but interesting wine list has lots of by-the-glass options. Oh, one last thing – it's part of the Nottingham-founded Heavenly Jukebox portfolio, and said jukebox lives up to its divine promise.
Babies and children welcome (until 6pm Sat, Sun). Entertainment: DJs occasional evenings; 4.30pm Sun. Separate room for hire, seats 30. **Map 5 P2.**

Kentish Town NW5

★ Highgate

79 Highgate Road, NW5 1TL (7485 8442). Tufnell Park tube/Kentish Town tube/rail. *Bar* **Open** noon-11pm Mon-Fri; noon-midnight Sat; noon-10.30pm Sun. **Main courses** £6.50-£9.50.
Restaurant **Main courses** £8.50-£14. **Service** 12.5%.
Both **Lunch served** 12.30-3pm Mon-Sat; 12.30-4pm Sun. **Dinner served** 6.30-10.30pm Mon-Sat; 6.30-10pm Sun. **Credit** AmEx, MC, V.

Beware first impressions. Filling the ground-floor space of a modernish office block the Highgate looks like a fitness centre from afar. Closer up, the vast open-plan space with busy bar counter just inside the door and then acres of vacant tables and chairs reminded us of a Marbella hotel lobby. The cut-glass chandeliers that hang from the claret-painted, industrial I-beam and breeze-block ceiling are a half-hearted stab at warmth and character. But forget all that and eat. The food is astoundingly good. Inventive too. Chicken liver parfait came with a slithery, rubbery chutney of runner beans (sounds odd, but tasted great), while another starter had a poached egg wreathed by baby leeks vinegarette (looked great, but tasted strange). Presentation peaked with a glacier of baked cod on a pebble beach of white beans and cockles, while top of the flavour charts was a crispy carapace of pork belly simmered in cider. Desserts are supposed to be good, but, really, we couldn't. Staff are cheerful. Plus, how many London restaurants boast a view of a kneeling camel – albeit fibreglass and belonging to an oriental carpet shop across the road?
Babies and children admitted (until 8pm). Bar available for hire. Booking advisable. Disabled: toilet. Separate room for hire, holds 150. Tables outdoors (3, pavement). **Map 26 A4.**

Junction Tavern

101 Fortess Road, NW5 1AG (7485 9400). Tufnell Park tube/Kentish Town tube/rail. **Open** noon-11pm Mon-Sat; noon-10.30pm Sun. **Lunch served** noon-3pm Mon-Fri; noon-4pm Sat, Sun.

Dinner served 6.30-10.30pm Mon-Sat; 6.30-9.30pm Sun. **Main courses** £7.50-£13. **Set lunch** (Sun) £12.50 2 courses. **Credit** MC, V.
Fortess Road is a grim location, but the JT is cosy inside. Front of house is the dining operation with open-plan kitchen – although the serving counter is so high all anyone can see is the heads of the chefs at work. Walls are claret, but otherwise bare, the off-white ceiling is high, and tables are reasonably spaced, so nobody feels cramped even if the place is pretty busy – which it usually is. The food doesn't aim for fireworks, but classic ideas and combinations are competently prepared. If we were going to be picky, we'd say that our roast lamb and new potato broth was a little light on meat, while the potato wedges that came with a char-grilled ribeye were oversalted. A starter of sautéed chicken livers with sherry vinegar was, however, excellent (the good news is this seems to be a standard on an otherwise frequently changing menu). The wine list, though cheap (mostly £11-£16), could use a little more excitement. Food can also be ordered in the large conservatory at the rear, which leads to a decent beer garden. Real ales include London Pride, Deuchars IPA and a regularly changing quirky guest ale.
Babies and children welcome. Booking advisable. Tables outdoors (15, garden). **Map 26 B4.**

Tufnell Park NW5

Dartmouth Arms
35 York Rise, NW5 1SP (7485 3267). Tufnell Park tube. **Open** 11am-11pm Mon-Fri; 10am-11pm Sat; 10am-10.30pm Sun. **Lunch served** 11am-3pm, **dinner served** 6-10pm Mon-Fri; **Meals served** 10am-10pm Sat, Sun. **Main courses** £7-£11. **Credit** MC, V.
How to define a gastropub? A pub that does food? But then they nearly all do, in some form or another. A pub that does food incorporating liberal amounts of rocket? That's closer it. Whatever the definition, it's probably stretching it to call the Dartmouth a gastropub, because this place is all kinds of things to all kinds of people. It's a micro bookstore. It's the setter of fortnightly pub quizzes and weekend venue for amateur club nights (bring your own records). It's a gathering point for sports fans who congregate under the TV for significant fixtures. It's a venue for regular wine tastings, and on Thursday it's a celebration of things Iberian with tapas platters and Spanish plonk. And, yes, it does food. Wednesday is steak night – an 8oz rib-eye with chips and a glass of red wine for £11 – but we prefer Sunday for exceptional roasts, chicken or beef, served with all the trimmings for eight quid. Otherwise, during the week expect well-made sandwiches, char-grilled vegetable stacks or toulouse sausage with mash. Beers include Badger, Adnams Bitter, and Hoegaarden, plus Aspall Cider, while wines are chosen with similar care. Maybe not a gastropub, but one of the best locals in London.
Babies and children welcome (before 8pm). Entertainment: open decks from 6pm Sat. Restaurant available for hire. **Map 26 A3.**

Lord Palmerston
33 Dartmouth Park Hill, NW5 1HU (7485 1578). Tufnell Park tube. **Open** noon-11pm Mon-Sat; noon-10.30pm Sun. **Lunch served** 12.30-3pm Mon-Sat; 1-4pm Sun. **Dinner served** 7-10pm Mon-Sat; 7-9pm Sun. **Main courses** £8.75-£13. **Credit** MC, V.
There's a school of thought that says the mark of a true aristocrat is shambolic dress and poor personal grooming. If you agree, then the Lord Palmerston is the genuine article – a real class act among a slew of gastro-pretenders. There's no open kitchen to establish credentials, nor even a designated dining area: it's just a big shabby pub with a Quaker meeting house austerity. Grab a table in the main bar, in the conservatory to the rear, or out on the forecourt; read the list of dishes off the barely decipherable blackboard; then place your order at the bar. The food is no-nonsense pub fare with a bit of Mediterranean dash (burgers, steaks, fish, all made with first-rate ingredients and prepared with flair, attention to detail and

generosity. Starters never seem to get much of a look-in, with only a couple of choices, but the main courses are so generous that going hungry is never an issue. Anyway, the puds are usually excellent; on a recent visit we had a slab of banoffi pie that was as light and creamy as (a light and creamy) cheesecake, plus a lovely raspberry brûlée, easy on the sugar. The place is always packed, mostly with locals who seem to have decided to bugger the trip to Waitrose for one day and nipped into the Lord P for supper instead. Sensible folk.
Babies and children welcome. Bookings not accepted. Separate rooms for hire, seats 35. Tables outdoors (5, garden; 13, pavement). **Map 26 B3.**

North West

Belsize Park NW3

Hill
94 Haverstock Hill, NW3 2BD (7267 0033/ www.geronimo-inns.co.uk). Belsize Park or Chalk Farm tube. **Open** 4-11pm Mon-Thur; noon-11pm Fri, Sat; noon-10.30pm Sun. **Lunch served** noon-3pm Fri, Sat. **Dinner served** 7-10pm Mon-Sat. **Meals served** noon-7pm Sun. **Main courses** £8.95-£15. **Credit** MC, V.
Sometimes a venue changes hands and you never notice; other times it hits you like a slap in the face with a poached sea bass. Such was the case when former grotty boozer the Load of Hay was reborn as the dandyish Hill. Now the Hill has changed hands again and the difference is hardly less striking. Gone are the fabulous funky design details of last year to be replaced with… well, very little. The Hill hasn't so much had a makeover as been gutted. What's happened to the cooking is even worse. From a fairly standard menu (duck, lamb, sea bass) comes fairly dismal fare. Salt and pepper squid was couched in inedible soggy batter. Curled shards of sea bass came with just six tuppenny-piece slices of fried potato plus mayo, while roundels of admittedly succulent lamb came with nothing other than a slag heap of lentils. While there is something to be said for simplicity, at these prices (up to £15 for mains) we felt cheated. Strange. because the new owners are Geronimo Inns, a company with plenty of experience in running top-class establishments. Perhaps it's just early days and things will improve – in the meantime, visit for the garden terrace and excellent König Ludwig weissbier.
Babies and children admitted. Booking essential weekends. Separate room for hire, seats 24. Tables outdoors (20, garden). **Map 28 C4.**

Hampstead NW3

★ Wells
2004 RUNNER-UP BEST GASTROPUB
30 Well Walk, NW3 1BX (7794 3785/www. thewellshampstead.co.uk). Hampstead tube. **Bar Open** noon-11pm Mon-Sat; noon-10.30pm Sun. **Lunch served** noon-3pm, **dinner served** 7-9.30pm daily. **Main courses** £8.95-£15.25.
Restaurant **Lunch served** noon-3pm daily. **Dinner served** 7-10pm Mon-Thur; 7-10.30pm Fri, Sat; 7-9.30pm Sun. **Set lunch** (Mon-Fri) £14.50 2 courses, £19.50 3 courses (Sat, Sun) £20 2 courses, £25 3 courses. **Set dinner** £24.50 2 courses, £29.50 3 courses.
Both **Service** 12.5%. **Credit** AmEx, DC, MC, V.
This leafy Hampstead backwater must be one of London's prettiest quarters, and the Wells is no disgrace to its surroundings. In fact, it cuts a very elegant figure with its smart exterior and stylishly simple black and white colour scheme inside. The ground-floor bar is where the cheaper menu operates, while upstairs a more formal dining space makes the most of some beautiful Georgian windows and offers a pricier modern British menu (three courses for £27.50; jerusalem artichoke soup; loin of hare with red cabbage and celariac purée; poached champagne rhubarb and vanilla rice pudding). We tried the bar menu. A starter of chilled pea soup with crispy parma ham was a wonderful summer dish spiked with garden-fresh flavours. A main course of wild boar and apple sausages was less breathtaking, but the house

burger served with fat chips and well-dressed salad proved to be juicy and extremely moreish. And while this is by no means an old-fashioned boozer, the atmosphere is such that you may also want to just pop in for a slurp of wine and a game on one of the stylish glass chess sets.
Babies and children welcome. Booking advisable. Disabled: toilet. No-smoking (restaurant). Separate room for hire, seats 12. Tables outdoors (6, patio). **Map 28 C2.**

Queen's Park NW6

Salusbury
50-52 Salusbury Road, NW6 6NN (7328 3286). Queen's Park tube/rail. **Open** 5-11pm Mon; noon-11pm Tue-Sat; noon-10.30pm Sun. **Lunch served** 12.30-3.30pm Tue-Sun. **Dinner served** 7-10.15pm Mon-Sat; 7-10pm Sun. **Main courses** £9.50-£16.50. **Set lunch** (Mon-Fri) £5 1 course incl 1 drink. **Credit** MC, V.
Just north of the unremittingly bleak urbanism surrounding Queen's Park station, Salusbury Road very suddenly goes all Hampstead, with a string of neat façades, a boutique bookshop, a fine food store and this very good gastropub. The pub is divided into two: the bar is intimate, more café-bar than boozer, and almost too small for all the chatter and curling cigarette smoke. The dining room is bigger, with an artfully stage-managed look of scuffed floorboards and chunky wooden furniture, all reflected in the two dozen or so mirrors that adorn the walls. The food is better than average, with lobster and rabbit supplementing steaks and lamb medallions. Presentation is excellent – prawns were served halved lengthways, and lobster was balled and on its back, with feelers and claws shooting up like some crustaceous floral arrangement. But the chefs could be a little more spirited with the spices: prawns, lobster and squid were all advertised as 'with chilli' – yet we couldn't taste any. Similarly, the promised lemon and thyme was absent from the bunny. Judging by the number of families and a table of four elderly matrons dining here on a recent Saturday night, safe but good-quality cooking wins custom in Queen's Park.
Babies and children welcome (before 7pm); high chairs. Booking advisable weekends. Tables outdoors (4, pavement).

St John's Wood NW8

Abbey Road Pub & Dining Room
63 Abbey Road, NW8 0AE (7328 6626). St John's Wood or Kilburn Park tube. **Open** 5-11pm Mon; noon-11pm Tue-Sat; noon-10.30pm Sun. **Lunch served** noon-3.30pm Tue-Sat; noon-4pm Sun. **Dinner served** 7-10.30pm daily. **Main courses** £9.50-£17. **Credit** AmEx, MC, V.
The third refurbishment in as many years sees a new name gracing the former Salt House and a lighter, more relaxed feel to the operation. Gone is the all-black exterior to be replaced by a less forbidding eau de nil, while inside the boudoir has been replaced by duck-egg blue paintwork and light pine furniture. The menu is less ambitious too, concentrating on basics such as rack of lamb, fillet of beef, salmon and sea bass. Basic, but beautifully executed. We greatly enjoyed starters of potato gnocchi with halved cherry tomatoes and melting chunks of mozzarella, and pan-fried squid with chilli: two unfussy dishes that let the flavours do the talking. Similarly, sea bass was baked whole, head and tail intact, and presented on a bed of mixed leaves. Lamb and mash were lifted by a lovely jus of an unidentifiable berry. We also appreciated the attentive service, with waiting staff who were there when needed, but otherwise out of your face (they operate by telepathy, we assume). Weather permitting, the prime dining spot is beneath the Parisian-styled awning over the decked terrace, from where you can observe the local media 'n' music folk in action, mobile in one hand, chardonnay in the other.
Babies and children welcome (before 7pm); high chairs. Booking advisable dinner. Separate room for hire, seats 24. Tables outdoors (12, terrace). **Map 2 D2.**

Global

There's a world to devour out there – and you needn't go beyond the M25. These restaurants specialise in cuisines rarely found in London. Some offer esoteric twists on more familiar cooking styles; others include ingredients that don't often find plate space in Britain. How about a braised elk for tea? Or a spot of kumera mash? Still other venues provide oases of a nation's culture, whether for homesick expats or culinary tourists. You don't need to be John Simpson to sample the flavours of downtown Kabul. Nor need you climb a mountain for a taste of the Alps. Go on, don those lederhosen – you could do würst.

Afghan

North
Islington N1

★ Afghan Kitchen
35 Islington Green, N1 8DU (7359 8019). Angel tube. **Lunch served** noon-3.30pm, **dinner served** 5.30-11pm Tue-Sat. **Main courses** £4.50-£6. **Service** 10%. **No credit cards.**
A recent redecoration has given Afghan Kitchen a slightly more clean-cut, trendier edge, but this popular little spot remains essentially the same. The dining areas (one upstairs, one down) are tiny, so guests crowd around communal tables. Sensibly, the menu is kept short; food is prepared in advance and reheated to order. There's plenty for vegetarians, including an appealing pumpkin with yoghurt and a delectable-looking slow-cooked aubergine dish. Our lentil dahl was nicely cooked, but suffered from being too long in the microwave. More impressive was a dish of kofta murgh, chicken meatballs (more like small patties) that were light and tender, served with fresh peas in a delicately flavoured sauce. Chicken in yoghurt was a gentle braise enhanced by a creamy sauce, which was enthusiastically wiped up with the accompanying flatbread. We were less convinced by Afghan mixed pickles, which, as well as being overwhelmingly vinegary, contained incongruous brussels sprouts. Staff can struggle to keep up the pace, but usually manage a friendly smile or two. The drinks list is very brief: just two bottles of red wine, two of white, plus a couple of bottled beers.
Babies and children admitted; high chairs. Booking advisable. Takeaway service. **Map 5 O2.**

Outer London
Southall, Middlesex

★ Kabul
First floor, Himalaya Shopping Centre, 65-67 The Broadway, Southall, Middx UB1 1LB (8571 6878/www.thekabulrestaurant.com). Southall rail. **Meals served** noon-midnight daily. **Main courses** £1.75-£7.99. **Credit** AmEx, MC, V.
Located on the first floor of a shopping centre that sells Punjabi outfits and glittery knick-knacks, Kabul quietly flies the flag for Southall's resident Afghan community. Decor includes hand-woven carpet hangings and fading memorabilia from Afghanistan's glory days, but it's the vivid blue upholstery that leaves a lasting impression – that and the ads for local businesses on tables. Best bets here are the rice-based pilaus. Qabuli murgh pilau,

a cardamom-infused chicken and rice dish, showered with plump fried raisins and shreds of tender carrot, won our approval for delicacy of flavour. Ashak (steamed dim sum-like crescents filled with warm, wilted spinach leaves) contrasted well with a topping of chilli-flecked yoghurt and dry-fried lamb mince. Less thrilling was showr-na-khot: boiled, bland chickpeas and potato slices that didn't boast any of the hoped-for vinegary tang. Still, at under a tenner a head, Kabul is a prime spot for budget comfort cooking.
Babies and children admitted; high chairs. Entertainment: Indian musicians 9pm Wed. No-smoking tables. Takeaway service; delivery service (within 8-mile radius).

Australian

Central
Piccadilly SW1

★ Osia
11 Haymarket, entrance on Orange Street, SW1Y 4BP (7976 1313/www.osiarestaurant.com). Piccadilly Circus tube. **Lunch served** noon-3pm Mon-Fri. **Dinner served** 5.30-10.45pm Mon-Sat. **Main courses** £15-£20. **Set meal** (lunch Mon-Fri, 5.30-7pm Mon-Sat) £19 2 courses, £23 3 courses. **Service** 12.5%. **Credit** AmEx, MC, V.
Not many restaurant menus come with a glossary, but unless you're familiar with ingredients such as quandong, rosella flower and wattleseed, you'll find the one at Osia damned handy. Aussie Scott Webster, chef and co-owner, makes use of a huge range of ingredients that you'll struggle to find this side of Wagga Wagga. But what does the food taste like? Judging from the meals we've had here, Webster's cooking is not about mere gimmickry. Each dish is carefully considered – from starters such as Celtic sea scallops with ironwood honey and maize purée (served with a bacon wafer and burnt butter vinaigrette), to eucalyptus lamb, served with kumera mash and green beans. What appears on the plate is balanced, with integrated flavours. Ingredients, from meat to fish to vegetables (many grown specifically for the restaurant), are of excellent quality. Imaginative vegetarian dishes are a plus, as is comfortable seating and a distinctive wine list (Australian and Kiwi bottles are particularly well chosen). For dessert, our hot Callebaut chocolate soup with vanilla and black pepper ice-cream was worth every calorie.
Babies and children welcome. Booking advisable. Disabled: toilet. Dress: smart casual. Vegetarian menu. **Map 17 K7.**

Austrian

West
Bayswater W2

Tiroler Hut
27 Westbourne Grove, W2 4UA (7727 3981/ www.tirolerhut.co.uk). Bayswater or Queensway tube. **Open** 6.30pm-1am Tue-Sat; 6.30pm-midnight Sun. **Dinner served** 6.30pm-midnight Mon-Sat; 6.30-11.30pm Sun. **Main courses** £9.70-£27.50. **Set dinner** £15.50 2 courses, £18.50 3 courses. **Cover** £1. **Service** 10%. **Credit** AmEx, DC, MC, V.

Where else in London can you find middle-aged men in lederhosen and Heidi maidens in dirndls? Tiroler Hut has been around since the 1960s (and has the fading photographs of minor celebs to prove it), yet its appeal remains, undaunted by such matters as tastefulness. This is an ironic party venue extraordinaire. The bunker-like underground space is tarted up to do a passing impression of an Alpine hut, and the host, Josef, plays accordion, keyboard and saxophone, banging out all the old favourites, 'Edelweiss' included. Guests are encouraged to sing along, foaming steins of beer in hand. Recruits from the audience lend a hand with the cacophonous cowbell show. The Austro-Hungarian cuisine is far better than it need be. We expanded our waistlines with proper leberknödel (liver dumpling) soup, Hungarian-style goulash (which needed a bit more sour cream) served with spätzle, a decent wienerschnitzel and some good, meaty bratwurst, served with not-too-sour sauerkraut. Any remaining gaps were filled by Kaiserschmarrn, an Austrian dessert of chopped pancake with plump raisins, topped with cream.
Babies and children admitted. Booking advisable; essential weekends (2 weeks in advance). Entertainment: cowbell show 9pm Wed-Sat. **Map 7 B6.**

Belgian

Central
Covent Garden WC2

Belgo Centraal
50 Earlham Street, WC2H 9LJ (7813 2233/ www.belgo-restaurants.com). Covent Garden or Leicester Square tube. **Meals served** noon-11pm Mon-Thur; noon-11.30pm Fri, Sat; noon-10.30pm Sun. **Main courses** £8.75-£17.95. **Set lunch** (noon-5pm) £5.95 1 course incl drink. **Service** 12.5%. **Credit** AmEx, DC, JCB, MC, V.
There was a time when you couldn't get a seat in this cavernous warehouse-deluxe basement without queuing. Times have changed. Yes, there are still crowds – mostly of the office party type – but this place has lost the plot. The waiters seemed more intent on goofing around than serving guests and the food was a let-down. Belgo made its name with high-quality moules frites. On our visit, the frites struggled to be average, while moules marinière traditionelle was woefully short on flavour; the main component was crudely chopped celery, there was little discernible flavour of the advertised wine or bacon, and the dish seemed quickly thrown together. Carbonnade flamande, beef braised in gueuze beer with apples and plums, was better, but we suspect it hadn't been freshly prepared. Both dishes arrived within five minutes of being ordered and the sauce on the carbonnade had congealed on top and was marked by burnt patches. In its favour, Belgo Centraal has one of the best beer lists in town, including seasonal beers, fruit beers, lambic and gueuze beers and bières blanches. Otherwise, don't bother.
Babies and children welcome; high chairs. Booking advisable. Disabled: lift; toilet. **Map 18 L6.**
For branches (Belgo Noord, Bierodrome) see index.

Burmese

Central
Edgware Road W2

★ ★ Mandalay
444 Edgware Road, W2 1EG (7258 3696). Edgware Road tube. **Lunch served** noon-2.30pm, **dinner served** 6-10.30pm Mon-Sat. **Main courses** £3.90-£6.90. **Set lunch** £3.90 1 course, £5.90 3 courses. **Credit** AmEx, DC, JCB, MC, V.

Mandalay has been a *Time Out* favourite for years. Who couldn't love the place? OK, so the Edgware Road location isn't terribly salubrious, and the decor does little to evoke 'the mysterious east', but the food is a revelation. Add to that the care paid to guests by the two brothers who run the place and you'll see why booking is essential. Burmese cooking combines elements of Thai, Indian and southern Chinese cuisines. Coconut and tomato provide the base for curries, while stir-fries are pepped up with soy sauce. Fresh coriander, mint and lemongrass play a part, and dishes are given extra depth by the likes of shrimp paste and fish sauce; they're made tangy with tamarind, lemon and lime and lent oomph with chillies. To start, calabash fritters, cooked in chickpea flour, are served with three sauces: tamarind, chilli and soy. Mokhingar, a slow-cooked fish dish in a coconut broth with rice noodles (a 'national dish' of Burma), has layer upon layer of flavour, while spicy bamboo shoot curry is enlivened with tomato and red chilli, served with coconut rice.
Babies and children welcome; high chairs. Booking essential. No smoking. Takeaway service. **Map 2 D4**.

Irish

Central
Marylebone W1

O'Conor Don
88 Marylebone Lane, W1U 2PY (7935 9311/ www.oconordon.com). Bond Street tube.
Bar **Open** noon-11pm, **meals served** noon-3pm, 6-10pm Mon-Fri.
Restaurant **Lunch served** noon-2.30pm, **dinner served** 6-10pm Mon-Fri. **Main courses** £9.95-£16. **Service** 12.5%.
Credit AmEx, MC, V.
Located above a pub in a quiet side street in genteel Marylebone, the O'Conor Don feels like a well-intentioned provincial restaurant. The dining room is done up in warm shades of red, with wooden floors, chintzy curtains and homey sideboards in which are tucked the odd bottle of whiskey. If you plan 36 hours ahead you can request whole honey-roast Irish gammon, whole poached salmon, beef wellington or chateaubriand for two or more. Sadly, we were spur-of-the-moment guests, so had to make do with the à la carte. The half-dozen Cuan oysters were firm, sprightly and more racy than our other starter, braised oxtail taken off the bone and served in filo pastry topped with carrot and parsnip jam. For mains, meaty beef and Guinness sausages were nicely flavoured, but served with lacklustre chips. More successful was a whole roast poussin, boned and stuffed with cashel blue cheese, spinach and pine nuts. Our dessert, rhubarb crumble with fresh custard, was rather watery and had a flaccid topping. Pleasant service helps make this an enjoyable hideaway, but don't expect culinary fireworks.
Babies and children admitted. Booking advisable. Entertainment: DJ 10pm Thur. Restaurant available for hire; all areas available for hire Sat, Sun. Separate bar for parties. **Map 9 G5**.

Scandinavian

Central
Knightsbridge SW7

Lundum's
117-119 Old Brompton Road, SW7 3RN (7373 7774/www.lundums.com). Gloucester Road or South Kensington tube. **Brunch served** 9am-4pm Mon-Sat; noon-1.30pm Sun. **Lunch served** noon-4pm daily. **Dinner served** 6-11pm Mon-Sat. **Main courses** £12.75-£21.50. **Set lunch** £12.50 2 courses, £15.50 3 courses. **Set dinner** £17.25 2 courses, £21.50 3 courses. **Service** 13.5%. **Credit** AmEx, DC, MC, V.

Afghan Kitchen. See p103.

Osia. See p103.

red cabbage and pickled cucumbers. The duck was cooked slowly at low temperature and was meltingly tender, while the huge and succulent meatballs did a quick disappearing act. The fairly priced wine list includes some great finds. The menu changes through the year, so look out for seasonal northern European ingredients.
Babies and children welcome; high chairs. Booking advisable brunch, dinner. Separate room for parties, seats 18. Tables outdoors (8, patio). Map 14 D11.

Marylebone W1

Garbo's

42 Crawford Street, W1H 1JW (7262 6582). Baker Street or Edgware Road tube/Marylebone tube/rail. **Lunch served** noon-3pm Mon-Fri, Sun. **Dinner served** 6-11pm Mon-Sat. **Main courses** £6.50-£13.50. **Set lunch** £10.95 2 courses, £11.95 3 courses; £12 smörgåsbord. **Set buffet lunch** (Sun) £13.95. **Cover** £1 (à la carte only). **Credit** AmEx, MC, V.
Garbo's feels a bit old-fashioned. The walls are decorated with black and white portraits of Swedish actresses (including, of course, Greta) and, rather incongruously, a stuffed elk's head. It's a calm, unfussy space made homey with a few Swedish knick-knacks. The menu lists both Swedish and 1970s-style continental dishes, but we stuck to the former and weren't disappointed. Gravadlax was properly made, firm and fresh, served with dill and sweet mustard sauce. Equally good was a selection of herring: a healthy portion of fish, arriving with chopped onion and crème fraîche. To follow, kalvrullader, thin slices of veal stuffed and rolled, comes with a punchy mustard sauce and lingonberry preserves on the side. A late-spring special of braised elk (with a flavour somewhere between venison and beef) is served in a slightly creamy sauce, with chanterelles, sautéed potatoes and redcurrant sauce. The cooking is competent, if somewhat staid, but we'd come back just for the herring and gravadlax, which couldn't be faulted. The short wine list isn't terribly imaginative, but it's not expensive.
Babies and children admitted; high chairs. Booking advisable. Separate room for parties, seats 35. Map 8 F5.

Swiss

Central

Soho W1

St Moritz

161 Wardour Street, W1F 8WJ (7734 3324/ www.stmoritz-restaurant.co.uk). Oxford Circus tube. **Lunch served** noon-3pm Mon-Fri. **Dinner served** 6-11.30pm Mon-Sat. **Main courses** £8.95-£16. **Service** 12.5%. **Credit** AmEx, DC, MC, V.
Fancy a trip back to the 1970s? You've come to the right place. Not that we're complaining: there's something comforting about St Moritz, with its twee cowbells and Alpine scenes hanging on the walls. Yet, as well as nostalgia, you'll find here London's most extensive list of Swiss wines, and the best fondues in town. The menu focuses on the cooking of German-speaking Switzerland, with rösti appearing in several dishes, as well as sausages such as bratwurst. Pizokel spätzle, or boiled flour-batter 'dumplings' (with bacon, cabbage, cream and sbrinz cheese), enjoyable though it was, may not have been the best pre-fondue choice, being incredibly rich and cheesy. Next, fondue 'moitié-moitié', a bubbling bowl of gruyère and vacherin cheese, served with bread and new potatoes, was heart-warmingly (or should that be artery-cloggingly) delicious. The only bum note was our other starter: a selection of unnaturally pink Swiss sausages. Desserts from the trolley are old-time faves such as carrot cake and chocolate mousse – or chocolate fondue for die-hard fondue fans.
Babies and children welcome; high chair. Book dinner. Separate room for parties, seats 30. Map 17 K6.

The best of London's handful of Scandinavian eateries. A family-run restaurant housed in an Edwardian building, Lundum's is comfortable and welcoming (and, since expanding into the property next door, spacious). The decor – huge mirrors, white linen and upholstered chairs – is decidedly more trad than fad. No Scandinavian minimalism here. Come for lunch if you're after typical Danish cooking; there's a fine selection of smørrebrød (open sandwiches) and marinated herrings, served the Danish way – with akvavit (a strong spirit). For those with herring problems, there's plenty of other fish, and, particularly in winter, some hearty meat dishes. At dinner, our sweet Danish waitress convinced us to try a house special, cured duck with mashed potatoes, and Danish meatballs with

Greek

Most of London's 'Greek' restaurants are in fact Greek-Cypriot. There's little change to report in their fortunes this year. **Lemonia**, **Vrisaki** and – on a good night – **Aphrodite Taverna** or **Andy's Taverna** are the places to go for straightforward, traditional Cypriot fare. The steady attrition of older, tired eateries whose proprietors take their pensions or bow to rises in rents and rates has declined, but it's still rare for a new venue to survive for more than a year or two. So farewell to Xenon in Battersea, hello to new hopeful **Greek Affair** in Notting Hill, and fingers crossed for **Retsina** in Primrose Hill (83 Regent's Park Road, NW1 8UY; 7722 3194; map 27 A1), due to emerge from a lengthy refit as we went to press.

Cutting-edge, metropolitan Greek (as opposed to Cypriot) fare, with ambitious wine-lists that rise above mass-produced plonk, is still pretty much the exclusive province of the **Real Greek** mini chain (which includes **Mezedopolio** and the **Real Greek Souvlaki & Bar**) and Dennis Marinakis' always-reliable **Café Corfu** in Camden. The Real Greek enterprise was set up by Theodore Kyriakou, but in the past year has been sold to a company created by David Page, former managing director of Pizza Express. Kyriakou and Page are planning to roll out a franchise based on the Real Greek Souvlaki & Bar concept. A branch has already opened on Bankside (Riverside House, 2A Southwark Bridge Road, SE1 9HA; 7620 0162) and two further sites have been secured in Soho.

Central

Clerkenwell & Farringdon EC1

The Real Greek Souvlaki & Bar
140-142 St John Street, EC1V 4UA (7253 7234/www.therealgreek.co.uk). Farringdon tube/rail. **Meals served** noon-11pm Mon-Sat. **Main courses** £3.85-£8.30. **Service** 12.5% for parties of 6 or more. **Credit** MC, V.
This offshoot of the original Real Greek (*see p108*) is a bar/restaurant concept that Theo Kyriakou is expanding into a chain. The industrial-chic decor features mock-mosque chandeliers and several periscope ventilators; seating is either at tables for two or at long counters. There's also a bar overlooking the kitchen. Roviés olives arrived as free nibbles, but mezédes platters are small – order four for two diners. Khtipiti wasn't very spicy, and had a rather chunkier texture than the traditional puréed variety. Mealy gigandes plaki were cooked to death; two tyrópitta were flavourful, but the filling was on the runny side. The flagship souvláki came wrapped in paper and slightly distressed pitta. The meat (pork chunks Armenian-style, and soutzoúkákia) was fine, though the tzatzíki consisted of runny yoghurt and coarse cucumber cubes. In general, flavours failed to meld together – which we've found to be a recurrent problem at the Real Greek. Being able to sample assorted exceptional Greek wines in 250ml or 500ml carafes is a bonus, however. Desserts perked us up: a Kymian fig and chocolate pot, and a nutty, almost filo-less own-made baklavá, with jumbo-sized latte coffees. We reckon that prices are rather high given our rather uneven meal.

Babies and children welcome; high chairs. Booking advisable. Disabled: toilet. Separate room for parties, seats 40. Tables outdoors (2, pavement). Takeaway service. **Map 5 O4**.

West

Bayswater W2

Aphrodite Taverna
15 Hereford Road, W2 4AB (7229 2206). Bayswater, Notting Hill Gate or Queensway tube. **Meals served** noon-midnight Mon-Sat. **Main courses** £8.50-£27.50. **Mezédes** £17 vegetarian, £19.50 meat, £27.50 fish. **Cover** £1. **Service** 10%. **Credit** AmEx, DC, JCB, MC, V.
On a balmy spring evening, Aphrodite's clientele included large numbers of tourists from nearby hotels. The much-prized outdoor seating area, fronting the affiliated sandwich bar next door, has been expanded, but these tables need to be booked – as does the interior. Aphrodite excels at starters: 'cover' nibbles (white bean salad, radishes, two kinds of olives) were great; extra mezédes of chunky houmous, loúntza (four slices interspersed with tomato slices) and manitária (huge mushrooms grilled, then doused with lemon and garlic oil) were generous, offsetting the slightly bumped-up prices. Mains were more mixed: presentation was much improved, with a garnish of fresh vegetables, and the starch (rice or potatoes) sensibly confined to a side dish, but a tender monkfish kebab was let down by whole grilled squid with the taste and consistency of cardboard. The wine list is fairly MOR, with Boutari and Cambas dominant among the Greek labels. Loutraki, the least distinguished Greek brand of mineral water, is served. The Brazilian waiting staff coped fairly well with the crush, presided over by ebullient proprietress Rosana, who pitches in, serving the mains and greeting regulars.
Babies and children welcome; high chairs. Booking advisable dinner. Tables outdoors (12, pavement). Takeaway service. Vegetarian menu. **Map 7 B6**.

Notting Hill W8

★ Greek Affair NEW
1 Hillgate Street, W8 7SP (7792 5226). Notting Hill Gate tube. **Meals served** 11am-11pm daily. **Main courses** £4.90-£9.50. **Unlicensed. Corkage** £1. **Service** 10%. **Credit** MC, V.
Greek Affair opened in 2003, opposite the Coronet cinema; it's a tiny place that manages to cram in seating on three levels, including a coveted roof terrace. The list of meze platters is extensive, with some rarely seen Cypriot or metropolitan-Greek specialities such as koúpes (cigar-shaped pastries with a meat filling) and kopanisti (a feta cheese spread) – both, alas, unavailable the night of our visit. We settled for mavromátika (black-eyed beans with olive oil, lemon and onions), kolokithokeftédes (courgette croquettes) and laderá. Mavromátika was a dull version, swimming in oil and with barely a fleck of the traditional onion or parsley. The croquettes, though resembling no rendition known in Greece, were a reasonable success; laderá consisted mainly of runner beans in a palatable sweet tomato sauce with cinnamon and onions. Main courses come starkly unadorned (we recommend ordering a side salad). Arní foúrnou (kléftiko) was a superior effort, though fish moussaka had a lemon-curdled, yoghurt-based béchamel. Desserts, unusually, are a strong point, including cheesecake and tiramisu, pastries such as galaktoboúreko and baklavá, semolina halva and karydópita (walnut cake). The latter was a

huge, rich chunk, not too sweet. Service by two charming central European waitresses was if anything over-attentive. Despite some uneven cooking, this is definitely a new venue worth watching. Greek Affair is unlicensed, but there's an off-licence 200m away on the high street.
Babies and children welcome. Booking advisable. No-smoking tables. Separate room for parties, seats 30. Vegetarian menu. **Map 19 C5**.

Shepherd's Bush W12

Vine Leaves
71 Uxbridge Road, W12 8NR (8749 0325). Shepherd's Bush tube. **Lunch served** noon-3pm, **dinner served** 5pm-midnight Mon-Thur. **Meals served** noon-1am Fri, Sat; noon-11.30pm Sun. **Main courses** £5.95-£14.95. **Set meal** £9.50 3 courses incl coffee (Mon-Thur, Sun), £13.95 3 courses incl coffee (no fish or steak), £17.95 3 courses incl coffee. **Mezédes** £9.95 mini, £13.95 mixed, £16.95 fish. **Service** 10% for parties of 4 or more. **Credit** AmEx, JCB, MC, V.
A makeover in 2003 has rendered this well-loved local less cosy, but its management and attentive service are unchanged. Prices seem marginally higher, though portions are large as ever. Among starters, kalámari rings seemed less than fresh (or perhaps the cooking oil needed changing), and loukánika arrived cut into little pieces as if for small children. Nevertheless, melitzanosaláta was a satisfyingly chunky version, and halloumi in a spicy crust also got the thumbs-up. A kotópoulo (chicken) lemonáta with mushrooms was enjoyable, but shish kofta – lamb mince on skewers – arrived overdone and dried out; despite its decent flavour, we couldn't finish it. Mineral water was served in glass bottles (a nice change from the usual downmarket plastic). The best label on a very modest wine list was an equally modestly priced, quaffable Calliga Ruby red. There's also house retsina at knockdown prices. We were too stuffed for dessert. Starters still tend to overshadow main courses, but for the quantity of food purveyed Vine Leaves represents pretty reasonable value.
Babies and children welcome; children's menu. Booking advisable weekends. No-smoking tables. Takeaway service. Vegetarian menu. **Map 20 B2**.

East

Shoreditch N1

Mezedopolio
14 Hoxton Market, N1 6HG (7739 8212/www.therealgreek.co.uk). Old Street tube/rail/26, 48, 55, 149, 243 bus. **Meals served** noon-10.30pm Mon-Sat. **Mezédes** £2.10-£6. **Service** 12.5%. **Credit** MC, V.
Leading restaurant the Real Greek (*see p108*) and its anteroom Mezedopolio now share an entrance at No.14; you'll be asked by bar staff where you intend to dine. Housed in a former Victorian mission hall, Mezedopolio retains quirky period features such as a stained-glass lancet window and marble commemorative plaques, with natural light from a translucent dome bathing parquet floors. A mezedopolio is to Greece what a tapas bar is to Spain; around 30 seasonally changing platters make up the menu here, and two diners will need at least seven to fill up. Kápari yahni were a bit disappointing – caper pods rather than pickled greens, well outnumbered by cocktail onions. Fáva was a thick, stand-to-attention version of the lentil, lemon and onion dip, while nicely breaded saganáki came with rather incongruous gherkin slices. Soutzoúki with a side dollop of htipiti were lovely, though the htipiti was overwhelmed by red pepper chunks (traditionally its hotness comes from natural fermentation). In contrast, the tyrokafterí cheese spread was bland, white and bereft of chilli. Spicy chicken livers were an unalloyed success, as were our desserts of fig-and-chocolate pot and authentically thick, Smyrna-style chocolate ice-cream.
Babies and children admitted. Booking advisable; essential weekends. Tables outdoors (8, pavement). **Map 6 Q/R3**.

★ The Real Greek

15 Hoxton Market, N1 6HG (7739 8212/ www.therealgreek.co.uk). Old Street tube/rail/ 26, 48, 55, 149, 243 bus. **Lunch served** noon-3pm, **dinner served** 5.30-10.30pm Mon-Sat. **Main courses** £12.90-£15.90. **Mezédes** £7.90-£8.60. **Service** 12.5%. **Credit** MC, V.

The Real Greek, a lodestar for the chattering classes of Shoreditch (and much further afield) offers classy mainland cooking, the like of which you won't find elsewhere in London. It shares singular premises (a former Victorian mission hall) with Mezedopolio (*see p107*). The bill for two, including restrained imbibing and service, can easily breach £90, or even £100 if one of the better wines from an eclectic Greek list is chosen. On a recent visit, we tried to spend less than £30 per person and settled on a meze combination (heftier than the diminutive individual mezédes), and one of the fagákia (midsized platters). The combo arrived with breaded lamb sweetbreads at the pinnacle of a mountain of casseroled peas, tasting just as they would in mainland Greece; cockles studding the 'foothills' seemed out of a jar, but a sturdy base of pork belly was delicious. For the fagáki, we were tempted by monkfish tail in fennel savóro, but plumped for courgette filo pie with a

dollop of sheep's yoghurt – and regretted it (the brioche-like pie was overcooked to rigidity at its edges). The dessert list has had an overhaul, though retains a couple of old favourites; tiramisu à la grecque cheered us up, a flawless confection with a ravaní (Greek syrup-sponge) base, served in a cappuccino cup. The range of beers is much improved, including draught Greek Alfa. The price of all the above, including beer and service? – £28.41 per head.

Babies and children admitted. Booking advisable. Separate rooms for parties, seating 8 and 20. Tables outdoors (6, pavement). **Map 6 Q/R3**.

North

Camden Town & Chalk Farm NW1

Andy's Taverna

81-81A Bayham Street, NW1 0AG (7485 9718/ www.andysgardenrestaurant.co.uk). Camden Town or Mornington Crescent tube. **Lunch served** noon-2.30pm Mon-Fri. **Dinner served** 6pm-midnight Mon-Fri; 5.30-11.30pm Sat.

Meals served 1-11pm Sun. **Main courses** £8-£14. **Mezédes** £13.95 per person (minimum 2). **Service** 10% for parties of 6 or more. **Credit** AmEx, DC, JCB, MC, V.

The slat-floored, white-walled courtyard was half-full, and there was a large, lively party inside under the beamed ceilings at Andy's – not too bad for a weekday lunch just before August Bank Holiday. The food wasn't bad either: fluffy, Turkish-style pide bread to scoop up a good rendition of houmous studded with chilli; and broad beans with artichokes, which, though they tasted as if they came out of a can, were made more appetising by heating and the addition of onion slivers. Among a generously sized mixed grill consisting of lamb chop, kebabs, chicken souvláki, loukánika and sheftaliá, only the latter was a little underdone. The house red, from Kambas in Attica, was more than drinkable. Service was courteous, if leisurely. A meal might include, as dessert, a fruit platter or coffees on the house. After some uneven review meals a few years ago, we're glad to see that Andy's is back on form.

Babies and children welcome; crayons; high chairs. Booking essential Fri-Sun. Separate rooms for parties, seating 30 and 40. Tables outdoors (7, garden). Takeaway service. **Map 27 D2**.

Menu

Dishes followed by (G) indicate a specifically Greek dish; those marked (GC) indicate a Greek-Cypriot speciality; those without an initial have no particular regional affiliation.

Afélia (GC): pork cubes, ideally from filleted leg or shoulder, stewed in wine, coriander and other herbs.

Avgolémono (G): a sauce made of lemon, egg yolks and chicken stock. Also a soup made with rice, chicken stock, lemon and whole eggs.

Baklavá: a pan-Middle Eastern sweet made from sheets of filo dough layered with nuts.

Dolmádes (G) or **koupépia (GC)**: young vine leaves stuffed with rice, spices and (usually) minced meat.

Fasólia plakí or **pilakí**: white beans in a tomato, oregano, bay, parsley and garlic sauce.

Garídes: prawns (usually king prawns in the UK), fried or grilled.

Gígantes or **gígandes**: white haricot beans baked in tomato sauce; pronounced 'yígandes'.

Halloumi (GC) or **hallúmi**: a cheese traditionally made from sheep's or goat's milk, but increasingly from cow's milk. Best served fried or grilled.

Horiátiki: Greek 'peasant' salad of tomato, cucumber, onion, feta and sometimes green pepper, dressed with ladolémono (oil and lemon).

Hórta: salad of wild greens, usually chicory or radicchio.

Houmous, hoúmmous or **húmmus (GC)**: a dip of puréed chickpeas, sesame seed paste, lemon juice and garlic, garnished with paprika. Originally an Arabic dish, not Hellenic.

Htipití: tangy purée of matured cheeses, flavoured with red peppers.

Kalámari, kalamarákia or **calamares**: small squid, usually sliced into rings, battered and fried.

Kataïfi or **katayfi**: syrup-soaked 'shredded-wheat' rolls.

Keftédes or **keftedákia (G)**: herby meatballs made with minced pork or lamb (rarely beef), egg, breadcrumbs and possibly grated potato.

Khtipití or **htipití**: tangy purée of matured cheeses, flavoured with red peppers.

Kléftiko (GC): slow-roasted lamb on the bone (often shoulder), flavoured with oregano and other herbs.

Kopanistí (G): a cheese dip with a tanginess that traditionally comes from natural fermentation, but is often boosted with chilli.

Koukiá: broad beans.

Loukánika or **lukánika**: spicy coarse-ground sausages, usually pork and heavily herbed.

Loukoúmades: tiny, spongy dough fritters, dipped in honey.

Loukoúmi or **lukúmi**: 'turkish delight' made with syrup, rosewater and pectin, often studded with nuts.

Loúntza (GC): smoked pork loin.

Marídes: picarel, often mistranslated as (or substituted by) 'whitebait' – small fish best coated in flour and flash-fried.

Melitzanosaláta: purée of grilled aubergines.

Meze (plural mezédes, pronounced 'mezédhes'): a selection of either hot or cold appetisers and main dishes.

Moussaká(s) (G): a baked dish of mince (usually lamb), aubergine and potato slices and herbs, topped with béchamel sauce.

Papoutsáki: aubergine 'shoes', slices stuffed with mince, topped with sauce, usually béchamel-like.

Pastourmá(s): dense, dark-tinted garlic sausage, traditionally made from camel meat, but nowadays from beef.

Pourgoúri or **bourgoúri (GC)**: a pilaf of cracked wheat, often prepared with stock, onions, crumbled vermicelli and spices.

Saganáki (G): fried cheese, usually kefalotyri; also means anything (mussels, spinach) made in a cheese-based red sauce.

Sheftaliá (GC): little pig-gut skins stuffed with pork and lamb mince, onion, parsley, breadcrumbs and spices, then grilled.

Skordaliá (G): a garlic and breadcrumb or potato-based dip, used as a side dish.

Soutzoúkákia or **soutzoúki (G)**: baked meat rissoles, often topped with a tomato-based sauce.

Soúvla: large cuts of lamb or pork slow-roasted on a rotary spit.

Souvláki: chunks of meat quick-grilled on a skewer (known in London takeaways as kebab or shish kebab).

Spanakópitta: small turnovers, traditionally triangular, stuffed with spinach, dill and often feta or some other crumbly tart cheese.

Stifádo: a rich meat stew (often rabbit) with onions, red wine, tomatoes, cinnamon and bay.

Taboúlleh: generic Middle Eastern starter of pourgoúri (qv), chopped parsley, cucumber chunks, tomatoes and spring onions.

Taramá, properly **taramósalata**: fish roe pâté, originally made of dried, salted grey mullet roe (avgotáraho or botárgo), but now more often smoked cod roe, plus olive oil, lemon juice and breadcrumbs.

Tavás (GC): lamb, onion, tomato and cumin, cooked in earthenware casseroles.

Tsakistés (GC): split green olives marinated in lemon, garlic, coriander seeds and other optional flavourings.

Tyrópitta (G): similar to spanakópitta (qv) but usually without spinach and with more feta.

Tzatzíki, dzadzíki (G) or **talatoúra (GC)**: a dip of shredded cucumber, yoghurt, garlic, lemon juice and mint.

The Real Greek Souvlaki & Bar. See p107.

★ Café Corfu

7 Pratt Street, NW1 0AE (7267 8088/ www.cafecorfu.com). Camden Town or Mornington Crescent tube. **Meals served** noon-10.30pm Tue-Thur, Sun; noon-11.30pm Fri; 5-11.30pm Sat. **Main courses** £7.95-£12.95. **Set meal** £16.75 3 courses, £20 4 courses. **Service** 12.5%. **Credit** MC, V.

The menu here seems to have pulled in its horns a bit from former years, and with crates of Alfa beer ('special promotion this month') being unloaded, it appears Café Corfu is going whole hog for the office-party market. Well it might, as the premises include an attractive bar area and cavernous back room. Service, at weekday lunchtime, verged on the unacceptable side of leisurely, but our doubts evaporated when the food finally arrived. Tyrokafteri (spicy cheese dip) was creamily authentic; spanakópitta was expertly executed both in the crust (a difficult feat) and the filling; squid rings in a pastry basket had not a trace of grease or superfluous batter. A main course of cod with pistachio boasted nicely caramelised onions, while our other choice, ragout of wild mushroom, was one of several appetising vegetarian dishes (despite having a dull portobello mushroom on top). Both mains were redolent of, but not overpowered by, spices and herbs. We rounded off a long lunch with lemonópitta (lemon cheesecake) with raspberry coulis. The Greek wine list is among the best in town; there's also a selection of ouzo and tsipouro (another raki-like spirit). Café Corfu may be settling into middle age, but it still wipes the floor with most London Greek eateries.
Babies and children welcome; high chairs. Booking advisable; essential weekends. Entertainment: belly dancer, DJ, dancing 9pm Fri, Sat; musicians 8pm Sun. No-smoking tables. Separate rooms for parties, seating 50-150. Tables outdoors (6, forecourt). Takeaway service. Map 27 D2.

Daphne

83 Bayham Street, NW1 0AG (7267 7322). Camden Town or Mornington Crescent tube. **Lunch served** noon-2.30pm, **dinner served** 6-11.30pm Mon-Sat. **Main courses** £7.50-£13.50. **Set lunch** £7.25 2 courses, £8.50 3 courses. **Mezédes** £12.50 meat or vegetarian, £16.50 fish. **Credit** MC, V.

At weekday lunch, the ground floor at Daphne was nearly full – a promising beginning. Encouraged by the friendly waiter, we stuck to the specials board (the best plan here): louví (black-eyed peas) were excellent stewed with greens (the usual Greek accompaniments are chopped onions and parsley), but 'crispy mushrooms' turned out to be batter-fried and rather soggy inside. We regretted ordering mince-filled artichokes rather than the more appropriate Lenten fare of angináres me koukiá (artichokes with broad beans). Mains garnered nul points for their startlingly desolate presentation, and were scarcely more sumptuous on the taste buds: stewed hare was nearly flavourless, and sea bass tasted a bit like trout. We consoled ourselves with ever-reliable coffees and loukoúmi, and a bottle of Monte Nero Kefallonian red, one of a respectable Greek wine list. Better luck next year?
Babies and children welcome; high chairs. Booking essential Fri, Sat. Separate room for parties, seats 50. Tables outdoors (8, roof terrace). Map 27 D2.

Lemonia

89 Regent's Park Road, NW1 8UY (7586 7454). Chalk Farm tube. **Lunch served** noon-3pm Mon-Fri; noon-3.30pm Sun. **Dinner served** 6-11.30pm Mon-Sat. **Main courses** £7.75-£12.95. **Set lunch** (Mon-Fri) £7.25 2 courses incl coffee, £8.50 3 courses. **Mezédes** £15 per person (minimum 2). **Service** 10% for parties of 10 or more. **Credit** MC, V.

On a Bank Holiday Monday night, Lemonia was as packed as ever, with a 45-minute wait for tables if you turned up without a booking. We stuck to the day's specials, and based on these we're happy to report that the quality of the cooking seems to have improved. Among starters, fish croquettes were course-grained, but fried just right – not too oily – with flecks of carrot and courgettes and a nicely presented dollop of skordaliá. Artichoke (yes, one) with koukiá (broad beans) arrived smothered in a pleasantly spicy tomato and oil sauce. Service was coping fairly well with the crowds, and there wasn't too long a wait for the mains, again catch of the day: tuna steak (ordered medium, arrived rare) and a smallish sea bass, with sides of spinach, okra and perfect chips. The Greek wine list remains one of the best in London; we were pleased with an organic white Laloudi from the Monemvasia region of the Peloponnese. Having assiduously avoided pitta, bulgur and any other starch, we were still too full to tackle anything other than a mint tea and bowl of strawberries for dessert. At about £75 for two with service, this isn't a cheap night out, but it's a pretty savoury one.
Babies and children welcome. Booking essential. Separate room for parties, seats 40. Vegetarian menu. Map 27 A1.

Limani

154 Regent's Park Road, NW1 8XN (7483 4492). Chalk Farm tube. **Lunch served** noon-3pm Sat. **Dinner served** 6-11.30pm Tue-Sat; 3.30-10.30pm Sun. **Main courses** £7.75-£14.50. **Mezédes** £14.50 meat or vegetarian, £17.50 fish, per person (minimum 2). **Credit** MC, V.

After a dismal experience last year, it was with some trepidation that we ventured back to Limani, the older sister of Lemonia (*see above*). With few expectations, we were pleasantly surprised: the staff (as ever, almost entirely non-Cypriot) seemed to have attended charm school in the interim, and most of the food was more than edible. Erratic service, however, remains a constant. Despite booking, our request to be seated in the airy upstairs conservatory (by far the best spot) was refused, though it was declared 'open' 15 minutes later. In addition, the wine list went missing; and we had to re-order a 'forgotten' item. Starters of okra yahní and halloumi were very good, what there was of them; portions seem to have shrunk. This trend continued with tender lamb lemonádo and rice, and moussakás. Horiátiki, when it finally arrived (well through the mains), was a let-down – far too much cabbage and no evidence of it being a summer salad. The brief wine list is stronger on French and South African labels than Greek or Cypriot, but we were pleased with a moderately priced bottle of Lafazanis Sillogi 2001 cabernet-agiorgitiko red. Despite its shortcomings, Limani remains buzzy, even on a weekday evening.
Babies and children welcome. Booking essential weekends. Separate room for parties, seats 30. Takeaway service. Map 27 A1.

Wood Green N22

Vrisaki

73 Myddleton Road, N22 8LZ (8889 8760). Bounds Green or Wood Green tube. **Lunch served** noon-4pm, **dinner served** 6-11.30pm Mon-Sat. **Main courses** £9.50-£18. **Mezédes** £18 per person (minimum 2). **Service** 10%. **Credit** AmEx, MC, V.

If old-fashioned tavernas are your thing, then Vrisaki will hit the spot. The restaurant (reached through a thriving kebab shop) has almost no natural light and no outdoor space – a disappointment on a sunny day, but no problem in the evening (when the place hits its stride). Inside, it's packed with dark wood furniture, rustic paintings showing idealised scenes of Cypriot life, fake plants and a small vase of carnations on every table. The menu and wine list are no-nonsense. There's limited choice on both, but everything you might expect is here. Drinks include Aphrodite white wine, Keo beer and a range of spirits (available by the bottle as well as the glass). The menu contains moussaká and kléftiko, but majors on grills and kebabs (lamb kebab came with salad and overcooked rice, yet apart from the last item, we couldn't fault it). A short list of meze features tahini, taramósalata, houmous, grilled halloumi and kalámari. All these were ordered and enjoyed with warm pitta; they were accompanied by various complimentary meze – gigandes, beetroot, potato salad, radishes – a nice touch, but there was no chance of going hungry even without these extras. One of the old school, aptly situated in a street that time forgot.
Babies and children welcome. Booking advisable; essential weekends. Takeaway service (8881 2920).

North West

Belsize Park NW3

Halepi

48-50 Belsize Lane, NW3 5AR (7431 5855). Belsize Park or Swiss Cottage tube. **Meals served** 4-11pm Mon; noon-11pm Tue-Sun. **Main courses** £7.50-£26. **Set lunch** £10 2 courses incl coffee. **Mezédes** £16.90 meat, £25 fish. **Cover** £1. **Credit** AmEx, DC, MC, V.

On a rainy spring evening, this 'Belsize Village' linchpin was uncharacteristically empty. One of our party was a strict vegetarian, and as it was Orthodox Lent, we hoped for some nistisima (Lenten, quasi-vegan) food on the menu. There was none, so we cobbled together a (mostly vegetarian) meze of houmous, halloumi, fasólia, goutsiá (broad beans fried with onions), ravioli and loukánika, plus a main of grilled quail and a side salad. Portions were more generous than we remembered, so we could have skipped a platter or two. Cooking too, was a notch or two up on past performances; our only complaint concerned a watery sauce for the ravioli. The quail, which had come painfully unadorned in the past, arrived well presented. A bottle of Keo D'Ahera red, one of the best mid-range Cypriot wines, and distressingly authentic plastic-bottled Ayios Nikolaos water accompanied the meal. Service left much to be desired: we asked for onion on the salad, and got none; asked for no ice or lemon in the water, and got both; and both coffees came *skéto* (unsweetened) despite being ordered *métrio* (medium sweet). One thing hasn't changed: a bracing bill of over £60 for two, despite us skipping dessert (mostly decadent ice-cream concoctions) and only having one bona fide main. *Babies and children welcome; high chairs. Booking advisable; essential weekends. Separate room for parties, seats 66. Takeaway service.* **Map 28 B3.** For branch see index.

St John's Wood NW8

Greek Valley

130 Boundary Road, NW8 0RH (7624 3217/ www.greekvalley.co.uk). Maida Vale or Swiss Cottage tube/16, 98, 139, 189 bus. **Dinner served** 6pm-midnight Mon-Sat. **Main courses** £7.50-£10.50. **Mezédes** £16.50 per person (minimum 2). **Credit** MC, V.
On a summer evening, we jumped at the chance to dine outside at one of the handful of pavement tables here, a relatively new perk. The menu, however, seemed unchanged from our first visit years ago. We started with mixed dips – houmous, taramósalata, tzatziki and melitzanosalata – and spanakópitta. The latter were acceptable, if more like Chinese spring rolls than Greek fare; enjoyment of the dips was hampered by pitta that tasted like cardboard. Moussakás had a rubbery top of béchamel sauce. Its flavour was OK, but there was nothing to counteract the richness: certainly not the handful of chopped iceberg and three tomato wedges that answered to the description of 'side salad'. Sis kófte (lamb-mince rissoles) were pleasantly spicy, but pilaf came with a dollop of Bisto-ish sauce at its centre. The wine-list is adequate, though we stuck to Keo beers. The promised dessert of Greek figs in cream turned out to be figs in syrup (which tasted tinned) with a few strawberries. Greek Valley hardly scales the peaks of culinary excellence, yet despite its shortcomings, survives as an adequate, reasonably priced local that's rarely ever more than half full.
Babies and children welcome; high chairs. Book weekends. Entertainment: Greek music 7.30pm Sat. Separate room for parties, seats 30. Tables outdoors (5, pavement). Takeaway service. **Map 28 A4.**

West Hampstead NW6

Mario's

153-155 Broadhurst Gardens, NW6 3AU (7625 5827). West Hampstead tube/rail/ 28, 139, C11 bus. **Lunch served** noon-3pm Thur. **Dinner served** 6-11pm Mon-Thur. **Meals served** noon-midnight Fri, Sat; noon-11pm Sun. **Main courses** £6.95-£13.95. **Mezédes** £14.95. **Service** 10% for parties of 8 or more. **Credit** AmEx, DC, MC, £TC, V.
After years of toying with the notion, we decided to sample the meze at this durable, candlelit, wooden-beamed Cypriot taverna. Portions seem to have diminished a bit since our last trip, but the half dozen or so cold platters – tahini, tzatziki, taramá, mavromátika (black-eyed beans with onions and oil), white beans in sauce, carrots, olives, chillies – were appetising enough, and the hot hors d'oeuvres that followed (meatballs, spanakópitta, calamares, marides) all passed muster, apart from some stringy, tasteless prawns. Mains consisted of a skewer or two of pork souvláki and a couple of lamb chops; it doesn't sound like much, but was perfectly adequate after the abundant starters. We'd no room for dessert. A vegetarian entrée of the day can be substituted for the meat course. The wine list is perfunctory, an assortment of MOR Greek and Cypriot bottles; we settled on large Keo beers and water. Service was friendly and attentive. In short, Mario's is a very good local (one-third full on a weekday night), but probably not worth a trip across town.
Babies and children welcome; high chairs. Book weekends. Separate area for parties, seats 35. Takeaway service. **Map 28 A3.**

Hotels & Haute Cuisine

In front of distinguished food professionals in 2004, Raymond Blanc announced that British consumers were ten years ahead of their French counterparts when it came to food – buying it, cooking it and eating out. So, we might know what we want when dining out – but do our chefs, waiters and restaurant managers?

It is evident that top restaurants are catering less to the needs of tourists and businessmen and more to Britain's home-grown foodies. Yet many establishments fail to recognise even the basic needs of their paying customers (efficient, polite service, for example), let alone more sophisticated desires (someone knowledgeable to tell us how a dish is made or what a wine is like, perhaps). Haute cuisine restaurants can no longer rely on old-fashioned elitism to draw people in, because the vast chasm of knowledge that previously existed between chef and diner is fast disappearing. Practically speaking, diners may still be unable to cook a piece of fish perfectly, but they certainly know if the chef's attempt is up to scratch.

Nonetheless, there's plenty of good news out there: less well known, more reasonably priced wines are on the increase, and set lunches continue to represent superb value (*see p111* **Best Lunch Deals**). London's haute cuisine is among the best in the world, and fierce competition keeps it bubbling away nicely. Highlights this year included the **Greenhouse** (which we have upgraded to a haute cuisine restaurant in 2004) and newcomers Gordon Ramsay's **Boxwood Café**, alongside such reliable stalwarts as the **Capital**, **Foliage**, **Pied à Terre** and the **Square**. However, to achieve and sustain long-term, world-beating brilliance, our restaurants need to be nicer to us, their patrons.

Central
City EC2

Bonds

Threadneedles, 5 Threadneedle Street, EC2R 8BD (7657 8088/www.theetongroup.com). Bank tube/ DLR. **Lunch served** noon-2.30pm, **dinner served** 6-10pm Mon-Fri. **Main courses** £17.50-£25. **Set lunch** £23.50 2 courses, £29.50 3 courses. **Service** 12.5%. **Credit** AmEx, DC, MC, V.
Due to its location in the City, Bonds is far livelier during the day than of an evening, when stockbrokers and *FT* readers have vacated the area. Inevitably this means that most midday patrons are male 50-year-olds in grey suits. Breaking up the capacious neutral space are four outsized lampshades, hanging like glowing stalactites from the ceiling. Down the centre of the room stomp their stalagmite counterparts – red glass vases speared with silk lilies and twigs. However, any real derring-do at Bonds is edible. There's a commendable and rare set vegetarian menu, a regular set meal and an à la carte. Dishes are peppered with goodies such as pigs' cheeks, smoked eel, bone marrow and frogs' legs aïoli. Not everything is at the culinary edge though, as five comforting semolina gnocchi demonstrated by bobbing like fat happy eggs in a rich cheese sauce along with fragrant sliced truffles, morels and diced tomato. Main-course skate was a rich roasted steak doused in rapier-sharp lime and caper

dressing: excellent with chunky, hearty bread. Set menus are simpler than the more adventurous and significantly pricier à la carte. A long wine list benefits from sexed-up tasting notes: no doubt a ploy to persuade banker-types to invest more daringly in their liquid lunches.
Disabled: lift; toilet. Dress: smart casual. No smoking. Separate rooms for parties, seating 9, 12 and 20. **Map 12 Q6.**

Embankment WC2

Jaan

Swissôtel London, The Howard, 12 Temple Place, WC2R 2PR (7300 1700/www.swissotel.com). Temple tube. **Lunch served** noon-2.30pm Mon-Fri. **Dinner served** 5.45-10.30pm daily. **Set lunch** £21 2 courses, £24 3 courses. **Set dinner** £28 2 courses, £31 3 courses, £39 5 courses, £45 7 courses. **Service** 12.5%. **Credit** AmEx, DC, JCB, MC, V.
Although it's busier than last year, there's room for more of us in this golden-hued restaurant overlooking a peaceful water garden at the Howard hotel. And it would be a shame to miss out. Jaan's French-Cambodian theme has settled more decidedly on the Asian side of the fence, producing deft, assured and fabulously light food with plenty of innovation to feast upon. This winning combination is appreciated by diners wanting to leave the table with some energy in reserve. Prices are distinctly fair for such cooking, and staff nice enough not to make the money-savers among us feel like Scrooge (though we'd like them to fill our glasses more often). Tuna and swordfish sashimi cut into a flat, alternating mosaic came drizzled with a zany lemon marmalade dressing and attention-grabbing salty caviar ice-cream. Water chestnut cappuccino was another great starter: ethereally silky, steamily fragrant and hiding an unbelievably velvety, truffle-infused wun tun. Main courses are on the small side, but with big flavours: wasabi-coated halibut on daikon radish was sweetly and surprisingly balanced by warm raisin sauce; black-skinned cod arrived on a tender medley of seafood with an aromatic green Thai-style curry emulsion that barely glossed the harmonious assembly. Desserts too are full of intriguing tastes and contrasting mouth-feels. Creamy black sesame seed panna cotta was topped with lychee granita the texture of powdered snow, and an edgy squirt of sour cherry juice. Lovely, unusual food in elegant surroundings.
Book dinner. Children admitted; high chairs. Disabled: toilet; ramp. Dress: smart casual. Entertainment: pianist in bar dinner daily. Restaurant available for hire. Tables outdoors (28, garden). Vegetarian menu. **Map 10 M7.**

Fitzrovia W1

★ Pied à Terre

34 Charlotte Street, W1T 2NH (7636 1178/ www.pied.a.terre.co.uk). Goodge Street or Tottenham Court Road tube. **Lunch served** 12.15-2.30pm Tue-Fri. **Dinner served** 6.15-11pm Mon-Sat. **Main courses** £27. **Set lunch** £21.50 2 courses, £26.50 3 courses. **Set dinner** £45 2 courses, £54.50 3 courses, £50-£65 8 courses. **Service** 12.5%. **Credit** AmEx, MC, V.
Pied à Terre goes out of its way to provide a realistically priced and completely relaxing gourmet experience: a fantastic achievement in the traditionally stony-faced world of haute cuisine. Staff make no distinction between celebrities (of which they see plenty) and the rest of us. If fine dining is an arena into which you've never ventured, then this intimate, softly lit restaurant is

an edifying place to start. The set lunch is great value and can be extended with dessert of the day or farmhouse cheese for just £5. Wine suggestions are listed under every dish to ensure you get the best possible match (a hefty tome is also offered, of course). Food is nothing short of heavenly. White bean and black truffle soup was all animal attraction, with crisp bacon lardons lurking in its fragrant depths. Roasted halibut was a fresh-tasting, beautifully crisped dish with braised lettuce, nut butter and some gritty cockles that didn't do anything for the texture of what was otherwise a cracking main course. Desserts from the à la carte menu are stunning, light and often fruity confections, such as poached pear presented in caramel-topped slices on a simple white platter with alternating patches of liquorice ice-cream and star anise cream. What's keeping you from a visit? *Babies and children admitted. Booking advisable; essential weekends. Dress: smart casual. No-smoking tables. Separate room for parties, seats 14.* **Map 9 J5.**

Holborn WC1

Pearl NEW

252 High Holborn, WC1V 7EN (7829 7000/ www.pearlrestaurant.com). Holborn tube. **Lunch served** noon-2.30pm Mon-Fri. **Dinner served** 6-10pm Mon-Sat. **Set meal** (noon-2.30pm, 6-7pm) £21.50 2 courses, £24.50 3 courses. **Set dinner** (7-10pm) £42.50 3 courses; (tasting menu) £45 5 courses (£72 incl wine). **Service** 12.5%. **Credit** AmEx, DC, JCB, MC, V.
QC has undergone a refurb and been relaunched as Pearl. Seating plan, bar and temperature-controlled wine store have been shuffled around to draw the eye away from the building's vast proportions and marble walls and pillars (the place was formerly a grand headquarters for Pearl Assurance). The art deco look has been replaced

Best Lunch Deals

Some restaurants offer fewer thrills with a set lunch than with à la carte dishes, but remember – these are among the best places to eat in the world: you're not going to go away disappointed. **Boxwood Café** (*see right*) doesn't have a set lunch, but prices are (relatively) low. Note that set lunch deals can change.

Allium
£17.50 two courses, £22.50 three courses. *See p114.*

Brian Turner Mayfair
£22.50 two courses, £25.50 three courses. *See p113.*

The Crescent
£20 two courses, £25 three courses – both with a half bottle of wine. *See p112.*

Jaan
£21 two courses, £24 three courses. *See p110.*

Pied à Terre
£21.50 two courses, £26.50 three courses. *See p110.*

Pearl
£21.50 two courses, £24.50 three courses. *See above.*

Putney Bridge
£18.50 two courses, £22.50 three courses (both Tue-Sat); £25 three courses (Sun). *See p116.*

by a softer palate of pearlescent pink, with zillions of crystals strung in curtains across the windows, from the ceiling and between drinking booths. To us, these looked less like sparkling pearls than depressing rain. This window treatment also does nothing to disguise the blinking traffic lights, Starbucks and dentist signs across the road. Stranger still is the table design, with a backlit circular glow in the centre becoming warm enough to melt the butter completely. The whole thing partially tipped over at one point, flinging a vase of flowers to the floor. 'Don't worry,' we were told, 'it has happened before.' Chef Jun Tanaka also remains. The finely judged, light Eurasian dishes that were coming along nicely at QC have been replaced by less interesting French cooking. Although everything was delicately presented, flavours and combinations were old school. Limosin veal on jerusalem artichoke gratin, and cannelloni of swiss chard, pine nuts and mousserons were both pleasant, yet unchallenging. Whether this subdued version of Tanaka's cooking will be more successful than his previous style remains to be seen. Staff operated with smooth proficiency. *Babies and children welcome (before 7pm); high chairs. Booking advisable. Disabled: toilet. Dress: smart casual; no jeans, T-shirts or trainers. No smoking. Separate room for parties, seats 12.* **Map 10 M5.**

Knightsbridge SW1, SW3

★ Boxwood Café NEW

The Berkeley Hotel, Wilton Place, SW1X 7RL (7235 1010/www.gordonramsay.com). Hyde Park Corner or Knightsbridge tube. **Lunch served** noon-3pm Mon-Fri; noon-4pm Sat, Sun. **Dinner served** 6-11pm daily. **Main courses** £13.50-£25. **Service** 12.5%. **Credit** AmEx, MC, V.
Is it a café, or is it a fine dining restaurant? The informal name and mouth-watering menu suggest the former, but the starched linen, silver leaf walls and dark lacquered furniture suggest the latter. We suggest you go and see for yourself, since Gordon Ramsay has again produced a fantastic place in which to eat and be pampered, only this time with considerably less stress on your wallet. Boxwood was created with family dining in mind; crowd-pleasing dishes and longer opening hours, seven days a week, encourage young restaurant-goers, but a typical weekday lunch sees nobody under the age of 30. Staff treat you as they would in a posh restaurant (a good thing), yet food is the kind of sublime home-cooking that, in your dreams, you'd whip together in moments for some exquisite heartthrob in the intimacy of your own kitchen (a very good thing). Croque monsieur, from among ten or so starters, was a comforting toasted sandwich – made stunningly lovely with brioche, smoked salmon, melting gruyère cheese and sunken pearls of sevruga caviar. Ramero peppers, another starter, were roasted until collapsibly sweet and soft; they came with teeny whole courgettes, roasted aubergine and feta, plus a sharp rocket salad. And, hurrah, we were allowed to have just starters and a few side dishes: spot-on chips, onion rings in a sensationally light batter, and perfectly steamed green beans with chopped shallots. This is the kind of cooking that ace chefs do on their days off: simple ingredients artfully and masterfully tossed together. *Babies and children welcome; children's menu; high chairs. Booking essential. Disabled: toilet. Dress: smart casual; no trainers or shorts. No smoking. Separate room for parties, seats 12-16.* **Map 9 G9.**

★ The Capital

22-24 Basil Street, SW3 1AT (7589 5171/7591 1202/www.capitalhotel.co.uk). Knightsbridge tube. **Bar Open** 11am-11pm daily. *Restaurant* **Breakfast served** 7-10.30am Mon-Sat; 7.30-10.30am Sun. **Lunch served** noon-2.30pm daily. **Dinner served** 7-11pm Mon-Sat; 7-10.30pm Sun. **Set breakfast** £12.50 continental, £16.50 full English. **Set lunch** £28.50 3 courses. **Set dinner** £48 2 courses, £55 3 courses, £68 7 courses. **Service** 12.5% (lunch, dinner). **Credit** AmEx, DC, JCB, MC, V.

By London standards the Capital's dining room is small and old-fashioned, and yet it's supremely elegant and considered. Set above pavement level and blessed with prettily etched floor-to-ceiling windows, the room is light-filled by day, intimate by night. Staff are, quite simply, in a class of their own when it comes to attending to diners' whims. It all comes down to detail; not one iota of comfort or food satisfaction is overlooked, from the daily delivery of fabulous dinner rolls and breakfast pastries from the hotel's own bakery, to the final mouthful of coffee and luxurious own-made petits fours in the evening. Lunch might start with an appetiser of risotto, formed into a table tennis-sized ball around a dot of mozzarella, fried in a crisp breaded shell and served on perky beetroot and bean salsa. At £28.50 for three courses, the set lunch isn't the cheapest in town, but is undoubtedly one of the most sophisticated and beautifully presented. Nor are portions large, but this somehow serves as an invitation to take your time and savour each mouthful with unusual deliberation. Grilled and marinated mackerel, one of five starters, was served in two parts: one, a shapely fillet balancing on a divine star anise-spiced tomato tapenade; the other, a lime-infused ceviche on microscopically diced, lemon-scented creamy potato salad. Vegetarians are not so generously served, but wild mushrooms, truffled gnocchi and cute fried quail eggs were delicious and surprisingly easy on the cream. No food education is complete without a visit to the Capital. *Booking advisable; essential weekends. Children over 10 admitted. Dress: smart casual; no jeans or trainers. Restaurant available for hire. Separate rooms for parties, seating 12 and 24.* **Map 8 F9.**

★ Foliage

Mandarin Oriental Hyde Park Hotel, 66 Knightsbridge, SW1X 7LA (7201 3723/ www.mandarinoriental.com). Knightsbridge tube. **Lunch served** noon-2.30pm, **dinner served** 7-10.30pm daily. **Set lunch** £25 3 courses (£32 incl wine). **Set meal** £47.50-£50 3 courses. **Service** 12.5%. **Credit** AmEx, DC, JCB, MC, V.
Foliage has to be one of London's best culinary secrets. It's not difficult to get a table at short notice, the atmosphere balances spiritedness with serenity, staff are impeccably responsive, at the weekend the restaurant lets its hair down enough to be family-friendly, and Chris Staines is a world-class chef (even managing it without a TV show). Added to all this, the pale, leafy-themed restaurant is open all week for lunch and dinner, and the menu du jour at £25 is an absolute steal, given its quality. So what will your palate be seduced by? Appetisers set the scene with their multi-faceted textures, temperatures and flavours, before a starter of foie gras parfait: cool, ultra-smooth paste sandwiching three wafer sails of toasted pain d'épice and, alongside, a hot pillow of pan-fried foie gras atop a butter-crisped cube of the same bread. Another finely executed comfort starter was fricassée of tiny wild mushrooms and lardons, with a soft egg and herby soldiers for dipping. One of the three main courses had run out by the time we ordered, but an alternative from the carte was immediately offered by way of replacement. So line-caught sea bass arrived with a light, divine medley of broad beans, peas and sweetcorn, while lusciously tender Welsh lamb was accompanied by puy lentils and horseradish-spiked white bean sauce. Squirm in childish pleasure at the array of breads, biscuits and fruit butter that comes with cheese, or splash out on a dessert such as black cherry soup with bitter almond ice-cream and goat's milk panna cotta. An inspiring restaurant. *Babies and children admitted; high chairs. Booking advisable. Disabled: toilet. Dress: smart casual. Vegetarian menu.* **Map 8 F9.**

Mju

The Millennium Knightsbridge, 16-17 Sloane Street, SW1X 9NU (7201 6330). Knightsbridge tube. **Lunch served** noon-2.30pm, **dinner served** 6-10.30pm Mon-Sat. **Main courses** £15-£22. **Set dinner** £45 6 courses (£70 with wine). **Service** 12.5%. **Credit** AmEx, DC, JCB, MC, V.

Tom Aikens. See p116.

Mju's low-key, vaguely oriental decor is losing its glossy newness. The kitchen has also settled down (after a few dodgy years), to produce sure-footed Eurasian cuisine. European influences are most apparent on the à la carte and menu du jour, where generous portions of pan-fried foie gras with miso-flavoured puy lentils might be served, or pheasant with herb gnocchi, Thai asparagus, girolles and black truffle. Those with a taste for adventure can experiment to their mouth's content by choosing from a popular lunchtime 'mezze' list and evening dégustation menus, which home-in on Japanese methods and ingredients. From the mezze menu, where two to three items are suggested per person, a salt-spiked salad of deep-fried soft-shell crab was a delight, contrasting with chilli-flecked mango and a melting square of slow-roast pork belly. Lobster with richly seasoned al dente glass noodles and copious amounts of wild mushroom was also aromatic and satisfying. After a long wait, the star of the show appeared: a plate of barely seared and mostly raw – deliberately so – Scottish Black Angus beef, thinly sliced and served at room temperature on a creamy truffle, rosemary and honey dressing, scattered with punchy mustard cress. At £6 the dish was an absolute bargain. Service was painfully slow. The waiters were fazed by 50 lunchtime diners who descended on them (presumably pre-booked), packing the room and drowning the conversation of a dozen couples already seated. We gave up on ordering dessert.
Babies and children admitted; high chairs. Booking advisable. Disabled: lift; toilets. No-smoking tables. Restaurant available for hire. **Map 8 F9.**

One-O-One

101 William Street, SW1X 7RN (7290 7101). Knightsbridge tube. **Lunch served** noon-2.30pm, **dinner served** 7-10.30pm daily. **Main courses** £22-£26. **Set lunch** £21.50 2 courses, £25 3 courses. **Set dinner** £70 7 courses. **Credit** AmEx, DC, JCB, MC, V.
Lunch is where the bargains are to be had at One-0-One, with two highly delicious courses costing just £21.50, as they have done for several years.

Nonetheless, every table was taken on our evening visit and, as if to demonstrate that low prices aren't everything, the top dishes rolling out of the kitchen were royal king crab legs from the Barents Sea (served one of six ways as a starter for £18.50), and whole wild sea bass in a Brittany sea-salt crust (one of chef Pascal Proyart's native speciality dishes) costing £49 per couple and accompanied by little other than a bit of de-boning drama at the table. Although the aim of One-0-One is to thrill us all to piscine pieces, one or two dishes are meat-led; think along the lines of duck three ways with morel and shallot mash, or Scottish beef with wild mushroom and bean fricassée. Yet fish is the thing, and our dover sole with roasted langoustines, spinach and chive mousseline was an innocent, milky fresh delight. Fillet of tapenade-encrusted sea bass was a more strident dish served on a fleshy bed of crushed purple potatoes, grilled baby artichoke and sauce barigoule – fantastic. Desserts are not among London's best, and service was on the slow if genuinely pleasant side, but there's something to be said for pouring your own wine occasionally. The aqua colour scheme is in need of an update; once this has been done, there might be no stopping One-0-One.
Babies and children welcome; high chairs. Booking advisable Thur-Sun. Disabled: toilet. Dress: smart casual. No-smoking tables. **Map 8 F9.**

Pétrus NEW

The Berkeley Hotel, Wilton Place, SW1X 7RL (7235 1200/www.marcuswareing.com). Hyde Park Corner or Knightsbridge tube. **Lunch served** noon-2.30pm Mon-Fri. **Dinner served** 6-11pm Mon-Sat. **Set lunch** £55 3 courses. **Set dinner** £55 3 courses, £70 tasting menu. **Credit** AmEx, MC, V.
We upset the sommelier at this plush, purple-velvet restaurant (formerly housing La Tante Claire), first by ordering an inexpensive (£18) half bottle from the huge leather-bound list, then by asking for a replacement because the white Crozes-Hermitage wasn't up to Louis Jadot's usual standards. To add insult to the sommelier's injury, we fell back on the

cheapest half bottle (£16) as a replacement – a good value and oft-underrated fragrant Loire white called Menetou-Salon. Understandably, wine waiters will always be more inspired by customers who spend thousands on the famous Château Pétrus, of which there is a mind-blowing amount here, but why look down on the rest of us? Once over this initial dispute (it was a very quiet one, as befits a velvet room, and ended with a grudging 'Well, I'll replace it since you don't like the style'), we settled down to some excellent food courtesy of Marcus Wareing. The seven-course tasting menu (including an amuse-bouche and pre-dessert, but not cheese and caviar – an extra £18) is not very different from a three-course dinner. From this latter arrangement, beef carpaccio was cleverly infiltrated with foie gras, adding a creamy depth to the tender red meat. Mackerel was generous in size yet pickled a degree too far, since anything tasted afterwards seemed under-seasoned by comparison. A main of roasted sea bream was on the wet and woolly side, but cheese and desserts were extraordinarily wonderful. Don't miss the silver bonbon trolley, which is wheeled around the room as if in a circus, full of awesome truffles, trembling fruit jellies and nut-packed nougats.
Babies and children welcome; high chairs. Booking essential. Dress: jacket preferred/smart. No-smoking. Separate room for parties, seats 16. Vegetarian menu. **Map 9 G9.**

Marble Arch W1

The Crescent

Montcalm Hotel, Great Cumberland Place, W1H 7TW (7402 4288/7723 4440/ www.montcalm.co.uk). Marble Arch tube. **Lunch served** 12.30-2.30pm Mon-Fri. **Dinner served** 6.30-10.30pm daily. **Set lunch** (incl half bottle of wine) £20 2 courses, £25 3 courses. **Set dinner** (incl half bottle of wine) £22.50 2 courses, £27.50 3 courses. **Credit** AmEx, DC, JCB, MC, V.
It's not exactly rocking at the Montcalm Hotel, but this genteel establishment, half obscured by shimmering plane trees, probably prefers it that

way. Given the hotel's proximity to Oxford Street, it is surprisingly quiet, yet avoids the overstuffed silence that blights many a hotel. Whether the Crescent will ever be in the same league as its neighbours in this section is questionable. Food is tame and firmly grounded rather than soaring to culinary heights. Given the static atmosphere and unpolished staff, the place seems determined to stay in the shadows. A wine list practically had to be begged into service; the waiter (there was only one on duty) looked shocked that anyone would consider a drink beyond the Chilean red or white that he sploshed into glasses at the beginning of the meal with no more enquiry than 'Red or white?' Still, we like the Crescent's easy-chair comfort. Best dish of the night was a haddock and crab cake, packed gently into shape and shallow-fried, resulting in a light, tasty, crusted-on-the-bottom dish. Medley of salmon, sea bass and langoustine came with lightly gingered couscous, while a pink noisette of lamb arrived atop a glossy, meaty jus streaked with smoky aubergine purée. Expect sparklers rather than fireworks, and go for lunch rather than listless dinner.
Babies and children welcome; high chairs. Booking advisable. Disabled: toilet. Dress: smart casual. No-smoking tables. Separate rooms for parties, seating 20 and 60. **Map 8 F6.**

Mayfair W1

Brian Turner Mayfair

Millennium Hotel Mayfair, 44 Grosvenor Square, W1K 2HP (7596 3444/www.millennium hotels.com). Bond Street tube. **Bar Open** noon-11.30pm Mon-Fri; 6-11.30pm Sat. *Restaurant* **Lunch served** 12.30-2.30pm Mon-Fri. **Dinner served** 6-10.30pm Mon-Sat. **Main courses** £12.50-£25. **Set lunch** £22.50 2 courses, £25.50 3 courses. **Service** 12.5%. *Both* **Credit** AmEx, DC, MC, V.
There's a relaxing sea theme going on at Brian Turner's: not the tropical aqua, but a palette of pebble grey/green more suited to London skies. Modern frameless canvasses of crashing surf on otherwise plain walls have their colours repeated in the comfortable decor, which we like. We also like the menu for its unashamedly British approach, the staff for their natural concern and quiet friendliness, the generous champagne glasses, and a host of other things that this plush hotel restaurant has got right. Yet the food doesn't always reach its target. From the set lunch (costing a few pounds more than last year), a lovely sounding salad of roasted pumpkin with rocket, citrus dressing and toasted cashew nuts tasted lacklustre; the 'roasted' pumpkin was more like boiled marrow, the rocket tasted of nothing, ditto the dressing; only the cashews were lush. Boneless skate wing with lacy potato cakes and creamed spinach was a good, fresh main course that lifted our spirits. But for dessert, how is a freestanding sturdy cylinder of cooked egg, minus pastry, a real British egg custard tart? Please, Mr Turner, all we want is good British food.
Babies and children admitted. Booking advisable. Disabled: toilet. Dress: smart casual. No-smoking tables. Separate room for parties, seats 45. Tables outdoors (5, terrace). **Map 9 G7.**

Le Gavroche

43 Upper Brook Street, W1K 7QR (7408 0881/ www.le-gavroche.co.uk). Marble Arch tube. **Lunch served** noon-2pm Mon-Fri. **Dinner served** 7-11pm Mon-Sat. **Main courses** £27-£39. **Minimum** £60 dinner. **Set lunch** £44 3 courses incl coffee, half bottle of wine, mineral water. **Service** 12.5%. **Credit** AmEx, DC, JCB, MC, V.
Given the popularity of Le Gavroche – after more than 20 years occupying these dark, clubby subterranean premises, and a further 15 before that in Chelsea – booking a table is easy as pie and only need be done a week or so in advance. What's more, reception staff are terribly polite, phone you back the day before to confirm, and don't demand a credit card number to secure the booking. If a restaurant as expensive as Le Gavroche can afford to risk no-shows, why can't others? And, yes, expensive is what your meal here will be. Set lunches have risen from £40 to £44, although this

includes pretty much everything – appetisers, water, half a bottle of wine per person, a three-course meal, coffee and petits fours – and is thus comparable to most establishments in this section. Otherwise, a typical main course will cost over £30, while starters and desserts weigh in at another £30 each. Still, for that you'll get some of the best food in London. From the set lunch a simple combination of asparagus, truffle shavings and parmesan was packed to the brim with flavour, but a tian of crab with tomato and balsamic dressing was a bit noncommittal. Fillet of poached veal, served cold with a creamy caper sauce and celeriac remoulade, was sensationally tender, beguilingly sweet and a very adult sophistication; almost equally good was a main of wild salmon trout with crackly thin ham and a meaty, thyme-infused jus. Dessert on this occasion could have been fabulous cheese, ices and sorbets, or a dense, orange-scented pudding of fine crêpes baked in egg custard. Adventurous diners may feel the set lunch doesn't exercise their taste buds as much as the carte, but either event leaves you wanting to visit more often.
Babies and children admitted. Booking essential. Dress: jacket; no jeans, shorts or trainers. No pipes or cigars. Restaurant available for hire. **Map 9 G7.**

Gordon Ramsay at Claridge's

Claridge's Hotel, 55 Brook Street, W1A 2JQ (7499 0099/www.gordonramsay.com). Bond Street tube. **Lunch served** noon-2.45pm Mon-Fri; noon-3pm Sat, Sun. **Dinner served** 5.45-11pm Mon-Sat; 6-11pm Sun. **Set lunch** £30 3 courses. **Set dinner** £55 3 courses, £65 6 courses. **Credit** AmEx, JCB, MC, V.
There are so many things we like about this beautiful hotel restaurant. Claridge's hosts some of the best food in the capital, and the most relaxed yet glamorous atmosphere. Opening hours are longer than most, so it's often possible to get a table without booking, even if this means delaying in the delightful bar or lounge areas for a short while (obviously, booking is sensible for busy times). The restaurant is also open for Sunday dinner, an absurd rarity in London. On this particular Sunday evening the calm peachy room was occupied by Mayfair locals, families, groups of single ladies-who-dine, courting couples and out-of-towners – not to mention a significant showing of chefs and food professionals from other restaurants, educating their palates. There are few better places to eke out the dregs of the weekend. Foie gras mousse and crostini accompany the browsing of menu and wine list, followed by a steaming cup of an artichoke and truffle-infused plaything. Starters begin in earnest with, perhaps, a sublime smoked eel and celeriac soup garnished with mouth-poppingly soft quail eggs (just as addictive, but much sexier than popping bubble wrap) or earthy chestnut tortellini with seared wild mushrooms and pumpkin velouté. Boiled beef was fantastically tender, three neat slabs served in their own consommé with tiny vegetables. Apple tarte tatin is justifiably one of chef Mark Sergeant's specialities, but two teaspoons of ice-cream alongside is just plain mean. One of London's master chocolatiers makes the salted caramels, rounding off an unmissable dining experience.
Babies and children welcome; high chairs. Booking essential. Disabled: toilet. Dress: smart/jacket preferred; no jeans or trainers. Separate rooms for parties, seating 10, 12 and 30. **Map 9 H6.**

★ Greenhouse

27A Hay's Mews, W1J 5NY (7499 3331). Green Park tube. **Lunch served** noon-2.30pm Mon-Fri. **Dinner served** 6.45-11.45pm Mon-Sat. **Set lunch** £28 2 courses, £32 3 courses. **Set meal** £55 3 courses. **Service** 12.5%. **Credit** AmEx, DC, MC, V.
Discovering the Greenhouse at the increasingly narrow end of Hay's Mews is an adventure in itself. On our visit, the arching bamboos and teak decking, which snake tropically from street to entrance, gleamed from a recent downpour. The idea is that this lush green outdoors follows

through into the restaurant, but we found the beige fabrics, terracotta leather chairs and walnut flooring more smart and sedate. Try to book a window table, to heighten the garden effect. Even more stimulating than the surroundings is the menu. The Greenhouse provides some genuinely exciting novelties: foie gras flavoured with espresso syrup and amaretto froth, for example; or English rare-breed beef with crispy polenta and beetroot relish; or Earl Grey-scented jelly and crumble. The tea menu alone goes down numerous paths: black, white or green tea, fermented or unfermented, fresh herbal infusions or dried flower preparations. In true haute cuisine manner a meal begins with a variety of appetite teasers, in this case a fine white asparagus panna cotta with a little raw salad of vinegared asparagus ribbons. Also sensational was a starter of braised and shredded oxtail in sticky jus on a slim flute of toasted french bread. Micro salad – minuscule herb tips and flowers – packed a surprisingly powerful punch alongside. Whole baby lobster was a generous main not for the faint-hearted: it was served sawn asunder with legs, scales and spiky bits akimbo over lurid saffron foam and buttered shredded leeks. Chef Bjorn van der Horst took over in May 2004, fresh from New York, following the restaurant's change of ownership and subsequent refurb. Watch your back, Gordon.
Babies and children admitted. Booking essential. Dress: smart casual. No-smoking tables. Separate room for parties, seats 10. **Map 9 H7.**

Angela Hartnett at the Connaught

The Connaught, 16 Carlos Place, W1K 2AL (7592 1222/www.gordonramsay.com). Bond Street or Green Park tube. **Breakfast served** 7-10.30am Mon-Fri; 7-11am Sat, Sun. **Lunch served** noon-2.45pm Mon-Fri; noon-3.15pm Sat, Sun. **Dinner served** 5.45-11pm Mon-Sat; 7-10.30pm Sun. **Set lunch** £30 3 courses. **Set dinner** £50 3 courses; (tasting menu), £70 6 courses. **Service** 12.5%. **Credit** AmEx, DC, MC, V.
London has got used to associating Angela Hartnett with the stately Connaught hotel. A weekday lunch saw the beautiful oak-panelled and clubby Menu dining room packed with a mix of older suits, middle-aged foodies and whip-thin 20-year-olds (the latter grazing on as little as possible). Happy anticipation fuelled the conversation. Staff were busy, yet not to the point of distraction. Menus are structured casually but carefully along British-Italian lines, with a scattering of seasonal victuals in between. A la carte and set menus are both dangerously tempting. Pumpkin and chestnut velouté demonstrated Hartnett's fondness for the rustic vegetables often under-used by mega-chefs, and proved her talent for coaxing out of them rare silky textures and aromatic undercurrents. The same is true for her farinaceous dishes – pasta, gnocchi, risotto and the like. At Menu these are mostly airy, finely crafted treasures suffused with herby fragrances and packed with surprisingly punchy flavours, as in jus-glossed ravioli filled with profoundly ducky spiced and shredded duck breast. Linguini with bottarga was overcooked and dull, but a waitress swiftly spotted and dealt with it without being asked. Shining like a beacon was a dessert of pineapple carpaccio, lime ice-cream, tiny sugared coriander leaves and a crumbly warm pineapple cake. The days of walking into the Connaught without a booking are over.
Babies and children welcome; high chairs. Booking essential. Disabled: lift; toilet. No-smoking Separate rooms for parties, seating 14 and 22. **Map 9 H7.**

Sketch: The Lecture Room

9 Conduit Street, W1S 2XZ (0777 4488/ www.sketch.uk.com). Oxford Circus tube. **Lunch served** noon-2pm, **dinner served** 7-10pm Mon-Sat. **Main courses** £45-£65. **Set lunch** £35 3 courses. **Set dinner** £80-£140 3 courses. **Service** 12.5%. **Credit** AmEx, DC, MC, V.
Once you've got over the annoyance of giving your credit card details in exchange for a booking, and swallowed the thought of a £50 cancellation fee

per person, you can lap up the tremendous style of this exquisite, lavishly decorated building. Funky is too tame a word to describe pictures that transmogrify into chairs, an electric-blue poetry-scrawled stairway, crystal-studded black washrooms with fairground music, and the padded muted and mirrored den of a dining room. Mourad Mazouz has transformed the former RIBA headquarters into a fantastic place to eat and be seen. Fantastic also are the prices: à la carte mains range from £45 to £70, starters are along the same lines, a cheese course is £30, dessert £28. The cheapest option is a five-course tasting menu for £80. Pascal Sanchez is head chef, although French wizard Pierre Gagnaire oversees menu construction. The extraordinary powers of pastry chef Etienne Irazoqui were revealed throughout. Portions were tiny at first, beginning with a bowl of white bean froth, black saké jelly, an asparagus spear and three thin slices of spiced duck breast. A pale fish course consisted of diced poached scallop meat between thin slices of mooli, over which the waiter poured a barely-there broth of artichoke and star anise. 'Main course' milk-fed veal was delicate and lovely. Then flavours and portions received a turbo-boost for some reason, dominated by a highly tasty cheese course and waves of no less than six desserts – with petits fours served in between them as 'palate fresheners'. The mirrors exacerbated the effect of a giddy number of waiters who work in an extremely formulaic manner, positioning plates and themselves at choreographed moments. Strange, but fun.

Babies and children admitted. Booking essential (no entrance without a table reservation after 5pm for non-members). Dress: casual. Entertainment: DJs 10.30pm-2am Mon-Sat (bar). Restaurant available for hire. Map 9 J6.

Le Soufflé

Hotel Inter-Continental, 1 Hamilton Place, W1V 0QY (7318 8577/www.london.interconti.com). Hyde Park Corner tube. **Lunch served** (not Aug) 12.30-3pm Tue-Fri. **Dinner served** 7-10.30pm Tue-Fri; 7-11.15pm Sat. **Main courses** £20.50-£28.50. **Set lunch** (not Aug) £19.50 2 courses, £23.50 3 courses. **Set dinner** £39.50 3 courses, £44.50 4 courses. **Credit** AmEx, DC, JCB, MC, V.

It's never going to escape its windowless confines deep below Park Lane, but Le Soufflé has seen significant improvements this year. Brighter lights, for one thing, which have transformed the parchment-toned dustiness of previous visits into an immediately more welcoming, lively room of fresh yellow and marine blue. Staff also seemed far more jovial and attentive despite, or perhaps because of, there being rather a lot of them for the eight punters present. The set lunch is cheaper and less static than before, allowing it to include more seasonal ingredients. Indeed, British asparagus cropped up everywhere in early summer: in baskets at the front of the restaurant, in starters, main courses and appetisers throughout each of the menus – and unfortunately on the bill as well, in the form of supplements that nullified the reduced set-meal prices. In this case, the wire-thin tender spears were served with rack of young lamb and nicely paired with goat's cheese gratin, to be followed a while later by a superbly flavoured and precisely cooked blueberry soufflé with palate-searing lime sorbet. À la carte meals are classically French – apart from a few dishes such as traditionally cured Scottish salmon, hand-carved at table – and might include best end of lamb with sweetbread boulin blanc, sautéed john dory with lyonnaise potatoes and confit garlic, or turnip velouté with truffle and honey.

Babies and children admitted (lunch); high chairs. Booking advisable. Disabled: toilet. Dress: smart casual. Entertainment: pianist and singer 7-10.30pm Wed-Fri; dinner dance Sat. No-smoking tables. Restaurant available for hire. Map 9 G8.

★ The Square

6-10 Bruton Street, W1J 6PU (7495 7100/ www.squarerestaurant.com). Bond Street or Green Park tube. **Lunch served** noon-2.45pm Mon-Fri. **Dinner served** 6.30-10.45pm Mon-Sat; 6.30-

9.45pm Sun. **Set lunch** £25 2 courses, £30 3 courses. **Set dinner** £55 3 courses; (tasting menu) £75 8 courses. **Service** 12.5%. **Credit** AmEx, DC, JCB, MC, V.

Like Claridge's (*see p113*), the Square is one of the few top London restaurants opening its doors on Sunday evening, and it's also one of our all-time favourite places to eat. Why? For being cool without being flash, efficient without being cold, and for its sheer deliciousness under the sensible, sensitive hand of chef Philip Howard. The fact that Howard can be found more frequently in his kitchen than in a recording studio or elsewhere is much evidenced by the consistently supreme quality of every mouthful you take, from the spiky tapers of anchovy-flecked pastry to start, through to the fathoms-deep chocolate truffles to finish. Along the way you might be treated to a sweet, sea-fresh salmon and lobster terrine served with dill cream and capers, or a meatier option involving pigeon breast and butter-smooth foie gras. The latter is served with a fantastic salad, arranged in a ring of bite-size pieces, jauntily flavoured with roasted hazelnuts and dried apricots. Veal served four ways allows the kitchen to show off a little (in an appealingly understated manner, of course), while a delicate fillet of wild salmon is more simply served and relies upon clarity of raw ingredients rather than complex cooking skills. At £25 for two courses and £30 for three, the Square's lunch menu isn't the cheapest in this section. The midday choice is limited to two starters, two mains and two desserts, but of these nothing will disappoint and much will exceed expectations.

Babies and children admitted. Booking essential. Disabled: toilet. Dress: smart. No cigars. Restaurant available for hire. Separate room for parties, seats 18. Map 9 H7.

Windows

Hilton Hotel, Park Lane, W1K 1BE (7493 8000/www.hilton.co.uk). Green Park or Hyde Park Corner tube. **Bar Open** noon-1.30am Mon-Thur; noon-2.30pm Fri; 5pm-2.30am Sat; noon-10pm Sun. *Restaurant* **Lunch served** 12.30-2.30pm Mon-Fri, Sun. **Dinner served** 7-10.30pm Mon-Thur; 7-11.30pm Fri, Sat. **Main courses** £26.50-£33.50. **Set lunch** £39.50, £42.50 3 courses, £45.50 4 courses incl half bottle of wine. **Set dinner** £59 5 courses. **Service** 12.5%. **Credit** AmEx, DC, MC, V.

Nothing much changes up on the 28th floor of the Park Lane Hilton. The views around London are inspiring enough to dine out on, but one of the in-house diversions is a buffet. Dominating the centre of the light-flooded room is a vast steel chiller cabinet stacked with plates of this and that. If your chosen menu is the £39.50 option, you take a plate and shuffle along the line as those before you hog all the giant prawns and asparagus and a waitress behind you busily fluffs up bowls of lettuce and straightens balls of mozzarella, just like an aged aunt plumping the cushion you've just vacated. Nevertheless, everything on the buffet was very fresh and tasty. Elsewhere, silver trolleys laden with the day's hunk of roasted flesh (rib of veal on Thursday, sea bass on Friday, for instance), farmyard cheeses or daintily tiered desserts are yoyo'd across the restaurant, displayed for diners to drool over (some customers get staff to pile up their plates for the second and third time). Windows will never win any value-for-money prizes, but you certainly needn't go home hungry. A more relaxing and less calorific arrangement is to order à la carte. Portions are smaller, delicately presented, prettily sauced and light in nature, as in crispy red mullet stuffed with black olives, or courgette risotto and gleaming red piquillo peppers. This style of dining is fine for groups, but lacks intimacy and panache.

Babies and children welcome: 50% discount for under-10s; high chairs. Booking advisable. Disabled: toilet. Dress: suit jacket; no jeans. Entertainment: live music 7pm-1.30am Mon-Sat (bar). No-smoking tables. Vegan dishes. Map 9 G8.

Piccadilly W1

The Ritz

150 Piccadilly, W1J 9BR (7493 8181/ www.theritzhotel.co.uk). Green Park tube. **Bar Open** 11.30am-11pm Mon-Sat; noon-10.30pm Sun. **Food served** noon-10pm daily. *Restaurant* **Breakfast served** 7-10.30am Mon-Sat; 8-10.30am Sun. **Lunch served** 12.30-2.30pm daily. **Tea served** (reserved sittings) 1.30pm, 3.30pm, 5.30pm daily. **Dinner served** 6-10.30pm Mon-Sat. **Main courses** £25-£56. **Set lunch** £39 (£45 from Nov 2004) 3 courses. **Set tea** £32. **Set dinner** (6-7pm, 10-10.30pm) £43 3 courses; (Mon-Thur) £60 4 courses; (Fri, Sat) £70 4 courses. *Both* **Credit** AmEx, MC, V.

It takes a brave team to renovate a hotel as revered as the Ritz, but the dining room is looking good. The faded, dated turquoise and salmon pink in this vast restaurant overlooking Green Park has subtly deepened to richer tones of garden green and cherry pink, while the stupendously excessive gold-leaf chandeliers, embellished with garlands of gilded flowers against a romantic mural, are fresh, strong and confident. Unlike most of its patrons, the Ritz is not a retiring venue. A new chef is at the helm, and the archaic and frankly unsettling old menu with its starters, entrées, fish courses, meat courses, farinaceous courses, soufflés and desserts ad infinitum (minus prices for the ladies) has gone. Phew. A much more navigable à la carte simply displays one page of starters, one page of main courses and a separate sheet for the three-course lunch of the day at £39 (£45 from Nov 2004). This gets you a light, modestly portioned meal for less than the price of most main courses on the carte. Vegetables were the order of the day when we visited: a salad packed to bursting with new-season asparagus, artichoke, beans (lima, french and peeled broad beans), peas, tiny carrots – 15 different vegetables in all – demurely served with a simple nut oil and balsamic dressing, but beautifully prepared, delicious and virtuous. Unfortunately, the same combination appeared warm in a vegetarian main course 'cassoulette'. Beef fillet, by way of excellent contrast, was sinfully meaty, deeply satisfying and accompanied by plenty of carbs and butter. Desserts are light, fruity, flirty and good for dieters, but all too easily cancelled out by a tiered stand of petits fours. Dining at the Ritz is iconic.

Babies and children welcome; children's menu; high chairs. Disabled: toilet. Booking advisable restaurant; essential afternoon tea. Dress: jacket and tie; no jeans or trainers. Entertainment: dinner dance Fri, Sat (restaurant); pianist daily. Separate rooms for parties, seating up to 22 & 55. Tables outdoors (8, terrace). Vegan dishes. Vegetarian menu. Map 9 J7.

Pimlico SW1

Allium NEW

Dolphin Square, Chichester Street, SW1V 3LX (7798 6888/www.allium.co.uk). Pimlico tube. **Lunch served** noon-3pm Tue-Fri; noon-2.30pm Sun. **Dinner served** 7-10.30pm Tue-Sat. **Main courses** £12.50-£24.10. **Set lunch** £17.50 2 courses, £22.50 3 courses. **Set meal** (6-7pm) £28.50 3 courses. **Set dinner** £32.50 3 courses. **Service** 12.5%. **Credit** AmEx, DC, MC, V.

Blue is the colour and footfall is the game at this discreet 1930s Pimlico restaurant, previously occupied by Gary Rhodes and now under the masterful care of Anton Edelmann (21 years at the Savoy) and head chef Peter Woods. Midnight-blue walls, carpets, banquettes and club chairs might seem too much of a good thing. However, when they're combined with shiny chrome, ship-shape bright white, an allium sculpture and tall, spiky flower displays, the effect is striking and likeably retro. As to footfall, there was a distinct lack of feet falling across the sea of blue on our visit. No doubt this will improve radically when London has caught on to Edelmann's light contemporary touch, which is designed to make us feel good about hotel dining. Initiative is shown in, for example, an exceptionally fairly priced (for London) wine list, ditto the food, and a pre-theatre meal that allows you to have two courses and then return after the show to linger over dessert until 11pm. Spring asparagus with herbed mascarpone was the sunny opposite of deep, sweet, caramelised allium tart with a foie gras garnish; both arrived dressed with amazingly fragrant and riotously green basil oil. Main courses were similarly lovely: seared fillet of john dory riding above gratinated fennel and a freckle of minute summer carrots, peas and peeled broad beans; and a heartier plate of roasted Buccleuch beef and yorkshire pudding, with lots more lush, delicately cooked vegetables. Unflashy

yet refined food such as this is the result of passionate but patient years spent slaving behind a hot stove. A worthwhile pleasure.
Babies and children welcome. Booking advisable. Disabled: toilet. No-smoking tables. Separate rooms for parties, seating 24 and 70. Vegetarian menu. **Map 15 J12**.

St James's SW1

L'Oranger

5 St James's Street, SW1A 1EF (7839 3774). Green Park tube. **Lunch served** noon-2.30pm Mon-Fri. **Dinner served** 6.30-10.30pm

Mon-Sat. **Main courses** £22-£29 (dinner). **Set lunch** £24 2 courses, £28 3 courses. **Service** 12.5%. **Credit** AmEx, DC, MC, V. Intimate, refined yet relaxed, L'Oranger is a special restaurant. The cooking has been excellent for several years, but, we are told, the arrival of a young French chef who has cooked at some of France's most revered eateries can only improve things further. Maître d' Thierry Tomasin, who also works at Aubergine (*see p116* – owned by the same company), ensures that front-of-house matters are smoothly attended to. Part of L'Oranger's success lies in the diversity of its diners: a multi-aged, multi-purpose bunch who

The Greenhouse. See p113.

might be rounding off a day at Wimbledon or Ascot, celebrating an anniversary, dining out with business colleagues or just chilling with family and friends. It's precisely this balance that produces the elusive attributes of ease and elegance. From the à la carte dinner menu came a stunning plate of jabugo ham, roasted artichoke hearts, salad and fine, creamy sage ravioli: a mammoth and superb starter. Less extrovert was a dish of buttered leeks, drowned at table by ladlefuls of creamy potato soup and garnished with a poached egg and single flake of smoked haddock. Nearly all main courses had roasted meat or fish at their hub, but we had no complaints over roasted pigeon with ultra-buttery pommes mousseline, and roasted lamb with aubergine caviar. Orange soufflés were the upstanding highlight of the meal: exquisitely crunchy with sugar around the edges; hot, citrous and dissolvingly creamy within; with icy fruit sorbet providing cool contrast. There's plenty of choice on the wine list around the £20-£30 mark too, so good feelings all round.
Children over 7 admitted. Booking essential. Dress: smart casual; no trainers. Separate room for parties, seats 22. Tables outdoors (6, courtyard). Map 9 J8.

South West
Chelsea SW3, SW10

Aubergine
11 Park Walk, SW10 0AJ (7352 3449). South Kensington tube/14, 345, 414 bus. Lunch served noon-2.15pm Mon-Fri. Dinner served 7-11pm Mon-Sat. Set lunch £32 3 courses incl half bottle of wine, mineral water, coffee. Set dinner £55 3 courses; (tasting menu) £72 7 courses. Service 12.5%. Credit AmEx, DC, JCB, MC, V.
Not much changes here, decor-wise, but the food and service have recovered from their disorientation of last year and a sense of direction has returned to both front- and back-of-house operations. Restaurant manager Thierry Tomasin is warm yet watchful, and followed by a team of proactive waiters who are almost beside themselves to get on with the job. The kitchen (under chef William Drabble) is again turning out confident, lightly sauced, multidimensional and interesting dishes, and their effect can be seen on more, and more contented, diners. Effort also seems to have been made to steady the relentlessly ascending prices of a fine meal in London; an extra course, wine, water and coffee have been added to the set lunch and, although a minimum charge still exists in the evening, this is now £55 for three courses instead of £50 for two. Saffron-scented red mullet escabeche from the lunch menu doubles as an appetiser in the evening, to be followed by generous starters such as creamy leek and filo tart with giant caramelised scallop slices and lemon beurre blanc, a supremely rich and filling combination. One of the inspired main courses was an assiette of pork: belly slices on creamed savoy cabbage and bacon, pan-fried loin on sweet onions, surprisingly tasty little strips of pig's ear breaded and deep fried, and an enchantingly aromatic tangle of pork shreds cooked in smoky tea and served alongside a refreshing square of tart apple. Lighter dishes include lemon sole with artichokes and confit lemon, and a dessert of red wine-poached pear with cool, tangy goat's cheese sorbet.
Babies and children admitted. Booking advisable; essential weekends. Dress: smart casual. No pipes or cigars. No-smoking tables. Map 14 D12.

Gordon Ramsay
68-69 Royal Hospital Road, SW3 4HP (7352 4441/3334/www.gordonramsay.com). Sloane Square tube. Lunch served noon-2pm, dinner served 6.30-11pm Mon-Fri. Set lunch £35 3 courses. Set meal £65 3 courses, £80 7 courses. Credit AmEx, DC, JCB, MC, V.
Those less passionate about fish than Mr Ramsay may be stuck for choice at his flagship enterprise, a stone's throw from the river in Chelsea. Six of the

eight starters contain fish, as do half the main courses. But that's where we stop being critical. Waiting staff really know what they're doing, treating every diner like royalty and discerning the difference between those with the whole day on their hands and others in for a working lunch. The former might be treated to tours of the kitchen and always to protracted descriptions of dishes (three people described our main course to us), while the latter are left more to themselves, staff just ensuring wine levels remain high. Uninspired by the set lunch menu, which, from peeking discreetly over the shoulders of others, looked beautiful but included too many household ingredients for our liking, we splashed out on the fish-led à la carte. Fat, orange langoustine tails were teamed with lengthily cooked glazed pork belly, lettuce purée and meaty jus in a tasty, substantial starter. Rather more elegant foie gras terrine came cleverly interlaced with paper-thin slices of smoked goose, which lifted the whole thing from its bed of buttery luxury and added a stimulating new dimension and smoky aroma. Sliced monkfish loin also exhibited wonderful cohesiveness, accompanied by scallops and delicate lobster cream sauce; it was brushed with said sauce during cooking, for subtle, tonal emphasis. Duck breast was excellently cooked, with a healthy degree of caramelisation, but in the end was just duck breast, prettily fanned over a roast potato. Every dessert leaving the kitchen looked sensational, but we were more than contented with our shiny, crisp cylinder of dark chocolate filled with caramel, coffee crisp mousse and white, gingery froth. If you haven't been here, start saving now. Book at least a month in advance and be prepared for a lengthy wait on the phone.
Booking essential. Children admitted. Dress: smart. No smoking. Vegetarian menu. Map 14 F12.

Putney SW15

Putney Bridge
Embankment, 2 Lower Richmond Road, SW15 1LB (8780 1811/www.putneybridge restaurant.com). Putney Bridge tube/14, 22 bus. Bar Open noon-midnight Mon-Thur; noon-2am Fri, Sat (last entry 11pm); noon-10.30pm Sun. Restaurant Lunch served noon-2pm Tue-Sat; noon-2.30pm Sun. Dinner served 7-10pm Tue-Sat. Main courses £19.50-£23. Set lunch (Tue-Sat) £18.50 2 courses, £22.50 3 courses; (Sun) £25 3 courses. Set dinner (tasting menu) £55 6 courses. Service 12.5%. Credit AmEx, DC, MC, V.
There's one disadvantage of a restaurant with floor-to-ceiling windows overlooking a waterscape: it can look bleak on a grey, leafless, coat-clutching day. But there's enough truly interesting food at the modern, split-level Putney Bridge to fire up the most inert of imaginations. The set lunch here is one of our favourite London bargains. Request a river view when you book; this is among the best places to watch the start of the annual Oxford-Cambridge boat race, champagne in hand and nibbles at elbow. Occasional hiccups in service are forgotten with the arrival of beguilingly fresh pastries: warm from the oven, thin as organza, and whipping the palate into a tantalising state of arousal. The simpler set lunch menu continued with a silky pale sea of potato soup, from which arose two islands of compliant herb chantilly and a poached egg. Introducing the à la carte meal was a refreshing dish of warm ricotta quenelles topped with beetroot dice, toasted hazelnuts and tender pea shoots. Roast free-range chicken with wild mushrooms did what it said on the menu, while rabbit was a more elaborate dish: a mini cast-iron casserole of confit meat and (more) wild mushrooms, topped with tarragon-laced mash – a witty and upmarket 'cottage pie'. Push the boat out for desserts, which are almost always sensational. Hot dark chocolate fondant with vanilla ice-cream was well executed, while coffee panna cotta delivered a fantastically intense coffee rush in a spellbindingly smooth wobbly format.
Babies and children admitted (lunch). Disabled: toilet. No smoking. Tables outdoors (15, riverside terrace).

South Kensington
SW3, SW7

1880 NEW
The Bentley Hotel, Harrington Gardens, SW7 4JX (7244 5555/www.thebentley-hotel.com). Gloucester Road tube. Dinner served 6-10pm Mon-Sat. Set dinner £45 3 courses; (tasting menus) £40-£58 5-10 courses. Credit AmEx, DC, MC, V.
Built in 1880, this place was transformed into an opulent hotel in 2003. Inside, the Bentley is bedecked in reflective gold and marble, thick pale carpets and silk wall panels, an effect that becomes more concentrated on descending to the subterranean restaurant. Here the ceilings are lower, the lights dimmer and the embellishments up close and personal. In the kitchen is Andrew Turner, whose complex system of grazing menus – set meals of between five and ten courses, costing £40-£58 – could have been lifted straight from restaurant 1887 at Browns Hotel (his previous post, currently undergoing a year-long makeover). Notes on the menu suggest this takes the stress out of ordering, but since each table must have the same set meal it also makes the kitchen's job easier. The 'seven courses for £46' option looked adventurous, and kicked off with rabbit velouté, confit pork spring roll and a shard of pastry stuffed with ginger, one of AT's signature dishes. Very tasty, very small. Next came a tiny glass of shredded lettuce and crab meat. After that arrived another signature dish of port-marinated foie gras with gingerbread and a teaspoon of salad, plus a shot of apple sorbet 'to be taken afterwards to cleanse the palate', all of which took longer for the waitress to describe than it took to eat. Fish and lamb courses rapidly arrived and rapidly disappeared, followed by nice French cheese and a stomach-curdling milk chocolate panna cotta covered in bitter orange jelly, which brought the grazing menu to a galloping finish. Too much happens on each plate, which spoils some great cooking and dining – and it all arrives at the table in a frantic blur. Ask for breaks between courses.
Babies and children welcome; high chairs. Booking advisable dinner. Disabled: toilet. Dress: smart casual; no trainers. No smoking. Separate rooms for parties, seating 10, 12 and 150. Vegetarian menu. Map 13 C10.

★ Tom Aikens
2004 RUNNER-UP BEST NEW RESTAURANT
43 Elystan Street, SW3 3NT (7584 2003/ www.tomaikens.co.uk). South Kensington tube. Lunch served noon-2.30pm, dinner served 7-11pm Mon-Fri. Set lunch £29 3 courses incl coffee. Set meal £55 3 courses incl coffee, £70 6 courses incl coffee. Service 12.5%. Credit AmEx, JCB, MC, V.
This is one sleek restaurant. That's not to say it's intimidating (staff are well-drilled and formal, but friendly) or overly fashionable (the decor is modern but classic in its clean lines and monochrome tones). Everything is choreographed beautifully: from the arrival of the champagne trolley – designed to tempt diners into an aperitif – to the array of petits fours and madeleines at the end, it's a smoothly oiled machine that paces the meal perfectly. From the very reasonably priced lunch menu (£29 for three courses, including coffee and petits fours), came a divine pea mousse with peas, pea shoots and parma ham, and borlotti bean soup, a light foaming broth topped with summer truffle and concealing foie gras mousse and beans. Mains couldn't quite hit these transcendental heights, but roast brill with artichokes, artichoke purée and mushroom duxelle, and duck confit with roast duck breast, sliced turnips, lentil purée and fried duck egg came close. To finish, roast apple, with apple sorbet, apple beignet and wafer-thin apple slices, was essence of apple in many forms; hard to choose between this and the cheese trolley, however. The £55 three-course set meal buys even more exalted haute cuisine, but given the generosity and skill of the set lunch, why upgrade?
Babies and children welcome. Booking essential dinner. Disabled: toilet. Dress: smart casual. No smoking. Vegetarian menu. Map 14 E11.

Indian

Supplying everything from mango Bellinis to madras curry takeaways, London's Indian restaurants cater to all tastes and pockets. At top-end Modern Indian venues, you might be treated to such fusion cuisine as herby rosemary nans, or french dressings flavoured with curry leaves, plus such conspicuous-consumption classics as chicken tikka flecked with gold leaf. Many dishes at these establishments will be unrecognisable to most Indian families. Far from the constraints of cultural expectation, Indian chefs in Britain have the freedom to innovate with local ingredients and to blend traditional recipes with western cooking techniques. Food is styled in the same way as carefully orchestrated Modern European cuisine. The results aren't always convincing, but, when the chef pulls it off, can be outstanding.

Newcomer **Rasoi Vineet Bhatia** in Chelsea is one of the latest of these new-wave Indian establishments, charging 24-carat prices for its superb food. Not quite as high-profile, restaurants such as the **Painted Heron** (now with two branches) deliver superbly executed meals inspired by pan-Indian flavours and careful spicing.

Yet the capital's Indian restaurants are not all about dressing up street food, engineering a maharajah's banquet, or giving mum's cooking a makeover. Affordable regional restaurants still hold their own, especially in areas that have sizeable Punjabi, Tamil and Gujarati communities, such as **Southall**, **Tooting** and **Wembley**. One of the best newcomers in this bracket is **Chai Pani** near Marble Arch. It specialises in providing vegetarian cooking from Rajasthan. For some of the best South Indian vegetarian food in town, try **Sagar** in Hammersmith; its dosais and idlis are quite the best in London.

Notable restaurants serving typically Bangladeshi, Nepali or Kashmiri cooking are thin on the ground, however. Many Brick Lane caffs have updated their image with light wooden furnishings, splashes of modern art and even an occasional salad bar, yet their cooking styles are rooted in the 1970s, and chefs have a tendency to dip into mass-produced masala pastes from a jar.

Old India hands might mourn the gradual demise of old-fashioned Indian caffs and canteens in favour of modern enterprises such as **Masala Zone**. Happily, though, the sun continues to shine on stalwarts such as the dearly loved, if somewhat frayed **India Club**, the **Indian YMCA**'s canteen and Southall's **New Asian Tandoori Centre**.

Central

Belgravia SW1

Salloos
62-64 Kinnerton Street, SW1X 8ER (7235 4444). Hyde Park Corner or Knightsbridge tube. **Lunch served** noon-2.30pm, **dinner served** 7-11.15pm Mon-Sat. **Main courses** £10.90-£14.90. **Set lunch** £12 2 courses, £16 3 courses. **Service** 12.5%. **Credit** AmEx, DC, MC, V. Pakistani

Basking in the goodwill of wealthy Belgravian locals, Pakistani diplomats and well-heeled expats, Salloos exudes understated elegance. Don't be put off by the dull ground-floor bar by the entrance – the first-floor restaurant is more inspiring. Furnishings have a colonial vibe, and staff, if a little aloof, maintain a 'family-retainer' charm. Geometric Islamic-style window grilles, chandeliers and a smattering of contemporary paintings add to the graceful character. Cooking is hearty, concentrating on marinated kebabs and regal curries. Succulent and tender tandoori lamb chops absorbed the tartness of garlic- and ginger-spiked yoghurt with deliciously smoky results. An outstanding pilau jehengiri (basmati rice simmered in a yakhni – cardamom-scented lamb stock) was delicate in flavour and enhanced by toasted cumin seeds. However, tarka dahl was bland, and in our experience, vegetarian preparations aren't the chef's strength. Yet these are minor gripes when matched against such a memorably meaty meal. *Booking advisable. Children over 8 years admitted. Dress: smart casual. Takeaway service.* **Map 9 G9**.

Fitzrovia W1

★ Indian YMCA
41 Fitzroy Square, W1T 6AQ (7387 0411/ www.indianymca.org). Great Portland Street or Warren Street tube. **Lunch served** noon-2pm Mon-Fri; 12.30-1.30pm Sat, Sun. **Dinner served** 7-8.30pm daily. **Main courses** £2-£5. **Credit** AmEx, JCB, MC, V. Pan-Indian

This spot isn't going to win any design awards. It is tucked away on the ground floor of a concrete block and bears all the hallmarks of an Indian canteen – there's even a water urn at the ready to replenish empty glasses. Sturdy plastic tableware, institutional furniture and a dated lino floor reinforce the utilitarian feel. Yet the canteen is a lifeline for homesick Indian students and a satisfyingly cheap choice for office workers. Cooking is simple and unpretentious, and dishes are made from scratch without formula pastes. It's standard thali fare with trimmings; we enjoyed a homely chicken curry with a mound of steaming rice. Equally satisfying was that mainstay of everyday Punjabi meals, mutter aloo – an onion- and tomato-based curry, studded with peas and diced potatoes; it was the real thing and worth mopping up with a soft chapati. Cooking isn't laden with chillies, and although masalas do occasionally get a little heavy, this remains one of London's cheerfully cheap unsung treasures. *Babies and children welcome. No smoking. Separate rooms for parties, seating 30 and 200. Takeaway service. Vegetarian menu.* **Map 3 J4**.

★ Rasa Samudra
5 Charlotte Street, W1T 1RE (7637 0222/ www.rasarestaurants.com). Goodge Street tube. **Lunch served** noon-3pm Mon-Sat. **Dinner served** 6-10.45pm daily. **Main courses** £6.25-£12.95. **Set meal** £22.50 vegetarian, £30 seafood, 4 courses. **Service** 12.5%. **Credit** AmEx, MC, V. South Indian

That Rasa Samudra – the seafood specialist of the small chain of Keralite restaurants – is among the best venues for Indian food in London, is beyond doubt. Yet what you won't get are the Modern Indian flourishes. Here, tradition triumphs over fusion; presentation owes nothing to nouvelle cuisine (neither do the hefty portions); and design statements are largely confined to the vivid pink frontage. Within is a collection of small rooms that foster intimacy between couples, yet might seem too poky for groups. For those of large appetite, we heartily recommend the set meals: both the vegetarian and the seafood feasts contain a good balance of curries and thorans (coconutty stir-fries). The feasts can be tailored to requirements, but always begin with Rasa's crisp, popadom-like snacks, served with delectable own-made chutneys. Next, make sure Samudra rasam soup is included: a wealth of seafood in a highly savoury stock. The talapia fish in the varutharachameen curry might be too soft for some, but we relished the accompanying lemon rice, a side dish of spicy potatoes, and the coconut, mustard seed and curry leaf flavourings peppered throughout the meal. Staff are alert and knowledgeable. Prices are high. *Babies and children welcome. Booking advisable. No-smoking tables. Separate rooms for parties, seating 15, 20 and 40. Takeaway service. Vegetarian menu.* **Map 9 J5**.

Knightsbridge SW3

Haandi
7 Cheval Place, SW3 1HY (7823 7373/ www.haandi-restaurants.com). Knightsbridge tube. **Lunch served** noon-3pm daily. **Dinner served** 6-11pm Mon-Thur, Sun; 6-11.30pm Fri, Sat. **Main courses** £6-£16. **Set lunch** £7.99-£13.99 incl soft drink. **Service** 12.5%. **Credit** AmEx, DC, JCB, MC, V. North Indian

With branches in Kampala, Nairobi and now Edgware, this upmarket nosherie – very haandi for Harrods – attracts affluent Indian families, well-heeled locals and adventurous tourists. The austere stairway hardly hints at the leafy maroon opulence to be found in the basement bar and airy dining room beyond. We found service polite, but, on occasion, slow. Still, we could watch the Nairobi-trained chefs at work. The food is Punjabi by way of East Africa, with thick, reduced sauces and plenty of lentils and vegetables. Aloo choley ki chat was a pleasing stir-fry of crisp potato pieces, chickpeas and vegetables with tamarind. Punjabi lamb shanks received an 'oooh', partly for its divine onion and mint relish. The haandi (a round-bottomed cooking pot) comes into its own for main courses, such as meaty, fiery rogan josh, and punjabi chicken curry (which got the thumbs-up from our Punjabi expat). A chilli garlic fish amritsari was well executed and tasty; the chef wasn't afraid to use green chillies. Haandi's version of vindaloo contains king prawns and coconut milk: an interesting idea and a pleasant dish, but patently not the classic Goan vindaloo we know. *Babies and children welcome; high chairs. Booking advisable weekends. Entertainment; pianist 6-10pm Mon-Thur. Restaurant available for hire. Takeaway service; delivery service.* **Map 14 E9**. **For branch see index.**

Best Indian

For political spice
Spot conniving backbenchers on heat at the superlative **Cinnamon Club** (*see p125*).

For nice rice
Zaika (*see p125*) does a mean mushroom biriani, **Deya** (*see p118*) has a fabulous fish version, while **Eriki** (*see p136*) is neat for rice 'n' meat.

For meat-free marvels
Try **Ram's** (*see p139*) for homely Gujarati cooking, **Rasa** (*see p136*) for coconutty Keralite cuisine, and **Sagar** (*see p125*) for South Indian dosais.

For new-wave flavours
Both branches of the **Painted Heron** (*see p126* and *p129*) score highly for adventurous food pairings.

For bargain street food
Head to Southall and drop in at the great-value **New Asian Tandoori Centre** (*see p141*).

Marble Arch W1

Chai Pani NEW

*64 Seymour Street, W1H 5BW (7258 2000/
www.chaipani.co.uk). Marble Arch tube.* **Lunch
served** noon-2.30pm Mon-Fri; noon-4.30pm Sat,
Sun. **Dinner served** 6-10.30pm daily. **Main
courses** £5-£7. **Buffet** (lunch, Mon-Fri) £8.
Thalis £6-£20. **Credit** AmEx, JCB, MC, V.
Rajasthani

This smart but homely vegetarian restaurant
decorated in Rajasthani motifs is unique in
London: it offers the rich and earthy desert cuisine
of the Marwaris, a merchant community of the
Shekhawati region in Rajasthan, northern India.
The menu makes abundant use of ingredients little
seen elsewhere, such as cluster beans, bottle gourd,
dried baby melon, desert berries and black salt.
Indeed some components, such as mangodi (sun-
dried lentil nuggets), gatta (spicy chickpea-flour
balls) and pithor (steamed chickpea-flour cakes)
keep recurring in various guises – from salads and
rice, to soups and curries. You need to be partial to
grains and lentils to enjoy a meal here. Dishes were
a mixed bunch on a recent visit: the hits included
moreish white pumpkin pakoras, rice and breads,
but the curries and desserts were variable. Spicing
had been toned down and lacked the customary
Marwari fieriness. Service fluctuated between slow
and overbearing – leading us to wonder whether
the newly extended, overly ambitious menu (now
featuring à la carte options as well as a variety of
'banquets') had overstretched the kitchen.
*Babies and children welcome; high chairs. Booking
advisable weekends. Disabled: toilet. Takeaway
service. Vegetarian menu. Vegan dishes.* **Map 8 F6**.

Deya NEW

*34 Portman Square, W1H 7BH (7224 0028/
www.deya-restaurant.co.uk). Bond Street
or Marble Arch tube.* **Lunch served** noon-
2.45pm Mon-Fri. **Dinner served** 6.30-10.45pm
Mon-Sat. **Main courses** £9.50-£14.50.
Set lunch £14.95 2 courses. **Set meal** £22-£40
5 courses (tasting menus). **Service** 12.5%.
Credit AmEx, JCB, MC, V. Modern Indian

Housed in an impressive listed building with large
Georgian windows, chandeliers and a high ceiling,
Deya evokes the colonial era. Sanjay Dwivedi – ex-
sous chef at Zaika (*see p125*), with whom Deya
shares owners – runs the kitchen, but the cooking
is more than just a Zaika II. We loved the amuse-
bouche teaser: rice mixed with mustard seeds,
curry leaves and yoghurt, topped with mint
chutney and spiced prawns. A mixed platter starter
had two outstanding bites – samosas, packed with
crab flakes speckled with sweetcorn; and succulent,
mellow chicken tikka – but the lamb patties were
dense and dry. Main courses were superb,
especially seafood biriani: perfectly cooked white
fish and king prawns, plus wilted mint leaves.
Spicy green chicken curry was another well-
orchestrated creation. We also enjoyed crisp stir-
fried broccoli, asparagus and sweetcorn, tossed
with crunchy cashew nuts, shreds of juicy coconut
and mustard seeds. However, black dahl had an
overriding flavour of acidic tomatoes. Desserts
were variable too: we liked the betel leaf filled with
mint and pistachio ice-cream, but the gelatine-
laden chocolate mousse on the same plate did it no
favours. Service was attentive yet unobtrusive.
*Babies and children welcome; high chairs.
Booking advisable. Dress: smart casual.
Vegetarian menu.* **Map 9 G6**.

Porte des Indes

*32 Bryanston Street, W1H 7EG (7224 0055/
www.pilondon.net). Marble Arch tube.*
Lunch served noon-2.30pm Mon-Fri; noon-
3.30pm Sun. **Dinner served** 7-11.30pm
Mon-Sat; 6.30-10.30pm Sun. **Main courses**
£9.90-£21. **Set buffet lunch** (Mon-Fri)
£19.90; (Sun) £22. **Set meal** £35 3 courses,
£38 4 courses. **Service** 12.5%. **Credit** AmEx,
DC, JCB, MC, V. Pan-Indian

The name is French for 'gateway to India': French
because of the French-Creole colonisation of
Pondicherry on India's east coast. Porte des Indes
is owned by the Blue Elephant group (which
majors in Thai restaurants). Chefs hail from across
India, and it's often the non-French-influenced
dishes that stand out. The menu incorporates
supposed Franco-Indian favourites such as pepper
crabs and beignets d'aubergine (roundels of fried
aubergine, stuffed with cheese and herb pâté), with
pan-Indian fare such as bombay chat, lucknowi
seekh kebab and parsi fish: said to be the chef's
speciality. This last dish offers lightly steamed
fillets of sole with a mint and coriander chutney
in banana leaf – and it works very well. Other
dishes didn't quite come off; a main course of
cassoulet de fruits de mer fell somewhere between
bouillabaisse and a simple Tamil fish stew. Prices
are high (starters up to £9, mains rising to £28 for
lobster), but service is attentive and the decor
spectacular, with lush tropical greenery, high
decorated ceilings and posh cane furniture. We
can vouch for the upmarket eat-all-you-can lunch,
which offers a good selection from the carte plus
salads, fruit and myriad own-made chutneys.
*Babies and children welcome; high chairs.
Booking advisable. Dress: smart casual.
Entertainment: music (Sun lunch). Restaurant
available for hire. Separate rooms for parties,
seating 10 and 14. Takeaway service. Vegetarian
menu.* **Map 8 F6**.

Mayfair W1

Benares

2004 RUNNER-UP BEST DESIGN

*12 Berkeley House, Berkeley Square, W1J 6AN
(7629 8886/www.benaresrestaurant.com).
Green Park tube.* **Lunch served** noon-2.30pm
Mon-Fri. **Dinner served** 5.30-10.30pm
Mon-Sat; 6-10pm Sun. **Main courses** £12-£15.
Set lunch £10 2 courses. **Set dinner** £37
(tasting menu). **Service** 12.5%. **Credit** AmEx,
DC, MC, V. Modern Indian

Appropriately located between a Bentley car
showroom and cashpoint machines, chef Atul
Kochhar's smart restaurant attempts a Mayfair
mock-up of the holy city, with a beautiful wooden
canoe, carvings of deities, and flower-filled water
pools representing the Ganges. On our visit, the
restaurant was populated by tourists, moneyed

Deya

Pan-Indian menu

Spellings of Indian dishes vary widely; dishes such as dopiaza or gosht may appear in several versions on different menus as the word is transliterated from (in this case) Hindi. There are umpteen languages and several scripts in the Indian subcontinent, the most commonly seen on London menus being Punjabi, Hindi, Bengali and Gujarati. For the sake of consistency, however, we have tried to use the same spellings throughout. The following are common throughout the subcontinent.

More food terms can be found in *An ABC of Indian Food* by Joyce P Westrip (Prospect Books).

Aloo: potato.
Ayre: a white fish much used in Bengali cuisine.
Baingan: aubergine.
Balti: West Midlands cooking term for karahi cooking (qv **North Indian menu**), which became all the rage a decade ago. Unfortunately, many inferior curry houses now apply the name to dishes that bear little resemblance to real karahi-cooked dishes.
Bateira, **batera** or **bater**: quail.
Bengali: Bengal, before Partition in 1947, was a large province covering Calcutta (now in India's West Bengal) and modern-day Bangladesh. 'Bengali' and 'Bangladeshi' cooking is quite different, and the term 'Bengali' is often misused in London's Indian restaurants.
Bhajia or **bhaji**: another name

for pakoras – vegetables dipped in chickpea flour batter and deep-fried.
Bhajee: vegetables cooked with spices, usually 'dry' rather than sauced.
Bhindi: okra.
Brinjal: aubergine (eggplant).
Bulchao or **balchao**: a Goan vinegary pickle made with small dried prawns (with shells) and lots of garlic.
Chana or **channa**: chickpeas.
Chapati: a flat wholewheat griddle bread.
Chat or **chaat**: various savoury snacks featuring combinations of pooris (qv), diced onion and potato, chickpeas, crumbled samosas and pakoras (qv), chutneys and spices.
Dahi: yoghurt.
Dahl or **dal**: a lentil curry similar to thick lentil soup. Countless regional variations exist.
Dhansak: a Parsi (qv) casserole of meat, lentils and vegetables, with a mix of hot and tangy flavours.
Dhaniya: coriander.
Ghee: clarified butter used for frying.
Gobi: cauliflower.
Gosht, **josh** or **ghosh**: meat, usually lamb.
Gram flour: chickpea flour.
Kachori: crisp pastry rounds with spiced mung dahl or pea filling.
Kadhi or **khadi**: yoghurt and chickpea flour curry.
Lassi: a yoghurt drink, ordered with salt or sugar, sometimes with fruit. Ideal to quench a fiery palate.
Machi or **machli**: fish.

Masala or **masaladar**: mixed spices.
Methi: fenugreek, either dried (seeds) or fresh (green leaves).
Murgh or **murg**: chicken.
Mutter, **muter** or **mattar**: peas.
Nan or **naan**: teardrop-shaped flatbread cooked in a tandoor (qv).
Pakora or **pakoda**: savoury fritters, an alternative name for bhajias (qv).
Palak or **paalak**: spinach; also called saag.
Paan or **pan**: betel leaf stuffed with chopped 'betel nuts', coconut and spices such as fennel seeds, and folded into a triangle. Available sweet or salty, and eaten at the end of a meal as a digestive.
Paneer or **panir**: Indian cheese, a bit like tofu in texture and taste.
Paratha: a large griddle-fried bread that is sometimes stuffed (with spicy mashed potato or minced lamb, for instance).
Parsi or **Parsee**: a religious minority based in Mumbai (Bombay), but originally from Persia, renowned for its cooking.
Pilau, **pillau** or **pullao**: flavoured rice cooked with meat or vegetables. In most British Indian restaurants, pilau rice is simply rice flavoured and coloured with turmeric or (rarely) saffron.
Poori or **puri**: a disc of deep-fried wholewheat bread; the frying makes it puff up like an air-filled cushion.

Popodom, poppadom, papadum or **papad**: large thin wafers made with lentil paste, and flavoured with pepper, garlic or chilli. Eaten in the UK with pickles and relishes as a starter while waiting for the meal to arrive.
Raita: a yoghurt mix, usually with cucumber.
Roti: a round, sometimes unleavened, bread; thicker than a chapati and cooked in a tandoor or griddle. Roomali roti (literally 'handkerchief bread') is a very thin, soft disc of roti.
Saag or **sag**: spinach; also called palak.
Tamarind: the pods of this East African tree, grown in India, are made into a paste that imparts a sour, fruity taste – popular in some regional cuisines, including Gujarati and South Indian.
Thali: literally 'metal plate'. A large plate with rice, bread, containers of dahl and vegetable curries, pickles and yoghurt relishes.
Vadai or **wada**: a spicy vegetable or lentil fritter; dahi wada are lentil fritters soaked in yoghurt, topped with tamarind and date chutneys.
Vindaloo: originally, a hot and spicy pork curry from Goa that should authentically be soured with vinegar and cooked with garlic. In London restaurants, the term is usually misused to signify simply very hot dishes.
Xacuti: a Goan dish made with lamb or chicken pieces, coconut and a complex mix of roasted then ground spices.

Indian families, Bollywood film stars, dating couples and Russian oligarchs. Pan-fried aubergine steaks stuffed with a crumbly potato and vegetable filling were pleasant yet under-seasoned. A trio of ginger- and basil-flecked chicken cake, mustard-marinated chicken kebab, and chicken nan had been more excitingly spiced, with the meat fresh and tender. Pindi chana (chickpeas in a tangy masala) is a speciality from Rawalpindi and is renowned for having extrovert spicing; the version here was a much quieter affair, however. Given Benares' status as a Modern Indian restaurant, its cooking is fairly conventional. There are no out-there flavour combinations and the kitchen doesn't try to show off. Service could be more polished, however; on our visit it ranged from flirty and entertaining to slow and incompetent.
Booking advisable dinner weekends. Dress: smart casual. No-smoking. Restaurant available for hire. Separate rooms for parties, seating 8, 16 and 20. Vegetarian menu. Map 9 H7.

★ Tamarind
20 Queen Street, W1J 5PR (7629 3561/ www.tamarindrestaurant.com). Green Park tube.
Lunch served noon-3pm Mon-Fri; noon-2.30pm

Sun. **Dinner served** 6-11.30pm Mon-Sat; 6-10.30pm Sun. **Main courses** £14.50-£22. **Set lunch** £14.50 2 courses, £16.50 3 courses. **Set meal** (6-7pm) £22 2 courses. **Service** 12.5%. **Credit** AmEx, DC, JCB, MC, V. North Indian
Dignified and luxurious, this elegant basement restaurant is synonymous with quality cooking, superlative service and a choice selection of wines. It's also a popular stomping ground for wealthy tourists and business folk on expense accounts. Crisp white table linen, speckled mirrors and muted lighting are enhanced by theatrical views of skewer-wielding chefs through the glass-fronted kitchen window. Chef Alfred Prasad cooks a selection of pan-Indian dishes. Saag aloo tikki – fried potato cakes stuffed with spinach and served with tamarind chutney – elevated a favourite snack to gourmet status with their delicate spicing and much-appreciated velvety-smooth texture. Dahl makhani (black lentils simmered with garlic, ginger and chillies, and enriched with cream, butter and tomatoes) was divine. Breads are light and soft, especially the roomali roti, which, when unfolded, is as large and thin as a handkerchief. There was the occasional disappointment; tari

gosht (chunks of lamb cooked in browned onion masala with mace and red chillies) had an overly thick sauce, more akin to home cooking than the expected fine-dining experience. Service remains spot-on, but chefs can't afford to be complacent given the competition.
Babies and children welcome (over 2 years); high chair. Booking advisable; essential dinner. Dress: smart casual. Restaurant available for hire. Takeaway service; delivery service. Map 9 H7.

Yatra
34 Dover Street, W1S 4NF (7493 0200/ www.barbollywood.net). Green Park tube.
Lunch served noon-3pm Mon-Fri. **Dinner served** 6.30-11pm Mon-Wed; 6-11.30pm Thur-Sat. **Main courses** £12.50-£19.50. **Set lunch** £9.95 2 courses incl drink, £12.95 3 courses incl drink. **Service** 15%. **Credit** AmEx, JCB, MC, V. Modern Indian
With its own basement club (the Bollywood Bar (popular with trendy young expats), and a menu priced to the expense account trade, Yatra attracts upmarket diners. We found the smart granite and earth-coloured dining room underused on a midweek evening; waiters were exceedingly attentive. The name of the game is Modern Indian

North Indian menu

Under the blanket term of North Indian cuisine, we have included dishes originating in the Punjab (both in Pakistan and the modern state of India), Kashmir and all points down to Hyderabad.

Southall (*see p140*) has some of London's best Punjabi restaurants, where breads cooked in the tandoor oven are often preferred to rice; marinated meaty kebabs are popular; and dahls are thick and buttery.

Bhuna gosht: a dry, spicy dish of lamb.
Biriani or **biryani**: a royal Moglai version of pilau rice, with meat or vegetables cooked together with basmati rice, spices and saffron. It's difficult to find an authentic biriani in London restaurants.
Dopiaza or **do pyaza**: cooked with onions.
Dum: a Kashmiri cooking technique where food is simmered slowly in a casserole (typically a clay pot sealed with dough), allowing spices to permeate.
Gurda: kidneys.
Haandi: an earthenware or metal cooking pot, with handles on either side and a lid.
Jalfrezi: chicken or vegetable dishes cooked with fresh green chillies – a popular cooking style in Mumbai.
Jhingri, **jhinga** or **chingri**: prawns.
Kaleji or **kalezi**: liver.
Karahi or **karai**: a small iron or metal wok-like cooking dish. Similar to the 'balti' dish made famous in Birmingham.
Kheema or **keema**: minced lamb, as in kheema nan (stuffed nan).
Kofta: meatballs or vegetable dumplings.
Korma: braised in yoghurt and/or cream and nuts. Often mild, but rich.
Magaz: brain.
Makhani: cooked with butter (makhan) and sometimes tomatoes, as in murgh makhani.
Massalam: marinated, then casseroled

chicken dish, originating in Muslim areas.
Moghul or **Mogul**: from the Moghul period of Indian history, used in the culinary sense to describe typical North Indian Muslim dishes.
Nihari or **nehari**: there are many recipes on the subcontinent for this long-simmered meat stew, using goat, beef, mutton or sometimes chicken. Hyderabadi nihari is flavoured with sandalwood powder and rose petals. North Indian nihari uses nutmeg, clove, dried ginger and tomato. In London, however, the dish is made with lamb shank (served on the bone).
Pasanda: thin fillets of lamb cut from the leg and flattened with a mallet. In British curry houses, the term usually applies to a creamy sauce virtually identical to a korma.
Paya: lamb's feet, usually served on the bone as paya curry (long-cooked and with copious gravy); seldom found outside Southall.
Punjabi: Since Partition, the Punjab has been two adjoining states, one in India, one in Pakistan. Lahore is the main town on the Pakistani side, which is predominantly Muslim; Amritsar on the Indian side is the Sikh capital. Punjabi dishes tend to be thick stews or cooked in a tandoor (qv).
Roghan gosht or **rogan josh**: lamb cooked in spicy sauce, a Kashmiri speciality.
Seekh kebab: ground meat, skewered and grilled.
Tak-a-tak: a cooking method – ingredients (usually meat or vegetables) are chopped and flipped as they cook on a griddle.
Tandoor: clay oven originating in north-west India in which food is cooked without oil.
Tarka: spices and flavourings are cooked separately, then added to dahl at a final stage.
Tikka: meat, fish or paneer cut into cubes, then marinated in spicy yoghurt and baked in a tandoor.

cuisine with risks. Starters of kebab on 'grass' (lemongrass) and aloo tikki were hard to fault, arriving with freshly made pickles that hit the wow factor. A Yatra salad consisted of a 25cm tower of grilled parmesan surrounded by a chunky tossed salad and tandoori prawn, and looked too good to eat – it wasn't, and was demolished in seconds. The trademark main course of railway lamb – an Anglo-Indian speciality – was ultra-savoury, with the meat and baby potatoes cooked in a rich, meaty sauce flavoured with curry leaf, black cumin and garlic: delicious. Less successful was the achari prawn, which was very similar to a standard tandooried shellfish (pickling spices hard to detect), accompanied by 'spicy mashed potato' that might have come from a recipe in *Family Circle*. Great when served in a curry house, but here (at £18.50), you expect, and usually receive, brilliance.
Babies and children welcome. Booking advisable. Disabled: toilet. Entertainment (Bar Bollywood): DJs Fri, Sat. Restaurant available for hire. Separate room for parties, seats 50.
Map 9 H7.

St James's SW1

Quilon
41 Buckingham Gate, SW1E 6AF (7821 1899/ www.thequilonrestaurant.com). St James's Park tube. **Lunch served** noon-2.30pm Mon-Fri. **Dinner served** 6-11pm Mon-Sat. **Main courses** £8-£23. **Set lunch** £12.95 2 courses, £15.95 3 courses. **Service** 12.5%. **Credit** AmEx, DC, MC, V. South Indian
Named after a coastal town in Kerala, Quilon is part of the Taj Group of Hotels-owned St James's Court Hotel. Its large dining room is decorated with a strange mishmash of colonial-style wicker chairs, pretty mosaics, a huge colourful mural, kitsch flower arrangements and a smart bar. We started with exquisitely fresh char-grilled scallops, and cauliflower sautéed in a tangy yoghurt batter, stunningly presented in a banana-leaf cone; both were moreish. A spicy curry of crab meatballs served with string hoppers was fine, but lacked oomph. Vegetable green curry in cashew, coconut and coriander sauce was mellow and dreamy, while

a raw mango curry was fine, if short on complexity. Malabar paratha wasn't the best we've tried either, though the red rice was exemplary and we also liked the flavoursome own-made pickles. In a soulless space frequented mainly by American tourists, we found the service overbearing. Quilon is charming, but expensive: it's possible to eat South Indian food that's just as good, if not better, elsewhere at lower prices.
Babies and children welcome; high chairs. Booking advisable. No-smoking tables. Takeaway service. Vegetarian menu. **Map 15 J9.**

Soho W1

★ Chowki
2-3 Denman Street, W1D 7HA (7439 1330). Piccadilly Circus tube. **Meals served** noon-11.30pm Mon-Sat; noon-10.30pm Sun. **Main courses** £5.95-£9.95. **Set meal** £10.95 3 courses. **Credit** AmEx, DC, MC, V. Pan-Indian
Chowki is a clever concept. An unflashy diner with red leather banquettes, it showcases three Indian regional cuisines each month at unfeasibly low prices. We visited shortly after it had received an award and several rave reviews in the national press. Big mistake, for although we were firmly told that bookings weren't necessary – or taken – the room was packed with dating couples, large groups, coachloads of tourists and a huge family party. When a table eventually became available, we were strongly encouraged to order a 'regional feast' (set menu) rather than mix and match. Some dishes were good (notably moong dahl with spinach, and prawn curry); others, such as spicy mussels, were merely OK. A Maharashtrian classic of rice flakes with coconut and peanuts was inexplicably replaced by layered steamed rice flour cakes that had a dried-out texture – a dish listed under Chettinad food, but in fact Gujarati in origin. In all, we found the flavours muted and underwhelming; the kitchen appeared to be having trouble coping with the sudden limelight.
Babies and children welcome; high chairs. Booking advisable. Vegetarian menu. **Map 17 K7.**

★ Masala Zone
9 Marshall Street, W1F 7ER (7287 9966/ www.realindianfood.com). Oxford Circus tube. **Lunch served** noon-3pm Mon-Fri; 12.30-3.30pm Sun. **Dinner served** 5.30-11pm Mon-Fri; 6-10.30pm Sun. **Meals served** 12.30-11pm Sat. **Main courses** £5.50-£11. **Thalis** £6-£11.50. **Service** 10%. **Credit** MC, V. Pan-Indian
Deserving its popularity, Masala Zone has Wagamama-fied Indian dining. Yet though you get the canteen vibe, the fast throughput and (at peak times) the queues, this isn't at the expense of authenticity. The mini chain is owned by the Chutney Mary group, and its great-value menu encompasses crisp Bombay beach snacks, meal-in-one plates, rare regional dishes (undhiyu, and lentil khichdi – a mushy rice mix – for instance) properly prepared curries and satisfying thalis. For dinner, a combination thali is a good way to go, allowing a choice of any two little pots of curry from the menu, plus a starter (perhaps aloo tikki chat: potato cake), two vegetable curries, raita, dahl, kuchumber (diced tomato and cucumber salad), popadoms and chutneys, a wholewheat chapati and rice. Lamb achari was a fine accompaniment to this, featuring a tangy, green-tinged sauce replete with freshly ground spices. Despite plentiful (multinational) staff, service became a touch disjointed during the Friday night rush. Otherwise, dining here – viewing the bustle of the open kitchen and the attractive primitive art murals – was a pleasure, aided by a palatable Sicilian (the house white).
Babies and children welcome; high chairs. Bookings not accepted. No smoking. Separate area for parties, seats 40. Takeaway service. Vegetarian menu. **Map 17 J6. For branch see index.**

★ Red Fort
77 Dean Street, W1D 3SH (7437 2115/ www.redfort.co.uk). Leicester Square or Tottenham Court Road tube. **Lunch served** noon-2.15pm Mon-Fri. **Dinner served** 5.45-11pm

Chai Pani. See p118.

Mon-Sat. **Main courses** £12.50-£20.
Set lunch £12 2 courses. **Set meal** (5.45-7pm)
£16 2 courses incl tea or coffee. **Service** 12.5%.
Credit AmEx, MC, V. North Indian

The former head chef here, Mohammed Rais, has
moved to Fulham's Darbar restaurant (*see p126*),
leaving the rest of the kitchen team to, ahem, hold
the fort. Winner of Best Indian Restaurant in *Time
Out*'s 2003 Eating & Drinking Awards, Red Fort
continues to attract a clientele of deep-pocketed
tourists and corporate types. Antique urns, red
sandstone walls and a sleek water feature at the
back of the restaurant lend a modern, almost zen-
like vibe to the place. It's no surprise that the
service never misses a beat; most of the Indian
staff have been poached from five-star hotels on
the subcontinent. Cooking remains inspired by the
regal traditions of Lucknow, and is characterised
by myriad, complex-tasting spice mixes. Winning
dishes included anaari champ – perfectly grilled
lamb chops, served in a delectable meaty jus,
spiked with star anise and tart pomegranate
powder. Avadhi gosht biriani (chunks of spiced
lamb, cooked in cardamom-scented yoghurt and
braised with saffron-streaked rice) would have
benefited from a lighter touch, though. Given time,
the Red Fort stands a good chance of regaining its
reputation as one of London's leading Indian
restaurants.
*Babies and children admitted. Booking advisable.
Vegetarian menu.* **Map 17 K6**.

Strand WC2

★ **India Club**

*Second Floor, Strand Continental Hotel,
143 Strand, WC2R 1JA (7836 0650). Covent
Garden, Embankment or Temple tube/Charing
Cross tube/rail.* **Lunch served** noon-2.30pm,
dinner served 6-10.50pm daily. **Main
courses** £3.50-£7. **Set meal** £12 4 courses
(minimum 2). **Unlicensed. Corkage** no charge.
No credit cards. Pan-Indian

Paying homage to wonky tables, mango-coloured
walls, strip lighting and velour-upholstered chairs,
this quirky, loveable spot brings small-town India
to the Strand. Pretty it isn't, but after more than 50
years of dishing out masala, the management has
sussed that customers aren't fazed by the
depressing climb up two flights of dingy stairs to
the caff. A loyal following of backpackers,
diplomats and office groups come here, not only
because the food is cheap, but because, on a decent
day, the cooking is soul-satisfyingly good. The
menu is listed in two columns: one side for non-
veg, the other for vegetarian dishes. We usually
order keema with peas; the richly spiced fried lamb
mince, studded with peas, is loaded with browned
onions, green chillies and tangy shreds of ginger
– perfect for mopping up with a griddle-cooked
chapati. Other reliable bets include chicken curry
– but vegetables tend to be oil-rich offerings, and
the dosais are no great shakes. Nattily dressed
waiters in spotless white uniforms are warmly
welcoming. Yes, the place needs dusting down, and
the fading sepia prints of yesteryear's Indian
notables help encapsulate it in a time-warp, but
we're not complaining.
Takeaway service. Vegetarian menu. **Map 10 M7**.

Victoria SW1

★ **Sekara**

*3 Lower Grosvenor Place, SW1W 0EJ (7834
0722/www.sekara.co.uk). Victoria tube/rail.*
Lunch served noon-3pm Mon-Sat; noon-
3.30pm Sun. **Dinner served** 6-10pm daily.
Main courses £5.95-£10.95. **Set lunch**
(Mon-Sat) £4.95 1 course. **Set buffet** (Sun)
£7.95. **Service** 10%. **Credit** AmEx, MC, V.
Sri Lankan

Central London's sole Sri Lankan diner is a
relaxing spot, despite its location on a busy road.
A yellow colour scheme, paintings, and wooden
flooring provide a laid-back, bistro-like setting. To
start, there's a choice of fish or mutton patties, or
South Indian vegetarian snacks. Sample the
'devilled dry fish' if you dare: lovely pungent
fishiness matched by fried onions, but with a chilli

heat of eye-watering power; bread is needed to temper the heat. Vadai were dull in comparison: dry, and served without relish. To follow, a huge portion of prawn kothu roti was an immense success: fresh from the pan, delicate strips of pasta-like bread, stir-fried with plenty of seafood and lip-smacking spices. Liquid was supplied by kiri hodi (spicy coconut gravy), garlicky dahl and the creamy coconut milk (mercifully unspiced) that accompanied a mighty log of pittu. Fish curry was meaty and appetising. Only the red onion sambol was a let-down (raw onions in lemon juice, when we'd hoped for them caramelised). In all, a highly satisfying – and inexpensive – meal.
Babies and children admitted; high chairs. Booking advisable. Restaurant available for hire. Takeaway service. Vegetarian menu. **Map 15 H9.**

Westminster SW1

★ The Cinnamon Club
The Old Westminster Library, Great Smith Street, SW1P 3BU (7222 2555/www.cinnamon club.com). St James's Park or Westminster tube. **Breakfast served** 7.30-9.30am, **lunch served** noon-2.30pm Mon-Fri. **Dinner served** 6-10.45pm Mon-Sat. **Main courses** £11-£26. **Set lunch** £19 2 courses, £22 3 courses. **Set dinner** £60 5 courses (£95 with wine). **Service** 12.5%. **Credit** AmEx, DC, JCB, MC, V. Modern Indian
A Westminster site and PR-savvy management might not augur well, but we were completely won over by the brilliance of our set lunch here. Chef Vivek Singh has put the Cinnamon Club at the forefront of Indian food in Britain. Classic dishes are cooked with due diligence, if unexpected twists (witness the flavour-suffused Hyderabadi biriani of beef, served with rich beef curry and raita); new creations are well judged (juicy tandoori swordfish was paired with a 'tomato lemon' sauce containing kaffir lime leaves); while regional rarities can be revelatory – as in a side dish of Rajasthani sangri beans: thin strips pepped up with wild berries. This, and a first course of lamb's sweetbreads (two lightly fried discs) with pungently spiced minced liver and a purple-hued version of coleslaw, were the most outstanding dishes on the daily changing set lunch menu, though nothing was amiss. Presentation showed further evidence of the highest culinary talent. The carte is expensive, featuring such ingredients as venison with pickling sauce. The setting (a conversion of a grand 19th-century library, with cinnamon-hued banquettes and crisp tablecloths) is peculiarly apt, evoking colonial splendour. The Club is within spitting distance of Parliament, and attracts Westminster's political elite. What a waste.
Babies and children welcome; high chairs. Booking advisable weekends. Disabled: toilet. Separate rooms for parties, seating 30 and 50. Vegetarian menu. **Map 16 K9.**

West

Chiswick W4

Woodlands
12-14 Chiswick High Road, W4 1TH (8994 9333/www.woodlandsrestaurant.co.uk). Stamford Brook tube. **Lunch served** noon-2.45pm, **dinner served** 6-10.45pm daily. **Main courses** £4-£7. **Thali** £14.50 4-5 dishes. **Service** 12.5%. **Credit** AmEx, DC, MC, V. South Indian
The latest branch to join the Woodlands chain is smartly decked out in burnt orange and brown walls, beige banquettes and stylish wooden tables. Elephant carvings and statues of Hindu deities also make their presence felt, though with restraint. Cooking remains resolutely South Indian and is, in the main, a decent rendition of home-style cooking. Upma (fried ground wheat, cooked with diced onions, crunchy cashew nuts, mustard seeds and chopped chillies) was as light as whipped mashed potato and deliciously creamy in texture. Not so memorable was onion and chilli uthappam (similar to a spiced, soft-based pizza): it was let down by undercooked fermented rice batter and a dense texture. Crisp dosais are above average, but we

found the potato masala accompaniment a shade too sweet. Sambar (tamarind-flavoured lentils, simmered with tomatoes and mixed vegetables) is a dependable choice: comfort cooking at its best. Service is slick and attentive, without being obtrusive. On our lunchtime visit, young families were made to feel especially welcome.
Babies and children welcome; high chairs. Booking advisable weekends. Restaurant available for hire. Separate room for parties, seats 40. Tables outdoors (2, pavement). Takeaway service. **Map 20 A4.**
For branches see index.

Hammersmith W6

★ ★ Sagar
2004 RUNNER-UP BEST VEGETARIAN MEAL
157 King Street, W6 9JT (8741 8563). Hammersmith tube/299 bus. **Lunch served** noon-2.45pm, **dinner served** 5.30-10.45pm Mon-Wed. **Meals served** noon-10.45pm Thur-Sun. **Main courses** £5-£10. **Thalis** £7.95-£11.45. **Credit** AmEx, DC, JCB, MC, V. South Indian vegetarian
This South Indian café is a relatively new arrival in Hammersmith, but is already a great draw for curious diners as well as the local Tamil community. Decor incorporates modern light wood tables and Indian artefacts (brass urns, statues of Hindu deities), giving a look of restrained elegance. Cooking – much of it hailing from the southern Indian state of Karnataka – is awe-inspiring and showcases the versatility of everyday vegetables, pulses and grains. Flavours are subtle yet well rounded. To do justice to the menu, order traditional South Indian specials; staff are happy to help with suggestions if need be. We fell in love with our masala dosai: a large thin pancake served with a bowlful of sambar (soupy lentils and vegetables flavoured with tart tamarind), and a generous dollop of mashed potato, fried with peppy mustard seeds and crackling curry leaves. Freshly made idlis (steamed rice and lentil cakes) were light and fluffy pillows, perfect for soaking in more sambar and accompanying with tongue-tingling coconut chutney.
Babies and children welcome; high chairs. Booking advisable. No-smoking tables. Takeaway service. Vegetarian menu. **Map 20 B4.**

Kensington W8

Utsav
17 Kensington High Street, W8 5NP (7368 0022/www.utsav-restaurant.co.uk). High Street Kensington tube. **Lunch served** 11.30am-3pm daily. **Dinner served** 6-11pm Mon-Thur; 6-11.30pm Fri, Sat; 6-10.30pm Sun. **Main courses** (lunch) £4.95-£5.95; (dinner) £9.75-£12.75. **Service** 12.5%. **Credit** AmEx, MC, V. Pan-Indian
The frontage is tiny, scarcely doing justice to this classy operation. Within, the long thin stalk of a dining space (on three levels) appears wider by dint of mirrors and is made attractive with cane chairs, bright lighting, rugs and, to the rear, vivid blue wall tiles. Staff are prompt, prompting us to try the AdiAdi beer from Bangalore (strongly flavoured, but not unpleasant). Utsav's menu offers food from across India. The vegetarian platter makes a good start to a meal: an alternative to the meaty tandooris. It includes cheese kurkuri (spiced cheese stuffed in a thin roti, rolled and deep-fried), cabbage vada, tandoori paneer and pani poori – all well presented and cooked with a light touch. To follow, the halibut allepy curry featured flaky fresh fish perfectly cooked in a tangy tomato, cocum (fish tamarind) and mustard seed sauce, served with coconut rice. Almost as good was the Hyderabadi lamb biriani: tender pieces of boneless lamb cooked with rose petal-scented rice in a sealed pot. Executive chef Gowtham Karingi (who has worked at Veeraswamy and Zaika) is a native of Hyderabad. So, accomplished cooking, but on our visit there were few punters to enjoy it.
Babies and children welcome; high chair. Booking advisable. No-smoking tables. Restaurant available for hire. Separate room for parties, seats 55. **Map 7 B8.**

★ Zaika
1 Kensington High Street, W8 5NP (7795 6533/www.zaika-restaurant.co.uk). High Street Kensington tube. **Lunch served** noon-2.45pm Mon-Fri, Sun. **Dinner served** 6.30-10.45pm Mon-Sat; 6.30-9.45pm Sun. **Main courses** £12.50-£19.50. **Set lunch** £15 2 courses, £18 3 courses. **Set meal** £38 6 courses, £58 9 courses (tasting menus). **Service** 12.5%. **Credit** AmEx, DC, JCB, MC, V. Modern Indian
Chef Vineet Bhatia has moved on to run his own place (Rasoi Vineet Bhatia; see p126), but Zaika remains as beautiful and glamorous as ever. The spacious dining room with a split-level bar is tastefully done up in shades of terracotta, charcoal and plum, and decorated with carved antiques and discreetly placed screens. A cheese platter included a cube of soft grilled paneer drizzled with mint sauce, almond-crusted paneer patty topped with tamarind sauce, and goat's cheese and 'smoked cashew' samosa with clove-flavoured pear chutney – all very elaborately executed. Wild mushroom biriani with fennel, ginger and red chillies resembled a cross between the classic Kashmiri gucci (morel mushroom) pilau and a traditional biriani; it was attractively presented with a pastry crust flecked with fennel, onion and watermelon seeds. The accompanying chana dahl was scrumptious, and the flavours worked surprisingly well together. Succulent grilled duck breast came with crisp fried okra, spicy mashed potatoes and tangy yoghurt sauce. We finished with a memorable fresh pineapple granita. Service throughout was slickly choreographed.
Babies and children welcome; high chair. Booking advisable. Dress: smart casual. Restaurant available for hire. **Map 7 C8.**
For branch (Zaika Bazaar) see index.

Sheen SW14

★ Sree Visakham NEW
180 Richmond Road West, East Sheen, SW14 8AW (8487 1331). Mortlake rail. **Lunch served** noon-3pm daily. **Dinner served** 6-11pm Mon-Thur, Sun; 6-11.30pm Fri, Sat. **Main courses** £5.90-£8.50. **Set lunch** £5.95 2 courses incl drink. **Set dinner** £25 2 courses (minimum 2). **Credit** JCB, MC, V. South Indian
The chef at this new venture used to work at Radha Krishna Bhavan (see p129), and it seems he took the menu with him. The same dishes appear, including wonderful appams: evenly browned on the outside, the interior pale and pock-marked like the moon. While it's great to see a South Indian restaurant in East Sheen, some of the dish preparation on our visit was haphazard. The tiny yellow lentils in the kappa – chunks of turmeric-yellow tapioca root, stir-fried with curry leaves – were rock-hard. And the salt lassi was oversalted and watery, tasting of little other than brine. We had much better luck with the kalan, a yellow coconut-rich sauce containing chunks of a marrow-like gourd; and with both a meen curry (fish steaks in a rich, orange-hued sauce) and a potato curry. The interior of this unit in a parade of shops has been decorated in startling crimson, carpet and walls. Tablecloths are golden. Coming complete with South Indian music (sounding like kazoo-players on coke), it's oddly evocative of hotel restaurants in small-town Kerala.
Babies and children welcome; high chairs. Booking advisable. Disabled: toilet. Takeaway service; delivery service (within 3-mile radius).

South West

Chelsea SW3, SW10

Chutney Mary
535 King's Road, SW10 0SZ (7351 3113/www.realindianfood.com). Fulham Broadway tube/11, 22 bus. **Lunch served** 12.30-2.30pm Sat; 12.30-3pm Sun. **Dinner served** 6.30-11pm Mon-Sat; 6.30-10.30pm Sun. **Main courses** £12.50-£24. **Set lunch** £16.50 3 courses. **Service** 12.5%. **Credit** AmEx, DC, JCB, MC, V. Pan-Indian

Service can be overbearing at this renowned establishment. Chutney Mary has two contrasting dining spaces: a bright, verdant conservatory out back, and a dark cavern of an interior with vibrant artwork, entirely lit by flickering candles. On this year's visit, our meal was disappointing. Prawns sautéed with asparagus, and another dish of asparagus stir-fried with freshly grated coconut, curry leaves and mustard seeds, didn't quite work as the flavour combinations were askew. However, a dish of three types of elaborately prepared vegetable patties was imaginatively executed and beautifully spiced. Lobster makhani was let down by a so-what tomato and brandy sauce. We had mixed feelings too, about a platter of vegetable and lentil dishes, and the bread basket, with some items (such as the delicately spiced black dahl) working better than others (cheddar-stuffed parathas). But don't miss the puddings, especially the exquisite, prettily presented almond halwa tarte. Overall though, Chutney Mary tries to be too flamboyant; it should focus on getting the basics right first.
Babies and children welcome; high chairs. Book dinner. Dress: smart casual. Entertainment: jazz Sun lunch. No-smoking tables. **Map 13 C13.**

★ The Painted Heron
112 Cheyne Walk, SW10 0TJ (7351 5232/ www.thepaintedheron.com). Bus 11, 19, 22, 319. **Lunch served** noon-2.30pm Mon-Fri. **Dinner served** 6-11pm Mon-Sat. **Main courses** £11-£18. **Thali** £12 3 courses. **Credit** AmEx, JCB, MC, V. Modern Indian
You get a feeling of space at this cream-painted, multi-roomed restaurant by the Thames. Staff are cordial too. Risks are taken on the regularly changing menu – starters might be calf's liver in tandoori marinade with mango, or crab with red onion and chilli in dosai pancake; mains could be wild boar jungle curry, or smoked chicken in crushed pepper cashew nut sauce – but the adventurous Modern Indian cuisine comes off brilliantly. Head chef Yogeth Datta served time with the Taj and Sheraton hotel groups in India, and arrived here via the ill-fated Tabla at West India Dock. A first course of hung yoghurt and aubergine cake with red onions was loosely packed together, crisp on the outside and bursting with flavour, while a main of tiger prawns in onion and tomato chutney sauce, served with (chopped) asparagus curry was impossible to fault. Unlikely ingredients and methods are combined with a skill that makes you wonder why everyone's not doing it. Prices aren't cheap (starters average £6.50; mains £11-£18), but never has the old adage been more true.
Babies and children welcome. Separate area available for hire, seats 25. Tables outdoors (6, garden). **Map 13 D13.**

Rasoi Vineet Bhatia NEW
10 Lincoln Street, SW3 2TS (7225 1881/ www.vineetbhatia.com). Sloane Square tube. **Lunch served** noon-3pm Mon-Fri. **Dinner served** 6.30-10.30pm Mon-Sat. **Main courses** £16-£22. **Set meal** £65 9 courses (tasting menu). **Service** 12.5%. **Credit** AmEx, JCB, MC, V. Modern Indian
Vineet Bhatia, formerly at Zaika (*see p125*), is one of Britain's foremost Indian chefs. His new restaurant near Sloane Square exudes quiet intimacy and subdued elegance. On our visit, the cooking was mostly spot-on, particularly a main course of lime-spiked chilli and ginger lobster, surrounded by a creamy moat of deliciously fishy sauce. Broccoli khichdi (risotto-style rice tempered with curry leaves) worked well as a restrained accompaniment. Yet sometimes Bhatia overdoes it. Rich black lentils, simmered with cream, butter and tomatoes came topped with buttery potato and cumin mash, and artfully arranged tandoori lamb slices. He should have stopped there, but this was crowned with deep-fried, batter-dipped asparagus spears: too much. Other creations include samosas stuffed with shiitake mushrooms, and coconut soup laced with truffle oil. Dessert – mango rice pudding layered between wafer-thin biscuits, topped with a brandy-snap basket filled with lemongrass ice-cream – was messy and fussy. After-dinner chocolates, crammed with Indian

mouth fresheners, is another wacky combination that tries too hard. So, a Bollywood blockbuster performance, but such flamboyance comes at a stonkingly high price.
Babies and children welcome. Booking advisable. Dress: smart casual. No smoking. Separate rooms for parties, seating 8 and 15. Vegetarian menu. **Map 14 F11.**

Vama
438 King's Road, SW10 0LJ (7351 4118/ www.vama.co.uk). Sloane Square tube then 11, 22 bus. **Lunch served** noon-3pm daily. **Dinner served** 6.30-11.30pm Mon-Sat; 6.30-10.30pm Sun. **Main courses** £6.25-£18.50. **Set buffet lunch** (Sun) £12.95. **Service** 12.5% for parties of 6 or more. **Credit** AmEx, DC, MC, V. Modern Indian
The ratio of serving staff to customers at Andy Vama's plush brown eaterie is impressively high, and service is spot on. Portions are quite small and prices high (starters cost up to £14.50), but the quality of cooking, and extras such as the wood-fired tandoor, make the experience worth it. The cuisine is Modern Indian, with first courses such as masala crab, makhmali kebab (roasted cheese and potato served with aubergine, onion and tomato compote), kali mirch ke tukre (cubes of chicken breast in a peppercorn and garlic crust) and rogani champen (tandoori baby lamb chops). Mains offer dishes as diverse as baingen ke turke (roasted baby aubergine), crab kofta curry and lobster tandoori. Spicing tends to be delicate: our til wale paneer tikka (tandooried cheese cubes in sesame seed and yoghurt coating) allowed every flavour its voice; and a main of coconut prawn curry zinged with mustard seed and curry leaf flavours. Only a slightly oversweet side dish of roasted baby aubergine failed to win high marks. The front terrace is awash with Chelsea socialites on warm nights, while the rear conservatory would seem to be the hot spot the rest of the time.
Babies and children welcome; high chairs. Book weekends. Entertainment: belly dancers by arrangement. Separate room for parties, seats 35. Tables outdoors (4, patio). **Map 14 D12.**

Colliers Wood SW19

★ Suvai Aruvi NEW
96 High Street Colliers Wood, SW19 2BT (8543 6266). Colliers Wood tube. **Open** 11am-midnight daily. **Main courses** £3.50-£10.25. **Unlicensed. Corkage** no charge. **No credit cards.** Sri Lankan
This little caff is in the Tamil heartland that lies between Colliers Wood and Tooting, and has a loyal following among local Tamils. A stream of customers come in for takeaway, and many know Arun, the proprietor, by name. The consequent chat can mean delays in table service, but there's a wall-mounted TV showing Tamil soaps and other programmes to pass the time. The prices are agreeably low, and portions generous, for one of the most extensive Sri Lankan menus in the area. The seeni sambol is perfection – a melted onion relish that's sweet, but well spiced too. String hoppers, made with Sri Lankan red rice, make a good foil to the fiery dishes, such as devilled mutton. This mouth-watering concoction has a slight anise tang at the back of the heat (you can ask for a milder version). We particularly liked the squid curry, the strips of squid so soft they resembled slow-cooked onion, served in a creamy pale-orange sauce thickened with yoghurt. With prices this low, it's very tempting to over-order just to experiment.
Babies and children admitted. Booking advisable. No smoking. Takeaway service. Vegetarian menu.

Fulham SW6

Darbar NEW
92-94 Waterford Road, SW6 2HA (7348 7373). Fulham Broadway tube. **Lunch served** noon-3pm, **dinner served** 6-11.30pm Mon-Sat. **Main courses** £9.50-£14.50. **Set lunch** £9.99 (vegetarian), £12.95 (non-vegetarian) 3 courses. **Service** 12.5%. **Credit** AmEx, MC, V. North Indian

We visited Darbar soon after it opened in 2003 and lamented its high prices, though couldn't deny the culinary talent. This time, the talent was still in evidence, yet main courses cost around a fiver less. Chef Mohammed Rais ran the Red Fort's kitchen (*see p121*) when it won a *Time Out* Award in 2003. Here his menu highlights recipes from the royal kitchens of Lucknow, and dum ('sealed in a pot') cookery. The samundari rattan biriani positively yodelled out the sweet flavours of seafood (plump prawns, meaty scallops, tender squid) once the dough lid on the earthenware pot had been broken. Almost equally accomplished was a starter of tava galauti kebab: mousse-light, minced lamb rissoles. There were some slips (stale popadoms; murg lababdaar, where the chicken breast chunks hadn't taken up the flavour of the tomato and dill sauce), but the set lunch was a steal – the non-veg option offers three juicy tikkas, then three full-flavoured curries, plus rice, bread and decent mango kulfi. The room was sparsely populated on a midweek lunchtime, with an avuncular maître d' in pinstripes in close attendance. Surroundings are stylish: shiny black granite flooring, ornate carvings on cream walls, partially frosted plate-glass windows. Pity about the King's Road traffic.
Babies and children welcome; high chairs. Booking advisable. Disabled: toilet. Dress: smart casual. Separate room for parties, seats 10. Vegetarian menu. **Map 13 B13.**

Raynes Park SW20

Cocum
2004 RUNNER-UP BEST CHEAP EATS
9 Approach Road, Raynes Park, SW20 8BA (8540 3250-8542 3843). Morden tube then 163 bus/Raynes Park rail. **Lunch served** noon-3pm Sun. **Dinner served** 5.30-11.30pm daily. **Main courses** £4-£8. **Service** 10%. **Credit** AmEx, DC, JCB, MC, V. South Indian
One year into its operation, Cocum still looks spick and span with its blond wooden flooring, lemon walls incorporating a frieze of line-drawn portraits, and Keralite artefacts (kathakali dancing mask, a model of a ceremonial river boat). Keralite cuisine encompasses a few meat dishes, but fish and vegetarian dishes provide the highlights. After a disappointing start (excellent chutneys, but accompanied by stale, popadom-like snacks), a scintillating kadal soup made swift amends: crab, fish, squid and mussels, finely diced and in a creamy coconut-milk stock. Vazhuthananga pori (aubergine fritters with tomato dip) was mundane in comparison. No complaints, though, about main courses of nadan meen curry (meaty fish in a coconut and cocum – 'fish tamarind' – sauce), mambazha pulissery (a soupy, yoghurt-based curry containing mango and green banana), and cheera parippu (dahl and spinach). Dessert was a sweet, cardamom-laced treat of rice pudding. Informative waiters helped the meal along.
Babies and children welcome; high chairs. Booking advisable weekends. Restaurant available for hire. Takeaway service; delivery service.

Southfields SW18

★ Sarkhel's
199 Replingham Road, SW18 5LY (8870 1483). Southfields tube. **Lunch served** noon-2.30pm Tue-Sun. **Dinner served** 6-10.30pm Tue-Thur, Sun; 6-11pm Fri, Sat. **Main courses** £6.95-£9.95. **Set lunch** £5 2 courses. **Thali** £9.95. **Credit** MC, V. Pan-Indian
In 2003 Sarkhel's extended next door to create Calcutta Notebook, a 'branch' that uses the same kitchen. But recent visits to both restaurants confirmed last year's findings – that the original Sarkhel's is still the jewel in the crown. Chef Udit Sarkhel's cooking is at its best when grounded in the north Indian dishes he cooked while head chef at the Bombay Brasserie (*see p127*). Take, for example, the lamb biriani: the was meat tender, the grains distinct, the spice aromas clear, and it was correctly served with a simple cucumber raita. That's not to say dishes from other regions aren't good too; we relished the lemon rice with cashew nuts, which transported us back to Kerala more

effortlessly than a flight to Trivandrum. A Parsi-style dish of tiger prawns cooked with pumpkin and aubergine was also just-so, sweet enough to bring a smile to the lips of any Parsi mother-in-law. While the food quality is unquestionably high and service appreciably better than at local competitors, don't expect the low bills you can find in nearby Tooting. Still, that's the price you pay for being on the 'right' (ie Wimbledon) side of the railway tracks.
Babies and children welcome; high chairs. Book Fri, Sat. Disabled: toilet. No-smoking tables. Takeaway service (8871 0808). Vegetarian menu.

South Kensington SW5, SW7

Bombay Brasserie

Courtfield Road, SW7 4QH (7370 4040/ www.bombaybrasserielondon.com). Gloucester Road tube. **Lunch served** 12.30-3pm, **dinner served** 7.30pm-midnight daily. **Main courses** £16-£21. **Minimum** (dinner) £25. **Set buffet lunch** £18.95 incl tea or coffee. **Service** 12.5%. **Credit** AmEx, DC, JCB, MC, V. Pan-Indian

The Bombay Brasserie was once a leading Indian restaurant, but its culinary standards have slipped a few notches. However, the opulent decor retains its colonial charm and remains a hit with wealthy tourists and corporate groups. Adorned with Raj memorabilia, the venue is a haven for old India hands. We prefer the light and airy conservatory with its leafy greens and comfy cane furniture to the more buttoned-down sombre dining hall. On our visit, cooking was hit and miss. High points included a deliciously juicy starter of mahi gandheri kebab (finely pounded fish, beaten with coriander and chillies and shaped around batons of sugar cane and lightly fried). Ringana nu shak (baby aubergines, simmered in a smooth peanut masala, spiked with blended tomatoes and sweet fried onions) was another admirable marriage of flavours and textures. Good news over: the main courses were sloppy and poorly executed. Lamb chettinad was let down by chewy meat and a thick

cloying masala, while a nondescript masala rendered our fish malabar more suited to a Kettering takeaway than a Keralite feast. Service, although well intentioned, becomes erratic when things get busy. Shame, as this is one of the best looking Indian restaurants in town.
Babies and children admitted; high chairs. Booking advisable; essential weekends. Dress: smart casual. Entertainment: pianist 9pm Mon-Fri; 12.30-3pm, 9pm Sun. No-smoking tables. Restaurant available for hire. Separate conservatory for parties, seats 150. Vegetarian menu. **Map 13 C10.**

Kare Kare

152 Old Brompton Road, SW5 0BE (7373 0024/www.karekare.co.uk). Gloucester Road tube. **Lunch served** noon-2.30pm daily. **Dinner served** 5.30-11.30pm Mon-Sat; 5.30-11pm Sun. **Main courses** £7.95-£14.95. **Set lunch** £9.95 4 courses incl tea or coffee. **Set meal** (5.30-7.30pm) £15.95 4 courses incl tea or coffee. **Service** 12.5%. **Credit** AmEx, DC, MC, V. Pan-Indian

Said to have been inspired by the New Zealand beach its name comes from, the '(Indian) Ocean' influence claimed here could be better expressed as featuring seafood and being Indian in style, rather than having anything to do with cuisine from a particular region. The decor is modern, with large picture windows and clean white lines. Regular exhibitions mean that ever-changing artwork dots the walls. Starters include gandaki crab (fried in breadcrumbs), paloong prawn pancake (served with spinach) and aloo jingha samosa, which – rather predictably – was heavier on the potato than the prawn. Practically everything we tried was timidly spiced. And a surprising number of dishes mentioned cornflower in their menu descriptions, an ingredient not usually associated with Indian cuisine. King prawns in a tomatoey sauce would have been far better with further reduction, and the signature dish of monkfish tikka masala was a good idea spoiled by its being spiced to appeal to European palates. Still, the largely well-heeled locals seemed to adore everything offered – and made sure everybody knew it. The place was so full on a

Friday night that tables were closer together than vacuum-packed sardines. Service was willing enough, but officious.
Babies and children welcome; children's menu; high chairs. Booking advisable. Separate rooms for parties, seating 26 and 30. Tables outdoors (3, pavement). Takeaway service; delivery service. **Map 13 C11.**

South

Norbury SW16

★ Mirch Masala

1416 London Road, SW16 4BZ (8679 1828/ 8765 1070). Norbury rail. **Meals served** noon-midnight daily. **Main courses** £3-£10. **Set buffet lunch** (noon-4pm Mon-Sat) £5.99. **Unlicensed. Corkage** no charge. **Credit** AmEx, JCB, MC, V. East African Punjabi

This simple, white caff serves some fine Punjabi (by way of East Africa) food, though service, like the decor, is a little rough and ready. After a fairly long wait for our bill, the young server disarmed us by saying: 'Sorry if you were waiting longer than we'd like, sir, we were carried away discussing the education question. What are your ideas?' Er…? The menu is divided into vegetarian and non-vegetarian 'warmers' (starters), 'steamers' (main courses) and 'coolers' (rice, breads, drinks). Warmers include robust and meaty kebabs, fish tikka, patra, and chilli paneer. Steamers can be either 'deigi' dishes (named after the small pot that rests inside a steamer) such as deigi dahl gosht – meat on the bone with lentils – or else cooked in a karahi, such as the deservedly popular karahi ginger chicken. Rice arrives in a lidded butter dish (very sensible), sauces are thick and much reduced, and nans don't come any lighter or crisper. Everything is cooked to your particular heat-setting (mild, medium or hot) and vegetarians have the option of Quorn. Fellow customers are as likely to include traditionally dressed Muslims as local office workers and couples on the low-key razzle.
Babies and children welcome; high chairs. Booking advisable. Takeaway service; delivery service (within 2-mile radius). Vegetarian menu. **For branches see index.**

Chowki. See p121.

Tooting SW17

Tooting has attracted a stream of smart, well-educated immigrants from the Indian subcontinent since the 1960s. The first arrivals came to study at the South West London College (which still specialises in accountancy, business and management studies). Some of these white-collar workers – Gujarati, Keralite, Pakistani, Tamil – stayed in the area, settled, and have raised families. The first South Indian restaurant, **Sree Krishna** (192-194 Tooting High Street; 8672 4250) opened in 1973.

Nowadays, there are Hindu temples, Asian video shops, mosques, a Sikh gurdwara and a score of little caffs and restaurants catering for the diverse Asian communities. The most interesting stretch of Tooting to explore on foot is between Tooting Bec and Tooting Broadway tube stations, though the Tamil cafés and shops continue down towards Colliers Wood tube.

In the late 1980s, a civil war between the Sinhalese majority and a minority of Tamil separatists in Sri Lanka created a wave of Tamil refugees – and many moved to the stretch between Tooting Broadway and Colliers Wood. Tooting is now home to around 30,000 Tamil people (of an estimated 100,000 living in London), which makes them the largest Asian community in the area.

★ ★ Banana Leaf NEW

190 Tooting High Street, SW17 0SF (8696 1423). Tooting Broadway tube. **Meals served** noon-11pm daily. **Main courses** £3.50-£5.75. **No credit cards.** Sri Lankan

Banana Leaf's menu is long – possibly too long, at around 100 items – but the cooking is among the best to be found in London's Sri Lankan caffs. Prices are shockingly cheap in comparison to those of central London. Crab curry costs a mere £3, but was the best dish we tried of several: a bowl of long crab limbs and shell, but with plenty of meat and an incredibly moreish, bisque-like sauce. One of the most expensive dishes (at a whopping £3.50) was the devilled mutton, the dry-roasted spices unusually, and pleasingly, mild. The South Indian and Sri Lankan breakfast dish, masala dosai, is served here on a real banana leaf, just as is still the case in some roadside cafés of South Asia. A batter of fermented rice and lentil flour is spread very thinly on a griddle and evenly fried, then filled with spiced potato and rolled into a giant tube, for £1.70. Seeni sambol (£1) is a sweet and spicy slow-cooked relish of caramelised onions; this version was very fresh and redolent of cinnamon, plus a touch of cardamom. Furnishings and service are basic. *Babies and children welcome. No-smoking tables. Takeaway service.*

★ Jaffna House

90 Tooting High Street, SW17 0RN (8672 7786/ www.jaffnahouse.co.uk). Tooting Broadway tube. **Meals served** noon-midnight daily. **Main courses** £2.25-£9. **Set lunch** (noon-3pm Mon-Fri) £4-£5 2 courses incl drink. **Credit** AmEx, MC, V. Sri Lankan

Jaffna House has started to attract more non-Tamil diners than ever, possibly something to do with it getting much press coverage after winning an award in summer 2004 as the UK's 'Best Sri Lankan Restaurant'. We wonder what first-timers will make of this tiny, unassuming café and dining room, with its amateurish service and cheap furnishings. The cooking is decent, though, and great value – a meal usually works out at around a tenner per head. Alongside the usual selection of Sri Lankan specialities are some surprises, such as beef curry (a Christian dish; in this case, strips of beef in a dark and rich sauce that reminded us of Vesta boil-in-the-bag days). More typical is fried string hoppers with mutton, the vermicelli chopped up and fried with eggs, chunks of full-flavoured mutton and a liberal dose of chilli. Dishes tend to be on the fiery side; the carrot sambol resembled coleslaw, apart from being laced with fresh green chilli. Remember to order a soothing lassi if you can't stand the heat. *Babies and children welcome. Booking advisable. Separate room for parties, seats 25. Takeaway service. Vegetarian menu.*

★ Kastoori

188 Upper Tooting Road, SW17 7EJ (8767 7027). Tooting Bec or Tooting Broadway tube. **Lunch served** 12.30-2.30pm Wed-Sun. **Dinner served** 6-10.30pm daily. **Main courses** £4.75-£6.25. **Thalis** £8.50-£16.25. **Minimum** £7. **Credit** MC, V. East African Gujarati vegetarian

Kastoori appears to attract more non-Asian customers than Asians. We can only assume this is because customers – especially vegetarians – travel from far and wide to eat here. It's certainly no reflection on the quality of the Thanki family's Gujarati-based vegetarian cooking. Savour, for example, the kachori: a spicy mung dahl and pea filling encased in pastry shells, served in an unusual vibrantly coloured sour/sweet yoghurt sauce. Or the sev poori: crisp, freshly fried pooris filled with diced potato and puffed rice, topped with sev the colour of Buddhist robes. The long, unusual and tempting 'Thanki family specials' are usually restricted to one dish per day, perhaps made of sweetcorn, mustard leaf or plantain, the last served in a sweet, tomato-based sauce. Even the oddest-sounding dishes are invariably good, such as the paneer stuffed with a dark coconut-and-spice mix, served in a buff-coloured, creamy pasanda sauce. Our only complaint concerns the 'passion juice', which is the colour of Fanta and tastes about as freshly juiced. *Babies and children welcome. Booking essential. Takeaway service. Vegan dishes.*

★ Lahore Karahi

1 Tooting High Street, SW17 0SN (8767 2477/www.lahorekarahi.co.uk). Tooting Broadway tube/133 bus. **Meals served** noon-

midnight daily. **Main courses** £5-£8. **Unlicensed. Corkage** no charge. **Credit** JCB, MC, V. Pakistani

Lahore Karahi is the best of the really cheap Indian restaurants that cluster around Tooting Markets. It makes no bones about being a fast-food joint – plate glass, bright lighting and wipe-clean tables do not make this an ideal spot for a hot date. Unless, of course, your beau adores dishes such as 'karela bitter melon gosht', with strips of bitter gourd cooked into submission with chunks of tender mutton over a hot karahi. Most dishes on display under the glass counter are good, but beware the so-called 'pilau rice', which is merely plain rice with a sprinkling of food colouring. The nan breads are a much better bet, freshly cooked in the tandoor by the entrance. For afters, consider the decadent falooda: a whole kulfi chopped up into a milk drink with vermicelli and tiny subja seeds (an Indian variety of basil, which become like frogspawn when soaked). It's little wonder the place is always bustling with a mix of people either eating in or collecting takeaways. *Babies and children welcome; high chairs. Booking advisable. Separate room for parties, seats 50. Takeaway service. Vegetarian menu.*

★ **Masaledar**

121 Upper Tooting Road, SW17 7TJ (8767 7676). Tooting Bec or Tooting Broadway tube/ 155, 219, 355 bus. **Meals served** noon-midnight daily. **Main courses** £3.50-£7.95. **Set lunch** (noon-6pm Mon-Fri) £2.95 1 course incl salad and rice. **Unlicensed. Corkage** no charge. **Credit** MC, V. East African Punjabi

The cooking is as good as ever, but we've detected a (further) deterioration in the standards of service at this hugely popular BYO restaurant. On our most recent visit of several in the past year, it took 20 minutes to persuade a waiter to take our order, and it was nearly an hour from our arrival to the first dishes arriving on the table. However, plenty of people seem prepared to put up with such nonchalant, sloppy service for dishes such as deigi gosht (a big lamb shank cooked almost to a mush in a wonderful sauce thick with yoghurt and onion); or the saabz achari (mixed vegetables with a mouth-watering blend of sour and sweet flavours, thanks to the use of pickling spices). All the 'Masaledar Specials' are excellent, including marage, a curry of red kidney beans in a meaty-tasting (but entirely vegetarian) stock. This goes well with mandazi, which are similar to triangular fried doughnuts but flavoured with fennel seeds. Masaledar's takeaway and delivery service is thriving; it seems the orders of eat-in customers now take second place. If you live locally, ordering a delivery probably makes more sense. *Babies and children welcome; high chairs. Booking advisable; essential weekends. Separate room for parties, seats 25. Takeaway service; delivery service (within 3-mile radius). Vegetarian menu.*

★ **Onam** NEW

219 Tooting High Street, SW17 0SZ (8767 7655). Tooting Broadway tube. **Lunch served** 11.30am-3pm, **dinner served** 6-11pm daily. **Main courses** £1.95-£6.95. **Service** 10%. **Credit** AmEx, JCB, MC, V. South Indian

The latest of Tooting's rash of South Indian restaurants, Onam is almost opposite the long-established (but, of late, complacent) Sree Krishna. The menu follows the precedents set by such earlier pioneers from Kerala. There's an extensive vegetarian selection; 'home-made' specialities; chicken, lamb or seafood curries; and 'exotic Cochin specialities' – which, bizarrely, is where chicken tikka masala is listed. Heading straight for the real dishes of Kerala, we found the cooking variable. One dish was memorably good, the meen curry: big chunks of kingfish cooked with the smoky, attractively sour flavour of cocum (aka fish tamarind). Less impressive was 'chicken 65', the chicken chunks smeared with red food colouring. Uthappam, which should be a light pancake, was leaden and scorched in places. It's best to stick to what the chefs know best: sambar, masala vadai and the appams were all up to par.

Babies and children welcome; high chairs. Booking advisable. Disabled: toilet. No-smoking tables. Takeaway service.

★ ★ **Radha Krishna Bhavan**

86 Tooting High Street, SW17 0RN (8682 0969/ www.sreekrishna.co.uk). Tooting Broadway tube. **Lunch served** noon-3pm daily. **Dinner served** 6-11pm Mon-Thur, Sun; 6pm-midnight Fri, Sat. **Main courses** £1.95-£6.95. **Thalis** (Sun) £5.95-£7.95. **Minimum** £5. **Service** 10%. **Credit** AmEx, DC, MC, V. South Indian

The name means house of the blue boy Krishna, and his main squeeze, Radha. Most people come here for the great value, the terrific food, and the truly memorable interior: orange sunsets, palm-fronded beaches, forest scenes and a full-size dummy of a Keralite kathakali dancer. But tear your eyes away from the gaudy decor to study the menu. Give the curry house dhansaks and kormas a swerve and stick to the Keralite dishes: that is, any of the 'specialities', plus the vegetable curries and dry vegetables. The 'Kerala tiffin specialities' include nadan dosai, a type of rice and lentil pancake cooked on a griddle. This version has a perfect texture, served with fresh green and red coconut chutneys and wonderfully sour-sweet sambar. The 'dry vegetables' are Keralite thorans: chopped and stir-fried al dente vegetables, flavoured with grated coconut and curry leaves. These are revelatory, especially if you're usually wary of cabbage or beetroot. Having eaten here many times, we can also vouch for the excellence of the appams, served with a choice of three curries. *Babies and children welcome. Booking advisable. Takeaway service; delivery service (within 3-mile radius). Vegetarian menu.* **For branch (Sree Krishna Inn) see index.**

Kennington SE11

The Painted Heron NEW

205-209 Kennington Lane, SE11 5QS (7793 8313/www.thepaintedheron.com). Kennington or Vauxhall tube. **Meals served** noon-2.30pm, 6-11pm Mon-Sat; 1-9pm Sun. **Main courses** £11-£17. **Set lunch** £10 1 course. **Service** 12.5%. **Credit** AmEx, JCB, MC, V. Modern Indian

Chelsea's Painted Heron (*see p126*) has a new branch. Zen-like in atmosphere, it provides a serene setting for well-heeled fans of regional Indian cookery. Light wood furnishings, candles on tables, and quietly efficient waiters add to the relaxed ambience. Chef Yogesh Datta supervises both restaurants, producing a daily changing menu. Culinary gems include marinades with mango, peppery pineapple pickles and nans showered with toasted red chilli shreds. Crab cake starters provided a mound of meaty flakes, flecked with mustard seeds and chopped chillies, crowned with a delicious crust of fried potatoes. Black tiger prawns, simmered in saucy, Bengali pickling-spice masala made a satisfying, complex-tasting curry; sweet-scented pandanus ('screwpine') essence, smoked mustard oil, and aromatic fennel seeds came through clearly, without overwhelming the prawns. Chilli beef, stir-fried with onions, tomatoes and peppers, was more a stew than the expected flash fry. No complaints about the taste, though – it was crammed with red chillies, chunks of green pepper, and shredded root ginger. Not all dishes hit the target; there was bitter-tasting black salt and too much sugar in the thin yoghurt

Sagar. See p125.

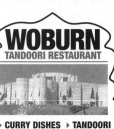

and cucumber raita. Nevertheless, the cooking – imaginative combinations without fussy garnishing – is generally notable.

Babies and children welcome. Booking advisable. No-smoking tables. Tables outdoors (25, garden). Takeaway service. Vegetarian menu. Map 16 M12.

Lewisham SE13

★ Everest Curry King

24 Loampit Hill, SE13 7SW (8691 2233). Lewisham DLR/rail. **Meals served** 11am-11pm daily. **Main courses** £3.95-£6.95. **Set meal** £3.95 3 courses. **Credit** MC, V. Sri Lankan

Attracting much local Sri Lankan custom, the oddly named Everest Curry King has become something of a fixture in Loampit Vale, also attracting celebrity diners we're told – though names were not forthcoming. There still appears to be no price list – but we've never heard of anyone getting a nasty surprise once the bill arrives. The place is tiny, filled with Formica-topped tables topped with jugs of water and various jars of condiment. The glass-fronted cabinet contains a variety of snacks, meat and vegetable dishes. Others can be prepared to order from the tiny kitchen at the rear. Plates are filled at the counter, microwaved to a furnace-like temperature, then carried quickly over to the table. Rapid turnover means the metal curry containers don't hold on to their contents for long. Expect all the usual Sri Lankan staples to be offered, plus specials such as liver and various permutations of vegetables and dahls. Spicing tends to be to Sri Lankan levels of chilli-heat, though delicious lassis are available to put out the fire.

Babies and children welcome. No smoking. Takeaway service. Vegetarian menu.

Madras NEW

244 Lewisham High Street, SE13 6JU (8852 6666). Lewisham DLR/rail/Ladywell rail/ 36, 47, 199 bus. **Lunch served** noon-3pm, **dinner served** 6-11pm daily. **Main courses** £2.25-£4.75. **Thalis** £6.95 (vegetarian), £7.50 (non-vegetarian). **Service** 10%. **Credit** AmEx, MC, V. South Indian

The former Sri Lankan-owned Green Cabin has been taken over by the people from the Madras in Manor Park, and has started serving South Indian food. The menu has retained the kothu roti dishes, but also includes specials such as poori masala, nine types of dosai, and mutton roll; local custom continues to be attracted by the madras, vindaloo and korma staples. Spicing is pretty authentic and the quality of cooking is above average. A masala dosai was big and light, made from properly fermented batter with that tell-tale slightly sour aftertaste; the filling was studded with mustard seeds and fresh curry leaves. Uthappam too passed muster, with a good complement of sliced chillies, tempered by the savouriness of tomato and onion. Chilli squid was far from rubbery, in a tangy, much-reduced sauce. A side dish of 'cabbage fried' (sic) was bland, however. The decor has been smartened up, with the serving area moved by the door (away from the kitchen), a coat of paint applied, and scenic Indian pictures installed. Service could have been more on the ball, but our waiter perked up once a manager-type arrived.

Babies and children welcome. Booking advisable. Takeaway service; delivery service (within 2-mile radius). Vegetarian menu.

East

Brick Lane and Banglatown may still be many people's idea of where to get that 'authentic curry experience', but those in the know avoid the pzazz and hard-sell and head further afield. These days only **Sweet & Spicy** remains from the time when the Lane was full of cafés catering to local Pakistani and Bangladeshi residents. Recent attempts by some restaurants to trumpet their Bangladeshi origins are to be applauded, although we've found so few people order special regional dishes that in many restaurants kitchen staff are sent out to buy ingredients like shatkora from the supermarket as (and if) they're ordered.

What the typical Brick Lane customer seems to want appears to include lots of beer, loud music and a korma or vindaloo not dissimilar to that served in any high street. And if a relatively inexpensive 'formula' curry is your thing, then look no further than Banglatown. But it's far better to try the numerous Pakistani-run cafés south of Commercial Road – although **New Tayyab** (and its daytime associate, **Tayyab Kebab House**) seem to have embarked on the same dumbing-down process as has occurred on Brick Lane.

Better still, visit Green Street (stretching from Barking Road in the south to Stratford Road, Forest Gate, in the north), a long thoroughfare peppered with good restaurants. Here you'll find meat that is slow-marinated and quickly grilled, and curries that are slow-cooked, thickly reduced and deliciously savoury. Go at the weekend to experience the bustling, cosmopolitan atmosphere that Brick Lane once enjoyed. Dozens of food shops sell all manner of exotic fruit and vegetables, mostly at ridiculously low prices. Don't expect this to be the enclave of just one ethnic group: expat Indians and Pakistanis and their British-born descendants coexist happily.

You'll find Moslem and Hindu shops and cafés side by side, street kulfi and mango sellers, and even (in summer, at least) kulfi-vans complete with chimes (they'll also sell you a Mr Whippy if pushed). Whether you try a tikka at one of two branches of **Mobeen**, **Lazzat Karahi** or a thali at pan-Indian vegetarian **Vijay's Chawalla**, you'll find yourself sitting among people enjoying their own cuisine. Pakistani-style grills are the speciality at a couple of branches of **Kebabish** (the largest is at 297 Green Street, E13 9AR; 8472 4036). There are also numerous sweet centres and a branch of the Gujarati vegetarian mini chain **Sakonis** (*see p143*).

South Indian menu

In recent years South Indian cuisine in London has come of age, with higher cooking standards and more sophisticated places serving varied regional specialities little known outside South India. The well-publicised expansion of both the **Woodlands** and the **Rasa** chains has played no small role in this.

Chefs tend to be from either Chennai (formerly Madras) or Kerala, but the one-year-old **Sagar** (*see p125*), which specialises in the famed vegetarian cuisine of Karnataka, has added a new dimension to South Indian dining in London.

Much of South Indian food consists of rice-, lentil- and semolina-based dishes. Fish features strongly in the non-vegetarian establishments, and coconut, mustard seeds, curry leaves and red chillies are widely used as flavourings.

Adai: fermented rice and lentil pancakes, with a nuttier flavour than dosais (qv).
Avial: a mixed vegetable curry from Kerala with a coconut and yoghurt sauce. Literally, 'mixture' in Malayalam (the language of Kerala).
Bonda: spiced mashed potatoes, dipped in chickpea flour batter and deep-fried.
Dosai or **dosa**: thin, shallow-fried pancake, often sculpted into interesting shapes – the very thin ones are called paper dosai. Most dosais are made with fermented rice and lentil batter, but variants include rawa (or rava) dosai, made with 'cream of wheat' semolina. Masala dosais come with a spicy potato filling. All variations are traditionally served with a lentil dahl (sambar, qv) and coconut chutney.
Gobi 65: cauliflower marinated in spices, then dipped in chickpea flour batter and deep-fried. It is

usually lurid pink due to the addition of food colouring.
Idli: steamed sponges of ground rice and lentil batter. Eaten with sambar (qv), and coconut chutney.
Kadala: black chickpea curry.
Kalan: a thin curry from the southern states made from yoghurt, coconut and mangoes; variants include moru kachiatu.
Kancheepuram idli: idli (qv) flavoured with whole black peppercorns and other spices.
Kappa: cassava root traditionally served with kadala (qv).
Kootu: mild vegetable curry in a creamy coconut and yoghurt sauce.
Kozhi varutha: usually consists of pieces of chicken served in a medium-hot curry sauce based on garlic and coconut – it is very rich.
Moilee: term used to describe Keralite fish curry.
Rasam: consommé made with lentils; it tastes both

peppery-hot and tamarind-sour, but there are many regional variations.
Sambar or **sambhar**: a variation on dahl (qv) made with a specific hot blend of spices, plus coconut, tamarind and vegetables – particularly drumsticks (a pod-like vegetable, like a longer, woodier version of okra).
Thoran: vegetables stir-fried with mustard seeds, curry leaves, chillies and fresh grated coconut.
Uppama: a popular breakfast dish in which onions, spices and, occasionally, vegetables are cooked with semolina using a risotto-like technique.
Uthappam: spicy, crisp pancake/pizza made with lentil and rice flour batter, usually topped with tomato, onions and chillies.
Vellappam: a bowl-shaped, crumpet-like rice pancake (same as appam or hopper, in Sri Lankan restaurants).

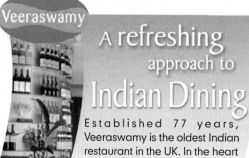

Brick Lane E1

★ Sweet & Spicy

40 Brick Lane, E1 6RF (7247 1081). Aldgate East or Whitechapel tube. **Meals served** 8am-10pm daily. **Main courses** £1.80-£5.50. **Unlicensed. Corkage** no charge. **No credit cards.** Pakistani

Plain in comparison to the snazzier Brick Lane cafés that attract City workers, Sweet & Spicy (est.1969) is furnished with functional white wall tiles, wipe-clean tables and old photos of Pakistani wrestlers. It's hardly surprising that the place is frequented mainly by Muslim men rather than Friday-night clubbers. Cooking isn't worthy of a Moglai feast, but it is basic and cheap. Chefs stand behind the self-service counter where calorie-laden curries are displayed alongside cochineal-coloured meat kebabs. Dishes are reheated in a microwave; this works sometimes, but not with the breads. Our nans were leathery – best to order rice instead. A chicken curry, scented with cloves and cardamom, quelled hunger pangs with its comforting and homely flavour. Tarka dahl, fiery with red chillies, must be lentil heaven for the Pakistani regulars who like their food pungently spiced.

Babies and children welcome. No smoking. Takeaway service; delivery service. **Map 12 S5**.

Leytonstone E11

Chandni

715 High Road, E11 4RD (8539 1700). Leytonstone tube. **Meals served** 5pm-midnight Tue-Sun. **Main courses** £2.50-£6. **Thali** £6. **Credit** AmEx, MC, V. Gujarati

Despite discovering a dirty fork on our table and a tasteless vegetable kofta curry in our thali, we generally have a lot of time for this mock-Tudor decorated, family-run vegetarian diner. Our final moan on what was overall a positive experience concerns the slightly soggy bhel pooris. We ignored the Chinese samosa (presumably bought-in) and wished we'd gone for mixed pakodas, which a neighbouring table pronounced excellent. Chilli paneer contained a mountain of velvet-soft cheese in a sauce that'd knock the socks off Zsa Zsa Gabor, and a side order of fried dahl almost had to be tied down. The thalis are good value, most dishes being scrumptious, especially the knockout aloo mutter we were surprised to discover. Stuffed paratha was enjoyable; tandoori roti even more so. Service was friendly and mostly on the ball, though we were never fully able to explain that it wasn't us who had dumped the fork on to the tablecloth. Just don't go expecting top-notch service or cooking – and at these prices you'd be mad to.

Babies and children welcome; high chairs. Booking advisable weekends. No-smoking tables. Takeaway service.

Upton Park E6, E7

★ Lazzat Kahari NEW

18 Plashet Grove, E6 1AE (8552 3413). Upton Park tube. **Lunch served** noon-2.30pm, **dinner served** 5pm-midnight daily. **Main courses** £3.95-£4.95. **No credit cards.** Punjabi

This small, smartly decorated diner was buzzing the Saturday we called in, with families and groups of Pakistani men cooing over the traditional Punjabi food that the four servers were rushing out. The rapid turnover meant the kitchen could hardly keep up with demand. The most popular dishes are sticks of shami kebab (rich and meaty), baby lamb karahi (on the bone) and chicken karahi special, which was practically clucking with joy, expertly spiced and awash with fresh methi leaves. The complimentary tomato, onion and cucumber salad produced on our arrival was bigger and better than many we've paid a fiver for; the dahl was savoury and properly tarka-ed; and the mixed vegetable curry had been deliciously reduced. Lazzat occupies the former site of a Chinese

Rasoi Vineet Bhatia. See p126.

restaurant, we were told; its new decor includes peach-coloured, mock-marble tiled walls, light wood tables and silver chairs. Think Austin Powers via Peshawar. Service was swift, friendly and helpful; we've never been offered extra curry to mop up our rice before.
Babies and children welcome; high chairs. Takeaway service.

★ Mobeen
224 Green Street, E7 8LE (8470 2419). Upton Park tube. **Meals served** 11am-10pm daily. **Main courses** £2-£5.50. **Credit** MC, V. Pakistani
Our advice is to visit this self-service caff at the weekend when food is likely to be fresher, tandoors smoking hot, and the place filled with swirling saris and noisy families with riotous kids. We landed up for Tuesday lunch and faced a bleak scenario of empty Formica tables, and tired-looking curries in the glass-fronted counter. Cooking is basic and orders are reheated in a microwave oven – fine for dahl, but certain death for breads. Safe bets are the meaty kebabs; we appreciated the chicken seekh kebab (spiced mince, shaped into a sausage and seared on a skewer) for its onion-rich flavour and juicy texture. Keema aloo (lamb mince and potato curry) was loaded with enough oil to fuel a power station. Smiling staff compensated for a hit-and-miss meal. Next time, we'll visit on a Saturday night and hope for a feast.
Babies and children welcome; high chairs. No smoking. Separate room for parties, seats 200. Takeaway service.
For branches see index.

★ Vijay's Chawalla
268-270 Green Street, E7 8LF (8470 3535). Upton Park tube. **Meals served** 11am-9pm daily. **Main courses** £4-£7. **Thalis** £6-£7. **Unlicensed. Corkage** no charge. **Credit** JCB, MC, V. Pan-Indian vegetarian
Popular with Green Street shoppers, this buzzy, no-frills caff is essentially a snack shop and fast-food joint rolled into one. The pink decor could do with sprucing up, and the plasma screens showing Bollywood films can be a distraction, but the food is the reason for dropping by. Ragada patties, a popular Gujarati snack consisting of stuffed spicy mashed potato balls with tamarind-flavoured chickpea and marrowfat pea sauce, were gutsily-spiced, with spot-on flavours. Sev khaman, another

Gujarati classic, featured cotton-soft, feather-light steamed cakes made with rice flour and split chickpea batter, unusually spiked with kewra (screwpine) essence. The dish was topped with tangy tamarind and yoghurt sauces and crunchy sev. Falooda contained what looked like a tropical fruit cocktail, but was otherwise creamy and delicious, and decorated with chopped pistachios. The menu offers an extensive range of Bombay street snacks and thalis. Flavours are punchy and multidimensional.
Babies and children welcome; high chairs. Disabled: toilet. No smoking. Takeaway service. Vegetarian menu.

Whitechapel E1

★ Café Spice Namaste
16 Prescot Street, E1 8AZ (7488 9242/ www.cafespice.co.uk). Aldgate or Tower Hill tube/Tower Gateway DLR. **Lunch served** noon-3pm Mon-Fri. **Dinner served** 6.15-10.30pm Mon-Fri; 6.30-10.30pm Sat. **Main courses** £9.95-£15.95. **Set meal** £25-£35 (minimum 2). **Service** 12.5%. **Credit** AmEx, DC, JCB, MC, V. Pan-Indian
Bombay-born Parsi chef-owner Cyrus Todiwala is famous for taking the best from the gamut of Indian cuisines and adding exciting twists. Expect the likes of venison and duck tikka, Goan wild boar sausages in a rich vindaloo sauce, seafood samosas and king scallops with ginger and chilli. Alongside are traditional Parsi dishes such as the (proper) dhansak: a rich, intense experience. The own-made chutneys and pickles served with pre-meal popadoms set the tone; you can't beat the turnip and mango. We were delighted to find a starter special of oyster bulchao (which married the crustacean's salty-sea flavours with the pickling spices); and a wonderful Goan-style pilau with scallops, tiger prawns, crab and mussels, served with 'saurac' (Goan red coconut curry). Even the side dish of kadhi with lentil dumplings was a work of art. Offhand service has been mentioned, but have always been well treated. This former magistrates' court has been comfortably decked out with traditional Parsi-inspired pink, purple, green and gold hangings, and attracts the expense-account crowd. Opened in 2003 and accessed via Magdalen Passage is the Ginger Garden, an al fresco dining area with outside tandoor (read 'barbecue') and snack menu.

Babies and children welcome; high chairs. Booking advisable. Disabled: toilet. Tables outdoors (8, garden). Takeaway service; delivery service (within 2-mile radius). **Map 12 S7**.

Kasturi
57 Aldgate High Street, EC3N 1AL (7480 7402/ www.kasturi-restaurant.co.uk). Aldgate tube. **Meals served** 11am-11pm Mon-Fri; 5.30-11.30pm Sat. **Main courses** £5-£10. **Credit** AmEx, MC, V. Pan-Indian
Kasturi – the name refers to the expensive deer musk used in perfumery – seems to be trying harder than most nearby Bangladeshi venues to escape the curry-house formula. The main dining room is long and thin, with a blond wood floor, cream paintwork, subdued lighting, and purple and white linen. Our waiters were eager to please if a little bewildered, as if they'd all just started. Starters include items such as fish samosa (mixed fish that was maybe too delicately spiced) and kadak kebab samarkand (minced lamb roll stuffed with cheese and grilled), as well as the usual onion bhajis and king prawn pooris. Similarly, the inevitable madras, vindaloo and dhansak staples are offset by 'chef's specials', such as jingha dum anarkhali (king prawns in a thick pomegranate and coconut sauce), gosht badami pasanda, and rann-e-buzkazi (for two persons), a whole leg of fire-roasted lamb. Occasionally, compromises aimed at appealing to western palates reduce Kasturi to the level of a high-street curry shop – as in the case of our bland mixed dahl tarka (supposedly cooked in the Bengali style, but without a hint of red chilli).
Babies and children welcome. Booking advisable. Disabled: toilet. No-smoking tables. Separate room for parties, seats 15. Takeaway service; delivery service. Vegetarian menu. **Map 12 S6**.

★ New Tayyab/ Tayyab Kebab House
83 Fieldgate Street, E1 1JU (7247 9543/ www.tayyabs.co.uk). Aldgate East or Whitechapel tube.
New Tayyab **Dinner served** 5-11.30pm daily. **Main courses** £3-£10.
Tayyab Kebab House **Lunch served** noon-5pm daily. **Main courses** £3-£4.
Both **Unlicensed. Corkage** no charge. **Credit** AmEx, MC, V. Pakistani

---

Gujarati menu

There has been a significant increase in the number of Gujarati eateries in London, mainly in Wembley, Neasden, Harrow and Kingsbury. These vegetarian, café-style establishments produce a hotchpotch of Gujarati, 'Punjabi-style' and 'South Indian' meals and snacks – as yet there are no really smart restaurants.

They tend to serve either East African-style Gujarati food (characterised by the presence of African vegetables such as cassava, strong seasonings and a heavy-handed use of tomatoes and sugar) or, if they're owned by Gujaratis from India, 'Surti' food, which features little-known vegetables such as purple yams and Indian broad

beans, and seasonings such as wild green garlic, fresh coconut, green chillies and coriander leaves. In reality, Surti food in London is not the real McCoy, and the mixture of fiery hot, tangy and overly sweet flavours can be an acquired taste.

On the whole, the standard of cooking in London's Gujarati establishments remains poor when compared to the real thing.

Bhel poori: a snack originating from street stalls in Mumbai, which contains crisp, deep-fried pooris, puffed rice, sev (deep-fried gram-flour vermicelli), chopped onion, tomato, potato and more, plus chutneys (chilli, mint and tamarind).
Farsan: Gujarati snacks.

Ganthia: Gujarati name for crisply fried savoury confections made from chickpea flour; they come in all sorts of shapes.
Mithi roti: round griddle-cooked bread stuffed with a cardamom- and saffron-flavoured lentil paste. Also called puran poli.
Mogo: deep-fried cassava, often served as chips together with a sweet and sour tamarind chutney; an East African Asian dish.
Pani poori: bite-sized pooris that are filled with sprouted beans, chickpeas, potato, onion, chutneys, sev and a thin, spiced watery sauce.
Patra: a savoury snack made of the arvi leaf (colocasia) stuffed with spiced chickpea flour batter, steamed, then cut into swiss-roll like slices.

The slices are then shallow-fried with sesame and mustard seeds.
Pau bhajee: a robustly spiced dish of mashed potatoes and vegetables, served with a shallow-fried white bread roll.
Puran poli: see mithi roti.
Ragda pattice or **ragada patties**: mashed potato patties covered with a chickpea or dried pea sauce, topped with onions, sev and spicy chutney.
Tindora: ivy gourd, a vegetable that resembles baby gherkins.
Undhiyu: a casserole of purple yam, sweet and ordinary potatoes, green beans, Indian broad beans, other vegetables and fenugreek-leaf dumplings cooked with fresh coconut, coriander and green chilli. A speciality of Surat.

For fans of standard curry-house fare, New Tayyab is top of the spice pops and a prime tourist attraction. Bold, brassy and very noisy, this dressed-up caff blasts Bollywood hits at full volume, has little elbow room on tables, and is favoured by trendy young things and boisterous groups. We can't understand what the fuss is about, because the cooking isn't much cop any more. Radioactive red chutneys, formula curry pastes, and kick-in chillies are hardly inspiring features of any menu. Only the piping-hot fluffy breads were worthy of recommendation. Burnt fried garlic in the dahl; boiled, watery potatoes in the saag aloo; and chana (chickpea) meat curry laced with mind-numbing chillies – all left us sorely disappointed. As for furnishings, despite the abundance of fake leafy greens, colourful artwork and surreal blue lighting, New Tayyab still has something of the street market about it. *Babies and children welcome; high chairs. Booking advisable. No-smoking tables. Separate room for parties, seats 60. Tables outdoors (8, garden). Takeaway service.* **Map 12 S6**.

North East

Stoke Newington N16

★ Rasa

55 Stoke Newington Church Street, N16 0AR (7249 0344/www.rasarestaurants.com). Stoke Newington rail/73, 243, 426 bus. **Lunch served** noon-3pm Sat, Sun. **Dinner served** 6-10.45pm Mon-Thur, Sun; 6-11.30pm Fri, Sat. **Main courses** £3.65-£6.85. **Set meal** £15.50 4 courses. **Service** 12.5%. **Credit** AmEx, DC, JCB, MC, V. South Indian vegetarian

Despite gaining several siblings, the original Rasa hasn't changed: the walls are still scarily pink; the idol of blue-skinned Krishna and a spicy incense aroma still greet you at the entrance; and the gentle South Indian hospitality is the same as always. Perhaps the only clues that Rasa has moved on in the world is a picture of the owner Das Sreedharan with Jamie Oliver, and a cosy new (and marginally less pink) extension at the back. All the Keralite classics are present and correct. The highlights of our visit were a delicious black-eyed bean thoran piled with wisps of freshly grated coconut; vegetable curry redolent of cinnamon and cardamom; mango and plantain curry spiked with shredded fresh ginger; and a perfectly cooked layered paratha. We've had disappointing meals here in recent months, but the only off-note this time was a tray of fried, crunchy snacks that seemed less than fresh, and slightly greasy aubergine fritters that tasted of stale cooking oil. Otherwise, we were pleased to find this iconic restaurant gloriously back on form. *Babies and children welcome. Booking essential weekends. No smoking. Takeaway service. Vegan dishes.* **Map 25 B1**. **For branches (Rasa Express, Rasa Travancore, Rasa W1) see index.**

North

Archway N19

★ The Parsee

34 Highgate Hill, N19 5NL (7272 9091/ www.theparsee.com). Archway tube. **Lunch served** noon-3pm Mon-Fri. **Dinner served** 6-10.45pm Mon-Sat. **Main courses** £10-£11.95. **Service** 10%. **Credit** AmEx, DC, MC, V. Parsee

Run by Cyrus Todiwala of Café Spice Namaste (*see p135*) fame, this elegant neighbourhood restaurant offers a warm welcome to customers, and serves authentic Parsi dishes in a cosy, yet contemporary setting. It's a natty spot, decked out with wooden flooring and tables, and pictures of notables from the Parsi community across the walls. Cooking is influenced by the mild fruity flavours of an Iranian heritage, tastefully embellished with Indian spices. Parsis love eggs – it's easy to see why. Masala no poro (a dressed-up omelette, cooked with meltingly soft sliced potatoes, toasted cumin and chillies) was splendid. The real star, though, was a main

course of jardaloo ma murghi (chicken curry with apricots). A classic wedding dish, this was a gorgeous marriage of rich dried apricots and sweetly scented cinnamon, combined with tender hunks of chicken and a dried red chilli masala. We especially liked the crunch of its sali topping (crisp-fried straw potatoes). Equally appealing was the gentle cumin spicing in the accompanying rice pilau. In the past we've had some variable meals here, but this time nothing could be faulted. *Babies and children welcome. Booking advisable. No-smoking tables. Restaurant available for hire. Separate room for parties, seats 20. Takeaway service; delivery service.* **Map 26 B1**.

Swiss Cottage NW3

★ Eriki

4-6 Northways Parade, Finchley Road, NW3 5EN (7722 0606/www.eriki.co.uk). Swiss Cottage tube. **Lunch served** noon-3pm Mon-Fri, Sun. **Dinner served** 6-11pm daily. **Main courses** £7.95-£11.95. **Set lunch** £6.95 1 course. **Service** 12.5%. **Credit** AmEx, JCB, MC, V. Pan-Indian

Mercifully, we are past the era where any top-class Indian restaurant felt the need to distinguish itself from a curry house by inventing high-falutin fusion dishes. Eriki exemplifies this new confidence; it cooks proper Indian food to extremely high standards. Witness the vegetarian panorama starters: five snacks ranging from delicate, crisp bhel poori to fresh-from-the-pan samosa and masala dosai. Duck, scallops and calamares all feature, but it's just as thrilling to sample classic dishes. Haandi gosht dum biriani showed the chef's mastery of the dum (sealed-in-a-pot) cooking style; every grain of rice was impregnated with intense meaty flavours, accentuated by cardamom and peppercorns. Tawa paratha was an outstanding disc of bread, and kali dahl a luxurious and mouth-watering bowl of

The Painted Heron, Kennington. See p129.

lentils. Desserts were relatively mundane, though mango ras malai was refreshing. Furnishings are suitably classy: carved screens, chunky wooden tables, brown leather banquettes, stylish cutlery, sumptuous orange or deep-pink walls. Partially frosted glass keeps out the worst of the Finchley Road. We ate a midweek lunch alone – a crying shame as such food deserves a full house. *Babies and children welcome. Booking advisable. Restaurant available for hire. Takeaway service. Vegetarian menu.* **Map 28 B4**.

North West

Kilburn NW6

Kovalam

12 Willesden Lane, NW6 7SR (7625 4761). Kilburn tube/98 bus. **Lunch served** noon-2.30pm daily. **Dinner served** 6-11.15pm Mon-Thur, Sun; 6-11.45pm Fri, Sat. **Main courses** £4.35-£7.95. **Set meal** (vegetarian) £18-£35, (non-vegetarian) £26-£48 serves 2-4. **Credit** AmEx, JCB, MC, V. South Indian

This lovely South Indian restaurant – which looks like a bog-standard tandoori with its pale pink walls, patterned carpet, padded chairs and artificial flowers – is renowned locally for its superior Keralite cooking. On our most recent visit, however, dishes were hit and miss. Malabar-style breadfruit curry, laced with cinnamon and black cardamom; green bean thoran packed with mustard seeds, red chillies, curry leaves and freshly grated coconut; and lemon rice – all these were sensational. However, avial, correctly cooked with traditional vegetables such as plantains and drumsticks, was marred by a too-sour yoghurt sauce that tasted slightly off. Uthappam was thick and fluffy, but a little bland; and poori masala had beautifully spiced mashed potato dolloped between two large, crisp poories, making it

★ Saravanas

77-81 Dudden Hill Lane, NW10 1BD (8459 4900/2400). Dollis Hill tube. **Meals served** noon-10.30pm Tue-Sun. **Main courses** £4.45-£7. **Thalis** £3.45-£6.95. **Set buffet lunch** (noon-3.30pm Fri, Sun) £4.75. **Credit** JCB, MC, V. South Indian vegetarian
One side is a dark and comfy bar, with Lloyd Loom-ish chairs and potted plants; the other is a bright, spick-and-span, pay-at-the-counter café (cream walls, blue tiled floor, Bollywood videos on the telly), where, oddly, no alcohol is allowed. Still, such is the quality of Saravanas's meat-free food that even carnivorous dipsomaniacs should be satisfied. Dishes are served on stainless-steel plates, just as in India. These include crisp or doughy starters, light meals (idli, uthappam), 20 or so vegetable curries and three thalis. Prices are such that we feasted with abandon, ordering special pakoda – freshly deep-fried vegetable chunks in a light batter, served with two dips (excellent garlic and chilli, and too-sweet tamarind) – then the most expensive main course, bombay thali at £6.95. This included palatable vegetable pilau rice, chapati, vadai and ten little pots ranging from piquant rasam to moreish potato masala and highly savoury sambal (with drumsticks). It easily outshone a lacklustre vegetable biriani served with yoghurt. Fresh juices (carrot, pomegranate) and a happy mix of customers increased our pleasure.
Babies and children welcome; high chairs. Booking advisable. Disabled: toilet. No smoking. Restaurant available for hire. Separate room for parties, seats 40. Takeaway service.

Outer London

Edgeware, Middlesex

Zanzibar NEW

113 High Street, Edgware, Middx HA8 7DB (8952 2986). Edgware tube. **Lunch served** noon-3pm Mon-Sat. **Dinner served** 5.30-11pm Mon-Thur; 6-11pm Fri, Sat. **Meals served** noon-10pm Sun. **Main courses** £5.45-£6.95. **Set lunch** £6.95 1 course. **Credit** AmEx, MC, V. Punjabi
Zanzibar's 1970s-style pub decor, complete with patterned carpet, dark wood fixtures and a bar, contrasts with East African artworks interspersed with Indian temple carvings. It's a quite sight. Decent Indian pub grub is served here, with genuine passion. There's a distinct Indo-African slant to the spicing; birianis are richer than usual, with more of a chilli kick. Although a little heavy with the masala, chicken biriani contained a generous amount of tender chicken pieces, and wasn't in the slightest bit oily. Breads are always freshly made, and go particularly well with the delicious dahl makhani (black lentils cooked with ginger, garlic, cream, tomatoes and dollops of butter). We weren't bowled over by the fish tikka; even though it was seared in a tandoor, the stodgy gram-flour batter didn't do it any favours. Zanzibar has become a firm favourite for Indian group bookings at weekends. Expect swirling silks, pints of bitter and blasts of Bollywood music to go with the Punjabi cooking. A true celebration of east-meets-west multiculturalism.
Babies and children welcome; high chairs. Book weekends. Disabled: toilet. Tables outdoors (5, garden). Takeaway service.

Harrow, Middlesex

The Charcoal Restaurent NEW

164 Greenford Road, Harrow, Middx HA1 3QS (8423 4222). Sudbury Hill tube. **Lunch served** noon-2.30pm Mon-Thur. **Dinner served** 5-midnight daily. **Main courses** £6-£10. **Set buffet (lunch)** £5.50. **Set meal** £12 4 courses. **Credit** AmEx, MC, V. North Indian
Located within roti-rolling distance of Sudbury Hill tube station, this family-run café has endeavoured to present a cosmopolitan appearance by showing off a large print of a scenic Mediterranean tourist destination across one wall. Otherwise, it's a dressed-up regular café, sporting ornately carved

---

inconvenient to tackle with either fingers or fork. There's an attentive new manager, and service was more professional than on previous visits.
Babies and children welcome. Booking advisable. Takeaway service; delivery service. Vegetarian menu. Map 1 A1.

★ Vijay

49 Willesden Lane, NW6 7RF (7328 1087/ www.vijayindia.com). Kilburn tube. **Lunch served** noon-2.45pm daily. **Dinner served** 6-10.45pm Mon-Thur, Sun; 6-11.45pm Fri, Sat. **Main courses** £3.50-£8. **Minimum** £6. **Credit** AmEx, MC, V. South Indian
Back in 1964 when Vijay first opened for business, South Indian cuisine was alien to a London where culinary inventiveness ended with gravy browning, canned orange juice and dried dates. Times may have changed, but Vijay's menu is still based around curry-house staples such as chicken tikka masala and chicken madras, with just a page of 'South Indian Specialities' to tempt the discerning. All dishes are entirely authentic, from the well-packed masala dosais, through the nutty sambar to the peppery rasam soup, with its addictive citrus and tamarind aftertaste. Our uthappam was exactly right, peppered with green chillies, tomato and onion in all the right proportions, and suitably spiced. Less impressive (but by no means terrible) was the avial, as some vegetables had gone soggy. The decor is comfortable, with a wooden ceiling and pictures of Hindu deities dotting the cream walls. Customers tend to be loyal and include the current mayor of London, pre-theatre diners (the Tricycle is a spin away) and celebrating couples. We've even spotted a pair of South African secret agents – at least that's what we thought they said.
Babies and children welcome. Booking advisable. Takeaway service; delivery service (within 3-mile radius). Map 1 A1.

Willesden NW10

Sabras

263 High Road, NW10 2RX (8459 0340). Dollis Hill tube/6, 52, 98, 260, 266, 297, 302 bus. **Dinner served** 6.30-10.30pm Tue-Sun. **Main courses** £4.50-£7.50. **Thalis** (6.30-8pm Mon-Thur, Sun) £6.50-£15.50. **Cover** 60p. **Service** 12.5%. **Credit** JCB, MC, V. Gujarati vegetarian
Operated by the Desai family since opening in 1973, Sabras has the look of a suburban garden centre from the outside. Inside, it's all clean white lines, with pictures of Hindu gods and (now rather dated) awards on the walls. On our most recent visit, we found the kitchen produced – with minor reservations – a good standard of cooking. The speciality is Surati cuisine, from Gujarat, though most Indian vegetarian styles are represented. Starters of well-executed Mumbai Beach appetisers, such as deluxe sev poori and bhel poori, sit side by side with Gujarati farsan (snacks) of the patra/samosa and banana methi gota kind. This last dish (fried, mashed green banana balls with fenugreek) is something of an acquired taste, but once acquired quickly becomes addictive. Dosais come in seven varieties, including sada (plain), masala and mysore-masala, which is a fiery but tasty version, the heat tempered by a sprinkling of crushed cashew nuts. Other dishes include fanasi-muthiya (green beans with aniseed and a type of semi-hard dumpling), spinach and corn paneer, and kashmiri kofta (savoury dumplings in a nutty vegetable sauce). Not everything comes off: the fresh shredded apple and onion chutney had a strange musty flavour, and the sambar was a little sweet and not sour enough. Service was generally helpful.
Babies and children welcome. Booking advisable. No-smoking tables. Takeaway service. Vegan dishes.

Sri Lankan menu

The cooking of Sri Lanka is most famed for its chilli heat, but there are many other subtleties to the cuisine. Like South Indian food, rice (rather than wheatflour bread) predominates, and coconut is used widely. Other facets are more reminiscent of Malaysian cooking – especially the sambols (fiery relishes and pickles, often served warm) and the use of dried fish.

Some dishes are uniquely Sri Lankan, notably string hoppers (rounds of steamed vermicelli noodles) and kuttu rotis (a biriani-style concoction made from pasta-like ribbons of bread). Kiri hodi or sothy (spicy coconut gravy) is a typical flavour, as are rich seafood curries (especially crab and squid). Although it is possible to get a standard chicken or lamb curry at all London's Sri Lankan restaurants, it is far more rewarding to order these distinctive dishes.

There are two main ethnic groups in Sri Lanka – Tamil and Sinhalese – and after decades of civil war, both communities are resident in London. Both groups run the capital's dozen or so Sri Lankan restaurants; there is little difference between the cooking styles, but some identical dishes have two names. Most are low-key establishments, spread throughout the Asian-populated outer boroughs, though the area around Tooting (see p128) and north-west London – especially the Ealing Road, Wembley (see p142) – are favourite districts. Only one restaurant, Sekara (see p123), is in central London. The cuisine is largely undiscovered by London's restaurant-going public, so it's still possible to get authentic, lovingly prepared Sri Lankan food at extremely low prices.

Ambul thiyal: sour fish curry cooked dry with spices.
Appam or **appa**: see hoppers.
Badun: black. 'Black' curries are fried; they're dry and usually very hot.
Devilled: meat, seafood or vegetable dishes fried with onions in a sweetish sauce; usually served as starters.
Godamba roti: flaky, thin Sri Lankan bread, sometimes wrapped around egg or potato.
Hoppers: confusingly, hoppers come in two forms, either as saucer-shaped, rice-flour pancakes (try the sweet and moreish milk hopper) or as string hoppers (qv). Also called appam.
Idiappa: see string hoppers.
Katta sambol: onion, lemon and chilli relish; fearsomely hot.
Kiri: white. 'White' curries are based on coconut milk and are usually mild.
Kiri hodi: coconut milk curry with onions and turmeric; a soothing gravy.
Kuttu roti, **kottu** or **kothu roti**: strips of thin bread (loosely resembling pasta), mixed with mutton, chicken, prawns or vegetables to form a 'bread biriani'; very filling.
Lamprais or **lumprice**: a biriani-style dish where meat and rice are cooked together, often by baking in banana leaves.
Lunnu miris: a relish of ground onion, chilli and maldives fish (qv).
Maldives fish: small, dried fish with a very intense flavour; an ingredient used in sambols (qv).
Pittu: rice flour and coconut steamed in bamboo to make a 'log'; an alternative to rice.
Pol: coconut.
Pol kiri: see kiri hodi.
Pol sambol: a mix of coconut, chilli, onions, maldives fish (qv) and lemon juice.
Sambols: strongly flavoured relishes, often served hot; they are usually chilli hot too.
Seeni sambol: sweet and spicy, caramelised onion relish.
Sothy or **sothi**: see kiri hodi.
String hoppers: fine rice-flour noodles formed into flat discs. Usually served steamed (in which case they're dry, making them ideal partners for the gravy-like kiri hodi).
Vellappam: appams (qv) served with vegetable curry.
Wattalappan or **vattilapan**: a version of crème caramel made with kithul palm syrup.

furniture, easy-wipe tables and an open kitchen near the back. Cooking is down to earth and pretty basic. Chapli kebab – a variation on a hamburger, made with pounded lamb – although a bit salty, did pack a punch with raunchy chillies and refreshing hints of ginger. Samosas, filled with mildly spiced diced vegetables, were also appreciated, but we weren't so sure about the radioactive red chilli sauce accompaniment. Mains are nothing to write home about; our chicken haandi curry and insipid-tasting methi aloo (karahi-fried potatoes with fenugreek greens) were heavy on oil, and low on flavour. The restaurant is overseen by eager-to-please staff. Despite our caveats, this is a convenient place to catch up on neighbourhood gossip over a kebab or two.
Babies and children welcome; high chairs. Booking advisable. Vegetarian menu.

★ ★ Ram's
203 Kenton Road, Harrow, Middx, HA3 0HD (8907 2022). Kenton tube. **Lunch served** noon-3pm, **dinner served** 6-11pm daily. **Main courses** £3.30-£4.50. **Thalis** £4.99 (lunch), £8.99 (dinner). **Set meal** £14.50 3 courses incl drink. **Credit** AmEx, DC, JCB, MC, V. Gujarati vegetarian
Making its presence felt on a drab road, Ram's brings a taste of Gujarati cooking to not-so-tropical Kenton. It's a squeaky clean, almost sanitised café, with walls emblazoned with colourful depictions of Hindu deities. Besides being ardently attentive to the mainly local Gujarati customers, the owner and son also take pride in explaining their style of cooking to first-time visitors. Heartily satisfying without being heavy, our meal was a near-perfect balance of flavours and textures. We loved the freshness of bhel poori made with diced red onion, puffed rice, and gram flour crispies, moistened with mint chutney and tangy tamarind sauce. Gujarati-style kadhi was a winner too; toasted gram flour, popped mustard seeds, red chillies and curry leaves were simmered with whipped yoghurt

and tamarind into a deliciously soupy curry, best enjoyed with plain boiled rice. Ram's prefers to let the careful spicing do the talking. An outstanding tribute to the region's cooking.
Babies and children welcome; high chairs. Booking advisable weekends. Disabled: ramp; toilet. No smoking. Restaurant available for hire. Takeaway service.

Rayners Lane, Middlesex

★ Eastern Fire NEW
430 Alexandra Avenue, Rayners Lane, Middx HA2 9TW (8866 8386). Rayners Lane tube. **Meals served** 6-11pm Mon-Thur; noon-midnight Fri, Sat; noon-11pm Sun. **Main courses** £3.50-£5. **Credit** AmEx, MC, V. Sri Lankan
Although the sign outside this modest, bring-your-own-alcohol venue boasts 'Malaysian and South Indian' food, the only Malaysian item on the menu is roti canai (flaky flatbread, here with an elegant stuffing of spring onion and scrambled egg). Apparently the Malaysian chef has left and been replaced by Sri Lankans. The menu isn't overly ambitious, but cooking is generally of a high standard. To start, a fiery rasam, crammed with red and green chillies, shredded ginger, curry leaves, coriander seeds, cherry tomatoes and fresh tamarind pods was unbelievably scrumptious. A golden-hued 'Sri Lankan dosai' had the delicious tang of well-fermented pan-fried rice and lentil batter. Next, string hoppers and pittu were both made with Sri Lankan red rice; the latter was light and fragrant. The accompanying kiri hodi and assorted sambols were jauntily spiced, and chicken and aubergine curries were aromatic with cinnamon, cardamom and star anise. Not all dishes are exquisite – some, like mutton roll, fish cutlet and devilled prawns, are merely workmanlike. The decor is bright, clean and fairly contemporary.
Babies and children welcome; high chairs.

Kathiyawadi NEW
434 Rayners Lane, Middx HA5 5DX (8868 2723). Rayners Lane tube. **Meals served** 5-11pm Mon-Fri; noon-11pm Sat, Sun. **Main courses** £4.75-£6.25. **Thali** £8.95. **Credit** AmEx, MC, V. Gujarati
One of London's few traditional and truly authentic Gujarati restaurants, Kathiyawadi showcases the hot and spicy cuisine of Kathiyawad, a dry and humid region in west Gujarat. Dishes are cooked with own-made yoghurt, white butter and butter-milk, balanced with a liberal use of chickpea flour. We enjoyed a 'weekend special' thali, featuring Gujarati classics given a Kathiyawadi twist, such as dark millet bread, stuffed bitter gourd, and mushy khichri (rice cooked with lentils). Undhyiu (casserole of aubergines, sweet potatoes, fenugreek dumplings, and a variety of green beans) was made in the Kathiyawadi style, with tomatoes and chilli powder replacing the more classic green masala. Unlike most Gujarati restaurants in London, whose menus are dominated by snacks and street food, this homely eaterie specialises in main courses and thalis. There's one drawback: as a result of the restaurant's immense popularity among the Gujarati community, it tends to get very crowded and noisy – and the din of Bollywood movies on plasma screens doesn't help either.
Babies and children welcome; high chairs. Booking advisable. Takeaway service. Vegetarian menu.

Papaya
15 Village Way East, Rayners Lane, Middx HA2 7LX (8866 5582). Rayners Lane tube/ H10, H12 bus. **Meals served** noon-midnight Mon-Sat; noon-11.30pm Sun. **Main courses** £6-£10. **Set lunch** £5.95-£7.95 2 courses. **Service** 10%. **Credit** MC, V. Sri Lankan
A huge papaya painted across one of the walls lends a quirky vibe to this modern-looking Sri Lankan restaurant. Smart, with its etched-glass frontage, bold blue walls and dinky bar, Papaya has an efficient service team, overseen, on our visit,

by an admirably well-informed Polish waitress. Cooking this time wasn't as outstanding as we've found it in the past. Hits included the spinach dahl, simmered with coconut milk and finished with fried onions and dried red chillies. We also enjoyed chicken kothu (shredded chicken fried with beaten egg, onions, red chillies and strips of chapati). However, our Sri Lankan chicken curry was let down by tough chunks of fried fowl and a mediocre masala. The main problem was a similarity of taste between dishes – a shame, as we've previously had some real treats here. As we went to press, Papaya had undergone a revamp and also gained two new chefs, so let's hope improvements are on the way.

Babies and children welcome; high chairs. Booking essential weekends. No-smoking tables. Restaurant available for hire. Takeaway service; delivery service. Vegetarian menu.

Richmond, Surrey

Origin Asia

100 Kew Road, Richmond, Surrey TW9 2PQ (8948 0509/www.originasia.co.uk). Richmond tube/rail/65, 391 bus. **Lunch served** noon-3pm daily. **Dinner served** 6-11pm Mon-Sat; 6-10.30pm Sun. **Main courses** £6.95-£14.50. **Set lunch** £6.99 (vegetarian), £7.99 (non-vegetarian) 3 courses. **Set buffet lunch** (noon-3pm Sun) £6.95-£10.95. **Credit** AmEx, DC, JCB, MC, V. Pan-Indian
When the sun shines we prefer to plump for one of Origin Asia's outdoor tables, where the atmosphere is more laid-back than in the indoor dining area. Four levels are crammed into the restaurant, but carefully placed mirrors save diners from feeling hemmed in. Office groups and well-heeled locals eat here. Cooking isn't always top grade, but there are a few tasty gems that shine out from a mainly average selection. Barrah champ madiri (lamb chops steeped in yoghurt with garlic, pounded chillies and rum, before being grilled over charcoal) rang the changes; the chops arrived with dinky little cutlet frills and an incongruous squiggle of mango purée sauce on the plate, but they tasted deliciously smoky and were meltingly soft in texture. Bhatti ka murgh (a heavyweight chicken curry, based on a tomato and ginger masala) was

too oily, and lacked the subtlety of delicate spicing. Other highlights included the light fluffy nans, layered parathas, and comforting Punjabi black lentil dahl. Staff are helpful.

Babies and children welcome; children's menu (buffet lunch Sun); high chairs. Booking essential at weekends). Restaurant available for hire. Tables outdoors (8, pavement). Takeaway service; delivery service (within 1-mile radius). Vegetarian menu.

Southall, Middlesex

Southall, the heart of Britain's Punjabi culture, has a more 'authentic' vibe these days than you'd find at most marketplaces on the Indian subcontinent. The Broadway is a one-stop thoroughfare for anyone in search of wedding caterers, street traders (offering all manner of goods), fruit and vegetable sellers, or glitter-laden party outfits. Visit during the weekend and you'll be welcomed by a riot of colourful chaos and a cacophony of honking car horns, bhangra beats and exuberant shouts in the earthy Punjabi vernacular.

Come here for such essentials of the Punjabi kitchen as huge bunches of sag, weighty marrows, and juicy seasonal mangoes from Pakistan. It's hard to resist the temptingly smoky aroma of the meat kebabs as you pass one of a score of takeaway joints, or to say no to calorie-laden jalebis as they are drained from a karahi outside **Moti Mahal** (94 The Broadway, UB1 1QF; 8571 9443).

If you've time, it's also worth exploring streets off the Broadway such as the Green, where restaurants remain true to their culinary roots and serve wholesome cooking at rock-bottom prices. Don't miss the **New Asian Tandoori Centre**, a favourite with Punjabi extended families. It consistently impresses with friendly service, piping-hot breads, fabulous chaats (spiced yoghurt and pastry snacks lashed with tamarind chutney), and the best churned lassis in town.

Known for their hard work and business savvy, Southall's Punjabis have improved their financial lot in recent years. Flashy cars, glitzy shopfronts and redecorated restaurants testify to newfound wealth. Refurbished **Madhu's**, with its shiny black granite interior, expansive plate-glass windows and pricey menu, exudes stylish affluence. It's a world far removed from Southall's street-life origins and a possible taste of future trends in the area.

Brilliant

72-76 Western Road, Southall, Middx UB2 5DZ (8574 1928/www.brilliantrestaurant.com). Southall rail. **Lunch served** noon-2.30pm Tue-Fri. **Dinner served** 6-11.30pm Tue-Sun. **Main courses** £6-£11. **Credit** AmEx, DC, JCB, MC, V. East African Punjabi
Hardly the glittering star it was a decade ago, Brilliant still manages to attract curious tourists and office groups. Its patterned carpet, heavy droplet chandeliers and functional table arrangements aren't show-stoppers, but the assortment of widescreen TVs blasting the latest in Bollywood hits adds some brash sparkle to the dated decor. Food isn't anything to trumpet; it's passable but unmemorable. Best of the bunch of dishes we sampled were the samosas, served piping hot and filled with mildly spiced potatoes. Keema mutter – minced lamb fried with onions, simmered with garam masala and ginger and dotted with peas – was let down by poor-quality meat and a heavy dose of oil. Vegetable koftas (fried marrow 'dumplings' cloaked in an appealing, onion-rich masala) were marred by raw-tasting gram flour mixed in with the koftas. Service, although polite, was a little slow. Our advice: stick to the tandoori meat kebabs rather than the curries.

Babies and children welcome; high chairs. Booking advisable weekends. No-smoking tables. Restaurant available for hire. Separate room for parties, seats 120. Takeaway service. Vegetarian menu.

Gifto's Lahore Karahi

162-164 The Broadway, Southall, Middx UB1 1NN (8813 8669). Southall rail. **Meals served** noon-11.30pm Mon-Thur; noon-midnight

Kathiyawadi. See p139.

Fri-Sun. **Main courses** £6-£10. **Unlicensed.**
Corkage no charge. **Credit** AmEx, DC, MC, V.
Pakistani
Gifto's, in its heyday, was a dependable destination
for top-quality meat kebabs, creamy dahls and the
lightest of Indian breads. It's still a landmark for
tourists and newcomers to the area, and is
distinguished by an expansive glassy frontage,
black and white tiled flooring, and rows of neatly
aligned tables. But the cooking isn't what it was.
On the plus side, chana masala (curried chickpeas)
was as perky as ever; we appreciated the nutty,
caramel tones of fried onions, spiked with tart
spices, shredded fried ginger and tomatoes. Breads
were a sad apology, though; we couldn't figure out
the difference between our nan and the tandoori
chapati – both were equally leathery, and cold.
Saag paneer was made with tinned mustard
greens: such a shame as the fresh stuff is available
at rock bottom prices just down the road. Food falls
way short of past excellence, and in the face of stiff
competition, Gifto's needs to buck up if it's ever to
reclaim the title of best caff in Southall.
Babies and children welcome; high chairs.
Takeaway service. Vegetarian menu.

Kashmir Tandoori [NEW]
157 The Broadway, Southall, Middx UB1 1LP
(8574 3505). Southall rail. **Main courses** £2-£7.
Credit AmEx, MC, V. North Indian
There isn't much about this place to enthuse fans
of Kashmiri cooking; it doesn't aim to shake the
world with royal renditions from a rich culinary
heritage. More of a canteen than a café, Kashmir
Tandoori serves up enormous portions of basic
grub, making it a suitable destination for students
and budget-diners. We appreciated the browned
onion and chilli masala in the keema mutter
(minced lamb curry, studded with peas), but did
need to siphon off extra oil before getting stuck in.
Chana masala, although hearty, was let down by
an overriding taste of bicarbonate of soda (used
when soaking chickpeas). Staff are charming, and
ardent in their desire to please. If you're after a
tummy-filling meal, opt for the dahls, kebabs and
a stack of hot breads.
Babies and children welcome; high chairs. Booking
advisable. No-smoking tables. Takeaway service.

★ Madhu's
39 South Road, Southall, Middx UB1 1SW
(8574 1897/www.madhusonline.com). Southall
rail. **Lunch served** 12.30-3pm Mon, Wed-Fri.
Dinner served 6-11.30pm Mon, Wed, Thur,
Sun; 6pm-midnight Fri, Sat. **Main courses**
£6-£12. **Set meal** £17.50-£20 16 dishes incl
tea or coffee. **Credit** AmEx, DC, MC, V.
East African Punjabi
This acclaimed eaterie, recently showered with
awards and accolades, stands out amid the heat
and dust of Southall. Long a favourite with local
Punjabi and Sikh families, Madhu's these days
attracts a younger, hipper mix of diners. Sprawled
over two floors, it sports a stylish, minimal look
with wood and granite flooring, large glass panels
on the wall, crisp white napery, and a tiny backlit
bar. Palak paneer was made with fresh
ingredients (not frozen spinach or supermarket-
variety cheese, as is often the case), and chole-
bhatura featured chickpea curry with soft, fluffy
pillows of deep-fried bread; however, we found the
smoky aromas and the pomegranate-laced spicing
of both dishes a little too similar and lacking the
customary pep of chilli. Sizzling lamb chops were
juicy with succulent meat, and pilau rice was
delightfully devoid of E-numbers. Some feel that
the revamped Madhu's has lost its bearings and
panders too much to western tastes, but our meal
was highly enjoyable and, despite a packed
restaurant, service couldn't have been sweeter.
Babies and children welcome; high chairs.
Booking advisable. Disabled: toilet. Dress: smart
casual. Restaurant available for hire. Separate
room for parties, seating 35. Takeaway service.

★ New Asian Tandoori Centre (Roxy)
114-118 The Green, Southall, Middx UB2 4BQ
(8574 2597). Southall rail. **Meals served** 8am-
11pm Mon-Thur; 8am-midnight Fri-Sun. **Main**
courses £3-£7. **No credit cards.** Punjabi
Although hardly upmarket, this spot is the number
one venue for home-style cooking favoured by
Punjabi families. Easy-wipe tables, functional decor
and a lengthy takeaway counter by the entrance
don't lend romance, but boisterous bonhomie
between staff and customers add a cosy appeal to

this expansive café. No one churns out lassi as well
as these guys; icy cold, sometimes flavoured with
mango, or left plain, these coolers make a
marvellous meal when accompanied by puffed
bhaturas (leavened deep-fried bread, similar to
pooris, but softer in texture) and sweet-sour
chickpeas. Stay with tried-and-tested dishes and
you usually won't be let down; street snacks such
as aloo tikki (potato cakes), papri chat (pastry discs
topped with yoghurt and tangy chutneys) and
butter chicken curry (flavoured with toasted cumin,
tomatoes and cream) are always dependable. Not
so hot are the birianis, which are tossed together in
much the same way as stir-fried rice in a karahi.
Staff are anxious to please and attentive.
Babies and children admitted; high chairs.
Booking advisable. Disabled: toilet. No smoking.
Separate room for parties, seats 60. Takeaway
service. Vegetarian menu.

Palm Palace
80 South Road, Southall, Middx UB1 1RD
(8574 9209). Southall rail. **Lunch served**
noon-3pm daily. **Dinner served** 6-11pm Mon-
Thur; 6-11.30pm Fri-Sun. **Main courses**
£3-£5.50. **Credit** AmEx, JCB, MC, V. Sri Lankan
Furnished with maroon upholstered chairs, red
tablecloths and a dinky bar, Palm Beach conforms
to the image of a 1970s curry house. Looks aren't
everything, though: staff are friendly (if not very
efficient), and cooking is, in the main, decent. Best
to order the typically Sri Lankan dishes; we didn't
regret trying the prosaic-sounding mutton ceylon,
which, when it finally arrived, tasted a lot better
than it read on the menu. Thin slivers of boneless
meat, simmered in a creamy coconut milk and
curry leaf masala, won our approval for their rich
and complex spicing. Appams (saucer-shaped
pancakes) made a good match with the soupy
curry, marred only because they were cold. Unlike
the mutton curry, potato ceylon (in common with
other vegetable dishes) was watery
potatoes and an oily, nondescript masala seriously
letting the side down. Affordable and cheery, Palm
Palace may not be a tropical paradise, but its
curries are popular and good value.
Babies and children welcome; high chairs.
Booking advisable weekends. Takeaway service.
Vegetarian menu.

Sweets menu

Walk into an Indian sweetmeat shop and you'll find a showcase filled with brightly coloured fudge-like blocks, soft cheese balls dunked in syrup, and rich sugary bites. Specialists make good use of relatively few ingredients, such as milk products, dried fruit, sugar and ghee. (Hindu sweet-makers, known as halwais, don't usually make anything containing eggs as these are considered non-vegetarian by many communities.) An essential feature of festivals and celebrations, Indian sweets are eaten throughout the day; they are not usually deemed puddings in the western sense.

Bengalis from Calcutta are generally credited with producing superb soft-cheese sweets, the best known of which are rasgullas and ras malai. The marzipan-like texture of pounded almond barfi is a classic sweetmeat served at weddings, and is sometimes sold topped with glistening wisps of silver leaf.

In recent years there has been a growing trend among more adventurous chefs in top-end restaurants to combine classic Indian flavours with western cuisine to form innovative desserts. Shining examples include the dried apricot ice-cream served at **Café Spice Namaste** (*see p135*) and the garam masala crème brûlée at **Chutney Mary** (*see p125*). On the flip side, many smaller establishments are buying in ready-made kulfis and pre-packed sweets from caterers; results, in the main, are underwhelming.

For traditional pan-Indian sweets, try **Ambala Sweet Centre**'s flagship store (112 Drummond Street, NW1; 7387 3521). Or, for a really wacky combination, try the chocolates flavoured with Indian aromatics at **Rasoi Vineet Bhatia** (*see p126*) .

Barfi: sweetmeat usually made with reduced milk, and flavoured with nuts, fruit, sweet spices or coconut.

Bibenca or **bibinca**: soft, layered cake from Goa made with eggs, coconut milk and jaggery.

Falooda or **faluda**: thick milky drink (originally from the Middle East), resembling a cross between a milkshake and a sundae. It's flavoured with either rose syrup or saffron, and also contains agar-agar, vermicelli, nuts and ice-cream. Very popular with Gujarati families, faloodas make perfect partners to deep-fried snacks.

Gajar halwa: grated carrots, cooked in sweetened cardamom milk until soft, then fried in ghee until almost caramelised; usually served warm.

Gulab jamun: brown dumplings, deep-fried and served in rose-flavoured sugar syrup, best served warm. A traditional Bengali sweet, now ubiquitous in Indian restaurants.

Halwa: a fudge-like sweet, made with semolina, wholewheat flour or ground pulses cooked with syrup or reduced milk, and flavoured with nuts, saffron or sweet spices.

Jalebis: spirals of batter, deep-fried and dipped in syrup, best eaten warm.

Kheer: milky rice pudding, flavoured with cardamom and nuts. Popular throughout India, where there are countless regional variations.

Kulfi: ice-cream made from reduced milk, flavoured with nuts, saffron or fruit.

Payasam: a South Indian pudding made of reduced coconut or cow's milk with sago, nuts and cardamoms. Semiya payasam is made with added vermicelli.

Rasgullas: soft paneer cheese balls, simmered and dipped in rose-scented syrup; served cold.

Ras malai: soft paneer cheese patties in sweet and thickened milk, served cold.

Shrikhand: hung (concentrated) sweet yoghurt with saffron, nuts and cardamom, sometimes with fruit added. A traditional Gujarati favourite, eaten with pooris.

green banana curry, and crisp dosais (rice and lentil pancakes) are a real treat. Spinach vada (savoury doughnuts made from roughly ground lentils, bitingly hot chillies, onion and chopped spinach) made a tempting teaser to our main course, and worked well with a dollop of fresh coconut and green chilli chutney. Vellapam (a hearty potato stew, spiked with green chillies and curry leaves) was served with saucer-like pancakes, light and golden on one side and deliciously soft on the other. Although we've had some memorable seafood dishes here in the past, this time our cochin prawn curry was let down by tough, chewy prawns and an overly rich coconut-based sauce. Service is polite, but staff aren't especially quick off the mark.
Babies and children welcome; high chairs. Booking advisable. No-smoking tables. Takeaway service; delivery service (within 3-mile radius on orders over £20).

Wembley, Middlesex

Ealing Road is changing. Yes, it still bustles and buzzes with Gujarati-owned businesses – notably food shops, greengrocers selling tindora and parval, and vegetarian fast-food cafés. There are still pavement stalls offering pani poori and bhel poori, jalebis straight out of frying pans, boxed mangoes in summer, and fresh sugar cane juice. Even the local ice-cream van remains, selling kulfis, lassis and faloodas.

Yet in recent years, more and more Sri Lankan, Tamil and Somali businesses have set up cafés and restaurants in the area, while Gujarati caterers and businesses are moving further north, to Harrow and Kingsbury. Ealing Road has thus become a real melting pot of different communities – and this is reflected in the area's hotchpotch of eateries. Sample and savour: during a short stroll you can now pick up a meat-free, garlic-free 'extra hot' pizza, followed by a Sri Lankan fish fry, with a finale of Somali sweetmeats.

Cinnamon Gardens
42-44 Ealing Road, Wembley, Middx HA0 4TL (8902 0660). Wembley Central tube/rail/79, 83, 297 bus. **Meals served** 11am-midnight daily. **Main courses** £4.99-£10. **Set lunch** £4.99 1 course. **Credit** MC, V. Sri Lankan
Although we get the impression that this café has seen more prosperous days, there's a quirky charm to its plastic tablecloths, peacock-green upholstered chairs, and heaps of fake greenery in the spacious premises. Idyllic murals depicting leaping gazelles and tropical havens don't quite transport customers from Wembley to Sri Lanka, but at least they try. On our Sunday lunch visit, there was barely a smattering of customers and the open-view kitchen looked a mite forlorn. Still, the staff were friendly and did their best to inject warmth. A huge mound of chicken kothu roti was well balanced, with fried pasta-like strips of soft bread, tender chicken pieces, squidgy sliced onions and slivers of mild green chillies. Devilled potato didn't deliver the goods, though – we were disappointed to see the chef shaking a bottle of branded chilli sauce on to the sliced potatoes, along with a fistful of chillies, sliced onions and green pepper chunks.
Babies and children admitted; high chairs. Booking advisable; essential weekends. Disabled: toilet. No-smoking tables. Separate room for parties, seats 120. Takeaway service. Vegetarian menu.

Jashan
1-2 Coronet Parade, Ealing Road, Wembley, Middx HA0 4AY (8900 9800/www.jashan restaurants.com). Wembley Central tube/rail. **Lunch served** noon-3.30pm, **dinner served** 6-11pm Mon-Fri. **Meals served** noon-11pm Sat, Sun. **Main courses** £3.50-£4.95. **Credit** AmEx, JCB, MC, V. Gujarati vegetarian
Plonked on the end of a row of small shops, this modern café stands out from the crowd with its expansive plate-glass frontage and smart demeanour. The light, airy furnishings are seasoned

Sudbury, Middlesex

★ Five Hot Chillies
875 Harrow Road, Sudbury, Middx HA0 2RH (8908 5900). Sudbury Town or Sudbury Hill tube. **Meals served** noon-midnight daily. **Main courses** £3.50-£9. **Unlicensed. Corkage** no charge. **Credit** MC, V. Punjabi
This cheerful caff dishes out straightforward cooking and no-frills service to an appreciative audience of mainly local Punjabi and Pakistani families. It's decked out with orange walls, green plastic chairs, green Formica tables, and a matching green carpet: subtlety, it seems, isn't a strength here. The chaotic atmosphere is more akin to a bustling Indian railway platform than a Sudbury café. Despite the noisy waiters, screaming kids and clanging pans, service never misses a beat and food arrives piping hot, without delay. Chicken tikka, steeped in yoghurt, garlic and ginger, was juicily tender and had a super lemony tang. Black lentil dahl was equally satisfying; our generous helping was treated to a hunk of butter, a dollop of cream and fried flecks of ginger – all

of which were mopped up with a delicious, flaky paratha. On the flipside, dishes tend to be salty.
Babies and children welcome; high chairs. Booking advisable. Disabled: toilet. Restaurant available for hire. Takeaway service. Vegetarian menu.

Twickenham, Middlesex

Pallavi
Unit 3, Cross Deep Court, Heath Road, Twickenham, Middx TW1 4QJ (8892 2345/4466/www.mcdosa.com). Twickenham rail. **Lunch served** noon-3pm daily. **Dinner served** 6-11pm Mon-Thur, Sun; 6pm-midnight Fri, Sat. **Main courses** £4.50-£7.95. **Service** 10%. **Credit** AmEx, MC, V. South Indian
Located on the first floor of a concrete-fronted shopping complex, Pallavi doesn't quite transport customers to Keralite heaven, but what it lacks in looks, it makes up for in the cooking. The carpet's a little worn, the fake greenery is dated, and the touristy knick-knacks past their sell-by date, but the food is fabulous. Culinary classics such as a tongue-tingling rasam (peppery soup), delicate

with tribal African artefacts and plenty of bold Bollywood colours. Jashan is more peaceful than other establishments in the area, with easygoing staff who are happy to let their young Gujarati customers linger over meals. Besides the usual pan-Indian vegetarian food, chefs try their hand at transcontinental curiosities such as spaghetti with curried peas, paneer steaks, and an Indian take on sweet and sour vegetables. We opted for some classic street snacks instead. A deliciously crunchy bhel poori starter (made with puffed rice, crisp-fried gram-flour strands and lashings of chilled tamarind sauce and mint chutney) won approval. Only our gobi mutter failed to please; the finely chopped cauliflower and peas, immersed in a weighty tomato masala, was way too heavy for our taste. Instead of lassi, try ordering the fresh lime soda (sweet or salted) – it's better than own-made lemonade and has more of a tangy kick.
Babies and children welcome; high chairs. Bookings not accepted weekend. No smoking. Tables outdoors (4, pavement). Takeaway service. For branch see index.

★ Karahi King

213 East Lane, North Wembley, Middx HA0 3NG (8904 2760/4994). North Wembley tube/ 245 bus. **Meals served** noon-midnight daily. **Main courses** £3.50-£12. **Unlicensed. Corkage** no charge. **No credit cards.** Punjabi
As far as neighbourhood restaurants go, Karahi King has done well by members of the local Indian community, who come here for feisty curries and hot breads. It is located amid a bland stretch of nondescript shops, but has made an attempt to dress itself up with rattan chairs, wooden tables and vertical blinds in the windows. The action happens by the steel-fronted counter where chefs stir sizzling masalas in capacious karahis, and give chapatis a twirl in the air before slapping them into the tandoor. Cooking, despite the theatrics, has its ups and downs. Samosas are consistently good; the lamb-filled versions were delicately spiced with pounded cardamom seeds, and encased in crisp pastry. Marinated meats usually deliver the goods too, and are a sight more healthy than the oil-laden curries and vegetable dishes. We were less than impressed with the butter chicken, which was little more than an everyday curry flavoured with a stick of sweet cinnamon and a dash of cream. Service always comes with a smile.
Babies and children welcome; high chairs. Separate room for parties, seats 60-80. Takeaway service. Vegetarian menu.

★ Sakonis

129 Ealing Road, Wembley, Middx HA0 4BP (8903 9601). Alperton tube/183 bus. **Breakfast served** 9-11am Sat, Sun. **Meals served** noon-10pm daily. **Main courses** £3.50-£7. **Set buffet** (noon-4pm, 7-9.30pm) £6.50-£8.99. **Service** 10%. **Credit** MC, V. Gujarati vegetarian
Many people agree that this branch of the small Sakonis chain is top when it comes to service and quality of cooking, though Harrow also gets honourable mentions. There's not a lot to distinguish it as far as decor goes; the utilitarian café is down a couple of steps after the takeaway snack counter, while the open kitchen is right at the back. The big draw is the reasonably priced menu and, of course, the top-notch cooking. The place is almost always busy with families and adventurous diners. We recommend getting in early – say just after noon – and elbowing your way towards the splendid buffet. We kicked off lunch with a teaser of papri chat: a yoghurt-based snack of crisp pastry discs, herby mint chutney and streaks of dark, gingery tamarind sauce. At the next counter, we picked up a hearty South Indian dosai, along with a ladleful of sambar. There are also excellent dahi wadas (soft lentil dumplings dunked in tart, chilli-flecked yoghurt). Prices are low, so you can have a meal, treat yourself to a tall glass of fresh-squeezed orange juice and still have change from a tenner. Small wonder that Sakonis is always bustling.
Babies and children welcome; high chairs. No smoking. Takeaway service. For branches see index.

International

Thanks to Britain's globe-trotting history, London is right at the cutting edge (or should that be the chopping board?) of intercontinental culinary innovation. All the ingredients are here: settlers from a wealth of nations, each group with its own gastronomic heritage; foodstuffs from around the planet, shipped or flown in to this European gateway; talented chefs, many from New World countries without the encumbrance of a centuries-old culinary canon; and, above all, a burgeoning restaurant-going population eager to experiment with new creations (partly due, no doubt, to Britain's national inferiority complex about its indigenous cuisine).

There is, of course, danger in having unrestricted access to a plethora of ingredients. In unskilled hands, fearful combinations and ludicrous assemblies can be brought into being. Yet under the light touch of a top chef – such as you'll find at the **Providores & Tapa Room**, **MVH** and **Cinnamon Cay**, among others – fusion food becomes a celebration of the best in multiculturalism.

Central
City EC4

Bar Bourse

67 Queen Street, EC4R 1EE (7248 2200/ 2211). Mansion House tube. *Bar* **Open** 11.30am-11pm Mon-Fri. *Restaurant* **Lunch served** 11.30am-3pm Mon-Fri. **Main courses** £14-£20. *Both* **Credit** AmEx, JCB, MC, V.
Being the only female in the restaurant apart from the waitresses is par for the course in the City, and Bar Bourse, a classy basement bar and lunch venue in one L-shaped room, is no exception. The atmosphere isn't a problem, however. Food and decor (discreet opulence is created with gold leaf, silk velour and hammered copper) are smart enough for business entertaining, yet casual enough to inspire diners to go jacketless. The menu contains such crowd-pleasers as asparagus with hollandaise, fish and chips, grilled lobster and coq au vin, but the kitchen also does the exotics well. An 'Asian plate' was an impressive display of prawn tempura, mini spring roll, sushi and rare tuna, all zingy with citrus and spices. Baby artichoke salad came with rocket, crunchy green beans, dill and a delicate mustard dressing. The menu allows you to order starter-size portions, typically of fish and pasta dishes; pea, mint and parmesan risotto was chock-full with fresh ingredients and sinfully rich. Lamb cutlets arrived still bloody, but were graciously whisked away for more searing. Nothing here is cheap, but prices aren't outrageous for the Square Mile, and the bar food is good value.
Babies and children admitted. Bar/restaurant available for hire. Book lunch Thur, Fri.
Map 11 P7.

Clerkenwell & Farringdon EC1

Vic Naylor Restaurant & Bar NEW

38-42 St John Street, EC1M 4AY (7608 2181/ www.vicnaylor.com). Barbican tube/Farringdon tube/rail.
Bar **Open** 5pm-1am Tue-Sat.

Restaurant **Meals served** noon-midnight Mon-Fri; 5pm-midnight Sat. **Main courses** £8-£15.50. **Service** 10% (for parties of 5 or more). **Credit** AmEx, MC, V.
This old-timer – in terms of the Farringdon dining scene, that is – was established in 1986. The bare brick walls and dark wood trimmings remain intact, but new life has been injected in the form of expanded premises and a new chef. Customers (mostly men in suits) seem to have taken kindly to such globally inspired dishes as seared duck breast on Thai spiced cabbage, and salt cod croquettes with romesco sauce and aïoli. We found the menu more of a mixed bag. Veal chop with broad beans and spinach was a very decent main, while Goan curry with pumpkin, chickpeas and spinach, served with naan bread, was slightly too close to a dish you might knock up at home. An international wine list and good-time vibe are pluses; the subterranean, scruffy loos are not. Service is slightly too laid-back; a meal here can take a long time, whether you want it to or not. There's also a separate bar, similarly decorated, offering a decent array of drinking options (wine, cocktails, bottled beer) and substantial snacks.
Babies and children admitted. Booking advisable.
Map 5 O5.

Covent Garden WC2

★ Le Deuxième

65A Long Acre, WC2E 9JH (7379 0033). Covent Garden tube. **Lunch served** noon-3pm, **dinner served** 5pm-midnight Mon-Fri. **Meals served** noon-midnight Sat; noon-11pm Sun. **Main courses** £11.50-£16. **Set meal** (noon-3pm, 5-7pm, 10pm-midnight Mon-Fri; noon-11pm Sun) £10.95 2 courses incl coffee, £14.50 3 courses incl coffee. **Service** 15%. **Credit** AmEx, MC, V.
As the name suggests, Le Deuxième (nearby Café du Jardin was the first) is essentially a French restaurant. Within the glass portals, all is serene. Starched white table linen, mink-coloured walls punctuated only by a huge amethyst rock and oriental flower arrangements set the scene. The menu is long, ambitious and includes some Italian/Asian-influenced dishes. The wine list is even longer. Prices are fair given the quality. Tian of crab was a perfect tower of spinach, crab, tomatoes, guacamole and cream, encircled by a ring of pesto, avocado and cream, which tasted as good as it looked. Heavily smoked goose breast came on a galette of wafer-thin potatoes, enlivened with pickled leeks and pumpkin seed oil. Pasta such as sage gnocchi can be had as a starter or a main. Rare grilled tuna was superb: simply served with choi sum, water chestnuts and a delicious sesame sauce. Grilled loin of venison was tender, and well matched with sweet and sour red cabbage and balsamic sauce. Only some sautéed potatoes – dark brown discs – and an apple tart on slightly soggy pastry were below par in an otherwise excellent meal. Staff are French and charming.
Babies and children welcome. Booking advisable.
Map 18 L6.

Fitzrovia W1

Archipelago

110 Whitfield Street, W1T 5ED (7383 3346). Goodge Street or Warren Street tube. **Lunch served** noon-2.30pm Mon-Fri. **Dinner served** 6-10.30pm Mon-Sat. **Main courses** £14-£19.50. **Set lunch** £15.50 2 courses. **Service** 12.5%. **Credit** AmEx, DC, JCB, MC, V.
Our bill at this restaurant read: '1 x frog, 1 x roo, 1 x scorpion = £43.50'. This sums up dining at Archipelago, which lures you in with an

assortment of floating plastic lotus blossoms, incense and a confusing doormat of loose gravel. The friendly staff take it all quite seriously. You don't have to eat expensive insects (we were assured locusts taste merely of their seasoning; like scorpion, which was just chocolate-with-a-crunch). Indeed, the quick lunch menu of global favourites such as tom yum soup, ceviche with soba noodles or red Asian vegetable curry is much better value at £15.50 for two courses. But surrounded by African fertility sculptures, peacock feathers and golden Buddhas, and seated in throne-like armchairs, you might let the exoticism go to your head. Kangaroo ('hot marsupial' – all à la carte dishes have irritating names) was wonderfully tender in its wine-based sauce; frog stew ('Jamaican Mountain Chicken') was a nice variation on Malaysian cooking, with copious cashew nuts, beautifully served in a banana leaf with coconut relish. The chef can cook; we just weren't convinced about the high prices.
Babies and children admitted. Booking advisable. No-smoking tables. Tables outdoors (2, patio). **Map 3 J4**.

Mash
19-21 Great Portland Street, W1W 8QB (7637 5555). Oxford Circus tube.
Bar **Open** 11am-2am Mon-Sat. **Bar snacks** (6-11pm) £2-£6.
Restaurant **Breakfast served** 7.30-11.30am, **lunch served** noon-3pm Mon-Fri. **Brunch served** noon-4pm Sat. **Dinner served** 6-11pm Mon-Sat. **Main courses** £9-£15. **Credit** AmEx, DC, MC, V.
Given its slightly tired, plastic-and-concrete design (reminiscent of 1970s municipal architecture) and its thudding music, Mash's appeal, we decided, must be the central location. That and the interesting beers brewed on site. Though the ground-floor bar is densely populated, the upstairs restaurant is rarely even half full, despite decent enough cooking and excellent service. The pizzas emerging from a wood-fired oven in the open kitchen are great crowd-pleasers (as they should be for around £10); we can recommend the mozzarella, cherry tomato, san daniele ham and rocket topping. An 8oz cote de boeuf (rump steak) came with watercress and skin-on chips; it was nice, if not great. Sea bass was carefully torn from its papillotte (paper bag) to reveal three sections of fish stuffed with spring vegetables. Additional vegetables cost £3, but it's the glasses of wine and desserts (£5.50 each) that really push up prices. Banana split was a lovely, childish mess of high-quality chocolate and vanilla ice-cream with chocolate sauce; oven-roasted plums with clotted cream tasted deliciously of citrus peel and cinnamon, yet these were both down-home dishes casually thrown together in cereal bowls.
Babies and children welcome; high chairs. Bar available for hire. Disabled: toilet. Dress: smart casual. Entertainment: DJs 10pm Thur-Sat. Separate room for hire, seats 28. Tables outdoors (8, pavement). **Map 9 J6**.

Spoon+ at Sanderson
50 Berners Street, W1T 3NG (7300 1444/ www.asiadecuba-restaurant.com). Oxford Circus or Tottenham Court Road tube. **Breakfast served** 6.30am-noon, **lunch served** noon-2.30pm, **dinner served** 6-11pm daily. **Tea served** 3-5pm daily. **Set teas** £19.50; £25 incl glass of champagne. **Main courses** £20-£36. **Service** 15%. **Credit** AmEx, DC, MC, V.
Burly men in black usually open the doors to guests entering this New York-style boutique hotel. Within, Spoon has a lozenge-shaped white bar usually packed with ageing DJs and other louche types. The dining room is white. The horseshoe-shaped leather banquettes are white. The sheer pretension of the place never fails to impress; and the pricing is ludicrous. Crab cakes, a pleasant little starter, cost £26. Beef fillet, the meat topped by a slice of foie gras and accompanied by a witty sheet of potato crisps, is £32. To be fair, these dishes made a much better meal than previous food we've experienced here. The organic cereals and beans, for example, are like eating cold porridge. This time, ceviche was a refreshing delight that worked

well with the little pots of caper condiment and fennel custard. Roast pigeon was excellent, its jus intense, but its 'turnip and vegetable shavings' were a bizarre mix of almost raw strips with a triangle of root saturated in balsamic. The wine list is terrifyingly expensive, but has a few OK bottles at around £30. In summer, sit outside in the central courtyard on benches strewn with pillows. In winter, thudding rock music inside means an evening of shouting.
Babies and children admitted; high chairs. Booking advisable. Disabled: toilet. Separate room for hire, seats 50. Tables outdoors (15, terrace). **Map 17 J5**.

Leicester Square WC2

Asia de Cuba
45 St Martin's Lane, WC2N 4HX (7300 5588/ www.asiadecuba-restaurant.com). Leicester Square tube. **Breakfast served** 7am-11am daily. **Lunch served** noon-2.30pm daily. **Dinner served** 6pm-midnight Mon-Wed; 6pm-12.30am Thur-Sat; 6-10.30pm Sun. **Tea served** 3-5pm daily. **Main courses** £14.50-£39.50. **Set meal** (lunch, pre-theatre) £25 bento box. **Service** 15%. **Credit** AmEx, DC, MC, V.
Like Spoon+ at Sanderson (*see above*), Asia de Cuba is a high-concept, high-volume, high-priced restaurant that not everyone will like – but if this is your kind of place, then the experience is a good one. Sweep past the giant chess pieces and gold molars masquerading as chairs in the lobby to a two-level dining room with vast pillars decorated with old books, stylish black and white photos or satin upholstery. The menu is hard to navigate, but received wisdom dictates two starters (both for sharing) followed by one main between two, with side dishes. 'Tunapica', a tartare of tuna with olives, dried blackcurrants, almonds and coconut, tasted good but looked off-puttingly like raw Christmas mincemeat. Coconut scallop ceviche was more successful, mixing the finely sliced seafood with yuzu, lime and tomatillo. Hacked lime and garlic duck was a huge portion of well-cooked meat sitting on pak choi. Desserts are hilariously vulgar (witness the jaw-dropping banana split, big enough for four); most are arranged skywards, like our priapic slice of Opera cake. It's nice to find an expensive restaurant that likes a joke.
Babies and children welcome; high chairs. Booking advisable. Disabled: toilet. No-smoking tables. Separate rooms for hire, seat 48 and 120. Vegetarian menu. **Map 18 L7**.

Marylebone W1

★ The Providores & Tapa Room
109 Marylebone High Street, W1U 4RX (7935 6175/www.theprovidores.co.uk). Baker Street or Bond Street tube.
Providores **Lunch served** noon-2.45pm daily. **Dinner served** 6-10.45pm Mon-Sat; 6-10pm Sun. **Main courses** £15-£22. **Cover** £1.50 (lunch Sat, Sun).
Tapa Room **Breakfast served** 9-11.30am Mon-Fri; 10am-3pm Sat, Sun. **Meals served** noon-10.30pm Mon-Fri; 4-10.30pm Sat; 4-10pm Sun. **Tapas** £1.50-£9.
Both **Credit** AmEx, MC, V.
Welcome to the refined upper reaches of fusion food, courtesy of New Zealanders Peter Gordon and Anna Hansen. There are two dining areas, both small and sparely decorated. The ground-floor Tapa Room (which is named after a bark cloth used in ceremonies in Polynesia, naturally) is the more casual space; it is open for posh breakfast fry-ups, brunchy snacks and global tapas. Upstairs, the Providores is a serene, clean-lined white room. Influences and ingredients from Asian, Middle Eastern and other cuisines appear, among them little-seen lemon myrtle, kumara and tamarillo. Some dishes read like an encyclopaedia of exotica, others are more straightforward – for example, two large hunks of perfect roast halibut came with sautéed artichokes, new potatoes and puy lentils, with sweetness provided by red onions, tartness by tarragon vinaigrette. Prices upstairs match the rarified cooking. Mains hover around £20, while a starter of smoky coconut and

tamarind laksa with green tea noodles (a densely flavoured affair) cost £9.50 for a small bowlful containing one fat prawn and one small dumpling made of chicken and hijiki (seaweed). The well-thought-out Kiwi wine list highlights a different New Zealand wine region every month.
Babies and children welcome. Booking essential (Providores); bookings not accepted (Tapa Room). Disabled: toilet. No smoking (Providores). **Map 9 G5**.

Pimlico SW1

Tate Britain Restaurant
Tate Britain, Millbank, SW1P 4RG (7887 8825/ www.tate.org.uk). Pimlico tube. **Breakfast served** 10-11.30am, **lunch served** 11.30-3pm, **afternoon tea served** 3-5pm daily. **Main courses** £12.50-£15.50. **Service** 12.5%. **Credit** AmEx, DC, MC, V.
This smart gallery restaurant – its four walls covered with a specially commissioned, amusingly entitled Rex Whistler mural, *The Expedition in Pursuit of Rare Meats* – is located in the basement at Tate Britain. On our latest visit, the place was thronging with mature diners spruced up in their Sunday best, but this is a surprisingly informal lunch spot, much helped by the businesslike, down-to-earth staff. The short but sweet menu changes regularly. It is scattered with British classics (we enjoyed a fantastic deep-fried sea bass with mushy peas and chips), yet is international in outlook. A starter of dressed Cornish crab with mayonnaise turned out to be marginally overdressed, though marinated smoked haddock with pickled cucumber and lime was well executed. Desserts are usually a high point, featuring well-turned-out, comforting classics like bread and butter pudding, apple crumble and cheesecake. Prices are highish – all starters are £6.50, mains £12.50, desserts £5.50 – but this place is recommended for a classy lunch. If you're off to Tate Modern, the Tate to Tate boat service, adorned with Hirstian multicoloured spots, awaits you outside on Millennium Pier.
Babies and children welcome; high chairs. Booking advisable. Disabled: toilets. No smoking. Tables outdoors (8, terrace). Vegan dishes. **Map 16 L11**.

Victoria SW1

Ebury Wine Bar & Restaurant
139 Ebury Street, SW1W 9QU (7730 5447/ www.eburywinebars.co.uk). Sloane Square tube/Victoria tube/rail.
Bar **Open** 11am-11pm Mon-Sat; noon-3pm, 6-10.30pm Sun.
Restaurant **Lunch served** noon-2.45pm daily. **Dinner served** 6-10.15pm Mon-Sat; 6-9.45pm Sun. **Main courses** £10-£19.50. **Set meal** (noon-2.45pm, 6-7.30pm) £12.50 2 courses. **Service** 12.5%. **Credit** AmEx, DC, MC, V.
An older, well-heeled crowd patronises the Ebury, where trompe l'oeil decor (of bookshelves, flowers and cartoon-like characters) makes for a cosy dining room and bar. On a weeknight, people were eating at every table. We liked the cheery atmosphere, genteel waitresses and fairly priced wines, taken from a long, intelligible list. Food is less inspiring – but somehow, from the battered tables, we had already intuited this. Sun-dried tomato, courgette and ricotta 'tart' was in fact a wedge of tasty and very eggy quiche. Fennel, orange and almond salad pleased with its crunchy, raw root veg, but the nut slivers resembled a garnish for rainbow trout. Next, we ordered roast rack of lamb, but the waitress 'pressed the wrong button', and out came calf's liver with ratatouille, the ensemble slightly marred by a puddle of orange-coloured oil. Grilled sea bream was another simple dish, prepared housewife-style with scattered anchovies and 'roasted' lemon on the side, to no purpose. Considering the lack of vegetables, mains are quite expensive for such pedestrian cooking. A £2 charge for bread was a further irritant. Locals presumably forgive all because of the great wine prices.
Babies and children admitted. Booking advisable. No-smoking tables. **Map 15 H10**.

Westminster SW1

The Atrium

4 Millbank, SW1P 3JA (7233 0032/www.simp sonsofmayfair.com). Westminster tube. **Lunch served** noon-3pm, **dinner served** 6-9.45pm Mon-Fri. **Main courses** £7.50-£14.95. **Service** 12.5%. **Credit** AmEx, DC, MC, V.
Effectively the politicos' canteen, the Atrium benefits from a lofty glass roof at the centre of a four-storey office building – but the decor resembles that of a 1970s hotel. Lunchtimes are moderately busy, evenings all but dead. Seeing the windowless, bland bar, we chose a table under the atrium. The waiter wasn't impressed, preferring guests to stay near his station. The menu is extensive. Pasta dishes, caesar salad and the like are geared to the quick-lunch crowd. Thai chicken soup is as exotic as it gets in a repertoire of modern, slightly heavy, European dishes. Caramelised scallops with baby spinach was nice, even if a velouté of chives seemed like overkill. Grilled artichoke and 'dried tomato' tart was a deliciously crisp, buttery pastry case filled with high-quality ingredients. Chump of lamb was

barely marinated, but tender, and came with pommes dauphinoises, rocket and pancetta. 'Roast curried cod' had a large fish sitting on mashed potato with a hint of curry powder, compensated by broad beans, good sticks of salsify, morels and another velouté, this time of ceps. Desserts, including rhubarb cheesecake, were more than competent. Few wines come by the glass, but the drinks list is extensive.
Book lunch. Disabled: lift; toilet. No-smoking tables. Separate rooms for hire, seat 12 and 24. **Map 16 L10**.

West

Kensington W8

Abingdon

54 Abingdon Road, W8 6AP (7937 3339). Earl's Court or High Street Kensington tube. Bar **Open** 12.30-11pm Mon-Sat; 12.30-10.30pm Sun.
Restaurant **Lunch served** 12.30-2.30pm Mon-Fri; 12.30-3pm Sat, Sun. **Dinner served** 6.30-10.30pm Mon, Sun; 6.30-11pm Tue-Sat. **Main courses** £11.75-£17.50. **Set lunch** (daily)

£13.95 2 courses; (Sun) £17.50 3 courses. **Service** 12.5%.
Both **Credit** AmEx, MC, V.
The Abingdon's L-shaped room means dining here can feel like sitting in a corridor. But this is a pleasant place, with efficient waiters and a brisk turnover. The bold kitchen attempts everything from espresso marinated lamb to red bream with Moroccan tagine, underpinned by bistro favourites like smoked haddock on spinach with parsley sauce. These refinements are only available on the pricey à la carte (Mon-Sat). At Sunday lunch you'll find a better deal but less exciting cooking. Corn and lemongrass soup was sweet, mildly spiced, with a blob of green pesto. Rare, tender Thai beef salad had all the expected spices (lemongrass, galangal). Roast chicken wasn't a great bird, but came in generous portions with good roast spuds, crisply steamed vegetables and bread sauce. Red mullet and salmon with chardonnay and dill sauce tasted bland, and creamy in a way that didn't suit fatty farmed salmon. For dessert, a brandy snap had been fashioned into a basket holding berries and toffee ice-cream. Good value at £26 each with a glass of wine; if we'd paid the £35-£40 it costs during the week we might not have been happy.

Asia de Cuba

Babies and children admitted; high chairs. Book dinner. Tables outdoors (4, pavement). Vegetarian menu. **Map 13 A9**.

Maida Vale W9

Otto Dining Lounge

215 Sutherland Avenue, W9 1RU (7266 3131/ www.ottodininglounge.com). Maida Vale tube.
Open 6pm-1am (last entry 11pm) Mon-Sat. **Meals served** 7-11pm Mon-Sat. **Main courses** £13.50-£19. **Service** 12.5%. **Credit** AmEx, MC, V.
More airport lounge than dining lounge, this glassy first-floor box offers striking views of, er, a petrol station. Such incongruity is brought even more sharply into focus by the sleek interior of black leather chairs, black-clad waiters and acres of empty carpet: not to mention empty tables. Yet the standard of cooking is high. The menu features European crowd-pleasers, from steak tartare to foie gras with brioche. Warm crab beignet was a trio of rough-textured patties served with onion marmalade. Rack of lamb was brilliantly accompanied by a purée of onions and garlic, with a neat circle of jus – and nothing else. Pricing is steep, with most starters around £7 and main courses topping £15, sans veg. We closed by sharing a chocolate and hazelnut brownie. As soon as we left, the blinds came down for the night.
Babies and children welcome (restaurant only). Booking advisable. Entertainment: DJ 9.30pm-1am Thur-Sat). Separate room for hire, seats 80. **Map 1 C3**.

Notting Hill W11

Rotisserie Jules

133A Notting Hill Gate, W11 3LB (7221 3331/ www.rotisseriejules.com). Notting Hill Gate tube.
Meals served noon-11pm daily. **Main courses** £5.75-£10.75. **Service** 10% (bills over £15). **Credit** AmEx, MC, V.

Anyone who has a craving for chicken and chips will find Rotisserie Jules hits the spot. There's a certain cynicism in the menu's proud proclamation, 'except for bread and ice-cream, everything we serve is prepared on the premises from scratch and without frozen products'. For this does not preclude reheating the soggy french beans that are brazenly on show in a display cabinet next to the mounds of salad, or using mediocre ingredients such as the super-sweet variety of corn on the cob. It's hard to be too picky at the price, however. A half chicken can serve two people at £6.75, with crispy french fries to accompany weighing in at a non-too-hefty £2. There's some attempt to flavour the chickens with a herby stuffing, which we appreciated. We didn't appreciate the unpalatable house white, or the caesar salad that turned out to be a heap of baby gem lettuce leaves and croûtons, sitting in a lake of thick sauce beneath enough powdered parmesan to fill a sandpit. We wondered about ordering the 'home made' chocolate mousse and apple tart, but decided not to risk it.
Babies and children welcome; children's menu; high chairs. Disabled: toilet. Takeaway service; delivery service (6-10pm Mon-Fri; noon-3pm, 6-10.30pm Sat; noon-10.30pm Sun). **Map 7 A7**.
For branch see index.

South West

Barnes SW13

★ MVH

5 White Hart Lane, SW13 0PX (8392 1111). Barnes Bridge or Mortlake rail/209 bus.
Bar **Open** 5pm-11pm daily.
Restaurant **Lunch served** noon-2.30pm Thur-Sun. **Dinner served** 6-10.30pm daily. **Set meals** £26 2 courses, £29 3 courses. **Service** 12.5%. **Credit** AmEx, JCB, MC, V.

Michael von Hruschka explores the wackier side of culinary innovation, but unlike many of his co-enthusiasts for fusion food, good taste wins through. Another reason to admire the man is his commitment to value. In a three-course menu costing £29, we counted five or six inter-course amuse-bouches, ranging from test tubes of citrussy green liquid propped in a bowl of sugar, through brilliant bonito soup with saffron, to vanilla yoghurt sprinkled with silver dust. There are no supplements (not even for foie gras) and 'trappings' such as truffled spring lettuce or honey lavender carrots come in at £2.50. Following barely cooked scallops in yuzu with thrillingly green flying fish roe and coriander, there was a wonderfully sweet and spicy dish of fallow buck steak with braised aubergine and beetroot purée. Other highlights were a green seafood curry with lime risottini and Thai basil, and jaggery with banana sauce, coconut ice-cream and quills of caramelised banana and chocolate. Good taste doesn't quite extend to the decor. The ground floor is sensibly stark and white, albeit with the odd painted nude; the upstairs bar is blood-red and the loos are pure kitsch. On our midweek visit, just one smiling, knowledgeable waiter coped admirably.
Booking advisable.

South Kensington SW3

The Collection

264 Brompton Road, SW3 2AS (7225 1212/ www.the-collection.co.uk). South Kensington tube.
Bar **Open** 5-11pm daily. **Bar snacks** £6-£28.
Restaurant **Dinner served** 6-10.30pm Tue-Sat. **Main courses** £7-£19.50. **Set dinner** £15 2 courses, £20 3 courses. **Service** 15%. **Credit** AmEx, MC, V.
A long, glass ramp takes you into the Collection's self-consciously stylish bar, a cavernous, black-painted room dominated by giant overhead

Bug Bar

screens showing looped catwalk shows. The bar crowd are all skinny 20-year-olds; on the mezzanine, restaurant customers tend towards middle age. Cooking is more than competent. Sweet potato and ginger soup was plain and refreshing; grilled goat's cheese on fig toast with a warm lentil salad was inspired in its use of sweet and tart. Among straightforward European food, several salads and some sushi, you'll find a few spicy dishes; red Thai chicken curry (medium hot) came with sticky rice and was authentically oily. Grilled blue-fin tuna was perfectly rare and sat on a pleasing mixture of jersey royals, wild garlic and boquerones (marinated anchovies), all of which were oily too. Overall, though, flavours were good. The wine list has steepish prices for all but the most pedestrian bottles. In comparison, desserts seem a steal. Local favourite, apparently, is the blueberry and white chocolate samosas and they got our vote even though we expected something sickly. Staff were friendly and low key – an improvement on the days when the Collection was packed most nights.
Booking advisable (restaurant). Disabled: toilet. Dress: smart casual. Entertainment: DJs 8pm daily. Separate room for hire, seats 50. **Map 14 E10.**

Wimbledon SW19

Light House
75-77 Ridgeway, SW19 4ST (8944 6338). Wimbledon tube/rail then 200 bus. **Lunch served** noon-2.30pm Mon-Sat; 12.30-3pm Sun. **Dinner served** 6.30-10.30pm Mon-Sat. **Main courses** £12-£15.50. **Set lunch** (Mon-Sat) £14 2 courses, £16.50 3 courses; (Sun) £18 2 courses, £23 3 courses. **Service** 12.5%. **Credit** AmEx, MC, V.
The cooking style has improved at this light, airy barn of a place. Instead of long lists of unpronounceable exotica, the menu now offers imaginative combinations of everyday ingredients. Beetroot, for example, comes roasted in a salad with blood oranges, walnuts and feta cheese. Risotto was made with barley instead of rice and had a wonderful aroma of crayfish; cherry tomatoes made nice padding. Sea bass seemed classically prepared with its salsa verde and olive oil mash, but even this was given extra zing with some garlic leaves. Squid and chorizo was a powerful dish, but with a little watercress on the side was not really enough as a main course. This is the dilemma in the restaurant's current incarnation; it lists dishes as 'antipasti', 'primi', 'secondi' and so on, but diners can find it hard to gauge portions. A side dish of roast new potatoes with chilli and lemon, though moreish, could have fed four. Desserts are few – strawberry ripple semi-freddo; chocolate mousse cake with pears poached in red wine – but good. In all, a deservedly popular place for Wimbledon's sophisticates, even if the decor is as bland as a manila envelope.
Babies and children welcome; children's menu (Sun); high chairs. Booking advisable weekends. Disabled: toilet. No-smoking tables.

South

Battersea SW8, SW11

Buchan's
62-64 Battersea Bridge Road, SW11 3AG (7228 0888). South Kensington tube then 49, 319, 345 bus. **Bar Open** noon-3pm, 5.30-11pm Mon-Sat; noon-3pm, 7-10.30pm Sun. **Main courses** £7.50-£8.95. *Restaurant* **Lunch served** noon-2.45pm daily. **Dinner served** 7-10.45pm Mon-Sat; 7-10pm Sun. **Main courses** £11-£17. **Set lunch** (Mon-Sat) £11.50 2 courses. **Set dinner** (Mon, Sun) £11.95 2 courses. **Service** 12.5%. *Both* **Credit** AmEx, DC, MC, V.
A friendly local set among semi-smart shops just south of Battersea Bridge. Blokes in blazers read newspapers at the bar; lunching mothers sit with their babies over rocket salad. The bar is light, with skylights at the back where a more formal dining area is distinguished by banquette seating and kilims stretched over the walls. Diners in the bar

can choose from any menu; as our waitress said, you're spoilt for choice. This is part of the problem, for food quality is variable. Daily specials struck us as hopelessly outmoded: anyone for parma ham with melon, or veal schnitzel with ham and cheese? Crab and parmesan tart from the à la carte was good, but the portion was minuscule. Linguine from the bar menu came with feta, asparagus and green beans, which was a nice mix, but the 'pesto' was a pool of oil flecked with herbs. The own-made burgers came recommended, and deservedly so, but we weren't impressed by pallid chips that tasted mass produced. Wines are available in two glass sizes, and service is obliging. Buchan's suited us fine as a pit stop, but it's not a destination restaurant.
Babies and children welcome; high chairs. Booking advisable. Separate room for hire, seats 60. Tables outside (4, pavement). **Map 21 B1.**

★ Cinnamon Cay
87 Lavender Hill, SW11 5QL (7801 0932/ www.cinnamoncay.co.uk). Clapham Junction rail then 77A, 137 bus. **Lunch served** noon-2.30pm, **dinner served** 6-10.30pm Mon-Sat. **Main courses** £9.50-£14.50. **Set meal** (Mon, Tue) £12 2 courses. **Service** 12.5%. **Credit** AmEx, DC, MC, V.
A sleek mecca of fusion food, Cinnamon Cay deserves to be better known. It's certainly popular locally; arrive late and you'll have to sit next to the open kitchen, where extractor fans add to the hubbub. Even vegetarians do well here. Pumpkin, coconut and lemongrass soup was an inspired blend of sweet and sour; a popadom acted as lid on the bowl. Green-lipped mussels came with tender octopus, chorizo and a salad full of caper berries. A main of roasted vegetables, couscous and goat's cheese was beautiful: the couscous made green with pesto and shaped into a cake-like wedge, topped by the veg, salad leaves and melting cheese. Sichuan pepper fillet was cooked to perfect rarity, its coating occasionally rendering the tongue pleasingly numb. This sat on a powerful stir-fry of baby carrot, courgettes, aubergines and chilli jam. The South-east Asian influences continue with desserts. Banana and sticky rice spring roll was sweet and nutty; the accompanying ginger ice-cream was fantastic. Staff are remarkably upbeat, given how busy they are. The bill came to £35 each, including a reasonable bottle of South African sauvignon. We're keen to return.
Babies and children welcome; high chairs. Booking advisable. Tables outdoors (5, patio).

Corum
30-32 Queenstown Road, SW8 3RX (7720 5445). Battersea Park, Queenstown Road or Clapham Junction rail/77, 137, 156 bus. **Bar Open** noon-3pm, 5pm-1am daily. **Bar snacks** 6pm-10pm daily. *Restaurant* **Lunch served** noon-3pm, **dinner served** 7-11pm Mon-Fri, Sun. **Meals served** noon-3pm, 7pm-midnight Sat. **Main courses** £8.95-£14.95. **Service** 12.5%. *Both* **Credit** AmEx, MC, V.
On a somewhat barren strip of Queenstown Road is the self-consciously cool, slate façade of Corum. The bar is popular – in summer doors open wide on to the street and low sofas encourage lounging – so being shown to the windowless dining room at the back feels like something of a banishment. Cooking can best be described as pedestrian, so that terse menu descriptions mean exactly what they say. Chilled tomato soup was a curious claret colour, and came with the unwise addition of slices of uninteresting mozzarella. The same cheese featured in a salad of figs, rocket and prosciutto, although the figs were excellent. Pan-fried rump of lamb came just how the chef wanted it (slightly overcooked), sandwiched between soggy sautéed potatoes and pea purée. A jus was suitably dark. Roasted aubergine and goat's cheese was a clumsy arrangement of thick slices, complete with rind. Big glasses of wine are good value and our waiter was eager to please, but the list of predictable puds (ice-cream, crème caramel, chocolate fondant) did not entice us to stay. For £30 a head in this neck of the woods, we expected a lot more.
Babies and children admitted (restaurant).

Book dinner Thur-Sat. Disabled: toilet. Tables outdoors (2, pavement).

Brixton SW2

Bug Bar
The Crypt, St Matthew's Church, Brixton Hill, SW2 1JF (7738 3366/www.bugbrixton.co.uk). Brixton tube/rail. **Lounge Bar Open** 5pm-midnight Tue-Sat; 1-9.30pm Sun. **Bug Bar Open** 7pm-2am Wed, Sun; 8pm-3am Thur-Sat. *Restaurant* **Dinner served** 5-11pm Tue-Thur; 5-11.30pm Fri, Sat. **Meals served** 1-9pm Sun. **Main courses** £8.95-£10.50. **Service** 12.5%. *All* **Credit** MC, V.
This darkly atmospheric bar, restaurant and nightclub seemed to have slid into mediocrity, but Bug's star is now on the rise again. An open kitchen plays to a youngish crowd with a mix of vegetarian dishes (cantonese mock duck with pancakes; miso risotto with crispy seaweed), Asian and Cajun-style mains and European starters. Presentation is paramount, with, say, squiggles of 'red pepper essence' filling a plate containing a few spears of asparagus nicely wrapped in courgette strips. Since decor is sparse, it's nice to have a picture on the plate. The only real disappointment is a penchant for sweetness and an absence of spicing. Where was the chilli in pan-fried chilli squid? The meat was certainly tender, but where were the North African flavours in lamb and apricot tagine? A brief wine list features mainly medium-dry wines to complement the cooking style; the cocktail list is far longer. Staff are cheery and efficient, making Bug a good place to pop into for one dish and a quick drink.
Babies and children admitted; booster seats. Book weekends. Disabled: ramp; toilet. Entertainment (Bug Bar): musicians, DJs weekends; poets and singers. No-smoking tables. Separate room for hire, seats 22. Tables outdoors (20, garden terrace). Vegan dishes. **Map 22 D2.**

Clapham SW4

Polygon Bar & Grill
4 The Polygon, SW4 0JG (7622 1199/www.the polygon.co.uk). Clapham Common tube/35, 37, 345 bus. **Lunch served** noon-2.30pm Mon-Fri; 11am-4pm, Sat, Sun. **Dinner served** 6-11pm Mon-Sat. **Main courses** £8-£15. **Set meal** (6-7.30pm Mon-Sat) £12.50 2 courses, £15 3 courses. **Service** 12.5%. **Credit** AmEx, MC, V.
It's got a great location, with a view of the leafy green just off Clapham's main drag spied through big, plate-glass windows. Inside, orange faux-leather banquettes and cobalt-blue chairs set the tone. Cool dudes perform the service. Polygon could be great, then, if it weren't for the face the food is misconceived, and thus way too expensive. A raviolo filled with aubergine and goat's cheese was very good, own-made pasta, yet the filling was overwhelmed by sour cream being dolloped on top. Baby octopus salad, the day's special starter, featured whole, tough cephalopod too heavily marinated in teriyaki sauce. Mains were slightly better. Tuna was excellent sashimi grade, but its flavour was lost under a crust of sesame seeds; artful squirts of 'lime chilli mayonnaise' (no lime or chilli discernible) and pungent salsa verde further muddled the flavours. Herb-crusted rack of lamb was similarly good meat, but sitting on a nasty mush of puréed aubergine. Poached plums were undercooked and came not with maple-walnut ice-cream, as listed, but blackcurrant sorbet. Clearly supplies were running out, as some of the cheaper wines were unavailable too. That left us with a bill of £90 and a feeling that this place should try harder.
Babies and children welcome; high chairs. Booking advisable. Disabled: toilet. **Map 22 A1.**

The Rapscallion
75 Venn Street, SW4 0BD (7787 6555/www.the rapscalliononline.com). Clapham Common tube. **Breakfast served** 10.30am- noon, **lunch served** noon-4pm Mon-Fri. **Brunch served** 10.30am-4pm Sat, Sun. **Dinner served** 6-11pm

Mon-Sat; 6-10.30pm Sun. **Main courses** £6-£11. **Service** 12.5%. **Credit** AmEx, DC, JCB, MC, V.
Cool cocktail connoisseurs patronise this small, minimalist bar. Yet there's no cocktail list on display, and on our visit the mixologist seemed too busy creating these potions to dispense water. Food quality at the Rapscallion is high; it's the service that lets the place down. Customers are asked to release their table within 90 minutes – a bit rich when it takes 30 minutes to get a drink. Our food orders were muddled; we were charged £3 for bread and olives, plus 25p for a tiny dish of unwanted oil. We felt so pressured to eat and go, we skipped starters, even though the spring rolls, tempura scallops and other Asian-influenced snacks looked good. A main of imam bayildi was an elegant tower of smoky puréed aubergine, red peppers, sultanas, a pesto of pumpkin seeds and pine nuts, and creamy goat's cheese. Blackened cod fillet came with sugar snaps and pink ginger, with a trail of wakame (seaweed); the components were sweet, crunchy and fresh in all the right ways. Lemon curd ice-cream was own-made and citrous; the nut biscotti that came with it were terrible. There are hefty mark-ups on many of the (albeit good) wines.
Babies and children welcome. Booking advisable. Tables outdoors (8, pavement). **Map 22 A2.**

The Sequel
75 Venn Street, SW4 0BD (7622 4222/www. thesequelonline.com). Clapham Common tube.
Bar **Open** 5pm-midnight Tue-Fri; 11am-midnight Sat, Sun.
Restaurant **Brunch served** 11am-4pm Sat; 11am-6pm Sun. **Dinner served** 6-11pm Tue-Thur; 6pm-midnight Fri, Sat; 6-10.30pm Sun. **Main courses** £9-£12. **Set meal** £14.50 2 courses. **Service** 12.5%.
Both **Credit** AmEx, DC, JCB, MC, V.
The Sequel, which is often half empty, is sister to the Rapscallion opposite (*see p147*), which is always full. Yet the cooking here is equally good. The menu is more Modern European than exotic; provençal fish soup, pastas and risottos, grilled steak, burgers, and fish with chips form the backbone. A starter of asparagus with a soft poached egg and lemon hollandaise was delicious. 'Mezze', a generous and colourful arrangement of vegetables, included a lettuce leaf holding russian salad that only a Hellmann's junkie would eat. Pan-fried Devon sea bass was fresh and perfectly cooked; olive mash was bland, but a ring of oil with concassé tomatoes and onion made up for the lack of flavour. Puy lentil rotolo (that's a mound to us) was nicely flavoured with stock and held together in a savoy cabbage leaf topped by halloumi and a dollop of onion marmalade. Lemon curd ice-cream was lovely; only its meringue 'cup' was dry and full of nut crumbs. In all, good value – unless you drink cocktails. The dining room is a mezzanine above the bar; sit on the banquettes for a decent view of the giant television screen showing classic movies.
Babies and children admitted. Booking advisable. Dress: smart casual. Tables outdoors (6, pavement). Takeaway service. Vegan dishes. **Map 22 A2.**

Waterloo SE1

Laughing Gravy
154 Blackfriars Road, SE1 8EN (7721 7055). Southwark tube/Waterloo tube/rail.
Bar **Open** noon-11pm Mon-Fri; 7-11pm Sat.
Restaurant **Meals served** noon-10pm Mon-Fri; 7-10pm Sat. **Main courses** £12.25-£15.95.
Both **Credit** MC, V.
Amiably scruffy is how this watering hole-cum-gastropub strikes us. Its unframed oil paintings and bare floorboards were clearly meant to evoke jazzy, boho chic, but Laughing Gravy's enduring popularity as a lunch spot has taken its toll. Things are quieter in the evenings. We chose two items off a blackboard: sesame goujons of swordfish, which were crunchy yet moist within; and char-grilled medallions of springbok (one of many exotic meats on the menu, another being bison tournedos with vodka, cranberry and rhubarb sauce). The springbok was somewhat chewy – but these are

On the South Bank
The Royal Festival Hall offers fine dining at the **People's Palace** (Modern European) or snacks at **Festival Square** (Cafés). Inside County Hall, choose from the **Four Regions** (Chinese), **County Hall Restaurant** (French) and newcomer **Ozu** (Japanese).

A taste of Tate
Choose from the **Tate Britain Restaurant** (International) or the **Tate Modern Café: Level 2** (Brasseries).

Somerset House
Gallic grandeur at the **Admiralty** (French) or summertime snacks at the **River Terrace Restaurant** (Cafés).

Trafalgar Square
Combine Italian art with Italian eats at the National Gallery's **Crivelli's Garden** (Italian). Atop the National Portrait Gallery is the **Portrait Restaurant** (Modern European) – or there's **Zoomslide Café** at the Photographers' Gallery.

Across town
Mix art with food at the following: **Blue Print Café** (Design Museum; Modern European); **Brew House** (Kenwood; Cafés) **Café Bagatelle** (Wallace Collection; Brasseries); **Delfina** (Delfina Gallery; Modern European); **RIBA Café** (RIBA; Cafés); **Searcy's at the Barbican** (Barbican; Modern European); and **Wapping Food** (Wapping Project; Modern European).

animals that run for a living, after all. Accompanying celeriac mash with redcurrant gravy was a delight. Guinea fowl came amply portioned as pan-fried breast and confit leg, but the 'lemon thyme scented jus' was bland. Cajun crayfish cocktail was a more successful, wittier dish, given extra zing with tequila and lime juice. The long list of desserts was equally varied: from 1970s throwbacks to inventive oddities. Belgian chocolate sponge pudding was a treat, though mascarpone, blueberry and vanilla flan came smothered in unnecessary butterscotch sauce. The wine list is modestly priced and has a good spread of bottles. No wonder locals like the place.
Babies and children welcome; high chairs. Booking advisable. Entertainment: jazz 7pm alternate Thur. Restaurant available for hire. **Map 11 O9.**

Waterloo Bar & Kitchen
131 Waterloo Road, SE1 8UR (7928 5086). Waterloo tube/rail. **Lunch served** noon-2.45pm Mon-Fri. **Dinner served** 5.30-10.30pm Mon-Sat. **Main courses** £9-£13. **Service** 10% for parties of six or more. **Credit** AmEx, DC, MC, V.
Just beyond the multi-restaurant Cut and the resplendent Old Vic theatre, you'll find this blank-looking eaterie. Admittedly, it has the exterior charm of a refrigerator, yet inside all is space, light and columns. On one side is the bar, with bare, old wooden tables; to the other is the restaurant, with white linen and some booths. The kitchen has no pretensions to fancy cooking. Soups, 'pitta pizzas', salads and a sharing platter of Cajun chicken, fried chorizo, olives, leaves and bread typify the starters – posh pub grub. Mains are homespun; portions are vast. Smoked haddock came with crushed new potatoes in a lovely grain mustard sauce, with a poached egg on top. Ribeye steak (unpleasantly charred on the outside) arrived with mediocre

chips, salad and a large roasted shallot. Desserts were nothing short of peculiar. Eton mess lacked meringue (it had run out, but no one confessed to this when we were ordering), so consisted of a mountain of whipped cream with strawberries hidden inside, sitting on a puddle of bright red strawberry coulis. But wines are good value and well chosen, so the bill is reasonable – which no doubt accounts for this venue's popularity with quiet youngsters looking for somewhere to eat, drink and chat near Waterloo station.
Babies and children admitted. Tables outdoors (3, pavement). **Map 11 N9.**

Tower Bridge E1

Lightship Ten
5A St Katherine's Way, St Katherine's Dock, E1W 1LP (7481 3123/www.lightshipx.com). Tower Hill tube. **Meals served** noon-10pm Mon-Fri; 6-10pm Sat; noon-8pm Sun. **Main courses** £10-£18.90. **Service** 12.5%. **Credit** AmEx, DC, MC, V.
This has to be one of London's most unusual, and irresistibly romantic, places to dine – in a beautifully restored Danish lightship, built in 1877 and now berthed at St Katherine's Dock. In fine weather you can eat on the upper deck (shame about next-door Starbucks marring the view), but our favourite spot is in the belly of the ship, where portholes, booth seating and a gentle rocking motion create an intimate atmosphere. The menu draws on various influences, but is anchored in Denmark, with fishy starters such as pickled herring and ballottine of gravlaks, followed by sturdy fish and meat dishes. We thoroughly enjoyed a richly flavoured roast duck accompanied by red cabbage, but were less sold on the heavy-going pork belly. For dessert, a warm waffle with berries and honeycomb ice-cream was a subtle pleasure, but an apple tart suffered from overzealous use of cinnamon. So fond are we of this restaurant, it pains us to concede that the quality of food was a little uneven on our most recent visit; but the unbeatable setting and the surprisingly reasonable prices do much to appease, as does the helpful service.
Book weekends. Entertainment: jazz 7-10pm Mon, Wed. Separate room for hire, seats 35. Tables outdoors (26, top deck). **Map 12 S8.**

Westcombe Park SE3

Thyme Restaurant & Bar
1A & 3 Station Crescent, SE3 7EQ (8293 9183/ www.thymerestaurant.co.uk). Westcombe Park rail.
Bar **Open** 5-11pm Tue-Sat.
Restaurant **Dinner served** 7-9.30pm Tue-Sat. **Main courses** £10.95-£12.95. **Credit** V.
A secluded backwater of handsome Victorian villas, Westcombe Park is just the locale for a smart neighbourhood eatery, and Thyme, set in two old shopfronts close to the station, is it. Decor is low key: stained-glass windows illuminate the façade; uninspired abstract paintings punctuate the white walls. Staff are bright and friendly. Our reservations about the place concern lazy cooking. A menu of five starters, five mains and three desserts should not be too taxing, especially when starters are often salad. A main of pan-fried chicken breast was the sort of dish you'd cook at home; it came with faintly gingery noodles, some coriander leaves and julienne carrot strips. Risotto-stuffed peppers featured lovely fresh peas, but the risotto was bland; mixed leaf salad on the side arrived without any form of dressing. Only a few wines are available by the glass, of which one (house red) was undrinkable. Apple crumble was made with, it seemed, just flour, butter, sugar and unsweetened apples, with ne'er a spice or oat considered. Cheese was a selection of average varieties, served with a glass of not very good port. Verdict: pretty average for the 'burbs.
Babies and children admitted. Booking advisable. No-smoking tables. Separate rooms for hire, both seats 35.

East
Bethnal Green E2

Perennial

110-112 Columbia Road, E2 7RG (7739 4556/ www.perennial-restaurant.co.uk). Bethnal Green tube then 55 bus. **Breakfast served** 8.30am-noon Sun. **Lunch served** noon-3pm Fri-Sun. **Dinner served** 7-11pm Tue-Sat. **Main courses** £10-£13. **Credit** AmEx, MC, V.

Running a bistro in a street that is famous for its Sunday flower market makes excellent business sense at weekends, but it must be a struggle during the week – unless yours is a destination restaurant. Perennial, alas, is not. It's ineffably cosy, in a shabby-chic way; on out visit, it had one perfectly sweet, slightly incompetent waiter and one chef working hard to produce passable dinner party food. The menu holds no real surprises (selections included sea bass en papillotte, steak and chips, bowls of mussels) and the wine list is brief and averagely priced. We started off well enough with fine roasted yellow pepper soup (though any hint of chilli was absent from the accompanying blob of 'chilli cream') and a sizeable salad of pears, roquefort and rocket. Venison in bitter chocolate sauce was a nice combination, especially with puréed parsnips and chestnuts, but the meat portion was huge and not tender. Barbary duck leg was good, but sat on acidic-tasting onions steeped in red wine. Dessert, an apple 'tarte tatin', was nothing of the sort, but rather a disc of flaky pastry with a neat assembly of bland, sweet fruit on top, and commercial ice-cream. We couldn't help wondering: will Perennial live up to its name?
Babies and children admitted. Book weekends. No-smoking tables. Separate room for hire, seats 30. Tables outdoors (6, garden). **Map 6 S3**.

Victoria Park E9

Frocks

95 Lauriston Road, E9 7HJ (8986 3161). Mile End tube then 277 bus. **Lunch served** noon-3.30pm, **dinner served** 6.30pm-midnight Tue-Sun. **Main courses** £11-£17. **Credit** AmEx, MC, V.

As Hackney institutions go, this friendly little dining room is up there alongside the Empire for the loyalty it inspires in customers. Timber cladding and twee wooden tables lend the place a country kitchen vibe that would feel preposterous elsewhere in Hackney, but seems perfectly attuned to the gentrified environs of Lauriston Road. Dishes here are typically Delia-esque, and while we wouldn't fault that per se, it's peculiar how the concise menu contrives to change with the season, yet play safe all year round. What the mains lack in creativity, though, they compensate for with robust portions and such reassuringly familiar combos as char-grilled steak with peppercorn sauce and chips, or veal escalope with gratin dauphinois. Our burnished chicken breast, sticky with honey and soy, edged towards the adventurous, but then pulled back with a surprisingly innocuous lime-scented couscous. To finish, Baileys and chocolate cheesecake landed a full-fat punch of sweet decadence, while crumbly orange and almond cake was pepped up with plum jam. It's not the WI, but you sense that same quality of matronly charm.
Babies and children welcome; high chair. Booking advisable weekends. Entertainment: singer Thur, Fri. No-smoking tables. Separate room for hire, seats 40. Tables outdoors (8, walled garden; 4, pavement).

Wanstead E11

Hadley House

27 High Street, E11 2AA (8989 8855). Snaresbrook or Wanstead tube. **Breakfast served** 10am-noon daily. **Lunch served** noon-2.30pm, **dinner served** 7-10.30pm Mon-Sat. **Meals served** 12.30-9pm Sun. **Main courses** £8.50-£15.95. **Set dinner** (Mon) £16.95 3 courses. **Credit** MC, V.

The Rapscallion. See p147.

Near the Essex border, Hadley House is a pleasant café-cum-restaurant with front terrace overlooking a green. From coffees and pâtisserie to lobster and wild mushrooms, the kitchen tries to turn out everything locals could desire. Evening menus struck us as pricey (£16.95 for mains); breakfasts and lunches are more generous, both in portion and price. At Sunday lunch, roasts come as vast pieces of meat. Roast pork (with proper crackling) was given a big hat of Yorkshire pudding, plus pease pudding and some tired carrots. Tomato tart had puff pastry filled with half fresh, half roasted tomatoes, a smear of pesto and some caramelised red onion, with congealed mozzarella on top; it came with a sizeable salad of rocket and so was excellent value. Similarly, an own-made burger was above average and arrived with fat yellow chips and salad. A large chicken leg was wrapped in parma ham and sage; it sat on pappardelle alleged to be in 'basil pesto cream', which was in fact a white wine sauce. Bread and olives are charged as extras, but wines are good value at less than £4 for very large glasses, making Hadley House a popular meeting place.

Babies and children welcome (lunch & Sun); high chairs. Booking essential. Tables outdoors (7, patio). Takeaway service (lunch only).

North

Islington N1

The Commissary

49-50 Eagle Wharf Road, N1 7ED (7251 1155/ www.holbornstudios.com). Angel tube/Old Street tube/rail. Apr-Sept **Breakfast served** 8-11.30am, **lunch served** noon-3.30pm, **bar snacks served** 4-10pm Mon-Fri. *Oct-Mar* **Meals served** 8am-8pm Mon-Fri. **Main courses** £3.75-£12.95. **Credit** MC, V.

The main problem about this arty studio-canteen is its restricted opening hours. Customers are buzzed in through an iron gate from the studios' car park, or can walk along the canal towpath. It's a lovely spot. Big glass windows on a huge, generally underused dining space allow you to look out over the canal. Sunny weather means you can sit on decking (that bobs up and down as people walk on it) next to the narrowboats as they pass by. Food quality is variable; the best bet is to have a look around you and see what others are eating. From a choice of only four main dishes, we scored with battered cod and chips: a fantastic version, with ultra-fresh fish and perfect chunky chips, served with capers and tartare sauce. Mixed vegetable salad contained some roasted root veg and a heap of leaves, but was pretty mediocre in truth; and a basket of bread featured dryish slices of baguette. The one dessert, upside-down pineapple cake, was soggy yet had dried-out fruit. Own-made mango sorbet on the same plate was excellent. Sandwiches, pasta and danish pastries are also offered. Most people seemed to be having a glass of wine – a good idea under the circumstances. So come and enjoy the view, but don't expect to be blown away by the food that's on offer.

Babies and children welcome; high chair. Disabled: toilet. No-smoking tables. Separate room for hire, seats 80. Tables outdoors (11, pontoon). **Map 5 P2.**

Frederick's

Camden Passage, N1 8EG (7359 2888/ www.fredericks.co.uk). Angel tube. Bar **Open** 11am-11pm Mon-Sat. *Restaurant* **Lunch served** noon-2.30pm, **dinner served** 5.45-11.30pm Mon-Sat. **Main courses** £11.50-£17.50. **Set meals** (lunch, 5.45-7pm) £12.50 2 courses, £15.50 3 courses, incl coffee. *Both* **Service** 12.5%. **Credit** AmEx, DC, JCB, MC, V.

Frederick's just carries on in its polished, quasi-French manner. At times the place seems to rest on its laurels, which is pretty galling considering the high prices. And the bad news is that our attempt to economise by exploring the set menu failed dismally. Roast cauliflower soup looked grand with

its hat of puff pastry, and the soup's flavour was intense, but over-salted: a fault of every dish we ordered. Fish, mussel and leek pie was another ceramic dish with puff pastry on top. Below was a very thin broth in which the fish and leeks floated. From the à la carte, a starter of spicy salt cod was merely average; a main of 'slow-roasted pork' turned out to be pork belly, consisting almost entirely of fat. We sent this back to the kitchen; it was replaced by a plate of lamb's kidneys cleverly skewered on rosemary twigs, but underdone despite our instructions ('not pink'). The accompaniment was a greasy piece of fried bread. The simple and cheap £5.95 kids' menu was a much better deal: fish goujons with chips, or pasta with tomato sauce, followed by some very nice sorbet. The room itself is pleasant enough: a big, airy white box with central potted tree, garish abstract paintings and an extension into a similar conservatory. The food needs work, though.

Babies and children welcome; children's menu (£5.95 lunch Sat); high chairs. Book weekends. No-smoking tables. Separate rooms for hire, seating 18 and 32. Tables outdoors (12, garden). **Map 5 O2.**

The Rotisserie

134 Upper Street, N1 3QP (7226 0122/ www.therotisserie.co.uk). Angel tube. **Lunch served** noon-3pm Wed-Fri. **Dinner served** 5-11pm Mon-Fri. **Meals served** noon-11pm Sat, Sun. **Main courses** £7.95-£15.95. **Set meal** £11.95 2 courses. **Credit** AmEx, DC, MC, V.

It is a curious disappointment that the rotisserie at the back of the dining room never seems to be in operation. The charcoal grill makes up for this deficiency, however, turning out plate after plate of chicken, prawns and steaks, all accompanied by the inevitable extruded potato chips. As long as you bear in mind that this mini-chain is the modern-day equivalent of the Berni Inn, then you can have an OK meal here. Fillet steak, for example, was well hung and well cooked, even if a side order of french beans was the teensiest portion we had ever seen, and tasteless to boot. Burgers are fine. Chicken caesar salad featured nicely grilled pieces of fowl on a bowl of cos lettuce, but pale, uninteresting tomato slices, scattered with strands of parmesan and unnaturally square croûtons. The dressing was agreeable. Our waiter recommended the malva sponge pudding with custard as the restaurant's best dessert. It was a wonderful nostalgia trip, being springy, sweet and exactly the shape of those served at old-time school dinners – with custard skin to match. Diners tend to be families and well-behaved boys looking to load up on carbs before a night out.

Babies and children welcome; high chair. Booking advisable weekends. No-smoking tables (not Sat). Tables outdoors (4, pavement). Takeaway service. **Map 5 O1.**
For branch see index.

Swiss Cottage NW3

Globe

100 Avenue Road, NW3 3HF (7722 7200/ www.globerestaurant.co.uk). Swiss Cottage tube/13, 31 bus. **Lunch served** noon-3pm Mon-Fri. **Dinner served** 6-11pm Mon-Sat. **Main courses** £9.50-£13.50. **Service** 12.5%. **Credit** MC, V.

A cabaret on Thursday nights is the weekly highlight at this conservatory-style restaurant much used by patrons of Hampstead Theatre. At other times, the atmosphere can seem lacking, and the artwork on the walls – bondage/vamp portraits framed with silver builder's tape – puzzling. Globe's owners are a couple of drag artistes; its camp waiters lend an otherwise sterile environment some character. The food is less outlandish. A chive blini formed a nice platform for a piece of (farmed) smoked salmon and sour cream, but aside from a circle of orange (chilli?) oil, some promised balsamic dressing was impossible to detect. Rocket salad with parmesan was just that; perfect, even if it might have been achieved by opening a packet of leaves. Sea bass consisted

of two sizeable fillets and some nicely roasted vegetables. Rump of lamb came with a mess of potatoes/sun-dried tomatoes and a lack of any trimmings; better service might have advised a side order. But we liked the wine and the bill, and reckon Globe is a better haven than nearby rivals on this thunderous intersection.

Babies and children admitted. Booking advisable. No-smoking tables. **Map 28 B4.**

North West

Queen's Park NW6

Hugo's

21-25 Lonsdale Road, NW6 6RA (7372 1232). Queen's Park tube/rail. **Meals served** 9.30am-11pm daily. **Main courses** £10.80-£14.80. **Service** 12.5%. **Credit** MC, V.

The quasi-industrial locality contributes much to the atmosphere of this backstreet bistro. On warm days, a wide frontage is open to the cobbled street and to the sounds of small manufacturers. Inside are church pews, old pine tables, jolly red fake flowers and an upright piano. Locals love Hugo's, and why not? It isn't too expensive, serves tea and coffee all day and has space for baby buggies. Service is so laid-back as to be dilatory. The menu isn't too ambitious, and its execution is no better than average. At weekends there's an all-day brunch menu offering salads, pasta, risotto, breakfasts, pancakes, soups and platters of meats and cheeses. Calamares with garlic mayonnaise was a nice little plate of battered squid rings. Hugo's organic beef burger was herby and well done, and came with cubed, skin-on chips and salad featuring pallid tomatoes. Steak pie contained good meat, but the fries were cold and the onion gravy had lumps of undissolved stock cube in it. The best thing about our meal was a basket of excellent olive focaccia that kept us going during the 45-minute wait for lunch. The cakes looked OK, but cost £4-£5 per slice.

Babies and children welcome; high chairs. Book dinner. Entertainment: dinner dance 8pm Thur; jazz 8.15-10.30pm Sun. No-smoking tables. Separate room for hire, seats 50. Tables outdoors (14, pavement). Takeaway service. **Map 1 A1.**
For branch see index.

★ Penk's

79 Salusbury Road, NW6 6NH (7604 4484/ www.penks.com). Queen's Park tube/rail. **Brunch served** 10.30am-3pm Sat; 10.30am-5pm Sun. **Lunch served** noon-3pm Mon-Fri. **Dinner served** 7-11pm Mon-Fri; 7-11.30pm Sat; 5-10.30pm Sun. **Meals served** 10.30am-11pm Sun. **Main courses** £9.95-£15.95. **Service** 10% for parties of 8 or more. **Credit** MC, V.

This slim strip of a place between the fancy food stores and the wacky interiors shops epitomises all that's best about Salusbury Road: it's small, personal and inexpensively decorated with brightly coloured walls and long mirrors. All of Penk's energies go into the food, and the result is big plates of wholesome, modern cooking, stylishly presented, and available at modest prices. Spiced roast tomato soup was our idea of a slimming starter – apart from the delicious fried croûtons, of course, and thick greek yoghurt. Monkfish gratin, by comparison, was a madly rich, buttery delight that was lent variety by shrimps and button mushrooms. Salads come in two sizes; we found the starter portion ample in the tuna version. The fish had been pot-roasted; its companions were butter beans, parsley, a soft boiled egg, rocket and aïoli. Grilled organic pork chop required some chewing, but the flavour was excellent and its accompanying gratin of jerusalem artichoke was superb. A great heap of salad came with the dish too. Caramelised lemon tart was the best dessert, but in truth there was nothing to complain about here, especially at £65 for two, including a bottle of very good Pouilly-Fumé. We'll definitely return.

Babies and children welcome; high chairs. Booking advisable. No-smoking tables. Separate room for hire, seats 16. Tables outdoors (3, pavement). **Map 1 A2.**

Italian

Downturn? What downturn? Whether it's confidence in the enduring popularity of Italian cuisine (ten new restaurants are included in this edition, and last year saw the debut of 11), or London's exorbitant rents, average prices in this sector are increasing well above the rate of inflation. Not so long ago an evening meal for two with reasonable wine and service would cost around £85; now you can expect total bills to hit the £100 mark even at run-of-the-mill venues. If you're up for fine dining or want to go to a particularly fashionable restaurant, expect to spend at least £130 for supper, and go easy on the aperitifs. It's too much. Someone should say something – and we just have. As is the case with restaurants in the **Hotels & Haute Cuisine** section (starting on p110), choosing a set menu at lunchtime can bring rewards, but only if the limited choice of dishes is mouth-watering.

On the plus side, regional Italian delicacies are increasingly easy to find, with the island cuisines and wines of Sardinia and Sicily vying with Tuscan food in the fashion stakes. Specialists are relatively scarce, but **Sardo** and the new **Sardo Canale** concentrate on the recipes of Sardinia, while **Giardinetto** has a forte in Genoese cooking (including vividly fresh pesto).

Central

Belgravia SW1

Como Lario
22 Holbein Place, SW1 8NL (7730 2954/9046/ www.comolario.uk.com). Sloane Square tube. **Lunch** served 12.30-2.45pm, **dinner served** 6.30-11.30pm Mon-Sat. **Main courses** £10-£15. **Cover** £1.50. **Credit** AmEx, DC, JCB, MC, V.
Last year's refurbishment brought Como Lario kicking and screaming into the late 1980s – which makes you wonder why it bothered. The lake scene mural has gone to be replaced by – now here's an original idea – framed black and white photographs of Marilyn Monroe, Maria Callas and Michael Caine. Food remains classic too, though we enjoyed the gimmick of wrapping mushroom risotto in parma ham. The buffalo mozzarella that came with grilled vegetables had the right milky quality. Although pasta with lamb ragù was a bland disappointment, a special of oven-baked sea bream with white wine and caper sauce was excellent. The house white is cheap and tastes it: not a savvy purchase. Previous visits had seen desserts desperately in need of improvement. The mascarpone mixture in our tiramisu had an otherworldly bright white colour, but overall tasted OK. Better was a tightly rolled pancake with marrons glacés and amaretti crumbs. Staff are sweet and kindly, but their bright red neckties all needed a trip to the dry cleaners: a little off-putting.
Babies and children welcome; high chairs. Booking advisable dinner. Dress: smart casual. Restaurant available for hire. Separate rooms for parties, seating 40 and 60. **Map 15 G11**.
For branch (Ziani) see index.

Il Convivio
143 Ebury Street, SW1W 9QN (7730 4099/ www.etruscagroup.co.uk). Sloane Square tube/ Victoria tube/rail. **Lunch served** noon-2.45pm, **dinner served** 7-10.45pm Mon-Sat. **Set lunch** £15.50 2 courses, £19.50 3 courses. **Set dinner**

£26.50 2 courses, £32.50 3 courses, £38.50 4 courses. **Service** 12.5%. **Credit** AmEx, DC, JCB, MC, V.
The large electric skylight at the rear of this long, thin, multi-layered restaurant is one of London's best-kept secrets. When open to the sun it creates a feeling of dining outdoors, without the noise or smog. Il Convivio's wine list hits the heights with expensive bottles, but prices start at a reasonable £12.50. Even more tempting is the menu based on prime ingredients, interesting combinations and elegant but not tricksy presentation. The stellar crab risotto with wilted mustard leaves had superb soupy texture: the artisan rice was a rich red from shellfish stock, while the greens had a good strong peppery taste. Other excellent seafood dishes included seared scallops with a warm salad of cucumber, watercress and preserved lemons, and pan-fried cod with liquorice and citrus sauce. Even classic combinations are prepared intelligently; a rich slab of tomato terrine with creamy burrata was a sophisticated take on the ubiquitous mozzarella and tomato salad. Dessert was a let-down, however – the fresh cherry compote served with panna cotta was disturbingly fizzy; it must have been delicious days earlier. Service, pleasant and unhurried for the most part, evolved to total lack of interest come bill time.
Babies and children welcome. Booking advisable dinner. Restaurant available for hire. Separate room for parties, seats 14. **Map 15 G10**.

Olivo
21 Eccleston Street, SW1W 9LX (7730 2505). Sloane Square tube/Victoria tube/rail. **Lunch served** noon-2.30pm Mon-Fri. **Dinner served** 7-11pm Mon-Sat; 7-10.30pm Sun. **Main courses** £13.50-£15. **Set lunch** £16.50 2 courses, £18.50 3 courses. **Cover** £1.50. **Credit** AmEx, DC, JCB, MC, V.
Vibrantly painted cement walls and bare floorboards give a timeless, modern look to this long-standing restaurant. However, they also seem to amplify the acoustics, so that Olivo sounds busy and buzzy (and slightly claustrophobic) even when only a few tables are occupied. The thrust of the menu is Sardinian, but subtly so. Char-grilled courgette salad with salted ricotta, rocket and truffle oil was an enchantingly light starter, though it is difficult to pass up Olivo's buttery spaghetti alla bottarga, or specials such as spaghetti with white truffle. Both our risottos, including a porcini-flavoured version from the specials board, were excellent, but the artichoke risotto was especially stunning: its dark olive colour and thick soupy texture indicating the rich intensity of vegetable flavour the kitchen had managed to imbue. A main of calf's liver came thickly sliced, with balsamic sauce and spinach. Desserts included almond semifreddo and a rich Italian cheesecake studded with candied citrus peel. The blissfully brief wine list emphasises Sardinian bottles, but we chose the 'wine of the month', a ripasso Valpolicella keenly priced at £19.50. Only the waitress spoiled our evening with her cavalier attitude. Still, although we were on a promise to leave before 8.45pm, we were not pushed out the door.
Children admitted. Booking advisable.
Map 15 H10.
For branch (Olivetto) see index.

City E1, EC3, EC4

Caravaggio
107 Leadenhall Street, EC3A 4AA (7626 6206/ www.etruscagroup.co.uk). Aldgate tube/Bank tube/ DLR/25 bus. **Lunch served** 11.45am-3pm, **dinner** served 6.30-10pm Mon-Fri. **Main courses**

£13.50-£18. **Set dinner** £23.50 2 courses, £28.50 3 courses. **Cover** £1.50. **Service** 12.5%. **Credit** AmEx, DC, JCB, MC, V.
A large former banking hall ornately decked with fabrics and art deco fittings, Caravaggio is a temple to 1980s excesses and expense-account lifestyles, but has notably endured in the competitive City environment. Our evening began poorly with dry, tasteless bread. Then the waitress failed to tell us that there was no cod or tuna available, and seemed irritated that we had failed to ascertain these facts by ESP. We consoled ourselves with starters of delicious smoked chicken consommé with diced veg and ricotta parcels, and trofie pasta with courgettes, pesto and crunchy crumbled stamens of saffron. However, main courses saw another turn for the worse. A murky green sauce served with sea bass, alpine ham and spinach looked particularly unappetising. Char-grilled liver resembled a slab of darkly striped milk chocolate; it was appalling, raw inside and veiny. We told the waiter it was terrible and all he did was spend the rest of the evening avoiding our table – no mean feat in such a sparsely populated restaurant. Very pleasant red wine for £25 (quite inexpensive in these parts) and an excellent dessert of ginger and pear millefoglie failed to remove the bitter taste from our mouths. If this restaurant wants to survive another recession, it needs to boost its performance.
Babies and children welcome. Booking advisable. Disabled: toilet. Dress: smart casual; no shorts. Restaurant available for hire. Separate area for parties, seats 30. **Map 12 R6**.

1 Blossom Street
1 Blossom Street, E1 6BX (7247 6530/ www.1blossomstreet.com). Liverpool Street tube/rail.
Bar **Open** noon-11pm Mon-Fri.
Restaurant **Lunch served** noon-3pm, **dinner served** 6-9pm Mon-Fri. **Main courses** £9.25-£16.50. **Set lunch** (noon-4pm) £25 2 courses, £30 3 courses.
Both **Service** (on food) 12.5%. **Credit** AmEx, DC, JCB, MC, V.
You can almost imagine Fagin and the Artful Dodger performing 'Consider Yourself' down these dark, antiquated streets on the edge of the City. Turn into the passage leading to this restaurant and you'll be greeted with a charming verdant courtyard and conservatory entrance that leads to the cavernous basement restaurant and bar. The place was populated with office groups on our evening visit, yet we sensed confusion over what the management was trying to achieve. Blossom Street looks like a comfortable, fairly classy 1990s venue for celebrating bonuses and takeovers, but the operation lacks sophistication – as evidenced by the badly written wine list, the budget-retailer-tasting bread, the foil-wrapped pats of butter on the table, the amateurish cooking and the lackadaisical service. There were no formalities such as changing cutlery, and no spoons provided for the pasta either. These dishes included a greasy mass of strozzapretti with prawns, cherry tomatoes and 'creamed courgettes', and linguine with clams – the volume of shellfish not compensating for their quality. Mint panna cotta was ill-conceived, while the chocolate and almond tart tasted soapy. Best was a main course of pork loin with good crackling and rosemary roast potatoes. Most horrific was the bill: over £120 for a dreary meal for two with inelegant wine.
Booking advisable. Disabled: lift; toilet. Dress: smart. Restaurant and bar available for hire. Separate rooms for parties, seating 6, 12 and 26. Tables outdoors (16, garden). **Map 6 R5**.

Refettorio NEW
Crowne Plaza Hotel, 19 New Bridge Street, EC4V 6DB (7438 8052). Blackfriars tube. **Lunch served** noon-2.30pm Mon-Fri. **Dinner served** 6-10.30pm Mon-Sat. **Main courses** £5.50-£17.50. **Service** 12.5%. **Credit** AmEx, MC, V.
This hotel restaurant makes a huge effort to import artisanal Italian ingredients and use them properly. With Giorgio Locatelli as the consultant chef, you're not going to find pineapple pizza on the menu. It's a surprise, then, to discover the 'refectory' is run by a subsidiary of Aramark, a

vast commercial catering empire. An impersonal, corporate feel permeated the place on our visit. Part of Refettorio's problem is the edge-of-City location, but if you're more interested in flavours than ambience, you won't be disappointed. Breads, for instance, are excellent. Cheeses and cold meats are also impressive: around 25 of each, including, for the connoisseur, lardo di colonnata (preserved lard, surprisingly moreish). The wine list is all-Italian. Prices throughout are set for the City. A fillet of cod, hardly a generous portion, pan-fried then placed on top of an insipid vegetable selection, cost £17.50. Bucatini pasta, served with an amatriciana sauce of onion, tomato and Italian bacon, cost £8 as a starter. We wanted to like Refettorio because it's clear there is serious intent behind the kitchen, but there is no Locatelli glamour or buzz, and the service was badly rehearsed. Which just goes to show that a successful Italian restaurant is about more than just getting the dishes right; hospitality and conviviality are vital ingredients.
Babies and children welcome; high chairs. Booking advisable. Separate room for parties, seats 70. **Map 11 O6**.

Clerkenwell & Farringdon EC1

Zetter NEW

86-88 Clerkenwell Road, EC1M 5RJ (7324 4455/ www.zetter.com). Farringdon tube/rail. **Breakfast served** 7-10.30am Mon-Fri; 7-11.30am Sat, Sun. **Lunch served** noon-2.30pm Mon-Fri; noon-3.30pm Sat, Sun. **Dinner served** 6-11pm Mon-Sat; 6-10.30pm Sun. **Main courses** £10.50-£17. **Credit** AmEx, DC, JCB, MC, V.
Within days of opening, the Zetter made it into *Condé Nast Traveller*'s list of the 50 coolest new hotels in Europe. So how does its restaurant match up? Formerly a warehouse for Zetter football pools, the restaurant, headed by ex-Moro chef Megan Jones, offers modern interpretations of Italian regional cooking. Decked out in cream and black, with huge picture windows overlooking St John's Square, the room curves around a black marble bar, where superior snacks are served. In the dining area, there's an ambitious, reassuringly short menu that changes monthly. A refreshing pear, chicory and pecorino sardo salad had the silky, unctuous sweetness of the fruit sinking into the assertive bitterness of red chicory. A main course of baked globe artichoke stuffed with ricotta and 'wild greens' was served with superb, delicate, fennel-flavoured lentils. Octopus with celery, lemon, olives and parsley looked picture-pretty, but lacked bite. Roman veal chop with parma ham and sage was overwhelmingly salty and had to be sent back – so we were offered complimentary desserts. Chestnut honey semifreddo had a heady, haunting floral flavour, but wasn't chilled and didn't gain anything by being served with a blood orange sorbet.
Babies and children welcome; children's portions; crayons; high chairs. Booking advisable. Disabled: toilet. Separate rooms for parties, seats 10 and 40. **Map 5 O4**.

Covent Garden WC2

Neal Street

26 Neal Street, WC2H 9QW (7836 8368). Covent Garden tube. **Lunch served** noon-2.30pm, **dinner served** 6-11pm Mon-Sat. **Main courses** £12.50-£21.50. **Set lunch** £21 2 courses, £25 3 courses. **Service** 12.5%. **Credit** AmEx, DC, JCB, MC, V.
While other established Italian restaurants in London are content with serving the same food that brought them success back in the 1960s and '70s, Neal Street's owners Antonio and Priscilla Carluccio (she is Terence Conran's sister) run a ceaseless campaign to seek out the most interesting Italian treats for diners. Take the new emerald-green olives from Puglia – juicy fleshy things that demonstrate that the olive really is a fruit – or the wonderful selection of fresh artisan breads brought to the table. No plastic packets of grissini here. Yet in seeking out the new, Neal Street does not forsake simplicity or tradition. Our

Latium

starter of lemon tagliolini from the set-lunch menu (a bargain at £25 for three courses, with an extensive choice) was perfect: toothsome al dente strands of egg pasta flavoured with lemon. Mixed mushroom risotto was slightly salty, but otherwise well flavoured and textured. A classic Sicilian stuffing of pine nuts and raisins was used to fill thin rolled slices of swordfish for a delightful main course. Crème brûlée with cherries was generous. Only strawberry tart with an unattractive port ice-cream melting at its side let the team down. There aren't many places where a celebrity chef comes to each table making sure customers are satisfied.
Babies and children welcome. Booking advisable. Dress: no shorts. Separate room for parties, seats 24. **Map 18 L6**.

Orso

27 Wellington Street, WC2E 7DB (7240 5269/ www.orso.co.uk). Covent Garden tube. **Meals served** noon-midnight daily. **Main courses** £8.50-£16. **Set lunch** (noon-5pm Sat, Sun) £18.50 2 courses, £20.50 3 courses, incl glass of champagne or cocktail. **Set meal** (5-6.45pm Mon-Sat) £16 2 courses, £18 3 courses incl coffee. **Credit** AmEx, MC, V.
We were saddened at the loss of Orso's sister restaurant Orsino in Holland Park, for we felt its airy dining room had the edge over this dark basement venue, where a repast always feels like a post-theatre meal, no matter what time you're eating. Orso's menu changes frequently, yet seemingly not at all, such is the intelligence of the blueprint, which sees rocket, pasta, shellfish, salads and pizzas combined this way and that. While an Italian version of the menu is included, this restaurant is more Venice Beach than Venetian, with its Hollywood pictures, smart, sassy staff and multicoloured seating. No wonder so many customers are American tourists. Wine is available by the jug, but this is really a place for beers and strong Bloody Marys. Deep-fried courgette flowers were filled with crab and mascarpone, and had an excellent crisp batter with no trace of oiliness. However, mussels with cream and fennel was disappointing, the shellfish tasting rubbery and old. The vegetables accompanying our nicely fatty rack of roast lamb with pesto were not so much grilled as cremated, while the green veg in a dish of flat pasta ribbons with moist chunks of pot-roast veal were unattractively grey. Orso retrieved its reputation with fabulous desserts of plum and almond tart, and flourless chocolate cake. The all-day dining policy is a terrific convenience, but we have found staff too happy to leave us to it during uncrowded periods.
Babies and children admitted; high chairs. Booking advisable. No-smoking tables. **Map 18 L7**.

Fitzrovia W1

Bertorelli

19-23 Charlotte Street, W1T 1RL (7636 4174/ www.santeonline.co.uk). Goodge Street or Tottenham Court Road tube.
Bar **Open** noon-11pm Mon-Sat.
Café **Meals served** noon-11pm Mon-Sat.
Main courses £7.50-£14.95.
Restaurant **Lunch served** noon-3pm Mon-Fri.
Dinner served 6-11pm Mon-Sat. **Main courses** £13.75-£16.50. **Set meal** £15.50
2 courses, £18.50 3 courses.
All **Service** 12.5%. **Credit** AmEx, DC, MC, V.
The first-floor restaurant in Bertorelli's flagship branch offers a more sedate and grown-up dining experience than does the bustling ground-floor café. A cover charge of £1.50 per person buys grissini, bread, olives and baci biscuits; when service is as friendly and efficient as on our visit, it seems unreasonable to begrudge the charge. Asparagus ravioli came with queen scallops and prawns, but there was no taste of asparagus in the filling. Nor could we detect celeriac in the celeriac mash said to accompany the roast chicken, although it was enjoyably flavoured with garlic, and the bird was tasty and juicy. A wonderful char-grilled beef fillet, sensibly modest in size, came with truffle oil and crunchy pickled vegetables with a pleasing tang. Desserts, including chocolate 'truffle' cake (nothing truffle about it), were a great disappointment; most supermarkets could have done better. However, the wine list impressively includes several bottles under £20, precisely targeted for the parties and office group
Babies and children welcome. Booking advisable. No-smoking tables. Restaurant available for hire. Separate rooms for parties, seating 18 and 40. Tables outdoors (5, terrace). Map 9 J5.
For branches see index.

Camerino

16 Percy Street, W1T 1DT (7637 9900/ www.camerinorestaurant.com). Goodge Street or Tottenham Court Road tube. **Lunch served** noon-3pm Mon-Fri. **Dinner served** 6-11pm Mon-Sat. **Set lunch** £17.50 2 courses, £21.50 3 courses, £25.50 4 courses. **Set dinner** £22.50 2 courses, £26.50 3 courses, £30.50 4 courses. **Service** 12.5%. **Credit** AmEx, DC, MC, V.
Formerly known as Paolo, this restaurant has been given a makeover that Laurence Llewelyn-Bowen would aspire to, with full-length red curtains, and white walls painted with a delicate black flower pattern reminiscent of embroidery. Plenty of threesomes were dining on our visit, underlining the convenience of the location for after-work and after-shopping meals. For starters, broccoli made a delicious alternative to predictable rocket in a dish of grilled squid and sweet chilli. Presentation was superb, as it was with a tuna carpaccio cleverly matched with shallots braised in sweet Marsala wine. The pasta list took in potato and chestnut gnocchi with walnut sauce, and buttery ravioli of beetroot and ricotta with poppy-seed dressing. Grilled eel with herbed bread coating made an appealingly unusual main course. Generous lamb shank was slowly cooked with balsamic, arriving stickily black on a bed of risotto-style farro. Most of the daily specials were based around foie gras and summer truffles, and demanded a supplement. The straightforward wine list includes four whites and four reds by the glass. We had no room for desserts (such as coconut tiramisu), and did not order coffees or liqueurs, yet the pleasant, attentive waiters brought petits fours regardless.
Babies and children welcome; high chairs. Booking advisable. Restaurant available for hire. Tables outdoors (2, pavement). Map 10 K5.

Carluccio's Caffè

8 Market Place, W1W 8AG (7636 2228/ www.carluccios.com). Oxford Circus tube. **Meals served** 7.30am-11pm Mon-Fri; 10am-11pm Sat; 10am-10pm Sun. **Main courses** £4.85-£10.95.
Credit AmEx, MC, V.
Although deservedly popular, this cleverly conceived luncheonette – the original West End branch of what has become a widespread chain – was a little dishevelled on our last visit. Busy staff were slow to bring menus, delivered an incorrect order, and a delay with the bill ruined any chance of the meal fitting into a lunch hour. But when food is so reasonably priced and delicious, such faults are easy to forgive. From the specials board we ordered red wine risotto, which came topped with zucchine fritte. Pasta of the day was a hearty plate of penne with courgettes. Although the menu features some staples, such as a choice of tasty antipasto platters, it changes periodically. Carluccio's rich, dark and dense chocolate torta is perfectly judged and well worth saving room for – same goes for the excellent coffees. We'd happily return; the flexibility of dining options and friendly casual environment is something London and the rest of the UK needs more of.
Babies and children welcome; children's menu; high chairs. Disabled: toilet. No-smoking tables. Tables outdoors (16, pavement). Takeaway service. **Map 18 J6.**
For branches see index.

Giardinetto

69 Charlotte Street, W1T 4BJ (7637 4907). Goodge Street tube. **Lunch served** 12.30-3pm Mon-Sat. **Dinner served** 6-10.30pm Mon-Sun. **Set meal** £24.50 2 courses, £29 3 courses. **Service** 12.5%. **Credit** AmEx, DC, JCB, MC, V.
Crazy paving and wild wallpaper bring a sense of kitsch to evenings at Giardinetto, a fun basement restaurant based on traditional Genoese cooking. Staff are endearingly keen to ensure guests love everything and have a good time. Having brought a complimentary welcoming glass of fizz to the table, our waiter recommended an off-list wine, Dolcetto d'Alba, as the best accompaniment for our meal, promising to take it back if we didn't enjoy it. Cold weather outside was sensibly reflected in a menu that featured plenty of chestnuts and chickpeas, but there were also lighter options such as steamed monkfish coated with pesto and tomato concasse, served with fennel salad. A special of wild boar sauce was offered either over vegetable ravioli or served as a main course with mashed potato. Dark green sheets of spinach and chestnut-flour pasta were given an otherworldly look when laced with the eerily bright fresh pesto that is Giardinetto's trademark. For dessert, we loved a first-rate tiramisu with plenty of cocoa powder ('different from all the others,' promised the waiter) and a crêpe filled with strawberries and pastry cream before being baked in the oven. It may not feature in glossy magazines, but, whereas other restaurants follow fashion, Giardinetto is like vintage Valentino.
Babies and children welcome; high chairs. Booking advisable. No-smoking area. Separate room for parties, seats 12. **Map 3 J5.**

Best Italian

Make like your favourite movie star at the following:

The Godfather

Enjoy old-fashioned charm and tradition at **La Famiglia** (see p163), **Neal Street Restaurant** (see p152) and **Riva** (see p162).

Sex & the City

Go glam and sexy at **Brunello** (see p160), **Cecconi's** (see p156) and **Isola** (see p155).

Wall Street

Deals follow meals at **Il Convivio** (see p151), **Alloro** (see p156) and **Latium** (see p153).

Friends

Chow down with your chums at **Emporio Armani Caffè** (see p155), **Zucca** (see p162) and **Aperitivo** (see p165).

Latium NEW

21 Berners Street, W1T 3LP (7323 9123/ www.latiumrestaurant.com). Oxford Circus tube. **Lunch served** noon-3pm Mon-Fri. **Dinner served** 6.30-10.30pm Mon-Fri; 6.30-11pm Sat. **Main courses** £11-£15. **Set meal** £21.50 2 courses, £25.50 3 courses. **Service** 12.5%. **Credit** AmEx, JCB, MC, V.
A partnership between a chef and a wine importer, Latium (Italian for Lazio) is housed on the site of a former fish! branch, conveniently central yet quietly removed from the passing trade. The black, white, dark wood and grey-covers decor is minimalist. Large retro photographs on the walls pay tribute to mama's country. A zucchini flower starter came with a perfect baby courgette attached, the petals stuffed with crab, and lying on a broad bean purée. Next: mixed seafood ravioli sprinkled with bottarga, a four-colour medley that came with instructions from the chef on the order in which the parcels should be eaten. Parma ham wrapped around pink roast pork fillet was a vividly salty main. Better was roast beef fillet stuffed with artichoke purée, served with roasted peppers and a good sticky gravy for which we were given sauce spoons. We closed with an accomplished rendition of pasticceria neapolitana, but few people find this heavy tart a mouth-watering choice, and while our vanilla bavarois had an excellent texture, the cherry sauce lacked fruity flavour. Latium's leather seating is attractive, but the banquettes are set too low, so even fairly tall people must eat with their arms up by their shoulders. Given our uncomfortable state, it was just as well the pleasant service was prompt, but never rushed.
Babies and children welcome; high chairs. Booking advisable weekends. **Map 17 J5.**

Passione

10 Charlotte Street, W1T 2LT (7636 2833/ www.passione.co.uk). Goodge Street or Tottenham Court Road tube. **Lunch served** 12.30-2.15pm Mon-Fri. **Dinner served** 7-10.15pm Mon-Sat. **Main courses** £10-£21. **Service** 12.5%. **Credit** AmEx, DC, JCB, MC, V.
In case you don't know: Passione's chef-patron Gennaro Contaldo has been an inspiration and mentor to Jamie Oliver. We don't share the loyal lad's enthusiasm, finding the cooking overrated and expensive, but the modestly chic and unintimidating interior, featuring beautiful framed photographs of food, is a pleasant lunchtime destination. Among Passione's best dishes are the light, fragrant ricotta and lemon ravioli, and soft, rich ice-cream flavoured with strawberry and limoncello. Straightforward roast rabbit with rosemary seems to be a popular order, no doubt because it is seldom offered elsewhere, but the version served on our most recent visit didn't have anyone rhapsodising. Outstandingly tender pointed pillows of ricotta dumplings were marred by the overwhelming flavour of a copious San Marzano tomato sauce, which tasted as if it took little but a can opener to prepare. Given this, plus the simple asparagus soup ordered as a starter, and a dreary white wine that cost around £25, we felt the bill of over £100 for two was outrageous.
Babies and children welcome. Booking advisable. Restaurant available for hire. Separate room for parties, seats 18. Tables outdoors (2, patio; 1, pavement). Map 10 K5.

★ Sardo

45 Grafton Way, W1T 5DQ (7387 2521/ www.sardo-restaurant.com). Warren Street tube. **Lunch served** noon-3pm Mon-Fri. **Dinner served** 6-11pm Mon-Sat. **Main courses** £8.90-£18.* **Credit** AmEx, DC, MC, V.
Sardo has acquired a reputation as the place restaurant reviewers go when they're spending their own money, as opposed to their publisher's. There are many popular, well-executed dishes on the menu (think grilled tuna with rocket and tomatoes), but it's best to order from the short list of daily specials on the blackboard, especially when fregola (Sardinian semolina pasta) and shellfish are involved. Alternatively, be guided by owner Romolo Mudu, who may have a couple of portions of something interesting available. He

visits Sardinia to source new ingredients and wines, and likes to try them out on choice patrons before launching them on the main menu. Our visit gleaned a tasty plate of wild boar prosciutto, and venison cooked perfectly, served with blue cheese sauce. Sweet creamy polenta made an unusual, but delicious and comforting finale. Sardo's fragrant breads and olives, charged at £3, are well worth the extra expense. Like the decor and service, they may be simple, but are done extremely well and without pretension.
Babies and children admitted. Booking advisable. No-smoking tables. Separate area for parties, seats 30. Tables outdoors (3, patio). **Map 3 J4.**

Knightsbridge SW1, SW3

Emporio Armani Caffè
191 Brompton Road, SW3 1NE (7823 8818). Knightsbridge tube. **Open** 10am-6pm Mon-Sat. **Breakfast served** 10am-noon Mon-Sat. **Lunch served** noon-3.30pm Mon-Fri; noon-4pm Sat. **Main courses** £11-£17. **Credit** AmEx, DC, JCB, MC, V.
Surely the only place in London with a menu held together by a band of beige bra-strap elastic, this stylish in-store café is renowned for its sexy Italian waiters strutting around the room like models down a catwalk. The Caffè's enduring popularity (you usually need to book) is thanks also to a clever, level-headed menu of flexible dining options including cocktail nibbles and afternoon tea. The wine list is sensibly brief too: four whites, four reds and a deep-pink rosé. Pan-fried john dory with cockle and brown shrimp risotto was a delicious dish that proved the kitchen is not afraid to innovate. Chicken supreme came with taleggio gnocchi that turned out to be a potato cake imbued with this fruity-flavoured cheese. Mushroom bruschetta with girolles and porcini, and balsamic roast vegetable salad laced with rocket were two appetisingly pretty starters. The great bread basket – featuring seeded, pepper-flavoured and white sliced varieties – was generously replenished by the careful, quietly attentive staff. A fridge breakdown meant there was no crème brûlée or ice-cream, so we consoled ourselves with choc-drizzled banana semifreddo, apple tart with thin, crisp pastry and good macchiato. This is great food and a great excuse to go shopping.
Babies and children welcome. Booking advisable. Disabled: toilet (in shop). **Map 14 E9.**

Floriana
15 Beauchamp Place, SW3 1NQ (7838 1500). Knightsbridge tube. **Lunch served** 12.30-3pm Mon-Fri; 12.30-3.30pm Sat. **Dinner served** 7-11pm Mon-Sat. **Main courses** £16-£20. **Set lunch** £15 2 courses, £19 3 courses. **Credit** AmEx, DC, JCB, MC, V.
A flock of graceful, black-suited, blonde waitresses greets visitors to this elegant restaurant, much more formal and tranquil than nearby San Lorenzo (*see below*). The decor and branding are subtly art deco, while dishes are classical, and presentation mostly modernist. The kitchen seems to like combining raw and cooked versions of the same ingredient in a dish, as witnessed in first-course salad featuring artichokes two ways, and a main course of olive-crusted bluefin tuna served with mandolin-shredded raw fennel and juicy grilled fennel. The generous log of prime fish was cooked perfectly medium rare. However, dish of the night (maybe of the year) was spaghetti with squid, green chilli, spring onions and herbs. Succulent, light, moreishly piquant, it made a discreet salute to Chinese cuisine without falling into any fusion traps. Excellent asparagus risotto, meanwhile, could not have been more traditional or authentic. Beautifully cherry-coloured Mandarossa rosé was full flavoured, complementing the warm weather and disparate dishes. Prices are at the high end, but Floriana is by no means poor value.
Babies and children welcome; high chairs. Booking advisable dinner. No-smoking tables. Restaurant available for hire. Separate room for parties, seats 25-45. Tables outdoors (4, pavement). **Map 14 F9.**

Isola
145 Knightsbridge, SW1X 7PA (7838 1044/ 1099). Knightsbridge tube. *Bar* **Open** 5pm-midnight Mon-Sat. **Snacks** £1.50-£8.50.
Restaurant **Lunch served** noon-3pm Mon-Fri; noon-3.30pm Sat. **Dinner served** 6-10.45pm Mon-Sat. **Main courses** £16-£25.
Both **Service** 12.5%. **Credit** AmEx, DC, MC, V.
Modern retro design (maybe *The Spy Who Loved Me*), low lighting, roomy tables and comfortably padded, lounge-style seats lend an intimate, sexy atmosphere to what is really just a cavernous open-plan basement. Isola's huge wine list, with scores by the glass, is seductive too, tempting you to spend more than you would perhaps like. We settled on an excellent Friuli red by Niedermeyer while greedily consuming lovely salty bread with olive oil – staff generously brought us more. The kitchen does not shy from using ingredients of fringe popularity; goat featured in a tasty tomatoey sauce for pappardelle. Another starter saw guanciale, a ham-like cut taken from pig's cheek, added to a salad served with scallops and capers. For mains, beef fillet came with foie gras and wonderfully tender gnocchi, while soft, creamy polenta provided a starchy bed for venison with cotechino sausages and fresh porcini. The apricot and almond tart was jalousie-style with puff pastry, rather than the typical fruits embedded in frangipane. Almonds also featured in another pleasing dessert of little chocolate fondants. Pleasant, efficient staff help make a visit something to look forward to – so why is Isola rarely crowded?
Babies and children welcome; high chairs. Booking advisable. Dress: smart casual. No-smoking area. Restaurant and bar available for hire. **Map 8 F9.**

San Lorenzo
22 Beauchamp Place, SW3 1NH (7584 1074). Knightsbridge tube. **Lunch served** 12.30-3pm, **dinner served** 7.30-11.30pm Mon-Sat. **Main courses** £17.50-£28.50. **Cover** £2.50. **No credit cards.**
It's a long time since dinner here cost under £1, but San Lorenzo wears its 41 years well. Warhol's 'Marilyn' and other Swinging Sixties art prints make the white tiled decor a time-warp treat, but the international roster of celebs who frequent the place are as hip and happening as Peter Sellers, Sophia Loren and the Stones were back in their day. Should Brad Pitt not be in town, expect large tables of It Girls ordering rocket salads and crudités with bagna cauda. We started simply: asparagus with olive oil and lemon, and rocket with parma ham and chilli oil. Sadly, much of the menu was unseasonal – wintry dishes with gorgonzola; rabbit with polenta. We could not resist the rich osso bucco with saffron risotto, but a more summery option was expensive turbot in a broth of oil, wine, basil and pachino tomatoes. The reasonably efficient service fell apart completely come dessert. Having waited too long to take our order, staff failed to mention that many options (ice-cream and sorbet dishes) were unavailable due to a broken freezer. Replacement plates of papaya and strawberries were generous, but the fruit would have benefited from a squeeze of lime. This rich person's canteen is enjoyable, but you'll pay gourmet prices for mediocre food.
Babies and children welcome; booster seats. Booking advisable Fri, Sat. Dress: smart casual; no shorts. Restaurant available for hire. Separate room for parties, seats 30. **Map 14 F9.**
For branch see index.

Zafferano
15 Lowndes Street, SW1X 9EY (7235 5800). Knightsbridge tube. **Lunch served** noon-2.30pm daily. **Dinner served** 7-11pm Mon-Sat; 7-10.30pm Sun. **Set lunch** £23.50 2 courses, £28.50 3 courses, £32.50 4 courses. **Set dinner** £29.50 2 courses, £37.50 3 courses, £41.50 4 courses. **Service** 12.5%. **Credit** AmEx, DC, MC, V.
There is an emerging sense that Zafferano, for a long time London's best Italian restaurant, is

resting on its bay leaves. Perhaps it's the lack of evolution on the menu. Dishes change seasonally, but otherwise it seems to rely on the classics established back when Giorgio Locatelli was head chef. Or maybe the staff are becoming over-confident given the persistently full room. Still, they handled our foolishly late arrival for dinner with grace; we were directed to the downstairs sitting room and presented with a plate of canapés and the menus. Well before the promised 20-minute waiting time was up, we were led to a table. So many dishes on the premium-priced menu required a supplement that it seemed a swizz to claim dinner was £37.50 for three courses. Osso bucco pasta parcels with saffron sauce is one reliable highlight that doesn't command a £5 surcharge, and the spring vegetable salad was delightful. The wine list features plenty of excellent bottles under £25. For romance, secure a table in the first room; the acoustics and layout of the second are more suited to business lunches and groups.
Babies and children welcome; high chairs. Booking essential, at least 1wk in advance for lunch, 4-6wks in advance for dinner. Dress: smart casual; no shorts (dinner). **Map 15 G9.**

Marble Arch W2

Al San Vincenzo
30 Connaught Street, W2 2AF (7262 9623). Marble Arch tube. **Lunch served** noon-3pm Mon-Fri. **Dinner served** 7-10pm Mon-Sat. **Main courses** £11.50-£18. **Credit** MC, V.
Nothing seems to dent the popularity of this long-standing restaurant. Perhaps it's the sense of domesticity that keeps customers returning, for dining here feels like eating in somebody's home. The menu is unwaveringly authentic, but expensive, especially given the lack of extras and special touches that turn eating out into a treat. On our visit, asparagus risotto lacked the intensity of buttery vegetable flavour required to make this dish a success. Herby grilled turbot, taken off the bone, also relied on simplicity, yet did so winningly, served with nothing but well-cooked broccoli florets. Hearts were broken when we learnt that the panettone bread and butter pudding was finished for the night, but consolation was found in a decent tiramisu. The desserts list also includes marzipan-stuffed dates, a rarely seen retro favourite. The short Italian wine list is uncomplicated and offers a satisfying range of prices.
Babies and children welcome; high chair. Booking advisable. Restaurant available for hire. **Map 8 F6.**

Marylebone W1

Caffè Caldesi
118 Marylebone Lane, W1U 2QF (7935 1144/ www.caffecaldesi.com). Bond Street tube. *Deli/bar* **Breakfast served** 8.30-11am Mon-Sat. **Meals served** 11am-11pm Mon-Sat; 10.30am-5pm Sun. **Main courses** £7-£9.50.
Bistro **Lunch served** noon-3pm, **dinner served** 6-11pm Mon-Sat. **Main courses** £9.50-£17.50.
Both **Service** 12.5%. **Credit** AmEx, JCB, MC, V.
Upstairs from this breezy café is a slightly more formal restaurant, where wooden tables are spaced wide apart on bare dark floorboards. Although the first-floor room is light and airy, the menu is not more grown up than that served below, and when crowded the venue isn't much more peaceful either (those floorboards). The menu offers around six starters, five or so classic pastas and a longer list of main courses based on meat, poultry and fish, so we were disappointed on our Sunday lunchtime visit to be handed a simpler 'brunch' menu of limited choice. Chicken salad with pesto dressing can easily be thrown together at home, and this version, although tasty and generous, was little better than a decent supermarket could have produced. Chocolate mousse and ricotta torta were the most tempting puds, and both arrived adequately prepared. The wine list starts at a reasonable £13.50, with the vast majority of

bottles under £30; it includes persuasive notes and helpful, vivid descriptions. Smiling, efficient staff brought excellent espresso to finish the meal. Caffè Caldesi is not sophisticated enough to be highly priced, but too expensive to be considered a bargain choice.
Babies and children welcome; high chairs; nappy-changing facilities. Booking advisable (bistro). Disabled: toilet. Restaurant and bar available for hire. Tables outside (7, pavement). Takeaway service (deli). **Map 9 G5**.
For branch (Caldesi Tuscan) see index.

Eddalino
10 Wigmore Street, W1U 2RD (7637 0789/ www.eddalino.co.uk). Bond Street or Oxford Circus tube. **Lunch served** noon-3pm, **dinner served** 6-10.30pm Mon-Sat. **Set lunch** £19.50 2 courses, £23 3 courses incl coffee. **Set meal** £27.50 2 courses, £34.50 3 courses, £38.50 4 courses. **Credit** AmEx, MC, V.
Andrew Lloyd Webber knows a good lunch, so we were interested to see him dining here during our weekday visit, when the restaurant attracted only three tables of customers. A pity, because the kitchen works hard at producing elegant, interesting food, and presenting it lavishly. A huge cheese trolley is something of a focal point amid the conservative decor, and even at lunch the chef sends out appetisers (a lovely collection of olives, caperberries and bread rolls with oil), amuse-bouches (white onion purée with basil oil), pre-desserts (chocolate and pistachio 'salami' with red fruit sauce) and petits fours (including apricot jam tarts and amaretti). It's a miracle we could manage three courses. Highlight of the meal was a wonderfully thick, lusciously tender veal chop. We also enjoyed pale-green courgette spätzle with speck and mushrooms, and aubergine puff pastry tartlet with tomato, mozzarella and a pretty ball of rocket on top. Chocolate fondant was expertly presented but overcooked, so that the centre was not molten, but we were revived with excellent espresso. Staff were attentive, gracious and really seemed to understand the chef's challenging menu.
Babies and children welcome; high chairs. Booking advisable. No-smoking tables. Restaurant available for hire. Separate area for parties, seats 30. Tables outdoors (2, pavement). **Map 9 H5**.

★ Locanda Locatelli
8 Seymour Street, W1H 7JZ (7935 9088/ www.locandalocatelli.com). Marble Arch tube. **Lunch served** noon-3pm Mon-Sat. **Dinner served** 7-11pm Mon-Thur; 7-11.30pm Fri, Sat. **Main courses** £16-£30. **Credit** AmEx, JCB, MC, V.
It may seem that, as the UK's foremost Italian chef, Giorgio Locatelli can do no wrong, but someone in this outfit certainly can. Locanda Locatelli was universally hailed when it opened in 2002, and tables were almost impossible to secure unless you were prepared to open next year's diary. In such a feeding frenzy, bouts of slow service were to be expected and forgiven, but after two and a half years, this problem should have been sorted out. Yet once again, we spent so long waiting for our main courses we could have fallen asleep on the seductively comfy banquette. That only one of the dishes – a main course of nasello in scabeccio (steamed hake with garlic and vinegar) – was truly impressive made matters all the more disappointing. Things started well enough: a reasonably priced bottle of prosecco, a creamy soup of chickpeas with strips of grilled squid, and a rich oxtail ravioli. Our other main, a plate of smoked venison with celeriac, was pleasing too. There were mixed views on whether desserts were delicious or simply interesting; the mango and strawberry lasagne actually included pasta layers, while the millefoglie had a curious parmesan aftertaste. Locanda Locatelli remains a highly enjoyable restaurant, but can do better.
Babies and children welcome; high chairs; nappy-changing facilities (in hotel). Booking advisable, well in advance. Disabled: toilet (in hotel). Dress: smart casual. **Map 9 G6**.

Mayfair W1

★ Alloro
19-20 Dover Street, W1X 4LU (7495 4768). Green Park tube.
Bar **Open** noon-midnight Mon-Fri; 6pm-midnight Sat. **Main courses** £8-£16.
Restaurant **Lunch served** noon-2.30pm Mon-Fri. **Dinner served** 7-10.30pm Mon-Sat. **Set lunch** £23 2 courses, £26 3 courses. **Set dinner** £27.50 2 courses, £31.50 3 courses, £35 4 courses. **Service** 12.5%.
Both **Credit** AmEx, DC, JCB, MC, V.
The discreet frontage gives few hints at the delights within this restaurant, and when you survey the conservative modern decor you are unlikely to gauge the flair in the kitchen – but Alloro is something of a dark horse that wins by

Best Restaurant Cookbooks

Just visited a restaurant, tasted something great, and want to recreate it at home? That's what the restaurant cookbook is for. Here are some of our faves.

The Cinnamon Club Cookbook
By Iqbal Wahhab & Vivek Singh (Absolute Press). From the creators of one of Britain's best Modern Indian restaurants (*see p125*).

Big Flavours & Rough Edges
By David Eyre & the Eagle cooks (Headline). Recipes from the pioneering Farringdon gastropub (*see p90*).

The Gate Vegetarian Cookbook
By Adrian & Michael Daniel (Mitchell Beazley). From one of London's finest veggie restaurants (*see p269*).

Casa Del Moro
By Sam & Sam Clark (Ebury Press). The bestselling *Moro: The Cookbook* from the much-praised Spanish restaurant (*see p237*) gets a follow-up, published in November 2004.

Nobu Now
By Nobu Matsuhisa (Quadrille). After *Nobu: The Cookbook* comes a second book (due out November 2004) from the master behind acclaimed Japanese restaurant Nobu (*see p175*).

The Real Greek At Home
By Theodore Kyriakou & Charles Campion (Mitchell Beazley). Pioneering modern Greek cooking. *See p108*.

River Café Cookbook
By Rose Gray & Ruth Rogers (Ebury Press). Four to choose from: yellow, blue, green and 'easy'; version 2 of 'easy' is due out in May 2005. *See p160*.

Sally Clarke's Book
By Sally Clarke (Grub Street). The subtitle says it all: 'Recipes from a Restaurant, Shop & Bakery'. *See p215*.

The Wagamama Cookbook
By Hugo Arnold (Kyle Cathie). Learn the secrets of the mega-successful noodle bar chain. *See p233*.

furlongs. Efficient, formal but friendly service is led by an entertaining maître d' who can talk at length about food, wine and anything else. Our preferred starter of deep-fried courgette flowers was unavailable, so we opted for a special of salty calamari and zucchine fritte. Dishes of roast rabbit (served in a huge bowl with numerous fresh peas) and lamb were well executed, and the soft tender gnocchi delightful. If this sounds too traditional, don't be fooled; there are flamboyant touches, especially when it comes to presentation. Puddings left a strong impression, particularly the wonderfully unusual almond bavarese. Wrapped up in a set-price package, with a wide choice of fine wines, a meal here is a gift to savour.
Babies and children admitted. Booking advisable. Restaurant and bar available for hire. Separate room for parties, seats 16. Tables outdoors (3, pavement). **Map 9 J7**.

Cecconi's
5A Burlington Gardens, W1S 3EW (7434 1500). Green Park tube. **Breakfast served** 8-11am Mon-Fri. **Brunch served** 10am-4pm Sun. **Lunch served** noon-3pm Mon-Fri. **Dinner served** 6.30-11.30pm Mon-Fri; 6.30-11.30pm Sat; 6.30-10.30pm Sun. **Main courses** £10-£27.50. **Service** 12.5%. **Credit** AmEx, DC, JCB, MC, V.
Sinking into the leather booths at this sexy, sophisticated restaurant gives a sense of excited anticipation. Cecconi's, after all, is one of London's best Italian restaurants. Or is it? Not if our last visit is indicative. Nothing was truly bad, but very little was anything special either. Here, a dish of Tuscan prosciutto, melon, figs and balsamic should be the most exquisite you can find, but the figs were so unripe they shouldn't have been on the menu. We would have been better ordering one of the carpaccios or tartares (a choice of monkfish, tuna, beef or royal black bream), each of which has its own specially matched dressing added with a flourish at tableside. Although the restaurant wasn't crowded, service was patchy, and our wine order wasn't taken until we were halfway through the starters. Desserts of panna cotta with strawberry and prosecco jelly, and chocolate tart with mint sorbet were fine but unmemorable. Cecconi's can do better.
Babies and children welcome; high chairs. Booking advisable. Disabled: toilet. **Map 9 J7**.

Sartoria
20 Savile Row, W1X 1AE (7534 7000/ www.conran.com). Oxford Circus or Piccadilly Circus tube.
Bar **Open** noon-11pm Mon-Sat; 6.30-10pm Sun. **Set meal** £12.95 2 courses, £16.95 3 courses.
Restaurant **Lunch served** noon-3pm Mon-Fri. **Dinner served** 6.30-11.30pm Mon-Thur; 5-11.30pm Fri, Sat; 6.30-10pm Sun. **Main courses** £15-£18.50. **Set meal** (6.30-8pm) £17.95 2 courses, £21 3 courses.
Both **Service** 12.5%. **Credit** AmEx, DC, MC, V.
Maybe we've been coming at the wrong times, but we can't think of an occasion when we've found Sartoria crowded, and those customers who were dining tended to be Japanese and American. It's a pity, for this is a fine, if pricey, restaurant. The grey fabric booth seating and spacious tables make the ambience sumptuously relaxing – all the better to enjoy reading the extensive Italian wine list. Service was patchy on our most recent visit, and we had trouble placing the wine order; later we waited an age for the bill to arrive. But the food was very pleasant indeed. Dishes are intelligently modern, sometimes disarmingly simple, and based on excellent ingredients. Cromer crab dressed with lemon and olive oil and served with a crisp bruschetta makes an unmissable starter, though the own-made filled pastas are excellent too. Typical main courses include lamb with stuffed baked tomatoes, and wonderful roast suckling pig flavoured with herbs and spices. For dessert, try a Venetian take on rice pudding, or something chocolatey. One of Conran's finest.
Babies and children welcome; high chairs. Booking advisable; essential lunch. Disabled: toilet. Entertainment: pianist 7-10pm Thur-Sat. Restaurant available for hire. Separate rooms for parties, seating 20 and 40. **Map 9 J7**.

Manicomio. See p160.

Piccadilly SW1

Quod

57 Haymarket, SW1Y 4QX (7925 1234/ www.quod.co.uk). Embankment or Piccadilly Circus tube/Charing Cross tube/rail. **Breakfast served** 8am-11.30pm Mon-Fri. **Afternoon tea served** 3-4.30pm, **meals served** noon-midnight Mon-Sat. **Main courses** £8.35-£16.75. **Set meal** (4-7pm, 10pm-midnight) £10.95 2 courses. **Service** 12.5%. **Credit** AmEx, DC, JCB, MC, V.

Subtle reworking of the colours, textures and artwork in this gigantic mezzanined space has resulted in a more intimate atmosphere at this restaurant, though the modern portraits are still bold and unusual. The front bar area works well as a casual eaterie and is handy for the cinema, theatre or occasions touristique. For once we enjoyed the opportunity to watch sport on a wide-screen telly. A woman dining nearby was careful to tell the waiter that her slow-roasted lamb shank was not up to the usual standard – he handled the complaint with good grace once he realised how many times she had eaten the dish in the past. The specials board offered a diversion from the standard 'Italian plus burgers and pizza' menu; duck with pak choi, mushrooms and a tasty gravy was executed with finesse. Pastas included good renditions of pappardelle with prawns, courgettes and cherry tomatoes, and potato gnocchi with gorgonzola and spinach sauce. Our Bloody Mary was powerful, though the celery salt was a little overpowering. To finish, greek yoghurt cake with crushed amaretti appealed, but in the end we opted to share a scrumptious plate of profiteroles with chocolate sauce. Service was relaxed and pleasant, though in a fairly uncrowded room staff seemed pleased to have the chance to watch TV too.
Babies and children welcome; children's menu; high chairs. Disabled: toilet. No-smoking tables. Restaurant available for hire. Separate rooms for parties, seating 10-120. **Map 17 K7**.

St James's SW1

Al Duca

4-5 Duke of York Street, SW1Y 6LA (7839 3090). Green Park or Piccadilly Circus tube. **Lunch served** noon-2.30pm Mon-Fri; 12.30-3pm Sat. **Dinner served** 6-11pm Mon-Sat. **Set lunch** £17.50 2 courses, £20.50 3 courses, £23.50 4 courses. **Set dinner** £20 2 courses, £24 3 courses, £28 4 courses. **Service** 12.5%. **Credit** AmEx, DC, MC, V.

Despite booking well in advance, we were made to wait for our lunchtime table at this fairly conservative contemporary restaurant. Waiting staff and kitchen seem to think themselves a cut above the competition. The menu offers a selection of classics – buffalo mozzarella and tomato salad, char-grilled chicken and wilted spinach, calf's liver with mash – plus several more intriguing combinations. A main course of pan-fried wild sea bass featured an excellent piece of fish, but this didn't sit well with the strong flavour of the accompanying swiss chard, nor with the two slices of thick salty bacon and the butter sauce that also came with it. However, orecchiette with broccoli, spicy sausage and pecorino worked well, as did a starter of smoked swordfish carpaccio. It took the waiter so long to take our dessert order that we weren't surprised when he returned some time later to tell us the kitchen had run out of chocolate and walnut tart. Banana panna cotta with liquorice caramel sauce was a satisfying replacement, though we also liked the sound of orange jelly with Grand Marnier zabaglione and mint granita. When the bill finally arrived, we were a little uncomfortable with the cost given the standard of food and the slow service.

Babies and children welcome. Dress: no shorts. Restaurant available for hire (Sun). **Map 17 J7**.

Shumi NEW

23 St James's Street, SW1A 1HA (7747 9380/ www.shumi-london.com). Green Park tube. **Lunch served** noon-2.45pm Mon-Fri. **Dinner served** 6.30-11pm Mon-Sat. **Main courses** £12-£20. **Set lunch** £19.50 2 courses, £23.50 3 courses. **Service** 12.5%. **Credit** AmEx, MC, V.

Shumi's pretentious opening gambit was a fusion of ciabatta and chopsticks. You can just imagine the planning meetings: 'Like, Japanese food is so fashionable now and, wow, carpaccio and sashimi are, like, both raw fish.' If the pictures of Posh Spice, Liam Gallagher, et al, lining the escalators up to the first-floor restaurant were also dumped, we could really go for this place. The cool, understated interior oozes relaxed glamour and beautifully complements the panoramic view of St James's. Staff are friendly, keen and efficient. The set lunch menu, with three dishes per course, offers excellent value plus the fun option of including a glass of wine matched to each dish. Mark-ups on wines vary; plenty were fairly priced given the location, others are pitched at those who want to flash their cash. A fabulously fresh pasta and bean

soup suited the warm weather. Pan-fried cod fillet came with lentils and pancetta, while tender sweet lamb loin was stacked on a round of polenta and topped with roasted peppers and a proud stalk of rosemary. Desserts included grappa panna cotta with caramelised oranges: nice and simple, but interesting. On the main menu, dishes are not just hip, but hip-and-thigh-conscious; still capable of pleasing the celebrity set, even though the Italian Nobu theme has bid 'sayonara'.

Babies and children welcome. Separate room for parties, seats 8. Tables outdoors (13, pavement). **Map 17 J8**.

Soho W1

Quo Vadis

26-29 Dean Street, W1T 6LL (7437 9585/ www.whitestarline.org.uk). Leicester Square or Piccadilly Circus tube. **Lunch served** noon-2.30pm Mon-Fri. **Dinner served** 5.30-11pm Mon-Sat. **Main courses** £10.50-£19. **Set meal** (lunch, 5.30-6.30pm) £14.95 2 courses, £19.95 3 courses. **Credit** AmEx, DC, JCB, MC, V.

An irreverent decor combining Hirst-esque art (including skeleton and butterfly collections), stained glass and clubby seating make Quo Vadis an amusing and comfortable restaurant to while away the evening. The menu blends classic and innovative Italian, but superb presentation skills lift the accomplished cooking to a higher realm. Sicilian salad arrived looking more like something from Barcelona thanks to its design – triangles of beetroot sitting on end, precise rectangles of ricotta and a mound of finely shredded spinach in the centre. A main of lamb with herb topping was presented as precise cubes of meat that tasted as good as they looked. Delicious tiny gnocchi came with smoked tomato and borlotti beans; there were just a few of the latter, but they were fat, mealy specimens. Mains went well with a Tuscan sangiovese, from a wine list that starts at £13.50

for Australian bottles, and takes in a number of French varieties too. Chocolate fondant was thick and hot, accompanied by mango sorbet. Ricotta chocolate terrine was glazed with orange caramel that, like all before it, could have been the work of Gaudi. The restaurant was packed, and the delightful staff strained a little to maintain full efficiency. A charming venue.

Children admitted. Booking advisable. Dress: smart casual. Separate rooms for parties, seating 12, 32 and 80. **Map 17 K6**.

Signor Zilli

40-41 Dean Street, W1V 5AB (restaurant 7734 3924/bar 7734 1853/www.zillialdo.com). Leicester Square or Piccadilly Circus tube.
Bar **Open** noon-midnight, **meals served** noon-11pm Mon-Sat. **Main courses** £7.50-£16.50.
Restaurant **Lunch served** noon-3pm Mon-Fri. **Dinner served** 6-11.30pm Mon-Sat. **Main courses** £7-£21.
Both **Credit** AmEx, DC, JCB, MC, V.

It may be good feng shui, but in a damp, dingy basement you really don't need an aquarium to add more water to the atmosphere. Zilli has done its best to make the downstairs dining area pleasant, but such a low-ceilinged, airless room is best used for storage, not supper. If you can't get a table in the frescoed upstairs dining room, open to the street, we'd suggest eating elsewhere. But the crowds that flock to this jumping joint clearly don't agree. The menu, while based on Italian cuisine, picks magpie-fashion from various food trends and is prone to listing items such as mango salsa. Zilli has clearly clocked the popularity of gastropubs, offering traditional cod and chips, Italian sausages with caramelised onions and mash, and steak with horseradish sauce. Fusion cooking has not escaped notice either, as exemplified in our salty crumbed sea bass with chunks of lemongrass, served on angel hair pasta with pesto and black olives. Pork rolls with gorgonzola sauce came with reasonable

Olivo. See p151.

chips, though it was a cauliflower soup with a gratinated camembert topping that was the surprising hit of the night. That, and a lovely Chianti for £18 from a short wine list that takes in France and Australia, as well as Italy.
Babies and children welcome; high chairs. Bar available for hire. Booking advisable (restaurant). Tables outdoors (4, pavement). **Map 17 K6**.

Vasco & Piero's Pavilion

15 Poland Street, W1F 8QE (7437 8774/ www.vascosfood.com). Oxford Circus, Piccadilly Circus or Tottenham Court Road tube. **Lunch served** noon-3pm Mon-Fri. **Dinner served** 6-11pm Mon-Sat. **Main courses** £9.50-£15.50. **Set meal** (lunch, 6-7pm Mon-Fri) £14.50 2 courses. **Set dinner** £21 2 courses, £25 3 courses. **Service** 12.5%. **Credit** AmEx, DC, JCB, MC, V.
How comfortable you find this restaurant depends on where you are sitting. Most of the tables for two are impossibly small and crammed in like sardine pâté. The chairs aren't very big either. No wonder tables turn over so frequently. However, there's no booting out patrons at a set hour – many have taken an after-work drink and are happy just to eat and go. Apart from the kitchen's infatuation with ginger (such as tuna carpaccio with avocado and ginger dressing), most dishes on the menu are pure Italian and no worse for it. A starter of spinach and ricotta pasta parcels with sage and butter sauce showed how delicious familiar recipes can be when done properly. Main courses tend to be simple affairs of meat, chicken and fish, accurately grilled, pan-roasted or fried, with a simple vegetable accompaniment such as broccoli or potatoes. The owners' Umbrian heritage ensures that chickpeas and lentils feature frequently, along with the delicious roast Umbrian ham, though the modest wine list roams throughout Italy.
Booking advisable. Children over 6 years admitted. Separate room for parties, seats 36. **Map 17 J6**.

Trafalgar Square WC2

Crivelli's Garden

National Gallery, Trafalgar Square, WC2N 5DN (7747 2869/www.thenationalgallery.com). Embankment, Leicester Square or Piccadilly Circus tube/Charing Cross tube/rail. **Lunch served** 11.30am-4pm daily. **Dinner served** 5.30-7.45pm Wed. **Main courses** £9-£13.50. **Set lunch** available during special exhibitions only; phone for details. **Service** 12.5%. **Credit** AmEx, JCB, MC, V.
We've had some excellent meals at this stylishly designed and comfortable, casual restaurant in the Sainsbury wing of the National Gallery, but in recent times have found Crivelli's to be not quite as good as it once was. Portions, especially for the starters and salads, are very generous, no doubt because most customers are not looking to run the whole three courses. That may also account for the rocket-with-everything menu – most people won't notice that it seems to appear a lot. Taleggio salad (with rocket) saw the orange rind of the cheese peeled away and the paste dusted with finely grated cheese so it looked like it was wearing a fluffy jumper. Grilled octopus salad would have benefited from better cleaning to help the seafood look more attractive. For mains, a large piece of chicken was vividly striped from the char-grill and served with tomatoes and, of course, rocket. Best of the lot was the vegetable lasagne, a pleasingly light combination of exotic mushrooms, asparagus, tomato and mozzarella. All wines are under £25 – we chose a yeasty, but reasonably quaffable pinot grigio. Dessert was a disappointing affair: a dry banana cake with unappealing, grey, sun-dried banana in the base, badly mismatched with coffee-flavoured sauce and ice-cream.
Babies and children welcome; children's menu; high chairs; nappy-changing facilities (in National Gallery). Disabled: toilet. No smoking. **Map 18 K7**.

Westminster SW1

Quirinale

North Court, 1 Great Peter Street, SW1P 3LL (7222 7080). St James's Park or Westminster tube. **Lunch served** noon-2.30pm, **dinner served** 6-10.30pm Mon-Fri. **Main courses** £12-£15. **Service** 12.5%. **Credit** AmEx, DC, MC, V.
While many restaurants talk about serving seasonal food, few are as faithful to the promise as Quirinale. This elegantly converted basement operation is deep in New Labour territory and heavy with the patronage of that party's apparatchiks. Winter sees lots of warming ingredients such as cabbage, mushrooms, chestnuts, chickpeas and polenta on the menu. Pizzocheri (ribboned buckwheat pasta) was served traditionally with savoy cabbage and potatoes, while orecchiette came with char-grilled scallops and pumpkin sauce. The scallops were divine, but the sweet-tasting sauce lacked a deep pumpkin flavour and might have benefited from use of the roasted vegetable. Also from the char-grill were finely etched curls of calamari, served with chickpea purée, decorative touches of herb emulsion and a chervil salad. Molten chocolate budino maintained the high standards, but apple cake with caramel was a little dry. From the wine list, Rubrato dei Feudi di San Gregorio 2001 was a keenly priced bottle endorsed by the maître d'; it matched perfectly the diverse range of dishes.
Babies and children admitted. Booking advisable. **Map 16 L10**.

Bayswater W2

★ Assaggi

First Floor, 39 Chepstow Place, W2 4TS (7792 5501). Bayswater, Queensway or Notting Hill Gate tube. **Lunch served** 12.30-2.30pm Mon-Fri;

1-2.30pm Sat. **Dinner served** 7.30-11pm Mon-Sat. **Main courses** £16.95-£19.95. **Credit** DC, MC, V.

Although based above a pub, this simply designed small room is a pleasure to dine in, with enchanting flower arrangements, well-kept window boxes and vibrant walls and artwork. Service hits the pitch-perfect note of being attentive yet unhurried, and it is a pleasure to listen to staff run through the day's menu and specials. The bread basket contained a simple sheet of carta di musica and two little squares of focaccia – just as well, because saving space for the wonderfully creamy, nutmeg-flavoured pure di patate should be a priority. Assaggi's menu does not change substantially from year to year and is not big on pasta, but there is a healthy choice of starters. On our visit, beautiful fresh scallops sat atop finely chopped salad with fregola pasta and a vivid-yellow saffron emulsion, while a special of white crab was served with a tangle of celery ribbons dressed with olive oil and lemon. Next, calf's liver was sprinkled prettily with deep-fried spring onions; it was expertly cooked, as was the grilled beef, which came with the thinnest of potato chips. For dessert, vanilla bavarese was doused with fine espresso, adding a surprisingly complex flavour. A substantial flourless chocolate cake had a reasonable dark chocolate taste and came with white chocolate ice-cream: good rather than superb, making it the exception here.
Babies and children welcome; booster seats. Booking advisable. **Map 7 B6.**

Chelsea SW3

Manicomio NEW

85 Duke of York Square, SW3 4LY (7730 3366/ www.manicomio.co.uk). Sloane Square tube. **Deli Open** 8am-7pm Mon-Fri; 10am-7pm Sat; 10am-6pm Sun. *Restaurant* **Lunch served** noon-3pm Mon-Fri; noon-5pm Sat, Sun. **Dinner served** 6.30-10.30pm Mon-Sat; 6.30-10pm Sun. **Main courses** £10.50-£19.75. **Service** 12.5%. **Credit** AmEx, JCB, MC, V.

We were greeted like old friends on our first visit to Manicomio, the main restaurant in the open-air shopping plaza carved from the Duke of York's territorial army barracks. Owned by Andrew and Ninai Zarach of Italian food import company Machiavelli Foods, it boasts a bar area and next-door deli in addition to the restaurant, which is already a hit with local families. Two of the most appealing starters – including pan-fried mackerel with carrots and peppers – were off the menu on our Sunday evening visit, so we opted to open with pastas. A divine dish of egg tagliatelle came with juicy stock sauce, strips of tender roast lamb and a hint of fresh mint. Seafood ravioli had a wonderfully textured filling of prawn chunks and white fish, the parcels doused with saffron and mussel sauce. Also delightful was a main of roast lamb with black olive crust and aubergine purée, but pan-fried dorade (bream) with cannellini beans and tomatoes didn't scale similar heights. Compensation was found in a smooth Umbrian red, astonishingly inexpensive given its quality. Slight undercooking of the almondy apricot clafoutis gave this dessert extra succulence, but our favourite was the chocolate and raspberry fondant with vanilla ice-cream. A clever, classy and convenient outfit.
Babies and children welcome; high chairs. Booking advisable. No-smoking tables. Separate room for parties seats 30. Tables outdoors (30, terrace). **Map 14 F11.**

Hammersmith W6

★ The River Café

Thames Wharf, Rainville Road, W6 9HA (7386 4200/www.rivercafe.co.uk). Hammersmith tube. **Lunch served** 12.30-3pm daily. **Dinner served** 7-9.30pm Mon-Sat. **Main courses** £23-£32. **Service** 12.5%. **Credit** AmEx, DC, MC, V.

Pray for sunny weather that allows you to sit in the courtyard on visits to the River Café. On colder, wetter days, patrons are crammed into the indoor dining area with only a foot or so between tables, and the cacophony is ear-splitting. But it's a small price to pay for dining at this highly enjoyable stalwart. The largest price you'll be paying is the bill. Main courses now hit £32 for the turbot (which, like many of the best dishes, comes from the wood-fired oven), but there are notably low prices on the enjoyably wide-ranging wine list. Two reds, a Valpolicella and pinot nero, are available chilled, the latter an excellent full-flavoured alternative to rosé and a fine match for our john dory with roast potatoes. Another main of three thick pieces of lamb, with salsa verde, wood-roasted aubergines and smashed cannellini beans was perfect and generous. Desserts included summer pud made with Valpolicella, a strawberry granita, signature chocolate nemesis, and a simple but sumptuous burned sugar caramel ice-cream. Apart from a delay with our wine order – we were halfway through starters before the bottle arrived – service on this visit was prompt, attentive and charming.
Babies and children welcome; high chairs. Booking essential. Disabled: toilet. Dress: smart casual. No cigars or pipes. Tables outdoors (15, terrace). **Map 20 C5.**

Holland Park W11

Edera

148 Holland Park Avenue, W11 4UE (7221 6090). Holland Park tube. **Coffee served** 10am-noon, **lunch served** noon-3pm, **dinner served** 6.30-11pm daily. **Main courses** £8.50-£14. **Set dinner** £21.50 2 courses, £25.50 3 courses. **Credit** AmEx, MC, V.

The 13th restaurant to join the A-Z group, Edera is a long thin property, very cleverly designed with staggered levels of seating creating intimate spaces. We found the menu on our lunchtime visit slightly too simple, but everything was beautifully presented. Efficient, disciplined staff appear with large trays of fancy plates, but otherwise there is little formality here. Four of the pasta dishes were suitable for vegetarians. A few dishes commanded supplements; for example, £2 for a generous portion of char-grilled sea bass with courgettes and aubergine. Calf's liver was thinly sliced and served with sweet, succulent, crisp onions and crunchy, salty pancetta. Starters included cauliflower soup with truffle oil, grilled vegetables, and asparagus with fried egg and parmesan crisps. We shouldn't have bothered with dessert – the grappa panna cotta with grapes poached in red wine syrup was dreary, and the chocolate almond cake did not taste chocolatey at all, especially when hammered with mint ice-cream. The appealing wine list starts at just £12.50 for a decent Sardinian white, and includes six of both colours by the glass.
Babies and children admitted. Booking advisable dinner. Restaurant available for hire. Separate room for parties, seats 12. Tables outdoors (4, pavement). **Map 19 B5.**

Ladbroke Grove W11

Essenza NEW

210 Kensington Park Road, W11 1NR (7792 1066). Ladbroke Grove tube. **Lunch served** 12.30-3pm Mon-Fri, Sun; noon-5pm Sat. **Dinner served** 6.30-11pm Mon-Fri; 6.30-11.30pm Sat; 6.30-10.30pm Sun. **Main courses** £13-£14.50. **Set lunch** £10 2 courses. **Service** 12.5%. **Credit** MC, V.

On a street that already houses two mid-priced Italian trattoria-style restaurants, it seems strange to open another, yet Essenza has acquired fans, especially among local families. Staff work hard to sell their favoured items on the specials list; wine selections are good value; and portions are generous. Tagliatelle with porcini and bacon sauce featured an abundance of lovely, fresh-tasting mushrooms and a succulent gravy. Saffron risotto with seafood arrived very quickly as a starter, but the homely texture was not off-putting and the chunks of squid, prawns and scallops were sweet and tender. Most of the main courses come from the char-grill: we enjoyed a huge plate of squid with chilli and rocket, as well as a special of medium-rare roast rack of lamb with moreish rosemary sauce. Dessert of chocolate fondant with chocolate and custard sauces was accurately cooked to give a rich and sumptuously oozy centre – such a grand finale that we wanted an encore. Service from the black-shirted Italian staff was perhaps a little too keen, but we prefer that to being left to flounder.
Babies and children welcome; high chairs. Booking essential Wed-Sun. Tables outdoors (2, pavement). **Map 19 B2.**

Mediterraneo

37 Kensington Park Road, W11 2EU (7792 3131). Notting Hill Gate tube. **Lunch served** 12.30-3pm Mon-Fri; 12.30-4pm Sat; 12.30-3.45pm Sun. **Dinner served** 6.30-11.30pm Mon-Sat; 6.30-10.30pm Sun. **Main courses** £12.80-£16.50. **Set lunch** £12.50 2 courses incl coffee. **Service** 12.5%. **Credit** AmEx, JCB, MC, V.

Tables are turned frequently and seamlessly in this popular trattoria, but even so staff seemed too anxious to take our order. Mediterraneo is a long-established high with Notting Hill's well-to-do, slightly trendy families. Almost nothing changes on the menu or in the decor from year to year – clearly a case of 'if it ain't broke…'. Rock oysters are a popular starter, available in sixes, nines or by the dozen. We ordered ribollita, a traditional Tuscan soup of beans, bread and curly black cabbage, but while it contained the proper cavolo nero, the dish was inauthentically watery. The list of main courses is based on the char-grill, and evocative of summer. We ordered polenta with porcini and shaved truffle; it had a wonderful aroma, but the porridge was oversalted, ruining the dish. Good points included excellent zucchine fritte, a huge wedge of rich and sweet chocolate mousse for dessert, and a nice rendition of panna cotta. You're also likely to find something satisfying on the broad wine list.
Babies and children welcome; high chairs. Booking advisable; essential dinner. Tables outdoors (3, pavement). **Map 19 B3. For branch (Osteria Basilico) see index.**

Kensington SW7, W8

Brunello NEW

Baglioni Hotel, 60 Hyde Park Gate, Kensington Road, SW7 5BB (7368 5700). High Street Kensington tube. **Breakfast served** 7-10.30am, **lunch served** noon-2.30pm, **dinner served** 7.30-10.30pm daily. **Set lunch** £18 2 courses, £23 3 courses, £26 4 courses. **Main courses** £11-£24. **Service** 12.5%. **Credit** AmEx, MC, V.

From the outside this looks like a nondescript west London hotel, but step through the doors and your eyes will be out of their sockets faster than a Ferrari off the grid. The open-plan bar, restaurant and foyer area is outrageously funky: gold leaf, velvet, ornate black glass chandeliers, massive arrangements of white flowers. Good-looking Italian staff swarm like bees around your soon-to-be-depleted wallet, swooning about the special starter of the day (fish soup with garlic bread), but failing to mention that it costs £22. The extensive wine list is fascinating; finding bottles under £25 a challenge in itself. But no one in the crowded restaurant seems to care – they are too busy enjoying the excellent food. The menu features plenty of luxury (quite unnecessary) ingredients, such as beluga caviar and black truffle. Halibut confit in olive oil was a wonderful piece of lightly cured and tender fish, sitting on soft sliced potato, with strands of raw fennel to add crispness. 'Modern style' veal milanese featured excellent juicy meat and was artfully presented, but still reminded us of breaded rissoles at school. Prices of desserts are so high we thought they were in lire; tropical fruit salad with passion fruit sorbet cost £10. However, we liked the sound of champagne mousse with peach jelly and moscato wine sabayon. Indeed, we liked an awful lot about this place – except the exorbitant bill.
Babies and children welcome; high chair. Book Fri, Sat. Tables outdoors (5, terrace). **Map 7 C9.**

★ Timo

343 Kensington High Street, W8 6NW (7603 3888/www.atozrestaurants.com). High Street Kensington tube. **Lunch served** noon-3pm Mon-Sat; noon-3.30pm Sun. **Dinner served** 7-11pm Mon-Sat; 7-10.30pm Sun. **Set lunch** £11 1 course, £18.50 2 courses, £21.50 3 courses, £24.50 4 courses. **Set dinner** £24.50 2 courses, £29.50 3 courses, £32.50 4 courses. **Service** 12.5%. **Credit** AmEx, DC, JCB, MC, V.
Extensive use of calming white, and some pretty, panoramic artworks bring a tranquil air to this sophisticated member of the A-Z restaurant group. Evenings tend to get busy, but lunchtimes may see as few as two or three tables of customers. Staff know what they are doing, yet tend to slack off at times; on a recent lunchtime visit, we had trouble finding anyone from whom to request the bill. However, Timo's delightful food and artful presentation more than compensate. We have fond memories of saffron gnocchi with prawns, broad beans and delightful nuggets of squid. Tuna tartare arrived as a piece of conceptual art, the fish shaped into a cone and the dressing balanced in an oriental spoon. Other typical starters include a grilled disc of goat's cheese served with green beans and roast peppers. Main courses can be as simple as medium-rare salmon fillet with wilted spinach, or sophisticated compilations with seductively sticky sauces. The generous cheese platter, impressively arranged on a slate board, makes cheese lovers feel wonderfully indulged. As with other restaurants under the clever ownership, Timo's wine list is crafted to suit all pockets.
Babies and children welcome. Booking advisable. No-smoking area. Restaurant available for hire. Separate room for parties, seats 18. **Map 13 A9.**

Maida Vale W9

Green Olive

5 Warwick Place, W9 2PX (7289 2469). Warwick Avenue tube. **Lunch served** 12.30-2.30pm Mon-Sat; 12.30-2.45pm Sun. **Dinner served** 7-10pm Mon-Sat. **Set lunch** £18 2 courses, £23 3 courses, £26 4 courses. **Set dinner** £21.50 2 courses, £26.50 3 courses, £30 4 courses. **Service** 12.5%. **Credit** AmEx, JCB, MC, V.
A small, intimate but airy dining room, Green Olive is serenely positioned on a quiet road, making it an ideal setting for a relaxing Sunday lunch or weeknight treat. Soft white curtains and pale creamy paintwork lighten the exposed brickwork walls hung with artistic black and white photographs. This restaurant is a long-time favourite, but service was disappointingly offhand on our most recent visit, and the cooking no more than competent, lacking its usual wow factor. The menu is an enticing read, and dishes of roast lamb fillet and potatoes, and roast cod with olive oil mash, though elegantly presented, give cosy satisfaction. Pastas feature classic ingredients combined inventively – witness aubergine ravioli with taleggio fondue, or the half-moon shaped parcels of goat's cheese and red pepper with amaretto sauce. Traditionalists will enjoy tagliatelle with wild mushrooms or linguine with seafood. There is an excellent cheese platter, where specimens can be sampled with mostarda di cremona, but it's hard to sacrifice beautifully presented desserts such as chocolate tart with frangelico ice-cream, or semifreddo with caramelised mango. It's surprising that this restaurant isn't busier, especially at weekends. Savour the tranquillity.
Babies and children admitted. Booking advisable. Restaurant available for hire. Separate area for parties, seats 16. **Map 1 C4.**

Notting Hill W8

The Ark

122 Palace Gardens Terrace, W8 4RT (7229 4024/www.thearkrestaurant.co.uk). Notting Hill Gate tube. **Lunch served** 12.30-3pm Tue-Sun. **Dinner served** 6.30-11pm Mon-Sat. **Main courses** £10-£18. **Set lunch** £12.50 2 courses, £15 3 courses. **Service** 12.5%. **Credit** AmEx, MC, V.
Everyone wanted to eat al fresco on our last visit to this curiously positioned restaurant on Notting Hill's one-way system, but the cute little decked area at front is, well, too cute and too little. With the pot plants not at their most verdant, we weren't comfortably shielded from the road and began to wonder whether we should have opted for the dimly lit, almost Japanese interior, with its sumptuous fabrics in hot pink and dove grey. Despite a use of traditional Italian ingredients and combinations, the Ark's menu reads like that of a modern, sophisticated restaurant, thanks to a willingness to look beyond clichés. There were classics, such as a trio of bruschetta with tomato, chicken liver and mushroom toppings, plus lovely ricotta, basil and lemon ravioli with globe artichoke sauce, but also new ideas such as pan-fried sea bass served on a 'stew' of spelt and cannellini beans. A still red wine served chilled was highly recommended by the conscientious waiter and bridged the disparate ingredients of our meal perfectly for £22. Chocolate fondant with a yellowy white centre was spoiled by a burned exterior, the taste of which no decorative dusting of icing sugar could hide, but there was lovely chilled rice pudding too, accompanied by warm poached figs and a sprinkle of cinnamon. Despite only a few choices per course, we had no trouble opting for the good-value £15 set menu for Sunday lunch.
Babies and children welcome; high chairs. Booking advisable. Restaurant available for hire. Tables outdoors (4, terrace). **Map 7 B7.**

Olympia W14

Cibo

3 Russell Gardens, W14 8EZ (7371 6271/2085/ www.ciborestaurant.co.uk). Shepherd's Bush tube/Kensington (Olympia) tube/rail. **Lunch served** noon-2.30pm Mon-Fri, Sun. **Dinner served** 7-11pm Mon-Sat. **Main courses** £10.50-£23.50. **Set lunch** (Mon-Fri) £15.50 2 courses; (Sun) £18.95 2 courses, £21.95 3 courses. **Service** 12.5%. **Credit** AmEx, DC, JCB, MC, V.
Don't let the bizarre taste in artwork put you off – everything else about this relaxed joint speaks of good sense. Modest prices transform into an impression of excellent value once the steady procession of freebies starts arriving at the table, which is roomy enough to hold packed bread baskets, dishes of olives and other appetisers, as well as the huge colourful plates on which starters and main courses are served. Fish and shellfish (cooked in various ways, but particularly with refreshing sauces of tomato, wine and herbs) are a strong point, but we opted for lamb cutlets with radicchio and balsamic sauce, and calf's liver, both proving the kitchen knows how to treat meat well too. For dessert, it's hard to pass up the assiette of chocolate puds, but if you're too full (as is likely because portions are big), you're sure to find something temptingly light in the wide choice of affogato-style ice-cream desserts. Indeed, the only problem we had with our meal was a language barrier with the young Italian staff.
Babies and children welcome; high chair. Booking advisable dinner. Dress: smart casual. Restaurant available for hire. Separate rooms for parties, seating 12 and 16. Tables outdoors (4, pavement).

Westbourne Grove W11

Zucca

188 Westbourne Grove, W11 2RH (7727 0060). Notting Hill Gate tube. **Brunch served** noon-3.30pm Sun. **Lunch served** 12.30-3pm Mon-Fri; 12.30-3.30pm Sat. **Dinner served** 7-11pm Mon-Sat; 7-10.30pm Sun. **Main courses** £7.75-£14. **Set lunch** (Mon-Fri) £12.50 2 courses, £14.50 3 courses. **Service** 12.5%. **Credit** MC, V.
Young TV producers with upper-class accents, record execs and other creative-industry types who enjoy talking loudly are the sort of people you expect to find in this enduring eaterie. Otherwise, Zucca quietly hums as the waitresses and kitchen staff efficiently go about their duties. Although the decor is several years old, the modern design (muted purple banquettes, beech wood and slate flooring) has proved to be classic, at least in the front room. The downstairs bar area is comparatively brash, with a vivid green colour scheme. The menu offers several large pizzas, reliable risottos and well-executed main dishes. For starters, pork loin gave an unusual twist to 'vitello' tonnato. In a rare departure from Italian flavours, there was a tasty dish of cod with chickpeas, chorizo and saffron. Belly pork was slow-roasted and served in a roll with pumpkin and radicchio. Ice-cream is invariably a good choice for dessert. On our visit, chocolate and whisky was the flavour of the day, presented in a comfortingly large bowl that makes you feel like the luckiest kid in the street. We also enjoyed a rhubarb and apple crumble, and a bottle of Firesteed from the helpfully annotated wine list. Zucca is a special restaurant, but you can come as you are.
Babies and children welcome; high chairs. Booking essential dinner; bookings not accepted lunch Sat. Restaurant available for hire. Separate room for parties, seats 40. Tables outdoors (7, pavement). Takeaway service. **Map 7 A6.**

South West

Barnes SW13

Riva

169 Church Road, SW13 9HR (8748 0434). Barnes or Barnes Bridge rail/33, 209, 283 bus. **Lunch served** noon-2.30pm Mon-Fri, Sun. **Dinner served** 7-11pm Mon-Sat; 7-9.30pm Sun. **Main courses** £11.50-£19.50. **Service** 12.5%. **Credit** AmEx, MC, V.
Are we picky? The owner sitting at the back of the restaurant reading a newspaper throughout Sunday dinner somehow degraded the experience of this otherwise discreet and elegant local. But, hey, that's the beauty of being your own boss. Some reviewers consider Riva the best Italian restaurant in London, but we've always found it patchy. A delightful starter plate included rocket salad with intense chewy chunks of bottarga, superlative vitello tonnato sprinkled with tiny capers, and sweet culatello ham with figs – the fruit marred by being fridge-cold. Penne all'amatriciana was no better than could be made at home. A special of turbot with lemon and rosemary came with lovely mash. Riva's gnocchi are usually very good, but ours, served with crab and creamy tomato sauce, were too chewy. The dessert list is substantial for an Italian restaurant and includes many fun variations on ice-cream. We went for the sbrisolona (cornmeal and almond cake) with heady vin santo-flavoured mascarpone, and pretty crescents of sweet milk gnocchi (perfectly textured) with a boozy honey butter sauce. The wine list is pleasingly brief, but, regrettably, only the house wines are available by the glass.
Babies and children admitted (lunch); high chairs. Booking essential dinner. No cigars or pipes. Tables outdoors (3, pavement).

Chelsea SW3

Daphne's

112 Draycott Avenue, SW3 3AE (7589 4257). South Kensington tube. **Lunch served** noon-3pm Mon-Fri; noon-3.30pm Sat; 12.30-4pm Sun. **Dinner served** 6.30-11.30pm Mon-Sat; 6.30-10.30pm Sun. **Main courses** £12.25-£26.75. **Set lunch** £15.75 2 courses, £18.75 3 courses. **Service** 12.5%. **Credit** AmEx, DC, JCB, MC, V.
A meal at Daphne's is like a house party at a glamorous aunt's estate, when she's invited lots of jolly 'gels', decent chaps and wealthy Americans. The menu is based around seasonal fresh produce; on our visit there was honey fungus, forest mushrooms and wild garlic in the risottos, and samphire not just in the octopus and potato salad, but also in a special of pasta salad with prawns and tomatoes. Roast suckling pig came with broad beans and a delicious fennel gravy. A rack of juicy spring lamb was perfectly cooked and served with a vibrant melange of spring onions, peas, artichokes and mint. Desserts were fun affairs, including a 'Casa Buitoni Eton Mess' featuring chestnut pieces and fresh strawberry sauce, and

indulgent chocolate cannoli with dark choc mousse filling, chocolate pastry and fresh strawberries. Everything was nicely cooked and served with a smile. Add the approachable wine list, and it's easy to see why old Daph is enduringly popular.
Babies and children welcome; high chairs. Booking advisable. Separate room for parties, seats 40. **Map 14 E10.**

Fulham SW10

La Famiglia
7 Langton Street, SW10 0JL (7351 0761-7352 6095/www.lafamiglialondon.co.uk). Sloane Square tube then 11, 22 bus/31 bus. **Lunch served** noon-2.45pm, **dinner served** 7-11.30pm daily. **Main courses** £10.50-£20.50. **Cover** £1.75. **Minimum** £18.50 dinner. **Credit** AmEx, DC, JCB, MC, V.
When there's a full house in the canopied courtyard out back, La Famiglia feels like a dishevelled tent at Henley Regatta, but it makes for a jolly knees-up of a night out. Popular owner Alvaro Maccioni keeps an eye on staff who are so practised and professional they could do it all with their eyes closed – but more likely they'll be winking flirtatiously. Gorgeous deep-fried artichoke slices on the seasonal specials list came with a mound of fresh pesto for dabbing: nice but unnecessary. New on the main menu was tasty maltagliati pasta with chunky walnut sauce, while summery ricotta and rocket ravioli wore a pastel-green cloak of mascarpone and rocket the texture of face cream. A lovely little dish of potato salad with red onion was recommended as an accompaniment to the dreamy vitello tonnato. To finish: something outrageously fattening from the dessert trolley, or ice-creams such as chocolate and pistachio served with petticoat-tail wafers so old-fashioned they were probably designed by Leonardo da Vinci. Robert De Niro hasn't given his view, but we suspect that, like us, he'd chose La Famiglia over San Lorenzo (*see p155*) any day.
Babies and children welcome; children's menu; high chairs. Booking advisable dinner and Sun. Separate room for parties, seats 30. Tables outdoors (30, garden). **Map 13 C13.**

Putney SW15

Enoteca Turi
28 Putney High Street, SW15 1SQ (8785 4449). East Putney tube/Putney Bridge rail/14, 74, 270 bus. **Lunch served** noon-2.30pm Mon-Sat. **Dinner served** 6.30-11pm Mon-Thur; 6.30-11.30pm Fri, Sat. **Main courses** £14-£17. **Set lunch** £12.50 2 courses. **Service** 12.5%. **Credit** AmEx, DC, MC, V.
A polished outfit offering Prada style at Putney prices, Enoteca Turi is decorated in mottled tones of rich terracotta and shantung gold, with stylish comfortable wood and leather chairs. Saying the wine list is comprehensive does not do it justice: the degree of annotation and cross-referencing makes the booklet an absorbing read; it's one of the best Italian lists in London, and includes some notably low mark-ups. Each dish on the main menu features a symbol indicating the best wine to accompany it, allowing us to ensure that at least one diner had an ideal match. Tenimenti Luigi D'Alessandro Cortona syrah 2002 from the Marche was recommended for the unusual dish of calf's liver with salad. The food came topped with paper-like ribbons of potato splashed with balsamic sauce. A special of beetroot and ricotta ravioli with poppy seed and butter sauce was sweet, earthy and nutty. Roast rack of lamb came tinged with pink; it was juicy and moreishly fatty, served with a gorgeous sticky jus and shredded courgette and mint salad. For desserts, the beautifully presented panna cotta was rubbery from too much gelatine. It arrived with a roasted nectarine highly spiced with star anise and cloves. The crocante chocolate tart was rich and accompanied by a lovely mandarin sorbet. Staff are pleasant, capable and discreet – and seemed genuinely surprised and grateful when we pointed out a mistake on the bill.
Babies and children admitted. Booking advisable. Disabled: toilet. No-smoking tables. Separate area for parties, seats 30.

Refettorio. See p151.

Edera. See p160.

South

Battersea SW8, SW11

Fabbrica NEW

153 Battersea Park Road, SW8 4BX (7720 0204). Vauxhall tube/rail then 44, 156, 344 bus/ Battersea Park rail. **Meals served** noon-3pm Tue-Fri; noon-5pm Sun. **Dinner served** 6.45-11pm Tue-Sat. **Main courses** £7-£12. **Set meal** £15.50 2 courses, £19 3 courses, £22.50 4 courses. **Service** 12.56%. **Credit** MC, V.

A stunning black diagonal partition cleverly divides this large dining room into more intimate areas than was conceived in the open-plan set-up of former residents. The disconcertingly dominant art has been replaced with a couple of low-key pictures, including a good abstract of Battersea Power Station. On our visit, a three-course dinner was £19 – and the limited-choice set menu was a decent £15.50 for two courses. We hope such tweaks will pull in the punters this venue deserves. The menu includes plenty of fish and seafood. Octopus 'mosaic' appealed, but we went for fregola pasta with seafood and a light, elegant terrine of tightly layered fresh tomatoes wrapped in a fine slice of aubergine. Lemon-flavoured potato gnocchi came with a vegetable sauce of carrot and courgette strips, making a scrumptious, healthy vegetarian dish. Lamb cutlets, very rare at the centre, were spread lightly with a black olive crust. After dessert, our waiter revealed that the strawberry and limoncello tiramisu was an experiment, but it had worked fine. The wine list offers inexpensive bottles from Friuli to Sicily, and the quality 'real Lambrusco' sparkling red from Emiglia Romagna, served chilled, proved a versatile bargain at £17. Highly enjoyable and very good value.
Babies and children welcome; high chair. Booking advisable.

Osteria Antica Bologna

23 Northcote Road, SW11 1NG (7978 4771/ www.osteria.co.uk). Clapham Junction rail/35, 37, 319 bus. **Lunch served** noon-3pm Mon-Fri. **Dinner served** 6-11pm Mon-Thur; 6-11.30pm Fri. **Meals served** 11am-11.30pm Sat; 11am-10.30pm Sun. **Main courses** £6.75-£16.50. **Set lunch** (Mon-Sat) £9.50 2 courses. **Cover** 90p. **Credit** AmEx, MC, V.

OAB has been serving the best Italian food on Northcote Road for so long it's beginning to look like an OAP, but the tables of Italians dining here suggest that reliability and authenticity are still appreciated. With wines starting at a very approachable £11, this is an ideal place for midweek get-togethers and lazy Sunday lunches. Make sure, though, that you get a table in the cosy front room rather than the desolate hindquarter. Expect to see unusual ingredients such as calf's tripe and goat on the menu, as well as the occasional historic Roman dish; we enjoyed the pairing of a sauce of celery, honey and garum (fish sauce) with venison meatballs. Also rarely seen in London restaurants are nibbles such as mortadella-stuffed olives coated in breadcrumbs and deep-fried – a nod to this venue's osteria tag, and a filling snack that, with the sizeable bread basket, obliterates the need for a starter. Soups are usually excellent, as was the case with our velvety celeriac soup from the specials board. Also pleasing was a dish of pasta rags with baked ricotta and a vegetable sauce based on carrots and zucchini. Desserts are hearty classics, such as tiramisu, panna cotta with strawberry sauce, and cappuccino semifreddo. Apart from trouble getting the bill (staff were too interested in chatting with friends), service is typically pleasant and efficient.
Babies and children welcome. Book dinner Fri, Sat. Restaurant available for hire. Separate areas for parties (Mon-Thur), seating 30 and 40. Tables outdoors (6, pavement). **Map 21 C4.**

Waterloo SE1

Loco

County Hall, 3B Belvedere Road, SE1 7GP (7401 6734/www.locorestaurants.com). Embankment or Westminster tube/Charing Cross or Waterloo tube/rail. **Meals served** noon-11pm Mon-Sat; noon-10.30pm Sun. **Main courses** £7.95-£14.50. **Service** 12.5%. **Credit** AmEx, MC, V.

Tony Allan seems to have a passion for chain restaurants, but unlike him (or the promotional bumf, at least) we're not convinced that Loco is significantly different from the Caffè Unos of this world. A bit more upmarket maybe, but essentially this is a restaurant for families, office groups, cheap dates and birthday parties. We admired the quality of pasta used in the ravioli, but other components (the bland swamp of tomato sauce, the firm meat-paste filling) were disappointing. Better was bruschetta of smoked salmon and rocket. Rubbery main-course venison was improved by creamy mash and delicious roast garlic cloves. A hunk of nicely cooked salmon came with salsa verde and a side dish of fine french beans (we could have had roast potatoes, rocket and parmesan salad, or spinach). Chocolate truffle and raspberry tart was made with excellent ingredients, but the filling was like cement. A generous portion of tiramisu came in a simple white bowl. The wine list, while cheap, is uneven, with no Italian reds between £20 and £30. Still, it's a handy spot if you're out and about on the South Bank.
Babies and children welcome; children's menu; crayons; high chairs. Booking advisable. Disabled: toilet. No-smoking tables. **Map 10 M9.**
For branches see index.

South East

Bermondsey SE16

Arancia

52 Southwark Park Road, SE16 3RS (7394 1751). Bermondsey tube/Elephant & Castle tube/rail then 1, 53 bus/South Bermondsey rail. **Lunch served** 12.30-2.30pm, **dinner served** 7-11pm Tue-Sat. **Main courses** £8.80-£9.20. **Set lunch** £7.50 2 courses, £10.50 3 courses. **Credit** AmEx, MC, V.

Empty on our Saturday lunchtime visit, apart from an elderly lady dining alone and noticeably enjoying her roast chicken dish, Arancia is rustic and simple. Even a fresh lick of vivid-orange paint cannot hide the general lack of finesse – exemplified by an inept but pleasant waitress, a lack of ice-cream, and a chef wandering casually out of the restaurant during service to buy milk. But at these prices, who cares? Salice Salento 2000 from Puglia at £14 showed the value to be found on the wine list. Main-course fish cakes, served with salsa verde and salad, were glistening golden, but heavy on the potato. Pork steak was impressively portioned, however, and lamb spiedini with roasted pepper salsa was tasty. We loved the mash. A plate of cheese came teetering with a large round of unadorned carta di musica, but featured good gorgonzola, while the typical blandness of ricotta cheesecake was lifted with stewed spiced pears. This is a great local geared neatly to its Bermondsey market.
Babies and children admitted; high chairs. Booking advisable evenings. Separate room for parties, seats 8.

Tower Bridge SE1

Cantina del Ponte

Butlers Wharf Building, 36C Shad Thames, SE1 2YE (7403 5403/www.conran.com). Tower Hill tube/Tower Gateway DLR/London Bridge tube/rail.

Lunch served noon-3pm daily. **Dinner served** 6-11pm Mon-Sat; 6-10pm Sun. **Main courses** £8.95-£14.95. **Set meal** (lunch, 6-7.30pm Mon-Fri) £11 2 courses, £13.50 3 courses. **Service** 12.5%. **Credit** AmEx, DC, JCB, MC, V.
Even if you didn't know already, the mirrors around the walls and the metallic boom that oblige everyone to shout to be heard, would tip you off that this is a Conran venue. Staff were friendly and helpful. The Cantina is smaller and more low-key than the grander Conrans, and the cooking style is classic Italian-rustic, including pizza. Dishes are quite simple and nicely done, although the larger mains scarcely justify their prices. Our starters were very pleasant: a simple risotto with al dente spring vegetables, and very tender, delicately flavoured beef carpaccio with rocket and tangy parmesan. Of the mains, veal ravioli with peas and mint was divertingly meaty, and scallops wrapped in pancetta with broad beans had an interesting mix of flavours, but neither was so special for the price. There's a substantial, overwhelmingly Italian wine, liqueurs and cocktail list. The Cantina attracts the Docklands lunch and after-work crowds. Maybe its biggest asset is the terrace on Butlers Wharf, which offers a great view of Tower Bridge.
Babies and children welcome; children's menu; high chairs. Booking advisable. Dress: smart casual. Restaurant available for hire. Tables outdoors (20, terrace). Takeaway service (pizza, noon-3pm, 6-10pm daily). **Map 12 S9.**

Tentazioni
2 Mill Street, SE1 2BD (7237 1100/ www.tentazioni.co.uk). Bermondsey tube/ London Bridge tube/rail. **Lunch served** noon-2.30pm Tue-Fri. **Dinner served** 7-10.45pm Mon-Sat. **Main courses** £13-£19. **Set dinner** £26 3 courses, £36 5 courses. **Service** 12.5%. **Credit** AmEx, MC, V.
Poised between Conran's Butlers Wharf development and the local housing estate, Tentazioni is a discreet, approachably elegant restaurant housed in a long thin warehouse with lots of open brickwork and contemporary art. The well-designed space includes a mezzanine level for intimate dining, though the front of the restaurant is the friendlier chamber. There's a choice of set menus, as well as à la carte dishes. The kitchen seems to take special pleasure in combining fruit and meat. Fillet steak came with pineapple sauce, as well as chanterelles and spinach. Honeyed duck was accompanied by caramelised figs and foie gras ravioli. We had gorgeous olives, nicely flavoured focaccia, plain carta di musica and rather dry ciabatta. Desserts were slightly off the mark – mint ice-cream was overpowered by a milk chocolate millefoglie; raspberry tart with crème anglaise was just too big. The wine list features ten 'wines to meditate on' (premium bottles); otherwise the list is succinct and has good, inexpensive bottles from Puglia and Basilicata. Staff were attentive, but not intrusive. A pleasurable if over-filling experience.
Babies and children welcome. Booking advisable dinner Fri, Sat. Restaurant available for hire. Separate room for parties, seats 24. **Map 12 S9.**

East
Shoreditch N1

Fifteen
15 Westland Place, N1 7LP (0871 330 1515/ www.fifteenrestaurant.com). Old Street tube/rail. **Trattoria Breakfast served** 8.30am-11pm Mon-Sat. **Lunch served** noon-3pm daily. **Dinner served** 6-10pm Mon-Sat. **Main courses** £12-£14.
Restaurant **Lunch served** noon-2.30pm daily. **Dinner served** 6.30pm-9.30pm Mon-Sat. **Main courses** £25-£29. **Set meal** £65 tasting menu.
Both **Service** 12.5%. **Credit** AmEx, MC, V.
Jamie Oliver's Fifteen was a hit the day it opened in November 2002; even now, getting a table in the restaurant requires much phone work (with recorded prompts from Jamie himself). It's expensive too (set dinner is £65 per head, and that's before wine or service). Yes, the profits go to a good cause (the Cheeky Chops Charity), but the

cost can dampen enthusiasm. To improve the PR own-goal that Fifteen restaurant has become, Oliver has converted the ground-floor lounge bar into the more affordable Trattoria. Only a third of tables are bookable (a week in advance); the remainder are kept aside for walk-ins. Trattoria has a simple Italian menu, less sophisticated than the restaurant downstairs (where a typical main might be pot-roast pork leg, wrapped in prosciutto, with green figs, borlotti and runner beans). So there's an antipasti plate, ravioli of artichoke and parmesan with a light butter broth, penne alla arrabiata, and mains such as calf's liver with Sicilian peaches, rocket, mint and balsamic vinegar. The cooking isn't without glitches, but there's less to go wrong here, and prices, while not bargain basement, are more palatable (though vegetables cost another £3). The cheapest option is to come for breakfast – Pete Gott's bacon sarnie can be yours for a scant £5.50.
Babies and children welcome; high chairs. Booking essential. Disabled: toilet (trattoria). Dress: smart casual. No smoking. **Map 6 Q3.**

North
Camden Town & Chalk Farm NW1

Aperitivo
30 Hawley Crescent, NW1 8NP (7267 7755/ www.aperitivo-restaurants.com). Camden Town tube. **Meals served** noon-11pm daily. **Main courses** £3.95-£9.50. **Service** 12.5%. **Credit** MC, V.
Aperitivo's cocktail of snacks and small dishes for sharing – or 'Italian tapas' as staff try to explain it – has proved intoxicating enough to open a sizeable branch in the centre of Camden. Unlike other mid-priced venues, this one sets gourmet standards for the kitchen to follow, and usually they are achieved. The menu presents a wide choice of dishes, such as spinach and ricotta ravioli; chunks of monkfish cooked with chilli, wine and garlic; scallops on pea purée; tiny veal meatballs; as well as nibbly bits such as a plate of bruschetta and dips. Our zucchine fritte were especially good. Indeed, the only disappointment was the selection of ices for dessert; combinations of pear and calvados, and citron with mint, sounded great but delivered little except bubblegum sweetness. Good tiramisu and excellent coffee restored our faith. The wine list is reasonably priced and includes several cocktails for after-work partying. Aperitivo's casual, all-afternoon, all-night mood is enhanced if you can successfully nab the sofas at the front, but for privacy head to one of the tables.
Babies and children welcome. Booking advisable. No smoking tables. **Map 27 C2.**
For branch see index.

Sardo Canale NEW
42 Gloucester Avenue, NW1 8JD (7722 2800/ www.sardo-restaurant.com). Camden Town tube. **Lunch served** noon-3pm, **dinner served** 6-10pm Tue-Fri. **Meals served** 10am-10pm Sat, Sun. **Main courses** £12-£18. **Service** 12.5%. **Credit** AmEx, DC, MC, V.
The reputation of the original Sardo (*see p153*) has grown so much over the past few years that owner Romolu Mudu has been able to open this vast new branch in chi-chi Primrose Hill. Sardo Canale is much more grown up than its parent. Customers are more affluent and the multi-roomed, spacious restaurant (on an unusual site) is imaginatively designed, the former canalside warehouse given a cool, modern look. There's industrial ducting, and a ripple of mosaic fills a fissure in a concrete wall (nothing structural, we hope). You'll also find outdoor tables and a conservatory, but no canal view. It's the quality of the ingredients that make Sardinian dishes shine, and Mudu imports many directly from that island, such as pane carasau, Sardinia's parchment-like crispbread. Mosciame di tonno – thin slices of sun-dried tuna, with a salty, pungent flavour – was simply presented with french beans and sun-dried tomato. Linguine al

granchio was perfectly al dente pasta with a sauce of fresh crab meat, good olive oil, plus parsley and chillies. There's also a choice of 35 Sardinian wines at fair prices, as well as other Italian bottles.
Babies and children welcome; high chair. Booking advisable. No-smoking tables. Separate room for parties, seats 30. Tables outdoors (5, canalside). **Map 27 B2.**

Vegia Zena
17 Princess Road, NW1 8JR (7483 0192/ www.vegiazena.com). Chalk Farm tube/274 bus. **Lunch served** noon-3pm, **dinner served** 7-11pm Mon-Sat. **Meals served** noon-10.30pm Sun. **Main courses** £10-£14. **Set lunch** (Mon-Fri) £5.95 1 course, £8.95 2 courses incl glass of wine or soft drink. **Credit** AmEx, DC, JCB, MC, V.
Friday night saw Vegia Zena buzzing with locals up for something a cut above a takeaway and telly. Over the years we've found service and cooking patchy at this dated, pink and pine-wood venue. This occasion saw both at their best, although the bog-standard bread basket leaves you in no doubt that impressing customers with the finest cuisine is not the priority here. Soup, risotto, fish and meat dishes of the day are offered. A rich, warming casserole with beef and carrots was pure comfort cooking that suited the wintry weather. There are Genoan and Ligurian touches on the menu, but for the most part it is all familiar stuff. Seared tuna with caponata was a well-proportioned, tasty dish. Thin chocolate cake with chocolate sauce concluded the meal nicely, though for something less rich, try lemon sorbet with limoncello, or vanilla gelato with Baileys, which are among the long list of ices. The wine list features several decent bottles under £20. Sitting upstairs is preferable to the basement, even though tables are small and close enough to hear more of your neighbours' conversation than you'd perhaps like.
Babies and children welcome; high chair. Booking advisable. Tables outdoors (12, garden; 3, pavement). **Map 27 B2.**

Crouch End N8

Florians
4 Topsfield Parade, Middle Lane, N8 8PR (8348 8348/www.floriansrestaurant.com). Finsbury Park tube/rail then W7 bus/91 bus.
Wine bar **Open** noon-11pm Mon-Fri; 11am-11pm Sat; 11am-10.30pm Sun. **Main courses** £6.50. **Set meal** £8.50 2 courses.
Restaurant **Lunch served** noon-3pm daily. **Dinner served** 7-11pm Mon-Sat; 7-10.30pm Sun. **Main courses** £9.20-£14.85.
Both **Credit** MC, V.
The sky-blue walls of this grown-up restaurant (secreted behind a noisy street-front bar) feature a regularly changing display of work by local artists. Staff are enthusiastic, their attitude adding to the air of smart but unpretentious comfort. The menu changes regularly, and a blackboard highlights daily specials. The kitchen likes to experiment, with dishes such as duck and mushroom ravioli made with poppy-seed pasta and served with a satin-smooth spinach sauce. Duck also featured in a main course with rhubarb and chilli sauce: a thick, luscious combination with welcome after-burn. Less inspired was a dish of Italian sausages with char-grilled polenta and flageolet bean 'casserole'; the bangers were terrific, the beans less so. Desserts were similarly patchy: we revelled in chocolate fondant with fine vanilla ice-cream, but thought a dollop of cinnamon mascarpone on the side of an acidic plum and frangipane tart was the best thing about it. Wines are reasonably priced and well described on the helpfully annotated list.
Babies and children welcome; high chairs. Booking advisable dinner. Separate rooms for parties, seats 15 and 40. Tables outdoors (8, patio).

Islington N1

Casale Franco
Rear of 134-137 Upper Street, N1 1QP (7226 8994). Angel tube/Highbury & Islington tube/rail. **Lunch served** noon-2.30pm Sat. **Dinner**

served 6-11.30pm Tue-Sat. **Meals served** noon-10pm Sun. **Main courses** £8.50-£17.50. **Cover** £1. **Credit** AmEx, JCB, MC, V.
You wouldn't guess from the main road and simple blackboard signpost, but this is an enormous, highly popular venue that in good weather spreads out over the courtyard of a Citroën garage. A former bakery, the restaurant bakes its own nourishing, seeded breads: heavy, but richly satisfying and homely. The waitress brought a dish of pickled and grilled vegetables while we waited for seafood risotto and a fiendishly hot gratin of asparagus with mozzarella and parmesan. Although several of the ingredients on the menu were listed as organic, many of the dishes seemed to be out of tune with the season – but we still enjoyed a main of velvety calf's liver with roast balsamic onions and dolcelatte-flavoured polenta. We anticipated that tuna loin with warm salad of new potatoes, green beans and salsa verde would be more summery, but the vegetables were not made into a salad at all, and the fish was swimming in butter sauce rather than green sauce. Dessert of the day was panna cotta with banana and coconut, but we were too full with bread, and instead drank good espresso. Service had a lackadaisical quality, though we enjoyed the proudly unpretentious vibe – reminiscent of Rome's al fresco side-street tratts and pizzerias.
Bookings not accepted. No-smoking tables. Restaurant available for hire (Mon). Separate room for parties, seats 50. Tables outdoors (32, courtyard). **Map 5 O1**.

Metrogusto
13 Theberton Street, N1 0QY (7226 9400/ www.metrogusto.co.uk). Angel tube. **Lunch served** noon-3pm Fri, Sat; 12.30-3pm Sun. **Dinner served** 6.30-10.30pm Mon-Thur; 6.30-11pm Fri, Sat; 7-10pm Sun. **Main courses** £10-£15.50. **Set lunch** £14.50 2 courses, £18.50 3 courses. **Service** 12.5%. **Credit** AmEx, JCB, MC, V.
'Progressive Italian cuisine' is how Metrogusto likes to describe its food, but this restaurant isn't poncey. Crammed with chunky wooden furniture (the chairs are a little too low for the tables) and bold modern art, it is an inviting, cosy space with friendly staff (though service-wise that's not every diner's experience, we hear) and customers. Our waiter, keen to ensure his advice on the reasonably priced red wine was accurate, went and checked with the manager before bringing the bottle. The menu offers plenty of exciting combinations, but also practical elements such as 'catch of the day' and 'butcher's cut of the day', both served with two vegetables. Fruit is a favourite ingredient in savoury dishes – grapes with calf's liver, peaches with duck breast, fig sauce with lamb cutlets – while cheese often features in the puds. Spelt flour and squash gnocchi came with a warning from the waiter that the wholegrain flour lent a distinctive texture to the dumplings, but the chewiness was tempered by the inclusion of tangy sorrel and fresh ricotta. We finished with a chocolate and almond cake and cold rice pudding, which had a boozy kick and was served with grilled banana. A distinctive and lovely local.
Babies and children welcome; high chairs. Booking advisable; essential weekends. No-smoking tables. Separate room for parties, seats 24. Tables outdoors (4, pavement). **Map 5 O1**.

North West
Golders Green NW2

Philpotts Mezzaluna
424 Finchley Road, NW2 2HY (7794 0455/ www.philpotts-mezzaluna.com). Golders Green tube. **Lunch served** noon-2.30pm Tue-Fri; noon-3pm Sun. **Dinner served** 7-11pm Tue-Sun. **Set lunch** £10 1 course, £15 2 courses, £19 3 courses, £23 4 courses. **Set dinner** £15 1 course, £22 2 courses, £25 3 courses, £30 4 courses, £35 5 courses. **Service** 12.5%. **Credit** AmEx, MC, V.
Chef-patron David Philpott uses Italian ingredients as a springboard for his own ideas, rather than adhering to nonna's cooking or regional traditions. His ribeye steak with gorgonzola-flavoured mash

and Barolo wine sauce is justifiably popular, and the regularly changing menu may feature unusual combinations such as calf's liver with orange and pickled walnut salad, or a bollito misto of chicken duck and pigeon served with salsa verde. Soon after ordering, we were proffered a tasty amuse-bouche of tuna-stuffed baby peppers. A massive portion of penne came with lovely smoked duck, but a tasteless sauce of root vegetable purée. Also huge was a roast chicken and saffron brasata served with grilled polenta, and a delicious gazpacho topped with mozzarella and basil. Roast peaches with apricot and amaretti gelato included a wonderful caramel sauce, but dolce di cioccolata proved to be simply chocolate mousse in a terrine shape. The well-priced wine list offers several bottles rarely seen elsewhere. This restaurant is very popular locally, despite its bland, tiled and fairly rudimentary interior, and a rather naff collection of carnival masks. Customers are sussed enough to know that decor only matters to a point, and that they don't have to travel into town or spend a fortune to enjoy quality cooking.
Babies and children welcome; high chairs. Booking advisable dinner Sat. Restaurant available for hire. Tables outdoors (3, terrace).

Villa Dei Siori
38 North End Road, NW11 7PT (8458 6344). Golders Green tube. **Lunch served** noon-2.30pm, **dinner served** 6.30-11pm daily. **Main courses** £11.50-£18.50. **Service** 12.5%. **Credit** AmEx, MC, V.
Experienced staff give a warm welcome at this long-standing local. The extensive menu is packed with old-fashioned dishes, not all of which are endowed with retro chic. Veal escalopes come with sauces of ham, sage and white wine, or porcini. Asparagus may be served with hollandaise, or topped with butter and parmesan for a gratin. This is also one of the few places you'll find crespelle (savoury pancakes), filled with ricotta and spinach. Grilled provolone cheese with garlic, chilli and balsamic vinegar; duck breast with balsamic sauce; and delicious saffron crème brûlée – all these were just groovy. We were only disappointed by our starter of Colchester crab salad; although it featured only white meat, the simplicity of the dish highlighted the dreary taste and texture of the crab. The decor may be as dated as the menu, but it has a lot of charm, not least thanks to the Michelangelo-style ceiling, complete with twinkling lights. The comfortable booth seating offers an ideal place to relax and enjoy the theatre of it all.
Babies and children welcome; high chairs. Booking advisable weekend. Entertainment: pianist 7.30-11pm Fri, Sat. Restaurant available for hire.

Hampstead NW3

Cucina
45A South End Road, NW3 2QB (7435 7814). Hampstead Heath rail/24, 168, C11 bus. **Lunch served** noon-2.30pm Mon-Sat; noon-3pm Sun. **Dinner served** 7-10.30pm Mon-Thur; 7-11pm Fri, Sat. **Set menu** £16.95 2 courses, £19.95 3 courses. **Service** 12.5%. **Credit** AmEx, MC, V.
Despite appearances – the stylish but comfortable decor, neat table settings and slanting-backed chairs are all entirely the same as last year – changes have been afoot at this well-established, popular Hampstead local. In place of a happily eclectic food range that wandered from the Mediterranean to the Pacific Rim, the menu is now solidly modern Italian, prepared by a chef from Pescara. Very superior own-made fresh pasta is one of Cucina's strong points. Other ingredients are impressively well sourced too: calamari salad with cumin dressing featured plump strips of first-rate, perfectly tenderised squid. While a carpaccio of zucchini with parmesan, lemon vinaigrette and pine kernels was less striking, its components were all very fresh. Saffron pappardelle with funghi had plenty of flavour, and black tagliolini with cuttlefish and squid was a satisfying mix, though with a strong peppery aftertaste. There's a limited choice of desserts (Italian or otherwise), but the wine list is international. Service is charming and attentive, and the set-price meals are good value.

Babies and children welcome; high chairs. Booking essential Fri, Sat. No-smoking tables. Tables outdoors (2, pavement). Takeaway service. **Map 28 C3**.

St John's Wood NW8

★ Rosmarino
1 Blenheim Terrace, NW8 0EH (7328 5014). St John's Wood tube. **Lunch served** noon-2.30pm Mon-Fri; noon-3pm Sat, Sun. **Dinner served** 7-10.30pm Mon-Sat; 7-10pm Sun. **Set lunch** (Mon-Thur) £14.50 2 courses, £19.50 3 courses. **Set meal** (lunch Fri-Sun; dinner daily) £22.50 2 courses, £27.50 3 courses, £32.50 4 courses. **Service** 12.5%. **Credit** AmEx, DC, MC, V.
The charming decked terrace at the front of this property has recently been enclosed with glass, cleverly making 18 more seats available for use all year round and allowing patrons to enjoy the benefits of outdoor dining indoors. Service on our visit was charmingly attentive. The menu promises a mix of classic dishes and innovative flavour combinations, and delivers all with spectacular presentation. A simple starter of mozzarella and grilled vegetables arrived as a perfect half ball of buffalo under a tender tomato petal, with char-grilled aubergine, courgettes, carrot and fennel making a pretty salad. A lobster pasta special was special indeed – moist chunks of lobster presented in a half shell with thick, ridged ribbons of pasta holding a luscious tomato sauce. For mains, a crumbed veal chop was beaten thin, but left on the bone. It was tasty, but outclassed by a perfect square of slow-roast belly pork on pure di patate with diced pumpkin, bright-green ribbons of savoy cabbage and truffled honey sauce. Desserts continued the classy standard: baked green apple with rum and raisin ice-cream, ginger-flavoured crème brûlée, and a Valrhona chocolate pudding with rosemary ice-cream – all truly scrumptious. With good merlot available cheaply by the glass, and excellent coffee to finish, this high-quality local is a wise choice.
Babies and children admitted; high chairs. Booking advisable dinner Fri-Sun. Restaurant available for hire. Separate room for parties, seats 20. Tables outdoors (7, terrace). **Map 1 C2**.

Outer London
Twickenham, Middlesex

A Cena
418 Richmond Road, Twickenham, Middx TW1 2EB (8288 0108). Richmond tube/rail. **Lunch served** noon-3pm Tue-Sun. **Dinner served** 7-11pm Tue-Sat. **Main courses** £12.75-£16. **Set lunch** (Tue-Sat) £10 2 courses, £12 3 courses. **Credit** AmEx, MC, V.
A sheet of paper listing the day's offerings effectively communicates A Cena's 'simple is best' policy. The decor is similarly devoid of pretension, consisting of white walls and dark wooden floors and tables, producing a modern bistro-via-gastropub look. You won't find flamboyant architectural presentation or twiddly garnishes with the robust food either, though dishes such as mackerel wrapped in pancetta, and duck breast with cherry sauce are well executed. The selection is sensitive to the needs of vegetarians. Expect an inspired combination of light ingredients in the risotto, as well as a few, simple, tasty pasta dishes. Highlight of our meal was a dessert of the day: seasonal rhubarb compote folded with thick, rich cream. It sounded too straightforward to order on a night out, but the waiter pressed us, saying the pastry chef had only just put it together; sure enough, the contrast of flavours was tremendous. Throughout the evening staff strove to be pleasant and businesslike (though we detected a hint of arrogance). Good points include the well-written and cleverly arranged wine list, which helpfully translates foreign bottle names into simple language, vividly describing the contents.
Babies and children welcome; high chairs. Booking advisable dinner Thur-Sat. Restaurant available for hire.

Japanese

Little Tokyo (located in and around Soho's Brewer Street) may not be getting any bigger, but the number of Japanese restaurants and range of postcodes they inhabit keeps growing. **Sapporo Ichiban** exemplifies this positive trend with its warm welcome, budget prices and pioneering Catford location. At the top end of the market, Knightsbridge's **Zuma** appears to have toppled **Nobu** as *the* Japanese restaurant in which to be seen, and is confident enough to have opened a second branch, **Roka**, in Fitzrovia. However, the best cooking and cutting is still to be found at modern **Tsunami** in Clapham, traditional **Café Japan** in Golders Green and the cheap but superb **Sushi-Hiro** in Ealing.

Perky little Greco-Japanese Kam-Pai bit the dust last year, but that surprising juxtaposition of Mediterranean with Japanese is now being practised by Italian restaurant Spighetta with its **Madama Butterfly** sushi bar. And we shouldn't forget the sterling work being done by those other mix-and-matchers: **Itsu** (*see p231* **Oriental**) and **Mju** (*see p111* **Hotels & Haute Cuisine**).

Umu (14-16 Bruton Place, W1J 6LX, 7499 8881/www.umurestaurant.com; Map 9 H7), offering classic and modern Kyoto food, arrived too late to be reviewed for this edition. **Nobu** is opening a new restaurant and lounge bar, in spring 2005, at 15 Berkeley Street, W1.

Central
Barbican EC1

Pham Sushi
159 Whitecross Street, EC1Y 8JL (7251 6336). Old Street tube/rail. **Lunch served** noon-3pm Mon-Fri. **Dinner served** 5-10.30pm Mon-Sat.

Main courses £4.50-£13.50. **Set lunch** £6-£12 2 courses. **Set dinner** £15-£25 6 courses. **Credit** MC, V.

Still close by the Barbican, Pham has moved a few doors away to larger premises. It's still bright and spotlessly clean, but the food this time around was disappointing, given past impressive performances. For lunch, we ordered the two-course £10 sushi menu and, à la carte, nasu dengaku (half an aubergine, sliced lengthways, grilled and topped with a sweetened miso sauce). The soup that started the meal, a clear vegetable broth laden with chunks of cabbage, shiitake and tofu, was bland. Then came the piping-hot nasu: far tastier, but not terribly easy to eat with the spoon provided. The sushi and sashimi were of decent quality and nicely arranged, but, like the soup, simply uninspiring. We regretted the absence of the precision instrument that is the tapered Japanese chopstick; here you get the thicker Chinese variety. All that said, the crowd of office workers were chowing down quite happily, and service was fine. If you live or work nearby, this diner is worth a try.
Babies and children welcome. Booking advisable. No-smoking tables. Takeaway service; delivery service (orders over £15). **Map 5 P4**.

Belgravia SW1

Feng Sushi
26-28 Elizabeth Street, SW1W 9RB (7730 0033/ www.fengsushi.co.uk). Victoria tube/rail. **Meals served** 11.30am-11pm Thur-Sat; 11.30-10pm Mon-Wed; noon-10pm Sun. **Main courses** £1-£13. **Set meal** £6.50-£15 bento box. **Credit** AmEx, DC, JCB, MC, V.

The Feng Sushi formula is now set: a pleasantly grey and beige colour scheme, fish tank decor and plasma TV screen; and a wide selection of maki and nigiri sushi, as well as Feng Sushi value boxes and a scattering of not-quite-Japanese offerings such as Japanese fish and chips, salmon fish cakes and vegetarian spring rolls. The service isn't quite Japanese either, as our waitress could cope only

with numbers and not names of dishes. High stools are gathered around roughly hewn wooden tables for those eating in, but home delivery is a major part of the business. Some of our sushi was unevenly constructed and tended to implode, and a seaweed salad was watery, but the inside-out tempura prawn rolls (good trend, this) were fresh and bright-tasting, a udon noodle soup with tempura served separately (another nice trend, for those who don't like sogginess) was honest and filling, while the California hand-roll was made with real fresh crab and not crabstick (please, can we turn this into a trend too). Fengs in Ken Church Street or Notting Hill might do better sushi, but any Feng seems to be a good Feng.
Babies and children welcome. Bookings not accepted. No smoking. Takeaway service; delivery service (orders over £10). Vegetarian menu. Vegan dishes. **Map 15 H10**.
For branches see index.

Bloomsbury WC1

Abeno
47 Museum Street, WC1A 1LY (7405 3211). Holborn tube. **Meals served** noon-10pm daily. **Main courses** £5.95-£39.60. **Set lunch** £6.50-£16 incl miso soup, rice. **Credit** AmEx, DC, JCB, MC, V.

The average pancake house might do well to take a leaf out of Abeno's book. Okonomiyaki, which means 'cooking what you like', makes a humble meal of vegetables and/or meat mixed with batter much more exciting by setting the action at your table. OK, the waitress does all the actual cooking – from mixing your ingredients and depositing them on the table-top hot-plate, to flipping your 'pancake' once the first side has browned nicely – but you get to decorate the result with a choice of mayo, fruit and vegetable sauce (sweeter than tonkatsu sauce), dried seaweed, shaved fish and chilli sauce. You could try the Kansai special of chicken, steak, prawn and asparagus for £39.80, but the remaining dishes at this authentic specialist are modestly priced; individual okonomiyaki cost £6-£10. Your comfort-food main can be accompanied by interesting side orders such as ika natto (squid and fermented soy beans) or avocado and tofu-filled gyoza. Alternatives include yaki soba and stranger dishes such as om soba and soba cooked with rice. The place was empty save for one customer on a weekday lunch – a shame, since the food is fresh, organic where possible, and hearty. Abeno deserves more.
Babies and children welcome; high chairs. Disabled: toilet. Takeaway service. **Map 18 L5**.

Pham Sushi

Chinatown W1, WC2

★ Misato

*11 Wardour Street, W1D 6PG (7734 0808).
Leicester Square, Oxford Circus or Tottenham
Court Road tube.* **Lunch served** noon-2.45pm
Mon-Fri; noon-3pm Sat, Sun. **Dinner served**
5.30-10.30pm daily. **Main courses** £4.90-£8.60.
Set lunch £5.40-£7 incl miso soup, rice &
pickles. **No credit cards.**

A canteen vibe and a predominantly Far Eastern
clientele: in these respects, Misato is a classic
Chinatown chop-shop. For the rest, it's the epitome
of nothing special. Behind a vivid green façade,
the elongated, beige-painted dining room is kitted
out with well-used, basket-bottomed chairs, and
tables whose tops are hidden beneath green and
white protective plastic. The grub is generously
served and cheap, for sure – all lunch meals cost
less than £7 – but it ain't terribly cheerful. The
short menu is, roughly speaking, one half bento
meals, one half things with rice: pork and ginger,
tofu steak, tonkatsu, teriyaki chicken and so on.
After a small dish of dressed cabbage and a bowl
of standard 'miso with tofu chunks', plates arrived
bearing their respective meats (in our case, fish and
chicken) beside eye-popping shovelfuls of rice and
chopped lettuce. If only there had been as much
flavour as poundage. The menu lists a brief array
of raw fish, but we wouldn't bet on it being
anything special. Still, there's obviously a market
for this sort of thing: Misato was virtually packed
on our visit.
*Babies and children admitted. Bookings not
accepted. No smoking. Takeaway service.*
Map 17 K7.

★ Tokyo Diner

*2 Newport Place, WC2H 7JP (7287 8777/
www.tokyodiner.com). Leicester Square or
Tottenham Court Road tube.* **Meals served**
noon-midnight daily. **Main courses** £3.90-
£12.90. **Set lunch** (noon-6.30pm) £4.90-£7.90
incl green tea, miso soup, rice. **Credit** JCB,
MC, V; no cheques accepted.

Tokyo Diner has become a bit of an institution
since opening its sliding doors back in 1992.
Deservedly so, as the place combines a funky,
casual atmosphere with good – if not challenging
– Japanese food. Service is swift and friendly,
though diners (there's usually an interesting mix
of Westerners and young Japanese) tend not to
linger long at the little tables. The menu is
unintimidating; there's a limited sushi list, plus
donburi dishes, bowls of soba and udon noodles,
bento boxes and the ever-popular katsu kare
(breaded deep-fried pork with curry sauce). You'll
even find instructions on how to eat sushi. Our
salmon teriyaki bento looked quite beautiful in its
red and black box, which also contained rice,
salmon sashimi, seaweed salad (though that was
fridge-cold and a bit bland) and sharp, crunchy
pickles. Aubergine age bitashi, cooked in a light,
slightly sweet broth and garnished with lotus root,
was subtle and satisfying, even if the miso soup
was short on excitement. Green tea and cans of
Japanese beer are the drinks of choice.
*Babies and children welcome. Bookings not
accepted Fri, Sat. No smoking (ground floor and
basement). Takeaway service.* **Map 17 K7.**

Zipangu

*8 Little Newport Street, WC2H 7JJ (7437 5042).
Leicester Square tube.* **Meals served** noon-11pm
Mon-Thur; noon-11.30pm Fri, Sat; noon-10.30pm
Sun. **Main courses** £4.50-£14. **Set lunch**
(noon-6pm) £6-£12 incl miso soup, rice & pickles.
Set dinner £9.50-£14 5 courses. **Credit** AmEx,
MC, V.

Billing itself as a 'Japanese Mother's Kitchen',
Zipangu serves up a mixed bag of sushi, braised
dishes, curry and noodles to a varied bunch of
backpackers, students and local office workers
who pop in for an eat-and-run lunch or stop by for
something to fill them up on the way home at
night. There are five tables in the ground-floor
dining room and seven in the basement (watch
your head). Decor is basic, verging on the
depressing, and service is lacklustre, but gets the

job done. The food was backpacker standard – it
won't kill you, but it won't make your day either.
The mixed sushi was competently produced,
although chilled tofu (hiya-yakko) was heavy and
dry, yakitori chicken was overcooked, and una-don
(grilled eel on a bowl of rice) tasted of nothing but
sweet sauce on something soft. The pork miso
ramen had a soggy, pallid, instant-noodle dullness,
in no way enlivened by half a hard-boiled egg with
grey rings around the yolk. Yes, it's cheap and fast,
but is that enough?
*Babies and children admitted. Bookings not
accepted Fri, Sat. Separate room for parties,
seats 15. Takeaway service.* **Map 17 K7.**

City EC2, EC4

City Miyama

*17 Godliman Street, EC4V 5BD (7489 1937).
St Paul's tube/Blackfriars tube/rail.* **Lunch
served** noon-2pm Mon-Sat. **Dinner served**
6-9.30pm Mon-Fri. **Main courses** £9-£25.
Set lunch £22-£25. **Set dinner** £35-£45.
Service 15%. **Credit** AmEx, DC, MC, V.

For a relatively formal City joint, Miyama put on
a surprisingly warm welcome, with a jolly greeter
who led us down from the ground-floor sushi and
teppan areas to the basement dining room. In this
small, overstaffed space, we were spared
claustrophobia by pale paintwork and
strategically positioned floor-to-ceiling mirrors,
leaving us to concentrate happily on devouring our
bountiful lunchtime trays amid a handful of
Japanese workers and broker types. Presumably
the Square Mile Bento is aimed at them. Both the
special set and the sashimi set lunch included
agedashidofu, cold soba with tempura sprinkled
in dipping broth, rice, miso soup, pickles and that
very 1980s teishoku accessory, a slice of melon. At
the heart of the special set were rich, fresh, tender
sardine tempura and succulent slices of tuna
tataki. The sashimi set centrepiece delivered a
satisfying mix of the usual tuna, salmon and sea
bream with less-common nori-garnished scallop
and turbot wings. A lovely bonus was the little
bowl of sunomono (vinegar-dressed 'salad'), which
included real crab with the typical cucumber-and-
wakame combo. No prizes for modernity here –
instead you get dated furnishings, traditional
dishes and good old-fashioned quality.
*Babies and children admitted. Booking advisable.
Separate room for parties, seats 10. Takeaway
service (pre-orders essential). Vegetarian menu.*
Map 11 O6.
For branch (Miyama) see index.

K-10

*20 Copthall Avenue, EC2R 7DN (7562 8510/
www.k10.net). Moorgate tube/rail.* **Lunch served**
11.30am-3pm, **dinner served** 5-9.30pm Mon-Fri.
Main courses £1-£5. **House wine** £12.50.
Credit AmEx, DC, JCB, MC, V.

White walls, blue neon highlights, black-clad staff
and some of the most iris-tightening colour
combinations you've ever seen – and that's just the
shirts and ties on the customers. City slickers make
up the majority of the lunchtime crowd at this
large basement diner, all lifting dishes off its long,
long conveyor belt with evident relish. Little
wonder: this is one of the best kaiten (K-10 –
geddit?) joints in town. Standards have been
reliably high whenever we've visited, breadth of
choice is excellent (stretching beyond standard
maki and nigiri to eel, octopus, gyoza, grilled and
breaded salmon, and artful concoctions of green
noodles and asparagus) and the ingredients shine
with freshness. The slices of seared tuna rolled in
black and white sesame seeds were tender as
heaven, although the tori kara-age was on the
tough side: a rare bum note. Desserts don't start
coming round until the end of the lunch hour and
include fruit salads and an un-Japanese crème
brûlée with a raspberry on top. Drinking water,
still and fizzy, is piped to every place setting – nice
touch – and the entrance has a takeaway counter.
*Babies and children admitted. Booking not
accepted. No smoking. Takeaway service;
delivery service (orders over £9 only). Vegan
dishes.* **Map 12 Q6.**
For branch see index.

Miyabi

*Great Eastern Hotel, Liverpool Street, EC2M
7QN (7618 7100/www.great-eastern-hotel.co.uk).
Liverpool Street tube/rail.* **Lunch served**
noon-2.30pm Mon-Fri. **Dinner served**
6-10.30pm Mon-Fri; 6-10pm Sat. **Main courses**
£6.50-£14. **Set lunch** £17-£25 incl miso soup,
rice & pickles. **Service** 12.5%. **Credit** AmEx,
DC, MC, V.

Very slick – dark wood panels from floor to ceiling,
chic tables and seating, a floor of dusky mineral
material, and an array of fine cloths on the backs
of the customers. Yup, City addresses like this suit
the suits down to the ground, which means that
at lunch you'll be an eavesdropper, willing or
otherwise, on conversations about money.
Speaking of lucre, prices here soar towards the
heavens. For instance, our sushi-sashimi-tempura
bento lunch, which was certainly pleasant but
hardly world-class, tipped the scales at £23. The
fish in the sushi and sashimi was slightly better
than average, the tempura light and crisp as you
please, but the sauce that came with the teriyaki
array was over-salted. The meal concluded with a
simple (or underwhelming: decide for yourself)
gathering of fresh fruit pieces. Staff appeared to
be struggling to keep up with the pace (an order
of tea was forgotten), although we were assured
Miyabi is calmer of an evening. This is one of
several restaurants in the Conran-owned Great
Eastern Hotel.
*Babies and children welcome. Booking advisable.
Disabled: toilet. Takeaway service (noon-2.30pm,
6-9pm Mon-Fri).* **Map 12 R6.**

Moshi Moshi Sushi

*Unit 24, Liverpool Street Station, EC2M
7QH (7247 3227/www.moshimoshi.co.uk).
Liverpool Street tube/rail.* **Meals served**
11.30am-10pm Mon-Fri. **Main courses**
£5-£11. **Set meal** £6-£14 2 courses.
Credit DC, MC, V.

We've never been greatly impressed by Moshi
Moshi, and being asked by the senior waitress to
fill in a customer feedback form when spotted
trying the new addition to the menu did nothing to
prompt warmer feelings. Clearly, MM keeps an eye
on the competition. The new dish in question was
similar to the seared slices of tuna rolled in sesame
seeds we'd sampled at K-10 some weeks
previously. They weren't bad, and this chain now
also puts a little more of the 'urchin, octopus, roe'
category of ingredients into its conveyor-belt
cargo. Even so, the place drops too many balls to
make the kaiten premier league: a waitress's sleeve
dragged over an array of sushi and fried chicken
that were so tough they could have been cooked
the day before; then there was the tasteless salmon,
stodgy rice, soggy gyoza... The new decor – foil-
wrapped pipes and futuristic dark wood pods for
the 'hot menu' tables – is just pointless swank. All
that said, the abekawa mochi (three coloured rice
cakes containing various sweet fillings) were
delicious. But would you come here just for
dessert? Probably not.
*Babies and children welcome. Disabled: toilet.
No smoking. Takeaway service; delivery service.
Vegetarian menu.* **Map 12 R5.**
For branches see index.

★ Noto

*2-3 Bassishaw Highwalk, off London Wall,
EC2V 5DS (7256 9433/www.noto.co.uk).
Moorgate tube/rail.* **Lunch served** 11.30am-
2.30pm, **dinner served** 6-9.45pm Mon-Fri.
Main courses £7.80-£9. **Set lunch** £7-£9.90
incl miso soup, rice. **Set dinner** £8.90-£22 incl
miso soup, rice. **Credit** JCB, MC, V.

Arm yourself with a compass and a cagoul before
setting out to find Noto amid the 'highwalks' of the
concrete carbuncle known as the Barbican. Your
(no doubt lengthy) journey will be rewarded.
There's a casual canteen-like feel to this little place,
with smiley, friendly service and a knockout menu
of well-prepared dishes. Set meals are a bargain.
The menu is lengthy, featuring yakitori, noodles,
curry, sushi and sashimi; but the list of specials is
not to be missed. Ika shiokara – umami-rich, salt-
cured, fermented squid – had a pleasingly firm
texture, while tempura of kisu (Japanese whiting)

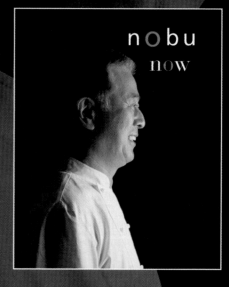

was everything that fried fish should be, the crisp casing enclosing perfectly steamed tender flesh. An Atkins-tastic dish of grilled fatty salmon needed a squeeze of lemon to cut through the richness, while maguro natto (raw tuna with fermented soy beans) was enhanced by a sprinkling of nori strips and a substantial nugget of wasabi: delicious. The drinks list runs to beer, some ordinary wines and half a dozen sakés, including the estimable Sho Chiku Bai brand, made in California. In terms of quality, presentation and price, Noto is pretty hard to fault.
Children welcome. No smoking (lunch). Takeaway service. **Map 11 P5.**
For branches (Harrods Sushi Bar, Noto Sushi) see index.

★ Yokoso Sushi

40 Whitefriars Street, EC4Y 8BH (7583 9656). Blackfriars tube/rail. **Meals served** 11am-10pm Mon-Fri. **Set meals** £7.50-£11.50 incl miso soup, rice. **Credit** AmEx, JCB, MC, V.
Tricky to find (there's just a sign and a doorway at street level), this butterscotch-walled basement kaiten diner was packed on our visit. The waiter bade us make haste to our seats, as if hordes of pursuing punters might elbow us out of contention for hanging around. The slightly juddering conveyor-belt aside (nothing a spot of oil can't fix, we presume), this is a smooth operation. There's not much in the way of fish, but what options we saw included yellowtail, something that looked like pale toro and – surprise! – salmon. Most of the rest of the plates paraded past bearing fried things: tasty gyoza (marred only by a slightly soggy wrap); flavourful, crisp chicken tonkatsu; not-bad breadcrumbed scallops; and slightly bland croquettes containing specks of minced beef. Edamame and the occasional yakitori also riffled by, interspersed with a growing number of desserts as the lunch hour passed. Price-wise, even customers pulling in more modest stipends than the prevailing City slickers will find the bill manageable. We tried to order beer, but were told the place no longer has a licence to serve booze.
Babies and children welcome. No smoking. Takeaway service; delivery service (within 1-mile radius on orders over £15).
Map 11 N6.

Clerkenwell & Farringdon EC1

Ginnan `NEW`

1 Rosebery Court, Rosebery Avenue, EC1R 5HP (7278 0008). Farringdon tube/rail/ 19, 38, 341 bus. **Lunch served** noon-2.30pm Mon-Fri. **Dinner served** 6-10.30pm Mon-Fri; 6-10pm Sat. **Main courses** £5.80-£8.
Set lunch £8.80 3 courses. **Set dinner** £18 4 courses, £25 5 courses. **Credit** AmEx, DC, JCB, MC, V.
Farringdon is undergoing extensive sushification, with Japanese eateries springing up like enoki mushrooms. One consequence is under-patronage for many venues, particularly at night – always a problem in this part of town. Ginnan (which has been around for a decade) was looking particularly hangdog on our visit. This appears to be an unloved enterprise; there's a sense of under-investment, most evident in the decor. The dining room feels like something out of a David Lynch film, and not in a good way. Many would-be diners must peer inside at the spinach-green cinema-lounge carpet, brown splash-back tiling and gloomy lighting, then make a break for the nearest cheery, halogen-lit sushi bar. Nevertheless, we found the service good, and some of the dishes were fine (mackerel grilled with salt was excellent: hot and moist with an edge of char), although others missed the mark (anchovy nigiri was an uncomfortable hybrid: part-tapas, part-sushi). The high point of our meal was the bill, but no-one eats out just to pay low prices. A restaurant in need of some care and attention, then.
Babies and children admitted. Booking advisable. Disabled: toilet. Takeaway service. Vegetarian menu. **Map 5 N4.**

Roka. See p172.

Menu

For a more comprehensive explanation and translation of the ingredients and dishes found in Japanese cuisine, Richard Hosking's *A Dictionary of Japanese Food: Ingredients & Culture* (Tuttle Publishing, $16.95) is highly recommended.

Agedashidofu: tofu (qv) coated with katakuriko (potato starch), deep-fried, sprinkled with dried fish and served in a shoyu-based broth with grated ginger and daikon (qv).
Amaebi: sweet shrimps.
Anago: saltwater conger eel.
Bento: a meal served in a compartmentalised box.
Calpis or **calpico:** a sweet soft drink derived from milk, similar in taste to barley water. Dilute to taste and serve ice-cold.
Chawan mushi: savoury egg custard served in a tea tumbler (chawan).
Daikon: a long, white radish (aka mooli), which is often grated or cut into fine strips.
Dashi: the basic stock for Japanese soups and simmered dishes. It's often made from flakes of dried bonito (a type of tuna) and konbu (kelp).

Dobin mushi: a variety of morsels (prawn, fish, chicken, shiitake, gingko nuts) in a gently flavoured dashi-based soup, steamed (mushi) and served in a clay teapot (dobin).
Donburi: a bowl of boiled rice with various toppings, such as beef, chicken or egg.
Edamame: fresh soy beans boiled in their pods and then sprinkled with salt.
Gari: pickled ginger, usually pink and thinly sliced; served with sushi to cleanse the palate between courses.
Gohan: rice.
Gyoza: soft rice pastry cases stuffed with minced pork and herbs; northern Chinese in origin, cooked by a combination of frying and steaming.
Hamachi: young yellowtail or Japanese amberjack fish, commonly used for sashimi (qv) and also very good grilled.
Hashi: chopsticks.
Hiyashi chuka: Chinese-style (chuka means Chinese) ramen (qv Noodles) served cold (hiyashi) in tsuyu (qv) with a mixed topping that usually includes shredded ham, chicken, cucumber, egg and beansprouts.
Ikura: salmon roe.

Izakaya: literally 'a place where there is saké'. A post-work drinking den frequented by Japanese businessmen, sometimes shabby, sometimes smart, and usually serving a wide range of food at reasonable prices.
Kaiseki ryori: a multi-course meal of Japanese haute cuisine that originally was followed by the Japanese tea ceremony.
Kaiten zushi: 'revolving sushi' (on a conveyor belt).
Katsu: breaded and deep-fried meat, hence tonkatsu (pork katsu) and katsu curry (tonkatsu or chicken katsu with mild vegetable curry).
Maki: the word means 'roll' and this is a style of sushi (qv) where the rice and filling are rolled inside a nori (qv) wrapper.
Mirin: a sweetened rice wine used in many Japanese sauces and dressings.
Miso: a thick paste of fermented soy beans, used in miso soup and some dressings. Miso comes in a wide variety of styles, ranging from 'white' to 'red', slightly sweet to very salty and earthy, crunchy or smooth.
Miso shiru: classic miso soup most commonly

containing pieces of tofu and wakame (qv).
Nabemono: a class of dishes cooked at the table and served directly from the earthenware pot or metal pan.
Natto: fermented soy beans of stringy, mucous consistency.
Nimono: food simmered in a stock, often presented 'dry'.
Noodles: second only to rice as Japan's favourite staple. Noodles are served hot or cold, dry or in soup, and are sometimes fried. There are many types, but the most common are: **ramen** (Chinese-style egg noodles), **udon** (thick white wheat-flour noodles), **soba** (buckwheat noodles), and **somen** (thin white wheat-flour noodles, usually served cold as a refreshing summer dish – hiyashi somen – with a chilled dipping broth).
Nori: sheets of dried seaweed.
Okonomiyaki: the Japanese equivalent of filled pancakes, whereby various ingredients are added to a batter mix and cooked on a hotplate, usually in front of diners.
Ponzu: usually short for ponzu joyu, a mixture of the juice of a Japanese citrus

---

Covent Garden WC2

Hazuki

43 Chandos Place, WC2 4HS (7240 2530/ www.sushihazuki.co.uk). Charing Cross tube/rail. **Lunch served** noon-2.30pm Mon-Fri. **Dinner served** 5.30-10.30pm Mon-Sat; 5.30-9.30pm Sun. **Main courses** £5.50-£18. **Set meals** £16-£40 3-8 courses. **Service** 10%. **Credit** AmEx, DC, JCB, MC, V.

Nicely placed as a post-show destination for both Covent Garden and South Bank audiences, Hazuki was seating customers right up to the 10.30pm watershed during our visit. Service was a little frazzled by this point, but the food coming out of the kitchen remained remarkably good. Our orders included fish cake tempura, sea bream nigiri sushi and pan-fried pork kimchi. This is a difficult combination to produce, since the tempura needs to be served instantly, the stir-fry piping hot and the nigiri at or a little below room temperature – but the kitchen handled the challenge well. The main menu is solidly Japanese, and though the specials edge towards oriental fusion, the best things we tasted were core dishes, including a spine-tinglingly good dobin mushi. To make maximum use of limited space, the restaurant is three-tiered: basement tables are fine; those at the glass-fronted entrance level are draughty; while the best are the four in the mezzanine, where vases of bamboo and dragon lilies take the edge off the spare decor. Draughts aside, the main drawback to this layout is that serving staff are often out of sight; ask for the bill with your last order.
Babies and children welcome. Booking advisable; essential dinner. Separate room for parties, seats 25. Takeaway service. Map 18 L7.

Fitzrovia W1

★ Ikkyu

67 Tottenham Court Road, W1T 2EY (7636 9280). Goodge Street or Tottenham Court Road tube. **Lunch served** noon-2.30pm Mon-Fri. **Dinner served** 5-10.30pm Mon-Fri, Sun. **Main courses** £6-£13. **Set lunch** £6.20-£9.60. **Set dinner** £6.10-£13.50. **Service** 10% (dinner only). **Credit** AmEx, MC, V.

If Suntory (now defunct) was the upmarket old warhorse of traditional Japanese restaurants in London, Ikkyu could justly claim to be its downmarket counterpart. Brisk but efficient service comes with a youthful smile. Maybe couples and groups won't feel special, but solo diners seated at the kitchen-in-your-face counter can blend in comfortably with the general bustle. The evening menu is an extensive affair of good solid staples in virtually all categories of Japanese cooking; lesser spotted variations include the likes of fermented soy beans, raw mountain yam and stewed intestine. Lunch boils down to a dozen or so sets (raw and grilled fish, katsu and tempura) and a modest list of sushi and sashimi. The tuna and salmon combo comprised four slices of each – fresh-tasting and simply presented, lounging against a pillow of springy daikon string. The tempura set lunch was almost too bountiful, with a brace of prawns, aubergines, green beans, sweet potato slices, green pepper, mushroom and onion jostling for space. The red-and-grey lino and black-beamed walls have seen better days, but there's nothing shabby about the food.
Babies and children welcome. Book dinner. No-smoking tables. Separate room for parties (tatami), seats 14. Map 4 K5.

Roka NEW

37 Charlotte Street, W1T 1RR (7580 6464). Goodge Street or Tottenham Court Road tube. *Bar* **Open/meals served** 5-11pm daily. *Restaurant* **Lunch served** noon-3pm Mon-Sat. **Dinner served** 5.30-11pm daily. **Main courses** £3.60-£21. *Both* **Service** 12.5%. **Credit** AmEx, MC, V.

When chef-restaurateur Rainer Becker followed his hit Knightsbridge debut with Roka, the question on critics' lips was: how does it compare with Zuma (*see p173*)? Although they share the same design genes (Japanese architects Super Potato), Zuma is windowless while Roka boasts acres of glass frontage. However, at both, chunky is the operative word. Roka uses great slabs of wood for its door and central counter, hefty ceramic serving dishes, even drinking glasses that are thick and attractively misshapen. In the food department, the key word is petite. Basic set lunches (such as tendon, £9) are filling and cheap, but ordering à la carte sends the bill rocketing when superb hotate in butter and ponzu (£8.90) number a mere two scallops, and 'skewered tiger prawns with yuzu chilli paste' (£14.30) proves to be just the one critter. Amid the tinkering with Japanese cuisine (Korean chilli and Western extras), the three-sashimi selection of tuna, salmon and sea bass stood out for its simple, fail-safe formula of fresh fish, tongue-tingling wasabi and quality soy sauce. The generously portioned, spicy battered squid was a bargain at £4.90, but too oily to finish. In contrast, passion fruit and cherry blossom cake with cherries and roasted pineapple ice-cream left us wanting more. For the buzz generated at Zuma, try the basement Shochu Lounge where the emphasis is on the Japanese

fruit (ponzu) and soy sauce, used as a dip, especially with seafood and chicken or fish nabemono (qv).
Robatayaki: a kind of grilled food, generally cooked in front of customers, who make their selection from a large counter display.
Saké: rice wine, around 15% alcohol. Usually served hot, but may also be chilled.
Sashimi: raw sliced fish.
Shabu shabu: a pan of stock is heated at the table and plates of thinly sliced raw beef and vegetables are cooked in it piece by piece ('shabu-shabu' is onomatopoeic for the sound of washing a cloth in water). The broth is then portioned out and drunk.
Shiso: perilla or beefsteak plant. A nettle-like leaf of the mint family that is often served with sashimi (qv).
Shochu: Japan's answer to vodka. It is colourless and distilled from a variety of raw materials including wheat, rice and potatoes.
Shoyu: Japanese soy sauce.
Sukiyaki: pieces of thinly sliced beef and vegetables are simmered in a sweet shoyu-based sauce at the table on a portable stove. Then they are taken out and

dipped in raw egg (which semi-cooks on the hot food) to cool them for eating.
Sunomono: seafood or vegetables marinated (but not pickled) in rice vinegar.
Sushi: combination of raw fish, shellfish or vegetables with rice – nearly always with a touch of wasabi (qv). Vinegar mixed with sugar and salt is added to the rice, which is then cooled before use. There are different sushi formats: **nigiri** (lozenge-shaped), **hosomaki** (thin-rolled), **futomaki** (thick-rolled), **temaki** (hand-rolled), **gunkan maki** (nigiri with a nori wrap), **chirashi** (scattered on top of a bowl of rice), and **uramaki** or **ISO maki** (more recently coined terms for inside-out rolls).
Tare: general term for shoyu-based cooking marinades, typically on yakitori (qv) and unagi (qv).
Tatami: a heavy straw mat, traditional Japanese flooring. A tatami room in a restaurant is usually a private room where you remove your shoes and sit on the floor to eat.
Tea: black tea is fermented, while green tea (ocha) is heat-treated by steam to prevent the leaves fermenting. **Matcha** is

powdered green tea, which has a high caffeine content.
Bancha is the coarsest grade of green tea which has been roasted; it contains the stems or twigs of the plant as well as the leaves, and is usually served free of charge with a meal. **Hojicha** is freshly toasted tea.
Mugicha is roast barley tea, served iced in summer.
Teishoku: set meal.
Tempura: fish, shellfish or vegetables dipped in a light batter and deep-fried. Served with tsuyu (qv) to which you add finely grated daikon (qv) and fresh ginger.
Teppanyaki: 'grilled on an iron plate', or originally 'grilled on a ploughshare'. In modern Japanese restaurants, a chef standing at a hotplate (teppan) is surrounded by several diners. Slivers of beef, fish and vegetables are cooked with a dazzling display of knifework and deposited on your plate.
Teriyaki: cooking method by which meat or fish – often marinated in shoyu (qv) and wine – is grilled and served in a tare (qv) made of a thick reduction of shoyu (qv), saké (qv), sugar and spice.
Tofu or **dofu:** soy beancurd used fresh in simmered or

grilled dishes, or deep-fried (agedashidofu), or sometimes eaten cold (hiyayakko).
Tokkuri: saké flask – usually ceramic, but sometimes made of bamboo.
Tonkatsu: see katsu above.
Tsuyu: a general term for shoyu/mirin-based dips, served both warm and cold with various dishes ranging from tempura (qv) through to cold noodles.
Unagi: freshwater eel.
Uni: sea urchin.
Wafu: Japanese style.
Wakame: a type of young seaweed most commonly used in miso (qv) soup and kaiso (seaweed) salad.
Wasabi: a fiery green 'mustard' often compared to horseradish, grated from the root of an aquatic plant. It is eaten in minute quantities (tucked inside sushi, qv), or diluted into shoyu (qv) for dipping sashimi (qv).
Yakimono: 'grilled things'.
Yakitori: grilled chicken (breast, wings, liver, gizzard, heart) served on skewers.
Zarusoba: soba (see noodles) served cold, usually on a bamboo draining mat, together with a dipping broth.
Zensai: appetisers.

---

equivalent of vodka in fruity variations or out-there flavours such as pine needle and catnip. A bit more Roka 'n' roll, then?
Babies and children welcome; high chairs. Booking advisable. Disabled: toilet. No smoking. Tables outdoors (6, pavement). Vegetarian menu. **Map 9 J5**.

Knightsbridge SW7

★ Zuma
5 Raphael Street, SW7 1DL (7584 1010/ www.zumarestaurant.com). Knightsbridge tube. **Bar Open** 5.30-11.30pm Mon-Sat; 5.30-10pm Sun. **Restaurant Lunch served** noon-2pm Mon-Sat; noon-2.30pm Sun. **Dinner served** 6-11pm Mon-Sat. **Main courses** £3.50-£28.50. **Set lunch** £8.50-£14.80. **Service** 12.5%.
Both **Credit** AmEx, DC, MC, V.
Has Zuma taken over from Nobu (*see p175*) as the capital's most glamorous dining spot? Possibly, if the wait (several weeks) for a reservation is anything to go by. Not to mention the strictly enforced two-hour table-turning system. On our most recent visit, the shoals of beautiful young fashion plates who had graced the immaculately designed restaurant when it opened had been usurped by groups of staid businessmen; air-kisses replaced by sombre handshakes. Still, the food remains compellingly good, helped by service that is well-informed and friendly (up until the two-hour deadline). The biggest problem remains what to choose from the extensive menu. Ingredients, as in our skewered scallops with green pepper and black bean sauce, are impeccable. Slivers of raw sea bass with yuzu, truffle oil and salmon roe, decorated with pretty shiso leaves, looked like a Cath Kidston print (but tasted better). Equally

impressive were miso-marinated lamb chops, which had a powerful Sichuan pepper kick. Only one dish, a rather dry roast-duck nori roll, disappointed. To drink, Zuma has some great saké-based cocktails, plus a very good saké list, as well as the country's first saké sommelier to guide you around it.
Babies and children welcome; high chairs. Booking essential. Disabled: toilet. Separate rooms for parties, seating 10 and 14. **Map 8 F9**.

Marylebone W1

Madama Butterfly NEW
43 Blandford Street, entrance inside La Spighetta, W1U 7HS (7486 7340). Baker Street tube. **Lunch served** noon-2.30pm Mon-Fri; 12.30-3pm Sat. **Dinner served** 6.30-10.30pm Mon-Thur, Sun; 6.30-11pm Fri, Sat. **Main courses** £6.90-£16.60. **Service** 12.5%. **Credit** AmEx, MC, V.
A strange one, this. You can sit in the terracotta-floored basement dining room of Italian restaurant La Spighetta (*see pXXX*), dining on sushi and sashimi (preceded by distinctly Mediterranean olives) prepared by a Chinese chef. Meanwhile, your nostrils are assailed by the smells of olive oil, pasta and basil wafting from the kitchen, and your ears pick up Italian banter between the waiting staff. Nevertheless, it was some damn fine sushi on rather pretty plates that arrived at our table, care of the Madama Butterfly sushi bar, which sits on the ground floor. Not everything was done by the book (beautifully tender, marbled toro on the nigiri was unnecessarily scored, a practice usually reserved for squid; tuna and scallop in the temaki were oddly diced rather than used in long strips), but

we couldn't fault the ingredients for texture and freshness. Our smiley Italian waiter even offered a suggestion; and the soft-shell crab maki was indeed worth ordering. Don't head here for a taste of Japan without first phoning ahead to check that the somewhat irregular sushi bar is open.
Babies and children welcome; high chairs. Booking advisable weekends. No-smoking tables. Takeaway service; delivery service. **Map 9 G5**.

Mayfair W1

★ Kiku
17 Half Moon Street, W1J 7BE (7499 4208/ www.kikurestaurant.co.uk). Green Park tube. **Lunch served** noon-2.30pm Mon-Sat. **Dinner served** 6-10.15pm Mon-Sat; 5.30-9.45pm Sun. **Main courses** £10-£28. **Set lunch** £12-£25 incl miso soup, rice & pickles. **Set dinner** £40-£60 incl miso soup, rice & pickles, dessert. **Service** 12.5%. **Credit** AmEx, JCB, MC, V.
A stone's throw from Nobu (*see p175*), Kiku is a little less exciting and not much cheaper than its glamorous neighbour. If you've seen *Lost in Translation*, the decor might seem to have a certain indefinable salaryman chic; if not, then not. There is something slightly Soviet about the functionality of company-account destinations like this. The food is of a high quality, however. This isn't a bad place to try kaiseki, sets of which begin at £42. Selections vary, but will always include a grilled, fried, steamed, boiled and raw dish plus soup; the way the chef plays around with these basic rules is what makes a kaiseki meal so enjoyable. Our Edo set featured turbot sashimi, dobin mushi, and light-as-air tempura. All was to the good apart

from a complimentary appetiser that may be the prototype for great dishes to come, but looked and tasted like a cube of steamed tofu someone had slipped on and surreptitiously scraped into a handy finger bowl: some compliment.
Booking advisable. Separate room for parties, seats 8. Takeaway service. **Map 9 H8**.

★ Nobu
Metropolitan Hotel, 19 Old Park Lane, W1K 1LB (7447 4747/www.noburestaurants.com). Hyde Park Corner tube. **Lunch served** noon-2.15pm Mon-Fri; 12.30-3pm Sat, Sun. **Dinner served** 6-10.15pm Mon-Thur; 6-11pm Fri, Sat; 6-9.30pm Sun. **Main courses** £5-£27.50 incl miso soup, rice & pickles. **Set lunch** £25 bento box, £25 sushi box, £50 chef's selection. **Set dinner** £70-£90 chef's selection incl green tea. **Service** 12.5%. **Credit** AmEx, DC, MC, V.
The bad news first: Nobu has unexpectedly unattractive features. The tables are small and packed, and the ratio of customers to square feet is emphasised by bright lighting and canteen noise levels. This isn't Le Gavroche, in other words, and at these prices you may feel entitled to more seclusion than Nobu is capable of offering. Now the good news: if you're here for the food, you won't spend long worrying about your earthly surroundings. The fusion of Japanese and Peruvian traditions is no longer novel, but is still capable of inspiring surprise and delight. Tuna tataki (petals of seared sashimi in ponzu sauce) was extraordinary. So too the lobster ceviche (nuggets of marinated flesh), the sugar snap tempura (hot little life-rafts of vegetable sweetness), and the wagyu beef (priced by the 25g; you'll need 100g for two people). To follow, the sorbets burst on the tongue like the last rounds in a firework display; this is one of the few Japanese restaurants where you really should try puddings. And everything else you can get your mitts on, for that matter. Nobu continues to offer some of the best cooking and culinary invention to be had in London – but you'll have to book well ahead. For the same menu, but a less scintillating atmosphere, visit sister restaurant Ubon in Docklands (34 Westferry Circus, E14 8RR, 7719 7800).
Babies and children welcome; high chairs. Booking essential. Disabled: lift; toilet. No-smoking tables. Separate room for parties, seats 14-40. **Map 9 H8**.

Sumosan
26 Albemarle Street, W1S 4HY (7495 5999/ www.sumosan.com). Green Park tube. **Lunch served** noon-3pm Mon-Fri. **Dinner served** 6-11.30pm Mon-Sat. **Main courses** £7.50-£22.50. **Set lunch** £19.50 incl miso soup, rice & pickles, dessert; £45 6 courses (maximum 4 people). **Set dinner** £65 8 courses (maximum 4 people). **Service** 12.5%. **Credit** AmEx, DC, MC, V.
This is sushi for the rich, corporate crowd – those pampered Kobe cattle, fed beer and massaged with saké, spring to mind. Sumosan's modern glamour is seductive, from the Venetian glass fishnet that tinkles over the glass street frontage, to the supremely comfortable banquettes and white Rosenthal china. The Nobu-influenced menu (yes, of course there is black cod with miso) is just as eye-catching, with its scattering of fusion specialities such as goose-liver sushi, tuna tartar with avocado and sevruga caviar, and barbary duck with lingonberry. The more traditional sushi and sashimi offerings are very good, and the salmon sashimi salad is fresh and light. Beyond sushi, however, the kitchen runs off the rails. A simple, single grilled squid was bland, and pricey at £14. Peking duck sushi was an expensive joke, and though a rare sighting of harusame noodles was welcome, they came as a nondescript Chinese stir-fry with itsy-bitsy pieces of beef and carrot. Any spell is soon broken by an uninterested service team, and waits (for menus, drinks and dishes) can be tedious.
Babies and children welcome; high chairs. Booking advisable. No-smoking tables. Separate area for parties, seats 30. Takeaway service. **Map 9 H7**.

Piccadilly W1

Benihana
37 Sackville Street, W1S 3DQ (7494 2525/ www.benihana.co.uk). Piccadilly Circus tube. **Lunch served** noon-3pm daily. **Dinner served** 5.30-10.30pm Mon-Sat; 5-10pm Sun. **Set lunch** £11.50-£15.50 5 courses. **Set dinner** £17-£23.75 6 courses. **Service** 12.5%. **Credit** AmEx, DC, JCB, MC, V.
Benihana, an international chain with three branches in London, has been around for donkey's years but is undeniably popular. And why not? The place is fun. Diners sit at large, half-moon-shaped teppanyaki tables and make their selection of meat and/or fish (teriyaki steak, tuna or chicken, prawns, filet mignon, lobster tails), after which the chefs claim centre stage. Knives are released from holsters, and vegetables and fish are sacrificed for the chefs to show off their (admittedly awesome) cutting skills. Pepperpots fly through the air, to squeals of delight from the youngsters. 'Japanese prawns,' prompts the chef. 'From Tokyo?' asks a guest. 'Fresh from Tesco.' The jokes are as corny as they are well-rehearsed, but who cares? This type of cooking is difficult to get wrong, as the chefs grill your choice of food to your liking. Ingredients are of decent quality (the steaks perhaps more than decent) and the food isn't bad value when you consider that most meals include onion soup, salad, a starter (prawns or California rolls), vegetables and rice. And you get some theatre chucked in too.
Babies and children admitted; high chairs. Booking advisable; essential Fri, Sat. Disabled: toilet. Separate room for parties, seats 10. Takeaway service (sushi). Vegetarian menu. **Map 17 J7**.
For branches see index.

St James's SW1

Matsuri
15 Bury Street, SW1Y 6AL (7839 1101/ www.matsuri-restaurant.com). Green Park tube. **Lunch served** noon-2.30pm Mon-Sat; noon-3pm Sun. **Dinner served** 6-10.30pm Mon-Sat; 6-9pm Sun. **Main courses** £10-£23 lunch, £13-£30 dinner. **Set lunch** £6.50-£42 incl green tea, miso soup, rice & pickles. **Set dinner** £35-£80 incl green tea, miso soup, rice & pickles, dessert. **Credit** AmEx, DC, JCB, MC, V.
All over the world, teppanyaki has been reduced to the status of a cheap sideshow, with comedic chefs tossing food into customers' mouths, and the whole thing played for laughs. Yet at this ten-year-old restaurant the venerable art of table-cooking is taken very seriously indeed. While there is still entertainment in watching the immaculately dressed grill chefs (best is Aksa, one of the few female chefs) go through their carefully choreographed rituals – slicing, flipping, tossing, seasoning, saucing, scraping and serving – there is respect shown for both their ingredients and their craft. So there's little wrong with a lean and clean-tasting 170g Scottish sirloin from the grill, boosted nicely by its creamy soy dipping sauce; or with a small, scorched grilled cod fillet from the kitchen. Unlike Matsuri's newer Holborn sibling, though, this branch is more of a grill specialist than an all-rounder. Hence it serves us right for ordering a combo platter of nigiri sushi and salmon maki that failed to sparkle, and agedashidofu (deep-fried beancurd) that was pasty. The basement dining room, like the food itself, is professionally put together, but borders on corporate blandness.
Babies and children welcome; high chairs. Booking advisable. Disabled: stair lift; toilet. No-smoking tables. Separate rooms for parties (teppanyaki), seating 8-18. **Map 17 J7**.
For branch see index.

Soho W1

Donzoko
15 Kingly Street, W1B 5PS (7734 1974). Oxford Circus or Piccadilly Circus tube. **Lunch served** noon-2.30pm Mon-Fri. **Dinner served** 6-10.15pm Mon-Sat.

Main courses £4.50-£28. **Set lunches** £6.50-£13 incl miso soup, rice & pickles, service. **Credit** AmEx, MC, V.
With its cosy, casual, woody, tavern feel, Donzoko is reminiscent of a Japanese izakaya – a friendly, no-frills neighbourhood bar – even if the neighbourhood happens to be Regent Street. As for the food, if it's made in Japan, it's probably made here, judging by the menu. The list runs through practically every type of Japanese cooking, including nimono (simmered dishes), yakimono (grilled), agemono (fried), sunomono (vinegared) and whatevermono. Such dishes are a mile away from formal, elegant kaiseki banquet cuisine, but prices are fair and the food is mostly likeable. The sushi is fine without making you gasp for joy; Donzoko udon with prawn, chicken and egg is hot and filling; and tori kara-age (fried chicken) is crisp and not oily, if a little heavy. One of Donzoko's strengths is a classic salt-grilled mackerel: two thick, moist planks of fish with bubbled skin that's as crisp as a rice cracker; what a way to get your omega-three essential oils! The ever-smiling staff are a delight, the kitchen pumps out the food, and the shochu (distilled spirit) cocktails can get you into a party mood, fast.
Booking advisable. Takeaway service. **Map 17 J6**.

Hi Sushi
40 Frith Street, W1D 5LN (7734 9688). Leicester Square, Piccadilly Circus or Tottenham Court Road tube. **Meals served** noon-11pm Mon-Thur; noon-11.30pm Fri, Sat; noon-10.30pm Sun. **Main courses** £4.50-£14. **Service** 10%. **Credit** MC, V.
Hi Sushi, not so high standards. On a summer midday visit we shared the ground-floor space with a pair of loud, foul-mouthed *Miami Vice* extras and a selection of 1980s pop tracks that Chris de Burgh wouldn't be caught dead listening to. Five minutes later, the profanities walked out (if only the music had decamped as well) and then there were 20: two punters (us), the chef, the waitress and 16 unoccupied stools. Poor show for a central establishment. On the subject of seating, said stools are all bolted to the floor just that bit too close to the counters. Still, in the unlikely event that the ground floor gets packed, there's seating of the table-and-chair variety in the basement. Our eight-piece sushi and sashimi sets each contained four passable nigiri and two surprisingly good pieces of toro, but the salmon was tasteless and all the fish was served too cold. Service was a touch brusque, but there's a touch of comedy in the menu: 'All our sushi are traditionally hand-prepared… not by ROBOT!' There's an all-you-can-eat promotion in the evening, should that appeal.
Babies and children admitted. Booking advisable weekends. No smoking area. Takeaway service. Vegetarian menu. **Map 17 K6**.
For branches (Koi, Tokyo City) see index.

★ Kulu Kulu
76 Brewer Street, W1F 9TX (7734 7316). Oxford Circus, Piccadilly Circus or Tottenham Court Road tube. **Lunch served** noon-2.30pm Mon-Fri; noon-3.45pm Sat. **Dinner served** 5-10pm Mon-Fri; 5-10pm Sat. **Main courses** £1.20-£3.60. **Credit** MC, V.
The name is a bit of Japanese onomatopoeia used when things are rolling smoothly: appropriate enough for a kaiten-zushi diner. However, service at this frills-free, wallet-friendly exponent of conveyor-belted meal delivery is not so much smooth as non-existent. Punters are waved to vacant seats and left to extract chopsticks and napkins from containers in front of them, find the nearest shoyu, wasabi and colour-coded price chart, and start grabbing; you even have to ask for a drinks menu. Still, KK's combo of simplicity, eccentricity and handy Soho location pulls 'em in, even if the grub on the move is really nothing exceptional: the usual salmon nigiri in large numbers, the usual maki, wan-looking chunks of tamago, mini salads, soup and the occasional temaki. Signs remind you that the clock is ticking at lunchtime. Diners are given a maximum of three-quarters of an hour to eat up and pack up, not that

this is the sort of place where you'd want to linger. We were tempted to stay put for the full 45 minutes just to see what happens after the deadline.
Babies and children welcome; high chairs. No-smoking tables. Takeaway service; delivery service. **Map 17 J7.**
For branch see index.

Ramen Seto
19 Kingly Street, W1B 5PY (7434 0309). Oxford Circus or Piccadilly Circus tube. **Meals served** noon-10pm Mon-Sat. **Main courses** £5-£8.50. **Set meals** £5-£8.50 incl miso soup, rice. **Credit** JCB, MC, V.
A fresh lick of paint, wood panelling and a change of furniture spruced up Ramen Seto in spring 2004. Service, however, remains the same: adequate, but not exactly accommodating. When we asked if miso ramen, served in a dish the size of a washing-up bowl, could be divided into two bowls (so we didn't have to keep swapping), the answer was a blank 'No'. Still, who's going to quibble when the portions are so large that a single main course could almost feed two? The menu appears long, but comprises variations on simple, basic dishes, mostly ramen or udon. There are also mountains of (slightly too squidgy) rice, with toppings such as katsu kare (breaded pork and curry sauce), or particularly pert tuna and (more flaccid) salmon sashimi. The lowest point was the shoddy tempura; the badly rendered batter didn't encase the vegetables, leaving them exposed to the hot oil. Cheap ingredients – celery, a boring English field mushroom – didn't help the dish either. Not a place for fine dining then, but Ramen Seto can hit the spot if you're ravenous and don't want to spend more than a tenner per head.
Babies and children welcome. Booking advisable weekends. Separate room for parties, seats 25. Takeaway service. **Map 17 J6.**

★ Ryo
84 Brewer Street, W1F 9TZ (7287 1318). Piccadilly Circus tube. **Meals served** 11.30am-midnight Mon-Wed, Sun; 11.30am-12.30am Thur-Sat. **Main courses** £5-£20. **Set meals** £6-£10. **No credit cards.**
Ryo is the Japanese equivalent of a greasy spoon, and if you bear that in mind, it's hard not to feel affectionate about the place. This is the kind of café beloved of Tokyo workers, who generally want nothing more out of lunch than a corner in which to relax with a newspaper, a cigarette and a daily special. You'll find better Japanese food of all descriptions elsewhere on Brewer Street, but perhaps nowhere else in London will you eat it in such unhurried, unpretentious surroundings. The decor is canteen-like, with faintly gothic overtones in the basalt-effect table-tops and the dark eating booths upstairs. The menu concentrates on noodles and dumplings, though also offers three sushi sets and one or two moments of pleasant wildness, such as baza-zushi (fish flakes, gourd strips, pickled red ginger, nori ribbons, shredded carrot, fried tofu strips and egg on sushi rice) which is bright pink, green and gold, like a bowl of edible neon. The gyoza are good, but noodle soups often contain too much residual cooking oil. Note that Ryo accepts no plastic. Order and pay for your food on entering.
Babies and children admitted. Separate room for parties, seats 30. Takeaway service. **Map 17 J7.**

★ Satsuma
56 Wardour Street, W1V 3HN (7437 8338). Piccadilly Circus tube. **Meals served** noon-11pm Mon, Tue; noon-11.30pm Wed, Thur; noon-midnight Fri, Sat; noon-10.30pm Sun. **Main courses** £8-£16. **Service** 12.5%. **Credit** AmEx, DC, JCB, MC, V.
Look no deeper than its skin, and Satsuma is unremarkably generic; it sports a shoddy-chic look (walls of rough concrete, one of coarse-hewn wood) combined with Wagamama-style communal tables. But when it comes to the food, this place stands out from the crowd. The sushi in the set lunch was plainly handmade and tasted excellent; the colour and texture of the fatty tuna, in particular, were spot on. (The fish supplier is the

renowned Atari-Ya.) As trimmings, we got two yakitori, a small seaweed salad and a bowl of miso soup. The latter two were also served with the kushiage set: a meal with features that wouldn't embarrass a restaurant three times as expensive – namely, ebi tempura with cornflakes instead of batter, and a shiso-leaf tempura doing duty as a small dish for the delicious salmon tataki. The breaded part of the menu included a slice of aubergine topped with a strip of salmon before frying – very nifty – plus vegetables and whitebait. Both menus concluded with sumptuously creamy vanilla ice-cream drizzled with espresso, and were fantastic value at £8.80 each. Staff were quick and efficient. There's plenty of seating if you take into account the large basement area.
Babies and children welcome; high chairs. Disabled: toilet. No smoking. Takeaway service. **Map 17 K6.**

★ Ten Ten Tei
56 Brewer Street, W1R 3PJ (7287 1738). Piccadilly Circus tube. **Lunch served** noon-2.30pm Mon-Fri; noon-4pm Sat. **Dinner served** 5-10pm Mon-Sat. **Set lunch** £6.50-£12 incl green tea, miso soup, rice & pickles. **Set dinner** £13.80-£17.80 incl green tea, miso soup, rice & pickles, dessert. **Service** 10% (dinner only). **Credit** JCB, MC, V.
Unpretentious, even tatty, this compendious restaurant with the catchily alliterative name is owned by the same people as kaiten diner Kulu Kulu (*see p175*) a few doors away. Compendious? When it comes to Japanese grub, you name it and the menu very probably has it: tempura, ramen, soba, udon (all available in multitudinous declensions), tonkatsu, oden (hotchpotch stew), sushi, sashimi, various Japanese beers, plum wine, saké… Rather surprisingly, the ground-floor dining room was sparsely populated when we arrived for a midweek lunch; just one customer sat at the counter and a few others at a handful of tables. We opted for the sushi and sashimi selection, which came generous, varied – nice to see akagai (ark shell) as well as the more familiar tuna, salmon and yellowtail – and nicely arrayed on a large, frosted, pedestalled glass dish. The fish was fresh, the rice good and tight. Chicken teriyaki had been well executed too. But a major disappointment were the gyoza: bland and mushy where they should have been tasty and crisp. Service was perfectly pleasant.
Babies and children welcome. Booking advisable. Takeaway service. **Map 17 J7.**

Yo! Sushi
52 Poland Street, W1V 3DF (7287 0443/ www.yosushi.com). Oxford Circus tube. **Meals served** noon-11pm Mon-Thur; noon-midnight Fri, Sat; noon-10.30pm Sun. **Main courses** £7.50-£10. **Credit** AmEx, DC, JCB, MC, V.
The original Yo! has had a refit, and – mm-mmm! – is it feeling pleased with itself? The double-track kaiten is still in situ, but the decor has been spruced up: new counter surfaces, cool stools topped with cranberry-coloured leather pouffes, new carpet and new slate floor tiles. The menu has been rethought too. The colour-coded plates now cost £1.50-£5, but the range of food on them is desperately narrow (salmon predominates). The new made-to-order specials cost £6.50-£9.50. Our 'spider roll' (a California roll containing, among other things, soft-shell crab tempura, yuzu tobiko and chilli mayonnaise) was too big to eat in one mouthful and didn't have much flavour. The staff had the mechanical moves of factory drones, and lacked knowledge about the food. When one was asked to identify a green leaf (it was shiso), he had to confer with his superior, who mis-described it as 'Japanese salad'. Still more dubious were the nuggets of, ahem, information in the menu: a mix of the blindingly obvious ('saké is rice wine') and nonsense (you're supposed to put nigiri in your mouth with the fish downwards, apparently – news to our Japanese dining companions).
Babies and children welcome. Bookings accepted (minimum 4 people). Disabled: toilet. No smoking. Takeaway service. Vegetarian menu. **Map 17 J6.**
For branches see index.

Ealing W5

★ ★ Sushi-Hiro
1 Station Parade, Uxbridge Road, W5 3LD (8896 3175). Ealing Common tube. **Lunch served** 11am-1.30pm, **dinner served** 4.30-9pm Tue-Sun. **Set lunch** £5-£14 incl miso soup, green tea. **Set dinner** £5-£14 incl green tea. **No credit cards.**
Design isn't a high priority at this modest little establishment, opposite Ealing Common tube. The plain white interior holds a sushi bar and a few tables. Nor does Sushi-Hiro have a wide-ranging menu: just sushi (nigiri, chirashi or maki) and sashimi. It's a restaurant for sushi purists, then, and the quality of food doesn't disappoint. The nigiri sushi involves small, delicate fingers of rice with ultra-fresh toppings such as surf clam, turbot, sea bass, salmon and several cuts of tuna. Our hamachi (yellowtail) sashimi was lusciously rich-textured. A lovely portion of horse mackerel was served in a shallow bowl with freshly grated ginger and finely chopped spring onion on a bed of green seaweed. There are a few 'new-style' maki such as squid shiso roll (not available on our visit) and scallop and cucumber roll, but well-made, traditional sushi is the forte. The food's good value too, with single nigiri costing 90p-£2.20. A huge glass of high-quality saké is a bargain at £5. Come armed with cash, as cheques and plastic aren't accepted, and the nearest cashpoint is a hike away.
Babies and children welcome; high chairs. Takeaway service.

Battersea SW11

★ Tokiya [NEW]
74 Battersea Rise, SW11 1EH (7223 5989/ www.tokiya.co.uk). Clapham Junction rail. **Lunch served** 12.30-3pm Sat, Sun. **Dinner served** 6.30-10.30pm Sat, Sun. **Main courses** £6.30-£16. **Set lunch** £7 3 courses. **Set dinner** £15-£18.50 5 courses. **Credit** AmEx, JCB, MC, V.
We love this place. It's Japanese-run, friendly and down to earth yet a deft observer of Japanese dining etiquette – and the food is first rate. We started with a cold, deliciously intense glass of umeshu (plum liqueur). Lemon-yellow walls, the roster for a sumo tournament, a couple of folk masks, a wooden floor and a hotchpotch of chairs create a homely vibe, while the menu covers much of the Japanese culinary map, and ends with a simple two-bottle wine 'list' (one red, one white) plus a few nationally specific tipples. The £13 sushi dinner set comprised ten pieces of sushi, each one different, all attractive, all fresh, all delicious. The morsel that tickled our fancy most? Seared salmon nigiri, topped with fine-chopped garlic that, the chef informed us, had been soaked in shoyu for six months. The salmon teriyaki menu (£16) brought two huge slices of salmon in a lovely sauce along with rice, miso shiru and salad. Some of the daily specials (deep-fried lemon sole in ponzu, for instance) sounded equally appetising. Our pretty waitress was amiable, and the chef sang out 'Hello! Evening!' to every new arrival.
Babies and children admitted. Booking advisable. Separate room for parties, seats 20. Takeaway service; delivery service. **Map 21 C4.**

Putney SW15

★ Chosan
292 Upper Richmond Road, SW15 6TH (8788 9626). East Putney tube. **Lunch served** noon-2.30pm Tue-Sat. **Dinner served** 6.30-10.30pm Tue-Sat; 6.30-10pm Sun. **Main courses** £3.30-£19.90. **Set lunch** £7.90-£13.90 incl miso soup, rice. **Set dinner** £17.90-£19.90 7 courses, £18.90-£24.90 bento box. **Service** 12.5%. **Credit** MC, V.
Small and unassuming though it looks from the outside, this is one of London's best spots for authentic Japanese food. Sleek and modern it isn't, however, with its profusion of varnished wood, potted plants and framed pictures hanging on brick

Ozu. See p179.

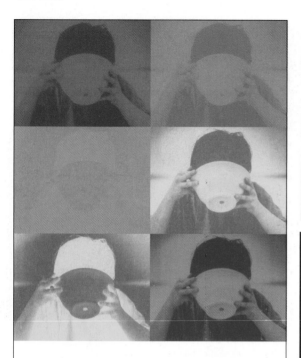
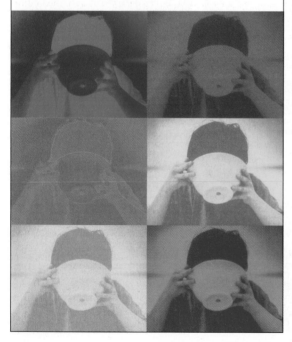

walls. The atmosphere is homey and comforting, but the food is serious. If you're on your own, nab a stool at the sushi counter and watch the chef work his magic; the range of fish is great, including the likes of ark shell, surf clam and wonderfully fresh uni. Daily specials might comprise grilled beef hearts and grilled salmon heads, but we opted for fried salmon skin served with a punchy ponzu sauce, and fried aubergine topped with minced pork in a savoury sauce. Sukiyaki, warm and comforting, came to the table ready-cooked in a heavy black pot brimming with beef, onion, carrot, cabbage, mushrooms and shirataki (konnyaku noodles), served with rice and a little dish of raw egg for dipping. Our neighbours' bento boxes looked pretty impressive too. Service is sweet, the food is nigh-on perfect and the saké list is good enough to impress connoisseurs.
Babies and children welcome. Separate area for parties, seats 22. Takeaway service.

Wimbledon SW19

Makiyaki
149 Merton Road, SW19 1ED (8540 3113/ www.makiyaki.com). South Wimbledon tube. **Lunch served** noon-3pm Mon-Sat. **Dinner served** 6-10pm Mon-Thur; 6-11pm Fri, Sat. **Main courses** £7.50-£14. **Set lunch** £7.50-£11.50 4 courses. **Set dinner** £19.50-£22.50. **Credit** MC, V.
You'd never guess from the grimy, residential exterior that there's a clean, welcoming, commercial enterprise here. As Makiyaki is run by Koreans, bulgogi and bibimbap rub shoulders on the menu with sushi, sashimi, noodles and tempura. Tables in the front (smoking) half of the restaurant contain hot-plates to accommodate lovers of yakiniku (barbecue, Seoul-style). On a Saturday lunchtime, all these tables were occupied and all had children at them (mercifully, only one was rowdy), and not a cigarette in sight. The ingredients in our order were fresh, the ceramic dishes pretty and portions plentiful, even if the salmon sashimi was a stubby cut and the tori kara-age underwhelmingly flavoured. Some things were fine if unremarkable, such as the nigiri sushi set, but the gyoza were well above average: dry, crisp parcels of moist, delicately seasoned pork. Our waitress didn't always understand our requests, but she kindly accommodated the off-carte demands of a three-year-old child for extra daikon string and sheets of nori. Seemingly stranded up a busy, dreary road (though just five minutes' walk from South Wimbledon tube), Makiyaki is clearly a family-friendly lunch option.
Babies and children welcome; high chairs. Booking advisable dinner Fri, Sat. No-smoking area. Takeaway service.

South

Clapham SW4

Tsunami
5-7 Voltaire Road, SW4 6DQ (7978 1610). Clapham North tube. **Dinner served** 6-11pm Mon-Thur; 6-11.30pm Fri. **Meals served** noon-11.30pm Sat. **Main courses** £6.95-£16.50. **Service** 12.5%. **Credit** AmEx, MC, V.
While you could question the wisdom of naming a restaurant after one of nature's sucker punches (a sea wave caused by an earthquake), the only evidence of mayhem visible from here might be a car wreck outside the fix-it shops across the street. Daylight, when available, pours in from a large skylight and even larger windows across satiny, dark-wood tables, chairs and chopsticks, white walls, tropical flowers and faux crocodile-skin banquettes the colour of Vuitton bags. Chic, no doubt, but thankfully the punters aren't all poseurs, and there's a healthy number of families. Tuna tataki in miso sauce, albeit costly (£9.95), was wonderful, and nasu goma (grilled aubergine) satisfyingly savoury. Vegetarian ju-ban served sizzling fiercely in a clay pot and grilled eel was well-presented indeed. But it's the little things we judge a restaurant by, and from that perspective Tsunami doesn't look so rosy: wine served in

Best Japanese

For sushi and sashimi
The roll-call includes **Café Japan** (*see p180*), **Chosan** (*see p176*), **Sushi-Hiro** (*see p176*) and **Sushi-Say** (*see p180*).

For kaiten-zushi
Moveable feasting at **K-10** (*see p169*), **Kulu Kulu** (*see p175*), **Moshi Moshi Sushi** (*see p169*), **Yokoso Sushi** (*see p171*) and **Yo! Sushi** (*see p176*).

For yakimono
Sample simple pleasures from the grill at **Donzoko** (*see p175*), **Ikkyu** (*see p172*), **Jin Kichi** (*see p180*) and newcomer **Roka** (*see p172*).

For modern Japanese
Traditional cuisine is given a twist at **Nobu** (*see p175*), **Roka** (*see p172*) and **Sumosan** (*see p175*), **Tsunami** (*see below*) and **Zuma** (*see p173*).

slightly grubby glasses; Western cutlery proffered twice when we were happy with chopsticks; and – failing the litmus test for any serious Japanese diner – too-dry rice. Hardly catastrophic, but a big wave away from the polished performance that earned Tsunami *Time Out*'s Best Japanese restaurant award in 2002.
Babies and children welcome. Booking advisable. Disabled: toilet. No-smoking tables. Takeaway service. **Map 22 B1.**

Waterloo SE1

Ozu NEW
County Hall, Westminster Bridge Road, SE1 7PB (7928 7766). Embankment or Westminster tube/Charing Cross or Waterloo tube/rail. **Lunch served** noon-3pm, **dinner served** 5.30-10.30pm Mon-Sat. **Main courses** £6.80-£15. **Set lunch** £10-£14 bento boxes. **Set dinner** £25.95 8 dishes incl saki and dessert. **Service** 12.5%. **Credit** AmEx, DC, JCB, MC, V.
Newcomer Ozu should be buzzing with people, delighted to discover somewhere on the South Bank that serves delectable food at a fair price, but the dining room was eerily quiet on our visit. Then again, it's not a place you stumble across, concealed in a distant corner of the County Hall building. A simply decorated room of japonoiserie, it has a glass-walled kitchen and western waiting staff. The menu covers the gamut of dishes found in the capital's better Japanese restaurants: deep-fried items, noodles, sashimi and sushi, grilled skewers, plus something unique to Ozu – 'kamado'. Kamado literally means 'kitchen range', but here it refers to the traditional ricepot dishes not previously seen in London. Arriving in wooden-lidded pots, the rice is cooked in a subtly flavoured stock, served with equally delicate toppings: quail egg, sansai ('wild vegetables') or snow crab. Other dishes were also done well. Tempura batter was light and crisp; a seaweed salad fresh and not too rockpool-odiferous; sushi rice was pert; and sashimi sharp-edged. Unusual textures and ingredients add interest: natto (fermented soy beans) was correctly stringy and slithery, and maguro yamakake – finely grated wild yam served with raw tuna – is certainly something you won't find in a Pret a Manger sushi pack.
Babies and children admitted. Booking advisable. Disabled: toilet. No-smoking tables. **Map 10 M9.**

South East

Catford SE6

★ Sapporo Ichiban
13 Catford Broadway, SE6 4SP (8690 8487). Catford rail. **Lunch served** noon-3pm Tue-Fri; noon-4.30pm Sat, Sun. **Dinner served** 6-10.30pm Tue-Sun. **Main courses** £5-£8. **Credit** AmEx, MC, V.

It is too easy to dismiss Sapporo Ichiban as being 'good for Catford'. Any area would be lucky to have such a pleasant, honest, hospitable and genuine neighbourhood restaurant in its midst. You can sit at modern café-style tables by the open kitchen and sushi bar, or at the more traditional tatami seating, and tuck into a menu that lists all the regulars: sashimi, sushi, teppanyaki, tempura, ramen, curry. Staff are keen, produce is decent, and the food is well-cooked – apart from the sashimi, obviously. While the sushi may not scintillate, it is very pleasant, and the quite mad 'fashion sandwich' of sushi rice, salmon, avocado and nori shaped into ritzy little triangles is fun and filling for £3.80. Two large skewers of tender yakitori are a bargain at £1.40; hiya-yakko (chilled tofu) is bright and fresh; the gyoza are good and solid; and the ramen with two big slabs of chicken katsu seems incredibly generous for £5. The best thing is the welcome when you arrive and the farewell when you leave; how rare, and how nice, is that?
Babies and children welcome. Booking advisable. Disabled: toilet. Takeaway service; delivery service (within 2-mile radius).

North

Camden Town & Chalk Farm NW1

★ Asakusa
265 Eversholt Street, NW1 1BA (7388 8533/ 8399). Camden Town or Mornington Crescent tube. **Dinner served** 6-11.30pm Mon-Fri; 6-11pm Sat. **Main courses** £5.50-£12. **Set dinner** £5.20-£19 incl miso soup, rice & pickles. **Service** 12%. **Credit** AmEx, MC, V.
The seedy decor remains unchanged, the basement stucco still as begrimed as the uncleaned wings of St Paul's. But either we were rumbled here, or the food at Asakusa has improved markedly since our last visit. A dish of yellowtail sashimi was as sweet as fruit; an order of sushi came beautifully presented and included good uni as well as unusual options from the à la carte menu, such as horse mackerel and ginger maki. The menu's emphasis on fried and grilled dishes shouldn't be taken as a sign that these are the best options; the highlights of our meal suggest that Asakusa is a surprisingly good place for raw produce. The notes handwritten in Japanese and stuck all over the walls here are not talismanic protections from death by stucco, but appendices to the printed menu; diners not shy about asking questions can do very well for themselves by getting the waitresses to translate. There's also a wide range of sakés to be sampled, which no doubt contributes to the very convivial, if down-at-heel atmosphere.
Babies and children welcome. Book dinner Fri, Sat. Separate room for parties, seats 20. Takeaway service. **Map 27 D3.**

North West

Colindale NW9

★ Oriental City Food Court
Oriental City, 399 Edgware Road, NW9 0JJ (8200 0009/www.oriental-city.com). Colindale tube/ 32, 142, 204, 303 bus. **Meals served** 10.30am-9.30pm Mon-Sat; 10am-8.30pm Sun. **Main courses** £3.50-£7.50. **No credit cards.**
In its original guise as Yaohan Plaza, this large shopping mall was enthusiastically billed as bringing all of Japan under one roof. These days, its appeal is more pan-oriental and the bustling food court serves up everything from Korean and Vietnamese to Malaysian and dim sum. The Japanese influence has shrunk to a sparsely stocked section in the supermarket, an excellent tableware shop (Utsuwa-no-Yakata) and four food stalls, the best of which is Noto Sushi (which also runs the Harrods sushi bar). The latter manages an old-fashioned sushi bar feel in spite of the conveyor belt, with particularly good tuna and salmon nigiri – although paying an extra quid for ginger seems a bit too Harrods. Noto Ramen

produces good, cheap bowls of ramen and udon, including a huge serving of tatsuta ramen with pork and some rather squishy gyoza. Less impressive was the bento box from the Atami stall, with its thickly crusted tempura, lacklustre sashimi and gluggy rice. Not what you would call destination dining, then.

Babies and children welcome; high chairs; nappy-changing facilities. Disabled: toilet. No-smoking tables. Takeaway service. Vegetarian menu.

Golders Green NW11

★ Café Japan

626 Finchley Road, NW11 7RR (8455 6854). Golders Green tube/13, 82 bus. **Lunch served** noon-2pm Sat, Sun. **Dinner served** 6-10pm Wed-Sat; 6-9.30pm Sun. **Main courses** £12-£16.50. **Set lunch** £8.20 bento box, soup. **Set dinner** £12-£17 bento box, soup. **Credit** (dinner) MC, V.

Despite two changes of ownership since opening in the mid 1990s, this former *Time Out* Eating & Drinking Award winner (Best Japanese, 1996) continues to keep Golders Greeners blissed out with a menu focusing on the raw end of the Japanese spectrum. A few years ago, chef-owner Koichi Konnai and his wife Kazuko decided to cut out the cooking (well, most of it) and concentrate on sushi and sashimi – to great effect. The quality cuts of fish are ultra-fresh and generously proportioned: stupendously in the case of the lunchtime chirashi sushi (Version A from a choice of three set sushis), which required a separate platter to bear its 'topping' of fatty tuna, salmon, sea urchin, salmon roe, cooked prawn, squid, octopus, marinated mackerel, bream, sea bass, clam, yellowtail and raw prawn. Keen to keep prices down, the Konnais accept cash only at lunchtime. Dining on a packed-out evening will cost a little more, but has the advantage of a longer menu and a specials list that usually offers some interesting diversions. On our way out we heard the chef tell a customer that black cod in miso was created here, not at Nobu. Whatever, Café Japan's version can definitely hold its own.

Babies and children welcome. Booking advisable. No-smoking. Takeaway service. Vegetarian menu.

Hampstead NW3

★ Jin Kichi

73 Heath Street, NW3 6UG (7794 6158). Hampstead tube. **Lunch served** 12.30-2pm Sat, Sun. **Dinner served** 6-11pm Tue-Sat; 6-10pm Sun. **Main courses** £5.30-£12.70. **Set lunch** £7.30-£13.80 incl miso soup, rice, green tea. **Credit** AmEx, DC, JCB, MC, V.

A very Hampstead sort of Japanese, this: clean, attractive, classy. It's of modest dimensions, with a small ground-floor room of counter and tables, and an even smaller tables-only basement; avoid the latter if possible. Not that Jin Kichi is an unpleasant place, quite the contrary. It's just that all it needs is a table of loudmouth Australians, like the bunch we had to endure, to spoil the mood. Decor-wise, simplicity (non-intrusive japonoiserie on the walls) and attention to detail (the double fugu fish emblem in the centre of the handsome dark blue dishes) are the watchwords; food-wise, very good presentation and ingredients. Cucumber and grilled eel in a ponzu dressing was fresh, tangy and delicious; the perfect agedashidofu was crisp and golden outside, melting inside, and made with first-class tofu. The sushi selection was fresh, tasty and artistic. Wind up with a shot of cold saké served in masu (small wooden boxes) with a side serving of salt. Jin Kichi has been in business for more than 15 years; we can see no reason why it shouldn't continue for at least as long again.

Babies and children admitted. Book Fri-Sun. Takeaway service. **Map 28 B2**.

Willesden NW2

★ Sushi-Say

33B Walm Lane, NW2 5SH (8459 2971). Willesden Green tube. **Lunch served** 1-3.30pm Sat, Sun. **Dinner served** 6.30-10.30pm Tue-Fri; 6-11pm Sat; 6-10pm Sun. **Main courses** £6.10-£18.90. **Set dinner** £18.20-£28.60 incl miso soup, rice & pickles, dessert. **Credit** AmEx, JCB, MC, V.

Long and as low-ceilinged as a Nissen hut, with wasabi-green walls and ersatz-lacquer spotlight gantries, Sushi-Say is an odd-looking fish, neither straight Japanese nor London fashionable. If you dine out for atmosphere, this may not be the place for you. On the other hand, no amount of dubious lacquer will disguise the fact that Sushi-Say is one of the most interesting Japanese restaurants in London. This is a good place for basics: a miso soup of balanced stock and quality tofu; edamame that reach the table al dente and piping hot (never trust a Japanese restaurant where they're served cold – if the edamame are prepared ahead of time, chances are other dishes will be too). Service is charming, the menu isn't overstretched and although the 'daily specials' seem to recur regularly, they're also reliable. Buri daikon (yellowtail and white radish in stock), for instance, was pure winter comfort food, the components simmered into sweet softness: a good example of the versatility of daikon. Also noteworthy is the single tatami seating area at the rear of the restaurant, available for bookings of four or more.

Babies and children welcome. Booking advisable. No smoking. Takeaway service.

Sapporo Ichiban. See p179.

Jewish

The joy of Jewish food is its variety. Jews, spread all over the world, took with them strict dietary laws and then adapted the specialities they found abroad. To be kosher a restaurant must be strictly supervised, adhering to the laws of what may be eaten (no shellfish or pork), how animals are killed, and what may be combined (separating dairy products from meat). Some venues offer Jewish favourites such as salt beef, but the meat is not kosher; such places might also serve desserts with cream. We've noted in the listings (in red) which places are not kosher.

There are two main strands of cooking: Ashkenazi from Russia and eastern Europe, and Sephardi, originating in Spain and Portugal. After the Inquisition, Sephardi Jews settled throughout the Mediterranean, in Iraq and further east. London used to have only Ashkenazi restaurants, most of which were in the East End, but now north-west London is full of Sephardi bakeries and cafés, specialising in the Middle Eastern food that you might find in Jerusalem. Not surprisingly, the highest concentration of eateries are around the Jewish area of Golders Green.

You can still get traditional chicken soup and knaidlach or fried latkes, but these are rarely as good as you'll find in the home. What the professionals do well are the meze (starters) and grilled meats. Jewish bread has always been good in London, but now the Israeli bakers have arrived. Added to their skill in making challah and bagels comes a knowledge of French pâtisserie, so they also turn out refined cakes and light pastries. Sweets in restaurants are less successful. Non-dairy ice-cream is a shadow of the real thing, so it's better to choose baklava or lockshen pudding. Jews tend to be less interested in drinking than eating, so although there may be wine, they expect and enjoy large platefuls. The menu may be Chinese, Iraqi, Israeli or Modern European, but portions will always be generous. As a Jewish grandmother would say: 'Enjoy!'

CAFÉS, BAKERIES & TAKEAWAYS

East

Brick Lane E1

Brick Lane Beigel Bake
159 Brick Lane, E1 6SB (7729 0616). Liverpool Street tube/rail/8 bus. **Open** 24hrs daily. **No credit cards. Not kosher**
Once part of a vibrant Jewish community, the Brick Lane bakery now serves local Bangladeshi residents and assorted night-time revellers. But the style hasn't changed. The bagels are boiled, then baked and the smell of rye bread and challah coming from the back of the bakery, day and night, wafts down the street. There are a few stools on which to perch, but most trade is in takeaways. The bakery is sited at the less colourful end of the street, though punters who walk on past the curry houses are rewarded with great-value bagels

generously filled with smoked salmon, salt beef or egg and onion. Don't leave without picking up some carrot or cheesecake at 60p a portion. *Takeaway service.* **Map 6 S4**.

Whitechapel E1

Rinkoff's NEW
79 Vallance Road, E1 5BS (7247 6228). Whitechapel tube. **Open** 7am-4.45pm Mon-Fri; 7am-3pm Sun. **No credit cards. Not kosher**
The original business was started in 1911 by Hyman Rinkoff from Russia. Now his grandsons are in charge; they've added a new café/deli to the existing bakery (with a mural of grandpa on the outside wall), in the hope of reviving the tradition of Jewish baking in the area. Whitechapel Market now sells saris and Asian foods rather than Jewish pickles, but the Rinkoffs have brought back a taste of the old Jewish East End. Smoked salmon and cream cheese bagels are as good as ever, with just the right chewiness. Chopped herring is a sweet reminder of Ashkenazi food, so too the cheesecake and creamy-topped carrot cake. There's also a range of fine deli produce (including beef salami) and fresh salads.
Babies and children admitted. No smoking. Tables outdoors (2, pavement). Takeaway service.
For branch see index.

North West

East Finchley NW11

Parkview NEW
56 The Market Place, NW11 6JP (8458 1878). East Finchley tube. **Meals served** 8am-6pm Mon-Fri; Sun. **Main courses** £4.50-£6.50. **Credit** (over £10) MC, V.
This corner café has two views, so you should choose to sit facing the park. By 1pm in summer, the tables outside (overlooking a garage) are full of mums with toddlers. Inside there's an older crowd, enjoying Israeli food. The service is pleasant yet distracted, so two main courses came five minutes apart. The bread and rolls (from local kosher bakeries) looked good, but mini borekas – warm and full of cheese or mushroom – made a better partner to the corn soup. The huge, toasted jerusalem bagel, topped with sesame seeds and filled with feta cheese, zatar and artichokes, was just what you might get in Ben Yehuda Street. Dessert cakes 'from the Holy Land' really do come from Israel, with dough for the pastries also flown in and baked on the premises. Parkview is worth a visit just for the chocolate cake: a dark base melting into a mousse, with white chocolate icing.
Babies and children welcome; high chairs. Kosher supervised (Beth Din). No smoking. Tables outdoors (7, pavement). Takeaway service.

Golders Green NW11

Café Also NEW
1255 Finchley Road, NW11 0AD (8455 6890). Golders Green tube. **Lunch served** noon-5pm daily. **Dinner served** 6-10pm Mon-Thur, Sat, Sun. **Main courses** £8.25-£12.95. **Set lunch** £9.95 2 courses. **Set dinner** £17.50 3 courses. **Credit** MC, V. **Not kosher**
If you've ever felt like browsing between courses, here's your chance. Joseph, the owner, also runs the Bookstore next door. As with the books, the café is 'mainly Jewish'; it serves only kosher fish and vegetarian dishes. The pale wood tables and glass front give an open feel and the food is equally light.

There are soups and pastas, but also modern salads such as mozzarella or seared tuna niçoise. Cold meze include taramasalata and a proper tabouleh, with more parsley and tomato than filling bulgar. These dishes are more successful than the solid, mainly fried hot hors d'oeuvres, though a half aubergine filled with onions and tomato was meltingly cheesy. Fish comes from the excellent Corney's fish shop, down the road; halibut and trout looked appealingly moist. To finish, carrot cake was more a hazelnut sponge with strips of carrot, but was light and warm and came with a strawberry sauce.
Babies and children welcome; high chairs. Booking advisable. No smoking. Tables outdoors (2, pavement).

Carmelli
128 Golders Green Road, NW11 8HB (8455 2074/www.carmelli.co.uk). Golders Green tube. **Open** 6.30am-1am Mon-Wed; 6am Thur-1hr before Sabbath Fri; 1hr after Sabbath Sat-1am Mon.* **No credit cards.**
At night much of this stretch of Golders Green (with 23 eateries in a few hundred metres) is buzzing with teenagers. They don't eat, but anyone who stands near Carmelli must be lured by the sweet smell of baking. Food to go is the only option; there's no seating. Everything is made on the premises and it shows – instead of tired-looking pastries or buns, there are trays of challah, rolls and bagels fresh from the oven. In this parev section there's also rye or black bread and biscuits and flans. On the right are hot savouries: pizza, borekas and wobbly quiche. The middle area is for serious cakes: luscious, fruit-topped sponges, cheesecakes or small eclairs oozing cream. Like the pâtisserie, the glazed danish pastries need to be eaten the same day – but is that a problem?
Kosher supervised (Beth Din and Kedassia).
For branch see index.

Daniel's Bagel Bakery
12-13 Hallswelle Parade, Finchley Road, NW11 0DL (8455 5826). Golders Green tube. **Open** 7am-9pm Mon-Wed; 7am-10pm Thur; 7am-1hr before Sabbath Fri.* **No credit cards.**
If you're in the area and want to meet a friend for a leisurely chat, Dan's Café is ideal. You'll be left alone with practically no attention from the waitress. From the all-day menu of pizza, salads and sandwiches we tried a mushroom soup and a savoury crêpe: both were over-salted and sprinkled with dried parsley. The pastries from the adjoining bakery are in a different league. We chose an almondy plum torte and an excellent sweet cheese danish to go with equally good espressos. From a big selection at the counter the apple strudel looked best, and there's an array of appealing rolls, bagels and loaves.
Kosher supervised (Beth Din).

Dizengoff's Fried Chicken NEW
122 Golders Green Road, NW11 8HB (8209 0232/www.dizengoffkosherrestaurant.co.uk). Golders Green tube. **Meals served** noon-midnight Mon-Thur, Sun; noon-1hr before Sabbath Fri; 1hr after Sabbath-midnight Sat. **Main courses** £3.99-£6.49. **No credit cards.**
Admittedly, Golders Green Road is not the Croisette in Cannes, but it's still fun to sit outside Dizengoff's and people-watch. Many unlikely customers find their way to this new takeaway modelled on KFC, to sample the kosher fast-food. There's a small American-style menu of fried chicken, burgers, wings and hot dogs. The place still seems to be in its experimental stage; the burgers were passable, and the recipe for honey-roast wings might not be the same from one week to the next. Chips are up (down?) to McDonald's standard. But the fried chicken was fine: crunchy, with a nice flavour and not too oily. The meal deals are good value, making this a useful stop for a quick meal. Don't say we told you, but you might want to finish your meal by popping into the Israeli fruit shop opposite.
Babies and children welcome; high chairs. Kosher supervised (Sephardi). No smoking. Tables outdoors (4, pavement). Takeaway service.

Hendon NW4

Bonjour NEW

84 Brent Street, NW4 2ES (8203 8848).
Hendon Central tube. **Meals served** 7am-
11pm Mon-Thur, Sun; 7am-6pm Fri.
No credit cards.
There's little to see (and nowhere to eat-in) at this
small Israeli-run bakery. It's all happening in the
back where staff bake several times a day, turning
out hot borekas, baguettes and croissants. The
flour is imported from France; the frozen dough
comes from Israel where Bonjour has hundreds of
outlets turning out their popular puffy pastries. If
Jews are like other people 'only more so', then the
rugelach here are like danish pastries 'only more
so'. The coffee or chocolate versions are sweet and
sticky – and huge bestsellers. If you just want
bread, you'll find it hard to choose between the
crusty tin loaves and the poppy- or sesame-
sprinkled challah.
Kosher supervised (Beth Din). Takeaway service.

Hendon Bagel Bakery

55-57 Church Road, NW4 4DU (8203 6919).
Hendon Central tube. **Open** 7am-11pm Mon-Wed;
7am-midnight Thur; 7am-6pm Fri; 11pm Sat-
11pm Sun. **No credit cards**.
Don't be put off by the gruff manner of the Israeli
owner at this great bakery; he supplies excellent
bread to his three north London cafés and shops.
Challahs and rye are especially good, with the
bagels coming a close third. Customers pack the
shop as the hot loaves come out of the oven; it's a
wonder they're not all sampling the little danish
pastries. The sweet cheese or cinnamon raisin
puffs are best eaten warm and not left to get cold.
If you're arranging a party in a hurry, pick up
platters of filled mini-bagels and rolls. The bakery
also does goujons of fish and borekas, exotic fruit
platters and tarts.
Kosher supervised (Federation).
For branches (Orli) see index.

Outer London

Edgware, Middlesex

Penashe NEW

60 Edgware Way, Mowbray Parade, Edgware,
Middx HA8 8JS (8958 6008/www.penashe.co.uk).
Edgware tube. **Meals served** noon-10pm Mon-
Thur, Sun. **Main courses** £2.95-£6.95. **Credit**
MC, V.
Under the name Penashe is the logo 'Kosher Food
Just Got Better'. The fast food here is modelled on
that of a New York deli. Inside you'll find high
stools and a large-screen TV, burgers and hot dogs.
The milkshake tastes strongly of pink, but the
meat is good. Best of all, it's freshly cooked, so
although it's fast food, you have to wait for tender
chicken wings or char-grilled beef in above-
average bread. Chips are chunky. We liked
Penashe's inspired idea of serving waffles with
maple syrup outside breakfast hours. If you're
aged about ten, you'll probably go for the slushies,
candyfloss or popcorn.
Babies and children welcome; children's menu;
high chairs. Kosher supervised (Beth Din).
No smoking. Takeaway service.

RESTAURANTS

Central

City EC3

★ Bevis Marks Restaurant

Bevis Marks, EC3A 5DQ (7283 2220/
www.bevismarkstherestaurant.com). Aldgate tube/
Liverpool Street tube/rail. **Lunch served** noon-
3pm Mon-Fri. **Dinner served** 5.30-7.15pm Mon-
Thur. **Main courses** £9.50-£15.90. **Service**
12.5%. **Credit** AmEx, MC, V.

The Restaurant shares a wall with Britain's oldest
surviving synagogue, built in 1701. From the airy
lattice-covered dining room you can see the old
chandeliers through the synagogue windows. The
setting is matched by fine-quality cutlery and
tablecloths, and pleasant, unobtrusive service. The
menu, which changes every few months, is
inventive – what might be termed Modern British/
Kosher. There's a nod towards tradition with
chicken soup and salt beef, but far better are the
dishes where the chef has made his mark. We
enjoyed braised ribeye steak with a red wine and
shallot jus, and a confit of duck with pomegranate
and walnut sauce. A tagine of lamb with apricot
and couscous looked tasty. There are also a couple
of fish or vegetarian dishes. From a good wine list
came a full-bodied Israeli cabernet sauvignon.
Curiosity (rather than hunger) made us try the
meltingly dark chocolate brownie. A pineapple-
based fruit salad with mango sorbet was better
than the non-dairy pistachio ice-cream. The
Restaurant and courtyard (not to be confused with
the heaving Bevis bar opposite) is deservedly full.
Book ahead and arrive early so you can see round
the synagogue first.
Babies and children admitted. Booking advisable
lunch. Disabled: toilet. Kosher supervised
(Sephardi). Restaurant available for hire. Tables
outdoors (4, courtyard). Takeaway service.
Vegetarian menu. **Map 12 R6**.

Marylebone W1

Reuben's

79 Baker Street, W1U 6RG (7486 0035).
Baker Street tube.
Deli/café **Open** 11.30am-4pm, 5-10pm Mon-Thur,
Sun; 11.30am-1hr before Sabbath Fri.
Restaurant **Lunch served** 11.45am-1hr before
Sabbath Fri. **Meals served** 11.45am-4pm,
5-10pm Mon-Thur, Sun. **Main courses** £10-£20.
Minimum £10 per person. **Credit** MC, V.
The ground-floor restaurant offers the likes of beef
wellington or chicken kiev at West End prices. To

Menu

Bagels or **beigels**: heavy,
ring-shaped rolls. The dough
is first boiled then glazed
and baked. The classic filling
is smoked salmon and cream
cheese.
Baklava: filo pastry layered
with almonds or pistachios
and soaked in scented syrup.
Blintzes: pancakes, most
commonly filled with cream
cheese, but also with sweet
or savoury fillings.
Borekas: triangles of filo
pastry with savoury fillings
like cheese or spinach.
Borscht: a classic beetroot
soup served hot or cold,
often with sour cream.
Calf's foot jelly (also called
petchah or **footsnoga**):
cubes of jellied stock,
served cold.
Challah or **cholla**: egg-rich,
slightly sweet plaited bread
for Sabbath.
Chicken soup: a clear, golden
broth made from chicken
and vegetables.
Chopped liver: chicken or
calf's liver fried with onions,
finely chopped and mixed
with hard-boiled egg and

chicken fat. Served cold,
often with extra egg and
onions.
Chrane or **chrain**: a pungent
sauce made from grated
horseradish and beetroot,
served with cold fish.
Cigars: rolls of filo pastry
with a sweet or savoury
filling.
Falafel: spicy, deep-fried
balls of ground chickpeas,
served with houmous and
tahina (sesame paste).
Gefilte fish: white fish
minced with onions and
seasoning, made into balls
and poached or fried; served
cold. The sweetened version
is Polish.
Houmous: chickpeas puréed
with sesame paste, lemon
juice, garlic and oil.
Kataifi or **konafa**: shredded
filo pastry wrapped around
a nut or cheese filling,
soaked in syrup.
Kibbe, kuba, kubbeh or
kobeiba: oval patties,
handmade from a shell
of crushed wheat (bulgar)
filled with minced meat, pine
nuts and spices. Shaping and

filling the shells before frying
is the skill.
Knaidlach or **kneidlach**:
dumplings made from matzo
meal and eggs, poached until
they float 'like clouds' in
chicken soup. Also called
matzo balls.
Kreplach: pockets of noodle
dough filled with meat and
served in soup, or with
sweet fillings, eaten with
sour cream.
Latkes: grated potato mixed
with egg and fried into crisp
pancakes.
Lockshen: egg noodles
boiled and served in soup.
When cold, they can be
mixed with egg, sugar and
cinnamon and baked into
a pudding.
Matzo or **matzah**: flat
squares of unleavened
bread. When ground into
meal, it's used as a coating
for fish or schnitzel to make
it crisp.
Parev or **parve**: a term
describing food that is neither
meat nor dairy.
Rugelach: crescent-shaped
biscuits made from a rich,

cream cheese pastry, filled
with nuts, jam or chocolate.
Popular in Israel and America.
Salt beef: pickled brisket,
with a layer of fat, poached
and served in slices.
Schnitzel: thin slices of
chicken, turkey or veal,
dipped in egg and matzo
meal and fried.
Schwarma or **shwarma**:
layers of lamb or turkey,
cooked on a rotating spit,
served with pitta.
Strudel: wafer-thin pastry
wrapped around an apple
or soft cheese filling.
Tabeet: traditional Iraqi
Sabbath dish of chicken
and rice.
Tabouleh: cracked wheat
(bulgar) mixed with ample
amounts of fresh herbs,
tomato and lemon juice,
served as a starter or salad.
Viennas: boiled frankfurter
sausages, served with chips
and salt beef.
Zatar: a spice mixture,
popular in Israel, made from
wild thyme, sesame seeds
and red berries of the
sumac tree.

sample traditional chopped liver and chicken soup, head upstairs, where the food is less expensive (though not cheap). Help yourself from the deli and cheerful staff will bring grills or desserts to the table. What to choose? Don't expect the taste of home-cooked food. The soup is fine, but the matzo balls were too firm. Latkes are so huge they lose the crispness of a freshly fried pancake. The salt beef sandwich in good rye bread would be better if the fat-police hadn't got to it; trimming off the fat takes away some of the flavour. But you can hardly go wrong with chops or steak, as long as you double-specify how rare you want them. Desserts were disappointing: a fruit salad billed as 'the talk of the town' had a few exotic fruits in a bed of chopped apple; and strudel came reheated on a drizzle of chocolate syrup. Our advice: choose the sandwiches. You won't go away hungry.
Babies and children welcome; high chairs. Booking advisable (restaurant). Kosher supervised (Sephardi). No-smoking tables. Tables outdoors (3, pavement). Takeaway service. Map 3 G5.

Six-13
19 Wigmore Street, W1U 1PH (7629 6133/ www.six13.com). Bond Street or Oxford Circus tube. **Lunch served** noon-3pm Mon-Thur. **Dinner served** *Summer* 5.30-10.30pm Mon-Thur; (prepaid only) from 7.30pm Fri. *Winter* 5.30-10.30pm Mon-Thur. **Main courses** £17-£24. **Set meal** (lunch) £20 2 courses; £24.50 3 courses. **Credit** AmEx, MC, V.
This smart, modern restaurant has a minimalist turquoise interior and offers well-crafted cuisine. We started with a good seared tuna and fashionably mounded terrine of ocean trout. While many kosher restaurants simply grill their steaks, Six-13 offers tender cuts of beef or duck with sour cherry or red wine jus. The staff even expect you to order it rare – unheard of in eastern Europe. A fruity 'cassia' of lamb came with a tagine-like sauce. So much for the successful innovations. Houmous with chicken liver pâté, and chunks of salt beef in the bean and barley soup, were less harmonious. The bland avocado soup had a smidgen of olive tapenade instead of the billed salmon caviar, while a lamb burger (surely something special at £18.50?) was a heavy, unseasoned patty on an unhappy layer of aubergine and coleslaw. The non-Jewish chef has worked hard on dairy-free desserts like coconut mocha parfait and chocolate torte, but incorporating the already sweetened parev cream into ices needs a master touch. Six-13 aims high. There's much to praise here, but perfection is to be found on a higher plane.
Babies and children welcome; high chairs. Kosher supervised (Beth Din). Separate room for parties, seats 22. Takeaway service; delivery service. Map 9 H6.

North West

Golders Green NW11

Bloom's
130 Golders Green Road, NW11 8HB (8455 1338). Golders Green tube. **Meals served** noon-10.30pm Mon-Thur, Sun; noon-3pm Fri. **Main courses** £7.50-£17.50. **Credit** AmEx, DC, MC, V.
The old-timers sit at the back of the restaurant waiting for it to get busy. These are the waiters. They might have been trained by a Jewish grandmother ('I've given you an extra bit of chopped liver; if you don't want the lockshen you can have another matzo ball'), and ours told us he'd been working for Bloom's for 39 years. There was hardly time to take in the mural – a fanciful impression of a Jewish street – when the starters arrived. Liver, egg and onion came with matzo crackers and rye bread. Perfect. Steaming chicken soup was overflowing with knaidlach and kreplach, the sheer quantity of the balls and meat-filled noodle dough making up for a slight lack in taste. On to the speciality salt beef, a hefty portion with enough fat to give it a taste rating of 8/10. Barbecued chicken also scored well, but the latke was too solid. Instead of apple strudel or sorbets, the only dessert we could manage was a refreshing

Bevis Marks Restaurant

bowl of fruit salad. And walking past the deli on the way out, we couldn't resist a takeaway lockshen pudding. We should have quit while ahead.
Babies and children welcome; children's menu; high chairs. Kosher supervised (Beth Din). Tables outdoors (2, pavement). Takeaway service.

Dizengoff's
118 Golders Green Road, NW11 8HB (8458 7003/www.dizengoffkosherrestaurant.co.uk). Golders Green tube. **Meals served** noon-midnight Mon-Thur, Sun. *Winter* **Dinner served** 6-11.30pm Sat. **Main courses** £12-£15. **Credit** MC, V.
Named after the famous street in Tel Aviv, Dizengoff is decorated with photographs of the city's cafés and markets. It's an ideal venue for an Ashkenazi to eat with Sephardi friends: the one could order chopped liver, hearty soups and warming puddings, the others might enjoy the spicier Middle Eastern specialities. Service is prompt and cheery; a bowl of olives and pickles was brought immediately to the table. For starters, there are six types of houmous, filo cigars, crisp kibbe, and aubergine slices, which came in a rich, oily tomato sauce. On a weekday lunchtime the kitchen was busy turning out large portions of meat with excellent rice or chips. The schnitzel was a generous cut of juicy chicken in matzo meal, crisp on the outside, but braised lamb shank was less appealing in its watery sauce. The chef who cooks the grilled meats and takeaway schwarma seems to come from a different school from the one who prepares the underseasoned and overcooked vegetables. If you have room, go for a large square of warm, honey-soaked baklava or the lockshen pudding, unusually light and tasting faintly of apple and cinnamon.
Babies and children welcome; high chairs. Book weekends. Kosher supervised (Sephardi). Tables outdoors (3, pavement). Takeaway service.

La Fiesta NEW
239 Golders Green Road, NW11 9PN (8458 0444). Brent Cross tube. **Lunch served** noon-3pm Mon-Thur. **Dinner served** 6-10.30pm Mon-Thur, Sun. **Main courses** £7.50-£22. **Set lunch** £12.50 3 courses incl coffee, tea or soft drink. **Credit** AmEx, MC, V.
Ask for a table by the window for a view into the bustling life of this religious part of Golders Green. La Fiesta is busy too. Unusually, it offers Argentinian-Jewish food (though the steaks are British), with music from a South American duo. As ever, the quantity almost makes up for lapses in flavour. To start, we skipped over pastry empanadas and went for soups and a vegetable brochette. Chicken soup was standard, but the tomato and red pepper soup was pleasantly hot in both senses. Grilled vegetables (with too many tomatoes) on two skewers was, again, a generous

helping. Lamb and beef (asado ribs) are served over white-hot coals, so unless you like well-done meat, order them rare, because they continue cooking on the coals. The flavour? Nothing spectacular, but enlivened by a well-spiced chimi churri sauce (a dip of parsley, garlic, onion and chilli). What would you expect from an Argentinian crêpe? We ordered apple and cinnamon, but the version drizzled with caramel was better. Forget the whipped cream or ice-cream; in a kosher meat restaurant both are non-dairy.
Babies and children welcome; high chairs. Booking advisable dinner. Kosher supervised (Beth Din). No-smoking tables. Separate area for parties, seats 90. Takeaway service.

Met Su Yan NEW
134 Golders Green Road, NW11 8HP (8458 8088/www.metsuyan.co.uk). Golders Green tube. **Lunch served** noon-3pm Sun. **Dinner served** 6-11pm Mon-Thur, Sun. **Main courses** £10.95-£15.95. **Set meal** £19.50 2 courses, £25-£29.50 3 courses, £39.50 4 courses. **Credit** AmEx, MC, V.
At first glance this seems like a run-of-the-mill Chinese restaurant, but closer inspection of the embossed menu on the elegant wooden tables reveals a secret. 'Metsuyan' in Hebrew means 'excellent' and the food here is kosher Chinese. Instead of pork, there's lamb, but does it have enough of what Jews call *ta'am* or taste? The Imperial hors d'oeuvres delivered crunch and flavour with good sesame chicken toast, marinated lamb spare ribs and skewered chicken in a spicy satay sauce. In contrast, West Lake beef soup, though full of peas, egg and pieces of meat, lacked the punch of a good consommé. Rice and crispy noodles made a nice foil for the sweet chilli sauce of the crispy shredded beef, but aromatic duck with pancakes and hoisin sauce was dry. Having chosen (wisely) more fried dishes than the blander steamed food, we didn't order dessert fritters. Next time we'll try tuna or salmon in black bean sauce, or opt for the vegetarian selection. Service was pleasant, if a little retiring.
Babies and children welcome; high chairs. Booking advisable. Kosher supervised (Federation). No smoking. Takeaway service.

★ Solly's
148A Golders Green Road, NW11 8HE (ground floor & takeaway 8455 2121/first floor 8455 0004). Golders Green tube.
Ground floor **Lunch served** noon-3pm Fri. **Meals served** noon-11pm Mon-Thur, Sun; 1hr after Sabbath-1am Sat. **Main courses** £10-£15. **Set meal** £22 3 courses.
First floor **Dinner served** 6.30-11.30pm Mon-Thur, Sun. *Winter* 1hr after Sabbath-midnight Sat. **Main courses** £8.50-£15. **Set dinner** £22 3 courses.
Both **Credit** AmEx, MC, V.

The dreary side entrance to this first-floor restaurant leads to a staircase hung with oriental carpets. Upstairs, the decor resembles that of a faded harem. Yet the traditional Lebanese Sephardi food draws the crowds. Anyone who has eaten in Jerusalem will recognise the style: simple grilled meats and brilliant pitta bread, freshly baked in the on-view oven. Main courses of boneless chicken or lamb kebabs came with a pile of fat chips or Iraqi-style rice, the grains perfectly cooked, with vermicelli for contrast. Starters were outstanding; a mixed plate of hot hors d'oeuvres (£12 for two people, but enough for three or four) included blackened chicken wings, cinnamon-scented meat kibbe, minced meat filo cigars and falafel. Forget the solid fried balls and dip the rest into the creamy houmous, pleasantly oily and with whole chickpeas. Only the greediest will be able to tackle dessert: nut-filled pastries soaked in syrup. While you wait for the bill (which can take time), enjoy a glass of fresh mint tea. Downstairs, there's a large café/takeaway, with shining new wood and sizzling schwarmas.
Babies and children welcome; high chairs. Booking advisable (upstairs). Kosher supervised (Beth Din). No-smoking tables. Separate room for parties, seats 100. Takeaway service.

Hendon NW4

Isola Bella Café NEW
63 Brent Street, NW4 2EA (8203 2000/ www.isolabellacafe.com). Hendon Central tube. **Meals served** 8am-11pm Mon-Thur, Sun; 8am-4pm Fri. **Main courses** £10-£18. **Set lunch** £15-£18 3 courses. **Credit** AmEx, DC, MC. V.
Strictly kosher dairy restaurants are rare in London, so Isola Bella's bright tables, topped with old maps of the world, are crowded morning and evening. There's one word to describe the menu: gigantic. From breakfast dishes of croissants and eggs, through a lunch menu of soups and sandwiches, you reach number 349 before you get to the end. Expecting Italian from the name, we were surprised also to find many Thai dishes. Both cuisines are competently executed: cheese ravioli had a good mushroom sauce; stir-fried noodles with wun tun and cashews came with plenty of vegetables, including oyster mushrooms and al dente green beans. Gigantic also applies to the portions; all the plates could easily be shared between two. There's no wine, but while you decide between a dozen different coffees you can drool over the super-rich desserts: layers of meringue, mousse, white chocolate, ganache and the like. One pudding, aptly named Himalaya, even fitted in a layer of tiramisu and praline. Service comes from smiling but amateurish and slow waitresses.
Babies and children welcome; children's menu; high chairs. Booking advisable. Kosher supervised (Beth Din). No smoking. Separate room for parties, seats 70. Takeaway service. Vegetarian menu.

Mama's Kosher Restaurant & Takeaway NEW
53 Brent Street, NW4 2EA (8202 5444). Hendon Central tube. **Meals served** 11am-11.30pm Mon-Thur, Sun; 11am-5pm Fri (1pm in winter). **Main courses** £8-£16. **Set lunch** (Mon-Fri) £7.99 1 course incl drink. **Credit** AmEx, MC, V.
The long room with café-style tables at recently opened Mama's was buzzing by 8.30pm. The owner, who'd flown in his mother from Israel to instruct the chefs in the art of Iraqi Sephardi cooking, offered new customers small dishes of starters on the house. These included falafel that had just been fried and a herby tabouleh; both tasted homemade. The main-course specialities, kibbe with okra or beetroot, were as they should be, though there could have been more meat in the semolina dumplings. Mama's had also got the tabeet right; a group of Iraqis at a nearby table were nodding approval. As in many new restaurants, service and timing were patchy. Iced water was brought instantly to the table, but the main courses (one was sent back as it was cold) were put down before the starters had been

cleared. All was forgiven with the gift of a vanilla cake and a surprisingly good parev chocolate pudding with chocolate sauce.
Babies and children welcome; booster seats; children's menu. Booking advisable. Kosher supervised (Federation). No smoking. Tables outdoors (1, pavement). Takeaway service.

Sami's Kosher Restaurant
157 Brent Street, NW4 4DJ (8203 8088). Hendon Central tube. **Lunch served** noon-3pm, **dinner served** 5pm-midnight Mon-Thur. **Meals served** 1hr after Sabbath-1am Sat; noon-midnight Sun. **Set lunch** £9.95 2 courses, £12.95 3 courses. **Main courses** £11.95-£14.50. **Credit** MC, V.
This corner café is an enigma. The owner is no longer called Sami. The linen tablecloths lead you to expect a sophistication quite at odds with the yellow plastic benches and fake plants. But the food is good. Service was, shall we say, distracted: the waitress simply forgot to bring the starters we ordered. So one enormous main course of lamb schwarma and chips arrived, followed later by a rib steak with rice. It was all well cooked, though the steak was disappointingly thin. Enjoying the excellent red cabbage that came with it, we were then presented with our starters: tahina and rice kibbe. Both were faultless, the kibbe handmade with a crisp shell and chicken filling. To make up for her mistake, the waitress offered us complimentary bread: a large puffy pitta. We couldn't finish everything on our plates, so sat for a while over a glass of fresh mint tea and then decided to attempt dessert. Fruit salad in a large bowl with plenty of pineapple and mango was refreshing, while three warm pieces of baklava and kataifi made a sweet ending to an enjoyable, if disorganised, meal.
Babies and children welcome; children's menu; high chairs. Kosher supervised (Beth Din). No smoking. Takeaway service.

St John's Wood NW8

Harry Morgan's
31 St John's Wood High Street, NW8 7NH (7722 1869/www.harryms.co.uk). St John's Wood tube. **Meals served** 11.30am-10pm Mon-Fri; noon-10pm Sat, Sun. **Main courses** £8.95-£11.50. **Service** 12.5%. **Credit** AmEx, MC, V. Not kosher
In this gilded street of boutiques and brasseries, it must be sheer nostalgia that takes folk back to Harry Morgan. The place has had a stylish revamp and the well-lit art on the white walls is attractive. At the back is a long display of wine bottles, but most of the customers don't seem to want wine with their kosher food. There are sandwiches and filled bagels, chicken soups and gefilte fish, yet most popular is the salt beef, which comes lean or not, regular or large. We ordered old-fashioned calf's foot jelly to start, deliciously wobbly and patterned with hard-boiled egg. We also had a glass of tangy cold borscht, before tackling a hefty main course of fried haddock. The fish boasted fresh moist flakes inside a crisp skin, but the mash was woeful and the latke a bit too stodgy. Desserts were a treat: a cinnamony apple strudel and a creamy cheese blintz, both adorned with not-too-sweet fruit sauce and a cape gooseberry. Too bad it took 20 minutes to get the bill from an otherwise pleasant waitress.
Babies and children welcome; high chairs. Booking advisable (taken on weekdays only). Tables outdoors (5, pavement). Takeaway service. **Map 2 E2.**

Outer London

Edgware, Middlesex

★ Aviv
87-89 High Street, Edgware, Middx HA8 7DB (8952 2484/www.avivrestaurant.com). Edgware tube. **Lunch served** noon-2.30pm Mon-Thur, Sun. **Dinner served** Winter 5.30-11pm Mon-Thur, Sat, Sun. Summer 5.30-11pm Mon-Thur, Sun. **Main courses** £9.95-£12.95. **Set lunch** (noon-2.30pm Mon-Thur) £8.95 2 courses. **Set meals** £14.95, £18.95, 3 courses. **Service** 10%. **Credit** AmEx, MC, V.

In recent years both the bright airy space and the menu have expanded at Aviv. Keen to try out more adventurous offerings, we strayed from the successful Israeli specialities and found some of the dishes disappointing. Barbecued spare ribs were stewed and the roast fillet of duck was masked by an over-sweet honey sauce. Starters of chopped liver, houmous and falafel, aubergine or meat cigars are what to order here. Grilled sole was fresh, even on a Monday, but slightly greasy. A char-grilled rib steak was faultless – rare and tender, with excellent chips. Lamb cutlets with a jacket potato were less pleasing. A glass of house red from a wide selection of Israeli and French wines restored our spirits. Even though portions were large we decided to try the desserts. Passing up a non-dairy tiramisu, we chose a too-cinnamony apple crumble and a sticky toffee pudding that needed more sauce and could have done without the non-dairy vanilla ice-cream. Service was welcoming, with smiling staff who kept their eyes on the tables. Aviv is great value and, if you stick to the less exotic dishes, worth the trip.
Babies and children welcome; children's menu; high chairs. Booking essential. Kosher supervised (Beth Din). No smoking. Tables outdoors (14, patio). Takeaway service.

★ B&K Salt Beef Bar
11 Lanson House, Whitchurch Lane, Edgware, Middx HA8 6NL (8952 8204). Edgware tube. **Lunch served** noon-3pm, **dinner served** 5.30-9.15pm Tue-Sun. **Main courses** £4-£9.50. **Unlicensed. Corkage** no charge. **Credit** MC, V. Not kosher
B&K is easy to miss, tucked away in a quiet parade far from the bright lights of Edgware. But for over 20 years those in the know have been coming here for the cheerful banter and the salt beef. Everything else is peripheral; it's the pickled meat that draws the crowds. The chopped liver is good, though it's no longer made with chicken fat; egg and onion is a bit coarse, the onion sliced instead of minced. For the beef you need to be hungry: someone with an outsize appetite will finish the 12 slices and the pile of chunky chips or crisp latkes on a large side plate. Despite such generous portions, prices are half those you'd pay in the West End or Golders Green. Another option is the strangely named continental salad, of celery, peppers and marinated cabbage. Tempted by the own-made lockshen pudding, we found the taste of orange juice rather odd. But then, we'd only come for the beef.
Babies and children welcome; high chairs. Bookings not accepted. No smoking. Takeaway service (11.30am-9.15pm).

Stanmore, Middlesex

★ Madison's Deli
11 Buckingham Parade, Stanmore, Middx HA7 4ED (8954 9998). Stanmore tube. **Lunch served** noon-3pm, **dinner served** 5.30-10pm daily. **Main courses** £4.95-£9.95. **Set lunch** £5.95 2 courses. **Credit** MC, V. Not kosher
An interesting mix of old-style deli food and shining bright decor have made Madison's a favourite among Stanmore shoppers. The Jewish connection is evident, from the matzo crackers on the table to the huge portions. Chopped liver was creamy but a bit bland, while the poached gefilte fish was perfect. The combination of soft, sweet fish and chrane with a kick is just what Jews from Poland would expect. The large menu also offers salt beef: the slices of lean meat, with two viennas filling up the plate, were, in the main, tender and tasty. A side order of sweet and sour cabbage was a bit soupy. Falafel and houmous, served with a good salad, gherkins and pitta, was what it should be, with the spicy balls freshly fried. Encouraged by the reasonable prices, we went on to dessert. The cheesecake was toffee-sweet, but the cube of hot lockshen pudding reinforced the view that Madison's has got it right – food with the taste you'd expect, at low prices.
Babies and children welcome; children's menu; high chairs. Booking advisable. Disabled: toilet. No-smoking tables. Takeaway service.

Korean

This year's Korean section is much-expanded, up from 13 restaurants listed last year to 18, a large proportion of which are new. Could it be that Londoners are finally catching on to the fact that Korean establishments offer some of the most excitement, pound for pound, of any restaurants in the capital?

Korean food, with its hot, sour, chillies-by-the-handful flavours, does take a bit of getting used to – yet it's easy to get hooked. It's a fun way to eat too. Many of the restaurants have built-in barbecues, and servers will cook marinated beef, pork, chicken, squid or prawns right at your table. The cuisine shares some characteristics with Chinese and Japanese cooking, but the flavours tend to be more intense and gutsy. Korean food without red chilli, which lends colour and punch to many of the dishes, is simply unthinkable. Garlic is used liberally, as is sesame oil, while pickles, such as kimch'i, add sour notes. No meal is complete without noodles or rice (rice cooked in a hot stone bowl is not to be missed).

There are two main parts of town to head for if you want to give Korean cooking a whirl: Soho and New Malden. A handful of new Korean places have opened up in Soho in the past year; our pick of the newcomers is **Nara**, with **Woo Jung** and the re-opened (and rather pricier) **Jin** not far behind.

London's sizeable Korean community is centred round New Malden, to the south-west. This is where to go for a real taste of what Korean food is all about. Generally, restaurants fall into two categories: no-frills cafés and upmarket venues with correspondingly higher prices. For the former, **Jee's**, **You-Me**, **Yeon-Ji** and **Hamgipak** will deliver the goods for a very modest outlay of cash. Alternatively, the swish interiors and accomplished cooking at **Asadal**, **Han Kook** or **MiGa** can't fail to impress.

Woo Jung NEW
59 St Giles High Street, WC2H 8LH (7836 3103). Tottenham Court Road tube. **Meals served** noon-midnight Mon-Sat; 5pm-midnight Sun. **Main courses** £6-£8. **Set meal** £10-£30. **Credit** MC, V.
Of the trio of tiny Korean restaurants that huddle in the shadow of Centrepoint, Woo Jung is the friendliest and best organised. The menu is far more extensive than the restaurant's compact size might suggest – dozens of rice dishes, noodles, soups, stews, barbecues, and more tongue-tingling pickles than Peter Piper picked. We've had only one dud dish in several visits during the past year; all the others have been carefully prepared using fresh, high-quality ingredients. Set meals are particularly good value if you're befuddled by choice (all cost under £10). First to arrive might be a pert, mouth-watering plate of panch'an: beansprouts, grated daikon and spinach, plus a separate plate of excellent kimch'i. Next might come ellipses of tempura-like fried courgette with a piquant soy dip; miso soup; and a bowl of perfect-consistency rice. All this arrives before the main course, which is usually something simple such as a pork stir-fry, the pork belly striated with tasty fat and served in a moreish chilli sauce. Ordering à la carte is also rewarding.
Babies and children admitted. Takeaway service.
Map 18 K6.

Menu

Chilli appears at every opportunity on Korean menus. Other common ingredients include soy sauce (different to both the Chinese and Japanese varieties), sesame oil, sugar, sesame seeds, garlic, ginger and various fermented soy bean pastes (chang/jang). Until the late 1970s eating meat was a luxury in Korea, so the quality of vegetarian dishes is high. Try bibimbap – steamed rice topped with seasoned or pickled veg and (or without, if preferred) a fried egg.

Given the spicy nature and the overall flavour of Korean food, drinks such as chilled lager or the vodka-like soju are the best matches. However, a wonderful non-alcoholic alternative that is always available, although not listed on the menu, is barley tea (porich'a). It has a light dry taste that perfectly matches Korean food, and is served free of charge at many of the restaurants listed.

Korean restaurants don't generally offer desserts. The few that do usually serve half an orange or some watermelon at about the same time as the bill.

There are several variations in the spelling of Korean dishes; we have given the most common.

Bibimbap or **pibimbap**: rice, veg and meat with a raw or fried egg dropped on top, often served on a hot stone.
Bokum: a stir-fried dish, usually with chilli.
Bulgogi or **pulgogi**: slices of marinated beef barbecued at the table and sometimes rolled in a lettuce leaf and then eaten with vegetable relishes.
Chapch'ae, **chap chee** or **jap chee**: mixed vegetables and beef cooked with transparent vermicelli or noodles.
Cheon or **jon**: the literal meaning is 'something flat'; this can range from a pancake containing vegetables, meat or seafood, to thinly sliced vegetables, beancurd and so on, in a light batter.
Chigae or **jigae**: a hot stew containing fermented bean paste and chillies.
Gim or **kim**: dried seaweed, toasted and seasoned with salt and sesame oil.
Gu shul pan: a traditional lacquered tray with nine compartments containing individual appetisers.
Hobak chun or **hobak jun**: sliced marrow in a light egg batter.
Jjim: fish or meat stewed for a long time in soy sauce, sugar and garlic.

Kalbi, **galbi** or **kalbee**: beef spare ribs, marinated and barbecued.
Kimch'i, **kimchi** or **kim chee**: pickled vegetables, usually chinese cabbage, white radishes, cucumber or greens, served in a small bowl with a spicy chilli sauce.
Kkaktugi or **kkakttugi**: pickled radish.
Koch'ujang: a hot red bean paste.
Kook, **gook**, **kuk** or **guk**: soup; Koreans have an enormous variety of soups, from consommé-like liquid to meaty broths with noodles, dumplings, meat or fish.
Ko sari na mool or **gosari namul**: cooked bracken stalks dressed with sesame seeds.
Mandu kuk or **man doo kook**: clear soup with steamed meat dumplings.
Na mool or **namul**: vegetable side dishes.
Ojingeo pokkeum: stir-fried squid in chilli sauce.
P'ajeon or **pa jun**: flour pancake with spring onions and (usually) seafood.
Panch'an: side dishes; they usually include pickled vegetables, but may also comprise tofu, fish, seaweed or beans.
Pap, **bap**, **bab** or **pahb**: cooked rice.

Pindaetteok, **bindaedok** or **bindaedoek**: a mung bean pancake.
Pokkeum or **pokkm**: stir-fry; cheyuk pokkeum is a pork stir-fry with lots of chilli sauce; yach'ae pokkeum is a vegetable stir-fry, etc.
Shinseollo, **shinsonro**, **shinsulro** or **sin sollo**: 'royal casserole', a meat soup with seaweed, seafood, eggs and various vegetables, all cooked at the table.
Soju or **shoju**: a strong Korean rice spirit, often drunk as an aperitif.
Teoppap or **toppap**: 'on top of rice' – for example, ojingeo teoppap is squid on rice.
Toenjang: seasoned (usually with chilli) soy bean paste.
Tolsot bibimbap: tolsot is a sizzling hot stone bowl that makes the bibimbap (qv) a little crunchy on the sides.
Tteokpokki: bars of compressed rice (tteok – rice cake) fried with veg and sausages in a chilli sauce on a hot-plate.
Twaeji gogi: pork.
T'wigim, **twigim** or **tuigim**: fish, prawns or vegetables dipped in batter and deep-fried until golden brown.
Yukhoe, **yukhwoe** or **yuk hwe**: shredded raw beef, strips of pear and egg yolk, served chilled.
Yukkaejang: spicy beef soup.

Fitzrovia W1

Han Kang

16 Hanway Street, W1T 1UE (7637 1985).
Tottenham Court Road tube. **Lunch served**
noon-3pm, **dinner served** 6-11pm Mon-Sat.
Main courses £6.50-£28. **Set lunch** £6.50
3 courses. **Credit** AmEx, MC, V.
If you're after a calm, smoke-free oasis, look
elsewhere. It seems that a large segment of
London's Korean student population comes here
for a quick bite (one-dish set menus with rice and
soup range from £5 to £6.50) and a pack or two of
fags at lunchtime. In the evening, the atmosphere
is less frenetic. Table-top barbecues are a forte,
including the likes of topside beef, strip loin, pork
and kimch'i and seasoned marinated chicken. The
menu is extensive, which didn't help our post-pub
decision-making skills. We finally settled on a
sweet/spicy dish of soy-cooked eel, served on a
mound of rice with spring onion, thin batons of
ginger, chilli, sesame seeds and enough raw garlic
to keep Dracula at bay on the journey home. A dish
of sautéed squid with vegetables in a spicy sauce
was fresh, tender and crunchy in all the right
places. Service tends to be brisk; instead of being
served kimch'i, we had to ask for pickles, which,
though crunchy and good, came to the table tooth-
numbingly cold. Even so, the cooking at Han Kang
usually hits the spot.
Babies and children welcome; high chair. Separate
room for parties, seats 20. Takeaway service.
Map 17 K5.

Mayfair W1

Kaya

42 Albemarle Street, W1X 3FE (7499 0622/
0633). Green Park tube. **Lunch served** noon-
3pm Mon-Sat. **Dinner served** 6-11pm daily.
Main courses £7.50-£17. **Set lunch** £12-£15
1 course. **Cover** £1 dinner. **Service** 15%.
Credit JCB, MC, V.
Korean restaurants don't often do 'smart'.
Convivial, comfortable, informal – yes, but posh,
no. Kaya is an honourable exception to the rule,
with its pervasive sense of calm and order and its
easy-on-the eye surroundings. The restaurant has
had a minor face-lift since last year; there's some
new lighting and crockery, and opera now plays
instead of traditional Korean music. The menu has
also had a few tweaks, although we were pleased
to see that old favourites such as jellyfish and
seafood in mustard sauce remain in place. For
aficionados, the 'chef's specials' section is where to
find the most interesting dishes (sadly, there was
no sea slug with sesame on our visit, but you may
have better luck). We were impressed with a light,
flavourful broth containing meatballs, prawn, crab,
beef, chicken and peppers, served in a steamboat
(similar to Japanese shabu-shabu), as well as the
plump deep-fried oysters and barbecued kalbi.
Service is of a consistently high standard. Some of
the prices are steep (and how can a £1 a head cover
charge be justified?), but Kaya is a very civilised
place in which to enjoy refined Korean cooking.
Babies and children admitted. Booking advisable.
Separate rooms for parties, seating 8 and 12.
Takeaway service. Vegetarian menu. **Map 9 J7.**

Soho W1

Jin NEW

16 Bateman Street, W1D 3AH (7734 0908).
Oxford Circus or Tottenham Court Road tube.
Lunch served noon-3pm, **dinner served**
6-11pm Mon-Sat. **Main courses** £8-£38. **Set**
lunch £7.50-£10 5 dishes. **Set dinner** £30-£35
6 courses incl barbecue. **Service** 10%. **Credit**
AmEx, MC, V.
To say that Jin had been in need of radical cosmetic
surgery for some time is an understatement. At
last, the deed has been done, and the restaurant
has emerged from the bandages looking younger
and slicker, with black marble tables and leather
seating. On the downside, prices seem to have risen
accordingly. If you want to splash out on the likes
of shark's fin, or house specials such as braised
sea cucumber with pork or minced shrimp

(£29/£30), this could be the place to do it. Prices at
lunchtime are easier on the wallet, ranging from
£7.50 to £10. Our stir-fried pork with kimch'i and
tofu was artfully served, with carved vegetables
and a careful arrangement of ingredients.
Barbecued beef loin, served with a side dish of
lettuce-leaf wraps that were too frilly to wrap well,
was seasoned with a sesame-edged marinade. The
classic Korean summer dish of poussin – stuffed
with rice, dried red dates and dried chestnuts
before being simmered in a light broth flavoured
with ginger, ginseng and lots of garlic – was a
treat. The set menus make a good introduction to
Korean cuisine.
Babies and children admitted. Booking advisable
weekends. Separate room for parties, seats 10.
Takeaway service. **Map 17 K6.**

Myung Ga

1 Kingly Street, W1B 5PA (7734 8220). Oxford
Circus or Piccadilly Circus tube. **Open** noon-3pm,
5.30-11pm Mon-Sat; 5-10.30pm Sun. **Set lunch**
£9.50-£12.50 2 courses. **Set dinner** £25-£35
3 courses. **Credit** AmEx, DC, MC, V.
A stone's throw from Liberty and the
pedestrianised shopping district off Regent Street,
Myung Ga is a great place to rest tired feet (without
stressing the wallet too much further). The decor
(heavy black tables, beige walls and blue carpet) is
oddly suburban, but the atmosphere is relaxed.
The menu holds few surprises, with a fairly
extensive range of rice and noodle dishes,
barbecues and stir-fries. The cooking is competent,
but on our most recent visit the menu didn't list the
house specials that had intrigued us in the past.
Cucumber pickle, stuffed with grated radish, was
hot, sour and crunchy, while a piquant starter of
pork belly stir-fried with kimch'i arrived sprinkled
with sesame seeds. To follow, our server stoked up
the gas barbecue sunk into the table-top, then
cooked some nicely flavoured pieces of marinated
chicken for us. We wrapped these in lettuce leaves
and dipped them in a light, soy-based sauce before
devouring. Service was an improvement on
previous visits: super-polite and professional.
Babies and children admitted. Booking advisable.
No-smoking tables. Separate room for parties,
seats 14. **Map 17 J6.**

★ Nara NEW

9 D'Arblay Street, W1F 8DR (7287 2224).
Oxford Circus or Piccadilly Circus tube. **Lunch**
served noon-3pm Mon-Sat. **Dinner served**
5-11pm daily. **Main courses** £6.50-£40.50.
Set lunch £6.50. **Set dinner** £7.50. **Credit**
MC, V.
Our pick of the new Korean restaurants that have
opened in and around Soho in the past year or so.
Nara bills itself as a Japanese and Korean
restaurant, but it's the Korean dishes that are the
stars. The long, rather plain room is given a touch
of urban funk by a black marble bar and a purple
back-lit wall. Food is the main attraction, and it has
never failed to deliver on any of our visits. Even
standard dishes such as tolsot bibimbap are
superlative versions, with layers of flavour (thin
strips of cloud ear fungus were a nice touch) and
perfectly cooked rice. Cuttlefish cooked in spicy
sauce sounded simple, but had a wonderful smoky
flavour that enhanced the tender pieces of sesame-
seed-dusted cuttlefish, mushrooms and vegetables.
Squid and pork barbecue, cooked at the table in a
massive cast-iron pan, came with a lip-smacking
sweet-salty-spicy sauce. At lunch, prices are great
value. As well as beer and saké, drinks include
cinnamon punch, served on ice with a few pine nuts
sprinkled on top.
Babies and children welcome; high chairs.
Map 17 J6.

Ran

58-59 Great Marlborough Street, W1F 7JY
(7434 1650). Oxford Circus tube. **Lunch served**
noon-3pm Mon-Sat. **Dinner served** 6-11pm
daily. **Main courses** £5.90-£12. **Set lunch**
£5.50-£9.95. **Set dinner** £17-£30. **Credit** JCB,
MC, V.
Ran is one of the older generation of Soho Korean
restaurants. It's generally a good, solid choice, with
polite staff and a simple, monochrome interior

with huge black and white prints hung on the
walls. Lunch set menus are pretty good value,
ranging from £4.50 for tteokpokki (rice cakes with
chilli sauce), to £10.50 for grilled lemon sole with
soy sauce. The evening menu is extensive – in fact,
you may need to sit and study the long list of rice,
noodle, barbecue and fried dishes. Some of the
most interesting are the casseroles, which are
cooked on a hob at the table and are large enough
for two or three to share. Our cod and vegetable
casserole with 'shells' was a delicate fish stock with
tofu, onion, beansprouts, white fish (not,
incidentally, cod), mussels and lots of fiery fresh
green chilli. The 'shells' turned out to be large fish
trimmings, which gave the stock its flavour. Less
successful was a barbecue of chilli and saké-
marinated prawns; although the huge tiger prawns
looked impressive, the flesh was watery and
mushy – no thanks. Successes, however, are more
frequent than disasters.
Babies and children welcome; high chairs. Booking
advisable. Separate room for parties, seats 12.
Takeaway service. **Map 17 J6.**

Acton W3

Mijori NEW

41 Churchfield Road, W3 6AY (8896 0202).
Acton Central rail. **Dinner served** 6-11pm Mon-Sat. **Main courses**
£6-£9. **Set dinner** £17-£28 8 dishes. **Credit**
MC, V.
Tucked away a couple of streets north of unlovely
Acton High Street, Mijori is an oasis of Korean
cooking. Quite apart from being undiscovered,
however, the place seems to be a destination
restaurant for clued-up locals; diners at tables to
either side of us were deep in conversation about
food and drink. A crisp, sweet and hot side dish of
grated carrot got things off to a good start. Next
came three gorgeous large prawns, deep-fried
tempura-style in the lightest, crispest batter, served
with a soy and sesame dip. A light, ungreasy
version of bindaedok was pleasantly squidgy and
contrasted well with a smallish portion of kimch'i
bokum bap (fried rice with kimch'i). Tenderloin
barbecue (cooked in the kitchen; there are no table-
top barbecues) was served on a bed of onions, with
sesame oil and salt for dipping. The only let-down
was an unexciting, plain dish of grilled salmon
with mushrooms and beansprouts. Service is
charm personified and the food meets high
expectations. Neophytes will be put at ease by a
menu that explains how to order a Korean meal,
and set menus are sensibly chosen.
Babies and children admitted; high chairs.
Booking advisable. Takeaway service.

Raynes Park SW20

★ Cah Chi

34 Durham Road, SW20 0TW (8947 1081).
Raynes Park rail/57, 131 bus. **Lunch served**
noon-3pm, **dinner served** 5-11pm Tue-Fri.
Meals served noon-11pm Sat; noon-10.30pm
Sun. **Main courses** £4.50-£14. **Set dinner** £15
3 courses. **No credit cards.**
We're not sure what the Korean is for *gemütlich*, the
German word that expresses so well the sense of
homely comfort that some places exude. Whatever
it is, that sensibility certainly applies to Cah Chi,
which consistently rates among our favourite
Korean restaurants. Partly it's the atmosphere.
Everyone is made to feel at home here, and there
are usually families and groups of friends chatting
and having a good time. The owners seem keen to
show off Korean food and offer helpful advice on
the menu. And then, of course, there's the food,
which is stunning. A meal here always includes a
few forms of table-top cooking, as in tteokpokki
(pressed rice cakes) with vegetables and noodles,
cooked with chilli sauce. The signature dish is soon
dae, black pudding made with rice vermicelli, and
cooked in various ways (or served as is). The
panch'an deserve special praise too, for both

Nara

quality and variety. Don't miss the sticky soya beans cooked in a sweet sauce, or the zippy pickled squid. Cah Chi is licensed to sell beer, or you can bring your own wine.
Babies and children welcome; high chairs. Booking essential. Separate room for parties, seats 18. Takeaway service.

North
Finchley N3

Yijo
1 Station Road, N3 2SB (8343 3960/ www.yijo.co.uk). Finchley Central tube. **Dinner served** 6-11pm daily. **Main courses** £6.50-£18. **Set meals** £13-£25 per person (minimum 2). **Service** 12.5%. **Credit** AmEx, DC, JCB, MC, V.
A yellow awning marks Yijo out from among the shopfronts opposite Finchley Central tube station. Inside, there's Classic FM playing, a fuss-free white-walled interior, and wafts of fragrant smoke rising from the central barbecue, just inside the front door. If you're a chilli-phobe, Yijo could make an unscary introduction to Korean food; the dishes here are far less spicy than most we've tried in London. We kicked off with two panch'an: crunchy chunks of mooli in a not-too-hot chilli sauce, and stuffed cucumbers with garlic. A soft cylinder of slow-cooked aubergine followed, the top finished in spicy-salty miso and chopped green onions. Chogye bokum ('stir-fried' scallops) were actually sautéed, served in scallop shells with a light broth. The classic galbi (sweetish thin-cut beef short ribs with the bone in) were marinated, then cooked on the barbecue. Salted grilled mackerel didn't get the taste buds tingling, though. Helped by keen staff and an easily decipherable menu, Yijo provides a walk on the mellow side of Korean cooking.
Babies and children welcome; high chairs. Book weekends. Takeaway service.

North West
Golders Green NW11

Kimchee NEW
2004 RUNNER-UP BEST CHEAP EATS
887 Finchley Road, NW11 8RR (8455 1035). Golders Green tube. **Lunch served** noon-3pm Tue-Fri; noon-4pm Sat, Sun. **Dinner served** 6-11pm Tue-Sun. **Main courses** £6.50-£8.50. **Set lunch** £6.50 6 dishes. **Credit** JCB, MC, V.
New, clean-cut and well run, Kimchee is a praiseworthy ambassador for Korean food in Golders Green. Main courses for dinner cost about £7, but lunchtime set meals are a steal at around £6 and cover most bases: rice, soup, main course and various kimch'i. You won't need extra side dishes, though it's worth paying £6.50 for two to share the excellent pa jun seafood pancake. All our dishes arrived in rapid succession, brought by quiet, helpful staff. Bokum udon featured thick, silky al dente noodles with strips of pork; budae chige had beancurd, spam-like ham and tender beef in a tomato and chilli-based soup, with egg noodles adding another textural dimension. Furnishings are predominately wooden, with tables displaying coils of rope beneath glass tops. Lighting from behind wooden faux cupboards adds to the neat, functional but relaxing feel. The house red wine (a smooth vin de pays merlot) is a corker too.
Babies and children admitted; high chairs. Booking essential Fri-Sun. No-smoking tables. Takeaway service. Vegetarian menu.

Outer London
New Malden, Surrey

★ Asadal
180 New Malden High Street, New Malden, Surrey KT3 4EF (8942 2334/8949 7385). New Malden rail. **Meals served** noon-11pm Mon-Fri;

noon-11pm Sat; 5-11pm Sun. **Main courses** £7-£25. **Set dinner** £15 2 courses, £50 per person (minimum 2) 5 courses. **Service** 10%. **Credit** MC, V.
We reckon that some of the best-value food in all London can be found in New Malden, at the area's many Korean restaurants. Asadal isn't quite the exception to the rule on price, but it has some of the priciest Korean food outside Mayfair. Is it worth it? We'd say so. More formal than most restaurants in the area, it's a first-date kind of place. The lengthy menu is peppered with expensive ingredients such as abalone. Portions are generous. Our panch'an were huge helpings of ko sari (blanched bracken shoots) and kimch'i. Deep-fried oysters weren't as light and fine as we remember them, but Asadal's beef bulgogi is an excellent version, the meat marinated in soy, sugar, garlic and sesame and cooked by white-shirted staff at your table. Wrap it up in lettuce leaves, add some koch'ujang and enjoy. Our rice cake and dumpling soup was mildly soothing: a well-flavoured chicken stock thick with tteokpokki cut into thin slices and light, well-flavoured meat dumplings. Fish dishes such as cuttlefish casserole and fried cod in beaten egg are a highlight.
Babies and children admitted; high chairs. Takeaway service.

★ Hamgipak
169 High Street, New Malden, Surrey KT3 4BH (8942 9588). New Malden rail. **Meals served** 11am-10pm daily. **Main courses** £5-£20. **Credit** MC, V.
Tiny Hamgipak is a mere slip of a place, boasting just five tables and a few high stools perched near the stylish glass frontage, but it has design credentials. Slate floors, blond wood and clever lighting give the interior a contemporary feel. The menu is extensive and well-translated; it has much to excite interest as well as the taste buds. Fish is a forte, from grilled saury to barbecued croaker, lightly steamed and fried pollock, and (our

favourite) preserved sea crab. Meat eaters might be more inclined towards pork belly or beef barbecues or Japanese-style tonkatsu (deep-fried breaded pork cutlet). We were extremely pleased with our fish roe stew, which came in a light, slightly smoky-flavoured broth with tofu, mooli, mushroom and slices of fresh green chilli to give it kick. Zol myun (sticky noodles, served cold) arrived with an assortment of finely sliced vegetables, plus a pot of spicy red koch'ujang to mix in. Pickles such as kimch'i and crunchy baby cucumbers stuffed with grated mooli, are zippily fresh. Service is laid-back but friendly.
Babies and children admitted. No smoking. Takeaway service.

Han Kook NEW

Ground Floor, Falcon House, 257 Burlington Road, New Malden, Surrey KT3 4NE (8942 1188). Raynes Park rail. **Lunch served** noon-3pm Mon, Tue, Thur, Fri. **Dinner served** 6-11pm Mon, Tue, Thur, Fri. **Meals served** noon-11pm Sat, Sun. **Main courses** £5.90-£27.90. **Set meal** £10 4 dishes (minimum 2). **Credit** MC, V.
A smart new place that opened in 2003, Han Kook is located in what looks like a business centre. However, the interior sheds its suburban skin and transforms into a chic restaurant with wooden screens, lots of greenery, and waitresses clad in traditional Korean costume. To one side is a raised platform with low tables, where diners sit on cushions on the floor. The menu lists hot-pots (16 types) and barbecues galore; this is the place to come with a large party, as many of the dishes are designed for sharing. One such is pickled skate wing with boiled pork wrapped in chinese cabbage: a bright mound of chilli-red skate wing, another mound of sliced pork belly, blanched cabbage leaves, two sauces for dipping and, just in case it isn't spicy enough, some green chillies and a handful of raw garlic cloves. Surf 'n' turf Korean style. Drinks include a tea made of dried persimmons flavoured with cinnamon, but we went for the alcoholic option: soju, a strong white spirit in which fresh cucumber had been macerated, served in a silver teapot. Just the thing to tame a chilli and garlic fire.
Babies and children welcome; high chairs. Booking essential Fri, Sat evenings.

Jee's

74 Burlington Road, New Malden, Surrey KT3 4NU (8942 0682). New Malden rail. **Lunch served** noon-3pm, **dinner served** 5-11pm Tue-Sun. **Main courses** £5-£8. **Set meals** £12-£20. **Credit** MC, V.
Jee's is a solid neighbourhood canteen, with rustic wooden tables, piles of free Korean-language newspapers and a general hustle and bustle. It's one of a number of Korean restaurants along this suburban stretch, and is always buzzing. The menu is extensive, with everything from dumpling soups to warming fish and meat casseroles, cooked at the table, plus a selection of barbecues and 'special dishes' such as teriyaki eel. Service can be erratic, and language a problem, but the quality of the cooking – and the fair prices – ensure that Jee's overcomes minor gripes. Our leek pancake was crisp and hot, if a bit overcooked. Chapch'ae (a generous plate of clear noodles with pork, courgette, carrot, onion and capsicum) was a meal in itself. Kalbi (beef short ribs, with the marinated meat carefully removed from the bone) is grilled at the table and cut with scissors into succulent bite-size pieces. You can tell a lot about a restaurant from the quality of panch'an offered. The selection at Jee's (nutty beansprouts, sour-hot daikon and chilli-spiked cabbage) is just like the rest of the food: fresh, zesty and generously portioned.
Babies and children welcome. Takeaway service.

★ MiGa NEW

79-81 Kingston Road, New Malden, Surrey KT3 3PB (8942 1811). New Malden rail. **Lunch served** noon-3pm, **dinner served** 6-11pm Mon-Sat. **Main courses** £6-£12. **Set dinner** £87-£89 (for 4 people). **Credit** MC, V.

Kimchee. See p187.

MiGa's inconspicuous white frontage gives on to an airy, clean, pale-toned space. To one side of the restaurant, three large tatami-style rooms are screened off by slatted wood screens. Here, low tables are surrounded by cushions and diners sit cross-legged. The rest of the restaurant has large, rectangular tables. Food is served off stylish plates and bowls. MiGa specialises in Korean 'fusion' food, which means many of the dishes have a Chinese or Japanese influence, as well as a bit of West Coast USA (such as Santa Barbara-style prawns). The cooking is top-notch, from panch'an (our firm-textured dried squid in a chilli-based sauce went down a treat) to starters such as whelks with ultra-fine beansprouts served in a miso-based sauce, or homey beancurd soup with rice, which was based on an excellent beef stock. On a hot summer's evening, a dish of elastic vermicelli noodles with chilli-spiked raw skate wing, cooled by ice cubes, worked well. Staff are happy to explain what the dishes are like, though it seems difficult to choose badly here.
Babies and children welcome; high chairs. Booking advisable. Separate room for parties, seats 30. Takeaway service.

★ ★ Yeon-Ji
106 Burlington Road, New Malden, Surrey KT3 4NS (8942 7184). New Malden rail. **Meals served** noon-10pm Mon-Sat; 5.30-10pm Sun. **Main courses** £5.50-£7. **No credit cards.**
What this plain-looking little storefront restaurant lacks in design sense, it more than makes up for in cooking talent. There's not much to say about the chunky wooden furniture (seven tables in all) and the plain beige walls, but the cooking? Well, that's another story. This isn't fancy food; the menu is one of those perspex numbers that stands on top of the table. The list isn't as extensive as you'd find at some other New Malden spots, and service is likely to be from the same woman who cooks your food – but what food! Spicy cod cheek and vegetable casserole featured plump, fibrous chunks of cod, dunked in flour and deep-fried, served in a stew with beansprouts, onion, water convolvulus, and red and green pepper: all wrapped up in a spicy-salty red koch'ujang-based sauce, sprinkled with sesame seeds. Chapch'ae is found in most Korean eateries, but this (meatless) version, based on stretchy potato-flour noodles, with shredded cloud ear mushrooms, oyster mushrooms, carrots and cabbage, had a wonderful woodland flavour. Portions are big, prices low. For home-style Korean cooking, we love Yeon-Ji.
Babies and children admitted. Takeaway service.

★ You-Me
96 Burlington Road, New Malden, Surrey KT3 4NT (8715 1079). New Malden rail. **Meals served** 11.30am-10.30pm Mon, Wed-Sun. **Main courses** £5.90-£13. **Set lunch** £11.90 6 dishes. **Credit** MC, V.
You-Me is among the cosiest of the clutch of family-run restaurants in New Malden. There's a small room at the front, plus a larger room at the back that's the site of frequent family gatherings. Waitresses wear air hostess-style uniforms and are efficient at guiding customers through the flash, newly printed menus (with good English translations). The selection, from barbecues to stir-fries and one-dish dinners, is impressive. On our visit, just about everyone was tucking into jajang myun – noodles with black bean sauce, a house speciality – but we headed straight for the list of chef's specials. Sadly, braised sea cucumber wasn't available, but braised minced beef balls (flying-saucer-shaped succulent rounds) arrived cooked in a savoury-spicy sauce of koch'ujang with loads of vegetables, sesame seeds and more fiery red chillies. A wintry dwenjang chigae (bean paste stew, packed with tofu, potatoes, mushrooms, soya beans and pork) helped cool the fire, as did limitless pots of barley tea. The food is always good, but portions tend to be large, so don't get carried away.
Babies and children welcome; high chairs. Separate room for parties, seats 6. Takeaway service.

Malaysian, Indonesian & Singaporean

After a long period during which London's Malaysian restaurants seemed stuck in a rut, things are changing. You'll now find much more diversity. For cheap, tasty pit-stop eating – whether a bowl of laksa or a plate of nasi lemak – try recent arrivals **C&R Café** and **Malaysia Kopi Tiam**. Both of these Soho eateries successfully recreate the simple, coffee house style of diners prevalent in Singapore and Malaysia. One step higher in the gastronomic echelon are restaurants such as **Mawar**, **Malay House** and **Satay House**, which produce more ambitious menus yet manage to keep about them an authentically laid-back atmosphere.

An increasing number of restaurants are also catering for the upper end of the market. Hats off to long-lasting **Singapore Garden**, which continues to serve excellent versions of Singaporean and Malaysian dishes – from chilli crab and satay to tauhu goreng and Hainanese chicken rice. **Nyonya**, with its elegant decor and carefully composed menu, also takes the Malaysian dining experience up a notch. **Champor-Champor** is another sophisticated venue that stands out both for its exotic ambience and the creativity of its Malaysian-fusion menu.

If you've never tried Malaysian food, it's well worth experimenting at some of the low-priced cafés. Classic dishes to try include laksa (a highly garnished noodle soup in a rich coconut broth), roti canai (layered fried flatbread served with a curry dipping sauce), satay (of course) and kangkong blachan (water spinach, stir-fried with shrimp paste and chilli). See the menu box (*p190*) for more guidance.

Central

City EC4

Singapura
1-2 Limeburner Lane, EC4M 7HY (7329 1133/www.singapuras.co.uk). St Paul's tube/Blackfriars tube/rail. **Meals served** 11.30am-10.30pm Mon-Fri. **Main courses** £8.25-£13.75. **Set meals** £20-£25 per person (minimum 2). **Service** 12.5%. **Credit** AmEx, DC, MC, V.
A short stroll from St Paul's Cathedral, Singapura is very much a City restaurant. It's a sleek, spacious venue with floor-to-ceiling windows and white walls. Smartly dressed business people filled the place on our lunchtime visit. Despite the restaurant's name, the menu is South-east Asian rather than Singaporean, offering Indonesian, Malaysian and Thai dishes. Larb (minced chicken tossed in a chilli-dressing), prettily presented in lettuce leaves, made a pleasant starter. Gado gado arrived covered in a flavourful peanut sauce. Beef rendang (garnished with shredded lime leaves) had a rich, thick, coconut gravy and an authentic chilli-kick, though the meat itself was on the dry side. Service, befitting the location, was professional and dishes arrived promptly. In all, a smooth-running operation, though prices are aimed at expense-account diners.
Babies and children admitted. Booking advisable lunch. Disabled: toilet. Tables outdoors (15, pavement). Takeaway service; delivery service. Vegetarian menu. Vegan dishes. **Map 11 O6.**
For branches see index.

Edgware Road W2

★ Mawar
175A Edgware Road, W2 2HR (7262 1663). Edgware Road tube. **Buffet Meals served** noon-10.30pm Mon-Sat; noon-10pm Sun. **Set meal** £4.25-£5.25 1 course. *Restaurant* **Dinner served** 6-10.30pm daily. **Main courses** £5-£9. **Unlicensed. Corkage** no charge. **Service** 10%. *Both* **Credit** (over £10) AmEx, MC, V.
Despite its basement location, Mawar has a loyal following and was brimming with customers (mostly Malaysian) on our Saturday night visit. The subterranean dining room, with green walls adding an aquatic feel, was abuzz with chattering diners. Evening visitors can choose from the bargain cafeteria set-up (£5 for rice with servings of three dishes) or à la carte (only offered for dinner). We opted to sit in the carpeted restaurant area rather than the brighter adjacent café space, and enjoyed courteous service. Beef satay, though a little chewy, had a pleasant lemongrass flavour – and the deliciously fluffy roti canai was fantastically fresh. For mains, mee goreng (fried noodles) really hit the spot, while ikan bakar (a whole mackerel coated in spice paste) was moist and packed with flavour. Sadly, the kueh (Malaysian cakes) had sold out, so we consoled ourselves with sago gula melaka (flavoured with pandan leaf) and comforting bubor pulot hitam (sweet, coconutty black rice). A notable venue for low-priced, highly flavoured food.
Babies and children welcome; high chair. Booking essential weekends. No-smoking tables. Takeaway service; delivery service on orders over £20. **Map 8 E5.**

Marylebone NW1

Rasa Singapura
Regent's Park Hotel, 154-156 Gloucester Place, NW1 6DT (7723 6740/www.regentspark hotel.com). Baker Street tube/Marylebone tube/rail. **Lunch served** noon-3pm, **dinner served** 6-11.30pm daily. **Main courses** £5.50-£25. **Set meals** £14.50-£30 3 courses. **Service** 12.5%. **Credit** AmEx, DC, JCB, MC, V.
Although it is housed in a hotel basement, Rasa Singapura's dining room – with its conservatory-style glass roof and hanging baskets of plastic plants – is surprisingly light and pleasant. The menu features a good number of Singaporean classics as well as more generic Chinese food. Our meal began poorly, with an insipid and oily chicken satay served with a dull sauce. Happily, things picked up considerably with the main courses: an ample portion of Hainanese chicken rice, hay mee soup (noodles in a good prawn-flavoured broth), and Nonya beansprouts sprinkled with small cubes of salt fish. Presumably the hotel caters for Malaysian and Singaporean visitors to London – it's a shame there weren't any other diners on our visit, to create some atmosphere.
Babies and children welcome; high chairs. Booking advisable. No-smoking tables. Takeaway service: delivery service (within 2-mile radius). Vegetarian menu. **Map 2 F4.**

Soho W1

★ C&R Café
3-4 Rupert Court, W1D 6DY (7434 1128). Piccadilly Circus tube. **Meals served** noon-11pm daily. **Main courses** £4-£6. **Set meals** £12 vegetarian, £16 per person (minimum 2). **No credit cards.**

Discreetly located on a Soho alleyway, C&R Café was pleasantly busy when we popped in for a late Sunday lunch, with diners ranging from families to groups of Chinese students. The simple but colourful decor (yellow walls, blue Formica table-tops) added to the cheery atmosphere. The extensive menu offers several Malaysian and Singaporean classics. Singapore laksa was a huge bowlful of fine noodles, swimming in a tasty (if not that spicy) coconut milk broth, impressively and generously garnished with fish cakes, chicken, beansprouts and a couple of succulent prawns. Disappointingly, Hainanese chicken rice was served without the bowl of light chicken broth we'd expected. On the plus side, it consisted of a large portion of well-flavoured, if rather dry, rice and tender poached chicken. We couldn't resist sampling a cooling ice kacang. This was a colourful affair and (despite an unorthodox sprinkling of cocoa powder) contained both palm nuts and azuki beans, scoring highly for authenticity. An inexpensive and enjoyable meal.
Babies and children welcome. Booking not accepted weekend eves. Takeaway service. Vegetarian menu. **Map 17 K7**.

★ **Malaysia Kopi Tiam**
9 Wardour Street, W1D 6PF (7434 1777). Leicester Square tube. **Meals served** 11am-11pm daily. **Main courses** £4.90-£5.50. **Service** 10%. **Credit** MC, V.
Among the hustle and bustle of Soho, Kopi Tiam retains a mellow vibe. The decor is cheerfully kitsch (apricot-hued walls, stained-glass windows and a skylight); service is efficient and prices are low. On our visit the place was filled with Malaysian students, all enjoying a colourful array of assorted soft drinks. One-dish dining is the name of the game here, so we went for nasi lemak. Served on a plastic banana leaf plate, this proved to be a generous mound of coconut rice, surrounded by ikan bilis in a sweet peanut sauce, acar (pickled vegetables), chicken curry, half a hard-boiled egg and a scattering of fried peanuts – in short, the real thing. To follow, ice kacang was good too, though kidney beans instead of azuki let the dish down slightly. Nevertheless, this unpretentious place offers great pit-stop dining.
Booking advisable weekends. No-smoking tables. Takeaway service. Vegetarian menu. **Map 17 K7**.

Melati
21 Great Windmill Street, W1D 7LQ (7437 2745). Piccadilly Circus tube. **Meals served** noon-11.30pm Mon-Thur, Sun; noon-12.30am Fri, Sat. **Main courses** £5.65-£8.95. **Set meals** £20-£23.50 per person (minimum 2). **Service** 10%. **Credit** AmEx, MC, V.
Melati's, housed in a tall, narrow town house, is a veteran of London's South-east Asian dining scene. Purple and sage-green walls, framed prints of tropical animals and birds, and a scattering of oriental artefacts create a cosy atmosphere. Pleasant, efficient staff brought our lunch with commendable promptness: freshly fried roti canai with a tasty gravy, and a huge portion of char kway teow (stir-fried rice noodles), flavoured with tiny shrimps and strips of fish cake. Star of the show, however, was the nasi lemak (which had seemed pricey). It turned out to be a splendidly generous affair: a mound of coconut rice topped with a fried egg, served with fried ikan bilis and peanuts, ikan bilis in chilli sambal, acar (pickled vegetables), two huge prawns and a chunk of fried mackerel. Melati's standards seemed to have slipped in recent years, so it's great to see the old place back on form.
Babies and children admitted. Book dinner Fri, Sat. Separate rooms for parties, both seating 40. Takeaway service. Vegetarian menu. **Map 17 K7**.

West
Ladbroke Grove W10
★ **Makan**
270 Portobello Road, W10 5TY (8960 5169). Ladbroke Grove tube. **Meals served** 11.30am-9.30pm daily. **Main courses** £3.50-£6. **No credit cards.**
Sandwiched between a pitta bread bar and a sausage and mash café on this famous market street, Makan serves up homely Malaysian food and is a great option for a quick bite. Decor is basic but cheery. Around 20 dishes are displayed behind a glass counter, including noodles, vegetable dishes, mackerel in soy sauce, chicken padang and huge curry puffs. Behind the scenes, in a kitchen painted fluorescent green, two Malay chefs can be glimpsed busily at work. Freshly cooked dishes,

ranging from Singapore laksa to nasi lemak, are also offered. We opted for roti canai. A few minutes later, two freshly fried flatbread were brought to our table, served with a spiced dahl gravy: a tasty lunch and gratifyingly good value.
Babies and children admitted. No-smoking. Takeaway service. Vegetarian menu. Vegan dishes. **Map 19 B2**.

Notting Hill W11
Nyonya
2A Kensington Park Road, W11 3BU (7243 1800/www.nyonya.co.uk). Notting Hill Gate tube. **Lunch served** 11.30am-3pm, **dinner served** 6-10.30pm Mon-Fri. **Meals served** 11.30am-10.30pm Sat, Sun. **Main courses** £5.50-£8.50. **Credit** AmEx, DC, MC, V.
Elegantly housed in a half-moon-shaped dining room, with aesthetically understated decor, Nyonya is a civilised venue for lunch. On our visit it had pulled in a crowd of predominantly Chinese-Malaysian diners, tucking in with gusto. The restaurant's name refers to a specific Chinese-Malay strand of South-east Asian cuisine, but the menu fails to offer several of the classic Nonya dishes. Service was charming and our prettily presented food – which included prawn-studded Penang char kway teow (stir-fried rice noodles), beansprouts with salt fish (skimpy on the salt fish), lemak prawns in a tasty sauce, sambal fish (deep-fried mackerel in a tame sambal sauce) and sambal okra – was authentically flavoured, yet low in chilli heat. Our main gripe was with the small portion sizes. Highlight of the meal was the dainty assortment of Nonya kueh, Malay cakes composed from coconut and cassava and flavoured with pandan leaf.
Babies and children welcome; high chair. Booking advisable dinner Mon-Fri, weekends. No smoking. Takeaway service. **Map 7 A7**.

Paddington W2
★ **Satay House**
13 Sale Place, W2 1PX (7723 6763). Edgware Road tube/Paddington tube/rail. **Lunch served** noon-3pm, **dinner served** 6-11pm daily. **Main courses** £5-£18.50. **Set meals** £13.50, £18, £25 per person (minimum 2). **Service** 10%. **Credit** AmEx, MC, V.

Menu

Here are some common terms and dishes. Spellings can vary.

Acar: assorted pickled vegetables such as carrots, beans and onions, which are often spiced with turmeric and pepper.
Assam: tamarind.
Ayam: chicken.
Bergedel or **pergedel**: a spiced potato cake.
Blachan, **belacan** or **blacan**: dried fermented shrimp paste; it adds a piquant fishy taste to dishes.
Bumbu bali: a rich, chilli-hot sauce from Bali.
Char kway teow or **char kwai teow**: stir-fry of rice noodles with meat and/or seafood with dark soy sauce and beansprouts. A Hakka Chinese-derived speciality of Singapore.
Chilli crab: fresh crab, stir-fried in a sweet, mild chilli sauce.

Daging: beef.
Ebi: shrimps.
Gado gado: a salad of blanched vegetables with a peanut-based sauce on top.
Galangal: also called lesser ginger, Laos root or blue ginger, this spice gives a distinctive flavour to many South-east Asian dishes.
Goreng: wok-fried.
Hainanese chicken rice: poached chicken served with rice cooked in chicken stock, a bowl of light chicken broth and a chilli-ginger dipping sauce.
Ho jien: oyster omelette, flavoured with garlic and chilli.
Ikan: fish.
Ikan bilis or **ikan teri**: tiny whitebait-like fish, often fried and made into a dry sambal (qv) with peanuts.
Kambing: actually goat, but in practice lamb is the usual substitute.
Kangkong or **kangkung**: water convolvulus, often

called water spinach or swamp cabbage; an aquatic plant often steamed and used in salads with a spicy sauce.
Kari: curry.
Kecap manis: sweet dark Indonesian soy sauce.
Kelapa: coconut.
Kemiri: waxy-textured candlenuts, used to enrich Indonesian and Malaysian curry pastes.
Kerupuk: prawn crackers.
Laksa: a noodle dish with either coconut milk or (as with Penang laksa) tamarind as the stock base; it's now popular in many South-east Asian cities.
Lemang: sticky Indonesian rice that is cooked in bamboo segments.
Lenkuas: Malaysian name for galangal (qv).
Lumpia: deep-fried spring rolls filled with meat or vegetables.

Masak lemak: anything cooked in a rich, red spice paste with coconut milk.
Mee: noodles.
Mee goreng: fried egg noodles with meat, prawns and vegetables.
Mee hoon: rice vermicelli noodles.
Murtabak: an Indian-Malaysian pancake fried on a griddle and served with a savoury filling.
Nasi goreng: fried rice with shrimp paste, garlic, onions, chillies and soy sauce.
Nasi lemak: coconut rice on a plate with a selection of curries and fish dishes topped with ikan bilis (qv).
Nonya or **Nyonya**: the name referring to both the women and the dishes of the Straits Chinese community. See peranakan below.
Otak otak: a Nonya (qv) speciality made from eggs, fish and coconut milk.

Stepping into this tucked-away restaurant, with its pale pink walls and prints, is rather like entering someone's living room. A well-established eatery, Satay House is authentically Malaysian – from its pleasantly relaxed ambience to the unmistakable smell of freshly fried blachan (shrimp paste) wafting from the kitchen. Satay and roti canai, chosen from the extensive menu, got our meal off to a promising start. The stars of the show, though, were the wonderfully flavourful ikan masak kecap (a great chunk of mackerel in a rich, soy sauce gravy) and the kangkong belacan (water spinach stir-fried with chilli and shrimp paste), both of which overshadowed the simply spiced ayam percik (chicken curry) in its turmeric-yellow gravy. Tempted though we were by the prospect of such desserts as sago gula melaka or ice kacang, we admitted defeat and left feeling mighty satisfied. *Babies and children welcome: high chairs. Book weekends. Separate room for parties, seats 35. Takeaway service.* **Map 8 E5.**

South

Brixton SW9

Satay Bar
447-450 Coldharbour Lane, SW9 8LP (7326 5001/www.sataybar.co.uk). Brixton tube/rail. **Bar Open** noon-11pm Mon-Thur, Sun; noon-2am Fri; 1pm-2am Sat. *Restaurant* **Lunch served** noon-5pm Mon-Fri; 1-5pm Sat, Sun. **Dinner served** 6-11pm daily. **Main courses** £5-£7. **Set meal** (rijsttafel) £13.95 per person (minimum 2). **Service** 12.5%. **Credit** MC, V.
With only a handful of diners present, this large bar-restaurant felt hollow and gloomy on our lunchtime visit, though it remains a popular evening drinking spot. Sadly, the food failed to redeem the lack of atmosphere. Satay, swamped in lacklustre peanut sauce, set the tone of the meal. Main courses, including a large portion of laksa (noodle soup in a coconut-milk broth) and a fish curry, were equally uninspired, and made for a very bland lunch. In the past we've been impressed by the way that Satay Bar, despite operating primarily as a bar, had produced decent food, but, judging from our latest visit, kitchen standards have fallen. Let's hope for an upturn.

Babies and children admitted (restaurant). Book weekends. Disabled: toilet. Tables outdoors (7, covered porch). Takeaway service. **Map 22 E2.**

South East

London Bridge & Borough SE1

★ Champor-Champor
62-64 Weston Street, SE1 3QJ (7403 4600/ www.champor-champor.com). London Bridge tube/rail. **Lunch served** by appointment Mon-Sat. **Dinner served** 6.15-10.15pm Mon-Sat. **Set meals** £19.90 2 courses, £24.90 3 courses. **Service** 12.5%. **Credit** AmEx, JCB, MC, V.
Since our last visit, this relative newcomer to the Malaysian dining scene has doubled in size, expanding sideways into the premises next door. Thankfully, there has been no loss of atmosphere. The decor in the new dining room is as striking as ever, incorporating a gold lacquer bar, a large, serene Buddha and an extraordinary scarlet cow. There's even an ingenious mezzanine, ideal for tête-à-tête dining. The food is as carefully composed as the surroundings, beautifully presented on ceramic and wooden dishes. It tastes as good as it looks (and there's plenty of choice for vegetarians; Champor-Champor was a finalist for Best Vegetarian Meal in *Time Out*'s 2003 awards). To start, tender roast squid in a palm sugar dressing, and a deliciously textured green mango salad went down well. Mains didn't disappoint either, yielding a rich roast duck and longan (a lychee-like fruit) curry and a beautifully balanced Laotian warm beef salad, served with kaduk rice (sticky rice wrapped in fragrant kaduk leaves, which impart a distinctive flavour) and a water-chestnut curry. Unable to resist desserts, we sampled soy bean and vanilla pudding, creatively served with sugared tempeh, and a dainty pandan kaya (coconut curd) trifle. For cutting-edge Malaysian cuisine, Champor-Champor (a Malay expression that roughly translates as 'mix and match') is the place.
Babies and children admitted; high chair. Booking essential. Disabled: toilet. Separate room for parties, seats 8. **Map 12 Q9.**

Georgetown
10 London Bridge Street, SE1 9SG (7357 7359/ www.georgetownrestaurants.co.uk). London Bridge tube/rail. **Lunch served** noon-2.30pm, **dinner served** 5.30-11pm daily. **Main courses** £7.75-£22. **Service** 10%. **Credit** AmEx, DC, MC, V.
Housed in a hotel by London Bridge station, Georgetown boasts dainty decorations inspired by the colonial Malaya of Somerset Maugham rather than the tropical beach-hut look – so instead of batik you'll find potted palms, chandeliers, tablecloths and cut-crystal glasses. The restaurant is named after the main town of the island of Penang, and the menu emphasises the multi-cultural nature of Malaysian cuisine, offering Indian, Chinese and Malay dishes. Presentation is distinctly westernised. On our lunchtime visit we took advantage of the set lunch menu in preference to the more elaborate à la carte. Ikan goreng, to start, was a rather neutered dish, consisting of a breaded white fish fillet coated with a mildly spiced tomato sauce. Kambing (lamb), however, was tender and tasty, served with a delicious al dente green-bean sambal and an excellent roti. Polite service added to an enjoyable dining experience.
Babies and children welcome; high chairs. Booking advisable. Disabled: toilet. No-smoking tables. **Map 12 Q8.**

North

Camden Town & Chalk Farm NW1

Singapore Sling
16 Inverness Street, NW1 7HJ (7424 9527). Camden Town tube. **Bar Open** noon-midnight daily. *Restaurant* **Meals served** noon-11pm Mon-Thur, Sun; noon-11.30pm Fri, Sat. **Main courses** £4.50-£15. **Set buffet** (noon-5pm daily) £6.50. **Set meals** £15-£23 3 courses. **Service** 10%-12.5%. **Credit** MC, V.
Atmospherically decked out in rich colours, with dark wooden furniture and colourful hangings, Singapore Sling is undoubtedly a pleasant spot. On a weekday evening, the upstairs bar was buzzing and, during the course of our meal, the

---

Panggang: grilled or barbecued.
Peranakan: refers to the descendants of Chinese settlers who first came to Malacca (now Melaka), a seaport on the Malaysian west coast, in the 17th century. It is generally applied to those born of Sino-Malay extraction who adopted Malay customs, costume and cuisine, the community being known as 'Straits Chinese'. The cuisine is also known as Nonya (qv).
Petai: a pungent, flat green bean used in Malaysian cooking.
Poh pia or **popiah**: spring rolls. Nonya or Penang popiah are not deep-fried and consist of egg or rice paper wrappers filled with a vegetable and prawn medley.
Rempah: generic term for the fresh curry pastes used in Malaysian cookery.

Rendang: meat cooked in coconut milk: a 'dry' curry.
Rijsttafel: an Indonesian set meal of several courses; it means 'rice table' in Dutch.
Rojak: raw fruit and vegetables in a spicy sauce.
Roti canai: a South Indian Malaysian breakfast dish of fried round, unleavened bread served with a dip of either chicken curry or dahl.
Sambal: there are several types of sambal, often made of fiery chilli sauce, onions and coconut oil; it can be served as a side dish or used as a relish. The suffix 'sambal' means 'cooked with chilli'.
Satay: there are two types – terkan (minced and moulded to the skewer) or chochok ('shish' – more common in London) – Beef or chicken are the traditional choices, though prawn is now often available too. Satay is served with a rich spicy sauce made with onions, lemongrass, galangal,

chillies in tamarind sauce, sweetened and thickened with ground peanuts.
Sayur: vegetables.
Soto: soup.
Soto ayam: a classic spicy Indonesian chicken soup, often with noodles.
Sotong: squid.
Tauhu: tofu, beancurd.
Tauhu goreng: deep-fried beancurd topped with beansprouts tossed in a spicy peanut sauce, served cold.
Telor: egg.
Tempeh or **tempe**: an Indonesian fermented soy bean product. Similar to tofu, it has a more varied texture and can look like peanut butter.
Terong: aubergine.
Tersai or **trassie**: alternative names for blachan (qv).
Udang: prawns.

Desserts

Bubor pulut hitam: black glutinous rice served in coconut milk and palm sugar.

Cendol or **chendol**: mung bean flour pasta, which is coloured and perfumed with the essence of pandan (screwpine) leaf and served in a chilled coconut milk and palm sugar syrup.
Es: ice; a prefix for the multitude of desserts made with combinations of fruit salad, agar jelly cubes, palm syrup, condensed milk and crushed ice.
Es kacang: shaved ice and syrup mixed with jellies, red beans and sweetcorn.
Gula melaka: palm sugar, an important ingredient with a distinctive, caramel flavour added to a sago and coconut-milk pudding of the same name.
Kueh or **kuih**: literally, 'cakes', but used as a general term for many desserts.
Pisang goreng: banana fritters.

ground-floor restaurant filled up with a cool, cosmopolitan crowd. Though Malaysian cooking is prominent, the menu is pan-Asian, including several Thai dishes. Given the friendly service and nice vibe, it's a shame the food was a let-down. Tough, oily satay with an insipid sauce made an unpromising starter. Main courses were better, but not impressive; chicken rendang lacked depth of flavour and the prawn sambal was too sugary. The okra Penang blachan and the roti were tasty, yet the pisang goreng dessert (an oily fried banana) also disappointed. Not our top choice for good Malaysian cooking.
Babies and children welcome (restaurant). Entertainment: pianist 7.30-10.30pm Thur-Sun. Restaurant. Tables outdoors (2, pavement). Takeaway service. **Map 27 C2**.

Crouch End N8

Satay Malaysia
10 Crouch End Hill, N8 8AA (8340 3286). Finsbury Park tube/rail then W7 bus. **Dinner served** 6-10.45pm Mon-Thur, Sun; 6-11.45pm Fri, Sat. **Main courses** £3.80-£8.90. **Set dinners** £11-£13 per person (minimum 2). **No credit cards**.
With its batik drapes and a bar illuminated by fairy lights, this small restaurant has the vibe of a relaxed local. A steady stream of diners flowed through the doors on our weekday evening visit: impressive in competitive Crouch End. The menu is Chinese-oriented – a fact reflected in the tame spicing. Beef rendang was tender though missing the requisite breadth of flavours; mee goreng, while pleasant enough, again didn't pack much of a zesty punch. Steamed whole sea bass with tamarind, ginger and spring onion was the high point of the meal: thoughtfully served off the bone, and set off well by a side order of stir-fried baby pak choi. Reasonable prices and upbeat service play a large part in Satay Malaysia's lasting appeal.
Babies and children welcome. Book weekends. Takeaway service. Vegetarian menu.

Swiss Cottage NW6

★ Singapore Garden
83A Fairfax Road, NW6 4DY (7624 8233). Swiss Cottage tube. **Lunch served** noon-2.45pm daily. **Dinner served** 6-10.45pm Mon-Thur, Sun; 6-11.15pm Fri, Sat. **Main courses** £6-£15. **Set lunch** (Mon-Fri) £7.50 2 courses. **Set meals** £20-£32.50 per person (minimum 2). **Minimum** £10. **Service** 12.5%. **Credit** AmEx, DC, MC, V.
On a Friday evening this veteran high-class Swiss Cottage restaurant was positively humming with a cosmopolitan crowd. Diners ranged from affluent Chinese businessmen to large family groups with small children seated around big tables. The menu is predominantly Chinese, but also offers several Singaporean classics rarely found in London. Tender chicken satay with a flavourful peanut sauce made a promising start. Our feast continued with ho jien (a rich omelette generously studded with oysters – a Singapore hawker stall favourite), authentically spiced Malaysian chicken curry in a fine-tasting coconut-milk gravy, and tauhu goreng (fried beancurd topped with beansprouts tossed in a salty-sweet nutty dressing), all washed down with Tiger beer and chendol. What consistently impresses about Singapore Garden is the breadth of the menu and how carefully executed each dish is. Polite, efficient service, combined with cooking of this calibre, explain its continuing success.
Babies and children welcome; high chairs. Booking advisable. Separate rooms for parties, seating 6 and 100. Tables outdoors (4, pavement). Takeaway service; delivery service. **Map 28 A4**.

Turnpike Lane N8

Penang Satay House
9 Turnpike Lane, N8 0EP (8340 8707). Turnpike Lane tube/29 bus. **Dinner served** 6-11pm Mon-Sat. **Main courses** £4-£8.50. **Set meals** £11.90, £13.50 per person (minimum 2). **Credit** MC, V.
Why can't we all have a neighbourhood restaurant like Penang Satay House? Attracting a loyal local

Malay House

following, it's often crowded at weekends. On the weekday evening we visited, diners ranged from courting couples to a large group of teenage girls celebrating a birthday. The menu offers a mixture of Chinese and Malay dishes. To start, satay scored a bullseye: tender, lemongrass-flavoured chicken served with a tasty sauce and cubes of compressed rice, onion and cucumber. Next, char kway teow was a generous portion of stir-fried fresh rice noodles, tossed with garlic, shrimps, egg, and beansprouts; it produced an authentic chilli glow. Okra sambal arrived nicely stir-fried and spiced. Service was polite and efficient. It's not hard to see why this place continues to thrive.
Babies and children welcome; high chairs. Booking essential. Takeaway service; delivery (within 2-mile radius on orders over £10). Vegetarian menu. Vegan dishes.
For branches (Penang Express) see index.

For branches (Penang Express) see index.

Outer London
Croydon, Surrey

Malay House
60 Lower Addiscombe Road, Croydon, Surrey CR0 6AA (8666 0266). East Croydon rail then 197, 312, 410 bus. **Lunch served** noon-3pm Fri.
Dinner served 6-11pm Tue-Sat. **Meals served** 1-9pm Sun. **Main courses** £3.80-£9. **Set lunch** (Fri) £5.25 2 courses. **Buffet** (Sun) £7. **Unlicensed. Corkage** £1 per person. **Credit** MC, V.
The location of this small, friendly restaurant may be uninspiring, but it's a pleasant place in which to dine. The simple decor, including an eye-catching painting of paddy fields and batik trimmings, and amicable service make for a mellow atmosphere. The menu offers a good cross-section of Malaysian classics. Our satay – six generous skewers of deliciously caramelised, turmeric-coloured chicken served with a large bowl of rich peanut sauce – was very much the real thing. Next came roti canai, accompanied by a fiery chicken curry and a simply superb dahl, complete with curry leaves and potato chunks. Standards were so impressive we couldn't resist trying the Malaysian kueh. These coconut-dusted, pandan-flavoured glutinous rice cakes arrived in a pool of palm sugar syrup and had exactly the right salty-sweet flavour. Lunchtime diners were distinctly thin on the ground when we visited; let's hope Croydon locals appreciate what a gem they have on their doorstep.
Babies and children welcome: high chairs. Booking advisable Fri, Sat. Takeaway service; delivery service. Vegetarian menu.

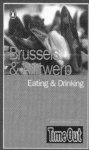

Mediterranean

Central

City EC3

Royal Exchange
Grand Café & Bar
*The Royal Exchange, EC3V 3LR (7618 2480/
www.conran.com). Bank tube/DLR.* **Breakfast
served** 8-11am Mon-Fri. **Meals served**
11.30am-10pm Mon-Fri. **Main courses** £6.50-
£14.50. **Service** 12.5%. **Credit** AmEx, DC,
MC, V.
A café-bar with an unquestionably grand setting,
in the atrium-courtyard of the old Royal Exchange
(now a classy shopping mall). There's a central
counter and bar surrounded by tables, all with the
unmistakable Conran stamp, while the colonnades
on either side host strikingly sleek mezzanine
cocktail bar areas above the shops. The menu
mainly offers seafood, cold food and a few dishes
that can be simply grilled or pan-fried behind the
bar. Star billing goes to the plutocratically priced
luxury foods (oysters, caviar, champagne). Passing
over these titbits, we tried a very refreshing,
smooth gazpacho, and nicely presented but rather
dull grilled asparagus with hollandaise sauce.
Presenting sophisticated food given such restricted
kitchen facilities doesn't always come off: in brie
with roasted vegetables, the mixed peppers, red
onion and other veg were satisfyingly juicy, but the
cheese tasted as if it had come straight from the
fridge. Langoustine mayonnaise was an
impressively large portion, but the shellfish were
not the best, and again served ultra-cold. The staff,
though, were likeably attentive, and this is
certainly a stylish venue. Not surprisingly, it's
popular for City working lunches.
*Babies and children admitted (restaurant).
Bookings not accepted. Disabled: toilet. Dress:
smart casual. Entertainment: DJ 11pm Fri.*
Map 12 Q6.

Soho W1

Aurora
*49 Lexington Street, W1F 9AT (7494 0514).
Oxford Circus tube.* **Lunch served** 12.30-
3pm Mon-Sat. **Dinner served** 6.30-10pm
Mon, Tue; 6.30-10.30pm Wed-Sat. **Main
courses** £11.95-£13.50. **Service** 12.5%.
Credit MC, V.
Occupying one of the more venerable 18th-century
houses in old Soho, Aurora has at the back a tiny,
plant-lined patio (aka yard): a tranquil spot for
open-air eating. Inside, the snug, comfortable
dining room has decor quirky enough to suit the
area – original fittings combined with vaguely
decadent deep-red walls and baroque gold lilies.
The fashionably eclectic menu is quite short, but
has several nice touches. Confit of tuna with
sweetcorn and avocado salad and basil
mayonnaise was freshly flavoured, and fried
halloumi with rocket and shallot salad was also
satisfying, if over-salted. In a main of duck breast
with sweet potato purée, purple sprouting broccoli
and salsa verde, the slightly under-flavoured meat
was less of a hit than the excellent fresh veg,
including delicious sweet potato mash. The day's
pasta dish, ravioli with spinach and ricotta, was
great, raised out of routine by careful cooking and
a touch of nutmeg in the ricotta. There's also a
moreish range of fruity desserts, and a short,
unadventurous wine list. Service is laid-back, but
not unfriendly.
*Babies and children admitted. Booking advisable.
Separate room for parties, seats 18. Tables
outdoors (10, courtyard).* **Map 17 J6.**

West

Brook Green W6

Snow's on the Green
*166 Shepherd's Bush Road, W6 7PB (7603 2142/
www.snowsonthegreen.co.uk). Hammersmith tube.*
Lunch served noon-3pm Mon-Fri. **Dinner
served** 6-11pm Mon-Sat. **Main courses**
£10.50-£16. **Set meal** £12.50 2 courses,
£16.50 3 courses. **Service** 12.5% for parties
of 6 or more. **Credit** AmEx, DC, MC, V.
Snow's has been up and running for over a decade,
becoming a reliable local favourite, but there's no
sign of it getting jaded. The large space, discreetly
decorated in whites and beiges, and the odd Bill
Brandt nude, is still fresh and airy, the staff keen
and attentive. The imaginative food scores highly
too, nearly always giving an original – but well-
judged – twist, even to familiar dishes. A spring
salad of baby spinach, dolcelatte, peas and pine
kernels was bright and refreshing; a similarly
fresh, well-assembled caesar salad came with
crispy chicken wings. From a varied list of mains
(though nothing for vegetarians), crispy confit of
pork with jerusalem artichokes, potato confit and
field mushrooms was unusually rich and powerful,
with delicious crunchy crackling and full-flavoured
meat; seared scallops with herb risotto featured
sweet, quality seafood and just-so, finely flavoured
rice. For dessert, panna cotta came with a cleverly
spiced winter-fruit mix of preserved pears,
peaches, apples and more. The wine list provides
plenty of options. It's not hard to see why Snow's
remains popular.
*Babies and children welcome; high chair. Separate
rooms for parties, seating 15 and 26. Tables
outdoors (2, pavement). Vegetarian menu.*
Map 20 C3.

South West

South Kensington SW7

Bistrot 190
*190 Queensgate, SW7 5EU (7581 5666).
Gloucester Road or South Kensington tube.*
Bar **Open** 4pm-1am daily.
Bistro **Meals served** 7am-11.30pm Mon-Fri;
7.30am-midnight Sat; 7.30am-11.30pm Sun.
Main courses £10.50-£14.95. **Service** 12.5%.
Credit AmEx, DC, MC, V.
Part of the Gore, a small but grand Kensington
hotel, Bistrot 190 has giant arching windows, lofty
ceilings, opulent flower arrangements and an orgy
of Victorian prints. Well-heeled tourists and the
local international crowd dine here, but this is one
of the area's most relaxing retreats, and service is
charming and attentive. On our last visit, the food,
broadly Franco-Italian in style, was very impressive.
A tartlet of aubergines, field mushrooms and goat's
cheese with marjoram and balsamic dressing
offered a great balance of fresh ingredients, with
a lovely woody flavour from the mushrooms; a
caesar salad had plenty of fat, juicy boquerones
instead of the more usual salted anchovies. Mains
were quite rich, but just as good: a nicely smoky-
flavoured leg of rabbit with pancetta, broad beans
and spinach; and a risotto with more of the
excellent field mushrooms. Best of all was an
inventive dessert of delicate poached rhubarb with
mango and ginger ice-cream. Accessories such as
the fresh bread are finely done too. The wine list is
substantial and pricey. Not cheap, but a nice place.
*Babies and children welcome; high chairs. Booking
advisable. No-smoking tables (restaurant).
Separate room for parties, seats 24.* **Map 8 D9.**

South East

Crystal Palace SE19

★ Numidie
*48 Westow Hill, SE19 1RX (8766 6166/
www.numidie.co.uk). Gypsy Hill rail.* **Lunch
served** noon-4pm Sun. **Dinner served** 6.30-
10.30pm Tue-Sun. **Main courses** £7.25-£12.50.
Service 10% for parties of 6 or more. **Credit**
MC, V.
Numidie was surprisingly quiet on a midweek
evening – goodness knows why. True, the decor is
nothing to write home about (dark and slightly
shabby), but the place has an extremely laid-back,
no-nonsense French air, enhanced by an eclectic
mix of Arab and Gallic music; whoever selected a
French rendition of 'Doing the Lambeth Walk' has
a wry sense of humour. But when it comes to the
food, the chef is deadly serious. We could find
virtually no faults on our visit. Tender garlicky
baby squid stuffed with crab in a fragrant olive-oil
dressing, and gently spiced, moist, grilled filleted
sardines, were followed by excellent tagines served
with couscous. This was Mediterranean cooking
with true flair. Seafood tagine had generous
chunks of cod, sea bass, scallops, prawns and
mussels: all cooked to perfection in a light fish
broth. A tagine of lamb shank, peas and
artichokes was also a winning dish, in a tasty
reduced sauce with a hint of cumin and ginger.
Poached pear in red wine with almond paste
stuffing came in a pool of melted balsamic ice-
cream, but was tasty nonetheless.
*Babies and children welcome; high chairs.
Booking advisable. No-smoking tables. Separate
room for parties, seats 20.*

East

Shoreditch EC2

★ Cantaloupe
*35 Charlotte Road, EC2A 3PB (7613 4411/
www.cantaloupegroup.co.uk). Old Street tube/
rail/55 bus.* **Open** 11am-midnight Mon-Sat;
11am-11.30pm Sun. **Lunch served** noon-3pm
Mon-Fri. **Dinner served** 6-11.30pm Mon-Fri;
7-11.30pm Sat. **Main courses** £9-£16. **Service**
12.5%. **Credit** AmEx, DC, JCB, MC, V.
You reach Cantaloupe's restaurant, at the hub of
trendy Shoreditch, through the packed bar. The
menu is a fashionable Spanish-North African mix
of dishes that often sound very busy. The dining
area is brilliantly designed so you can eat in cool
comfort unharassed by music from the bar (except
maybe when DJs arrive at weekends). Service is
an exceptional blend of friendliness and efficiency.
Even the busiest dishes are cleverly balanced, and
comprise excellent, mainly organic ingredients.
The 'Spanish plate' is recommended for two, but
we were helpfully told it would do fine for three:
a platter of first-rate Spanish meats (jamón
ibérico, chorizo, salchichón), manchego cheese,
boquerones (marinated anchovies), tortilla, olives
and capers. Moqueca (king prawns, calamares,
mussels and chicken braised with peppers, garlic,
tomatoes, cashews and coconut milk, with moros
y cristianos – rice and beans) was full of goodies,
imbued with a lovely smooth flavour from the nuts
and coconut. Char-grilled chermoula swordfish
had succulent fish served with wonderfully minty
tabouleh. To finish, apple and vanilla crema
catalan tasted great. Drinks are reasonably priced
too. This is a class act.
*Babies and children admitted. Booking advisable.
Disabled: toilet. Entertainment: DJ 8pm Fri, Sat.*
Map 6 R4.

★ Eyre Brothers
*70 Leonard Street, EC2A 4QX (7613 5346/
www.eyrebrothers.co.uk). Old Street tube/rail.*
Lunch served noon-3pm Mon-Fri. **Dinner
served** 6.30-11pm Mon-Sat. **Main courses**
£13-£25. **Service** 12.5%. **Credit** AmEx,
DC, MC, V.
A winning combination of Shoreditch stylishness
(inventive lighting, long dark-wood banquettes), a
friendly atmosphere and highly enjoyable food

Royal Exchange Grand Café & Bar

pleasant, but didn't have a real teriyaki flavour. Two vegetarian mains – courgette gratin with parmesan and mozzarella; and potato and walnut gnocchi with gorgonzola and basil – both featured heavy, chewy cheese sauces, after which the Marine Ices sorbets were very welcome. Service is charming but often slow. There's also a dubious practice of putting 'service not included' on the bill yet adding a 10% 'cover charge'. Mesclun's regulars must overlook these foibles.
Babies and children admitted; high chairs. Booking advisable. Vegetarian menu. Vegan dishes. **Map 25 C1**.

North
Islington EC1

Café Med
370 St John Street, EC1V 4NN (7278 1199). Angel tube. **Meals served** noon-11pm Mon-Sat; noon-10.30pm Sun. **Main courses** £7.95-£13.75. **Set lunch** (noon-5pm Mon-Sat) £9.95 2 courses. **Set meal** (5-7pm Mon-Sat) £11.95 2 courses. **Service** 12.5%. **Credit** AmEx, MC, V.
The baroque decor of the Café Meds, with deep-red walls, bronze pillars and sleek-lined bar areas, sets out to impress. It produces an aura of early 1990s flashiness, but also creates airy, comfortable and discrete spaces for diners, drinkers and coffee-takers. Open kitchens add to the mix. Char-grilled meat, fish and (a few) veg possibilities are centrepoints of the pretty standard modern-bistro menu. Food has its ups and downs. In pan-fried prawns with leeks, shallots and chilli, adequate main ingredients were overpowered by a crude tomato sauce. Caesar salad was just dull, and side-salads limp and over-priced. Mains were better: corn-fed chicken came with tangy lemon aïoli and Café Med's usual giant bowl of chips; char-grilled swordfish arrived with delicious roasted mixed veg, though the fish was unexciting. Best of all was a moreish espresso affogato of vanilla ice and coffee – resembling an old-fashioned American ice-cream float. Generous portions are another plus, and there's a varied choice of drinks. Service (on a quiet day) was friendly and helpful.
Babies and children welcome; children's menu; high chairs. Booking advisable. Disabled: toilet. **Map 5 O3**.
For branches see index.

North West
Hampstead NW3

Base
71 Hampstead High Street, NW3 1QP (7431 2224/www.basefoods.com). Hampstead tube. **Lunch served** noon-4pm daily. **Dinner served** 7-10.45pm Tue-Sat. **Main courses** £9.95-£15.95. **Credit** AmEx, DC, MC, V.
A den of 1980s chic – white walls, red banquettes, discreet artwork – Base has an easy-going feel that's appreciated by the well-heeled Hampstead regulars. It's a café-bistro by day, with breakfasts, juices and sandwiches, and serves a full restaurant menu from 7pm. Staff are French-Moroccan, and the food style is busy, quite rich and French-ish, with global touches (so there's crispy duck with hoi sin sauce, as well as pasta). We started with a tomato and parmesan tart made excellent by the use of flavoursome tomatoes, and crab spring roll with sweet and sour sauce (superior batter, routine filling). The day's fish special, roast sea bass with rosemary, warm mustard and chive potatoes, was pleasant but unexceptional. Pan-fried beef fillet with potato rösti, quenelle of horseradish, onions and shiitake mushrooms had decent meat somewhat overwhelmed by the other ingredients. Desserts tend to be fruity and creamy; the short wine list includes some Moroccan labels. Staff are welcoming; less friendly are the charges for side orders: £3.25 for a meagre saucer of spinach.
Babies and children welcome; high chairs. Booking advisable lunch, weekends. No-smoking tables. Takeaway service (noon-4pm Mon-Fri). Vegetarian menu. Vegan dishes. **Map 28 B2**.
For branches see index.

makes Eyre Brothers a benchmark among newer London restaurants. The brothers themselves (Robert and David) grew up in Mozambique, and the head chef is from Portugal, so Portuguese-based dishes feature strongly, along with Spanish and modern-eclectic recipes. Ingredients are outstanding. Roast morcilla with red onion and potato torta gave us the real taste of Iberian black pudding, rich and punchy; pan-roasted asparagus came with a smooth, delicious Catalan romesco sauce. Of our mains, grilled king scallops with chilli, garlic and lemon was a fine platter in which the hot spice was skilfully balanced with the delicate seafood, but this was outshone by a fabulous beef rib steak, ideally cooked and served with a refined (possibly overly so) mix of tomatoes, red peppers, wild garlic and salt-baked potatoes. Desserts include great sorbets in flavours such as champagne and grapefruit. The wine list is as well thought out as the menu. Our only grumble was with the slow service.
Babies and children admitted. Booking advisable. Disabled: toilet. No-smoking tables. Restaurant available for hire. **Map 6 Q4**.

North East
Stoke Newington N16

Mesclun
24 Stoke Newington Church Street, N16 0LU (7249 5029/www.mesclunrestaurant.com). Angel tube then 73 bus. **Open** noon-11pm Mon-Sat. **Main courses** £8.80-£13.50. **Set lunch** £8.50 2 courses, £11.50 3 courses. **Service** (dinner) 10%. **Credit** AmEx, MC, V.
With a few years on the clock, this little restaurant is clearly a local favourite, as witnessed by busy tables early in the week. The eclectic menu and wine list are 100% organic, and there's plenty for vegetarians (a mesclun is a kind of provençal salad, although the version here lacks all the classic ingredients). The decor is simple and slightly rustic, with earthy abstract art around the walls. Food, though, seems a mixed bag. The best that we tried was a starter of scallops with confit of pork and cabbage sauce: an original and enjoyable surf-and-turf combination. Chicken teriyaki with coriander, spring onion and noodle salad was quite

Middle Eastern

London's Middle Eastern restaurants come in two broad flavours: Iranian and Lebanese, corresponding to the two great cuisines of the region (for the flavours of neighbouring Turkey and North Africa, see p257 and p223 respectively). Lebanese dining is essentially about meze. The typical meal involves a table of these small hors d'oeuvres shared between all, with grilled meats (lamb or chicken) arriving at the end. Again, these dishes are placed centrally for everybody to tuck into. Dessert options rarely extend beyond the honey-soaked nutty pastries that are generically known as baklava. The food is ideally accompanied with a glass of arak, an aniseed liquor like pastis, although the Lebanese also produce some decent wines, notably under the Ksara label.

Iranian restaurants are almost solely about kebabs: lamb or chicken, fillet or minced. These are sometimes supplemented with a daily special, which is typically a stew of some description. That's about as far as the options extend. The marinated and tenderised meat comes with mounds of fluffy, saffron-stained long-grain rice, a grilled tomato and vast discs of taftun, a chapati-like bread. It's a working-class meal and London's best Iranian restaurants are all modest affairs.

The healthy nature of much Middle Eastern food – lots of salads, pulses and puréed veg – seems to be proving a hit with Londoners and Lebanese 'fast-food' outlets such as **Ranoush** and **Al-Dar** are expanding across the city. (For super-fresh falafel, try takeaway joint **Maoz** at 43 Old Compton Street, W1D 6HG; 7851 1586/ www.maoz.nl). Meanwhile, we are also seeing a shift from tradition to experimentation, exemplified by exciting newish venues **Aziz** and the remodelled **Fakhreldine** – although it doesn't always come off.

Central
Belgravia SW1

★ Noura
16 Hobart Place, SW1W 0HH (7235 9444/ www.noura-brasseries.co.uk). Hyde Park Corner tube/Victoria tube/rail. **Meals served** noon-midnight daily. **Main courses** £9-£17. **Set lunch** (noon-6pm) £14.50 2 courses incl coffee. **Set meals** £14.50-£29 per person (minimum 2) 3 courses incl coffee. **Credit** AmEx, DC, MC, V. Lebanese
A short stroll from Victoria, on an impersonal stretch of road, Noura's exterior is distinctly imposing. Inside is a stylishly spacious restaurant, filled at lunchtime with a smart business crowd. The decor and fittings are distinctly contemporary, a world away from the hotel-lounge style of design that smart Lebanese restaurants in London tend to go for. Warm bread, served with a flourish by one of a team of waiters, set the scene for an upmarket meal. The extensive menu features all the classics plus, refreshingly, a number of less familiar items. Grazing on meze is strongly recommended; our selection took in rich and spicy muhamara (mixed spicy nuts), zingy tabouleh and smooth lamb-topped houmous. Dishes that stood out included deliciously fresh fatayer, aromatic mana'eesh (thyme-topped flatbread) and delicate samke harra (white fish with a ratatouille-style

tomato topping). Above-average pastries and aromatic Lebanese coffee made a classic ending. A class act – even if the service, although efficient, lacked polish.
Babies and children welcome; high chairs. Booking advisable; essential dinner. Disabled: toilet. No-smoking tables. Takeaway service; delivery service. **Map 15 H9.**
For branch see index.

Edgware Road W1, W2

★ Al-Dar
61-63 Edgware Road, W2 2HZ (7402 2541/ www.aldar.co.uk). Marble Arch tube. **Meals served** 8am-1am daily. **Main courses** £7.50-£9.50. **Set meze** £8-£10. **Service** 10%. **Credit** AmEx, MC, V. Lebanese
Occupying a prime site on Edgware Road, this flagship branch of the Al Dar chain is a spacious establishment divided into two parts. On one side is a tearoom, filled with Lebanese men smoking and chatting; on the other is a large, smart restaurant, decked out in yellow and orange stripes, with gold-tiled pillars. We ate in the latter. A long glass counter along one wall featured an appetising array of dips, salads, pastries and meat kebabs, plus pyramids of fresh fruit. We started with meze, ranging from houmous shawarma to parsley-laden tabouleh, while enjoying delicious fruit cocktails. Baby okra in tomato sauce, and fuul medames swimming in garlicky liquor were particularly tasty, but fatayer (spinach pastries) were rather dull. We also squeezed in a plateful of baklava and cardamom-scented Lebanese coffee. Less formal and glitzy than other Lebanese restaurants in London, Al-Dar impresses with its smooth-running service and tasty food.
Babies and children welcome; high chairs. Takeaway service; delivery service. **Map 8 F6.**
For branches see index.

★ Kandoo
458 Edgware Road, W2 1EJ (7724 2428). Edgware Road tube. **Meals served** noon-midnight daily. **Main courses** £5.60-£10. **Unlicensed. Corkage** no charge. **Service** 10%. **Credit** MC, V. Iranian
At the wrong end of the Edgware Road is this modest, inconspicuous Iranian restaurant serving honest, good-quality kebabs and Persian stews. The respectable if slightly dull interior is complemented by a spacious walled garden at the back, a pleasant place to eat in summer (green plastic garden furniture notwithstanding). In the front picture window is a large, bulbous, mosaic-covered oven for on-site bread-making. From a list of typical starters (yoghurt dips, salads, feta with sabzi), we chose salad shirazi, everyday salad ingredients cut into tiny cubes, with a piquant dressing and covered with a dusting of dried herbs, along with mast-o-musir, a yogurt dip with garlic (this version used extremely thick, cream-like yoghurt). Hot, paper-thin bread straight from the oven made a great accompaniment. Kandoo offers a roster of Persian stews throughout the week – the day we visited it was lamb and green beans cooked in a spicy tomato sauce. We couldn't resist the kebabs, though. Chelo kebab koobideh was two skewers of juicy, minced lamb, flavoursome and pink on the inside, served with rice done the Persian way (a half and half mixture of plain boiled and saffron rice, best eaten with a knob of butter and a dusting of warm, red sumac spice – fabulous). The restaurant doesn't have a licence, but customers are welcome to bring their own alcohol. There's not much for vegetarians.

★ Maroush
21 Edgware Road, W2 2JE (7723 0773/ www.maroush.com). Marble Arch tube. **Meals served** noon-midnight daily. **Main courses** £12-£22. **Set meal** £21-£35 (minimum 2). **Cover** (noon-10.30pm) £2. **Minimum** (after 10.30pm) £48 incl £7.50 cover. **Credit** AmEx, DC, MC, V. Lebanese
There really is nowhere quite like Maroush. This branch of the successful London chain is housed in a handsome and spacious dark red basement (there's a café area upstairs), that's just made for after-dark. Meze dishes are always super-fresh and beautifully presented. Classic dishes like houmous and a zingy tabouleh had fresh, strong, distinctive flavours. Chicken livers in a lemon sauce melted in the mouth. Falafel were crisp on the outside, soft on the inside and not greasy, served with thin tahina sauce. A shared mixed grill, ample for two, consisted of a variety of well-cooked meat: lamb, liver, chicken, minced lamb. Instead of the more usual complimentary cakes that are served with coffee, we were presented with a sumptuous bowl of fresh fruit. What really distinguishes this branch of Maroush, though, is its weekend programme of entertainment. Lounge and Arabic classics from a succession of singers, two top-class belly dancers, plus some of the international cast of diners on the dancefloor, made for an atmosphere that was charged at times, lively to say the least and neither entirely Arab nor English. Cosmopolitan, really.
Babies and children admitted (lunch). Booking essential after 10pm Fri, Sat. Dress: smart casual. Entertainment: musicians 9.30pm-2am nightly; belly dancer (phone for details). Separate room for parties, seats 100. Takeaway service. **Map 8 F6.**
For branches see index.

Patogh
8 Crawford Place, W1H 5NE (7262 4015). Edgware Road tube. **Meals served** 1pm-midnight daily. **Main courses** £6-£12. **Unlicensed. Corkage** no charge. **No credit cards.** Iranian
Patogh is set over two narrow floors, just off the Edgware Road. The ground-floor dining area is dominated by an open-plan kitchen with a huge grill around which three chefs busily tend an array of kebabs. The upstairs room, with its ruggedly distressed plaster walls, offers a calmer (and cooler) dining area. For starters, the 'special' Persian bread turned out to be an absolutely huge sesame seed-topped crunchy flatbread, with which we nibbled at the mixed meze, including mouth-puckeringly sour pickles and dollops of houmous and yoghurt-based dips, washed down with a jugful of sour dogh (Persian yoghurt drink) flavoured with dried mint. Main courses of minced chicken and minced lamb kebabs, both served with rice, were a letdown – harshly flavoured, with rather too much onion, and an unpleasantly oily texture. Despite these reservations, however, Patogh was positively brimful with diners, perhaps attracted more by the lively atmosphere than the so-so food.
Book weekends. Takeaway service. **Map 8 E5.**

★ Ranoush Juice Bar
43 Edgware Road, W2 2JR (7723 5929/ www.maroush.com). Marble Arch tube. **Meals served** 8am-3am daily. **Main courses** £3-£10. **No credit cards.** Lebanese
Part of the Maroush chain, Ranoush is an Edgware Road institution, serving fast food Lebanese style, to eat in or take out, along with a large variety of fruit juices to the (mainly Arabic) passing foot traffic. It's pretty hectic most of the time: behind the counter gangs of chefs turn out shawarma sandwiches by the dozen; orders are shouted; and takeaways dispatched to waiting flunkeys. Lights are bright, and seating space on the marble-topped tables or wall counters is at a premium. The standard of food is fine for a café. Good-quality Lebanese standards such as houmous, tabouleh, green beans with tomatoes, and chicken livers in citrusy sauce are served alongside the shawarmas (as sandwiches in pitta bread or in a bowl). But

Fakhreldine

fruit juices are on the small side – Al-Dar (*see p197*) a few doors down does much larger juices – service is brusque to say the least and the atmosphere hardly relaxing. A good place to grab a snack and see a slice of Arab London life, but not somewhere to linger.
Babies and children welcome. Takeaway service; delivery service. **Map 8 F6.**
For branches see index.

Marylebone W1, NW1

Al Fawar
50 Baker Street, W1U 7BT (7224 4777/ www.alfawar.com). Baker Street tube. **Meals served** noon-midnight daily. **Main courses** £12.50-£13.90. **Set meal** £25 3 courses incl coffee and dessert. **Cover** £2 (à la carte). **Credit** AmEx, DC, JCB, MC, V. Lebanese
Al Fawar asserts its identity with a large mural of a snow-covered cedar of Lebanon on one wall. On another is an oasis scene, and in the front window a mosaic fountain arrangement. The carpet is deep red and the tablecloths are white – and there are plenty of them. Add the black-suited staff and the result is pretty formal, albeit with touches of kitsch. On a recent visit diners were outnumbered by staff, so we did feel rather scrutinised, but they were pleasant and the food was of a high standard. Some great meze dishes included manakeesh jibneh (grilled halloumi on pitta with a dusting of herbs); foul akhdar bil zeit (called foul moukala elsewhere: broad beans cooked with a thin, zingy sauce with lashings of coriander – this version was a little bit squidgy but still tasted good); falafel, which were spot-on – crisp on the outside and not greasy inside; and a light and tangy tabouleh. A mixed grill and a shish taouk were both generous portions with juicy, perfectly cooked meat. Arabic

coffee and mint tea came with a plate of complimentary (and fresh) cakes. It was a nice touch to end a pleasant meal.
Babies and children welcome; high chairs. Book dinner. Dress: smart casual. Separate area for parties, seats 130. Takeaway service; delivery service (within 3-mile radius). **Map 9 G5.**

★ Ali Baba
32 Ivor Place, NW1 6DA (7723 7474/5805). Baker Street tube/Marylebone tube/rail. **Meals served** noon-midnight daily. **Main courses** £8-£10. **Unlicensed. Corkage** no charge. **Service** 10%. **No credit cards.** Egyptian
It's just as well that Egypt has its pyramids because the place is never to going wow anyone with its cuisine. So what keeps us going back to Ali Baba, one of a handful of London restaurants to specialise in the underwhelming food of the pharaohs? Novelty, that's what. The novelty of stepping from a street in London straight into a backroom in Cairo. The place couldn't be more Egyptian – a scruffy single room with patterned carpet, plastic flowers and a 22-inch set in the corner permanently tuned to Arabic TV. The menu features Cairo classics such as fuul, falafel (the Egyptian type with chopped parsley and black-eyed beans) and koshari (pasta, rice, black lentils and caramelised onions served with a thin but spicy-hot tomato sauce). You'll also find molokhia, a soup of stewed leaves that has the consistency of snot – the 11th-century ruler of Cairo, Al-Hakim, found the stuff so revolting he had it banned. Mains are grilled meats: kebabs, kofte or chops. Customers tend to be expat Egyptians or Brits who were once expats in Egypt – folk in thrall to nostalgia rather than their taste buds. Booze is not served, but there is an off-licence round the corner.

Babies and children admitted; high chairs. Booking advisable. Separate room for parties, seats 25. Takeaway service; delivery service. **Map 2 F4.**

Fairuz
3 Blandford Street, W1H 3AA (7486 8108/ 8182). Baker Street or Bond Street tube. **Meals served** noon-11.30pm Mon-Sat; noon-10.30pm Sun. **Main courses** £9.95-£18.95. **Set meze** £17.95. **Set meal** £24.95 3 courses. **Cover** £1.50. **Credit** AmEx, DC, MC, V. Lebanese
Perhaps the most welcoming of London's Lebanese restaurants (a notoriously starchy bunch) and consequently packed for lunch and dinner. But while the fold-back frontage with pavement seating and a Mediterranean-flavoured interior of lemon yellow and duck-egg blue entice passing trade, it's the quality of the food that's built up Fairuz's following. The menu is standard Lebanese with an expansive offering of around 50 hot and cold meze. Some are better than others: light, fluffy falafel come with a little pot of tahina; chicken livers deliver a sharp little kick courtesy of a marinade of lemon and pomegranate juice, but calamari were oily and the houmous had an unwelcome cheesy aftertaste. We usually gorge on multiple meze, re-ordering as necessary, but of the mains farouj mousakhan is a stand-out – a duvet of flatbread filled with chicken pieces smothered in fried onions and parsley and baked in the oven. Fairuz has a more style-conscious sibling with the same name (itself a homage to Lebanon's most popular diva) over on Westbourne Grove, where the cooking is every bit as good but the atmosphere is… what was that word again? Starchy.
Babies and children admitted; high chairs. Book dinner. Takeaway service. **Map 9 G5.**
For branch see index.

Levant
Jason Court, 76 Wigmore Street, W1U 2SJ (7224 1111/www.levantrestaurant.co.uk). Bond Street tube.
Bar **Open** noon-1am daily.
Restaurant **Meals served** noon-11.30pm Mon-Fri. **Dinner served** 5.30-11.30pm Sat, Sun. **Main courses** £11.25-£25. **Set lunch** (noon-6pm Mon-Fri) £12.50 2 courses. **Set dinner** £24.50-£35 3 courses. **Service** 15%.
Both **Credit** AmEx, DC, JCB, MC, V. Lebanese
Levant aims at oriental fantasy. Scattered rose petals cover the dramatic lamp-lit stairs leading to the basement eating area, where low tables, wooden carved screens and Moroccan lanterns make up the furnishings – all very *Sheltering Sky*. The Arabic music is loud, and the atmosphere partyish, with diners egged on by staff and the occasional belly dancer. This approach appeals mainly to a younger generation of diners in search of a good night out. (When booking, you're told to prepare for the possibility that the table may be required for a second sitting – no one has booked the table, but the restaurant is keeping its options open.) The menu stretches from Moroccan-style tagines to European-influenced dishes with a Lebanese slant (salmon kebab) to classic Lebanese meze and grills. Most of the food was well cooked and presented, with some careful little touches. Baba ganoush came decorated with pomegranate seeds. Sambousek were tasty cheese parcels in soft pastry that melted in the mouth, and chicken liver was a generous portion with plenty of zing. Lamb shawarma was good if unremarkable. However, with the loud music and lack of space, it all seemed a bit frenetic (or maybe we're just too old).
Booking advisable. Entertainment: belly dancer 8.30pm. Separate area for parties, seats 12. Takeaway service. **Map 9 G6.**
For branch see index.

Mayfair W1

Al Hamra
31-33 Shepherd Market, W1Y 7HR (7493 1954/ www.alhamrarestaurant.com). Green Park or Hyde Park Corner tube. **Meals served** noon-11.30pm daily. **Main courses** £14-£20. **Minimum** £20. **Cover** £2.50. **Credit** AmEx, DC, JCB, MC, V. Lebanese

If you ever have the good fortune to be invited to dinner by the under-secretary of the embassy of an Arabian state, chances are this is where you will be brought. Al Hamra is the grand old dame of London's Levantine restaurants, and has the role of club-cum-canteen for the Middle Eastern diplomats whose residences and workplaces dot the surrounding streets. It's a strangely claustrophobic place that, with its low ceiling, strip windows and formal table settings, feels like a cruise ship dining room. The food is excellent. Order from a traditional menu led by what can be a bewildering array of hot and cold meze – a nervy American couple at a table beside us, plainly novices at this game, took almost an hour to settle on their order. They needn't have worried. Of the half-dozen dishes we tried – including fried beid ghanem, or 'lamb's eggs' (testicles) – everything was first class, particularly the 'cheese salad' (shinklish in Arabic), which is chopped tomato, parsley and onion with tangy aged cheese. Mains were a disappointment by comparison, but that's Lebanese cuisine for you. There is a £20 minimum spend per head – for regulars that's tipping money. *Babies and children welcome; high chairs. Book dinner. Tables outdoors (24, terrace). Takeaway service; delivery service (orders over £20).* **Map 9 H8.**

★ Al Sultan

51-52 Hertford Street, W1J 7ST (7408 1155/ 1166). Green Park or Hyde Park Corner tube. **Meals served** noon-midnight daily. **Main courses** £10-£12. **Cover** £2. **Credit** AmEx, DC, MC, V. Lebanese
Very much a classic Mayfair Lebanese, Al Sultan comes complete with a prim interior – mirrored arches, pastel colours, impressive floral arrangements – hypnotic Lebanese piped music playing in the background, and a team of professional, uniformed waiting staff. Within minutes of arriving an appetising selection of lettuce leaves, radishes, carrot and cucumber batons, plus olives, landed on the table. Such was the spread of meze on offer that we decided to stick with these, rather than opting for the grilled meat mains. Standards in the kitchen are high, and we browsed happily on smooth, rich houmous

garnished with lamb and pine nuts, tasty manakeesh (thyme-topped flatbread); parsley-rich tabouleh, deliciously sour fatayer, and broad beans. Whitebait were admirably crisp and moreish, while batrakh (smoked fish roe) was luxuriously rich. Service managed to combine efficiency with courtesy, adding to a smooth-as-silk dining experience. Well worth visiting for an accomplished taste of Lebanese cuisine.
Babies and children welcome; high chairs. Book dinner. Tables outdoors (4, pavement). Takeaway service; delivery service (within 2-mile radius on orders over £35). Vegetarian menu. **Map 9 H8.**

Fakhreldine

85 Piccadilly, W1J 7NB (7493 3424/ www.fakhreldine.co.uk). Green Park tube. **Meals served** noon-midnight daily. **Main courses** £13-£20. **Set lunch** £25 3 courses incl coffee. **Service** 12.5%. **Credit** AmEx, DC, JCB, MC, V. Lebanese
How we thrilled to this place when it reopened in summer 2003 after a dramatic makeover. And after penning a rave review, how we looked forward to a return visit. Well, now we've returned and, sad to say, something equally drastic, not to say tragic, has occurred: the kitchen has been stricken with ageusia. How else to explain it? In a mixed meze selection, the tabouleh was drenched in lemon juice, an honest mistake, perhaps, but houmous prepared with rose water must have been deliberate – and the results are highly unpleasant. Fillet of beef and sea bream both came soaked in pomegranate juice. The meat put up game resistance, but the fish was wholly obliterated. Our waitress was sympathetic and confided that another dish on the menu was done with essence of orange blossom and tasted like washing-up liquid. Otherwise, we love this place: the decor of stained oak and stone greys is gorgeous, staff are lovely and the views of Green Park are London at its most enchanting. So, all's not lost. We were told that the menu is about to undergo major changes, so one hopes things may soon improve. Here's hoping that the chefs get their sense of taste back.
Babies and children welcome; high chairs. Booking advisable. Takeaway service; delivery service. **Map 9 H8.**

West

Bayswater W2

★ Al Waha

75 Westbourne Grove, W2 4UL (7229 0806/ www.waha-uk.com). Bayswater or Queensway tube. **Meals served** noon-midnight daily. **Main courses** £9-£18. **Set lunch** £12.50 5 courses. **Set dinner** £21-£25 3 courses incl coffee. **Cover** £1.50. **Credit** MC, V. Lebanese
Ranged over two levels, painted a mellow yellow and furnished with plenty of greenery, Al Waha manages to create an impression of spaciousness in quite a small area. Staff are serene but efficient, the atmosphere subdued but relaxed. This is Lebanese dining at its best: quality meze and meat dishes, white tablecloths, a huge bowl of salad vegetables to snack on or dip, but none of the accompanying frosty formality of some London Lebanese restaurants. The meze list is the usual long affair. We couldn't find a bad word to say about the items we tried: a delicately fragrant foul moukala (broad beans cooked in lemon and oil, served with coriander); down-home bamia bil zait (literally, okra with oil, actually served in a tomato sauce); a lovely manakeesh jibneh (warmed cheese on pitta bread, spread with a dusting of mellow dried herbs); fatayer (spinach pastries); and a creamy baba ganoush. A main course shish taouk was tender chicken cooked to a T, and plenty for two. A light Lebanese Kefraya rosé was a perfect accompaniment.
Babies and children admitted (until 7pm); high chairs. Booking advisable; essential dinner. Tables outdoors (4, patio). Takeaway service; delivery service. **Map 7 B6.**

★ Fresco

25 Westbourne Grove, W2 4UA (7221 2355). Bayswater or Royal Oak tube. **Meals served** 9am-11pm daily. **Main courses** £5.95-£7.95. **Set meze** £9.95. **Credit** MC, V. Lebanese
This bustling, cheery café is a jewel, and a million miles away from London's stuffier Lebanese establishments. Walls are bright yellow, and huge coloured photos of fruit give a clue as to the place's

---

Menu

See also the menu boxes in **North African** (starting on p223) and **Turkish** (starting on p257).

Meze

Baba ganoush: Egyptian name for moutabal (qv).
Basturma: smoked beef.
Falafel: a mixture of spicy chickpeas or broad beans ground, rolled into balls and deep fried.
Fatayer: a soft pastry with fillings of cheese, onions, spinach and pine kernels.
Fattoush: fresh vegetable salad containing shards of toasted pitta bread and sumac (qv).
Fuul or **fuul medames**: brown broad beans that are mashed and seasoned with olive oil, lemon juice and garlic.
Kalaj: halloumi cheese on pastry.
Kibbeh: highly seasoned mixture of minced lamb, cracked wheat and onion, deep-fried in balls. For meze

it is often served raw (**kibbeh nayeh**) like steak tartare.
Labneh: Middle Eastern cream cheese made from yoghurt.
Moujadara: lentils, rice and caramelised onions mixed together.
Moutabal: a purée of char-grilled aubergines mixed with sesame sauce, garlic and lemon juice.
Muhamara: spiced and crushed mixed nuts.
Sambousek: small pastries filled with mince, onion and pine kernels.
Sujuk: spicy Lebanese sausages.
Sumac: an astringent and fruity-tasting spice made from dried sumac seeds.
Tabouleh: a salad of chopped parsley, tomatoes, crushed wheat, onions, olive oil and lemon juice.
Torshi: own-made pickled vegetables.
Warak einab: rice-stuffed vine leaves.

Mains

Shawarma: meat (usually lamb) marinated then grilled on a spit and sliced kebab-style.
Shish kebab: cubes of marinated lamb grilled on a skewer, often with tomatoes, onions and sweet peppers.
Shish taouk: like shish kebab, but with chicken rather than lamb.

Desserts

Baklava: filo pastry interleaved with pistachio nuts, almonds or walnuts, and covered in syrup.
Konafa or **kadayif**: cake made from shredded pastry dough, filled with syrup and nuts, or cream.
Ma'amoul: pastries filled with nuts or dates.
Muhallabia: a milky ground-rice pudding with almonds and pistachios, flavoured with rosewater or orange blossom.

Om ali: bread and butter pudding.

IRANIAN DISHES

Ash-e reshteh: a soup containing noodles, spinach, pulses and dried herbs.
Kashk-e badejan: baked aubergines mixed with herbs.
Kuku-ye sabzi: finely chopped fresh herbs mixed with eggs and baked in the oven.
Masto khiar: yoghurt mixed with finely chopped cucumber and mint.
Masto musir: shallot-flavoured yoghurt.
Mirza ghasemi: crushed baked aubergines, tomatoes, garlic and herbs mixed with egg.
Sabzi: a plate of fresh herb leaves (usually mint and fennel) often served with a cube of feta.
Salad olivieh: a bit like a russian salad, with chopped potatoes, chicken, eggs, peas and gherkins, plus olive oil and mayonnaise.

raison d'être. All manner of fruit combinations are juiced to order and served in pint-sized glasses – banana, strawberry and orange was a glorious gunge. You can have single juices, milkshakes and healthy vegetable juices too. Meze dishes sit behind the glass counter and are served in generous portions, microwaved where necessary. They come as sandwiches in pitta bread – falafel, halloumi and so on, combination plates, and individual dishes served in bowls, along with plenty of bread. Some of the food is a tad more rough and ready than that in elite establishments, but this is really only discernible in presentation; everything tastes good. A filling portion of falafel comprised no fewer than five large globes (we had to take three of them away with us); batata harra and a tangy tabouleh were similarly generously portioned. While there is a brisk trade in takeaways, tables get filled too. Service is in the hands of cheerful young people. *Babies and children welcome; high chairs. Bookings not accepted. Takeaway service (within 2-mile radius). Vegetarian menu.* **Map 7 B6**.

Hafez

5 Hereford Road, W2 4AB (7221 3167/7229 9398). Bayswater tube/328 bus. **Meals served** noon-midnight daily. **Main courses** £6-£14.50. **Service** 10%. **No credit cards**. Iranian
This small restaurant located on a Bayswater side street offers a chance to sample homely Iranian food in pleasantly low-key surroundings. A pavement table was the perfect option for a hot summer's day – especially given that the inside of the restaurant is dominated by a magnificent tiled bread oven blasting out heat. The fruits of this device were soon in evidence; we tucked into fine, freshly baked Persian flatbread, furnished with a tasty yoghurt and shallot dip. Also good was sabzi-o-paneer, a slab of smooth, white, salty cheese served with radishes and a large handful of fragrant tarragon and mint. The main courses, though simple, were tasty: generous portions of tender grilled lamb fillet and minced lamb kebabs,

served on a mound of light, fluffy rice. We finished with mint tea and the usual plateful of small, fantastically sweet, syrup-soaked pastries, and left feeling very content indeed. *Babies and children welcome; high chairs. Tables outdoors (4, pavement). Takeaway service; delivery service.* **Map 7 B6**. **For branch see index**.

Kensington W8

Phoenicia

11-13 Abingdon Road, W8 6AH (7937 0120/ www.phoeniciarestaurant.co.uk). High Street Kensington tube. **Meals served** noon-midnight daily. **Main courses** £10.95-£15. **Minimum** £16.80 dinner. **Set meze** £16.80, £24.95, £30.95. **Set lunch** (12.15-3pm Mon-Fri) £9.95 2 courses, £11.95 3 courses. **Set buffet** (12.15-2.30pm Sat) £12.95; (12.15-3.30pm Sun) £14.95. **Cover** £1.90. **Credit** AmEx, DC, JCB, MC, V. Lebanese
Smart but quite subdued, Phoenicia is the place for a classic menu of Lebanese dishes (including a meze list as long as your arm), produced to a consistently high standard. The surroundings are rather bland, with magnolia walls and a few potted plants, but the food is anything but dull. On a recent visit we tried a creamy moutabal served with a little well of olive oil in the middle and a sprinkling of pomegranate seeds, warak einab (stuffed vine leaves), a fresh fattoush salad (lettuce, tomato, cucumber, onion and fresh herbs in dressing, with a scattering of sumac and pieces of crisp toasted pitta bread) and batata harra (fried potatoes with peppers – a little too squashy, perhaps, but still tasty). A main-course shish taouk (chicken kebab) was well cooked and unusually spicy. Staff are formal, unobtrusive and polite; they, together with thoroughly pleasant food and a light Lebanese rosé, made for a relaxing eating experience. *Babies and children welcome; children's menu; high chairs. Book weekends. Dress: smart casual.*

No-smoking tables. Separate room for parties, seats 30. Takeaway service; delivery service. **Map 7 A9**.

Olympia W14

Alounak

10 Russell Gardens, W14 8EZ (7603 7645). Kensington (Olympia) tube/rail. **Meals served** noon-midnight daily. **Main courses** £5.60-£11. **Unlicensed. Corkage** no charge. **Service** 10%. **Credit** MC, V. Iranian
Alounak is a bright, cheerful, family-friendly establishment ten minutes' walk from High Street Kensington. As with most Iranian restaurants its menu is a paean to marinated meats served with mounds of rice. Take it or leave it. (Although you can substitute bread or salad for the rice.) Vegetarians not accommodated. There is the option of fish, which comes in a single variety: grilled, marinated sea bass, served whole with head and tail intact, skin blackened and its flesh yellowed by saffron. Absolutely gorgeous. Starters include the usuals, such as mirza ghasemi (char-grilled aubergine with fried onion and garlic), halim bademjan (mashed char-grilled aubergine with onions, herbs and walnuts) and salad olivieh (a Persian potato salad with shredded chicken). All of these, plus houmous, olives and chillies, come as part of a mixed starter deal (good value at £8.90). Service is never less than friendly; how could it be otherwise when the owner is nearly always present, sat with friends at a table in the front room beneath an artificial palm tree. *Babies and children welcome (lunch only); high chairs. Booking advisable. Takeaway service; delivery service.* **For branch see index**.

★ Chez Marcelle

34 Blythe Road, W14 0HA (7603 3241). Kensington (Olympia) tube/rail. **Meals served** 5-10pm Tue-Thur; noon-10pm Fri-Sun. **Main courses** £7-£9.50. **No credit cards**. Lebanese

Hafez

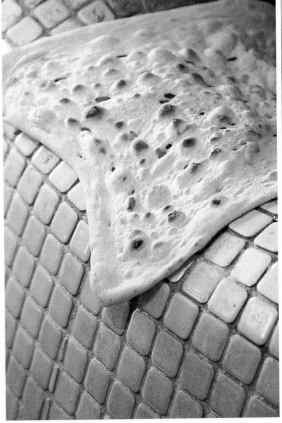

Tucked away in a side street next to Olympia's huge exhibition halls, this small restaurant, simply decorated with stripped pine floorboards and pale green walls, offers a welcome antidote to corporate impersonality. Marcelle herself presided over our lunch with charm and a firm motherliness, announcing that she would mix chickpeas into our fuul medames 'because they're very nice together' and adding dates and figs to our dessert as they're 'very good for you'. The kitchen at the back produced a medley of tasty meze dishes: a plateful of sizzling sujuk (spiced sausage), robustly flavourful broad beans, tabouleh, houmous and a tasty arayes (minced meat sandwiched between flatbread). To drink: tangy, freshly squeezed lemon juice. A generous plateful of dainty sweet pastries and dried fruits, together with refreshing mint tea, rounded off a pleasant meal. Weekend lunchtimes can be rather quiet, but Chez Marcelle does brisk business during the evenings.
Babies and children welcome. Booking advisable. Separate room for parties, seats 40. Takeaway service. Map 20 C3.

★ ★ Mohsen
152 Warwick Road, W14 8PS (7602 9888). Earl's Court tube/Olympia tube/rail. **Meals served** noon-midnight daily. **Main courses** £12-£15. **No credit cards**. Iranian
Rather miraculously, considering its location on traffic-congested Warwick Road opposite a huge DIY superstore, Mohsen manages to strike a holiday note. White walls, terracotta tiles and round blue tables evoke a Mediterranean feel, while the restaurant extends through to an al fresco dining area, complete with plants, colourful carpets and chirping caged songbirds. A charming waiter was quick to provide the most delicious, dimpled, sesame seed-topped Persian flatbread, freshly baked in a smart steel oven by the window, together with aromatic herbs, salty cheese, shallot-infused yoghurt and a rich aubergine and walnut dip. The starters were so tasty we were almost reluctant to move on; luckily, the mains also turned out to be excellent. Kebab koobideh was a classic piece of Persian cooking at its simple but delicious best: tender grilled minced lamb with a mound of fluffy rice. Dish of the day was a tender, subtly spiced lamb shank served with rice flavoured with dill and broad beans. With cooking as good as this, no wonder our lunchtime visit saw a steady stream of predominantly Iranian customers.
Babies and children welcome. No-smoking tables. Tables outdoors (2, yard). Map 13 A10.

Yas
7 Hammersmith Road, W14 8XJ (7603 9148). Olympia tube/rail. **Meals served** noon-4.30am daily. **Main courses** £6-£30. **Service** 10%. **Credit** AmEx, DC, MC, V. Iranian

As the elder statesman of Iranian dining in London, Yas is a little more upmarket than most of its compatriots, but not by too much. It boasts a smart maître d', but otherwise is a modest place with a warm interior of deep orange walls and a heavy doughy smell emanating from a large clay oven. The menu is kebabs, kebabs and kebabs, but beautifully done, plus a variety of specials (mainly stews). While portions are enormous, it would be a shame to miss out on the starters, especially the kashk-e bademjan (puréed aubergine with chopped mint and a smear of pungent, runny goat's cheese), and kuku-ye sabzi (a wedge of puffed-up omelette with heaps of parsley, coriander and dill). Masto musir – a bowl of creamy yoghurt studded with diced, crunchy shallots – is a great accompaniment to meat. Yas is unusual for an Iranian restaurant in that it's licensed, and unusual for a London restaurant in that it's open until 4.30am.
Babies and children admitted. Booking advisable. Takeaway service.
For branch see index.

Paddington W2

Levantine
26 London Street, W2 1HH (7262 1111). Paddington tube/rail. **Meals served** noon-midnight daily. **Main courses** £4.25-£19. **Set meze** (lunch) £8.50-£15. **Set meze** (dinner) £19.50-£27.50. **Service** 12.5%. **Credit** AmEx, MC, V. Lebanese

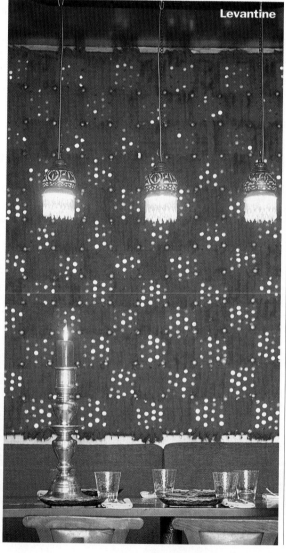

Levantine

Levantine is one of those restaurants where dim lighting, lanterns, loud music and fun fun fun combine to make someone's ersatz oriental fantasy. For such a venue, you could say that Levantine's look is quite low key: deep orangey-red walls, low tables and chairs, some lanterns. Actually, the loos are a highlight: darkened stairs lead down to a lamp-lit mosaic pool filled with rose petals. Though the decor nods towards North Africa, the food is mainly Lebanese: a good meze selection, with kebabs to follow. The meat set menu promised an astonishing 19 dishes. Very small portions, we imagined – but we imagined wrong. Dishes came on a kind of raised tray (placed on our low table, that was quite high and rather uncomfortable). First came dips, including lovely, creamy baba ganoush and houmous. Highlights among the multitude of dishes that followed were spicy Armenian sausages, batata hara, okra with tomato, kibbeh, meatballs, chicken and lamb kebabs (all in little bowls). It was professional, top-class stuff, but way too much – and this set meal is for a minimum of two people. Such excess somehow encapsulates what is wrong with such places: food is way down the agenda, subsumed to the forced merriment of the staff, the music and the belly dancer.
Babies and children admitted. Booking advisable. Entertainment: belly dancer 9pm daily. Vegetarian menu. **Map 8 D6.**

Shepherd's Bush W12

★ Abu Zaad
29 Uxbridge Road, W12 8LH (8749 5107). Shepherd's Bush tube. **Meals served** 11am-11pm daily. **Main courses** £3.90-£6.90. **Credit** MC, V. Syrian
Situated on a corner of bustling Uxbridge Road, Abu Zaad offers a rare chance to sample Syrian food in London. Cheerfully decorated with framed illuminated transparencies of Damascan scenes, this friendly, spacious restaurant pulled in a steady stream of predominantly Middle Eastern customers during our lunchtime visit. Within minutes of seating, an affable young waiter had taken our order and returned with freshly squeezed fruit juices. A trio of dishes – broad beans in yoghurt, an aubergine dip and deliciously tasty, freshly cooked aris (minced lamb sandwiched between flatbread) – got the meal off to a great start. The mains weren't as tasty: 'meat with freekah' proved to be a huge portion of smoky freekah (roasted green wheat), topped with tender but bland lamb and a yoghurt dip, while chicken with aubergine was lacklustre. Excellent baklava and fragrant mint tea, however, made a delicious close. Considering the amount of food consumed, the bill was remarkably reasonable and we left feeling cheered and replete.
Babies and children welcome; high chairs. Book weekends. No-smoking tables. Separate room for parties, seats 25. Takeaway service. **Map 20 B2.**

South West

Balham SW12

Dish Dash
11-13 Bedford Hill, SW12 9ET (8673 5555). Balham tube/rail. *Bar* **Open** 10.30am-11pm Mon-Fri; 10.30am-11pm Sat, Sun. *Restaurant* **Meals served** 5-11pm Mon-Fri; 10.30am-11pm Sat, Sun. **Main courses** £7.50-£11.25. **Service** 12.5%. **Credit** MC, V. Iranian
The Goodge Street original has closed, but the Balham branch appears to be prospering. Location counts for much of this: the High Road end of Bedford Hill now boasts a cluster of aspirational bars that serve bar food to bright young things, and Dish Dash matches this demographic perfectly. Although the menu claims it 'draws influence' from Persia, this is primarily a theme bar with a good list of cocktails, modish music and a (soundless) flat-screen TV. The dishes are not too complicated, nothing too challenging for the young staff to prepare – quite unlike the complexity of real Persian food, in other words. A lamb khoresh

was served with 'jewelled rice', which was garnished with just five – yes, five – barberries. The lamb stew was OK, though the flavours of the dried limes, cinnamon, rose petals and apples advertised on the menu were hard to detect. Likewise the joojeh (chicken) kebab; the best versions are slowly marinated, but this one appeared as ill-acquainted with its marinade as Ayatollah Khomeini was with the *Playboy* mansion. Dish Dash is fine for a lively night out, but look elsewhere for real Persian cooking.
Babies and children admitted: high chairs. Book weekends. Disabled: toilet. No-smoking tables. Separate room for parties, seats 30. Tables outdoors (4, pavement). Takeaway service. Vegetarian menu.

Fulham SW6

Aziz
24-32 Vanston Place, SW6 1AX (7386 0086). Fulham Broadway tube. **Lunch served** noon-3pm Mon-Fri. **Dinner served** 6pm-midnight Mon-Fri. **Meals served** noon-midnight Sat; noon-11pm Sun. **Main courses** £7-£14. **Set lunch** (Mon-Fri) £10 2 courses. **Service** 12.5%. **Credit** AmEx, MC, V. Modern Middle Eastern
Our last visit to Aziz would best be described as good in parts. The place looks good: a modern space with a lounge area with divan seating and low tables, plus a bar along one side of the room. But off-key service (things kept arriving at the wrong times, or waiters disappeared) combined with duff dishes, left us uncomfortable and dissatisfied. The menu spans the region, with dishes from Spain, North Africa, the Levant and Iran. Mechouia, a North African-style cooked green pepper salad with tomato and onions was nicely flavoured, though not extraordinary. Pickled boquerones with chilli (pickled fish on a cocktail stick with slices of kebab shop-style chilli pepper) was salty but otherwise tasteless. Chickpea and white bean salad suffered from undercooked beans and a lack of flavour. Mains took a better turn. Chicken tagine was great, and shank of lamb with a tomato sauce flavoured with dried limes was a generous portion, served with luxurious 'jewelled rice' – with raisins and pistachios. Sort out the service, rationalise the menu and Aziz could be back on form.
Babies and children welcome; high chairs. Booking essential weekends. Disabled: toilet. Tables outdoors (6, pavement). Takeaway service (deli). **Map 13 A3.**

South Kensington SW7

Al Bustan NEW
68 Old Brompton Road, SW7 3LQ (7584 5805). South Kensington tube. **Meals served** noon-10.30pm daily. **Main courses** £11.50-£16. **Set meal** (lunch Mon-Sat; noon-10.30pm Sun) £10 3 courses. **Credit** AmEx, DC, JCB, MC, V. Lebanese
A recent meal at this South Ken restaurant was hit and miss. First, it's not cheap (£85 for two people, without wine, is pretty steep). Second, the decor is bland, with even blander artworks. Third, service was delivered by a curious mix of friendly and offhand waiters. Thankfully, the food is up to scratch: chef Ina'am Atalla cooks up a steady stream of Lebanese dishes, including charcoal grills and dishes labelled 'traditional home cooking'. A mix of hot and cold meze featured flavoursome houmous, zingy fresh tabouleh and crisp yet fluffy falafel. Arayes (flatbread filled with spiced minced meat, then toasted) were an acquired taste (the spicing verging on sweet), but one we'd happily acquired by the time we'd finished ploughing through them. For mains, lamb shawerma was spot-on, with excellent-quality meat, while prawns in tomato sauce were also good, the spicing perfectly judged. Rice with lentils went well with everything. The clientele was a mix of Middle Eastern diners, Western couples and tourists – all of whom seemed to be enjoying the food as much as we were.
Babies and children welcome. No-smoking tables. Takeaway service; delivery service. **Map 14 D10.**

South

Battersea SW8

The Village
34 Queenstown Road, SW8 3RX (7720 1161). Battersea Park or Queenstown Road rail. **Meals served** 11am-midnight Tue-Sun. **Main courses** £8.25-£9.45. **Set meze** £15 per person (minimum 2). **Cover** £1. **Service** 10% for parties of 4 or more. **Credit** MC, V. Lebanese
This well-established South London outpost of classic Lebanese cuisine serves high-quality food in surroundings reminiscent of a '70s Swiss chalet (or is it a Greek taverna?). In any case, decor is lots of pine combined with white Artexed walls. Whatever the drawbacks of this decorating scheme, it does lend a summery aspect to the room, which suits the food well. Freshness is key with meze, and at the Village you can hear plenty of chopping going on behind the scenes. The result: a finely textured tabouleh (lemony and full of herby flavour); a fatttoush salad also had that just-chopped taste and was served with a sprinkling of warm sumac spice; baba ganoush (moutabal), meanwhile, was beaten to a creamy consistency. A juicy shish taouk finished off a good summer lunch. Our only complaints were that we missed the bowl of salad vegetables that generally appears on the table at the beginning of a Lebanese meal; and the cover charge represented only one tiny saucer of olives.
Babies and children welcome; high chairs. Booking advisable; essential dinner. Disabled: toilet. No-smoking tables. Takeaway service; delivery service (within 2-mile radius).

East

Brick Lane E1

★ Hookah Lounge NEW
133 Brick Lane, E1 6SB (7033 9072). Shoreditch tube/8 bus. **Meals served** 11am-10.30pm Mon-Thur, Sun; 11.30am-midnight Fri, Sat. **Meze** £2.50-£6.90. **Set meze** £6.95. **Credit** (over £10) AmEx, MC, V. Lebanese
Part vintage emporium (chandelier, standard lamps, kitsch orientalist paintings), part den of eastern exotica (low seating, cushions, arabesque accoutrements), everying in Hookah Lounge looks as if it came out of an attic – and the place has charm by the bucketful. The menu lists soft drinks with an eastern touch, including mint tea and hibiscus (both available hot or iced); a big selection of coffees; original cocktails (lots of mint, lemon juice and vodka); wine and beer; plus 14 meze and

a few additional set dishes. You can smoke a hookah too, if you like. We made up a lunch from a few meze plates. OK, so they didn't have the finesse that top restaurant chefs would apply to the same dishes: tabouleh came with parsley stalks and big chunks of leaf; grilled halloumi seemed warmed rather than grilled; batata hara had a lot of grease with it. But the tabouleh was herby and superbly fresh, and the potatoes packed a good chilli punch. Add a laid-back atmosphere and pleasant staff and you have a very pleasant retreat from the bustle of Brick Lane.
Booking advisable. Takeaway service. Vegetarian menu. **Map 6 S4.**

North

Camden Town & Chalk Farm NW1

Le Mignon
98 Arlington Road, NW1 7HD (7387 0600). Camden Town tube. **Meals served** noon-midnight daily. **Main courses** £9.50-£18.50. **Service** 12.5%. **Credit** MC, V. Lebanese
The name is French, but the restaurant is Lebanese. It's moved to a new site – though it's hard to tell since it's only a couple of doors from its former location. Still a tiny space, Le Mignon is now a bit more formal with stone-clad walls and tables set with pink cloths, roses and candles. Thankfully, the cooking is the same – good, going on very good. Of the meze we tried, the stand-out was fattoush, a green salad with shards of crisp bread given zing with lemon juice and sumac. Fatayer (fried pastry triangles stuffed with lemon-drenched spinach) and sambousek (fried pastry pockets of minced lamb and pine kernels) actually enhanced our appetite for the mains. These were lahma meshwi, a tumulus of rice layered with thin strips of lamb under a heavy fall of almonds, cashews and pine nuts; and farouj meshwi, small pieces of charcoal-blackened chicken under a blanket of sliced onions and red and green peppers. A great little neighbourhood restaurant, well worth braving the winos and other substance-influenced streetfolk of Camden.
Babies and children admitted (daytime). Booking advisable. Tables outdoors (4, pavement). Takeaway service. **Map 27 D3.**

North West

Kilburn NW6

★ Beirut Cellar
248 Belsize Road, NW6 4BT (7328 3472). Kilburn Park tube. **Meals served** noon-11pm Tue-Sun. **Main courses** £6.50-£8. **Set meal** £15 2 courses incl coffee (minimum 2). **Cover** £1. **Credit** MC, V. Lebanese
Don't be put off by the humdrum location, somewhat depressing name, or unreconstructed decor (complete with ersatz stone walls); this cosy Lebanese restaurant definitely has its heart in the right place. On a quiet Sunday lunchtime a friendly waiter made us feel genuinely welcome, offering advice on what the eight-year-old in our party might enjoy and ensuring it was ordered at once, ahead of the adults. A basket of complimentary salad vegetables and a bowl of olives added to the hospitable reception. Dishes arrived as they were ready, so silky houmous with cubes of grilled lamb and a refreshing tabouleh kicked off the meal. Hot meze dishes featured chunks of spicy Lebanese sausage, four freshly fried kibbeh with a lamb and pine nut filling, and finger-lickingly tasty jawaneh (grilled chicken wings with a seriously garlicky sauce). A generous portion of char-grilled chicken kebab was a winner: the meat moist and tender, with a delicate cinnamon flavour. To round off, complimentary cashew-filled, pistachio-dusted baklava (very fresh) and a strong shot of Lebanese coffee. A real neighbourhood gem.
Babies and children welcome. Booking advisable. No-smoking tables. Separate room for parties, seats 45. Takeaway service; delivery service (within 2-mile radius). **Map 1 B1.**

Modern European

A number of iconic Mod Euro restaurants have served their final meal since the last edition, among them Conran's mega operation Mezzo (transforming into Cuban/Latin American joint Floridita in October 2004), the Sugar Club, Pharmacy and 192. That's not to say the scene is moribund; there's always been a lot of coming and going in one of London's most fashionable and fought-over cuisines.
The biggest opening of the year has been Jeremy King and Chris Corbin's lastest creation, the **Wolseley**, on a prime Piccadilly spot; garnering a huge amount of press attention, it also picked up the Best New Restaurant trophy in *Time Out*'s Eating & Drinking Awards 2004. The Square Mile is home to four new arrivals – the **Chancery**, **Lanes**, **Novelli in the City** and wine specialist **Vivat Bacchus** – while elsewhere there's the **Hoxton Apprentice** (where Prue Leith advises on the menu) and the **Burlington** (sibling of lovely East Sheen stalwart **Redmond's**).

Central

Barbican EC2

Searcy's
Level 2, Barbican, Silk Street, EC2Y 8DS (7588 3008/www.searcys.co.uk). Barbican tube. **Lunch served** noon-2.30pm Mon-Fri. **Dinner served** 5-10.30pm Mon-Sat. **Set meal** £21 2 courses, £25 3 courses. **Service** 12.5%. **Credit** AmEx, DC, JCB, MC, V.
First-timers at this restaurant and lounge bar in the Barbican arts complex are usually surprised at quite how appealing it is. Soft lighting, subtle design, a fine view (over the lake, fountains and St Giles' church) and extremely warm and efficient staff are an attractive blend. The food is worth having too. Not every dish we tried worked, but most did: standouts were a richly flavoured pumpkin soup followed by poached sea bass with sorrel sauce (both from the bargain 'performance' menu); also hitting all the right buttons was glazed fillet of Irish beef with braised celeriac, spinach and périgueux (madeira and truffle) sauce, with a baked vanilla cheesecake with strawberries and cream making a nice flourish at the end. Less pleasing was a dish of best end of lamb with piperade, new-season garlic and niçoise tapenade, which managed to be both too fatty and yet almost tasteless. Overall, though, this is a gem that should be much busier than it is. A further plus – classy bar snacks are served in the handsome lounge area.
Booking advisable. Dress: smart casual; no trainers. No-smoking tables. **Map 11 P5.**

City E1, EC2, EC3, EC4

Aurora
Great Eastern Hotel, 40 Liverpool Street, EC2M 7QN (7618 7000/www.aurora.restaurant.co.uk). Liverpool Street tube/rail. **Lunch served** noon-2.30pm, **dinner served** 6.45-10pm Mon-Fri. **Main courses** £15.50-£29.50. **Set lunch** £28 3 courses. **Set meal** (tasting menu) £50 6 courses, £70 6 courses with wine. **Service** 12.5%. **Credit** AmEx, MC, V.
Many Conran spots have become 'destination' restaurants for reasons other than the food. Not this one. Granted, like the hotel in which it's situated, the formal, gracious Aurora is a real looker: witness the stained-glass dome over the middle of the room and the decadent bar to one side. But the food is easily good enough to divert attention away from the decor and back towards the plate. Roasted sea scallops, served with deceptively light dots of black pudding and a creamy garlic sauce, were the perfect appetite-whetter for a beautiful milk-fed veal cutlet almost overshadowed by the gnocchi, girolles and madeira velouté that ringed it. In another meal, we followed a clear lobster soup with tarragon and tomato (fragrant and complex), with a saffron risotto with asparagus, broad beans and morels that came as close as possible to justifying its £16.50 price tag (though prices are very high). Desserts – a chocolate fondant cake, and 'lemon three ways' (sorbet, jelly, biscuit) – were unimpeachable, as were the amuse-gueules and petits fours. The slow ballet of the service was a delight from start to stop. At lunchtime, Aurora is dominated by City folk giving their expense accounts a thorough workout; in the evening, the mix of diners is surprisingly, pleasingly egalitarian for such a high-end place.
Babies and children admitted. Booking advisable. Disabled: toilet (in hotel). **Map 12 R6.**

The Chancery NEW
9 Cursitor Street, EC4A 1LL (7831 4000/ www.thechancery.co.uk). Chancery Lane tube. **Lunch served** noon-2.30pm, **dinner served** 6-10.30pm Mon-Fri. **Main courses** £12-£16. **Service** 12.5%. **Credit** AmEx, DC, JCB, MC, V.
A new sister to the Clerkenwell Dining Room (*see p207*), the Chancery occupies a City corner site and resembles a wine bar that's had an IKEA makeover: simple, clean, yet welcoming. Its menu, Modern European without being faddish, is something of a corker. There's some tower-building and drizzling with the starters, but it's not so trend-chasing that the dishes look as daft as your mum browsing in Top Shop. Fresh peas and vinaigrette dressing, around some à point scallops on white sweet potato purée, helped balance the dish, rather than just being there for decoration; and the braised oxtail, served marshmallow-sized wrapped inside a skin of caul fat, provided a contrast of depth of flavour to the subtlety of the scallop. You'll find more substance where it matters, in the main courses. Braised pork cheeks were rich and fleshy, served in the Alsatian way with a pleasantly acidic choucroûte (sauerkraut), crisp leaves of pancetta-like Alsace bacon, and a chewy lardon. Pudding – strawberry shortbread – consisted of two wafer-thin discs, held apart by utterly fresh strawberries and vanilla ice-cream, with a lustrous strawberry coulis. Its excellent food and well-judged service are secrets that deserve to be shared.
Babies and children welcome; high chairs. Booking essential. No-smoking tables. Separate room for parties, holds 20. **Map 11 N6.**

The Don
The Courtyard, 20 St Swithin's Lane, EC4N 8AD (7626 2606/www.thedonrestaurant.com). Bank tube/DLR.
Restaurant **Lunch served** noon-2.30pm, **dinner served** 6.30-10pm Mon-Fri. **Main courses** £12.20-£22.95.
Bistro **Lunch served** noon-3pm, **dinner served** 6-10pm Mon-Fri. **Main courses** £8.95-£13.95.
Both **Service** 12.5%. **Credit** AmEx, DC, MC, V.
As is the way in the City, both the cellar-based bistro and the ground-floor restaurant at this former port-and-sherry warehouse are heaving at

lunchtimes and tranquil in the evening. On our most recent visit, we ate dinner in the bistro. Staff were near-perfect – attentive when needed, out of sight when not required. And the menu was a wonderful late-summer read: chilled pea soup with minted créme fraîche; risotto of asparagus, peas and broad beans; croustade of duck eggs with wild mushrooms and truffles. Alongside puddings such as banana tarte tatin with rum and raisin ice-cream, there's a French rarebit (toasted reblouchon on potato and garlic bread). Stand-out dishes were warm goat's cheese mousse with mixed leaves – a featherlight confection; and a flavour-packed grilled lamb burger with caramelised onions and frites. The cellar is decorated in an unfussy way – it's smart, but hasn't lost its brickwork; the restaurant is a more starched affair. As you'd

expect, the wine list is a hefty tome, but there are affordable bottles. The Don is an unshowy haunt, but one with a lot more to shout about than many more established City names.

Children over 10 years welcome. Booking essential. Dress: smart casual. Separate room for parties, seats 24. **Map 12 Q7**.

Lanes NEW

East India House, 109-117 Middlesex Street, E1 7JF (7247 5050/www.lanesrestaurant.co.uk). Liverpool Street tube/rail.
Bar **Open** 10am-11pm Mon-Fri.
Restaurant **Lunch served** noon-3pm, **dinner served** 5.30-10pm Mon-Fri. **Main courses** £12.50-£18.50. **Set dinner** £15 2 courses, £20.50 3 courses. **Service** 12.5%. **Credit** AmEx, DC, JCB, MC, V.

Lanes restaurant and bar opened in autumn 2003, its owners intent on providing a more relaxed venue (though with serious food) than is the City norm. And they've succeeded. Walk in at ground-floor bar level, where drinks and light meals are served (there's a big screen too); pass through and climb a few steps to the dining room (beyond which there's another room, for private functions). Both spaces are decorated in an understated way, with wooden floors, cream walls and dark red panelling. Food, by New Zealander Hayden Smith, rarely strikes a duff note, although oven-roast tomato salad with nut dressing was a bit underwhelming. Fish features prominently – a summer salad had scallops, king prawns, salmon and calamares alongside asparagus and parmesan – but there's ribeye, braised rib and horseradish potato for die-

Lanes

hard City gents. Tomato salad apart, everything we tried was a success: most notably a flavour-packed cauliflower soup with pommery mustard; a divinely succulent fillet of roast halibut with fennel, asparagus and pancetta-wrapped potatoes; and a chocolate marquis that looked as good as it tasted. Drinks run from cocktails (in the bar) to a shortish wine list that includes quite a choice of champagnes. Staff are an easy-going bunch, but efficient and friendly: very much in keeping with the tone of the whole venture.

Bar & restaurant available for hire (weekends). Book lunch. Disabled: toilet. Separate room for parties, seats 28. **Map 12 R6.**

Novelli in the City NEW

London Capital Club, 15 Abchurch Lane, EC4N 7BW (7717 0088/www.londoncapitalclub.com). Cannon Street tube/Bank tube/DLR. **Lunch served** noon-2.30pm, **dinner served** 5.30-9.30pm Mon-Fri. **Main courses** £17-£20. **Set meal** £16.25 2 courses, £18.50 3 courses. **Credit** AmEx, MC, V.

This very slick modern brasserie occupies part of the London Capital Club, honorary patrons of which include an Earl, a Baroness, a Lord and a clutch of mere Sirs. And yet, while the surroundings are undoubtedly upper-crust, the basement dining room is open to non-members, and the three-course lunch menu rapide (£18.50) is one of the best bargains in the City. Star chef Jean-Christophe Novelli has had fluctuating fortunes from previous ventures in London (and is currently based at Brocket Hall in Hertfordshire), but his latest enterprise deserves success. From a choice of three starters and three mains, we began with a seared chunk of tuna accompanied by a crunchy grilled cheese cup containing coriander and rocket, and slices of raw beef with aniseed seasoning. Then followed herb risotto – tasty and well made if unexciting – and juicy poached chicken breast with a bean and onion fricassee. The dessert list was somewhat more extensive; we opted for the nougat glâcé and delightful shimmery-trembly champagne jelly with summer fruits. There's a good wine list, with each and every choice available by the glass. The waiters are so solicitous, it's almost funny. Novelli's dining room is a masterpiece of spot lighting, mirrors, dark wood tables and clean lines: almost as clean and shiny, indeed, as the bald pates of some of the diners.

Children over 8 years admitted. Booking essential. Dress: smart casual. Separate rooms for parties, seating 6-70. **Map 12 Q7.**

Prism

147 Leadenhall Street, EC3V 4QT (7256 3888/ www.harveynichols.com). Monument tube/ Bank tube/DLR.
Bar **Open** 11am-11pm Mon-Fri. **Food served** 11.30-3pm, 6-10pm Mon-Fri. **Main courses** £6-£13.
Restaurant **Lunch served** 11.30am-3pm, **dinner served** 6-10pm Mon-Fri. **Main courses** £17.50-£22.
Both **Service** 12.5%. **Credit** AmEx, DC, JCB, MC, V.

Prism is a true City restaurant, which means that if you want company while you're dining, you're best off visiting for lunch. On the Friday night we stopped by, the action at this Harvey Nicks operation was, we were told, just like that of any other Friday night – which is to say, the restaurant was extremely quiet. Indeed, the lack of customers was exaggerated by the grand, pillared hall (formerly the Bank of New York): a space that hardly aids intimacy at the best of times. Still, if you're not here for a business lunch, when the place is busier, there's something peculiarly romantic about having these imposing surroundings, and these excellent staff, all to yourself, especially when the food is so damn good. A crab and mango salad was set off beautifully by the accompanying coriander; a warm asparagus starter was simpler, and only marginally less successful. Mains were even better: an immaculate portion of rabbit was nevertheless eclipsed by a stunning piece of roast cod, as melt-in-the-mouth tender as we've ever tasted. A subtle bread and butter pudding rounded things off very nicely. A most impressive operation.
Disabled: toilet. Separate rooms for parties, seating 20 and 40. **Map 12 Q6.**

Terminus Bar & Grill

Great Eastern Hotel, 40 Liverpool Street, EC2M 7QN (7618 7400/www.terminus-restaurant.co.uk). Liverpool Street tube/rail.
Breakfast served 7-11am Mon-Fri; 7.30-11am Sat, Sun. **Lunch served** noon-4pm daily. **Dinner served** 5-10.30pm Mon-Fri; 5-10pm Sat, Sun. **Main courses** £9.50-£15. **Service** 12.5%. **Credit** AmEx, DC, MC, V.

Rather smarter than the grub dished up at the George pub, yet some way below the high-class Aurora (*see p204*), Terminus is the Great Eastern Hotel's concession to those City boys whose expense accounts are impressive, but by no means overwhelming. It's a breezy place in the Conran ilk, the decor clean, crisp and modern; but when the business lunchers and after-work drinkers come in, the ambience grows pacier and the din becomes quite offputting. The hurried nature, sadly, also extends to the food. Cream of cauliflower and chive soup managed to be both watery and oily at once; better, if still far from perfect, was a morass of baked eggs, mushrooms and chorizo. The mains were ordinariness personified: a plump beef rump (accompanied by excellent chips) and a fillet of sea bass dished up with some garlic mash. All told, Terminus is fine, but of the Great Eastern's myriad eating options, this appears to be the weakest.
Babies and children welcome; high chairs. Booking essential lunch Mon-Fri. Disabled: toilet. No-smoking tables. **Map 12 R6.**

Vivat Bacchus NEW

47 Farringdon Street, EC4A 4LL (7353 2648/ www.vivatbacchus.co.uk). Chancery Lane tube or Farringdon tube/rail.
Bar **Open/snacks served** noon-11.30pm Mon-Fri.

The Chancery. See p204.

Restaurant **Lunch served** noon-2.30pm, **dinner served** 6.30-9.30pm Mon-Fri. **Main courses** £12-£18. **Set meal** (noon-2.30pm, 6.30-7pm) £13.50 2 courses, £15.50 3 courses. **Service** 12.5%.
Both **Credit** AmEx, MC, V.

Vivat Bacchus, located in a brick cellar near Smithfield Market, is sibling to Brown's restaurant in Rivonia, near Johannesburg. It is named after one of South Africa's top wines, made by Veenwouden. Since opening in 2003, VB has earned a name in wine-loving circles for its wine list and relatively low mark-ups. Guests who show more than a passing interest in the excellent choice are likely to be shown to the cellar, which holds some distinctive bottles from France, California, Australia – and, of course, South Africa. Despite the heritage of the owners and chefs, however, most dishes on the succinct menu (such as seared scallops with crushed peas, alsace bacon and vinaigrette of girolles; or goat's cheese and red onion tart) have their roots firmly in Europe. There are the occasional South African touches, as in grilled ostrich medallions with butternut pithiviers and macerated cherries. The cooking is pretty good, although timings aren't always spot on. You like cheese? If so, head for the walk-in cheese room that's filled with well-kept (mainly European) specimens and choose your own. Service is well informed and friendly.
Babies and children admitted. Booking advisable. Disabled: toilet. Dress: smart casual. No-smoking tables. Separate room for parties, seats 45.
Map 11 N5.

Clerkenwell & Farringdon EC1

Clerkenwell Dining Room
69-73 St John Street, EC1M 4AN (7253 9000/ www.theclerkenwell.com). Farringdon tube/rail.
Lunch served noon-2.30pm Mon-Fri. **Dinner served** 6-11.30pm Mon-Fri; 7-11.30pm Sat. **Main courses** £12-£16. **Set meal** £14 2 courses, £17 3 courses. **Service** 12.5%.
Credit AmEx, DC, JCB, MC, V.
Previously a Stephen Bull outpost, then a Belgo Bierodrome, the CDR opened in 2001. With considerable talent to back it up – executive chef Andrew Thompson and manager Zak Jones both boast L'Escargot on their CVs – it deserves to do well. We complained of a lack of ambience last year, but this time the bar and narrow dining room were lively and atmospheric. The menu offers comfort food with flair. Scallops were slightly small, but went well with tender pork belly. Tuna loin was high quality, though the spicing (cumin, fennel and coriander seeds) wasn't particularly to our taste. A main of john dory with bacon, lentils, mushroom and artichoke purée was a winning combo, if an ingredient too far. However, braised short rib of beef was outstanding, arriving with subtle horseradish mash. Desserts lifted standards even higher – feather-light beignets (aka fritters), maple ice-cream and chocolate waffles. What were we thinking of, ordering just one portion? Staff were professional yet down to earth, suggesting the lowest-priced wine as an accompaniment. On the downside, à la carte prices are a touch high (especially desserts, which come in at £7).
Babies and children welcome. Booking advisable. Separate room for parties, seats 50. Vegetarian menu. **Map 5 O4.**

Smiths of Smithfield
67-77 Charterhouse Street, EC1M 6HJ (7251 7950/www.smithsofsmithfield.co.uk). Farringdon tube/rail.
Ground-floor café **Meals served** 7am-5pm Mon-Fri; 10am-5pm Sat; 9.30am-5pm Sun. **Main courses** £3.50-£6.
Cocktail bar **Snacks served** 5.30-11pm Mon-Wed; 5.30pm-1am Thur-Sat.
Dining Room **Lunch served** noon-3pm Mon-Fri. **Dinner served** 6-11pm Mon-Fri; 6-10.45pm Sat. **Main courses** £9.50-£11.50.
All **Credit** AmEx, DC, MC, V.
Staying true to its roots as a former market store, Smiths retains an industrial, New York warehouse feel, with exposed bricks, reclaimed wood, metal

tubing and raw concrete. Of the four storeys, the ground floor is the most laid-back, serving breakfast, brunch and other casual fare to a steady stream of punters. The next level up is a cocktail and champagne bar, with plush red leather booths. The second-floor Dining Room, where we ate, is based around a central mesh gallery, overlooking the champers bar. The Top Floor restaurant (*see p42*) on the third floor serves posh British food. Quality is high; organic or additive-free ingredients are used where possible, and chef John Torode oversees the menu. Think comfort food with a twist, with a nod to the orient. A starter of mozzarella, beetroot and marinated anchovy salad was good quality, though little more than the sum of its parts. One main (diver-caught scallops with black pudding, mash and mustard sauce) worked better on paper than in practice. There wasn't much black pudding, and the scallops were just studded on top of the mash. Smiths beef burger with cheddar cheese and Old Spot bacon was fine, though the burger eventually became a mulch. For dessert, vanilla ice-cream, hot chocolate fudge sauce and honeycomb were overly sweet. Service was a bit ditzy, if well-meaning. Noise levels mean this isn't the place for a heart-to-heart. We've a bigger gripe, though – if you're going to get the heavy mob to move us on at 11pm, please don't serve us a £7 cocktail two minutes beforehand.
Babies and children welcome; high chairs. Booking advisable. Disabled: toilet. Entertainment: DJ 8pm Wed-Sat. Separate room for parties, seats 26. Takeaway service.
Map 5 O5.

Covent Garden WC2

Axis
One Aldwych, 1 Aldwych, WC2B 4RH (7300 0300/www.onealdwych.com). Covent Garden or Embankment tube/Charing Cross tube/rail.
Lunch served noon-2.45pm Mon-Fri. **Dinner served** 5.45-10.45pm Mon-Fri; 5.45-11.30pm Sat. **Main courses** £11.95-£21.95. **Set meal** £16.75 2 courses, £19.75 3 courses. **Service** 12.5%.
Credit AmEx, DC, JCB, MC, V.
Axis is one of two places to dine in One Aldwych hotel (the other is Indigo; *see below*). You can start with cocktails in the intimate balcony bar while taking in the impressive modernist mural that provides focus to the otherwise minimalist surroundings of the basement space. The menu adopts a classic Modern European stance, with a few tempting options for vegetarians. For starters, steamed asparagus with parmesan shavings had a subtle hint of lemon, while quail was succulent and tasty. The grilled section encompassed, on our visit, both organic salmon and sea bass, alongside venison cutlets served with a cheesy mash and lightly crunchy spring vegetables. Hay-baked leg of lamb with rosemary jus arrived with a delicious crust and just a hint of pink. Desserts offer an innovative assortment of flavours: pistachio soufflé with hot chocolate sauce was lovely and fluffy, although baked peach and lemon sorbet was a little on the bitter side. Service was professional, allowing for a relaxing evening in chilled surroundings. A good spot for pre- and post-theatre meals and business dinners.
Babies and children welcome; high chairs. Booking advisable. Disabled: toilet (in hotel). Entertainment: jazz 8pm Tue, Wed (menu £39.50 3 courses incl cocktail and service). Restaurant available for hire. Vegetarian menu. **Map 18 M7.**

Bank Aldwych
1 Kingsway, WC2B 6XF (7379 9797/ www.bankrestaurants.com). Holborn or Temple tube.
Bar **Open** 11.30am-11pm Mon-Sat; 11.30am-10pm Sun. **Meals served** 5.30-11pm Mon-Fri; 5.30-11pm Sat; 5.30-9.30pm Sun.
Restaurant **Breakfast served** 7.30-10.30am Mon-Fri. **Brunch served** 11.30am-3pm Sat, Sun. **Lunch served** noon-3pm Mon-Fri. **Dinner served** 5.30-11pm Mon-Sat; 5.30-9.30pm Sun. **Main courses** £10.80-£21. **Set meal** (lunch, 5.30-7pm, from 10pm) £12.50 2 courses, £15 3 courses. **Service** 12.5%.
Both **Credit** AmEx, DC, MC, V.

This place is as impressive as it was when it opened in 1996. The vast chandelier, the huge bar area where cocktails are supped, the mirrored walls along the chef's station, beyond which is the cool dining area with red leather bucket seats and crisp linen – all can still make the heart race in anticipation of a chic and rewarding dining experience. Staff are friendly, immediately asking whether a high chair was needed for a little 'un, and efficient. Perhaps that was the problem. Starters arrived what seemed like moments after we ordered. A good, if not especially inventive, menu included firm asparagus with a delicious truffle mousseline sauce and perfectly cooked poached egg. Delicate seared tuna with miso dressing was sensational, pairing well with tart pickled daikon. Equally speedily delivered mains were mixed: organic salmon with broccoli and the same mousseline sauce was a well cooked, if unexciting dish, while roast cod was underdone and gained nothing from its accompanying sea of houmous, though the anchoyade and caper dressing was better. Desserts are mostly of the sorbet and cheese school, plus a fine sticky toffee pudding. A page of wines covers all bases, with a few half-bottles available.
Babies and children welcome; children's brunch menu; high chairs; nappy-changing facilities. Booking advisable. Disabled: toilet. Entertainment: jazz 11.30am-3pm Sat, Sun. Separate room for parties, seats 28.
Map 10 M6.

Indigo
One Aldwych, 1 Aldwych, WC2B 4RH (7300 0400/www.onealdwych.com). Covent Garden or Embankment tube/Charing Cross tube/rail.
Breakfast served 6.30-11am, **dinner served** 6-11.15pm daily. **Lunch served** noon-3pm Mon-Fri; 12.30-3pm Sat, Sun. **Main courses** £13.95-£21. **Set dinner** (6-7pm, 10-11.15pm) £16.75 2 courses, £19.75 3 courses. **Service** 12.5%. **Credit** AmEx, DC, JCB, MC, V.
Set on the mezzanine overlooking the lively lobby bar, Indigo is the more low-key of the two restaurants at One Aldwych (the other is Axis; *see above*). There were virtually no other diners when we arrived on a Saturday night, though the place started to fill up later with the post-theatre crowd. The room makes a nice setting, with the requisite crisp linen and big vases of lavish flowers. Food is described as 'creative Modern European', and places an emphasis on organic produce. Starters include plump crab cakes, accompanied by well-dressed rocket, but a curiously bland sweetcorn, pear and coriander relish. Mains were a mixed bag. Salmon raviolini with walnut cream sauce (which, like salads, came from a 'create your own' section) was shy on fish, though the combination of flavours received a thumbs-up. Monkfish with summer vegetables was overcooked, with the veg drowned in butter. Duck was better: an excellent piece of meat cooked just so, with a portion of excellently judged spiced butternut squash on the side. Service was well meaning, but obtrusive (we were offered bread four times). Also, staff steered us towards an expensive Chablis. At least we finished on a high note in the form of apple tarte tatin with organic cinnamon ice-cream, and chocolate fudge cake with raspberry sorbet (a brilliant combination of sweet and sour).
Babies and children welcome; high chairs. Booking advisable. Disabled: toilet (in hotel). Separate rooms for parties, seating 45 and 48.
Map 18 M7.

The Ivy
1 West Street, WC2H 9NQ (7836 4751/ www.caprice-holdings.co.uk). Leicester Square tube.
Lunch served noon-3pm Mon-Sat; noon-3.30pm Sun. **Dinner served** 5.30pm-midnight daily. **Main courses** £9.25-£35. **Set lunch** (Sat) £19.50 3 courses; (Sun) £22 3 courses. **Cover** £2 (lunch). **Credit** AmEx, DC, JCB, MC, V.
It may be among the world's most famous restaurants – and notorious for its ages-in-advance booking policy – but attention to detail had slipped slightly on our latest trip to the Ivy. While the welcome was warm as ever, there wasn't much eye

THE BRITISH MUSEUM

illuminating world cultures

court*restaurant*
Level 6, The Great Court

Open daily from 12.00 Noon • Lunch & afternoon tea
Party planning service available
Dinner: Thursday, Friday & Saturday until 21.00

Information & reservations
020 7323 8990 or visit
www.digbytrout.co.uk
email: courtrestaurant@digbytrout.co.uk

contact from staff. Also, the ventilation system isn't always up to scratch, meaning smoke can waft from neighbouring tables. We chose from the relatively bargain set lunch menu, and weren't disappointed (though the £2 cover charge for lunch is annoying). Starters were outstanding. Butternut squash soup with Thai spices was smooth, creamy, with perfectly balanced spices. Potted salmon featured creamy chunky fish; even the toast and pickled cucumber that came with it were superb. Mains let the side down faintly. Roast beef was flavoursome, but too fatty in places; roast spuds were chewy rather than crunchy. A huge piece of roast chicken was gorgeous, with perhaps the best stuffing we've tasted, but the skin had sagged somewhat. For dessert, staff wouldn't let us change crème fraîche for custard as an accompaniment to our sticky toffee pudding. Their refusal to budge paid off: the sourness of the cream worked well with the sweetness of the moist, perfectly spiced pud. Even cheesecake was a masterpiece: served like a scoop of ice-cream, surrounded by plump juicy berries in a raspberry sauce. One last quibble: the celeb quotient was paltry. Still, you can't have everything.
Babies and children admitted; high chairs. Booking essential, several weeks in advance. Separate room for parties, seats 60 (minimum 25). **Map 18 K6**.

Thyme

The Hospital, 24 Endell Street, WC2H 9RD (7170 9200/www.thymeandspace.com). Covent Garden tube. **Lunch served** noon-2.30pm, **dinner served** 6-10.30pm Mon-Sat. **Set lunch** £25 3 courses. **Set dinner** £45 3 courses. **Set meal** £60 6 courses (tasting menu). **Service** 12.5%. **Credit** AmEx, MC, V.
As we went to press, Adams Byatt and Oates had closed their well-regarded Clapham restaurant and were about to move to Dave Stewart's central London art space, the Hospital (with opening scheduled for October 2004). Their new home will be located on the first floor of the contemporary photography gallery, with an 80-seat restaurant, a lounge bar and a private dining room. Hopefully, Thyme's fine cooking will survive the transfer into town. The old formula of providing solely starter-sized portions has already bitten the dust, and Thyme will now concentrate on producing standard three-course meals. A visit in the closing days of the Clapham venture provided a light soup of langoustines with roast shallot and (under-cooked) garlic butter tortellini; an excellent, earthy terrine paysanne, with marinated foie gras, trompettes, teeny braised carrots and pain Poilâne; and tender pot roast rump of veal with fondant potato, jerusalem artichoke purée and meat juices. Desserts included honeycomb nougat glacé with bitter chocolate sorbet and passion fruit. Good stuff; fingers crossed it stays that way.
Babies and children admitted. Booking advisable. **Map 18 L6**.

Knightsbridge SW1

The Fifth Floor

Harvey Nichols, Knightsbridge, SW1X 7RJ (7235 5250/www.harveynichols.com). Knightsbridge tube.
Café **Breakfast served** 10am-noon, **lunch served** noon-3.30pm, **dinner served** 6-10pm Mon-Sat. **Brunch served** 11am-4pm Sun. **Tea served** 3.30-6pm Mon-Sat; 4-6pm Sun. **Main courses** £9.50-£15
Restaurant **Lunch served** noon-3pm Mon-Thur; noon-3.30pm Fri, Sun; noon-4pm Sat. **Dinner served** 6-11pm Mon-Sat. **Main courses** £15-£24. **Set dinner** £19.50 3 courses. **Service** 12.5%.
Both **Credit** AmEx, DC, JCB, MC, V.
The food, decor and staff at Harvey Nicks's Fifth Floor restaurant are all classier than most of the clientele, judging by the motley assortment dining here on a weekday evening. Gaze instead on the white, space-age decor (the walls are fibre optic-lit, and change colour slowly) and the nattily attired staff (white suits), and savour dishes that have a little more imagination than most. The menu changes daily, but always includes a couple of

user-friendly options such as an antipasto and charcuterie plate, followed by a steak. More typical are starters such as roast scallops with beetroot dressing, caramelised chicory, apple and radish salad; or white asparagus wrapped in pancetta with shimeji mushroom, black truffle and cauliflower velouté. Mains such as roast cod with crushed new potatoes, sweet and sour cherry tomatoes, black olives, parsley and caper salad deliver brilliantly complementary flavours. Needless to say, all this doesn't come cheap (the cod, for example, was £19) – and vegetables cost extra (Jersey royals £4). Staff are professional, but unstuffy, and the sommelier in particular is refreshingly down-to-earth; one of the tricks up his sleeve is a choice of wine flights (taster selections to try before you buy).
Babies and children welcome; high chairs. Booking advisable. Disabled: lift; toilet. Tables outdoors (15, café terrace). Vegetarian menu. **Map 8 F9**.

Marylebone W1

Blandford Street

5-7 Blandford Street, W1U 3DB (7486 9696/ www.blandford-street.co.uk). Baker Street or Bond Street tube. **Lunch served** noon-2.30pm Tue-Sun. **Dinner served** 6.30-10.30pm Mon-Sat. **Main courses** £11-£17.50. **Service** 12.5%. **Credit** AmEx, DC, MC, V.
There's something rather bland about Blandford Street these days. Despite a good location in the heart of Marylebone Village, it was almost empty on our midweek visit, and the rather dated design – mirror walls, unappealing artworks – doesn't overcome the shortcomings of an awkward space. Frosty air-conditioning, and slightly supercilious staff didn't help the atmosphere either. The menu is appealing, making good use of carefully sourced seasonal ingredients, and the restaurant is keen to emphasis the extra effort put in; for example, all the pasta, ice-creams and sorbets are made in-house. But something's amiss. The individual elements in a starter of white bean salad with grilled halloumi, aubergine purée and flatbread were tasty, but little attempt had been made to meld them into a cohesive dish. Our mains – dorset crab risotto with grilled red mullet and red peppers, and roast milk-fed lamb with carrots, onion, courgette and basmati rice – were pleasant enough, but lacking thrills (and a portion of the lamb was undercooked and had to be sent back). Portions were small for the price (most mains top £14; side orders are £3.50 each). Desserts tend toward the calorific – Valrhona chocolate pudding with chocolate sauce and peanut butter ice-cream, say, or rum and raisin crème brûlée – and are generally well executed. The international wine list is helpfully detailed, but offers few bargains.
Babies and children welcome. Booking advisable lunch. Dress: smart casual (dinner). No-smoking tables. Separate area for parties, seats 18. Tables outdoors (3, pavement). **Map 9 G5**.

Orrery

55 Marylebone High Street, W1M 3AE (7616 8000/www.orrery.co.uk). Baker Street or Regent's Park tube. **Lunch served** noon-3pm daily. **Dinner served** 7-11pm Mon-Sat; 7-10.30pm Sun. **Main courses** £16.50-£30. **Set lunch** £23.50 3 courses. **Set dinner** (Sun) £30 3 courses incl glass of champagne. **Set meal** £55 6 courses (tasting menu); £85 with wine. **Service** 12.5%. **Credit** AmEx, DC, JCB, MC, V.
This top-of-the-line Conran outlet sets out purposefully to offer luxury: from the smiling greeters to the cigar list and giant digestifs trolley. The long space is white, airy and (of course) sleek. The haute-cuisine cooking is refined and extremely delicate, with much use of froth in line with current fashion, but whether the results are special enough to match the very high prices is questionable. Both a tomato consommé amuse-gueule, and a frothy raspberry pre-dessert were exquisite. Of our first courses, velouté of spring garlic with parmesan, rocket and chive oil was superb, infused with multi-layered flavours; crab ravioli with an étuvée of leeks and grapefruit was

perhaps too subtle; and stuffed baby artichokes with asparagus and quails' eggs was surprisingly bland. Mains – Somerset lamb with roast saddle, braised shank and baby vegetables; beef fillet with lyonnaise onions; and a risotto of spring vegetables, pea shoots and parmesan foam – were elaborately presented and had their high points, but failed to thrill. Opulent desserts showed a return to form. Abundant staff mill about with a great deal of restaurant theatrics, and the head sommelier is a helpful guide to the giant wine list – but a mix-up over wines was surprising in a restaurant with these aspirations. Orrery seems to promise more than it delivers.
Babies and children welcome; high chairs. Booking essential. Disabled: toilet. Tables outside (12, roof terrace). **Map 3 G4**.

Villandry

170 Great Portland Street, W1W 5QB (7631 3131/www.villandry.com). Great Portland Street tube.
Bar **Open** 8am-11pm Mon-Fri; 9am-9pm Sat. **Breakfast served** 8am-noon Mon-Sat. **Lunch served** noon-3.30pm Mon-Fri; noon-3pm Sat. **Snacks served** 5-11pm Mon-Fri; 5-9pm Sat. **Snacks** £5.50-£10.
Restaurant **Lunch served** noon-3pm Mon-Fri. **Dinner served** 6-10.30pm Mon-Sat. **Main courses** £10.50-£22.
Both **Service** 12.5%. **Credit** AmEx, DC, MC, V.
Beyond Villandry's bar (which can get lively at night) is an airy, spacious restaurant that exudes calm, with huge picture windows, and white walls and tablecloths. The setting is perfect for the food, which is great but not flashy. Tip-top, carefully sourced ingredients are matched and prepared with flair (and so they should be, with main course prices pushing £20). Much of the food is Mediterranean with a twist – swordfish wrapped in speck with white bean purée, rosemary and spinach, say; or black olive and sun-dried tomato gnocchi with rocket and parmesan salad. There can often be a robust edge too; on a warm evening, we found a shortage of summery options. After a starter of super-soft scallops came a main of perfect salt beef and carrots. Other dishes – smoked black pudding, puy lentils and onion gravy; confit pork belly with shredded vegetables, noodles and ginger – are in a similar vein. Puds are divine concoctions such as pear, blackberry and whisky trifle, or lemon curd tartlet with plum sauce. Staff are pleasant and professional.
Babies and children welcome; children's menu (restaurant); high chairs. Booking advisable (restaurant). No smoking (restaurant). Tables outdoors (13, pavement). Takeaway service (shop). **Map 3 H5**.

Mayfair W1

Berkeley Square Café

7 Davies Street, W1K 3DD (7629 6993/ www.theberkeleysquare.com). Bond Street tube. **Lunch served** noon-2.30pm Mon-Fri. **Dinner served** 6-10pm Mon-Sat. **Set meal** £16.95 2 courses, £19.95 3 courses. **Set dinner** £45 3 courses, £49.50 7 courses. **Service** 12.5%. **Credit** AmEx, DC, MC, V.
Don't be fooled by the casual title: this 'café' falls squarely into the posh restaurant category, both in terms of wallet damage and the smart interior. Decor is simple but fresh, with white linen and stylish lime-green details (and a fashionable green awning outside). Prices are eye-catchingly high – the two- and three-course set dinner costs £45 and £49.50 respectively – so we were expecting some pretty impressive food. By and large, that is what we got. To begin, a solid Cornish crab risotto came with a well-judged plum tomato sorbet and frozen olive oil, while globe artichoke arrived with fresh-as-a-daisy mizuna salad, dotted with orange and celeriac. We'd have been more than happy with our mains – fillet of Aberdeen Angus beef with ceps, asparagus, cherry tomatoes and madeira dressing, and Welsh Black Mountain organic chicken with carrot and tarragon salad and a light pea sauce – had the food not reached us lukewarm. In the end, it was the nectarine tarte tatin (for two) with almond ice-cream that stole the show – it

was a generous portion for two, but we couldn't have left any on the plate. Other (minor) criticisms concerned a slight lack of atmosphere and some blips in the otherwise efficient service. There's a swish art deco bar downstairs.

Babies and children welcome. Booking advisable lunch. No-smoking tables. Separate room for parties, seats 30. Tables outdoors (8, terrace). **Map 9 H7.**

Langan's Brasserie

Stratton Street, W1J 8LB (7491 8822/ www.langansrestaurants.co.uk). Green Park tube. **Meals served** 12.15-11.45pm Mon-Fri. **Dinner served** 7pm-midnight Sat. **Main courses** £12.50-£18.50. **Cover** £1.50. **Service** 12.5%. **Credit** AmEx, DC, JCB, MC, V.

You go to Langan's for the buzz, the sense of being in a distinctly metropolitan 'London restaurant'. It has a feel you just don't get in your neighbourhood eaterie – a combination of noise, crowds, space, the odd celeb (far fewer than in years past), gleaming table settings, bustling (but not very organised) waiters in long white aprons, and an opulent decor of antiques and eclectic artwork. Although the restaurant was only created in the 1970s, its look already seems like a bit of 'old London'. Meanwhile, the food is ordinary, and assembled with notable lack of finesse. A caesar salad was made with iceberg instead of cos lettuce, and covered in far too much dressing; field mushrooms with bacon and Lancashire cheese were pleasant, but no more than that. Langan's 'British brasserie' menu has always included old English faves, and its cod and chips was, indeed, a big (but ordinary) portion of fish and chips. Grilled swordfish came with an enjoyable honey and mustard dressing, but the fish was bland and the accompanying mixed veg, soaked in butter sauce, were reminiscent of old-fashioned British hotel food. The wine list is perfunctory. Still, the crowds keep coming, whether suited lunchers, couples celebrating something, young City types getting loudly jarred, or families of tourists looking for city life.

Babies and children welcome; booster chairs. Booking advisable; essential dinner. Entertainment: band 10.30pm Wed-Sat. **Map 9 H7.**
For branches see index.

★ Nicole's

158 New Bond Street, W1Y 9PA (7499 8408). Bond Street or Green Park tube. **Bar Open** 10am-10.45pm Mon-Fri; 10am-6pm Sat. **Meals served** 11.30am-5.30pm Mon-Sat. **Main courses** £9-£12.50.
Restaurant **Breakfast served** 10-11am Mon-Fri; 10-11.30am Sat. **Lunch served** noon-3.30pm Mon-Fri; noon-4pm Sat. **Afternoon tea served** 3-6pm Mon-Sat. **Dinner served** 6.30-10.30pm Mon-Fri. **Main courses** £12.50-£22. **Cover** (noon-4pm, 6.30-10.45pm Mon-Sat) £1. **Minimum** £15.
Both **Service** 15%. **Credit** AmEx, DC, JCB, MC, V.
Located in the basement of the Nicole Farhi boutique, and opposite Donna Karan, Nicole's is a magnet for ladies who lunch. If you've the time and the cash to 'do' lunch in style, then we'd certainly recommend you do so here, as Nicole's is producing some of London's best Modern European cuisine: adventurous, without ever tipping over into the ridiculous, and brimming with delicate flavours. We started with a tangy gazpacho with a subtle, floating crab and avocado salad, and a perfect prosciutto salad with grilled peaches and almonds. Mains were equally faultless: a melt-in-the-mouth seared beef fillet served with ginger and lentil salad, and ultra-delicate braised halibut with a rich camargue rice salad and tomato salsa. The desserts were, in the local dialect, 'to die for'; gorgeous ice-cream, and a densely satisfying strawberry and vanilla cheesecake. Prices are predictably high, but we were pleasantly surprised to find an agreeable cabernet sauvignon for £15.50. Nicole's is bustling at lunchtime, but you're likely to find the place empty in the evening.

Babies and children admitted. Booking advisable lunch. No-smoking tables. Restaurant available for hire. **Map 9 H7.**

noble rot

3-5 Mill Street, W1S 2AU (7629 8877/ www.noblerot.com). Oxford Circus tube. **Lunch served** noon-3pm Mon-Fri. **Dinner served** 6-11pm Mon-Sat. **Main courses** £16-£28. **Set lunch** £16.50 2 courses, £19.75 3 courses. **Service** 12.5%. **Credit** AmEx, DC, JCB, MC, V.
As oenologists will know, noble rot refers to a benign fungus that grows on grapes, giving sweet wines their flavour. There's certainly nothing rotten about this posh restaurant, with its swanky modern decor, fashionable members' bar and luxurious ingredients. Our latest meal got off to an inspired start with a beautifully rich ajo blanco soup and nicely seasoned dorset crab, with a disconcertingly sweet sorbet of avocado, lobster essence and white tomato. Both mains – ribeye with salsify, black truffles and porcini mushrooms; and new season lamb with a cassoulet of summer beans – were succulent successes. Desserts were superb too: roasted white peach with lavender honey and crème fraîche sorbet, and white chocolate frozen cake with an intensely fruity raspberry sorbet. The wine list offers little under £30, but the house Côtes du Rhône at £19 was satisfactory. On paper, there's little we can fault at noble rot; it offers suave, efficient service and imaginative food, in sleek surroundings. But as an overall dining experience, we feel it lacks charisma. Maybe this can be attributed to the barking expense-accounters, the weak lounge-pop soundtrack or the generic decor (high-backed chairs, black and white framed photos). But with such impressive food, we're hoping that character will develop with time.

Babies and children welcome. Booking advisable. Separate room for parties, seats 40. Tables outdoors (6, terrace). **Map 9 H6.**

Sketch: Gallery

9 Conduit Street, W1S 2XG (0870 7774488/ www.sketch.uk.com). Oxford Circus tube. **Dinner served** 7-10.30pm Mon-Sat. **Main courses** £18-£22. **Service** 12.5%. **Credit** AmEx, DC, MC, V.
Mourad Mazouz and Pierre Gagnaire's Sketch opened to a cacophony of press attention in 2003, partly as a result of its striking design (a bizarre mix of futuristic space age and retro salon), partly for being (then) the most expensive restaurant in London. Or, at least, one element of it: the top-floor Lecture Room (*see p113*). There are also two bars (East and West), a tea room serving exquisite pâtisserie (Parlour at Sketch; *see p300*) and the Gallery, a more informal – and cheaper – restaurant on the lower ground-floor. Not that it's cheap, with plenty of mains topping £20. It really is a gallery by day, transforming into an eating space at night, though ambient video artworks still pulse silently as you dine. The celebrity quotient and shock value may have lessened, but the decor remains a winner, and novelty remains in the likes of gnocchi with dried ceps and 'scents of Costa Rica'. Oriental and European flavours and ingredients mingle – witness shiitake with chicken mousse, edamame, asparagus salad, lemon grass and black pepper chilled broth (a starter) or lamb with beetroot cake, prunes and hazelnuts (a main) – though you can also get simpler dishes, such as pan-fried fillet of beef. Service can still be frosty.

Booking essential. Dress: smart casual. Entertainment: DJs 11.30pm-2am Mon-Sat. Restaurant available for hire. **Map 9 J6.**

Sotheby's Café

Sotheby's, 34-35 New Bond Street, W1A 2AA (7293 5077). Bond Street tube. **Breakfast served** 9.30-11.30am, **lunch served** noon-3pm, **afternoon tea served** 3-4.45pm Mon-Fri. **Main courses** £12.50-£17. **Set lunch** £15.50 2 courses. **Set tea** £5.25. **Credit** AmEx, DC, MC, V.
A small roped-off area on the ground floor forms the café at Sotheby's auction house. It's surprisingly cosy – with soft leather banquettes, black and white photos of classic film stars, and the day's newspapers – and all but refreshingly friendly for such a highfalutin' establishment. What's more, the food is a delight, both in terms of presentation and taste. A short selection of lunch dishes is buttressed by breakfast and tea menus.

Celery soup with celery crackers, or linguine with crab, petits pois, lemon chilli and garlic might be followed by caramelised onion puff pastry tartlet with spinach, girolles, béarnaise sauce and french bean salad, or a lobster club sandwich. Top marks went to seared tuna with ruby chard and avocado, tomato and black bean salsa, and meringue with pistachio ice-cream and raspberries. Our only gripe was that a large slice of Kirkham's Lancashire cheese (served with plum chutney, grapes and biscuits) arrived too cold for the flavour to emerge. But we imagine that complaints are few and far between among the mix of art dealers, tourists and well-heeled shoppers who form the core clientele.

Babies and children welcome. Booking essential lunch. Disabled: toilet. No smoking. **Map 9 H6.**

Piccadilly W1

★ The Wolseley **NEW**

2004 WINNER BEST NEW RESTAURANT
160 Piccadilly, W1J 9EB (7499 6996/ www.thewolseley.com). Green Park tube. **Breakfast served** 7-11.30am Mon-Fri; 9-11.30am Sat, Sun. **Lunch served** noon-2.30pm Mon-Fri; noon-3pm Sat, Sun. **Tea served** 3-5.30pm Mon-Fri; 3.30-6pm Sat, Sun. **Dinner served** 5.30pm-midnight Mon-Sat; 5.30-11pm Sun. **Main courses** £8.75-£26. **Cover charge** £2. **Credit** AmEx, DC, JCB, MC, V.
The handsome new venture from Jeremy King and Chris Corbin, the team who made the Ivy such a stellar success, is a surprisingly egalitarian affair. The long opening hours mean that everyone can get in at short notice, even if just for breakfast, tea or a cocktail accompanied by superior bar snacks (smoked salmon and brioche toasts, tartine of anchovy and shallots). And the sizeable, brasserie-style menu is a crowd-pleasing list that really does have something for everyone. Whether it's a simple omelette aux fines herbes with frites, half a dozen oysters, marinated herring with potato salad, wiener schnitzel or fillet steak au poivre – it's all there, immaculately executed and delivered with panache. The style of the place (a high-ceilinged homage to European grand cafés, created out of what was once a car showroom) is a winner too; and the details are a constant pleasure (rough-woven linen tablecloths, a wonderful range of silvery teapots, slightly offbeat wine and water glasses). And the waiting staff seem pleased to see all their customers; only a chosen few diners receive visitations from one or other of the owners, but for the rest of us the warm service and relaxed vibe more than suffice. Prices are very reasonable for the quality and spectacle involved, although it's a shame that a £2 cover charge is added. Overall though, a wonderful addition to London dining.

Babies and children welcome; high chairs; toys. Disabled: toilet. Takeaway service. Vegan dishes. **Map 9 J7.**

St James's SW1

The Avenue

7-9 St James's Street, SW1A 1EE (7321 2111/ www.egami.co.uk). Green Park tube. **Bar Open** noon-11pm Mon-Sat; noon-10pm Sun. **Restaurant Brunch served** noon-3.30pm Sun. **Lunch served** noon-3pm Mon-Sat. **Dinner served** 5.45pm-midnight Mon-Thur; 5.45pm-12.30am Fri, Sat; 5.45-10pm Sun. **Main courses** £11-£17.50. **Set meal** £17.95 2 courses, £19.95 3 courses. **Service** 12.5%. **Credit** AmEx, DC, MC, V.
With its cavernous all-white dining space, high noise levels and thrusting vibe, the Avenue feels like a throwback to the mega-restaurants of the 1990s. That it has survived (since December 1995) is testament to a continuing market for big, buzzy, business-oriented eateries; that it is thriving is thanks to the professionalism of its staff and a well-conceived menu that rarely fails to deliver. Lunch is great value. On our last outing a simple salad of baby gem, feta and sun-dried tomatoes was laden with chunks of cheese, while risotto nero with saffron chilli squid was agreeably sharp and creamy. You can only respect a restaurant with a signature dish of fish fingers and chips,

particularly when the fish is as flavoursome and firm and the batter as light, crispy and grease-free as the Avenue's. Salt beef with bubble and squeak is another fine example of superior nursery food. The theme continues with the dessert menu: spotted dick, and rhubarb and hazelnut crumble. *Babies and children welcome. Disabled: toilet. Entertainment: pianist 8pm Sat.* **Map 9 J8**.

Le Caprice

Arlington House, Arlington Street, SW1A 1RT (7629 2239/www.caprice-holdings.co.uk). Green Park tube. **Lunch served** noon-3pm Mon-Sat; noon-4pm Sun. **Dinner served** 5.30pm-midnight Mon-Sat; 6pm-midnight Sun. **Main courses** £12.50-£25. **Cover** £2. **Credit** AmEx, DC, MC, V. This long-time haunt of the old-school fashionable shows no sign of falling from its des-res(ervation) perch. Now immune to the vicissitudes of hip, it still generates a sense of excitement. How? It can't be the site (concrete block), the decor (upmarket Pizza Express, art deco mirror version), or the glamorous clientele (not a plunging neckline in sight). It could be the expensive, but not exorbitant modern brasserie food, which at its best is heavenly, but can plunge to mere mortal standards on the more complex dishes. Perhaps best not to dissect: suffice to say that even if you're given the worst seats in the house, you're not just eating a meal but taking part in a piece of social theatre, from eyeing (but not ogling) famous diners to admiring the far from dumb waiters' servile

superiority. Book ahead, dress nice and enjoy. Oh, and the food. Crab with celeriac remoulade: fresh and flavoursome. Spaghettini with rock shrimps, chilli and parsley: actually quite unpleasant. Pea soup with ricotta: we've had better. Ribeye steak: we haven't had better and don't expect to, ever. A mixed bag, but is that why you're here? *Babies and children welcome; high chairs. Booking essential, several weeks in advance. Entertainment: pianist 7pm-midnight daily. Vegetarian menu. Vegan dishes.* **Map 9 J8**.

Quaglino's

16 Bury Street, SW1Y 6AJ (7930 6767/ www.conran.com). Green Park tube. Bar **Open** 11.30am-1am Mon-Thur; 11.30am-2am Fri, Sat; noon-11pm Sun. *Restaurant* **Lunch served** noon-3pm daily. **Dinner served** 5.30-11.30pm Mon-Thur; 5.30pm-12.30am Fri, Sat; 5.30-10.30pm Sun. **Main courses** £12.50-£22.50. **Set meal** (noon-3pm, 5.30-6.30pm daily) £17 2 courses, £19 3 courses. **Service** 12.5%. *Both* **Credit** AmEx, DC, JCB, MC, V. Though the discreet outside entrance gives little away, first-time visitors will be wowed by the sheer size and opulence of this Conran restaurant, with its high ceilings, painted columns and, at the far end, a flamboyant 'crustacea altar' displaying a wealth of marine life. The brasserie-style menu, with a British slant, is big on seafood. We were enthused by the huge portion of langoustines

mayonnaise – each one perfectly fresh and sweet, accompanied by a moreish mayo. For mains, the (21-day aged) Glen Fyne ribeye steak with béarnaise had a full flavour, while pan-fried halibut with celeriac mash and wild mushrooms (from the specials menu) seemed a touch dry, although the fantastic accompanying mash made amends. Quag's is anything but subdued, thanks to a combination of up-for-it groups of diners (several hen parties were dining on our visit) and live music; the resulting noise echoes around the cavernous dining room to deafening effect. No place, then, for an intimate meal: not least because conversation between close tables seems to flow almost as freely as the wine. Unusually for an expensive Mayfair restaurant, plenty of families tuck in here. Service from the army of waiters is fast and efficient, if not very personalised and somewhat over-zealous in terms of topping up wine glasses. *Babies and children welcome; children's menu; high chairs. Booking advisable. Disabled: toilet. Entertainment: musicians daily (call for details). Separate room for parties, seats 44 (7389 9619).* **Map 17 J7**.

Soho W1

Alastair Little

49 Frith Street, W1D 4SG (7734 5183). Leicester Square or Tottenham Court Road tube. **Lunch served** noon-3pm Mon-Fri. **Dinner served** 6-11.30pm Mon-Sat. **Main courses** £16.50-

The Wolseley

The Restaurants

£21.50. **Set lunch** £29 3 courses. **Set dinner** £38 3 courses. **Service** 12.5% for parties of 8 or more. **Credit** AmEx, JCB, MC, V.

The man himself is no longer wielding the pans, but Little's guiding principles of simplicity and quality remain paramount at this iconic Soho culinary beacon (which celebrates its 20th birthday in 2005). The ever-evolving menu is always finely tuned to the season, and gently inventive. Oysters, for instance, are paired with spicy sausage and soda bread; a smoky quail comes speckled with five-spice and served with cucumber, soy, ginger and wasabi. Recently sampled spring main courses included a rich chump of lamb paired with a sharp greek salad and creamy boulangère potatoes; sea bass fillets were complemented by fennel, rösti and a butter and cucumber sauce with super-sweet tiny brown shrimps. Desserts are often as simple as a perfect crème brûlée, or vanilla ice-cream with a glass of raisiny, chocolatey Pedro Ximenez sherry poured over the top. Service is always on the ball, yet agreeably relaxed. Our only minor criticism is the ordinariness of the setting – a box of a room, a scuffed wooden floor, cream walls hung with (on our last visit) surf-inspired artworks (for sale), and a burnt sienna ceiling hung, wildly over-the-top, with 45 individual light fittings. Still, the food's the thing here, and, on that basis, Alastair Little is faultless.
Babies and children welcome. Booking advisable. Separate room for parties, seats 25. Tables outdoors (2, pavement). Map 17 K6.

★ Andrew Edmunds
46 Lexington Street, W1F 0LW (7437 5708). Oxford Circus or Piccadilly Circus tube. **Lunch served** 12.30-3pm Mon-Fri; 1-3pm Sat, Sun. **Dinner served** 6-10.45pm Mon-Sat; 6-10.30pm Sun. **Main courses** £7.95-£13. **Service** (over £50) 12.5%. **Credit** MC, V.
Thank heaven, some places never change. This gloriously unselfconscious slither of a restaurant has long thumbed its nose at decorative and culinary fashion. The interior suggests 'passé wine bar meets gentleman's club': it's cramped (the basement even more so than the ground floor), lined with dark wooden pew seating and (heavens!) wood-chip wallpaper hung with Gillray-era political cartoons. The food is superior peasant fare: simple, hearty and fairly priced, yet perfectly pitched and cooked with aplomb. We demolished a huge portion of pork rillettes, served with toasted walnut and raisin bread; and a salad of feta, chicory, pear and walnut that proved a winning blend of salty, sweet and bitter flavours, together with creamy, crisp, crumbly and crunchy textures. To follow, a comfortingly earthy rare duck breast and puy lentil stew was cut through by a spiky, caper-laced salsa verde, while squid and chorizo stew with white wine, tomatoes and potatoes was intoxicatingly smoky: a heavenly surf 'n' turf combo. Desserts are similarly straightforward: a fruit crumble; a light, eggy lemon tart; or nutmeg ice-cream, perhaps. The whole Andrew Edmunds package is sealed by the smiling, utterly chilled staff who radiate inclusiveness – turn up in a suit or in jeans, you'll feel equally at home. A Soho gem.
Babies and children welcome. Booking advisable; essential weekends. Tables outdoors (2, pavement). Map 17 J6.

Circus
1 Upper James Street, W1F 9DF (7534 4000/ www.egami.co.uk). Piccadilly Circus tube. *Bar* **Open/meals served** noon-1am Mon-Wed; noon-3am Thu, Fri; 6pm-3am Sat. **Main courses** £3.50-£12. **Admission** (after 11pm) £5 Mon-Sat.
Restaurant **Lunch served** noon-3pm, **dinner served** 5.45pm-midnight Mon-Fri. **Main courses** £6-£18.80. **Set meal** (lunch, 5.45pm-midnight Mon; 5.45-7.15pm, 10.30pm-midnight Tue-Sat) £14.50 2 courses, £16.50 3 courses. **Service** 12.5%. **Credit** AmEx, DC, MC, V.
Set in the old Granada Television building, the cool and minimalist dining room at Circus tries hard to retain its image as the quintessential media lunch spot. By night, though, the plate-glass walls make it hard to hide the fact that diner numbers appear

Hoxton Apprentice. See p221.

to have dropped in recent years (on a Thursday evening, the place was half-empty). Still, chef Richard Lee's boldly flavoured offerings are hard to fault. His acclaimed starter of smoked haddock risotto with a poached egg was simply a masterpiece – a rich, golden yolk oozed through every cranny of the chewy, intense risotto. Chilled avocado and prawn soup with tomato salsa was a simple and effective use of top-notch ingredients. To follow, Gressingham duck with butternut squash and pumpkin purée seemed an odd choice for late spring, but worked marvellously. Monkfish with crab and tarragon risotto, on the other hand, suffered from a timid approach to seasoning, and a dessert of 'wild' strawberry and ginger arctic roll was stodgy and came with a dauntingly heavy custard sauce. Every London restaurant of this kind has its shelf-life, and Circus was launched with its fair share of self-regard back in 1997.
Babies and children welcome. Booking advisable. Entertainment: DJ (bar) 9pm-3am Thur-Sat. Separate room for parties, seats 16. Map 17 J6.

Strand WC2

Adam Street
9 Adam Street, WC2N 6AA (7379 8000/ www.adamstreet.co.uk). Charing Cross tube/rail. **Lunch served** noon-2.30pm Mon-Fri. **Dinner served** (members only) 6-11pm Mon-Sat. **Main courses** £9-£17.90. **Set lunch** £14.50 2 courses, £17.50 3 courses. **Service** 12.5%. **Credit** AmEx, MC, V.
It may be a private members' club, but banish all thoughts of a stuffy, smoky venue full of braying ex-army types. Not only is Adam Street none of these, it's open to the public for lunch. Lucky us. Prices are high, but with starters beginning at £6, mains starting at a not-extortionate £14.50 and a sensibly priced set lunch, it's possible not to overspend. And even if you do, the experience will justify the cost. First, there's the setting – underground vaulted rooms in a building designed

by Robert Adam, done up 21st-century style (red carpet, comfy banquettes, art on the walls). Then there's the food. We were bowled over by the terrine of the day (foie gras, duck, chicken, ham hock and apricots, wrapped in parma ham), the flavours combining beautifully. Chicken caesar salad was as good as a salad gets, bursting with fresh anchovies, pan-fried croûtons, parmesan and soft-boiled eggs, and coated in dressing. Delectable. Mains follow the comfort food theme: fish and chips, roast beef, shepherd's pie and so on. Roasted chicken with herbs (cooked to order) was outstanding, plump and juicy, but could have done without the weird veg combo (chopped tomatoes, smashed potatoes, cabbage). Neither did herb-crusted sea bass disappoint. Desserts proved too hard to resist. Pear and apple crumble with vanilla custard and mixed berry sorbet was a triumph of complementary textures and flavours. Service is entirely professional and not in the least stuffy; and the wine list is well chosen.
Babies and children admitted (lunch). Booking advisable. Separate room for parties, seats 45. Map 18 L7.

Trafalgar Square WC2

The Portrait Restaurant
National Portrait Gallery, St Martin's Place, WC2H 0HE (7312 2490/www.searcys.co.uk). Leicester Square tube/Charing Cross tube/rail. **Open** 10am-5pm Mon-Wed, Sat, Sun; 10am-9pm Thur, Fri. **Lunch served** 11.45am-2.45pm Mon-Fri; 11.30am-3pm Sat, Sun. **Tea served** 3-5pm daily. **Dinner served** 5.30-8.30pm Thur, Fri. **Main courses** £11.95-£17.95. **Service** 12.5%. **Credit** AmEx, JCB, MC, V.
Perched on top of the National Portrait Gallery's modern extension, this Searcy's-run restaurant is popular with visitors to the glut of nearby cultural institutions. One wall of the long thin space is all window, so that everyone gets a view over the roofscape towards Trafalgar Square. Demurely

decorated in shades of grey, white and black, the room can be noisy when full, thanks to the hard surfaces and low, angled ceiling. Starters included endive, walnut, roquefort and pea salad (good, but you'd be hard-pressed to do it badly); and grilled goat's cheese sitting on a salad of aubergine, tomato, raisins and pine nuts (a dry layer of toast added nothing to the dish). Mains of duck breast with creamed cabbage, bacon and madeira sauce, and salmon with peas and potatoes were judged pleasant. Best was the poached smoked haddock – high-quality fish, perfectly cooked – with a gooey-yolked egg and buttery sauce. Pecan toffee tart was a sticky treat, accompanied by an odd-tasting banana beer ice-cream. The wine list is reliable, and service well meaning, if slightly scatty. In short, the creation of a worthy apprentice rather than a masterpiece.
Babies and children welcome; high chairs. Booking advisable. Disabled: lift; toilet. No-smoking tables. **Map 18 K7.**

Westminster SW1

Bank Westminster

45 Buckingham Gate, SW1E 6BS (7379 9797/ www.bankrestaurants.com). St James's tube.
Bar **Open** 11am-11pm Mon, Tue; 11am-1am Wed-Fri; 5pm-1am Sat.
Restaurant **Lunch served** noon-3pm Mon-Fri. **Dinner served** 5.30-11pm Mon-Sat. **Main courses** £15.95-£21.50. **Set lunch** £12.50 2 courses, £15 3 courses. **Service** 12.5%.
Both **Credit** AmEx, DC, MC, V.
It can all get a bit frantic at this Bank branch during the lunchtime rush hour – a fact that betrays the shortage of decent dining options in Westminster. On our visit, would-be diners were contained in a holding pattern before being conducted to a table by a harassed maître d'. Service was distracted. Our zealous waiter kept trying to remove plates before we'd finished eating; and the food arrived at unpredictable temperatures.

On the whole, however, the kitchen remains eclectically creative, turning out a range of innovative dishes flavoured from the four corners of the globe: from nasi goreng with satay sauce, Scottish ribeye with sauce béarnaise or Thai red curry risotto with squid, to cumberland sausages with swede and black peppercorn mash. It's all much less oddball than it sounds. Prices are on the steep side, but there's an excellent prix fixe lunch and dinner option. And the setting (with a semi-circular glass wall overlooking an internal courtyard) is entertaining.
Babies and children welcome; high chairs. Booking advisable. Disabled: toilet. Separate room for parties, seats 50. Tables outdoors (4, terrace). **Map 15 J9.**

West

Chiswick W4

The Burlington NEW

1 Station Parade, Burlington Lane, W4 3HD (8995 3344/www.theburlington.org.uk). Chiswick rail. **Lunch served** noon-2pm Tue-Sun. **Dinner served** 6.30-10pm Mon-Sat; 7-9.30pm Sun. **Main courses** £9.75-£18.50. **Set lunch** (Tue-Fri) £12.50 2 courses, £15 3 courses. **Credit** MC, V.
Acclaimed East Sheen restaurant Redmond's (*see p217*) has spawned a sister restaurant: a smart yet informal bistro with a light, summery interior and an open-view kitchen. To start, a warm salad was crammed with crisp jerusalem artichokes and interesting mushrooms such as enoki, but it contained too much frilly lettuce drenched in balsamic vinegar and arrived without the advertised green beans; the hazelnut oil in the dressing was indiscernible too. Better was a silky, mousse-like duck liver parfait cut through with sharp red onion marmalade. Goat's cheese and spinach tart was a small disc of pastry, topped with spinach and two substantial slabs of grilled goat's cheese. Too unctuous for a main course, it came with yet more balsamic-sodden frilly lettuce. Our other main consisted of tender breast of wood pigeon, velvety seared foie gras, nutmeggy polenta and caramelised chicory – all practically drowning in balsamic 'jus'. A chocolate tart (like a chocolate mousse inside a thin pastry wall) came with caramel ice-cream overwhelmed with rosemary. Despite our misgivings, we liked the Burlington; chatty, friendly service was a definite plus. But overall we found the food very rich. Moreover, too many strong, gutsy ingredients combined with a heavy-handed use of balsamic vinegar meant the cooking lacked balance; the addition of something plain, uncooked or vibrant in each dish would have helped round out the flavours.
Babies and children welcome; high chairs. Booking advisable weekends. No-smoking tables. Restaurant and garden available for hire. Tables outdoors (9, garden).

Ealing W5

Gilbey's

77 The Grove, W5 5LL (8840 7568/ www.gilbeygroup.com). Ealing Broadway tube/rail. **Lunch served** noon-2.30pm Tue-Sun. **Dinner served** 7-10pm Tue-Sat. **Main courses** £9.95-£17.95. **Set lunch** (Tue-Sat) £8.95 2 courses; (Sun) £12.95 2 courses. **Set dinner** (Tue-Thur) £12.95 2 courses. **Service** 12.5%.
Credit AmEx, DC, MC, V.
Though it's slightly off the main drag, many an Ealingite beats a path to Gilbey's in the hope of some decent Modern European tucker and, during the summer, a table in the pretty conservatory at the back. That said, the restaurant might benefit if a few stayed away – in particular, the table of diners who neglected to switch off their incessantly ringing mobile phones. Food is generally well presented and flavoured. The signature dish of cornish crab and prawn tian was a tasty starter (if a little stingy on the crab front). A beautiful red mullet terrine with pimiento sauce consisted of a scrumptious pairing of chunky fish pieces with a piquant coulis. Perfectly seared tuna with an anchovy vinaigrette, atop a salad niçoise, made a

substantial main course. Grilled monkfish tail, which arrived on a pile of pak choi with chillies, was a delicious combination. The great-value wine list offers many decent bottles for around £11. Our only disappointment was dessert; walnut bread pudding wasn't nearly naughty enough: practically healthy, in fact, arriving as it did with no cream. The cheeseboard, on the other hand, was a treat and included a lovely applewood smoked.
Babies and children welcome; half-price children's portions; high chairs. Booking advisable dinner; essential weekends. No smoking (conservatory). Separate room for parties, seats 30. Tables outdoors (5, garden; 2, patio).

Gloucester Road SW7

L'Etranger

36 Gloucester Road, SW7 4QT (7584 1118/ www.etranger.co.uk). Gloucester Road tube.
Brunch served noon-3pm Sun. **Lunch served** noon-3pm Mon-Fri. **Dinner served** 6-11pm Mon-Sat; 6-10pm Sun. **Main courses** £12-£20. **Set meal** (noon-3pm, 6-7pm Mon-Fri) £14.50 2 courses, £16.50 3 courses. **Service** 12.5%.
Credit AmEx, MC, V.
Behind a long, curved frontage and lavender blinds, this acutely stylish restaurant has a surprisingly small and intimate interior. Its customers (most of them male on our visit) looked very contented to be here. The light is subdued, the walls are white and flannel-grey. The regulars come back for the attentive service and the exceptional French-turning-Japanese food. Take, for instance, the snails with black truffles, hefty ceps and cantal cream, where the skewered snails are in a tempura batter – delicious. Or the pink, tender tamarind-glazed duck with rhubarb and ginger marmalade, served on white rectangular plates and eaten with chopsticks. Promotional postcards on the tables depict caramelised cod. Sample it and you may want to send your own card with a 'wish you were here to share it' message; the thick slab of fish, rich and intense, is served alongside sushi rice wrapped in a leaf with a black sesame crust. Raspberry macaroons missed the Japanese treatment (if you ignore the black sesame ice-cream that arrived with it), while crème brûlée came in wasabi, green tea and liquorice flavours (of which the wasabi worked best). None of this comes cheap, though, and some dishes are a little cheeky – can a starter with 16 balls of beluga arranged on four pieces of yellowtail sashimi justify a £14.50 price tag?
Babies and children welcome: high chairs. Book dinner. Dress: smart casual. Restaurant available for hire. Vegetarian menu. **Map 13 C9.**

Hanwell W7

Clock

130-132 Uxbridge Road, W7 3SL (8810 1011/ www.clock-restaurant.co.uk). Boston Manor tube.
Bar **Open/meals served** 5-11pm Tue-Sun.
Main courses £4.50-£10.
Restaurant **Lunch served** noon-3pm Fri, Sun. **Dinner served** 5pm-midnight Tue-Sat. **Main courses** £12.50-£16.75. **Service** 12.5%.
Both **Credit** AmEx, JCB, MC, V.
The monthly changing menu at this west London restaurant is popular with locals. Tables and chairs are gastropub-simple, but chandeliers, mirrors and linen napkins, along with good service, give a more upmarket flavour. So too do elaborate dishes such as velouté of cos lettuce, prawn and scallop dumplings, lumpfish caviar and truffle oil. A starter of spiced okra with fresh pasta, yellow lentils and coriander pesto was delicately spiced and texturally pleasing. Tartare of salmon and yellowfin tuna with avocado looked pretty, but the sesame and lemon dressing lacked the necessary punch to bring the dish alive. Main courses combined traditional French cuisine with funky Mediterranean touches; roasted sea bass with crushed new potatoes came with dinky sage beignets. Rolled loin of deliciously tender lamb on a wedge of gratin dauphinois arrived with a dollop of aubergine caviar. Portions were generous, making side dishes unnecessary, but the innovative puddings had to be tried; goat's cheese

and ginger cheesecake with confit pink rhubarb was deliciously refreshing. The Chilean sauvignon blanc house wine is very reasonable, but there's plenty to explore higher up the wine list. The adjoining bar area has its own (cheaper and simpler) menu: meze, soup and pizzas typically. *Babies and children welcome; children's menu; high chairs; nappy-changing facilities. Booking advisable. Disabled: toilet. Dress: smart casual. Restaurant available for hire. Tables outdoors (5, patio garden).*

Kensington W8

Babylon

The Roof Gardens, 7th Floor, 99 Kensington High Street, W8 5ED (7368 3993/ www.roofgardens.com). High Street Kensington tube. **Lunch served** noon-3pm Mon-Fri, Sun. **Dinner served** 7-11pm Mon-Sat. **Main courses** £11-£20. **Set lunch** (Mon-Fri) £14 2 courses, £16 3 courses; (Sun) £18.50 2 courses, £21 3 courses. **Service** 12.5%. **Credit** AmEx, DC, JCB, MC, V.
The arrival of head chef Oliver Smith in October 2003 has really turned things around for the once-struggling Roof Gardens. Gone are the tired and tasteless standbys of the old regime, replaced by such delights as a chilled carrot and orange soup with lemon thyme and crème fraîche – a sort of sweet gazpacho in orange. Another starter of warm asparagus, egg, parmesan, truffle and cep oil was simple buttery innocence on a plate. There are still some missed cues, such as corn-fed chicken breast with artichoke and crisp prosciutto that featured one succulent, tender piece of meat next to a lump of unpalatable flesh that tasted as if it had been boiled. The amateurish service staff are still here too, and still obviously preoccupied with their modelling careers. But the very chic, 'Brady Bunch house meets airport VIP lounge' design scheme is a pleasant distraction from any culinary blindspots. And hats off to Smith, whose desserts at least are truly a cut above. An £8 selection plate gives you a taste of all five creations, but we say go straight for the luscious espresso crème brûlée or the chilled sticky Thai rice pudding with coconut chips, mango and ginger sauce. Finally there's that view: sweeping vistas across south London and a garden full of yawning flamingos. Can that really be beaten?
Babies and children welcome; children's menu; entertainer; high chairs (Sun only). Booking advisable. Disabled: lift; toilet. Separate room for parties, seats 14. Tables outdoors (15, balcony). **Map 7 B9**.

★ Clarke's

124 Kensington Church Street, W8 4BH (7221 9225/www.sallyclarke.com). Notting Hill Gate tube. **Brunch served** 11am-2pm Sat. **Lunch served** 12.30-2pm Mon-Fri. **Dinner served** 7-10pm Tue-Sat. **Main courses** (lunch) £14-£16. **Set dinner** £32-£36 2 courses; £48 4 courses incl coffee, truffles and service. **Credit** AmEx, DC, JCB, MC, V.
Sally Clarke's delightful dining room celebrated its 20th anniversary in 2004. Back in 1984 – when she first started serving Californian-inspired dishes with an emphasis on simple, freshly sourced ingredients presented with the minimum of fuss – her style was unique in London. Since then, it has been honed, developed and emulated by countless others. Thankfully, Clarke and her team of chefs have remained consistent and the many regulars here (several of whom pop in to dine solo at lunchtime) would attest to her success. The surroundings are simple and the choice, famously, limited to a dozen or so dishes for lunch and a set no-choice menu at dinner. Fish and meat arrive daily from specialist suppliers: perhaps some Welsh lamb, served char-grilled with mushrooms and a glossy red wine and rosemary glaze. A salad of buffalo mozzarella with spiced aubergine, roasted red peppers, black olives and pine nuts is made with cheese specially flown over from Naples. To finish, there might be some soft vanilla meringue served with pineapple ice-cream and passion fruit sauce, or brioche and butter pudding with an apricot sauce. A similar amount of care

has gone into selecting the wine list, which features over 200 Californian, French and Italian bottles, many sourced from lesser-known producers. *Babies and children welcome; high chair. Booking advisable; essential weekends. No smoking.* **Map 7 B7**.

Kensington Place

201-209 Kensington Church Street, W8 7LX (7727 3184). Notting Hill Gate tube. **Lunch served** noon-3.30pm daily. **Dinner served** 6.30-11.45pm Mon-Sat; 6.30-10.15pm Sun. **Main courses** £14-£18.50. **Set lunch** (Mon-Fri) £18.50 3 courses; (Sun) £21 3 courses. **Service** 12.5%. **Credit** AmEx, DC, JCB, MC, V.
A fixture since the late 1980s – with formerly trend-setting decor to prove it – Kensington Place has never ceased to pull in the crowds. It is a restaurant that many people swear by: from celebrity diners to the more anonymous, of all ages. It also generates radically contrasting opinions; lunchers seem more consistently contented than dinner diners. Our recent evening meal was disappointing, mainly because of lacklustre ingredients. A chicken and goat's cheese mousse was far the best, smooth and very subtle. In risotto with girolles, on the other hand, the mushrooms were flavourless, and an exaggerated butteriness seemed to have been added to compensate. The restaurant has a fresh fish shop attached, but saffron-fried monkish and prawns featured very dull fish and saffron seasoning, and only the excellent prawns and some good spinach added some zest. Venison cutlets with cherries came with a deliciously rich wine gravy, though the meat was almost bizarrely lacking in flavour for game. Things only really picked up with a great, freshly made, soufflé-like chocolate mousse with coffee ice-cream. Staff are (mostly) professional and helpful, but given how full the Place gets, they often struggle to keep up.
Babies and children welcome; high chairs. Booking advisable; essential weekends. Disabled: toilet. Separate room for parties, seats 45. **Map 7 B7**.

Launceston Place

1A Launceston Place, W8 5RL (7937 6912/ www.egami.co.uk). Gloucester Road or High Street Kensington tube. **Lunch served** 12.30-2.30pm Mon-Fri, Sun. **Dinner served** 7-11.30pm Mon-Sat; 7-10.30pm Sun. **Main courses** £17.50-£19.50. **Set lunch** £15.50 2 courses, £18.50 3 courses; (Sun) £22.50 3 courses. **Service** 12.5%. **Credit** AmEx, DC, JCB, MC, V.
In a neat and genteel corner of Kensington sits this neat and genteel restaurant, with conservatively comfortable decor that could belong to a country-house hotel: a style that's evidently appreciated by affluent local diners. Service is charming, and not at all snooty or fussy. And the food is very impressive, with dishes – British/European based, but with a few global/Far Eastern touches – that are designed to be enjoyed, not just to dazzle. To start, one of the house standards, twice-baked goat's cheese soufflé with spiced plums, was a most pleasant fruity-and-cheesy combination; truffle mozzarella with tomato and beetroot salad featured delicious, crumbly cheese and (very unusual, this) truly excellent beetroot. Of our mains, roast duck breast with kumquat and ginger and a shiitake mushroom spring roll was nicely done, but the star dish was grilled tuna with salsa verde: an exceptional, meltingly soft piece of perfectly presented fish that needed only the slightest cooking. We finished with a generously fruity, traditional summer pudding with cream. The wine list isn't huge, but it's ample. Launceston Place is no fashion leader, yet it remains an exceedingly pleasant spot for a relaxing meal.
Babies and children welcome; children's portions. Booking advisable. Dress: smart casual. Separate rooms for parties, seating 14 and 30. **Map 7 C9**.

The Terrace

33C Holland Street, W8 4LX (7937 3224/ www.theterracerestaurant.co.uk). High Street Kensington tube. **Lunch served** noon-2.30pm Mon-Sat; noon-3pm Sun. **Dinner served** 6.30-11pm Mon-Sat. **Main courses** £11.50-£20. **Set lunch** (Mon-Fri) £14.50 2 courses, £17.50

3 courses. **Set brunch** (noon-3pm Sat; noon-3.30pm Sun) £17.50 2 courses, £21.50 3 courses. **Service** 12.5%. **Credit** AmEx, JCB, MC, V.
You may well find duffers discussing diplomatic postings in former outposts of the Empire, but there's nothing intrinsically stuffy about this small Kensington local. The setting is entirely agreeable, with beige walls, large windows on two sides and a mini, shrub-enclosed front terrace whence the restaurant takes its name. The set lunch comprised two starters: a delicate dish of chilli, garlic and tarragon tiger prawns; and a piquant char-grilled chicken salad. To follow, own-made merguez sausages on herb mash was a fine Iberian variation on bangers and mash, while poached fillet of organic salmon with red onion, savoy cabbage and yoghurt cucumber dressing was perfectly light. Papaya and apricot bread pudding with vanilla ice-cream was too tempting to resist, and continued the theme of re-spun classics. Prices rise quite steeply for the more ambitious a la carte numbers, but sophisticated cooking is guaranteed across the board. Add to that good wines by the glass from a modest but classy wine list, and service that is as warm as the kitchen's own bread.
Babies and children welcome; children's portions; high chairs. Booking advisable. No smoking (terrace). Tables outdoors (7, terrace). **Map 7 B8**.

Ladbroke Grove W10

Number 10 NEW

10 Golborne Road, W10 5PE (8969 8922/ www.number10london.com). Ladbroke Grove or Westbourne Park tube. **Bar Meals served** 10am-10.30pm Mon-Fri; 11am-10.30pm Sat; 11am-10pm Sun. *Restaurant* **Lunch served** noon-3pm Mon-Sat; noon-4pm Sun. **Dinner served** 6-10.30pm Mon-Sat; 6-10pm Sun. **Main courses** £12-£17.75. **Set meals** £15.50 2 courses, £18.50 3 courses. *Both* **Credit** AmEx, DC, JCB, MC, V.
Formerly the Prince Arthur pub in an up-and-coming part of Portobello, Number 10 has been restored as a live music venue. There's a bar on the ground floor, a restaurant on the first, and a private members' club at the top. We kicked off with excellent gin and tonics in the bar, which is resplendent with retro swirly-patterned carpet, red velvet curtains, disco balls (and disco belles) and opulent chandeliers. Here, bands play five or six times a month. Classical music is performed in the restaurant, which is decorated with striking, monochrome wallpaper and glass drop curtains. On our visit, a harpist and cellist were drowned out by a boisterous group of trustafarians celebrating a birthday (staff coped admirably). Head chef Julien Maisonneuve's menu reinterprets Modern European classics. Twice-baked stilton soufflé had a dense, cakey texture, but was overcooked and needed more stilton; its classic pairing with pears and port jus meant the flavours worked well, though. Tunisian-style filo pastry parcel, with cumin and paprika-spiced butternut squash, was served lukewarm, yet tasted fine. We also liked the broadly east European flavours of 'very fresh' scallops with honey and lemon chicory, and succulent chicken breast with cucumber and beetroot. For dessert, 'home made jaffa cake' tasted divine. Brunch, lunch and afternoon tea are also offered. Enjoyable? Certainly. Pretentious? Unquestionably. But it's all done with wit, charm, and tongue firmly in cheek.
Babies and children welcome: children's menu; high chairs. Booking advisable. Entertainment: bands 9pm Thur-Sat. Separate room for parties, seats 40. Tables outdoors (7, pavement). Vegetarian menu. **Map 19 B1**.

Maida Vale W9

The Vale

99 Chippenham Road, W9 2AB (7266 0990). Maida Vale or Westbourne Park tube. **Brunch served** 11am-3pm Sun. **Lunch served** 12.30-2.30pm Tue-Fri. **Dinner served** 7-11pm Mon-Sat. **Main courses** £8.50-£14. **Set lunch** £12 2 courses, £15 3 courses. **Set dinner** £15 2 courses, £18.50 3 courses. **Service** 12.5%. **Credit** DC, JCB, MC, V.

Every neighbourhood could do with one of these: a pleasant, sensibly priced local that offers no-nonsense, brasserie-style cooking in laid-back surroundings. The Vale occupies a rambling, glass-roofed corner site on the border between Maida Vale and West Kilburn. It features wooden floors, paper tablecloths and a flexible menu that changes twice a day. There are soups and salads (perhaps minted summer minestrone, or a salad with gorgonzola, chicory, pear and walnuts), as well as a choice of pasta dishes available in large or small sizes (pappardelle with braised lamb shank, pea and mint, for example; or asparagus, potato and mozzarella lasagne). More substantial mains might include roast sweetbreads with olive oil mash and sautéed baby artichokes, fillet of halibut 'en papillote' with new potatoes and lemony butter sauce, or a classic sirloin served with chips and béarnaise. There's a lengthy wine and drinks list that includes a range of eaux de vie to go with your coffee.
Babies and children welcome; children's portions; high chairs. Booking advisable. No-smoking tables. Separate rooms for parties, seating 14, 22, 32 and 40. Map 1 A3.

Olympia W14

Cotto
44 Blythe Road, W14 0HA (7602 9333). Hammersmith or Shepherd's Bush tube/ Kensington (Olympia) tube/rail. Lunch served noon-2.30pm Mon-Fri. Dinner served 7-10.30pm Mon-Sat. Set lunch £13.50 2 courses, £16.50 3 courses. Set dinner £17 2 courses, £19.50 3 courses. Service 12.5%. Credit AmEx, JCB, MC, V.
Cotto is handily located if you've just had a long day exhibiting at Olympia, but a bit out of the way to attract much passing trade. The decor is pleasant enough, if a little white and sterile (some flowers would help), and the standard café-restaurant muzak (Lemonjelly, Air, St Germain) is unobtrusive. The varied dinner menu is excellent value (two courses £17, three £19.50; some dishes have a supplement). Our sautéed razor clams needed a less overpowering chorizo as accompaniment, while the potato and truffle tortellini hit the spot. Corn-fed chicken with garlic for mains came with a fresh foie gras; and a pot-roasted rump of veal had just the right blend of artichokes, spinach, plus a caper, parma ham and anchovy relish. The wine list is a high-quality mixture of Old and New World wines, not prohibitively priced. Poached pear and dates with spiced filo and praline was an excellent way to finish. The lack of fellow diners or any repartee from the lonely waiter gave our evening a ghostly edge, but the quality-to-price ratio is hard to fault.
Babies and children welcome: high chairs. Separate room for parties, seats 35. Tables outdoors (4, pavement). Map 20 C3.

Shepherd's Bush W6, W12

Brackenbury
129-131 Brackenbury Road, W6 0BQ (8748 0107). Goldhawk Road or Hammersmith tube. Lunch served 12.30-2.45pm Mon-Fri; 12.30-3.30pm Sun. Dinner served 7-10.45pm Mon-Sat. Main courses £9-£16. Set lunch (Mon-Fri) £12.50 2 courses, £14.50 3 courses. Service 12.5%. Credit AmEx, MC, V.
Runner-up in the Best Local Restaurant category of the *Time Out* Eating & Drinking Awards in 2003, this consistent, high-quality performer hasn't let standards slip. The Brackenbury is an old-fashioned establishment that caters for a well-heeled and aged crowd. You won't have trouble finding a cosy corner in the split-level dining room, and there's a covered terrace (on a quiet street) for dining al fresco. The service is spot on: attentive without being overbearing. There's usually a choice of eight starters and mains, including the trademark omelette. On our most recent visit, both starters – black tiger prawns, globe artichoke, guacamole and crispy fennel salad; and mozzarella salad with parmesan tuile – were on the money.

Main courses (roasted hake, chorizo, potato and caper hash, with saffron aïoli; and pan-fried sea bass fillet, fennel, samphire and lemon salad, with salsa rouge) balanced delicate flavours and substance perfectly. Portions were at the right end of nouvelle cuisine. Desserts of iced white chocolate parfait with passion fruit sauce, and banoffee cheesecake with caramel sauce were again subject to fault. A bill of £70 (including wine and service) for such quality puts plenty of other London establishments to shame. We left wishing the Brackenbury was on our street.
Babies and children welcome; high chair. Booking advisable. Tables outdoors (7, patio). Map 20 B3.

Bush Bar & Grill
45A Goldhawk Road, W12 8QP (8746 2111/ www.bushbar.co.uk). Goldhawk Road tube. Bar Open noon-11pm Mon-Sat; noon-10.30pm Sun. Restaurant Lunch served noon-3pm Mon-Sat; noon-4pm Sun. Dinner served 5.30-11.30pm Mon-Sat; 6.30-10.30pm Sun. Main courses £8.50-£17. Set lunch (Mon-Sat) £12.50 2 courses, £15 3 courses; (Sun) £15 2 courses, £17 3 courses. Both Service 12.5%. Credit AmEx, MC, V.
It's easy to miss the entrance to what used to be a warehouse-like watering hole for Aussies, but is now a favoured haunt of BBC folk who work close by. The Bush Bar & Grill has a spacious feel, with two bar areas (one curtained-off, which can be booked) and a leafy outside space. The menu features chunky salads and a range of meat and fish, with an emphasis on carefully sourced, seasonal, free-range or organic produce. Chef Wayne Dixon seems to have improved things in the kitchen after our disappointing last visit. A delicately flavoured starter of crab and spiced avocado set the tone, while a main of Blenheim lamb was a lovely cut of meat, cooked to perfection. Haddock fish cakes were munchable rather than memorable. Despite the 'would rather be anywhere but here' air of the staff, service was attentive. Snacks and decent cocktails are available in the bar area, and there's a weekend brunch menu (on our visit, children could eat for free on a Sunday).
Babies and children welcome; children's menu (Sat, Sun); high chairs. Booking advisable Fri, Sat. Disabled: toilet. Separate room for parties, seats 50. Tables outdoors (9, courtyard). Map 20 B2.

Barnes SW13

★ Sonny's
94 Church Road, SW13 0DQ (8748 0393). Barnes Bridge rail/209 bus. Café Open 10.30am-6pm Mon-Sat. Lunch served noon-4pm Mon-Sat. Main courses £3.95-£9.
Restaurant Lunch served 12.30-2.30pm Mon-Sat; 12.30-3pm Sun. Dinner served 7.30-11pm Mon-Sat. Main courses £10.75-£16. Set lunch (Mon-Sat) £13 2 courses, £16.50 3 courses; (Sun) £21 3 courses incl coffee. Set dinner (Mon-Thur) £16.50 2 courses, £19.50 3 courses. Service 12.5%. Credit AmEx, MC, V.
This polished neighbourhood restaurant has been satisfying the culinary appetites of Barnes locals for years. It's a modern, clean-lined white space (the back room is nicer than the front), as suitable for dinners à deux as it is for family gatherings. The whole operation is run with professional ease, from the well-judged wine list to the artfully presented Mod Euro concoctions delivered from the kitchen by cordial staff. The menu makes good use of seasonal ingredients, offering (in summer) the likes of salad of marinated girolles with apricot, pecorino and pea shoots: a light yet flavour-packed starter. Main courses might include tender pork loin with nutty camargue red rice and marinated cranberries. Another main of pan-fried sea bass came swimming in lobster-flavoured minestrone, the latter meeting with a mixed reaction, though the fish was perfect. The set dinner is limited, but good value considering most à la carte mains cost £14-plus. Desserts – such as

inventive sorbets or vanilla soufflé with chocolate brownie ice-cream – are always delectable. The wine list provides bubbly options for those in a celebratory mood: but the food is enough to create that.
Babies and children welcome; high chairs. Booking advisable (restaurant). Restaurant available for hire. Separate room for parties, seats 22.

Chelsea SW3

Bluebird
350 King's Road, SW3 5UU (7559 1000/ www.conran.com). Sloane Square tube then 11, 19, 22, 49, 319 bus. Bar Open 11am-11pm Mon-Thur; 11am-12.45am Fri-Sat; 11am-10.45pm Sun. Restaurant Brunch served noon-3.30pm Sat, Sun. Lunch served 12.30-3.30pm Mon-Fri. Dinner served 6-11pm Mon-Sat; 6-10pm Sun. Main courses £12.95-£25. Service 12.5%. Credit AmEx, DC, JCB, MC, V.
When we booked, the receptionist at this Conran restaurant told us that tables taken before 8pm could only be occupied for 1 hour 45 minutes, after which they might have to be vacated for later diners. That is shorter than we usually spend over three courses, and makes for an unrelaxing meal. Unfortunately, the food was too hit and miss to relieve the tension, and overcast skies (visible on a summer's evening through the large skylight) made the spacious white dining room feel small. Ham hock terrine had a foie gras tube down the middle like a gala pie; though the accompanying piccalilli complemented the ham, it smothered the liver. Crab and avocado – arranged in layers of brown, white and green – was fresh enough, yet unexciting. Things started to look up with tender suckling pig, which came with a good robust apple sauce, but the fragment of crackling on top was partly burnt. Strongly flavoured sea bass was nicely firm, but small, its 'garlic tapenade' more of an oil dressing. The highest point came with figs cooked in port, served with pecorino ice-cream – excellent and well balanced. The low point was a pistachio tart, accompanied by a compote of plums containing four tooth-cracking pieces of shrapnel-hard shell. Bluebird was busy, yet wasn't, for us, a very enjoyable experience, and the rather tense staff didn't look happy either.
Babies and children welcome; children's menu (weekends); high chairs. Disabled: toilet. Entertainment: DJs Fri, Sat. Separate rooms for parties, seating 15 and 42. Map 14 D12.

Fulham SW6

★ The Farm [NEW]
18 Farm Lane, SW6 1PP (7381 3331/ www.thefarmfulham.co.uk). Fulham Broadway tube/11, 14, 211 bus. Bar Open noon-11pm Mon-Sat; noon-10.30pm Sun. Meals served noon-10pm Mon-Sat noon-9.30pm Sun. Main courses £3-£9.50. Restaurant Lunch served noon-3pm daily. Dinner served 6-10.15pm Mon-Sat; 6-9.30pm Sun. Main courses £9-£17. Service 12.5%. Both Credit AmEx, JCB, MC, V.
The Farm's owner, Tom Etridge, has been associated with Golborne House, the Waterway, the Wells (see p102) and the Ebury (see p92) – all different, yet all loosely described as 'gastropubs'. But don't expect bare boards and a blackboard menu here. The Farm's 1930s shell has been expensively rebuilt, panelled in dark oak wainscot, with luxurious leather seating and coolly modern chrome fireplaces. Chef Paul Merrett used to work at the Greenhouse (see p113), where he held a Michelin star, and his mastery of flavour, timing and presentation is still very apparent. Although the dishes – fish cakes, chicken caesar salad, chocolate fondant – may sound or be familiar, the rendition of them is exemplary. Scallop on black pudding was served with a pea purée and onion gravy; you'll find no better version. Terrine of rabbit and foie gras with apple jelly and celeriac remoulade was sublime. A main course of cumin-spiced rump of lamb was cooked perfectly pink, served with herby tabouleh and smoked aubergine. Puddings are elaborately garnished with swirls of coulis and colour, but it's not just all show: plum

The Restaurants

tart with a lemongrass and black pepper sorbet also had kick. Anything else we liked? The wine list, although there's not much below £20; more choice by the glass would help too. Service was unfailingly gracious, even under pressure.
Babies and children welcome; children's portions. Booking advisable. Disabled: toilet. Dress: smart casual. **Map 13 A13.**

Mims

541A King's Road, SW6 2EB (7751 0010). Fulham Broadway tube or West Brompton tube/rail/11, 22 bus. **Lunch served** 12.30-3pm, **dinner served** 6.30-11pm Tue-Fri. **Meals served** 12.30-11pm Sat; 12.30-10.30pm Sun. **Main courses** £7.50-£11. **Set lunch** £7.50 2 courses. **Set dinner** £14 2 courses. **Service** 10%. **Credit** MC, V.
While neighbouring restaurants were crowded, we had this place to ourselves, save for an optimistic rough sleeper who wandered in and asked us for cigarettes before requesting chicken and chips. The waiter was as welcoming to him as he was to us. As for why the place was empty, it may partly have been the worn decor, but there was also something disconcerting about the presentation of the food – not contemporary, but not retro. Crab ravioli arrived as a vertical cone of mousse with a sheet of pasta draped over, dressed with a ginger and coriander sauce and a slab of seared salmon to the side. Tasty scallops came with a (vertical) stick of fennel, surrounded with tangy caramelised red onion. For mains, tender roast duck was again three-dimensional with its accompanying honeyed carrots, salsify and sweet potato stacked like building bricks (this was also the substitute for our neighbour's chicken and chips, and was rightly pronounced delicious). A generous portion of monkfish (vertical) was cooked to perfection with spinach, chilli and garlic. Puddings were more than competent; pear tarte tatin was hot, fresh and caramelised, the tiramisu was rich and surrounded with powdered chocolate. There's nothing wrong with the quality, but presentation has to change or it is hard to see Mim's surviving.
Babies and children admitted: high chair. Booking advisable. Disabled: toilet. **Map 13 C13.**

Putney SW15

Phoenix Bar & Grill

162-164 Lower Richmond Road, SW15 1LY (8780 3131). Putney Bridge tube/22, 265 bus. **Lunch served** 12.30-2.30pm Mon-Sat; 12.30-3pm Sun. **Dinner served** 7-11pm Mon-Thur; 7-11.30pm Fri, Sat; 7-10pm Sun. **Main courses** (Sun) £19.50 3 courses. **Set meal** (7-7.45pm Mon-Thur, Sun) £13.50 2 courses, £16.50 3 courses. **Service** 12.5%. **Credit** AmEx, MC, V.
Come the weekend, the Phoenix is the sort of place that well-heeled locals dress up for. The sense of occasion that a meal here creates makes it feel very 'London', despite the leafy location. Sister restaurant to Sonny's (*see p216*) in Barnes, it shares the same spare, clean, white-walled architectural look and professional approach to front-of-house. Former consultant chef Franco Taruschio has moved on, but the Modern European menu retains an Italian accent, with cavolo nero, bresaola (cured on the premises) and pancetta turning up on the frequently changing menu. Generally, the cooking is well handled. The bresaola came thinly sliced, strewn with rocket leaves and parmesan shavings. It didn't exactly hum with flavour, yet was pleasingly delicate. Less successful was pappardelle with venison and wild mushroom ragù. The ingredients suggest full-on, bosky sexiness, but the dish didn't quite deliver on the promise. Making up for the lapse was moist, succulent roast suckling pig with rosemary potatoes and apple compote: full-flavoured and rib-sticking. Italianate desserts – such as panna cotta with winter fruits, and panettone bread and butter pudding – are made all the more attractive by some well-chosen sweet wines and grappas by the glass.
Babies and children welcome; children's menu (Sun); crayons; high chairs. Booking essential summer; advisable winter. Disabled: toilet. No-smoking tables. Tables outdoors (14, terrace).

The A Bar & Restaurant. See p222.

Sheen SW14

★ Redmond's

170 Upper Richmond Road West, SW14 8AW (8878 1922/www.redmonds.org.uk). Mortlake rail then 337 bus, or 33 bus. **Lunch served** noon-2.30pm Sun. **Dinner served** 6.30-10.30pm Mon-Thur; 7-10.30pm Fri, Sat. **Set lunch** (Sun) £19 2 courses, £23 3 courses. **Set meal** (6.30-7.45pm Mon-Thur) £12.50 2 courses, £15 3 courses. **Set dinner** £27.50 2 courses, £31 3 courses. **Service** 10% for parties of 6 or more. **Credit** JCB, MC, V.
Redmond's core clientele may be middle-class and middle-aged, but there's nothing middle-of-the-road about this husband-and-wife operation. Courteous, attentive service; a relaxed atmosphere; tastefully subdued decor: everything speaks of the confidence that comes from doing something well for many years. The set dinner is shortish (five starters, six mains and desserts apiece), but everything appeals. Ingredients are high quality and change with the seasons. Murmurs of appreciation greeted the fresh clear flavours of smoked haddock tartare with chive crème fraîche. For mains, roast cod peeled into fat, juicy flakes atop pak choi, perfect mash and lemony puy lentils: an excellent combination. Tagliatelle had a moreishly rich mushroom sauce. The only duff note came with the over-perfumed vanilla and orange sauce accompanying nicely cooked chicken breast and baby leeks. The savoury/sweet combo of pear tarte tatin lined with basil leaves, with red pepper ice-cream on the side, was not a full-on success, but deserves points for inventiveness. Best of all were the fantastically intense flavours of lime mousse and raspberry sorbet. Oenophiles are in for a treat too; the lengthy wine list is helpfully detailed and regular wine-related events are held. Long may Redmond's continue to crest the wave of classy neighbourhood dining.
Babies and children welcome; high chair. Booking advisable; essential weekends. No-smoking. Restaurant available for hire.

South Kensington SW3

Bibendum

Michelin House, 81 Fulham Road, SW3 6RD (7581 5817/www.bibendum.co.uk). South Kensington tube. **Lunch served** noon-2.30pm

Mon-Fri; 12.30-3pm Sat, Sun. **Dinner served** 7-11.30pm Mon-Sat; 7-10.30pm Sun. **Main courses** £19-£42. **Set lunch** (Mon-Fri) £28.50 3 courses. **Service** 12.5%. **Credit** AmEx, DC, MC, V.
The original figurehead of the good ship Conran remains an attractive venue. The spectacular dining room, on the first floor of the Michelin building – above the Bibendum Oyster Bar (*see p74*) – has a real sense of occasion, dominated by the original 1930s rich blue Michelin Man stained-glass windows. Service, if not entirely seamless, is both crisply efficient and welcoming. The food doesn't shy away from the rich and robust; a warm salad of quail included a powerful mix of figs, fried prosciutto and a madeira ravioli (really, more like a pastry). For something lighter, a lettuce hearts and summer vegetable salad featured excellent ingredients, even if they were served too cold. For mains, monkfish, a special of the day, came with a luxuriant lobster sauce and chives, while grilled rabbit with stuffed artichokes was another no-holds-barred combination, almost like a rabbit mixed grill. In a restaurant like this, the various pampering extras can count as much as main dishes towards justifying the £60-a-head price tag, and a dessert of vodka, watermelon and mint granita and the extravagant petits fours didn't disappoint. The wine list is immense, mainly French and suitably pricey.
Babies and children welcome; high chair. Booking essential, 2 weeks in advance for dinner. Dress: smart casual. **Map 14 E10.**

South

Balham SW12

Lamberts

2 Station Parade, Balham High Road, SW12 9AZ (8675 2233/www.lambertsrestaurant.com). Balham tube/rail. **Lunch served** 11am-3pm Sat. **Dinner served** 7-10.30pm Tue-Sat. **Meals served** 11am-9pm Sun. **Main courses** £11-£17. **Set menu** (Tue-Thur) £14 2 courses, £17 3 courses. **Service** 12.5%. **Credit** JCB, MC, V.
Balham, once the butt of jokes, is now des-res territory and has a clutch of good restaurants to prove it. We've visited Lamberts regularly since it opened, and have been quite positive about the

Inc Bar & Restaurant

place, but usually with a few reservations. Recently though, Lamberts seems to have climbed the league table. The white walls, chocolate banquettes, linen tablecloths and glass frontage are crisp and clean. Service is friendly but professional and enthusiastic. Better yet, the menu and wine list are put together with evident care. It isn't often we see the likes of Herdwick mutton on the menu, so following a starter of succulent smoked eel with pickled beetroot, we had to try it. The full-flavoured meat was tender, even though cooked rare, and was served with a variety of tiny vegetables, herbs and a meltingly soft potato cake. Also getting a nod of approval was a whole black bream served with a smooth aubergine purée and more baby vegetables: fennel, in this case. Desserts tend to be simple, such as strawberries with panna cotta. Paintings by local artists are exhibited on the walls. The list of after-dinner drinks, including some top armagnacs and single-malt whiskies, provides the perfect excuse to linger.
Babies and children welcome; children's menu (weekends), high chair. Booking advisable. No-smoking tables. Restaurant available for hire.

Battersea SW11

Niksons
172-174 Northcote Road, SW11 6RE (7228 2285). Clapham Junction rail.
Bar **Open** 5-11pm Mon-Thur; noon-11pm Fri, Sat; noon-10.30pm Sun.
Restaurant **Brunch served** noon-3pm Sun. **Lunch served** noon-3pm Fri, Sat. **Dinner served** 6-10pm Mon-Sat; 7-10pm Sun. **Main courses** £10-£15.50. **Set brunch** (Sun) £15.50 2 courses, £17.50 3 courses. **Service** 12.5%.
Both **Credit** AmEx, DC, MC, V.
Northcote Road is not short of a restaurant or a few dozen, but Niksons, located towards the southern end, is far from the madding crowd. It's a proper neighbourhood restaurant, catering for both drinkers and diners, and is several notches above the chain-dominated standard of the area. The kitchen doesn't aim for culinary fireworks, instead offering a short menu with plenty of flavour appeal. A starter of wild salmon cured with vodka and forest berries was served in beautiful pink rosettes, while poached foie gras and truffle, with jelly and brioche, was a generous-sized, meltingly tender portion. There can be ups and downs: veal 'saltimbocca' showed no signs of the expected sage and parma ham, the veal instead enclosing a sun-dried tomato and some mild cheese. Not an improvement on the original. However, an assorted seafood 'pie' had us singing the chef's praises. This time, the variation on the theme worked, the 'pie' being a thin, crisp crust served atop beautifully cooked prawns, red mullet and tender scallops enveloped in a rich, buttery sauce. Service on our visit was ditzy, with long waits for menus, bread, drinks and food. The place is popular, so book.
Babies and children welcome; high chairs; nappy-changing facilities. Booking advisable. Disabled: toilet. Separate room for parties, seats 30. Tables outdoors (4, pavement). **Map 21 C5.**

★ Ransome's Dock
35-37 Parkgate Road, SW11 4NP (7223 1611). Battersea Park rail/19, 49, 319, 345 bus.
Brunch served noon-3.30pm Sun. **Meals served** noon-11pm Mon-Fri; noon-midnight Sat. **Main courses** £10.50-£20. **Set meal** (noon-5pm Mon-Fri) £14.75 2 courses. **Service** 12.5%. **Credit** AmEx, DC, JCB, MC, V.
Long-established as a prime destination for lovers of good food, Ransome's Dock has a dedicated following. Perched on the edge of a small inlet off the Thames, it's a friendly place, with interested, knowledgeable staff and an unstuffy attitude. Ingredients are well chosen, organic where possible; fish is mostly from sustainable resources. The short, monthly changing menu is the sort that's likely to inspire lengthy bouts of indecision; every dish sounds appealing. We finally settled on a daily special of grilled squid and prawns with chermoula (a spicy, herby Moroccan marinade), with baby salad leaves. The kitchen shows an instinct for flavour combinations, but dishes are kept agreeably simple. Plump, juicy Norfolk smoked eel fillets, served atop a cloud-light buckwheat pancake topped with crème fraîche, had us begging for the recipe. For main courses, small slices of English veal were pan-fried and served with tiny pasta shells with fresh peas, pancetta and mascarpone. A dessert of 'ice-cream and jelly' was a sophisticated version: the jelly flavoured with gooseberry, muscat grape and elderflower; the sphere of vanilla ice-cream rich and creamy. The wine list, overseen by owner Martin Lam, is outstanding for its range – and good value. We can't wait to go back.
Babies and children welcome; high chairs. Booking advisable. No-smoking tables. Tables outdoors (12, terrace). **Map 21 C1.**

Tooting SW17

Rick's Café
122 Mitcham Road, SW17 9NH (8767 5219). Tooting Broadway tube. **Lunch served** 12.30-3pm daily. **Dinner served** 6.30-11pm Mon-Sat; 6.30-10.30pm Sun. **Main courses** £6-£12. **Set lunch** (Sun) £10.95 2 courses. **Service** 12.5%. **Credit** MC, V.
With its rough and ready raw-plaster walls and simple wooden tables, Rick's Café has a fuss-free atmosphere. The menu is short (about eight starters, seven main courses) but appealing, and changes frequently. On our most recent visit, there was a Spanish feel to the dishes, with the likes of salt cod croquettes with aïoli, tuna and tomato empanada, and a Spanish charcuterie plate. Our salt cod croquettes were hot and tender, maintaining the fibrous texture of the fish. Less impressive was a main course of seared tuna with couscous salad, wasabi and soy; though the dish was well conceived, the tuna was tough and stringy, and the couscous soggy. You can't go wrong with sausages, though, and Rick's bangers hail from nearby Merton Abbey (which was once a mill on the River Wandle); they are served with buttery mash, mushrooms and gravy. The kitchen comes into its own for desserts. We fought over the last mouthful of bramble and bramley crumble, with a beautifully crunchy topping and a scoop of quality organic ice-cream. Most of the wines cost under £25, but there are a few pricier examples on the 'bin ends' list should you want to make the most of a night out in hip and happening Tooting.
Babies and children welcome; children's portions; high chairs. Book dinner and weekends. Disabled: toilet.

Waterloo SE1

Oxo Tower Restaurant, Bar & Brasserie
8th Floor, Oxo Tower Wharf, Barge House Street, SE1 9PH (7803 3888/www.harvey nichols.com). Blackfriars or Waterloo tube/rail.
Bar **Open** 11am-11pm Mon-Sat; noon-10.30pm Sun.
Brasserie **Lunch served** noon-3.15pm Mon-Sat; noon-3.45pm Sun. **Dinner served** 5.30-11pm Mon-Sat; 6-10.15pm Sun. **Main courses** £10.25-£17. **Set meal** (lunch, 5.30-6.45pm Mon-Fri) £16.50 2 courses, £21.50 3 courses.
Restaurant **Lunch served** noon-2.30pm Mon-Sat; noon-3pm Sun. **Dinner served** 6-11pm Mon-Sat; 6.30-10pm Sun. **Main courses** £17.50-£26. **Set lunch** £29.50 3 courses.
All **Service** 12.5%. **Credit** AmEx, DC, JCB, MC, V.
There's something of the production line about the Brasserie at Oxo Tower: diners are processed through their allotted time slot in an efficient if rather soulless fashion, with the industrial noise levels a further incentive to eat up and go. The view is impressive; the food mostly delivers; and the place is certainly lively – but if you require a little peace and quiet when you're eating serious food (and paying about £50 a head for a meal with wine), look elsewhere. The modern menu has a strong element of fusion about it: witness crispy marinated sesame seed tofu with cucumber and lotus root salad, followed by roast halibut with fried sweet potato, steamed pak choi, yellow

coconut curry sauce and chilli jam. Dishes look just so, and are punchily flavoured. Sometimes too much so: twice-cooked pork was rather swamped by the accompanying coriander and chilli. In the restaurant, the style is broadly similar, although there are more luxury ingredients (and accordingly high prices): on our visit, a warm salad starter of quail, smoked duck, foie gras and truffle was £13.50; to follow, seared scallops with roast butternut squash and Sri Lankan spiced lentils was £25.50. A cheaper way of seeing what all the fuss is about is to opt for a drink in the busy bar.
Babies and children welcome; children's menu; high chair. Booking advisable. Disabled: lift; toilet. Entertainment: pianist/singer 7.30pm daily (brasserie). Restaurant available for hire. Tables outdoors (27, restaurant terrace; 34, brasserie terrace). **Map 11 N7.**

The People's Palace
Royal Festival Hall, South Bank Centre, SE1 8XX (7928 9999/www.peoplespalace.co.uk). Embankment tube/Charing Cross or Waterloo tube/rail. **Lunch served** noon-3pm Mon-Sat. **dinner served** 5.30-11pm Mon-Sat; 5.30-8pm Sun. **Main courses** £12.50-£17. **Set lunch** £14 2 courses, £18 3 courses. **Set meal** (5.30-7pm Mon-Sat; Sun) £18 2 courses, £23 3 courses. **Service** 12.5%. **Credit** AmEx, DC, MC, V.
With its floor-to-ceiling windows and 1950s-style furnishings inside the landmark Royal Festival Hall, the People's Palace offers one of the best river views in the capital. A shame, then, that the restaurant doesn't have the same pulling power as its building (there aren't, after all, that many dining options on the South Bank), but the atmosphere was staid on a Friday night. The RFH (and thus the restaurant) is closing for 18 months from July 2005, and perhaps this has slowed momentum. Still, there are pleasures to be had from the menu, which co-opts ingredients from cuisines as diverse as Indian, Middle Eastern and Thai. Starters include frogs' legs with garlic mousse, a creamy warm stilton and red onion tart, and sautéed squid (slightly rubbery), which went surprisingly well with 'Bengal gram dhansak', a thick, cumin-flavoured lentil sauce. Mains produced the good (lamb with pumpkin mash and mint pesto) and the not so good (overcooked sea bream with crab mash that was spoiled by a very buttery caper sauce). For afters, sublime iced ginger parfait and roast pear combined well, but the (unadvertised) sponge cake and chocolate were unnecessary. Service was thorough, if charmless. Let's hope the operation finds new direction after the closure.
Babies and children welcome; children's menu; high chair. Booking advisable. Disabled: lift; toilets. No-smoking tables. Separate room for parties, seats 40. **Map 10 M8.**

South East

Blackheath SE3

Chapter Two
43-45 Montpelier Vale, SE3 0TJ (8333 2666/ www.chaptersrestaurants.co.uk). Blackheath rail. **Lunch served** noon-2.30pm Mon-Sat; noon-3pm Sun. **Dinner served** 6.30-10.30pm Mon-Thur; 6.30-11pm Fri, Sat; 6.30-9pm Sun. **Set lunch** (Mon-Sat) £14.50 2 courses, £18.50 3 courses. **Set dinner** (Mon-Thur, Sun) £16.95 2 courses, £19.95 3 courses; (Fri, Sat) £23.50 3 courses. **Service** 12.5%. **Credit** AmEx, DC, JCB, MC, V.
The appointment of Trevor Tobin (a protégé of Hywel Jones) as head chef at Chapter Two in 2004 has brought new life to an old Blackheath fave. There's now a greater precision and consistency in a menu of neatly conceived and confidently executed crowd-pleasers. Most impressive is the pricing, which provides exceptional value for food of this quality. A recent summer lunch offered starters of an evocatively mediterranean raviolo of crab with white onion purée and a splash of earthy bouillabaisse, and a perfectly balanced dish of honey-roast quail with celeriac and apple remoulade and hazelnut vinaigrette. To follow, a meltingly tender piece of poached and roasted

Landes chicken came with runner beans, baby onions and carrot purée, while a silky slab of roast salt cod was successfully paired with braised fennel and leek, pommes lyonnaise and, unusually, chicken jus. Save a space for desserts, such as a faultless vanilla panna cotta with a trio of blueberries (compote, muffin and milkshake) or warm coconut and poppy seed cake with white chocolate anglaise and a salad of raspberries.
Babies and children welcome; high chairs. Booking advisable. Disabled: toilet. No-smoking.

Dulwich SE21

Belair House
Gallery Road, SE21 7AB (8299 9788/ www.belairhouse.co.uk). West Dulwich rail. **Lunch served** noon-3pm daily. **Dinner served** 7-10.30pm Mon-Sat. **Set lunch** (Mon-Sat) £27 3 courses. **Set dinner** £32 3 courses. **Service** 12.5%. **Credit** AmEx, DC, JCB, MC, V.
Sam and Sallyanne Hajaj took over Belair House in 2002, giving a gentle revamp to the elegant 1785 building and introducing occasional guest chefs and music (Monday evening 'soft jazz'). We've had doubts about whether the quality of food has matched the smart, high-ceilinged setting (which can feel soulless when empty) or justified the lofty prices. This year's Sunday lunch caused the worries to resurface. Our waiter was alternately friendly and offhand (cooing over babies, then whisking away a misunderstood wine order with the alarming words, 'cabernet sauvignon is a white grape…'). Food, while rarely poor, wasn't exciting enough to warrant a tag of £27 for three courses. Moroccan- and French-trained chef Zak El Hamdou specialises in pâtés and terrines – two appeared on the list of four starters (the duck, prune and armagnac version had an agreeably gutsy, earthy tang). Lentil and spinach soup was fine, but nothing you couldn't knock up at home. Of the mains, roast beef with Yorkshire pud featured quality slices of rare meat, but the promised caramelised vegetables weren't particularly caramelised. Panache of fish was a nice hunk of red snapper and a thin, uninteresting slither of tuna on 'spring beans' – in fact, a dull mix of rice and pulses. Desserts didn't improve matters; pineapple tatin was OK, but would have benefited from being served warm.
Babies and children welcome; high chairs. Booking essential weekends. Disabled: toilet. Restaurant available for hire. Tables outdoors (10, terrace).

Greenwich SE10

Inside
19 Greenwich South Street, SE10 8NW (8265 5060/www.insiderestaurant.co.uk). Greenwich rail/DLR. **Brunch served** 11am-2.30pm Sat. **Lunch served** noon-2.30pm Wed-Fri; noon-3pm Sun. **Dinner served** 6.30-11pm Tue-Sat. **Main courses** £10.95-£16. **Set meal** (lunch, 6.30-8pm) £14.95 2 courses, £17.95 3 courses. **Credit** MC, V.
Providing a breeze behind Greenwich's gentle rise to stylishness, Inside resembles a less expensive version of the bar-restaurant you'd find in a boutique hotel. Though it's sited on an unremarkable parade of shops, within there's thick white linen, decent art on the walls, aluminium tables and a slow but serious attitude to service. It's posh, but only a bit posh. You are made to feel like a welcome guest, and the ambience is quiet, almost music-free, protective and private. The menu is one of those where you want to try everything. If the scallops on risotto (only three, but so succulent, so pungent) and lean lamb kebab for starters, and the mains of sea bass and trout are a fair indication of the quality, then this place is well worth a trip downriver. Everything smelled wonderful; herbs are used generously and wisely. The trout, which can be monotonous, was tasty and charred round the edges to give those shifts of moisture fish needs. An unmissable brownie and a satisfactory raspberry pavlova sealed the meal perfectly. You can get a good sauvignon blanc for £18 (the waitress's tip; she knew her wine). A top neighbourhood restaurant.

Babies and children welcome. Booking advisable. Disabled: toilet. No-smoking tables.

Greenwich SE10

Inc Bar & Restaurant [NEW]
2004 RUNNER-UP BEST DESIGN
7 College Approach, SE10 9HY (8858 6721/ www.incbar.com). Cutty Sark DLR/177, 180, 286 bus. **Bar Open** 5pm-midnight Mon-Thur, Sun; 5pm-1am Fri, Sat. **Tapas served** 6-10pm daily. **Tapas** £3-£5. *Restaurant* **Meals served** 6-10pm daily. **Main courses** £10-£17. **Service** 12.5%. *Both* Credit MC, V.
Situated near the *Cutty Sark*, next to Greenwich Market, this is a spacious venue housing two bars and a bar-restaurant. Love him or loathe him, Laurence Llewelyn-Bowen has been involved in its design. There are some beautiful touches: the fruity montage of rock slices that front the main Pit Bar, the naughty wallpaper in the seductive Divan Bar, the swirly carpet in the more ancestral Larry's Bar, the pronounced grain of the zebrano wood, the multitude of fireplaces, and the Starck-inspired 'Heaven' and 'Hell' toilets (pink and white for girls, black and steel for boys). Other elements don't work so well, such as the diagonally-laid floor boards (why?), the sketch of LLB, or the display of antique clocks (a little unoriginal for Greenwich). As for the food, highlights on the menu included an unfeasibly light, herby goat's cheese soufflé with a Ramsay-esque 'truffle cappuccino'. Other dishes on our visit were either bland, salty or burnt. Service was enthusiastic, but ultimately poor. It's probably wisest to visit this place for the great-value cocktails and the bar snacks, and to gawp at the surroundings.
Babies and children admitted. Booking advisable. Dress: smart casual; no caps. Entertainment: DJs 9pm-1am Sat. Vegetarian menu.

London Bridge & Borough SE1

Bermondsey Kitchen
194 Bermondsey Street, SE1 3TQ (7407 5719). Bermondsey or Borough tube/London Bridge tube/rail. **Brunch served** 11.30am-3.30pm Sun. **Lunch served** noon-3pm Mon-Fri; 11.30-3.30pm Sat. **Dinner served** 6.30-10.30pm Mon-Sat. **Main courses** £9-£13. **Service** 12.5% for parties of 6 or more. **Credit** DC, MC, V.
A powerful aroma hit us upon entering this bistro – a little bit smoky, a little bit woody. It set our taste buds to full alert in anticipation of what was to follow. We were not disappointed. Starters were superb: cod fritters that were salty and delicious, finished with a creamy dollop of aïoli; and a white anchovy salad with giant capers perfectly mellowed by crunchy leaves and quails' eggs. After such an opening, mains struggled to make an equal impression, but were fine nonetheless. A rich seafood paella and a side dish of spinach (served Catalan-style, with pine nuts and currants) were tasty, but a dish of 'roast suckling pig' was a little bland, and arrived hacked to pieces on the plate. The kitchen, far from being tucked away in the background, is right in the middle of the action, staffed by two black-shirted chefs who sizzle and stir in full view of the simply decorated, wood-and-maroon restaurant. Where restaurant meets bar, there are deep leather sofas for relaxed eating, giving the Bermondsey Kitchen the chameleon-like ability to suit all occasions, whether it be drinking, relaxing or fine dining.
Babies and children welcome; high chairs. Booking advisable. Disabled: toilet. No-smoking tables. Restaurant available for hire.

Cantina Vinopolis
1 Bank End, SE1 9BU (7940 8333/ www.cvrestaurant.co.uk). London Bridge tube/rail. **Bar Open** 10am-11pm Mon-Sat; noon-4pm Sun. *Restaurant* **Lunch served** noon-3pm Mon-Sat; noon-4pm Sun. **Dinner served** 6-10.30pm Mon-Sat. **Main courses** £8.50-£19. **Service** 12.5%. **Credit** AmEx, DC, JCB, MC, V.

The Restaurants

A paean to the grape, Vinopolis houses an interactive wine museum, a shop, a wine bar (natch) and Cantina – an enormous restaurant. The exposed-brick space has tables and chairs set a little too close together for an intimate dinner à deux, but it's fine for a post-work chow with colleagues. Presumably this was why the place was full of suits the night we visited. The regularly changing menu offers six starters, six salads and pasta dishes, and more than ten main courses. While vegetarians might quibble, omnivores are well catered for. Things started well on our visit with an excellent beef carpaccio, generously spread with tapenade, and perfectly married with confit tomatoes, capers, rocket and parmesan. Less impressive was unremarkable parma ham with equally unexciting celeriac remoulade. A ribeye steak with a stonking béarnaise arrived with the recommended side dish of oversized (and not so great) chips. Well-cooked grilled tuna was overwhelmed by (more) tapenade, but was accompanied by an enjoyable and sizeable salad niçoise. There's a disappointing lack of budget wines, but the Tantalus proved a fine Australian red. The finale wasn't so thrilling, a dessert of pear and almond tart with vanilla ice-cream proving too stodgy to finish.
Babies and children admitted. Booking advisable. Disabled: toilet. No-smoking tables. Restaurant available for hire. Separate room for parties, seats 80-100. **Map 11 P8.**

Delfina

50 Bermondsey Street, SE1 3UD (7357 0244/ www.delfina.org.uk). London Bridge tube/rail. **Lunch served** noon-3pm Mon-Fri. **Dinner served** 7-10pm Fri. **Main courses** £9.95-£12.95. **Service** 12.5%. **Credit** AmEx, MC, V.
Opened ten years ago, Delfina is a part-gallery, part-eaterie, and manages to perform both roles with aplomb. Tables are well spaced (we didn't notice the nearest diners were smokers), and the decor is a soothing palette of white, pale green and navy, with tasteful wall art. The relaxed, informal atmosphere is boosted by friendly and informative staff, who help you around Maria Elia's innovative, monthly changing menu. A starter of a huge, tender scallop in pancetta came with a rich white bean aïoli. Our other choice, sardine with polenta, was a substantial (if fiddly to bone) fish on a pile of creamy, chillified cornmeal; it went well with the accompanying tart green tomatoes. A crisp but fruity Rioja from Delfina's own vineyard made a fine accompaniment. Fish of the day was a firm and chunky Australian yellowfin, grilled and served with a slightly vinegary salad. Equally well-cooked barramundi came on a zingy bed of pomelo, peanut and beanshoot salad – but we could have done without the horrid dried shrimps. Dessert (we could only manage one between two) was a dream: a huge chocolate tart topped with a poached pear, and basil and coconut sorbet. In all, Delfina is a treat for the senses.
Babies and children welcome. Booking advisable. Disabled: toilet. No-smoking tables (on request). Separate rooms for parties, seating 12 and 30 (7564 2400). **Map 12 Q9.**

Tower Bridge SE1

Blueprint Café

Design Museum, 28 Shad Thames, SE1 2YD (7378 7031/www.conran.com). Tower Hill tube/Tower Gateway DLR/London Bridge tube/rail/47, 78 bus. **Lunch served** noon-3pm daily. **Dinner served** 6-11pm Mon-Sat. **Main courses** £12.50-£22. **Service** 12.5%. **Credit** AmEx, DC, MC, V.
The fact that the Blueprint has, at least aesthetically, aged better than some of Terence Conran's other restaurants has little to do with what's in it (the decor is plain, almost forgettable) and everything to do with what lies just outside. Location, location, location, goes the mantra, and the Blueprint has it: on the first floor of the Design Museum, with huge windows looking out over the river towards Tower Bridge. Given such a setting, the kitchen can't compete. However, it actually does pretty well, the food as refreshingly unfussy as the descriptions on the plain-speaking menu. Among the starters were razor clams and mojama (salt-cured tuna), two relative curios we'd certainly order again, and a plate of overcooked asparagus, poached egg and parmesan, which we wouldn't. Mains were a mixed bunch: roast middle-white pork and a tender roast loin of rabbit impressed, but the monkfish was overseasoned and the onglet arrived lukewarm. Nonetheless, aside from the dreadful but typical acoustics (Conran restaurants have long mistaken 'noise' for 'atmosphere'), our main complaint was with the consistently slow service. Still, at least there's something to look at while you're waiting.
Babies and children admitted; high chair. Booking advisable dinner. Disabled: toilet (in Design Museum). Restaurant available for hire. Tables outdoors (4, terrace). **Map 12 S9.**

Le Pont de la Tour

Butlers Wharf Building, 36D Shad Thames, Butlers Wharf, SE1 2YE (7403 8403/ www.conran.com). Tower Hill tube/Tower Gateway DLR/London Bridge tube/rail/47, 78 bus. **Bar & grill Lunch served** noon-3pm, **dinner served** 6-11pm daily. **Main courses** £12.50-£19.50. **Set lunch** £13.95 2 courses, £16.95 3 courses.
Restaurant **Lunch served** noon-3pm daily, **dinner served** 6-11pm daily. **Main courses** £12.50-£35. **Set lunch** £29.50 3 courses. **Both Service** 12.5%. **Credit** AmEx, DC, JCB, MC, V.
If you've never been to this Conran restaurant, you could be forgiven for wondering whether you'd walked into the right place. Distinctly lacking the brashness of some of its more talked-about stablemates, Le Pont de la Tour is an oasis of understated decor and seamless service, with every detail informed by a more civilised era in London's dining history. From the Brylcreemed sommelier and encyclopaedic wine list to the mellow piano jazz, no effort has been spared in

keeping noisy bankers and tousled ad execs at the gate. So has the empire finally struck out? Yes and no. Our starters consisted of unimpeachably fresh seafood, flavoured so subtly that we felt they lacked sparkle. Tuna carpaccio with beetroot and sevruga caviar, for instance, needed a sharper tang to lift it. But our main courses left us nearly speechless. Roast venison, as tender and juicy as any we've tried, was served with a 'ventrèche boulangère' – a sort of baked bacon concoction. A bouquet of veal sweetbreads quivered and wiggled atop a potato hash before it melted straight on to the palate. Desserts were hit and miss: tarte tatin was a standard affair, but a simple caramel soufflé with caramel ice-cream (a miracle in monochrome) was unforgettable.
Babies and children welcome; high chairs. Booking advisable. Entertainment: pianist 7pm daily (bar & grill); duos and trios 7pm Thur-Sat. Separate room for parties, seats 20. Tables outdoors (22, terrace). Map 12 S8.

East

Shoreditch N1

Cru Restaurant, Bar & Deli
2-4 Rufus Street, N1 6PE (7729 5252/ www.cru.uk.com). Old Street tube/rail. **Brunch served** noon-3.30pm Sat, Sun. **Lunch served** noon-3pm Tue-Fri. **Dinner served** 6-10.30pm Tue, Wed, Sun; 6-11pm Thur-Sat. **Main courses** £9.50-£15.50. **Set lunch** £10 2 courses, £14 3 courses. **Service** 12.5%. **Credit** AmEx, MC, V.
A real Hoxton place, this. Cru's large space has been put to multipurpose use: there's a bar at the front with comfy chairs; an open kitchen on one side; and tall racks of wine divide the space further. The 'deli' is little more than a few loaves of bread in the window. There's art on the white walls, wooden floors and quite a lot of noise. Food is best described as eclectic Mediterranean, with a welcome lack of fussiness, but, truth be told, the eating didn't live up to the menu on a recent visit. Spanish omelette was a perfectly fine rendition, yet nothing you wouldn't find in a Spanish tapas bar (for much less than £6.50). Grilled sardines tasted old and the accompanying red pepper salsa lacked flavour. Char-grilled steak with watercress, mushroom and onion confit was much better – tender meat cooked as requested, with a confit that had bite. Grilled halibut with mediterranean vegetables failed to rise above the banal, however. The menu seems well thought out and is unafraid to be original (smoked chicken salad with pink grapefruit and balsamic vinegar), to look beyond the Med (lamb brochette on wild rice and sultanas with minted yoghurt), or to offer new takes on classics (chicken breast stuffed with taleggio cheese on chorizo and tarragon bean stew). But nothing really impressed us. Staff were a pleasant and professional lot.
Babies and children welcome: high chairs. Booking advisable. Disabled: toilet. No-smoking tables. Takeaway service (deli). Map 6 R4.

Hoxton Apprentice NEW
16 Hoxton Square, N1 6NT (7739 6022/ www.hoxtonapprentice.com). Old Street tube/rail. **Bar Open** noon-11pm Tue-Sun. *Restaurant* **Lunch served** noon-4pm, **dinner served** 7-10.30pm Tue-Sun. **Main courses** £4.50-£7.50. **Credit** MC, V.
Hoxton Apprentice is not a Fifteen (*see p165*) wannabe, though the charity behind it does share the same aim – to give disadvantaged people a step on to the jobs ladder. Without Jamie Oliver's millions behind it, this place is a curious mixture of good-looking interior, simple menu and surprisingly polished service. Trustee Prue Leith (founder of Leiths School of Food & Wine) was dining here on both our visits; she advises on the menu, which resembles posh gastropub fare. The restaurant was fully booked, yet only half full; limiting customer numbers prevents a new kitchen from becoming overloaded. This allowed our dishes to arrive in good time, carefully prepared.

The Burlington. See p213.

A starter of white bean salad with chorizo and mint was a straightforward assembly, as was a salad of crab, prawns, and grated coconut (though pomegranate seeds didn't complement the other components). Our main courses were serviceable, if not worth a long journey. Pork ribs were served in a sweet marinade of honey, soy and garlic; and a slightly dry but high-quality sirloin steak came with roasted vine tomatoes and mustard hollandaise. Desserts included chocolate tart and vanilla panna cotta. The wine list is brief, but contains good bottles at fair prices. In many ways, the Apprentice is better than Fifteen: it's more democratically priced, you can get a table with relative ease, and it's not done for the cameras.
Babies and children welcome. Booking advisable. Disabled: toilet. No-smoking tables. Separate room for parties, seats 40. Tables outdoors (6, pavement). Map 6 R3.

Wapping E1

★ Wapping Food
Wapping Hydraulic Power Station, Wapping Wall, E1W 3ST (7680 2080). Wapping tube/ Shadwell DLR. *Bar* **Open** noon-11pm Mon-Sat; noon-6pm Sun. **Main courses** £4.50-£7.50. *Restaurant* **Brunch served** 10am-12.30pm Sat, Sun. **Lunch served** noon-3pm daily. **Dinner served** 6.30-11pm Mon-Fri; 7-11pm Sat. **Main courses** £11-£19. **Service** 12.5%. *Both* **Credit** AmEx, DC, MC, V.
For an inner-city restaurant, the setting really can't be bettered: Wapping Food is housed in what was a hydraulic pumping station, and is surrounded by a gallery space. Diners are dwarfed by the dimensions, but the friendliness of the staff means there's no chance of urban alienation here. The daily changing menu is a mix of easy-going (selection of Spanish charcuterie, caperberries and olives, or buffalo mozzarella, roast peppers, mixed leaves and pine nuts) and slightly more involved Modern European cooking (organic leg of lamb with warm salad of artichoke, beet leaves and Agen prunes). Not everything worked on the summer evening of our most recent visit. A couple of dishes – seared scallops with piquillo peppers, morcilla and preserved lemon beurre blanc; and mushroom duxelle tartlet, sautéed morels and golden beetroot with baked garlic – just didn't hang together, although the individual ingredients were nice enough. Better was an assembly of smoked finnan brandade with crostini, baby capers, shallots and parsley. As long as the food is at least this good (and it's frequently better), Wapping Food is a must-visit destination – there's really nowhere else like it in London.
Babies and children welcome; high chairs. Disabled: toilet. Entertainment: performances and exhibitions (phone for details). Tables outdoors (20, garden).

North

Camden Town & Chalk Farm NW1

★ Odette's
130 Regent's Park Road, NW1 8XL (7586 5486). Chalk Farm tube/31, 168 bus. **Lunch served** 12.30-2.30pm daily. **Dinner served** 7-11pm Mon-Sat. **Main courses** £14-£23. **Set lunch** £16.50 2 courses, £18 3 courses. **Service** 12.5%. **Credit** AmEx, JCB, MC, V.
Expect to find yourself in a reflective mood as you take your seat amid what must be one of London's finest collections of gilded mirrors. This USP of Odette's cosy decor, along with its elegantly simple tables covered in starched white cloths, has proved a successful formula for many years now and, despite a refurb in 2003, the management has made no attempt to change it. Quite right too: this Primrose Hill bolt-hole always has been, still is and looks set to remain a charming, shamelessly romantic place in which to enjoy some decent bistro cooking. Prices are set to the meridian of NW1, which means you may end up shelling out £25 for a main course of roasted tronchon of turbot with tartare sauce and deep-fried parsley, say – but it's a rare dish that disappoints. A starter of risotto of dorset crab with lobster coral butter, chilli, tomato-scented olive oil and basil is typical of the light, uncluttered house style, while sturdier mains, such as pot-roasted milk-fed loin of veal, sticky with its own pan juices, provide some clout. Puddings are sinful, service is sophisticated and wines are plentiful.
Babies and children admitted. Booking essential. Restaurant available for hire. Separate rooms for parties, seating 8 and 30. Tables outdoors (3, conservatory). Map 27 A1.

Islington N1

Lola's
The Mall Building, 359 Upper Street, N1 0PD (7359 1932/www.lolas.co.uk). Angel tube. **Lunch served** noon-2.30pm Mon-Fri; noon-3pm Sat; noon-4pm Sun. **Dinner served** 6-11pm Mon-Sat; 7-10pm Sun. **Main courses** £12.50-£18.50. **Set meal** (6-11pm Mon-Thur; 6-7, 10-11pm Fri, Sat) £12.50 2 courses, £15.50 3 courses. **Service** 12.5% for parties of 5 or more. **Credit** AmEx, DC, JCB, MC, V.
Lola's is an oasis of serenity in the heart of the Angel. Its feng shui-ed appearance (high ceiling, parquet flooring, tan suede banquettes, large picture window) is matched by a dedication to the clever combining of flavours from Brian Sparks (who became head chef in spring 2004), and by discreet, friendly service from the staff. A pre-starter of tomato and feta consommé was sweet and tangy, with just a hint of sharpness. A tuna

tartare starter contained melt-in-the-mouth fish and a fine combination of salty caviar and tart apple slices; another dish of pear, roquefort and almond salad was sweet but well matched. Other less fruity starters could include the likes of duck three ways with turnip remoulade, or grilled langoustines and shellfish 'brûlée'. A main of Welsh lamb with confit of shoulder, served with stuffed piquillo pepper, was first class: a chunky, pink, moist dome of perfect meat, with robust confit and vivid pepper. Stuffed darne of sea bass with salmon tortellini and braised lettuce was equally successful, if less dramatic. This was followed by a tiny pre-pudding cupful of the best apple crumble ever, and an irresistible passion fruit brûlée with white chocolate mousse.
Babies and children welcome; high chairs.
Booking advisable. Dress: smart casual. Separate room for parties, seats 16. **Map 5 O2**.

Seraphin NEW

341-342 Upper Street, N1 0PB (7359 7374/ www.seraphin-n1.com). Angel tube/Highbury & Islington tube/rail. **Breakfast/lunch served** 10am-4pm Mon-Sat. **Dinner served** 5.30-11pm Mon-Thur; 5.30pm-midnight Fri, Sat. **Meals served** 12.30-9pm Sun. **Main courses** £10-£18.50. **Set lunch** £10 2 courses incl coffee. **Set dinner** £15 2 courses incl glass of wine. **Service** 12.5%. **Credit** AmEx, DC, MC, V.
Our visit to this light, fresh, almost minimalist new restaurant – with sweeping bar that added an art deco faux-Hollywood touch – was enjoyable, mainly due to the sunniest waitress, Constance, who sorted out the glitches from the kitchen with unfailing good humour. There's a shortish, formula-type lunch menu; if you choose any starter and main, the price comes down to £10.95 (including coffee) – and £2 reduction on a dessert. The red pepper soup had a mere hint of the supposed bacon; soggy croûtons lurked beneath the surface. A 'classic' caesar salad arrived with chicken (not ordered) and contained undercooked croûtons and bacon bits rather than anchovies: all on a tasteless heap of shredded lettuce. A minuscule square of mahi mahi fish was perfectly cooked, though the bed of swiss chard looked suspiciously like spinach. Linguine with tiger prawns proved to be a great choice, deliciously simple. Raspberry crème brûlée was well executed (though took an unconscionable time to arrive). The pricey wine list had little choice by the glass; an irritation at lunchtime. The chef's real talent, it seems, lies in his dinner menu (obviously the result of a creative writing course), which features incredible combinations of ingredients in each dish. An entertaining place, in spite of patchy food, but only if time is not an issue.
Babies and children welcome: children's portions; high chairs. Booking advisable. Disabled: toilet. Entertainment: live jazz (call for dates). No-smoking tables. Separate room for parties, seats 35. Tables outdoors (11, patio). Takeaway service. Vegan dishes. **Map 5 O2**.

North West
West Hampstead NW6

Walnut

280 West End Lane, NW6 1LJ (7794 7772/ www.walnutwalnut.com). West Hampstead tube/rail. **Dinner served** 6.30-11pm Tue-Sun. **Main courses** £9.50-£12.95. **Credit** DC, JCB, MC, V.
As you enter this likeable local (sited by a small green at the top of West End Lane), the semi-open kitchen is above and in front of you, presiding over the restaurant from a kind of white-walled mezzanine. The dining space, in mellow white and tan shades, is pleasantly cool, although minimalist fittings mean it can get noisy at busy times. The menu is a suitably eclectic modern mix. The daily specials are worth investigating; on our last visit, a delicious crayfish salad featured loads of fresh, finely flavoured seafood amid bright, varied greens and radish. A starter from the main menu, grilled chorizo with pine nuts, and endive and watercress

salad, was also enjoyable, although could have been more generously supplied with nuts. Original takes on trad-British dishes feature strongly, as in nicely tangy wild boar and apple sausages with mash, and port and onion gravy, and an excellent vegetarian dish of intriguingly herby aubergine and sorrel sausages with mash and mustard sauce. Salmon and cod fish cakes were equally moreish, packed with good fish and served with a delicate lemon and thyme mayonnaise. Desserts are fairly traditional, and there's a functional but generously priced wine list. Friendly staff add to the comfy atmosphere, and help draw in the regulars.
Babies and children welcome; children's portions; high chairs. Booking advisable weekends. No-smoking tables. Restaurant available for hire. Separate room for parties, seats 20. Tables outdoors (4, pavement). Vegetarian menu. **Map 28 A2**.

Outer London
Kew, Surrey

★ The Glasshouse

14 Station Parade, Kew, Surrey TW9 3PZ (8940 6777). Kew Gardens tube/rail. **Lunch served** noon-2.30pm Mon-Sat; 12.30-2.45pm Sun. **Dinner served** 7-10.30pm Mon-Thur; 6.30-10.30pm Fri, Sat; 7.30-10pm Sun. **Set lunch** £17.50 3 courses; (Sun) £25 3 courses. **Set dinner** £32.50 3 courses; (tasting menu) £45. **Service** 12.5%. **Credit** AmEx, MC, V.
Two sides of this wedge-shaped dining room are glass. On warm days, the windows at the sharp, street end are thrown open and light floods on to the white and honey walls, making everyone look ten years younger. On the whole, the diners are old enough to appreciate this benefit almost as much as they do the warm atmosphere and great food. The place is packed and everyone seems delighted to be here, including the effective and unfussy staff. Unusually for such a busy room, the volume never gets too loud, making the venue surprisingly intimate. You couldn't ask more of the warm squab pigeon salad (topped with an egg that was flavoured with truffles before being deep-fried in yolk-yellow batter: delicious), or the thick slices of home-cured bresaola. Other dishes were substantial and pretty: pink lamb with saffron sauce could only be described as very appetising (as was the accompanying confit lamb croquette – like an upmarket fish finger); and the two pieces of pork fillet looked and tasted appealing, with a prune and bacon roll between them, stacked on a fine apple tart. To finish, we sampled a perfect selection of cheeses (described with verve by an enthusiastic waiter), and an exceptional apricot and almond tart. A treat.
Babies and children welcome (lunch); children's menu; high chairs. Booking essential. No smoking.

Twickenham, Middlesex

The A Bar & Restaurant NEW

93 Colne Road, Twickenham, Middx TW2 6QL (8898 8000). Twickenham or Strawberry Hill rail. **Breakfast served** 10am-noon Sun. **Lunch served** noon-5pm Sun. **Dinner served** 7-10pm daily. **Tapas served** noon-10pm Tue-Thur. **Main courses** £11.95-£15.95. **Tapas** £4.50-£7.95. **Set meal** (Sun) £12.95 2 courses, £15.95. **Service** 10% for parties of 6 or more. **Credit** AmEx, DC, MC, V.
The A Bar & Restaurant lives up to its name – everything on our recent visit was A-grade. Situated behind Twickenham Green, the former Duke's Head boozer is now a smart restaurant with wooden floors, leather upholstery and vivid Warholesque pop art on the walls. Confusingly also known locally as Austin's, the place has a buzzy atmosphere; on our visit, well-heeled locals were knocking back wines and beers with obvious enjoyment. Head chef Michael Jackson's self-assured cooking is infused with clean, uncluttered flavours and vibrant Mediterranean colours. We loved everything we tried: fresh breads with tangy, herby olives and sharp, creamy aïoli; scallops with zingy mango, lime,

chilli and mint salsa; perfectly pink, pesto-topped tuna with warm niçoise salad; full-flavoured carrot and orange soup; and portobello mushroom stuffed with cream cheese and spinach (still beautifully emerald-green in colour), baked in a filo pastry parcel and dolloped with roasted tomato and red pepper sauces. Service from the mature waiting staff was very knowledgeable. Not merely a restaurant with beer pumps, then, but a true local.
Booking advisable. Dress: smart casual; no hats. Tables outdoors (5, garden).

Brula
2004 RUNNER-UP BEST LOCAL RESTAURANT
43 Crown Road, Twickenham, Middx TW1 3EJ (8892 0602/www.brulabistrot.co.uk). St Margaret's rail. **Lunch served** 12.30-2.30pm, **dinner served** 7-10.30pm Mon-Sun. **Main courses** £9.50-£13.75. **Set lunch** £10 2 courses, £12 3 courses. **Credit** MC, V.
This long-standing establishment is the epitome of a fine neighbourhood restaurant. Intimate and homely, it dishes up tasty fare to a loyal local clientele (there wasn't a seat free on a Tuesday night). Rough cream walls, stained-glass windows and pew seating provide a French bistro feel, as does the shortish, weekly changing menu (foie gras and snails both appear). More earthy tastes are also offered, such as braised collar of ham with carrots, leeks and parsley sauce: a fine combo of melting meat and stew-like vegetables. Desserts – perhaps banana and ginger frangipane with crème fraîche, crème brûlée or good cheese – are enjoyable. A few fluffs (feeble frites, overcooked sea bass served with a beetroot and anchovy salad that didn't come off) meant that the cooking wasn't quite up to the high standards of our past experience, but perhaps the kitchen was overstretched by the demands of a full house. The set-price lunch menu (£10 for two courses, £12 for three) is a real bargain, and there's no faulting the decent wine list, genuinely friendly service and overall feeling of bonhomie.
Babies and children welcome. Booking advisable. Separate room for parties, seats 10. Tables outdoors (3, pavement).

★ McClements

2 Whitton Road, Twickenham, Middx TW1 1BJ (8744 9610). Twickenham or Whitton rail/ 33, 110, 267, 281, 290, 490, 904, 942 bus. **Lunch served** noon-2pm daily. **Dinner served** 6.30-10pm Mon-Thur; 6.30-10.30pm Fri, Sat. **Set lunch** £19.50 3 courses. **Set dinner** (Mon-Thur) £35 3 courses incl wine. **Set meal** £48 3 courses, £60 8 courses. **Service** 10%. **Credit** AmEx, MC, V.
On a nondescript street next to Twickenham station, McClement's unassuming frontage gives little hint of the culinary delights that lie within. It won a Michelin star in 2004, and prices have risen to similarly stellar heights: the three-course set dinner is now a sobering £48. This buys you masterful combinations of flavours and textures, artistically styled under chef Daniel Woodhouse. For starters: mousse-like lobster ravioli with a delicate mini black pudding and solitary lobster claw in a rich, foamy sauce; and carrot in multiple forms - jelly, pickled strips and oven-baked wholes. Clever, but very carroty. For mains: meltingly tender venison (a tad rare for our taste) well matched with intense, meaty girolles and a bulb of creamy roast garlic; and succulent john dory, accompanied by fennel ragout, fennel salad and potato cake in fish velouté. Desserts were the masterstroke, though. Rhubarb wrapped around a thick lemon posset looked too pretty to eat with its spear of white meringue – but we forced ourselves. Even better was almond pudding in a pool of malted milk with a slippery pistachio mousse and honeycomb tuile. Bonuses come in the form of fabulous bread, an impressive wine list and deft, friendly service. The space is smartly serene, in shades of chocolate and cream, with soft lighting. McClement's can be quiet early in the week, but you'll need to book come the weekend.
Babies and children welcome. Booking advisable. Disabled: toilet. No-smoking.

North African

For North African read Moroccan (in London, Tunisian and Algerian cooking doesn't get much of a look in). As a cuisine, it's practical and unfussy. The overriding principle is to throw all the ingredients into a pot then leave to cook slowly.

Prime exhibit is the signature dish of tagine (also spelled tajine), which is essentially a stew of meat (usually lamb or chicken) and vegetables slow-cooked over a charcoal fire. Olives, tangy preserved lemon, almonds or prunes are typically added for flavouring. The name tagine describes both the food and the pot it's cooked in – a shallow earthenware dish with a conical lid that traps the rising steam and stops the stew from drying out. The other defining local staple is couscous, which again is the name of the basic ingredient (granules of processed durum wheat) and of the dish; the couscous is slow-cooked and accompanied with a rich meat or vegetable stew.

The standard Moroccan menu rarely strays much beyond these two items, except for perhaps some grilled brochettes (kebabs). Starters take the form of hot and cold small dishes, called salads, but which are more usually spiced purées of carrots, peppers, aubergine, tomatoes and the like. Briouettes are little envelopes of paper-thin ouarka (filo) pastry wrapped around ground meat, rice or cheese and deep-fried. Bastilla is ouarka pastry filled with a mixture of shredded pigeon (often replaced by chicken), almonds and spices.

Moroccan wine can be very drinkable, especially the vin gris, a type of dry rosé produced in the region around Meknes. Meals are finished off with mint tea and pastries, and nine times out of ten the soundtrack seems to be a Maghrebi chillout CD called *Arabesque*, put together by the guys at Momo (*see below*).

Central

Leicester Square WC2

Souk
27 Litchfield Street, WC2H 9NJ (7240 1796/ www.soukrestaurant.net). Leicester Square tube. **Meals served** noon-11.30pm Mon-Thur, Sun; noon-2am Fri, Sat. **Main courses** £7.95-£8.95. **Set meal** £15 3 courses incl mint tea. **Service** 12.5%. **Credit** AmEx, MC, V.
Souk's popularity – and it is popular, particularly with celebratory groups – has nothing to do with the food. In fact, judged on the food alone, Souk is a disaster. We ordered two starters, a grilled aubergine and potato salad, and a warm roast pepper and tomato salad, and it's no exaggeration to say that we couldn't tell the two apart. The lamb in a lamb tagine was hard and crusty, and any taste was smothered under a blizzard of icing sugar. The couscous royal was at least edible. So what's the appeal? Set dressing. Souk's interior is pure oriental fantasy: a ground-floor dining room filled with silky cushions and filigree lanterns plus a troglodytic brick-lined basement with a ceiling draped in black sheets, kilim-covered benches and a bazaar's worth of trinketry. North African staff sport flowing jellabas, there's belly dancing several evenings a week and the air is heavy with the sweet scent from glass-bowled waterpipes. We admit that it's all fabulous and fun in its own

hokey way – if you just concentrate on the booze rather than the food then you'll be all right. *Babies and children admitted. Booking essential. Entertainment: belly dancing 11pm Fri, Sat. Separate room for parties, seats 40. Vegetarian menu.* **Map 18 K6**.

Marylebone W1

★ Original Tagines
7A Dorset Street, W1H 3SE (7935 1545/ www.originaltagines.com). Baker Street tube. **Lunch served** noon-3pm, **dinner served** 6-11pm daily. **Main courses** £9.50-£11.95. **Set lunch** £10 2 courses. **Credit** MC, V.
One of London's very best Moroccan restaurants, Original Tagines eschews the gimmicky kasbah decoration so popular elsewhere and instead concentrates on what goes on in the kitchen. The menu is firmly traditional (couscous and tagines), but the cooking and presentation are very much contemporary. Instead of the mounded food common elsewhere, portions are modest. A couscous lamb kedra was a lovely light thing with the meat balanced on a bed of semolina grains, topped with caramelised onions and raisins and a dusting of icing sugar. This means that you can indulge in some starters (the menu includes varieties of briouettes, salads and a few rarities such as sautéed kidneys) and desserts (try the rice pudding with orange blossom) and not finish the meal feeling like an overstuffed boa constrictor. Original Tagines is also notable among North African restaurants in that it recognises the existence of vegetarians. There's a reasonable, almost exclusively Moroccan wine list with wallet-friendly prices, and we appreciate the footnote to the menu reminding customers that 'Gratuities [are] to be awarded for good service only.' *Babies and children welcome; high chairs. Booking advisable. Tables outdoors (5, pavement). Takeaway service.* **Map 3 G5**.

Mayfair W1

★ Momo
25 Heddon Street, W1B 4BH (7434 4040/ www.momoresto.com). Piccadilly Circus tube. **Lunch served** noon-2.30pm Mon-Sat. **Dinner served** 7-11pm Mon-Sat; 7-10.30pm Sun. **Main courses** £14.50-£19.50. **Set lunch** £17 2 courses, £20 3 courses. **Service** 12.5%. **Credit** AmEx, DC, MC, V.
Sketch continues to hog the limelight, but restaurateur Mourad Mazouz's earlier London venture, Momo, is still a real winner. It's simply gorgeous, decked out like Rick's Café Américain (of *Casablanca* fame) with wooden-screen windows, hanging brass lanterns and plenty of large tables filled every night with chatty action and a smattering of exotic-looking types including imposing Nubians and chic North Africans. If the staff, who are kitted out in custom-designed kasbah pop art T-shirts, appear to be chosen more for their looks than their attentiveness to customers, well, that only adds to the glamour. The menu supplements the standard tagines and couscous of Morocco with dishes such as baked cod, duck breast and sea bass. It's all very good if not quite as exceptional as you might hope. Not that this seems to bother anyone. The true allure of Momo is that, despite it being ten years ago that Madge opted to celebrate her birthday here, it still feels like the place to be. It's got style, it's got class, it's got attitude. It's Maroc 'n' roll, man. *Babies and children welcome. Booking essential. Separate room for parties, seats 80. Tables outdoors (7, terrace).* **Map 9 J7**.

Mô Tea Room
23 Heddon Street, W1B 4BH (7434 4040/ www.momoresto.com). Piccadilly Circus tube. **Open** noon-11pm Mon-Wed; noon-midnight Thur-Sat. **Meals served** noon-10.15pm Mon-Wed; noon-11.15 Thur-Sat. **Main courses** £3.50-£5. **Service** 12.5%. **Credit** AmEx, DC, MC, V.
We've long loved the Tea Room, little sister to Momo next door. It's a glitzy, even glamorous place hung with so many lanterns and chandeliers that it seems like a Maghrebi version of John Lewis's light fittings department. In addition to the lanterns are kaftans, raffia bags, T-shirts, jewellery, antiques and books, all of which are for sale. There's been a little smartening up in the past year, including moving the serving area to create more space and buying in new, uniform (but still Moroccan) furniture. It's still exotic and seductive – until you come to eat. Gone are the wonderful spicy sandwiches of old, replaced by a selection of meze, plus three wraps. We were wholly underwhelmed. The houmous had the consistency of mashed potato, goat's cheese was goat's cheese and just that, and a meat-filled pancake was dry and so small it wouldn't have satisfied a gnat. (The mixed peppers were fine, however.) Added to which the 'fresh' orange juice came from a carton. Somebody has taken their eye off the ball. One hopes the management will get its act together because this used to be such a great place for lunch. As it stands, it's only of interest to anyone contemplating buying a bit of fancy brass to hang from the ceiling. *Babies and children admitted. Bookings not accepted. Tables outdoors (3, terrace).* **Map 17 J7**.

Oxford Street W1

Momo at Selfridges NEW
2nd Floor, Selfridges, 400 Oxford Street, W1C 1JT (7318 3620/www.momoresto.com). Bond Street tube. **Breakfast served** 10am-noon, **lunch served** noon-3pm, **meze served** 3-7pm Mon-Sat. **Main courses** £8-£17.50. **Set meal** £17 2 courses, £20 3 courses. **Service** 12.5%. **Credit** AmEx, DC, JCB, MC, V.
How absurd is this: a faux-kasbah complete with sheesha room (sealed and air-conditioned to prevent straying smoke) inside an Oxford Street department store? The answer is 'very'. Even stranger is that, instead of going for the type of snacks offered at sibling venue the Mô Tea Room, this venture is a mini Momo. So expect fussy taster dishes such as the Momo kemia (kemia means tapas in Moroccan) – an artful presentation of two

The Restaurants

filled savoury pastries, some mashed aubergine and a mixed pepper salad – very pretty but unexceptional in taste and not much food for £8.50. Otherwise, it's full-blown fare such as merguez couscous with lamb brochettes or medallions of rump lamb on sweet potato mash, which again look splendid but fail to measure up taste-wise. Is this really the kind of food anyone wants to eat in a concourse surrounded by shoppers? We do, however, love the cocktail bar, a glamorous four-square affair with plenty of bar counter seating. Our advice: forgo the heavy dishes and pull up a stool, order a cocktail and gorge on spiced olives.

Babies and children welcome; children's menu. Bookings not accepted Sat. Disabled: toilet. No-smoking. Map 9 G6.

Piccadilly SW1

Saharaween NEW

3 Panton Street, SW1Y 4DL (7930 2777). Leicester Square or Piccadilly Circus tube. **Meals served** noon-1am daily. **Main courses** £7-£9. **Unlicensed**. **Corkage** no charge. **Credit** MC, V.

The grisly surrounds of Leicester Square are the last place you'd expect to find an enchanting restaurant, but this new Moroccan-and-beyond eaterie was instantly bewitching. The interior of billowing drapes, colourful cushions and carved brass table-tops – a common aesthetic in North African restaurants – is attractively realised. In the basement, low seats and pillows amass to create a floor-level lounge, a comfortable and attractive den for shisha pipe smoking (a booze licence has been applied for). Food and drinks are crafted with the same careful-eyed expertise. From the first sip of a forest fruit blend to the last sip of a sweet mint tea, our meal was close to flawless. A meze bowl of various dipping delights was just as it should be. Chicken tagine with olives and preserved lemon was a superb rendition of the classic flavour combination, and a selection of grilled meats – chicken, skewered lamb and an unusually good merguez sausage – was also delicious, served with a light vegetable stew and perfect couscous. And it's good value too.

Babies and children welcome. No-smoking tables. Separate room for parties, seats 40. Tables outdoors (2, pavement). Takeaway service. Map 17 K7.

West

Bayswater W2

Couscous Café

7 Porchester Gardens, W2 4DB (7727 6597). Bayswater tube. **Meals served** noon-11pm Mon-Thur, Sun; noon-midnight Fri, Sat. **Main courses** £9.95-£15.95. **Service** 10%. **Credit** AmEx, MC, V.

Queensway is more noted for its Lebanese restaurants (and even more so for its Chinese ones), but just a few steps off the main drag, down the side of Whiteley's, the Couscous Café has been quietly winning over fans to the North African eating experience. It's a humble little place (tiled floor, tiled tables, low bamboo ceiling, lots of knick-knacks and rugs – a sort of tiki hut in the souk) driven by the personality of the owner, who does the rounds of the handful of tables explaining the menu and expounding the delights of his Moroccan wine list, about which he's hugely knowledgeable. Not that the menu needs much explanation. Starters are limited to harira (a vegetable soup enriched with lamb stock and lentils), borek (spicy minced meat in filo pastry on a bed of chopped red cabbage, shallots and olives) or a meze selection to share (for two or four people). Mains are tagines or couscous. The latter comes as a DIY assemblage with a dish of couscous, a bowl of chickpeas and raisins, and a pot of meat, potatoes, courgettes and carrots in a broth. Mix to taste, then consume.

Babies and children admitted. Booking essential. Tables outdoors (2, pavement). Vegetarian menu. Map 7 C6.

Hammersmith W6

Azou

375 King Street, W6 9NJ (8563 7266). Stamford Brook tube. **Lunch served** noon-2.30pm Mon-Fri. **Dinner served** 6-11pm daily. **Main courses** £7-£13. **Set meal** £12.50-£15 3 courses. **Service** 12.5%. **Credit** MC, V.

A casual restaurant with a café-like ambience, Azou brings a splash of brightness to an otherwise dour stretch of King Street. It's a pleasant place – bright (brash even), with dusky ochre walls the colour of Marrakech, and a whitewashed ceiling billowing with stripy cloth – although it might be improved by blinds to cut out the traffic thundering by on the other side of the picture windows. Food is no-frills Moroccan served in excessively large portions. You really don't need starters here, although we're often tempted by the chakchouka, a Moroccan salad of tomato, peppers and onions, and the brik, a scrunched brittle pastry filled with tuna, potato and runny egg, which tastes pleasingly like old-fashioned fish cakes. Mains are a choice between couscous or tagine; of those we tried, dishes with lamb were good but the chicken was a little dry. Two corner areas at the rear are nicely padded with floor cushions, which is presumably where overstuffed eaters collapse until they're ready to attempt the journey home. You could do worse than while away the time with a sheesha (waterpipe) – £5 here compared to the £9 or £10 almost everywhere else.

Babies and children admitted. Booking advisable. Entertainment: belly dancing (phone for details). Takeaway service. Vegetarian menu. Map 20 A4.

Fez

58 Fulham Palace Road, W6 9BH (8563 8687). Hammersmith tube. **Meals served** noon-midnight daily. **Main courses** £6.50-£9.95. **Set lunch** £6.50-£8.95 2 courses. **Set meal** £12.95 2 courses. **Meze** £22.95-£24.95. **Credit** MC, V.

There are two types of North African restaurants in London: the ones with the striped rugs on the walls and sequinned throw cushions everywhere, and the ones that do good food. Fez is a bit of both. It's a small place crammed with things with tassles and tarnished ethnicky glitter and glitz, all of which makes it a big hit with parties and anyone who's ever travelled with a Lonely Planet guide or bought a Claude Challe CD. In fact, it can get so busy that reservations are a must towards the end of the week. However, apart from some

Momo at Selfridges. See p223.

The owner of this unpretentious restaurant (Adam is his son) is from Djerba in Tunisia, so dishes are Tunisian in origin. The cooking favours liberal use of harissa and tomato purée instead of meat stock, and there's also a bias towards seafood rather than lamb and chicken. It gets packed, especially at the weekend. The choice is extensive, and we're happy to report that we've never had a bad dish. A major massacre of marine life resulted in the mound of garlic sautéed prawns masquerading as a starter, while the brik au thon (a brittle pastry filled with tuna, potato and egg) came slotted into a scored lemon. Fish is fresh: the mullet was a monster served with a lovely tessia garnish of chopped peppers and egg in an edible pastry cup. Stuffed squid had a greenish tinge, which made them look like super-sized olives, but they tasted wonderful. For dessert, the own-made almond tart is great. Adam's is also a child-friendly place; the owner took our three-year-old off into the kitchen for a look around, giving mum and dad a bit of space to actually enjoy the food (instead of just picking it up off the floor).
Babies and children welcome. Book weekends. Separate room for parties, seats 24. Vegetarian menu. Map 20 A1.

South West
Gloucester Road SW7

Pasha
1 Gloucester Road, SW7 4PP (7589 7969/ www.pasha-restaurant.co.uk). Gloucester Road tube/49 bus. **Lunch served** noon-3pm Mon-Sat. **Dinner served** 6-11pm Mon-Sat; 6.30-10pm Sun. **Main courses** £9.75-£16.75. **Service** 15%. **Credit** AmEx, DC, MC, V.
Pasha takes North African cuisine as its staring point, but then heads off in intriguing and unusual directions. The humble borek is transformed by stuffing with mushroom and goat's cheese and glazing with pomegranate juice before being served on a bed of chopped walnuts and figs, while spicy harissa is added to mayonnaise to create a sharp accompaniment to crispy peppered squid. This is sophisticated stuff that is to normal Moroccan cuisine what smoked salmon and gratin dauphinoise is to fish and chips. Indulge in delights such as the brochette d'Essaouira (named after the Moroccan Atlantic coast fishing port), in which hunks of tuna, swordfish, salmon and tiger prawns marinated in chermoula are skewered together and laid upon a speed bump of chopped peppers spiked with bits of marinated lemon. (Never mind that the fish for which Essaouira is renowned is the sardine.) The restaurant itself is a classy affair with pale yellow and mustard striped plaster walls, and carved stucco door frames seductively lit by flickering tea candles. Our only complaint would be with the staff. Their supercilious manner and lack of proficiency did not, once again, encourage us to pay the 'optional' 15 (!) per cent service charge.
Babies and children admitted. Book weekends. Separate room for parties, seats 18. Vegetarian menu. Map 7 C9.

South
Clapham SW4

Kasbah
73 Venn Street, SW4 0BD (7498 3622). Clapham Common tube. **Dinner served** 4-11.30pm Mon-Sat; 3-10.30pm Sun. **Main courses** £8.75-£12.95. **Credit** MC, V.
On a grey Saturday evening Kasbah was aglow with candles and subtle lighting – a much more enticing prospect than on a previous daylight visit, when the wooden tables and plain walls looked bare and slightly shabby. The place soon filled up with cheery diners, many on first-name terms with the friendly staff. Moroccan beer was the choice of many, but our ubiquitous Meknes rosé, Gris de Guerrouane, was as delicious as ever. Not so the food. Too many rules were broken. A spicy aubergine dish was served very hot, when it cried out to be eaten lukewarm; grilled prawns were tired and tough. Seafood tagine featured the same

geographically misplaced Lebanese meze as starters (soggy stuffed vine leaves and so forth), the Moroccan main dishes are solid to excellent. Choose between a couple of tagines and half a dozen types of couscous. The latter are zesty affairs, enlivened with raisins, browned onions and cinnamon, and heaped in deep white plates. Fez is a favourite with the native staff at the Moroccan tourist office, who we suppose must know a thing or two about North African cuisine.
Babies and children admitted. Booking advisable. Entertainment: belly dancers Fri, Sat (phone for details). Takeaway service; delivery service (orders over £25 only). Map 20 C4.

Ladbroke Grove W10

★ Moroccan Tagine
95 Golborne Road, W10 5NL (8968 8055). Ladbroke Grove or Westbourne Park tube/23 bus. **Meals served** noon-11pm daily. **Main courses** £5.50-£7.90. **Credit** MC, V.
The prices have crept up a little with the arrival of fancy new laminated menus, but otherwise this remains a no-frills, Moroccan caff, well sited among the halal butchers and cumin-scented grocer shops on Golborne Road, London's hunting ground for

all things North African. Belying the humble setting, the food is superb – couscous, tagines and grilled meats – all prepared by genial, bearded Hassan, a Berber from the mountains of Morocco. The olives that come as a complimentary starter are particularly good; they're imported and then specially marinated to Hassan's own recipe. You can buy a little bag of them to take away. Beyond that, anything with merguez – meaty, fierce little sausages – is recommended, or go for the grilled sardines served with rice and salad. No alcohol is served, but for a hit of something potent after you've eaten we suggest nipping down the street to the Portuguese Oporto café for a bica (espresso) and a custard tart.
Babies and children welcome. Book weekends. No-smoking tables. Tables outdoors (4, pavement). Takeaway service. Map 19 B1.

Shepherd's Bush W12

Adam's Café
77 Askew Road, W12 9AH (8743 0572). Hammersmith tube then 266 bus. **Dinner served** 7-11pm Mon-Sat. **Set dinner** £10.50 1 course incl mint tea/coffee, £13.50 2 courses, £15.50 3 courses. **Service** 10%. **Credit** AmEx, MC, V.

lifeless prawns, mussels and salmon in a overly tomato puréed sauce. Couscous royale looked promising – with a chunk of tender lamb, good grilled merguez and chicken drumstick– but the couscous was uncharacteristically drenched with butter and there was no separate watery stew to moisten it or take away the aroma. Good on atmosphere, but the cooking needs more rigour. *Babies and children welcome. Booking advisable Fri, Sat. Separate room for parties, seats 26. Tables outdoors (2, pavement). Vegetarian menu.* **Map 22 A2**.

North
Finsbury Park N4

★ Yamina
192 Stroud Green Road, N4 3RN (7263 6161). Finsbury Park tube/rail then 210, W3, W7 bus. **Dinner served** 6-11.30pm Tue-Fri. **Meals served** noon-11.30pm Sat, Sun. **Main courses** £4.50-£8. **Service** 10%. **Credit** MC, V.

Menu

See also the menus in **Middle Eastern** and **Turkish**.

Bastilla or **pastilla**: an ouarka (qv) envelope with a traditional filling of sliced or minced pigeon, almonds, spices and egg, baked then dusted with cinnamon and powdered sugar. In the UK chicken is often substituted for pigeon.
Brik: minced lamb or tuna and a raw egg bound together in paper-thin pastry, then fried.
Briouats or **briouettes**: little envelopes of deep-fried paper-thin ouarka (qv) pastry; these can have a savoury filling of ground meat, rice or cheese, or be served as a sweet flavoured with almond paste, nuts or honey.
Chermoula: a dry marinade of fragrant herbs and spices.
Chicken kedra: chicken stewed in a stock of onions, lemon juice and spices (ginger, cinnamon), sometimes with raisins and chickpeas.
Couscous: granules of processed durum wheat. The name is also given to a dish where the slow-cooked grains are topped with a meat or vegetable stew like a tagine (qv); couscous royale usually involves a stew of lamb, chicken and merguez (qv).
Djeja: chicken.
Harira: thick lamb and lentil soup.
Harissa: very hot chilli pepper paste flavoured with garlic and spices.
Maakouda: spicy potato fried in breadcrumbs.
Merguez: spicy, paprika-rich lamb sausages.
Ouarka: filo pastry.
Tagine or **tajine**: a shallow earthenware dish with a conical lid; it gives its name to a slow-simmered stew of meat (usually lamb or chicken) and vegetables, often cooked with olives, preserved lemon, almonds or prunes.
Zaalouk or **zalouk**: a cold spicy aubergine, tomato and garlic dip.

With a view straight into the kitchen from the balcony, a low babble of conversation, Arabic music and a warm welcome from the eponymous owner, Yamina has a homely feel. The vivid red walls and bright rugs are all attractively lit by coloured Moroccan lamps. Seating, over three levels, is on comfy banquettes at bare wood tables – the lower space is ideal for a laid-back party. The no-nonsense traditional cooking is streets ahead of much fancier places; combined with friendly service and very reasonable prices, this makes Yamina pretty much the ideal local. The mixed mezze platter, stars of which were garlicky aubergine caviar, simple cooked carrot salad with just a hint of gingery vinegar, and pasta salad lifted by a zingy lemon and dill dressing, are highly recommended. Sizzling tagines of chicken with lemon and olives, and lamb, almond and prunes (sweet without being sickly) lived up to their promise: meat cooked to perfect tenderness in intense, gloppy sauces – just right for soaking up with decent Turkish-style bread. Portions are generous – no room for puddings, but fragrant fresh mint tea was the ideal digestif.
Babies and children welcome; high chair. Booking advisable Fri, Sat. No-smoking tables. Separate room for parties, seats 30. Takeaway service.

Islington N1

Fez NEW
70 Upper Street, N1 0NU (7359 1710/ www.fez-islington.co.uk). Angel tube. **Meals served** noon-11pm daily. **Main courses** £7.25-£28. **Credit** MC, V.
Fez seems to suffer a little from its Upper Street location. The heavy studded wooden door and artily lit entrance promise a degree of sophistication that is slightly dashed by the presence of large youthful parties who repair to the downstairs school disco-ish bar. Initial impressions were of friendly if inexperienced service, appealing cocktails, a reasonably priced wine list, soothing music – yet somehow we feared for the food. The mezze kemia (in rather small portions) featured serviceable versions of salade mechouia, zaalouk, briouats with cheese, and cucumber salad, but it was the mains that won us over. The sauce of the tagine de rouget fruit de mer was intensely rich, like a much reduced bouillabaise. Couscous brochette d'agneau provided generous skewers of succulent, tender lamb with a very good couscous, correctly presented with the vegetable broth and harissa served separately, to be added to taste. Pancake with honey and almonds, not of the traditional spongy variety, but tasty nonetheless, went down well with fresh mint tea. Light terracotta walls, henna lamps, studded mirrors and rattan furniture have a comfortable yet smart feel. Definitely worth a repeat visit.
Babies and children welcome. Booking advisable. Tables outdoors (3, pavement). Vegetarian menu. **Map 5 O2**.

Maghreb
189 Upper Street, N1 1RQ (7226 2305/ www.maghrebrestaurant.co.uk). Highbury & Islington tube/rail. **Meals served** 6-11.30pm Mon-Thur; noon-11.30pm Fri-Sun. **Main courses** £5.95-£11.95. **Set lunch** (Fri-Sun) £7.95 2 courses. **Service** 12.5% for parties of 6 or more. **Credit** AmEx, JCB, MC, V.
On previous visits to Maghreb we'd loved the opulence of the stylish, bright decor against dark-wood furniture, the luscious silk lanterns, the fairly formal but pleasant service and the general vibe of the place – but the food had been slightly disappointing. This time, all seems to have come right; even the Moroccan in our party praised the authenticity of the well-executed traditional dishes. The extensive menu includes more 'fusion' choices than most Maghrebi places, including imaginative fish dishes, but we stuck with the trad. Zaalouk, aromatic with rough-crushed coriander, cumin and chilli, had my friend transported back to his mother's kitchen. Chicken tagine with preserved lemons and olives was equally well received. Chicken and vegetable couscous – lovely

fluffy couscous and flavoursome stew – didn't come with separate extra sauce and harissa, but both arrived promptly once requested. The extensive wine list has far more Moroccan choices than is usual, and the tempting dessert menu features baghrir (spongy pancakes with honey) and Moroccan rice and almond pudding as well as the usual pastries. Considering its location and upmarket atmosphere, Maghreb is also very reasonably priced.
Babies and children welcome; high chairs. Booking advisable. No-smoking tables. Restaurant available for hire. Separate areas available for parties, seating 38 and 44. Takeaway service. **Map 5 O1**.

North West
Camden Town & Chalk Farm NW1

Moroccan Flavours NEW
94 Camden Road, NW1 9EA (7485 7879). Camden Town tube/Camden Road rail. **Dinner served** 6-11.30pm Mon-Sat; 5-11pm Sun. **Main courses** £6.95-£13.50. **Set dinner** £15 3 courses incl mint tea. **Service** 10%. **Credit** MC, V.
Previously known as Osmani, this small local came highly recommended – the patron assured us that only the name had changed. The decor features the ubiquitous red-hued blankets and rugs, coloured glass lamps and silver teapots. Those customers on the tapestry banquettes were sitting pretty, but equal numbers were perched on rather too small stools. Music was strictly traditional and played at just the right volume. Mixed starters were neither very good nor very Moroccan – carrot salad, houmous, moutabal, tabbouleh and a nutty falafel (better than the rest). Couscous with chicken was fine, but a tagine of lamb and prunes with roasted apples was a disaster. The meat was lean and tender, but instead of the richly sweet sauce that should characterise this dish, it swam in a watery, greasy liquid with an overpowering taste of icing sugar. Quite horrid. Oranges and dates in orange flower water and mint tea couldn't rescue things, but the place was full so clearly gets it right for some.
Babies and children admitted. Booking advisable. Entertainment: belly dancer Sat. Tables outdoors (4, pavement). Takeaway service. **Map 27 D2**.

Hampstead NW3

★ Safir
116 Heath Street, NW3 1DR (7431 9888/ www.safir-restaurant.co.uk). Hampstead tube. **Meals served** noon-midnight daily. **Main courses** £8.85-£17.50. **Set meal** £10.99 2 courses incl glass of wine. **Credit** MC, V.
Arriving at Safir work-weary on a midweek evening, we found ourselves transported to a serene, relaxing world of comfortable divans, soothing music and friendly service. Jewel-hued, striped satin upholstery, traditional green and yellow tenting and a heavy, studded wooden door lend the place a sense of opulence that is mirrored by the classic traditional cuisine. Safir could certainly teach some other London Moroccan restaurants a thing or two. Simplicity is the key, with skilful spicing to bring out the essence of the meat or vegetables. Carrot chermoula (just-cooked carrot with fresh coriander and the slightest hint of spiced vinegar dressing) and tender pan-fried sardines, packed with a herby stuffing, led the way. Mains were even better: the sauce in lamb and prune tagine cooked down to a perfect, sweet but not cloying glop; succulent baby chicken mhamer – rubbed with spices, then fried before being baked – also came with a sauce of perfect intensity. There are several Moroccan bottles on a reasonably priced wine list and, given Safir's Hampstead location and excellent food and service, even the bill was a pleasant surprise.
Babies and children welcome; high chairs. Book Fri, Sat, dinner Sun. Entertainment: belly dancer 8pm Thur-Sat; band 7.30pm Fri. Separate room for parties, seats 25. Takeaway service. **Map 28 C1**.

Yamina

Oriental

In London, oriental cuisine – eastern Asian food from more than one specific country – began to take shape in the late 1980s. In those days it was barely a coherent cooking style. More often, you'd find Chinese-owned establishments producing classic dishes from Malaysia, Thailand or Vietnam as food from those countries had its turn in the fashion spotlight. To this list was added a routine batch of stir-fries.

In more recent years a distinctive cuisine has developed, which incorporates styles and ingredients from across the region. The pioneer was **Wagamama**, with its canteen-style noodle bars serving healthy oriental nosh at low prices. It spawned many imitators, but of late a smarter set of eateries has emerged with the opening of **East@West** and **Taman Gang**: contemporary restaurants that incorporate ingredients from Europe as well as the Orient to form a 'Modern Asian' style.

One recent newcomer – which opened too late to earn a separate review – is the central London branch of **dim t** (32 Charlotte Street, W1T 2NQ, 7637 1122). A better-looking and more conveniently located version of the Hampstead original, it offers excellent and innovative dim sum, as well as a create-your-own-dish noodle menu.

For explanations of specific dishes or ingredients, see the menu boxes in the relevant sections elsewhere in the guide.

Central

City EC4

Silks & Spice
Temple Court, 11 Queen Victoria Street, EC4N 4UJ (7248 7878). Mansion House tube/Bank tube/DLR. **Meals served** 11.30am-10.30pm Mon-Fri. **Main courses** £5.50-£20. **Set meals** £16 3 courses, £17.50 3 courses (vegetarian), £25 4 courses. **Service** 12.5%. **Credit** AmEx, DC, JCB, MC, V.
Not much remains of the Silks & Spice chain, which led us to approach this capacious, tucked-away City branch with relatively low expectations. More fool us: it's not going to win any awards, sure, but our above-par lunch led us to wonder what on earth must have gone wrong elsewhere. A mixed platter cherry-picked a number of staples from the starter menu: duck spring rolls, caramelised spare ribs, chicken gyoza and the like. Nothing too tricky, granted, but the execution was very good. It was a similar story with the generous Thai red curry and pad Thai. A couple of ropy desserts didn't sully the experience too much either. At lunchtime, the clientele is besuited, but the atmosphere is relaxed (reflecting, perhaps, the good-value menu) and the service is highly efficient. However, our bill arrived stapled to a flyer promoting the early-evening happy hour at the restaurant's Temple Bar, which, with '2 for 1 all bottled beerss [sic] & not forgetting the ladeez [sic] – 2 for 1 Breezers all flavours!!', offered a terrifying glimpse at how the atmosphere must change when the local bankers [sic] knock off work.
Babies and children welcome. Booking advisable; essential for parties. Disabled: toilet. Dress: smart casual. Entertainment: DJs 10.30pm Thur, Fri. Separate room for parties, seats 25. Takeaway service. Vegetarian menu. **Map 11 P6**.
For branches see index.

Clerkenwell & Farringdon EC1

Cicada
132-136 St John Street, EC1V 4JT (7608 1550/ www.cicada.nu). Farringdon tube/rail.
Bar **Open** noon-11pm Mon-Sat.
Restaurant **Lunch served** noon-3pm Mon-Fri. **Dinner served** 6-10.45pm Mon-Sat. **Dim sum served** noon-3pm, 6-10pm Mon-Sat. **Main courses** £8-£14. **Service** 12.5%. **Credit** AmEx, DC, MC, V.
Seven years after opening on a then-dreary stretch of road, Will Ricker's buzzy pan-Asian bar-restaurant is still going strong. Drinkers take the area nearest the door (where bar snacks are available), while diners get a series of handsome booths and tables and a larger menu of Thai-, Chinese- and Japanese-influenced dishes. Most, but not all of these, hit the spot: a starter of chilli-salt squid was rubbery, but vegetable tempura (baby sweetcorn, avocado, sweet potato) were tenderly under-battered, and the wrap-it-yerself beef san choy bau deceptively moreish. Mains were also mixed. Chilli-crusted tofu with ong choi (water spinach) and black bean sauce was fairly uninteresting, the tofu served in a huge slab that had failed to absorb much flavour. Fillet beef toban yaki was cooked with great care and skill, but its side order of rice had clearly been sitting around for a while. Still, ginger cheesecake was rich but not overwhelming, service was matey and efficient, the ambience is fashionable while never oppressive, and the bill was entirely reasonable. Ricker's empire now extends to Ladbroke Grove (E&O; *see p231*), Shoreditch (the Great Eastern Dining Room; *see p232*) and Chelsea (Eight Over Eight; *see p231*).
Babies and children admitted. No-smoking tables. Separate room for parties, seats 75. Tables outdoors (6, pavement). **Map 5 O4**.

Covent Garden WC2

★ East@West [NEW]
2004 RUNNER-UP BEST VEGETARIAN MEAL
13-15 West Street, WC2H 9NE (7010 8600/ www.egami.co.uk). Leicester Square tube.
Bar **Open** 5.30pm-2am Mon-Sat.
Restaurant **Dinner served** 5.30pm-midnight Mon-Sat. **Main courses** £9-£40. **Credit** AmEx, DC, MC, V.
Australian chef Christine Manfield has quickly established a funky but seriously classy dining spot here. Her esteemed background on the other side of the world (notably at the award-winning Paramount restaurant in Sydney) creates the foundation for a modern Asian menu. Pass through the shiny chic decor of the bar (which is an impressive destination spot in its own right) to the first-floor restaurant, an elegant, sparsely decorated space that's beautifully lit. It's the setting for 'tastes' such as asparagus tempura served with lotus root, wasabi avocado cream and toasted seaweed; or steamed halibut fillet and foie gras with porcini mushrooms in a soy ginger broth; or sweet grilled eel with steamed pork, chilli-salt squid and black ink noodles. These are like tapas in that you order several of them, but it is suggested that you take them individually and sequentially; in the evening there are wines matched to each dish. Finish with the likes of a caramel, honeycomb and hazelnut chocolate ice-cream pyramid, and reflect on the passion put into each and every one of these taste sensations – whatever happens, you certainly won't be bored.

Babies and children welcome. Booking advisable. Disabled: toilet. Entertainment: DJ 10pm Thur-Sat. Separate room for hire, seats 22. Vegan dishes. Vegetarian menu. **Map 18 K6**.

Fitzrovia W1

Bam-Bou
1 Percy Street, W1T 1DB (7323 9130/ www.bam-bou.co.uk). Goodge Street or Tottenham Court Road tube.
Bar **Open** 6pm-1am Mon-Sat.
Restaurant **Lunch served** noon-3pm Mon-Fri. **Dinner served** 6-11.30pm Mon-Sat. **Main courses** £9.80-£14. **Service** 12.5%.
Both **Credit** AmEx, DC, MC, V.
This French-Vietnamese Fitzrovia gem has a distinct colonial feel, thanks to its dark wood antique furniture, stone ornaments, traditional Vietnamese paintings and muted colour scheme. The varied, if not especially inventive, menu contains lots of healthy, steamed-not-fried options. Light, crispy prawn spring rolls made an above-average starter, being generously stuffed with vibrant-looking prawns and greens. For mains, steamed sea bass with herbs had a light texture and a clean, delicate flavour, while chicken with cashew nuts was good too, if a little bland. All the accompanying vegetables were of excellent quality, and a dessert of three mini crême brûlées (passion fruit, mango and vanilla) was sublime: light and flavourful without being overly sweet. Exceptionally polite and relaxed staff, and a fine (but pricey) wine selection added to the experience. There's also a bar upstairs.
Babies and children admitted (restaurant only). Booking advisable; essential lunch and weekends. Separate rooms for parties, seating 12, 14 and 20. Tables outdoors (4, terrace). **Map 10 K5**.

Crazy Bear [NEW]
26-28 Whitfield Street, W1T 7DS (7631 0088/ www.crazybeargroup.co.uk). Goodge Street or Tottenham Court Road tube. **Lunch served** noon-3pm Mon-Fri. **Dinner served** 6-11pm Mon-Sat. **Main courses** £7-£18.50. **Set lunch** £8 1 course. **Set meal** (tasting menu) £25 8 dishes, £30 10 dishes. **Service** 12.5%. **Credit** AmEx, MC, V.
This new oriental restaurant and bar (a branch of an Oxfordshire gastropub) adopts an enthusiastic approach to design. There's an art deco theme to the ground-floor restaurant, while the basement bar is stunning, with padded leather booths the colour of scarlet lipstick, and a 1947 Murano chandelier on the staircase. The team of half a dozen male and female chefs from Thailand – plus a British pastry chef – is successful in putting an unorthodox spin on conventional flavours and dishes. The main focus is Thai, but there are influences from Chinese, Vietnamese, Malaysian and Japanese cuisines. Dishes include a sassily spiced red curry with tender pieces of beef; crisp vegetables encased in lacy egg pancake wrap (a fine rendition of Vietnamese banh xeo); tofu stir-fried with crunchy cashews and peppers; and a lively and aromatic vegetable 'yellow curry'. Gai lan (chinese broccoli) and morning glory (aka Thai water spinach) were perfectly cooked. Even if you don't eat puddings, try the salted pistachio and peanut butter caramel with chocolate and thyme 'sorbet' – it's extraordinarily cloying and moreish.
Booking advisable. Dress: smart casual. **Map 4 K5**.

Knightsbridge SW1

★ Pan Asian Restaurant
The Paxton's Head, 153 Knightsbridge, SW1X 7PA (7589 6627). Knightsbridge tube.
Pub **Open** 11am-11pm Mon-Sat; noon-10.30pm Sun.
Restaurant **Lunch served** noon-3.30pm, **dinner served** 5.30-10.30pm Mon-Fri. **Meals served** noon-10.30pm Sat; noon-9pm Sun. **Main courses** £6-£8.
Both **Credit** MC, V.
Don't be put off by the scruffy entrance, located at the side of a Knightsbridge pub. This first-floor restaurant is a haven of style. Pistachio-green

walls, smart wooden furniture and large, pretty windows are matched by chilled background music. Seating is communal, around three large, low, square tables, with additional seating at the small bar if you don't fancy sharing. Service is slightly erratic and our beers were warm, but prices are very reasonable – especially for this part of town. The South-east Asian food is hit and miss. Our starters were very disappointing: Vietnamese spring rolls were dripping in oil, while yakitori chicken lacked much flavour. Nasi goreng followed; the highlight of the meal, it was a large portion with plenty of crunchy fresh vegetables, a sweet chilli sauce and a fried egg on top. Chicken breast yellow curry was pleasant too, though the sauce tasted as if it had come out of a jar. A reasonable meal, but this is not a restaurant to go out of your way for.
Babies and children welcome. Booking advisable. Separate room for parties, seats 48. Takeaway service. **Map 8 F9**.

Mayfair W1

Taman Gang NEW
141 Park Lane, W1K 7AA (7518 3160/ www.tamangang.com). Marble Arch tube. **Lunch served** noon-2.30pm Tue-Fri. **Dinner served** 6.30-11pm Mon-Thur, Sun; 6.30-midnight Fri, Sat. **Main courses** £12.50-£45. **Set lunch** £20 3 courses. **Service** 15%. **Credit** AmEx, JCB, MC, V.
A basement location is de rigueur among fashionable restaurants these days, but Taman Gang's discreet street-level entrance gives little hint of what lies inside. Charming, attractive staff ushered us downstairs into a low-lit dining room, complete with alcove dining areas. White orchids, carved stonework, candles and water features evoke a tropical fantasy. The pricey menu offers refined pan-oriental dishes, with luxurious ingredients such as beluga caviar, lobster and diver scallops to the fore. A dim sum platter, however, turned out to be a sad, flabby, overcooked affair that would have shamed any self-respecting Chinatown restaurant. A main of monkfish medallions and asparagus benefited from a tasty champagne butter sauce, though the tiny asparagus spears lacked flavour. Grapefruit and yuzu lemon chicken was simply dull – a deep-fried, crumbed chicken fillet served with a sticky, citrus-flavoured sauce – but stir-fried pea shoots made a satisfying side dish. Fellow diners comprised large parties of besuited young men, with the group nearest to us continually shouting loudly for more wine, 'the best you've got'. Too disheartened for dessert, we left and ascended to the real world. Flashy style over substance, without a doubt.
Babies and children welcome. Booking essential. Disabled: toilet. Entertainment: DJ nightly. Vegan dishes. **Map 9 G6**.

Soho W1

Itsu
103 Wardour Street, W1F 0UQ (7479 4790/ www.itsu.co.uk). Piccadilly Circus tube. **Meals served** noon-11pm Mon-Thur; noon-midnight Fri, Sat; 1-10.30pm Sun. **Main courses** £1.95-£3.45. **Credit** AmEx, MC, V.
The main problem with conveyer-belt cuisine is that without a chef's touch to proportion portions, it's very easy to eat too much. Which is exactly the point: the longer you sit there, the more often the belt goes round and the higher your bill rises. The standard of food at Itsu is fine, with the sushi, soups and salads looking just as enticingly fresh as they're meant to, and tasting just so – in keeping with the tradition of a venture thought up by the man behind Pret A Manger. There are five colour-coded price ranges travelling on the belt, plus a list of hot dishes that you can order from the staff, who descend at the press of a button. Seared fillet of beef with shallot sauce was gorgeously rare; hot spicy edamame popped in the mouth. Fruit drinks were a bit of a disappointment, but a decidedly un-Japanese crème brûlée went down well. Itsu is best experienced in pairs; the side-by-side seating does not encourage conversation among groups and the few four-seater booths are always full.

Babies and children admitted. Bookings not accepted. No smoking. Takeaway service. **Map 17 K6**. **For branches see index**.

West

Bayswater W2

I-Thai
The Hempel, 31-35 Craven Hill Gardens, W2 3EA (7298 9001/www.the-hempel.co.uk). Bayswater, Queensway or Lancaster Gate tube. **Lunch served** 12.30-6pm Mon-Thur; 12.30-2pm Fri, Sat. **Dinner served** 7-10.30pm Mon-Sat. **Main courses** £17. **Set lunch** £15-£20. **Service** 12.5%. **Credit** AmEx, DC, JCB, MC, V.
Located in the softly lit basement of the minimalist Hempel hotel, I-Thai has a Japanese accent that creates a formal yet tranquil mood (think black wooden tables, sliding white paper screens and branches of pink blossom). The menu, though, is less harmonious, made up of a curious amalgam of Thai, Japanese and Italian dishes, resulting more in identity-confusion than fusion. Quality is inconsistent. Sushi, to start, was distinctly average, but green curry with lime rice and Thai basil was very good indeed, with vibrant, flash-cooked vegetables and a robustly flavoured sauce. Seafood hot-pot with lotus noodles was disappointingly bland (and unnervingly pricey at £17). The meal comes with efficient service, and a range of amuse-bouches and palate-refreshers are served between courses. Desserts were accomplished, with an Italian bias. Several days after our visit we were alarmed to discover that an item had been erroneously added to our bill after we had signed the debit card slip. The error was swiftly sorted out once the manager was alerted, but this was a black mark against I-Thai.
Babies and children welcome; high chairs. Booking advisable. Disabled: toilet. Separate room for parties, seats 35. **Map 7 C6**.

Ladbroke Grove W11

★ E&O
14 Blenheim Crescent, W11 1NN (7229 5454/ www.eando.nu). Ladbroke Grove or Notting Hill Gate tube. **Bar Open** noon-11pm Mon-Sat; noon-10.30pm Sun. **Dim sum** £3-£6.50. **Restaurant Lunch served** noon-3pm Mon-Sat; 1-3pm Sun. **Dinner served** 6-10.30pm Mon-Sat; 6-10pm Sun. **Main courses** £6-£21.50. **Service** 12.5%. *Both* **Credit** AmEx, DC, MC, V.
Sister to the Will Ricker-owned restaurants Great Eastern Dining Room (*see p232*), Cicada (*see p229*) and Eight Over Eight (*see below*), E&O – much like its extraordinarily attractive siblings – is one hip and stylish restaurant. Cream walls, huge circular lampshades and dark wood slatted walls create a simple, oriental feel that is reflected in the interesting pan-Asian menu. The small bar (with its range of spirits on ceiling-suspended glass shelves) is always packed – Gwyneth Paltrow was there the night we visited – but the food is the highlight. Take a seat at one of the brown leather banquettes and browse the glossary at the back of the menu to help make your choice. Roasted coconut and pomegranate betel leaves (beautifully presented on a pretty plate) were extremely fresh and minty. Tender and deliciously marinated spicy lamb followed, with a crunchy salad of papaya and mango. Chicken pad Thai was also a tasty, if less adventurous, choice. Service is admirably efficient, with staff more than happy to advise on what to order. E&O is deservedly popular, so booking is crucial.
Babies and children welcome. Booking essential weekends. Separate room for hire, seats 10-18. Tables outdoors (5, pavement). Vegan dishes. **Map 19 B3**.

Uli
16 All Saints Road, W11 1HH (7727 7511). Ladbroke Grove or Westbourne Park tube. **Dinner served** 6.45-11.15pm Mon-Sat. **Main courses** £6.50-£9. **Service** 12.5%. **Credit** MC, V.
All Saints Road may be getting more upmarket, but Uli continues to serve quality Asian fare in modest surroundings and has become a firm favourite among locals. Its stir-fried turnip cakes, baked fish, five-spice pork rolls, Mongolian lamb, and beef in black bean sauce all have their advocates. And the service with a smile from the friendly Singaporean owners invariably brightens proceedings. Despite its small size (booking is advisable), Uli doesn't feel too cramped or lack air and there's a patio garden for warm evenings. Deep-fried soft-shell crab with accompanying curls of chilli starred on our visit, while the beef in black bean sauce was as reliable as ever. Staff are always happy to recommend combinations and there are usually some daily specials. A tiny, titillating slice of baked ice-cream for dessert amplified the sweet taste we had in our mouths on departure.
Babies and children admitted. Booking essential. Restaurant available for hire. Tables outdoors (6, patio). Takeaway service. Vegetarian menu. **Map 19 B2**.

Maida Vale W9

Southeast W9
239 Elgin Avenue, W9 1NJ (7328 8883). Maida Vale tube/31 bus. **Meals served** 4-11pm Mon-Wed; noon-11pm Thur-Sat; noon-10pm Sun. **Main courses** £7-£8. **Credit** AmEx, MC, V.
Southeast W9 has a pleasant ambience, more café than restaurant with its white walls, simple furniture and attentive but not intrusive service. The menu offers a Thai/Malaysian/Vietnamese mix, including such stalwarts as chicken satay, gado gado and pad Thai. Prices are fair and portions generous. The standout starter was tod man pla, a delicious, densely layered Thai fish cake served with fresh pickles. To follow, sousi pa (spicy coconut fish) was enjoyable enough, but, as one of the most expensive dishes on the menu, should have done more for the palate. Ped makam (grilled duck breast in tamarind) from the specials list was a real disappointment, the duck lacking texture and flavour. Steamed rice was fine, but the roti bread was tired and unappetising. There's also the usual selection of one-dish rice and noodle meals – barbecued pork on rice, Singapore fried noodles, spicy seafood noodle soup – which at around £6 a pop offer reasonable value for those in search of sustenance in Maida Vale.
Babies and children welcome. Booking advisable. No-smoking tables. Takeaway service. **Map 1 C3**.

South West

Chelsea SW3

Eight Over Eight
392 King's Road, SW3 5UZ (7349 9934/ www.eightovereight.nu). Sloane Square tube then bus 11, 22. **Lunch served** noon-2.45pm Mon-Fri; noon-4pm Sat. **Dinner served** 6.15-10.45pm Mon-Fri; 6.15-11pm Sat; 6.15-10.30pm Sun. **Main courses** £8-£20. **Service** 12.5%. **Credit** AmEx, DC, MC, V.
Occupying the site of a former pub on the King's Road, Eight Over Eight is an oasis of minimalist style. Part of the trendy E&O mini chain (*see above*), it has cream walls plus chocolate-brown suede banquettes that are frequently adorned with west London's young and beautiful. The elegant bar area at the front offers a fine range of cocktails, and is often buzzing. Staff are young, friendly and eager to explain the eclectic pan-Asian dishes, but there's a glossary of terms at the back of the menu should you want to go it alone. To start, prawn and chive dumplings were light and bursting with filling, while carpaccio of tuna with chilli and lemon was so beautifully thin it melted on the tongue. For mains, scallop, coconut and kaffir leaf curry was hot and creamy; crispy-skin chicken was slightly dry, though the skin was satisfyingly crunchy. We finished an enjoyable meal with a rich and creamy chocolate honeycomb mochi. As with its siblings, you'll need to book.
Babies and children welcome. Booking advisable. Dress: smart casual. Separate room for hire, seats 12. **Map 14 D12**.

Fulham SW6

★ Zimzun
Fulham Broadway Retail Centre, Fulham Road, SW6 1BW (7385 4555/www.zimzun.co.uk). *Fulham Broadway tube.* **Meals served** noon-10.30pm Mon-Thur, Sun; noon-11pm Fri, Sat. **Main courses** £5.50-£7.95. **Set lunch** £5.95 2 dishes. **Service** 12.5%. **Credit** MC, V.
If Zimzun were on a street, it would be constantly heaving. Stuck as it is in a shopping centre, staff often outnumber diners. This is truly a shame, because decor, ambience and service are better than at most canteen-style noodle bars. Walls are a sumptuous dark red, and the teak tables come adorned with mini ponds on which float flowers and candles. Which just leaves the food: a broad range of South-east Asian one-course meals of noodles, stir-fries, grills, salads and curries whose huge portions do little to compensate for their flavour. Grilled duck with pak choi and tamarind sauce was heavy and hard-going, while vegetarian noodle soup was delicate to the point of blandness. Side dishes were better, yet still hit and miss: coconut mangetout were crisp and delicious, vegetable spring rolls overly greasy. But a good selection of Asian beers (Asahi, Singha, Siam), a short but decent wine list, enticing soft drinks (try the Passion Delight for dessert) and a good-value lunch set menu make Zimzun worth a visit.
Babies and children welcome. Booking advisable weekends. Disabled: toilet. No-smoking tables. Takeaway service. **Map 13 B13.**

South

Balham SW12

★ The Paddyfield
4 Bedford Hill, SW12 9RG (8772 1145). *Balham tube/rail.* **Dinner served** 6-11pm daily. **Main courses** £4.50-£6.95. **Unlicensed**. **Corkage** £1. **No credit cards.**
A long yellow room full of simple tables, this is an unpretentious place for a quick bite rather than somewhere to linger. A small menu offers standard Vietnamese and Thai favourites – all easy on the wallet – and there's a bustling takeaway trade. We started with summer rolls in translucent rice paper, which were light and herby, if a little rubbery; and a papaya salad that was pleasant but lacking in the promised fiery heat. Vietnamese vermicelli with seafood, a big dish flavoured with fish sauce and lime, was lukewarm and again missing a kick. Vegetable pad Thai was better, but best of all were the desserts: sticky rice pudding with black-eyed beans had a lovely consistency and wasn't too sweet, while pancakes filled with coconut and rolled in sesame seeds were a treat.
Babies and children welcome. Booking advisable weekends. No smoking. Takeaway service.

Brixton SW9

★ New Fujiyama
7 Vining Street, SW9 8QA (7737 2369/ www.newfujiyama.com). Brixton tube/rail. **Meals served** noon-11pm Mon-Thur, Sun; noon-midnight Fri, Sat. **Main courses** £5.10-£6.70. **Service** 10%. **Credit** MC, V.
With its bright red interior, this very popular Brixton eaterie resembles a lacquered box. The long tables are made for sharing, and the place was packed with a young crowd by 8pm on our midweek visit, which means it can get very noisy – something not helped by the loud music policy. However, a vast menu and very reasonable prices create a winning formula, and the separation of smokers and non-smokers into different rooms works well (the smokers get the atmospheric bonus of regular live jazz). Choose from lots of variations on a few themes: soup noodles, pan-fried noodles, curry noodles and some rice dishes, many of them vegetarian and with the option of wholemeal noodles for the health-conscious. We tried curry udon, a huge bowl of thick noodles in spicy coconut curry sauce with angel fish, ginger, lemongrass and mint; and yaki udon, fried noodles with chicken, prawns, fish cakes, vegetables and

pickled ginger. Both were full of fresh flavours. Sides of edamame and prawn dumplings were fine too – no mystery as to this place's popularity then.
Babies and children welcome; high chairs. Booking advisable. No-smoking area. Separate rooms for parties, seating 14-35. Takeaway service; delivery service (7737 6583). **Map 22 E2.**

Waterloo SE1

Inshoku
23-24 Lower Marsh, SE1 7RJ (7928 2311). *Waterloo tube/rail.* **Lunch served** noon-3pm Mon-Fri. **Dinner served** 6-10.30pm Mon-Sat. **Main courses** £8-£15. **Set lunch** £4-£8 2 courses. **Set dinner** £10-£30 3 courses. **Credit** AmEx, MC, V.
Forgoing the Day-Glo Tokyo-by-numbers decor favoured by many sushi houses, Inshoku is a disarmingly spacious and simply laid out café-restaurant on Lower Marsh, Waterloo's eclectic and bedraggled answer to Berwick Street. Revelling in the amount of space left between tables, and choosing to ignore the six-month-out-of-date soy sauce bottle plonked on our table, we were pleased, if not overwhelmed by the sushi. This is served in various set options or can be ordered à la carte. Much better was a staggeringly satisfying seafood ramen noodle soup, so dense it was better eaten with chopsticks than a spoon. No complaints about the salmon teriyaki either. Service was friendly, with the manager taking the opportunity of a lull in service to nosh down a treat supplied by the partially open kitchen. In an area of town where there's a surprising amount of choice (especially on The Cut, just over the road), Inshoku holds its own. It also does takeaways: worth noting if you're a local with a hankering for raw fish.
Babies and children welcome; high chairs. Booking advisable Thur, Fri. Takeaway service; delivery service (within 3-mile radius). Vegetarian menu. **Map 10 M9.**

South East

Herne Hill SE24

Lombok
17 Half Moon Lane, SE24 9JU (7733 7131). *Herne Hill rail.* **Dinner served** 6-10.30pm Tue-Thur, Sun; 6-11pm Fri, Sat. **Main courses** £6-£7.95. **Service** 10%. **Credit** MC, V.
Herne Hill's most popular restaurant continues to pack in the punters (a trifle too cosily perhaps: claustrophobics and those wanting an intimate dinner à deux beware). There's a vague New England chic to the tiny interior; only a tasteful scattering of carved wood ornaments and a reclining Buddha give away Lombok's culinary leanings. The menu roams freely throughout South-east Asia, and includes authoritative versions of all your faves – chicken satay, Thai green and red curries, Singapore fried noodles and the like – but also less common dishes. Of the starters, we particularly liked the delicacy of chicken wrapped in pandan leaves and the punch of mussels in a fiery Thai broth. The sourness of tamarind worked well with the richness of roast duck in the logically named tamarind duck; mixed seafood hot-pot with vermicelli featured squeaky-fresh crab, squid and prawns; and even a dish as dull-on-paper as chicken with cashews and pineapple was lively and surprisingly tasty. It's the freshness of the ingredients and cleanness of the flavours that distinguishes Lombok's food, and this even extends into the short dessert menu; papaya and mango sorbet with fresh mango was the perfect palate cleanser.
Babies and children welcome. Book weekends. Takeaway service. Vegetarian menu.

East

Shoreditch EC2

Great Eastern Dining Room
54-56 Great Eastern Street, EC2A 3QR (7613 4545/www.greateasterndining.co.uk). Old Street tube/rail/55 bus.

Ground-floor bar **Open** noon-midnight Mon-Fri; 6pm-midnight Sat. **Main courses** £4.50-£10.50. *Below 54 bar* **Open** 7.30pm-1am Fri, Sat. **Main courses** £4.50-£10.50. *Restaurant* **Lunch served** 12.30-3pm Mon-Fri. **Dinner served** 6.30-10.45pm Mon-Sat. **Main courses** £9-£14.50. **Service** 12.5%. *All* **Credit** AmEx, DC, MC, V.
Once heralded as cutting-edge, the Great Eastern's seamless interior of unembellished neutrals feels conventional now – replicated as it has been by style bars throughout London. The ground-floor entrance bar has been known to be only half full come Saturday night, a clear indication that the fashion set has moved on. That said, the dining room gets booked to capacity, and sometimes attracts families: a rarity on this particular drag. It all boils down to whether you're prepared to compromise on service (you can encounter a distracted reception and a haphazard approach to table-clearing) in the name of a good feed. The pan-Asian dishes have improved of late, being varied, appetising and attractively presented. Dim sum, sushi and tempura are available as starters; chicken and snowpea gyozas, and avocado and sweet potato tempura each came with delicately flavoured dipping sauces. A main of soft-shell crab, ginger and rocket salad had a good ratio of meat to leaves, and the house dish of beef fillet toban yaki was well executed, if basic in scope. Fine food – shame about the staff.
Babies and children admitted. Booking advisable Thur-Sat. Dress: no suits (downstairs Thur-Sat). Entertainment: DJs 9pm Fri, Sat. **Map 6 R4.**

North East

Stoke Newington N16

Barracuda
125 Stoke Newington Church Street, N16 0UH (7275 0400). Stoke Newington rail/73 bus. **Dinner served** 6.30-11pm Mon-Thur, Sun; 6.30-11.45pm Fri, Sat. **Main courses** £7.50-£11.50. **Service** 10%. **Credit** AmEx, DC, MC, V.
Mottled paint effects – one room daubed crimson, the other turquoise – and sundry stencilled images mean this Pacific Rim local resembles a *Changing Rooms* makeover casualty. True to form, the menu itself is more ambitious quick-fix than concerted effort at solid craftsmanship. Thai steamed dumplings were like spam's eastern cousin, with the stuffing being a pale pink amalgam of minced pork, chicken and shrimp. A main of lamb was passable – the tamarind sauce subtle enough, though the accompanying coconut rice was overly sweet. Spicy snapper proved a guilty pleasure, the fish barely noticeable under a crackling shell of thick, crispy batter, and served atop a big portion of un-oriental mash encircled by sweet Thai sauce. Desserts extend only as far as sorbet, ice-cream or the omnipresent banoffi pie; given that service can be slow and offhand, it's probably not worth lingering to try them out. The variable quality is comparable to your average takeaway, but prices are somewhat steeper.
Babies and children welcome; high chairs. Booking advisable. Entertainment: jazz 9pm Fri, Sat. Restaurant available for hire. Separate room for parties, seats 35. Tables outdoors (9, garden). Takeaway service. Vegetarian menu. **Map 25 B1.**

★ Itto
226 Stoke Newington High Street, N16 7HU (7275 8827). Stoke Newington rail/67, 73, 76, 106, 149, 243 bus. **Lunch served** noon-3pm, **dinner served** 5-11pm Mon-Sat. **Main courses** £3.70-£6. **No credit cards**.
No-frills dumpling and noodle bars might exist cheek by jowl in the centre of town, but in Stoke Newington Itto is a refreshingly useful anomaly. Little effort has been expended on decor, so the interior feels small and boxy despite the potentially space-enhancing prospect of pale green walls, but some thought has gone into devising a low-cost menu that neatly covers all bases. There are around 50 dishes, many with a choice of ramen, udon, ho fun or thin egg noodles. A main of Singapore noodles was more piquant than we'd expected, making the vegetable soup noodles – a deep bowl

of savoury broth awash with tofu, beansprouts, peppers and mushrooms – seem comfortingly mild in comparison. Sides of vegetable dumplings, and chilli and pepper tofu were nondescript, resorting to liberal pools of oil and sauce to generate interest. That said, you easily get out for under a tenner per head, so Itto shapes up as excellent value.
Babies and children welcome; high chairs. No smoking. Takeaway service. **Map 25 C1**.

North

Camden Town & Chalk Farm NW1

Wagamama

2004 RUNNER-UP BEST FAMILY RESTAURANT
11 Jamestown Road, NW1 7BW (7428 0800/ www.wagamama.com). Camden Town tube. **Meals served** noon-11pm Mon-Sat; noon-10pm Sun. **Main courses** £5.50-£9.25. **Set meals** £10.50-£11.50 2 dishes & drink. **Credit** AmEx, MC, V.
Everyone's a bit blasé about noodle bars – a high-street staple nowadays – but it pays to remember that Wagamama is one of the originals, and one of the best. And one of the most successful too, with 20 branches in London alone and outlets as far afield as Australia and Dubai. A gleaming, smoke-free environment, perky staff and a wholesome menu are appealing – especially for families – though not everyone likes the communal tables and resultant noise. The menu is divided by style rather than into starters and mains, so choose from headings such as ramen, kare noodles, rice, sauce, side dishes and so on. One of the most popular dishes is yaki soba, with its fiery ginger and garlic flavours alongside ramen noodles, still-crisp fried vegetables, chicken and shrimps. Other meat and vegetarian ramen dishes come in an ocean of stock, with ladles. For kids, there's chicken katsu (chicken breast fried in breadcrumbs) with dipping sauce, rice and shredded cucumber, or vegetarian or chicken noodle dishes for just £3.50. To drink, choose from raw juices, beer, wine, saké – or drown yourself in gallons of free green tea.
Babies and children welcome: children's menu; high chairs. Disabled: toilet. No smoking. Takeaway service. Vegan dishes. **Map 27 C2**.
For branches see index.

Hampstead NW3

★ dim T café

3 Heath Street, NW3 6TP (7435 0024/ www.dimt.co.uk). Hampstead tube. **Meals served** noon-11pm daily. **Main courses** £5.95-£8.95. **Credit** MC, V.
Tucked away among the maternity shops and galleries on Heath Street, this fast-paced, sleek local eaterie is dim sum and then some. Come for Sunday lunch and see it in all its Hampstead glory, as polo-necked couples with rectangular glasses pile into the purple-accented dining room, clutching newspapers and baby toys. Dim sum is the name of the game here, with intense morsels of steaming delight arriving in steady succession; pork and chicken with sticky rice wrapped in a giant lotus leaf was an unforgettable highlight. This was one of the first restaurants in London to serve dim sum, and it's still among the best (though the Charlotte Street branch now offers real competition). There are also ten kinds of oriental tea, and noodle dishes cooked your own way – choose your meat, your noodle and your sauce, then say how you want it done. Pork and yellow egg noodle, with a chilli sauce in a tom yum broth, was a huge bowl of exciting flavours. There's an à la carte menu too, though Japanese warm chicken wasabi salad was disappointing. As for dessert, dim T's chocolate wun tuns with coconut ice-cream are the stuff of local legend.
Babies and children admitted; high chairs. Booking advisable; essential dinner. No-smoking tables. Separate room for hire, seats 30. Tables outdoors (2, pavement). Takeaway service. **Map 28 C2**.
For branches see index.

East@West. See p229.

Primrose Hill NW3

★ ★ Café de Maya

38 Primrose Hill Road, NW3 3AD (7209 0672). Chalk Farm tube/31 bus. **Breakfast served** (English) 7.30am-3.30pm, **dinner served** 6-11pm daily. **Main courses** £4-£6.25. **Service** 10%. **Credit** MC, V.
Wonky furniture, hanging plants, outré paintings and photos and triangular artefacts covering every inch of wall space, plus a precarious-looking rack of CDs, are just a few of the 'touches' that lend this old Primrose Hill favourite the feel of a student commune with a kitchen. But what a kitchen it is, serving fresh, well-seasoned South-east Asian grub at scrupulously fair prices. A starter of chicken satay was moist and tender, and came with an intense and creamy peanut sauce. Crispy duck pancakes were delightfully sticky, sweet and fresh-tasting. A heaving bowl of Singapore laksa followed, bursting with meat, veg, egg and noodles. Thai chicken curry held just the right balance between smooth and spicy – an uncommon feat. Sadly, we were far too full after all this to face banana fritters, but the pineapple and mango sorbet was better than most we've had. If the crowd of locals and regulars is anything to go by, do what they do: come here hungry and come here often.
Babies and children welcome; high chairs. Booking advisable weekends. Disabled: ramp. No-smoking tables. Restaurant available for hire. Tables outdoors (2, pavement). Takeaway service; delivery service (within 3-mile radius). Vegetarian menu. **Map 28 C5**.

North West

Queen's Park NW6

★ Café Asia NEW

16 College Parade, Salusbury Road, NW6 6RN (7372 1404). Queen's Park tube/rail/ Brondesbury Park rail. **Lunch served** noon-3pm Mon-Fri. **Dinner served** 6-11.30pm Mon-Sat. **Main courses** £4.50-£9.50. **Set lunch** £4.50 1 course incl bread, rice and salad. **Credit** AmEx, DC, JCB, MC, V.
Café Asia has taken over the site of the suddenly defunct Orange, Lemon & Lime restaurant. Sri Lankan, Thai and Malaysian dishes dominate the menu (Vietnamese favourites are promised soon). Execution and presentation are homely. The substantial main courses cost £8.50 on average. Tom yum soup (served in a small cereal bowl) was fiercely hot and fragrant. Sri Lankan curry (choose from chicken, lamb or vegetable) and king fish curry both came with the same army of accompaniments: mini popadoms, yellow rice,

coconut dahl, lots of lettuce, tomatoes and cucumber, plus curried cauliflower and broccoli. Charming service and fresh sauces compensate for a lack of authenticity around the edges. Among the delightful puds are rarely seen Sri Lankan faves, such as wattalappan – a wobbly, crème caramel-like offering made from coconut, palm sugar and cashew nuts. Sago pudding was equally enjoyable: a dollop of vivid green 'frog spawn' on a syrup of palm sugar with coconut milk. There's also excellent own-made lime ice-cream. With a couple of beers, this feast set us back £35.
Babies and children welcome; high chairs. Booking advisable. Disabled: toilet. Separate room for hire, seats 30. Tables outdoors (3, pavement). Takeaway service; delivery service (within 2-mile radius). Vegetarian menu.

Outer London
Barnet, Hertfordshire

★ Emchai
78 High Street, Barnet, Herts EN5 5SN (8364 9993/www.emchai.co.uk). High Barnet tube.
Lunch served noon-2.30pm Mon-Thur; noon-3pm Fri-Sun. **Dinner served** 6-11pm Mon-Thur; 6pm-midnight Fri, Sat; 5-10pm Sun. **Main courses** £4.90-£6.50. **Credit** MC, V.
Behind a frosted-glass frontage so discreet as to be easy-to-miss, Emchai opens out into a spacious dining room, simply but strikingly decorated with turquoise and purple walls. The pan-oriental menu ranges from one-dish meals, such as Japanese-style noodle soup or Singapore laksa, to Malaysian classics including gado gado and beef rendang. We opted for deliciously crisp 'salt and spicy soft-shell crab' (a dish that lived up to its name with its salty-chilli flavouring), and steamed edamame. For mains, mee goreng, generously sprinkled with sliced red chilli, had an authentic hawker-stall flavour, while prawns with asparagus and lily buds was a delicate dish, again nicely cooked. Polite, attentive service, which saw complimentary prawn crackers and a chilli dipping sauce arrive on our table within moments of sitting down, added to a highly pleasurable dining experience.
Babies and children welcome; high chairs. Disabled: toilet. No-smoking tables. Restaurant available for hire. Takeaway service.

Kingston, Surrey

Cammasan
8 Charter Quay, High Street, Kingston upon Thames, Surrey KT1 1NB (8549 3510/www.cammasan.com). Kingston rail.
Meinton noodle bar Lunch served noon-3pm, **dinner served** 5.30-11pm Mon-Fri. **Meals served** noon-11pm Sat, Sun. **Main courses** £5.50-£8.90. **No credit cards.**
Chaitan restaurant **Minimum** £15. **Main courses** £5.50-£30. **Set meals** £13.90-£21 3 courses. **Service** 10%. **Credit** MC, V.
Cammasan bagged its spot on posh Charter Quay way back, and has resolutely remained. There are two dining spaces. The ground-floor Meinton noodle bar serves a variety of curries and stir-fries to punters with a film to catch or a pub to visit; it is usually the busier of the two. Upstairs is the more formal Chaitan restaurant, where the menu is very similar to Cammasan's older sibling, China Royal, at the north end of Kingston – which has always been something of a winner with locals. There are influences from Malaysian, Thai and (predominantly) Chinese cuisines. From the generous set menu options, a platter of crispy seaweed, prawn toast, sweet and sour wun tun and spring rolls made for an ample but can't-really-go-wrong starter. Crispy aromatic duck was less greasy than we've had elsewhere; chicken with cashew nuts in a yellow bean sauce was moreish; and fiery sichuan prawns were tender. It's not mind-blowing stuff, but the cooking is decent enough and staff are friendly.
Babies and children welcome; high chairs. Booking advisable. Disabled: toilet. Dress: smart casual (Chaitan). Restaurant available for hire. Tables outdoors (30, terrace). Takeaway service.
For branch (China Royal) see index.

Portuguese

If you think the cooking of Portugal is just poor man's Spanish cuisine, you haven't eaten enough Portuguese food. Despite sharing the Spanish love for chorizo-style sausages (chouriço), dry cured ham (presunto) and salt cod (bacalhau), the Portuguese have developed a cooking style that has a character, a culture and a cachet all its own. Take the famous arroz (rice) dishes that appear on practically every Portuguese menu. While they are often compared to paella, they are, in fact, far soupier, with the rice used almost as a thickening agent.

Portuguese cooking is in essence a peasant cuisine: the food of farmers and fishermen. Pork, sausages and charcuterie figure prominently, as does an abundance of fresh fish and seafood and olive oil (azeite). There's a strong tradition of charcoal-grilled fish and meats. The hearty bean stews from the north and the thick bready soups (açordas) are also worth trying, as is the coastal speciality of caldeirada, Portugal's answer to bouillabaisse. Garlic, lemon juice, wine and wine vinegar are much used in marinades, with favoured spices being piri-piri (hot peppers, often used to flavour oil in which chicken is basted) and, for the cakes, cinnamon – both the latter showing the culinary influence of Portugal's colonial past. To finish, there is always a lush arroz doce (rice pudding), a wobbly pudim flan (crème caramel) or the world's most loved custard tart, the deliciously scorched pastel de nata.

The heartland of Portuguese dining in London is in the south, notably around Vauxhall and Stockwell, where there seems to be a never-ending supply of friendly neighbourhood drop-in bars with a casual café, an ever-present TV screen and a more formal restaurant attached. In west London, particularly around Golborne Road, the Portuguese flag still flutters as locals divide themselves into those who take their coffee and cake at **Oporto** and those who prefer **Lisboa**. Top-end Portuguese restaurants are thin on the ground, but the recently refurbished and re-energised **O Fado** in Knightsbridge serves up old-fashioned charm and carefully cooked Portuguese classics with a side serving of soul-stirring fado music that has to be good for the digestion.

PASTELARIA

West
Ladbroke Grove W10

Lisboa Patisserie
57 Golborne Road, W10 5NR (8968 5242). Ladbroke Grove or Westbourne Park tube/ 23, 52 bus. **Open** 8am-8pm Mon-Sat; 8am-7pm Sun. **Credit** MC, V.
If London isn't overcome with one giant urge for pasteis de nata – those delectable Portuguese egg custard tarts invented in Lisbon's 16th-century Jeronimos monastery – you can't blame Lisboa. With three other deli/pâtisseries throughout London, the firm is doing its best to spread the word. This, the original branch, contains the

bakery. Plans are afoot to move to bigger premises across the road early in 2005. In the meantime, come for the decor, which consists of dinky little brides, grooms and choirboys preening on top of decorative cakes. Two Cimballi machines pump out very good bicas (espressos) and galãos (milk coffees) and can barely keep up with the permanent crowd of local reprobates, out-of-work actors and slumming-it Notting Hill types. Overly squishy minced meat croquettes were no highlight, but the rolls and sandwiches are fresh and cheap, and the variety of Portuguese cakes is vast, including pasteis de nata, bolos de arroz, orange and coconut tarts, and castanha de ovo, a blobby rich egg cake. Locals sit at the outside tables, tourists inside, but if you get a seat anywhere, you're doing well.
Babies and children welcome. Tables outdoors (3, pavement). Takeaway service. **Map 19 B1.**
For branches see index.

Oporto Patisserie
62A Golborne Road, W10 5PS (8968 8839). Ladbroke Grove or Westbourne Park tube/23, 52 bus. **Open** 8am-7pm daily. **No credit cards.**
We wouldn't mind betting that the sign writer responsible for the big sign outside this popular cake and coffee stop was Irish. Either that or there's a town called O'Porto somewhere in County Cork. However, judging from the white tiles, the big tall glasses of galão (milky coffee) and the number of people tucking into pasteis de bacalhau and chouriço sandwiches, Oporto is more spiritually linked to Portugal's second largest city. In the old days you had to resort to fisticuffs to get a table here. Now the place seems to have lost a little of its mojo, with a smaller selection of brought-in cakes huddling in the long glass counter. The coffee is a little harsh, the rolls (egg salad, schnitzel, ham and cheese) are fairly unremarkable, but on a good day, the pasteis de nata are damn fine. There are now more tables out on the pavement for discreet people-watching.
Babies and children welcome: high chair. Tables outdoors (3, pavement). Takeaway service. **Map 19 B1.**

South
Vauxhall SE1

Café Madeira
46A-46B Albert Embankment, SE1 7TN (7820 1117). Vauxhall tube/rail. **Open** 7am-7pm daily. **Credit** MC, V.
The long lunchtime queue snaking out of the front door speaks volumes about the quality and the prices at this insanely popular Vauxhall bakery, café and sandwich shop. There's a tremendous variety of food to choose from. It seems a shame to go for jacket potatoes when there are various breads from the bakery that can be filled on the spot with everything from schnitzel to tuna salad or parma ham and peppers. We loved our toasted madeira bread with sliced chouriço sausage and melted cheese. Then again, for £4.50 you can help yourself to one of the specials of the day from the hot buffet; these could include chilli con carne, roast pork with roast potatoes, or a prawn and mussel-strewn paella that's far too good for the price. We were also taken with the deep, fresh, almost creamy vegetable tortilla, and the vast range of freshly baked Portuguese cakes – another thumbs up for the pasteis de nata. You can sit in the plain but practical café inside or take a table in the sun outside, and stock up from the decent Portuguese deli and wine shop next door.

Babies and children welcome. Disabled: toilet. No-smoking tables. Separate room for parties, seats 15. Tables outdoors (10, pavement). Takeaway service. Vegan dishes. **Map 16 L11**.

RESTAURANTS

Central

Knightsbridge SW3

O Fado
49-50 Beauchamp Place, SW3 1NY (7589 3002). Knightsbridge or South Kensington tube. **Lunch served** noon-3pm, **dinner served** 6.30pm-1am daily. **Main courses** £7.20-£14.50. **Cover** £1.50. **Service** 12.5%. **Credit** AmEx, JCB, MC, V.

Menu

Açorda: a bread stew, using bread that's soaked in stock, then cooked with olive oil, garlic, coriander and an egg. Often combined with shellfish or bacalhau (qv).

Amêijoas à bulhão pato: clams with olive oil, garlic, coriander and lemon.

Arroz de marisco: soupy seafood rice.

Arroz de tamboril: soupy rice with monkfish.

Arroz doce: rice pudding.

Bacalhau: salt cod; soaked before cooking, then boiled, grilled, stewed or baked, and served in myriad variations.

Bifana: pork steak, marinated in garlic, fried and served in a bread roll.

Caldeirada: fish stew, made with potatoes, tomatoes and onions.

Caldo verde: the classic soup of finely sliced spring cabbage in a potato stock, always served with a slice of chouriço (qv).

Caracois: boiled snails, eaten as a snack with beer.

Carne de porco alentejana: an Alentejo dish of fried pork, clams and potato.

Cataplana: a special copper cooking pan with a curved, rounded bottom and lid.

Chouriço assado: a paprika-flavoured smoked pork sausage cooked on a terracotta dish over burning alcohol.

Cozido à portuguesa: the traditional Sunday lunch of Portugal – various meats plus three types of sausage, cabbage, carrots, potatoes and sometimes white beans, all boiled together.

Dobrada: tripe stew.

Feijoada: bean stew, cooked with pork and sausages.

Pastel de bacalhau: salt cod fish cake.

Pastel de nata: a rich egg custard tart made with crisp, thin, filo pastry.

Piri piri or **peri peri**: Angolan hot red pepper.

Pudim flan: crème caramel.

Sardinhas assadas: fresh sardines, roasted or char-grilled.

Things were looking bleak for local Portuguese aficionados when those two Beauchamp Place stalwarts – O Fado and Caravela – closed their doors early in 2004. At least O Fado has opened them again, under the same management and in modestly pretty basement rooms, but with a new spring in its step. The menu contains all the old favourites, along with the occasional sighting from the past (crêpe à la chef, stuffed with shellfish and brandy sauce; melon with prawn and cocktail sauce). But if you feel like a simple grilled whole fish, some garlicky clams fragrant with coriander, or some seared, searingly hot spring chicken piri-piri, you're in the right place. Best of all are the arroz dishes: soupy rice stews of seafood, monkfish or prawns brought to the table steaming in huge cast-iron pots. Heart-wrenching fado music is still played every night from Tuesday to Friday, and service is still old-fashioned, bow-tied and hard-working in a very nice, homely way.
Babies and children welcome. Booking advisable; essential dinner weekends. Entertainment: guitarists 8pm Tue-Sat. Separate room for parties, seats 75. **Map 14 F9**.

West

Westbourne Grove W2

Nando's
63 Westbourne Grove, W2 4UA (7313 9506/ www.nandos.co.uk). Bayswater tube. **Meals served** noon-11.30pm Mon-Thur, Sun; noon-midnight Fri, Sat. **Main courses** £4.95-£8. **Credit** JCB, MC, V.
Nando's trademark peri-peri chicken may not be corn-fed, but the restaurant's sense of humour certainly is. Waitresses wear 'Chicks rule' T-shirts; paper napkins bear the message 'Wipe that smile off your face', and 'How did we rate?' cards are headed 'Did we cluck up?'. This two-floor cantina is one of around 100 Nando's in Britain and one of 400 around the world, so it's hardly surprising that the place has the anonymous, automated feel of a fast-food chain. Chickens are pre-marinated and pre-cooked, before being flame-grilled to order; salads are pre-washed and pre-packed; and sauces are decanted into large squeezy bottles. Place your order at the counter, then help yourself to crockery, cutlery, sauces and bottomless soft drinks and frozen yoghurts. Salads, vegetarian offerings and steak rolls play supporting roles to the chicken, which is spiced according to taste, served whole, halved, quartered, as a burger or in pitta. It's a far cry from the scorched, sizzling, salt-grilled chickens of traditional Portuguese peri-peri joints, but prices are low, the chips aren't bad and the Lagosta vinho verde is drinkable. And it's a good choice for families.
Babies and children welcome; children's menu; high chairs; toys. Bookings not accepted. No-smoking tables. Takeaway service. Vegetarian menu. **Map 7 B6**.
For branches see index.

South

Brixton SW2

The Gallery
256A Brixton Hill, SW2 1HF (8671 8311). Brixton tube/rail/45, 109, 118, 250 bus. **Dinner served** 7-10.30pm Tue-Sun. **Main courses** £8.50-£14. **Credit** AmEx, MC, V.
Stepping into this nondescript takeaway chicken joint with its black-and-white tiled floor, plain brick counter and well-worn waiting seats, you'd be forgiven for thinking 'whoops, wrong place!'. But push the door marked 'Restaurant', and you enter a parallel universe: a quirky, cantina-style restaurant encased in colourful murals, with a wooden gallery that looks down on the dining floor. Staff are friendly enough, servings are big and our fellow diners seem contented. There's the usual array of grilled meat, fish and, of course, chicken, plus several variations on bacalhau, as well as more unusual dishes such as chicken curry old Goa style. The Gallery is best known for its cataplana dishes – cooked and served in the

O Moinho. See p236.

famous Portuguese hinged copper cooking pot. Our version, with chicken, clams and chouriço, took an age to arrive. The chicken was overcooked, the sauce was just oil, and the clams were inedibly gritty. Some piri piri chicken, spare ribs and grilled lamb chops from the takeaway counter would have been a better idea.
Babies and children welcome; high chairs. Book weekends. Takeaway service (12.30-11pm Tue-Sat; 12.30-10.30pm Sun). **Map 22 D3**.

Stockwell SW8, SW9

Bar Estrela
111-115 South Lambeth Road, SW8 1UZ (7793 1051). Stockwell tube/Vauxhall tube/rail. **Meals served** 8am-midnight daily. **Main courses** £7.50-£12. **Credit** AmEx, DC, MC, V.
'No topless!!! Keep shirts on!' reads the handwritten sign that greets you as you step into Bar Estrela. It obviously works, as all customers – the Portuguese men drinking at the bar, the younger local crowd eating in the terrazzo-floored café to the right, and the older, more genteel lot in the formal restaurant to the left – do indeed keep their shirts on. We can only imagine the sign is intended for (male) sun lovers who fill the front pavement tables in summer. Estrela is a friendly, something-for-everyone place with a typical London-Portuguese greatest-hits menu that runs from tapas-style dishes to a full-on paella or whole grilled sea bass. From the specials list a dish of steamed clams was harsh with garlic and low in clam flavour, while a main course of grilled quail served with both chips and rice lacked any character of the grill. On the plus side, crumbed whitebait were oil-free and crunchy, grilled sardines were impeccably fresh, and a nicely gloopy stew of chouriço, pork and broad beans (favas à portuguesa) was the sort of thing you could eat any and every night of the week.
Babies and children welcome; high chairs. Booking advisable. Disabled: toilet. No-smoking area. Tables outdoors (10, pavement). Takeaway service. **Map 16 L13**.

O Cantinho de Portugal
135-137 Stockwell Road, SW9 9TN (7924 0218). Stockwell tube/Brixton tube/rail/2, 322, 325, 355 bus. **Bar Open** 11am-11pm daily.

Restaurant **Meals served** noon-midnight daily. **Main courses** £4-£9.50. **Credit** AmEx, MC, V. *Both* Closed 1st 3wks Aug.

A typical neighbourly Portuguese bar and restaurant, with television screens everywhere, a pumping bar, a buzzy café (serving tapas-style snacks) and a more sedate restaurant to the side. The main dining room holds few decorative surprises: pink tablecloths, carnations in vases and a refrigerated cabinet with the usual chocolate mousses, rice puddings and pudim flans. Most dishes are enormous, so you might want to share a starter: perhaps some mussels in white wine, or a huge pot of cold, yet flavourful octopus salad. The seafood rice is deservedly popular, but we were also impressed by the simple, honest dishes listed as daily specials, including a hearty pile-up of liver and bacon and an extremely likeable rabbit and pea stew, flavoured with the odd slice of chouriço and flanked by two cliff faces of rice and chips. The wine list is better than the norm too. When a gent at the next table spilled gravy on his sleeve, the waiter came running up with a cloth and spot remover. Now that's what we call service. *Babies and children admitted; high chairs. Booking advisable. Disabled: ramp, toilet.* **Map 22 D1.**

Grelha D'Ouro

151 South Lambeth Road, SW8 1XN (7735 9764). Stockwell tube/Vauxhall tube/rail. **Breakfast served** 7am-noon, **lunch served** noon-6pm, **dinner served** 6-11pm daily. **Main courses** £4.50-£5.50 lunch, £7.50-£12.35 dinner. **Tapas** £3-£4. **Credit** MC, V.

A hastily stuck up bath towel emblazoned with the Oporto FC logo might seem strange decor for a popular neighbourhood tapas bar, café and restaurant, but it was excusable given that the Portuguese team had won the Champions League the night before. No wonder then that everyone was in such good humour. In the more casual area at the front, a local young Portuguese crowd were toying with tapas, coffee and Portuguese beers while glancing at the TV sets over the bar. In the back restaurant, it's another story altogether with double-clothed tables and bright red carnations in vases. You can order prawn cocktail or melon and parma ham if you must; otherwise, pretend you're in Oporto with a generous serving of feijoada de marisco (bean and seafood stew). The deep-fried calamares were surprisingly tender and crisp, and the crisp-skinned little sardines straight off the charcoal grill were the real thing. Offal lovers might be disappointed with the 'chicken gizzards', however, which turn out to be chicken wings. The food is honest and hearty, whether you want just a snack or a full-on victory celebration. *Babies and children welcome; high chairs. Booking advisable weekends. No-smoking tables. Separate room for parties, seats 100. Takeaway service. Vegetarian menu.* **Map 16 L13.**

O Moinho

355A Wandsworth Road, SW8 2JH (7498 6333). Stockwell tube/Vauxhall tube/rail/77, 77A bus. **Tapas served** 10am-11pm daily. **Main courses** £6.50-£9.50. **Credit** MC, V.

Most of the locals tend to end their meals here with a snifter of Macieira (Portuguese brandy). Do likewise. It makes a fine finish to a modest but filling dinner that kicks off with good fresh crusty bread served with olives and little sachets of tuna and sardine pâté. Pizza and pasta are popular orders, as are 1960s throwback dishes like gratinated scallops, prawn cocktails and simple, grilled steaks. Far better, however, is to throw yourself into one of the homely seafood stews, such as arroz de tamboril (monkfish rice), or a veritable bathtub of açorda, a soupy bready gruel studded with prawns, mussels and clams that's so big it could feed a family of four for a week. The large, airy bar-café area to the right segues into a large, airy restaurant area to the left. Both spaces look pretty much the same, except the café tables are bare, and the restaurant tables are double-clothed. The walls of the restaurant are adorned with handsome azulejo tiles, while the café walls are hung with football sweaters bearing names like Postiga and Oliveira. Your choice. *Babies and children welcome; high chairs. Booking advisable. Separate area for parties, seats 50. Tables outdoors (5, pavement). Takeaway service.*

North

Camden Town & Chalk Farm NW1

Pescador

23 Pratt Street, NW1 0BG (7482 7008). Camden Town or Mornington Crescent tube/24, 29 bus. **Dinner served** 6-11pm Tue-Fri. **Meals served** 1-11pm Sat; 1-10pm Sun. **Main courses** £9.50-£16. **Credit** JCB, MC, V.

Don't let the colourful picture of the Italian seaside town of Portofino on the wall fool you. This place is all Portuguese, from its vinho verde to its copper cataplana (used for cooking the house special of mixed seafood for two). With its yellow walls, tealight candles, bud vases and cushioned bistro chairs, Pescador is a simple, pretty neighbourhood fish restaurant blessed with sparkling service thanks to a personable young waiter who will implore you not to leave anything on the plate, as the chef tends to get upset. He had no need to worry. The golden pasteis de bacalhau (football-shaped potato and salt cod fritters) were the best we've had in London; a whole grilled sea bass with head left on as requested ('any preference for eye colour?' asked the waiter) was fresh, moist and everything a grilled fish should be; and the arroz de marisco (soupy rice loaded with prawns, squid, clams, mussels and fish) was Portuguese comfort food. That said, we left the limp beans, lifeless boiled potatoes, lacklustre salad and Lurpak butter sachets. Sorry, chef. *Babies and children welcome; high chairs. Booking advisable; essential weekends. Takeaway service.* **Map 27 D2.** **For branch see index.**

Spanish

London's Spanish restaurants have a bit of an image problem, tending to be pigeonholed either as rowdy tapas bars or dated sangria-and-flamenco joints, forever stuck in some 1970s time-warp, when a package holiday to the Costa del Sol was the last word in exotic. True, both of these exist – and we've culled some of the more dismal examples this year – but there are a few very good, long-serving restaurants such as **Cambio de Tercio** and **Navarro's**, and also some deservedly popular, reliable neighbourhood eateries, including **Laxeiro** in Bethnal Green and **Rebato's** in Vauxhall. A new breed of hip, high-quality restaurants has also emerged in the past few years, showcasing the best of modern Spanish cuisine and design, notable among them **Moro** and tapas-only **Fino**. We lament the passing this year of Gaudí in Farringdon; the capital's Spanish dining scene is poorer for its loss.

Central
Bloomsbury WC1

Cígala
54 Lamb's Conduit Street, WC1N 3LW (7405 1717/www.cigala.co.uk). Holborn or Russell Square tube. **Lunch served** noon-10.45pm Mon-Fri; 12.30-10.45pm Sat. **Main courses** £10-£17. **Tapas** £2-£8. **Set lunch** (Mon-Fri) £15 2 courses, £18 3 courses. **Set tapas** £18 5 dishes. **Credit** AmEx, DC, MC, V.
One of a cluster of restaurants on Lamb's Conduit Street, Cígala is a slick, modern operation with crisp white and pine decor. Despite the trendy aesthetics, the menu keeps things surprisingly traditional and unshowy. It offers a daily changing roster of classic starters and mains, such as tasty, deep-fried padrón peppers, fish served a la plancha (grilled) and delicious salt-cured serrano ham, all simply but effectively prepared with robust ingredients, and accompanied by crusty, own-made bread. The extremely thorough Spanish wine list is reasonably priced in the main, with a handful of vintages by the glass, and an admirable selection of sherries and cavas. We found the staff efficient and knowledgeable, and the prices, though not extreme, are in line with the chic surroundings. Note: tapas – spanning meat, fish, veg and a section dedicated solely to cheese – are served in the basement or on the pavement tables, but if it's not busy, staff may let you order tapas in the main restaurant.
Babies and children welcome; high chairs. Bar available for hire. Booking advisable. Tables outdoors (10, pavement). **Map 4 M4**.

City E1, EC3

Barcelona Tapas Bar y Restaurante
15 St Botolph Street, entrance at 1 Middlesex Street, EC3A 7DT (7377 5222/0845 4900512/ www.barcelona-tapas.com). Aldgate tube/Liverpool Street tube/rail. **Meals served** 11am-11pm Mon-Fri. **Tapas** £2.95-£13.95. **Service** 12.5%. **Credit** AmEx, DC, MC, V.
Though the name is boring and typical of a chain restaurant, there is, in fact, little to fault about the atmosphere of these tapas hangouts. Nicely run-down and dim, they exude a lived-in functionality and, behind the scenes, wily wine selectors, sharp waiters and good tapas chefs are busy delivering commendable food and drink. The tortillas, always

a good litmus test, are just that little bit creamy, as they ought to be, and the seafood comes lightly breaded, fresh and moist. Of the mains, the habas catalanas stew was rich, with the big broad beans soft but not overboiled; equally exciting was the pincho – pork with chillis, soaked in a red wine-based sauce. The wine list is long and yields heavy reds and fruity whites, served by the glass in the tapas spirit. The desserts, in particular the massive Gran Torres liqueur-laced tiramisu with mascarpone, are a fecund area. Carajillo coffee, generously infused with cognac, brings the night to a satisfying close, just as in everyone's favourite city – except five hours too early. The Tapas Club (free to join) has special meal nights and offers – so ask if there are any on when you arrive.
Babies and children welcome; high chairs. Booking advisable lunch. Restaurant available for hire. Separate floor for parties, seats 80. **Map 12 S6**.
For branches see index.

Mesón Los Barriles
8A Lamb Street, E1 6EA (7375 3136). Aldgate East tube/Liverpool Street tube/rail. **Lunch served** noon-4pm Sun. **Meals served** 11am-11pm Mon-Fri. **Closed** 3 wks Aug. **Tapas** £2.50-£21.90. **Credit** AmEx, JCB, MC, V.
Wander over to this food bar-resto tucked into the corner of Spitalfields Market on a Tuesday and you'll be hard-pressed to imagine it draws its inspiration from the bustling barrels-and-hams tapas bars of Seville. Ambience apart, several of the tapas were pretty good: tender squid rings, hot and tasty button mushrooms in garlic, and a big plate of crispy salmon were all popular. On the sloppier side were a boring chicken, its promised spicy 'salsa' merely a dollop of mayonnaise, and the manchego cheese, which lacked the sweaty bite of the original. A preponderance of empty shells in our clam dish meant more searching than savouring. In fact, some of the seafood on display looked tiny and none too fresh. Both the baked items and the cold desserts were poor: the cheesecake we tasted was soured, the almond tart boring. Even the hazelnut ice-cream – a 'Vesuvio' – lacked flavour. On the upside, service was fast and friendly, there was a good supply of bread, and for £20 you can get an excellent Marqués de Riscal or equivalent Riojan red or white.
Babies and children welcome; high chairs. Booking advisable. Separate room for parties, seats 60. Tables outdoors (5, market). **Map 12 R5**.
For branch see index.

Clerkenwell & Farringdon EC1

Anexo
61 Turnmill Street, EC1M 5PT (7250 3401/ www.anexo.co.uk). Farringdon tube/rail/55, 243 bus.
Bar **Open** 11am-1am Mon-Thur; 11am-2am Fri; noon-2am Sat; (summer only) 2pm-midnight Sun. *Restaurant* **Brunch served** (summer only) 2pm-midnight Sun. **Lunch served** noon-2.30pm Mon-Fri. **Dinner served** 6-11pm Mon-Sat. **Tapas served** 11am-11pm Mon-Sat; 2-11pm Sun. **Main courses** £6.50-£12.50. **Tapas** £2.95-£5.25. **Set lunch** £7.50 2 courses, £9.50 3 courses.
Both **Credit** AmEx, MC, V.
We like the idea of Spanish tapas in Farringdon, and we were even more pleased to find a two-for-one Monday tapas deal in progress on our latest visit. Anexo is in a fine location (close to the tube station and adjoining Turnmills), and comes complete with a large TV (for sport), DJs, sassy

waitresses and a buzzy atmosphere. We opted for around five or six dishes between two, and were treated to a tasty and well-cooked selection of Spanish sausage (cooked in red wine), spicy potatoes, tender prawns and ham croquettes – only an octopus dish was rather too trying on the teeth. Fresh bread and olive oil does a good job of mopping it all up, and a largely continental and well-priced wine list (or cocktails) does an even better job of washing it all down. There's a Mediterranean à la carte menu for more discerning diners with more cash to spend – but that might not be quite so much fun.
Babies and children welcome (lunch only). Booking advisable dinner. Entertainment: DJs (top floor) from 8pm Thur-Sat. Restaurant available for hire. Separate floor available for parties. Tables outdoors (6, pavement). **Map 5 N4**.

★ Moro
34-36 Exmouth Market, EC1R 4QE (7833 8336/www.moro.co.uk). Farringdon tube/rail/ 19, 38 bus.
Bar **Open** 12.30-11.45pm Mon-Fri; 6.30-11.45pm Sat (last entry 10.30pm).
Restaurant **Lunch served** 12.30-2.30pm Mon-Fri. **Dinner served** 7-10.30pm Mon-Sat. **Main courses** £13.50-£17.50. **Service** 12.5% for parties of 6 or more.
Both **Credit** AmEx, DC, MC, V.
With praise from all sides, a top-selling cookbook and near-permanently busy tables, Moro has set the style for restaurants offering an imaginative English take on Mediterranean food traditions – in this case, from Spain and North Africa. Chef duo Sam and Sam Clark have kept standards impressively high since Moro opened in 1997, the cornerstone being the use of prime-quality authentic ingredients, inventively combined, but without ever wasting their essential flavours. A salpicón de mariscos made a delightful summer starter; fattoush salad with crisp Moroccan bread, tomatoes, herbs and other veg was just as bright. Moro's wood-fired oven and charcoal grill come into play with the mains, and, while there are great fish choices, we were especially impressed by the superb meats: wood-roasted pork with potato, pepper and onion salad, and char-grilled lamb with leeks, yoghurt and mint. To finish, we couldn't resist the fabulous Malaga wine and raisin ice-cream. Tapa-sized dishes are available too, at the bar. Service has remained as bright as the food, but it needs be said that the combination of crowds and Moro's stylishly stripped-down design make this one of London's noisiest restaurants. We've noticed that wine prices have been climbing – the list is a fine selection of often-unusual Spanish and other labels, but there's little under £23.
Babies and children welcome; high chairs. Booking essential. Disabled: toilet. Tables outdoors (6, pavement). **Map 5 N4**.

Fitzrovia W1

★ Fino
2004 RUNNER-UP BEST NEW RESTAURANT
33 Charlotte Street, entrance on Rathbone Street, W1T 1RR (7813 8010). Goodge Street or Tottenham Court Road tube. **Lunch served** noon-2.30pm Mon-Fri. **Dinner served** 6-10.30pm Mon-Sat. **Tapas** £5-£15. **Set tapas meal** £17.95 6 tapas. **Credit** AmEx, MC, V.
It may be in a basement, but this stylish Spanish restaurant and bar is anything but gloomy. The pale wood fittings and smart lighting, helped by the sheer spaciousness of the premises, create a buzzy, congenial atmosphere. The small mezzanine bar is even busier. An immensely appealing menu lists tapas that runs all the way from caperberries and toasted almonds (£1.80 a portion) to foie gras with chilli jam at £15.50. It's such a good read that greed will lead you to order too many dishes of the order of crispy fried squid rings, piping hot piquilla croqueta, moreish spicy pimientos de padrón, luscious duck breast with tapenade, patatas bravas (with classy spicy dip served separately), and grilled asparagus with manchego shavings. There are classic (£17.95 per person) and gourmet (£28 per person) selections (for two or

PASSION BEYOND REASON

CERVEZA DE PASIÓN

more) if you really can't make a choice from what is a pretty substantial list. Desserts run from a shot of crema catalana foam to a chocolate brownie with pistachio ice-cream; there's a choice of manchego, picos or goat's cheese too. All in all, much-needed contemporary addition to London's moribund Spanish dining scene.
Babies and children welcome; high chairs. Booking advisable. Disabled: lift; toilet. **Map 9 J5**.

Navarro's

67 Charlotte Street, W1T 4PH (7637 7713/ www.navarros.co.uk). Goodge Street or Tottenham Court Road tube. **Lunch served** noon-3pm Mon-Fri. **Dinner served** 6-10pm Mon-Sat. **Tapas** £1.50-£14.50. **Service** 10%. **Credit** AmEx, DC, MC, V.
Despite the relatively recent arrival of fresh and fancy competition round the corner in the shape of Fino (*see p237*), Navarro's continues to hold its own as one of the most enjoyable mid-range Spanish restaurants in London. The cheerful interior – dark wood and Moorish tiles – is often heaving, so you may have to book, but it's not just the atmosphere that draws a crowd. Generously sized tapas are the order of the day: on our latest visit we sampled a hearty lentil stew with chorizo and vegetables, a crisp ensalada betica (lettuce, beans, onion and avocado), some incredibly moreish bombas de patatas (deep-fried mash and veg with a garlicky tang) and a less successful monkfish in a saffron and brandy sauce on a bed of fried aubergines. Having gone for what turned out to be a highly ambitious seven tapas between two, we were too full for dessert, but sweet dishes run along traditional Spanish lines (crema catalana, flan de huevo). The choice is rich, and the standard of ingredients and cooking is usually high; service is upbeat and friendly. Wash it all down with a robust, reasonably priced Rioja. A fantastic place and, even better, no stuffed shirts.
Babies and children welcome; high chairs. Booking advisable. **Map 3 J5**.

Mayfair W1

El Pirata

5-6 Down Street, W1J 7AQ (7491 3810/ www.elpirata.co.uk). Green Park or Hyde Park Corner tube. **Meals served** noon-11.30pm Mon-Fri; 6-11.30pm Sat. **Main courses** £10-£13.50.

Tapas £2.50-£8. **Set tapas meal** £8, £13.75, £17.50. **Service** 10%. **Credit** (over £10) AmEx, DC, JCB, MC, V.
El Pirata does justice to its Mayfair surroundings, with faux leather tablecloths, repro Picassos on the wall and a stylish mirrored bar. The atmosphere is lively and welcoming, and the clientele more varied than you'd expect for the area, with a few lone lunchers and couples mixed in with the office crowd. The tapas menu is lengthy, with plenty of fish and vegetarian options, and generous set menus can help keep prices down. Culinary triumphs on our latest visit included boquerones (marinated anchovies) in a perfectly balanced garlic and vinegar sauce; fresh, not-too-greasy sardines; and featherlight pan con tomate (a bargain at £1.25). Less successful were gambas pil pil, which came with burnt garlic, and an artificial-tasting arroz con pollo, while patatas bravas were, well, weird – like chips with a bland tomato sauce. To end on a sugar high, choose from the likes of crème brûlée, rice pudding or fried banana with honey and ice-cream. Fans of Spanish wine take note – the list features some stunners. Not the place to come for a culinary extravaganza, then, but for a good-value meal – rare in these parts – with a buzz, you could do considerably worse.
Babies and children welcome. Booking advisable dinner. Separate room for parties, seats 65. Tables outdoors (4, pavement). Takeaway service. **Map 9 H8**.

Piccadilly W1

Mar i Terra

17 Air Street, W1B 5AF (7734 1992/ www.mariterra.co.uk). Piccadilly Circus tube. **Lunch served** noon-3pm, **dinner served** 5-11pm Mon-Fri. **Meals served** noon-11pm Sat. **Tapas** £1.50-£13.50. **Service** 10%. **Credit** AmEx, DC, MC, V.
We had high hopes for this mini chain of tapas bars in light of last year's glowing review, but a recent visit to its Soho outpost was disappointing. The decor is attractive – modern, with dark wood and blue walls – the atmosphere laid-back and the welcome friendly, despite the place being discouragingly quiet on a Friday night (though it did fill up later). As for the tapas, they're split between traditional and modern. We chose mainly from the former list, and weren't overly impressed.

Patatas bravas were fine – fresh, with a spicy kick; both prawns and chicken in garlic were merely average, lacking the necessary garlic zing; and deep-fried medallions of monkfish were dull, verging on the unpleasant, with an overriding flavour of burnt garlic (plus, the portion simply wasn't bit enough to justify the £5.75 price tag). On the other hand, chorizo in wine stood out, boasting rich flavours, and moreish garlic bread was another winner. Wishing to prolong the feel-good factor, we ordered chocolate brownie with walnuts, pine nuts and raisins. Sadly, it didn't do the trick, being hot, steamy and under-sugared. There's only one type of beer (Estrella Damm), but the wine list, by contrast, cries out to be explored. We are hoping that this underwhelming visit was just a one-off blip.
Babies and children welcome. Booking advisable. Restaurant available for hire. Separate room for parties, seats 8. **Map 17 J7**.
For branches see index.

Pimlico SW1

Goya

34 Lupus Street, SW1V 3EB (7976 5309/ www.goyarestaurants.co.uk). Pimlico tube. **Lunch served** noon-3pm, **dinner served** 6-11.30pm daily. **Main courses** £12-£15. **Tapas** £3-£7. **Credit** DC, JCB, MC, V.
We found an appealingly unusual mix of diners at this popular Pimlico haunt. Discreet pinstriped politicians mixed happily with animated young Europeans and locals in the buzzy upstairs bar, while downstairs in the restaurant a heavy Monday evening calm prevailed. Sitting upstairs, we enjoyed a series of dishes from the tapas menu, including marinated anchovies, grilled baby squid, prawns in olive oil, garlic and chilli, a house speciality of mixed shrimp and crab salad, bean casserole with Spanish sausage and lots of olives. None was spectacular, but all were adequate, and the house red is a tasty Rioja. The Spanish staff are charming and efficient despite not having great English, making this a useful spot in an otherwise quiet area.
Babies and children welcome; high chairs. Booking advisable Mon-Fri. No-smoking tables. Tables outdoors (10, pavement). Takeaway service. **Map 15 J11**.
For branch see index.

Moro. See p237.

Soho W1

Café España

*63 Old Compton Street, W1D 6HT (7494 1271).
Piccadilly Circus or Leicester Square tube.*
Meals served noon-midnight Mon-Sat; noon-11pm Sun. **Main courses** £4.95-£12.95. **Tapas**
£2.20-£5.95. **Credit** JCB, MC, V.
Café España packs 'em in every night, despite
being the antithesis of trendiness in terms of
atmosphere and decor (think sooty brass wall
lamps, naff boot-fair pictures and dark maroon
carpets). Its popularity can be explained by the
exceptionally friendly staff, and the extensive and
staunchly traditional menu that pulls in homesick
Spaniards, as well as tourists and Soho bohos. We
went down the tapas route; three per person was
ample. The dishes arrived disconcertingly quickly,
and presented few surprises: this is bog-standard
fare, although appetising enough and in huge,
good-value portions. Spanish tortilla, saffron rice,
and garlic bread were all good choices; the patatas
bravas, prawns, and manchego cheese plates were
less successful, being generous in size but really
quite bland. We witnessed (several times) staff
putting bread from half-empty baskets into those
destined for new customers. Still, such behaviour
doesn't seem to trouble the loyal patrons.
*Babies and children welcome. Bookings not
accepted. Restaurant available for hire. Separate
room for parties, seats 30. Map 17 K6.*

West

Brook Green W6

Los Molinos

*127 Shepherd's Bush Road, W6 7LP (7603
2229). Hammersmith tube.* **Lunch served**
noon-3pm Mon-Fri. **Dinner served** 6-10.45pm
Mon-Sat. **Tapas** £3.50-£7.90. **Service** 10%.
Credit AmEx, DC, JCB, MC, V.
You'd have to be a cold-hearted curmudgeon not to
be charmed by this pretty little tapas bar.
Everything is spick and span, with salmon pink
walls covered with a colourful array of ceramics,
a central bar and smartly varnished wooden
furniture. The young waiting staff are ultra-
friendly. The lengthy tapas menu (three dishes per
person is probably enough) offers plenty for
vegetarians and seafood fans, as well as standard
meaty options (lamb kidneys in sherry, meatballs
in a carrot and wine sauce, sautéed chicken livers)
and a few daily specials. The food is fresh and good
quality, if not mind-blowing. Patatas bravas came
in a nicely spicy if slightly watery sauce;
garbanzos (chickpeas) were flavoured with
spinach and cumin; grilled squid (a la plancha) was
tender; and there was lots of good chewy bread to
mop up stray juices. To drink, there's Iberian beers
and a reasonable Spanish wine list (though little
by the glass). Finish with a strong cafe con leche,
a traditional dessert (arroz con leche, crema
catalana) or palate-cleansing lemon sorbet. No
surprise that it was buzzing on a midweek night,
complete with kids running about way past their
bedtime in true Spanish style.
*Babies and children welcome; high chairs. Booking
advisable dinner Fri, Sat. Restaurant available
for hire. Separate room for parties, seats 45.
Vegetarian menu. Map 20 C3.*

Ladbroke Grove W10

Galicia

*323 Portobello Road, W10 5SY (8969 3539).
Ladbroke Grove tube.* **Lunch served** noon-3pm
Tue-Sun. **Dinner served** 7-11.30pm Tue-Sat;
7-10.30pm Sun. **Main courses** £7-£12.
Tapas £2.50-£6. **Set lunch** £7.50 3 courses;
(Sun) £8.50 3 courses. **Credit** AmEx, DC, MC, V.
Pass the market and keep on walking along
Portobello Road and you'll finally reach this little
slice of Spain, with an interior that looks like it
hasn't been touched since the 1970s. There's a
small bar at the front, a larger room at the back and
an upstairs (empty on our most recent visit). The
gruff waiters will usually turn on the charm just
enough to find you a seat. The menu offers

standard Spanish staples at reasonable prices. You
can chomp on a filling selection of tortilla,
albóndigas, chorizo in wine, and patatas bravas
while quaffing a reasonable bottle of Rioja, and not
feel out of pocket. The main menu features mainly
northern Spanish dishes – usually not too heavy –
and the pulpo a gallego is recommended. Quality
espresso can then speed you on your way. Not
really a destination restaurant, but certainly a
decent spot to visit to avoid other more aspirational
establishments in the locale and get some true
Spanish flavour.
*Babies and children welcome. Booking essential
weekends. Map 19 B1.*

Maida Vale NW6

Mesón Bilbao

*33 Malvern Road, NW6 5PS (7328 1744). Maida
Vale tube.* **Lunch served** noon-3pm Mon-Fri.
Dinner served 6-11pm Mon-Thur; 7-11.30pm
Fri; 6-11.30pm Sat. **Main courses** £9.95-£11.75.
Tapas £2.50-£6.50. **Credit** MC, V.
Our Spanish guest proclaimed, 'this is
Fuenterabbia standard' (her home in the
gastronomic Basque country) – high praise indeed.
Behind the unprepossessing exterior of this cosy
bar lies a true Spanish enclave complete with
pictures of favoured football teams, castanets and
other artefacts, as well as blackboard menus of
tapas, fish and meat. Tapas of the day included
fabada, morcilla, grilled squid and pimientos. The
last two won our votes, especially the succulent,
perfectly seasoned squid, which was clearly ultra-
fresh and light years away from the all-too-
common rubbery pods. Sweet and aromatic
piquillo peppers, grilled with slivers of garlic, were
another success. An impressive selection of fish,
including bass, swordfish and salmon, made for
some tough decisions. Bacalao vizcaina,
traditionally served in a tomato sauce, was one
happy choice, while clams with rice was a
sensational dish – masses of tiny clams resting on
a delicious pile of rice infused with the clam juices.
More than satisfied, we managed to resist the not
particularly Spanish desserts. Pleasant service,
wines and sherries by the glass, and the prospect
of an authentic paella invites a rapid return visit.
*Babies and children welcome; high chairs.
Booking advisable dinner Fri, Sat. Tables
outdoors (2, pavement). Map 1 A3.*

Paddington W2

Los Remos

*38A Southwick Street, W2 1JQ (7723 5056/
7706 1870). Edgware Road, Lancaster Gate or
Paddington tube/rail.*
Tapas bar **Open** noon-midnight Mon-Sat.
Tapas £1.95-£8.50.
Restaurant **Lunch served** noon-3pm, **dinner
served** 7-11.45pm Mon-Sat. **Main courses**
£7.50-£16. **Set lunch** £9.95 3 courses incl coffee.
Service 10%.
Both **Credit** AmEx, DC, JCB, MC, V.
None of your fancy schmancy modern tapas bar
stuff here. Los Remos is pure retro: we're talking
naff wallpaper, pink tablecloths and an old-
fashioned bar, the sort of place where the (hard)
bread comes with curls of butter, rather than olive
oil. There's a ground-floor restaurant and a
basement tapas bar, but you can choose from the
'restaurant' or 'tapas' menu in both; we ate from
the latter, with mixed results. Meatballs were tasty
and fresh; Spanish omelette was fine, if slightly
over-oniony; but the 'jumbo' (read: slightly bigger-
than-average) scampi, encased in a delicate batter
and smothered in a light lemon and butter sauce,
was the real highlight. On the down side, patatas
bravas were dismal (dry, in a watery tomatoey
sauce). As if straight out of *Fawlty Towers*, there's
a sweet trolley for desserts. But by this time we
were done with the food and content to listen to the
guitarist strumming his stuff (Friday and
Saturday night, in the restaurant). Service is
slightly weary, though never brusque. We can't say
we'd rush back, but with a varied clientele,
including a local Spanish contingent, Los Remos
is obviously doing something right.

Best Spanish

For nueva cocina

For a new slant on old favourites, try
Fino (*see p237*), **Moro** (*see p237*)
or **Cambio de Tercio** (*see p242*).

For tapas

Stay trad at **El Parador** (*see p245*),
Los Molinos (*see below*), **Navarro's**
(*see p239*), **Mesón Bilbao** (*see below*),
Tendido Cero (*see p242*), **Rebato's**
(*see p243*) and **Laxeiro** (*see p244*).

For a party

Break out the sangría at **Mesón
Don Felipe** (*see p243*), **Lomo** (*see
below*), **El Rincón Latino** (*see p243*)
and **Café Loco** (*see p245*).

*Babies and children welcome. Disabled: toilet.
Dress: smart casual (restaurant). Entertainment:
guitarist 8pm Fri, Sat. No-smoking tables.
Restaurant available for hire. Separate rooms for
parties, seating 22 and 50. Vegetarian menu.
Map 8 E5.*

South West

Fulham SW6, SW10

Lomo

*222-224 Fulham Road, SW10 9NB (7349 8848/
www.lomo.co.uk). South Kensington tube then
14 bus.* **Dinner served** 5pm-midnight daily.
Tapas £2.95-£7.95. **Set meal** £6.95 paella
incl glass of wine. **Service** 12.5% for parties
of 6 or more. **Credit** AmEx, JCB, MC, V.
Owned by Julian Richer of Richer Sounds fame,
this Fulham Road eaterie is no discount store, but
the maverick businessman's touch is detectable in
a few appealing quirks. Screenings of Spanish
films on Sunday afternoons, for instance, and a
wallet-friendly early dinner combo of a plate of
paella and a glass of cava. The place fills up early,
thanks to popular happy-hour deals. Most of the
seating is on bar stools around small round tables,
with a few larger dining tables at the back. A
substantial menu offers all the usual favourites,
and the food, swiftly served, is good quality. We
sampled chorizo maniero, cooked in red wine with
peppers, tasty (if a tad chewy) steamed octopus, a
successful plate of mixed charcuterie with
manchego, quince and olives, and a huge portion
of deep-fried whitebait. Desserts range from crema
catalana to (oddly) banoffee pie. Service is
extremely charming and capable.
*Babies and children welcome. Bookings not
accepted after 8.30pm. Entertainment: guitarist
8-10pm Mon-Thur; Spanish films 6pm Sun.
Separate area for parties, seats 30. Vegetarian
menu. Map 13 C12.*

Olé

*Broadway Chambers, Fulham Broadway, SW6
1EP (7610 2010/www.olerestaurants.com).
Fulham Broadway tube.*
Tapas bar **Open** noon-3pm, 5-11pm Mon-Sat.
Tapas £1.55-£6.
Restaurant **Meals served** noon-10.30pm daily.
Main courses £6.50-£10.50. **Service** 10%
for parties of 6 or more.
Both **Credit** AmEx, DC, JCB, MC, V.
The shout of 'olé!' is all about flamboyance and
skill, thrown at agile matadors or footballers
stringing together effortlessly smooth passes.
Which makes us wonder why it was chosen as the
moniker for this understated restaurant. A
narrow bar brightened with mirrors leads to a
small dining area with bare white walls and
polished pale wood furniture. The place looks cold
and unfinished rather than stylishly minimalist,
but, fortunately, the menu is more imaginative,
combining simple dishes (calamares, octopus, cold
meats, cheeses) with more creative ones (shredded
confit of duck with serrano ham rolls, beef with
date and sun-dried tomato sauce). A moist tortilla

The Restaurants

with smoky chorizo was faultless. Juicy grilled langoustines and tender discs of pork fillet with mustard were also good, though the artistically arranged salad and vegetable accompaniments were oily even by Spanish standards. Two traditional staples were disappointing: patatas bravas were pale and powdery, and albóndigas were dry. While conversation among diners – smart couples, well-groomed twentysomethings, a family – went some way to creating a convivial atmosphere, it was surprisingly quiet for a Saturday night. Overall, more OK than Olé.
Babies and children welcome. Book weekends. Disabled: toilet. Restaurant/bar available for hire. **Map 13 B13.**

Putney SW15

La Mancha

32 Putney High Street, SW15 1SQ (8780 1022/ www.lamancha.co.uk). Putney Bridge tube. **Meals served** noon-11pm Mon-Thur; noon-11.30pm Fri, Sat; noon-10.30pm Sun. **Main courses** £8.85-£12.95. **Tapas** £3.95-£6.95. **Set lunch** (noon-2.45pm) £7.95 2 courses. **Credit** AmEx, DC, JCB, MC, V.
The welcoming warmth of La Mancha transported us from a grey Tuesday evening in Putney to a sunnier place. Ochre walls, dark wood furniture and soft lighting were cosy, and the friendly Spanish staff added to the relaxed atmosphere. We cracked open a fruity white Gran Viña Sol, as holiday classic 'Guantanamera' played. A guitarist took over later, perched on the stairs to the first-floor restaurant. Below him, an after-work crowd lined the bar and filled the sprawling dining area. La Mancha's menu doesn't pay particular tribute to the eponymous region's cuisine, taking inspiration from all over the Iberian peninsula. A platter of octopus sprinkled with paprika was superb, as were the rich, dark slices of calf's liver in balsamic vinegar. Spicy beef and chorizo meatballs were also good. Less impressive were swordfish fillets dowsed in too much oil, a stodgy triangle of tortilla, and patatas bravas made soggy by an overdose of salsa picante. Moist tarta de santiago (almond cake) washed down with syrupy moscatel left us on a high, though. The food may be variable, but the good dishes are very good and the robust Spanish flavour of the place makes it well worth a visit.
Babies and children welcome; high chairs. Entertainment: guitarist 8.30-11pm Mon-Sat. Separate room for parties, seats 60.

South Kensington SW5

★ Cambio de Tercio

163 Old Brompton Road, SW5 0LJ (7244 8970/ www.cambiodetercio.com). Gloucester Road or South Kensington tube. **Lunch served** 12.30-2.30pm daily. **Dinner served** 7-11.30pm Mon-Sat; 7-11pm Sun. **Main courses** £13.50-£15.50. **Service** 12.5% for parties of 6 or more. **Credit** AmEx, DC, MC, V.
It's a mystery. Occasionally someone reports having a bad experience at Cambio de Tercio. In the interests of science we've really tried to have one too, but every meal we've had there has been great, sometimes wonderful and, most recently, it's been on a new high. Some complaints seem to come from people who think that all Spanish restaurants should serve generic paella at £7 a head. Not here: this place serves some of the most sophisticated modern Spanish cooking in London. Immediately outstanding on our last visit were the true, rich flavours of every dish, with nothing lost (as so often) to over-elaboration. Spanish classics are not forgotten, they are done exceptionally well: perfectly tender fried calamares came with 'alioli blanco y negro' (garlic mayonnaise and subtle black squid's ink); serrano ham croquetas successfully combined creaminess with the strong flavours of the ham. Beef solomillo with artichokes and boletus mushrooms was a superb, perfectly cooked piece of meat, and a beautifully textured supreme of hake came with a delicate patty of leeks and other veg. Finally: a wholly original, fabulously refreshing thyme and lemon ice-cream. The wine list offers a vast array of fine modern Spanish labels. Service is individual, and also charming and helpful.
Babies and children admitted. Booking advisable dinner. Restaurant available for hire. Separate room for parties, seats 22. Tables outdoors (3, pavement). **Map 13 C11.**

Tendido Cero

174 Old Brompton Road, SW5 0BA (7370 3685/ www.cambiodetercio.co.uk). Gloucester Road or South Kensington tube. **Tapas served** noon-11pm daily. **Tapas** £4.50-£6. **Set tapas meal** £25 per person incl soft drink, water & coffee. **Unlicensed. Corkage** £2. **Service** 12.5%. **No credit cards.**
This tapas-bar offshoot of Cambio de Tercio (*see above*) across the street follows the same style, with a sleekly modern space in black with dashes of vivid Spanish colour, and black-clad waiters who are generally charming (but can get pushed when the bar fills up, as often happens). The upmarket tapas reflect Cambio's style too, and also use fine ingredients, though with a little less refinement. The addictive ham croquetas are exactly the same as over the road, and a generous mixed salad included subtly flavoured rice. Wild asparagus flash-fried in olive oil was also first-rate. A classic potato tortilla and a platter of mixed Spanish meats (chorizo, salchichón and pork loin) were not quite so impressive, and the tortitas (pancakes) stuffed with tuna and prawns offered too few of the promised prawns. Overall, though, the six tapas made a very enjoyable combination and, unusually for a tapas bar, there are some great desserts, especially the deliciously fresh tarta de santiago almond tart with berries and ice-cream. Inexplicably (since it does have a bar), Tendido has no alcohol licence, so take your own wine.
Babies and children welcome. Booking advisable dinner Tue-Sat. Restaurant available for hire. Tables outdoors (5, pavement). **Map 13 C11.**

Los Molinos. See p241.

South

Battersea SW11

Castilla

82 Battersea Rise, SW11 1EH (7738 9597). Clapham Junction rail. **Dinner served** 5.30-11pm Mon-Thur; 5.30-11.30pm Fri, Sat. **Main courses** £7.90-£14. **Tapas** £1.90-£8.50. **Set tapas meal** £10-£15. **Service** 10%. **Credit** AmEx, JCB, MC, V.

After 13 years under the management of its León-born owner, Castilla has been revamped for sale. The extension of the restaurant and the new red-brick bar clash somewhat with the heraldic tapestries and barrel-ends, but, still, innovation is needed here. Certainly, the menu needs overhauling. There's nothing exactly wrong with the tortilla, the peppery paellas, the shellfish starters and assorted fried tapas, but nothing is scintillating, and few items are worth savouring. The fideua (paella with noodles) is typical – it came recommended, but was weak in saffron, poorly stocked with clams and monkfish and ultimately monotonous. Plenty of good £15-£18 Riojan and Navarran reds can distract from the dull grub, but we can see little here to encourage a return visit. The music, which ranged from Pixies to Gotan Project and then switched to a flamenco number and '80s US rock, was hilariously unsuitable. One final warning: descend on Castilla on a wet Tuesday and you may well be alone and, with the new open-plan bar, it really does feel like a tomb. *Babies and children welcome; high chairs. Booking advisable dinner Thur-Sat. Restaurant available for hire. Separate room for parties, seats 35.* **Map 21 C4.**

Clapham SW4

El Rincón Latino

148 Clapham Manor Street, SW4 6BX (7622 0599). Clapham Common tube. **Dinner served** 6.30-11.30pm Mon-Fri. **Meals served** 11am-11.30pm Sat; 11am-10.30pm Sun. **Main courses** £9.95-£13.95. **Tapas** £3.20-£5.20. **Service** 10% for parties of 6 or more. **Credit** AmEx, JCB, MC, V.

Tapas here seem to bring out the Latino in Clapham's normally stiff, Sloanesque society – drop in for a slice of jamón serrano on a Friday night and you can't move for heaving, sweating bodies, shouting gangs of hysterical twenty-somethings and, somewhere in the background, strains of salsa or flamenco. The food on offer isn't half bad, though: there are South American bites such as empanadas and banana chips, as well as all the classic croquettes, cured ham, seafood snacks and pungent cheeses typical of a rustic Spanish menu. Little creativity goes into the standard dishes – lamb chops, 'granny-style' meat balls, cod in sauce and the like – but nothing offends, and there's plenty of good wine, sherries and cocktails. Asking for a dessert or coffee sometimes feels over-formal in the bar-room setting (which can get too noisy to talk and too busy to go to the loo), but the manchego cheese with membrillo is a murderously nice combination, and sweet moscatel is served alongside. If you want to focus on food and drink, go in the week. *Babies and children welcome; high chairs. Booking essential dinner. Disabled: toilet. Vegetarian menu (tapas).* **Map 22 B1.**

Vauxhall SW8

★ Rebato's

169 South Lambeth Road, SW8 1XW (7735 6388/www.rebatos.com). Stockwell tube.
Tapas bar **Open** 5.30-10.45pm Mon-Fri; 7-11pm Sat. **Tapas** £2.95-£5.50.
Restaurant **Lunch served** noon-2.30pm Mon-Fri. **Dinner served** 7-10.45pm Mon-Sat. **Set meal** £17.40 3 courses.
Both **Credit** AmEx, DC, MC, V.
It's not often you see an old, traditional restaurant on the up, but this Vauxhall stalwart was positively heaving on a Wednesday night. It's an artful combination: coolly efficient middle-aged staff from Spain, quick service of a zillion different dishes, new flamenco on the record player and, when we asked for an extra cognac, it came – and was presented on the house. The good thing is, between all these stage and set elements, the food was great: mouthwatering chipirones, sublime

albóndigas (meatballs), nicely roasted kidneys in sherry, and a delicate main dish of plaice. Of course, the wine had all the stamping red anger of an angry bull, and the sherries were served on arrival, and, when we didn't know what to ask for, the maître d' was forceful in his recommendations. Like bullfighting and flamenco, all the charm here is restrained and edgy, but we were totally seduced. (Some readers may recall how an MI6 employee left his laptop here some years back after a meal that became just too relaxing.) Cheesecake was only OK, and the oranges in Gran Marnier and caramel were better in the mind than on the table – but this is a deeply satisfying restaurant experience. Long may it last. *Babies and children welcome. Booking essential (restaurant).* **Map 16 L13.**

Waterloo SE1

Mesón Don Felipe

53 The Cut, SE1 8LF (7928 3237). Southwark tube/Waterloo tube/rail. **Meals served** noon-11pm Mon-Sat. **Tapas** £2.25-£4.75. **Service** 10%. **Credit** MC, V.
Mesón Don Felipe gets so crammed that even the in-house entertainment – a Spanish guitar player, natch – has to avoid the hustle-bustle by perching precariously on top of a cupboard in one corner of the box-like restaurant. This cheerful but cramped tapas joint is not the place for a romantic soirée (grab a table along the side if you do come as a pair). Instead, it's best experienced as part of one of the raucous groups that pack the place out every night, sharing plates of authentic tapas, glugging down jugs of sangria and forcing everybody else at the table to get up when they need to go to the toilet. The atmosphere and South Bank-friendly location are clearly the main draw, but the food's not bad either: excellent crispy calamari and a delicious broad bean and cured ham salad were the highlights of our latest visit, with only a rather limp artichoke salad letting the side down. The wine list is all Spanish and good. *Babies and children welcome. Booking advisable (not accepted after 8pm). Entertainment: guitarist 8.30-11pm daily. Takeaway service.* **Map 11 N8.**

Kennington SE11

The Finca

185 Kennington Road, SE11 4EZ (7735 1061/ www.thefinca.co.uk). Kennington tube/rail. Bar **Open** noon-midnight Mon-Wed, Sun; noon-1am Thur-Sat. *Restaurant* **Lunch served** noon-4pm, **dinner served** 6-11.30pm Mon-Fri. **Meals served** noon-11.30pm Sat, Sun. **Tapas** £3.25-£7.95. **Service** 10%. **Credit** MC, V.

On the one hand, the Finca is a down-to-earth taberna, aptly equipped with swirling ceiling fans and a menu featuring traditional Spanish staples such as rabo de toro (oxtail stew) and pulpo (octopus). But there is also an element of modern chic to this expansive venue. There are banquettes strewn with white cushions, above which psychedelic patterns are projected on to the wall, while low-key Spanish guitar music forms a soothing soundtrack. In the simply furnished dining area, groups of friends and after-work drinkers tucked into white ceramic bowls of patatas bravas and garlic prawns. The food is uncomplicated and neatly presented, with artistic drizzles of garlicky olive oil a favourite garnish, but none of our choices really shone. Lamb chops were tender but served with sticky, lumpy, mashed potato, mackerel fillets were rather dry and a small tortilla was light but over-laden with potato. Better were chunks of smoky chorizo in cider, a verdant mound of sautéed spinach peppered with pine nuts and raisins, and thick, deep-fried slices of manchego cheese. Overall, it is the friendly Spanish staff and easy-going atmosphere that are the highlights at the Finca, with the food generally playing second fiddle.

Babies and children welcome. Booking essential. Entertainment: DJ 8pm-1am Thur-Sat. Separate room for parties, seats 60. Vegetarian menu.

Bethnal Green E2

★ Laxeiro

93 Columbia Road, E2 7RG (7729 1147/ www.laxeiro.com). Bethnal Green tube/Liverpool Street tube/rail/8, 26, 48, 55 bus. **Lunch served** noon-3pm, **dinner served** 7-11pm Tue-Sat. **Meals served** 9am-3pm Sun. **Tapas** £2.95-£9.50. **Credit** AmEx, DC, MC, V.

Tiny and informal, Laxeiro is a lively number, adored by bohemian locals who swing by time and again for the pleasingly varied blackboard menu of traditional tapas. This being the gritty heart of east London, the warm, Mediterranean-inspired decor was never going to offer a substitute for the freewheeling haze of a late-night Spanish bar – Columbia Road is pretty enough but imposing towerblocks and housing estates encroach on all sides – yet the cheesy muzak, sunny Spanish-speaking staff and plentiful Rioja invariably raise everyone's spirits as the night wears on. Apart from gloriously garlicky paella (for two), tapas are the only option, but some are more substantial than you'd imagine; dishes such as barbecued tuna and garlic prawns are approaching main-course size, and – at £9.50 and £7.50 respectively – so are the prices. Cheaper tapas tend to be smaller, and thus better for dipping into a wide range of flavours: barbecued sardines, beef in pepper sauce, pork fillet, pimientos, patatas bravas, chorizo in wine – the quality was consistently high. Recommended. *Babies and children welcome. Booking advisable; essential weekends. Tables outdoors (2, pavement). Takeaway service.* **Map 6 S3**.

Leytonstone E11

Elche

567-569 Leytonstone High Road, E11 4PB (8558 0008). Leytonstone tube. **Lunch served** 12.30-2.30pm Tue-Sat. **Dinner served** 6.30-11pm Mon-Thur; 6.30pm-midnight Fri, Sat. **Meals served** 12.30-10pm Sun. **Main courses** £8.50-£15. **Tapas** £2.50-£5. **Set tapas meal** £12. **Set buffet** (12.30-4pm Sun) £12 incl half bottle of wine or sangria. **Credit** AmEx, JCB, MC, V.

Some things, such as the joyously rip-roaring flamenco nights and the comic coat of arms propped up by the door, just don't change at this Spanish old-timer. Others do. Which in the case of the tapas, is a pity: the menu itself has the same seafood specialities (monkfish, whitebait, squid, sardines – you name it, it's here) and incredible breadth as ever, but on our most recent visit everything tasted mediocre at best. A warm artichoke salad wasn't improved by the addition of mint dressing; lamb cutlets were OK, but had an insipid rosemary sauce. Salmon steak fared better, though the accompanying 'vegetables' turned out to be ratatouille. Even the pan con tomate, usually so flavoursome it belies its simplicity, was oily and slightly charred. To finish, a small square of tarta de manzana got the soft caramelised apples just so, but was let down by a soggy, compacted pastry base. What seemingly can't be bettered, though, is the service, so open and friendly that it feels churlish to criticise anything else.

Babies and children welcome; half-price Sun buffet; high chairs. Booking advisable; essential dinner Fri, Sat. Entertainment: flamenco 8.30pm Fri. Restaurant available for hire. Separate room for parties, seats 30. Takeaway service.

Tendido Cero. See p242.

North

Camden Town & Chalk Farm NW1

Bar Gansa

2 Inverness Street, NW1 7HJ (7267 8909/ www.gansa.co.uk). Camden Town tube. **Open** 10am-midnight Mon-Wed; 10am-1am Thur-Sat; 10am-11pm Sun. **Main courses** £5-£19.50. **Tapas** £3.25-£4.50. **Service** 10% before 5pm; 12.5% after 5pm. **Credit** MC, V.

It's easy to dismiss Bar Gansa as just another grotty Camden dive, filled with a noisy, itinerant population of people who would rather be in Amsterdam – and in many ways, it is exactly that. But it's not all backpackers and ganja-worshippers here, and the owners are clearly keen to class themselves a cut above their Inverness Street neighbours, with a warm, orange-accented dining room and a reasonable standard of cooking. Unfortunately, tapas tend to turn up a little on the lukewarm side: lamb skewers (pinchitos morunos) and their chicken counterparts (pinchito de pollo) should both have made their entrances with an audible sizzle, but just didn't. A mountain of gambas al pil-pil, by contrast, were both peppery and garlicky, and something called 'tumbert' (aubergine stacked with tomatoes, potato and cheese) was an unexpected delight. A generous stack of smoked fish atop a cylinder of fresh avocado was also quite pleasant, if a little too redolent of advance refrigeration. It's all a long way from the back-street bars of Madrid, but come on a Monday and let the flamenco musicians take your mind off the mediocrity. Trust us: at £3 to £4 a plate, you can forgive a lot.
Babies and children welcome. Booking advisable weekends. Entertainment: flamenco 8-11pm Mon. Tables outdoors (2, terrace). **Map 27 C2**.

El Parador

245 Eversholt Street, NW1 1BA (7387 2789). Mornington Crescent tube. **Lunch served** noon-3pm Mon-Fri. **Dinner served** 6-11pm Mon-Thur; 6-11.30pm Fri, Sat; 6.30-9.30pm Sun. **Tapas** £3-£5.80. **Service** 10% for parties of 5 or more. **Credit** MC, V.

For years, one thing has distinguished El Parador from the constellation of dreary north London tapas joints it has to compete with: its proprietors actually care about the food. Dishes always have an earnest, home-made quality to them, and ingredients are generally fresh and well chosen. A plate of higadillos – chicken livers pan-fried with sherry, grapes and balsamic vinegar – was a moist and dribbly treat. Salteado de gambas was another highlight – beefy, spirited tiger prawns livened up with chillies, padrón pepper and caraway seeds. As for some of the more conventional items, patatas bravas came closer to their Spanish namesake than many we've tried, but a tortilla Española was a little on the bland side. With the majority of tapas in the £4 range, though, and a decent wine list, there is really little to complain about. For those fed up with the loud, smoky sangria pits that pass for Spanish restaurants across so much of the capital, El Parador, with its cosy back garden and family-run charm, continues to be a rare treat.
Babies and children welcome. Bookings accepted for 3 or more only. Separate room for parties, seats 30. Tables outdoors (10, garden). Vegetarian menu. **Map 27 D3**.

Jamón Jamón

38 Parkway, NW1 7AH (7284 0606). Camden Town tube. **Meals served** noon-11.30pm Mon-Thur, Sun; noon-12.30am Fri, Sat. **Tapas** £2-£6.95. **Set meal** (Mon-Fri) £6.95 2 tapas & soft drink. **Service** (over £40) 10%. **Credit** AmEx, DC, MC, V.

The ham's so good here, they named it twice – at least that's what they'd like you to believe. Jamón Jamón's earth-coloured walls are entirely blank but for the words 'jamón jamón' cast in shadows above every table, and the menus proudly bear the slogan 'where jamón is king' (it all starts to feel a little Orwellian after a while). So is this rambunctious Camden local with its delightful retractable roof feature really a little piece of hog heaven? Well, yes and no. A 'tabla' (a sort of large wooden paddle) of jamón serrano bore ham that was well textured but lacking the flavour of a really top cut. We got over it fairly quickly, though, when the tapas arrived. Chorizo in red wine sauce featured top-notch sausage cooked to perfection in a moreish broth; gambas a la plancha were fat, dribbly and satisfying. Boquerones en vinagre, on the other hand, were a disappointment – a plate of limp anchovies on iceberg lettuce. Lamb chops were also a little on the tough side. A very un-Spanish dessert selection includes items such as tiramisu and a plain strawberry cheesecake. House Rioja was sickly-sweet and too young, while the slow, nearly absent service bordered on farce at times. We're all for mañana, but a three-hour tapas meal? Por favor.
Babies and children welcome: high chairs. Booking advisable dinner and weekends. Vegetarian menu. **Map 27 C2**.
For branches (La Siesta, Tapeo) see index.

Crouch End N8

La Bota

31 Broadway Parade, Tottenham Lane, N8 9DB (8340 3082). Finsbury Park tube/rail then 91, W7 bus. **Lunch served** noon-2.30pm, **dinner served** 6-11.30pm Mon-Fri. **Meals served** noon-11.30pm Sat, Sun. **Main courses** £6.50-£11.95. **Tapas** £1.80-£4.50. **Credit** JCB, MC, V.

This is a proper local-standby tapas bar, with generally enjoyable food and a comfortable atmosphere that are appreciated by all and sundry – families, couples, after-work snackers, or noisier, partying groups on weekend nights. There's a sizeable list of mainly classic tapas, but the ones to go for are the daily specials chalked up on a board – perhaps the likes of fresh chocos madrileños (cuttlefish grilled with garlic). Good use of punchy Spanish flavours – such as garlic – is the trademark at La Bota. Other tapas from the main menu – ensaladilla rusa, patatas alioli, chistorra sausages cooked in cider – were less distinctive, but still pleasant, even if the potatoes were not as liberally spread with garlic mayonnaise as we remembered from other visits. While tapas are the main event, the menu also offers a few more substantial dishes, and there's a decent choice of Spanish wines, beers and liqueurs. Service tends to be deadpan but efficient, in a very traditional Spanish bar kind of way.
Babies and children welcome: high chairs. Booking advisable dinner Fri, Sat. Takeaway service.

Harringay N4

La Viña

3 Wightman Road, N4 1RQ (8340 5400). Harringay rail/29, 341 bus. **Meals served** 5pm-midnight Mon-Sat; 5-10.30pm Sun. **Main courses** £7.50-£10.50. **Tapas** £3-£5. **Credit** AmEx, MC, V.

On its own on the corner of one rung of the Harringay Ladder – a rarity amid the area's overwhelmingly Turkish eateries – this likeable little tapas restaurant has a solid local following. Warm, quietly welcoming service is one major asset. Comfortable seating and an unfussily attractive decor, with its consignment of the obligatory Spanish-rustic paintings and knick-knacks, but no kitsch overkill, make this an easy place to settle in for as long as you need to. The tapas-heavy menu offers few surprises, but prices are very reasonable. As usual in budget tapas bars, the cooking has its highs and lows: the best dishes are nicely fresh and lively; others have a bland feel. Albóndigas (meatballs) were rich and meaty, and fried calamares and habichuelas de la casa (green beans with lemon juice, garlic and onion) also hit the right notes. Pinchitos morunos were oddly made with chicken rather than pork, but were still tasty, and only the strangely soup-

like bacalao con garbanzos (salt cod with chickpeas) got the thumbs down. Wines are as decently priced as the food, and whites and rosés are kept nicely cold. Monday and Tuesday are special 'paella nights'.
Babies and children welcome; high chairs. Booking advisable; essential dinner. No-smoking tables. Restaurant available for hire (Sun).

Muswell Hill N10

Café Loco

266 Muswell Hill Broadway, entrance on Muswell Hill, N10 2QR (8444 3370). Highgate tube then 43, 134 bus. **Dinner served** 6pm-midnight Mon-Sat (open until 2am); 3pm-11pm Sun. **Main courses** £7-£11.95. **Tapas** £2.50-£5.50. **Service** 12%. **Credit** AmEx, DC, MC, V.

Café Loco has worked hard to cultivate its krazy-kool image over the years, with sultry primary colours and an open-all-hours DJ-driven weekend routine. Perhaps it was the bank holiday, then, but we were surprised to find it pleasantly free of the sangria- and fag-fuelled rowdiness of previous visits. Friendly, if slightly vapid, service and an unpretentious atmosphere make it a prized alternative to some of the area's newer and brasher arrivals, if not exactly a foodie's paradise. All the usual suspects of the tapas world are on offer here – from pimientos rellenos to tortilla Española – with little in the way of experimentation or unique regional specialities. Patatas bravas, for example, were dry and served in a timid chilli sauce. Manchego cheese, layered with tomato and oregano, was pleasing, but had all the personality of an in-flight meal. A plate of jamón serrano, by contrast, was noticeably first-class. We never made it to dessert, sadly, as 10pm was deemed too late an hour for it. As Muswell Hill has grown up and shed some of its scruffy self-image, has this much-loved Café lost just a bit too much of its Loco?
Babies and children welcome (until 9.30pm). Booking essential dinner Fri, Sat. Dress: no tracksuits or caps. Entertainment: DJ 10pm-2am Wed-Sat. Restaurant available for hire. Takeaway service.

Outer London

Richmond, Surrey

Don Fernando's

27F The Quadrant, Richmond, Surrey TW9 1DN (8948 6447/www.donfernando.co.uk). Richmond tube/rail. **Lunch served** noon-3pm Mon, Tue. **Dinner served** 6-11pm Mon, Tue. **Meals served** noon-11pm Wed-Sat; noon-10pm Sun. **Tapas** £3-£6.50. **Credit** AmEx, JCB, MC, V.

Spanish tiles covering every available surface of this large and lively restaurant, combined with friendly and efficient staff, alert you to the fact this is an authentic Spanish restaurant presided over by a Spanish family who know a thing or two about restaurants and food. The Izquierdo family from Andalucia set up shop here 14 years ago and do a roaring trade, with a wide-ranging menu of tapas, main courses, paellas and a great wine list. We opted for tapas and soon had a table groaning with griddled squid with garlic, freshly marinated anchovies, butterfly king prawns with chilli sauce, tortilla, meatballs, monkfish and ham kebabs, vegetable croquettes and fried potatoes. Verdicts were unanimous: the fish and seafood were generally better than the meat, though the squid was chewy enough to suggest it could have been fresher. Sauces tasted ready-made and the vegetables dishes were particularly disappointing, with the few they had being bland in flavour and small in size. Desserts failed to make amends; only two of an uninspired choice were own-made. Despite such shortcomings, with a great wine and sherry list, cold Cruzcampo beers and an ambience that was warm as the evening outside, we left happy enough.
Babies and children welcome; high chairs. Bookings not accepted. No-smoking tables. Separate area available for parties, seats 100. Tables outdoors (4, pavement).

Thai

Thai food is rivalling Indian and Chinese as Londoners' favourite (budget) Asian cuisine. Every other pub in the capital seems to have bolted on a Thai restaurant in the past few years, following the success of pioneers like **Churchill Thai Kitchen**. Yet quantity hasn't been matched with a general rise in quality. Too many of the newer, Anglo-Thai venues swap cheap substitutes for authentic ingredients (garden peas for pea aubergines is the most common money-saver), with the resultant food akin to a chillified version of a Chinese takeaway. We've culled several such second-rate establishments from the section this year.

Not all London's Thai trends are dispiriting, though, with Alan Yau's **Busaba Eathai** exemplifying a exciting and more modern approach to budget dining. And at the other end of the price spectrum, London has one of the very best exponents of 'Royal Thai' cuisine in David Thompson at **Nahm**; plus stylish **Nipa** and **Patara**.

Don't expect chopsticks at a Thai restaurant: Thai food is usually eaten with a fork and spoon, although fingers are acceptable if that's most convenient.

Central

Belgravia SW1

★ Nahm

The Halkin, Halkin Street, SW1X 7DJ (7333 1234/www.halkin.como.bz). Hyde Park Corner tube. **Lunch served** noon-2.30pm Mon-Fri. **Dinner served** 7-11pm Mon-Sat; 7-10pm Sun. **Main courses** £19.50-£21.50. **Set lunch** £18-£26 2-4 courses. **Set dinner** £47 4 courses. **Credit** AmEx, DC, JCB, MC, V.

The old cliché 'never judge a book by its cover' is nowhere more appropriate than at this gem of a restaurant inside the Halkin hotel. For despite a dull, slightly odd interior featuring muted gold surfaces and net curtains, David Thompson's award-spangled interpretation of the 'Royal Thai' cuisine of ancient Bangkok is among the best you'll find in the UK. Nahm's £47 set dinner – an extraordinarily generous banquet – showcases old, forgotten Thai recipes given a modern twist with Michelin-pleasing ingredients such as white asparagus and foie gras. Dishes – such as rabbit and coconut salad with lemongrass and chilli jam, red curry of Middle White pork, and mixed Thai vegetable salad with tamarind and palm sugar – are cooked with astonishing skill and understanding; the perfectly judged balance of sweet, sour, hot and salty flavours reveals its depth in degrees. Nahm is not just a great restaurant, it's a phenomenon – and dining here is a humbling and memorable experience. One for true aficionados of Thai cuisine.

Book dinner. Disabled: toilet. Dress: smart casual; no shorts. No pipes or cigars. Separate room for parties, seats 36. Vegetarian menu. **Map 9 G9**.

City EC2

Nakhon Thai ![NEW]

10 Copthall Avenue, EC2R 7DJ (7628 1555/ www.nakhonthai.co.uk). Moorgate tube. **Meals served** 11.30am-10pm Mon-Fri. **Main courses** £5-£19. **Set meal** £19.95-£24.95 3 courses. **Service** 12.5%. **Credit** AmEx, MC, V.

With oriental knick-knacks on white walls, wooden furniture scattered on wooden floors and potted palms aplenty, this restaurant's 'Thai beach hut stranded in the City' look wouldn't appear amiss in a tourist brochure. We found spring rolls, tofu satay, chicken satay, pork dumpling, and beef stir-fried with asparagus prettily presented and carefully prepared using top-notch ingredients – but underseasoned and lacking personality. A mild green vegetable curry (made with golf-ball aubergines) was pleasantly redolent of fresh herbs and spices, and the Thai fragrant rice was exemplary. Puddings aren't a strong point: expect offerings of the pancake and banana fritter variety. This is a handy lunch spot if you work nearby (the set lunch is a steal), but the spice, spunk and spirit of real Thai cooking was lost in translation.

Babies and children admitted. Booking advisable. No-smoking tables. Separate room for parties, seats 15. Takeaway service. **Map 12 Q6**.

Fitzrovia W1, WC1

★ Busaba Eathai

22 Store Street, WC1E 7DS (7299 7900). Goodge Street or Tottenham Court Road tube. **Meals served** noon-11pm Mon-Thur; noon-11.30pm Fri, Sat; noon-10pm Sun. **Main courses** £5.10-£9.80. **Service** 10% for parties of 5 or more. **Credit** AmEx, JCB, MC, V.

This is a shared-table, bench-seating, no-smoking, no-booking restaurant. Sound familiar? This Thai Wagamama was created by Alan Yau, who also created the original Wagamama and now runs top Chinese restaurants Hakkasan (*see pxxx*) and Yauatcha (*see pxxx*). The dark wood and walls turn Busaba into a photo-negative version of its pale cousin; it evokes the Asia of opium dens, not bullet trains. But there is more to the place than just a nifty idea and some striking design. The excellent Thai menu was created with the help of David Thompson (of Nahm fame; *see above*), and although Thompson is no longer involved, standards remain remarkably high. Such interesting ingredients as wing beans, wood-ear mushrooms, morning glory and rose apple are abundantly used; there is no cheap ingredient substitution with carrots or cabbage. Portions are generous. But most of all, you find the thrilling balance of flavours that distinguishes real Thai cooking: the sour, salt, sweet, and especially the spicy. The best dishes? Far too many to mention; but if you haven't tried the prawns pomelo and peanuts served on betel leaves, you've not lived. There's a popular branch on Wardour Street in Soho, and a third is planned for spring 2005 at 8-13 Bird Street, W1T 6BW.

Babies and children welcome. Bookings not accepted. Disabled: toilet. No smoking. Separate room for parties, seats 12-20. Tables outdoors (12, pavement). **Map 4 K5**.

For branch see index.

Thai Metro ![NEW]

38 Charlotte Street, W1T 2NN (7436 4201). Goodge Street or Tottenham Court Road tube. **Meals served** noon-11pm Mon-Fri; 1-11pm Sat; 1-10.30pm Sun. **Main courses** £5.50-£10.95. **Set lunch** £5.50 1 courses, £7.50 2 courses, £9.50 3 courses. **Service** 10%. **Credit** AmEx, MC, V.

Charlotte Street has become even more of a restaurant hotspot in recent years, but Thai Metro remains hugely popular, despite being not particularly special (it moved just up the street, to larger, brighter premises, at the end of 2003). Perhaps it's because the food is fresh and filling, the staff are amiable, the central location always guarantees a buzz, and it's good value for money. The menu-by-numbers lists all the expected favourites, including stir-fries, curries, soups, noodles and snacks. Succulent, mildly seasoned chicken wings, and fluffy tempura vegetables were our starters of choice: both were perfectly acceptable. Beef stir-fried with pak choi and mushrooms had a good balance of flavours, and warm, gingery undertones. A stir-fry of crunchy peppers, pineapple and cashew nuts appealed more because of its texture than its taste. In fine weather, diners spill on to the pavement seating, and you may have to queue.

Babies and children admitted. Booking advisable. Tables outdoors (7, pavement). Takeaway service. Vegetarian menu. **Map 9 J5**.

King's Cross WC1

★ Paolina

181 King's Cross Road, WC1X 9BZ (7278 8176). King's Cross tube/rail. **Lunch served** noon-3pm Mon-Fri. **Dinner served** 6-10pm Mon-Sat. **Main courses** £3.45-£7.50. **Unlicensed. Corkage** 50p. **No credit cards**.

'Cheap and cheerful' may be a cliché, but it's a term that seems to have been coined especially for this café, with its clashing furniture, artificial flowers and an open-view kitchen. The food is as basic as the decor, but it comes in portions too big to finish and prices are very low. Sweetcorn cake with sweet and sour sauce was dense and clunky, not light and spicy as it should be. Fried squid, which also came with a sweet and sour sauce, was a little too chewy. Beef mussaman curry, crammed with potatoes and peanuts, was creamy and well spiced. Vegetable green curry was jam-packed with a variety of vegetables in a coconutty sauce flecked with green chilli and coriander. The dishes are really more 'Chinese style' than 'Thai style'. However, people don't come to Paolina expecting a gourmet experience; it's more a refuelling place for local workers and travellers in King's Cross, and service is chatty and good-natured.

Babies and children admitted. Booking advisable dinner. Takeaway service. Vegetarian menu. **Map 4 M3**.

Marylebone W1

Eat-Thai.net

22 St Christopher's Place, W1U 1NP (7486 0777/www.eatthai.net). Bond Street tube. **Lunch served** noon-3pm, **dinner served** 6-10.30pm daily. **Main courses** £7.25-£17.95. **Set lunch** £8.95 2 courses. **Service** 12.5%. **Credit** AmEx, MC, V.

With its widely spaced, linen-draped tables, displays of Thai sculpture and white-walled basement, Eat-Thai.net offers a soothing respite from the bustle of Oxford Street. On our visit, the varied customers included thirtysomethings on casual dates and a smattering of Thais. The range of dishes is vast and impressive (though the layout of the menu is disorganised and difficult to read). We had no complaints what came out of the kitchen: ingredients were fresh, and flavours were reassuringly diverse and satisfying. Beer is the best accompaniment; avoid the insipid Thai wine that just doesn't do this food justice. The set menu was a fabulous feast. Highlights were the crisp and delicate herb tempura (deep-fried morning glory leaves, orchid, basil and betel leaves) and pao peay sod (a rice paper roll stuffed with crabmeat, prawn and herbs), followed by delicately spicy sai aua (Chiang Mai sausage) and moo muk kha (pork marinated with galangal and coriander root). Service was charming and timely. So, good cooking, but you pay West End prices for it.

Babies and children welcome. Booking advisable. No-smoking tables. Separate area for parties, seats 24. Takeaway service. **Map 9 H6**.

Mayfair W1

★ Patara

3&7 Maddox Street, W1S 2QB (7499 6008). Oxford Circus tube. **Lunch served** noon-3pm, **dinner served** 6.30-10.30pm daily. **Main courses** £10.95-£16.95. **Set lunch** £11.95 2 courses, £14.95 3 courses. **Service** 12.5%. **Credit** AmEx, DC, MC, V.

Oozing style and sophistication by the ice-bucket-load, Patara doesn't have to try too hard by garnishing its dishes with mountains of orchids, curly parsley and elaborately carved fruit and veg. The self-assured cooking speaks for itself. A tangy salad of green mango featured crisp, juicy shreds of fruit enlivened with chilli and lime. Steamed dumplings in assorted colours, from lilac to pale golden, were stuffed with prawn, chicken and pork – with some fillings working better than others. Grilled black cod with ginger and pickled yellow bean sauce was a scrumptious version of an old classic. Pineapple and tofu red curry had an intriguing mix of hot, sour, spicy and fruity flavours. More tofu featured in a delightfully piquant stir-fry with green beans, chillies and lime leaves. Puddings, such as banana tart and coconut custard pancakes, are rich and generously portioned. Overall we found the cooking a touch too sweet, but the soothing, earthy-hued interior, smiling staff and a buzzy crowd contributes to a highly enjoyable dining experience.
Babies and children welcome. Booking advisable. No-smoking tables. Vegetarian menu. **Map 9 J6**. **For branches see index.**

Soho W1

★ **Soho Thai**

27-28 St Anne's Court, W1F 0BN (7287 2000). Tottenham Court Road tube. **Lunch served** noon-3pm, **dinner served** 6-11.30pm Mon-Sat. **Main courses** £5.95-£6.25. **Credit** AmEx, MC, V.

The Soho outpost of the Thai Square chain has the not unlikeable feel of a Thai travel agent: air-conditioned and scrupulously clean, with big printed boards of Buddha in various states of fuzzy-gold nirvana. It's cosy nevertheless, and does a convivial lunch trade (no thrusting Sohoites here) around its clusters of wooden tables and chairs. The food is freshly prepared and quickly served, but only narrowly surpasses the 'authentic' Thai cuisine now offered by many London pubs. Spicy fish cakes, although slightly greasy, came with a good dipping sauce; chicken green curry needed a thicker broth and was shot through with too much fresh chilli, but did the job well enough. The menu does venture out of oriental (rice, noodles, curry) territory too, although our nicely grilled lamb cutlets came with a bitter-tasting hot chilli sauce

Nakhon Thai

that had a strange sandy texture thanks its ground garlic and pepper. Service is friendly, on the whole – one waiter was topping up glasses of tap water without being asked – and prices are reasonable. *Booking essential weekends. No-smoking area. Takeaway service. Vegetarian menu.* **Map 17 K6.**

West

Bayswater W2

★ Nipa
Royal Lancaster Hotel, Lancaster Terrace, W2 2TY (7262 6737/www.royallancaster.com). Lancaster Gate tube.
Bar **Open** 11am-11pm Mon-Sat; 11am-10.30pm Sun.
Restaurant **Lunch served** noon-2pm Mon-Fri.
Dinner served 6.30-10.30pm Mon-Sat. **Main courses** £8.50-£13.50. **Set meal** £25-£28 4 courses; khantoke (lunch, 6.30-7.30pm) £14.90. **Both Credit** AmEx, DC, MC, V.
This smart restaurant inside the Royal Lancaster Hotel feels like the inside of a wood-panelled jewel box adorned with woven gold and maroon tableclothsclothes, patterned carpet and an array of golden Thai knick-knacks. Service can be hit and miss – we were kept waiting a long time before being brought the menu and drinks, then suddenly overwhelmed with over-attentive waiters. Don't let this put you off, though, because Nipa's food has an amazing clarity of flavours. Minced prawn and chicken tartlets boasted impossibly light, flaky pastry with a tasty filling, and sweetcorn cake (although slightly overdone) was zinged up with fresh curry paste. Vegetable green curry revealed sparkling layers of flavours, in turn subtle and fiery, and a lively mixed seafood stir-fry was packed with perfectly cooked fresh prawns and squid. Nipa is the Thai community's choice for special-occasion dining; on our visit, apart from a few, mainly Thai customers it was nearly empty. If you love Thai food, and haven't been yet, what are you waiting for?
Babies and children welcome; high chairs. Booking essential Fri, Sat. Disabled: toilet. Dress: smart casual. Takeaway service. Vegetarian menu. **Map 8 D6.**

Tawana
3 Westbourne Grove, W2 4UA (7229 3785/ www.tawana.co.uk). Bayswater tube. **Lunch served** noon-3pm, **dinner served** 6-11pm Mon-Sat. **Meals served** noon-10pm Sun. **Main courses** £5.25-£17.95. **Set meal** £15.95 2 courses. **Minimum** £10. **Service** 10%. **Credit** AmEx, DC, MC, V.
Excellent service is the main draw here. Super-fresh ingredients, frequently flown in from Thailand, are another plus; otherwise, the interior of tiled floors, wooden furniture and white tablecloths is fairly modest. Deep-fried pork with noodles was a little heavy and greasy, but tofu fried with ginger, spring onions and chillies was delightful, with a satisfyingly meaty texture. The menu, other than interesting noodle dishes, includes a range of salads, seafood and curries. Dishes aren't elaborately garnished, but are presented more attractively than in many neighbourhood Thai restaurants. Don't miss the puddings: exotic fresh fruits such as rambutans are brought in little containers for you to choose, then assembled by staff with some flourish. Tawana is one of the largest suppliers of Thai foodstuffs in London; see for yourself at the nearby Tawana Supermarket and Oriental Deli.
Babies and children welcome. Booking advisable. Separate room for parties, seats 50. Takeaway service. Vegetarian menu. **Map 7 B6.**
For branches (Thai Hut, Thai Kitchen) see index.

Chiswick W4

★ Bedlington Café
24 Fauconberg Road, W4 3JY (8994 1965). Chiswick Park or Turnham Green tube then E3 bus. **Meals served** 8am-2pm Mon-Sat.

Dinner served 6-10pm Mon-Sat; 6-9.30pm Sun. **Main courses** £3.95-£6.50. **Service** 10% for parties of 10 or more. **No credit cards**.
This once-iconic, family-owned café is now looking grubby, with a dirty lino floor and tables that need a good wiping down. Food is cheap and generously portioned, but disappointing in taste. Tofu stir-fried with green beans in black bean sauce featured a meltingly soft mound of fried tofu, but otherwise the dish lacked authentic flavours, and was more like a sloppy Chinese stir-fry. Vegetable fried rice, and noodles fried with chicken were both crammed with too many vegetables, and had little in the way of flavour. The dishes, although freshly prepared, were bulked up with onions and tomatoes and, in a near-empty restaurant, both the chef and the waiter looked fed up. The café still serves English breakfast, and has a small selection of specialities from Laos and Esarn, but otherwise it's resting on its laurels. The yellowing walls are plastered with rave reviews – which date back to the mid 1990s and even the '80s.
Babies and children welcome. Booking advisable weekends. Disabled: toilet. No smoking. Tables outdoors (4, pavement). Takeaway service; delivery service (within 2-mile radius). Vegetarian menu.

★ Thai Bistro
99 Chiswick High Road, W4 2ED (8995 5774). Turnham Green tube/27, 237, 267 bus. **Lunch served** noon-3pm Mon, Wed, Fri-Sun. **Dinner served** 6-11pm Mon-Sat; 6-10.30pm Sun. **Main courses** £5.95-£7.95. **Service** 12.5% for parties of 5 or more. **Credit** MC, V.
Owned by leading Thai chef and cookery writer Vatcharin Bhumichitr, this smartish, simply decorated restaurant with wooden bench seating aims to showcase recipes from his cookery books, most notably his ground-breaking classic *Thai Vegetarian Cooking*, published in the early 1990s. For starters, Thai vegetable samosas, golden triangles of crisp filo pastry containing a somewhat indistinct curried vegetable filling, were acceptable, but rather unconvincing. A stir-fry of chicken and vegetables was pepped up with lots of chilli and basil, and had clean, uncomplicated flavours. More chilli and basil featured in a dish of garlicky aubergine in yellow bean sauce. Service was warm, friendly and chatty. However, if you're familiar with Bhumichitr's writing, and expect the dishes to reproduce the recipes in his books, you may be disappointed.
Babies and children welcome. Booking essential Fri, Sat. No smoking. Tables outdoors (4, garden). Takeaway service. Vegetarian menu.

Kensington W8

Papaya Tree
209 Kensington High Street, W8 6BD (7937 2260). High Street Kensington tube. **Lunch served** noon-3pm, **dinner served** 6-11pm daily. **Main courses** £6.95-£9.95. **Set lunch** £4.50-£6 1 course. **Set dinner** £18-£23 3 courses. **Service** 15%. **Credit** AmEx, DC, JCB, MC, V.
This basement restaurant has a light, simple interior, complete with polished wooden floors and elaborately arranged white napery. Although the staff are friendly enough, on our visit orders were sometimes confused or forgotten. The menu, with the likes of som tam (green papaya salad – not the best version here, as it was too bland and soggy) and spring rolls (crisp, well filled), is pretty conventional. The best dishes are the curries; a well-flavoured red chicken curry and authentically spiced vegetable penang curry were the the highlights. Vegetables stir-fried with chilli and basil had a nice kick to them, but were otherwise fairly standard, and steamed rice and egg noodles were merely OK. This is unadventurous Thai food, and likely to appeal to those who like their oriental flavours predictable and unchallenging.
Babies and children admitted; high chairs. Booking advisable. No-smoking tables. Takeaway service; delivery service (7644 6666). Vegetarian menu. **Map 7 A9.**

Maida Vale W9

★ Ben's Thai
Above the Warrington, 93 Warrington Crescent, W9 1EH (7266 3134). Maida Vale or Warwick Avenue tube. **Lunch served** noon-2.30pm, **dinner served** 6-10.30pm daily. **Main courses** £5-£7.50. **Service** 10%. **Credit** MC, V.
Situated on the first floor of the immensely popular Warrington pub, this unassuming Thai dining room is packed with a boisterous young crowd lining their stomachs with hot and spicy fare in between pints. The decor is kitschly ornate – if a little tatty – with high ceilings and patterned carpets. The food comes in massive portions with obvious flavours. Sweetcorn cakes and prawns in rice pastry (effectively prawn spring rolls) were chunky and a little greasy, but had tasty dipping sauces. Chicken stir-fried with cashew nuts and chilli, and tofu with chilli and basil were big on both colour and heat. Pad Thai noodles and mixed fried rice were loaded with assorted vegetables and yet more chilli. Don't expect sophistication – but if your idea of a lively ambience is a noisy room, and you like your Thai food outgoing and wallet-friendly, Ben's is a reliable choice.
Babies and children admitted. Booking advisable; essential dinner. No-smoking tables. Takeaway service. Vegetarian menu. **Map 1 C4.**

Notting Hill W8

★ Churchill Thai Kitchen
Churchill Arms, 119 Kensington Church Street, W8 7LN (7792 1246). High Street Kensington or Notting Hill Gate tube. **Meals served** noon-9.30pm Mon-Sat; noon-8pm Sun. **Main courses** £5.85. **Credit** AmEx, DC, MC, V.
The Thai restaurant tucked away at the back of this pretty pub is so full of lush greenery that the effect is akin to a walled indoor garden. The ceiling is covered with overgrown potted plants, and butterflies in frames fill every inch of space on bare brick walls. Alongside British comfort food such as shepherd's pie and apple crumble is a very basic menu of Thai restaurant standards. Red chicken curry was fiery with succulent meat, and the solitary veggie option of sweet and sour vegetables came with a gloopy sauce reminiscent of Chinese takeaways. Dishes are served with mountains of rice, without any of the frou-frou garnishes associated with Thai restaurant cooking. The only adornment is the 'English garden' surroundings; otherwise, this is simple and unsophisticated Thai fare, as interpreted for the elderly colonial types who make up the core of the customer base.
Babies and children welcome. Book evenings. No-smoking. Tables outdoors (9, pavement). **Map 7 B7.**

Shepherd's Bush W12

★ Esarn Kheaw
314 Uxbridge Road, W12 7LJ (8743 8930). Shepherd's Bush tube/207, 260, 283 bus. **Lunch served** noon-3pm Mon-Fri. **Dinner served** 6-11pm daily. **Main courses** £4.95-£8.95. **Credit** AmEx, DC, MC, V.
If we were judging this restaurant by its cooking alone, it would have gained a red star. However, the experience of sampling some of the best Thai food in London was marred by rude service in an overcrowded restaurant; food that took too long to arrive; decor and toilets that could do with refurbishment; and somewhat small portions. But the wonderful array of lesser-known dishes from Esarn, a north-east region of Thailand, really sparkle with their spot-on spicing and are cooked by a talented chef. We loved the crisp, hot and juicy som tam (green papaya salad), and gutsily spiced Thai sausages. Catfish cooked with coriander and lime is something of an acquired taste, but a hot-pot of tofu, glass noodles and spring onions was full of vibrant flavours and contrasting textures. The huge menu does offer Thai restaurant standards such as green and red curries – but if you order those, you'd be missing the point.
Babies and children welcome. Booking advisable. Takeaway service. **Map 20 B1.**

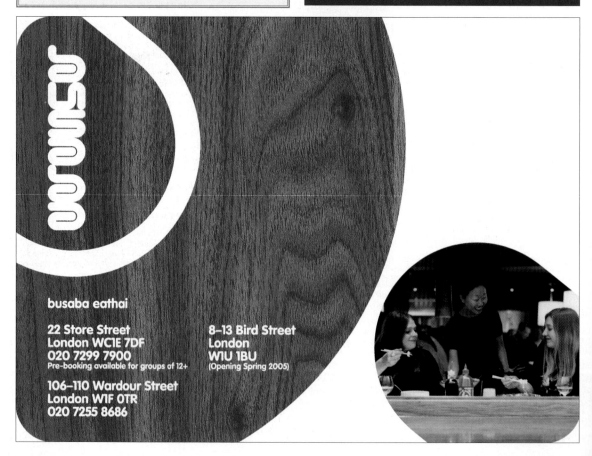

South West

Fulham SW6

★ Blue Elephant

4-6 Fulham Broadway, SW6 1AA (7385 6595/ www.blueelephant.com). Fulham Broadway tube. **Lunch served** noon-2.30pm Mon-Fri; noon-4pm Sun. **Dinner served** 7pm-midnight Mon-Thur; 6.30pm-midnight Fri, Sat; 7-10.30pm Sun. **Main courses** £10.60-£28. **Set meals** £33-£39 3-4 courses. **Set buffet** (lunch Sun) £22 adults, £11 children. **Service** 12.5%. **Credit** AmEx, DC, MC, V.

After an over-eager greeting, you are led to a table through a huge crowded space – at which point any hope of privacy evaporates. The interior of the Elephant, filled with abundant foliage, ponds, bridges, waterfalls and Thai ornaments, is full-on – and a little too slick, corporate and packaged. The food, however, is delicious and surprisingly good value. A mixed platter of starters brought such delights as succulent chicken legs; plump, well-filled spring rolls; crisp, spicy sweet corn cakes; and stuffed baby corn wrapped in pastry – each with a different dipping sauce. We followed this with the khantoke platter, which included a distinctively spiced mussaman curry, beautifully flavoured aubergine and okra in chilli paste, and beef stir-fried with basil. Some dishes were too mouth-scorchingly hot, but there's clearly a great deal of skill in the kitchen, the presentation is pretty, and the vegetarian menu is remarkable. Still one of London's memorable dining experiences. *Babies and children welcome; high chairs. Booking advisable. Disabled: toilet. Dress: smart casual; no shorts. Entertainment: children's activities Sun (phone for details). Takeaway service; delivery service. Vegetarian menu.* **Map 13 B13**.

Sugar Hut

374 North End Road, SW6 1LY (7386 8950/ www.sugarhutfulham.com). Fulham Broadway tube. **Dinner served** 7-11.30pm Tue-Thur, Sun; 7pm-midnight Fri, Sat. **Main courses** £9.50-£19.50. **Set meal** £28.50-£34 4 courses (minimum 2). **Service** 12.5%. **Credit** AmEx, MC, V.

A favourite with celebrities, Sloanes and hip young things, this dark cavern of a bar with dim lighting and low seating makes for an interesting discovery – you feel as though you're being let into a secret. The enchanting and sexy interior, done up with Asian and Moroccan ornaments including funky light fittings and luxurious curtains, has a nightclubby feel. Indeed, the place is host to a variety of live acts such as loud R&B bands and Elvis impersonators, and can get very crowded. From an elegant, pared-down menu, we sampled an average pad Thai and a more successful pork with orange. There are also platters available to share, but food really isn't the point of this place. Sugar Hut is popular for group dining, and ideal for beautiful people in search of beautiful cocktails; the food is of secondary consideration. *Babies and children welcome. Booking advisable weekends. Dress: smart casual. Entertainment: musicians 9pm Thur-Sun. Vegetarian menu.* **Map 13 A13**.

South

Clapham SW4

★ Pepper Tree

19 Clapham Common Southside, SW4 7AB (7622 1758). Clapham Common tube. **Lunch served** noon-3pm Mon-Fri. **Dinner served** 6-10.30pm Mon; 6-11pm Tue-Fri. **Meals served** noon-11pm Sat; noon-10.30pm Sun. **Main courses** £4-£6. **Service** 10% for parties of 8 or more. **Credit** JCB, MC, V.

The plain, spacious dining room has communal wooden-bench seating and large windows that open on to a traffic-laden street overlooking Clapham Common. The outside tables are popular in summer, and at weekends the place is favoured by groups of locals. Tofu satay featured very soft, fresh, grilled tofu marinated in an Indonesian-style

Blue Elephant

coconut and turmeric sauce; it was somewhat let down by an underwhelming peanut dipping sauce. Ba mee noodles were stir-fried with lots of fresh, crunchy vegetables and pepped up with basil and chilli. Chicken red curry was fiery and came with a deliciously gloopy sauce. Pepper Tree's food is fresh, cheap, generously portioned and served with a smile – but don't expect complex flavours and garnishes; this is a strictly no-frills joint.
Babies and children welcome; high chairs. Bookings not accepted dinner. No smoking. Takeaway service. **Map 22 A2**.
For branch see index.

South East
Blackheath SE3

Laicram
1 Blackheath Grove, SE3 0DD (8852 4710). Blackheath rail. **Lunch served** noon-2.30pm, **dinner served** 6-11pm Tue-Sun. **Main courses** £4.50-£13.90. **Service** 10%. **Credit** AmEx, MC, V.

A modest restaurant tucked away in a blink-and-you'll-miss-it side street, Laicram is nonetheless extraordinary popular with locals. It must be the prices (very low) rather than the food (average), or perhaps it's the charming, attentive service that does the trick. The interior, bedecked with wood carvings and plants, is cute but looks slightly worn. From a fairly standard menu peppered with a number of surprises, we liked the creamy chicken and coconut tom kha gai soup, spiked with the green, almost herbal undertones of galangal. Perfectly cooked steamed sea bass with ginger and spring onions was a delicate dish, but deep-fried battered mushrooms were bland. A red vegetable curry aromatic with lemongrass and spices was more robust, though, as were stir-fried noodles with beef, eggs and vegetables. If you enjoy Thai sweets, don't miss the dessert trolley overflowing with such goodies as dainty coconut custard with yellow bean and palm sugar, served in attractive cups made of pandanus leaves.
Babies and children welcome (until 8pm). Booking essential Fri, Sat. Takeaway service. Vegetarian menu.

London Bridge & Borough SE1

Kwan Thai
The Riverfront, Hay's Galleria, Tooley Street, SE1 2HD (7403 7373/www.kwanthairestaurant. co.uk). London Bridge tube/rail. **Lunch served** 11.30am-3pm Mon-Fri. **Dinner served** 6-10pm Mon-Sat. **Main courses** £10-£14. **Set lunch** £7.95-£8.95 2 courses. **Set dinner** £20-£28 per person (minimum 2) 3 courses. **Credit** AmEx, DC, MC, V.

Situated next to the River Thames, Kwan Thai benefits from a wonderful location, surrounded by London landmarks (HMS *Belfast*, Tower Bridge, London Bridge) and the bustle of shops. As a result, it gets very busy and lively; thankfully, service is slick and professional. In general, the food is pretty good. To start, tom kha gai (chicken soup in a hot, sour and creamy coconut broth) had dazzling layers of flavours, foregrounded by ginger, galangal and lime leaves. Vegetable spring rolls were perfect: the pastry crisp and flaky, the

Menu

We've tried to give the most useful Thai food terms here, including variant spellings. However, these are no more than English transliterations of the original Thai script, and so are subject to considerable variation. Word divisions vary as well: thus, kwaitiew, kwai teo and guey teow are all acceptable spellings for noodles.

Useful terms
Khantoke: originally a north-eastern banquet conducted around a low table while seated on traditional triangular cushions – some restaurants have khantoke seating.
Khing: with ginger.
Op or **ob:** baked.
Pad, pat or **phad:** stir-fried.
Pet or **ped:** hot (spicy).
Prik: chilli.
Tod, tort, tord or **taud:** deep-fried.
Tom: boiled.

Starters
Khanom jeep or **ka nom geeb:** dim sum. Little dumplings of minced pork, bamboo shoots and water chestnuts, wrapped in an egg and rice (wun tun) pastry, then steamed.
Khanom pang na koong: prawn sesame toast.
Kratong thong: tiny crispy batter cups ('top hats') filled with mixed vegetables and/or minced meat.
Miang: savoury appetisers with a variety of constituents (mince, ginger, peanuts, roasted coconut, for instance), wrapped in betel leaves.
Popia or **porpia:** spring rolls.

Tod mun pla or **tauk manpla:** small fried fish cakes (should be lightly rubbery in consistency) with virtually no 'fishy' smell or taste.

Soups
Poh tak or **tom yam potag:** hot and sour mixed seafood soup, sometimes kept simmering in a Chinese 'steamboat' dish.
Tom kha gai or **gai tom kar:** hot and sour chicken soup with coconut milk.
Tom yam or **tom yum:** a hot and sour consommé-like soup, smelling of lemongrass. **Tom yam koong** is with prawns; **tom yam gai** with chicken; **tom yam hed** with mushrooms.

Rice
Khao, kow or **khow:** rice.
Khao nao: sticky rice, from the north-east.
Khao pat: fried rice.
Khao suay: steamed rice.
Pat khai: egg-fried rice.

Salads
Laab or **larb:** minced and cooked meat incorporating lime juice and various other ingredients such as ground rice and herbs.
Som tam: a popular cold salad of grated green papaya.
Yam or **yum:** refers to any tossed salad, hot or cold, but it is often hot and sour, flavoured with lemon and chilli. This type of yam is originally from the north-east of Thailand, where the Laotian influence is greatest.
Yam nua: hot and sour

beef salad.
Yam talay: hot and sour seafood salad (served cold).

Noodles
Generally speaking, noodles are eaten in greater quantities in the north of Thailand. There are many types of **kwaitiew** or **guey teow** noodles. Common ones include **sen mee:** rice vermicelli; **sen yai** (river rice noodles): a broad, flat, rice noodle; **sen lek:** a medium flat noodle, used to make pad Thai; **ba mee:** egg noodles; and **woon sen** (cellophane noodle): transparent vermicelli made from soy beans or other pulses. These are often prepared as stir-fries.
The names of the numerous noodle dishes depend on the combination of other ingredients. Common dishes include:
Khao soi: chicken curry soup with egg noodles; a Burmese/Thai dish, sometimes referred to as the national dish of Burma. Not to be confused with khao suay (steamed rice).
Mee krob or **mee grob:** sweet crispy fried vermicelli.
Pad si-ewe or **cee eaw:** noodles fried with mixed meat in soy sauce.
Pad Thai: stir-fried noodles with shrimps (or chicken and pork), beansprouts and salted turnips, garnished with ground peanuts.

Curries
Thai curries differ quite markedly from the Indian

varieties. Thais cook them for a shorter time, and use thinner sauces. Flavours and ingredients are different too. There are several common types of curry paste; these are used to name the curry, with the principal ingredients listed thereafter.
Gaeng, kaeng or **gang:** the generic name for curry. Yellow curry is the mildest; green curry (**gaeng keaw wan/kiew warn**) is medium hot and uses green chillies; red curry (**gaeng pet**) is similar, but uses red chillies.
Jungle curry: often the hottest of the various curries, made with red curry paste, bamboo shoots and just about anything else at hand.
Massaman or **mussaman:** also known as Muslim curry, because it originates from the area along the border with Malaysia where many Thais are Muslims. For this reason, pork is never used. It's rich but mild concoction, with coconut, potato and some peanuts.
Penang, panaeng or **panang:** a dry, aromatic curry made with 'Penang' curry paste, coconut cream and holy basil.

Fish & seafood
Hoi: shellfish.
Hor mok talay or **haw mog talay:** steamed egg mousse with seafood.
Koong, goong or **kung:** prawns.
Maw: dried fish belly.
Pla meuk: squid.

filling well seasoned and generous. We also enjoyed a dish of salmon steamed in banana leaves, in a coconut custard laced with curry paste and fresh coriander. Another favourite was pad Thai, which was generously studded with prawns, eggs, beansprouts and peanuts, and served (unusually) with tamarind sauce. Aubergine fried with eggs, basil and chilli was not so impressive, with rather 'so what' flavours. The food is quite expensive for what it is, but it's all carefully made and full of flavour. In summer, take advantage of the expansive riverside terrace.

Babies and children welcome; high chairs. Booking advisable. No-smoking tables. Separate room for parties, seats 50. Tables outdoors (20, riverside terrace). Takeaway service. Vegetarian menu.
Map 12 Q8.

New Cross SE14

Thailand
15 Lewisham Way, SE14 6PP (8691 4040). New Cross or New Cross Gate tube/rail. **Lunch served** noon-2.30pm Tue-Fri. **Dinner served** 5-11.30pm Tue-Sun. **Main courses** £4.95-£10. **Set meal** (noon-2.30pm, 5-7pm) £3.95 2 courses; £10 2 courses incl glass of wine. **Credit** MC, V.
The cooking of Esarn (in the north-east of Thailand) and Laos, with its emphasis on frugal ingredients pepped up with large amounts of chilli, isn't for everyone. It's honest and homely – read simple and unsophisticated – and is an acquired taste even for those Thais not native to the region. This small eaterie, as its ceiling maps indicate, is one of very few restaurants in London to specialise in the cuisine of this area. Forget about the cramped space and the granny-flat decor: your time will be better spent studying the unusual menu, or asking the helpful staff about specials of the day. Light, aromatic minced pork cakes were laced with lemongrass and served with a tasty peanut sauce. We also enjoyed a refreshing

mixed fruit salad, fired up with hot and sour sauces and spices. Both stir-fried bamboo shoots, and a Laotian speciality of fried aubergine came with an abundance of fresh herbs. Charcoal-grilled chicken marinated with whole peppercorns was garlicky and very tasty; traditional sticky rice made an ideal accompaniment.
Babies and children welcome. Booking essential Fri, Sat. No smoking. Takeaway service; delivery service (within 3-mile radius). Vegetarian menu.

South Norwood SE25

★ ★ Mantanah
2 Orton Building, Portland Road, SE25 4UD (8771 1148/www.mantanah.co.uk). Norwood Junction rail. **Lunch served** noon-3pm, **dinner served** 6-11pm Tue-Sun. **Main courses** £5.75-£8.50. **Set dinner** £16 3 courses, £20 4 courses, per person (minimum 2). **Credit** AmEx, DC, MC, V.
Mantanah would undoubtedly be very busy were it more centrally located; sadly, on our visit, it wasn't patronised by many locals. Dishes showcase fresh ingredients flown in weekly from Thailand, and everything is cooked to order. Staff are Buddhist, and don't eat meat for part of the year, so there's plenty of choice for vegetarians on the extensive menu – which also caters for people with food allergies. All the dishes we tried were excellent. We were delighted by light and crispy batter-fried shredded pumpkin, and even more so by shredded chicken and banana flower salad: the hot and tangy coconut dressing contrasted well with shreds of roasted coconut, dried chillies and crispy shallots. Beef was perfectly cooked with a touch of red wine and chilli, and given crunch from green beans and beansprouts. Also excellent was fruity mock duck curry with pineapple and Thai pea aubergines: delightfully creamy and exquisitely spiced. Dishes are given fun names such as 'Cinderella's Best Friend', and the interior is homely and cheery.

Babies and children welcome. Booking advisable. Takeaway service; delivery service (within 2-mile radius). Vegetarian menu.

East

Bethnal Green E2

★ Thai Garden
249 Globe Road, E2 0JD (8981 5748/www.the thaigarden.co.uk). Bethnal Green tube/ rail/8 bus. **Lunch served** noon-2.45pm Mon-Fri. **Dinner served** 6-10.45pm daily. **Main courses** £4.50-£6.95. **Set meal** (noon-2.45pm, 6-7.30pm) £7.50 2 courses. **Set dinner** £16-£20 3 courses. **Service** 10%. **Credit** MC, V.
Vatcharin Bhumichitr, chef and author of an acclaimed Thai vegetarian cookery book (and owner of Thai Bistro; *see p249*), helped his cousin set up Thai Garden many moons ago. It was London's first Thai vegetarian and seafood restaurant, and was ahead of its time with an imaginative menu of rarely seen dishes. Sadly, standards appear to have slipped. Mushroom larb (a salad-like snack) was sprinkled with khao kua, a common Thai ingredient not often seen on London menus, made by dry-frying uncooked rice until golden and grinding it into a coarse powder that is sprinkled on dishes like a spice; the version here comprised chewy, uncooked grains of rice that marred rather than accentuated the delicacy of other ingredients. Other dishes such as som tam (here with added crabsticks and carrots) and a main course of stir-fried scallops came piled on heaps of lettuce leaves, giving them the appearance of salad. Fried potato discs with mushroom and vegetables were fine, if a little unexciting. Overall, we found the flavours muted and one-dimensional, and the once-cheerful blue and pink decor is now looking rather worn.
Babies and children welcome; high chairs. Booking essential weekends. No-smoking tables. Separate room for parties, seats 14. Takeaway service; delivery service. Vegetarian menu.

Nid Ting. See p256.

Docklands E14

Elephant Royale
Locke's Wharf, Westferry Road, E14 3AN (7987 7999/www.elephantroyale.com). Island Gardens DLR. **Meals served** noon-10pm Mon-Thur, Sun; noon-10.30pm Fri, Sat. **Main courses** £4.80-£19.50. **Set meal** £19.50-£27.50 4 courses. **Set buffet** (noon-4pm Sun) £14.50. **Service** 12.5%. **Credit** AmEx, DC, MC, V.
The lush tropical decor, complete with a bamboo hut bar, exotic plants and flowers, wooden bridge above a fish pond, and an outside terrace overlooking Greenwich, is either beautiful or tacky, depending on your point of view. It does have a romantic ambience, however, enhanced by smiling, traditionally attired staff handing out orchids for the ladies. From a somewhat limited menu, lettuce-wrapped chicken was beautifully flavoured, and benefited from great-quality meat, while a delicious tom yam soup was aromatic with an abundance of lemongrass. Duck in tamarind sauce was swamped with too much sauce, but a green curry was outstanding – one of the best we've tasted. Desserts such as sweet potato and chestnut pudding are also worth a try. The Sunday lunch is immensely popular, although the musicians can be a bit too loud. Many people count this as their favourite Thai restaurant; not all the dishes are exquisite, but it's certainly well worth a visit.
Babies and children welcome; high chairs. Booking essential. Disabled: toilet. Entertainment: band 7pm Wed-Sat. No-smoking tables (Mon-Fri). Tables outdoors (19, patio). Takeaway service. Vegetarian menu.
For branch see index.

North

Archway N19

★ Charuwan
110 Junction Road, N19 5LB (7263 1410). Archway or Tufnell Park tube. **Lunch served** noon-3pm Tue-Fri. **Dinner served** 6-11pm daily. **Main courses** £4.30-£8.95. **Service** 10%. **Credit** AmEx, MC, V.
Named after the daughter of the proprietor, this charming neighbourhood restaurant is decorated with kitsch ornaments and souvenirs. On a sultry day, a hot and sour cucumber salad with a strong chilli kick was welcome and refreshing. Minced chicken on toast was nothing special, and potatoes with mushrooms and vegetables in a 'house special' gingery brown sauce was pleasant enough, but didn't set our pulses racing. Steamed sea bass with ginger and preserved plums featured fresh fish, and was almost Japanese in flavour and simplicity. Our favourite was rice fried with spring greens from the specials menu: a bowlful of vibrant, verdant flavours of spring. Bananas in coconut milk was flecked with nutty toasted sesame seeds, but was too sloppy.
Booking advisable. Children over 5 years admitted. Takeaway service. Vegetarian menu. **Map 26 B2.**

★ Nid Ting
533 Holloway Road, N19 4BT (7263 0506). Archway or Holloway Road tube. **Dinner served** 6-11.15pm Mon-Sat; 6-10.15pm Sun. **Main courses** £4.25-£9.50. **Set dinner** £15 2 courses incl coffee. **Credit** AmEx, DC, JCB, MC, V.
A popular and pleasant local with smiling staff in traditional clothing, Nid Ting is filled with ornaments and plants, and has a split-level dining area with a lovely wooden bar. To start, deep-fried beancurd with sweet chilli dip was fine, if a little unexciting; much tastier was a zingy pork and seafood salad with cucumber and fresh coriander in a chilli and peanut dressing. Next, duck curry with pineapple and coconut managed to be creamy, tangy and fiery all at once. Other dishes were competent if lacking in authenticity, such as stir-fried vegetables with soy beans that featured supermarket-style (rather than traditional Thai) mixed vegetables. Beancurd fried with chilli and basil was tasty but unchallenging. This is a handy neighbourhood Thai if you live in the area, but the cooking does pander to western tastes.

Babies and children welcome; high chairs. Booking essential Fri, Sat. Separate room for parties, seats 25. Takeaway service. Vegetarian menu. Map 26 C2.

Camden Town & Chalk Farm NW1

★ Lemongrass
243 Royal College Street, NW1 9LT (7284 1116). Camden Town tube. **Dinner served** 6-10.30pm Mon-Thur, Sun; 6-11pm Fri, Sat. **Main courses** £4.80-£7.90. **Set dinner** £14.80-£15.80 per person (minimum 2). **Credit** JCB, MC, V.
Appropriately enough, this small, neat restaurant has lemongrass-coloured walls. The food is hard to categorise, but could be loosely termed 'modern Cambodian and oriental with French influences'. To start, mango, chilli, red onion and coriander salad was refreshingly tangy. Leek cakes – shredded leek and oriental greens stuffed in dim sum-like rice flour pastry, steamed and then shallow-fried – were scrumptious; they also looked pretty, garnished with fresh carrot, cucumber pickle and pineapple pieces. Chilli lemon steak was cooked perfectly medium-rare, and pepped up with chilli and lemon as well as garlic, onions and fresh coriander. Asparagus stir-fried with garlic butter and cracked pepper was unusual, and came in a generous pile. There was also an intriguing dessert made with deep-fried bread coated in sugar syrup, served with fresh pineapple and strawberries. Service was extraordinarily friendly. One of our most surprising and delightful experiences of the year.
Babies and children welcome. Booking advisable weekends. No smoking. Vegetarian menu. **Map 27 D1.**

Islington N1

Thai Square
349 Upper Street, N1 0PD (7704 2000/ www.thaisq.com). Angel tube. **Lunch served** noon-3pm Mon-Fri. **Dinner served** 6-11pm Mon-Thur; 6-11.30pm Fri. **Meals served** noon-11.30pm Sat; noon-10.30pm Sun. **Main courses** £5.95-£11.95. **Credit** MC, V.
This attractive Upper Street restaurant is part of the ever-expanding Thai Square/Thai Pot chain. The colourful decor features golden dragons and Buddhas, funky artwork and stunning fresh flower arrangements – a shame then to receive tatty, food-splattered menus. To start, vegetable spring rolls were made with wheat-flour rather than the advertised rice-flour pastry, and were a bit bland. Grilled squid salad was better, with tender, fresh squid atop frilly lettuce drizzled with spiky chilli sauce. Goong pow (spicy char-grilled jumbo prawns on a very slender bed of pak choi) – was tasty, but came with so much lettuce that the dish looked like a salad. Vegetable jungle curry was crammed with fresh veg, including pea and golf-ball aubergines, but was thin and soup-like in consistency. Puddings of pineapple sorbet and banana in coconut milk were disappointing. Service from trendy young staff was friendly, though rushed.
Babies and children welcome. Booking advisable Fri, Sat. Disabled: toilet. Takeaway service. Vegetarian menu. **Map 5 O2.**
For branches (Thai Pot, Thai Square) see index.

North West

Golders Green NW11

★ Bangkok Room NEW
756 Finchley Road, Temple Fortune, NW11 7TH (8731 7473/www.bangkokroom.co.uk). Golders Green tube. **Lunch served** noon-3pm, **dinner served** 6-11pm daily. **Main courses** £6.95-£7.95. **Set lunch** £3.50 vegetarian, £3.95 meat 1 course. **Credit** MC, V.
This recently opened neighbourhood restaurant is somewhat eccentric: its decor is a combination of stylish (lots of terracotta and wrought iron), kitsch (cute toys and pictures of the Thai royal family) and the downright bizarre (ceiling light holders fashioned from bleached rubber plant leaves).

Further 'original' touches include a chatty, spiky-haired proprietor, who doubles up as waiter and occasional chef, and a menu that combines Thai restaurant standards with specialities from Esarn, Koh Samui and Chiang Mai. To start, banana flower salad with dried shrimps had an interesting texture and was loaded with fresh mixed herbs. A platter of vegetarian starters was hit and miss, comprising slightly burned stuffed pastry bags, average spring rolls and enthusiastically spiced sweetcorn cakes. From a list of daily specials, salmon in choo-chee curry paste was subtly spiced, with strong herbal overtones. Vegetables stir-fried with eggs and curry powder were surprisingly tasty. Definitely not your typical local.
Babies and children welcome; high chairs. Booking advisable. Tables outdoors (4, garden). Takeaway service. Vegetarian menu.

Outer London

Harrow, Middlesex

★ Thai Café
12 Mason's Avenue, Harrow, Middx HA3 5AP (8427 5385). Harrow & Wealdstone tube/rail. **Dinner served** 6-11pm daily. **Main courses** £4-£5. **Unlicensed. Corkage** no charge. **No credit cards.**
This cheap and cheerful café, with checked tablecloths and potted plants, is so popular with Harrow locals that our friendly waitress seemed genuinely baffled as to why she had never seen us before. She combined professional efficiency with a homely warmth, and appeared to be on first-name terms with all the diners, enquiring after their holidays and health. We started with sesame-studded prawn toast, beancurd satay with chilli dip, tempura-style vegetables and stuffed chicken wings – all good, but very basic, and lacking bite. Sizzling chilli beef was more exciting, however: fiery in terms of both taste and temperature. A stir-fry of mushrooms was very meaty and garlicky, and vegetable fried rice was packed with a variety of crunchy, colourful vegetables. The cooking here is honest, well intentioned and freshly cooked to order – just don't expect any razzmatazz.
Babies and children welcome. Booking advisable Fri, Sat. No-smoking tables. Takeaway service. Vegetarian menu.

Kingston, Surrey

Ayudhya
14 Kingston Hill, Kingston upon Thames, Surrey KT2 7NH (8546 5878/www.ayudhya kingston.com). Kingston rail. **Lunch served** noon-2.30pm Tue-Sun. **Dinner served** 6.30-11pm Mon-Sat; 6.30-10.30pm Sun. **Main courses** £5.95-£9.95. **Credit** MC, V.
Ayudhya takes its name from the ancient capital of Thailand, and is of historical interest itself – at more than 20 years old, it's one of the longest-lived Thai restaurants in the country. It looks it too, with a dark interior of carved wood, portraits of Thai grandees, and a Buddhist altar so garishly decorated it wouldn't look out of place in a Khao San Road tuk-tuk. As a new wave of groovier, cheaper Thai restaurants have overtaken Ayudhya in volume of customers, this old-timer has stood its ground, not cutting corners and preparing dishes just as they might be done in Thailand. That's not to say the cooking is faultless, however – we found a lack of 'harmony of the flavours' (what the Thais call 'rot chart'). Too much frisée lettuce lines the plates, disguising the sometimes meagre portions; and flavours tend towards the two-dimensional, often too sweet and citrous. A som tam had all the right ingredients present and correct, but lime juice dominated. Likewise in a moreish salad of roasted aubergine – deliciously smoky when chopped up with plenty of fresh herbs, red onion and chilli – but the dominant flavours were of lime juice and chilli. Pork with green beans and red curry paste was sweet and salty. But it's still the best Thai in the area.
Babies and children welcome. Booking advisable. Separate rooms for parties, both seat 30. Takeaway service. Vegetarian menu.

Turkish

The past year has been rough at the top of the market, with the loss of both the luxurious Chinatamani and Raks near Piccadilly, and cut-backs in the previously unstoppable expansion of the Sofra chain. There is a noticeable anxiety about pulling in the customers throughout the West End, hence the trend for customer-grabbing waitresses who lurk outside restaurants. However, Turkish restaurants continue to spread across north and central London. Many of the most authentic – and the best – are cafés in the centres of Turkish and Kurdish immigration around the Dalston/Stoke Newington borders and Green Lanes. For an evening out, the widest range is in nearby Islington – İznik, Pasha and Sedir are recommended – but outposts are popping up on many high streets throughout the city.

There is far more to Turkish cuisine than simple grilled kebabs, and many specialise in stews, fish or pide (Turkish pizzas). Such a rapidly expanding scene means restaurants come and go, improve and decline at a dizzying rate, so we've added plenty of new entries this year. Forget the tired cliché of late-night greasy döners for soaking up booze, and instead sample one of the world's great cuisines.

Central

Edgware Road W1

Safa

22-23 Nutford Place, W1H 5YH (7723 8331). Edgware Road or Marble Arch tube. **Meals served** noon-midnight daily. **Main courses** £7.50-£16. **Set meal** £10.50, £14.50 meat, £19.50 fish, 2 courses. **Service** 10%. **Credit** JCB, MC, V.
With its combination of Turkish and Iranian cuisine, Safa fits in well in an area famed for Middle Eastern restaurants. The bread oven wasn't working on our visit, which was a pity as the wafer-thin Iranian bread is one of the best reasons for visiting here. Starters of crispy bread with pine nuts and peynirli börek made up somewhat for this disappointment, though the börek was slightly over-fried. Mains came with excellent rice and salad, but both the ucler (mixed grill) and sultani (an Iranian speciality with filleted lamb) were a bit bland. Desserts, however, were unequivocally wonderful; muhallebi (milk pudding with pistachio and rosewater) and Iranian saffron ice-cream. Turkish coffee is a fine version too, and not over sweet. Quiet, heavy matting and white tablecloths lend a sedate feel to proceedings, and water trickles through a rockery of artificial flowers at the back. The waiters were friendly and helpful. Overall, our meal was a bit of a let-down, especially as Safa has excelled in the past.
Babies and children welcome. Booking advisable weekends. Restaurant available for hire. Tables outdoors (5, pavement). Takeaway service; delivery service. **Map 8 F5.**

Fitzrovia W1

Istanbul Meze

100 Cleveland Street, W1P 5DP (7387 0785/ www.istanbulmeze.co.uk). Great Portland Street or Warren Street tube. **Meals served** noon-11pm Mon-Fri. **Main courses** £7-£12. **Set lunch** £7.90 2 courses. **Set dinner** £10.90 2 courses. **Set meal** £15 4 courses. **Credit** AmEx, MC, V.

Just around the corner from Great Portland Street tube station, this small restaurant has a basement wine bar, with musicians playing in the evening. On the ground floor, a copper-covered grill fills the back of the small interior, and a couple of tables nestle outside on the pavement. While waiting to order, diners are plied with fat black olives, chillies and carrot. The house red (Turkish Villa Doluca) costs £2.50 a glass. There's a changing soup of the day: classic Turkish lentil when we visited. For starters, a mixed cold meze included ıspanak tarator, a bland houmous, aubergine and a kısır-type salad, accompanied by warm pitta bread. To follow, we ate a very satisfying lamb iskender, made with köfte and a great splodge of yoghurt. The waitresses brought around a big pan of chilli sauce with ritual seriousness. To finish, a very decent Turkish coffee was accompanied by small Turkish delights. While it would hardly stand out on Upper Street, Istanbul Meze is still recommended, bringing authentic Turkish dishes to an otherwise starved area.
Babies and children admitted. Book weekends. Entertainment (wine bar): guitarists from 6pm Mon-Sat; DJ Fri, Sat. Separate room for hire, seats 30. Tables outdoors (4, pavement). Takeaway service. Vegetarian menu. **Map 3 J4.**

★ Özer

5 Langham Place, W1B 3DG (7323 0505). Oxford Circus tube.
Bar **Open** noon-11pm daily.
Restaurant **Meals served** noon-midnight daily. **Main courses** £8.70-£15.70. **Set lunch** (noon-7pm) £9 2 courses. **Set dinner** (7-11pm) £11 2 courses. **Service** 12.5%.
Both **Credit** AmEx, DC, MC, V.
Özer deservedly remains one of the premier Turkish restaurants in central London. Although large and usually busy, it still employs a waitress to run out and entice in anyone who stops to glance at the menu. By the entrance is a bar, behind which is the spacious red-walled restaurant, with black-uniformed staff flitting around. The manager's mobile number was displayed on our table in case anyone wanted to complain. It seemed a little unnecessary, as there was nothing to complain about, especially with big marinated olives and extra-smooth houmous already supplied. Neither had we any quibbles with a starter of broad beans in yoghurt; it was fresh, tasty and well presented. The high quality continued into the main courses. The menu is varied enough to satisfy a wide range of tastes; it includes grills and stews, meat, fish and vegetarian dishes. We enjoyed mücver, which was served with falafel to offer complementary flavours; it came with excellent basmati rice and vegetables. Tandir (shoulder of lamb) was a big portion of meat that was slightly too dry and salty, although this was lessened by the kumquat and lime with which it was served.
Babies and children welcome; children's menu; high chairs. Disabled: toilet. No-smoking tables. Tables outdoors (5, pavement). Takeaway service. **Map 2 H5.**

Holborn WC1

Ottomans [NEW]

54 Red Lion Street, WC1R 4PD (7430 2880/ www.ottomansrestaurant.co.uk). Holborn tube. **Lunch served** noon-3pm Mon-Fri. **Dinner served** 6-11pm Mon-Sat. **Main courses** £8.50-£14.95. **Set lunch** £9.95 2 courses, £14.95 3 courses incl tea or coffee. **Credit** AmEx, MC, V.
Modern and upmarket, Ottomans seems almost embarrassed to be a Turkish restaurant. It has a more generally Mediterranean feel, with tasteful

abstract pictures adorning the walls. However, you'll still find many classic dishes here, including iman bayıldı. The restaurant specialises in large mezes (vegetarian, meat or fish, starting at around £12), which make a tasty all-in-one meal. Flatbread and olive oil were provided while we waited for food to arrive; good job too, since said wait wasn't short. We hope this was because each dish was being freshly made. For starters, squid fried in batter came nicely presented, with a lot of light batter and a chilli sauce. A main course of excellent köfte was served on a metal skewer, accompanied by fresh salad and fries (rather than the more traditional rice). Another sign of the internationalisation is the lack of Turkish coffee.
Babies and children welcome. Booking advisable lunch. Separate room for parties, seats 30. Takeaway service; delivery service. **Map 10 M5.**

Marylebone W1

Grand Bazaar

42 James Street, W1N 5HS (7224 1544). Bond Street tube. **Meals served** noon-11pm daily. **Main courses** £9-£10. **Set lunch** £5.95 2 courses. **Set dinner** £8.50 mixed meze. **Credit** AmEx, MC, V.
Lamps and incense burners hang from the ceiling; tables are small and the atmosphere is smoky; all this might be uncomfortable, but at least it provides the feel of an authentic Istanbul bazaar. We began our meal with houmous kavurma: a very smooth puréed dip studded with pine nuts and juicy nibbles of lamb. Avocado tarama (half an avocado filled with tarama) came as a very generous portion. Pide is charged extra (an increasingly common occurrence in central London). For mains, Grand Bazaar special kebab was a hearty mix of pirzola, beyti and şiş, though none of the individual components was exceptional. Similarly, the sauce covering the chicken harem kebab was unremarkable. Desserts, however, were above criticism: a nice, light, rose-watered sütlaç (rice pudding) and baklava. It's also worth trying the Turkish spirits (mint, rose or gold, at £2.50 a go) and the fine Turkish coffee. Despite the small tables and variable food quality, there's an enjoyable feel to this place.
Babies and children welcome; high chairs. Booking advisable. Tables outdoors (16, pavement). Takeaway service. **Map 9 G6.**

Mayfair W1

Sofra

18 Shepherd Market, W1Y 7HU (7493 3320/ www.sofra.co.uk). Green Park tube. **Meals served** noon-midnight daily. **Main courses** £7.95-£14.45. **Set lunch** (noon-6pm) £8.95 2 courses. **Set dinner** (6-11pm) £11.95 2 courses. **Cover** £1.50. **Service** 12.5%. **Credit** AmEx, MC, V.
This upmarket restaurant has large windows giving a fine view of the Mayfair street outside. The decor favours white (paintwork, tiles and tablecloths) and, like the clientele, is somewhat more opulent than you'd find in your average Turkish caff. Each table sports a single rose. If this branch of Sofra gets busy (and it does), you might be unlucky enough to find yourself crammed into the basement. The complimentary houmous was good, but had been left standing in the dish. By contrast, kalamar tarator was most appetising: tender squid marinated in vodka and served with an exceptionally nutty tarator. For mains, try the kul basti, very tender lamb with beautiful basmati rice and a roast vegetable salad. The fine, fresh chilli sauce also deserves a mention. The meal was accompanied by incomparable pide. Sofra has cut back of late, closing some of the branches it opened in 2003. The firm may have been overstretching itself – crowding restaurants and skimping on basics – but on this showing it seems to be consolidating, focusing on where its reputation was built.
Babies and children welcome; high chairs. Booking advisable. Separate room for hire, seats 14. Tables outdoors (10, pavement). Takeaway service. Vegetarian menu. **Map 9 H8.**
For branches see index.

Chiswick W4

Andy's Kebab House

3-4 Bedford Park Corner, Turnham Green Terrace, W4 1LS (8994 3953). Turnham Green tube. **Meals served** noon-midnight daily. **Main courses** £7.50-£8.90. **Set meal** £14.50 4 courses. **Cover** 50p. **Credit** JCB, MC, V.
Though fronted by a takeaway kebab place, Andy's doesn't come across as a typical Turkish restaurant and looks very English. It also seems very small, but there's a larger room upstairs, with blue walls, heavy white tablecloths, chandeliers and a good view of the green across the road. We began with pleasantly spicy barbunga pilaki (haricot beans and celery), but a dish of mitite köfte (meatballs) was too oily and fatty. For mains, Chiswick kebab (lokma by any other name) was highly enjoyable, served with rice, a traditional slice of döner and a non-traditional and unnecessary portion of chips. Vegetarian dishes include stuffed vine leaves, lots of fresh and well-made dolma with chips, and the vegetarian platter – a kind of vegetable moussaka, and good with it. Meals were served with quite acceptable olives and pitta, rather than pide. For all its minor faults, Andy's makes a fine local.
Babies and children welcome. Restaurant available for hire. Separate room for hire, seats 50. Takeaway service.

Notting Hill W11

Manzara

24 Pembridge Road, W11 3HL (7727 3062). Notting Hill Gate tube. **Breakfast served** 8am-noon, **lunch served** noon-6pm, **dinner served** 6-10.30pm daily. **Main courses** £6.75-£9.85. **No credit cards.**
Manzara calls itself Mediterranean, but has a largely Turkish menu. That doesn't stop the place serving non-Turkish dishes such as sandwiches and organic burgers, and selling a large range of cakes and gateaux. It specialises in pide (Turkish pizzas), which are becoming an increasingly common meal around London. A small, select wine list is also offered (organic wine is promised soon). Dolma, from the general menu, was a little stodgy and came with a small tray of pitta bread. The mixed kebab with chicken, shish and spicy köfte, however, was wonderful: enormous chunks of high-quality meat, cooked well. Staying Turkish, we tried the baklava and were pleased with the choice. Manzara may not be worth travelling great distances to, but it's fine for a meal if you're in the area (the management seems to concur with this view, as it has installed uncomfy chairs and tables worthy of a fast-food joint).
Babies and children welcome; high chairs. Restaurant available for hire. Tables outside (2, pavement). Takeaway service. **Map 7 A7**.

West Kensington W14

Best Mangal

104 North End Road, W14 9EX (7610 1050/ www.londraturk.com). West Kensington tube. **Meals served** noon-midnight daily. **Main courses** £7-£16. **Set meal** £16 2 courses, £18 3 courses, incl soft drink. **Credit** MC, V.
You'll find this decent, workman-like oçakbaşı restaurant hiding behind the narrow entrance of a busy takeaway. Prices reflect the no-nonsense, very plain furnishings (grey tiles and cream walls). For starters, patlıcan esme (puréed aubergine) was fine, but could have been tangier. It arrived with saç bread, plus nice fresh pide. A main course pilav üstu döner was very filling (indeed, it spilled off the large plate) and came with a big salad, lots of average rice and fillet döner (enjoyable, if rather fatty). The staff were bubbly and jokey, yet had to double on takeaway duty, which meant they weren't totally on the ball. The choice of desserts is limited, though our baklava was fine. At these prices the erratic quality of the cooking can be excused, as when Best Mangal gets it right, the food is really pretty good.

Babies and children welcome; high chairs. Booking advisable. Takeaway service. Vegetarian menu. For branch see index.

Southfields SW18

Kazans **NEW**

607-609 Garratt Lane, SW18 4SU (8739 0055/ www.kazans.com). Earlsfield rail/44, 77, 270 bus. **Lunch served** noon-3pm, **dinner served** 5-11pm daily. **Main courses** £6.50-£12.95. **Credit** AmEx, MC, V.
Popular with young couples, Kazans has a modern feel with purple walls and a wooden floor. The front opens up; there's jazzy, funky music; and palms in pots blow in the breeze (a shame that the noisy traffic spoils the tranquillity). This south London haunt is so far from the usual Turkish restaurant zones that kebabs are called 'brochettes', and burgers and other non-Turkish dishes are served. The venue pushes itself as a Turkish and Mediterranean bar and meze joint (it has no Turkish wine, but does offer a range of meze dishes as main courses). Börek were beautifully crisp layers of fine filo pastry around good feta cheese. İskender consisted of great chunks of lamb in a rich sauce. The meat was a little gristly, though, and arrived atop a bed of pitta rather than pide. Still, there's high-quality baklava for dessert. Kazans is a welcome new development and deserves success.
Babies and children welcome; high chairs. Booking advisable weekends. Disabled: toilet. Separate rooms for hire, seat 30 and 50. Tables outdoors (4, pavement). Takeaway service.

Battersea SW11

Adalar

50 Battersea Park Road, SW11 4GP (7627 2052). Battersea Park or Queenstown Road rail. **Meals served** 5pm-midnight daily. **Main courses** £7.50-£8.50. **Set dinner** £14.25 per person (minimum 2) 3 courses incl coffee. **Credit** MC, V.
Its name means a group of islands, but Adalar is an island very much out on its own in Battersea. It's rarely busy, and prices seem quite high, but that may be due to the location. Mixed meze included an exceptional bakla (delectable broad bean pâté), along with very good patlıcan esme (smoky puréed aubergine), tarama, houmous and kısır. The hot sigara börek was light and crisp, yet slightly oily, which isn't ideal. Moussaka was the only vegetarian main course (though fortunately the dish was light and most agreeable). Yoğhurtlu şiş was very tasty. To finish, there's a varied choice of excellent baklavas. Adalar has an enjoyable atmosphere for a quiet night out; locals should use it before they lose it.
Babies and children welcome; high chairs. Booking advisable weekends. Separate room for hire, seats 30.

Camberwell SE5

★ Tadim Café

41 Camberwell Church Street, SE5 8TR (7708 0838). Denmark Hill rail/12, 171 bus. **Meals served** 8am-11pm Mon-Thur, Sun; 8am-midnight Fri, Sat. **Main courses** £3.50-£5. **No credit cards.**
The decor hasn't changed in the past few years, still featuring large pastel murals of Turkish scenes. The plastic sheeting covering the bright tablecloths is starting to warp at the edges, but locals know what to expect from this rest-stop. Tadim is an unpretentious local café with a pâtisserie counter out front. The limited menu includes fish and chips, as well as a selection of Turkish dishes. Kısır was fresh and tangy, served with a large chunk of fresh baked bread (not pide, but nice). Shish kebab came with both rice and

chips; it would have been better to dump the chips and work on a livelier salad. The shish was unusual in being grilled fillet rather than cubes of meat, but an even more offbeat dish is kadin budu (literally 'ladies' thighs'), but, in practice, lamb patty fried in egg and flour). Tadim is a decent outpost of Turkish cooking, providing an alternative to the after-pub kebab houses that still dominate south London.
Babies and children admitted. No-smoking tables. Takeaway service. **Map 23 B2**.

London Bridge & Borough SE1

Tas

72 Borough High Street, SE1 1XF (7403 7200/ www.tasrestaurant.com). London Bridge tube/rail. **Meals served** noon-11.30pm Mon-Sat; noon-10.30pm Sun. **Main courses** £4.95-£14.45. **Set meal** £7.95-£9.95 per person (minimum 2) 10 meze; £18.50 per person (minimum 2) 3 courses. **Service** 12.5%. **Credit** AmEx, MC, V.
The flagship branch of the Tas mini chain is probably the Waterloo one, but that might change with the launch of a new concept, Tas Gurme: a restaurant-deli-wine bar combination due to open in autumn 2004. Apart from Tas Pide (which has a classically derived decor, and specialises in Turkish pizza), all branches have a similar look. Modern and rather chic, with designer chairs, wooden floors and polished fittings, this Borough High Street outlet manages to pack in plenty of people without ever seeming overcrowded. The airy no-smoking basement helps. Start with a plentiful portion of midye corbasi (mussels with celery, coriander and ginger) or tasty grilled hellim. Move on to kagita kilic baligi – a great swordfish steak with red peppers and potatoes, cooked in foil in a rich sauce bursting with flavour. Apple dolma (two baked apples stuffed with mulberry rice) makes an interesting veggie option. Some dishes, such as the mulberry rice, are rather bland. Piped music was played during our meal, though musicians often perform in the evenings. The decent wine list includes French, Turkish and New World selections. Next door is a café-pâtisserie offering takeaway Turkish meze and salads, alongside croissants and pasta. Tas Pide of Farringdon Road, EC1, is currently closed for renovations, but is due to reopen in February 2005.
Babies and children welcome; high chairs. Separate room for hire, seats 100. Takeaway service. **Map 11 P8**.
For branches see index.

Shoreditch E2, EC1

Shish

313 Old Street, EC1V 9LE (7749 0990/ www.shish.com). Liverpool Street/Old Street tube/rail.
Bar **Open** 5pm-midnight Mon-Sat; 5-10.30pm Sun. **Snacks served** £2.75-£5.75.
Restaurant **Meals served** 11.30am-11.30pm Mon-Fri; 10.30am-11.30pm Sat; 10.30am-10.30pm Sun. **Main courses** £3.95-£10.95.
Both **Service** 12.5%. **Credit** AmEX, DC, JCB, MC, V.
This is the second branch of Shish, which calls itself a 'Silk Road' restaurant and covers cuisine from Turkey to Indonesia. There's a bar in the basement, plus a first-rate juice bar in the main restaurant; try the striped mixed fruit juice. Water pumps (for unlimited still or sparkling water at £1 a head) dominate the long bar. Staff also serve wine and a range of bottled beers (Japanese, Belgian, Czech, but no Turkish). There's a fixed 'silk route' choice of dishes, plus a shifting menu (Middle Eastern when we visited). Meat kibbeh (baked meatballs) made an exciting starter from the Middle Eastern menu, while, to follow, chicken with apricot and ginger from the main menu is highly recommended. This came with a sharp tangy sauce, a small salad and a good portion of wonderful basmati rice. The restaurant has something of a canteen feel, yet was less busy than

Tadim Café

19 Numara Bos Cirrik. See p262.

we expected. In the past, Shish has seemed to emphasise the decor above the food, but this wasn't the case on our most recent visit.
Babies and children welcome; children's menu; high chairs. Bookings not accepted for parties of fewer than 9 (restaurant). Disabled: toilet. Entertainment: world music 10pm Wed; DJs 8pm Thur, Fri. No smoking (restaurant). Tables outdoors (6, pavement). Takeaway service. Vegetarian menu. Vegan dishes. **Map 6 R4.**
For branch see index.

★ Tas Firin NEW

160 Bethnal Green Road, E2 6BG (7729 6446). Bethnal Green or Liverpool Street tube/rail then 8 bus. **Meals served** noon-11.30pm daily. **Main courses** £5-£7.50. **No credit cards.**
A corner-café (not part of the Tas chain) with shiny metal seats and big windows giving a panoramic view of Bethnal Green Road, Tas Firin serves Turkish pizza, stews and all the basic grills. Both hot and cold starters are available. Try the mercimek, an appetising and filling lentil soup, which came with two wedges of lemon. For mains, beyti took a while to arrive and was a little charred round the edges. The meat used to make the mince was a bit fatty too, though it was put together with fresh garlic and spices and came with good rice, salad and bread. Pizzas can be topped with onions, spices, lamb, chicken, egg, Turkish sausage or even potato. This may not be up to the standard of the best cafés in Dalston and Green Lanes, but it's a nice authentic eaterie; locals should pay a visit.
Babies and children welcome. Booking advisable. Takeaway service. **Map 6 S4.**

North East

From Dalston Kingsland rail station up the A10 to Stoke Newington Church Street, many shop signs appear in Turkish, rather than English. A recent sprinkling of Polish delicatessens has yet to dent the area's Anatolian feel. A large section of this community comes from south-east Turkey, and many are Kurdish. Endless bargain oçakbaşı caffs serve high-quality food at rock-bottom prices, and you'll find more variety in the cuisine here than on Green Lanes.

None of the following establishments gets a full review, but only because the area is a cornucopia of choice. On Stoke Newington Road: **Best Tava** (No.17) is good for güveç; **Taka** (No.23) for fish; **Turku** (No.79) for meze with folk music; and **Aziziye** (Nos.117-119) occupies the basement of an intricately tiled mosque. Elsewhere are: **Dervish Bistro** (15 Stoke Newington Church Street); **Sölen** (84 Stoke Newington High Street); **Özlem** (Unit 1, Prince George Road); and **Yeni Umut 2000** (6 Crossway). Also keep an eye out for the ever-popular **Best Turkish Kebab** (125 Stoke Newington Road), a takeaway with an absurdly large döner rotisserie and a permanent queue, and pâtisserie **Öz Anteplier** (30 Stoke Newington Road), which sells perfect baklava.

Dalston E8, N16

Istanbul Iskembecisi

9 Stoke Newington Road, N16 8BH (7254 7291). Dalston Kingsland rail/76, 149, 243 bus. **Meals served** noon-5am daily. **Main courses** £6.50-£9.95. **Set lunch** (noon-5pm) £5 2 courses. **Set meal** (5pm-5am) £9.50 2 courses. **Credit** MC, V.
Retaining a vaguely regency look, this remains the closest Dalston or Stoke Newington has to an upmarket Turkish dining establishment, and stands out from the cheerful vulgarity of much of the competition. There's a bar at the back, pastel shades on the walls, real flowers on the tables and a varied wine list. The large menu ranges from the tripe soup that gives the restaurant its name (which translates as 'Istanbul tripe house') through to a decent selection of vegetarian dishes. The mixed meze is well worth ordering for starters, providing an enjoyably disparate batch of dishes, including mitite köfte,

Menu

It's useful to know that in Turkish 'ç' and 'ş' are pronounced 'ch' and 'sh'. So şiş is correct Turkish, shish is English and sis is common on menus. Menu spelling tends to be enthusiastic rather than consistent, so expect wild variations on everything given here. See also the menu boxes in **Middle Eastern** (p199) and **North African** (p226).

Cooking equipment

Mangal: brazier.
Oçakbaşı: an open grill under an extractor hood. A domed saç is put over the charcoal for making paper-thin bread.

Soups

İşkembe: finely chopped tripe soup, an infallible hangover cure.
Mercimek çorbar: red lentil soup.
Yayla: yoghurt and rice soup (usually) with a chicken stock base.

Meze dishes

Arnavut ciğeri: 'albanian liver'– thinly sliced or cubed lamb's liver, fried then baked.
Barbunya: spicy kidney bean stew.
Börek or **böreği**: fried or baked filo pastry parcels with a savoury filling, usually cheese, spinach or meat. Commonest are **muska** or **peynirli** (cheese) and **sigara** ('cigarette', so long and thin).
Cacik: diced cucumber with garlic in yoghurt.
Çoban salatası: 'shepherd's' salad of finely diced tomatoes, cucumbers, onions, perhaps green peppers and parsley, sometimes with a little feta cheese.
Dolma: stuffed vegetables (usually with rice and pine kernels).

Enginar: artichokes, usually with vegetables in olive oil.
Haydari: yoghurt, infused with garlic and mixed with finely chopped mint leaves.
Hellim: Cypriot halloumi cheese.
Houmous: creamy paste of chickpeas, crushed sesame seeds, oil, garlic and lemon juice.
Imam bayıldı: literally 'the Iman fainted'; aubergine stuffed with onions, tomatoes and garlic in olive oil.
Kalamar: fried squid.
Karides: prawns.
Kısır: usually a mix of chopped parsley, tomatoes, onions, crushed wheat, olive oil and lemon juice.
Kizartma: lightly fried vegetables.
Köy ekmeği: literally 'village bread'; another term for saç (qv).
Lahmacun: 'pizza' of minced lamb on thin pide (qv).
Midye tava: mussels in batter, in a garlic sauce.
Mücver: courgette and feta fritters.
Patlıcan: aubergine, served in a variety of ways.
Patlıcan esme: grilled aubergine puréed with garlic and olive oil.
Pide: a term encompassing many varieties of Turkish flatbread, served with most meals. Confusingly, also refers to Turkish pizzas (heavier and more filling than lahmacun, qv).
Pilaki: usually haricot beans in olive oil, but the name refers to the method of cooking not the content.
Piyaz: white bean salad with onions.
Saç: paper-thin, chewy bread prepared on a domed saç over a charcoal grill.
Sucuk: spicy sausage, usually beef, less often lamb.

Tarama: cod's roe paste.
Tarator: a bread, garlic and walnut mixture; **havuç tarator** adds carrot; **ıspanak tarator** adds spinach.
Yaprak dolması: stuffed leaves.
Zeytin: olive.

Main courses

Alabalik: trout.
Balik: fish.
Güveç: stew, which is traditionally cooked in an earthenware pot.
Hünkar beğendi: cubes of lamb, braised with onions and tomatoes, served on an aubergine and cheese purée.
İçli köfte: balls of cracked bulgar wheat filled with spicy mince.
İncik: knuckle of lamb, slow roasted in its own juices. Also called kléftico.
Karni yarik: aubergine stuffed with minced lamb and vegetables.
Kléftico: see incik.
Mitite köfte: chilli meatballs.
Sote: meat (usually), sautéed in a tomato, onion and pepper (and sometimes wine) sauce.
Uskumru: mackerel.

Kebabs

Usually made with grilled lamb (those labelled **tavuk** or **piliç** are chicken), served with bread or rice and salad. Common varieties include:
Adana: spicy mince.
Beyti: usually spicy mince and garlic, but sometimes best-end fillet.
Bıldırcın: quail.
Böbrek: kidneys.
Çöp şiş: small cubes of lamb.
Döner: slices of marinated lamb (sometimes mince) packed tightly with pieces of fat on a vertical rotisserie.
Halep: usually döner (qv) served over bread with a buttery tomato sauce.

İskender: a combination of döner (qv), tomato sauce, yoghurt and melted butter on bread.
Kaburga: spare ribs.
Kanat: chicken wings.
Köfte: mince mixed with spices, eggs and onions.
Külbastı: char-grilled fillet.
Lokma: 'mouthful' (beware, there's a dessert that has the same name!); boned fillet of lamb.
Patlıcan: mince and sliced aubergine.
Pirzola: lamb chops.
Şeftali: seasoned mince, wrapped in caul fat.
Şiş: cubes of marinated lamb.
Uykuluk: sweetbread.
Yoğhurtlu: meat over bread and yoghurt.

Desserts

Armut tatlısı: baked pears.
Ayva tatlısı: quince in syrup.
Baklava: filo pastry interleaved with minced pistachio nuts, almonds or walnuts, and covered in sugary syrup.
Kadayıf: cake made from shredded pastry dough, filled with syrup and nuts or cream.
Kazandibi: milk pudding, traditionally with very finely chopped chicken breast.
Kemel pasha: small round cakes soaked in honey.
Keşkül: milk pudding with almonds and coconut, topped with pistachios.
Lokum: Turkish delight.
Sütlaç: rice pudding.

Drinks

Ayran: a refreshing drink made with yoghurt.
Çay: tea.
Kahve or Turkish coffee: a tiny cup half full of sediment, half full of strong, rich, bitter coffee. Offered without sugar, medium or sweet.
Rakı: spirit, aniseed flavour.

---

kalamari, falafel, mücver and hellim. For main courses, levrek (grilled sea bass), makes a fine option. The inegöl köfte – spiced meatballs with rice and salad – was praiseworthy, even if was ever so slightly overdone. For dessert, kazandibi, tasty Turkish crème caramel, contrasted with the not-at-all-Turkish tart tatin (with apple and lots of chocolate). The Turkish coffee is as excellent as you'd expect in this area, while the staff are serious and attentive.
Babies and children welcome; high chairs. Book Fri, Sat. Takeaway service. **Map 25 B4.**

Mangal Oçakbasi
10 Arcola Street, E8 2DJ (7275 8981/ www.mangal1.com). Dalston Kingsland rail/76, 149, 243 bus. **Meals served** noon-midnight daily. **Main courses** £6.50-£11.50. **No credit cards**.

Despite ever-growing competition in the area, the original Mangal goes on doing exactly the same thing – and is much appreciated for it. People who are after restaurant trappings (like menus) go to Mangal II around the corner (*see below*); those who just want a top-quality grill, venture down a dark sidestreet to Mangal (there's now a local theatre opposite to liven things up a bit). Once through the tiny entrance and past the display of raw kebabs, you'll find a plain, clean, grey-tiled café. Locals know that Mangal produces outstanding grills; they also know it's worth asking for dishes not on display (such as stew or lahmacun). Cold starters of houmous and cacik are also available: big portions served on a side plate. Bread is good and plentiful, though not warmed. Pirzola (lamb chops) came without rice, but with a large fresh salad.

Such cooking looks so easy, you wonder why every restaurant can't produce it. Staff may seem uninterested, but this is a small place so they'll soon notice you and are happy to help make choices. Mangal is no longer as cheap as it once was, but that's only relative to ridiculously cheap Dalston prices.
Book weekends. Takeaway service. **Map 25 C4.**

Mangal II
4 Stoke Newington Road, N16 8BH (7254 7888). Stoke Newington rail/76, 149, 243 bus. **Meals served** noon-1am daily. **Main courses** £7-£12. **Set meal** £12.50-£14 per person (minimum 2) 2 courses. **No credit cards**.
This well-loved local restaurant with its neutral green walls and vaulted blue ceiling is a step upmarket from the original Mangal café (*see above*),

and from the Mangal Turkish pizza shop across the way at No.27. But it's still casual enough for family outings on a Sunday afternoon, and prices remain keen. The restaurant is usually busy with a mixed and noisy local crowd. For starters, both arnavut tatlısı (liver) and kalamar (fried squid with russian salad) were fine, the liver notably juicy – though the kitchen has taken to supplying slices of lemon that are so skinny they're more picturesque than practical, proving almost impossible to squeeze satisfyingly. Starters are accompanied by both pide and saç bread. For mains, lokma kebab (medallions of lamb held together with cocktail sticks) was exceptional, while the flavours of individual spices and garlic could be discerned in the wonderful yoğhurtlu adana. Service was always friendly and relaxed, but not particularly fast.
Babies and children admitted; children's portions; high chairs. Book weekends. No-smoking tables. Takeaway service. **Map 25 C4**.

★ ★ 19 Numara Bos Cirrik
34 Stoke Newington Road, N16 7XJ (7249 0400). Dalston Kingsland rail/76, 149, 243 bus. **Meals served** noon-midnight daily. **Main courses** £5-£8. **Credit** MC, V.
This oddly named café and takeaway is usually busy, with lots of coming and going. That's no surprise; this is a tremendous place. Its secret is simple: enormous portions of perfect grills. Though a full range of starters is also offered, only the truly starving should indulge. Once a grill is ordered, a large salad and cold starters will be brought – usually onion in chilli, and onion in pomegranate and turnip sauce – plus warm bread. (Wonderful fresh bread, both saç and pide, heated over the grill, comes in an endless supply.) We chose a succulent beyti, made from minced, spiced lamb; and keynali pide, a Turkish pizza with spicy lamb paste, tomato and chilli. It's a close call, but this place remains the best grill on the strip – and this strip is unequalled in London for great

Turkish cafés. To drink, Turkish tea and ayran are plentiful, or there's Efes beer; wine can be brought in. An exceptional favourite.
Babies and children welcome. Booking advisable. Takeaway service. **Map 25 C4**.

★ Sömine
131 Kingsland High Street, E8 2PB (7254 7384). Dalston Kingsland rail/76, 149, 243 bus. **Meals served** 24hrs daily. **Main courses** £3.50-£5.50. **No credit cards**.
Very much a local Turkish café, Sömine is full of Dalston folk drinking tea and eating a shifting variety of common (and less common) Turkish dishes. A couple of women sit on a raised platform at the back of the café making flatbread stuffed with spinach and potato. There's no printed menu, and the available dishes – usually a range of criminally cheap stews – are chalked on the wall. While we were waiting for the main course, a plate of pickled vegetables was provided, including a deadly chilli. It's worth coming here just for the manti (one of the more unusual dishes); this homely offering of meat and dumplings varies around Turkey, but is served here in the central Turkish style: lots of little dumplings stuffed with lamb, covered in thick yoghurt, with spicy/sour red seasoning sprinkled on top. Unusually in Turkish cooking, no vegetables are included in the manti, but it's tasty and filling. As at all traditional cafés, Turkish tea and bread are supplied and topped up at no extra charge. This is also a good place to try staples such as the yoghurt drink, ayran.
Babies and children welcome. Takeaway service; delivery service. **Map 25 B4**.

Hackney E8

★ Anatolia Oçakbasi NEW
253 Mare Street, E8 3NS (8986 2223). Hackney Central rail/48, 55, 253, 277, D6 bus. **Meals served** 11am-midnight daily. **Main courses** £4.50-£9.80. **Corkage** £3.50. **Credit** (£1.50 charge) MC, V .

Big, but café-like, with a popular takeaway, Anatolia certainly hasn't suffered from its move down the road in 2003. However, the open-plan look means the takeaway (and winter winds) can impose on seated diners. Mixed meze had a touch of cold starters about it (tarama, houmous, dolma, cacik and the like). If anything, there were too many choices, putting the dips in danger of blending together on the plate. Halep (slices of döner kebab served over bread with a buttery tomato sauce) was a fine big portion, if slightly too tomatoey; roll shish (kebab rolls of lamb fillet around onion and cheese) was highly satisfying too, but the cheese tends to melt and drip out of the lamb – which may explain the rarity of the dish. A bottle of house red is £9.10 (you can bring your own, but there's a £3.50 corkage charge). It's good to see a decent Turkish eaterie in Hackney.
Babies and children welcome; children's menu (noon-6pm Sat, Sun). Booking advisable weekends. Disabled: toilet. No-smoking tables. Takeaway service. Vegetarian menu.

Newington Green N16

★ Beyti
113 Green Lanes, N16 9DA (7704 3165). Bus 141, 341. **Meals served** noon-midnight daily. **Main courses** £4.50-£10. **No credit cards**.
Beyti stands out from a crowd of similar-looking Turkish eateries along this stretch of Green Lanes by offering variations on the standard menu (the emphasis is on northern Anatolian cuisine). Mixed meze starters of cacik, patlıçan esme and falafel may have been routine choices, but they were all noticeably fresh and tasty. More unusual was a main course of akçabat köfte, a Black Sea speciality that varies the spicing in the mince. Tavuk beyti (minced chicken kebab) is a commonly found dish, but here it is served wrapped in saç bread. Each day a different selection of stews is offered, and the menu includes an appetising collection of fish dishes. Everything was

accompanied by beautiful fresh, hot pide (replenished without our having to ask) and a good fresh salad (lots of red cabbage). One or two super-sweet desserts are on the menu, as well as Turkish beverages such as ayran. Staff are friendly and chatty, and the walls are decorated with snapshots of grinning customers. An interesting alternative to the local norm.

Babies and children welcome. Booking advisable. Restaurant available for hire. Tables outdoors (2, pavement). **Map 25 A4.**

★ Sariyer Balik

56 Green Lanes, N16 9NH (7275 7681). Bus 141, 341. **Meals served** 5pm-1am daily. **Main courses** £6.50-£10. **No credit cards.**
This outstanding fish restaurant is a little off the beaten track, but it's worth the effort. The interior is tiny (though there's more seating in the basement) and painted black. Fishing nets are suspended from the ceiling; from these hang a variety of stuffed fish and oddments, including a flashing blue cable. A Turkish Villa Doluca light white wine went well with everything, although raki is always popular with the clientele. A starter of mussels, marinated in beer and deep-fried, was gloriously full of flavour. It came with toasted chunks from a loaf of bread rather than the more common pide, but that's not a complaint – it was good bread. Pan-fried anchovies were a succulent revelation. Bream was also excellent, though it wasn't our first choice: both mackerel and mullet were off (options vary according to the availability). To accompany the main courses, a large shredded salad came lightly dressed with a slight sour tang from a particularly tasty vinegar. Nothing was too fancy or pretentious; in short, the food was simply perfect.

Babies and children welcome; high chairs. Booking advisable. Separate room for hire, seats 60. Takeaway service. **Map 25 A4.**

Stoke Newington N16

★ Bodrum Café NEW

61 Stoke Newington High Street, N16 8EL (7254 6464). Stoke Newington rail/73, 76, 149, 243 bus. **Meals served** 7am-9pm daily. **Main courses** £5-£7.50. **Set lunch** £4.99 2 courses incl coffee. **No credit cards.**
This popular café changed hands last year, but hasn't altered much. The caff food is decent enough (particularly the English, Turkish and vegetarian breakfasts), but the Turkish meals are usually outstanding, if slightly more erratic than of old. Starters of sak suka (aubergine and potato salad) and patlıcan esme (puréed aubergine dip) were both fresh and tasty. Mains of çöp şiş (small cubes of grilled lamb) and izgara tavuk (chicken breast marinated in milk) were beautifully prepared and accompanied by excellent rice and crisp salad. The set lunch consists of a choice of any available Turkish cold starter, one set meat or vegetarian main course and a tea or coffee for £4.99: great value. Service can be slow when things are busy, but the atmosphere is enjoyable; the clientele is extremely mixed, from Stoke Newington revolutionaries to police officers from the station a few doors down.

Babies and children welcome; high chairs. Booking advisable. Separate room for hire, seats 30. Tables outdoors (4, pavement). Takeaway service. Vegetarian menu. **Map 25 B2.**

★ Café Z Bar

58 Stoke Newington High Street, N16 7PB (7275 7523). Stoke Newington rail/73, 76, 149, 243 bus. **Meals served** 8am-9pm daily. **Main courses** £4.50-£7.50. **No credit cards.**
This venue continues to provide a mix between a café, bar and restaurant, with hints of gallery and cultural centre thrown in. Don't be put off by the café menu in the window; from noon onwards, a limited but perfectly acceptable restaurant menu is offered, with a commensurate wine list. There's a recently expanded basement area too, for evening concerts and events. The light, airy, noisy ground floor also hosts a shifting exhibition of paintings

Café Z Bar

and photos. On to the food. Complimentary olives were chillied and succulent. Muhamara made an interesting starter: a tasty, red, walnut paste that had the texture of houmous and was served with plentiful pide. A main course of çop şiş was tender and juicy. As well as grills, a range of Turkish pizzas and vegetarian dishes is available (plus café food, served with chips, during the day). Costa coffee is offered alongside Turkish coffee and tea, and freshly squeezed apple, orange or carrot juice. We're still impressed by Z Bar.

Babies and children welcome; high chairs. Book weekends. Entertainment: jazz 8pm Thur. Separate room for hire, seats 50. Tables outdoors (2, pavement). Takeaway service. **Map 25 C2.**

North

Finchley N3

Izgara

11 Hendon Lane, N3 1RT (8371 8282). Finchley Central tube. **Meals served** noon-midnight daily. **Main courses** £5.95-£11.95. **Set meal** £14.75-£16.95 (minimum 2) 3 courses. **Credit** MC, V.
Though spacious and popular with locals, Izgara is not all it could be. It has a sunny yellow decor, with smoking and no-smoking areas. The night we visited, smoke was drifting between the two, but that may have been down to malfunctioning air-conditioning, which the staff were trying to fix. Service was generally rushed; waiters seemed confused and made small errors. We started with a fresh, tasty melon, but piyaz (haricot beans with onion) was bland and left unfinished. Bıldırcın (quail) had a fine flavour and came with a hearty salad. Vegetarian islim tava (aubergine wrapped around peppers, with mushrooms and courgettes in a tomato sauce) was acceptable, though supplied with rice rather than the requested salad. For dessert, armut tatlısı (pear stuffed with walnuts and covered in cream) was worth a try, yet hardly classic. Izgara has a larger range of Turkish dishes than many restaurants, but it's a shame the service and cooking isn't more consistent.

Babies and children welcome; high chairs. Booking advisable weekends. Disabled: toilet. No-smoking tables. Takeaway service. **For branch see index.**

★ The Ottomans NEW

118 Ballards Lane, N3 2DN (8349 9968). Finchley Central tube. **Meals served** noon-10.30pm daily. **Main courses** £6.90-£10.50. **Set lunch** £5.50 2 courses. **Set dinner** (Mon-Thur, Sun) £9.95 3 courses. **Credit** JCB, MC, V.

With a light, wooden interior and enormous mural of a waterside scene dominating one wall, the Ottomans doesn't come across as a traditional Turkish café (though it does have a selection of mood-enhancing incense burners). However, the menu sticks with traditional favourites. A lunch special costs a very reasonable £5.50 for a starter and main course. Patlıcan esme (puréed aubergine) was good, smoky and nicely textured, though came with only one piece of warm pitta. Inegöl köfte had an enjoyable, well-spiced taste, yet the portion was far from large; it was served with salad and rice – and another half a pitta. Ottomans is well worth visiting, but a basket of pide would be an improvement on the measly bread situation. That's one Turkish tradition that certainly should be kept.
Babies and children welcome; children's menu; high chairs. Book weekends. No-smoking tables. Takeaway service. Vegetarian menu.

Finsbury Park N4

★ Yildiz Restaurant

163 Blackstock Road, N4 2JS (7354 3899). Arsenal tube. **Meals served** noon-11pm Mon-Sat; 2-11pm Sun. **Main courses** £4-£12.65. **Set meal** £7.95-£11.50 3 courses. **No credit cards**.
This thin restaurant nestles behind a takeaway (with tasteful fairy lights flashing round the walls). It is licensed, despite a big sign in the window telling you to bring your own wine. Olives and chillies are provided while you browse the menu; this isn't an exclusively Turkish list, having a wider Mediterranean feel and containing lots of steaks. Starters of Turkish sucuk (small samosas filled with diced spicy sausage and mushrooms) were a joy, though the aubergine slices in the aubergine börek (pastry with feta cheese) were slightly too oily. The house special, sliced chicken breast rolled around spinach and mushrooms, was extremely palatable, but the halep (döner served over bread with a buttery tomato sauce, in this case with mushrooms) was absolutely outstanding.

Baklava and Turkish coffee were also thoroughly satisfactory. A recommended destination for a cheap but satisfying night out.
Babies and children admitted. Book weekends. No-smoking tables. Takeaway service.

Harringay N4

Green Lanes in Harringay developed as a Cypriot area, with a mix of Greek and Turkish that remains. However, the area's character is shifting; many of the newer arrivals from Turkey are Kurds, and this is reflected in the restaurants. Numerous cheap and vibrant oçakbaşı cafés line the street, several open 24 hours. Few are licensed, but almost all will let you bring your own alcohol.

There's not much to distinguish most of these places from one other, but the following are worth a look (Green Lanes street numbers are given in brackets; numbers under 100 are on Green Lanes Grand Parade): **Tara** (No.6), which has a more Middle Eastern feel; **Gökyüzü** (No.27); **Yore** (No.29), which specialises in seafood; **Gaziantep** (No.52); **Diyarbakır** (No.69); **Harran** (No.399); **Öz Sofra** (No.421); **Yayla** (No.429); **Mangal** (No.443), which wins the prize for the best sign, a psychedelic wonder; **Mizgin** (No.485); Bingöl (No.551); and **Selale** (2 Salisbury Promenade). The menus rarely stray from the standard grills, güveç and pide (both bread and pizza), but the food is high quality, fresh and very cheap. There are also plenty of pâtisseries, mostly Turkish, which produce a frightening variety of wedding cakes, as well as breads and confectionery.

Erenler NEW

64 Grand Parade, N4 1AF (8802 3263). Manor House tube/29, 141, 341 bus. **Meals served** noon-1am Mon-Thur, Sun; noon-2am Fri, Sat. **Main courses** £6-£8.50. **Set lunch** £8.50

3 courses. **Set dinner** £17.50 4 courses; £22 4 courses incl wine (minimum 2). **Credit** AmEx, JCB, MC, V.
It's difficult to decide on which is the pick of all the similar and generally very good Turkish cafés that are found along this stretch of road, but Erenler demands attention. It is slightly more of a restaurant than many of its local rivals, and is licensed. There's a standard oçakbaşı grill at the front, and the menu largely sticks to the usual selections of grilled meat and fish, stews, plus some vegetarian dishes. We began with excellent mücver (deep-fried courgette with feta). While the yaprak dolması (stuffed vine leaves) wasn't freshly made, it was still pleasant. We moved on to the chef's special of minced lamb köfte with mashed aubergine, and halep (slices of döner in a rich butter and tomato sauce), both of which were first rate. The wonderful fresh warm pide deserves a mention of its own. Excellent value.
Babies and children welcome; high chairs. Booking advisable Fri, Sat. No-smoking tables. Takeaway service. Vegetarian menu.

★ Serhat

403 Green Lanes, N4 1EU (8342 9830). Manor House tube. **Meals served** 8am-11pm daily. **Main courses** £4-£7.50. **Unlicensed. Corkage** no charge. **No credit cards**.
Like many along this strip, Serhat is a basic café, though none the worse for that. The bright 'ethnic' tablecloths are covered with thick sheets of perspex for easy wiping, and the place is packed with a local Kurdish and Turkish crowd. Olives, onion and radish are supplied to munch upon while you choose your food. Five stews are made each day, mostly variations on lamb with differing spices and vegetables. All the standard kebabs are available too. We started with lahmacun (a 'pizza' of minced lamb on thin pide bread with salad), which was a fair rendition, though not perfect. Mercimek (lentil) soup was excellent. A main course iskender (a combination of döner, tomato sauce, yoghurt and melted butter on bread) and tavuk beyti (spicy minced chicken and garlic) were

Zara. See p266.

both basic but well prepared, the beyti coming with a sizeable salad and very good rice. This is one of several cafés on Green Lanes worth travelling to for authentic, cheap Turkish food.
Takeaway service.

Highbury N5

★ İznik

19 Highbury Park, N5 1QJ (7354 5697).
Highbury & Islington tube/rail/4, 19, 236 bus.
Meals served 10am-4pm Mon-Fri. **Dinner served** 6.30pm-midnight daily. **Main courses** £7.50-£9.50. **Service** 10%. **Credit** MC, V.
İznik has barely changed in the past few years, and there are no complaints about that. The cluttered interior is divided by carved wooden screens, and the patterned tiles typical of the city of İznik are still in place. There are warm orange walls and masses of lamps and candles. The only niggle, and it is a minor one, is that staff continue to serve pitta bread rather than Turkish pide with meals. Mücver (grated courgette and feta cheese mixed and fried) had a beautiful texture, and came with fresh kısır. Dolma were crisp and piquant, flavoured with fresh dill. For mains, tavuk beğendi (chicken in aubergine sauce) had a gloriously smoky flavour, and was served with good basmati rice. Kuzu firinda (oven-cooked lamb) was mouth-wateringly tender. Mains came with a beautiful salad, including sweet pepper seeds, small, sharp-tasting peppers, and olives. Desserts are very sweet (of course). Armut tatlısı (pear with chocolate and pistachio) was probably too big a portion, but ekmek kadayıf, a very sweet 'cake', was exemplary. Strongly recommended all round.
Babies and children admitted. Booking essential weekends. Takeaway service.

Islington N1

Angel Mangal

139 Upper Street, N1 1QP (7359 7777).
Angel tube. **Meals served** noon-midnight daily. **Main courses** £6.95-£12.95. **Set lunch**

£5.50 2 courses. **Set meal** £16.25 per person (minimum 2). **Cover** £1. **Credit** MC, V.
This large open-plan restaurant is decorated with stained-glass panels, carpets and Ottoman etchings. A copper grill at the back dominates the space. The menu ranges wider than at some restaurants in the area, and contains a decent choice of Turkish pizzas and vegetarian dishes. For starters, kasar pane (little squares of deep-fried cheese with a garlic dipping sauce) remains a favourite, though patlıcan soslu (aubergine salad with onions and tomatoes) is ace too. Our mains were also excellent: halep (grilled, spicy, mince kebab with onions, tomatoes and butter sauce) and mantarlı tavuk (chicken with mushrooms, tomatoes, peppers, onions and garlic, with a white sauce). We were served a large fresh salad, and fresh garlic and chilli sauces were at hand. The wine list features Turkish and New World choices, and includes food-pairing recommendations. Our waitress was rather strident, but helpful too. It seemed a little unfair that Angel Mangal wasn't full on a Saturday night, despite the queues outside another nearby Turkish restaurant.
Babies and children welcome; high chairs.
Booking advisable. Tables outdoors (2, pavement).
Takeaway service. Vegetarian menu.
Map 5 O1.

Alaturca NEW

127 Upper Street, N1 1QP (7226 3222).
Angel tube/Highbury & Islington tube/rail.
Meals served 10am-11pm Mon-Thur, Sun; 10am-midnight Fri, Sat. **Main courses** £7.95-£11.95. **Set lunch** £5.95 2 courses. **Set dinner** (6-11pm) £13.95 3 courses. **Credit** MC, V.
The latest Turkish addition to the Upper Street restaurant strip, Alaturca is up against stiff competition and the verdict is: 'could try harder'. The helpful waiters and ethnic odds and ends are all in place, but the menu is not extensive. Bread is served cold and is not freshly made. Odd lighting leads to the restaurant being split into pools of bright light and near darkness. On the plus side, there's nothing wrong with the food. Starters of

sucuk izgara (Turkish sausage) and buffalo string (baby prawns in spicy breadcrumbs) were perfectly acceptable. Tavuk tadir (chicken mildly curried with potato, carrot and courgette) was an interesting diversion from the usual staples, and came with fine basmati rice. The more traditional iskender was made with fillet lamb and yoghurt and couldn't be faulted. Alaturca would be a welcome addition to almost any other street in London, but the competition on Upper Street casts a harsh light on its minor faults.
Babies and children welcome; high chairs.
Booking advisable Fri, Sat. Disabled: toilet.
Tables outdoors (3, pavement). Takeaway service.
Map 5 O1.

Gallipoli Again

120 Upper Street, N1 1QP (7359 1578/
www.gallipolicafe.co.uk). Angel tube. **Meals served** 11am-11pm daily. **Main courses** £4.95-£9.95. **Set lunch** £12 3 courses.
Set dinner £13.50 3 courses incl coffee. **Service** 10% for parties of 10 or more. **Credit** MC, V.
Gallipoli now has three outlets, all on Upper Street, and they are the most popular Turkish restaurants in Islington. At Gallipoli Again, the front window opens on to the street in good weather, but the interior is always in shadow. Sit as close to the front as possible; the back section can get cramped and uncomfortable and has an unappealing corrugated plastic roof. A charge is made for bread that, while acceptable, isn't the fresh hot pide any Stoke Newington café would provide for free. The place is always busy, but service is slow. The food isn't at all bad, however, and prices are generally very reasonable. A bottle of Turkish house red costs £9.95. Dolma was tangy and fresh, but the portion of succulent albanian liver was simply too large. For mains, Gallipoli kebab came with tender portions of kanat, köfte, shish and tavuk, while the chicken in the tavuk Gallipoli had been tenderised by marination in milk. Both were accompanied by a salad with a heavy dressing. This is a popular spot with young locals and parties itching for the chance to sing and dance on tables.

*Babies and children welcome; high chairs.
Booking advisable. Tables outdoors
(5, pavement). Takeaway service.* **Map 5 O1.**
For branches see index.

★ Gem

*265 Upper Street, N1 2UQ (7359 0405).
Angel tube/Highbury & Islington tube/rail.*
Meals served noon-11pm; Mon-Sat; noon-
10.30pm Sun. **Main courses** £5.50-£8.
Set lunch £5.45 3 courses, £7.45 4 courses.
Set dinner £8.45 3 courses, £10.95 4 courses,
£22.45 5 courses incl wine or beer. **Service**
10% for parties of 6 or more. **Credit** MC, V.
The owners of this restaurant have a Kurdish
background; much of the time you'll find a woman
baking qatme (distinctive, Kurdish stuffed
flatbread) just inside the door. Three types are
offered: cheese, spinach and slightly spicy potato.
Try them all at £1 each; portions are small, so get
lots or have another starter too. A more substantial
first course is kahaldi: a big plate of salad, spicy
sucuk sausage and feta. From the standard mezes,
the very beautifully textured mücver, with kısır on
the side, can't be faulted. A main course şiş kebab
was wonderful: good meat, well grilled and served
with salad. More unusual was tavuk göğsü
(chicken with cheese and chips), which was tasty,
but pretty heavy. A fair choice of vegetarian dishes
is offered. Complimentary baklava and ice-cream
were served, with no skimping on quality. Gem's
walls are painted an attractive burnt orange, and
the atmosphere is enjoyable, aided by attentive and
helpful staff. There's a separate dining room in the
basement. Good food at low prices.
*Booking advisable weekends. Children welcome;
high chairs. Separate room for hire, seats 70.
Takeaway service. Vegetarian menu.* **Map 5 O1.**

★ Pasha

*301 Upper Street, N1 2TU (7226 1454). Angel
tube/Highbury & Islington tube/rail.* **Lunch
served** noon-3pm Mon-Fri. **Dinner served**
6-11.30pm Mon-Thur; 6pm-midnight Fri.
Meals served noon-midnight Sat; noon-11pm
Sun. **Main courses** £7.50-£13.95. **Set meal**
£12.95 per person (minimum 2) meze selection,
£18.95 3 courses incl dessert and coffee. **Cover**
£1. **Service** 10% for parties of 6 or more.
Credit AmEx, DC, MC, V.
Pasha deservedly retains its position at the top of
the range in Islington. While we browsed the menu,
small portions of complimentary olives and
delicious pide and pitta were brought for us to
munch on. A first course of sardines wrapped in
vine leaves tasted deliciously moist and tender;
sucuk (sausage) was beautifully spiced and well
above the Turkish restaurant average. To follow,
kağit kebab (lamb in thyme and garlic sauce)
arrived foil-wrapped and piquant. Patlıcan kebab
was unusually presented; customarily, alternating
slices of aubergine and köfte are grilled on a
skewer, but here a bed of mashed potato was filled
with a stew of aubergine and lamb. Very tasty it
was too. For dessert, angelic fırın sütlaç (rice
pudding with the aroma and flavour of rosewater)
was perfect, while chocolate mousse was light and
fluffy. Pasha is dark and very busy; waiters rushed
around at such a rate, we worried they'd start
crashing into things.
*Babies and children admitted. Booking advisable
weekends. Tables outdoors (3, pavement).
Takeaway service.* **Map 5 O1.**

Sedir

*4 Theberton Street, N1 0QX (7226 5489).
Angel tube/Highbury & Islington tube/rail.*
Meals served 11am-11.30pm Mon-Thur;
11.30am-midnight Fri, Sat; 11.30am-11.30pm
Sun. **Main courses** £7.95-£11.95. **Set lunch**
£7.95 2 courses incl coffee. **Set meze** (11.30am-
6pm daily) £11.95 per person (minimum 2);
(6pm-midnight Fri, Sat) £13.95 per person
(minimum 2). **Cover** 60p. **Service** 10% for
parties of 6 or more. **Credit** AmEx, JCB, MC, V.
Spread across two floors, with a couple of tables
outside on a quietish sidestreet off Upper Street,
Sedir has pastel-coloured walls to lighten what is
a rather crowded interior. Enormous prints of
European paintings of the Ottoman court cover

the walls. A waitress lurks outside to pounce on
people browsing the menu and drag them inside,
which slightly spoils the otherwise sedate
atmosphere. A notable wine list includes Turkish,
New World and European selections. The wide-
ranging menu includes much fish and a number of
unexpected dishes. Ispanak (spinach) pancake was
quite heavy, perhaps a little too reminiscent of
lasagne for a starter, but the tabouleh was fresh
and light. Tavuk sedir (chicken in white wine sauce
with mushrooms and broccoli, served with basmati
rice) was fine, but not as special as a superb islim
kebab; strips of aubergine around the edge held in
the juices of the melting lamb. The bread was
perfectly crisp (though it's a pity we were charged
extra for it). There's a varied choice of desserts,
from trad Turkish to apple crumble. A fine place
for an evening out.
*Babies and children welcome; high chair. Booking
essential dinner. Separate room for hire, seats 50.
Tables outdoors (4, pavement). Takeaway service.*
Map 5 O1.

Muswell Hill N10

Bakko

*172-174 Muswell Hill Broadway, N10 3SA
(8883 1111). Highgate tube then 43, 134
bus.* **Meals served** noon-10.30pm daily. **Main
courses** £6.90-£15.50. **Set lunch** (noon-4pm
Mon-Fri) £6.90 3 courses. **Set meal** £13.50 per
person (minimum 2). **Credit** AmEx, MC, V.
Bakko (a Kurdish term for a village elder) has a
low arched ceiling and brick walls that suggest a
peasant household. The menu is quite varied –
though this isn't a good place for vegetarians. Pasa
meze (feta cheese grated with lots of chilli) made
a pleasantly unusual starter. Some main courses
also flirt with the unexpected – try Bakko köfte, a
large meat patty stuffed with a layer of spinach
and cheese, with rice and salad. The walls are
decorated with pictures of Kurdish women baking
flatbread, but what comes with the meal is very
ordinary pitta. The range of desserts is not
typically Turkish either, including chocolate
gateaux and fruit salad. You'll find decent Turkish
coffee, but also Illy for those wanting something
more familiar. Staff remain friendly and attentive.
Bakko has improved and is hitting its stride,
making it a worthwhile local restaurant, but there's
still room for improvement. At the very least, a
restaurant proclaiming its Kurdish roots should be
serving fresh Kurdish bread.
*Babies and children welcome; high chairs.
Book weekends. No-smoking tables.
Vegetarian menu.*

North West

Golders Green NW11

Baran

*748 Finchley Road, NW11 7TH (8458 0515).
Golders Green tube.* **Meals served** noon-
midnight daily. **Main courses** £7-£9.50.
Set meal £12 per person (minimum 2) 5 meze
incl coffee. **Credit** MC, V.
A long, narrow restaurant with a takeaway by the
door, Baran is stepped on three levels. Assorted
carpets hang on the walls, and there are also tables
on the wide pavement outside. The venue might be
developing a slightly run-down feel, but the food
is good. The menu consists of standard Turkish
grills. For starters, kısır was rather heavy, but had
an attractive nutty taste. Next, sarma lamb beyti
came wrapped in saç bread with runny yoghurt.
Our only complaint concerned the accompanying
'salad': a paltry half tomato. Finish with a fine
Turkish coffee and complimentary Turkish
delight. Service is friendly.
*Babies and children admitted. Booking advisable.
No-smoking tables. Separate room for parties,
seats 40. Takeaway service.*

Beyoglu NEW

*1031 Finchley Road, NW11 7ES (8455 4884).
Golders Green tube/82, 160, 260 bus.* **Meals
served** noon-midnight daily. **Main courses**
£6.50-£10. **Set dinner** £12-£13.75 3 courses
incl coffee. **Credit** MC, V.

A move across the road hasn't affected Beyoglu's
status as the best of the little cluster of Turkish
restaurants in Temple Fortune. The venue is light
and spacious, with new chairs and intricately
patterned decorations. The very un-Turkish music
playing suggests a relaxed attitude towards
authenticity. Service is helpful and attentive, but
not oppressive. Sigara börek were good, crisp and
chunky, filled with cheese and spinach. Bamya
(okra in olive oil with tomato, mushrooms and
peppers) – also available as a vegetarian main –
was appetising too, with the flavour of the okra
blossoming. These starters were accompanied by
saç bread, as well as some rather nice pide. Next,
our main course kul basti was an enormous lamb
steak with thyme, served with fluffy rice and salad.
The dessert menu is limited, but the sütlaç is
excellent. Nice, typically powerful Turkish coffee
comes with complimentary top-range Turkish
delight. Highly recommended.
*Babies and children welcome; high chairs.
Book weekends. No-smoking tables. Tables
outdoors (2, pavement). Takeaway service.
Vegetarian menu.*

Hampstead NW3

★ Zara

*11 South End Road, NW3 2PT (7794 5498).
Belsize Park tube/Hampstead Heath rail.*
Meals served 11.30am-11.30pm daily.
Main courses £6.50-£9.50. **Service** 10%.
Credit JCB, MC, V.
It's a compliment to say that Zara is much like a
restaurant from the Turkish areas of north-east
London, transported to Hampstead and moved
slightly upmarket (such luxuries as correctly
spelled menus, for instance) – though prices remain
very reasonable. In summer, the window opens up
and a couple of tables are plonked on the pavement.
Benches with cushions run along the walls of the
compact interior, which is divided into smoking
and no-smoking areas. Turkish themed pictures
(for sale) hang on the walls. The food is excellent:
mitite köfte were perfectly fried balls of minced
lamb; muska börek had an exceptional texture. To
follow, hünkar beğendi was stewed lamb in a rich
and heavy sauce of cheese and aubergine, while
tavuk iskender came with chunks of chicken rather
than slices of chicken döner. Both were cooked to
perfection. An appealing range of Turkish desserts
is offered, along with Italian-style ice-creams.
Turkish tea and coffee are supplied on request.
Unpretentious, efficient, ideal.
*Babies and children welcome; high chairs. Book
weekends. No-smoking tables. Tables outdoors
(3, pavement). Takeaway service. Vegetarian
menu.* **Map 28 C3.**

Willesden NW2

★ Mezerama

*76 Walm Lane, NW2 4RA (8459 3311).
Willesden Green tube.* **Dinner served** 5pm-
midnight Mon-Fri. **Meals served** 12.30pm-
midnight Sat, Sun. **Main courses** £6.50-£11.95.
Set lunch £6 1 course incl glass of wine or
soft drink. **Credit** AmEx, DC, MC, V.
Despite discarding the Turkish restaurant clutter
in favour of plain walls in lilac and pale green, plus
a distinctive round mirror, Mezerama doesn't stray
far from traditional Turkish cooking. Much effort
is put in to make diners new to Turkish food feel
at home, with dishes named in English and
described in full on the menu. Complimentary
houmous and bread were supplied on arrival. Our
starters were mouth-watering: musga börek (crisp
filo pastry triangles with parsley and feta), and
bulgar köfte (light, crisp meatballs). We moved on
to a haddock with tomato herb crust, coated in
thin lemon slices, with a subtle white wine and
lemon sauce; it was served with chips (though they
were superior chips). Lamb yoğhurtlu (mixed köfte
and shish) was beautifully done and came with a
fresh salad. This restaurant keeps improving and
deserves to be much better known.
*Babies and children welcome; high chairs. Booking
advisable; essential Fri, Sat. Restaurant available
for hire. Takeaway service. Vegetarian menu.*

Vegetarian

The winner of the Time Out Best Vegetarian Meal award in 2004 was **Manna** in Chalk Farm; runners-up were **Eat & Two Veg** (also listed in this section), **East@West** (Oriental; *see p229*), **Morgan M** (French; *see p88*) and **Sagar** (Indian; *see p125*). Regrettably, this year has seen a drop in the number of exclusively vegetarian venues in the capital, but non-meat eaters still have options in other cuisines. For vegetarian Gujarati and South Indian restaurants, see the **Indian** section, starting on p117. For more restaurants that make a special effort for vegetarians and vegans, look under **vegetarian food** in the **Subject Index**, starting on p394.

Central

Barbican EC1

Carnevale
135 Whitecross Street, EC1Y 8JL (7250 3452/ www.carnevalerestaurant.co.uk). Barbican tube/ Old Street tube/rail/55 bus. **Lunch served** noon-3pm Mon-Fri. **Dinner served** 5.30-10.30pm Mon-Sat. **Main courses** £9-£12. **Minimum** (noon-2.30pm Mon-Fri) £5.50. **Set meal** (noon-3pm Mon-Fri, 5.30-7pm Mon-Sat) £12.50 3 courses. **Service** 12.5% for parties of 5 or more. **Credit** MC, V.
This cosy Mediterranean restaurant, deli and takeaway is a favourite with local workers, who especially love the tiny covered courtyard, all bare brick and trailing plants. The initially intrusive sounds of the extractor fan are soon filtered out as you dine. Staff weave between the tables with a basket of delicious breads and olive oil to dip while you wait for your meal. The excellent-value set menu might involve the likes of smooth spinach soup, followed by pennette with creamed wild mushrooms and, to round off, a drink or one of the tempting desserts. À la carte prices are steeper, with starters at £4.95 and mains £11.50. Corn peppers stuffed with potato and herbs, served with roasted fennel, was enjoyable, while the caramelised blood orange tart with own-made Amaretto ice-cream was divine – a winning combination of warm and cold, rich and bittersweet. Organic soft drinks and wine include Sedlescombe, a pleasant dry white from Sussex.
Babies and children welcome. Booking advisable. Tables outdoors (3, conservatory). Takeaway service. Vegan dishes. **Map 5 P4**.

City EC2

★ The Place Below
St Mary-le-Bow, Cheapside, EC2V 6AU (7329 0789/www.theplacebelow.co.uk). St Paul's tube/ Bank tube/DLR. **Breakfast served** 7.30-11am, **lunch served** 11.30am-2.30pm, **snacks served** 2.30-3.30pm Mon-Fri. **Main courses** £5.50-£7.50. **Unlicensed Corkage** no charge. **Credit** MC, V.
An oasis of calm in the City, this is an ideal spot for breakfast before facing the office. Browse the morning papers with fortifying toasted oat porridge with maple syrup and cream, fruit salads or muesli. Good, strong Illy coffee is a bargain 80p. If you visit at non-peak dining times, you may even have the atmospheric crypt dining room, with its impressive domed ceiling, columns and alcoves, to yourself – and get £2 off main-course prices as well. The soups with own-made bread are satisfying, sometimes sublime (fennel, green pea and mint deserves special mention), as is the daily changing choice of quiche. Other freshly made hot dishes include pasta with walnut pesto, roast butternut squash and parmesan shavings. Leafy salads, a 'healthbowl' (wholegrain brown rice, puy lentils and seasonal vegetables, with sesame and ginger dressing) and filled ciabatta rolls are also available. Leave space for the Valrhona chocolate brownies and fluffy muffins.
Babies and children admitted. No smoking. Tables outdoors (24, churchyard). Takeaway service (7.30am-3.30pm). Vegan dishes. **Map 11 P6**.

Covent Garden WC2

★ Food for Thought
31 Neal Street, WC2H 9PR (7836 9072). Covent Garden tube. **Breakfast served** 9.30-11.30am, **dinner served** 5-8.30pm Mon-Sat. **Lunch served** noon-5pm daily. **Main courses** £3-£6.50. **Minimum** (noon-3pm, 6-7.30pm) £2.50. **Unlicensed. Corkage** no charge. **No credit cards.**
The antithesis of the ultra-trendy, wallet-bashing boutiques and shoe shops of Neal Street, FfT is unpretentious, reliable and great value. Diners share tables in the small narrow basement (if you're lucky, the little alcoves at the back may be free) to enjoy a daily changing, globally inspired menu. Lunchtime takeaway queues can be long and dishes sometimes run out, but this is a testament to the enduring popularity of the place. There's always a soup (Thai spinach and coconut, say), stir-fry, quiche and chunky salads, plus specials such as aubergine and fennel timbale, layered with rice and a rich tomato sauce, and topped with melted cheese. Risotto-filled portobello mushrooms, Moroccan tagine or Indonesian curry and noodles may also feature, and fruit crumbles, cakes and scones are available. Produce is GM-free, with vegan and wheat-free options. Appealing, inviting and just a little bit boho, it's no surprise that FfT has remained a much-loved Covent Garden institution for three decades.
Babies and children welcome. Bookings not accepted. No smoking. Takeaway service. Vegan dishes. **Map 18 L6**.

★ Neal's Yard Bakery & Tearoom
6 Neal's Yard, WC2H 9DP (7836 5199). Covent Garden tube. **Meals served** 10.30am-4.30pm Mon-Sat. **Main courses** £3.50-£4.35. **Minimum** (noon-2pm Mon-Fri, 10.30am-4.30pm Sat) £1.50. **No credit cards.**
Situated in a corner of Neal's Yard – since forever, it seems – this is a little slice of the original, alternative Neal's Yard spirit amid the Covent Garden flashiness. No hip menus and decor here, just delicious, healthy veggie and vegan food – at unbelievably low prices, given the location. The downstairs bakery sells wonderful organic bread (a loaf and some cheese from the fantastic selection at Neal's Yard Dairy around the corner makes the basis of a lovely picnic). You'll also find massive, salad-laden sandwiches, scones and cakes; the latter sweetened by a high fruit content rather than sugar. Tasty seed-topped baps filled with beany burgers or roast vegetables (smoky aubergine and sweet red pepper) are similarly huge. The daily changing menu includes own-made soups (puy lentil, vegetable and barley, for example) and hot dishes such as risottos and Thai curry. Take your meal or a pot of tea upstairs to relax at rustic wooden tables; there's a great view over the colourful yard below.
Babies and children welcome. No smoking. Takeaway service (10.30am-5pm Mon-Sat). Vegan dishes. **Map 18 L6**.

Neal's Yard Salad Bar
1, 2, 8 & 10 Neal's Yard, WC2H 9DP (7836 3233/www.nealsyardsaladbar.co.uk). Covent Garden tube. **Meals served** Summer 8am-9pm daily. Winter 10am-9pm daily. **Main courses** £8.25. **No credit cards.**
Location, location, location: that's the main draw of NYSB. Serving vegetarian and vegan fare for more than 20 years, the outlet has spread over that time, so that now most of the outdoor eating area in this charming corner of Covent Garden is sandwiched between NYSB premises. It's a lovely spot, so it's a shame that the menu doesn't live up to the high expectations and prices. The salad bar and 'takeaway station' offers only five, unexciting choices; on our visit, carrot and mushroom, turnip and red onion, pasta with sweetcorn, beansprout and celery, and a green salad consisting almost entirely of shredded iceberg lettuce, plus a few pieces of lollo rosso. Specials didn't impress either: aubergine cheese bake was more filling than satisfying, and pumpkin polenta pie was dry and flavourless, possibly because of wheat- and yeast-free ingredients. Better to choose from the range of snacks, cheese breads, cakes, gooey puds, shakes and strange Brazilian juices with an authentic taste of the tropics.
Babies and children welcome. Tables outdoors (11, courtyard). Takeaway service. Vegan dishes. **Map 18 L6**.

★ World Food Café
First floor, 14 Neal's Yard, WC2H 9DP (7379 0298). Covent Garden tube. **Meals served** 11.30am-4.30pm Mon-Fri; 11.30am-5pm Sat. **Main courses** £4.85-£7.95. **Minimum** (noon-2pm Mon-Fri; 11.30am-5pm Sat) £5. **Credit** MC, V.
The clue is in the name: from colourful framed prints on the whitewashed walls and world music soundtrack to the menu, global influences abound at this cheery café. Large wooden tables by the huge windows overlook the veggie mecca of Neal's Yard; otherwise seating is on tall stools around a bar circling the open kitchen. Choose from a daily soup or salad special, a 'light' meal or a heartier option. Prices are fair, and portions generous and well presented. Dishes are themed by country, so you might find Thai yellow curry, Moroccan tagine, Indian thali or Sri Lankan mallung. West African sweet potatoes and cabbage in a ginger, garlic, cayenne and ground nut sauce, served with rice and salad, was a warming and mellow dish. The Middle Eastern meze platter – aubergine cooked in herbs, mashed carrot salad, tabouleh, a lovely light houmous, and toasted pitta bread – was a feast of fresh ingredients, subtly spiced. Finish with a fresh fruit lassi, own-made cake or mango and cardamom ice-cream from India.
Babies and children welcome; high chairs. No smoking. Takeaway service. Vegan dishes. **Map 18 L6**.

Marylebone W1

Eat & Two Veg
2004 RUNNER-UP BEST VEGETARIAN MEAL
50 Marylebone High Street, W1U 5HN (7258 8599/www.eatandtwoveg.com). Baker Street tube. **Meals served** 8am-11pm Mon-Fri; 9am-11pm Sat; 10am-10.30pm Sun. **Main courses** £6.50-£9. **Credit** AmEx, DC, MC, V.
Eat & Two Veg doesn't look like your stereotypical veggie restaurant; it's styled like a contemporary diner, with maroon banquettes, turquoise Formica tables, exposed brickwork and an open kitchen. The bar by the entrance serves a decent range of wines and cocktails. It's a popular hangout for those who want to enjoy hearty breakfasts, hangover lunches and on-the-go dinners with friends, without having to sift through a meat-oriented menu. Omnivores might even be pleasantly surprised by the dishes that use soya protein as a meat substitute. From vibrant salads (poached pear, beet and toasted almonds), to faux-meat comfort food (Lancashire hotpot), with burgers, mega-sandwiches and pasta in between, it's hard to think of a time of the day when you couldn't swing by and find something you like on

The Restaurants

the menu. It's not the height of fine dining, but anywhere you can enjoy a boozy reunion with mates and a breezy Sunday brunch with your kids can't be a bad thing.

Babies and children welcome: children's menu; high chairs. Booking advisable. Disabled toilet. No-smoking tables. Area available for parties, seats 35. Takeaway service. Vegan dishes. **Map 3 G4.**

Soho W1

★ Beatroot

92 Berwick Street, W1F 0QD (7437 8591). Oxford Circus, Piccadilly Circus or Tottenham Court Road tube. **Meals served** 9.15am-9.30pm Mon-Sat. **Main courses** £3.15-£5.15. **No credit cards.**

More fast-food outlet than venue for a lingering lunch, Beatroot does have some seating outside and benches inside, but most customers just grab and go. Prices are low and the food is hearty, plus the smoothies and juices really hit the spot. The zingy 'vitalizer' (carrot, apple, ginger) is well-named, but if fresh-squeezed froth isn't your thing, there are iced teas and fizzy pop in the fridge. Ten daily changing hot dishes are offered, such as shepherd's pie, sag aloo, falafel, tofu stir-fry, lentil lasagne or spanish omelette with chunky potatoes. Salads are another good option, and come without an oilslick of dressing that unpleasantly masks the taste (and freshness) of the ingredients – pasta salad, beetroot, tabouleh and green leaves are all tasty. Just pick your combination, choose a box size, and the staff will cram as much into the carton as you would yourself; there's no stinginess here. You could also have quiche, soup or a slice of own-made cake. Delicious, healthy, on-the-move eating, with minimal packaging and waste.

Babies and children welcome. No smoking. Tables outdoors (2, pavement). Takeaway service. Vegan dishes. **Map 17 J/K6.**

Mildred's

45 Lexington Street, W1F 9AN (7494 1634). Oxford Circus or Piccadilly Circus tube. **Meals served** noon-11pm Mon-Sat. **Main courses** £6.25-£7.95. **Service** 12.5%. **No credit cards.**

Small and snug but light and cheery, Mildred's is closely packed with tables and gets crowded at peak times – don't come with shopping bags or a child's buggy. Diners return time and again to enjoy the winning combination of tasty food (and big portions), good service and a relaxed and unpretentious atmosphere in the heart of Soho. Daily specials might feature pistachio and goat's cheese risotto, a spicy and sharp fennel and chickpea tagine, or divine roasted apple and shortbread galette with sticky toffee sauce. Vegan and wheat-free options are clearly marked on the menu. Burgers are huge and imaginative (broccoli, poppyseed and lime being one example), and served with possibly the best chunky chips on the planet. Another winning hot dish is the rich, mellow puy lentil and red wine casserole with roasted veg, melted goat's cheese and sweet potato fries. Calorie-counting diners may prefer an energising detox salad with organic tofu. Drinks are largely organic, and include Fairtrade coffee, juices, smoothies, wine and champagne.

Babies and children welcome. No smoking. Tables outdoors (2, pavement). Takeaway service. Vegan dishes. **Map 17 J6.**

Plant

47 Poland Street, W1F 7NB (7734 7528/ www.plantfooddrink.co.uk). Oxford Circus tube. **Meals served** 8am-11pm Mon-Thur; 8am-7pm Fri; noon-9pm Sun. **Main courses** £4.50-£11.50. **Service** (restaurant) 10%. **Credit** AmEx, JCB, MC, V.

This modish Soho café offers healthy sandwiches, soups and salads, plus breakfast options such as bagels, wraps, and organic scrambled eggs and own-made, low-sugar baked beans. There's also a smart restaurant at the back – although we've found it almost empty on previous visits, and some of the fancily described dishes are more successful than others. Perhaps the new all-you-can-eat buffet lunch deal will bring in more diners:

£7.50 for a choice of ten salads and six hot dishes freshly made daily. Everything is vegetarian or dairy-free; try the delicious (vegan) aubergine parmigiana, creamy shepherd's pie made with veggie mince, or mild chickpea curry. Salad options include 'tofu Thai', roast vegetables, and olive and bean. Among evening à la carte mains are seared asparagus and houmous wrapped in spelt (wheat-free) pancakes, and vegetable protein 'meatballs' with rice or spaghetti. It's a pleasant (if rather pricey) place, and staff are jolly.

Babies and children admitted. No-smoking. Takeaway service. Vegan dishes. **Map 17 J6.**

★ Red Veg

95 Dean Street, W1V 5RB (7437 3109/ www.redveg.com). Oxford Circus or Tottenham Court Road tube. **Meals served** noon-10pm Mon-Sat; noon-7pm Sun. **Main courses** £2.85-£3.55. **No credit cards.**

Red Veg's menu features mugshots of Marx and Che alongside nuggets and burgers, but you won't find anything as naff as a 'Lenin lentil loaf' here – the revolutionary flag these guys are flying is in the name of fast food without exploitation. GM- and meat-free, with vegan versions on request, offerings include three-bean wraps, breaded mushrooms, spicy potato wedges and falafel with salad and dipping sauce. However, it's the burgers that steal the show. The hickory-smoked veg version with monterey jack cheese (generously garnished with crisp lettuce, red onion and tomato) was well-textured and satisfyingly chewy, with a delicious smoky flavour. Also good are the 'mushroomVeg' with Swiss cheese, and 'chilliVeg'. Stuffed jalepeño peppers and baby corn 'firesticks' didn't deliver the spicy kick we'd hoped for, but still beat chain burger side orders hands down for interest. Food is cooked to order, so the small premises can become crowded with waiting customers.

Babies and children welcome. Takeaway service. Vegan dishes. **Map 17 K6.**

West

Hammersmith W6

★ The Gate

51 Queen Caroline Street, W6 9QL (8748 6932/ www.gateveg.co.uk). Hammersmith tube. **Lunch served** noon-2.45pm Mon-Fri. **Dinner served** 6-10.45pm Mon-Sat. **Main courses** £7.95-£13. **Service** 12.5% for parties of 6 or more. **Credit** AmEx, MC, V.

The Gate's younger sibling (in Belsize Lane) closed in 2004, but this trendsetting restaurant – with a bright, sunny interior that comes alive with flickering candlelight in the evenings – still has much to shout about. Diners are still flocking to this branch in their droves, and chef-proprietors Adrian and Michael Daniel have just published an acclaimed cookery book. The pair are renowned for their love of mushrooms; little wonder, then, that truffle risotto cake topped with unusual wild mushrooms was the highlight of our meal. But all the dishes we tried were inventive, inspiring and, above all, fresh and flavoursome: fresh fig and goats' cheese tart with rocket and walnut salad; aubergines layered with mushroom mousse; and stuffed artichoke accompanied by broad beans and ricotta. The cooking shows a real grasp of Middle Eastern, Mediterranean and Asian ingredients and techniques – and we found the flavours particularly well judged and self-assured. In a city that is short of truly world-class vegetarian restaurants, the Gate isn't just a beacon of hope – it's the future.

Babies and children welcome; high chair. Booking essential. Tables outdoors (12, courtyard). Vegan dishes. **Map 20 B4.**

Shepherd's Bush W12

★ Blah Blah Blah

78 Goldhawk Road, W12 8HA (8746 1337). Goldhawk Road tube/94 bus. **Lunch served** 12.30-2.30pm, **dinner served** 7-11pm Mon-Sat. **Main courses** £9.95. **Unlicensed. Corkage** £1.25 per person. **No credit cards.**

This lilac-hued, romantically lit restaurant has been working with 'new concepts', and now offers some of the most outstanding vegetarian fare in London. From an imaginative global menu, try such starters as spicy, sweet and savoury plantain fritters, or a sophisticated artichoke, butternut squash and dolcelatte tart. Follow with tortilla crammed with interesting ingredients such as yams, sweet potatoes and beguilingly smoky pasilla chillies. Or how about stuffed, couscous-coated aubergine with beetroot and chickpea relish? Salsas, sauces and other accessories are especially noteworthy, and desserts such as light passion fruit pavlova perk up the palate. The restaurant says it's aiming for 'cleaner Japanese and Asian flavours' on the menu, and a cookery school is also on the cards. Elaborate, labour-intensive preparation; gorgeous presentation; clear, precise flavours; a lively ambience, and the high regard in which customer feedback is held all go towards making this a superior vegetarian restaurant that's truly in a class of its own.

Babies and children welcome. Booking advisable. Separate room for parties, seats 35. Vegan dishes. **Map 20 B2.**

South West

Wimbledon SW19

★ Service-Heart-Joy

191 Hartfield Road, SW19 3TH (8542 9912). South Wimbledon tube/Wimbledon tube/rail. **Meals served** 8am-5pm Mon-Thur; 8am-9pm Fri; 9am-5pm Sat. **Main courses** £1.95-£6.95. **No credit cards.**

This sunshine-coloured café lives up to its name as the immensely friendly service is delivered with real heart and joy. The ambience balances Zen-like tranquillity with buzziness, in a small but cheerful space filled with plants and images of Buddha. The menu comprises breakfast dishes, including veggie sausages and bacon, and pancakes; paninis and sandwiches, including one with cashew butter for vegans; Indian platters with daily changing curries; Italian platters with lasagne and garlic bread; casseroles and bakes; and delicious own-made cakes such as a nicely spiced nutmeggy carrot cake. On our visit, 'Greek-style quiche' from a specials menu was made with good pastry and filled with goat's cheese, olives, tomatoes and spring onions – a combination that worked a treat. It's good wholesome food, and prices are cheap too.

Babies and children welcome. No-smoking. Tables outdoors (2, pavement). Takeaway service. Vegan dishes.

South

Clapham SW4

★ Cicero's on the Common

2 Rookery Road, SW4 9DD (7498 0770). Clapham Common tube/35, 37, 88, 155, 345, 355 bus. **Meals served** 10am-6pm daily. **Main courses** £5.50-£6. **Unlicensed. Corkage** no charge. **No credit cards.**

The best thing about this café is its location on Clapham Common. The small, colourful interior is lit with lanterns, while the outside sports multicoloured glass-and-mirror murals. More colour features in seats and benches in the ramshackle courtyard (which could do with sprucing up). The menu lists breakfast dishes, burgers, salads, pasta and cakes such as lemon and poppy seed, carrot, and chocolate. Specials of the day might include Brazilian black-eyed bean soup, or a meze platter with halloumi, plantain, dolmades and Lebanese bread. A spinach and cottage cheese tart had an agreeable nutmeggy filling, but the wholemeal pastry was dry and stodgy. Worse, it was served on chipped crockery. Cicero's doesn't have to try too hard because it gets busy in fine weather; unfortunately, as a result, it just doesn't try hard enough.

Babies and children welcome; children's menu; high chairs; toys. No smoking. Tables outdoors (20, courtyard). Takeaway service. Vegan dishes. **Map 22 A2.**

Crystal Palace SE19

Domali

38 Westow Street, SE19 3AH (8768 0096/ www.domali.co.uk). Gypsy Hill rail. **Meals served** 9.30am-10.30pm daily. **Main courses** (9.30am-6pm Mon-Fri) £3.90-£4.90; (6-10.30pm Mon-Fri; 9.30am-10.30pm Sat, Sun) £5.90-£9.90. **Service** 10% for parties of 6 or more. **Credit** MC, V.

This cosy, homely café has a rambling garden at the back, complete with outdoor heater. The long breakfast menu plus the huge range of toasties and sandwiches appear to be the strengths; otherwise, choosing between 'specials' and 'favourites' could be confusing. To start, wild mushroom pâté and houmous were OK, if a little too smooth. Broad bean falafel, spiked with coriander and served with pitta and a chilli-tomato sauce, was flavourful. We were surprised to see ribbolita on the menu – this classic Tuscan bean and cabbage stew rarely features in veggie restaurants. This version was packed with vegetables and topped with cheese: inauthentic, but pleasant. Children's portions are available, and the chunky chips are fabulous, but please note: the 'chargrilled farmhouse bread' served with many main dishes is just good ol' toast. *Babies and children welcome; high chair. Booking advisable; bookings not accepted daytime Sat, Sun. Entertainment: DJ 7pm Sun. No-smoking tables. Tables outdoors (8, heated garden). Takeaway service. Vegan dishes.*

Bethnal Green E2

★ The Gallery Café

21 Old Ford Road, E2 9PL (8983 3624). Bethnal Green tube/8, 388 bus. **Meals served** 8.30am-3.30pm Mon, Wed-Fri; 8.30am-3pm Tue; 10.30am-5pm Sat. **Main courses** £3-£5.50. **Credit** MC, V.

Run by the London Buddhist Centre (as is its nearby sister operation, Wild Cherry; *see below*), the Gallery Café is situated in a spacious, sparsely decorated basement, with picture windows at the back overlooking a beautiful private garden. Quiches, salads, pastas, sandwiches and cakes are on offer. A large meze platter included standard houmous; tangy dolmades; flavoursome Turkish imam bayildi, dolloped with yoghurt; a sublimely spiced, Moroccan-inspired carrot and feta salad; and wonderful Greek-style courgettes with mint. All the dishes were delicious, and came with generous chunks of ciabatta. Helpful service and a charming little courtyard at the front overlooking a church makes this ideal for a drop-in lunch. *Babies and children welcome; high chairs. No smoking (indoors). Tables outdoors (14, patio, conservatory). Takeaway service. Vegan dishes.*

★ Wild Cherry

241-245 Globe Road, E2 0JD (8980 6678). Bethnal Green tube/8, 388 bus. **Meals served** 11am-4pm Mon; 11am-7pm Tue-Fri; **Main courses** £2.90-£5.25. **Unlicensed. Corkage** £1. **Credit** MC, V.

There's nothing wild about this cherry: run by the nearby London Buddhist Centre, it's as calm and sedate as they come. Diners queue up for freshly prepared hot and cold meals, including salads, sandwiches and quiches, before heading to the canteen-like dining area or the sprawling garden. It was too hot for the delicious-sounding African curry with plantains; instead we sampled a lovely pasta salad enlivened by almonds and fresh coriander, and a vibrant salad of ruby chard, beetroot and hazelnuts. For mains, large, crispy vol-au-vents came packed with every type of green vegetable you can imagine, and flavoured with fresh basil and mustard seeds, plus a creamy green vegetable sauce. Service was good-natured, and most customers appeared to be regulars. *Babies and children welcome; high chairs. No smoking. Tables outdoors (9, garden). Takeaway service. Vegan dishes.*

Camden Town & Chalk Farm NW3

★ Manna

2004 WINNER BEST VEGETARIAN MEAL
4 Erskine Road, NW3 3AJ (7722 8028/ www.manna-veg.com). Chalk Farm tube. **Brunch served** 12.30-3pm Sun. **Dinner served** 6.30-11pm daily. **Main courses** £8.95-£12.75. **Set dinner** (6.30-7.30pm) £13.25 2 courses. **Credit** MC, V.

Tucked round the corner from posh Primrose Hill's main drag, Manna is an unpretentious mix of the veggie world's old and new. Decorated simply with lots of wood and candles, the place has a café atmosphere and the spicy scent of a classic health food shop. Laid-back, friendly staff bring a mix of international dishes to your table presented in trendy stacks or elegant dressings, quite unlike the slabs of organic goo you might have encountered 20 years ago. Starters include the 'tortilla tower' (layers of spinach, red pepper and potato omelettes with melted smoked cheddar) and flautas – corn tortilla tacos with black refried beans and smoky tofu filling served in a tangy sauce. Mains offer a mix of Indian and Mediterranean dishes, including Majorcan baked aubergine, and whisky barbecue marinaded grilled tofu, which is served on garlic mash with onion rings and is comfort food of the most sophisticated order. Organic ice-creams, fruit crumbles and cheeses make up much of the dessert list and continue the whole menu's attention to detail, including a wide range of vegan and gluten-free options. However, Manna achieves this without ever sacrificing imagination and taste for goodness or principle. *Babies and children welcome; high chairs. Booking advisable. No smoking. Tables outdoors (2, pavement; 2, conservatory). Takeaway service. Vegan dishes.* **Map 27 A1.**

Vietnamese

Vietnamese food might not be as well established in London as it is in Paris, but delicious and authentic (and cheap) dishes are available if you know where to look. The best hunting ground is in Hackney, home to one of the largest Vietnamese communities in Britain: up to 4,000 at the last count. Some are ethnic Chinese who left northern Vietnam after the 1979 Sino-Vietnamese war; others are southern Vietnamese who fled the communist takeover in 1975. The vast majority came to the UK in 1979, when the Conservative government offered homes to 20,000 Vietnamese boat people from Hong Kong.

The An-Viet Foundation, a charity helping the boat people adjust to their new lives in London, opened a very basic canteen in a residential street in Dalston; **Huong Viet** quickly became known for its fresh, authentic food. Some of its staff later opened **Viet Hoa** at the southern end of Kingsland Road. Nowadays, Viet Hoa is surrounded by Vietnamese restaurants of varying quality; of these, **Sông Quê** and **Loong Kee** are particularly recommended. **West Lake** in Deptford is a notable outpost. Restaurants in more salubrious areas may be more glamorous, but they tend to be Chinese-run and are seen as less authentic by the Vietnamese themselves.

Most restaurants offer a range of standard Chinese dishes, but it's best to head for the Vietnamese specialities. Vietnamese cookery makes abundant use of fresh, fragrant herbs such as mint and Asian basil, and refreshing, sweet-sour dipping sauces known generically as nuoc cham. Look out for spices such as chilli, ginger and lemongrass, and crisp root vegetables pickled in sweetened vinegar. These fresh, piquant seasonings and raw vegetable ingredients create a taste experience that is entirely different from Chinese cuisine.

Some dishes are steamed or stir-fried in the Chinese manner; others are assembled at the table in a way that is distinctively Vietnamese. Order a steaming bowl of pho (rice noodles and beef or chicken in an aromatic broth), and you'll be invited to add herbs, chilli and citrus juice as you eat. Crisp pancakes and grilled meats are served with herb sprigs, lettuce-leaf wraps and piquant dipping sauces. Toss your cold rice vermicelli with salad leaves, herbs and hot meat or seafood fresh from the grill. All these dishes offer an intriguing mix of temperatures, tastes and textures.

Aside from the pronounced Chinese influence on Vietnamese culinary culture through the ages, there are hints of the French colonial era (for example, in sweet iced coffee and the use of beef) and echoes of neighbouring South-east Asian cuisines. Within Vietnamese cooking itself there are several regional styles; the mix of immigrants here means you can sample some of them in London. The food of Hanoi and the north – try West Lake and Loong Kee – is known for its plain, no-nonsense flavours and presentation. The former imperial capital Hue and its surrounding region are famed for a royal cuisine and robustly spicy soups; look out for Hue noodle soups (bun bo Hue) on some menus.

The food of Saigon and the south is more elegant and colourful in style, and makes great use of fresh herbs and vegetables.

Central

Soho W1

Saigon

45 Frith Street, W1D 4SD (7437 7109). Leicester Square tube. **Meals served** noon-11.30pm Mon-Sat. **Main courses** £5-£13.75. **Set meals** £16.18 per person (minimum 2). **Service** 10%. **Credit** AmEx, DC, MC, V.

French colonial Vietnam is the vibe being evoked here, with revolving ceiling fans, dark wood furnishings and gracious hostesses in traditional dress. It's all faded grandeur though – the place is spick and span, but our white linen tablecloth had more than one hole in it. The menu is relatively short (compared to the Shoreditch Vietnamese epics), but includes a number of must-order items, notably green papaya and pickled cucumber salad, and squid balls served with herbs and lettuce (both starters). Mains feature a few pot-simmered dishes (chicken with shredded ginger and fish sauce, for example), plenty of stir-fries and the odd fish dish (grilled sea bass with garlic, spring onion and soy), but only three versions of pho (beef, chicken and seafood). Drinks run from wine to saké, but there's no Vietnamese beer (Tiger or Tsingtao are the choices). Very much a safe option, but you could do a lot worse in Soho, for a lot more money.
Babies and children admitted. Separate rooms for parties, seating 40 and 50. Vegetarian menu. **Map 17 K6.**

South East

Deptford SE8

★ ★ West Lake

207 Deptford High Street, SE8 3NT (8305 6541). Deptford rail. **Meals served** noon-10pm daily. **Main courses** £3-£6. **Unlicensed. Corkage** no charge. **No credit cards.**

A pilgrimage to this tiny café in Deptford is always a pleasure, thanks to the absolutely lovely staff and the authentic dishes from northern Vietnam (the place is named after a lake in Hanoi). A piquant, crunchy salad of lotus stems, shredded carrot and mooli, topped with shrimp, made a refreshing start. The 'crisp shrimp pastry' was irresistible, with its naturally sunset-coloured combination of whole shrimp, sweet potato batons and rice-flour batter. From a selection of tempting noodle soups came one topped with 'mung' vegetable (pale, spongy taro stems) and little fish patties, gently soured and sublimely fragrant with dill. Stir-fried goat with rice vermicelli, and a peppery prawn and tomato stir-fry were also delicious. The dining room is simple, adorned with a few Vietnamese knick-knacks (including beautiful flower-patterned china and wooden chopsticks tipped with mother-of-pearl). Take your own booze.
Babies and children admitted. Book weekends. Takeaway service.

East

Shoreditch E2

★ ★ Au Lac NEW

104 Kingsland Road, E2 8DP (7033 0588). Old Street tube/rail/26, 48, 55, 67, 149, 242, 243 bus. **Lunch served** noon-3pm Mon-Fri. **Dinner served** 5.30-11.30pm Mon-Thur; 5.30pm-midnight Fri. **Meals served** noon-midnight Sat; noon-11.30pm Sun. **Main courses** £3.50-£7.80. **Set dinner** £10 2 courses; £14.50 2 courses (minimum 2). **Credit** AmEx, MC, V.

This classy spot more than measures up to the stiff Shoreditch competition. Still the newcomer on the block, it can be quiet, but the smiling staff bubble with suggestions as to the best places to sit in the large, elegant room. They also draw attention to the high points of the extensive menu. Our starters were all first-rate: fresh rolls with a deliciously cool minty stuffing of prawns, lettuce and vermicelli, in a sweetish hoi sin sauce; crispy pancakes filled with chicken and other goodies, the flavours and textures oozing through an extra wrapping of lettuce leaves, all to be dunked in a chilli fish sauce; and six pieces of char-grilled quail (just squeeze your lemon into the salt and pepper mix, and start dipping). Main courses range from frogs' legs to goat, with plenty of vegetarian dishes in between. Crispy sea bream with a fruity tamarind sauce, and crunchy ung choi (water spinach) stir-fried in garlic were both fine. Chicken with lemongrass and coconut was the one disappointment, its flavours hiding beneath the batter. As a whole though, top marks for Au Lac.
Babies and children welcome; high chairs. Entertainment: pianist 8-10pm Fri. Takeaway service. Vegetarian menu. **Map 6 R3.**

Hanoi Café

98 Kingsland Road, E2 8DP (7729 5610). Old Street tube/rail/26, 48, 55, 67, 149, 242, 243 bus. **Main courses** 12.30-11.30pm daily. **Main courses** £3.70-£10.50. **Set lunch** £3.80. **Set meal** £5.50-£7.50 3 dishes. **Service** 10% dinner. **Credit** AmEx, MC, V.

The small scale and simplicity of this Vietnamese café make it good for a low-key lunch or supper. Most dishes are listed only by their English names, and the restaurant is not a particular favourite among local Vietnamese. Food is fresh and tasty, but lacks the sharp, brilliant flavours of Sông Quê (see p272) up the road. Best was the bun rieu cha ca: a mellow, spicy soup of rice noodles and golden-fried fish cakes, served with a scattering of shredded lettuce and beansprouts and a sharp squeeze of lime. Paddyfield pork, a dark, treacly stew, was enticingly aromatic but slightly oversalted, while the goi (Vietnamese salad) was a refreshing tumble of vinegar-pickled raw veg and toasted peanuts. Desserts include some interesting Vietnamese sweetmeats, but they aren't especially well done. Still, we enjoyed the home-cooked feel of the food, and service was friendly.
Babies and children welcome; high chairs. Restaurant available for hire. Takeaway service. **Map 6 R3.**

★ Loong Kee

134G Kingsland Road, E2 8DY (7729 8344). Old Street tube/rail/26, 48, 55, 67, 149, 242, 243 bus. **Lunch served** noon-3pm Mon-Fri. **Dinner served** 5-11pm Mon-Thur; 5pm-midnight Fri. **Meals served** noon-midnight Sat; noon-11pm Sun. **Main courses** £3.50-£5.50. **Unlicensed. Corkage** no charge. **No credit cards.**

This unassuming café is known in the Vietnamese community for its northern Vietnamese food, especially the freshly made rice pasta, which has a lovely texture. We skipped the main part of the menu, which lists the usual Sino-Viet roll-call, and dived straight into the Vietnamese specials on the last page. 'Steamed spring rolls' – actually sheets of slithery rice pasta interleaved with a smattering of minced pork and cloud-ear fungus, served with shredded lettuce and a garlicky fish sauce dip – were delightful. A bowlful of pho was so aromatic we could smell it from the other end of the room. It was delicious too, with slurpable ribbons of rice noodles, slices of beef and a scattering of basil leaves and beansprouts. The greyish hue of the minced pork sausage, a kind of Vietnamese spam, was unappetising, but it tasted fine. Grilled prawns were OK, but not particularly fresh. Staff are amiable, and food is extremely cheap.
Babies and children welcome; high chairs. Booking advisable. Separate room for parties, seats 20. Takeaway service. **Map 6 R3.**

★ ★ Sông Quê

134 Kingsland Road, E2 8DY (7613 3222). Old Street tube/rail/26, 48, 55, 67, 149, 242, 243 bus. **Lunch served** noon-3pm, **dinner served** 5.30-11pm Mon-Sat. **Meals served** noon-11pm Sun. **Main courses** £4.40-£5.60. **Set meal** £8.50-£14.50 per person (minimum 2). **Credit** AmEx, MC, V.

Despite all the plaudits heaped upon it, Sông Quê has resisted the temptation to ratchet up the prices. Deep-fried tofu costs just £2, and even the massive, totally addictive pancakes served with herbs and dipping sauce are very decently priced (the tofu version costs £4; the prawn and chicken one is £4.80). Ignore the Chinese-oriented dishes and concentrate on the fresh clean tastes exemplified by fresh rolls with pork and herbs, or grilled beef wrapped in betel leaves, served with dipping sauce – an absolute knock-out. Richly satisfying pho is a speciality (lovingly described on the menu as 'a delicious meal for breakfast, lunch and even dinner'), with well over 20 types offered, including rare sliced steak, tendon and tripe; mixed seafood; and hot and spicy beef and pork. The functional decor is not much to write home about, the lighting is bright and the basement is very curious indeed (a glorified, ramshackle storage space that you must pass through to reach the loo), but Sông Quê is still a must-visit Vietnamese in an increasingly crowded market.
Babies and children welcome; high chairs. Booking advisable. No-smoking tables. Takeaway service. **Map 6 R3.**

Viet Hoa

70-72 Kingsland Road, E2 8DP (7729 8293). Old Street tube/rail/26, 48, 55, 67, 149, 242, 243 bus. **Lunch served** noon-3.30pm Mon-Fri; 12.30-4pm Sat, Sun. **Dinner served** 5.30-11pm Mon-Fri; 5.30-11.30pm Sat, Sun. **Main courses** £3.50-£8.50. **Service** 12.5%. **Credit** MC, V.

Like most of its neighbours, the cool and airy canteen-style Viet Hoa packs in the punters by offering a multitude of exotic taste sensations, all with minimal fuss, formality or expense. Go in a group to sample a wide range of starters (often the best part of a Vietnamese meal), from melt-in-the-mouth deep-fried aubergine to smoky and aromatic grilled beef wrapped in betel leaves. The delicate glass noodles, coriander and tofu of the summer rolls were offset by a rich, satay-style peanut sauce. Tilapia with green mango was a delight – the fish succulent beneath its hard skin, and the sweet chilli sauce conjuring up the tropics. But there was an overall sweetness about many dishes that is almost as reminiscent of the Caribbean as the Orient, and we missed the subtler, more earthy flavours to be found in some other Vietnamese restaurants. We also missed the usual generous green bundles of lettuce, mint and coriander in which to wrap the spring rolls. Viet Hoa is still an enjoyable bargain, but there are signs of a few corners being cut.
Babies and children welcome; high chairs. Booking advisable; essential dinner. No-smoking tables. Takeaway service. **Map 6 R3.**

Tay Do Café NEW

65 Kingsland Road, E2 8AG (7729 7223). Old Street tube/rail/26, 48, 55, 67, 149, 242, 243 bus. **Lunch served** 11.30am-3pm, **dinner served** 5pm-midnight daily. **Main courses** £2.10-£8.50. **Unlicensed. Corkage** no charge. **Credit** MC, V.

This smart, attractive little café appeared to be on the crossover between shifts on our visit. A slew of Vietnamese people were just finishing their meals, and trendy young Hoxtonians were drifting in to replace them. An enticing menu and fresh, vibrant food explains the cross-cultural popularity. Excellent starters included a sparkling green papaya salad topped with prawns and pork, and 'fresh rolls' – translucent rice pancakes stuffed with shredded mooli, aromatic herbs and coconutty minced prawn. Spicy squid was crisp and delicious. A large bowlful of 'special northern white noodle soup' topped with thinly sliced beef was fairly good. The dining room is spruce and gently lit, its walls adorned with Vietnamese pictures and enormous multicoloured lobsters. Only the very poor service lets the place down. Our waiter gave confused and contradictory information about the menu, messed up our order and then tried to pretend he hadn't. Another waitress was offhand and slapdash.
Babies and children welcome; high chairs. Takeaway service. Vegetarian menu. **Map 6 R3.**

Wanstead E11

Nam An

157 High Street, E11 2RL (8532 2845). Wanstead tube. **Lunch served** noon-2.30pm Wed-Sun. **Dinner served** 6-11.30pm daily. **Main courses** £5-£6.50. **Set meals** £20-£35 per person (minimum 2) 4 courses. **Service** 10%. **Credit** AmEx, JCB, MC, V.

An oasis of oriental opulence just yards from the A12 interchange, Nam An has fresh flowers on every table, carved teak furniture, a fountain with huge goldfish and even an antique cycle rickshaw. The soothing, exotic atmosphere is more typical of a theme restaurant in a five-star Asian hotel than somewhere the average Vietnamese family is likely to go. But the food is as beautifully presented as the restaurant itself – and most of it tastes pretty good. Grilled scallops with peanuts, chilli and garlic made a wonderful appetiser. There was lots of prawn in the prawn paste on sugar cane. Chicken with lemon leaf, however, was bland and vaguely soapy in taste. But if you're looking for an impressive place to take your date on an evening out in Wanstead, you could certainly do far worse.
Babies and children welcome; high chairs. Booking advisable. Disabled: toilet. No-smoking tables. Separate room for parties, seats 26. Takeaway service. Vegetarian menu.

North East

Dalston N1

★ Huong-Viet

An Viet House, 12-14 Englefield Road, N1 4LS (7249 0877). Bus 67, 149, 236, 242, 243. **Lunch served** noon-3.30pm Mon-Fri; noon-4pm Sat. **Dinner served** 5.30-11pm Mon-Sat. **Main**

Menu

Below are some Vietnamese specialities. Note that spellings can vary.

For enticing recipes and information about Vietnamese food culture, look for *Pleasures of the Vietnamese Table* by Mai Pham, a Californian restaurateur of Vietnamese origin. It's published in the US by HarperCollins, but is available in the UK.

Banh cuon: steamed rolls of fresh rice pasta, sometimes stuffed with minced pork or shrimp (reminiscent in style of Chinese cheung fun, a dim sum speciality).
Banh xeo: a large pancake made from a batter of rice flour and coconut milk, coloured with turmeric and traditionally filled with prawns and pork. To eat it, tear the pancake apart with your chopsticks, roll the pieces with sprigs of herbs in a lettuce leaf, and dip in nuoc cham (qv).

Bun: rice vermicelli, served in soups and stir-fries. These are also eaten cold, with raw salad vegetables and herbs, a nuoc cham (qv) dipping sauce, and a topping such as grilled pork or prawns, all of which are tossed together at the table.
Bun pho: flat rice noodles used in soups and stir-fries, usually with beef.
Cha gio: deep-fried spring rolls. Unlike their Chinese counterparts, the wrappers are made from rice rather than wheat flour, and pucker up deliciously after cooking.
Chao tom: grilled minced prawn on a baton of sugar cane, usually served with rice vermicelli, cucumber, pickles and herbs.
Goi: Vietnamese salad made from raw, crunchy vegetables and herbs, perhaps accompanied by chicken or prawns, with a sharp, perky dressing.
Goi cuon (often translated as 'fresh rolls' or 'salad rolls'):

cool, soft, rice-paper rolls usually containing prawns, fresh herbs and rice vermicelli, served with a thick, beany dip scattered with roasted peanuts.
Nem: the north Vietnamese name for cha gio (qv).
Nom: the north Vietnamese term for goi (qv).
Nuoc cham: the generic name for a wide range of dipping sauces, based on a paste of fresh chillies, sugar and garlic that is diluted with water, lime juice and the ubiquitous fish sauce, nuoc mam (qv).
Nuoc mam: a pale or clear liquid derived from fish that have been salted and left to ferment. It's the essential Vietnamese seasoning, used in dips and as a cooking ingredient.
Pho: the most famous and best-loved of all Vietnamese dishes, a soup of rice noodles and beef or chicken in a rich, clear broth flavoured with aromatics. It is served

with a dish of fresh beansprouts, red chilli and herbs, and a chunk of lime; these are added to the soup at the table. Though now regarded as quintessentially Vietnamese, pho seems to have developed as late as the 19th century in northern Vietnam, and may owe its origins to French or Chinese influences. Some restaurants, such as Sông Quê, offer many different versions of this delicious, substantial dish.
Rau thom: aromatic herbs, which might include Asian basil (rau que), mint (rau hung), red or purple perilla (rau tia to), lemony Vietnamese balm (rau kinh gioi) or saw-leaf herb (ngo gai).
Tuong: a thick dipping sauce based on fermented soy beans, enlivened with hints of sweet and sour, and often garnished with crushed roasted peanuts.

courses £4.20-£6.90. **Set lunch** £6 2 courses incl soft drink. **Service** 10% (12.5% parties of 5 or more). **Credit** JCB, MC, V.

Tucked away in a Vietnamese community centre, this former canteen for refugees has led the way in attracting Islingtonians to the eastern delights of Dalston. Queues and closely packed tables (go in a group and get a round one) add to the community atmosphere. The red-walled interior is softened by candles and flowers, the staff are friendly and the food satisfying. Steamed rolls (banh cuon) are a recent addition to the menu: soft, almost flat, translucent pancakes that slide down effortlessly. Equally scrumptious was the less elegant but more imposing-looking stuffed squid – big white sacs bulging with minced pork, prawn, carrot and vermicelli, garnished with fiery red chillies and swimming in a piquant tomato sauce. The traditional pho was light and fresh-tasting, while barbecued aubergine was fragrant with sesame seeds but oil-heavy. Hot and spicy lamb wasn't very lamb-like; Vietnam isn't exactly famous for its sheep, so you might be better sticking with the excellent steamed fish.

Babies and children welcome; high chairs. Booking advisable; essential weekends. Disabled: toilet. Separate room for parties, seats 25. Takeaway service. Vegetarian menu.

Hackney E8

Green Papaya

191 Mare Street, E8 3QE (8985 5486/ www.greenpapaya.co.uk). Bus 48, 55, 253, 277, D6. **Dinner served** 5-11.30pm Mon-Sat; 5-11pm Sun. **Main courses** £5-£8. **Credit** DC, JCB, MC, V.

No noodle caff, this, but a casual modern restaurant beloved of its hip South-east Asian and semi-arty Hackneysider clientele. Green Papaya is hitting its seven-year itch with congenial vibe intact, but its decor in need of some attention (except for the lovely non-smoking conservatory at the back). The menu has expanded over the years, perhaps beyond the kitchen's capabilities. Starters are the strength, with no duds and several delights, including spicy squid, banana flower salad, a truly fine bahn tom (sweet potato and prawn pancakes) and, when on the specials menu, spicy Vietnamese sausages. Avoid main courses that involve sauce. Better are the big soup bowls, rice and noodle dishes and marinated proteins – satay chicken is excellent. Puddings, never a main feature, seem to have fallen off the menu altogether. Which is a shame, as the durian ice-cream was exceptional.

Babies and children welcome; high chairs. Book weekends. No-smoking tables. Tables outdoors (5, garden). Takeaway service.

★ Hai-Ha

206 Mare Street, E8 3RD (8985 5388). Hackney Central rail/48, 55, 253, 277, D6 bus. **Lunch served** noon-3pm daily. **Dinner served** 5.30-11.30pm Mon-Fri; 5.30pm-midnight Sat, Sun. **Main courses** £3.50-£5.50. **Unlicensed**. **Corkage** no charge. **No credit cards**.

Always bright, breezy and basic (customers are addressed as 'mate'), this Vietnamese version of a transport caff used to make up for any lack of refinement with its good food and quick service. But, alas, those days are gone. The long, canteen-style tables were mainly unoccupied on the night we visited, but the staff sat at their own table in the corner, eating watermelon and ignoring our attempts to order. Service did improve, but successive dishes didn't. Prawn on sugar cane tasted mainly of flour; crispy sweet potato tasted of deep-fried batter. Of the lettuce-wrapped starters, the lamb was good, but minced chicken, prawn and bamboo shoots had no discernible flavour at all. And the salad consisted of almost nothing but lettuce. Fresh herbs (normally a Vietnamese tour de force) only appeared when we got to the sliced goat meat – a popular dish among male drinkers, we were told. One thing Hai-Ha remains, however, is cheap.

Babies and children admitted. Booking advisable Fri, Sat. Takeaway service; delivery service (within 2.5 mile radius).

Sông Quê

Tre Viet [NEW]

251 Mare Street, E8 3NS (8533 7390). Hackney Central rail/48, 55, 253, 277, D6 bus. **Meals served** 11.30am-11pm daily. **Main courses** £4-£10. **Unlicensed**. **Corkage** no charge. **No credit cards**.

Opened towards the end of 2003, this is another brightly lit Vietnamese eaterie, just along from Hai-Ha and Green Papaya (for both, *see above*); on current form, it is out-performing both of them. The extensive menu has everything from Chinese-style dishes to items so hardcore they aren't even translated. It includes a good choice of pho (hot and spicy beef, for example), and a staggeringly long list of starters. From this, pancakes with prawn, chicken or tofu, served with herb-packed salad and a clean-tasting dipping sauce, are an absolute must-have; they spill over the edges of the plate. Smaller appetites might prefer salt and pepper squid or fresh rolls with prawns and herbs. The zingy salads are worth trying too. Mains run from the likes of frogs' legs with lemongrass and chilli to chicken with ginger and spring onion, with much to choose in between. A recent highlight was stir-fried ung choi with beancurd and chilli: a deeply savoury dish of water spinach. Diners are a mixed bag of locals, Vietnamese and otherwise, and the atmosphere is welcoming but low-key. Prices are

Huong-Viet. See p272.

pretty cheap to start with, and the BYO policy keeps costs down further. A welcome addition to the area, though service needs to improve.
Babies and children welcome; high chairs. Booking essential weekends. Disabled: toilet. Separate room for parties, seats 30. Takeaway service.

North

Camden Town & Chalk Farm NW1

★ ★ Bluu Grass

6 Plender Street, NW1 0JT (7380 1196). Mornington Crescent tube. **Lunch served** noon-3pm Mon-Fri. **Dinner served** 5-11pm Mon-Sat. **Main courses** £4.90-£5.60. **Set lunch** £4.30-£5 2 courses. **Credit** AmEx, DC, MC, V.
A bright-looking café with wipe-down surfaces and irritating MOR pop, made one of the best places to eat in Camden by dint of lovely staff and superior food. There's more of a French influence on this menu than in most London Vietnamese places. Frogs' legs fried in butter, for example, and a satisfying, rich and very savoury beef casserole (served with french bread or rice), not to mention a list of very French puddings. Not that you'll make it to dessert stage, so generous are the portions. Even if you stick with such light starters as a zingy salad or juicy rice-paper wrapped rolls with dipping sauce, you'll be stymied by such mains as noodles, herbs and tofu cooked in chilli and lemongrass, or one of the bowls of pho (beef slices and meatballs, or fish balls, squid and prawns). Staff are charming, and attentive – we

dropped a chopstick and had only just retrieved it from the floor by the time a waiter had appeared with a replacement set. A refreshing alternative to Camden's many also-rans.
Babies and children welcome. No-smoking tables. Separate room for parties, seats 50. Tables outdoors (4, terrace). Takeaway service; delivery service (free over £10). **Map 27 D3**.

Viet Anh

41 Parkway, NW1 7PN (7284 4082). Camden Town tube. **Lunch served** noon-4pm, **dinner served** 5.30-11pm daily. **Main courses** £3.95-£7.95. **Service** 10% (on bills over £15, evening only). **Credit** MC, V.
The welcoming smile of the manageress of this small and bustling café was as bright and fresh as the sky-blue walls and the fluffy clouds on the ceiling. She explained that her husband and her father in the kitchen came from different parts of Vietnam, so between them had the country's culinary specialities well covered. These included delightfully fresh-tasting prawns sprinkled with sesame seeds and wrapped in a leaf that's similar to lotus leaf; you dip this in a tangy sauce then wrap it again in lettuce. Chinese-style steamed dumplings were a bit heavy on the dough, but the more typically Vietnamese spring rolls were suitably well packed and crunchy. Main courses come with rice, noodles or vermicelli. Lemongrass monkfish seemed initially boring, but a quick stir of the juices hiding at the bottom transformed it into something altogether fruitier and sharper. Tofu with chinese broccoli in rice noodle soup was dreamily aromatic. Another beancurd dish, featuring galangal, came with a powerful, peanutty curry sauce. It's all a tad pricier than the Shoreditch equivalent, but a welcome option in Camden.

Babies and children admitted; high chair. Book dinner. No-smoking tables. Tables outdoors (2, pavement). Takeaway service. **Map 27 C2**.

Islington N1

★ Viet Garden

207 Liverpool Road, N1 1LX (7700 6040). Angel tube. **Lunch served** noon-3.30pm Mon-Sat; noon-3.30pm Sun. **Dinner served** 5.30-11pm Mon-Thur, Sun; 5.30-11.30pm Fri, Sat. **Main courses** £4.50-£6.90. **Set lunch** (Mon-Fri) £5.50 2 courses. **Service** 12.5%. **Credit** AmEx, MC, V.
The cooking here doesn't match up to that of Sông Quê (*see p272*), these days the gold standard for London's Vietnamese food, but some dishes were good. Golden pancake was lacking in crispness; it arrived with a slightly mean pile of lettuce leaves and herbs, and the onion in the pork and prawn filling was almost raw. Summer rolls were pleasant but unremarkable. A couple of dishes were garnished with stale roast peanuts, spoiling the taste and mouth-feel of the food. After these disappointing starters, however, beef wrapped in betel leaves was juicy and seductive, with a dark, caramelised taste; and spicy bun hue soup with snaking rice noodles and juicy prawns (served with the usual scattering of beansprouts and purple basil and a wedge of lemon) was enjoyable. The highlight was a delicious, mellow pork stew with fried hard-boiled duck eggs, served with a plate of clean, crisp beansprouts and fresh red chilli. Viet Garden is a simple place, with pale walls and basic tiled floors. Staff are delightfully friendly.
Babies and children welcome; high chairs. Book weekends. Takeaway service. **Map 5 N1**.

The Restaurants

Eating on a Budget

Budget

More bargain-priced restaurants can be found elsewhere in the guide, indicated by ★. The most comprehensive guide to budget-eating in the capital is Time Out's *Cheap Eats in London* (£6.99), containing details of more than 700 eateries offering meals at under £20 a head.

Central

Clerkenwell & Farringdon EC1

Little Bay
171 Farringdon Road, EC1R 3AL (7278 1234). Farringdon tube/rail. **Meals served** 10am-midnight Mon-Sat; 10am-11pm Sun. **Main courses** £5.45-£7.95. **Credit** MC, V.
One could be forgiven for thinking that this smart, friendly bistro on Farringdon Road has slipped into the budget section via some monumental clerical error. A huge bowl of juicy mussels – drizzled in an addictive garlic sauce that had us eagerly mopping up the remains with bread – for less than £3? Believe it. All starters cost £2.95; all mains are £7.95. A hefty dish of ribeye steak with creamed celeriac was a little over-rich, but the chips cooked in goose fat were sublime: melting, moreish and certain to appear on our Death Row wish-list (those planning to remain eating a little longer might want to share just one filling bowl between two). When a three-course meal with wine totals about £20 a head, you might assume a mistake has been made. But don't make a stealthy dash for the door just yet: Little Bay equals little bill.
Babies and children admitted. Tables outdoors (2, pavement). **Map 5 N4.**
For branches see index.

Covent Garden WC2

Hamburger Union NEW
4-6 Garrick Street, WC2E 9BH (7379 0412/ www.hamburgerunion.com). Covent Garden tube. **Meals served** 11.30am-9.30pm Mon, Tue, Sun; 11.30am-10.30pm Wed-Sat. **Main courses** £3.95-£9.95. **Credit** MC, V.
Hamburger mega-chains provide an easy option in the tourist jungle that is Covent Garden, but this new Garrick Street venture offers a pleasing alternative to the fast-food superpowers. Although less substantial than the towering offerings at the Fine Burger Co (*see p279*), Union burgers make a filling treat and, at £3.95, are a lot cheaper. However, we were disappointed not to be asked how the meat should be cooked – surely a criminal oversight in a gourmet burger joint – and the result was a 'well-done', flavour-drained patty. So specify if that's not your preference. Other variations fared better: a lemony chicken sandwich and a garlicky mushroom burger were firstrate. Free of brand-imposed intimidating clowns and golden arches, the dining area sets new style standards for hamburger joints: sleek wooden benches, a compact bar, framed artwork and – gulp – diners enjoying a glass of wine with their fries.
Babies and children welcome; high chairs. Bookings not accepted. No smoking. Takeaway service. Vegan dishes. **Map 18 L7.**
For branch see index.

Leicester Square WC2

Gaby's
30 Charing Cross Road, WC2H 0DB (7836 4233). Leicester Square tube. **Meals served** noon-midnight Mon-Sat; noon-10pm Sun. **Main courses** £3.60-£9. **No credit cards.**
Popular with the pre-theatre crowd, this West End stalwart is ideal for a filling meal before curtain-up or for a takeaway at lunch. The menu, with specials and a choice of wines marked on a blackboard, offers Jewish favourites like salt beef and a range of Middle Eastern salads. Starters such as tabouleh, ful medames and the crispiest falafel were good and, for a vegetarian, a better choice than a main course of heavy rice-filled peppers with lentils. For meat-eaters, the bean and barley soup was strong and chunky, while fried chicken livers came with clean-the-plate chips (though we could have done with more fried onions). Salt beef sandwich on rye bread was generously stuffed. You won't starve here, but service is erratic and some dishes arrived five minutes apart. Desserts from the deli counter were variable: the cheesecake rather dry, but the almond twist was a solid option; best was the flaky apple strudel.
Babies and children admitted. No-smoking tables. Takeaway service. **Map 18 K7.**

Soho W1

Café Emm
17 Frith Street, W1V 5TS (7437 0723/ www.cafeemm.com). Leicester Square or Tottenham Court Road tube. **Lunch served** noon-2.30pm daily. **Dinner served** 5.30-10.30pm Mon-Thur, Sun; 5.30pm-11.30pm Fri; 5-11.30pm Sat. **Main courses** £5.95-£8.95. **Service** 10% for parties of 6 or more. **Credit** AmEx, MC, V.
Dishes at Café Emm are simply prepared and presented, almost to the point of perversity: a plate of poached haddock, spinach and carrot mash arrived as a disarming three-colour plate of mess that hardly set our mouths watering. But it tasted fine, as did an equally unattractive hunk of lamb in lentil jus. Starters too were reasonably tasty, but lacking in adventure. None of this seems to have affected Emm's popularity though, probably due to the reasonable prices and sprightly atmosphere. Tables are packed with bantering groups, and eager staff did their best to accommodate a long line of diners that snaked out of the doors from about 8pm. The queue lasted all evening: clearly a lack of culinary drama does not necessarily translate into a lack of punters.
Babies and children admitted. Bookings not accepted for dinner. Tables outdoors (2, pavement). **Map 17 K6.**

Centrale
16 Moor Street, W1V 5LH (7437 5513). Leicester Square or Tottenham Court Road tube. **Meals served** noon-10.30pm Mon-Sat. **Main courses** £3.75-£7.50. **Minimum** £3.50. **Unlicensed. Corkage** 50p. **Service** 10%. **No credit cards.**
This is a bring-your-own-booze, share-your-table, cut-the-bread-yourself affair. And don't plan on using the facilities, because there aren't any. But Centrale – for all its Formica tables, tube lighting and whirring fans – has a charm all its own. Chattering groups pack into the tight booths for no-nonsense budget eating, Soho-style. Our starter platter of mixed meat and cheese was a marvel of inconsistency (delicious thick-cut salami teamed with – eek! – triangles of boring cheddar), but gigantic. 'Are you ready for part two?' asked the friendly waitress. Only just, replied our stomachs, with well-placed caution: mains of spaghetti bolognese and lasagne were monstrous in size, but very satisfying. The bill was cheerfully cheap (most dishes hover around the fiver mark) and we were in and out within 45 minutes, making this a useful pre-show spot.
Babies and children welcome. Bookings not accepted. Takeaway service. **Map 17 K6.**

Pierre Victoire
5 Dean Street, W1D 3RQ (7287 4582). Leicester Square or Tottenham Court Road tube. **Meals served** noon-11pm Mon-Wed, Sun; noon-11.30pm Thur-Sat. **Main courses** £8.90-£13.90. **Set lunch** £6.90 2 courses. **Set dinner** (4.30-7pm) £8.90 2 courses. **Credit** AmEx, DC, MC, V.
Stripped-wood furniture and very low lighting give this high-ceilinged yet cosy brasserie a definite Gallic authenticity. At first we were a little overwhelmed by the loud live piano (any attempt at conversation had to be replaced by mime), but it was hard not to get caught up in the jaunty mood. Food was pleasant, if not awe-inspiring. A generous hunk of swordfish had a satisfying meaty flavour, but rubbery texture; similarly, lamb steak was rich and well seasoned but a little tough. A shame, as prices are fairly high (most mains cost £10-£14) and the quality of dishes only just surpassed cheaper offerings from the likes of Café Rouge. Still, convincing decor and a lively atmosphere make this a worthy attempt to import a chunk of Paris to Soho.
Babies and children admitted; high chairs. Entertainment: pianist 7.45pm daily. Restaurant available for hire. Separate room for parties, seats 25. Tables outdoors (4, pavement). **Map 17 K6.**

Stockpot
18 Old Compton Street, W1D 4TN (7287 1066). Leicester Square or Tottenham Court Road tube. **Meals served** 11.30am-11.30pm Mon, Tue; 11.30am-midnight Wed-Sat; noon-11pm Sun. **Main courses** £3.40-£5.50. **Set meal** (Mon-Sat) £5.65 2 courses; (Sun) £5.95 2 courses. **No credit cards.**
Think of this as a vending machine for sturdy, homely time classics: a fast, efficient source of familiar food that arrives quickly and without ceremony. The vast, hand-scrawled menu reads like an index of post-war British favourites: lamb cutlets, liver and onions, cottage pie, gammon and chips. Almost all dishes cost under a fiver, and when you throw in starters and desserts for less than £2 each, the Stockpot proves itself scandalously affordable. Food is prepared without flair, but conveys that unmistakeable home-cooked feeling, even down to the brown-rimmed plates that could have been plucked straight from grandma's kitchen cabinet. The place isn't without its faults – tables are packed tight and staff are rushed by weight of numbers – but these are indicative of an enduring popularity that has established the Stockpot as a much-loved Soho institution for solid and reliable comfort food.
Babies and children welcome. Tables outdoors (2, pavement). Takeaway service. **Map 17 K6.**
For branches see index.

Trafalgar Square WC2

Café in the Crypt
Crypt of St Martin-in-the-Fields, Duncannon Street, WC2N 4JJ (7839 4342/www.stmartin-in-the-fields.org). Embankment tube/Charing Cross tube/rail. **Lunch served** 11.30am-3pm Mon-Sat; noon-3pm Sun. **Dinner served** 5-7.30pm Mon-Wed, Sun; 5-10.15pm Thur-Sat. **Main courses** £5.95-£7.50. **Set meal** £5.25 soup and pudding. **No credit cards.**
This cavernous self-service café is hidden in the centuries-old crypt below St Martin-in-the-Fields church, minutes from the National Gallery, the Mall and other key sights. A daily-rotating menu offers large salad platters (probably best to avoid the over-dry veggie tartlet), as well as more substantial options such as salmon fillet with new potatoes and cabbage, doled out to tray-carrying diners by uniformed staff. It's more than a little school-dinnerish (bread and butter pudding with lumpy custard – oh, the memories), but the food isn't the main reason to visit. Sitting amid the curved stone pillars or in an cosy alcove along the far wall, the atmosphere is incomparable. Soft classical music, a subtle candle-lit ambience and the singularity of the environment make this a subterranean must-visit spot that, if slightly let down by the food, remains an inimitable London experience.
Babies and children welcome; high chairs. No-smoking tables. Restaurant available for hire. Separate room for parties, seats 70. **Map 18 L7.**

South West

Chelsea SW3

Le Shop `NEW`

329 King's Road, SW3 5ES (7352 3891). Sloane Square or South Kensington tube. **Meals served** 10am-midnight daily. **Main courses** £5-£20. **Set lunch** £6.95 2 courses incl drink. **Service** 10% for parties of 4 or more. **Credit** MC, V.
This is an unpretentious little bistro, with bare brick walls, wooden floors and French posters dotted about. Located as it is just across the street from Conran's Bluebird, the contrast couldn't be more obvious. The main selling point, aside from the prices, are the excellent galettes – thin, buckwheat pancakes wrapped around fillings such as chicken, mushrooms and sweetcorn, or smoked salmon, sour cream and caviar – cooked to order in the open kitchen. Prices are low, but go up quickly as you add on extras. Other options include pasta dishes and daily specials, but plenty of people pop in just for a cappuccino and a dessert crêpe filled with things like stewed apple or bananas and butterscotch. Divine.
Babies and children welcome. Booking advisable. Takeaway service. Vegetarian menu.
Map 14 D12.

South

Battersea SW11

★ Fish in a Tie

105 Falcon Road, SW11 2PF (7924 1913). Clapham Junction rail. **Lunch served** noon-3pm, **dinner served** 6pm-midnight Mon-Sat. **Meals served** noon-11pm Sun. **Main courses** £5.95-£8.95. **Set meal** £6 3 courses. **Service** 10% for parties of 5 or more. **Credit** MC, V.
'This is the most divine monkfish I have ever tasted,' an American man boomed to his wife, the waiter, the owner and pretty much the entire restaurant on our visit. He wasn't far off: the fish dishes are fantastic at this homely, bizarrely named bistro. A chunky piece of swordfish came with a tasty pesto dressing, while our plate-sized sea bass (speared with sprigs of rosemary) was one of the freshest-tasting we've found in London. For such quality of produce, Fish in a Tie is startlingly cheap: most mains are £5.95, and the expansive specials list tops out at £8.95. Interesting meats such as ostrich steak provide an alternative to all the fish, but it would be a mistake to pass up such a selection of sea-plucked delights.
Babies and children welcome; high chairs. Booking advisable. Separate rooms for parties, seating 25 and 40. **Map 21 C3**.

★ Gourmet Burger Kitchen

44 Northcote Road, SW11 1NZ (7228 3309/ www.gbkinfo.co.uk). Clapham Junction rail/ 49, 77, 219, 345 bus. **Meals served** noon-11pm Mon-Fri; 11am-11pm Sat; 11am-10pm Sun. **Main courses** £4.95-£7.25. **Credit** MC, V.
Standing proud at more than half a foot high, Gourmet Burger Kitchen's burgers are Scooby snacks to be proud of. The meat is 100% Aberdeen Angus Scotch beef, shaped into thick patties and cooked to your liking (medium-rare to well done), served in a sourdough roll topped with sesame. You'll need two hands to eat them. The toppings are pretty imaginative too. This being a NZ-owned mini-chain, we'd recommend the Kiwiburger, topped with beetroot, egg, pineapple, cheese, salad and relish. Other toppings include smoky barbecue sauce, fresh garlic mayo, pesto and many other tempting ingredients. Chicken, lamb and chorizo are also available, while veggies can feast on falafel or aubergine and goat's cheese burgers. Oh, and don't forget the chips, which are golden on the outside and fluffy in the middle: near perfect. For drinks, choose from milkshakes, soft drinks, coffee, tea, beer (top billing goes to Steinlager from New Zealand) or wine. Service is unfailingly polite.
Babies and children welcome; children's portions; high chairs. No smoking. Tables outdoors (4, pavement). Takeaway service. **Map 21 C4**. **For branches see index.**

Hamburger Union

HAMBUR

E Pellicci. See p280.

rather well. Tables tucked into hidden crannies make ideal spots for romantics, minor celebrities and adulterers keen to enjoy a cosy meal away from unwanted eyes. The menu follows a similar budget formula to Le Mercury (*see below*) and Little Bay (*see p276*) – one price for starters (£2.95), one for mains (£7.95) – but the quality of the cooking is a notch above both. Lamb with paprika potato mash was delicious, as was salmon with fresh green beans. Puds in particular are well worth a space-saving effort: a juicy poached pear with a fantastically creamy cinnamon brûlée was so enjoyable it should surely be illegal. Take a trip to LMNT pronto; walk like an Egyptian if you must. *Babies and children welcome. Entertainment: opera 8pm Sun. Tables outdoors (6, garden).* **Map 25 C5.**

North

Camden Town & Chalk Farm NW3

Marine Ices
8 Haverstock Hill, NW3 2BL (7482 9003). Chalk Farm tube. **Lunch served** noon-3pm, **dinner served** 6-11pm Mon-Fri. **Meals served** noon-11pm Sat; noon-10pm Sun. **Main courses** £6.10-£11.35. **Credit** MC, V.
Seventy years old and run by the three grandsons of the original owner, this popular ice-cream parlour and restaurant has recently welcomed a great grandchild to the staff. Clearly *la famiglia* is valued highly here. Perhaps that's why it's so popular with families: on our visit there were plenty of such gatherings, sprinkled around both the traditionally decorated gelaterie and the restaurant. Pizzas, pastas and salads are on offer in the latter, but it's the desserts that draw. Whether lavished with sauces and toppings in a novelty glass or served as a simple scoop astride a wafer, the ice-cream is something special. Although one can feel spoiled for choice with ice-cream these days (every chocolate-bar brand has its own freezer incarnation, after all), there are more than 20 Marine flavours on offer, and they still hold their own against the big boys – even after 70 years.
Babies and children welcome; high chairs. No-smoking tables. Takeaway service. **Map 27 B1.**

Islington N1

Le Mercury
140A Upper Street, N1 1QY (7354 4088). Angel tube/Highbury & Islington tube/rail. **Meals served** noon-1am Mon-Sat; noon-11.30pm Sun. **Main courses** £5.95. **Credit** AmEx, JCB, MC, V.
While other ventures fight for survival on restaurant-saturated Upper Street, Le Mercury has carved itself a valued place in the heart of locals by virtue of its simple, well-priced menu. Across-the-board pricing (starters £3.45, mains £5.95) allows frugal diners to forgo laborious price comparisons and get down to choosing what they actually want to eat. A good thing, as the menu is varied and the food excellent: well-presented, flavoursome French fare that far exceeded our expectations. Limited space means it gets a little claustrophobic when busy, although the huge windows help. One corner table, tucked against wall and window, directly faces on to the street: to some, a good people-watching spot; to others, a hands-on taster of life as a zoo animal. But Le Mercury is undeniably cosy, and candlelit tables make it relatively romantic. Wine is reasonable and dishes are just about substantial enough to share, if such a thing appeals.
Babies and children admitted. Book weekends. Separate room for parties, seats 52. **Map 5 O1.**

★ S&M Café
4-6 Essex Road, N1 8LN (7359 5361). Angel tube. **Breakfast served** 8am-noon Mon-Fri; 9am-noon Sat, Sun. **Meals served** noon-11pm daily. **Main courses** £5.95-£6.95. **Service** 12.5% for parties of 6 or more. **Credit** DC, MC, V.

East

Docklands E14

Hubbub
269 Westferry Road, E14 3RS (7515 5577). Mudchute DLR/D7 bus. **Lunch served** noon-2.30pm Mon-Fri; 11am-5pm Sat, Sun. **Dinner served** 5-10.30pm Mon-Fri; 6-10.30pm Sat; 6-10pm Sun. **Main courses** £3.90-£10. **Credit** MC, V.
Home to eye-grating 'concept' flats and eerie children's playgrounds that have probably never seen a child, the Isle of Dogs is far from pretty. It also seems to be The Land That London Transport Forgot. Try to ignore such disadvantages, though, because Hubbub is a real gem. The name is misleading: this airy loft space is actually extremely tranquil, and the perfect place for a relaxed weekend brunch. All the cooked breakfast staples make an appearance (sausage, eggs, bacon: you know the drill), plus some old-time stalwarts such as eggs benedict and florentine. Our favourite was the scrambled eggs special: a hefty plate of

creamy eggs, chopped smoked salmon and sprinkled dill atop three buttery toasted muffins. Sandwiches and bar nibbles are also available, but don't miss the excellent breakfasts.
Babies and children admitted (until 9pm). Disabled: lift; toilet. Separate room for parties, seats 150. Tables outdoors (6, courtyard). Takeaway service. Vegetarian menu.

North East

Hackney E8

★ LMNT
316 Queensbridge Road, E8 3NH (7249 6727/ www.lmnt.co.uk). Dalston Kingsland rail/ 236 bus. **Open** noon-11pm Mon-Sat; noon-10.30pm Sun. **Main courses** £5.45-£7.95. **Credit** MC, V.
There's not just an eLeMeNT of Egyptian decor at this Hackney eaterie; it's more a style obsession taken to theme-park extremes. Woven papyrus blinds, wall-carved hieroglyphics, a glittering Tutankhamen bust… it sounds like design overkill, but the result is fun and actually works

S for sausage and M for mash – just to ward off any misunderstandings. This is about comfort eating; a pick 'n' mix of pick-me-up food. Select your S (from a choice of 12 or so, including veterans like the cumberland and gourmet fancies such as wild boar), throw in some M (we recommend the creamy, perfect, traditional mash) and finish with one of three gravies. The result is served *Beano*-style, with sausages poking cutely out of a generous mash mountain. Alternative options include mash-accompanied pies and casseroles, plus a few salads and an all-day breakfast. This is food that invites a smile: even the most hardened depressive will find themselves humming 'Walking on Sunshine' as they leave. The Islington branch of this growing mini-chain is a lovely-looking gem, with a vintage 1920s blue-and-chrome interior (the previous occupant was much-loved caff Alfredo's).
Babies and children welcome; children's menu; high chairs. Tables outdoors (3, pavement). Takeaway service. Vegetarian menu. **Map 5 O1**.
For branches see index.

Muswell Hill N10

Fine Burger Company
256 Muswell Hill Broadway, N10 3SH (8815 9292). Highgate tube then 43, 134 bus. **Meals served** noon-11pm daily. **Main courses** £4.95-£8.20. **Service** 10%. **Credit** AmEx, MC, V.
A tenner for burger and chips? Expensive, yes, but don't be put off. These are no burger-van squirrel-meat nasties or production line McPatties; these are fine burgers. Served in chunky ciabatta buns with colourful salad on white plates, we debated whether to gorge ourselves immediately or halt proceedings for an impromptu photoshoot. Bantering staff convey a huge variety of burgers from an open kitchen into the restaurant: a lofty, modern space that seems as well suited to beer-supping trendies as it does to milkshake-slurping family-of-four. In addition to six takes on the standard 6oz beef burger – including a punch-packing stilton number – the menu tempts with chicken, lamb and fish varieties, and two vegetarian alternatives. Rich, chunky chips (encouragingly golden brown rather than yellow) add further credence to the 'fine' tag. A tenner for burger and chips? You'll hand it over gladly.
Babies and children welcome; children's menu; high chairs; toys. No-smoking tables (daytime). Takeaway service. **For branches see index.**

North West

Kilburn NW6

★ Small & Beautiful
351-353 Kilburn High Road, NW6 2QJ (7328 2637). Kilburn tube/Brondesbury rail/16, 32 bus. **Lunch served** noon-3pm, **dinner served** 6pm-midnight Mon-Fri. **Meals served** noon-midnight Sat; noon-11pm Sun. **Main courses** £4.25-£8.85. **Set meal** (noon-midnight Mon-Thur, Sun; noon-7pm Fri, Sat) £5.50 2 courses. **Service** 10% for parties of 7 or more. **Credit** MC, V.
Small and Beautiful: a conundrum certain to keep you occupied while you eat. Small and beautiful dishes? No: mains such as pesto cod and spaghetti marinara are definitely well-presented, but hardly small. Portions, in fact, are very generous. Small and beautiful surroundings? No, again: the two-room layout makes for a relatively spacious restaurant, and the decor – bare brick walls and wood-panelled floors – is functional rather than beautiful. A small and beautiful menu? Hardly. As well as a chunky list of regulars and specials, there's a set meal at an astonishing £5.50 for two courses and a nicely priced wine list. Titular confusion reigns, then, but the food is easier to classify. Put simply, it's great. The Tiger Island, in particular – an enormous bowl of garlicky mussels topped with meaty prawns and squid in a tomato sauce – will have you forgetting your own name, let alone the restaurant's.
Babies and children welcome; high chairs. Booking advisable weekends. No-smoking tables. Restaurant available for hire. Vegan dishes.

DAYTIME VENUES

Central

Bloomsbury WC1

Goodfellas
50 Lamb's Conduit Street, WC1N 3LH (7405 7088). Chancery Lane or Holborn tube. **Meals served** 8.30am-5pm Mon-Fri; 10am-5pm Sat. **Main courses** £3.39-£4.25. **No credit cards.**
Despite a prime spot, Goodfellas – with its delightfully uncool yellow-on-maroon sign – has doggedly resisted trendification. It's been here long enough to earn a bit of stubbornness, as evidenced by the legions of loyal fans that descend on the café for US-inspired breakfasts, ciabatta sandwiches and buffet lunches. The buffet offers both hot and cold dishes: on our visit the salads were fresh and colourful, but the hot dishes looked staid and heat-lamped to within an inch of their lives. Better were the fruit juice blends: a tall, iced glass of 'M&M' (mango and melon) is perfect refreshment on an outdoor seat at one of the streetside tables or in the back garden. Should the weather not oblige, stools by the window are the ideal place from which to observe the fashion brigade catwalking outside.
Babies and children admitted. Bookings not accepted. No-smoking tables. Separate room for parties, seats 60. Tables outdoors (3, pavement). Takeaway service. Vegetarian menu. **Map 4 M5.**

King's Cross WC1

Konstam NEW
109 King's Cross Road, WC1X 9LR (7833 5040/ www.konstam.co.uk). King's Cross tube/rail. **Meals served** 7.30am-4pm Mon-Fri; 8.30am-4.30pm Sat, Sun. **Main courses** £5-£8. **Credit** MC, V.
This tiny café is in a windswept, industrial-feeling part of King's Cross, but brave the duststorms and juggernauts because it's as cute as a button. The lunch menu is short but interesting, on our visit offering salads and quiches, plus more unusual dishes such as fennel soup or mackerel escabèche – the cool, lightly spiced, marinated flesh served heaped on chunky toast. Sandwich fillings are hearty and appealing and include the likes of roast pork loin; aïoli and little gem lettuce; or ox tongue with grain mustard and rocket. Tiramisu was vast and alcoholic. Prices are great too.
Babies and children welcome. Bookings not accepted. No smoking. Restaurant available for hire (evenings). Tables outdoors (2, pavement). Takeaway service. Vegan dishes. **Map 4 M3.**

Soho W1

Carlton Coffee House
41 Broadwick Street, W1F 9QL (7437 3807). Tottenham Court Road or Leicester Square tube. **Meals served** 7am-5.30pm Mon-Fri; 8.30am-6.30pm Sat. **Main courses** £4.80-£7. **Unlicensed. Corkage** £2. **No credit cards.**
Broadwick Street – a surprisingly clean stretch of Soho – plays host to more than one Italian café, but this is easily the best: a bouncy team of staff, imported Italian music and a seemingly permanent bustling crowd give Carlton a fun atmosphere that nudges it ahead of the competition. Panini are made to order from a long list of fillings that includes chicken escalope, parma ham and various Italian cheeses. For a more substantial meal, bowls of pasta and sauce are a bargain at around a fiver. Our pasta florentine was a delight: a combination of spinach, strips of smoked salmon and cream served in just the right quantity. A good place at which to pause and take a break from Soho's relentless parade of record shops and road-cleaners, trendies and traffic wardens. Oh, and the coffee's not bad either.
Babies and children welcome. Tables outdoors (4, pavement). Takeaway service; delivery service. **Map 17 J6.**

Star Café
22 Great Chapel Street, W1F 8FR (7437 8778). Tottenham Court Road tube. **Meals served** 7am-4pm Mon-Fri. **Main courses** £4.55-£7.25. **Credit** MC, V.
A corner-building hotspot, perfect for the allsorts of Soho in search of a good, solid meal and a friendly, unthreatening vibe. The hot food menu contains five or six rotating mains, which generally include such reliable faves as steak pie and chips or pan-fried salmon with new potatoes. It's filling stuff, but not exactly gourmet fare: on our visit, vegetables were flavour-drained and lukewarm. Extravagant mounts and signs cover the walls, while red and white checked tablecloths and bright red floor tiles complement the jovial, game-for-a-laugh decor. A counter at the entrance dispenses well-made sandwiches to those who don't have time to stop and appreciate the light-hearted atmosphere and substantial, if not perfect, plated food.
Babies and children admitted. Booking advisable. No-smoking tables. Separate room for parties, seats 35. Takeaway service; delivery service. **Map 17 K6.**

Thanks for Franks
26 Foubert's Place, W1V 1HG (7494 2434). Oxford Circus tube. **Open** 7am-6pm Mon-Sat; 11am-5pm Sun. **Main courses** £4.60-£5.50. **Minimum** (noon-2.30pm) £2.95. **No credit cards.**
Location may not be everything, but it certainly hasn't hurt this friendly café near Carnaby Street. Sandwiches are the prime remit, and there's a huge range to choose from, both in terms of fillings (hot and cold) and breads – our favourite was the US-style pretzel roll. Cooked breakfasts are solid, satisfying and served all day. The decor is clean-cut and pale blue, with a hint of New York diner thrown into the mix. Tables are overseen by psychedelic-era portraits of John, Paul, George and Ringo; if the Fab Four aren't to your liking, the clump of tables outside makes for a choice lunchtime spot. Prices are pleasantly cheap, so if you've haemorrhaged a dangerous amount of money into the neighbouring clothes shops, you can thank Frank when the lunch bill arrives.
Babies and children welcome. Tables outdoors (6, pavement). Takeaway service. **Map 17 J6.**

South

Clapham SW4

Abbevilles
88 Clapham Park Road, SW4 7BX (7498 2185/ www.fstabbevilles@btopenworld.com). Clapham Common tube/35, 37 bus. **Meals served** 9.30am-3.30pm Mon-Fri. **Main courses** £5.50. **No credit cards.**
Located in the leafy surrounds of Clapham Common, Abbevilles is not just a very reasonably priced bistro, but also an enterprise that gives people with mental disabilities the opportunity to participate in the management of a restaurant. Starters were hit and miss: a plate of gravadlax was tasty and served in abundance, but a selection of prawn in various filo wrappings was the stuff of Chinese takeaways. The same inconsistency afflicted the mains: a salad of chicken, avocado and new potatoes was disappointingly bland, but a colourful tuna dish with grilled vegetables looked – and tasted – great. Prices cannot be faulted, however; with two starters and two mains rolling in at well under £15, this philanthropic eaterie proves to be a worthy lunch spot.
Babies and children welcome; high chairs. Disabled: toilet. No-smoking tables. Separate room for parties, seats 50. Tables outdoors (16, garden). Takeaway service. **Map 22 B2.**

CAFFS

The humble caff: a British institution to rival the Royal family, EastEnders and endless gripes about the weather. Here are a few of our fave not-so-greasy spoons, all of which stand head and shoulders (or should that be bacon, eggs and a mug of tea?) above the competition. Better hurry though, as old-time cafés are increasingly under threat as the modern chains take over; for more gems, visit lovingly detailed (and regularly updated) website **www.classic cafes.co.uk** or get a copy of Adrian Maddox's *Classic Cafés* (Black Dog Publishing).

South
Waterloo SE1

Perdoni's
18-20 Kennington Road, SE1 7BL (7928 6846). Lambeth North tube/Waterloo tube/rail. **Meals served** 7am-6.30pm Mon-Fri; 7am-2.30pm Sat. **Main courses** £4.50-£6.50. **No credit cards**.
Not an interior to rival other period classics such as Pellicci's (*see below*; Perdoni's brown and beige colour scheme hasn't aged so well), but this Lambeth caff is friendly and bustling nevertheless. Fry-ups, sandwiches and chunky desserts such as cherry pie wait to be devoured, plus there's a selection of salads, pasta, meaty grills and other Italian dishes. Prices are reasonable (most mains between £4-£7), which helps explain Perdoni's all-day popularity: even at five minutes to closing, it was packed with customers.
Babies and children welcome. No-smoking tables. Tables outdoors (6, pavement).

South East
Greenwich SE3

Gambardella
47-48 Vanbrugh Park, SE3 7JQ (8858 0327). Bus 53. **Meals served** 7am-5.30pm Mon-Fri; 7am-2.30pm Sat. **Main courses** £2.50-£4.20. **Unlicensed. No credit cards.**
Authentic 1960s swivel stools, white tiled floors and caff-standard Formica tables form the basis of an interior that has slowly evolved over the last 70 years. Family-run since its inception, Gambardella offers all the fried usuals in portions that would sate even the hungriest of low-trousered builders. Friendly staff, classic decor and extremely filling breakfasts: walk it off around Greenwich Park.
Babies and children welcome. No-smoking area.

East
Bethnal Green E2

★ E Pellicci
332 Bethnal Green Road, E2 0AG (7739 4873). Bethnal Green tube/rail/8 bus. **Meals served** 6.30am-5pm Mon-Sat. **Main courses** £4.20-£7.40. **Unlicensed. No credit cards.**
'Now where's my chicken pie,' said one hungry punter as he strolled in, rubbing his hands together. It's easy to see why this classic caff inspires such dogged loyalty from regulars: the wood-panelled, low-ceilinged interior is welcoming, homely and the perfect environment in which to enjoy some top-notch breakfasts and pie-style lunches (including the aforementioned chicken number). Service is the kind of friendly you don't experience often in the capital, and prices are reasonable. We can't praise this Bethnal Green legend highly enough.
Babies and children admitted.

North
Camden Town & Chalk Farm NW1

Mario's Café
6 Kelly Street, NW1 8PH (7284 2066). Camden Town tube/Kentish Town tube/rail. **Meals served** 7.30am-4pm Mon-Sat. **Unlicensed. Corkage** £1.50. **No credit cards.**
Discreetly tucked into a small room under someone's staircase, Mario's is a real treasure. A huge menu offers a wide variety of cooked breakfast staples, as well as 'proper' lunches (such as chicken milanese or gammon steak), salads and ciabatta sandwiches. The work of local photographers hangs on the walls. On our visit, portraits of old men in dodgy wigs were a source for banter and giggles between loyal regulars and a very friendly owner. First-class.
Babies and children welcome. **Map 27 D1.**

Eating on a Budget

Pie & mash

As London's working-class communities continue to sell up and shift out to outer boroughs, so the eateries that nourished them must transform, relocate or die. London's boozers have in the main trodden the transformation route, making the most of their Victorian interiors, yet jettisoning their pickled eggs for parma ham, their Ben Truman for Bourgogne Aligoté.

No such compromise has, and perhaps can, be made by London's time-honoured caterers to the workers: the pie and mash shops. They stick resolutely to providing food that has altered little since the middle of the 19th century: potatoes (a wedge of glutinous mash), pies (minced beef and gravy in a watertight crust), eels (jellied and cold, or warm and stewed) and liquor (an unfathomable lubricant loosely based on parsley sauce). Escalating eel prices mean that many places only serve pie and mash. Vinegar and pepper are the preferred condiments, a fork and spoon the tools of choice.

A choice bunch of these establishments remains as handsome bulwarks to the process, resplendent with tiled interiors, marble-topped tables and worn wooden benches. The oldest and most beautiful pie and mash

shop is **Manze's** on Tower Bridge Road, established in 1902, though **F Cooke** of Broadway Market, the **Kellys'** and the **Harrington's** shops all date from the early 20th century. Visit these family-run businesses while you can, for each year another one closes, and with it vanishes a slice of old London. Relish the food, the surroundings, the prices (you'll rarely pay more than a fiver) and also your dining companions: Londoners to the core, not yet seduced by the trashy allure of the international burger chains.

None of these shops serves alcohol; all offer takeaways.

WJ Arment
7 & 9 Westmoreland Road, SE17 2AX (7703 4974). Elephant & Castle tube/rail/ 12, 35, 40, 45, 68A, 171, 176, 468 bus. **Open** 10.30am-5pm Tue, Wed; 10.30am-4pm Thur; 10.30am-6.15pm Fri; 10.30am-6pm Sat. **No credit cards**.

Bert's
3 Peckham Park Road, SE15 6TR (7639 4598). Bus 21, 53, 78, 172, 177, 381. **Open** 11.30am-1.30pm, 4.30-6.30pm Tue, Thur, Fri; 11.30am-1.30pm Wed; 11.30am-1.30pm, 4.30-6pm Sat. **No credit cards**.

Castle's
229 Royal College Street, NW1 9LT (7485 2196). Camden Town tube/Camden Road rail. **Open** 10.30am-3.30pm Tue-Fri;

10.30am-4pm Sat. **No credit cards. Map 27 D1.**

Clark's
46 Exmouth Market, EC1R 4QE (7837 1974). Farringdon tube/ rail. **Open** 10.30am-4pm Mon-Thur; 10.30am-5.30pm Fri; 10.30am-5pm Sat. **No credit cards. Map 5 N4.**

Cockneys Pie & Mash
314 Portobello Road, W10 5RU (8960 9409). Ladbroke Grove tube. **Open** 11.30am-5.30pm Tue-Thur, Sat; 11.30am-6pm Fri. **No credit cards. Map 19 B1.**

F Cooke
9 Broadway Market, E8 4PH (7254 6458). Bus 55, 106, 236. **Open** 10am-7pm Mon-Thur; 10am-8pm Fri, Sat. **No credit cards**.

F Cooke
150 Hoxton Street, N1 6SH (7729 7718). Old Street or Liverpool Street tube/rail/ 48, 55, 149, 242, 243 bus. **Open** 10am-7pm Mon-Thur; 9.30am-8pm Fri, Sat. **No credit cards. Map 4 R2.**

AJ Goddard
203 Deptford High Street, SE8 3NT (8692 3601). Deptford rail/Deptford Bridge DLR/ 1, 47 bus. **Open** 9.30am-3pm Mon-Fri; 9am-3pm Sat. **No credit cards**.

Harrington's
3 Selkirk Road, SW17 0ER (8672 1877). Tooting Bec or Tooting Broadway tube. **Open** 11am-9pm Tue, Thur, Fri; 11am-2pm Wed; 11am-7.30pm Sat. **No credit cards**.

G Kelly
414 Bethnal Green Road, E2 0DJ (7739 3603). Bethnal Green tube/rail/ 8 bus. **Open** 10am-3pm Mon-Thur; 10am-6.30pm Fri; 9.30am-4.30pm Sat. **No credit cards**.

G Kelly
526 Roman Road, E3 5ES (8980 3165). Mile End tube/ Bow Road rail. **Meals served** 10am-2.30pm Mon-Thur; 10am-6.30pm Fri; 10am-5.30pm Sat. **No credit cards**.

S&R Kelly
284 Bethnal Green Road, E2 0AG (7739 8676). Bethnal Green tube/rail/8 bus. **Open** 9am-2.30pm Mon-Thur; 9am-5.30pm Fri; 10am-3.30pm Sat. **No credit cards**.

L Manze
76 Walthamstow High Street, E17 7LD (8520 2855). Walthamstow Central tube/rail. **Open** 10am-4pm Mon-Wed; 10am-5pm Thur-Sat. **No credit cards**.

Manze's
204 Deptford High Street, SE8 3PR (8692 2375). Deptford rail/Deptford Bridge DLR/1, 47 bus. **Open** 9.30am-1.30pm Mon, Thur; 9.30am-3pm Tue, Wed, Fri, Sat. **No credit cards**.

M Manze's
87 Tower Bridge Road, SE1 4TW (7407 2985/ www.manze.co.uk). Bus 1, 42, 188. **Open** 11am-2pm Mon; 10.30am-2pm Tue-Thur; 10am-2.15pm Fri; 10am-2.45pm Sat. **No credit cards**.

Fish & Chips

Central

Barbican EC1

★ Fish Central

149-151 Central Street, EC1V 8AP (7253 4970).
Angel or Barbican tube/Old Street tube/rail/
55 bus. **Lunch served** 11am-2.30pm, **dinner**
served 4.45-10.30pm Mon-Sat. **Main courses**
£4.95-£10.90. **Credit** AmEx, MC, V.
There has been a tasteful makeover at this popular
diner, adding a zinc-topped serving area, bare
wooden flooring and light aubergine walls. We
hadn't booked and were lucky to get a spot at the
window, overlooking the shabby arcade outside.
Lines of parked black taxis hinted at the core
clientele, but the presence of a couple of suave
coiffured ladies to our left suggested that Fish
Central could be leading the gentrification of this
corner of Clerkenwell. The inclusion on the long
paper menu of own-made bread (only 50p), fresh
market vegetables of the day, scamorza, salad
niçoise, brill cooked in sea salt, skate wings and
roast cod point to higher ambitions. Own-made
fish soup was brown and delicious; spinach and
ricotta ravioli was remarkably good too. Our
battered haddock and cod were both faultless, with
rustic-looking golden chips and mushy peas that
were brilliantly savoury and sweet at the same
time. The wine list is worth a look, starting at just
£1.90 a glass (£7.95 a bottle). Somewhere to take
the boss, mother-in-law or bank manager.
Babies and children welcome; children's portions;
high chairs. Booking advisable. Tables outdoors
(10, patio). Takeaway service. **Map 5 P3**.

Bloomsbury WC1

North Sea Fish Restaurant

7-8 Leigh Street, WC1H 9EW (7387 5892).
Russell Square tube/King's Cross tube/rail/
68, 168 bus. **Lunch served** noon-2.30pm,
dinner served 5.30-10.30pm Mon-Sat. **Main**
courses £7.90-£16.95. **Credit** AmEx, MC, V.
There's something deliciously old-fashioned about
this chintzy diner that makes it a firm favourite
with visiting Americans, artisans and local
academics. The decor – dark wood beams, stippled
walls and red velvet upholstery – brings to mind
Carry On Up the Khyber, Carnaby Street and
Eamonn Andrews. The waitresses tend to be
eastern European, combining efficiency with a
matronly smile. Starters of fish cakes (big and
fishy) and scampi (sweet and succulent) were hard
to fault, as were the golden haddock and cod that
followed. Battered fish comes in two sizes: jumbo
and standard, and the standard was jumbo enough
for us. Own-made tartare sauce, mushy peas and
baskets of first-rate chips are the accompaniments,
with the sweets menu offering the likes of apple
crumble and trifle.
Babies and children admitted. Book dinner.
Separate room for parties, seats 35. Takeaway
service (until 11pm). **Map 4 K4**.

Covent Garden WC2

Rock & Sole Plaice

47 Endell Street, WC2H 9AJ (7836 3785).
Covent Garden tube. **Meals served** 11.30am-
11pm Mon-Sat; noon-10pm Sun. **Main courses**
£8-£14. **Credit** MC, V.
The Hassan family has been comparatively recent
arrivals, but there has been a chippy on this site
since 1871. In clement weather the outside seats
get thronged – and the young waiting staff shoo
away takeaway customers hoping to rest their legs.

Taramasalata, Efes Turkish beer and pitta point
to the family's Turkish roots, but the name of the
game is good old-fashioned British fish and chips.
This will either be brilliant – which it is most of
the time – or disappointingly average. On the good
days, large portions of thick, creamy cod and
haddock come encased in just-right golden batter,
accompanied by crisp, rough-cut chips. The
impressive fish and whale mural in the basement
is worth a detour to the loo.
Babies and children welcome. Book dinner. Separate
room for parties, seats 36. Tables outdoors
(20, pavement). Takeaway service. **Map 18 L6**.

Holborn WC1

★ Fryer's Delight

19 Theobald's Road, WC1X 8SL (7405 4114).
Holborn tube/19, 38, 55 bus. **Meals served**
noon-10pm Mon-Sat. **Main courses** £1.30-£4.95.
Minimum £1.30. **Unlicensed. Corkage**
no charge. **No credit cards.**
Long a cabbies' favourite, this no-frills Formica-
clad chippy comes with low-watt lighting and
bum-numbing bench seating. The menu is short
but sweet: fish, chips and accompaniments, plus
more variations on the theme of sausages and
saveloys than you'd ever want to contemplate.
Everything – excluding the tea and bread and
butter – is deep fried and there's no stinting on
quantities. Battered fish overflows the plate, and
mounds of roughly hewn chips take up any
remaining space. Bread is thick and crusty, and the
tea is of the good old-fashioned spoon-supporting
style. The friers are perpetually at work; the banter
between them and the customers hardly lets up for
a second. If there's a finer place to spend an hour
or two, after which you emerge full and satisfied,
we don't know it. And if you spend more than six
quid, you're throwing it away.
Babies and children welcome. Takeaway service
(until 11pm). **Map 4 M5**.

Marylebone W1, NW1

Golden Hind

73 Marylebone Lane, W1U 2PN (7486 3644).
Bond Street tube. **Lunch served** noon-3pm
Mon-Fri. **Dinner served** 6-10pm Mon-Sat.
Main courses £4, (dinner) £5. **Minimum** (lunch)
£4, (dinner) £5. **Unlicensed. Corkage**
no charge. **Credit** AmEx, JCB, MC, V.
Pride of place in this beautifully preserved art deco
chippy goes to the gleaming stainless steel and
Bakelite fish fryer from F Ford of Halifax. Sadly,
it's no longer in use; the frying's done in the rear
kitchen. The menu contains some unusual items:
we wonder whether deep-fried mussels in batter
have ever been served; we've certainly never seen
them. Fish cakes were also off the menu – a pity
because we often crave their fishy flakiness.
Scampi were fine as a replacement, and the main
course of haddock was as fresh and flaky as you'll
find anywhere. Chips the colour of proper lager
were done to a turn, and even the mushy peas
appeared on top form. Staff were warm and
personal, making sure we weren't left waiting.
Babies and children welcome; children's portions;
high chair. Booking advisable. Separate room for
parties, seats 24. Takeaway service. **Map 9 G5**.

Sea Shell

49-51 Lisson Grove, NW1 6UH (7224 9000/
www.seashellrestaurant.co.uk). Marylebone tube/
rail. **Lunch served** noon-2.30pm, **dinner served**
5-10.30pm Mon-Fri. **Meals served** noon-10.30pm
Sat. **Main courses** £6.75-£16. **Credit** AmEx,
JCB, MC, V.

Once London's most renowned fish and chip
restaurant, the Sea Shell has been under several
owners during the past couple of decades
(including the Rank Organisation) and appears
to have slipped from its pedestal. But on the Friday
night of our most recent visit the place was packed
out with groups of cabbies, tourists and
representatives of the blue rinse brigade; tables
were at a premium. The interior, with its dark wood
booths and green-upholstered chairs, rang to the
sound of happy diners. Own-made fish cakes were
delicious: a crispy shell around a well-seasoned ball
of fish and potato, nicely complemented by the
own-made tartare sauce. Sadly, it was downhill
from there. Our chips were OK, but our haddock
was slimy and undercooked, inside a coating of
batter that was on the verge of being burnt. All
around us people were ooing and ahhing over their
food, but we couldn't join in. Service was charming
if a little distracted. We left feeling we'd missed out
on the party.
Babies and children welcome; children's menu;
high chairs. Disabled: toilet. No-smoking tables.
Separate room for parties, seats 40. Takeaway
service. **Map 2 F4**.

Piccadilly, W1

Harry Ramsden's NEW

Regent Palace Hotel, Sherwood Street, W1A
4BZ (7287 3148/www.harryramsdens.co.uk).
Leicester Square or Piccadilly Circus tube.
Breakfast served 7am-10am, **dinner**
served 11am-11pm daily. **Credit** AmEx,
DC, MC, V.
Any rumbling you hear at this corporate franchise
showpiece is probably the sound of Mr Harry
Ramsden spinning in his grave. From the over-
crisp 'crispy coated mushrooms' starter to the tiny
portion of mushy peas in a minuscule paper
container, our experience at this new Piccadilly
outlet was pretty dreadful. The 'parsley fish cakes'
contained too much potato and not enough
flavour, and our portions of haddock were smaller
than you'd expect for £8.99 and dry, surrounded
by a rigid batter shell that overwhelmed the fish.
The cavernous dining room is popular with
tourists – who probably just don't know any better
– but you can have a much tastier (and cheaper)
meal at London's numerous independent fish and
chip restaurants.
Babies and children welcome: children's menu;
high chairs. Book weekends. Disabled: toilet.
No-smoking tables. Takeaway service.
Map 17 J7.

Victoria SW1

Seafresh Fish Restaurant

80-81 Wilton Road, SW1V 1DL (7828 0747).
Victoria tube/rail/24 bus. **Lunch served**
noon-3pm, **dinner served** 5-10.30pm Mon-
Fri. **Meals served** noon-10.30pm Sat.
Main courses £5.55-£16.95. **Credit** AmEx,
DC, MC, V.
There has been a paint-job and much of the
trinketry has gone (including the nets and glass
balls), but not much else has changed at this long-
established fish and chipperie. Situated just south
of Victoria rail station, just before Wilton Road
becomes Pimlico, Seafresh attracts characters
from a Joseph Connolly novel, American tourists
and commuters stopping off for a swift one on the
way home. Fish soup is a house speciality and
comes peppery and bursting with white fish
chunks, prawns, celery and baby mussels. Smoked
salmon, calamares, and avocado with prawns are
alternative first courses. The usual fish options
arrive in a tasty golden batter or can be grilled for
a few pence extra. Our haddock was all that was
expected of it, and was accompanied by thick,
crisp, golden chips and a fragrantly pickled
cucumber the size of a rugby ball (well, almost).
A neighbour's king prawn salad was huge,
containing enough greenery to hide a platoon of
soldiers. Puddings include Italian ice-cream, and
sherry trifle.
Babies and children welcome; high chairs.
Restaurant available for hire. Takeaway service.
Map 15 J10.

Costas Fish Restaurant

West

Bayswater W2

Mr Fish NEW

*9 Porchester Road, W2 5DP (7229 4161/
www.mrfish.net). Bayswater or Queensway tube.*
Meals served 11am-11pm daily. **Main courses**
£5.95-£11.95. **Set lunch** £6.25 incl mushy peas,
bread, coffee or tea. **Credit** AmEx, MC, V.

Judged on shopfront alone, Mr Fish looks to be one
of London's innumerable mediocre chippies. But
negotiate the unpromising entrance, duck 'n' roll
past a counter display of savelous and pre-
packaged pies, and slip into the restaurant at the
back. Then, and only then, will Mr Fish surprise
you. Fresh fillets of cod, haddock, plaice or rock
salmon (around £7.50 for large with chips) don't
just come battered; they can also be grilled,
poached, breadcrumbed or fried in matzo meal.
Matzo is the best option, encasing the fish in a thin,
crisp, mercifully ungreasy coating that enhances
rather than bludgeons the flavour within. Chips are
chunkily cut and clearly made from well-sourced
potatoes (not a mutant blackhead or green-eye in
sight), and the mound of mushy peas is thick,
satisfying and embedded with just enough
survivors of the mush cull to prove the stuff didn't
come out of a tin.
*Babies and children welcome: children's menu;
high chair. No-smoking tables. Takeaway service
(11am-midnight). Vegetarian menu.* **Map 7 C5**.

Notting Hill W8

★ Costas Fish Restaurant

*18 Hillgate Street, W8 7SR (7727 4310). Notting
Hill Gate tube.* **Lunch served** noon-2.30pm,
dinner served 5.30-10.30pm Tue-Sat. **Main
courses** £4.70-£7.90. **No credit cards**.

Not to be confused with next door's Costas Grill,
this small back-room restaurant is reached
through the takeaway counter, via the food
preparation area – there's confidence for you. (It
would appear traditional to offer a greeting in
Greek as you pass through.) The decor inside is
gratifyingly untrendy with pale walls, brown
banquettes and stone flooring. Cypriot touches
include the houmous and calamares starters,
retsina (for those with feelings of nostalgia and
robust palates) and baklava for pud. Fish can be

grilled or battered, standard or large. Our standard
cod was large enough for anyone not actively
engaged in the wrestling business, housed in a
dark-yellow batter, and flaky and perfectly white
inside. Chips were chunky and very good; the
mushy peas were well up to scratch too. Service
was very friendly and efficient, except for odd
moments when our east European waitress found
herself engrossed in reading. But maybe that only
happens at exam time.
*Babies and children welcome. Book dinner.
Tables outdoors (2, pavement). Takeaway service.*
Map 7 A7.

Geales

*2 Farmer Street, W8 7SN (7727 7528). Notting
Hill Gate tube.* **Lunch served** noon-3pm Mon-
Sat. **Dinner served** 6-11pm Mon-Sat; 6-10.30pm
Sun. **Main courses** £7.25-£11.50. **Cover** 50p.
Service 12.5% for parties of 5 or more. **Credit**
AmEx, MC, V.

Established in 1939 (maybe not the most opportune
year to start up a fresh food business), Geales can
be relied upon to serve up an exemplary plate of
cod with chips or new potatoes. Or haddock, plaice,
skate wing, salmon fillet – you get the idea. There's
a 50p cover charge and the own-made tartare sauce
costs 60p, but overall the experience makes this
worthwhile. Those wanting to splash out can opt
for oysters or Iranian oscietra caviar at £27.50 for
30g, though this does come with toast and chopped
egg. The 'house' salmon fish cakes exhibit plump
fishy savouriness, and the 'famous' fish pie is worth
a punt – as is the vegetarian version. Organic steak
of the day is the carnivore option. Fish is fried in
beef dripping, chips in vegetable oil. And at £2.50
a pint, the draught London Pride is cheaper than at
many of the local boozers; service is probably going
to be more attentive too.
*Babies and children welcome; children's menu;
high chairs. Book weekends. Tables outdoors
(4, pavement). Takeaway service.* **Map 7 A7**.

South

Wandsworth SW18

★ ★ Brady's

*513 Old York Road, SW18 1TF (8877 9599).
Wandsworth Town rail/28, 44 bus.* **Dinner
served** 6.30-10.30pm Mon-Sat. **Main courses**
£6.60-£8.75. **Service** 10%. **No credit cards**.

Treated to a tidy-up, a fresh coat of primrose-white
paint and an extra skylight, Brady's has smartened
up, but retains its unique, slightly dotty
atmosphere. Personal service from the owner and
his family, plus food of the highest standard, make
this one of the most amiable dining experiences in
town. Anyone eschewing the starters must be mad:
potted shrimps, packed into chilli and lemon
flavoured butter, are irresistible; dressed crab (if
available) is a meaty taste-bomb; and salmon fish
cakes come packed with flaky pink flesh. And
there's more. Choose from the board menus and
dive in. Main course portions aren't huge, but if
you want three courses (recommended), restraint
like this is essential. Plaice in batter was
flavoursome and extremely fresh, complemented
admirably by the choice of five herb-flavoured
mayonnaises and chips that were chunky, golden
and very potatoey. The wine list is brief but hits
the spot, though we think Czech Budvar the perfect
fish and chip accompaniment. Quibbles? The
mushy peas are a tad sweet for our taste, and the
bench seats are uncomfy. Puds might include a
divinely built apple crumble or a thick, sticky
treacle sponge. Yum all round.
*Babies and children welcome; children's portions.
Bookings not accepted. Takeaway service.*
Map 21 A4.

Waterloo SE1

★ ★ Masters Super Fish

*191 Waterloo Road, SE1 8UX (7928 6924).
Waterloo tube/rail.* **Lunch served** noon-3pm
Tue-Sat. **Dinner served** 5.30-10.30pm Mon;
4.30-10.30pm Tue-Thur, Sat; 4.30-11pm Fri.
Main courses £7-£13. **Credit** MC, V.

Platefuls of fresh, golden-battered fish, mountains
of brown chips and free own-pickled onions and
gherkins are the speciality of this well-regarded
chip shop. With its exposed brickwork, green-
clothed tables and mahogany woodwork it looks a
little like a set from *Minder*, but so what? Super
Fish is invariably packed with cabbies, plus a
healthy smattering of local families and Old Vic
theatregoers. You sit down to a complimentary
prawn threesome – four, if you're lucky – and a
bowl of french bread. Starters might include
dressed Cromer crab (go for it!), whitebait,
calamares and fish soup. Leave room for the main
event: our haddock was huge, suitably crisp and
golden outside, and creamily white and flaky

within. Mushy peas were wonderful. And when was the last time you tasted the luxury of homemade pickles? Puds are of the apple pie type, but we've never had the space to try one. Service is attentive and comes with a smile, making this place (on a good day) one of London's finest. *Babies and children welcome; high chair. Book weekends. Takeaway service. Map 11 N9*.

South East
Dulwich SE22

★ **Sea Cow** NEW
2004 RUNNER-UP BEST LOCAL RESTAURANT
37 Lordship Lane, SE22 8EW (8693 3111). East Dulwich rail/176, 196 bus. **Meals served** noon-11pm Tue-Sat. **Main courses** £7-£10. **Credit** MC, V.
Sea Cow adopts a refreshingly simple approach to the business of eating fish. At the front is the wet fish counter with its gleaming mounds of ice; next to that the fryer, where you can order takeaway portions; and beyond that some hefty wooden tables and bench seating if you want to eat in. The look is modern, all clean lines and bare walls. The menu keeps it simple too, with 15 or so dishes ranging from yer basic cod and chips through the more exotic delights of tilapia and bluefin tuna to crab cakes with salad and lime mayo. You'll pay a couple of quid more to eat in, but prices are still great value; whole sea bass costs a mere £9. Perfectly cooked and super-fresh (thanks to daily deliveries from Billingsgate), it came unadorned save for wedges of lime and lemon. Extras include good fat chips, fresh leafy salads and upmarket minted mushy peas. Fast-working, friendly staff keep things moving nicely. Sea Cow is more a glorified chippy than a full-blown restaurant (and better ventilation might lessen the smell from the fryer), but it does the job admirably.
Babies and children welcome; children's menu. Booking essential for parties of 8 or more. No smoking. Takeaway service. Map 23 C4.

Herne Hill SE24

★ **Olley's**
67-69 Norwood Road, SE24 9AA (8671 8259/ www.olleys.info). Herne Hill rail/3, 68 bus. **Dinner served** 5-10.30pm Mon, Sun. **Meals served** noon-10.30pm Tue-Sat. **Main courses** £7.65-£18.25. **Credit** AmEx, MC, V.
A railway arch in Herne Hill isn't the obvious place to find one of the best chip shops in town, but that's what you get here. Following the success of Mr Niazi's enterprise, all London seems to have erupted in a rash of Olley's (spellings vary), but this is the one that wins awards. Apparently it was supposed to look like a Dickensian caff, but the exposed brickwork, rough plaster and bare beams has more of Torremolinos about it. Despite the joke names ('Lord Archer's Experience', 'Guy Dimond Experience') the food is a cut above the norm. Starters include Neptune's Punchbowl (creamy fish soup), prawn cocktail and specials. Chips are pre-blanched then fried in groundnut oil for a two-tone crunchy shell and soft inside; we're told the batter for the fish is kept cold to ensure a crisp, even coating. It seems to work: 'Lord Archer' (cod, chips, mushy peas) was impossible to fault; grilled skate – there's steamed, too – without optional coriander, paprika, garlic and olive oil paste, was fresh and perfectly cooked. Staff are ridiculously friendly and helpful, tempting us with puddings (apple pie, gourmet ice-creams) we couldn't even attempt.
Babies and children welcome; children's menu; high chair. Booking advisable. Tables outdoors (6, pavement). Takeaway service. Map 23 A5.

Lewisham SE13

★ **Something Fishy**
117-119 Lewisham High Street, SE13 6AT (8852 7075). Lewisham rail/DLR. **Meals served** 9am-5.30pm Mon-Sat. **Main courses** £2-£6. **No credit cards**.

This basic blue and white decorated café is only open during the day, catering to the busy market trade. Fish and chips shares the spotlight with eels, pie and mash – but let's not go there. Order from the counter, where prices are ludicrously low, and park yourself on a plastic bucket seat to enjoy the experience. Upstairs is a slightly posher sit-down restaurant called Blighty's, with the same menu plus sandwiches and soups, but that's for the nobs. Expect fish that's white, boneless and flaky, in a crisp and golden batter. Almost a crime to squirt tartare sauce (from a packet, sadly) or ketchup on to it, you'd think – but such heresy is accepted in SE13 and the squirting goes on unabated. Chips tend to be pale and chunky, but this side of flabby. Puddings of the spotted dick and chocolate sponge variety fight it out with knickerbocker glories and ice-cream and jelly. It's like being at the seaside.
Babies and children welcome; children's menu; high chairs. Bookings not accepted. Tables outdoors (4, pavement). Takeaway service.

North East
Dalston E8

Faulkner's
424-426 Kingsland Road, E8 4AA (7254 6152). Dalston Kingsland rail/67, 76, 149, 242, 243 bus. **Lunch served** noon-2pm Mon-Fri. **Dinner served** 5-10pm Mon-Thur; 4.30-10pm Fri. **Meals served** 11.30am-10pm Sat; noon-9pm Sun. **Main courses** £8.50-£13. **Minimum** £4. **Credit** AmEx, JCB, MC, V.
The look is traditional: chunky wooden furniture, cream walls dotted with Victorian fishing and Billingsgate photographs. You can almost believe that the fish were heading for Faulkner's when the pictures were taken – but not so, this thriving restaurant and takeaway is a relatively recent arrival on Kingsland Road. Starters include own-made, flavour-packed fish cakes in a crispy shell, along with specials such as smoked salmon, potted shrimps or expertly pickled herring. The fish is so fresh it practically leaps from the table, served in golden batter (or grilled), with strapping chunky chips, robust mushy peas and own-made tartare sauce that'd do credit to the finest kitchen. Comfort staples such as cherry pie, sherry trifle and spotted dick are among the puds. Service comes from matronly waitresses who keep the place ticking over nicely. Hard to beat, especially east of town.
Babies and children welcome; children's menu; high chairs. Bookings not accepted. Disabled: toilet. No-smoking tables. Separate room for parties, seats 25. Takeaway service. Map 6 R1.

North
Finchley N3

Two Brothers Fish Restaurant
297-303 Regent's Park Road, N3 1DP (8346 0469). Finchley Central tube. **Lunch served** noon-2.30pm, **dinner served** 5.30-10.15pm Tue-Sat. **Main courses** £8.15-£18.15. **Credit** AmEx, MC, V.
A good place for families and for celebrity-watching of the minor kind: one of the brothers was fawning over Richard Littlejohn the last time we passed along. It's rare to find this bright, breezy restaurant anything less than buzzing. The decor is cheery in a Californian kind of way, and the LED digital display that tracks orders keeps lone diners occupied between courses. Pick of the starters are Tony's arbroath smokies – a pleasant grilled concoction of smoked haddock, cream, cheese and fresh tomato – and a flavour-packed fish soup. Our plaice was cooked to perfection, with plenty of fishy juice flowing between the firm flakes, and the batter (matzo is an option) crisp and golden. Chips could hardly be faulted, while the mushy peas could put Finchley on the mashed legumes map. Busy as it was, staff were on the ball and congenial, with the wait between courses amazingly brief.
Babies and children welcome; high chairs. Bookings accepted lunch only. No-smoking tables. Takeaway service (until 10pm).

Muswell Hill N10

★ **Toff's**
38 Muswell Hill Broadway, N10 3RT (8883 8656/ www.toffsfishrestaurant.co.uk). Bus 43, 134. **Meals served** 11.30am-10pm Mon-Sat. **Main courses** £8.95-£17.50. **Set meal** (11.30am-5.30pm Mon-Sat) £7.50 2 courses. **Credit** AmEx, DC, JCB, MC, V.
Toff's dining room is a cordoned-off area beyond the takeaway zone, decorated with sepia photographs of Victorian fish markets, signed celebrity snaps and the odd gold disc. Think dark wood and cream plasterwork and you'll have the idea. The nationality of the ownership can be guessed from the presence of calamares, Greek salad and taramasalata on the menu. The name is an abbreviation of the founder's surname: Toffali. If you can, try the fish soup: thick and delicious, but not always available. The usual suspects (cod, haddock, rock salmon) come in huge portions, overflowing the plate and threatening to take over the table. Batter or matzo, grilled or fried – the options are numerous. Haddock was expertly cooked, white and flaky in a crisp, golden batter, while chips came big and yellow. Fruit flan, apple pie and similar puddings are apparently offered, but we've never had enough room left to find out.
Babies and children welcome; children's menu; high chairs. Bookings not accepted. No-smoking tables. Takeaway service.

North West
Golders Green NW11

★ **Sam's**
68-70 Golders Green Road, NW11 8LM (8455 9898). Golders Green tube. **Meals served** noon-10pm daily. **Main courses** £4.50-£10. **Unlicensed. Corkage** no charge. **Credit** MC, V.
The Jewish influence is obvious, with gefilte fish, falafel and cracked wheat starters, and lockshen pudding for dessert. Sam's is a veritable fish and chip palace, promising 'kosher' fish (though it's not supervised). It has chandeliers, gold-coloured chairs and crisp white linen on long rows of tables. To fill a restaurant this size would appear difficult, but we've usually found it a hive of munching activity. And that's not counting the busy next-door takeaway. In the restaurant, you get a free side salad to kick off, then, after the exemplary gefilte, it's straight into the fish. Grilled, battered or fried in matzo meal, it's your choice. The matzo option is good: lighter than batter and a favourite with the middle-aged couples who provide the diner's core clientele. Chips are very chip-like and the dill-soaked wallies are out of this world.
Babies and children welcome; children's menu; high chairs. Booking advisable. Disabled: toilet. No-smoking tables. Takeaway service.

West Hampstead NW6

Nautilus
27-29 Fortune Green Road, NW6 1DT (7435 2532). West Hampstead tube/rail then 328 bus. **Lunch served** 11.30am-2.30pm, **dinner served** 5-10pm Mon-Sat. **Main courses** £8.50-£17.50. **Credit** JCB, MC, V.
Operated by a Cypriot family, Nautilus is an old-style chippy with a menu that's brief but refreshingly trad. Starters include grapefruit halves, smoked salmon and prawn cocktail, but we normally ignore these and jump straight into main courses. Fish is either grilled or deep fried in matzo meal, which gives a golden, crisp, almost tempura-like coating. There was nothing to complain about with our fried haddock, and it came with chips that could have starred in an ad for the Spud Council. No mushy peas – you can't have it all – but wally and Cyprus beer made everything right with the world. The decor is clean and crisp, with bright paintwork and occasional framed prints. The clientele tends towards NW6's older residents, assisted by gangs of large families. All appear desperately keen to keep room for the (bought-in) ice-cream desserts, though we'd rather pig out on the fish.
Babies and children welcome; high chair. Booking advisable weekends. Takeaway service.

Pizza & Pasta

London's pizza and pasta scene is inevitably dominated by the chain restaurants, but there's also a number of one-off restaurants offering a more individual dining out experience. Notable among these this year are **Rocket**, **Italian Graffiti** and **Story Deli**, which was runner-up in the Best Cheap Eats category in *Time Out*'s 2004 Eating & Drinking Awards.

It's also worth remembering the better class of takeaway outfit, such as mini chain **Basilico** (www.basilico.co.uk), which currently has four London locations – Lavender Hill (0800 389 9770); Fulham Road (0800 028 3531); Finchley Road (0800 316 2656) and East Sheen (0800 096 8202). If you're in Soho, there's the exemplary **Malletti** (26 Noel Street, W1 3RD; 7439 4096).

For more restaurants serving pizzas and pasta, see the **Italian** section, starting on p151, and **The Americas**, starting on p30.

Central

Covent Garden WC2

Café Pasta
184 Shaftesbury Avenue, WC2H 8JB (7379 0198/www.pizzaexpress.com). Covent Garden tube. **Meals served** noon-11.30pm Mon-Sat; noon-11pm Sun. **Main courses** £5.25-£14.95. **Credit** AmEx, DC, MC, V.
Straddling the corner wedge of Shaftesbury Avenue and Monmouth Street, this Pizza Express-owned offshoot is well placed for Covent Garden shoppers and evening meals with mates. It's a pleasant space, with neutral tones, marble-topped tables and easy-on-the-ear music, but closely packed furniture and a fast turnover of tourists makes it feels more like a transient fuel stop than a place to while away an evening. Starters include pan-fried spicy Italian sausage with rocket: plenty of leaves, nicely dressed, and a sausage that was succulent without being fatty – just not especially spicy. The pizzas are about what you'd expect from Pizza Express – but to be picky, the base on ours was uneven, with some parts so thin the topping collapsed when we attempted to lift a slice. Pasta dishes fared better, including a very good fettucine with fresh-tasting salmon strips, red onion and asparagus chunks in a creamy sauce. A pity that service was slow and without a smile.
Babies and children welcome; children's portions; high chairs. Bookings accepted only for parties of 6 or more. Tables outdoors (13, pavement). Takeaway service. **Map 17 K6**.
For branches see index.

Euston NW1

Pasta Plus
62 Eversholt Street, NW1 1DA (7383 4943/ www.pastaplus.co.uk). Euston Square tube/Euston tube/rail. **Lunch served** noon-3pm Mon-Fri. **Dinner served** 5.30-11pm Mon-Sat. **Main courses** £6.50-£15.50. **Service** 10%. **Credit** AmEx, DC, MC, V.
On a rather grotty side street behind Euston station, Pasta Plus's blue neon sign and scruffy pillars either side of the entrance only add to the seedy impression. Inside, however, it's another story, bright and fresh with a pretty view on to a well-kept garden. Staff are friendly and the white walls, check tiled floor and bright, framed posters provide a contemporary European feel. The menu focuses on pasta dishes, with numbers by each

dish corresponding to a recommended wine. We started with a very tasty bruschetta: lovely bread, with drizzled olive oil and plenty of fresh tomato. Main courses of ravioli and spaghetti with ragu were less exciting; both were rather tasteless and lacked seasoning. Portions are large. A reliable choice if you're looking for a quick meal before boarding the train.
Babies and children welcome; high chairs. Booking advisable. Tables outdoors (26, conservatory). Takeaway service. **Map 4 K3**.

Fitzrovia WC1, W1

Amaretto NEW
116 Tottenham Court Road, W1T 5AJ (7387 6234). Warren Street tube. **Lunch served** noon-3pm Mon-Fri. **Dinner served** 6-11pm Mon-Sat. **Main courses** £7-£14. **Credit** MC, V.
For a central London alternative to the ubiquitous chains, try this family-run restaurant at the north end of Tottenham Court Road. Don't expect a cutting-edge experience – the look is bright and old-fashioned, with walls and tablecloths in pink and white, and an amateurish mural of the Florence skyline on the back wall – while the long menu (26 pastas, 18 pizzas, 16 meat dishes) offers trad faves from spaghetti bolognese to veal escalope. Portions are substantial (you'd be hard-pressed to manage three courses) and the cooking homely. Pizzas are better than average – crispy base, generous topping. The pasta in linguine alla scoglio was slightly undercooked and the sauce a tad oily, but it came loaded with clams and mussels, with a gentle chilli kick. Spaghetti bolognese was an authentically rich and meaty affair. Desserts hold no surprises – tiramisu, crème caramel, some enticing-looking fruit tarts – and drinks include house wine at a bargain £2.75 a glass plus excellent, ice-cold Italian lager. Safe territory for business lunches, or sustenance while shopping.
Booking advisable. Disabled: toilet. Separate room for parties, seats 25. Tables outdoors (2, pavement). Takeaway service. **Map 3 J4**.

★ ASK
48 Grafton Way, W1T 5DZ (7388 8108/ www.askcentral.co.uk). Warren Street tube. **Meals served** noon-11.30pm daily. **Main courses** £4.95-£7.70. **Service** 10% for parties of 8 or more. **Credit** AmEx, DC, JCB, MC, V.
This central London branch of the successful pizza and pasta chain is geared to office workers – so lunch is a brisk affair (we felt a little rushed). Two floors (ground and basement) are divided by a spiral staircase; the basement gets lots of light thanks to a glass half-ceiling, but the ground floor is the more appealing space. The decor is classic pizza parlour – white walls with splashes of colourful art, tiled floors, bare tables – as is the menu and drinks list. Judging by the quality of our most recent meal, the 170-strong ASK chain seems to have slipped behind Pizza Express in the quality stakes. Starters of bruschetta topped with fresh tomatoes, red onion and basil, and mozzarella, tomato and basil salad were adequate, but suffered from barely ripe tomatoes and second-rate mozzarella. Mains came in decent portions, but were also a bit so-what: best of the bunch was fusilli al rustica, a nicely spicy chicken, roast veg, mozzarella and pasta dish baked in the oven; tagliatelle all'arrabbiata only had taste thanks to lots of fresh green chilli, and a stromboli pizza had soggy dough. Drown any savoury sorrows in cookies and cream cheesecake or banoffi pie, and hope that ASK manages to rise above the level of humdrum soon.

Babies and children welcome; high chairs. Disabled: toilet. Tables outdoors (5, pavement). Takeaway service. **Map 3 J4**.
For branches see index.

★ Pizza Express
7 Charlotte Street, W1T 1RF (7580 1110/www. pizzaexpress.co.uk). Goodge Street or Tottenham Court Road tube. **Meals served** 11.30am-midnight Mon-Sat; 11.30am-11pm Sun. **Main courses** £4.95-£7.80. **Credit** AmEx, MC, V.
With nearly 100 branches in London alone, you're never far from a Pizza Express. Which is no bad thing; it's reliable, fairly priced and good for families. The Charlotte Street branch feels more like a one-off restaurant than a cog in a chain; it's an airy and attractive space, with white walls adorned with colourful paintings, stylish blond wood furniture, a concrete and metal staircase that spirals up to the first floor, and a fold-back glass frontage opening on to a small cordoned-off seating area on the front pavement. Some new dishes have been introduced for 2004: the 22-strong list of pizzas now includes frutti di mare (seafood, tomato, no cheese); gorgonzola, mozarella and tomato; and a version with asparagus, parma ham and egg, as well as old faves (the cheapest, the margherita, is only £4.95). Salad niçoise was a bit on the small side but tasty enough; a napoletana pizza was crispy and oozy in all the right places, with a fair sprinkling of anchovies and capers – and good value at £5.45. Desserts – along the lines of summer pudding, or chocolate fudge cake and ice-cream – are perfectly palatable. Not the most scintillating food, but a very useful standby.
Babies and children welcome; children's menu. Disabled: toilet. No-smoking tables. Tables outdoors (5, pavement). Takeaway service. **Map 9 J5**.
For branches see index.

★ Prezzo NEW
98 Tottenham Court Road, W1T 4TR (7436 5355/www.prezzoplc.co.uk). Tottenham Court Road tube. **Meals served** noon-11.30pm daily. **Main courses** £5.95-£8. **Credit** AmEx, DC, JCB, MC, V.
Pizza and pasta form the backbone of this Prezzo's menu, though chicken plays a big part too. It comes from the rotisserie (quarter, half or whole), can be oven-baked or grilled, and even makes an appearance on some of the pizzas. We settled for the vesuvio, with a nicely spicy topping of pepperoni sausage, red chilli, mozzarella and tomato. Decently sized, and with a thin but crispy base, this pizza was the best dish from a selection that otherwise couldn't rise above the chain norm. Penne arrabbiata was one-dimensional, a mixed salad a bit limp, and starters of bruschetta and deep-fried mozzarella with pomodoro sauce failed to shine. Still, prices are very reasonable for the centre of town, and the softly lit room, dark tan furnishings and terracotta walls offer an instant and soothing refuge from the hustle of Tottenham Court Road. One of the smaller pizza chains, Prezzo now has 22 branches across the south of the country, including five in central London.
Babies and children welcome; children's menu. Booking advisable. No-smoking tables. Takeaway service. **Map 3 J4**.

★ Ristorante Olivelli Paradiso
35 Store Street, WC1E 7BS (7255 2554/ www.ristoranteparadiso.co.uk). Goodge Street or Tottenham Court Road tube. **Meals served** noon-midnight Mon-Sat. **Main courses** £7-£9.30. **Credit** AmEx, DC, MC, V.
It's not every restaurant that can boast the Marx Brothers, Danny Kaye and Mae West as former diners. But then Ristorante Olivelli Paradiso, part of a London mini chain, does date back seven decades. It remains so popular that, when packed, the back end of the narrow room can feel a little claustrophobic, but nobody seems to mind too much – they're too busy chatting and chowing down. Dishes are an interesting mix of classics and more inventive fare (including a few Sicilian specialities, as a nod to the owners' heritage). Reliable old spag bol was a winner, with a rich sauce of good-quality meat. From the pizzas, the paradiso wasn't perfect, with an uneven base and

chewy crust, but the topping was fresh and in good proportion. If you've still got room for dessert, choose from the usual suspects (tiramisu, panna cotta) or more imaginative creations such as semifreddo taormina (mango sorbet and coconut ice-cream with meringue). A reliable stop-off.
Babies and children welcome; high chairs. Booking advisable. No-smoking tables. Separate room for hire, seats 80. Takeaway service. **Map 4 K5**.
For branches (Pizza Paradiso) see index.

Strada
9-10 Market Place, W1W 8AQ (7580 4644/ www.strada.co.uk). Oxford Circus Tube. **Meals served** noon-11pm Mon-Sat, noon-10.30pm Sun. **Main courses** £5.95-£13.95. **Service** 12.5%. **Credit** AmEx, MC, V.
This modish, capital-wide chain has been expanding at a gentle rate, presumably in the hope of maintaining standards. Going on our visit to the Fitzrovia branch, spread over two handsome floors and a chunk of pavement, it seems to be working, but not quite as well as we'd hoped. A starter of polenta with a mushroom sauce was edible without being memorable, and while the pizzas for which the chain is famed were well above average (we tried the ham-topped speck and the simpler bufala, both cooked in a wood-burning oven), they were also a little under-topped. A shame, as the ingredients are about as fresh as you'll find in any London pizzeria. The stinginess also extended to the lower-than-advertised level of chilli applied to the gamberoni starter and the vongole veraci main. The former was watery and tasteless, though the latter was rather better, certainly good enough to survive its underspicing. Service was speedy if a little ditzy, but the complimentary filtered water delivered immediately to every table garners the place a huge pile of brownie points.
Babies and children welcome; high chairs. No-smoking tables. Tables outdoors (16, pavement). **Map 17 J6**.
For branches see index.

Zizzi
33-41 Charlotte Street, W1T 1RR (7436 9440/ www.zizzi.co.uk). Goodge Street or Tottenham Court Road tube. **Meals served** noon-11pm Mon, Sun; noon-11.30pm Tue-Sat. **Main courses** £5-£8. **Service** 10% for parties of 8 or more. **Credit** AmEx, DC, JCB, MC, V.
Zizzi's stylish surroundings (lots of wood, warm ochre tones, low-key lighting; even the toilets are classy) make it a hit with Charlotte Street's trendy media types. Spacious enough for large groups, this is also a smart venue for intimate or family gatherings. Alongside carbonara, smoked salmon and mixed seafood pastas you'll find a flavour-packed penne della casa – marinated chicken, gorgonzola, broccoli, goat's cheese and roasted peppers in a cream sauce – and meat dishes like escalope of veal and roasted herb-crusted salmon. We couldn't fault the pizzas, which emerged from the roaring wood-burning oven with a lovely smoky flavour and aroma, and were deliciously crispy with a few bubbly burnt bits on the edges to pop. Our contadino (roasted peppers, aubergine, goat's cheese, mushrooms) had the perfect amount of topping. Wines are largely Italian, prices are good, and service is friendly and efficient. A good option among the high-street chains.
Babies and children welcome; high chairs. Booking advisable. Disabled: toilet. No-smoking tables. Tables outdoors (5, pavement). Takeaway service. **Map 9 J5**.
For branches see index.

Marylebone W1

La Spighetta
43 Blandford Street, W1U 7HS (7486 7340). Baker Street tube. **Lunch served** noon-2.30pm Mon-Fri. **Dinner served** 6.30-10.30pm Mon-Thur, Sun; 6.30-11pm Fri, Sat. **Main courses** £6.90-£12.90. **Service** 12.5%. **Credit** AmEx, MC, V.
In a large and slightly cavernous white-painted basement, La Spighetta's fabulous food more than makes up for what it lacks in atmosphere. Service is friendly and efficient and there's a good selection

of specials, as well as a tempting range of pizzas and pastas. The aroma from the wood-burning oven as you walk down the stairs is absolutely divine. To start, we tried an excellent swordfish carpaccio (from the specials list): it was beautifully delicate, with a tangy lemon dressing. A pizza fra calzone was satisfyingly large and bursting with cheese, tomatoes, spinach and ham. Pan-fried veal escalope – also a special – was an interesting layered dish with a potato tart at the bottom. Prices are reasonable, portions are large and the location, just off Marylebone High Street, is a bonus. Unusually, the premises also house a sushi bar on the ground floor (*see p173* Madama Butterfly).
Babies and children welcome; high chairs. Booking advisable. No-smoking tables. Tables outdoors (2, pavement). Takeaway service (pizzas). **Map 9 G5**.

Mayfair W1

★ Rocket NEW
4-6 Lancashire Court, off New Bond Street, W1Y 9AD (7629 2889/www.rocketrestaurant.co.uk). Bond Street or Oxford Circus tube. **Lunch served** noon-3pm, **dinner served** 6-11pm Mon-Sat. **Main courses** £7.50-£13.50. **Credit** AmEx, MC, V.
Rocket ups the ante for modern pizzerias. Its competitive prices rival the familiar chains, but as a one-off it has bags more personality. The ground floor is a chic little style bar that in no way hints at the soaring, almost ecclesiastical dining space upstairs. It scores highly on looks (a rich, lambent woody finish throughout, set off by funky orange velour upholstery) and does even better with the food. Starters of battered baby squid in chilli sauce and pâté-like scallops were both superb. Pizzas come with outsized bases that hang over the edges of the plates, making it fiendishly difficult to eat with decorum. In fact, one is easily big enough for a couple to share. Going on our experience, diners can be a bit rah-rah, but the staff are lovely.
Babies and children welcome. Booking advisable. Separate rooms for hire, seat 10 and 28. **Map 9 H6**.

Soho W1

★ Italian Graffiti NEW
163-165 Wardour Street, W1F 8WN (7439 4668). Oxford Circus tube. **Lunch served** 11.45am-3pm, **dinner served** 5.45-11.30pm Mon-Fri. **Meals served** 11.45am-11.30pm Sat. **Main courses** £6-£14. **Credit** AmEx, DC, MC, V.
With fires crackling in the hearth and its big windows overlooking bustling Wardour Street, this cosy, friendly Italian eaterie is simply adorable. Food is fresh and good, and the staff are almost absurdly friendly. Pizzas baked in a wood-fired oven are a house speciality, while starters such as the ensalata del mar are quite big enough for a main course, stacked with fresh prawns, squid and mussels in a delicate lemony dressing. The pasta is exceptionally fresh – the gnocchi in crema tomato sauce was tender and light, and tortellini, in a tangy, rich pesto sauce, was equally excellent. Booking is essential at peak times, as a crowd of loyal regular after-workers tends to fill the place until about 9pm.
Babies and children welcome; high chairs. Booking advisable. Takeaway service. **Map 17 K6**.

Kettner's
29 Romilly Street, W1D 5HP (7734 6112/ www.kettners.com). Leicester Square or Piccadilly Circus tube. **Bar Open** 11am-1am Mon-Sat; 11am-10.30pm Sun. **Restaurant Meals served** noon-1am Mon-Sat; noon-midnight Sun. **Main courses** £8.50-£16.50. **Service** 12.5% for parties of 7 or more. **Credit** AmEx, DC, MC, V.
This old trouper – opened in 1867 and now part of the Pizza Express stable – looks a treat. It's a great place to go if your budget won't stretch too far but you fancy a bit of class (plump pink banquettes, a pianist, lots of mirrors and sparkling glassware). There are various dining rooms, plus a champagne bar (obviously, avoid this one if you're counting the pennies). The atmosphere isn't stuffy, and the menu is resolutely populist (not only pizzas but

also burgers). Ingredients are good quality – a buffalo mozzarella and tomato salad starter had beautifully creamy cheese; and tuna in a main-course niçoise salad was succulent and lightly seared, the french beans nice and snappy. Pizzas cut the mustard too – not too outré ingredients on fairly crispy bases; we tried the contadino (artichokes, capers, olives, red onions, rocket, garlic, mozzarella and tomato), but there are old favourites such as American hot and fiorentina too.
Babies and children welcome; high chairs. Booking advisable. Entertainment: pianist 1-3.30pm, 6pm-midnight daily. Separate rooms for hire, seats 5-80 (phone 7287 6180). **Map 17 K6**.

Spiga
84-86 Wardour Street, W1V 3LF (7734 3444). Leicester Square, Piccadilly Circus or Tottenham Court Road tube. **Lunch served** noon-3pm Mon-Sat. **Dinner served** 6-11pm Mon, Tue, Sun; 6pm-midnight Wed-Sat. **Main courses** £8-£14. **Service** 12.5%. **Credit** AmEx, DC, MC, V.
A busy Sunday afternoon saw people of all ages crowding into Spiga, a small yet sophisticated chain. The main menu includes 11 pizza – another was offered as a special – plus six or so pastas that extend from familiar classics with tomato, basil and chilli to specialities such as duck and fonduta cheese ravioli, and home-made chestnut tagliatelle with porcini. Meaty main courses include venison loin with polenta, and rib-eye steak with artichokes. A pizza golosa was a huge offering topped with mozzarella, spinach, Tuscan salami and parmesan. We also enjoyed calzone filled with mozzarella, roast ham and mixed mushrooms. Peroni is one of the best accompaniments for pizza, but Spiga's wines by the glass include a £4 Montalcino described as 'a beast of a wine'. To finish: chocolate and banana soufflé, and a dish of 'caramelised fruit' that turned out to be mincemeat writ large with apples, prunes and dried figs served with yogurt ice-cream. A very handy venue offering casual dining with a sprinkle of class.
Babies and children welcome; high chairs. Booking advisable. Disabled: toilet. Restaurant available for hire. **Map 17 K6**.
For branches see index.

West

Maida Vale W9

★ Red Pepper
8 Formosa Street, W9 1EE (7266 2708). Warwick Avenue tube. **Lunch served** 12.30-3pm Sat; 12.30-3.30pm Sun. **Dinner served** 6.30-11pm Mon-Sat; 6.30-10.30pm Sun. **Main courses** £8-£17. **Credit** JCB, MC, V.
On a pretty street in leafy Maida Vale, Red Pepper is a great local. With tables on the pavement and both a ground floor and a basement, it can squeeze in an impressive number of diners, defying its apparently small floor space. The effect is cramped but cosy, with friendly staff adding to the intimate, café feel. The menu is mainly pizzas and pastas, though there was an interesting choice of meat and fish specials chalked up on a blackboard. We started with a generous rocket and parmesan salad. To follow, tagliatelle with duck ragoût and parmesan was delicious. It was well presented in a large bowl with deliciously shredded duck in a light tomato sauce. The calzone, from the wood-fired pizza oven in the basement, was equally good. Prices are reasonable, service friendly and the food is excellent, which explains why the place was packed on a Monday night.
Babies and children admitted. Booking advisable. Tables outdoors (5, pavement). Takeaway service (pizzas). **Map 1 C4**.

South West

Fulham SW6, SW10

★ Calzone
335 Fulham Road, SW10 9TW (7352 9797). Fulham Broadway tube/14, 414 bus. **Meals served** noon-11.30pm daily. **Main courses** £5.50-£8.75. **Credit** AmEx, MC, V.

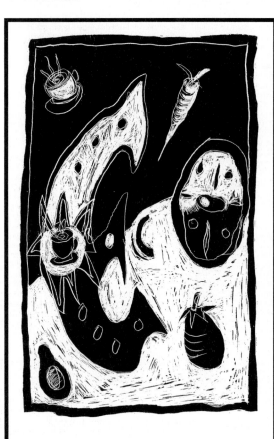

eco

162 Clapham High Street,
London SW4 7UG
020 7978 1108

4 Market Row, Electric Lane,
Brixton SW9 8LD
020 7738 3021

www.ecorestaurants.com

In an area buzzing with eateries and where the local takeaway is sushi, Calzone is relatively inconspicuous and surprisingly good. From a rather standard menu, fusilli aglio e olio, incorporating crisp broccoli florets, red onion and generous chunks of pancetta, was simple yet satisfying. Star of the evening was an antipasto misto, billed as mixed cold meats and cheese, but in fact a delightfully varied plate of olives, artichoke hearts, salami, parma ham, chorizo, chilled tomato, basil and garlic salsa, various cheeses and a piping hot bruschetta drizzled in garlic olive oil. On the quiet Monday night of our visit, diners enjoyed a balmy evening, and locals stopped by to chat to the warm and laid-back staff, confirming that this is the place for a simple, fulfilling, comfortable meal. It's nothing to write home about, but therein lies the appeal.
Tables outdoors (5, pavement). Takeaway service.
Map 14 D12.

Napulé
585 Fulham Road, SW6 5UA (7381 1122).
Fulham Broadway tube. **Lunch served** 12.30-3.30pm Sat, Sun. **Dinner served** 6.30-11.30pm Mon-Sat; 6.30-10.30pm Sun. **Main courses** £8-£16. **Service** 12.5%. **Credit** MC, V.
The queue outside, the glowing fire in the stone pizza oven and the stunning array of antipasto dishes, buffet-style, that greets diners at this packed Fulham restaurant raise expectations that, sadly, are not met. Antipasto misto from the buffet was randomly selected by the waiter, with no enquiry as to individual preference; portions were small and served on chipped plates. The evening special – linguine alla Sophia Loren: fillet of sea bass with mussels and cherry tomatoes – was an excellent choice, but there was a long wait for our other main. A vegetariana pizza, served on a wooden raised tray for ease of sharing, was burned around the edges and soggy in the middle. Mini Italian pastries looked beautiful, but tasted bland. It was a shame because service was well meaning, the atmosphere bubbling and the decor rustic and warm. With a little more focus on the food, Napulé could be a very pleasant evening out.
Babies and children welcome; high chairs.
Booking advisable. **Map 13 A13.**
For branches (Made in Italy, Mare Chio, Santa Lucio) see index.

South
Battersea SW11

C Notarianni & Sons
142 Battersea High Street, SW11 3JR (7228 7133). Clapham Junction rail/45, 249, 319 bus.
Lunch served noon-2.45pm Tue-Fri. **Dinner served** 6.15-11pm Mon-Sat. **Main courses** £4.90-£12. **Minimum** £5 after 8pm. **Service** 10% for parties of 5 or more. **Credit** MC, V.
This charming, unpretentious restaurant occupied by the Notarianni family since the 1930s is decorated with bygone advertisements, old-style diner furniture and a great jukebox that plays music from the '50s to date. The menu features a wide range of crispy-based pizzas with generous toppings, and a few calzone options. Expect plenty of Italian standards: the pizza-shaped garlic bread served with a choice of fresh tomatoes or anchovies makes a tasty starter for two or an accompaniment to one of the many pasta dishes. The amatriciana di sergio, a tomato-based dish with pecorino cheese, speck and chilli needed more sauce to cover the large bowl of bucatini, but was still flavoursome. Larger dishes featuring trout, sea bass or veal are also available, served with fresh vegetables and smothered with similar sauces.
Babies and children welcome; high chairs. Booking advisable Fri, Sat. Tables outdoors (2, pavement). Takeaway service (dinner). **Map 21 B2.**

Brixton SW9

★ Neon
71 Atlantic Road, SW9 8PU (7738 6576/ www.neonbrixton.co.uk). Brixton tube/rail.
Dinner served 6-11pm Tue-Fri. **Meals served** noon-11pm Sat; noon-10.30pm Sun. **Main courses** £6.95-£14.95. **Service** 12.5%. **Credit** DC, MC, V.
The name, the logo and the garish scarlet façade might lead the wary to imagine this is just another fly-by-night 'lounge bar' attempting to gentrify Brixton. But not at all – far from being an afterthought or adjunct to imported beers, food is what Neon is about and the attentive service would grace far fancier establishments. The same kind of care goes into the thin, well-oiled, oven-baked pizzas, which use a good, strong tomato sauce on the base, smothered with classic toppings. The pastas and other Italian standards – ranging from pork belly and meatballs to risottos and salt cod – are, perhaps, even better than the pizzas, and are anything but the preambles to a main you tend to get in older London Italian eateries and in Italy itself. All are good to look at, hot, seasoned to perfection, and light and summery in that Tuscan way. Tiramisu and ice-cream are the best desserts, and there's a satisfactory wine list. Oh, and Neon is not even that red inside; the feng shui-ish layout and basic banquettes provide a novel setting for these hearty, richly seasoned Med meals.
Babies and children admitted. Restaurant available for hire. Separate area for hire, seats 35. Takeaway service. **Map 22 E2.**

Clapham SW4

★ Eco
162 Clapham High Street, SW4 7UG (7978 1108/www.ecorestaurants.com). Clapham Common tube. **Lunch served** noon-4pm, **dinner served** 6.30-11pm Mon-Fri. **Meals served** noon-11.30pm Sat; noon-11pm Sun. **Main courses** £5.40-£10.50. **Service** 12.5% for parties of 5 or more. **Credit** AmEx, MC, V.
Loud, trendyish (with ochre walls and twisted cast-iron lamps) and full of groups of brash thirtysomethings, from one angle this is your archetypal Clapham restaurant. Scrape below the surface, though, and you'll discover warm and competent staff, plus an extensive menu characterised by fresh ingredients and tried-and-tested combinations (as well as a few unusual ones, such as wild boar and fennel spaghetti). Mains are generous, so you may not want a starter – though we'd recommend the plate of asparagus and pancetta. A fiorentina and a smoked salmon and spinach pizza for main courses, created in the open-plan kitchen, were both good: huge, with suitably crisp bases, generous toppings and the right ratio of mozzarella to tomato sauce. Our only gripe was the overload of fish on the smoked salmon option. There are also numerous pasta dishes and a good selection of vibrant salads. If they could just turn the music down, this would be a good all-rounder.
Babies and children welcome; high chairs. Booking advisable; essential weekends. No-smoking tables (daytime). Takeaway service. **Map 22 A2.**
For branch see index.

★ Verso
84 Clapham Park Road, SW4 7BX (7720 1515). Clapham Common tube. **Dinner served** 6-11.30pm Mon-Sat; 4-11.30pm Sun. **Main courses** £5.90-£12. **Credit** MC, V.
Verso – now with a fashionable blue frontage and shiny lemon interior – is your quintessential neighbourhood restaurant, run by a young and friendly team. Being off the main thoroughfare, it's often quieter than other Clapham establishments, but this in no way indicates inferior quality; on the contrary, it's consistently reliable. Things got off to a good start with a well-chosen wine list and complimentary bread with olive oil. Mains are divided into pizza, pasta, fish and meat dishes. We were particularly impressed by the grigliata di pesce, a large plate of grilled prawns, squid, salmon and sea bass, carefully arranged on a bed of rocket: filling, fresh and excellent value. A napoletana pizza was good too, with the right amount of anchovies, olives and herbs. Any quibbles we had were minor (salad dressing a little too vinegary, pizza base not quite crispy enough). The dessert menu throws up few surprises, but the tiramasu and panna cotta shouldn't be missed.

Babies and children welcome; children's portions; high chairs. Disabled: toilet. Tables outdoors (6, pavement). Takeaway service. **Map 22 B2.**

Elephant & Castle SE1

★ Pizzeria Castello
20 Walworth Road, SE1 6SP (7703 2556).
Elephant & Castle tube/rail. **Meals served** noon-11pm Mon-Thur; noon-11.30pm Fri. **Dinner served** 5-11.30pm Sat. **Main courses** £4.70-£10.30. **Credit** AmEx, DC, MC, V.
For the uninitiated, the maze of underpasses around the far from salubrious Elephant & Castle roundabout may seem daunting, but perseverance will be rewarded. Pizzeria Castello is worth the trip: it's a warm, welcoming restaurant in a most unlikely place, and all the better for it. The surroundings are simple and comfortable, and service comes with beaming smiles. From a selection of Italian classics, tagliatelle marinara was an enormous, steaming bowl of tender pasta with squid, baby octopus and masses of prawns, seasoned with fresh herbs. Pizzas are decent as long as you stick to the simpler combinations. Desserts include glorious gelato creations and Italian traditionals. The restaurant does a roaring trade in takeaway and was extremely busy on the weekday night of our visit – testament to the good food, great value and lively atmosphere.
Babies and children welcome; high chairs. Booking advisable. Takeaway service. **Map 24 O11.**

Walworth SE17

★ La Luna
380 Walworth Road, SE17 2NG (7277 1991).
Bus 12, 35, 40, 45, 68, 68A, 171, 176. **Lunch served** noon-3pm, **dinner served** 6-11pm Tue-Sat. **Meals served** noon-10.45pm Sun. **Main courses** £6-£13. **Set lunch** £5.50 1 course incl coffee. **Service** 10% for parties of 6 or more. **Credit** AmEx, JCB, MC, V.
A testosterone-heavy team of friendly enough waiters, a stone oven in the centre, rustic plates, and pictures of the home country on lemon sorbet-coloured walls give this Italian joint an air of authenticity. And pizzas follow suit, with large, crispy bases and fresh-tasting toppings amply sprinkled with herbs. There are also plenty of pasta options (with mainly tomato- and seafood-based sauces), several meat and fish dishes, and daily specials. Low points come in the form of side orders: the flat garlic bread had a bitter, burned garlic taste, and an anaemic-looking tomato salad was covered with an unappetising gloopy beige dressing. Note too that the wine list is basic. For dessert, tiramasu was generous and enjoyable. Our advice: keep things simple by sticking to the mains (especially the pizzas) and La Luna – set in the gastronomic desert that is the Walworth Road – can be a unexpectedly good and unpretentious option for an easy-going meal.
Babies and children welcome; high chairs. Booking advisable. Separate room for hire, seats 30. Tables outdoors (2, pavement). Takeaway service.

South East
Camberwell SE5

Mozzarella e Pomodoro **NEW**
21-22 Camberwell Green, SE5 7AA (7277 2020). Elephant & Castle tube/rail then 12, 35, 45, 68, 176, 185 bus. **Lunch served** noon-3pm Mon-Fri. **Dinner served** 6-11.30pm Mon-Sat. **Meals served** noon-11pm Sun. **Main courses** £5.25-£23.95. **Set lunch** (Mon-Fri) £7.50 2 courses incl coffee. **Credit** AmEx, JCB, MC, V.
On what is arguably one of south London's busiest and ugliest corners, Mozzarella e Pomodoro has given a bit of hope to Camberwell's kebab- and curry-weary citizens. When packed – on Fridays and Saturdays – there's quite a lively vibe to this airy, unpretentious space, and the Italian and Colombian waiters are always affable and helpful. There's enough on the menu to make four or five visits without repeating. The food is classic Italian and pasta dishes are always good, as are the thin pizzas (though the crust could be a little crispier).

Eating on a Budget

Carpaccio was not as slender and tender as it can be, and the parmesan didn't quite kick enough for the contrast you need, but mains of veal and lamb chops with rosemary were excellent. The waiters recommended £40 wines – as they might – but an £18 cabernet sauvignon was dark and fruity; avoid the house wine, which is one-dimensional and acidic. Classic desserts include ravishing profiteroles. Freshly cut tulips sat on every table, and there's something of the New York neighbourhood Italian about everything – but they should sort out the music, as the fast salsas alternating with dentist muzak just don't cut it.
Babies and children welcome; high chairs. Booking advisable Fri, Sat. Separate room for hire, seats 120. Takeaway service. **Map 23 A2**.

East Dulwich SE22

Upstairs at the EDT NEW

First Floor, East Dulwich Tavern, 1 Lordship Lane, SE22 8EW (8693 1817). East Dulwich rail/40, 176, 185 bus. **Lunch served** noon-4pm Sun. **Dinner served** 6-10.30pm Mon-Sat. **Main courses** £6.95-£11.95. **Credit** MC, V.
Teal walls, draped curtains, dimmed lighting, huge paper lanterns and palms create a civilised dining space above this popular pub. Patronised by thirtysomething locals in the know, it's often busy; if you have to wait for a table, do so in the trendy adjacent bar. Dishes are upmarket pizza joint fare, and interesting enough, with a choice of eight pizzas (napoletana and quatro formaggi sit beside the more novel 'Marittima Upstairs' with tiger prawns and spinach) and a smaller selection of pasta dishes and main-course salads. The pizzas are large, with crispy bases and fresh toppings. A big plateful of linguine with gorgonzola, spinach, pine kernels and walnuts was nicely creamy and flavourful, if not especially memorable. A chicken caesar salad was, again, OK save for the rather dry texture of the meat. A robust liqueur affogato for dessert was much more striking. Good, friendly service nudges this place into the slightly-better-than-average category – although we found a small piece of gravel in our side salad, the waitress was extremely apologetic and swiftly knocked the item off the bill.
Babies and children welcome; children's portions; high chairs. Booking advisable. Takeaway service. **Map 23 C4.**

East

Brick Lane E1

★ ★ Story Deli NEW

2004 RUNNER-UP BEST CHEAP EATS
3 Dray Walk, The Old Truman Brewery, 91 Brick Lane, E1 6QL (7247 3137). Liverpool Street tube/rail. **Meals served** 8am-7pm daily. **Main courses** £2-£7.50. **Unlicensed. Corkage** no charge. **Credit** AmEx, MC, V.
If there is such a look as 'industrial rustic' this acutely trendy deli-cum-pizzeria has managed it. Behind huge plate-glass windows you'll find exposed brickwork, a mezzanine kitchen (reached by stairs lined with flour sacks), and a couple of vast old tables seemingly pinched from a baronet's scullery. Diners sit communally around one of the big tables, perched on cardboard box-stools; the other table displays bowls of salad and quiches. Otherwise the menu consists of breakfasts, the odd special (a whopping, strongly flavoured kedgeree topped with a feather-light herb omelette), pizzas and alluring cakes and tarts. Service is casual (and occasionally shambolic). Pizzas are superb, with bubbly thin bases, high-quality tomato and mozzarella toppings, and top-notch extras such as thinly sliced spicy sausage. Indeed, the food is of such a great standard that to serve it in cardboard boxes or greaseproof paper (whether you're eating in or taking away) can surely only be some sort of post-industrial ironic joke.
Babies and children welcome; high chair; toys. Disabled: toilet. No smoking. Tables outdoors (10, pavement). Takeaway service; delivery service. Vegetarian menu. Vegan dishes. **Map 6 S5.**

Wapping E1

Il Bordello

81 Wapping High Street, E1W 2YN (7481 9950). Wapping tube/100 bus. **Lunch served** noon-3pm Mon-Fri. **Dinner served** 6-11pm Mon-Sat. **Meals served** 1-10.30pm Sun. **Main courses** £7.75-£22.95. **Credit** AmEx, DC, MC, V.
Little changes at this smarter-than-average Italian, and little needs to. The only other decent eateries in Wapping are a chain (Smollensky's, just down the road) and a destination (Wapping Food, a few streets away), and so the noisy, jovial Il Bordello has long stood unchallenged as Wapping's reigning neighbourhood restaurant. It makes the most of its near-monopoly status: tables are packed tightly together in the tidy, busy and slightly '80s-looking room, and with (for example) bruschetta at £4.95, the menu's clearly aimed at those living in the pricey warehouse conversions opposite rather than the estates around the corner. The food, on the whole, is pretty good: spaghetti alle vongole was generous and very decent, and a bicycle-wheel-sized four seasons pizza was thin, crispy and copiously topped. However, some very cheap-tasting tuna on the mixed appetisers platter and a rather unappealing desserts fridge were both indicative of a restaurant that doesn't do any more than it needs to in order to keep the money rolling in. Service comes courtesy of greying Italian gentlemen with amusingly matter-of-fact manners.
Babies and children welcome. Booking essential. Disabled: toilet. Takeaway service.

North East

Stoke Newington N16

Il Bacio

61 Stoke Newington Church Street, N16 0AR (7249 3833). Stoke Newington rail/73 bus. **Lunch served** noon-2.30pm Tue-Fri; 12.45-4.30pm Sat, Sun. **Dinner served** 6-11.15pm daily. **Main courses** £6.50-£15.95. **Service** 12.5% for parties of 6 or more. **Credit** MC, V.
Il Bacio opened less than a decade ago, but, if you ignore the modernish decor, this place feels like a real throwback. It's the kind of Italian restaurant that sprung up all over in the 1970s: family-owned and enthusiastically staffed, boasting a simple menu (mostly pizzas, with some pastas and a few more expensive entrées) and competitive prices. The food, as you might expect, is decent without being outstanding, but it makes up in quantity for what it lacks in quality. Our mushroom risotto and sapore d'estate pizza (anchovies, olives, egg) were both ordinary and both vast. Better were the starters – a fresh salad and a moreish plate of goat's cheese baked with pears – and the cheery service; worse was the excruciating Italian pop that soundtracked our dinner. One welcome touch: although Il Bacio attracts a lot of noisy parties, its layout means that there's plenty of separation between them and the thirty- and fortysomething couples who otherwise keep the place busy. There's also an Il Bacio café and deli a little further along Church Street.
Babies and children welcome; high chairs. Booking advisable. Separate room for hire, seats 50. Tables outdoors (3, pavement). Takeaway service; delivery service. **Map 25 B1.**
For branch see index.

North

Islington N1

★ La Porchetta

141 Upper Street, N1 1QY (7288 2488). Angel tube. **Dinner served** 5.30pm-midnight Mon-Thur. **Meals served** noon-midnight Fri-Sun. **Main courses** £4.90-£8.50. **Credit** MC, V.
First impressions of La Porchetta are not good – the basement's ascetic, the tables are crammed together, the grimy toilets are those one-piece all-metal affairs you find in public lavs and the acoustics are abysmal. But by the time we left, we'd been won over by the friendliness of the very competent staff and a dining experience that's as

close to the bustle of a Neapolitan pizzeria as you're likely to find outside Italy. The emphasis here is very much on friends enjoying an evening together around food. The vast menu includes a wide variety of meat-free pasta dishes and pizzas, but starters of tuna and canellini bean salad and insalata tricolore were acceptable rather than inspired. These were followed by a capricciosa pizza that overhung the plate and a pretty, perfectly al dente risotto primavera. Both lacked the punch of truly top-rate ingredients, but failed to dent our enjoyment of this authentic slice of Italian life.
Babies and children welcome; high chairs. Bookings accepted only for parties of 5 or more. Takeaway service. **Map 5 O1.**
For branches see index.

North West

West Hampstead NW6

La Brocca

273 West End Lane, NW6 1QS (7433 1989). West Hampstead rail/139, C11 bus. **Bar Open** noon-11pm daily. **Lunch served** noon-4pm Mon-Fri; noon-4.30pm Sat, Sun. **Main courses** £5.95-£10.95. **Restaurant Dinner served** 6.30-10.30pm Mon, Sun; 6.30-11pm Tue-Sat. **Main courses** £6.95-£10.95. **Both Credit** AmEx, JCB, MC, V.
With so many eateries along this strip you might think you'd get a table here any night of the week, but booking is essential because crowds of young locals love the generous platefuls of flavour-packed food. The small galley kitchen knocks out a constant stream of amply covered crisp-based pizzas and overflowing dishes of pastas that are the house specialities. There's also a blackboard list of daily specials ranging from ribeye steak and fish to a good vegetarian selection. Dishes included a hearty bowl of asparagus and parmesan soup, and squid on an intensely seasoned salad, served with a bowl of chilli jelly. Lobster and ricotta ravioli in a tomato and courgette brandy sauce was another big taste sensation. Saffron and salmon risotto with delicious cherry tomatoes came with taleggio cheese drooped over it – possibly one ingredient too many. In short: fairly priced good eating, plus an interesting worldwide wine list and bright service.
Babies and children admitted. Entertainment: jazz duo (bar) 8.30-11pm Thur. Tables outdoors (5, patio). **Map 28 A2.**

Outer London

Kingston, Surrey

★ La La Pizza

138 London Road, Kingston upon Thames, Surrey KT2 6QJ (8546 4888). Kingston rail. **Lunch served** noon-2.30pm Tue-Sat. **Dinner served** 6-11.30pm Mon-Sat. **Main courses** £4.20-£8.50. **Service** 12.5% for parties of 5 or more. **Credit** MC, V.
Walking into this charming restaurant about ten minutes' walk out of Kingston is like walking into an Italian history lesson. There are postcards and photos of eminent Italian people and places dotted around, a mural of the Roman-built Pont du Gard on one wall, and a long list of pizzas with names that nod to famous Italians. A Pinza, named after the Italian bass opera singer, came with a generous spread of egg, bacon, cheese, mushrooms and onions to match his lung power. Another meatier creation – with asparagus, cured beef, ham, bacon and pepperoni – was a little oily, but artfully presented. Not so a starter of whitebait, which, though tasty, looked hastily thrown together. Although pizza is where La La's heart is, there are also a couple of specials and pasta options, with a choice of sauces. Wines are well priced, and remain faithfully Italian. Shame about the lemon sorbet (inside a real lemon), which was rock-solid and tasted as if it had just come out of the freezer.
Babies and children welcome; high chairs. Booking advisable. Tables outdoors (6, garden). Takeaway service.

Eating on a Budget

Sarastro Restaurant

The Show After the Show

Located in the heart of theatreland can be found one of London's most spectacular restaurants. Sarastro is not only a treat for the palate but for the eyes and ears as well. Dine in the flamboyant operatic surroundings and feast upon the fine array of Mediterranean dishes.

Every Sunday matinee and Sunday and Monday evenings there are live opera performances from up and coming stars, not only from the Royal and National Opera Houses but from all over the world. Sarastro is ideal for pre and post-theatre dining with a menu available at £12.50. Also available for lunch every and all day.

Private function room for all occasions (for up to 150 guests) available.

126 Drury Lane, London. WC2
Tel. 020 7836 0101   Fax. 020 7379 4666
www.sarastro-restaurant.com   Email. reservations@sarastro-restaurant.com

On the Town

Brasseries

If you want a full-blown meal in the middle of the afternoon, you need a brasserie. Bridging the divide between the formality of a restaurant and the coffee-and-sandwich option of a café, brasseries offer a more laid-back approach to eating out – but not at the expense of the food. And they're often the best places for a lazy, lingering weekend brunch.

Central

City EC4

Just The Bridge
1 Paul's Walk, Millennium Bridge North Side, EC4V 3QQ (7236 0000/www.justthebridge.com). St Paul's tube/Blackfriars tube/rail. *Bar* **Open** *Easter-Sept* 11am-10pm Mon-Sat; 11am-4.30pm Sun. *Oct-Easter* 11am-10pm Mon-Fri. **Main courses** £4.80-£11.80. *Restaurant* **Lunch served** *Easter-Sept* noon-3pm daily. *Oct-Easter* noon-3pm Mon-Fri. **Dinner served** *Easter-Sept* 6-10pm Mon-Sat. *Oct-Easter* 6-10pm Mon-Fri. **Main courses** £9.80-£13.80. **Service** 12.5%.
Both **Credit** AmEx, DC, JCB, MC, V.
Despite the superb location a hop, skip and jump from the north end of the Millennium Bridge, and floor-to-ceiling windows that look across to Tate Modern, Just The Bridge was empty on our Friday evening visit. Weekday afternoons, it's another matter, when City types flock to this brasserie to dine on the outside terrace or rack up expenses at the attached bar. The pinstripe brigade probably digs the 1980s decor (a reminder of the glory days) and a menu equally beholden to the past: not quite retro, but certainly not Modern European. Mixed starters scored highly for their perfect mini beef satay and lush, spicy vegetable 'bow ties', but the accompanying seaweed was dreadful. For mains, oriental fish cakes were fine, though jambalaya was filling rather than exciting. The same could be said of Eton mess and sticky toffee pudding – perfunctory, solid, dependable, but no thrills to be had. The house red was a decent tipple, but Just The Bridge is best experienced as a refuelling point after a tiring tour round the Tate or St Paul's rather than a destination in its own right.
Babies and children welcome. Booking advisable Wed-Sat. Disabled: toilet. Restaurant and bar available for hire. Tables outdoors (11, terrace). **Map 11 O7**.

Clerkenwell & Farringdon EC1

Brasserie de Malmaison [NEW]
Malmaison, 18-21 Charterhouse Square, EC1M 6AH (7012 3700/www.malmaison.com). Barbican tube/Farringdon tube/rail. **Brunch served** 11am-3pm Sun. **Lunch served** noon-2.30pm Mon-Sat. **Dinner served** 6-10.30pm daily. **Main courses** £10.95-£15.95. **Set lunch** £12.95 2 courses, £14.95 3 courses. **Set dinner** £15.95 2 courses, £17.95 3 courses. **Service** 12.5%. **Credit** AmEx, DC, JCB, MC, V.
Glossy stone, tall vases of orchids in a row and a fireplace of pebbles set the tone at this ultra-modern hotel, hidden behind a Victorian façade. There's just one eaterie – the Brasserie. Yet prices are lower than the average hotel restaurant, running from £10.95 for risotto of spring vegetables to £15.95 for, say, pan-fried skate wing on a garlic purée with pea velouté. All the brasserie staples are here (though the menu changes seasonally). Starters are soups, fancy salads and

tricky little tarts. We liked the way baby onion tarte tatin was studded with the creamy glazed onions like a buttery puzzle, and celery and chestnut soup was nicely spiced with nutmeg. Calf's liver and bacon was tender (liver) and crispy (bacon), and was presented on a neat circle of celeriac. Monkfish sat on a circle of jerusalem artichoke purée, garnished with sticks of roasted salsify; the colours were pale, but the flavour gratifying. Desserts follow timeworn paths (perhaps the cooking occasionally errs towards the formulaic). Chocolate fondant and brioche bread and butter pudding were warm, sweet and scented with vanilla. Most wine bottles cost less than £20.
Babies and children welcome; high chairs. Booking advisable. Disabled: toilet. Separate room for hire, seats 12. **Map 5 O5**.

★ Flâneur Food Hall
41 Farringdon Road, EC1M 3JB (7404 4422). Farringdon tube/rail. **Open** 9am-10pm Mon-Sat; 9am-6pm Sun. **Brunch served** 9am-4pm Sat, Sun. **Lunch served** noon-3pm Mon-Fri. **Dinner served** 6-10pm Mon-Sat. **Main courses** £8.50-£15.50. **Service** 12.5%. **Credit** AmEx, DC, JCB, MC, V.
This food hall restaurant charms immediately with its Wonderland atmosphere and enthusiastic staff. It's a handsomely converted warehouse with an element of whimsy in the improbably tall shelves and shapely wooden tables, interspersed haphazardly between cabinets of sensual cheeses and toothsome deli goods. The food is impeccably fresh, so picnic-style dishes such as a charcuterie or cheese plate (with great bread) are a default order, but the menu, though simple, is more than an assembly of provisions. It's mod-Med food in the current seasonable vernacular, and someone in that kitchen can cook. A delicate yoghurt and cucumber soup had been scented as much as flavoured with garlic and mint; feta risotto was both generous and intense; and the salmon (on a potato salad) was first class in quality and cooking. Dessert is inescapable, either to eat in or take out; cake-baking smells seduce you as you dine. To judge by the deli display, all are delicious – imaginative, indulgent flavour combinations in solid rounds. Both dark chocolate tart with crystallised ginger, and the banana walnut cake looked good; the moist chocolate cake tasted it too. Not surprising that baker Wendy Amagh is developing something of a following.
Babies and children welcome. Booking advisable. No smoking. Takeaway service. **Map 5 N5**.

Covent Garden WC2

Café des Amis
11-14 Hanover Place, WC2E 9JP (7379 3444/ www.cafedesamis.co.uk). Covent Garden tube. *Bar* **Open** 11.30am-11pm Mon-Sat. **Snacks served** 11.30am-10.30pm Mon-Sat. *Restaurant* **Meals served** 11.30am-11.30pm Mon-Sat. **Set meal** (11.30am-5pm, 5-7pm, 10-11.30pm) £13.50 2 courses, £16 3 courses. **Main courses** £13.50-£24. **Service** 12.5%. *Both* **Credit** AmEx, DC, MC, V.
Tucked down an alley between Long Acre and the Royal Opera House, this smart brasserie and wine bar is a handy retreat from the intensity of the tourists, shoppers and buskers of Covent Garden. The bar's design is clean-lined and contemporary, with stripped floorboards, purplish-brown chairs and attractive glass screens, including a striking red wall behind the bar. The à la carte menu offers such brasserie staples as oysters, chicken caesar salad, ribeye steak, rump of lamb, and calf's liver, but is pricey, with most mains topping £15, so

plenty of customers opt for the good-value prix fixe – especially as it's available practically all day. Some dishes are offered in small or large portions so you can adjust according to appetite or wallet. The set meal produced a pleasant greek salad starter (oddly topped by a dollop of houmous) followed by a main of char-grilled swordfish; avocado salsa went well with the strongly flavoured fish, but cold couscous and a barely discernible gazpacho dressing added little. Best of the lot was the dessert: a warm slab of chocolate and pecan tart with vanilla ice-cream. Portions aren't massive, and the cooking is competent rather than exciting, but this is a pleasant (air-conditioned) spot. Service was effortlessly smooth and proficient.
Babies and children admitted. Booking advisable (restaurant). Separate room for hire, seats 60. Tables outdoors (10, courtyard). **Map 18 L6**.

Palm Court Brasserie
39 King Street, WC2 8JD (7240 2939). Covent Garden tube/Charing Cross tube/rail. **Meals served** noon-11.30pm Mon-Wed; noon-12.45am Thur-Sat; noon-10.30pm Sun. **Main courses** £9.75-£13.95. **Set meal** (not available 7.30-10pm Fri, Sat) £9.95 2 courses, £11.95 3 courses. **Service** 12.5%. **Credit** AmEx, DC, JCB, MC, V.
One of a great many restaurants around Covent Garden catering to the shopping and sightseeing masses, Palm Court Brasserie stands out a little from the crowd for being decent value, for its bright, pseudo-'palm court' interior, and for fast, on-the-ball service. The multi-choice menu includes traditional English nosh (shepherd's pie), French brasserie classics (moules frites) and international favourites (burgers, pastas). To start, deep-fried camembert with fig and pistachio compote was spoilt by the cheese being far too mild. By contrast, organic beef hamburger with melted cheese, bacon and fries was one of London's better burgers, having juicy meat and tasty accompaniments. Toulouse sausages with garlic mash and a mustard sauce was more humdrum, and rather crudely put together. To finish, seville orange and polenta cake with pine nut mascarpone seemed closer to an old English treacle pud than anything Italian, but was a nice plate of comfort food. The wine and drinks list is limited, with prices quite steep (though not unusual for the area). Palm Court is, though, a decent port in a storm.
Babies and children welcome; high chairs. Booking advisable Fri, Sat. Entertainment: pianist 9.30pm Thur-Sat. No-smoking tables. Separate room for hire, seats 50. **Map 18 L7**.

Fitzrovia W1

RIBA Café
66 Portland Place, W1B 1AD (7631 0467). Great Portland Street tube. **Meals served** 8am-5pm Mon-Fri; 9am-3.30pm Sat. **Set meal** (Mon-Fri) £11.95 1 course, £15.95 2 courses, £19.95 3 courses. **Credit** AmEx, DC, MC, V.
The first floor of the Royal Institute of British Architects building has a coffee bar and brasserie space, run by Milburns catering company, which serves breakfasts, sandwiches and salads, plus a full lunch menu. This changes weekly, but features Modern European classics such as pan-fried calf's liver or roasted cod, followed by the likes of raspberry meringue. It's worth ordering from this menu, as at lunch it gives access to the roof terrace (booking strongly advised). French windows open on to 25 tables surrounded by zinc planters filled with (appropriately) architectural plants, garden heaters and sun umbrellas. At other times of the day you can sit out here and order from the café menu, but do so with care – roast pepper wrap with fruit salsa and salad produced a cardboard-textured wrap containing a smear of avocado and what tasted liked boiled peppers, served with lacklustre green leaves. Tuna niçoise was better, but still pretty average. A great setting, let down by uninspired corporate catering.
Babies and children welcome; high chairs. Booking advisable. Disabled: lift, toilet. No smoking. Tables outdoors (25, terrace). Separate rooms for hire, seat 10-400. **Map 3 H4**.

Leicester Square WC2

Browns

82-84 St Martin's Lane, WC2N 4AA (7497 5050/www.browns-restaurants.com). Leicester Square tube. **Meals served** noon-11.30pm Mon-Sat; noon-10.30pm Sun. **Main courses** £7.95-£16.95. **Set meal** (noon-6.30pm, 10-11pm Mon-Sat) £10.95 2 courses. **Credit** AmEx, DC, MC, V.

Despite (or perhaps because of) its innate tackiness, the cavernous dining room of this chain's flagship West End restaurant is regularly packed to the rafters. Whether it's the cheap pre-theatre menu, the range of salads and pasta dishes alongside more typical brasserie fare, or the combination of piped jazz muzak and plastic potted plants – something has kept tourists and local office workers flocking here for more than 30 years. Our last visit was underwhelming. Soup of the day, a bland smoked salmon bisque, came with an inedible gloop of soggy croûtons. Pork pâté with apricot chutney was fine, but lacked both meaty texture and garlicky flavour. Entrecôte steak ordered rare (a staple of any good brasserie) arrived a charcoaled slab of chewy meat. Juicier beef chunks filled the 'Browns classic' Guinness, steak and mushroom pie, but came swimming in thin school-dinner gravy. For pud, lemon tart was a gaudy slice of yellow stodge streaked with bright strawberry sauce. Thankfully, a helpful young waiter brought some much-needed enthusiasm to an otherwise uninspiring evening.
Babies and children welcome; children's menu; high chairs. Bookings accepted only for parties of 5 or more. Disabled: toilet. No-smoking tables. Separate rooms for hire, seats 10-250. **Map 18 L7.** *For branches see index.*

Marylebone W1

Café Bagatelle

The Wallace Collection, Manchester Square, W1U 3BN (7563 9505). Bond Street tube. **Morning coffee served** 10am-noon Mon-Sat. **Lunch served** noon-2.30pm, **afternoon tea served** 2.30-4.30pm daily. **Main courses** £10.50-£16.35. **Credit** AmEx, MC, V.

The menu is slightly pricier – and offers less choice – than you might expect at this Marylebone museum café. But the surroundings – a light and airy glassed-in courtyard with pink hues, palms and well-spaced tables – are most appealing. The café is open for morning coffee and afternoon tea, but it's at lunchtime that tables are hotly fought over (booking is highly recommended). The set lunch, which offers three courses, is worth its £19.95 tag. From this, we bravely opted for some pan-fried salmon, which came with what was unfortunately billed as 'pee and mint purée'. It tasted far better than such a description suggests. From the main menu, pork with apple and parsnip mash, steamed sea bass with spring herbs and broad beans, and chicken breast spiced with paprika and rosemary and served with chickpea, avocado and red pepper salsa, are typical of an eclectic but essentially Modern European menu. Don't miss a tour of the equally eclectic and satisfying Wallace Collection afterwards.
Babies and children welcome; high chairs. Disabled: toilet. No smoking. Restaurant available for hire (evenings only). **Map 9 G5.**

★ No.6

6 George Street, W1U 3QX (7935 1910). Bond Street tube. **Breakfast served** 8am-noon, **lunch served** noon-3pm, **snacks served** 3-6pm Mon-Fri. **Main courses** £10.50-£14.50. **Minimum** (noon-3pm) £14. **Credit** MC, V.

Small but complete, No.6 is a beguiling sort of place. It's a deli-cum-café, with a counter at the front dispensing pastries, tarts, slices of quiche and other tempting delicacies. The space is light and airy, furnished with a few stripped pine tables and chairs and fresh flowers. Excellent bread, unsalted butter and olives arrive at the table together with the menu: a daily changing list offering half a dozen choices in each course. It's all

kept very simple; a few fresh ingredients are carefully put together with the minimum of fuss but maximum flavour. Delicately perfumed courgette and basil tart came with a glossy side salad of mixed leaves. A heartier main course of grilled lamb cutlets was served with aubergines, rocket and rosemary-roasted potatoes. Another main – an exceedingly light and fluffy goat's cheese soufflé – was cleverly brought down to earth by a beetroot and walnut salad. Puddings are equally rewarding, whether apple tart with ginger ice-cream, or a creamy amaretto cheesecake. Service is charming and prompt, though you'll want to linger over lunch.
Babies and children welcome; high chairs. Booking advisable. No smoking. Restaurant available for hire. Takeaway service. **Map 9 G5.**

Mayfair W1

Truc Vert

42 North Audley Street, W1K 6ZR (7491 9988/ www.trucvert.co.uk). Bond Street or Marble Arch tube. **Meals served** 7.30am-10pm Mon-Sat; 9.30am-4pm Sun. **Main courses** £10-£15. **Cover** £1. **Credit** AmEx, MC, V.

Ironically, as dining tables have gradually eased out the deli counter and shelves at this Gallic deli/restaurant, the food seems to have lost some of its edge. Beating a retreat from the Oxford Street hurly-burly on a recent lunchtime, we tried some disappointingly dry and salty crab cakes, served with a frisée salad and tomato salsa, followed by gamy duck breast teamed with pumpkin, green beans and stilton, which turned out to be something of a sledge-hammer combo. Sea bass fillets came with oil-drenched peppers and courgettes and overpowering amounts of rosemary. Even banana cheesecake was sickly sweet, buried beneath a heavy dusting of cocoa powder. We've been fans of the formula here in the past, which offers simple, home-style cooking with a Mediterranean slant, and hope the Truc returns to form. Staff remain charming and distant.
Babies and children welcome; high chairs. Booking advisable. No smoking. Tables outdoors (4, pavement). Takeaway service. **Map 9 G6.**

Piccadilly W1

Zinc Bar & Grill

21 Heddon Street, W1R 7LF (7255 8899/www.conran.com). Piccadilly Circus tube. *Bar* **Open** noon-11pm Mon-Sat. *Restaurant* **Meals served** noon-11pm Mon-Sat. **Main courses** £9.50-£15.50. *Both* **Credit** AmEx, DC, JCB, MC, V.

The Conran-run Zinc chain supposedly offers a modern British take on Parisian brasserie bonhomie. However, our most recent visit to this, the West End flagship, found the restaurant lacking both in chic hedonism and gastronomic delights. An antipasti board piled high with mozzarella, marinated vegetables, rocket and parmesan – although fun to pick at – was let down by the staleness of some ingredients. A main of goat's cheese and spinach pithiviers was a soggy puff pastry parcel stuffed with rocket as well as spinach, and not enough cheese. Sea bream en papillote was much better; the juicy steamed fish was strewn with crispy strips of red and yellow peppers and covered in a rich buttery sauce. Desserts – white chocolate and almond pudding,

Mosaica@the lock. See p298.

Balham Bar & Kitchen

the bottle. Salmon fillet was fresh and simply cooked, but an accompanying salad of rocket, sun-dried tomatoes and artichoke was sopping wet and vinegary. Rib of beef with asparagus, mangetout, and oyster mushrooms, in a red wine sauce, was so-so; although the vegetables were fresh, the meat was fatty, and the dish lacked harmony. Pommes frites, though, were tasty and hot, and a vanilla crème brûlée dessert certainly passed muster. Staff, dressed in black and white, have rather forced smiles, but are nevertheless efficient. A lively spot for some French nosh at any time of the day, but really too commercial to feel truly bohemian. *Babies and children admitted (before 7pm). Book dinner. Music (jazz 4-6pm Thur; chillout jazz 4-6pm Sun). Tables outdoors (9, pavement).* **Map 17 K6.**

Randall & Aubin
14-16 Brewer Street, W1F 0SG (7287 4447). Piccadilly Circus tube. **Meals served** noon-11pm Mon-Sat; 4-10.30pm Sun. **Main courses** £7-£18. **Service** 12.5%. **Credit** AmEx, DC, JCB, MC, V.
Don't expect to have a quiet meal at this Soho joint, what with the sound system set at a relentlessly high level and the constant stream of traffic along grimy Brewer Street. It retains many of the fittings from its previous incarnation as a much-loved deli, with white-tiled walls, globe lights and venetian blinds. It can be a cramped experience, with seating on uncomfortable high stools at narrow marble counters. The menu majors on fish and seafood, with everything from rock oysters (£8.50 for a half-dozen reasonable specimens) to a fruits de mer platter (£26 per head, minimum two). A salad of tuna niçoise was a bit of a DIY number with a thick slice of tuna atop separate piles of ingredients and a pot of dressing on the side, but fresh and tasty. There are plenty of other options too, among them caesar salad, eggs benedict, fish cakes, roast chicken, sausages and butter bean mash, calf's liver, plus soups, filled baguettes and even Iranian sevruga caviar (presumably for Soho ad creatives celebrating a big win). Service was friendly but somewhat slapdash. *Babies and children welcome. Bookings not accepted. Takeaway service.* **Map 17 K6. For branches see index.**

Westminster SW1

★ ★ The Vincent Rooms NEW
2004 WINNER BEST CHEAP EATS
Westminster Kingsway College, Vincent Square, SW1P 2PD (7802 8391/www.westking.ac.uk). St James's Park tube/Victoria tube/rail. **Lunch served** noon-1.15pm Mon-Fri. **Main courses** £6.50-£8.50. **Set meal** *Escoffier room* £20 3 courses incl coffee. **Credit** MC, V.
Celebrated chefs (Jamie Oliver included) have trained at Westminster Kingsway College, and the Vincent Rooms is where the mettle of current students is tested. Pretty lustrous metal too, judging by our meal in the brasserie. In this capacious, handsome hall a three-course meal with wine costs around £18, dinner is a few quid more, and there's also a fine dining set-price option served in the Escoffier room for £20. The daily changing brasserie menu provides ample choice of Modern European cuisine, cooked and devised (under supervision) by students. To start, chicken and cashew terrine was a triumph of texture and taste. To accompany it with 'Asian salad' (a Thai-style jumble) produced an intercontinental clash of flavours, but it's easy to forgive such slips for £3.50. Next, moist, fresh brill rested atop a black sludge of pungent squid ink risotto, surrounded by broad bean and sage dressing: bold flavours, classy ingredients, cooked and presented with care. A luxurious chocolate and pistachio marquise confirmed the high-class trend. Service, though a trifle gauche, came from friendly, alert, black-clad students. Staff, pupils and a few clued-up Londoners dine here, relishing the first-class cooking at lower-second prices. *Babies and children welcome; high chairs. Booking advisable. Disabled: toilet. No smoking. Separate room for hire, seats 30. Vegan dishes.* **Map 15 J10.**

---

panna cotta with berry compote – made a fine if uninspiring end to a decidedly average meal. What really disappointed was the restaurant's lack of ambience (only a quarter full on a Friday night) and amateurish service; it took half an hour for a bottle of vin de pays d'Oc house white to arrive. *Babies and children welcome; high chairs. Booking advisable. Disabled: toilet. Separate room for parties, seats 40. Tables outdoors (9, pavement).* **Map 17 J7. For branch see index.**

Soho W1

Balans
60 Old Compton Street, W1D 4UG (7437 5212/ www.balans.co.uk). Leicester Square tube. **Meals served** 8am-5am Mon-Thur; 8am-6am Fri, Sat; 8am-2am Sun. **Main courses** £8-£12. **Service** 12.5%. **Credit** AmEx, MC, V.
Situated on Soho's main drag, Balans pulls in a smart, lively and mainly gay crowd to match its slick, funky interior. Big mirrors, metal chairs, black wood and zebra prints provide the setting for background house music beats. The concept is based on New York-style cafés, with a diverse menu offering grazing and brunch-type food such as caesar salad, thyme and onion tart, or steak sandwiches, along with more substantial dishes (pasta, T-bone steak, grilled tuna). The quesadilla was fine: a flour tortilla stuffed with cheese and served with mango salsa and sour cream. Corn-fed

chicken with grilled vegetables and salsa verde was good too, although neither main course was especially memorable. Ingredients, though, are fresh, and dishes well put together. Side orders (such as fat chips) provide enjoyable pre-drinking nosh. Plus there's a plenitude of desserts, and a huge drinks list, with lots of cocktail and pitcher options. Service is friendly and competent. *Babies and children admitted. No-smoking tables. Takeaway service.* **Map 11 K6. For branches see index.**

Café Bohème
13 Old Compton Street, W1D 5JQ (7734 0623/ www.cafeboheme.co.uk). Leicester Square tube. **Open** 8am-3am Mon-Sat; 8am-10.30pm Sun. **Meals served** 8am-2.30am Mon-Sat; 8am-10.30pm Sun. **Main courses** £6-£15. **Set meal** (noon-7pm) £10.50 2 courses, £12.50 3 courses. **Cover** (Fri, Sat) £3 10-11pm, £4 after 11pm. **Service** 12.5%. **Credit** AmEx, DC, MC, V.
This well-known, Parisian-style brasserie manages to avoid blatant clichés, achieving a relatively authentic ambience. Both the music and the customers give Bohème its Soho edge. The extensive menu consists of classics such as moules marinière (the speciality), omelettes, caesar salad, boeuf bourguignon and whole dover sole. Prices reflect the location rather than the cooking, although the prix fixe (before 7pm) is good value. There's a wide variety of side dishes and daily specials, and several wines by the glass as well as

West

Ladbroke Grove W11

Electric Brasserie

191 Portobello Road, W11 2ED (7908 9696/ www.electricbrasserie.com). Ladbroke Grove tube. **Open** 8am-midnight Mon-Sat; 8am-11pm Sun. **Meals served** 8am-11pm Mon-Fri; 8am-5pm, 6-11pm Sat; 8am-5pm, 6-10pm Sun. **Main courses** £9.50-£15. **Service** 12.5%. **Credit** AmEx, MC, V.
In essence a posh American diner conjoined to the Electric Cinema, this is a fashionable beacon for Notting Hill all-comers. The food is good if not great, just as the prices are up there if not extortionate. Variety is the name of the game. The venue is decked out in red leather, chrome and wood fittings, with a marginally more formal dining area to the rear. Southern European starters cover pasta, ravioli and foie gras, while mains include veal cutlet in roquefort butter, and roast sea bream with roast fennel and sun-blushed tomatoes. Alternatively, there are 'small plates' such as sautéed chorizo, potted crab and 'aubergine bialdi' (sic) – a gorgeous aubergine, onion and yoghurt mulch on a wooden platter. Sandwiches and burgers include a lobster BLT; heartier dishes such as beef wellington for two take an extra 30 minutes' cooking time. The food is a little too pan-global, but a steamed toffee pudding was great by any cultural yardstick.
Babies and children welcome; high chairs. Booking advisable. Disabled: toilet. Tables outdoors (7, pavement). **Map 19 B3**.

Notting Hill W11

★ Notting Hill Brasserie

92 Kensington Park Road, W11 2PN (7229 4481). Notting Hill Gate tube. **Lunch served** noon-3pm, **dinner served** 7-11pm Mon-Sat. **Main courses** £17-£21.50. **Set lunch** £14.50 2 courses, £19.50 3 courses. **Service** 12.5%. **Credit** AmEx, MC, V.
If you think brasseries offer simple, inexpensive food, you're in for a surprise at this bourgeois den of culinary purity. There's a small bar where a jazz band plays, producing the feel of a 1920s luxury liner. The tables in each of the small, porcini-mushroom-emulsioned rooms are laid with linen and furnished with upholstered armchairs. This is one of the smartest restaurants du jour in Notting Hill. Chef Mark Jankel doesn't disappoint. Among the eight starters was a beautifully rich osso bucco ravioli with cep purée. A similar number of mains included pan-fried fillets of john dory with a ragoût of baby artichokes and white beans; and roasted duck breast on a bed of roasted vegetables infused with an intense, sticky sauce. All dishes are presented with a flourish, but none was more elegant than a poached pear interleaved with brandy snap discs alongside a mini egg of pear sorbet and a puff of Pernod cream. The wine list is aimed at a discriminating palate, yet the house options aren't pricey or anything less than good quality. It's pushing it to call this place haute cuisine, but then it's pushing it to call this place a brasserie.
Babies and children welcome; high chairs. Booking advisable. Entertainment: jazz and blues musicians 7pm-midnight Mon-Sat. Separate rooms for hire, seat 8 and 40. **Map 7 A6**.

South West

Barnes SW14

The Depot

Tideway Yard, 125 Mortlake High Street, SW14 8SN (8878 9462). Barnes Bridge or Mortlake rail/209 bus. **Open** 10am-11pm Mon-Sat; 10am-10.30pm Sun. **Lunch served** noon-3pm Mon-Sat; noon-4pm Sun. **Dinner served** 6-11pm Mon-Sat; 6-10.30pm Sun. **Main courses** £9.95-£15.50. **Set meal** (lunch Mon-Fri, dinner Mon-Thur, Sun) £12 2 courses. **Service** 12.5%. **Credit** AmEx, DC, MC, V.
This riverside establishment manages effortlessly that laid-back brasserie vibe. With gleaming woodwork and well-spaced tables, it's best visited in the day or at sunset for sweeping views over the Barnes bend of the Thames. The menu makes good use of seasonal ingredients, and prices are fair for this upmarket neighbourhood; there's also a limited but bargain-priced two-course set menu. Gruyère and sweet onion tart, and grilled goat's cheese atop a fresh-tasting salad of chicory, radicchio and beetroot salad were excellent starters. Mains offer the likes of calf's liver and bacon, pork fillet, and salmon fish cake – a comforting treat, with a poached egg and mustard hollandaise sauce. Blackened tuna was nicely cooked, pink inside, crisp and sweet on the outside, but sweetcorn and artichoke salsa made a dull accompaniment. Shoestring chips were ace. Puds are always a highlight: moist orange and almond cake, perhaps, or velvety vanilla panna cotta with tangy rhubarb compote. An amenable wine list (with 16 options by the glass, including bubbly), good coffee and proficient service all add to the class of the operation.
Babies and children welcome; children's menu; crayons; high chairs. Booking advisable. No-smoking tables. Tables outdoors (10, patio).

Chelsea SW1, SW3, SW6

Blue Kangaroo NEW

555 King's Road, SW6 2EB (7371 7622/ www.the bluekangaroo.co.uk). Fulham Broadway/Sloane Square tube then 11, 19, 22 bus. **Meals served** 9.30am-7pm Mon-Fri; 9.30am-8.30pm Sat, Sun. **Main courses** £8-£16. **Credit** AmEx, MC, V.
It may be the most sprog-centric restaurant in London, but a family meal at the Blue Kangaroo is far from the ketchup-smeared purgatory that parents might fear. For a start, the food is prepared with enormous care, from diligently sourced ingredients. Though not flashy, it is uniformly good. Children, if they want nuggets, get own-made, free-range ones; salmon fish cakes are made with the wild variety and sausages are organic. The children's menu costs £4.95 with a drink. Grown-ups should try those fish cakes in a larger size, or the excellent butternut risotto, creamy wild mushroom tagliatelle or grilled chicken in ciabatta (adult dishes cost £6.95-£10). Puddings are comforting – pecan nut pie, treacle sponge, tarte tatin. The wine list has also been assembled with some care and includes a number of bottles well priced for the family budget. Undoubtedly the feature young children like best about this lively, otherwise simply appointed place is that it sits on a whole basement of play apparatus; diners pay about £3 to set the kids loose here. The play area can be monitored via plasma screen or the obliging staff, who were saintly on our visit.
Babies and children welcome: children's menu (£4.95); high chairs; toys. Booking advisable (weekends). Disabled: toilet. No smoking. Vegan dishes. **Map 13 C13**.

Cheyne Walk Brasserie NEW

50 Cheyne Walk, SW3 5LR (7376 8787). Sloane Square tube. **Breakfast served** 11am-1pm Sat, Sun. **Lunch served** noon-3pm daily. **Dinner served** 7-10pm Mon-Sat. **Main courses** £9-£29.50. **Set lunch** £16.95 2 courses, £19.95 3 courses. **Service** 12.5%. **Credit** AmEx, MC, V.
Style and substance mingle pleasingly in this Chelsea eaterie, fashioned from a former pub by way of a French restaurant. Style is provided by airy nouveau-classicism organised about a central barbecue with sky-blue banquette seating. Completing the francophile feel, polished wooden floors contrast with pretty chandeliers and cut-glass sidelights. And that's just the restaurant. The first-floor cocktail lounge, set with fin-de-siècle chaises longues, overlooks the Thames between Battersea and Albert Bridges. The substance is classic French brasserie food, majoring in grilled red meat and fish. Sirloin steak was a choice piece of meat, served ruby in the middle and barbecued on the outside. In contrast, scallops in a creamy cardamom and aniseed sauce with celeriac mash was ordinary. Despite mains costing about £20, side dishes were required, but the likes of stir-fried veg provided little relief from richness. Desserts are typified by crème brûlée or moelleux au chocolat. Smart enough for a sommelier, the wine list is an absorbing collection of French varieties with a commendable range by the glass. Service too was charming, but don't expect much change out of £100 for dinner for two.
Babies and children welcome; crayons; high chairs. Book dinner. **Map 14 E12**.

The Market Place

Chelsea Farmers' Market, 125 Sydney Street, SW3 6NR (7352 5600). South Kensington tube/11, 19, 22, 49 bus. **Meals served** Apr-Sept 9.30am-9pm Mon-Fri; 9.30am-7pm Sat, Sun. Oct-Mar 9.30am-4.30pm daily. **Main courses** £8-£12. **Service** 12.5%. **Credit** AmEx, MC, V.
The Sloaney garden party season runs all year on this alternately sun- and rain-drenched terrace. The Market Place is sited in the middle of a mini shopping village just off the King's Road near the old Town Hall. In summer it's a great draw for the Bolly-swilling toffs, and also serves as a déclassé pit-stop for the kind of ladies who plan plastic surgery over coffee and cake. The menu is reliable, indulging little change in content or quality year on year. Portions are ample. Starters range from paprika squid salad to a generous buffalo mozzarella and parma ham salad. Mains hover just over £10; they include a fair but pricey chicken caesar salad, and a much more reasonable sirloin steak and fries. Desserts pander to the tastes of prep school boys (we're talking good stodgy sponge puddings). The wine selection is fair and glass sizes are large, encouraging a conviviality that is shared by the gregarious waiters.
Babies and children welcome; high chairs. Bookings not accepted. Tables outdoors (35, patio). **Map 14 E12**.

Top Floor at Peter Jones

Sloane Square, SW1W 8EL (7730 3434/www.john lewis.com). Sloane Square tube. **Meals served** 9.30am-7pm Mon-Sat; 10am-4pm Sun. **Main courses** £3.50-£13.50. **Credit** AmEx, MC, V.
If John Lewis ran motorway service station restaurants, this is how they would be: popular self-service canteens that aren't designed to clog your arteries. Occupying the summit of the sleekly renovated Peter Jones at Sloane Square, the Top Floor offers magnificent views of London towards Kensington Gardens, along with a mid-range hot and cold buffet. The cold salads (tuna niçoise, charcuterie and suchlike) are covered with cellophane and regularly replaced, so they're always fresh. Hot food (rack of lamb or poached salmon, for instance) is displayed ready-cooked and taken away to be heated when given the nod by a desiring customer. Desserts such as lemon cake with blueberry topping are top stodge, going perfectly with good machine-generated coffee. There's a small selection of wine, including champagne. Never knowingly undersold, silver service is now available on the second floor in a bijou cocktail bar of a restaurant just the other side of women's lingerie. Here one may enjoy, in carpeted exclusivity, luncheons of gnocchi, oriental belly of pork and rhubarb crème brûlée.
Babies and children welcome; children's menu; crayons; high chairs. Bookings not accepted. Disabled: toilet. No smoking. **Map 14 F11**.

South

Balham SW12

Balham Bar & Kitchen NEW

2004 RUNNER-UP BEST LOCAL RESTAURANT
15-19 Bedford Road, SW12 9EX (8675 6900/ www.balhamkitchen.com). Balham tube/rail. **Open** 8am-11pm Mon-Sat; 8am-10.30pm Sun. **Main courses** £7-£25. **Credit** AmEx, MC, V.
Balham trendy? It seems unlikely, but the success of this gleaming brasserie – the latest venture from the Soho House Group, owners of the Soho House club and Portobello Road's popular Electric Brasserie (*see above*) – shows changes are afoot down south. It's a smart black and white affair, with eating and drinking spaces arranged cleverly around a large central pewter bar. Chatty couples

and matey groups (all young, all trendy, all noisy) occupied the marble- and metal-topped tables or squishy black leather banquettes (good for lounging, bad for eating). The fold-back frontage comes in handy when Balham is balmy. With sandwiches and salads, starters, mains, small plates, seafood and breakfast, the menu caters for every appetite. Steak, cumberland sausages, smoked haddock and other brasserie staples all appear, plus some more unusual dishes (tasty red snapper with baba ganoush). Not everything was up to scratch (crispy squid was uncrispy, pea and mint risotto undercooked), but this is a bar as well as a kitchen, with a wide-ranging drinks list that includes some impressive cocktails. And the locals are obviously delighted to have such a modish establishment so close to home.
Babies and children welcome (before 6pm). Disabled: toilet. Function room. No-smoking area.

Battersea SW11

The Lavender
171 Lavender Hill, SW11 5TE (7978 5242). Clapham Junction rail. **Open** noon-11pm Mon-Sat; noon-10.30pm Sun. **Lunch served** noon-3pm Mon-Fri; noon-4pm Sat. **Dinner served** 7-11pm Mon-Sat; 7-10.30pm Sun. **Main courses** £7.50-£12.80. **Service** 12.5%. **Credit** AmEx, MC, V.
This cosy, lavender-fronted brasserie, with endearingly mismatched tables and chairs, emits a welcoming hum. On a Sunday evening, the place was positively buzzing with young locals filling up on generous (but delicately presented) portions of solid, comfort food. The daily changing menu chalked up on the blackboard is inviting and varied in style, featuring mainly European fare with occasional Asian flourishes. Our meal started well, with quality bread and olives, followed by an excellent spinach and smoked haddock bavarois with poached egg and hollandaise sauce. Mains yielded a good, if not outstanding leek, asparagus and wild mushroom ravioli with spinach and cream sauce, and a decent Sunday roast. Desserts were mixed: some rather watery sorbets and an outstanding banoffee pie with white chocolate ice-cream. Service is smooth and youthful.
Babies and children welcome; high chairs. Booking advisable. Tables outdoors (6, patio). **Map 21 B3.** *For branches see index.*

Clapham SW4

Metro
9A Clapham Common South Side, SW4 7AA (7627 0632/www.metroclapham.co.uk). Clapham Common tube. **Meals served** *Summer* 6-11pm Mon, Tue; noon-11pm Wed-Sat; noon-10pm Sun. *Winter* 6-11pm Mon-Fri; noon-11pm Sat; noon-10pm Sun. **Main courses** £9-£13. **Service** 12.5%. **Credit** MC, V.
It may not look like much from the outside, but this brasserie harbours an utterly charming tented area out back, adorned with fairy lights, candles and ample foliage. Shame, then, that our latest visit was marred by chaotic service and so-so food. For starters, smoked salmon was simple and tasty, but a disappointing roasted vegetable tart suffered from hard pastry. Mains of cheesy risotto and chicken breast with pancetta were nice enough, without blowing us away. Our main complaint was with the service – over-familiar and under-effective. As the place filled up, near-chaos ensued: our table was curiously laid for main courses while we awaited desserts and it took us half an hour to catch the waitress's attention and then about the same length of time to receive the bill. Still, most of the almost exclusively twentysomething diners seemed to be having a fine old boozy time. And our Rioja was good and fairly priced.
Babies and children welcome (lunch). Booking essential. Tables outdoors (25, garden). **Map 22 A2.**

Newtons
33-35 Abbeville Road, SW4 9LA (8673 0977). Clapham South tube. **Lunch served** noon-4pm daily. **Dinner served** 7-10.30pm Mon-Thur; Sun;

7-11pm Fri, Sat. **Main courses** £9.50-£15. **Set lunch** (noon-3pm Mon-Sat) £8 2 courses, £10.50 3 courses. **Set dinner** (7-11.30pm Mon-Sat; 7-10.30pm Sun) £15 2 courses. **Set meal** (noon-7pm Mon-Sat) £5 1 course. **Service** 12.5%. **Credit** AmEx, MC, V.
There's a real neighbourly feel to this professionally run French-style joint on chi-chi Abbeville Road. Diners are as comfortable eating on their own as in groups. There's something very European about the look: plain wooden chairs and tables, painted brickwork, starched tablecloths, gleaming glasses and several pleasant outside tables. The food's impressive; regular diners had clearly come for the good-value set meal, but the à la carte is worth a look. Melon, goat's cheese and mangetout salad was a lovely summery starter made with flawless ingredients; pan-fried foie gras with grilled figs and bruschetta was smooth and delicious, well worthy of the waitress's irritatingly chirpy 'please enjoy'. Mains were just as good: char-grilled dorade with spicy chorizo, olives and chillies was a winning combination of tastes, the chorizo infusing the fish with its kick; and duck confit with sweet potatoes was spot-on. Appetising-looking puddings included baked chocolate and ricotta cheesecake, summer pudding and pear tarte tatin. A classy local act.
Babies and children welcome; children's menu; crayons; high chairs. Booking advisable. No-smoking tables. Separate room for hire, seats 30. Tables outdoors (8, terrace). **Map 22 A3.**

South East

Bankside SE1

Bankside
32 Southwark Bridge Road, SE1 9EU (7633 0011/www.bankside restaurants.co.uk). Mansion House or Southwark tube/Blackfriars or London Bridge tube/rail.
Brasserie **Lunch served** noon-3pm Mon-Fri. **Main courses** £3.50-£7.
Restaurant **Lunch served** noon-3pm daily. **Dinner served** 6-10.15pm Mon-Thur; 6-10.30pm Fri, Sat; 6-9.30pm Sun. **Main courses** £7.50-£11.50. **Service** 12.5%.
Both **Credit** AmEx, DC, MC, V.
Run by one of Ken Clarke's former private chefs, Bankside does a brisk trade with account managers and office workers from the City. The food – a moderately priced, though ultimately uninspiring mix of modern British and international cuisine – is served within trendy departure lounge surroundings: all nondescript grey banquettes and soft-focus lighting. For starters: a huge bowl of leek and potato soup, and a slice of chicken liver pâté with brioche toast; both were comfortingly rich and full in flavour yet had little to separate them from a Marks & Spencer's meal. The ribeye steak was a slab of muscular meat that came with thickly seasoned chunky chips. Of the several fish dishes offered, grilled trout was tender and juicy, but as it came without any sauce or flavouring the dish lacked culinary chutzpah. Whisky and marmalade bread and butter pudding sounded the most exciting of the desserts, but was disappointingly plain. On the plus side, staff are attentive and efficient, and the perfectly palatable house wine is sold in cheap, large carafes, ensuring that eating at Bankside is a pleasant, if forgettable, experience.
Babies and children welcome; high chairs. No-smoking tables. Brasserie available for parties, seats 40. **Map 11 P8.**

Tate Modern Café: Level 2
Second Floor, Tate Modern, Sumner Street, SE1 9TG (7401 5014/www.tate.org.uk). Southwark tube/London Bridge tube/rail. **Breakfast served** 10-11.30am, **lunch served** 11.30am-3pm daily. **Afternoon tea served** 3-5.30pm Mon-Thur, Sun; 3-6pm Fri, Sat. **Tapas served** 6-9.30pm Fri, Sat. **Main courses** (lunch) £7.95-£11. **Set lunch** £9.50 2 courses, £12.50 3 courses. **Service** 12.5%. **Credit** AmEx, DC, MC, V.
Hungry Tate Modernists can find sustenance in this spacious café-restaurant, and take a break from staring at art by staring at the riverbank

through the floor-to-ceiling windows. Three menus (breakfast, lunch and afternoon) are offered during the day, plus tapas on late-opening nights. The bare floorboards and simple black-painted furniture are looking a bit scuffed these days, as well they might considering the volume of art-lovers piling through the doors – though staff manage to cope pretty well with the hordes. Prices are quite high (£2.50 for a small bowl of indifferent chips, £6.25 for a toasted crumpet with asparagus), but there's plenty of scope for snacks and light meals, from soups and sandwiches to salads and cakes. Green pea soup with parmesan was a generous summery bowlful; feta, tomato, olive and mint salad was small but tasty, while a cheddar and chutney sandwich was too heavy, made with unexciting bread. Best are probably the tempting cakes (almond and vanilla, say) and desserts (spiced pear charlotte with cinnamon custard). To drink, choose from teas and coffees, smoothies, juices, a well-selected wine list or a batch of beers and cider. There's also a smarter, table-service restaurant on level seven.
Babies and children welcome; crayons; high chairs. Disabled: toilets. No smoking. **Map 11 O7.**

Crystal Palace SE19

Joanna's
56 Westow Hill, SE19 1RX (8670 4052/ www.joannas.uk.com). Crystal Palace or Gipsy Hill rail. **Open** 10am-11.15pm Mon-Thur; 10am-11.30pm Fri, Sat; 10am-10.30pm Sun. **Brunch served** 10am-6pm daily. **Meals served** noon-11.15pm Mon-Thur; noon-11.30pm Fri, Sat; noon-10.30pm Sun. **Main courses** £5.95-£17.95. **Credit** AmEx, MC, V.
After an inauspicious start – the maître d' offered us outdoor seats where there was an unpleasant aroma – a visit to this discreetly smart bistro slowly transformed itself into a very pleasant long lunch. Decked out in wood, mirrors and glass, with little snugs and bright window seats (only for those who reserve, mind), Joanna's is very popular with Palace families doing a spot of shopping. All the food, from basic but tasty sausage and mash to a roasted red onion tart, comes piping hot and carefully prepared. The fancier foreign bites (satays, thai crab cakes, feta salads) are worth sampling for starters. Main courses – a burger with cheese and bacon, and haddock with peas and chips – were outstanding. The fairly priced wine list (a peppery Argentinian Torrontes was just £16.50) means you might feel flush enough for the chocolate nemesis, which lives up to its name in calories and cholesterol, but seems light and airy while you're eating it.
Babies and children welcome (before 8pm); children's menu; high chairs. No-smoking tables. Separate room for hire, seats 6. Tables outdoors (5, patio).

East Dulwich SE22

The Green
58-60 East Dulwich Road, SE22 9AX (7732 7575/www.greenbar.co.uk). East Dulwich rail/37, 185 bus. **Open** 10am-11pm daily. **Breakfast served** 10am-noon, **lunch served** noon-5pm, **dinner served** 6-11pm daily. **Main courses** £9.95-£11.95. **Set lunch** £7.95 2 courses, £10.95 3 courses; (Sun) £13.95 3 courses. **Service** 10%. **Credit** AmEx, MC, V.
The setting, on a main road opposite a building site off East Dulwich's old common (Goose Green), and the standard spare decor and sofa interior might put you off this newish bar-restaurant-music venue. Don't let them: the Green's Med-Arab kitchen prepares wonderful lamb and cheese dishes, the drinks list has a great range of £15-£20 wines plus a decent selection of well-mixed cocktails, and the front-of-house is managed by charming waiters. Grading the starters, it was hard to choose between a fantastic goat's cheese on focaccia with peppers, and an aromatic slice of brie in breadcrumbs with plum purée. For a main course, stick with the tender lamb; its subtle flavours were far more stimulating than the heavily seasoned char-grilled chicken. Fresh sprigs

On the Town

of rosemary and thyme on all dishes add good looks and flavours. There's a big terrace on the wide pavement, with lots of chrome chairs under a green canopy. You can happily ignore the traffic – which fades anyway by 8pm. This is a dead zone early in the week, and the restaurant is a cavern when empty, but there's jazz on Tuesdays and Thursdays and weekend crowds can bring a buzz to the large open space.
Babies and children welcome; children's menu; high chairs. Disabled: toilet. Entertainment: music 8-11pm Tue, Thur. Booking advisable. No-smoking area. Separate room for hire, seats 39. Specialities: cocktails. Tables outdoors (12, terrace). **Map 23 C3.**

Greenwich SE10

Bar du Musée NEW
17 Nelson Road, SE10 9JB (8858 4710/www.bar dumusee.com). Cutty Sark DLR. **Brunch served** 11am-4pm Sat, Sun. **Lunch served** noon-5pm Mon-Fri. **Dinner served** 6-11pm daily. **Main courses** £11-£16. **Service** 12.5%. **Credit** MC, V.
Flickering candles, wrought-iron fittings and dark-wood furniture characterise the drinking area of the Bar du Musée (taken over and recently refurbished by the new Inc Bar & Restaurant). There's a vast new conservatory at the back, a large garden – providing a welcome retreat from the touristy bustle of central Greenwich – and even a deli next door. Downstairs, the atmosphere is cosy, with a roaring fire in winter and snug little booths. The feel is akin to a gentlemen's club: think mahogany, leather, low lighting and soft jazz. Maritime themed portraits and prints crowd the walls. The menu is short but varied. To start, choices included chilled cucumber soup with chervil, and wild mushroom gnocchi in truffle oil topped with brie. A main of sea bass on a bed of crushed jersey royals, with caperberries and asparagus spears, was divine. In contrast, pan-fried monkfish on pak choi was bland and swimming in coriander oil. The meal concluded on a high with a delicately flavoured lime and ginger crème brûlée. Service can be brusque, but was friendly and attentive on our visit. There's an extensive if unexciting wine list.
Babies and children welcome; high chairs. Booking advisable. Separate room for hire, seats 24. Tables outdoors (22, garden).

North East
Newington Green N16

Cava Bar
11 Albion Road, N16 9PS (7923 9227/www. cavabar.com). Canonbury rail/73, 141 bus. **Bar Open** 4-11.30pm Mon, Tue; noon-midnight Wed-Fri; 10am-midnight Sat; 10am-11.30pm Sun. **Restaurant Meals served** 4-11pm Mon, Tue; noon-11pm Wed-Fri; 10am-11.30pm Sat; 10am-11pm Sun. **Main courses** £6.95-£13.95. **Set meal** (4-6.30pm Mon-Fri) £10 2 courses. **Both Credit** MC, V.
More eye-catching style-bar than accomplished bistro, Cava is aiming above its reach – even though executing such moderately priced, mainly Mediterranean cooking should be pretty simple. Staff are pleasant, but not entirely up to speed; they tend to muddle through, asking you even simple questions more than once. Ordering eggs benedict and the surf 'n' turf one Sunday lunchtime seemed to tax everyone, from the lackadaisical waiter who twice asked how we wanted the steak done (medium rare, so hardly unusual), to the chef who poached the eggs until they lost all trace of runniness. A side order of spinach with garlic and parsley butter was fine, but we couldn't help but notice how virtually every other customer was ploughing through the all-day fry-up. Seeing their plates loaded with bangers, beans, tomatoes, mushrooms and toast, we realised they'd made a canny choice. If you come here to eat, stick with brekkie, or else keep your expectations modest.
Booking advisable Fri-Sun. Restaurant and bar available for hire. Tables outdoors (7, terrace). **Map 25 A4.**

Best Waterside
For a different kind of water with your meal, head for the following:

Riverside
There are tables by the Thames at **Kwan Thai** (Thai) near London Bridge or further west at the **Depot** (*see p295*), **Putney Bridge** (Hotels & Haute Cuisine), **Ransome's Dock** (Modern European), the **River Café** (Italian),**Riverside Vegetaria** (Vegetarian) and the **Ship** (Gastropubs).

Canalside
It can be tricky to find, but the **Commissary** (International) rewards with lovely views of Regent's Canal.

Dockside
Plenty of options in Docklands, including **Elephant Royale** (Thai), **Royal China Docklands** (Chinese) and newcomer **Yi-Ban** (both Chinese). There's also **Aquarium** (Fish) in St Katherine's Dock.

On a boat
For the ultimate in river dining, climb aboard **Lightship Ten** (International). **The Lobster Pot** (Fish), meanwhile, is only decorated like the inside of a boat, so might suit the seasick.

North
Camden Town & Chalk Farm NW1

Café Delancey
3-7 Delancey Street, NW1 7NL (7387 1985). Camden Town tube. **Meals served** 9am-11.30pm Mon-Sat; 9am-10pm Sun. **Main courses** £9.50-£15.50. **Credit** MC, V.
A venerable 1980s survivor, Café Delancey is claimed to be where such novelties as rösti were popularised in London. Decor in the bright and roomy multi-chambered interior (with a logo and artwork peculiarly obsessed with playing footsie) has scarcely changed over the years; neither has the menu, mostly of brasserie classics, grills and salads. Our evening meal was decent and fairly priced, if unexceptional. A salade gourmande of baby spinach, bacon, parmesan, croûtons and vinaigrette was a pleasant mix, and goat's cheese salad came with a smooth, enjoyable dressing, although the cheese itself was a bit sticky. To follow, the house's own-recipe pork sausages were nicely meaty, but also quite bready, while an entrecôte steak au poivre vert was a hefty piece of meat without much flavour. The famous rösti now seems to come as an odd kind of patty, rather like a Spanish tortilla. The drinks list is quite weak on wines but strong on everything else. It might be better to stick with the smaller (and cheaper) snacks, such as steak sandwiches, or the ever-popular weekend breakfasts and brunch.
Babies and children welcome. Book dinner weekends. Separate room for hire, seats 60. Tables outdoors (4, pavement; 4, garden). **Map 27 D3.**

★ Heartstone
106 Parkway, NW1 7AN (7485 7744). Camden Town tube. **Breakfast served** 8.30am-noon Tue-Fri. **Meals served** noon-9pm Tue; 8.30am-9pm Sat; 10am-4pm Sun. **Main courses** £9.50-£15. **Service** 12.5%. **Credit** MC, V.
There's no avoiding the word: this is a very mellow spot – bright, calm and decorated in whites and mauves. Heartstone is as female in mood and appearance as dark-wood steakhouses are male; trendy ladies lunch here, sometimes making the place resemble a wholefood Harvey Nichols. Staff are, well, mellow, and ultra-friendly. Organic food is presented with a clever, modern sense of style.

The menu is mainly vegetarian (with generous sandwiches as well as starters and mains), but there are always some non-veg options such as the great house burgers, as well as fish or meat specials. This kind of wholefood cooking depends on the use of high-quality fresh ingredients, and the kitchen doesn't disappoint in this department. A spinach, apple and pumpkin salad starter was lovely, crisp and crunchy, with a just-right, tangy dressing. Next came some of the best falafels we've ever had: crisp and delicately minty, served with freshly made houmous and another great, varied salad. Dessert maintained the pattern: a fruit salad with first-rate strawberries and mango. The drinks of choice are the invigorating fresh smoothies and imaginative juice combos; there are also organic wines and beers, such as the excellent Beer Station lager. Very refreshing. Very mellow.
Babies and children welcome; high chairs. Book dinner. No smoking. Takeaway service. Vegetarian menu. **Map 27 C3.**

Crouch End N8

Banners
21 Park Road, N8 8TE (8348 2930). Finsbury Park tube/rail then W7 bus. **Meals served** 9am-11.30pm Mon-Thur; 9am-midnight Fri; 10am-4pm, 5pm-midnight Sat; 10am-4pm, 5pm-11pm Sun. **Main courses** £8.95-£11.50. **Set meal** (10am-6pm Mon-Fri) £6.95 2 courses. **Credit** MC, V.
Crouch End has the reputation of being home to a certain modern London stereotype (in their mid-thirties, possibly pushing a pram, copy of the *Guardian* tucked under one arm), and this local institution fits well with the idea. Banners caters cleverly to all needs: progressive parents and their tots gather here by day, getting through huge quantities of coffee, crayons and colouring books; older Crouch Enders mingle at night, amid the mock-beach bar decor (including globetrotting accoutrements from a Brazilian flag to North Korean posters). The menu is suitably global, to match. There's a large children's section, plus snacks, sandwiches, salads, burgers, jerk chicken, Thai or Sri Lankan fish dishes, and Greek standards like lamb kleftiko. Food is perky and tasty rather than subtle. It comes in big portions, often with many different things on the same plate. The giant drinks list runs from juices and shakes to wines, cocktails (especially Daiquiris, Mojitos and the like, to go with the tropical image), speciality coffees and a varied choice of rums and beers. Service often feels vaguely chaotic, but that's all part of the show. Banners is nearly always packed, yet it's often not as cheap as the laid-back buzz might suggest.
Babies and children welcome; children's menu (until 7pm); crayons; high chairs. Booking advisable at weekends.
For branch see index.

Muswell Hill N10

Café on the Hill
46 Fortis Green Road, N10 3HN (8444 4957/ www.cafeonthehill.com). Highgate tube then 43, 134 bus. **Breakfast served** 8am-4pm, **lunch served** noon-4pm, **dinner served** 6.30-10.30pm daily. **Main courses** £7.95-£12.95. **Credit** MC, V.
Café on the Hill is very Muswell Hill: a community standby much appreciated by locals (especially women), who meet to mingle and talk over matters from (on our recent survey) Wayne Rooney to local schools and the insides of the publishing business. It looks more like a comfortable modern café than a restaurant; many people come just for coffee and chat. Nevertheless, there's an enterprising food range, beginning with breakfasts (from full traditional and BLTs to pancakes and croissants), continuing with enjoyable lunch choices (salads, snacks, panini), then a quite ambitious evening menu, with globetrotting dishes such as Vietnamese chicken curry, or baked sea bass with sweet potato and a ginger and citrus sauce. Ingredients are predominantly organic, and used inventively, especially in spicy and herby sauces.

On the Town

A regular from the lunch menu – char-grilled chicken skewers with chunky chips, salad and red pepper sauce – hits the spot, with good, lively lettuce and fresh flavours. To drink, there's a short but useful choice of wines, spirits and beers, plus juices and an extensive range of coffees and teas. Add welcoming service and decent prices, and it's easy to see why this place is so popular.
Babies and children welcome; high chairs; toys. Entertainment: jazz 8pm Tue. Tables outdoors (4, pavement).

★ Giraffe
348 Muswell Hill Broadway, N10 1BJ (8883 4463/www.giraffe.net). East Finchley tube then 102 bus. **Meals served** 9am-10.45pm Mon-Sat; 9am-10.15pm Sun. **Main courses** £6.95-£12.95. **Set meal** (5-7pm Mon-Fri) £6.95 2 courses; (7-11pm Mon-Fri) £9.95 2 courses. **Service** 12.5%. **Credit** AmEx, JCB, MC, V.
The Giraffe chain has struck a chord with London diners, and this large branch (opened spring 2004) has continued the pattern. Queueing is near-inevitable at weekends, when no bookings are taken, but staff try to ensure the wait is painless. An appealing balance is maintained; chirpy, attentive service helps make the restaurants family-friendly, but they're also comfortable locals for unaccompanied adults. An eclectic menu gives plenty of choice: brunch dishes such as pancakes or a full-English fry-up, salads, dips and snacks, burgers, several vegetarian choices, Tex-Mex burritos, steaks, daily specials and Asian-oriented dishes like thai chicken or miso and lime-grilled salmon, followed by crowd-pleaser puddings (cheesecakes, brownies, ice-cream). The Giraffe house salad was full of good things: avocado, mushrooms, artichoke hearts and great beetroot. The coarse-cut chips were moreish, the classic burger was juicy and flavoursome, and the ranch-style tostada, if hardly made with the promised 'Mexican sausage' (it looked like Spanish chorizo) was also enjoyable. There's a varied drinks list too: yummy mixed-fruit smoothies, teas or coffees, cocktails and decent wines. Our burger could have come in a better, less spongy, bun, but that's the only change we'd make.
Babies and children welcome; children's menu; crayons; high chairs. Booking not accepted lunch weekends. No smoking. Tables outdoors (3, pavement). Takeaway service.
For branches see index.

Tottenham Hale N17

★ Mosaica@the lock NEW
Heron House, Hale Wharf, Ferry Lane, N17 9NF (8801 4433). Tottenham Hale tube/rail. **Lunch served** noon-2.30pm Tue-Fri, noon-3.30pm Sun. **Dinner served** 7-10pm Tue-Sat. **Main courses** £13.50-£15.50. **Service** 10% for parties of 6 or more. **Credit** AmEx, MC, V.
Urban regeneration must be good if it brings us places like this. Mosaica@the lock is an offshoot of Wood Green's greatly praised Mosaica@the factory, only still further off the usual tracks by a canal in Tottenham Hale. The space, in the ground floor of a college, is large, light and airy, with an open kitchen and comfy seating. The menu offers around six starters, a few more mains, and kid-size dishes, with several pasta options among the modern-eclectic range. High-quality ingredients are put together with flair. Starters were full of fresh flavours; charred asparagus with balsamic and parmesan featured perfect, peak-season asparagus. For mains, a 'seafood risotto' was misnamed; instead of the usual prawns and mussels it contained juicy chunks of sea bass and salmon, plus scallops, in a great rich stock. Grilled swordfish with chicory was just as enjoyable, with highly original use of the veg. Desserts aren't neglected either, and the day's special, an 'iced plate', was a scrumptious combination of own-made toffee and raspberry-whip ice-creams and lemon sorbet. The short wine list has decent bottles at low prices. Service is both friendly and helpful.
Babies and children welcome; children's menu (Sun); high chairs. Booking advisable. No-smoking tables. Tables outdoors (8, garden).
For branch see index.

Cafés

You're never far from a cappuccino in London, now that the coffee chains – Starbucks, Caffè Nero, Coffee Republic, Costa Coffee and their ilk – seem to have a branch on every street corner and in every ex-bank. But if you want an alternative to cookie-cutter homogeneity, rest assured that the capital still has a healthy selection of cafés and pâtisseries where you're guaranteed a serving of character and individuality along with your latte.

CAFÉS, PÂTISSERIES & TEAROOMS

Central
City EC4

De Gustibus
53-55 Carter Lane, EC4V 5AE (7236 0056/ www.degustibus.co.uk). St Paul's tube/Blackfriars tube/rail. **Open** 7am-5pm Mon-Fri. **Main courses** £4.95-£7.25. **Licensed. Credit** MC, V.
Better known as one of the UK's leading bakers, De Gustibus makes artisan breads for restaurants and luxury loaf lovers, but they also run cafés. This branch is looking a little dated, mind, with its ragged yellow walls and bentwood chairs, but the quality of the bread is indisputable. Choose from a huge range including olive or tomato ciabatta, crusty white and sourdough, and pair with fillings such as pesto chicken, roasted vegetables, prawns and plenty of cheeses, including mozzarella, brie and cheddar. A huge doorstop of granary bread, crammed with smoked mozzarella and salad, was wonderfully fresh and tasty. Less impressive were the little sides of coleslaw and grated carrot, which both tasted less than morning fresh. For a sweeter tooth, there are muffins, croissants and brownies. On the way out, stock up on a six-day sourdough to see you through the week.
Babies and children admitted. No smoking. Takeaway service. **Map 11 O6.**
For branches see index.

Clerkenwell & Farringdon EC1

De Santis
11-13 Old Street, EC1V 9HL (7689 5577). Barbican tube/Farringdon tube/rail/bus 55. **Open** 8.30am-11pm Mon-Fri. **Main courses** £3-£8.50. **Licensed. Credit** MC, V.
Since July 2002 this elegant café has been bringing the fine art of Milanese panini-making to the heart of the City. The method is simple: quality ingredients (own-made bread, fresh vegetables, specialities imported from Italy) in well-judged combinations (praga ham, brie and own-made pork and duck pâté or bresaola, fontina and incredibly rich caprino al vino blanco with rocket and an enlivening dash of lemon) – at good prices. The menu also covers tartine, cold platters to share, pizza and pasta, as well as good wines that are available by either the glass or the bottle. Of the puddings, a crêpe with berries and cream was delicious, if a touch stodgy. Staff prepare the food in a stainless steel island in the middle of the floor, and while the tall stools and dark-wood tables are so sleek they purr, they don't demand you be on your best behaviour.

Babies and children welcome. Entertainment: jazz occasional Fri evening. Restaurant available for hire. Separate room for hire, seats 45. Tables outdoors (12, courtyard). Takeaway service; delivery service. **Map 5 O4.**

feast
86 St John Street, EC1M 4EH (7253 7007/ www.feastwraps.com). Farringdon tube/rail/ 55, 505 bus. **Open** 7.30am-4.30pm Mon-Fri. **Main courses** £2.40-£5.25. **Licensed. Credit** (over £10) AmEx, MC, V.
Feast bears all the trappings of a typical sandwich bar – big front window; a counter area that stretches most of the way along a thin room; and a half-hearted seating area at the back. Busy staff work to keep the lunchtime queues down, serving up packed wraps, filled bagels, salads, coffee and juices. Wraps are the speciality and come in many combinations – the 'moroccan' contains couscous mint salad, roast veg and harissa dressing; the hot 's&m' has speciality sausage, horseradish mash and caramelised onions; 'chilled out' has salsa crème fraîche, avocado and chedder. There's no skimping on portions: our hot breakfast wrap came with ham (they were out of bacon), scrambled eggs, mushrooms, tomatoes and onions. Delicious though it was, its sheer size had us beat. The decor is clean and simple, staff are eager to please, and music is tolerable. A good place to know about.
Babies and children welcome. No smoking. Takeaway service. **Map 5 O5.**

Covent Garden WC2

★ Kastner & Ovens
52 Floral Street, WC2E 9DA (7836 2700). Covent Garden tube. **Open** 8am-5pm Mon-Fri. **Main courses** £3.75-£4.25. **Unlicensed. No credit cards.**
This unassuming little storefront at the Royal Opera House end of Floral Street isn't, strictly speaking, a café; the four or five chairs around a single table at the back of the room constitute the only seating, so more or less everyone takes their food away. Still, the 'moveable feast' prepared by Anne-Marie Kastner and Sue Ovens and their team is far too good for this guide to ignore because of mere semantics. On the left-hand table you'll find the savouries, ferried up at regular intervals from the basement kitchen: soups, hot dishes (casseroles, pies, bakes and even kedgeree), quiches, salads, impeccable breads and a few sandwiches. To the right, meanwhile, sit a vast and inviting array of sweet things; while we've by no means sampled every offering, it's hard to believe anything tops the chocolate-caramel-coconut crunch. Don't be surprised if your planned quick snack becomes a three-course meal, or if you find yourself returning at the earliest possible opportunity for seconds.
Babies and children admitted. No smoking. Takeaway service. **Map 18 L6.**

Mode
57 Endell Street, WC2H 9AJ (7240 8085). Covent Garden tube. **Open** 9am-11pm Mon-Sat. **Main courses** £4.50-£6.90. **Licensed. Credit** AmEx, DC, JCB, MC, V.
Mode's tangible popularity is due more to its location, just yards from the shops of Shorts Gardens and Neal Street, than its food, which is pretty ordinary. Still, this small café is a pleasant place to while away a lunch hour. The menu in the small upstairs room is anchored by pizzas; thin-crusted stomach-liners that do the job with neither frill nor fuss. You're probably better off with a

The Wolseley. See p301.

salad or one of the small range of sandwiches, made with ciabatta bread and filled generously. The high turnover of customers and the apparent inexperience of the staff resulted in service that was erratic but at least came with a smile. The downstairs room, available to hire, comes dressed in bargain-basement Moroccan chic.
Babies and children admitted; high chairs. Booking advisable. No-smoking tables. Separate room for hire, seats 30. Tables outdoors (4, pavement). **Map 18 L6**.

★ Paul
29 Bedford Street, WC2E 9ED (7836 3304). Covent Garden tube. **Open** 7.30am-9pm Mon-Fri; 9am-9pm Sat, Sun. **Main courses** £3.50-£7.25. **Licensed. Credit** MC, V.
Popular with students, well-dressed shoppers and young families, this flagship café combines Parisian style with a friendly and informal atmosphere. Admire rows of picture-perfect pastries, beautiful breads and savoury tarts in the shop window, or sit in the café behind the shop and watch bakers at work through the glass-fronted kitchen. Opulent chandeliers, plenty of dark wood and depictions of battle scenes provide a typically French slant to the decor. Dishes are more likely to be substantial snacks than hearty meals, but the cooking is unpretentious and quite delicious. Carré soleil – an open puff pastry tart, crammed with tomatoes, courgettes and warm emmenthal, was memorable for wafer-thin layers of nut-brown pastry and perfect filling. Don't forget to sink a fork into the dreamy pâtisserie selection – the chocolate éclairs and raspberry tarts are divine.
Babies and children welcome; high chairs. No smoking. Takeaway service. **Map 18 L7**.
For branch see index.

Fitzrovia W1

Apostrophe
216 Tottenham Court Road (entrance in 20/20 optical shop) or 9 Alfred Place, W1T 7PT (7436 6688/www.apostropheuk.com). Goodge Street or Tottenham Court Road tube. **Open** 7.30am-6pm Mon-Fri; 8.30am-5pm Sat, Sun. **Unlicensed. Credit** MC, V.
Navigate the beauticians and rows of posh specs to find this sleek little boulangerie and pâtisserie at the back of the 20/20 optician's shop (there's also an entrance on Alfred Place). A light and airy space with smart, chunky, dark wood tables and stools along one wall, plus a couple of tables outside, it's a mellow retreat from frenetic Tottenham Court Road. Classy sandwiches made with artisan breads and fine fillings include tuna mayo and green beans or avocado, tomato, rocket and cheese. There's also a range of good savoury and sweet tarts and pastries, excellent coffees and a few freshly squeezed juices (a mix of orange and carrot is recommended). You can buy breads to take away. Prices are on the high side, but the mousse-like dark chocolate tart was worth every penny of its £2.60 eat-in price. Apostrophe is a mini chain, with a bigger branch on St Christopher's Place.
Babies and children welcome. Takeaway service. **Map 4 K5**.
For branches see index.

Leicester Square WC2

Zoomslide Café
The Photographers' Gallery, 5 Great Newport Street, WC2H 7HY (7831 1772/www.photo net.org.uk). Leicester Square tube. **Open** 11am-5.30pm Mon-Wed, Fri, Sat; 11am-7.30pm Thur; noon-5.30pm Sun. **Main courses** £1.65-£4.25. **Licensed. No credit cards.**
Tucked away in one of the two Photographers' Gallery buildings on Great Newport Street, Zoomslide Café doubles as an exhibition space, its two large communal tables ringed by selections from the gallery's current show. The range of food served in this curious but agreeable atmosphere – bring a copy of the *Guardian* to blend in – is small: the handful of sandwiches are joined in the glass-fronted chiller cabinet by four fresh salads (greek, tuna, pasta, and apple with fennel and celery), which you can mix and match into bowls of two different sizes depending on your appetite. Desserts, all made in-house, include banana cake and some extremely tempting flapjacks. A good little hideaway from the maddening crowd.
Babies and children welcome; high chairs; nappy-changing facilities. Disabled: toilet. No smoking. Takeaway service. **Map 18 K6**.

Marylebone W1

Bean Juice
10A St Christopher's Place, W1U 1NF (7224 3840). Bond Street tube. **Open** 7.30am-7.30pm Mon-Fri; 10am-6.30pm Sat; 11am-6.30pm Sun. **Main courses** £1.95-£3.45. **Unlicensed. Credit** MC, V.
This friendly little juice bar makes a handy retreat from shopper-rammed St Christopher's Place. Sit outside on one of the few pavement tables or in the multicoloured back room, decked out with blond wood tables and chairs, purple walls and a squishy bright red sofa scattered with lime and pink cushions. There's a limited selection of designer healthfood in a chiller cabinet, mainly pre-packaged salads (greek, niçoise, spinach) and sandwiches (tuna, mangetout, beansprouts and soy sauce on rather heavy rye bread), plus fruit and a few flapjacky cakes. Drinks are the forte, from coffees and infusions to freshly squeezed juices and elaborate smoothies. Prices are highish – a 16oz Date Alexander smoothie, comprising fresh dates, banana, almond, nutmeg and skimmed milk cost £3.50 – but it was almost a meal in itself. Chirpy staff add to the relaxed vibe.
Babies and children welcome. No smoking. Tables outdoors (5, pavement). Takeaway service. **Map 9 H6**.

★ La Fromagerie
2-4 Moxon Street, W1U 4EW (7935 0341/ www.lafromagerie.co.uk). Baker Street or Bond Street tube/ Marylebone tube/rail. **Open** 10.30am-7.30pm Mon; 8am-7.30pm Tue-Fri; 9am-7pm Sat; 10am-6pm Sun. **Main courses** £6.50-£13.50. **Unlicensed. Credit** AmEx, MC, V.

Yauatcha. See p302.

Ladies who lunch adore the informality of communal dining at this highbrow cheese shop, deli and café. After you've splashed out on pricey cheese and bags of posh muesli, take a pew on a boarding school-style bench by one of two sturdy tables – it's often a tight squeeze. The eating area also offers quality breakfasts of the unpasteurised butter, brioche and granola variety. If tea and cake are more your thing, drop in around five for a quiet cuppa and a flavoursome wedge of marmalade cake. Despite the frosty reception meted out by austere waitresses, the food is worth waiting for. Salads are sound choices – on our visit, we enjoyed for a delectable plate of baked Wiltshire blue pumpkin with roasted red onions, portobello mushrooms, radicchio and pecorino rosso cheese. Soups are hearty, breads are brill – only the snooty staff are difficult to stomach. The original shop in Highbury is also worth a visit.
Babies and children welcome. Bookings not accepted. Café available for hire (evenings only). No smoking. Takeaway service. **Map 3 G5**.
For branch see index.

Quiet Revolution
28-29 Marylebone High Street, W1V 4PL (7487 5683). Baker Street or Marylebone tube/rail. **Open** 9.30am-5.30pm Mon-Sat; 12.30-4.30pm Sun. **Main courses** £5.95-£9.95. **Licensed. Credit** MC, V.
Marylebone isn't short of fancy bijou cafés, and Quiet Revolution is one of the fanciest. A big square space located around the back room of a cosmetics shop, the café has large shared tables in the centre of the room, a couple of smaller tables on one side and a bench in front of the big window, plus a bookshelf filled with veggie magazines and art books. Food is health-conscious, and set at prices that could hardly be termed giveaway (£4 for orange juice), but beautifully prepared, fresh and organic. As well as daily specials such as falafel with a big helping of salad, there are soups, omelettes and sandwiches (roasted veg on sourdough), plus loads of juices. When a customer on our table complained that her fine-looking salad was 'tired', staff dealt with her professionally (and we don't mean a shot through the forehead). Clientele is posh; prices deter the riff-raff.
Babies and children welcome. No smoking. Tables outdoors (6, pavement). Takeaway service. **Map 9 G5**.

Pâtisserie Valerie at Sagne
105 Marylebone High Street, W1U 4RS (7935 6240/www.patisserie-valerie.co.uk). Baker Street or Bond Street tube/ Marylebone tube/rail. **Open** 7.30am-7pm Mon-Fri; 8am-7pm Sat; 9am-6pm Sun. **Main courses** £6.95-£8.25. **Licensed. Credit** AmEx, MC, V.
It's hard to walk past this branch of the Pâtisserie Valerie chain without marvelling at the fine window display of towering cakes. Inside are fake pillars, weighty chandeliers and walls painted with murals of bountiful garden scenes – all terribly eccentric, but in an endearing way. Service was superlative on our visit: a lone waiter managed to keep his eye on a packed café without letting anybody down. Toasted ciabatta, filled with melted mozzarella, roasted red peppers and mediterranean veggies, although passable, was let down by a shortfall in seasoning. Pastries didn't get off the starter's block, though: an overly sweet chocolate éclair was cloying, and the rum baba, although tastefully dunked in boozy syrup, was crowned with a blob of unappealing custard. Next time we'll play safe and stick with the straightforward fruit gateaux.
Babies and children welcome; high chairs. Bookings not accepted. No-smoking tables. Tables outdoors (3, pavement). Takeaway service. **Map 9 G5**.
For branches see index.

Mayfair W1

★ Parlour at Sketch
9 Conduit Street, W1S 2XZ (0870 777 4488/ www.sketch.uk.com). Oxford Circus tube. **Breakfast** served 8am-noon, **lunch served** noon-2.30pm, **afternoon tea/snacks served** 3-10.30pm Mon-Sat. **Main courses** £3.50-£10. **Licensed. Credit** AmEx, DC, MC, V.

A haunt of the wealthy, Sketch makes top billing when it comes to celebrity spotting and conspicuous entertaining. More accessible is the intimate Parlour café located on the ground floor of the Grade II-listed Georgian building. The dazzling display of elegant and perfectly executed pâtisserie showcases razor-sharp pastry edges, glossy chocolate glazes and the lightest of fruit-based mousses. Imaginative flavour combinations include miniature pastry tartlets filled with mandarin marzipan and orange cream, crowned with glistening grapefruit segments. It's open for breakfast, lunch and supper, but we found the à la carte choices a tad underwhelming – there's not a lot to say about bland leafy salads, and smoked salmon sandwiches. A more substantial roast chicken anointed with green herby sauce was let down by dry, overcooked meat. Better to drop in for afternoon tea and sink into cake heaven with a pot of aromatic coffee, a fragrant infusion or wickedly indulgent hot chocolate.
Babies and children welcome. Bookings accepted lunch only. Café available for hire, seats 35. Takeaway service. **Map 9 J6**.

Victory Café
Basement, Gray's Antiques Market, South Molton Lane, W1K 5AB (7499 6801). Bond Street tube. **Open** 10am-6pm Mon-Fri. **Main courses** £2.75-£4.95. **Unlicensed. No credit cards.**
Hidden in the basement of Gray's Antiques Market is this quirky gem. The vibe is deliciously retro; the decor is a pastiche of post-war Britain, with mock ads for Bovril and Brylcreem on the walls. The jukebox is equally nostalgic, spinning everything

Internet cafés

Virtual services come before victuals in the majority of internet cafés, so don't expect anything more than surfing fuel.

BTR
39 Whitfield Street, W1T 2SF (7209 0984). Goodge Street tube. **Open** 10.30am-2am Mon-Thur; 10.30am-4am Fri, Sat. **Internet access** £1/30mins. **No credit cards.** **Map 3 J5**.

Café Internet
22-24 Buckingham Palace Road, SW1W 0QP (7233 5786). Victoria tube/rail. **Open** 8am-10pm Mon-Fri; 9am-8pm Sat, Sun. **Internet access** £1/15mins; £1.50/30mins; £2/hr. **No credit cards.** **Map 15 H9.**

easyInternetcafé
9-13 Wilton Road, opposite Victoria Station, SW1V 1LL (7241 9000/www.easyeverything.com). Victoria tube/rail. **Open** 8am-late daily. **Internet access** metered access 50p-£2/hr depending on demand; day pass £3; month pass £20. **No credit cards.** **Map 15 H10.**
For branches see index.

Surf.Net Web & Winebar
13 Deptford Church Street, SE8 4RX (8488 1200/www.surfnet.co.uk). Deptford DLR/rail/47, 53, 177 bus. **Open** 11am-8pm Mon-Thur; 11am-6.30pm Fri; 11am-4.30pm Sat. **Internet access** £1/hr; free for 1hr with food. **No credit cards.**

from Bing to Burt Bacharach. Despite the Victory gaining new owners in the past year, the menu remains old school. The all-day English breakfast provides organic, free-range eggs and the gorgeous chips are hand-cut; bangers and mash are top notch too. Mascarpone cheese graces the (own-made) quiche. There's also healthy stuff: carrot and parsnip soup, fresh wholemeal bread and decent salads. Made-to-order sandwiches and pastries – such as baked lemon cheesecake with a wonderful cookie crust – are also specialities. Staff are laid-back, as are the eclectic clientele.
Babies and children admitted. Bookings not accepted. No-smoking tables. Restaurant available for hire. Takeaway service; delivery service. **Map 9 H6**.

Piccadilly W1

La Madeleine
5 Vigo Street, W1S 3HF (7734 8353). Green Park or Piccadilly Circus tube. **Open** 8am-7pm Mon-Sat; 11am-6pm Sun. **Main courses** £5.25-£10.95. **Licensed. Credit** AmEx, MC, V.
This French-accented café has been a fixture on the fringes of Mayfair for years, established back in the days when Paris was still an exotic, faraway dream and Brits were easily pleased by any dish they didn't have to prepare themselves. These days, we're all better travelled and demand more from our eateries than ever, but the plainly decorated La Madeleine hasn't really tried to adapt. The menu covers innumerable bases, with salads and sandwiches joined by steak, snacks and even a few spaghetti plates. Prices vary wildly (£7.50 or thereabouts for the salads is reasonable, £5.95 for egg mayonnaise most certainly isn't), as does quality. Our goat's cheese salad was generously portioned but clumsily tossed; indeed, you're probably best off sticking to the sweet things that line the windows and tempt passers-by inside from this noisy street. Service was… well, French.
Babies and children welcome. Book lunch. No-smoking tables. Tables outdoors (3, pavement). Takeaway service. **Map 17 J7.**
For branch (Fileric) see index.

★ The Wolseley NEW
2004 WINNER BEST NEW RESTAURANT
160 Piccadilly, W1J 9EB (7499 6996/www.the wolseley.com). Green Park tube. **Breakfast** served 7-11.30am Mon-Fri; 9-11.30am Sat, Sun. **Lunch served** noon-2.30pm Mon-Fri; noon-3pm Sat, Sun. **Tea served** 3-5.30pm Mon-Fri; 3.30-6pm Sat, Sun. **Dinner served** 5.30pm-midnight Mon-Sat; 5.30-11pm Sun. **Main courses** £8.75-£26. **Cover charge** £2. **Credit** AmEx, DC, JCB, MC, V.
Housed in a former car showroom and bank, the Wolseley – the latest offspring of top restaurateurs Chris Corbin and Jeremy King – has fast become one of London's prized dining spots. The art deco interior recreates pre-war grandeur with vaulted ceilings, grand pillars, polished marble and weighty chandeliers. Despite the opulence, the vibe is friendly, and customers are welcome to enjoy food from the café menu without having to book. It's open from breakfast onwards, and the afternoon tea ritual is truly memorable. A superb selection of fresh finger sandwiches, filled with smoked salmon, succulent chicken pieces and sliced cucumber, said so much about stylish simplicity. Also scrumptious were dainty French cakes, excellent macaroons and almond meringues.
Babies and children welcome; high chairs; toys. Disabled: toilet. Takeaway service. Vegan dishes. **Map 9 J7**.

Soho W1

Amato
14 Old Compton Street, W1D 4TH (7734 5733/ www.amato.co.uk). Leicester Square, Piccadilly Circus or Tottenham Court Road tube. **Open** 8am-10pm Mon-Sat; 10am-8pm Sun. **Main courses** £3.75-£8. **Licensed. Credit** AmEx, DC, MC, V.
At one end of the café a large picture of Marilyn Monroe sets the theme, while art deco posters across the other walls add splashes of colour. The

window might be a showcase for towering, multi-tiered cakes, but inside warm hues of maroon-coloured tabletops and dark wood chairs provide an easy-going informality. Take your pick from calorie-laden cakes, tarts and rich breads, or go all out for the substantial pastas or quiche. Service is welcoming, no matter how small the order. Coffee brims with the dark-roasted flavour of quality beans. Accompaniments aren't always so reliable: an almond-filled croissant, although crisp and puffed, was a tad oily. Puff pastry palmiers – crisp-baked flat pastry whirls sweetened with crunchy sugar – could have done with more time in the oven to provide that characteristic caramel-tasting bite.
Babies and children welcome. Takeaway service.
Map 17 K6.

Bar Italia

22 Frith Street, W1V 5PS (7437 4520/www.bar italiasoho.co.uk). Leicester Square, Piccadilly Circus or Tottenham Court Road tube. **Open** 24hrs Mon-Sat; 7am-4am Sun. **Main courses** £3.20-£8. **Licensed. Credit** (noon-3am only) AmEx, DC, MC, V.
Still going strong after 55 years, Bar Italia is part of the Soho furniture. All walks of life come here to chat, sip coffee and people-watch. It's open round the clock most days (and gets very busy from midnight onwards), but it can be hard to get a pavement table no matter when you come. The bar is extremely characterful, with a long counter and stools for perching; the left-hand side is more bog-standard café. We're pleased to report that the food is getting better, and though prices aren't the lowest in town, at least you get bags of atmosphere. A recent meal featured excellent panini, including a special of hot cumberland sausage, tomato, shallots and mustard mayo, and a huge, crisp, well-topped rocket, parma ham and mozzarella pizza. A vastly superior choice to the ubiquitous chain cafés. Long may it last.
Babies and children welcome. Tables outdoors (4, pavement). Takeaway service. **Map 17 K6.**

★ Maison Bertaux

28 Greek Street, W1V 5LL (7437 6007). Leicester Square, Piccadilly Circus or Tottenham Court Road tube. **Open** 8.30am-8pm daily. **Main courses** £1.30-£2.90. **Unlicensed. No credit cards.**
Furnished with wonky tables and chairs that have seen better days, this Soho institution cocks a snook at bourgeois tastes. Friendly staff are cheerfully chatty with customers, many of whom belong to the arty/boffin brigade. No written menus either – what you get is what you see. It's quite a sight, though: French pâtisserie, freshly baked breads and flavoursome savouries. A quiche lorraine, still warm from the oven, was encased in crumbly pastry, enriched with a creamy custard filling and tastefully flecked with bits of bacon. Top marks to the Paris Brest gateau, too with its luscious nutty praline and cream filling, sandwiched between two choux pastry rings. Coffee is strong, and the lemon tarts are fabulous. This spot gets seriously busy at teatime; best to drop in for breakfast and a buttery croissant.
Babies and children welcome. No-smoking tables (ground floor). Tables outdoors (3, pavement). Takeaway service. **Map 17 K6.**

Pâtisserie Valerie

44 Old Compton Street, W1D 4TY (7437 3466/ www.patisserie-valerie.co.uk). Leicester Square, Piccadilly Circus or Tottenham Court Road tube. **Open** 7.30am-8.30pm Mon, Tue; 7.30am-9pm Wed-Fri; 8.30am-9pm Sat; 9.30am-7pm Sun. **Main courses** £3.75-£7.95. **Licensed. Credit** (over £5) AmEx, DC, MC, V.
Indulgent cakes, marzipans and typically French breads provide a feast for the senes at this landmark Old Compton Street pastry shop and café. Decor is a throwback to the 1950s: Formica tables, walls embellished with arty cartoons from the same era. Pâtisserie Valerie is a favourite with shoppers and local workers and can get busy; for a quieter setting, avoid the often cramped and somewhat gloomy ground floor and head for the

more airy (but noticeably less atmospheric) space on the first floor. The menu offers a decent choice of sandwiches and grilled snacks, as well as all-day breakfasts, pastas and salads. Ciabatta filled with spicy chicken, roasted peppers, melted cheese and guacamole was a resounding success, let down only by a bland salad accompaniment. We had a few gripes – the insipid coffee was a downer, and the signature white and dark chocolate mousse cake didn't make the grade. Service gets harried when the place fills up.
Babies and children admitted. Takeaway service.
Map 17 K6.
For branches see index.

Yauatcha NEW

2004 RUNNER-UP BEST DESIGN
15 Broadwick Street, W1F 0DE (7494 8888). Oxford Circus tube. **Open** 9am-11pm Mon-Sat; 9am-10.30pm. **Set tea** £19. **Unlicensed. Service** 12.5%. **Credit** AmEx, MC, V.
Chinese newcomer Yauatcha has already made a mark in London for serving tasteful dim sum in its basement restaurant (*see p57*). There's also a chic teahouse and pâtisserie located on the spacious ground floor. (Don't expect builders' tea here – we're talking rare Chinese and exotic Taiwanese varieties.) Blue-glass walls, chill-out music and low seating lend an air of classy serenity, while a semi-opaque window along one wall gives customers a fuzzy view of chefs switching on food mixers and doing their thing with rolling pins in the kitchen. The effect is quite surreal. The beautifully presented cakes and pastries, although inspired by French tradition, are given an oriental twist. This doesn't always work: the cakes we tried were sweet and overly creamy. Expect curiosities such as lashings of lychee spirit, Assam tea creams and mandarin coffee-soaked sponges – it's very much an acquired taste. Service is patchy but it's a nice place in which to meet friends.
Babies and children welcome. Booking essential. Disabled: toilet. No smoking. Takeaway service.
Map 17 J6.

Strand WC2

River Terrace Restaurant

Somerset House, Strand, WC2R 1LA (7845 4623/www.somerset-house.org.uk). Embankment or Temple tube/Charing Cross tube/rail. **Open** *Summer* (in good weather) noon-10pm Mon-Sat; noon-6pm Sun. **Closed** winter. **Main courses** £12-£13. **Minimum** £12 (noon-3pm). **Licensed**. **Service** 12.5%. **Credit** MC, V.

The setting is not quite as delightful as the name implies. The River Terrace Restaurant is indeed on a terrace by the river, but the name obscures the fact that between the two – out of sight, but not out of earshot – is the Victoria Embankment. The music piped in from invisible speakers is intended to drown out the traffic noise, but only draws attention to it. Still, this al fresco café, perched on a raised wooden floor and hemmed in by discreet glass walls on an otherwise public terrace behind Somerset House, is a smooth operation. We enjoyed a refreshing bowl of gazpacho and a fresh, skilfully compiled Terrace salad (chickpeas, avocado, green beans); warm options include spit-roasted chicken. Our main grumble is the cost: our salad, the cheapest main on the menu, was £13.50. Indeed, at these prices, you can see why clued-up local workers simply bring sandwiches to the public tables that sit just yards from the café. Between lunch and dinner, there's an appealing (and more affordable) mix of snacks on offer. *Bookings not accepted. Disabled: toilet. Tables outdoors (20, terrace).* **Map 10 M7**.

West

Ladbroke Grove W11

★ Books for Cooks

4 Blenheim Crescent, W11 1NN (7221 1992/ www.booksforcooks.com). Ladbroke Grove tube. **Open** 10am-6pm Tue-Sat. **Unlicensed**. **Credit** MC, V.

Tucked away at the back of this well-known shop is a tiny haven offering wholesome, country-style food. Chefs create a daily changing menu, often inspired by the volumes sold at the shop; expect dishes to embrace global flavours. You can't book, menu options are limited and food often runs out – so it's best to take your chances and get in early if it's lunch you're after. Despite it's tiny size, the café has a lot going for it. The open kitchen and café are bathed in light streaming down from rooftop windows, and the pleasantly chatty service team complement the bright and breezy atmosphere. Creamy lentil soup was surprisingly light in texture, and worked well with delicious red onion focaccia bread. A crisp filo tart main course, filled with savoury custard, mushrooms, sweet potato and spinach, was a shade too stodgy. Order wine by the glass – it's served rustic-style in glass tumblers, and it works. *Bookings not accepted. Disabled: toilet. No smoking.* **Map 19 B3**.

Westbourne Grove W11

202

Nicole Farhi, 202 Westbourne Grove, W11 2RH (7727 2722). Notting Hill Gate tube. **Open** 10am-6pm Mon, Sun; 8.30am-6pm Tue-Sat. **Main courses** £5.50-£12.50. **Licensed**. **Service** 12.5%. **Credit** AmEx, DC, JCB, MC, V.

A surprising combination of the industrial and the rustic in a clothes shop, 202 is where the beautiful people of Westbourne Grove go for brunch. Simple wooden tables and chairs nestle against huge, exposed silver vents and a glass and chrome bar, while smartly aproned waiters glide around smoothly. There's also a small garden and a few outside tables. Food is high class and on the pricey side. From the Sunday brunch menu, we enjoyed a seriously good salad of warm goat's cheese with prosciutto, figs, toasted pistachios and rocket, and a flawless grilled rump steak with potato hash, finishing with lovely rhubarb tart and apple crumble from the specials board. Popular with well-heeled families, this is a stylish place to stop (and shop). The fact it's licensed helps the mood.

Babies and children welcome. Bookings not accepted. No smoking. Tables outdoors (14, pavement). **Map 7 A6**.

Tom's Delicatessen

226 Westbourne Grove, W11 2RH (7221 8818). Notting Hill Gate tube. **Open** 8am-7pm Mon-Sat; 9am-5pm Sun. **Main courses** £6.95-£9.75. **Unlicensed**. **Credit** MC, V.

It's hard not to be charmed by the beautifully packaged sweets and goodies from all over the world that welcome you at the entrance of this small café/deli. Nostalgic posters celebrate foodie design classics such as HP sauce, and traditional marble café tables combine with 1930s lampshades and pretty paintwork to create a stylish, retro feel. Be prepared to wait for a table and expect to share it – so much charm in such cramped surroundings makes this a very popular destination for tourists as well as shoppers and locals. Tom's legendary eggs benedict/florentine are lovingly prepared with real hollandaise and perfectly poached eggs, and the US diner-influenced menu offers elaborate toasted sandwiches, salads and breakfasts, plus good cakes and freshly squeezed juices. There are also classy takeaway sandwiches, and lots of tempting treats in the deli.

Babies and children welcome. No smoking. Tables outdoors (4, garden; 2, terrace). Takeaway service (daytime). **Map 7 A6**.

Maida Vale W9

Raoul's

13 Clifton Road, W9 1SZ (7289 7313). Warwick Avenue tube/6 bus. **Open** 8.30am-10.15pm Mon-Sat; 9am-10pm Sun. **Main courses** £8.50-£15. **Minimum** £3.95. **Licensed**. **Credit** AmEx, MC, V.

Chic Maida Vale favourite Raoul's draws an international crowd. The feel is stylish, with 1930s-inspired decor, brown leather banquettes and lots of mirrors. In summer, pavement tables catch the sun and look very inviting. The daytime menu offers a vast range of breakfasts, sandwiches and snacks, including kippers, bagels, fry-ups and salads, as well as smoothies, while in the evening there's a smaller menu of steaks, burgers and a few specials. A chorizo sandwich came with lots of rocket and very tasty sausage; eggs benedict was fine, if not notable. Good coffee and cakes, along with speedy service, make this a classic European-style café. The recently expanded and refurbished deli across the street sells lots of delicious things to take away, plus good coffee, fresh juices and fine pastries to eat at the few tables out front or in the cute enclosed garden at the back.

Babies and children welcome; high chairs. No-smoking tables. Tables outdoors (13, pavement & patio). Takeaway service (until 6pm). **Map 2 D4**.

Shepherd's Bush W12

Bush Garden Café NEW

2004 RUNNER-UP BEST FAMILY RESTAURANT
59 Goldhawk Road, W12 8EG (8743 6372). Goldhawk Road tube. **Open** 8am-6pm Mon-Sat; 9am-2pm Sun. **Main courses** £4-£5. **Licensed**. **Credit** AmEx, MC, V.

Just walking into this amiably staffed, attractive wholefood café and grocery makes your tummy rumble. With its shelves of organic pastas, sauces, wines and treats and chilled counter full of bright salads, quiches, pies and pastries, it's always time for lunch. There's plenty of space for children, especially out in the garden with its playhouse and rainproof canopy. Indoors, the white tongue-and-groove walls and mismatched furniture exude a busy household air. The food is cooked with enormous flair. A simple carrot and coriander soup was a warming dose of colour and spice; chicken and sweet potato broth was even more satisfying. Salads are laden with quality items at very ordinary prices. The children's menu offers nursery food such as beans or eggs on toast, with organic chocolate or cake for afters.

Babies and children welcome: children's menu; high chairs; toys. No smoking. Tables outdoors (6, garden). Takeaway service. Vegetarian menu. **Map 20 B2**.

South

Battersea SW11

Boiled Egg & Soldiers

63 Northcote Road, SW11 1NP (7223 4894). Clapham Junction rail. **Open** 9am-6pm Mon-Sat; 9am-4pm Sun. **Main courses** £4.95-£9.95. **Licensed. No credit cards.**

This café on family-friendly Northcote Road is a promising breakfast spot: a huge menu boasts everything from healthy morning treats to stodgy hangover fare, complete with hair-of-the-dog cocktails. The simple, primary-coloured decor is reminiscent of Ikea's kiddie-room department, while the few outside tables are perfectly positioned for sunny days. Combos include the 'posh breakfast' of smoked salmon and a glass of bubbly, full fry-ups, variations on the boiled egg and soldiers theme, plus classics such as cucumber sandwiches and Marmite on toast. Freshly squeezed orange juice is standard and the menu promises quality, but we were a bit disappointed with airline-style scrambled eggs and soggy toast, although a steak sandwich was fine. It's a popular place and great for kids – next time, though, we'll go for the Battersea cream tea instead of eggs. *Babies and children welcome; children's menu; high chairs. Tables outdoors (3, pavement; 8, garden). Takeaway service.* **Map 21 C4**.

Waterloo SE1

Festival Square

Ground floor, Royal Festival Hall, South Bank Centre, SE1 8XX (7928 2228/www.digby trout.co.uk). Embankment tube/Charing Cross or Waterloo tube/rail. **Open** 9am-10pm Mon-Fri; 11.30am-10pm Sat; 11.30am-9pm Sun. **Main courses** £7.95-£9.95. **Set meal** (11.30am-4pm, 7.30-9pm) £10 2 courses. **Licensed**. **Credit** AmEx, MC, V.

Considering the paucity of decent dining options on the South Bank, this sleek café-bar (run by Digby Trout) on the south side of the Royal Festival Hall is an asset. Or, at least, its location is – and the generous outside seating area is the perfect drinking spot for culture-goers in warmer weather. A shame, then, that the food is so disappointing. The menu offers mains such as grilled squid with couscous, penne with roast tomatoes and pesto, and cold poached salmon with (undercooked) mustardy potato salad. There are also 'bites' priced by quantity (£2.75 each, three for £6.95, six for £13.25): a useful device, though the results are mediocre, with supermarket-standard houmous, lacklustre chips and a weird-tasting goat's cheese pâté. Note that the good-value set dinner (£10 for two courses) doesn't operate until 7.30pm despite the menu clearly saying 7pm, an irritating error for which our offhand waiter was barely apologetic. The café will remain open while the RFH undergoes renovations from 2005. *Babies and children welcome; high chairs. Booking advisable. Disabled: toilet. No-smoking tables. Tables outdoors (60, terrace). Takeaway service.* **Map 10 M8**.

South East

London Bridge & Borough SE1

★ Konditor & Cook

10 Stoney Street, SE1 9AD (7407 5100). London Bridge tube/rail. **Open** 7.30am-6pm Mon-Fri; 8.30am-4pm Sat. **Main courses** £2.10-£4.75. **Unlicensed. Credit** AmEx, MC, V.

This is one of our favourite mini chains. The inside is minimalist, with bare floorboards, bench seating, and tables outside in good weather. Staff are professional rather than chatty. Sandwiches, in a variety of imaginative combos (including veggie and vegan), are great value at around £2.75. Tandoori chicken with leaves and cucumber on granary bread was moist and fresh, with properly marinated chicken. Bacon, onion and gruyère tart was also spot on. Other hot dishes include soups,

On the Town

Bush Garden Café. See p303.

pizzas, vegetarian tagine and kedgeree. Even the drinks are well thought-out, including coffees, smoothies and juices from the Innocent range, plus organic fizzy juices. Whatever you do, save room for something sweet: K&C's cakes, tarts and biscuits are deservedly legendary. Brownies, treacle tarts, raspberry and coconut slices, and Curly Whirly (chocolate and vanilla) cake – all have gone straight to our hips recently (dieters beware). Trust us, whatever you choose, you won't be disappointed.
Babies and children admitted. Tables outdoors (2, pavement). Takeaway service. **Map 11 P8. For branches see index.**

Shoreditch E2

★ Frizzante@City Farm NEW

2004 WINNER BEST FAMILY RESTAURANT
Hackney City Farm, 1A Goldsmith's Row, E2 8QA (7739 2266/www.frizzanteltd.co.uk). Liverpool Street tube then 26, 48 bus. **Open** 10am-4.30pm Tue-Fri; 10am-5.30pm Sat, Sun. **Main courses** £5-£7. **Unlicensed. Corkage** no charge. **No credit cards.**
Sensitive souls may hesitate to order the grilled chicken skewers out of respect for the Afro-feathered bantams pecking around outside Hackney City Farm's delightful Italian café. Be assured they are delicious, as was everything else we sampled on the frequently changing menu. Location is all, of course, especially when you've brought a young family for lunch, and this place has built-in baaing, lowing, clucking and grunting entertainment, as well as a tiny slide in the garden

by the outdoor eating area. From the frantic farmhouse kitchen come all-day breakfasts (free-range eggs as standard) or light-lunch choices, such as pumpkin and spinach pie, salad niçoise, spaghetti with mussels, chicken skewers with golden fried potatoes, and glorious own-made gnocchi with mushroom sauce. The ultra-thin kids' pizzas have a bubbling topping of mozzarella and tomato sauce, and the own-made pesto or tomato sauce served with the pasta is delicious. A great place to know about, especially if you have kids.
Babies and children welcome: children's menu; high chairs; toys. Bookings not accepted Sun. Disabled: toilet. No smoking. Separate room for parties, seats 40. Tables outdoors (8, garden). Takeaway service. Vegetarian menu. Vegan dishes. **Map 6 S3.**

Jones Dairy Café

23 Ezra Street, E2 7RH (7739 5372). Bethnal Green tube/26, 48, 55, 149, 243 bus. **Open** 9am-3pm Fri, Sat; 8am-3pm Sun. **Main courses** £2-£5. **Unlicensed. No credit cards.**
On Sunday mornings, when the Columbia Road Flower Market is in full bloom, this adorable little operation gets overrun by green-fingered locals well aware that it has the best bread in the area and the finest bagels this side of Brick Lane. On Fridays and Saturdays, though, it's a far more sedate operation, dishing up daisy-fresh brunches to in-the-know locals sat around a large farmhouse table or, in summer, on the peaceful street outside. The menu is tiny, but you can't really go wrong with any of it: kippers, quiche, an omelette or two, usually some soup. The coffee is excellent too, and if you can avoid filling yourself up on the breads (easier said than done), you'd be a fool not to try the cheesecake. A shop, tucked around the corner,

offers a wider range of breads, a worthwhile selection of cheeses and a small assortment of other picnic-friendly temptations.
Babies and children welcome; high chair. No smoking. Tables outdoors (2, pavement). Takeaway service. **Map 6 S3.**

Stoke Newington N16

Blue Legume

101 Stoke Newington Church Street, N16 0UD (7923 1303). Stoke Newington rail/73 bus. **Open** 9.30am-6.30pm daily. **Main courses** £4.95-£6.95. **Licensed. Credit** MC, V.
The prettily mediterranean Blue Legume, replete with murals and no-smoking conservatory, has been going for a few years now (no mean feat in Stokey, where cafés come and go with more frequency than the 73 bus), and its appeal seems to be as strong as ever. This is doubtless due to a wide-ranging menu that offers a great choice of all-day breakfasts and mains for meat-eaters, veggies and vegans. The great-value counter dishes are what most people go for. Including the likes of spinach and feta lasagne, a range of galettes and a sumptuous (and huge) chickpea and tahini burger, these come with five salads that can also be bought on their own. But don't overlook the specials: own-made wild mushroom tortellini with sugar snap peas and olives in a sauce of fresh tomatoes, garlic, white wine and olive oil was fantastic. Or just while away an hour with a white cherry tart or chocolate muffin cheese cake and a ginger pressé, ice-cream berry smoothie or fresh apple juice – bliss.
Babies and children welcome; high chairs. Tables outdoors (4, pavement). Takeaway service. **Map 25 B1.**

Highgate N6

Café Mozart

17 Swains Lane, N6 6QX (8348 1384). Gospel Oak rail/214, C2, C11, C12 bus. **Open** 8am-10pm Mon-Fri; 9am-10pm Sat, Sun. **Main courses** £6.75-£12.50. **Licensed. Credit** MC, V.
Located near Parliament Hill Fields, charmingly old-fashioned Café Mozart holds its own against a clutch of cafés competing for the attention of well-heeled locals. Regulars come here for the Viennese pastries, hearty breakfasts, brasserie lunches and suppers. Mozart-related memorabilia enhance the wood-pannelled decor, while subdued classical music adds to the cosy, casual ambience. We enjoyed a wholesome goulash of spiced paprika vegetables studded with waxy potatoes and chunks of red pepper and carrots, mopping up the sauce (redolent of softened onions and spiced tomatoes) with a handy hunk of rye bread. Our gold star went to the mouth-watering puff pastry tart topped with chewy baked plums. Service is friendly and attentive. When the sun shines, sit outside and soak in the aroma of brewed coffee wafting out from the café.
Babies and children welcome; high chairs. Book dinner. No smoking inside. Tables outdoors (8, courtyard). Takeaway service.

Islington N1

★ Ottolenghi NEW

287 Upper Street, N1 2TZ (7288 1454). Angel tube or Highbury & Islington tube/rail. **Meals served** 8am-11pm Mon-Sat; 9am-7pm Sun. **Main courses** (lunch) £7-£11; (dinner) £11-£14.50. **Credit** MC, V.
Ottolenghi is the second branch of the busy Notting Hill deli/café of the same name. You could just order a takeaway, but then you'd miss out on the pristine, all-white modernist interior with its long communal dining tables and space-age chairs. Then there's the food. Choose from breakfast dishes (granola or pastries), cakes, sandwiches and other savouries, all made on the premises. The breads, created by renowned master baker Dan

Lepard, include focaccia, rye, huge grissini and an excellent sourdough. Among the marvellous French-style creations are rich and intensely flavoured lemon and mascarpone tarts with polenta crusts, or fruit tarts made on bases of packed crumble and almond cream. More substantial dishes (which change daily) could be loosely described as southern Mediterranean, using influences from Iran to Morocco. Stunningly displayed, they're a riot of colour and form. Roasted butternut squash is a vibrant orange, flecked with nigella seeds, chilli, and fresh tarragon. Rings of squid are curiously pink and served with fennel bulb, parsley and fennel seeds. Freshness and vibrancy of flavour are key. A great addition to Upper Street.
Babies and children welcome; high chairs. Booking advisable evening. No smoking. Takeaway service. **Map 5 O1.**
For branch see index.

North West

Kilburn NW6

★ **Baker & Spice** NEW
75 Salusbury Road, NW6 6NH (7604 3636/ www.bakerandspice.com). Queen's Park tube. **Open** 7am-8pm Mon-Fri; 7am-7pm Sat; 8.30am-5pm Sun. **Licensed. Credit** MC, V.
Every neighbourhood should have a branch of Baker & Spice. Primarily a bakery, delivering daily batches of boule de meule, rye, cholla or San Francisco sourdough, plus a range of irresistible

cakes and tartes, it also produces plats du jour, soups, salads and platefuls of assorted other goodies to be eaten in or taken away. There's an open kitchen at the back of the tiny shop and up to ten diners share space at a central wooden table laden with jars of own-made jams, marmalade, chutneys and an oversized arrangement of flowers. Staff are enthusiastic and helpful. The only drawback is that greed is bound to win over budget in the end (especially if you indulge in the rather pricey house wine).
Babies and children admitted. No smoking. Tables outdoors (3, pavement). Takeaway service. **Map 1 A2.**
For branches see index.

St John's Wood NW8

Maison Blanc
37 St John's Wood High Street, NW8 7NG (7586 1982/www.maisonblanc.co.uk). St John's Wood tube. **Open** 8am-7pm Mon-Sat; 9am-6.30pm Sun. **Main courses** £5-£8. **Unlicensed. Credit** MC, V.
Modern, light and cheery, this bakery-pâtisserie is an informal meeting place, suited to young families as well as the overwhelmingly wealthy local residents and shoppers that make up the neighbourhood. Glass shelves boast jars of confiture, chocolates and bagged biscuits, while substantial snacks, inspired by French classics, are crammed with tasty flavour combinations. Thumbs-up to a fresh-tasting filling of chicken breast, roasted mushrooms, basil and onion. Tarts,

sandwiches and a soup of the day also provide sustenance, although standards of preparation aren't always top notch. We absolutely loved the chocolate éclairs and light-textured St Michel cheesecakes topped with glazed blackcurrants, but were left rather unimpressed with the 'extreme' chocolate mousse cake, which was let down by over-whipped cream. Service is good-natured, and the atmosphere laid-back.
Babies and children welcome; high chairs. No smoking. Takeaway service. **Map 2 E2.**
For branches see index.

Swiss Cottage NW3

Camden Arts Centre NEW
Corner of Arkwright Road & Finchley Road, NW3 6DG (7472 5516/www.camdenarts centre.org). Finchley Road tube/Finchley Road & Frognal rail. **Meals served** 10am-5.30pm Tue, Thur-Sun; 10am-8.30pm Wed. **Main courses** £2.95-£5.95. **Credit** MC, V.
Camden Arts Centre has recently surfaced after a £4 million refit and is all spare walls and sharp planes, tricked out in fashionable materials. The café, which fills a corner of the ground floor and spills out into a garden, is nicely soothing. For the menu, think sandwiches and well-priced platters of fresh mezze or a daily special such as plump, juicy salmon and dill fish cakes. There are plates of Italian cold cuts or French cheeses from La Fromagerie – £6.50 each with a glass of wine or beer – toast with marmite, and Kit-Kats. To drink, there's wine, cold beers and good coffee. Add to

---

Hotel teas

For a quintessential English experience, head to one of London's posher hotels to indulge in the ritual of a formal afternoon tea. It can be an expensive business, and you'll have to dress smartly, but when everything is as it should be – fresh and interesting sandwiches, hot crumpets, rivers of refreshing teas, and extravagant cakes – this is a great way to spend an afternoon. Just don't expect to want any supper, and book well in advance.

If you just want tea without the fancy cakes, **Fortnum & Mason** has a Rare Tea Bar on the mezzanine level above the main shopfloor, round to the left. There's an outstanding selection of rare teas to try – Sri Lankan, Indian, Chinese, even Nepalese, at £5.95 per pot. Cheaper blends cost from £2.75. It's a good place to rest your feet and try out a brew before making a purchase of a smartly packaged tin of the stuff downstairs.

Basil Street Hotel
8 Basil Street, SW3 1AH (7581 3311/www.thebasil.com). Knightsbridge tube. **Tea served** 3.30-5.30pm daily. **Set teas** £10.50-£16.50. **Credit** AmEx, DC, MC, V.
Babies and children admitted. No-smoking tables. **Map 8 F9.**

Claridge's
Brook Street, W1K 4HA (7629 8860/www.claridges.co.uk). Bond Street tube. **Tea served** 3-5.30pm daily. **Set teas** £30.25; £38.50 incl glass of champagne. **Cover** (if not taking set tea) £3. **Service** 10%. **Credit** AmEx, DC, MC, V.
Babies and children welcome; high chairs. Disabled: toilet. Entertainment: musicians 3-6pm daily. **Map 9 H6.**

The Connaught
16 Carlos Place, W1K 2AL (7499 7070/www.the-savoy-group.com). Green Park tube. **Tea served** 3-5.30pm daily. **Set teas** £18-£24; £30 with glass of champagne. **Credit** AmEx, JCB, MC, V.
Babies and children welcome; high chairs. **Map 9 H7.**

The Dorchester
53 Park Lane, W1A 2HJ (7629 8888/www.dorchesterhotel. com). Hyde Park Corner tube. **Tea served** 3-6pm, **high tea served** 3-8pm daily. **Set teas** £23.50; £29.50 incl glass of champagne; £32 high tea. **Credit** AmEx, DC, JCB, MC, V.
Babies and children welcome; high chairs. Disabled: toilet. Entertainment: pianist 3-11pm Mon-Sat; 3-7pm Sun. **Map 9 G7.**

Fortnum & Mason
181 Piccadilly, W1A 1ER (7734 8040). Green Park or Piccadilly Circus tube. **Tea served** 10am-5.30pm Mon; 3-5.30pm Tue-Sat; noon-5pm Sun. **Set teas** £19.50; £21.50 high tea.

Minimum £19.50. **Service** 12.5%. **Credit** AmEx, DC, JCB, MC, V.
Babies and children welcome; high chairs. Disabled: lift; toilet. Dress: smart casual; no shorts. **Map 17 J7.**

The Lanesborough Hotel
Hyde Park Corner, SW1X 7TA (7259 5599/www.lanes borough.com). Hyde Park Corner tube. **Tea served** 3.30-6pm Mon-Sat; 4-6pm Sun. **Set teas** £26-£34. **Minimum** £9.50. **Credit** AmEx, DC, MC, V.
Babies and children welcome; high chairs. Disabled: toilet. **Map 9 G8.**

Le Meridien Piccadilly
21 Piccadilly, W1J 0BH (7734 8000/www.lemeridien.com). Piccadilly Circus tube. **Tea served** 3-6pm daily. **Set teas** £12.50; £25; £30 incl glass of champagne. **Minimum** £12.50. **Credit** AmEx, DC, JCB, MC, V.
Babies and children admitted. Booking advisable. Disabled: lift; toilet. **Map 17 J7.**

Le Meridien Waldorf
Aldwych, WC2B 4DD (7836 2400/www.lemeridien.com). Covent Garden tube. **Tea served** 3-6pm daily. **Set teas** £14.95; £19.95 incl glass of champagne. **Credit** AmEx, DC, MC, V.
Babies and children welcome; high chairs. Disabled: toilet. **Map 18 M6.**

The Ritz
150 Piccadilly, W1J 9BR (7493 8181/www.theritzhotel.co.uk).

Green Park tube. **Tea served** (reserved sittings) 1.30pm, 3.30pm, 5.30pm daily. **Set tea** £32. **Credit** AmEx, MC, V.
Babies and children welcome; high chairs. Disabled: toilet. Booking essential. Dress: jacket and tie; no jeans or trainers. **Map 9 J7.**

The Savoy
Strand, WC2R 0EU (7836 4343/www.the-savoy.com). Covent Garden or Embankment tube/Charing Cross tube/rail. **Tea served** 2.30-5.30pm Mon-Thur; 2-6pm Fri-Sun. **Set teas** (Mon-Fri) £24; (Sat, Sun) £27. **Credit** AmEx, DC, JCB, MC, V.
Babies and children welcome; high chairs. **Map 18 L7.**

Spoon+ at Sanderson
50 Berners Street, W1T 3NG (7300 1444/www.spoon-restaurant.com). Oxford Circus or Tottenham Court Road tube. **Tea served** 3-5pm daily. **Set teas** £19.50; £25 incl glass of champagne. **Service** 15%. **Credit** AmEx, DC, MC, V.
Babies and children admitted; high chairs. Booking advisable. Disabled: toilet. **Map 17 J5.**

Threadneedles
5 Threadneedle Street, EC2R 8AY (7657 8080). Bank tube/DLR. **Tea served** 3-5.30pm Mon-Fri. **Set teas** £21.50-£29. **Service** 12.5%. **Credit** AmEx, MC, V.
Booking advisable. Disabled: toilet. Dress: smart casual. **Map 12 Q6.**

that upmarket newspapers and magazines, plus some art books, and you have a hangout in which to calmly while away the day.
Babies and children welcome; children's menu; high chairs. Disabled: toilet. No smoking. Tables outdoors (5, garden). Takeaway service. **Map 28 B2**.

Outer London
Kew, Surrey

Kew Greenhouse
1 Station Parade, Kew, Surrey TW9 3PS (8940 0183). Kew Gardens tube/rail. **Open** 9am-6.30pm Mon-Fri; 9-7.30pm Sat, Sun. **Main courses** £6-£7.50. **Licensed. No credit cards.**
A popular spot with daytrippers to Kew Gardens as well as locals, this is a delightfully old-fashioned café near Kew Gardens station. There's plenty of seating on the pavement outside, while the airy interior, all green and white, resembles a National Trust tea room, with a foliage-packed conservatory at the rear. To eat, there's quiche, salads, toasted sarnies and sturdy meals of the pie variety (shepherd's, steak), plus scones, pastries, huge cakes and ice-creams from Marine Ices. Prices are on the high side: £1.40 for a regular coffee, £7.75 for steak pie and salad. Greenhouse pie contained roasted celeriac, sweet potatoes and parsnips with butter beans and dahl inside a lattice pastry case (both vegetables and pastry were a bit tough), accompanied by a few cold potatoes and a dull salad of kidney beans and diced carrots. Disappointing; better to stick to a drink and one of the luscious-looking cakes.
Babies and children admitted; high chairs. No-smoking tables. Tables outdoors (25, piazza). Vegetarian menu.

PARK CAFÉS

At the time of writing, **Oshobasho** café in Highgate Woods was temporarily closed for an unspecified period; we hope it reopens soon. For upmarket dining in bucolic surroundings, there's newcomer **Inn the Park** (*see p45*) in the middle of St James's Park.

West
Chiswick W4

Burlington's Café
Chiswick House, off Burlington Lane, W4 2RP (8987 9431). Turnham Green tube/Chiswick rail. **Open** *Apr-Oct* 10am-5pm daily. *Nov-Mar* 10am-4pm Wed-Sun. **Main courses** £2.50-£6.50. **No credit cards.**
In stark contrast to the grandeur of Chiswick House, Lord Burlington's Palladian masterpiece, the café in the house's grounds is set in a rather run-down pavilion. Where lichen and peeling paintwork hold a certain charm in the sculpted and landscaped gardens, the café just feels a bit dingy. Brown plastic chairs and floral print plastic tablecloths don't lift the mood. The food is simple: full English breakfasts, bacon rolls, sarnies and a few pasta dishes. Toasted wholemeal ciabatta with chicken and avocado was enjoyable, while very large slices of fresh cakes looked appealing. Burlington's also offers lollies, ice-creams and free dog biscuits. Parents can chat over a coffee knowing the kids are playing safely on the green in front of the café.
Babies and children welcome; children's menu; high chairs. Disabled: toilet. No smoking. Tables outdoors (15, patio). Takeaway service.

Kensington W8

The Orangery
Kensington Palace, Kensington Gardens, W8 4PX (7376 0239). High Street Kensington or Queensway tube. **Open** *Mar-Oct* 10am-6pm daily. *Nov-Feb* 10am-5pm daily. **Main courses** £5.95-£10.95. **Set teas** £6.75-£14.75. **Credit** MC, V.

Afternoon tea at the Orangery in Kensington Gardens is a civilised affair. Fresh flowers and neatly trained citrus trees soften the vast, white and otherwise imposing interior of Corinthian pillars, stone garlands and Grecian statues. A Garden Party tea consisted of delicate little cream cheese and cucumber sandwiches, and a fruit scone with jam and clotted cream from an enormous pile displayed enticingly near the entrance. Orangery cake was a delicious citrus iced sponge (not one for the calorie-conscious but very refined). For lunch, expect potted shrimp and smoked salmon, along with some traditional English hot dishes. Unfortunately, our visit was spoiled by a rude manager, and a 40-minute wait while tables sat uncleared and the whole staff focused on a pre-booked party of tourists. Once inside, however, the service was impeccable.
Babies and children welcome; children's menu; high chairs. Disabled: toilet (in Palace). No smoking. **Map 7 C8**.

South West
Wandsworth SW18

Common Ground
Wandsworth Common, off Dorlcote Road, SW18 3RT (8874 9386). Wandsworth Common rail. **Open** *Summer* 9.30am-6.30pm daily. *Winter* 9am-6pm daily. **Main courses** £3.50-£9. **Credit** MC, V.
Common Ground is not cheap, but it's popular – and for good reason. There's a considerable choice of breakfasts (continental and English), jacket potatoes, sandwiches made with the freshest bread, melts and a few choice mains. The selection of cakes is mind-boggling and not to be missed. Salmon and dill tart of the day came with a large plate of mediterranean salad (£3 extra), while a chicken salad sandwich was packed with rocket, delicately flavoured with lemon, and was prepared to order. The café is quietly child-friendly, with a kids' menu and plenty of room for buggies and high chairs. Among low leather sofas in the back room a corner is given over to a children's play area. The light, bright conservatory is the choice place to sit. A haunt of minor celebs and monster baby-buggies, common it ain't.
Babies and children welcome; children's menu; high chairs; nappy-changing facilities. No-smoking tables. Separate room for hire, seats 100. Tables outside (15, patio). Takeaway service.

South East
Dulwich SE21

Pavilion Café
Dulwich Park, SE21 7BQ (8299 1383). West Dulwich rail. **Open** *Summer* 9am-5.45pm daily. *Winter* 8.30am-dusk daily. **Main courses** £2.50-£6.50. **No credit cards.**
This cool, clean, welcoming space is just what you'd hope to find down Dulwich way. The glass-fronted pavilion, decorated with striking contemporary art (for sale) and large bunches of fresh flowers, can be opened up on hot days, with plenty of tables inside, though it's a bit of a squeeze outside. The café has a relaxing vibe even when busy. Sweets, lollies, ice-creams, English breakfasts and the usual sandwiches and cakes are available, but the Pavilion goes a step further than your average park café, with the likes of orange-blossom and ginger cake, and tender pork marinated with rosemary, served in flatbread with salad and apple and cinnamon sauce. Produce is free-range and locally sourced.
Babies and children welcome; children's menu; high chairs. Disabled: toilet. No smoking. Takeaway service.

Greenwich SE10

Pavilion Tea House **NEW**
Greenwich Park, Blackheath Gate, SE10 8QY (8858 9695). Greenwich DLR/rail/Blackheath rail. **Open** 9am-6pm Mon-Fri; 9am-7pm Sat, Sun. **Main courses** £2.50-£7.25. **Credit** MC, V.

Recently extensively refurbished, the Pavilion Tea House has been transformed into a wonderfully light, bright space, with fast, friendly service and a satisfyingly wide selection of good-quality dishes and snacks. Hot food includes breakfasts, grilled salmon, soups with crusty bread, and warm onion tart; a tuna niçoise salad made with seared tuna steak was enormous, and beautifully presented. Bread and butter pudding, sherry trifle and cream teas provide comfort. You can sit inside where the design is reminiscent of nearby Vanbrugh Castle, upstairs with a lovely view of the park through huge, partly stained-glass windows, or outside in the spacious garden next to the rose beds. Be warned, you'll have to work for your refreshments as the café sits next to the Royal Observatory on a very steep hill (though you can walk or drive in from the Blackheath end of the park). Don't forget to get your 'cup cake' loyalty card stamped and also fill in an evaluation card – for every one completed, a donation is made to the Royal Parks Education programme for local kids.
Babies and children welcome; high chairs. Disabled: toilet. No smoking. Tables outdoors (15, garden). Takeaway service.

North West
Golders Green NW3

Golders Hill Park Refreshment House
Off North End Road, NW3 7HD (8455 8010). Golders Green tube. **Open** 10am-6pm daily. **Main courses** £3-£7. **No credit cards.**
Always a choice spot for freshly made ice-cream, this Italian-run café was spruced up since last year. The menu is well presented, the glasshouse interior is bright and clean, service is patient and friendly, and there's a good selection of cakes and drinks. The savoury menu includes a long list of salads and pasta dishes, plus a kids' menu. The entrance to the service area is decorated with a selection of early 20th-century prints of the park and the surrounding area. Hanging baskets add to the lovely setting of the popular terrace – which is certainly what makes this café a great refreshment spot and a place to meet and to linger.
Babies and children welcome; high chairs. Disabled: toilet. Entertainment: jazz and folk Tue evenings; brass band 2.30-5pm Sun. No smoking. Tables outdoors (60, terrace). Takeaway service.

Hampstead NW3

Brew House
Kenwood, Hampstead Lane, NW3 7JR (8341 5384). Archway or Golders Green tube/210 bus. **Open** *Apr-Sept* 9am-6pm (7.30pm on concert nights) daily. *Oct-Mar* 9am-4pm daily. **Main courses** £2.95-£9.95. **Credit** MC, V.
The Brew House has a wonderful English country-garden feel; it's located in an old stable block of Kenwood House, with large outdoor tables set amid glorious flower beds and massed hanging baskets. Inside are high ceilings, lightly frescoed walls and quaint village-style signposts that point out the cake stand (as if you could miss the huge chunks of carrot cake, pineapple pavlova, scones, and gooseberry and nettle cheesecake) and guide you around the jam-packed service area. The food fits the theme perfectly, with an emphasis on locally sourced produce. Leek, chickpea and sage soup was served with hunks of fresh wholemeal bread; free-range pork, ginger and spring onion sausages with a delicious apricot and red onion chutney came with potatoes and lightly cooked veg. Efforts have been made to accommodate the many visitors, but be prepared to use your elbows. Beady-eyed, tray-laden visitors mill around on the lookout for an empty table, and do not encourage diners to linger.
Babies and children welcome; high chairs; nappy-changing facilities. Disabled: toilet. No smoking. Restaurant available for hire. Separate room for hire, seats 100. Tables outdoors (100, garden & terrace). Takeaway service. **Map 28 C1**.

Bars

Here we list the cream of the London bar scene. One old favourite, the **Shoreditch Electricity Showrooms** (39A Hoxton Square, N1 6NN; 7739 6934; map 6 R3) was under new management and facing a refit as we went to press. Some of the more interesting beers and cocktails had already been axed, but this has always been a winning venue, so let's hope any other changes are for the better. For more bar reviews, consult the latest edition of *Time Out Pubs & Bars* (£8.99). For pubs serving good food, *see* **Gastropubs**, starting on p90. For the best of London's unabashed boozers, *see* **Pubs**, starting on p315.

Central

Bloomsbury WC1

AKA

18 West Central Street, WC1A 1JJ (7836 0110/ www.akalondon.com). Holborn or Tottenham Court Road tube. **Open** 6pm-3am Tue-Fri; 7pm-5am Sat; 10pm-4am Sun. **Food served** 6pm-midnight Tue, Wed; 6pm-1am Thur, Fri; 7pm-1am Sat. **Main courses** £2.50-£10. **Admission** £3 after 11pm Tue; £5 after 10pm Thur; £5 after 9pm, £7 after 10pm Fri; £10 after 9pm Sat; varies Sun. **Credit** AmEx, DC, JCB, MC, V.
Well established but far from complacent, this pre- and post-club DJ bar (the End is next door) is one of the classiest yet least pretentious operations in town. Everything in its brazenly barren, two-floor industrial space (once a Victorian sorting office) is done with style and panache. The drinks – dispatched from a zinc counter running most of the long length of the downstairs space, dotted with curved-back seats and candlelit tables – are of sublime quality. The shooters are imaginative (a Highbury's Burning of layered absinthe and Goldslager Kummel set aflame), and the dozen champagne cocktails (under £10) and Martinis (£7) are of an equally high standard. The whisky menu (Tennessee, rye and bourbon selections) is impeccable, as are the bottled beer options (including Belgian Brugs and Grimbergen, and Russian Baltika); the food (salt and pepper squid in batter) is a cut above most. Oh yes, and 20 types of champagne, right up to a £195 Louis Roederer Cristal '95. Settled, sassy club nights (Underwater, Harlem Nights, The Players) are interspersed with private promotions – always phone ahead.
Bar available for hire. Disabled: toilet. Entertainment: DJs 10pm daily. Separate areas for hire, holding 10-100. **Map 18 L6**.

Covent Garden WC2

Detroit

35 Earlham Street, WC2H 9LD (7240 2662/ www.detroit-bar.com). Covent Garden or Leicester Square tube. **Open** 5pm-midnight Mon-Sat. **Dinner served** 5-10.30pm Mon-Sat. **Main courses** £9.75-£13.50. **Set meal** (5-8pm) £7 incl cocktail and bar snack. **Service** 12.5%. **Credit** AmEx, DC, MC, V.
Without pretence or price hikes, this sandy cavern of a bar has been offering discerning, trendy punters a superb, extensive range of cocktails for the best part of a boozy decade. The house speciality may be the Martini – more than a dozen of them at under £7 – but there are numerous alternatives to consider. While you do, a solid soundtrack of club sounds sweeps over you, wafting from the futuristic, imposing bar counter and creeping into the intimate low-lit alcoves at the back of the bear cave, allowing for both conversation and occasional head nods to the rhythm. Generous happy hours make cocktails inevitable, though avoidance is eased by an excellent selection of beers (Asahi, Duvel, Pilsner Urquell). Attempts at temperance can be assisted by zingy, fruity 'tails of the non-alcoholic variety. Tasty platters too.
Bar available for hire. Booking advisable. Dress: smart casual. Separate areas for hire, holding 40 and 80. **Map 18 L6**.

Lowlander

36 Drury Lane, WC2B 5RR (7379 7446/ www.lowlander.com). Covent Garden or Holborn tube. **Open** noon-11pm Mon-Sat; noon-10pm Sun. **Meals served** noon-10pm daily. **Main courses** £8.95-£12.95. **Snacks** £3.50-£6.75. **Set meal** £12.95 2 courses, £16.95 3 courses. **Credit** AmEx, MC, V.
Continental dining and Benelux brews still bring in parties of punters to this neatly logoed beer hall. Motifs of the dandy dozen draughts are cleverly displayed above an impressive phalanx of tall, shiny pumps that stand guard on the handsome bar counter. The two-score of bottled varieties range from the fruit-flavoured to the monastic, the wacky to the wheaty, outlined in deferential detail in a drinks menu that also bears the flying beer-froth house logo. Space is allowed for a more than adequate choice of wines and cocktails, while the food menu features hearty Belgian standards and well-known dishes of Dutch dairy provenance. Seek out the prix-fixe lunchtime deals if you can, when bar space is not at such a premium. By the evening, the closely stacked rows of communal tables will fill quickly, the attractive mezzanine enclave invariably booked weeks in advance. Service is snappy.
Babies and children admitted. Booking advisable. No-smoking tables. Separate room for hire, seats 27. Tables outdoors (5, pavement). **Map 18 L6**.

Edgware Road W2

★ Salt Whisky Bar **NEW**
2004 RUNNER-UP BEST BAR
82 Seymour Street, W2 2JB (7402 1155/www.salt bar.com). Marble Arch tube. **Open** noon-1am Mon-Sat; noon-midnight Sun. **Lunch served** noon-3pm Mon-Sat; noon-3pm Sun. **Dinner served** 6-10.30pm Mon-Sat. **Main courses** £7.50-£8.95. **Service** 12.5%. **Credit** AmEx, MC, V.
Until this year, Edgware Road (aka Little Beirut) was always somewhere you went for a late-night shwarma sandwich and a hit of bitter Arabic coffee. Since the arrival of modish style bar Salt, it's now the place for some of the capital's best whisky cocktails. It's a looker, with wood and dark leather banquettes and an accommodatingly shaped bar counter with a top fashioned from underlit perspex.

Salt Whisky Bar

On the Town

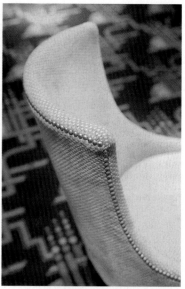

American Bar.
See p310.

But, of course, the main attraction is the back shelves racked with whisky galore; not just Scottish but Irish whiskeys, American rye, bourbon and Tennessee whiskeys, and even some bottles of the Japanese stuff, just for the hell of it. Connoisseurs will have a field day (especially if they have a spare £12,000 for a bottle of 1937 Glenfiddich), but novices can have fun with the cocktails, particularly the signature selection that includes odd ingredients such as plums, ginseng and maple syrup. For non-whisky drinkers there are also Daquiris, Bellinis, Martinis, champagne cocktails and a kaleidoscope of other spirits.
Babies and children welcome. Entertainment: DJs 8pm daily. Separate room for hire, seats 40-60. Tables outdoors (5, terrace). Map 8 F6.

Fitzrovia W1

★ Hakkasan

8 Hanway Place, W1T 1HD (7907 1888). Tottenham Court Road tube.
Bar **Open** noon-12.30am Mon-Wed; noon-1.30am Thur-Sat; noon-midnight Sun.
Restaurant **Lunch served** noon-3.15pm Mon-Fri; noon-4.30pm Sat, Sun. **Dinner served** 6-11.30pm Mon-Wed, Sun; 6pm-12.30am Thur-Sat. **Dim sum** £3.50-£16. **Main courses** £11.50-£40.
Both **Service** 13%. **Credit** AmEx, MC, V.

One of London's best non-members cocktail bars, Hakkasan can be picked out from the seedy gloom of its back alley dogleg location by cobalt-blue street signs, presumably there to help the last five taxi drivers on the planet unaware of its presence. An incense-scented staircase leads down to an impossibly polite reception, where you're gestured past a sumptuous and very highly regarded Chinese restaurant (*see p56*) to the cocktail counter, separated by a wooden partition whose slats throw odd shadows over the back bar. Despite the narrow space twixt counter and divide, everything has the calm efficiency of first-class travel by an award-winning Asian airline. All cocktails cost £8, plus 13 per cent, and once one arrives you wonder why you ever spent more than £9.04 on a cocktail anywhere else. Ginger, coriander, kumquat, lemongrass, nashi pears and rose-petal syrup fuse sublimely with Ketel, Matusalem, rice wines and ginseng spirits, from a simple four-column list of 40 champagne cocktails, Martinis, long drinks and short drinks. Snacks don't sully the experience; six sakés, hot or cold, just might heighten it. Oh yes, and there's one beer, Japan's Yebisu, at £4.50 a bottle.
Booking advisable; essential dinner. Disabled: toilet. Dress: smart casual. Entertainment: DJ 9pm daily. Restaurant available for hire. Separate area for hire, seats 65. Map 17 K5.

Long Bar

Sanderson Hotel, 50 Berners Street, W1P 3AB (7300 1400). Oxford Circus or Tottenham Court Road tube. **Open** noon-12.30am Mon-Sat; noon-10.30pm Sun. **Meals served** noon-11.30pm Mon-Sat; noon-10pm Sun. **Dim sum** £3-£25. **Service** 12.5%. **Credit** AmEx, DC, MC, V.
On the surface, little has changed at the Long Bar since its spectacular arrival as part of the Starck-inspired Sanderson Hotel. The Dali-esque eyeball seatbacks counterpoint the long, oblong island bar counter of silver, white and glass, while billowy curtains part to reveal the occasional dog portrait and a Japanese water garden of rare tranquillity. And the cocktails remain pricey (£9-£11) and praiseworthy. Highballs, champagne cocktails and Martinis: they're all a marvellous mixture of high-end, fresh ingredients, not least the Wyborowa lemon, Polstar cucumber and apple juice in the Sanderson, mixed with freshly crushed grapes and brown sugar. Creams, Chambords and champers are all taken and shaken with classic aplomb. Scratch the surface, though (metaphorically, of course) and you might find that the more 'interesting' celebs have moved on, perhaps discouraged by the disadvantages of an open-door policy at an establishment of such quality. The very decor itself, if not dated, seems dimmed by

Starck's delicious adjoining lobby. And staff-client banter is functional, very nearly curt. Right now, how many of us mere mortals are thinking: 'So long, Long Bar'?

Babies and children welcome (terrace); high chairs. Bookings not accepted. Disabled: toilet. Entertainment: DJs 7pm-12.30am Wed-Fri. Tables outdoors (20, terrace). Map 17 J5.

Market Place

11 Market Place, W1W 8AH (7079 2020/ www.marketplace-london.com). Oxford Circus tube. **Open/food served** 11am-midnight Mon-Wed; 11am-1am Thur-Sat; 1-10.30pm Sun. **Tapas** £2.50-£5.50. **Admission** £7 after 11pm Fri; £3 8-11pm, £7 after 11pm Sat. **Credit** AmEx, MC, V.
Of the small cluster of fashionable, funky spots forming a tentative scene behind Oxford Circus, the Market Place is the least distinctive, but would stand head-and-shoulders over the competition in most other pockets of the West End. Even if the jokey slogans branded on the wooden decor grate more than a little, there's no doubting the quality of the fare here – it is, after all, one of the Cantaloupe Group, also owners of Cargo and the Cantaloupe (*see p195*) itself. Drink options are varied: the bottled beers list features Mexican Dos Equis beer or litre bottles of Cruzcampo, plus Morland's Old Specked Hen; Erdinger Weissbier and Budvar are on draught. A decent Rioja will set you back £17, and the shooters and cocktails are regularly augmented, recently by a bloodbath shot of Sauza Hornitos tequila and crème de fraise, and a Sazerac 'tail of Buffalo Trace bourbon, Rémy Martin and a hint of absinthe. Distinctive flavours of the Med, the Middle East and Latin America inform an eclectic all-day food selection of platters and casseroles. Downstairs has a bar that hosts regular DJ happenings.
Bookings not accepted. Disabled: toilet. Entertainment: DJs 8pm daily. Tables outdoors (8, terrace). Map 9 J6.

Nordic

25 Newman Street, W1T 1PN (7631 3174/ www.nordicbar.com). Tottenham Court Road tube. **Open** noon-11pm Mon-Fri; 6-11pm Sat. **Lunch served** noon-3pm Mon-Fri. **Snacks served** 5.30-10pm Mon-Sat. **Main courses** £6.25-£7.95. **Service** 12.5%. **Credit** AmEx, MC, V.
Nordic is the successful offspring of a dedicated young management team, which picked up on the neat idea of a Scandinavian theme bar, ran with it, and are now making a tidy living out of private parties while allowing the rather splendid basement bar to run itself. The lounge is accessed from an alleyway off Percy Street, and is dominated by a mural triptych of Max von Sydow necking Akvavit; the dining area (accessed from a staircase in Newman Street) sports arty photos of obscure Scandinavians and racks of tourist brochures. Between them stands a bustling, narrow bar counter. The key is the drinks menu: an excellent range of vodkas (six flavours of Icelandic Polstar and Norwegian Christiania), draught Danish Faxe and Red Erik beers, bottled Swedish Crocodile and Finnish Lapin Kulta beers, plus Swedish Kopparbergs cider. There's also a fun selection of shooters and cocktails (Lapp Dancer, Dyslexic Tobogganist) that use high-end vodkas and schnapps. An authentic smörgåsbord of 30 small dishes can be ordered in all kinds of combinations. Skol!
Booking advisable. Separate room for parties, seats 50. Map 17 J5.

★ The Social

5 Little Portland Street, W1W 7JD (7636 4992/ www.thesocial.com). Oxford Circus tube. **Open/food served** noon-11pm Mon, Tue; noon-midnight Wed-Fri; 1pm-midnight Sat. **Snacks** £3.30-£6.20. **Credit** AmEx, MC, V.
The formula for this bar has become so successful that it has spawned imitators as far away as Bondi Beach. But for the time being, the Social has got to be one of the few venues in London where you can order a bottle of Bollinger to accompany your spaghetti hoops on toast. By day, the small street-level bar plays student caff, with Heinz and HP bottles plonked on each of its five rounded booth

tables (square pies are a speciality, plus comfort food such as fishfinger sarnies). But it's not just about grub for apprentice gasfitters. A varied range of drinks includes fairly priced cocktails (such as a Social of Frangelico hazelnut and Teichenne butterscotch schnapps), threefer shooters and unusual beers (Estonian A Le Coq) to complement the standard draughts. An array of classic New York punk photos on the walls (the exhibition changes but music photography is normally the key) and a Heavenly Jukebox hint at a high standard of music appreciation, and lo! come evening, the one-time *Time Out* DJ Bar of the Year kicks in downstairs. Hip but not hurting; accept no substitutes.
Babies and children admitted (until 5pm). Entertainment: DJs Mon-Sat; occasional bands Mon; £4). Map 9 J5.

Knightsbridge SW1

★ Blue Bar

The Berkeley, Wilton Place, SW1X 7RL (7235 6000/www.the-berkeley.co.uk). Hyde Park Corner tube. **Open/meals served** 4pm-1am Mon-Sat. **Tapas** £5.50. **Service** 12.5%. **Credit** AmEx, DC, JCB, MC, V.
One of the best and most stylish hotel bars in town, the Berkeley's Blue Bar is tucked away to the left of the lobby as you walk through the modest main entrance, itself tucked away in an elegant off-Knightsbridge passage. The original Lutyens interior has been exquisitely transformed into a three-space lounge for classy relaxation, in which clusters of cool leather armchairs are surrounded by periwinkle-blue walls, with touches of stucco and decorative hints of another era. Manning the narrow bar counter are staff of the type who wear starched white, alert to your wishes while blending in perfectly with the tableau. Like good referees, you don't notice them until they're needed. Average cocktail prices sit in the two-figure bracket, but your cooler, cocktail classic or Martini will come with its own leather coaster and a cotton napkin, just in case the complimentary honey-coated nuts or marinated olives the size of practice rugby balls demand a delicate dab of the lip. Paid-for snacks are categorised into 'modern' and 'sweet', and are basically a mix of Thai and tapas.
Bookings not accepted. Disabled: toilet. Map 9 G9.

Mandarin Bar

Mandarin Oriental Hyde Park, 66 Knightsbridge, SW1X 7LA (7235 2000/www.mandarin oriental.com). Knightsbridge tube. **Open** 11am-2am Mon-Sat; 11am-10.30pm Sun. **Food served** 11am-11.30pm Mon-Sat; 11am-10.30pm Sun. **Snacks** £7-£13. **Admission** £5 after 11pm daily. **Credit** AmEx, DC, MC, V.
Imaginatively conceived by Hungaro-American design guru Adam Tihany, this destination hotel bar attracts a cosmopolitan, moneyed clientele otherwise jaded with the everyday chintz of the world's capitals. Even three years after its inception, coinciding with the complete overhaul of this luxury Knightsbridge hotel a century after its foundation, the Mandarin still feels fresh. Come here every day for a month and you'll still find surprises in its drinks menu, as cool and comprehensive as any in London. Along with the cocktail list, there are any number of vodkas, whiskies and liqueurs, even beers – far too many for such a modest four-square bar counter to contain. It's all done with mirrors. No spirit bottles, shakers or shake-makers, no rehearsed twirl of cocktail jug sully the open space around the counter area; instead, everything is mixed behind a coloured back-lit glass partition, and presented – voilà! – with gusto and a genuine smile to your small, brown marble table. Arrive early if you want to grab one of two secluded seating niches. If there are no spare seats (the staff can bring one if space allows), it'll be an undignified two-deep at the bar counter, your attention grabbed by the competent jazz trio otherwise easily chatted over.
Disabled: toilet (in hotel). Dress: smart casual. Entertainment: jazz trio 9pm Mon-Sat, 8pm Sun. Map 8 F9.

Marylebone W1

Low Life

34A Paddington Street, W1U 4HG (7935 1272/ www.lowlifebar.com). Baker Street tube. **Open** noon-11pm Mon-Fri. **dinner served** 5-9.30pm Mon-Fri. **Main courses** £4.50-£7.50. **Credit** AmEx, MC, V.
A popular party bar in a busy side road that links Baker Street with Marylebone High Street, its main basement area done out in the multi-toned flame-coloured spray paint of youth clubs of yore, Low Life does the simple things right. Its musical policy is positively inclusive, recognisable breakbeats the norm, open-deck nights (Mondays) an abnormal attraction. Its furniture – semicircular banquettes and small square pouffes, in intimate clusters – is low-key enough to be graced by many a bejeaned bottom, but not so seedy as you'd be afraid to venture to the toilets. Its drinks are mixed, in the main, with premium spirits, but kept at a graded price (£6 for one, £11 for two, £15 for three, and so on). A cold bottle of Russian Baltika is the beer of choice. Its 'lite bites' have plenty of zingy elements, and even its menu, adorned with Marvel comic characters, hits the right note with its overall offbeat tone. There are also far worse spots in town to strike up fresh sparks or fan the old flames of love than a prime tiny alcove here, though be aware that it will be filled with mainly twentysomethings eying up their prey.
Bar available for hire (6pm-1am Sat). Entertainment: open decks 5-11pm Mon; DJs 6.30pm Tue, Thur, Fri; bands 7pm Wed. Tables outdoors (4, pavement). Map 3 G5.

Mayfair W1

Trader Vic's

Hilton Hotel, 22 Park Lane, W1K 4BE (7208 4113/www.tradervics.com). Hyde Park Corner tube. **Bar Open/food served** noon-1am Mon-Thur; noon-3am Fri; 5pm-3am Sat; 5-11.30pm Sun. **Main courses** £8-£11. **Restaurant Lunch served** noon-5pm Mon-Fri. **Dinner served** 6pm-12.30am Mon-Sat; 6-11.30pm Sun. **Main courses** £18-£22. **Both Service** 15%. **Credit** AmEx, DC, JCB, MC, V.
Rarely is a chain bar to be recommended, but such is the pedigree of the London branch of Polynesian-themed Trader Vic's that it deserves mention in its own right. The original outpost was established in Oakland, California, in 1934 by former waiter Victor 'Trader Vic' Bergeron, who found an enthusiastic market for his potent cocktails and Americanised versions of Polynesian food. The cocktails really took off after the war, when GIs returning from the Pacific were looking for some R&R beyond the familiar pissy beers they had left behind as boys; ergo fun, strong cocktails at the tiki bar. Trader Vic's opened in the basement of the Park Lane Hotel around the time that Elvis's *Blue Hawaii* was topping the album charts and filling the cinemas, and the kitsch levels (stuffed sharks, dugout canoes, serving girls in native garb) have not wavered from über-ridiculous ever since. The cocktail list doesn't understand the meaning of understated, and when your drink arrives, piled so high with exotic fruit you don't know whether to slurp it or ask it to dance, it will knock your head off. Not cheap (15 per cent service, plus room for a gratuity on the slip), but invariably fun.
Babies and children welcome; high chairs. Booking advisable. Disabled: toilet (in hotel). Dress: smart casual. Entertainment: musicians 10.30pm daily. Separate room for hire, seats 50. Takeaway service. Map 9 G8.

Oxford Street W1

Eagle Bar Diner

3-5 Rathbone Place, W1T 1HJ (7637 1418/ www.eaglebardiner.com). Tottenham Court Road tube. **Open** noon-11pm Mon-Wed; noon-midnight Thur, Fri; 11am-1am Sat; 11am-6pm Sun. **Meals served** noon-11pm Mon-Wed; noon-11.30pm Thur, Fri; 11am-midnight Sat; 11am-6pm Sun. **Main courses** £4-£8.75. **Credit** MC, V.

The Eagle has landed. Grabbing rave reviews when it opened in October 2002, the US-style brunch-to-bedtime operation has consolidated its position as one of the prime (if not *the* prime) dine-and-drink spots along the busy, hazy border between Soho and Noho. The opening hours may be more generous, the DJs more dynamic and staff more cocktail-savvy, but in essence, the Eagle is the same extremely cool, almost postmodern slice-of-the-States diner it was the day it hatched. Two sides of high-backed green snugs with brown, slatted sofas in front face a long zinc bar. Cocktails drinkers enjoy the novelty of choosing their own premium brand to go with the classics, including WL Weller 19-year-old bourbon, Ketel One and Grey Goose. Even the standard cocktails are mixed with Myer's, Mount Gay and the like. There are interesting variations on Glenfiddich, alcoholic milkshakes and the better US microbrewery beers (Brooklyn, Liberty, Anchor Steam). DJs man the decks from Thursday to Saturday. For the food (and milkshakes – a crucial part of its culinary appeal) side of the operation, *see p31.*
Babies and children welcome (until 8pm Thur-Sat). Disabled: ramp; toilet. Entertainment: DJs from 8pm Thur-Sat. Takeaway service. **Map 17 K6**.

Soho W1

Alphabet
61-63 Beak Street, W1F 9SS (7439 2190/ www.alphabetbar.com). Oxford Circus or Piccadilly Circus tube. **Open** noon-11pm Mon-Fri; 5-11pm Sat. **Lunch served** noon-4pm, **dinner served** 5-9pm Mon-Fri. **Main courses** £6.90-£8.50. **Service** 12.5%. **Credit** AmEx, JCB, MC, V.
A Soho standard. Many of the media darlings are doing lunch elsewhere and some of the urban barflies have buzzed off to seek other nectar, but still this tatty-yet-trendy two-floor bar thrives. Seven years young, its iconic slice of Soho street-tangle floor art scuffed by a thousand shoe soles, Alphabet is as comfy as an old denim jacket. The main ground-level bar is spacious, with a scattering of zinc-topped tables and, near the picture windows giving out on to Soho streetlife, the occasional sofa. Art of some description decorates the walls. The skylighted bar counter features an open kitchen, which produces a whole mess of above-average bar food. Bottled beers are the norm – pick from Belgian, Czech or Japanese – and there's two dozen or so New World wines to choose from. The cocktails are acceptable, if unadventurous. Downstairs, DJs play as the weekend approaches, and on any given night there is an infective level of energy amid a more avid drinking fraternity than upstairs.
Babies and children admitted (until 5pm). Entertainment: DJs 7.30pm Thur-Sat. Separate room for hire, seats 25. **Map 17 J6**.

Lab
12 Old Compton Street, W1D 4TQ (7437 7820/ www.lab-bar.com). Leicester Square or Tottenham Court Road tube. **Open** 4pm-midnight Mon-Sat; 4-10.30pm Sun. **Snacks served** 6pm-midnight Mon-Sat, 6-10.30pm Sun. **Snacks** £5.50-£13.50. **Credit** AmEx, MC, V.
A bar that was essential to the process that popularised quality cocktail mixing at the turn of the millennium, the Lab has met with hundred-fold success – which has since been performed in many mid-range bars all over London. And despite the cramped, two-storey conditions, Lab's irreverent signage (Blokes and Bitches on the toilet doors), retro decor (dots, swirls, browns and oranges) and fearsome mixing (music and cocktails) mean it's still a pleasure to pull up a stool here and flick open its drinks menu, dolled up with dynamic images of the Soho that inspired it (how many other local bars do as much justice to their surroundings?). Run your fingers down the long contents list and consider a Collins in any number of fruit flavours (stretching as far as lychee and morello cherry) or a Caipirinha of similar persuasion. The 'Hall of Fame' stars a truly awesome Soho Iced Tea, the 'Hall of Shame' a set of imaginative non-alcoholic concoctions. Ketel One and Chivas Regal get

sloshed about with abandon before an appreciative audience of female-dominated party people. Three cheers for the Lab!
Entertainment: DJs 9pm Mon-Sat. **Map 17 K6**.

★ Milk & Honey NEW
2004 WINNER BEST BAR
61 Poland Street, W1F 7NE (7292 9949/0700 655469/www.mlkhny.com). Oxford Circus tube. **Open/food served** *Non-members* 6-11pm Mon-Fri; 7-11pm Sat. *Members* 6pm-3am Mon-Fri; 7pm-3am Sat. **Snacks** £5-£15. **Credit** AmEx, DC, MC, V.
Billed as London's most secret bar, Milk & Honey oozes exclusivity. It has the unmarked door and ring-for-entry arrangement of a Prohibition-era speakeasy. It also has strict house rules enforced on a three-strikes-and-out basis; 'No name-dropping, no star fucking. No hooting, hollering, shouting or other loud behaviour. No fighting, play-fighting, no talking about fighting. Gentlemen will remove their hats. Hooks are provided.' The interior is fantastic: a Jazz Age affair of dimly lit booths, a low ceiling covered in diner-style aluminium and a business-like corner bar area, lit like an Edward Hopper painting. Staff are the absolute model of professionalism and the cocktails they prepare are sublime (and not too outrageously priced at £7-£8.50). The list fills just one double-spread of a pocket-sized menu, but if you can't find what you want on there then you probably ought to be drinking at the Frog & Ferret. Discounting the caviar and oysters, bar snacks barely total up to half a dozen choices, but they're fantastic, particularly the spicy fish cakes, which beat hands down any we've tried elsewhere. And the best thing of all? Anyone can visit. Just phone in advance and make a reservation.
Booking essential. Separate room for hire, holds 60. **Map 17 J6**.

★ Player
8 Broadwick Street, W1F 8HN (7494 9125/ www.thplyr.com). Oxford Street or Tottenham Court Road tube. **Open** 5.30pm-midnight Mon-Wed; 5.30pm-1am Thur, Fri; 7pm-1am Sat. **Meals served** 6-11pm Mon-Fri; 7-11pm Sat. **Main courses** £6-£11. **Admission** £3 after 10pm Fri, Sat. **Credit** AmEx, MC, V.
This one-time members' only bar has been a Soho landmark since joining the Match Bar fellowship, with its cast-iron guarantee of cocktail quality. Its infancy as a West One shebeen – basement space, conspiratorial alcoves – keeps up the Player's cachet as providing the backdrop for doing something you shouldn't really be doing; meanwhile, mixers with the best pedigree in town keep the cocktail classics coming from the modest bar counter by the small entrance at the bottom of the staircase. Sleek retro stylings remain intact and pristine. Small pins of light pick out the low brown furniture – giving you the impression that you are being shown to your seat before the main feature starts. When you do cast a glance over the drinks list, you'll find cocktails (£5.75-£10) categorised by the quality of spirit kicking around inside them: standard vodka or Grey Goose? That is the question. On admission-charging DJ and comedy nights, it may be the former. But don't worry – you'll be back.
Bar available for hire. Booking advisable. Entertainment: comedy 7pm 1st Sun of mth; DJs 8pm Thur-Sat. **Map 17 J6**.

Strand WC2

American Bar
Savoy Hotel, Strand, WC2R 0EU (7836 4343/ www.the-savoy.co.uk). Embankment tube/Charing Cross tube/rail. **Open** 1pm-1.30am Mon-Sat. **Drinks served** 4pm-midnight Mon-Thur; 4pm-1am Fri; 2pm-1am Sat. **Snacks served** 1-5pm Mon-Sat. **Snacks** £7-£14. **Credit** AmEx, DC, JCB, MC, V.
This pioneering cocktail bar dating from the pre-war era has attracted three generations of celebrity custom, as depicted by the framed photographs and caricatures of writers, directors and film stars on the walls. Smart dress is still required – the waiter in the Bogart-white jacket runs his eyes over

each guest – in order to blend in with the authentic art deco interior and the classy location on the first floor of the Savoy. The bar gained global renown during Prohibition, when a moneyed clientele from across the Atlantic demanded a higher standard of drink than was common in London at the time. Britain's first Martini was mixed here, by bar legend Harry Craddock, who compiled an entire Savoy cocktail book in 1930. Its classic era was after the war, when head bartender Peter Dorelli, who retired in 2003, would concoct masterpieces in cocktail form for the rich and famous. Today's drinks list reflects this heritage, with 12 champagne cocktails, 20 cocktails, ten long drinks and every conceivable whisky. It would be churlish, though, not to order a vodka Martini, by most accounts the best in town, and reflect on a century of champion drinking.
Dress: smart; no denim or trainers. Entertainment: pianist/vocalist 7pm-midnight Mon-Thur; 7pm-1am Fri, Sat. **Map 18 L7**.

Lobby Bar
1 Aldwych, WC2B 4RH (7300 1070/www.one aldwych.com). Covent Garden or Embankment tube/Charing Cross tube/rail. **Open** 11am-11pm Mon-Sat; 11am-10.30pm Sun. **Snacks served** 5.30-10pm Mon-Sat. **Snacks** £4-£35. **Service** 13.5%. **Credit** AmEx, DC, JCB, MC, V.
An oasis of cool and calm a world away from the whizzing traffic taking the bend of the Aldwych outside, the Lobby Bar of the One Aldwych hotel occupies a huge high-ceilinged space flooded with natural light from arched windows. Sitting guard in an undersized boat between the doormen and the bar area is a stooping carved rower with huge oars that resemble vaulting poles. It's the only nod toward the bizarre in a bedrock of formalised behaviour. The chattily deferential staff, the towering flowers reflected in the pristine back-bar mirrored glass, the library hush – it could be 2004, it could be 1924. The selection of fare, though, is pure 21st-century: Martinis and Manhattans, customer-chosen from six premium gins, eight premium vodkas or five premium bourbons, with or without olives of two types, or silver-skinned onions. Martinis alone run to nearly 30 varieties. Bar food after 5.30pm includes fish sushi and oscietra caviar for thrice the price of a circa-£9 cocktail. Taste comes at a price.
Babies and children welcome; nappy-changing facilities (in hotel). Bookings not accepted. Disabled: toilet (in hotel). **Map 18 M7**.

West

Chelsea SW3

Apartment 195 NEW

195 King's Road, SW3 5ED (7351 5195/ www.apartment195.co.uk). Sloane Square tube/11, 22 bus. **Open** 4-11pm Mon-Sat. **Tapas served** 4-10.30pm Mon-Sat. **Tapas** £5-£11. **Service** 12.5%. **Credit** AmEx, DC, MC, V.
It's been some time since there was anything on the King's Road to get the blood racing, but this place does it. Or at least does it for around 50 per cent of the population; the other half might not be so excited by the idea of being served quality booze by women who appear to have been dressed by Agent Provocateur. But the surroundings are sexy too – a dimly lit, high-ceilinged room filled with soft leather seating, warmed by open fires and lightened by camp, candy-coloured comic-book paintings of Barbarella babes and pistol-packing cowboys. Cocktails are the core of a drinks list strong on Martinis, Mojitos, Caipirinhas and bubbly stuff (£7-£9.50); the list includes the Lord of the Rings (42 Below vodka, kiwi juice and apple juice – 100% New Zealand). Beers are limited to two bottled lagers. Wine drinkers do better, and there's decent bar food tailored to deep pockets, something that the King's Road is rarely short of. *Book weekends. Dress: smart casual; no caps or trainers. Separate rooms for hire, seat 8 and 25. Vegetarian menu.* **Map 14 E12.**

Notting Hill W11

Trailer Happiness NEW

2004 RUNNER-UP BEST DESIGN
177 Portobello Road, W11 2DY (7727 2700). Ladbroke Grove or Notting Hill tube. **Open** 5-11pm Tue-Fri; 6-11pm Sat. **Food served** 6-10.30pm Tue-Sat. **Credit** AmEx, MC, V.
Low and laid-back with a discernable '60s vibe, this basement Tiki bar does lounge with a capital L. Owner Jonathan Downey – the man with the golden touch that's behind Match (*see p314*), Milk & Honey and Player (for both, *see p310*) – has taken the stark space that was previously the underwhelming Canvas and, on minimum budget, created what he describes as 'a retro-sexual haven of cosmopolitan kitsch and faded trailer park glamour'. Prime spot is clearly 'the den', an intimate alcove overlooked by a giant image of Tretchikoff's exotic 'Chinese Girl'. However, the main bar space is decidedly pedestrian and a few kitsch pics, shagpile carpet and a bead curtain do not a make this good enough to win Best Design. But there are some absolutely killer (and very good-value) cocktails, thanks to 'Bartender of the Year' Michael Butt and 'king of cocktails' Dale DeGroff. The Tiki specials are some of the fruitiest, frothiest, most luridly coloured, knockout concoctions going. Food is sensibly snacky and seemed appealing, though the kitchen had been chomped clean on the night of our visit. *Entertainment: DJs 8pm Thur-Sat.* **Map 19 B3.**

Lonsdale

44-48 Lonsdale Road, W11 2DE (7228 1517/ www.thelonsdale.co.uk). Notting Hill Gate or Westbourne Park tube. **Open** 6pm-midnight Mon-Sat; 6-11.30pm Sun. **Meals served** 6.30-11.30pm Mon-Sat; 6.30-11pm Sun. **Main courses** £7-£12. **Service** 12.5%. **Credit** AmEx, MC, V.
The *Time Out* Best Bar of 2003 is set in a quiet, residential street a world away from the Notting Hill beloved by London's slackers and slummers. If its stylishly plain frontage doesn't clue you in, then the strictly smart doorstaff ('Have you booked?') might. This is a serious joint, for serious people with serious money to spend. Quality is all. Once you find a spot at the bar counter, or on one of the brown, candlelit semi-circular banquettes, you will swiftly be handed a directory of consumables displaying immaculate taste and attention to detail. The cocktails (£8) are concocted with high-end spirits (Ketel One vodka, in particular), some having been graced with the house trademark: a Lonsdale Mary is a 'classic Bloody with fresh basil leaves'; a Lonsdale Lemonade consists of Buffalo Trace bourbon shaken with fresh lime, Triple Sec and fresh pomegranate juice. (£14-£75) are categorised according to a full range of adjectives, while the food list would put a five-star hotel bar in Dubai to shame, the plate of Spanish charcuterie, including a jamón jabugo aged five years, or the marinated Welsh black beef enhanced by chilli, lime, crisp noodles, sugar snaps and holy basil. Musicians get a Sunday night slot – heaven help the jazzer who hits a bum note, because this place is as deadly efficient as the Prague metro whose sci-fi interior its walls vaguely resemble. *Booking advisable. Disabled: toilet. Entertainment: DJs 9pm Fri, Sat; jazz 8.30pm Sun. Separate room for hire, seats 30.* **Map 7 A6.**

Westbourne Grove W2

★ Tom & Dick's NEW

2004 RUNNER-UP BEST BAR
30 Alexander Street, W2 5NU (7229 7711/ www.tomanddicks.com). Royal Oak tube. **Open** 6.30pm-midnight Mon-Sat; 11am-3pm, 6.30-10.30pm Sun. **Lunch served** 11am-3pm Sun. **Dinner served** 6.30pm-midnight Tue-Sat; 6.30-10.30pm Sun. **Credit** MC, V.
What was Harry's (Social Club) is now Tom & Dick's, a luscious yet homely little drinking haunt where auction-house furniture, hand-painted antique silk wallpaper and assorted curios conspire to create an atmosphere that's two parts camp to one splash of calculated cool. Wafted with incense and lit by tea candles and brass lanterns it's the front room boudoir of a batty old friend who once danced cabaret in Bombay. It's even got a hearth rug in front of the tiny bar counter. Bless. When first opened in late 2003 the place had its shortfalls – the food and drink – and still we loved it. Now that it has a fruity cocktail menu (the drinks are big on apples, berries and citrus) and excellent spicy Indian snacks (coconut prawns, spicy minced lamb kebabs, deep-fried scallops), we adore it even more. Add changing displays of art, and a gorgeous set of upstairs rooms, which are used for occasional Sunday afternoon movies but are otherwise for hire. If *Time Out* had an Audrey Hepburn Award for the Kookiest Best Bar, this would have been the winner. *No-smoking area upstairs.* **Map 7 B5.**

South West

Battersea SW11

★ Dusk NEW

2004 RUNNER-UP BEST BAR
339 Battersea Park Road, SW11 4LF (7622 2112/www.duskbar.co.uk). Battersea Park rail. **Open** 6pm-12.30am Mon-Thur; 6pm-1.30am Fri, Sat. **Food served** 6-10.30pm daily. **Credit** MC, V.
Pub makeovers are a dime a dozen – and most of the time they're not even worth that. Good then to see someone getting it so right. What was the GII gastropub is now a sophisticated cocktail bar with a sultry cocoa paint job and chocolate upholstery, low lighting and flickery candles. At the long, sleek bar counter the beer pumps are gone, replaced by upended silver shakers, sheaves of fresh mint and

Trailer Happiness

black boxes of straws and stirrers, utensils to aid the posse of black-shirted bartenders in their preparation of the 60 or more mixed drinks listed on the menu. This features some excellent concoctions, including a selection of 'uniquely Dusk' cocktails created by the house mixologists (particularly fine if you're a fan of vodka and fruits). Bar snacks are simple platters of grilled or fried nibbles, made with care. A good wine list, two-for-one drink deals early in the week and DJs toward the weekend, as well as a generous membership scheme, help ensure that this is currently the best little bit of classy neighbourhood boozing south of the river (with south of the river prices – cocktails £6 – to boot).
Entertainment: DJs 9pm Wed-Sat. Separate room for hire, seats 90. Tables outdoors (10, terrace). **Map 15 H13.**

Clapham SW4

Arch 635

15-16 Lendal Terrace, SW4 7UX (7720 7343/ www.arch635.co.uk). Clapham North tube/ Clapham High Street rail. **Open** 5pm-midnight Mon-Thur; 5pm-1am Fri; 4pm-2am Sat; 4pm-midnight Sun. **Credit** (over £10) MC, V.
As arch as so many arriviste bars in Cla'am might be, the good ol' 635 is as honest as the day is long. Perhaps it's because the interior is so plain (bare brickwork, exposed piping, standard leather sofas), perhaps it's the standard selection of beers, perhaps it's even the regular rattle of train wheels over the railway arch itself or, more probably, it's the people who make the Arch so attractive. No Gavins and Pippas, wearing rugby shirts with the collars turned up, that make Clapham so abysmally unbearable. Here it's everyday locals who make up the numbers, loudly chatting up potential bedfellows over the noisy soundtrack of the songs of the day, shooting pool and watching Sky Sports. It almost gives Clapham a good name.
Disabled: toilet. Entertainment: DJs 9pm Fri, Sat; 8pm Sun. Separate areas for hire, hold 20-80. **Map 22 B1.**

Exhibit B NEW

13 Old Town, SW4 0JT (7498 5559). Clapham Common tube.
Bar **Open** noon-11pm Mon-Sat; 11.30am-10.30pm Sun. **Lunch served** noon-3pm Mon-Sat; 12.30-4pm Sun. **Snacks served** 3-9pm Mon-Sat; 4-9pm Sun. **Main courses** £3.50-£5.90. **Snacks** £4-£5.70.
Restaurant **Meals served** 7-10.30pm daily. **Main courses** £9.50-£13.50. **Service** 12.5%.
Both **Credit** MC, V.
This new Clapham Old Town bar and restaurant is a branch of Balham's Exhibit (12 Balham Station Road, SW12 9SG; 8772 6556) – a swish coffee and cocktail bar next to Balham station – but this version is more ambitious than the original. It's a vast, concrete space decorated with vibrant patches of colour, texture and pattern that prevent it from looking too much like a multistorey car park. The extensive drinks list of nitrokeg beers, bottled mixers, cocktails and a dozen wines by the glass is certainly varied; most people should find something of interest. Behind a red glass wall is a quieter dining area; rösti topped with rack of pork (£13.50) was a knockout dish. Service was rather shambolic on our visit, but it was early days.
Babies and children welcome (until 6pm). Booking advisable. Disabled: toilet. No smoking (restaurant). **Map 22 A1.**

South

Brixton SW2, SW9

Brixton Bar & Grill NEW

15 Atlantic Road, SW9 8HX (7737 6777/ www.bbag.me.uk). Brixton tube/rail. **Open** 4.30pm-1am Tue-Thur, Sun; 4.30pm-3am Fri, Sat. **Food served** 6pm-midnight Tue-Thur, Sun; 6pm-1am Fri, Sat. **Tapas** £3-£6. **Service** 12.5%. **Credit** MC, V.
Here's a surprise: a trendy new Brixton bar that's put as much effort into the food and drink as it does into the music policy. (More, in fact.) Solicitous,

super-friendly bar staff? Check. Interesting bottled beers? Check. Grown-up cocktails made by bartenders who know what they're doing? Definitely. Well-chosen wine list, with a good selection by the glass? You bet. Even the bar snacks are exquisitely prepared – beetroot fritters with yoghurt and watercress; moist but tiny lamb cutlets with yoghurt mint sauce. Simple snacks are available for those on a smaller budget, a generous bowl of green olives and bread with tapenade or spicy chorizo cost between £1.50 and £3 each. Be warned that the DJs in the rear of this railway arch get loud on Friday and Saturday evenings – but then that's the Brixton we know and love.
Booking not accepted. Disabled: toilet.
Entertainment: 8pm Fri-Sun. Separate room for hire, seats 20. Tables outdoors (4, pavement). Vegetarian menu. **Map 22 E1.**

Fridge Bar

1 Town Hall Parade, Brixton Hill, SW2 1RJ (7326 5100). Brixton tube/rail. **Open** 6pm-2am Mon-Thur; 6pm-4am Fri; 8pm-4am Sat; 8pm-3am Sun. **Admission** £5-£10 after 10.30pm Fri, Sat; £3 occasional Sun. **Credit** (over £10) MC, V.
As crucial to Brixton as hash smoke and crazy people outside the station, the venerable Fridge Bar broke the mould of pre-club venues to become a destination bar in its own right. Silly opening hours and the new fashion for getting blind blotto on absinthe were the conduits in this transition, and have generated a pretty loyal fan base. Even a recent spring clean, and expanded entertainment – theme nights along with DJs and live acts – cannot diminish the fact that the Fridge is still stuck in a mid-1990s time-warp – chasing absinthe at 3am still feels like a wonderfully illicit thing to do. The erotic paintings are still there, as are the penny-chew colours surrounding them, and the service is still bovine at best. As if to bring things full circle, admission prices to the main bar after hours or of a weekend are now approaching the kind of figure you'd pay to get into a club anyway – but without the sense of communal naughtiness.
Dress: no trainers (weekends). Entertainment: DJs 10pm daily; salsa 8pm Tue. Tables outdoors (4, pavement). **Map 22 D2.**

Waterloo SE1

★ Baltic

74 Blackfriars Road, SE1 8HA (7928 1111/ www.balticrestaurant.co.uk). Southwark tube.
Bar **Open/snacks served** noon-11pm daily.
Restaurant **Lunch served** noon-3pm Mon-Fri. **Dinner served** 6-11.15pm Mon-Sat. **Meals served** noon-10.30pm Sun. **Main courses** £9.50-£14. **Set meal** (noon-3pm, 6-7pm) £11.50 2 courses, £13.50 3 courses. **Service** 12.5%.
Both **Credit** AmEx, MC, V.
Most bars with international cultural themes are a tacky mess. Baltic is a jewel. Hidden behind a bland exterior across from Southwark tube station, this is a treasure trove of rarities. First, Seth Stein's design is breathtaking. It comprises a long, thin bar area of cool alcoves, banquettes and button stools, subtly lit, backdropped by bright art and lined with a glass-fronted, amber wall. The restaurant (*see p68*) at the far end, with its huge, glass-topped atrium and gorgeous fibre-optic amber chandelier accentuates the wow factor. Second, there's the drinks menu, featuring almost every vodka known to Poles, and some known to Siberians. Each one is used in the house variety of cocktails, one Baltic-flavoured one for every more recognisable one, the house named after its source material, for instance, roza (rose petal), prunella (plum) and jarzebiak (rowanberry). Solitary vodkas come in 25cl or 50cl shots or by the bottle, possible chasers for Polish EB, Czech Zatek or Estonian A Le Coq beers. Third, there's superb food to go with them, including blinis of smoked salmon or oscietra caviar, fish cakes, shashlik and golonka (Polish roast pork shank served with a sauerkraut salad). Breathtakingly brilliant.
Babies and children welcome; high chair. Booking advisable dinner. Disabled: toilet. Entertainment: jazz 7-10pm Mon, Sun. Separate room for hire, seats 30. Tables outdoors (5, courtyard). **Map 11 O8.**

East

Brick Lane E1

Vibe Bar

The Old Truman Brewery, 91-5 Brick Lane, E1 6QL (7377 2899/www.vibe-bar.co.uk). Aldgate East tube/Liverpool Street tube/rail. **Open** 11am-11.30pm Mon-Thur, Sun; 11am-1am Fri, Sat. **Meals served** 7-11.30pm Tue-Thur; 6-10pm Fri, Sat; noon-10pm Sun. **Main courses** £4-£8. **Credit** AmEx, DC, MC, V.
Occupying Ben Truman's former Black Eagle brewery in the heart of Brick Lane, the Vibe Bar has been flying the flag for underground entertainment for the best part of ten years, its laid-back main bar area a major hangout for local DJs and musicians. Here, where ginormous speakers make a clear and deep din, a hatch of a bar dispenses standard bottled beers while scruffy types lounge about on skip furniture, with a piano and exotic paintings providing a suitable backdrop. DJs and live bands share the weekly bill of entertainment. Upstairs, cards and obscure Indian parlour games are played by groups gathered from every corner of the globe. Most of the year the cobbled terrace is open too, with beer garden tables arranged in an orderly fashion; this spot allows respite if the basslines become too relentless inside. Internet access is also on offer if you get here early enough.
Entertainment: DJs 7pm Mon, Wed-Sat; bands 7.30pm Tue, Sun. Tables outdoors (70, heated courtyard, marquee). Separate room for hire, holds 150. **Map 6 S5.**

Shoreditch E1, E2, EC2

Bar Kick

127 Shoreditch High Street, E1 6JE (7739 8700/ www.cafekick.co.uk). Old Street or Liverpool Street tube/rail. **Open** noon-11pm Mon-Wed, Sun; noon-midnight Thur-Sat. **Lunch served** noon-3.30pm, **dinner served** 6-11pm Mon-Fri. **Meals served** noon-midnight Sat; noon-11pm Sun. **Main courses** £4-£12. **Credit** MC, V.
Could this be London's most enjoyable bar? Bar Kick is the broader, younger sibling of Café Kick, the original Exmouth Market venue that established the concept of a continental-style bar complete with table football (the proper kind, made by René Pierre), obscure Latin and Euro beers, Portuguese snacks, zinc bar counter and exotic advertising. Big enough to accommodate a World Cup's worth of national flags on the ceiling, Bar Kick has sufficient space for a dining area – and the food goes a step beyond snacks, to say the least. The well-travelled German chef insists on the finest Sicilian olive oil, Serrano ham from Aragon, mozzarella from Campagna and other choice ingredients, for a changing menu of superb stews, salads and mains, finished off by Helsett Farm organic Cornish ice-cream. Bottled beers include Belgian Liefman's Kriek and Duvel, Jenlain (usually only seen in late-opening corner shops in France), Krombacher in two sizes and the Portuguese standards of Sagres and Superbock. The new range of Kick cocktails at both venues is equally welcome: Daiquiris and Martinis prepared with as much attention to detail as everything else in this thoroughly commendable operation.
Babies and children welcome (lunchtime only). Disabled: toilet. Entertainment: film nights 8pm Mon, Tue; table football tournaments 7pm last Thur of mth. No-smoking tables. Separate basement area available for hire, holds 150. Tables outdoors (4, pavement). **Map 6 R4.**
For branch (Café Kick) see index.

dreambagsjaguarshoes

34-36 Kingsland Road, E2 8DA (7729 5830/ www.dreambagsjaguarshoes.com). Old Street tube/rail. **Open** 5.30pm-1am daily. **Meals served** 5.30pm-midnight daily. **Main courses** £3-£6. **Credit** MC, V.
Not quite as balls-out bare-all as when it burst on to the scene in 2002, dreambags (named after the original two stores whose signs still hang over the doors) has begun to accommodate a clientele more

Loungelover

comfortable with itself on recognisable furniture. Hell, the downstairs lounge could almost pass for chic. Back on dry land, it's still barren walls, bare radiators, challenging art by local gnash merchants and a heart-warmingly radical soundtrack. Cushions or no cushions, the drinks at least have always been striking, and they're still served from the bare corner bar area, with offerings chalked up in a handwriting style similar to Jack The Ripper's *From Hell* letter dateline. Draught Staropramen and Grolsch, or bottled Duvel, Chimay, Grimbergen, Bitburger, Liefman (cherry and raspberry), Dos Equis, Asahi and Tiger can be chased by a hefty raft of vodkas, or there's a wine list (in the £12-£15 range) and even Breton cider. Spiky, but with a smile.
Bar available for hire. Entertainment: DJs 8pm Wed-Sun. **Map 6 R3.**

★ Home

100-106 Leonard Street, EC2A 4RH (7684 8618/ www.homebar.co.uk). Old Street or Liverpool Street tube/rail. **Bar Open** 5.30pm-midnight Mon-Sat. **Snacks served** 5.30-10pm Mon-Sat. **Snacks** £2.50-£6. *Restaurant* **Lunch served** 12.30-3pm, **dinner served** 7pm-midnight Mon-Sat. **Main courses** £8-£15. **Service** 12.5%.
Both **Credit** AmEx, DC, JCB, MC, V.
There certainly is no place like Home, one of the true Hoxton originals and still a pack leader in London's 'cool' quarter. Home does the simple things right. Downstairs from the restaurant, a spruce basement bar features four intimately lit rooms and one bright room, where attentive, cute waiting staff roam and an unobtrusive bar is quietly busy. Tables are at perfect height with the low, brown seating; each one is set with a menu proposing classic or champagne cocktails, modern Martinis, long and short drinks, Mules, Mojitos and shooters in the £6 range, plus five acceptable wines of each colour (three by the glass). The bar snacks are delicate but pricey: a sharing platter of prosciutto, gorgonzola, salami and bread cost £6. The beers (bottled Asahi, Budvar and Staropramen) could be improved, as could the music on occasion, but overall, this is as good as it was when it was pretty much the only game in town.
Booking advisable. Disabled: toilet. Entertainment: DJs 9pm-midnight Thur-Sat. Separate rooms for hire, seat 15 and 70. Vegetarian menu. **Map 6 R4.**

★ Loungelover

2004 WINNER BEST DESIGN
2004 RUNNER-UP BEST BAR

1 Whitby Street, E1 6JU (7012 1234/www.lounge lover.co.uk). Liverpool street tube/rail. **Open** 6pm-midnight Mon-Thur; 6pm-1am Fri; 7pm-1am Sat. **Meals served** 6.30-10.30pm Tue-Fri; 7-11pm Sat. **Main courses** £9.90-£14.50. **Service** 10%. **Credit** AmEx, MC, V.
A year after it opened Loungelover remains a shrine to high campery and high times. Flashing its bloomers at the self-conscious street style of surrounding Shoreditch, it fills a former butcher's store with painted fairground gallopers, gaily coloured anatomical models, a decaying doll's house, stuffed small mammals and heaven knows what else. A half-dozen visits on and we're still spotting new things. All of this would be only so much set dressing if the drink and food part of the operation didn't work, but, of course, it does. The cocktail list has been overhauled (and shrunk) since opening, but the drinks remain true to the venue: fruity, quirky confections (all £8-£9) such as a Smooth Criminal of bourbon with cherry purée and vanilla liqueur, or the Loungelover, which is champagne a-fizz with lemon and vanilla. Chilli 'n' Chocolate struck us a taste too far, but you have to admire the verve. Bar snacks are limited but the kitchen also turns out a fuller menu to be eaten at the cartwheel-like tables at front of house. Prime lounging territory is the crimson-tinted boudoir at the rear, where the sensation is like sitting for LaChapelle. It's a bar in which the feel-good factor kicks in even before the alcohol hits.
Booking advisable. Disabled: toilet. **Map 6 S4.**

Smersh

5 Ravey Street, EC2A 4QW (7739 0092/ www. smershbar.com). Liverpool Street or Old Street tube/rail. **Open** 5pm-midnight Mon-Fri; 7pm-midnight Sat. **Credit** (over £10) AmEx, DC, MC, V.
Few dank cellars named after a wing of the KGB could ever be considered sympathetic, but this rather splendidly idiosyncratic DJ bar is as friendly and unpretentious as it gets in these parts. True, there is a theme – 'Smersh' originally meant 'Death to Spies', so the walls are papered with Soviet propaganda and the toilets with old copies of the GDR state broadsheet in English officialese. But it's touches like pictures of Serge Gainsbourg and Who bassist John Entwistle that win the day, just

the kind of nonsense that would decorate a subversive's bedroom in the old days way out East. The musical offerings are enthusiastically programmed – country & western one night, northern soul another – while a range of Polish vodkas (try the rare Siwucha), compatriot Brok beer and the excellent German König Pilsener provide a drink selection most Hoxton bar-owners should envy. Smersh – Slava!
Bar available for hire (Sat). Entertainment: DJs 7pm Mon-Sat. **Map 6 Q4.**

Sosho

2 Tabernacle Street, EC2A 4LU (7920 0701/ www.sosho3am.com). Moorgate or Old Street tube/rail. **Open** 11.30am-10pm Mon; 11.30am-midnight Tue; 11.30am-1am Wed, Thur; 11.30am-3am Fri; 7pm-3am Sat. **Food served** noon-11pm Mon-Fri; 7-11pm Sat. **Snacks** £6-£12. **Credit** AmEx, DC, JCB, MC, V.
An award-winning member of the Match family, Sosho's shape and style would set it a class apart in any company. A cool, wide corridor leads to a wide communal area comprising a bar counter, glitterball and gas station mural, with a raised area at the back overlooking the bar for more intimate chat. A downstairs lounge is used for private do's and special events. The drinks menu is the same Dale DeGroff humdinger generic to the Match chain, changing according to season. Many of the mixes (all around £6) are original: try Sam Jeveons' Spacific Martini made with 42 Below vodka or DeGroff's own Perfect Agave with Cuervo Tradicional, lychee, strawberries and home-made ginger beer. Those are just the tip of a cool iceberg of stirred and shaken delights. Match's own wines comprise the bulk of a modest list, while beers are limited to bottles of Proof Kölsch or Pilsen, Bitburger and Union. Entrance fees are charged on DJ nights, such as Friday's Weekending or Saturday's Mindfluid. There are superior bar snacks and dinners too.
Babies and children welcome (daytime only). Disabled: toilet. Entertainment: DJs 9pm Wed-Sat. Separate room for hire, holds 120. **Map 6 Q4.**

Tea NEW

56 Shoreditch High Street, E1 6JJ (7729 2973). Liverpool Street or Old Street tube/rail. **Open** 9am-11pm Mon-Fri; 6.30-11pm Sat; 11am-10.30pm Sun. **Meals served** 9am-10pm Mon-Fri; 6.30-10pm Sat; 11am-10pm Sun. **Main courses** £3.50-£8. **Service** 12.5%. **Credit** MC, V.
This cavernous, ground-floor warehouse space is basically the works canteen for the inhabitants of the Tea building's studios and offices, a louche bunch of local creative and media types. As such, it has a pleasant ebb and flow of custom and an appealingly local feel, though there's plenty of room for allcomers in its design-differentiated areas – a deli, a sit-down eating space, and a bar space – very low-key stylish in the concrete-industrial mode. You can get a few beers and a dozen or so wines, but here the cocktail really is king. We sampled more than was wise, and found not a dud: almost chef-like consideration is given to the mixology, with subtle, seasonal combinations and lightness embraced. Favourites were the Bethnal Green Tea (orange pekoe, many spirits, lemon and champagne), the East End Sour, with orgeat and egg white, and the watermelon Martini – all good value at £5.50-£6. Food comes in various forms: international snacks, deli sandwiches and modern caff classics, plus an American-esque breakfast/Sunday brunch. There isn't a vast amount of seating in the bar, but that's all to the good for the standing customers, who pack the place when the DJ plays at weekends.
Booking advisable. Disabled: toilet. No-smoking tables. **Map 6 R4.**

North

Camden Town & Chalk Farm NW1

Bar Vinyl

6 Inverness Street, NW1 7HJ (7681 7898/ www.vinyl-addiction.co.uk). Camden Town tube. **Open** 11am-11pm Mon-Sat; 11am-10.30pm Sun.

Lunch served noon-4.30pm daily. Dinner served 5.30-9pm Mon-Thur, Sun; 5.30-8pm Fri, Sat. Main courses £3.95-£6.95. Credit (over £10) MC, V.

How apt for Camden's finest bar to name itself Vinyl. But whereas much of Camden's trade is provided by musical nostalgia – sad men in leather jackets leafing through stacks of old singles at the nearby market – this slice of vinyl is anything but history. The BV is owned by Finger Lickin' Records, whose DJs play superclubs around the world, and was a pioneer in the early stages of the DJ bar phenomenon. It still boasts a fine set of decks, squeezed into its narrow street-level interior, and a record shop below. The last of a trio of terraced bars along pedestrianised, stall-cramped Inverness Street, the Vinyl offers Budvar, Grolsch, Caffrey's and Guinness to its high-fidelity fanbase, perched on red leatherettes and surrounded by the kind of vibrant colour patterns used for '60s record sleeves. If the walls ever get too scuffed, they could cover them thrice over with the piles of flyers stacked up by the main door. The open kitchen at the back, while hardly adventurous, does a decent job of pastas and fry-ups.
Babies and children welcome (before 5pm). Entertainment: DJs 8pm Wed-Fri; all day Sat, Sun. Record shop: 11.30am-7.30pm daily. Tables outdoors (2, pavement). Map 27 C2.

Islington N1

Embassy Bar
119 Essex Road, N1 2SN (7226 7901/ www.embassybar.com). Angel tube/38, 56, 73 bus. Open 4pm-midnight Mon-Thur, Sun; 4pm-2am Fri, Sat. Admission £3-£4 after 9pm Fri, Sat. Credit AmEx, MC, V.
This eternally trendy retro Tardis of a bar shines like a lighthouse amid the scrubbed pine hulks of pricey gastropubs infecting N1. True, the Embassy has its downsides. On busy nights, posing round the horseshoe bar that dominates proceedings can be akin to spending three hours standing beside tube doors as they open and close in rush hour, and even the introduction of DJ nights downstairs has done little to ease congestion. The cocktails are average at best (despite the nice use of Smiths' song titles to describe them). Still, the Embassy is truly a jewel of a bar. The horseshoe counter is ringed by neat swivel bar chairs, and the studded black leather banquettes are comfort itself if you're here on a quiet night. The music is just right, whatever and whenever it happens to be. And more than anything, it feels like the HQ of some secret society, whose initiation rites involve frequent attendance. Everyone seems to know everyone else, or at least do a good job of faking it. Join the gang – maybe they've even got a rota going for occupying the bar chairs.
Bar available for hire. Entertainment: DJs 8pm Thur, Sun; 9pm Fri, Sat. Map 5 P1.

Medicine Bar
181 Upper Street, N1 1RQ (7704 9536/ www.medicinebar.net). Angel tube/Highbury & Islington tube/rail. Open 5pm-midnight Mon-Thur; 5pm-2am Fri; 2pm-2am Sat; 2pm-midnight Sun. Admission £4 after 9.30pm Fri, Sat. Credit MC, V.
This mothership of a successful three-venue operation combines the best features of both pub and bar. Decorative echoes of a Victorian public house – the intricately carved back bar, the beautiful bay window – mesh nicely with the louche, lounge feel towards the back of the main bar. The music and drinks, though, reflect 21st-century mores, with the club sounds and standard cocktails drawing a young up-for-it crowd combing the candlelight for meaningful eye contact. The back area, signposted by a huge poster of Cassius Clay in boyhood, suits intimacy; the summer-only sideyard is a right-angle of respectable reunion. Weekend nights can be impossibly crowded, despite a reasonably hefty entrance charge. Apart from that, this is one of the best prescriptions for a good time anywhere north of City Road.
Entertainment: DJs 8.30pm Thur-Sun. Function room. Tables outdoors (4, pavement). Map 5 O1.
For branch see index.

Pubs

Despite a spate of recent conversions, London still contains a wealth of pubs. Yet too often these are mere links in a much-replicated chain, with mass-produced knick-knacks, ropy beers and well-scrubbed management – all supplied by head office. Below we list a selection of the city's most cherished and unique drinking dens. For more of the best, consult the latest edition of *Time Out Pubs & Bars* (£8.99).
For pubs that specialise in food, see **Gastropubs**, starting on p90.

Central

Aldwych WC2

Seven Stars
53-54 Carey Street, WC2A 2JB (7242 8521). Chancery Lane, Holborn or Temple tube. Open 11am-11pm Mon-Fri; noon-11pm Sat. Lunch served noon-3pm, dinner served 5-9pm Mon-Sat. Credit AmEx, MC, V.
Winner of the Best Pub category in the 2003 *Time Out Eating & Drinking Awards*, this perfect, unspoilt little boozer is tucked away behind the Royal Courts of Justice, adjacent to a legal wigmaker's. The only significant change in recent years came following the arrival of landlady Ms Roxy Beaujolais, who created a more adventurous bistro-style menu, painted the rough plasterwork yellow and added a smattering of framed legal-theme movie posters. Built in 1602, the pub began life as the Leg & Seven Stars, after a Dutch maritime flag; its thin dark wooden beams and narrow settles are pretty much the genuine article. The two doors are marked 'General Counter' and 'Private Counter', although these days all that stands between them is a thin partition. You'll invariably find groups of thesps and lawyers in residence, downing real ales (there are usually three different ales available on tap) or wines from a list that wouldn't disgrace a decent country hotel.
Free house: Adnams Broadside £2.70; Harveys Sussex Best £2.70. Map 10 M6.

Bloomsbury WC1

★ Lamb
2004 RUNNER-UP BEST PUB
94 Lamb's Conduit Street, WC1N 3LZ (7405 0713/www.youngs.co.uk). Holborn or Russell Square tube. Open 11am-11pm Mon-Sat; noon-4pm, 7-10.30pm Sun. Lunch served noon-2.30pm daily. Dinner served 6-9pm Mon-Thur, Sat. Credit AmEx, MC, V.
Built in around 1730 over William Lamb's river conduit, this celebrated pub is the central London flagship for Wandsworth's Young's brewery. It's an outstanding Grade II listed structure, and the decor is carefully restored Victorian (sympathetically done in the 1960s), complete with opulent green upholstery, an original mahogany bar edged with etched-glass snob screens, and matching windows and mirrors. The three drinking areas are wood-panelled, with walls practically groaning under the weight of framed portraits of Victorian theatricals. The pulchritudinous polython by the main door will play music in return for a donation to charity – at least it makes a change from a Coldplay-spewing jukebox. Coming as it does from Young's, the beer is beyond reproach, and there's a no-smoking area for those who value their lungs.
Young's: Young's Bitter £2.35; Waggledance £2.50. No-smoking tables. Separate room for parties, seats 25. Tables outdoors (3, patio; 3, pavement). Map 4 M4.

City EC4

Tipperary
66 Fleet Street, EC4Y 1HT (7583 6470/ www.tipperarypub.co.uk). Blackfriars tube/rail. Open 11am-11pm Mon-Fri; noon-6pm Sat, Sun. Food served 11am-10pm Mon-Fri; noon-5.30pm Sat, Sun. Credit MC, V.
The former Boar's Head was built in 1605 with stone recycled from the dissolved Whitefriars Monastery. As a result, it was one of the few Fleet Street buildings to survive the Great Fire. In 1639, the Dublin brewing firm of SG Mooney took over, making this London's first Irish-themed boozer. In its time, the tall, narrow, three-storey pub was the first in London to sell both bottled and then draught Guinness. The present name comes from the famous World War I song; it was adopted after a dozen or so of the thousands of Fleet Street printers shipped to the trenches returned in one piece. Today the Tipp is in good shape, having been restored in the 1960s to 18th-century glory, using the original fittings, by Suffolk's Greene King brewery. Antipodean serving staff pour well-kept Greene King IPA, plus the odd drop of Guinness for tourists who still believe the blarney.
Greene King: Greene King IPA £2.45; Abbot £2.70. Babies and children welcome. Games (fruit machine). Separate room for hire, seats 28. TV. Map 11 N6.

Clerkenwell & Farringdon EC1

★ Jerusalem Tavern
55 Britton Street, EC1M 5UQ (7490 4281/ www.stpetersbrewery.co.uk). Farringdon tube/rail. Open 11am-11pm Mon-Fri; 5-11pm Sat; 11am-6pm Sun. Food served noon-3pm Mon-Fri; 6-10pm Sat; noon-4.30pm Sun. Credit MC, V.
Despite its seemingly authentic appearance, this tiny little pub was restored less than a decade ago to what the place would have looked like when it was built in 1720 – er, had it originally been a tavern. The walls are ragged and set off by old white tiles, a chunky wooden floor, sturdy mismatched furniture and cosy panelled cubicles. The tiny bar area in the alcove that separates the small front drinking bar from the even smaller rear part serves lagers, wines and suchlike, plus the full range of usually wonderful and often unusually flavoured beers from St Peter's Brewery in Suffolk. Over 20 come in dinky green bottles and there are about half a dozen on draught. We usually head straight for Best Bitter, Old Style Porter or Suffolk Gold, leaving the cinnamon and apple to more adventurous drinkers. If you've ever wondered how many people can be crammed into a tiny boozer, come here on practically any night and experience it first hand.
St Peter's Brewery: Best £2.40; Fruit Beer £2.40. Bar available for hire (Sat, Sun only). No piped music or jukebox. Specialities (fruit beers). Map 5 O4.

Covent Garden WC2

Lamb & Flag
33 Rose Street, WC2E 9EB (7497 9504). Covent Garden tube. Open 11am-11pm Mon-Thur; 11am-10.45pm Fri, Sat; noon-10.30pm Sun. Lunch served noon-3pm daily. No credit cards.
One of London's oldest pubs, the Lamb & Flag – named after the chivalric heraldry symbol for John the Baptist – was built in 1623. Thanks to a link with bare-knuckle boxing, it was allegedly once

Elgin

known as the Bucket of Blood, though we take that with a pinch of snuff. Architects know it as one of London's oldest remaining wooden-framed buildings; the rest of us as a rather fine boozer. The interior hasn't changed much since Georgian times (give or take a wooden partition or two) and the place is thick with old wooden beams and panelling, plus accumulated artefacts. Real ale is the drink of choice for most of the office workers, off-duty cops and tourists who flock here. In addition to the complete Young's range, you can expect the likes of Bombardier and Courage Directors. In 1679 John Dryden was duffed up outside and, as consolation, the upstairs Brit-grub restaurant has been named in his honour. Imagine how proud his dear old mum would have been. *Free house: Young's Bitter £2.60; Young's Special £2.70. Babies and children admitted (mornings only). Entertainment: jazz 7.30-10.30pm Sun. No piped music or jukebox. Restaurant.* Map 18 L7.

Holborn EC1

Ye Old Mitre

1 Ely Court, Ely Place (at the side of 8 Hatton Gardens), EC1N 6SJ (7405 4751). Chancery Lane tube/Farringdon tube/rail. **Open** 11am-11pm Mon-Fri. **Food served** 11am-9.30pm Mon-Fri. **Credit** AmEx, MC, V.

Although documentary evidence goes back to 1546, there's some confusion as to the Mitre's actual age, largely because it was completely rebuilt in the 18th century using the original materials and plans. Unperturbed by the loss of a century or two, tourists and after-work lawyers enjoy navigating the warren of wood-panelled rooms with low-beamed ceilings and exposed stonework. The name comes from the building's original purpose as servants' quarters for the Bishops of Ely, whose London palace stood roughly where St Ethelreda's

Church now is. Expect three or four real ales, maybe including Tetley, Burton and something from Adnams of Southwold. Wine-lovers have been known to applaud the brief but bountiful list. *Spirit Group: Tetley Bitter £2.30; Adnams £2.55; Burton Ale £2.60. Function room. Games (cribbage, darts). No piped music. Tables outdoors (barrels, pavement).* Map 11 N5.

West

Hammersmith W6

Dove

19 Upper Mall, W6 9TA (8748 5405). Hammersmith or Ravenscourt Park tube. **Open** 11am-11pm Mon-Sat; noon-10.30pm Sun. **Food served** noon-2.30pm, 5-9pm Mon-Sat; noon-4pm Sun. **Credit** AmEx, MC, V.

Anoraks will already know that the *Guinness Book of Records* insists that this ancient riverside pub has the smallest bar in England, at 3.12sq m: just enough room for three men and a dog, or four dogs and a man if you prefer. The rest of us (unlikely to fit inside, especially if we all arrive at once) are more interested in soaking up the historic atmosphere and the quite stunning riverside views from the terrace. Then there's the superbly kept Fuller's ales. Yum. Built some time in the 17th century as a private house – the archives are hazy – the premises were transformed into the Dove Coffee House in 1796. Most of what we see today dates from that time. Lovers of dark wood panelling, flagstones and low lighting will be in their element. Past regulars have included actor Trevor Howard, Graham Greene, William Morris and the poetic genius wot wrote the words to 'Rule Britannia', James Thomson. *Fuller's: London Pride £2.55; ESB £2.65. No piped music or jukebox. Tables outdoors (15, riverside terrace).* Map 20 A4.

Ladbroke Grove W11

★ Elgin

2004 RUNNER-UP BEST PUB

96 Ladbroke Grove, W11 1PY (7229 5663). Ladbroke Grove tube. **Open** 11am-11pm Mon-Sat; noon-10.30pm Sun. **Meals served** noon-10pm daily. **Credit** AmEx, MC, V.

One of London's grander boozers and now bristling with urban chic, the Elgin was reborn after a dodgy few years as a Firkin. When built in 1851, it was all that stood in Ladbroke Grove aside from a Poor Clares convent. William Dickinson acquired the pub in 1892 and decorated it in the lavish gin palace style that later ensured its listed status, adding his initials at every opportunity. There are three bars, arranged around a central serving area, with tall, gangly windows at the front. Most of today's punters take the carved mahogany, elaborate stained glass, etched mirrors and decorative tiles for granted. Take a look: you'll not find better this side of the 1890s. Big-screen TVs make the pub a popular venue for major sporting events, but those more interested in the four or five real ales and well-chosen Belgian beer selection can usually find a nook or cranny in which to hibernate and tut-tut at the canned music. *Spirit Group: Adnams £2.40; Charles Wells Bombardier £2.40; Tetley Bitter £2.40. Babies and children welcome. Entertainment: Elvis 8pm first Fri of mth. Tables outdoors (12, pavement).* Map 19 B2.

South West

Colliers Wood SW19

★ Sultan

2004 WINNER BEST PUB

78 Norman Road, SW19 1BT (8542 4532). Colliers Wood tube. **Open** noon-11pm Mon-Sat; noon-10.30pm Sun. **Credit** MC, V.

After suffering a direct hit during World War II, this backstreet brick boozer was rebuilt some time in the 1950s. Architects and pub quiz swots will know all about the unusual pre-cast concrete window surrounds and the four tall chimney stacks that mount each corner. Inside are two ground-floor bars, including a saloon named after Ted Higgins, the first actor to play Walter Gabriel in *The Archers*. Decor epitomises the no-nonsense school of local pubbery, with scrubbed wooden furniture and aged Turkish-style carpets. A friendly, family-run pub, the Sultan is now sole London outpost of Salisbury's Hop Back brewery, so the beers are wonderful, with regular and seasonal brews such as GFB, Entire Stout, Thunderstorm and Summer Lightning. Look out too for the annual September beer festival. To the rear is a pleasant terrace-cum-garden, venue of regular summer barbecues. Weekly quizzes, community events and a Wednesday Beer Club ensure that there's something going on for everybody. There's even an in-house Old English sheepdog called Dylan and a cat for those desperate for intelligent company. Every neighbourhood deserves a Sultan – or at least one of its own-made sultana sponges with custard. *Hop Back: GFB £1.85; Summer Lightning £2.20. Disabled access: toilet. Tables outdoors (11, patio).*

Parsons Green SW6

★ White Horse

1-3 Parsons Green, SW6 4UL (7736 2115). Parsons Green tube. **Open** 11am-11pm Mon-Sat; 11am-10.30pm Sun. **Food served** noon-3pm, 6-10pm Mon-Fri; 11am-10pm Sat, Sun. **Credit** AmEx, MC, V.

The Fulham/Chelsea/Parsons Green triangle can boast many good pubs, but none more popular than the White Horse. You get a choice of six or seven decent real ales (including Highgate Dark Mild, Harveys Best Bitter and Rooster's Ranger), every Trappist beer produced by a Belgian (or Dutch) monk, plus loads of other rather fine European and North American brews. Oenophiles will appreciate a wine list that stretches to almost

On the Town

80, a quarter of which are available by the glass. Although decked out with the currently in-vogue bare board, bench and sofa look, there's no hiding that this is a fine late-Victorian establishment. Outside, on the well-organised seated and heated terrace on the green, fairy lights glitter in the trees and sensible locals fervently pray that heaven comes with decent beer and maybe a more comfortable bench.
Mitchell's & Butler's: Harveys Sussex £2.40; Adnams Broadside £2.50; Rooster's Yankee £2.50. Babies and children admitted. Function room. No-smoking area (restaurant). Tables outdoors (30, garden).

South East

Deptford SE8

Dog & Bell

116 Prince Street, SE8 3JD (8692 5664). New Cross tube/rail/Deptford rail. **Open** noon-11pm Mon-Sat; noon-3.30pm, 7-10.30pm Sun. **Food served** noon-2.30pm, 6-9pm Mon-Fri. **No credit cards.**
The village boozer is alive, well and tucked away in a Deptford side street. Here you'll find regular pickle-making competitions and pub quizzes. The three compact drinking areas include a small 'games' room, where darts, board games, dominoes, shove ha'penny and bar billiards may be played. Most of the army of local musicians, thespians, artisans, market traders and intellectuals – a loose term to include staff and students from nearby Greenwich University and Goldsmiths College – who frequent the pub try for a table in the raised drinking area, with its hanging hops and chunky furniture. The place is something of a local Camra favourite; there are invariably four or five real ales on tap, including Fuller's London Pride and ESB and guests from far-flung British breweries. Who could refuse a pint of Dorothy Goodbody's Wholesome Stout?
Free house: Fuller's London Pride £2.25; Fuller's ESB £2.75. Tables outdoors (6, garden).

Greenwich SE10

★ Greenwich Union

56 Royal Hill, SE10 8RT (8692 6258). Greenwich DLR/rail. **Open** 11am-11pm Mon-Sat; noon-10.30pm Sun. **Meals served** 12.30-10pm Mon-Fri; 12.30-8pm Sat, Sun. **Credit** MC, V.
The amalgam of all that's best in the traditional pub and the modern bar, plus decent micro-brewed beers, makes the former Fox & Hounds/McGowans a welcome addition to Greenwich's vibrant boozing scene. Meantime Brewery's Alastair Hook trained in Munich, so the emphasis

here is on lager. His repertoire encompasses such delights as chocolate and raspberry beers, White, Golden (a traditional Pilsner), Amba and Union. Although all house beers are unpasteurised, the sole totally 'real ale' is Blonde Ale, a mouth-wateringly delicious pale, contract-brewed – we are led to believe – by Rooster's of Knaresborough, Yorkshire. The pub's flagstone floor and wood panelling remain, boosted by modern art, yellow and orange paintwork and on-the-ball staff who seem to regard this as their pub. Just try getting a seat in the child-friendly garden at peak hours.
Meantime Brewery: Blonde Ale £2.30; Union Lager £2.70. Babies and children welcome (before 9pm). Tables outdoors (12, garden).

London Bridge & Borough SE1

★ Royal Oak

44 Tabard Street, SE1 4JU (7357 7173). Borough tube/London Bridge tube/rail. **Open** 11.30am-11pm Mon-Fri. **Food served** noon-2.30pm, **dinner served** 6-9.30pm Mon-Fri. **Credit** MC, V.
Appearing on an increasing number of lists as London's finest pub, this smart corner establishment has plenty going for it. For a start, it's the only London tenancy of Harveys of Lewes – a particularly praiseworthy brewery – and the full range of four superb regular ales, ranging from Mild to Armada, is augmented by seasonal brews. Knots in May (a hoppy mild) and liquorice-like winter Porter are two of our favourites. Food is simple: own-made British pies and dinner-plate steaks, plus the odd rabbit casserole and veggie lasagne. The two compact bars are separated by a large wooden serving area, the whole space resplendent in carved mahogany, etched glass and ornate mirrors. A wood-panelled upstairs function room is much in demand for real ale groups, book launches and readings from Chaucer.
Harveys: Sussex Mild £2.10; Sussex Best £2.40. Disabled: toilet. Separate room for parties, seats 20. **Map 11 P9.**

East

Brick Lane E1

Pride of Spitalfields

3 Heneage Street, E1 5LJ (7247 8933). Aldgate East tube. **Open** 11am-11pm Mon-Sat; noon-10.30pm Sun. **Lunch served** noon-2.30pm Mon-Fri; 1-5pm Sun. **No credit cards.**
Recovered and well restored after a fire-bomb attack, this cosy pub now comes with a slightly thicker carpet but the same banquettes, sewing-

machine tables and Victorian photographs on the wall. The main bar's not much larger than an average front room, with a smaller antechamber where Spitalfields' arty types tend to congregate and discuss the spiralling costs of photographic paper. Overall, the clientele is a mirror of the area, encompassing students, pensioners, business folk, traders, artists and those simply waiting for the right employment opportunity to come along. Real ales are well kept and inexpensive, with a range of three that's likely to include London Pride and ESB from Fuller's, plus Crouch Vale Woodham IPA.
Free house: Crouch Vale Best Bitter £2.30; Fuller's ESB £2.40. Babies and children welcome. Tables outdoors (4, pavement). **Map 12 S5.**

Limehouse E14

Grapes

76 Narrow Street, E14 8BP (7987 4396). Limehouse DLR/rail. **Open** noon-3pm, 5.30-11pm Mon-Fri; noon-11pm Sat; noon-10.30pm Sun. **Food served** noon-2pm, 7-9pm Mon-Sat; noon-3.30pm Sun. **Credit** AmEx, MC, V.
Although the present building dates from 1720, there has been a pub here since 1583. Charles Dickens wrote about it in *Our Mutual Friend*, thinly disguising it as the Six Jolly Fellowship Porters. Though other boozers claim the honour, the description of the uneven, rickety pub that begins Chapter Six points to Narrow Street's finest. There has obviously been a tidy-up and a major renovation since those days, and the sinking wooden platform on the river is now a fetching veranda. Still, the staircase that leads up to the fish restaurant creaks and groans deliciously, the etched windows let in near-magical shafts of light and you get the idea that the Inimitable himself might still be scratching away in a corner, staining his pages with drops of Burton Bitter.
Spirit Group: Adnams £2.40; Bass £2.35; Burton £2.45. Restaurant available for hire.

Wapping E1

Prospect of Whitby

57 Wapping Wall, E1W 3SH (7481 1095). Wapping tube. **Open** 11.30am-11pm Mon-Sat; noon-10.30pm Sun. **Food served** *Pub* 11.30am-10pm Mon-Sat. *Restaurant* noon-3pm, 7-10pm Mon-Fri; 7-10pm Sat; noon-3pm Sun. **Credit** AmEx, DC, MC, V.
The former Devil's Tavern was built around 1520, last remodelled in 1777, and has since become a popular tourist attraction and riverside landmark. The first fuchsia ever to enter the country was exchanged for a noggin of rum here in 1780, and in 1953 an armed robbery took place on a party being held upstairs, resulting in a villain called Scarface (better known as Robert Harrington-Saunders) being hanged after shooting one of his pursuers. The pewter-topped counter (resting on wooden casks), flagstones, low ceilings, giant timbers, fireplaces and pebbled windows are wonderfully preserved. They add to an atmosphere that's unique, even in these well-sailed waters. A small terrace makes a good waterside drinking spot. The two or three real ales offered might include Fuller's London Pride and Young's Special.
Spirit Group: London Pride £2.50; Old Speckled Hen £2.60. Babies and children welcome (dining area). Function room. No-smoking area. Restaurant. Tables outdoors (7, garden).

North

Euston NW1

Head of Steam

1 Eversholt Street, NW1 1DN (7383 3359). Euston tube/rail. **Open** 11am-11pm Mon-Sat; noon-10.30pm Sun. **Lunch served** noon-2.30pm Mon-Fri; noon-3pm Sat. **Dinner served** 5-8pm Mon-Fri. **Credit** MC, V.
The people behind Head of Steam made a name for themselves 'oop north (Huddersfield, Scarborough, Blackpool) by turning railway bars into friendly, customer-led oases. Expect a wide selection of real ales and own-cooked food, in

Prospect of Whitby

Royal Oak

addition to the usual sandwiches, muffins and pots of tea. Here, the idea's roughly the same. Despite its concrete-block setting, the Head of Steam has the feel of a local, with a wealth of railway and London Underground memorabilia, a raised no-smoking area, bar billiards and up to nine real ales, usually including a mild, a cider and an occasional perry (cider made from pears). If there's a better way to await a delayed train, let us know.
Free house: Banks's Original Bitter £2; Hop Back Summer Lightning £2.40. Babies and children welcome. No-smoking area. **Map 4 K3.**

Harringay N4

★ Salisbury Hotel NEW
2004 RUNNER-UP BEST PUB
1 Grand Parade, Green Lanes, N4 1JX (8800 9617). Manor House tube then 29 bus. **Open** 2pm-1am Mon-Wed; noon-2am Thur-Sat; noon-midnight Sun. **Food served** 6-10pm Mon-Thur; noon-3pm, 6-10pm Fri, Sat; noon-4pm Sun. **Credit** MC, V.
This huge, three-storey (plus attic) boozer was a pub in decline before it was taken over by the small but seemingly worthy pub chain Remarkable Restaurants – whose other premises include the Swimmer at the Grafton Arms (*see right*). Some £2m was duly spent on renovation. Thanks to these efforts, the Salisbury now looks as good as it did when Scottish developer John Cathles Hill first designed and built the place in 1899. The main entrance in Green Lanes is a riot of decorative ironwork and intricate mosaics, leading through to three bars, around a central serving area. The flecked black stone pillars are made of Norwegian

larvikite. Cubby holes of carved mahogany offer discrete nooks for naughty noodling. At the side is a sturdy-looking billiard room, now transformed into a dining area lined with tables and illuminated by an impressive skylight decorated with floral motifs. Beers include real ales from Fuller's of Chiswick, as well as Litovel and Zubr Czech lagers, and Hoegaarden.
Free house: Fuller's London Pride £2.60; Fuller's ESB £2.70. Babies and children welcome (restaurant only). Disabled: toilet. Entertainment: jazz 8.30pm Sun. Function room. Restaurant.

Holloway N7

Swimmer at The Grafton Arms
13 Eburne Road, N7 6AR (7281 4632). Holloway Road tube or Finsbury Park tube/rail. **Open** noon-2.30pm, 5-11pm Mon-Thur; noon-11pm Fri, Sat; noon-10.30pm Sun. **Lunch served** noon-2pm Sat; noon-3pm Sun. **Dinner served** 6-9.30pm Mon-Sat. **Credit** MC, V.
A happy cross between a locals' haunt and a destination boozer, the Swimmer is one of those rare chain pubs (Remarkable Restaurants again, owners of the Salisbury Hotel – *see left*) that seem to get practically everything right. The jukebox is eclectic, the beer selection encompasses cask-conditioned brews from Ridleys of Chelmsford, plus European favourites like Zubr and Litovel, and the staff combine friendliness and efficiency in equal measure. There's only one small bar; even with the front terrace in full swing, it wouldn't take a platoon of marines to fill the place. The interior is tarted-up Victorian: cream and black paintwork, a long serving area and an open kitchen.

Free house: Fuller's London Pride £2.50; Fuller's ESB £2.80. No-smoking area. Tables outdoors (15, patio).

Islington N1

★ Wenlock Arms
2004 RUNNER-UP BEST PUB
26 Wenlock Road, N1 7TA (7608 3406/ www.wenlock-arms.co.uk). Old Street tube/rail/ 55 bus. **Open** noon-midnight Mon-Sat; noon-10.30pm Sun. **Food served** noon-9pm daily. **No credit cards.**
Pub companies spend millions on designers and market research trying to recreate the 'unique pub', little realising that rough diamonds like the Wenlock evolve organically, provided the management gives more than a damn. These premises were built in 1835 and are named after the now-defunct Wenlock Brewery. The excellent beer selection is what elevates this small, traditional, single-bar boozer above the herd. You'll find up to eight real ales on tap at any one time, plus a mild, a real cider or perry, and one or two Belgian specialities. Food is limited to 'real' pasties and hot 'sandwedges', while the decor is simple, traditional and plain. Drinkers plonked on stools around the bar can be hard to manoeuvre around in their 'this is my local' kind of way, but the bar staff are keen enough to ensure you'll not go thirsty for long. Incidental delights include the 'Fat Controller's' Thursday night quiz.
Free house: Crouch Vale Brewer's Gold £2.20; Pitfield EKG £2.20. Babies and children welcome. Entertainment: jazz 9pm Fri, Sat; 3pm Sun. Separate room for parties, seats 25. **Map 5 P3.**

Wine Bars

London's wine bar scene is dominated by the chains – **Balls Brothers, Corney & Barrow, Jamies** and **Davy's** – which tend to cater for younger customers than the traditional, independently run wine bars. In general, the scene is pretty stagnant, so it's pleasing to see the arrival of **Putney Station**, an addition to the successful – and very reasonably priced – Brinkley's chain.

Below are the best of the capital's wine bars; **Kettners** in Soho (*see p285*) also has a great champagne bar. For more choices, see the latest edition of the *Time Out Pubs & Bars Guide* (£6.99). For where to buy wine, see **Drink Shops**, starting on p357. For advice on learning more about wine, see the feature starting on p14.

Central

Bloomsbury WC1, WC2

Grape Street Wine Bar

224A Shaftesbury Avenue, WC2H 8EB (7240 0686). Holborn or Tottenham Court Road tube. **Open** 11am-11pm Mon-Fri. **Lunch served** noon-3.30pm, **dinner served** 5-10pm Mon-Fri. **Main courses** £6.95-£12.95. **House wine** £10.50 bottle, £2.65 glass. **Credit** AmEx, MC, V.
Away from the melee, Grape Street is a modestly attired spot at the less frantic end of Shaftesbury Avenue. It's one of those places worth keeping at the back of your mind: a central London venue where you can usually find a seat for a quiet natter. Furnishings focus on the matter in hand, with bottles, corks, prints and grape-inspired lamps providing decoration. Not much changes here, so the wine list remains ample rather than lengthy. It tends to favour the more popular grape varieties (chardonnay, sauvignon blanc, merlot, cabernet). Prices are about average, even given the central location. To eat, there's a choice of typical British wine bar food, plus main-course daily specials and a list of snacks designed to accompany wine.
Babies and children admitted. Separate room for parties, seats 20. Tables outdoors (2, pavement). **Map 18 L6.**

Vats Wine Bar

51 Lamb's Conduit Street, WC1N 3NB (7242 8963). Holborn or Russell Square tube. **Bar Open** noon-11pm Mon-Fri. *Restaurant* **Lunch served** noon-2.30pm, **dinner served** 6-9.30pm Mon-Fri. **Main courses** £9.95-£14.95.
Both **House wine** £13.50 bottle, £3.75 glass. **Service** 12.5%. **Credit** AmEx, DC, MC, V.
This narrow wine bar is very highly regarded by its regular patrons. The front part, built with roughly the same dimensions as the average living room, and decked out in pale wood panelling and a dark green ceiling, is the main drinking area. Then comes the dining area, and beyond that a very pleasant inner sanctum that's frequently used for parties and launches. Food is a feature – a mix of traditional and modern, Brit and European, full meals and snacks – that might include half a roast Sussex pheasant, a stilton, brie and cheddar platter, risotto, and salmon fish cakes. The long wine list centres on France and has much that will please dabblers and connoisseurs alike; highlights include plenty of half bottles and wines by the glass, a hefty choice of vintage fizz and some brilliant (though premium-priced) Bordeaux.
Babies and children admitted. Booking advisable restaurant. Separate room for parties, seats 40. Tables outdoors (4, pavement). **Map 4 K4.**

Truckles of Pied Bull Yard

Off Bury Place, WC1A 2JR (7404 5338/ www.davy.co.uk). Holborn or Tottenham Court Road tube.
Café/bar **Open/snacks served** 11am-10pm Mon-Fri; 11am-3pm Sat. **Snacks** £4.95-£6.
Restaurant **Lunch served** 11am-3pm, **dinner served** 5-9pm Mon-Fri. **Main courses** £7.95-£13.95. **Set lunch** £13.95 2 courses, £16.95 3 courses.
Both **Credit** AmEx, DC, MC, V.
The best thing about dignified, olde worlde Truckles is its setting – in a vast, characterful courtyard alongside an emporium of rare cameras and the London Review bookshop, and opposite the British Museum. It's tucked off the main street, so often surprisingly empty, even on sunny days. Truckles is part of the extensive Davy's chain of sawdust-floored wine bars, which specialise in several own-label wines and Davy's Old Wallop ale served in pewter tankards. The ground-floor is firmly set in the 21st century, with vibrant colours, parquet flooring, furniture leaning towards minimalism, and express lunches politely despatched without ceremony. The downstairs Ale & Port House Bar upholds the traditional image that Davy's (established 1870) successfully cultivates, with scuffed wood, sawdust and signs proclaiming 'Skeffington's Vintage Port', and food of the stilton-and-courgette tart variety. The wine list isn't extensive, but is adequate and fairly priced. Own-label bottles are to the fore: Davy's Australian chardonnay comes from Bimbadgen Estate, Hunter Valley; its blanc de blanc fizz hails from Seyssel, in the Savoie region of France.
Babies and children admitted. Bar/restaurant available for hire. Booking advisable. Dress: smart casual. No-smoking tables. Tables outdoors (15, courtyard).
For branches (Davy's) see index.

City EC2, EC4

Balls Brothers

6-8 Cheapside, EC2V 6AN (7248 2708/ www.ballsbrothers.co.uk). St Paul's tube. **Open** 11am-10pm Mon-Fri. **Lunch served** 11.30am-3pm, **snacks served** 5-9pm Mon-Fri. **Main courses** £4.25-£7.50. **House wine** £16 bottle, £3.80 glass. **Credit** AmEx, DC, MC, V.
Few branches of the big Balls Brothers chain can hope to match the location of this bar: opposite St Paul's Cathedral, and with a paved outdoor drinking terrace. Inside, the ground floor is a grand affair with high ceilings and arched windows. Downstairs is a traditional cellar wine bar with dark wooden furniture, oak panelling, alcoves and framed prints on the walls. Food is of the basic sandwich and snack variety, but the wine list is worth serious consideration. Ball Brothers is also a wine merchant's, so the choice is extensive. Many bottles are matured in the firm's cellars, particularly the range of more modestly priced clarets and burgundies. The accent is on France, with labels including Pouilly-Fumé from Jean Pabiot et Fils, and Château Haut-Bailly, Graves. Louis Roederer is among the wide choice of champagnes. There's also plenty of choice from the New World, including wine from award-winning producers such as Grant Burge from Australia's Barossa Valley.
Children admitted (garden only). Separate area for parties, seats 70. Tables outdoors (16, courtyard). **Map 11 O6.**
For branches (Balls Brothers, Bar Under the Clock) see index.

Corney & Barrow

19 Broadgate Circle, EC2M 2QS (7628 1251/ www.corney-barrow.co.uk). Liverpool Street tube/rail. **Open** 7.30-11pm, **breakfast served** 7.30-11am, **meals served** noon-10pm Mon-Fri. **Main courses** £6-£13. **House wine** £11.95 bottle, £3.25-£3.95 glass. **Credit** AmEx, DC, MC, V.
Flagship of the swanky, City-based chain, this branch of C&B curls around the circumference of Broadgate Circle. It's a corridor-like glass-fronted space, flooded with natural light during the day. By the windows are high tables around which young, self-assured City types sit on dark-blue stools. Outside there are heated canopies; in winter you get a bird's-eye view of the ice rink. Food is served throughout the day: breakfast, a modern brasserie menu during the day (from posh sandwiches and warm salads to main courses such as chicken breast stuffed with halloumi, chorizo hash and roasted red pepper jus) and an evening selection of bar bites. The drinks list is modified every couple of months, but is laudably user-friendly. Wines are ordered by grape variety, with helpful, concise tasting notes. Chocapalha 2000 from Estremadura, Portugal, for example, is: 'a temptress of a wine, with pepper dark chocolate and vanilla cream'. The choice is large yet unintimidating, and bottles are sourced from an admirably wide spread of countries.
Booking essential. Disabled: toilet; lift. Restaurant and bar available for hire. Tables outdoors (30, balconies and terrace). **Map 12 Q5.**
For branches see index.

Jamies at the Pavilion

Finsbury Circus Gardens, EC2M 7AB (7628 8224/www.jamiesbars.co.uk). Liverpool Street or Moorgate tube/rail. **Bar Open** 11am-11pm, **lunch served** 11am-3pm, **snacks served** 6-9pm Mon-Fri. **Snacks** £1.75-£15.95. *Restaurant* **Lunch served** 11am-3pm Mon-Fri. **Main courses** £9.95-£16.95. *Both* **House wine** £13 bottle, £3.25-£4.50 glass. **Service** 12.5%. **Credit** AmEx, JCB, MC, V.
An oasis from the City's grim finance factories, this branch of the Jamies chain is located in a pavilion that's also the clubhouse for the City of London Bowling Club. Best viewed in summer, the venue is surrounded by an emerald bowling green and a circle of trees and shrubbery: you could be in the wilds of East Grinstead. The wine list changes three times a year, with advice on new labels being provided by Willie Lebus of Bibendum (*see p358*). The choice is well thought-out and pretty evenly split between Old World and New. Sensibly ordered by grape variety, the selection includes several wines for less than £20: Alamos Mendoza cabernet sauvignon 2002 from Argentina (£19.50); and Pierre Sparr Reserve pinot blanc 2002 from Alsace (£18.50), for instance. Almost all the wines are available by the glass, making Jamies a good spot for experimentation. Prices are a little above average, but that's only to be expected given the location, and the clientele of youngish, besuited City workers who flock here at lunchtime and after work. To eat, there are shared snack plates, sandwiches and more substantial main courses.
Bookings not accepted for parties of fewer than 6 (bar). Dress: smart casual. Restaurant and bar available for hire. **Map 12 Q5.**

La Grande Marque

47 Ludgate Hill, EC4M 7JU (7329 6709/ www.lagrandemarque.com). St Paul's tube/ Blackfriars tube/rail. **Open** 11.30am-9.30pm Mon-Fri. **Lunch served** 11.30am-3pm, **snacks served** 5-8pm Mon-Fri. **Main courses** £4.70-£6.50. **Snacks** £3-£5. **House wine** £14 bottle, £4 glass. **Credit** AmEx, DC, JCB, MC, V.
There can be absolutely no doubt that the speciality here is champagne. Bottles of the stuff line the windows and fill just about every nook and cranny of this grand, former City bank headquarters, built in 1891. The name is an old French term, signifying a champagne brand of superior quality. Inside, you'll find the swishest of swish drapes, a marvellous moulded ceiling, subtle lighting, a pleasing tiled floor and enough chunky

dark wood to keep Noah in business for some time. Fine wines and champers are a given (there's a separate section for the real wallet-busting bottles), but you'll also find an abundance of well-chosen and wide-ranging vins ordinaires.
Separate room for parties, holds 50. **Map 11 O6**.

El Vino

47 Fleet Street, EC4Y 1BJ (7353 6786/ www.elvino.co.uk). Chancery Lane tube or Temple tube/Blackfriars tube/rail.
Bar **Open** 8.30am-9pm Mon; 8.30am-10pm Tue-Fri.
Restaurant **Open** noon-3pm Mon-Fri. **Meals served** 8.30am-8pm Mon; 8.30am-9pm Tue-Fri. **Main courses** £8.50-£12. **Service** 12.5%.
Both **House wine** £13.50 bottle, £3.40 glass.
Credit AmEx, JCB, MC, V.
El Vino opened in 1879 and scarcely seems to have changed since, though it no longer attracts as many old-school journalists following the departure of the national press from Fleet Street. Lawyers, however, still flock to its well worn but comfortable interior, feeling at home in the slightly clubby atmosphere. In the basement is a staunchly traditional restaurant, where steak and kidney pie can be followed by spotted dick and custard. As you might expect, the wine list has a forte in claret, port, burgundy and champagne. Yet thanks to the choice of styles, vintages and prices, the selection appeals to a wide range of imbibers. The New World isn't overlooked either, with plenty of antipodean interest. A recent big seller was Dancing Sun sauvignon blanc 2003 from New Zealand. El Vino has an off-licence attached, so you can take home a bottle of your favoured tipple.
Booking advisable. Dress: smart casual; no trainers. Separate room for parties, seats 40. Takeaway service. Vegetarian menu. Tables outdoors (2, pavement). **Map 11 N6**.
For branches see index.

Clerkenwell & Farringdon EC1

Bleeding Heart Bistro & Tavern

Bleeding Heart Yard, off Greville Street, EC1N 8SJ (7242 8238/www.bleedingheart.co.uk). Farringdon tube/rail.
Tavern **Open** 7.30am-11pm Mon-Fri. **Lunch served** noon-3pm, **snacks served** 3-6pm, **dinner served** 6-10pm Mon-Fri. **Main courses** £7.95-£12.95. **Snacks** £4-£8. **House red**

£11.75 bottle, £2.95 glass. **House white** £14.25 bottle, £3.50 glass.
Bistro **Lunch served** noon-3pm, **dinner served** 6-10.30pm Mon-Fri. **Main courses** £7.45-£13.95. **House red** £19.95 bottle, £4.95 glass. **House white** £16.45 bottle, £4.15 glass.
Restaurant **Lunch served** noon-2.30pm, **dinner served** 6-10.30pm Mon-Fri. **Main courses** £11.95-£19.95. **House red** £19.95 bottle, £4.95 glass. **House white** £16.45 bottle, £4.15 glass.
All **Service** 12.5% for parties of 6 or more.
Credit AmEx, DC, MC, V.
There's a choice of two quite distinct venues at Bleeding Heart. The Tavern is an historic old pub now owned by Adnams brewery. It dates from 1746 and is a softly lit, congenial spot. As well as Adnams ales, you'll find a well-chosen batch of more than 450 wines here, several available by the glass. The choice includes a selection from the firm's own vineyard in Hawkes Bay, New Zealand. On the ground floor an appetising menu of British food includes starters such as Cromer crab with citrus salad, and main courses from the spit (roast ale-fed suckling pig) or grill (organic salmon with an olive oil and green herb sauce) with more intricate creations served in the smart, intimate cellar restaurant (roasted fillet of monkfish with feve beans and saffron potatoes, say). Separate from all this is the Bleeding Heart Bistro, hidden round the corner and across a cobbled courtyard. It's an exceedingly French place where classic Gallic cuisine has been given a contemporary nudge (so grilled sea bream come with confit fennel and aïoli sauce). A dozen wines in the bistro can be ordered by the glass.
Booking advisable. Dress: smart; no shorts, jeans or trainers (restaurant). Separate rooms for parties, seating 30-40. Tables outdoors (15, terrace). **Map 11 N5**.

Cellar Gascon

59 West Smithfield, EC1A 9DS (7796 0600). Barbican tube/Farringdon tube/rail. **Open/ meals served** noon-midnight Mon-Fri.
Tapas £5-£6. **House wine** £15.70 bottle, £4 glass. **Service** (food) 12.5%. **Credit** AmEx, JCB, MC, V.
We like this place. Located next to French restaurant Club Gascon (*see p78*), the Cellar's highly original and beautifully designed bar is the embassy for Gascon wines in London, lining up an impressive and intriguing list of 120 wines exclusively from said south-western region of France. But instead of the expected rural look, the

interior is pure metropolitan chic, with leather scoop bar stools, banquettes and elegant copper hanging lamps. Black-clad French waiters smoulder away behind the bar and turn out to be entirely knowledgeable and happy, nay eager, to guide novices through lesser-known areas of winery such as Irouléguy and Pacherenc. A lip-smacking selection of 35 foodie dégustations includes more familiar regional classics such as foie gras, while traditional aperitifs and digestifs such as Floc de Gascoigne, as well as a huge selection of cognac and armagnac, complete the Gasconomic experience.
Bookings not accepted. Bar available for hire. **Map 11 O5**.

Covent Garden WC2

Café des Amis

11-14 Hanover Place, WC2E 9JP (7379 3444/ www.cafedesamis.co.uk). Covent Garden tube.
Bar **Open** 11.30am-11pm Mon-Sat. **Snacks served** 11.30am-10.30pm Mon-Sat.
Restaurant **Meals served** 11.30am-11.30pm Mon-Sat. **Main courses** £13.50-£24. **Set meal** (11.30am-5pm, 5-7pm, 10-11.30pm) £13.50 2 courses, £16 3 courses. **Service** 12.5%.
Both **House wine** £13 bottle, £3.40 glass.
Credit AmEx, DC, MC, V.
Reached down a quiet side street, Café des Amis sports a narrow terrace out front where pavement tables are set up in summer. Inside, a recent refurbishment has given both the chic, ground-floor brasserie (*see p292*) and basement wine bar a more contemporary feel. The wine bar features banquette seating with plush upholstery, low-level coffee tables and a circular wooden bar. A light menu of bar snacks, and an extensive continental cheeseboard (including some splendidly pungent specimens) are available throughout the day. Local office workers flock here after a day on the treadmill. They wind down with a quaff of something from the varied list of easy-drinking wines (about half the collection is available by the glass). Prices are around the West End average, though there's a decent choice of bottles for under £20: the Portuguese Tuella Douro 1997 costs £14.25, while the Lindauer Brut fizz from New Zealand is £18.50. Fine wine buffs should examine the selection of aged bottles.
Babies and children admitted. Booking advisable (restaurant). Separate room for parties, seats 60. Tables outdoors (10, courtyard). **Map 18 L6**.

Corney & Barrow

On the Town

Leicester Square WC2

Cork & Bottle

*44-46 Cranbourn Street, WC2H 7AN
(7734 7807). Leicester Square tube.* **Open**
11am-11.30pm Mon-Sat; noon-10.30pm Sun.
Main courses £4.50-£12.95. **House wine**
£15 bottle, £3.50 glass. **Credit** AmEx, DC, JCB,
MC, V.

One of those eccentric little places that make
London special, the Cork has been maturing nicely
since 1971 in an inconspicuous basement tightly
squeezed between purveyors of sex and kebabs,
right behind the glare of Leicester Square. Here,
down a narrow staircase hung with old
champagne adverts and press cuttings, long-time
owner Kiwi Don Hewitson has built an
underground world of wine. 'Life's too short to
drink boring wine,' quoth Don. 'The Thoughts of
Chairman Don' are broken down region by region
(France is encyclopaedic, Spain somewhat
neglected), and written with grit and gusto. The
list is updated at regular intervals. About a dozen
options are served by the glass, and staff will be
delighted to offer suggestions. Beside the bar
counter, there's a display of meats and cheeses, and
chalked-up plats du jour. The food is excellent, the
atmosphere intimate (cosy alcoves a speciality) and
the prices reasonable.
*Babies and children welcome. Bookings accepted
until 6.30pm. No-smoking area (daytime).
Separate room for parties, seats 12.*
Map 18 K7.

Soho W1

Shampers

*4 Kingly Street, W1B 5PE (7437 1692).
Oxford Circus or Piccadilly Circus tube.* **Open**
11am-11pm Mon-Sat (*Aug* closed Sat). **Meals
served** noon-11pm Mon-Sat. **Main courses**
£8.75-£13.50. **House wine** £11.50 bottle,
£3.25 glass. **Service** 12.5%. **Credit** AmEx,
DC, JCB, MC, V.

Tweeds and wines. In a nutshell (or grape skin),
that's what you're getting at this reassuringly
unchanging wine bar just off Regent Street. More
specifically, you've also got blazers, Barbours,
business shirts and the odd mohair jumper. As for
the wines, there are 166 to choose from: in racks,
on shelves, in fridges – all impeccably chosen and
admirably wide-ranging. So for every stalwart
such as Beaujolais Villages, there's an intriguing
number like the red Château Musar from Lebanon,
described in the helpful menu as 'mighty
idiosyncratic'. Every month also sees ten or so new
additions; when we visited, the new arrivals
included, among others, a sparkling number from
Sussex Downs vineyard Breaky Bottom and a
pricey Barolo Roggeri 1997. Although the country-
style green paint and terracotta tiling in the stand-
up bar at the back is pleasant, the provincial feel
is slightly contrived and the social cross-section
somewhat fuddy-duddy. The food – standard-issue
wine bar dishes such as terrines, anchovies, cold
cuts and cheeses – looked appetising, and was
being lapped up in the front dining area by a group
of chattering fiftysomethings.
*Babies and children welcome. Booking advisable.
Restaurant and bar available for hire. Separate
room for parties, seats 50. Tables outdoors
(3, courtyard).* **Map 17 J6**.

Strand WC2

Gordon's

*47 Villiers Street, WC2N 6NE (7930 1408/
www.gordonswinebar.com). Embankment tube/
Charing Cross tube/rail.* **Open** 11am-11pm Mon-
Sat; noon-10pm Sun. **Meals served** noon-10pm
daily. **Main courses** £6.95-£8.95. **House wine**
£11.50 bottle, £3.20 glass. **Credit** AmEx, MC, V.
Atmospheric subterranean Gordon's is ideally
located for commuters heading to or from Charing
Cross station. The building, once home to Samuel
Pepys and Rudyard Kipling, became a bar in 1890.
At the bottom of the stairs is a food bar offering
cold cuts, cheeses, salads and suchlike, but turn

left to a warren of grime-encrusted brick alcoves
– at head-knocking height to make getting around
that bit more interesting. Don't count on finding a
seat; in summer, tables in the courtyard are at a
premium. Wines are mainly French, but Chile,
Argentina, Australia, South Africa and even India
(Grovers sauvignon blanc, £12.95) are
represented. Bottles start at a reasonable £11.50,
with plenty of options under £20. You'll also find
sherries, ports and madeiras. Customers tend to be
a mix of Rumpole-style wine buffs and shoppers
and local workers popping in for a reviving glass
before they head home.
*Babies and children welcome. Bookings not
accepted. Tables outdoors (10, terrace).*
Map 18 L7.

Victoria SW1

Tiles

*36 Buckingham Palace Road, SW1W 0RE
(7834 7761). Victoria tube/rail.* **Open** noon-
11pm Mon-Fri. **Lunch served** noon-2.30pm
Mon-Fri, **dinner served** 5.30-10pm Mon-Fri.
Main courses £7.95-£13.95. **House wine**
£11.50 bottle, £3 glass. **Service** 12.5%.
Credit AmEx, DC, JCB, MC, V.
This commendably simple and unpretentious two-
floor continental wine bar and eatery has been
dedicated to the pleasures of the palate for more
than 20 years. Choose from the cosy,
Mediterranean-style ground-floor bar, or the funky
basement lounge bar with squashy sofas and
subtle lighting. Two rosés, 20 reds and 20 whites
are each given a one-line recommendation in a clear
wine list. Many bottles can be sampled by the
glass; the list includes a crisp South African chenin
blanc, a Chilean carmenère or an easy Sacchetto
pinot grigio. For special occasions, Tiles keeps a
classic collection, such as a Burgundian Nuits St
Georges from Bouchard Père et Fils or a
Chambolle-Musigny 1998 from Georges Roumier,
in the £40 range. The kitchen isn't shabby, either,
with imaginative and well-priced mains,

On the Town

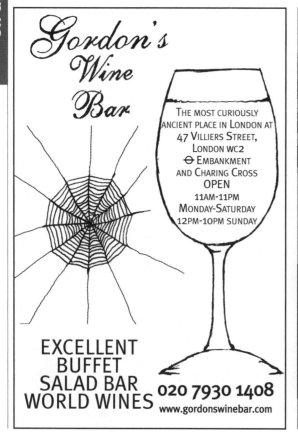

including fish cakes (the speciality) or the likes of sun-dried tomato and leek risotto.
Booking advisable. Restaurant available f or hire. Separate room for parties, seats 60. Tables outdoors (6, pavement).
Map 15 H10.

West

Holland Park W11

Julie's
135-137 Portland Road, W11 4LW (7229 8331/www.juliesrestaurant.com). Holland Park tube.
Bar **Open** 9am-11pm Mon-Sat; noon-10pm Sun. **Lunch served** 12.30-2.45pm Mon-Sat; 12.30-3.30pm Sun. **Afternoon tea served** 3-6.30pm daily. **Dinner served** 7-10.45pm Mon-Sat; 7-10pm Sun. **Main courses** £10-£17.
Restaurant **Lunch served** 12.30-3pm Sun. **Dinner served** 7-11.30pm Mon-Sat. **Main courses** £10-£17.
Both **House wine** £16 bottle, £4 glass. **Service** 12.5%. **Credit** AmEx, JCB, MC, V.
Tucked away down a residential street in leafy Holland Park, this long-standing wine bar attracts a stream of well-heeled regulars, drawn by the feel-good atmosphere, cheerful staff and eclectic Indian/Arabesque-inspired decor. Expect fringed curtains, slightly battered little tables and random artworks stuck wherever there's space for a knick-knack. French options dominate the shortish wine list, but it also ranges further afield to the likes of Chile, Australia, New Zealand and California, and includes a few fine wines and five champagnes (starting at Ellner Epernay NV for £30 a bottle). Next door is the charming and popular restaurant of the same name, offering European dishes that use organic produce 'whenever possible'. Julie's is also a family-friendly spot, with even a crèche in operation on Sunday afternoons. If you've imbibed too much to get home safely, you can always stagger the short distance to the eccentric Portobello Hotel, under the same ownership as Julie's and a fave with visiting rock stars.
Babies and children welcome; children's menu (Sun); crèche (1-4pm Sun); high chairs. Booking advisable. Separate rooms for parties, seating 12, 16, 24, 35 and 45. Tables outdoors (12, pavement). **Map 19 B5.**

Kensington W8

Whits
21 Abingdon Road, W8 6AH (7938 1122/ www.whits.co.uk). High Street Kensington tube.
Open noon-2.30pm, 5.30pm-11pm Tue-Sat. **Lunch served** 12.30-2.30pm, **dinner served** 5.30-10pm Tue-Sat. **Main courses** £10.50-£16.50. **House wine** £11.95 bottle, £3 glass. **Service** 12.5%. **Credit** AmEx, DC, MC, V.
Goolies has changed hands and, in a highly commendable move, been renamed Whits. The new owners have spruced the place up, making what was already a rather swish venue still more attractive. A handsome oval skylight brightens the daylight hours; the ground-floor drinking area also features back-lit niches, plush banquettes and a long and becoming wooden bar. Up a few steps is the smart mezzanine restaurant, where lunch might be halibut and salmon fish cakes with buttered spinach, parsley and champagne sauce. Roast grouse with poached plums and poitrine fumé is among the elaborate and pricey main courses for dinner. The wine list is well liked by Kensington's opulent vinophiles. It contains a fair assortment of styles, with plenty of choice under the £20 mark and a dozen or so options by the glass. A 2002 gewürztraminer from Paul Zinck goes for £16.50.
Children admitted. Booking advisable.

Shepherd's Bush W12

Albertine
1 Wood Lane, W12 7DP (8743 9593). Shepherd's Bush tube. **Open** 11am-11pm Mon-Fri; 6.30-11pm Sat. **Meals served** noon-10.30pm

Mon-Fri; 6.30-10.30pm Sat. **Main courses** £5.50-£7.50. **House wine** £10.90 bottle, £2.80 glass. **Credit** MC, V.
Situated two minutes from Shepherd's Bush tube, this compact, long-established wine bar is a nicely placed spot, and much appreciated by locals – it can get pretty crowded. It doesn't look much from the outside, and reworked church pews and solid wooden tables make for an interior that's sturdy and not particularly comfortable, but the comprehensive collection of quaffable treats more than compensates. With over 60 wines under £30 a bottle to choose from, the needs of most tastes and wallets are met. Prices start at a very reasonable £10.90 a bottle, with plenty of options available by the glass. Handwritten wine lists are flaunted on the walls, and the menu offers inexpensive bistro food, and an impressive cheese board. Staff are friendly and knowledgeable.
Booking advisable for large parties. Separate room for parties, seats 28. **Map 20 B2.**

South West

Earlsfield SW18

Willie Gunn
422 Garratt Lane, SW18 4HW (8946 7773). Earlsfield rail. **Open** 11am-11pm Mon-Sat; 11am-10.30pm Sun. **Meals served** 11am-11pm Mon-Sat; 11am-10pm Sun. **Main courses** £9.50-£15. **House wine** £11 bottle, £3.25 glass. **Service** 12.5%. **Credit** AmEx, MC, V.
Demurely decked out with a lilac colour scheme, carefully chosen pictures, and candlelit tables in the front bar and rear dining room, Willie Gunn is among Earlsfield's smartest venues. Locals are well catered for, with a full English breakfast served every weekday and brunch at weekends, from 11am to 1pm. Then the regularly changing menu kicks in, offering fixtures like sausages and mash, and specials such as skate wing with deep-fried capers and celeriac mash. There's also a range of bar snacks and an alluring collection of unpasteurised cheeses. To drink, there's Pilsner Urquell on tap, plus various bottled lagers and a sizeable wine list. This starts at £11 a bottle, though rises substantially for the fine wines. A popular choice for the cooler months is likely to be the Tulbagh merlot from South Africa at £15.50 a bottle.
Babies and children welcome; high chairs. Booking advisable. Tables outdoors (4, pavement).

Fulham SW10

Wine Gallery
49 Hollywood Road, SW10 9HX (7352 7572/ www.brinkleys.com). South Kensington tube then 14, 345 bus. **Lunch served** noon-4pm, **dinner served** 7-11.30pm daily. **Main courses** £7.50-£11.50. **House wine** £7.50 bottle, £2.50 glass. **Service** 10%. **Credit** AmEx, DC, JCB, MC, V.
The oldest link in the Brinkley's chain (the wine merchant's head office is next door), the Wine Gallery has maintained its popularity over the decades with a smart-casual set of locals. Such folk probably don't lose sleep over the cost of a bottle of Gevrey-Chambertin, but Brinkley's doesn't take advantage. Wines are supplied at retail prices, so even if you decide to splash out with a bottle of Bolly, you won't part with more than £35 (compare that with City wine bars). More modest tipples on the large, French-led list include a premier cru Chablis (Beauroy, 2000) for £15, and a Norton malbec (2003) from Argentina for just £8.50. The venue includes a bar area where woodiness is leavened by splashes of colourful art on the walls; a popular, multi-roomed restaurant; pavement tables under an electronic canopy; and a small, pretty garden. The brasserie-style menu encompasses the traditional (cottage pie with peas) and the contemporary (grilled cod with puy lentils, rocket and tomato sauce).
Booking advisable; essential Thur-Sat. Separate rooms for parties, seating 20-50. Tables outdoors (15, garden; 3, pavement). **Map 13 C12.**

Putney SW15

Putney Station [NEW]
94-98 Upper Richmond Road, SW15 2SP (8780 0242/www.brinkleys.com). East Putney tube.
Bar **Open/snacks served** noon-11pm Mon-Sat; noon-10.30pm Sun. **Snacks** £3.50-£7.
Restaurant **Meals served** noon-11pm Mon-Sat; noon-10.30pm Sun. **Main courses** £5-£15.
Both **House wine** £5 bottle, £3 glass. **Service** 10%. **Credit** MC, V.
Putney Station is the latest link in a small chain that includes wine bar/brasseries the Oratory (*see below*), the Wine Gallery (*see above*) and the Union Café. As with all Brinkley's outlets, the wine list is not only peppered with good producers, the mark-ups are negligible; barely more than off-licence prices. Fizz-lovers will appreciate that a bottle of Bolly costs only £35, while Laurent-Perrier NV is a mere £30 – you could pay nearly double these prices elsewhere. If you're a real connoisseur, how about an Isabel pinot poir 2002 from Marlborough at £22.50; or Cloudy Bay sauvignon blanc 2003 for £18.50? Besides top-flight New Zealand wines, the list is also strong on Australia and Burgundy, with all but the sparklers costing from as little as a fiver to £25. The menu attempts to cover all bases, offering pizzas, burgers and Thai fare. The look is sleek and contemporary, with big windows and a sweeping polished bar.
Babies and children welcome; high chairs. Booking advisable. Disabled: toilet. No-smoking tables. Separate room for parties, seats 35. Tables outdoors (4, pavement). Takeaway service.

South Kensington SW3

The Oratory
234 Brompton Road, SW3 2BB (7584 3493/ www.brinkleys.com). South Kensington tube.
Open/meals served noon-11pm Mon-Sat; noon-10.30pm Sun. **Main courses** £6-£14.50. **House wine** £7.50 bottle, £3.50 glass. **Service** 10%. **Credit** AmEx, MC, V.
Despite its moneyed locale, the Oratory (named after the nearby Brompton Oratory) has earned a place in wine lovers' hearts by dint of its low cost. Bottles are supplied at retail prices by the owners, wine merchant's Brinkley's. Hence you'll pay just £7.50 for a bottle of the house white (Caliterra 2003, a chardonnay/sauvignon blanc from Chile), while a bottle of Brinkley's Brut champagne is £18.50. Though the list doesn't change much, there's a reasonable choice of grape varieties – especially among the reds, which include Brunello di Montalcino 1998, a Col d'Orcia sangiovese (at just £27.50). You don't have to slum it here either: the venue has character aplenty, with furnishings producing a feel of fashionably faded grandeur. Glass chandeliers hang from high ceilings, and the walls (painted in gold and blue) are trendily disfigured by designer cracks. The menu is modern, eclectic and not too dear: grilled bruschetta with goat's cheese and a red pepper and red onion compote might precede thai chicken curry with lemon and poppy seed rice, with hot toffee cake for pud. In clement weather, the pavement seating soon fills up. And there's the rub: a sizeable proportion of south-west Londoners seems to head here in the early evenings. Booking ahead is essential, especially at weekends.
Babies and children welcome. Booking advisable. Tables outdoors (9, pavement).
Map 14 E10.

South

Waterloo SE1

The Archduke
Concert Hall Approach, SE1 8XU (7928 9370). Waterloo tube/rail.
Bar **Open** 8.30am-11pm Mon-Sat. **Meals served** 11am-11pm Mon-Sat. **Main courses** £3.95-£7.50.
Restaurant **Lunch served** noon-2.15pm Mon-Fri. **Dinner served** 5.30-11pm Mon-Sat. **Main courses** £10-£14.95. **Set meal** (noon-2.15pm, 5.30-7.30pm Mon-Fri; 5.30-7.30pm Sat)

£13.50 2 courses, £16.75 3 courses incl bread and coffee.
Both **House wine** £11.50 bottle, £2.95 glass. **Service** 12.5%. **Credit** AmEx, DC, MC, V.
This multi-levelled bar/restaurant is nestled under the arches of Hungerford Bridge, its name picked out in red neon – making it a doddle to spot as you walk from Waterloo station to the South Bank. Resembling a giant conservatory, with acres of glass and foliage in abundance, it's divided into various areas, including a laid-back mezzanine and ground-floor bar, an outdoor gravel patio, and a more formal restaurant on the uppermost level, beneath a high, bare-brick ceiling (hear those trains rumble). The wine list majors on easy-drinking European, plus some tempting New World numbers – and most bottles come in under £20. A pleasant Mandrarossa-Settesoli chardonnay from Sicily weighs in at £17.95, a good Rioja – say, Viña Ijalba – costs £18.25, and a better one – Viña Real Crianza – will set you back £21. Non-wine lovers won't suffer: there's Breton cider by the bottle and draught Paulaner. Oh – and if you're a mainstream jazz fan, stick around for the nightly sessions.
Babies and children welcome; children's menu (Sat). Bar available for hire. Booking advisable restaurant. Entertainment: jazz 8.30-11pm Mon-Fri; 8.30-11.30pm Sat. No-smoking areas. Separate rooms for parties, seating 35 and 45. Tables outdoors (11, pavement). **Map 10 M9**.

South East
London Bridge & Borough SE1

Wine Wharf
Stoney Street, Borough Market, SE1 9AD (7940 8335/www.winewharf.com). London Bridge tube/rail. **Open** 11.30am-11pm Mon-Fri; 11am-11pm Sat. **Meals served** noon-9.30pm Mon-Sat. **Main courses** £4.50-£9.95.
House white £13.50 bottle, £3-£3.50 glass. **House red** £15 bottle, £3.50-£4.25 glass.
Credit AmEx, DC, MC, V.
Tucked down a quiet backstreet, Wine Wharf – the wine bar for Vinopolis (the wine museum) – offers a suitably extensive and global selection of interesting wines. If you like to experiment, this is the place to do it – you can roam from an English gamay to a Uraguayan tannat. The young wine-savvy staff are friendly and fun, plus they always let you try before you commit to buy. Options by the glass (125ml and 175ml) are strewn all over the menu, meaning choice is exceptional and quality is tip-top. Uncommon wines abound; try a pinot noir from Oregon's Firesteed Winery (£31) for instance, or a Dr Unger, Gruner Veltiner, Kremstal, 2003 from Austria (£33.75). Unfortunately, despite all the above – and the attractively modish wharf-style interior of bare bricks, beams and metal – the place doesn't seem to be pulling in the punters. Shame. London's wine-lovers will lose a valuable resource if neglect forces the place out of business. The Modern European restaurant Cantina Vinopolis (*see p219*) is also on the site.
Babies and children welcome (until 8pm). Disabled: toilet. Restaurant and bar available for hire. Separate area for parties, seats 50. **Map 11 P8**.

North West
West Hampstead NW6

No.77 Wine Bar
77 Mill Lane, NW6 1NB (7435 7787). West Hampstead tube/rail. **Open** noon-11pm Mon, Tue; noon-midnight Wed-Sat; noon-10.30pm Sun. **Lunch served** noon-2.30pm Mon-Fri. **Meals served** noon-10.30pm Sat; noon-10pm Sun. **Main courses** £7.25-£14.50. **House wine** £11.45 bottle, £2.75 glass. **Service** 12.5%.
Credit MC, V.
Unlike many designer bars, the No.77 Wine Bar has an unpremeditated style that is exceptionally charming – the walls are lovingly hung with signed sports shirts, strange African carvings and naïve art. A labyrinth of different rooms, it creates

a cosy feel despite its fairly ample proportions. Sport is a focus both for design and events; the bar calls itself 'North London's Spiritual Rugby Home'. The wine list offers plenty of easy-drinking options from the familiar to the unusual, with plenty of options by the glass. The brasserie-style menu includes some fine burgers (such as the signature No.77 burger topped with smoked

cheddar, braised capiscum and onions, with fries). Tea lights sparkle on each table, illuminating the faces of the thirtysomething crowd, who obviously love the place in all its unpretentious glory. It's popular in the evenings, so it's wise to book.
Babies and children welcome. Booking advisable. Separate room for parties, seats 40. Tables outdoors (8, pavement). Map 28 A1.

Jamies at the Pavilion. See p320.

Parties & Shops

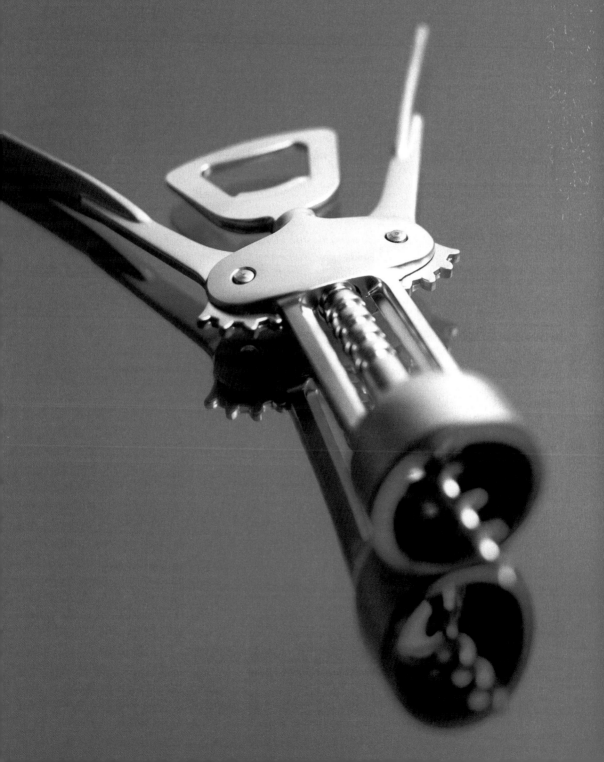

Eating & Entertainment

Comedy

It's often difficult to find a comedy venue that serves food and laughs of equal standard. There are, however, a few places that offer food of a higher quality than the standard old-style pub grub. South London has a choice between **Aztec Comedy** (First Floor, The Borderland, 47-49 Westow Street, SE19 3RW; 8771 0885) and **Up the Creek** (302 Creek Road, SE10 9SW; 8858 4581/www.up-the-creek.com). Over in Maida Vale there's the **Canal Café Theatre** (First Floor, The Bridge House, on the corner of Westbourne Terrace Road and Delamere Terrace, W2 6ND; 7289 6056/www.news revue. com; map 1 C5), while Shoreditch boasts the popular **Comedy Café** (66-68 Rivington Street, EC2A 3AY; 7739 5706/www.comedy cafe.co.uk; map 6 R4).

The best-known comedy club in London is probably Leicester Square's **Comedy Store** (1A Oxendon Street, W1Y 4EE; information 0870 060 2340/bookings Ticketmaster 7344 4444/ www.thecomedystore.co.uk; map 17 K7). Another fave is **Jongleurs Camden Lock** (Middle Yard, Camden Lock, Chalk Farm Road, NW1 8AD; 7564 2500/www.jongleurs.com; map 27 C1) – which has two other London branches, one in Battersea, the other in Bow.

For more up-to-date information on the capital's comedy clubs, see the Comedy section in the weekly *Time Out* magazine.

Dining afloat

Vessels for hire include canal cruisers from the **Floating Boater** (Waterside, Little Venice, Warwick Crescent, W2 6NE; 7266 1066/www. floatingboater.co.uk; map 1 C5); the **Leven is Strijd** (West India Quay, Hertsmere Road, West India Docks, E14 6AL; 7987 4002/www. theleven.co.uk), a classic Dutch barge, for views of Canary Wharf; and the **Elizabethan** (5 The Mews, 8 Putney Common, SW15 1HL; 8780 1562/www.thamesluxurycharters.co.uk), which is a replica of a 19th-century Mississippi paddle steamer that cruises from Putney to beyond the Thames Barrier.

The **Sunborn Yacht Hotel ExCeL** (Royal Victoria Dock, E16 1SL; 0870 040 4100) has good food but a conference-centre vibe, while the **RS Hispaniola** next to Hungerford Bridge (Victoria Embankment, WC2N 5DJ; 7839 3011/ www.hispaniola.co.uk; map 10 L8) is a popular party venue with a cocktail bar, disco area and a large restaurant. There's also **El Barco Latino** (see *p327*) and Danish-oriented **Lightship Ten** (see **International**).

If you want to hire a boat for a celebration, see the **Parties** section, starting on p331.

Dinner & dance

Break out that tux! Who said dinner dances were a thing of the past? Some of London's swankiest hotels still provide the opportunity for an evening bursting with glitz, glamour and gourmet food. Weekend dinner dances are offered at the River Restaurant of the **Savoy** (see *p45*; £49.50 Fri, £52.50 Sat), at the **Ritz** (see *p114*; £65 Fri, Sat), at the Hilton's **Windows** (see *p114*; £67-£80 Fri, Sat), and at the Conservatory restaurant in the **Lanesborough** (Hyde Park Corner, SW1X 7TA, 7259 5599/www.lanes borough.com, map 9 G8; £42.50 Fri, £48 Sat).

DIY

Blue Hawaii

2 Richmond Road, Kingston-upon-Thames, Surrey, KT2 5EB (8549 6989/www.blue hawaii.co.uk). Kingston rail. **Meals served** noon-3pm, 6pm-1am Mon-Sat; noon-1am Sun. **Set meal** £6.95-£10.95 unlimited barbecue. **Service** 10%. **Credit** AmEx, DC, MC, V.
Hawaiian Brian and his merry crew work hard to ensure a memorable night's entertainment; every night bands play requests and there are themed fancy dress parties on the last Saturday of each month. Food takes the form of an all-you-can-eat barbecue; choose your ingredients and watch them being cooked on a griddle. Diners leaving by 9pm pay £6.95, otherwise it's £10.95. Children under 12 eat for free.
Babies and children welcome; children's menu; high chairs; supervised play area (noon-3pm, not Wed). Book weekends. Disabled: toilet. Entertainment: music 8.30pm daily.

Mongolian Barbeque

12 Maiden Lane, WC2E 7NA (7379 7722/ www.themongolianbarbeque.co.uk). Covent Garden tube. **Meals served** noon-11pm Mon-Fri, Sun; noon-midnight Sat. **Set meal** £7.95 1 bowl, £9.95 starter & 1 bowl, £12.95 unlimited buffet. **Service** 12.5%. **Credit** AmEx, MC, V.
The barbecue experience on offer here goes like this: choose meat or seafood and vegetables from the large choice at the salad counter, add sauce as per the displayed recipe card suggestions, and then watch as a chef stir-fries your confused creation on a griddle. Repeat as often as desired. When crowded, this large venue has a fun vibe, with pitchers of beer or cheap and cheerful house wine to lubricate proceedings; otherwise, it can feel cavernous and lacking in atmosphere.
Map 18 L7.
For branch see index.

Tiger Lil's

270 Upper Street, N1 2UQ (7226 1118/ www.tigerlils.com). Highbury & Islington tube/rail/4, 19 bus. **Lunch served** Oct-June noon-3pm Mon-Fri. **Dinner served** 6-11pm daily. **Set lunch** £5.35 1 course. **Set dinner** £11.90 3 courses, £12.50 unlimited buffet. **Credit** AmEx, MC, V.
The premise of this DIY restaurant is much the same as its rivals – assemble your own raw ingredients from the huge selection that is available, choose a cooking oil and sauce, watch chefs then stir-fry them in a central cooking area – but the quality of the food is better than most. The tasteful modern interior is another plus point, and the regular bursts of flames from the woks make an impressive backdrop. A popular and child-friendly venue.
Babies and children welcome; high chairs. Disabled: toilet. Separate room for hire, seats 40.
For branches see index.

Dogs' dinners

Walthamstow Stadium

Chingford Road, E4 8SJ (8531 4255/ www.wsgreyhound.co.uk). Walthamstow Central tube/rail, then 97, 97A, 215, 357 bus. **Meals served** 6.30-9.30pm Tue, Thur, Sat. **Set meal** £18 3 courses. **Admission** *Popular enclosure* free Tue; £3 Thur, Sat. *Main enclosure* £6 Tue, Thur, Sat. Free under-15s. **Credit** MC, V.
There are many eating options here, from burger kiosks to ordering à la carte from the Paddock Grill, which has great views of the track. The Stowaway restaurant offers three courses for £18; this also includes admission and a programme. There are free lunchtime races (with half-price drinks) held on Monday and Friday each week; call ahead for details.
Disabled: toilet. Private boxes for hire, seats 25-200.

Wimbledon Stadium

Plough Lane, SW17 0BL (8946 8000/ www.wimbledonstadium.co.uk). Tooting Broadway tube/Earlsfield rail/44, 270, 272 bus. **Meals served** 7-9.30pm Tue, Fri, Sat. **Set meals** (Broadway) £25 3 courses; (Star Attraction) £28 3 courses. **Admission** Grandstand £5.50. **Credit** AmEx, MC, V.
The Broadway and Star Attraction restaurants offer a smarter dining alternative to the usual hot-dog stands, the latter being adjacent to the finishing line and the larger and more luxurious of the two. The set meal package includes a three-course menu, admission, programme and service, including waiters on hand to place bets for you. Expect such fare as steaks and tiger prawns, monkfish and salmon kebabs.
Disabled: lift; toilet. Separate rooms for parties, seating 28-120. Takeaway service.

Jazz & soul

Dorchester Bar

The Dorchester, 53 Park Lane, W1K 1QA (7629 8888/www.dorchesterhotel.com). Hyde Park Corner tube. **Open** 11am-11pm Mon-Sat; noon-10.30pm Sun. **Meals served** noon-11.45pm Mon-Sat; noon-10.30pm Sun. **Music** *Pianist* 7-11pm Mon-Wed; 7-10.30pm Sun. *Jazz band* 7-11pm Thur-Sat. **Credit** AmEx, DC, MC, V.
The Dorchester Hotel's restaurant bar serves up a menu of mainly Italian dishes in elegantly casual surroundings. In the evenings, the bar becomes a relaxed jazz venue, with a pianist providing soothing background tunes from Sunday to Wednesday, and a band playing livelier modern jazz the rest of the week.
Disabled: toilet. **Map 9 G7.**

Dover Street

8-10 Dover Street, W1S 4LQ (7629 9813/ www.doverst.co.uk). Green Park or Piccadilly Circus tube. **Open** noon-3.30pm, 5.30pm-3am Mon-Thur; noon-3.30pm, 7pm-3am Fri; 7pm-3am Sat. **Music** *Bands* 9.30pm Mon; 10.30pm Tue-Sat. *DJs* until 3am Mon-Sat. **Admission** £6 after 10pm Mon; £7 after 10pm Tue; £8 after 10pm Wed; £12 after 10pm Thur; diners only until 10pm, then £15 Fri, Sat. **Credit** AmEx, DC, MC, V.
Celebrating its 25th anniversary this year, the three bars and restaurant at Dover Street make it a favourite for classy corporate events and parties, hosting lively jazz bands as well as blues, swing, soul and funk. A new French chef has added Gallic touches to the Mediterranean menu, where you can expect the likes of steak and herb-crusted lamb. Check the website for band listings.
Booking advisable. Dress: no jeans or trainers.
Map 9 G7.

Jazz After Dark

9 Greek Street, W1D 4DQ (7734 0545/ www.jazzafterdark.co.uk). Leicester Square tube. **Open** 2pm-2am Mon-Thur; 2pm-3am Fri, Sat. **Music** 9pm-1.30am Mon-Thur; 10.30pm-2.30am Fri, Sat. **Admission** £3 Mon-Wed; £5 Thur; £8 (diners), £10 (non-diners) Fri, Sat. **Credit** AmEx, DC, JCB, MC, V.
The relaxed feel at this popular Soho haunt attracts twentysomethings with a passion for jazz and blues. Weeknights are more laid-back, with dinner jazz and soul on offer. The international menu (from French cuisine to Tex Mex and tapas) and impressive cocktail list help to prolong the night's entertainment for post-pub party people.
Map 17 K6.

Jazz Café

5-7 Parkway, NW1 7PG (7916 6060/www.jazz cafe.co.uk). Camden Town tube. **Open** 7pm-1am Mon-Thur; 7pm-2am Fri, Sat; noon-4pm, 7pm-midnight Sun. **Bar snacks served** 9.30pm-midnight daily. **Music** *Bands* 9-11.30pm Mon-Thur, Sun; 9-10.30pm Fri, Sat. *Club nights* 11pm-2am Fri, Sat. **Admission** £12.50-£25. **Credit** MC, V.
Renowned for its contemporary soul, R&B and acoustic rock acts, the Jazz Café attracts a wide selection of jazz junkies and more mature music connoisseurs, as well as fashionable youngsters for the weekend club nights. It's essential to book a table if you want to eat in the exclusive balcony restaurant (overlooking the performers), but dining is exclusive of ticket prices, and the food (Cajun salmon, baked cod) isn't that remarkable. The music's the thing, here.
Disabled: toilet. **Map 25 D2**.

Pizza Express Jazz Club

10 Dean Street, W1D 3RW (7439 8722/ www.pizzaexpress.com/jazz). Tottenham Court Road tube. **Meals served** noon-midnight daily. **Music** 9pm-midnight daily. **Admission** £15-£20. **Credit** AmEx, DC, MC, V.
The sound of the sax has been on the menu here since the company was founded in 1965. With appearances from legends such as Van Morrison to new stars like Diana Krall and Jamie Cullen, crowds still flock to the basement den. The Pizza Express standards make the dining part of the equation reliably enjoyable, and the atmosphere is always friendly. Musicians play nightly (check the website for details).
Map 17 K6.

Ronnie Scott's

47 Frith Street, W1D 4HT (7439 0747/ www.ronniescotts.co.uk). Leicester Square tube. **Open** 8.30pm-3am Mon-Sat. **Meals served** 8.30pm-1am Mon-Sat. **Music** 9.30pm-2am Mon-Sat. **Admission** (non-members) £15 Mon-Thur; £25 Fri, Sat. **Membership** £60/yr. **Credit** AmEx, DC, MC, V.
This Soho institution has been attracting jazz legends (as well as artists not strictly in the jazz field) since the 1960s and shows no signs of winding down. Reliable food is served into the early hours and there are three bars to choose from, as well as a disco upstairs holding salsa nights on Wednesday, Friday and Saturday, and 1970s soul and funk on Thursday.
Booking advisable. No-smoking tables.
Map 17 K6.

606 Club

90 Lots Road, SW10 0QD (7352 5953/www.606 club.co.uk). Earl's Court tube. **Open** 7.30pm-1am Mon-Wed; 8pm-1.30am Thur; 8pm-2am Fri, Sat; 8pm-midnight Sun. **Meals served** 7.30-11.30pm Mon-Wed; 8-11.30pm Thur; 8pm-12.30am Fri, Sat; 8-10.30pm Sun. **Music** 8pm-1am Mon-Wed; 9.30pm-1am Thur; 10pm-2am Fri, Sat; 9.30pm-midnight Sun. **Admission** *Non-members* £7 Mon-Thur; £9 Fri, Sat; £8 Sun. *Members (if dining)* £6 Mon-Thur; £8 Fri, Sat; £7 Sun. **Membership** £95 first yr; £60 subsequent yrs. **Service** 12.5%. **Credit** MC, V.
This smart Chelsea members' club only books British-based musicians. Each week around ten bands play nightly, with double bills scheduled from Monday to Wednesday. Non-members are admitted to the club, but can only purchase alcohol with a full meal. The global-accented menu changes daily, offering the likes of Scotch fillet steak and grilled Mediterranean prawns.
Map 13 C13.

Latin

Cuba

11-13 Kensington High Street, W8 5NP (7938 4137/www.barcuba.info). High Street Kensington tube. **Open** *Restaurant & bar* noon-2am Mon-Sat; 5pm-midnight Sun. *Club* 9.30pm-2am Mon-Sat. **Admission** £3-£10. **Credit** AmEx, DC, MC, V.
Live music, a happy hour offering potent rum cocktails, and Hispanic cuisine attract a young and vibrant crowd to this venue. Daily salsa and merengue dance lessons are offered in the basement club, where you can stay on to enjoy DJs spinning Latin grooves until 2am.
Babies and children admitted (lunch only).
Booking advisable Fri, Sat. Entertainment: dance classes 7.30-9.30pm Mon-Sat; 6.30-8.30pm Sun; occasional bands. **Map 7 C8**.

El Barco Latino

Temple Pier, Victoria Embankment, WC2R 2PP (7379 5496/www.elbarcolatino.co.uk). Temple tube. **Open** *Bar* 11am-3am daily. **Meals served** noon-11pm daily. **Set lunch** £6.50 buffet. **Set dinner** £15 2 courses, £25 3 courses incl glass of wine. **Admission** £5 after 10.30pm Fri; (non-diners) £5 Sat. **Service** 12.5%. **Credit** MC, V.
This former Thames barge seems an unlikely venue for late-night dancing, but it attracts a mixed crowd of Latin movers, less expert Brits and tourists keen to try out the steps and enjoy the party atmosphere. Free salsa lessons on Thursday

Globe. See p329.

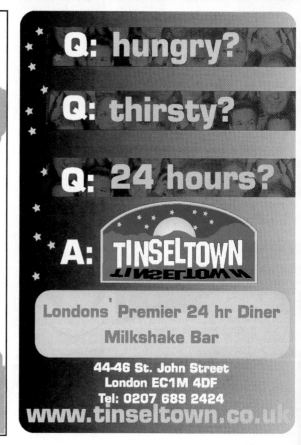

evenings should help those who are a bit dodgy on the dancefloor. Food consists largely of beef and chicken dishes; on Sundays, traditional Colombian fare is also offered.
Booking advisable weekends. Entertainment: occasional Latin bands. **Map 10 M7.**

Havana
17 Hanover Square, W1S 1HU (7629 2552/ www.fiestahavana.com). Oxford Circus tube.
Bar Open 5pm-2am Mon-Thur; 5pm-3am Fri, Sat; 6pm-1am Sun.
Restaurant **Meals served** 5pm-2am Mon-Sat; 6pm-midnight Sun. **Admission** first 100 people admitted free; £4 after that; £5 after 9pm Tue, Wed; £5 after 8pm Thur; £5 after 8pm, £10 after 10pm Fri, Sat. **Main courses** £9.95-£14.95. **Set dinner** (incl free entry to club) £19.95 3 courses. **Service** 12.5%.
Both **Credit** MC, V.
People who love dancing pack out this busy subterranean haunt, because it certainly doesn't attract anybody interested in food. While a salsa teacher barks out instructions, music thumps and couples try their best to follow. From Cuba to Spain, the Med to South America, Havana's lengthy menu wears its influences lightly, as most dishes are just cheapo blandness to the core. Most tuck into their tapas in the bar area – at least there they can soak up the fevered atmosphere and cop an eyeful of the frenetic swivelling and shaking.
Booking essential weekends. Dress: smart casual; no trainers. Entertainment: Latin bands; dance classes (phone for details). Restaurant available for hire. **Map 9 H6.**
For branch see index.

Salsa!
96 Charing Cross Road, WC2H 0JG (7379 3277/www.barsalsa.info). Leicester Square or Tottenham Court Road tube.
Bar Open 5.30pm-2am Mon-Sat; 6pm-12.30am Sun.
Restaurant **Meals served** 5.30-11pm daily. **Bar snacks served** 5.30pm-1.30am Mon-Sat; 5.30-11pm Sun.
Both **Music** *Dance classes* 7-9pm daily. **Admission** after 9pm £4 Mon-Thur; £2 after 7pm, £4 after 8pm, £8 after 9pm, £10 after 11pm Fri, Sat; £4 after 7pm Sun. **Credit** AmEx, MC, V.
Party people flock here in their droves to sample a slice of salsa spice; the (ear-splittingly loud) music plays well into the night. Latin American fare (char-grilled chilli ribs, enchiladas and so forth) and a substantial cocktail list add to the exotic spirit. Should you want to improve your dancefloor moves, evening classes are listed on the website.
Dress: no trainers or sportswear. **Map 17 K6.**

Music & dancing

Break for the Border
8 Argyll Street, W1F 7TF (7734 5776/www. bftb.com). Oxford Circus tube. **Open** noon-3am Mon-Sat; noon-11pm Sun. **Meals served** noon-2am Mon-Sat; noon-10pm Sun. **Main courses** £7-£14. **Admission** (non-diners) free Mon, Tue; £3 after 10pm Wed; £5 after 10.30pm Thur, Fri; £10 after 9.30pm Sat. **Credit** AmEx, MC, V.
Break For The Border's lively atmosphere (when it is busy) attracts a mixed clientele of up-for-it tourists, hen parties and office groups. DJs mixing cheesy chart tunes and old favourites rally the troops on to the dancefloor, where embarrassing encounters inevitably follow. Reasonably palatable Tex-Mex food provides fuel to get you through the night, but service in the past has ranged from friendly to indifferent and pushy – also beware an expensive drinks bill.
Entertainment: DJs 10pm Wed-Sat. **Map 9 J6.**

Costa Dorada
47-55 Hanway Street, W1T 1UK (7636 7139). Tottenham Court Road tube.
Tapas bar **Open** 7pm-3am Mon-Sat. **Tapas** £3-£12.50. **Set tapas meal** £20 per person (minimum 10).
Restaurant **Dinner served** 7.30pm-2.30am Mon-Sat. **Set dinner** £32.95 per person (minimum 10) 3 courses incl half bottle of wine and coffee.
Both **Service** 10%. **Credit** AmEx, DC, MC, V.

The Sports Café. See p330.

A visit to kitschy Costa Dorada can be a fun night out (when it's full). Raucous office party groups come to drink and watch the twice-nightly flamenco shows, staged in a gaudy mock-Spanish setting. Tapas, paella and steaks – all of which can be rather hit and miss – help to soak up the sangria. But you come here for the fiesta, not the food. It's late licence is another attraction.
Booking essential Fri, Sat. Entertainment: flamenco shows 9.30pm, 11.30pm Mon-Thur, 10pm, midnight Fri, Sat; music 8.30pm Tue-Sat. **Map 17 K6.**

Roadhouse
35 The Piazza, WC2E 8BE (7240 6001/ www.roadhouse.co.uk). Covent Garden tube.
Open 5.30pm-2.30am Mon; 5.30pm-3am Tue-Sat; 5.30pm-1am last Sun of mth. **Meals served** 5.30pm-1.30am Mon-Sat; 5.30pm-12.30am last Sun of mth. **Admission** (after 9pm) £5 Mon-Wed; £7 Thur; £10 Fri, Sat. **Credit** AmEx, DC, MC, V.
Roadhouse's Covent Garden location makes it a favourite venue for hen nights, with added attractions such as happy-hour cocktails. DJs and cover bands belt out hits from the past two decades ensuring a non-stop party atmosphere (ie: meat market). The menu includes the likes of grills, BBQ chicken wings, wraps and burgers.
Dress: smart casual. **Map 18 L7.**

One-offs

Elvis Gracelands Palace
881-883 Old Kent Road, SE15 1NL (7639 3961/ www.gracelandspalace.com). New Cross Gate tube.
Open 6pm-midnight Mon-Thur, Sun; noon-3pm, 6pm-midnight Fri, Sat. **Shows** 10pm-late Mon-Thur, Sun; 10pm Fri, Sat; also by arrangement. **Set meal** £16.50-£19; £15 vegetarian. **Service** 10%. **Credit** AmEx, DC, MC, V.
The food here is good-value, if formulaic, Sichuan and Peking cuisine; it's not especially exciting, but includes well-done favourites such as crispy aromatic duck, and there's a decent vegetarian menu. But as you can tell by the name, the main draw of this place is Paul Chan's shamelessly flamboyant and well-rehearsed Elvis tribute act on Friday or Saturday night. The relaxed atmosphere, friendly staff and familiar, catchy tunes will soon have you singing along too.
Babies and children admitted (lunch); high chairs. Booking advisable. No-smoking tables. Vegetarian menu.

Globe
100 Avenue Road, NW3 3HF (7722 7200/ www.globerestaurant.co.uk). Swiss Cottage tube/ 13, 31 bus. **Lunch served** noon-3pm Mon-Fri. **Dinner served** 6-11pm Mon-Sat; 7-10pm Sun. **Main courses** £9.50-£13.50. **Credit** MC, V.
Globe mostly operates as a straightforward restaurant serving decent international fare (for example, try baked herb-crusted cod or pan-fried duck breast), but two or three times a month the place is completely transformed with a full-on drag act and cabaret. The fabulously costumed Globe Girls perform several evening slots, singing and dancing their camp little hearts out. Friendly and charming staff help to ensure a great night out. Check the website for dates.
Booking advisable. No-smoking tables. Separate room for parties, seats 20. **Map 28 B4.**

La Pergola
66 Streatham High Road, SW16 1DA (8769 2646). Streatham Hill rail. **Lunch served** noon-3pm Mon-Sat. **Dinner served** 6-11pm Mon-Thur; 6pm-2am Fri, Sat. **Shows** 9pm-2am Fri, Sat; also by arrangement. **Set dinner** (Fri) £17 3 courses; (Sat) £22 3 courses. **Credit** AmEx, MC, V.
The King spotted in Streatham? Well, an Elvis impersonator, anyway. Half the entertainment here comes from watching your fellow diners sing and swivel along to the on-stage antics. Most people seem to arrive early, wolf down three courses of Italian grub and then get on with the serious business of drinking and dancing.
Booking advisable.

Just Around the Corner
446 Finchley Road, NW2 2HY (7431 3300). Finchley Road or Golders Green tube. **Meals served** 6pm-midnight Mon-Sat; noon-midnight Sun. **Credit** AmEx, MC, V.
London's only restaurant without prices invites you to pay what you think the meal was worth, with a similar pricing policy applying to the wine. Inspired, or an insane trading philosophy? The French-influenced menu features old-fashioned classics, and food and service are generally good – but not wanting to seem miserly can lead to overpaying for what is basically uncomplicated bistro fare. Still, this unconventional approach seems to work, pleasing both customers and proprietor alike.
Babies and children welcome; high chairs. No-smoking tables.

Parties & Shops

Rainforest Café

20 Shaftesbury Avenue, W1D 7EU (7434 3111/ www.therainforestcafe.co.uk). Leicester Square or Piccadilly Circus tube. **Meals served** noon-10pm Mon-Thur, Sun; noon-7.30pm Fri, Sat. **Main courses** £9.95-£15.95. **Service** 12.5% for parties of 6 or more. **Credit** AmEx, DC, MC, V.
A big hit with the nippers and extremely popular for kids' parties, this extravagant restaurant is filled with animatronic apes and elephants, cascading waterfalls and thunderstorm sound effects. Accessed via a safari-themed shopping area, your offspring will be whining for soft toys and T-shirts throughout their meal. The menu is geared to younger palates, but at adult prices; a few healthier, non-burger options can be found (Mediterranean polenta, for example), and there are some fantastically messy, fancy desserts.
Babies and children welcome; bottle-warmers; children's menu (£9.95); crayons; high chairs; nappy-changing facilities. No smoking. Separate rooms for hire, seat 11-100. **Map 17 K7.**

Sound

Swiss Centre, Leicester Square, W1D 6QF (7287 1010/www.soundlondon.com). Leicester Square tube. **Open** *Café* 10am-2am Mon-Sat; 10am-1am Sun. *Bar & restaurant* 5pm-3am Mon-Thur, Sun; 5pm-4am Fri, Sat. **Admission** *Bar & restaurant* £5 after 9pm, £10 after 10pm Fri; £5 after 9pm, £12 after 10pm Sat. **Service** 12.5%. **Credit** AmEx, MC, V.
The decor – leopard-skin seating, brightly coloured walls, velvet and diamanté everywhere – is the first thing that hits you when visiting Sound. Two main rooms, Club Sound and Sound Bar & Restaurant, are run as separate events every night except Saturdays, when the whole place operates as one huge club. The upstairs café serves pizzas and burgers, while the restaurant offers a grill menu, seafood and steaks.
Disabled: toilet. Dress: smart casual. **Map 17 K7.**

The Spitz

109 Commercial Street, E1 6BG (7392 9032/ www.spitz.co.uk). Aldgate East tube/Liverpool Street tube/rail. **Open** *Venue* 7pm-midnight Mon-Sat; times vary Sun, call to check. *Gallery* noon-7pm Mon-Fri; noon-5pm Sat; 11am-5pm Sun. *Bar & bistro* 10am-midnight daily. **Meals served** 10am-3pm, 5-10.30pm Mon-Sat; 10am-3.30pm, 6-9pm Sun. **Main courses** £10.55-£14.95. **Credit** MC, V.
Hip without being pretentious, Spitz is a great place to see an eclectic range of music (everything from avant garde electronica to country and western), as well as eat and drink. The Venue hosts interesting and diverse club nights and provides a live music programme that crosses genres; the gallery, Element 3, exhibits photo-journalistic work, and there's also a bar and bistro (with a lovely terrace overlooking Old Spitalfields market), which also showcases live jazz. The menu features cosy dishes like salmon fish cakes, goat's cheese roulade, sausage and mash, and pancakes – perfect for relaxed weekend brunches, or fuelling up before a night out.
Babies and children welcome (bistro); high chairs. Booking advisable Fri, Sat. Disabled: toilet. Entertainment: music Tue, Fri, Sat. Gallery and Venue available for hire. Tables outdoors (12, terrace). Vegetarian menu. **Map 12 R5.**

Twelfth House

35 Pembridge Road, W11 3HG (7727 9620/ www.twelfth-house.co.uk). Notting Hill Gate tube. **Open** *Bar* 10am-11pm Mon-Sat; 10am-10.30pm Sun. *Restaurant* 10am-10pm Mon-Fri; 10am-4pm, 6-10pm Sat; 10am-4pm, 6-9.30pm Sun. **Main courses** £10-£15. **Service** 12.5%. **Credit** MC, V.
Find out what the stars have in store for you while sipping a coffee or snacking on meze platters – this mystical and magical-themed café/restaurant offers astrological chart sessions for £25, and tarot card readings at £3 a question. The restaurant upstairs serves Modern British fare, such as roast monkfish and slow-cooked lamb shanks.
Babies and children admitted (restaurant only). Booking advisable. Restaurant available for hire. **Map 7 A7.**

Opera

Mamma Amalfi's

45 The Mall, W5 3TJ (8840 5888). Ealing Broadway tube/rail. **Meals served** noon-11pm Mon-Thur; noon-11.30pm Fri, Sat; noon-10.30pm Sun. **Main courses** £4.95-£12.95. **Service** 12.5%. **Credit** AmEx, MC, V.
Free operatic performances at this family-friendly trattoria start at 8.30pm on Sundays; non-diners may still enjoy the music with just a drink. The cooking is good-quality traditional Italian, including pizzas from a wood-fired oven and specialities such as pan-fried halibut and braised lamb shank. The Croydon branch offers operatic recitals on Friday evenings.
Babies and children welcome; children's menu; high chairs. No-smoking tables. Separate room for hire, seats 35. Tables outdoors (5, pavement). Takeaway service.
For branches (Amalfi's, Mamma Amalfi's) see index.

Sarastro

126 Drury Lane, WC2B 5QG (7836 0101/ www.sarastro-restaurant.com). Covent Garden or Holborn tube. **Meals served** noon-11.30pm daily. **Main courses** £7.50-£15.50. **Set lunch** (noon-6pm) £10 2 courses. **Set dinner** (from 6pm) £22.50 3 courses incl dessert and coffee. **Service** 12.5%. **Credit** AmEx, DC, MC, V.
Velvet drapes, statues and golden cherubs cover every inch of this opulent restaurant: suitable surroundings for the opera-based entertainment on offer, and quite a show-stealer. Young performers from the nearby national opera houses perform popular arias on Monday and Sunday evenings, and food is generally decent Turkish and Mediterranean fare. Reserve a balcony table overlooking your fellow diners to round off the theatrical experience. Service standards can slip during busy periods. New sister branch Papageno is equally flamboyant.
Babies and children admitted; high chairs. Booking advisable. Disabled: toilet. Entertainment: opera 1.30pm, 8.30pm Sun; 8.30pm Mon. No-smoking tables. **Map 18 M6.**
For branch (Papageno) see index.

Sports bars

Although it's not a sports bar as such, **Bodean's** (*see p33*), the excellent American barbecue restaurant in Soho, has become *the* venue of choice for expat Yanks catching up on baseball, hockey and American football. The TV screens are constantly tuned to NASN, the North American Sports Network.

Elbow Room

89-91 Chapel Market, N1 9EX (7278 3244/www. theelbowroom.co.uk). Angel tube. **Open** 5pm-2am Mon; noon-2am Tue-Thur; noon-3am Fri, Sat; noon-midnight Sun. **Meals served** noon-11pm daily. **Main courses** £5-£8. **Admission** £2 9-10pm, £5 after 10pm Fri, Sat. **Credit** MC, V.
A popular bar, pool lounge and club for dressed-up twentysomethings to come for a few frames of pool, a few snacks, a few drinks and then stay on for DJs later in the night. The 11 pool tables get booked up fast, but there are two decent bars with curved leather booths, and a VIP room at which to relax, and the menu of good burgers, fajitas, char-grilled skewers and light bites provides decent grub with which to line your stomach. Friday and Saturday nights are packed with punters out on the piss, on the pull, or both.
Disabled: toilet. Entertainment: DJs 9pm Tue-Sat; bands 9pm Sun. Separate room for hire, seats 30. **Map 5 N2.**
For branches see index.

The Sports Café

80 Haymarket, SW1Y 4TE (7839 8300/www.the sportscafe.com). Piccadilly Circus tube. **Open** noon-3am Mon-Wed, Fri; noon-2am Thur; 11am-3am Sat; noon-12.30am Sun. **Admission** £3 after 11pm Mon-Thur; £5 after 11pm Fri, Sat. **Main courses** £8.45-£15.95. **Credit** (bar & food) AmEx, MC, V.

A huge US-style establishment with more than 100 TV screens (from jumbo to elephantine) supplying a seemingly endless array of competitive sports, from football and rugby league to Formula One and tennis, and a ketchup-friendly menu favouring burgers, ribs, steak, wedges, pizza and the like. With four bars pulling in sports-loving revellers, it can become uncomfortably crowded and noisy during major tournaments, but there are also separate dining areas on each floor, plus pool tables, pinball machines and table football. After 10pm, DJs spin a mix of chart, techno and oldie favourites on the dancefloor to the rear.
Children admitted (until 6pm, dining area only). Disabled: toilet. Separate room for hire, seats 50. **Map 17 K7.**

24-hour eats

Tinseltown

44-46 St John Street, EC1M 4DT (7689 2424/ www.tinseltown.co.uk). Farringdon tube/rail. **Open** 24hrs daily. **Set lunch** £5 2 courses incl drink and 15mins internet access. **Credit** AmEx, DC, MC, V.
Clerkenwell clubbers, cabbies and late-night lost souls frequent this US-styled basement diner, a perfect stop-gap for good global fast-food (burgers, Cajun chicken) refuelling in the small hours. Cosy booth seating, internet access, music TV and top-notch milkshakes ease the bleary-eyed wait for the first tube home.
Internet access. **Map 5 O5.**

Vingt-Quatre

325 Fulham Road, SW10 9QL (7376 7224). South Kensington tube. **Meals served** 24hrs daily. **Main courses** £5.75-£14. **Service** 12.5%. **Credit** AmEx, MC, V.
As befitting its location, V-Q is a classy alternative to typical 24-hour joints, with Chelsea clubbers rather than late-night truckers filling the smart modern interior. Food ranges from salads and steak to char-grilled yellowfin tuna and posh pasta. **Map 14 D12.**

Views & victuals

The Tenth

Royal Garden Hotel, 2-24 Kensington High Street, W8 4PT (7361 1910/www.royalgarden hotel.co.uk). High Street Kensington tube. **Lunch served** noon-2.30pm Mon-Fri. **Dinner served** 5.30-10.45pm Mon-Sat. **Main courses** £15-£42. **Credit** AmEx, DC, MC, V.
The last Saturday of the month is Manhattan Night, when the 16-piece John Wilson Orchestra resurrects the glitz and glamour of the New York dinner-dance scene, playing 1950s big band classics. At £60, the entrance fee isn't cheap, but this includes a five-course dinner (better value than dining à la carte) and stunning views out over Hyde Park from the restaurant's tenth-floor windows. On other nights, the entertainment is less inspiring: a single pianist plonking out insipid show tunes.
Babies and children admitted (restaurant); high chairs. Disabled: toilet. Dress: smart casual. Entertainment: pianist 8.30pm Sat. **Map 7 B8.**

Vertigo 42

Tower 42, 25 Old Broad Street, EC2N 1PB (7877 7842/www.vertigo42.co.uk). Bank tube/DLR/Liverpool Street tube/rail. **Open/ meals served** noon-3pm, 5-11pm Mon-Fri. **Set lunch** (noon-3pm Mon-Fri) £15 3 courses. **Main courses** £9.50-£17.50. **Service** 12.5%. **Credit** AmEx, DC, JCB, MC, V.
The big attraction at this lounge bar – 590 feet (180 metres) above the pavement – is the stunning panoramic view over London's skyline. Smart City types come for champagne and oysters while taking in the sights. Some 18 floors down, Gary Rhodes' new restaurant, Rhodes Twenty Four (*see p42*), serves classic British fare. Due to security arrangements, prior booking is essential, and photo ID must be produced on arrival. It's also worth noting that last admission is at 10pm.
Bar available for hire. Booking essential. Dress: smart casual. No cigars or pipes. **Map 12 Q6.**

Parties

This new section is all about helping you find the unique venues, most efficient caterers, great entertainers and the best equipment to make your bash go with a bang. If you're planning an intimate dinner overlooking the London skyline, a wedding in a picturesque garden, a power lunch on the river, or a fun afternoon for the children, read on.

Venues

London is blessed with thousands of diverse venues. Here we've listed a broad choice of the best – from historic houses, museums and clubs to river boats and hotel hire. Many restaurants, gastropubs, bars and pubs also have separate rooms for hire for smaller parties; these are identified in the services provided after each review in the rest of the guide.

Boats

River Boat Party Cruises by ChilliSauce
49 Carnaby Street, W1F 9PY (0845 450 7450/ www.chillisauce.co.uk). **Phone enquiries** 9.30am-5.30pm Mon-Fri. **Credit** AmEx, MC, V.
ChilliSauce prides itself on its hen and stag weekends, although the company also caters for group and corporate events. Cruises generally start with a sit-down meal or buffet, followed by drinks and dancing. Prices vary.

Silver Fleet
Woods River Cruises, Wapping Pier, King Henry's Stairs, Wapping High Street, E1W 2NR (7481 2711/www.woodsrivercruises.co.uk).
Phone enquiries 9am-5.30pm Mon-Fri. **Credit** AmEx, MC, V.
Founded in 1947, this fleet caters for all kinds of private events, from a working lunch for 30 to a wedding party for 400. The firm also arranges combined parties and tours with riverside venues such as Tate Modern, the London Eye, Vinopolis, and the National Maritime Museum in Greenwich. Prices depend on which vessel you use, with a minimum hire requirement of three hours during the day, four hours in the evening.

Thames Leisure
Swan Pier, Swan Lane, London Bridge, EC4R 3TN (7623 1805/www.thamesleisure.co.uk). Monument tube/Cannon Street tube/rail.
Phone enquiries 9.30am-5.30pm Mon-Fri. **Credit** AmEx, MC, V.
Choose from five luxury vessels and prices that range from £190 to £460 an hour. This outfit claims to take on any kind of event – sightseeing cruise, corporate function, private party, luncheon or dinner cruise, birthday or business promotion. The website is worth a look.

Clubs

London is home to numerous bars and clubs, many of which cater for private parties. Below we've chosen a few of the smaller venues. If you want a superclub in which to dance the night away, try **Fabric** for drum 'n' bass paradise (77A Charterhouse Street, EC1M 6HJ; 7251 3090); **Elysium** for a glamorous, star-studded event (68 Regent Street, W1B 5EL; 7439 7770); **Ministry of Sound** for a classic night at the original superclub (103 Gaunt Street, SE1 6DP; 7740 8728); or **Pacha**

London, Victoria's answer to Ibiza clubbing (Terminus Place, SW1V 1JR; 7251 3090). None comes cheap, of course.

For more possible venues, see the annual *Time Out Pubs & Bars Guide* (£8.99) or the 'Nightlife' section of the weekly *Time Out* London magazine.

The Aquarium
256 Old Street, EC1V 9DD (7251 6136/ www.clubaquarium.co.uk). Old Street tube/rail.
Phone enquiries 10am-4pm Mon-Fri. **Credit** MC, V.
Living up to its name, this is the only bar/club in England with swimming facilities. The pool room comes as part of a package when hiring another of the function rooms, so choose from the lounge (with space for 50 people), the main room (350), the smaller back room (100), or the small VIP room (15). Buffet costs £5 to £20 a head; prices vary according to requirements

Castle
65 Camberwell Church Street, SE5 8TR (7277 2601). Oval tube/Denmark Hill rail/ 12, 35, 68, 176, 185, 345 bus. **Open** noon-midnight Mon-Thur; noon-2am Fri, Sat; noon-10.30pm Sun. **Credit** AmEx, DC, JCB, MC, V.
The Castle bar contains an upstairs room with a 70-person capacity, a self-contained bar and air-conditioning. It will provide DJs and equipment – hire costs £100, with no minimum spend. The larger downstairs room accommodates 200; prices depend on the night you choose, plus the extras you want. Buffets or canapés can be arranged.

The Cross
Arches, 27-31 King's Cross Goods Yard, N1 0UZ (7837 0828/www.the-cross.co.uk). King's Cross tube/rail. **Phone enquiries** 10am-6pm Mon-Fri. **Credit** MC, V.
Slap-bang in the middle of a run-down goods yard, the Cross has a capacity of 800, four bars and three dancefloors under seven bricked arches. It also boasts a wooden decked garden with heated umbrellas, an outside bar and tropical foliage. A catering and entertainment service is offered, including a free consultation for private events. Taxis will get you back home (or to work) the next morning when the Cross closes at 8am.

Leighton House. See p333.

Parties & Shops

RUMI

Hosting great parties, corporate events, providing the best DJ`s and creating the best ambience is essential for us at Rumi

Whether its your birthday or a formal corporate event Rumi will astound you with the level of service we provide and with a varied selection of drinks, from Vintage Champagne to Classic Cocktails and authentic Arabian/Lebanese fusion canapes and finger food .

We cater for private events and bookings all year round

Capacity: 140

Opening Times:
Tuesday - Saturday from 7pm - 1am
(a 2am extension can be arranged)

531 Kings Road • London SW10 0TZ

Tel: 020 7823 3362
E-mail: info@rumibar.com

CORPORATE EVENTS • LAUNCH PARTIES
LEAVING PARTIES • BIRTHDAYS • REUNIONS
ANNIVERSARIES • CHRISTMAS PARTIES

www.rumibar.com

" Soul receives from soul
that knowledge,
therefore not by book nor from tongue.
If knowledge of mysteries come
after emptiness of mind,
that is illumination of heart "

- Rumi 1207-1273

FUN TIMES COSY PLACE COOL PEOPLE HOT MUSIC WILD PARTIES A GREAT NIGHT OU

Best Party Websites

www.askginka.com
Source information and ideas for your wedding, especially religious and cultural details, themes and ideas. With over 14,000 links.

www.kids-party.com
A wealth of information for under-prepared parents with plenty of tips and ideas. You can search by region of the country.

www.net-weddings.co.uk
All you need for the big day, from designing your own veil to picking an organiser and buying/selling a second-hand wedding dress.

www.partypages.co.uk
Fairground rides, unusual venues, magicians, entertainers, bouncy castles and more, for adult and children's parties alike. Very user-friendly.

www.wedding-directories.com
Find all the wedding essentials, from cars to stationery, cakes to tiaras.

The Roof Gardens
99 Kensington High Street, W8 5SA (7937 7994/0870 780 9485/www.roofgardens.com). High Street Kensington tube. **Phone enquiries** 9am-6pm Mon-Fri. **Credit** AmEx, MC, V.
With one-and-a-half acres of open-air, themed gardens perched 100ft above Kensington's streets, the Roof Gardens is quite something. Trees, plants, pools and gardens surround the clubhouse. The venue can cater for almost anything – be it a wedding, private party, conference or product launch. An experienced functions and promotions team is on hand.

Zoo Bar & Club
13-17 Bear Street, WC2H 7AS (7839 4188/ www.zoobar.co.uk). Leicester Square tube. **Open** 10am-6pm Mon-Fri. **Credit** AmEx, DC, MC, V.
The glamorous and very central Zoo Bar hires out its VIP room (with space for 150 people) on a Tuesday; there's no hire charge, but a £1,000 minimum spend (including food) is required. On a Thursday, the minimum spend is £2,000 (again, including food).

Historic houses

Some of London's most dazzling stately homes and other historic venues are available to hire for events – at a price. Here's a choice selection. Please note, prices below might not include VAT or insurance.

Cabinet War Rooms
King Charles Street, SW1A 2AQ (7930 6961/ www.iwm.org.uk). St James's Park tube/Charing Cross tube/rail/3, 12, 88, 159 bus. **Phone enquiries** 9am-5pm Mon-Fri. **Credit** MC, V.
Follow in the steps of Churchill at the restored underground War Rooms, four of which can be hired for private dining, corporate hospitality or conferences, either during the day or evening. The Auditorium costs £1,500, the Plant Room £750, and the Switchboard Room (evenings only) £400. The Churchill Room, from which Winston directed wartime operations, costs £3,000. All rooms have air-conditioning. Should Armageddon strike, where better to be?

Chiswick House
Burlington Lane, W4 2RP (7973 3292/ www.english-heritage.org.uk). Turnham Green tube/Chiswick rail. **Phone enquiries** 9am-5pm Mon-Fri. **Credit** MC, V.
Designed by acclaimed Palladian architect Lord Burlington and built in 1729, Chiswick House (also known as Burlington House) has a capacity of 80 for dinner/dances (across three inter-linked rooms) and 130 for receptions. In summer, the house can be hired on Saturdays from 3pm onwards, on Mondays and Tuesdays for daytime events, and on evenings throughout the week from 6.30pm. Hire for a summer wedding costs £3,000 (plus VAT). The house is currently closed for refurbishment until June 2005.

Eltham Palace
Court Yard, off Court Road, SE9 5QE (8294 2577/www.english-heritage.org.uk/hospitality). Eltham rail then 161 bus. **Phone enquiries** 9am-5.30pm Mon-Fri. **Credit** AmEx, MC, V.
The palace, with its mix of art deco and medieval styles, caters for everything from buffet lunches to lavish receptions in the medieval Great Hall. Weddings work particularly well here, with the exclusive use of the art deco mansion, Great Hall, and grounds providing a beautiful backdrop for receptions. A drinks reception for 200 costs £2,000, while weddings on Saturdays in summer cost around £5,000. Events can be arranged on Mondays, Tuesdays and Saturdays, as the palace is open to the public on other days.

Kensington Palace
Kensington Palace State Apartments, Kensington Gardens, W8 4PX (0870 751 5184). Kensington High Street or Queensway tube. **Phone enquiries** 9am-5pm Mon-Fri. **Credit** MC, V.
Kensington Palace is open to the public during the day, so most events take place in the evening. However, some daytime receptions may be catered for in the North Drawing Room, which houses up to 50 people for £1,500. Evening hire of the entire palace costs £8,250, and includes use of the Queen's Gallery, a tour of the palace, and dinner in the Victorian Garden Rooms. There's also a formal garden with space for up to 80 people. For Kensington Palace Orangery, *see p335.*

Kenwood House
Hampstead Lane, NW3 7JR (8341 5384/ www.english-heritage.org.uk/hospitality). Golders Green tube then 210 bus. **Phone enquiries** 9am-5pm daily. **Credit** MC, V.
You can hire the Orangery Suite at this neo-classical house on the edge of Hampstead Heath for dinner or an intimate wedding. It has a capacity of 80 for dinner, and 120 for a reception. The servants' quarters, including the restaurant and old kitchen, can also be hired. Typical prices run between £2,000 and £3,500.

Leighton House
12 Holland Park Road, W14 8LZ (7603 1123/ www.rbkc.gov.uk/leightonhousemuseum). High Street Kensington tube/Kensington (Olympia) tube/rail. **Phone enquiries** 9am-5pm Mon-Fri. **Credit** MC, V.
Only available in the evenings, the entire house (formerly the studio/residence of Victorian painter Frederic, Lord Leighton) with private gardens and famously ornate Arab Hall can be hired from 6.30pm to 11pm at a cost of £2,100, or from 6.30pm to 9pm for £1,100. It holds 150 guests for a cocktail party, or 80 for a seated dinner. Note that prices don't include insurance.

Hotels

This is just an example of the many hotels across London with rooms available for hire.

London Hilton
22 Park Lane, W1K 1BE (7493 8000/ www.hilton.co.uk). Green Park or Hyde Park Corner tube. **Phone enquiries** 7am-7pm Mon-Fri. **Credit** AmEx, DC, MC, V.
The Hilton's Wellington Ballroom, with views over Hyde Park and Park Lane, has capacity for 250. Smaller rooms house parties of up to 100 people, while the imposing Grand Ballroom is famed for lavish 1,000-capacity parties. In 2001, the Banqueting Chef Award went to Anthony Marshall, the London Hilton's executive chef.

Lowndes Hotel
21 Lowndes Street, SW1X 9ES (7823 1234/ www.lowndeshotel.com). Knightsbridge tube. **Open** 9am-6pm Mon-Fri. **Credit** AmEx, DC, JCB, MC, V.
The ground floor contains the meeting room, known as the Library, overlooking the hotel's gardens. It can accommodate private receptions, or up to 18 people for dinner. Sound and video systems, and an audio-visual unit are also available for corporate events. Prices are charged on a half-day/full-day basis, regardless of whether your party takes place in the evening or day.

myhotel
11-13 Bayley Street, Bedford Square, WC1B 3HD (7907 4923/www.myhotels.co.uk). Tottenham Court Road tube. **Phone enquiries** 9.30am-6pm Mon-Fri. **Credit** AmEx, DC, JCB, MC, V.
There are three spaces available at the bijou, design-conscious myhotel. The East Room seats 12-15, with space for 25-30 standing. It costs £400 for a whole day. The slightly larger West Room costs £600 for 60-70 standing or 30 sitting. The myplace Penthouse will set you back £1,000 and comes with a terrace. Catering is also available, ranging from a variety of set menus to buffets and canapés. Prices don't include VAT.

Museums & galleries

Barbican
Silk Street, EC2Y 8DS (7382 7043/ www.barbican.org.uk). Barbican or Moorgate tube. **Phone enquiries** 9am-6pm Mon-Fri. **Credit** AmEx, MC, V.
The Barbican can be a somewhat impersonal space, but not so the Conservatory and Contemporary Garden Rooms: the two function spaces, both of which are airy and filled with beautiful plants and flowers. A drinks reception for up to 450 people can be held in both rooms. To hire the Conservatory for a sit-down meal costs £950, while a drinks reception is £1,500. The Garden Room seats 280 for a sit-down meal, with room hire starting from £1,300 for evening events (6-11.30pm). VAT and catering is extra.

Design Museum
28 Shad Thames, SE1 2YD (7940 8756/ www.designmuseum.org). London Bridge tube/ rail/Tower Hill tube/DLR. **Phone enquiries** 9.30am-5pm Mon-Fri. **No credit cards.**
This ultra-stylish museum near Tower Bridge offers the Riverside Hall and Contemporary Design Gallery for private events, and the Meeting Room for corporate presentations. The Riverside Hall (with riverfront terrace) can hold up to 250 guests; to hire it from 6.30pm to 11pm costs £2,500 (Mon-Thur) or £3,750 (Fri-Sun). The Gallery, with panoramic views, holds up to 150 guests and costs £4,000 during the week, £4,500 at the weekend.

Imperial War Museum
Lambeth Road, SE1 6HZ (7416 5392/ www.iwm.org.uk). Lambeth North tube/Waterloo tube/rail. **Phone enquiries** 9am-5pm Mon-Fri. **No credit cards.**
If you fancy schmoozing among shining guns and uniforms, head to this beautiful building (and former asylum) in Lambeth. It has six function rooms for day hire (7am-6pm), including the Boardroom (capacity 70, £700), the Georgian Boardroom (capacity 80, £700) and the Beaton Room (capacity 30, £400). The Main Atrium is available for evening hire, with space for 400; it costs £4,000 from 6.30pm until midnight. Visit the website for more details.

Institute of Contemporary Arts
12 Carlton House Terrace, SW1Y 5AH (7766 1413/7930 3647/www.ica.org.uk). **Phone enquiries** 10am-6pm Mon-Fri. **No credit cards.**
Housed in impressive premises on the Mall, the ICA has the Nash and Brandon rooms for hire, as well as a theatre, two cinemas and a New Media Centre. Catering (including trained technical staff)

Parties & Shops

Dunn's. See p341.

can be supplied for private parties, weddings or even theatre productions, but this isn't included in hire price. Prices for evening hire of the Nash and Brandon rooms is £1,600 from 6pm to 11pm, or £2,000 from 6pm to 1am.

National Maritime Museum

Romney Road, SE10 9NF (8312 6644/ www.nmm.ac.uk/hospitality). Cutty Sark DLR. **Phone enquiries** 9am-5pm Mon-Fri. **No credit cards**.
Two historic parts of the museum can be hired for evening receptions and dinners: the Queen's House (designed by Inigo Jones) and Royal Observatory (by Christopher Wren). The lecture theatre and parlours in the Queen's House are available for hire during the day. The Queen's House is licensed for civil wedding ceremonies and also welcomes christening parties.

Outdoor

Kensington Palace Orangery

Kensington Palace State Apartments, Kensington Gardens, W8 4PX (0870 751 5184). Kensington High Street or Queensway tube. **Phone enquiries** 9am-5pm Mon-Fri. **No credit cards**.
The Orangery, set in its own private gardens, features Queen Anne architecture, a Portland stone terrace and verdant lawns that provide a great setting for summer parties. Available only for evening events (7-10.30pm), it accommodates up to 150 for dinner in the summer, or 550 people for a reception. Hire will set you back £6,000 (plus VAT). The fee includes optional private views of the State Apartments and the Royal Ceremonial Dress Collection (no dressing up, though). For Kensington Palace itself, *see p333*.

The Orangery, Holland Park

Abbotsbury Road, W8 6LU (7603 1123/ www.rbkc.gov.uk/theorangery). Holland Park or Kensington High Street tube. **Phone enquiries** 9am-5.15pm Mon-Fri. **Credit** MC, V.
Situated in bucolic Holland Park, the Orangery (licensed for civil weddings) is available from 9am to 5pm or 6 to 11.30pm on any day for £850 (plus insurance). There's room for 150 people for a cocktail party, or 80 for a seated lunch or dinner. Private catering is provided by Searcy's.

Ranelagh Gardens

The Royal Hospital, Royal Hospital Road, SW3 4SR (7881 5298/www.chelsea-pensioners.co.uk). Sloane Square tube. **Phone enquiries** 9am-6pm Mon-Fri. **Credit** AmEx, DC, JCB, MC, V.
Home to the Chelsea Flower Show, the Ranelagh Gardens at the Royal Hospital, redesigned by landscaper John Gibson in 1860, are available for private and corporate marquees and garden parties all year round. The State Apartments, the Chapel and the Great Hall of the Royal Hospital can also be hired. See the website for prices and other information.

Royal Botanic Gardens

Entrances on Kew Green & Kew Road, Kew, Richmond, Surrey TW9 3AB (8332 5641/ www.kew.org). Kew Gardens tube/Kew Bridge rail. **Phone enquiries** 9am-5pm Mon-Fri. **Credit** MC, V.
London's premier botanical venue provides an exceptional backdrop for weddings, with provision for civil ceremonies and catering. Corporate events and luncheons can also be held at Kew's Cambridge Cottage or Temperate House. See the website for prices, which vary greatly depending upon function, time of year and group numbers.

Venues with a view

British Airways London Eye

Riverside Building, County Hall, Westminster Bridge Road, SE1 7PB (0870 220 2223/ www.londoneye.com). Westminster tube/Waterloo tube/rail. **Phone enquiries** 8.30am-8pm daily. **Credit** AmEx, DC, MC, V.
For unbeatable views of London's skyling, choose from a range of private capsule hires on the London Eye. Options include a 'champagne capsule', a 'private capsule', a 'Pimms and strawberries capsule' or a 'breakfast capsule', each with individual pricing. For example, a 'private capsule' is £350 plus £50 per bottle of champagne (minimum order two bottles). A 'Pimms and strawberries capsule' costs £350 plus £12.50 per person (minimum order 20 guests) and is available from 11am daily or noon on a Sunday. You can even get married here (from £1,700).

HMS Belfast

Morgan's Lane, Tooley Street, SE1 2JH (7403 6246/www.iwm.org.uk). London Bridge tube/rail. **Phone enquiries** 9am-5pm Mon-Fri. **Credit** MC, V.
Second World War cruiser HMS *Belfast* is permanently moored between London Bridge and Tower Bridge. There are four areas for hire: the Admiral's Quarters, the Ward Room (and Ante Room), the Gun Room Banqueting Suites and the Ship's Company Dining Hall. A full catering service is available.

Wellington Arch

Hyde Park Corner, W1J 7JZ (0870 780 4082/ www.english-heritage.org.uk). Hyde Park Corner tube. **Phone enquiries** 9am-5pm Mon-Fri. **Credit** MC, V.

Papageno RESTAURANT & BAR

'Where the show goes on for the theatre workers and goers'.

Prominently located in the heart of Covent Garden's theatreland, Papageno is dedicated to pre and post-theatre dining. Open all day, seven days a week; eat from an exclusive a la carte menu or special set theatre meals available at £12.50 throughout the day and pre-theatre. Enjoy live performances from a String Quartet every Sunday afternoon and Sunday & Monday evenings; however, adhoc appearances can happen from a variety of artistes!

Available for private functions, weddings, parties and other events for 100 guests or more, Papageno has one of London's most beautiful rooms with its own private entrance and bar.

"Seeing is believing"

29-31 Wellington Street, London. WC2
Tel. 020 7836 4444   Fax. 020 7836 0011
www.papagenorestaurant.com   Email. reservations@papagenorestaurant.com

Designed in 1825 as a grand entrance way to Buckingham Palace, the impressively lit Wellington Arch at Hyde Park Corner is available for hire during the day on Tuesdays and in the evenings throughout the week from 6.30pm. The Burton Room has access to exterior balconies and views over Hyde Park and Buckingham Palace, with a capacity of 36 for dinner, or 80 for a drinks reception. Hire costs around £2,750 (plus VAT).

Planners & entertainers

Organising a party can be a stressful business, with so many elements needing close attention to ensure the event runs without any hitches. So why not hire a professional?

General party planners

The Admirable Crichton
5 Camberwell Trading Estate, Denmark Road, SE5 9LB (7326 3800/www.admirable-crichton. co.uk). **Phone enquiries** 9.30am-5.30pm Mon-Fri. **No credit cards.**
Founded 21 years ago by Rolline Frewen and Johnny Roxburgh, and with a huge staff of chefs, food designers, waiting staff and party designers, this very fashionable and much-lauded outfit organises hundreds of parties, corporate events, Christmas bashes, bar mitzvahs, anniversaries, weddings... and anything in between. Prince Charles, Tiffany's, *Tatler*, the Royal Academy, the Almeida: the client list is awesome.

Crown Society
13 Bishopsgate, EC2N 3BA (7236 2149/ www.crowngroup.co.uk). **Phone enquiries** 8.30am-6pm Mon-Fri. **Credit** AmEx, DC, MC, V.
Established in 1978, Crown Society has provided the catering for high-profile corporate and private events throughout the UK, winning several awards in the process. The informative website is worth a look for ideas.

EventWise
The Coda Centre, 189 Munster Road, SW6 6AW (7386 5000/www.eventwise.co.uk). **Phone enquiries** 9am-6pm Mon-Fri. **Credit** AmEx, MC, V.
EventWise has created packages that range from summer parties to corporate team-building events. Case studies of past private parties can be viewed on the website.

Fortesqueue's Event Management
The Stables, Brook Farm, Logmore Lane, Wescott, Dorking, Surrey RH4 3JN (0870 901 0203/www.fqevents.com). **Phone enquiries** 8.30am-6pm Mon-Fri. **Credit** AmEx, JCB, MC, V.
Apart from corporate events, Fortesqueue's also organises complete party packages, summer and Christmas parties, and themed parties.

Hospitality Matters
Mill Lane Business Park, Mill Lane, Brigg, North Lincolnshire DN20 8NE (07000 399 0999/www.hospitalitymatters.co.uk). **Phone enquiries** 9am-5.30pm Mon-Fri. **No credit cards.**
Specialising in event management and the building of temporary structures, this company will manage and co-ordinate every aspect of party organising – from venue finding and event design, to travel and catering. Weddings, private functions and corporate entertainment are all covered.

Mask Event Design & Production
Studio 302, Lana House, 118 Commercial Street, E1 6NF (7377 8001/www.mask.co.uk). **Phone enquiries** 9am-6pm Mon-Fri. **No credit cards.**
Mask specialises in Christmas and summer parties. Its themed Christmas party packages are all inclusive, covering drinks, finger buffets and public liability insurance. Events are held in London locations.

Progressive Events
24 Carmichael Mews, SW18 3HJ (8874 7555/www.progressiveevents.co.uk). **Phone enquiries** 9am-5pm Mon-Fri. **No credit cards.**
This firm organises a multitude of parties, from seasonal entertainment to weddings and themed corporate functions, as well as low-key, intimate dinners. It can arrange all aspects: lighting, production, furniture, flowers and sound.

Theme Traders
The Stadium, Oaklands Road, NW2 6DL (8452 8518/www.themetraders.com). **Phone enquiries** 8am-6pm Mon-Fri. **Credit** AmEx, MC, V.
Themed parties are the speciality of this company, which has worked with everyone from the Beeb to Graham Norton. Weddings, summer balls, Christmas parties, corporate occasions: Theme Traders has done it all. Prices start at around £2,000 and the team takes care of everything from design to rigging.

Westend Events
61-63 Great Queen Street, WC2B 5DA (7404 4232/www.westendevents.co.uk). **Phone enquiries** 9am-6pm Mon-Fri. **Credit** MC, V.
From murder mystery dinners to casino nights and secret agent appearances, this firm specialises in theme nights. Medieval events and 1980s parties are also in Westend's repertoire.

William Bartholomew Party Organising
23 The Talina Centre, Bagleys Lane, SW6 2BW (7731 8328/www.wbpo.com). **Phone enquiries** 9am-5pm Mon-Fri. **No credit cards.**
Organising private parties, corporate events and weddings for 25 years all over the world (including Beirut, Washington, Switzerland and France), but primarily in London and the Home Counties, this company runs functions from a basic £50-a-head party to top celebrity get-togethers. A travelling disco with lighting and two DJs costs £850.

Kids' party planners

Adam Ants
8959 1045/www.adamantsparties.com.
Adam Ant stands and delivers the nuts and bolts of memorable parties: music and dancing, magic, balloon sculpture and general japery, all courtesy of a range of entertainers. The cost depends on the length of the party, but starts at £85 for one hour. Party accessories can be hired, including ball ponds and bouncy castles (from £45).

Kasimira
29 South Terrace, SW7 2TB (7581 8313/ www.kasimira.com). **Phone enquiries** 10am-6pm Mon-Fri. **Credit** MC, V.
Kasimira has a database of entertainers, face painters, magicians and other experts in the party field, all of whom have been interviewed, referenced and police checked. Ring for details of the firm's Harry Potter parties, with Quidditch lessons and potions classes.

Laurie Temple & the Party Wizard Company
8840 5293/www.thepartywizard.co.uk. **Phone enquiries** 24hrs daily. **No credit cards.**
Temple and his team of fellow entertainers offer magic, balloons, juggling, junior discos, puppetry, storytelling and face-painting. Themes vary from pop star discos to circus workshops where kids can learn to stilt-walk and spin plates. Party Wizard also offers full party organisation. Prices start at £100 an hour.

PK Entertainments
07771 546676/www.fairandfete.co.uk. **Phone enquiries** 24hrs daily. **No credit cards.**
What do you get for the kid who has everything? Well, an indoor fairground might be a start. If your house is large enough, PK can set up a basic package (from £200) in your living room, with mini bouncy castle, bucking bronco and stalls of the

pop gun variety; more spacious venues could even include a toboggan run. Outdoor events start at around £250 for 20 children. A fully blown fair can be built for roughly £500: roundabouts, swing-boats and all.

Puddleduck Parties
8893 8998. **Phone enquiries** 24hrs daily. **No credit cards.**
Stressful party preparations flow like water off Puddleduck's back; the firm can arrange entertainment, have the cake baked and sort out the goody bags. Party themes are aimed at children of all ages – teddy bears' picnics for the youngest, perhaps, or Batman birthdays for the heroically inclined. There's also the option of drama parties, sports parties and discos for older kids.

Splodge
7350 1477/www.planetsplodge.com. **Phone enquiries** 9am-5pm Mon-Fri. **Credit** MC, V.
The trained actors of Splodge – called 'Splodgas' – immerse groups of up to 20 kids in a choice of themed environments at either Battersea Park or Holland Park. Parties range from Bombay Dreams to girl band rehearsals, with extras such as stegosaurus sandwiches, face-painting and video footage of the big day (from £330). Parties last two hours, with craft activities optional. Prices start at £305 for a zoo party, which includes pony and carousel rides, party bags and a tent for the birthday lunch (food supplied by parents, although lunch boxes can be provided for £8.50 per child).

Twizzle Parties
8789 3232/www.twizzle.co.uk. **Phone enquiries** 9am-5pm Mon-Sat. **Credit** MC, V.
Twizzle puts on different events for different age groups: toddlers will enjoy a giant bubble-blowing party (£240); there are circus, princess and beach themes for small children, and a highly popular creepy-crawly party for their older siblings (£280). Wannabe pop stars can cut their own CD and music video in a real London recording studio (from £350 for two hours, with up to 16 kids) and take home a copy to play – repeatedly.

Parties & Shops

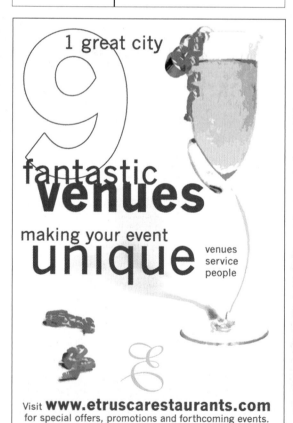

Entertainers

Cabaret Casino Associates

01932 455902/www.cabaretcasino.co.uk.
Phone enquiries 24hrs daily. **No credit cards**.
The guys at Cabaret Casino can transform your
venue (whether it be a lounge or a conference room)
into an authentic gambling den. Casino tables, slot
machines, professional croupiers and even a wheel
of fortune can be hired. Scalextric tracks and bingo
machines (complete with callers) are also available.

Dark Blues Management

*Puddephat's, Markyate, Herts AL3 8AZ (01582
842226/www.darkblues.co.uk).* **Phone enquiries**
9.30am-5.30pm Mon-Fri. **No credit cards**.
Dark Blues can source and provide a wide range
of entertainers, including jazz musicians, pianists,
tribute bands, DJs, magicians and fire-eaters.

Diamond Fun Casino

*1 The Byeways, Field Common Lane, Walton-
on-Thames, Surrey KT12 3QH (01932 888706/
www.diamondfc.com).* **Phone enquiries**
9am-5pm Mon-Fri. **No credit cards**.
Gambling entertainment for corporate functions,
weddings, charity events and various other
occasions is provided by this firm. Games include
black jack, roulette and poker. Players are given
'fun money' to gamble with. Prices start from £200
per table (and lower as more tables are hired); this
pays for a croupier, delivery and collection.

Discotech

*Studio 36, Building 56, Magnet Road, East
Lane Business Park, Wembley, Middx HA9 7RG
(0800 163712/www.discotech.co.uk).* North
Wembley tube/rail. **Open** 10am-6pm Mon-Sat.
Credit MC, V.
With its prices starting at under £200, Discotech
can provide the tunes for any celebration, complete
with a sound system, lighting and DJ. Karaoke
machines (with compère/operator) cost from
around £250, while portable dancefloors can be
arranged for £250 (plus VAT and rigging).

Function Junction

*7 Market Square, Bicester, Oxon OX26 6AA
(0800 0343232/www.functionjunction.co.uk).*
Phone enquiries 9am-6pm Mon-Fri. **Credit**
AmEx, MC, V.

Function Junction provides entertainment for
private parties, weddings and corporate events. A
huge array of talent is offered, from bands, jazz
and rock musicians, to top DJs and classical
performers. A four-piece rock band playing for two
hours costs £900.

Juke Box Junction

*12 Toneborough, off Abbey Road, NW8 0BL
(7328 6206).* **Phone enquiries** 9am-5pm
Mon-Fri. **No credit cards**.
Fancy a blast from the past? Michael Flynn has
two classic 1970s Seeburg jukeboxes for hire at
£275 per night. Hand over a £50 deposit, choose a
playlist of 50 records from Flynn's large collection
and enjoy a musical treat.

Latin Touch Entertainments

*Fatima Community Centre, Commonwealth
Avenue, W12 7QR (8740 9020/www.latin
touch.com).* White City tube. **Open** 10am-6pm
Mon-Fri. **No credit cards**.
Latin Touch can supply a wide variety of South
American music, from Cuban folk to Brazilian
salsa and Mexican jazz. Artists are based in the
UK, but the agency can also book well-known
Latin American stars to perform at private parties,
weddings and corporate bashes.

Nigel Round Management & Entertainment Agency

*119 Railway Road, Adlington, Chorley,
Lancs PR6 9QX (01257 480103/www.nigel
round.co.uk).* **Phone enquiries** 9am-5pm
Mon-Fri. **No credit cards**.
This established agency represents comedians,
hypnotists, tribute bands, children's entertainers,
ventriloquists and country & western singers.
Successful *Stars in their Eyes* look-alikes as well
as stars in their own right are on its books. Prices
start from £100 for a disco/karaoke.

Nostalgia Amusements

*22 Greenwood Close, Thames Ditton,
Surrey KT7 0BG (8398 2141/www.nostalgia-
hire.co.uk).* **Phone enquiries** 24hrs daily.
No credit cards.
An impressive selection of authentic vintage
amusements can be hired from this firm, including
pinball tables (from the 1930s), one-arm bandits
and classic jukeboxes. The Victorian amusement

parlour boasts a laughing policeman and
distorting mirrors, as well as attendants dressed
in period costume.

Sacconi String Quartet

*07941 053696/01634 826359/
www.sacconi.com.* **Phone enquiries**
10am-6pm daily. **No credit cards**.
This talented quartet provides music for various
occasions, from formal concerts and weddings to
private parties and corporate functions. It has even
played for the Queen. The group's flexible
repertoire includes work from composers and
bands as diverse as Puccini, the Beatles and the
Verve. Prices start at £350 for the first hour and
£50 for every hour thereafter.

Young's Disco Centre

*2 Malden Road, NW5 3HR (7485 1115/
www.youngsdisco.com).* Chalk Farm tube.
Open by appointment only Mon-Fri; 11am-5pm
Sat. **Credit** AmEx, MC, V.
Dancing queens (and kings) will find all they need
to get their groove on at Young's. A sound system
and DJ costs from £180 for a two-hour weekday
party (£250 at weekends); karaoke machines are
available from £80. Further refinements include a
smoke machine or industrial bubble-blower,
popcorn and candy-floss makers, and even fake
snow machines.

Kids' entertainers

For more ideas on how to entertain the kids in
your care, consult the latest *Time Out London
for Children* guide (£8.99).

Ali Do Lali

01494 774300. **Phone enquiries** 24hrs daily.
No credit cards.
After 30 years of perfecting his tricks and
illusions, Ali Do Lali can grip all ages with his
individual and quirky style of entertaining.
Younger party-goers are treated to storytelling and
more gentle trickery, while the fire-eating and the
sawing in half of parents is saved for older kids.
Prices vary.

Billy the Disco DJ

8471 8616/www.billythediscodj.co.uk. **Phone
enquiries** 9am-9pm daily. **No credit cards**.

Choccywoccydoodah. See p341.

Parties & Shops

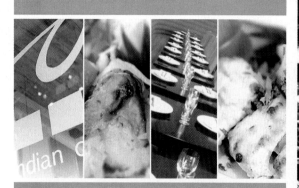

Billy's disco for party people aged four to 11 includes limbo contests, disco lights, pop quizzes and karaoke. It costs £150 for two hours.

Blueberry Playsongs Parties

8677 6871/www.blueberry.clara.co.uk. **Phone enquiries** 9am-5pm Mon-Fri. **No credit cards**.
An established parent-and-toddler music group with nine branches across the capital, Blueberry also sends its entertainers to kids' parties for 45 minutes of guitar-led singing, dancing and fun. Prices start at £75 for 20 children, and include balloons as well as a special present for the birthday boy or girl.

Chris Howell

7376 1083/www.christopherhowell.net. **Phone enquiries** 10am-8pm daily. **No credit cards**.
Chris is a member of the fast-talking school of American conjuring (and the Magic Circle), but that doesn't mean his shows go over the heads of younger audiences – far from it. Hour-long parties for four- to eight-year-olds weave through a story in which the kids play an active part, and there's balloon modelling to finish. Prices start at £85.

Juggling John

8938 3218/www.jugglersetc.com. **Phone enquiries** 9am-5pm Mon-Fri. **Credit** MC, V.
Juggling John – master of slapstick and mime – supplies unicyclists, stilt-walkers, storytellers and fire-eaters, and is himself available for children's parties in several guises, including Reggie the Raccoon, Ronnie the Robot and good old JJ. One- or two-hour shows start at £140.

Lee Warren

8670 2729/www.sorcery.org.uk. **Phone enquiries** 9am-10pm daily. **No credit cards**.
Warren's brilliant shows combine deft sorcery with audience participation. Boys and girls dress up to take part in stories, with plenty of conjuring, illusion and amusing calamity along the way. Lee's hour-long shows – aimed at four- to eight-year-olds – cost £110 for a home performance and £120 in a hired hall.

Little Blisters

8948 3874/www.childrensentertainment-surrey.co.uk. **Phone enquiries** 10am-6pm daily. **No credit cards**.
Actress Ava Desouza uses her dramatic skills to make parties sparkle for three- to seven-year-olds. As one of three characters – Flossie the Fairy, Sea Lily the Mermaid or Kitty the Magical Pussy Cat – she tells a story with plenty of visual trickery, singing and dancing. There are also games, prizes and face-painting.

Merlin Entertainments

8866 6327/www.merlinents.co.uk. **Phone enquiries** 9am-6pm daily. **No credit cards**.
Choose from a long list of performers, from caricaturists and comedy waiters to fortune tellers and fire eaters. Prices start at £115 for a one-hour performance, or £145 for a more interactive, two-hour show. Merlin also organises circus and clown workshops or parties, for six-year-olds upwards.

Fireworks

Dynamic Fireworks

Unit 18, Peartree Business Centre, Stanway, Colchester, Essex CO3 0JN (01206 762123/www.dynamicfireworks.co.uk). **Phone enquiries** 9.30am-4.30pm Mon-Fri. **Credit** MC, V.
Dynamic organises professionally fired shows (from £1,000), complete with an expert on hand to oversee proceedings. Staff can also arrange smaller events on request, but if you'd rather go it alone, you can choose from a wide range of individual fireworks, including cakes, fountains, rockets and mines. Mail order is available.

Fantastic Fireworks

Rocket Park, Pepperstock, Luton, Beds LU1 4LL (0800 511511/www.fantastic-fireworks.co.uk). **Phone enquiries** 8.30am-5.30pm Mon-Fri. **Credit** MC, V.

Glasgow, Manchester, Leeds and Liverpool all saw in the New Year with a firework display organised by Fantastic. Staff will run any type of celebration, including wedding parties, Bonfire Night celebrations and corporate bashes (prices start at £800 plus VAT). The Luton shop also carries a full range of fireworks. Mail order is available.

Le Maitre

6 Forval Close, Wandle Way, Mitcham, Surrey CR4 4NE (8646 2222/www.lemaitreltd.com). **Phone enquiries** 9am-5.30pm Mon-Fri. **Credit** MC, V.
The largest pyrotechnic company in Europe, Le Maitre has an impressive reputation and client list. Although it specialises in indoor spectacles, the firm can also arrange outdoor displays. Prices start at £1,000, but the sky really is the limit.

Caterers & equipment

Many party planners (*see p337*) also offer catering and equipment hire.

Cakes

The Cake Studio

8878 2066/www.thecakestudiolondon.co.uk. **Phone enquiries** 9am-5.30pm Mon-Fri. **No credit cards**.
The Cake Studio has an astonishing range of cake designs: contemporary, classic, futuristic or just plain wacky. Wedding cakes are delivered to the venue on the day, and prices include delivery in central London (deliveries outside the capital are charged by distance, at 65p per mile).

Choccywoccydoodah

47 Harrowby Street, W1H 5EA (7724 5465/www.choccywoccydoodah.com). Edgware Road or Marble Arch tube. **Open** 10am-6pm Wed-Fri; 11am-6pm Sat; or contact Brighton branch daily on 01273 329462. **Credit** MC, V.
Ignore the terrible name, Choccywoccydoodah is here to make real your most indulgent dreams. Its delightful creations are layered with fresh Belgian truffles and coated in plain, milk or white chocolate; the chocolate can even be dyed to match your party's colour scheme. Eight to ten portions cost from £19.50; £90 buys up to 70 portions.

Dunn's

6 The Broadway, N8 9SN (8340 1614/www.dunns-bakery.co.uk). Finsbury Park tube/rail then W7 bus/Crouch Hill rail/41, 91 bus. **Open** 7am-6pm Mon-Sat. **Credit** MC, V.
This highly respected traditional English baker makes cakes of the highest quality, in a huge number of prepared designs, including 3-D football pitches and snooker tables. Bespoke designs can be iced on to order, and a new line in impressive photo-quality images is selling like, er, hot cakes. Basic cakes start at £20.

Suzelle Cakes

26 Replington Road, SW18 5LR (8874 4616/www.suzellecakes.com). Southfields tube/39, 156 bus. **Open** 9am-5pm Mon-Sat. **Credit** MC, V.
Suzelle provides everything from a modest 'minicake' to an impressive culinary edifice for a big birthday bash. You can get a commemorative edible decorative plaque to go on top of the cake, which can then be removed and kept as a souvenir.

Caterers & catering equipment

All in Good Taste

433 Harrow Road, W10 4RE (8969 6333/www.allingoodtaste.ltd.uk). **Phone enquiries** 8am-4pm Mon-Fri. **No credit cards**.
This small, experienced company offers budget cocktail and buffet catering, with prices starting at £6.75 a head for the likes of melon balls wrapped in salami, and prawn and pork wun tuns. You can follow suggested menus or get a custom-made. Dietary need are taken into account.

At Home

40 High Street, Cobham, Surrey KT11 3EB (7649 9695/www.athomecatering.com). **Phone enquiries** 9am-5.30pm Mon-Sat. **Credit** AmEx, MC, V.
This outfit provides food for corporate and private parties, offering a number of different menus including canapés, seasonal lunch and dinner menus, and a Thai dinner party menu designed by chef Michael Caines. Three-course party menus start at £40 per person. It's more than just food, though: At Home also has a party-planning service – they'll also sort out the venue, marquee, lighting, theme, flowers, music and staff.

Creative Canapés

7 Southwell Gardens, SW7 4SB (7244 0782). **Phone enquiries** 9am-7pm Mon-Fri. **No credit cards**.
Specialising in finger buffets, Creative Canapés provides an elegant and unusual selection of nibbles for small or big bashes. Typical options include Asian (sesame soy beef skewers and tandoori chicken kebabs), classic (caviar blinis and toad in the hole), Mediterranean (crab and brandy tartlets and paella croquettes) and dessert canapés (chocolate pots with with kiwi, raspberry and lime mousse and blueberry tartlets).

Gorgeous Gourmets

Gresham Way, SW19 8ED (8944 7771/www.gorgeousgourmets.co.uk). Wimbledon Park tube. **Open** 8.30am-5.30pm Mon-Fri; 9am-noon Sat. **Credit** MC, V.
Bone china, linen, cutlery, glassware, candlesticks kitchen and cooking utensils – whatever you need, this gourgeous lot should be able to supply it. The neatly designed website makes ordering easy.

Just Hire Catering

Unit 5, Davenport Centre, Renwick Road, Barking, Essex IG11 0SH (8595 8877/www.justhirecatering.com). Upney tube. **Open** 9am-5.30pm Mon-Fri. **Credit** MC, V.
Just Hire's experienced staff provide an extensive range of tables, glassware, seating, bone china and colour co-ordinated tablecloths and napkins. Cutlery and china come shrink-wrapped for hygiene, and serving, bar and kitchen equipment is also available.

Florists

Lavender Green

17-18 Bridgewater Way, Windsor, Berks SL4 1RL (7808 7065/www.lavendergreen.co.uk). **Phone enquiries** 9am-5.30pm Mon-Fri. **Credit** AmEx, MC, V.
Lavender Green creates displays for both corporate and private clients, offering original designs and good value for money. The company has been used by many of London's top museums, including the Design Museum, the V&A and the National History Museum. Weddings and parties are catered for, with table-centre arrangements costing £35-£250, bouquets £85-£150 and free-standing pedestals £250-£450.

Serenata Flowers

117 Munster Road, SW6 6DH (0800 083 8880/www.serenataflowers.com). Fulham Broadway or Parsons Green tube. **Open** 9am-6pm Tue-Sat. **Credit** AmEx, MC, V.
Striking contemporary designs for weddings, parties, banqueting and corporate events. Order online with options according to colour, variety, price or style.

Sophie Hanna Flowers

Arch 48, New Covent Garden Market, SW8 5PP (7720 0841/www.sophiehannaflowers.com). **Phone enquiries** 8.30am-4.30pm Mon-Fri. **Credit** MC, V.
Sophie Hanna is a prized flowerseller in New Covent Garden Market, catering for weddings, themed events and all kinds of celebrations. Table displays start from £30, bridal bouquets from £60 and pedestals from £150. Candlesticks, vases, glassware and other props are also available.

Parties & Shops

The wonder of waxy's...

Renowned as London's Premier Irish Bar, Waxy O'Connor's is celebrated for its excellent food and customer service

food and Drink

4 bars on 7 levels offer a unique and friendly environment in the heart of the West End.
Bar food served daily.

The **Dargle Restaurant** serves a selection of à la carte meals including seafood dishes, vegetarian options and more traditional preferences. Open from 5.30pm.

Sports

Live coverage of all major sporting events.

music

Every Sunday night
Live Traditional Session in the Cottage Bar
Monday and Tuesday
Live music in the Church Bar

We also host performances from Guest Artists throughout the year.

Function rooms available for hire
www.waxyoconnors.co.uk

Tel: 020 7287 0255 Fax: 020 7287 3962
E-mail: london@waxyoconnors.co.uk
14 - 16 Rupert Street, Leicester Square, London W1D 6DD

Serenata Flowers. See p341.

Ice sculptures

Duncan Hamilton Ice Sculptor
5 Lampton House Close, SW19 5EX (8944 9787/ www.icesculpture.co.uk). **Phone enquiries** noon-5pm Mon-Fri. **No credit cards**.
Duncan Hamilton and his team have been working with ice for more than 25 years. Advertising and publishing shoots, films, parties, corporate get-togethers – Hamilton's hand-sculpted creations have appeared at them all. Miniature sculptures start at £80-£100, while larger pieces tend to be around £1,000. Prices include consultation, design, lighting, delivery within London and collection of equipment (usually the following day).

Ice World London
1 Ethelburga Street, SW11 4AG (7801 0606/ www.icesculptures.co.uk). Clapham Junction rail then 319 or 345 bus. **Open** 8am-6pm Mon-Sat. **Credit** AmEx, MC, V.
Fancy a dragon made out of ice? Check out Ice World's website, which has extensive photographs of sample work, including animals, novelty and Christmas designs, plus some very unusual drinking luges. Choose from myriad designs for weddings, anniversaries, themed parties or any social occasion, costing from £55 to £2,000.

Marquees

Alfred Bull
Unit 2C, Cathedral Hill Industrial Estate, Guildford, Surrey GU2 7YB (01483 575492/ www.alfredbullmarquees.co.uk). **Phone enquiries** 8.30am-6pm Mon-Fri. **No credit cards**.
This venerable firm ('supplier of marquees and awnings for over 100 years'), based in Guildford, specialises in creating classy tents for weddings and other celebrations. Marquees are available in various widths and any length. Party versions can have starlit ceilings, coloured linings and flat or pleated walls. Wedding marquees come with a broad choice of colours and styles, but your own ideas can also be accommodated.

Berry Marquees
Barnett Wood Farm Buildings, Barnett Wood Lane, Leatherhead, Surrey KT22 7DY (01372 379814/www.berrymarquees.com). **Phone enquiries** 8am-6pm Mon-Fri. **No credit cards**.
Clients of this well-established outfit have included M&S and Nat West. Services including a free site evaluation and, for larger events, a site supervisor (at a charge of £24 per hour) to keep your party running smoothly.

Field & Lawn Marquees
Units A58-A60, New Covent Garden Market, SW8 5EE (7622 1988/www.fieldandlawn.com). **Phone enquiries** 8am-5pm Mon-Fri. **Credit** JCB, MC, V.
Field & Lawn is one of the UK's premier marquee hire companies. Weddings, graduation balls, award ceremonies and corporate shindigs are all covered. Marquees start from 2m in width up to 30m, in pretty much any length you want. Furniture , lighting, flooring and entertainment can be arranged. Prices begin at £500.

Sunset Marquees
Welsbach House, Broomhill Road, SW18 4JQ (8741 2777/www.sunsetmarquees.com). **Phone enquiries** 24hrs daily. **No credit cards**.
A basic 3m by 3m pop-up marquee starts at £190, but there are numerous possibilities, with flexible configurations, and double- and triple-decker options. Lighting, heating, tables, chairs and flooring cost extra.

Vehicle hire

Drewitt Carriages
36 Hazon Way, Epsom, Surrey KT19 8HN (01372 727153). **Phone enquiries** 24hrs daily. **No credit cards**.
For that old-fashioned sense of style, hire a wedding carriage. They come in two styles: pulled by horses (hoods are available in case of rain), or driven by costumed staff. Guests can be taken from home to the ceremony and reception. The service covers London and the south-east.

Hanwells of London
86-91 Uxbridge Road, W7 3SU (7436 2070/ http://hanwells.net). Hanwell rail. **Open** 9am-7pm Mon-Fri; 9am-5pm Sat;11am-4pm Sun. **Credit** AmEx, DC, MC, V.
A Rolls-Royce Silver Seraph or Bentley Arnage with chauffeur costs £85 per hour, or £65 for a Rolls-Royce Silver Spur or Bentley Turbo R. Unusually, you can also drive the car yourself – a Rolls-Royce Silver Seraph for a day is £500. There is a minimum of four hours' hire.

Roberts Car Hire
50 Broadway, SW1H 0RG (7152 4050/ www.rocar.co.uk). **Phone enquiries** 8.30am-6pm Mon-Fri. **Credit** AmEx, JCB, MC, V.
Roberts' fleet includes plenty of flash cars (Mercedes, Bentley), limousines and people carriers. Stretch limos come with leather seats, heating and air-con, a bar and TV/radio/DVD/CD. Bilingual chauffeurs and Blue Badge guides are available if you need sightseeing help.

Savile Executive Cars
5B Russell Gardens, W14 8EZ (7751 1100/ www.savilecars.co.uk). **Phone enquiries** 8am-8pm daily. **Credit** AmEx, JCB, MC, V.
A reliable place to hire posh wedding cars, complete with leather upholstery, air-conditioning and mobile phones. Weddings, birthdays, sightseeing and airport transfers are all catered for. A stretch limo costs £250 for the first three hours, then £45 for every subsequent hour.

Videos

Institute of Videographers
PO Box 625, Loughton, Essex IG10 3GZ (0845 7413626/www.iov.co.uk). **Phone enquiries** 9am-5pm Mon-Fri. **Credit** MC, V.
Acting as a regulatory body for production companies and independent producers alike, the IoV can send you a free guide on what to look for when choosing a videographer and can recommend a list of professionals. Useful tips on filming styles and costs can also be obtained.

Shops

Unusual extras add those important finishing touches to a great party. The shops below provide costume and suit hire, and children's party necessities for a fantastic bash.

Costumes & dress hire

Angels
119 Shaftesbury Avenue, WC2H 8AE (7836 5678/www.littleangels.co.uk/ www.fancydress.com). Leicester Square or Tottenham Court Road tube. **Open** 9am-5.30pm Mon-Fri. **Credit** AmEx, MC, V.
Costumes that look like they've come straight out of a film, from *Braveheart* to *Chicago*, are to be found in this multistorey fancy dress den. Elizabethan outfits contrast with rock 'n' roll clobber. Prices to hire a complete outfit start at £82.25, with a £100 refundable deposit required. Mail order is also available.

Escapade
150 Camden High Street, NW1 0NE (7485 7384/ www.escapade.co.uk). Camden Town tube. **Open** 10am-7pm Mon-Fri; 10am-6pm Sat; noon-5pm Sun. **Credit** AmEx, MC, V.
Though it's only a small space, Escapade has over 2,000 costumes for hire, with everything from the classic clown outfits to straightlaced period designs. But the merchandise doesn't stop there – latex heads of Richard Nixon and Prince Charles

sit alongside a small selection of fireworks, a huge choice of wigs (from £5) and novelty items (edible undies, anyone?). Costume hire ranges from £30 to £35 for four days, with a refundable £50 deposit.

J&M Toys

46 Finsbury Drive, Wrose, Bradford, W Yorks BD2 1QA (01274 591887/www.jandmtoys.co.uk). **Phone enquiries** 9am-5.30pm Mon-Fri. **Credit** MC, V.

J&M Toys' costume catalogue is organised by profession: firemen, traffic wardens with lollipops, and enough medical outfits and paraphernalia to kit out a hospital. The owners are medieval enthusiasts, so there also are regal robes, Robin Hood lincoln greens, and a comprehensive range of knights' armour. It's all surprisingly cheap: most outfits cost little more than £15, with discounts on group purchases. Orders are taken via the website, by post or by fax.

Moss Bros

27-28 King Street, WC2E 8JD (7632 9700/ www.mossbros.com/hire). Covent Garden tube. **Open** 9am-6pm Mon-Wed, Fri, Sat; 9am-7pm Thur; 11am-4pm Sun. **Credit** AmEx, DC, JCB, MC, V.

Moss Bros is still a reliable choice for suits for most traditional events, ranging from dinner suits to various types of wedding attire, morning suits, black tie and Royal Ascot wear. A two-piece, three-button dinner suit starts at £33, with a Ted Baker suit for £65. Stores are located all over the UK, with 14 outlets in London alone.

Party supplies

Balloon & Kite Company

613 Garratt Lane, SW18 4SU (8946 5962). Tooting Broadway tube/Earlsfield rail. **Open** 9am-6pm Mon-Fri; 9am-5.30pm Sat. **Credit** AmEx, MC, V.

The name says it all. Balloons in rubber or foil (£1 or £2.99 apiece), bearing images of bright-eyed characters; names can be added to happy birthday versions while you wait (£3.25 each). There's also a nice line in paper tableware and banners for the more popular party themes, while kites (from £10) make for good last-minute gift. Presents for loot bags start at around 99p, including yo-yos, bracelets and other small toys. Delivery in London for orders over £10.

Circus Circus

176 Wandsworth Bridge Road, SW6 2UQ (7731 4128/www.circuscircus.co.uk). Fulham Broadway tube. **Open** 10am-6pm Mon-Sat. **Credit** AmEx, MC, V.

Circus Circus will supply everything that's needed to bring a kids' party to life, from the background music to the decorations. They'll even bake the cake, blow up the balloons and bring the entertainer to your home. Individual items are available for those who trust their own event co-ordination skills, including costumes from £10.99, invitations, bouncy castles and balloons.

Harlequin

254 Lee High Road, SE13 5PR (8852 0193). Hither Green rail/Lewisham rail/DLR/21, 261 bus. **Open** 10am-5.30pm Mon, Tue, Thur-Sat; 10am-1pm Wed. **Credit** MC, V.

This is a great little shop with a good range of children's costumes for sale, including plenty of characters from well-loved fables – Snow White, Peter Pan, Cinderella. Prices start at £9.95 and rise to £28 for elaborate animal suits. For parents on a budget, there are costume kits for £3.95: the pirate kit, for example, contains a patch, bandana, moustache and earring.

Hill Toy Company

Unit 1, The Tavern, Lower Green, Higham, Bury-St-Edmonds, Suffolk IP12 6NL (0870 607 1248/www.hilltoy.co.uk). **Phone enquiries** 10am-4pm Mon-Fri. **Credit** MC, V.

The Hill Toy Company has a great range of toys and games, as well as an excellent selection of outfits. Forget realism: most of the costumes –

The Non-Stop Party Shop

from the Indian brave's get-up (£24.95) to the unbelievably huggable, all-in-one lamb suit (£21.95) – are designed to make kids look cute, and do so with style. The accessories list runs from impressive-looking medical kits to wigwams, and the online ordering system is very good.

Just Balloons

7434 3039/www.justballoons.com. **Phone enquiries** 9am-6pm Mon-Fri. **Credit** AmEx, JCB, MC, V.

A thoroughly misleading name for a store that offers the complete party package – bunting, bubble blowers, face paints, party poppers – but one which gives a good indication of the inflatable empire lying behind these tiny doors. Foil balloons come in a range of styles (from £2.95), and novelty balloons – animal-shaped foils or floating pieces of fruit – can be had from £4.99 a pop. Balloons can also be printed with personalised messages, although more extravagant types may want to immortalise a memorable moment with a printed photograph balloon.

Mexicolore

28 Warriner Gardens, SW11 4EB (7622 9577/www.pinata.co.uk). **Phone enquiries** 8am-8pm Mon-Sat. **Credit** (website only) MC, V.

Children bored with pinning a tail on the donkey might prefer to smash the thing to pieces. Such gratifyingly violent antics are a traditional feature of a Mexican Christmas, and are becoming increasingly popular at children's parties in this country. The lovingly decorated target, a piñata, is made of papier mâché and can be filled with fruit, sweets or small toys. Piñatas are available in various animal forms, from a fish (£15.95) to an elephant (£41.95).

The Non-Stop Party Shop

214-216 Kensington High Street, W8 7RG (7937 7200/www.nonstopparty.co.uk). High Street Kensington tube. **Open** 9.30am-6pm Mon-Sat; 11am-5pm Sun. **Credit** MC, V.

Everything your party needs, from bubble machines (£29.95) to sparkly 'happy birthday' banners, is sold here. A 'party time' box filled with novelty items like bangers, masks and hooters will set you back £19.99. There's also an extensive stock of cards. Mail order available.

Oscar's Den

127-129 Abbey Road, NW6 4SL (7328 6683/ www.oscarsden.com). Swiss Cottage tube/ West Hampstead tube/rail/28, 31, 139, 189 bus. **Open** 9.30am-5.30pm Mon-Sat; 10am-2pm Sun. **Credit** AmEx, JCB, MC, V.

Oscar's Den is an Aladdin's cave of party-related paraphernalia, and has an excellent reputation. Celebrations cater for individual budgets, and services run from face paints to year-round firework displays. Bouncy castles (from £40) and big toys (seesaws, slides, pedal-cars and more, from £10) are permanently for hire, and individual items are always on sale.

Party Superstore

268 Lavender Hill, SW11 1LJ (7924 3210/ www.partysuperstore.co.uk). Clapham Junction rail/39, 77, 345 bus. **Open** 9am-6pm Mon-Wed, Fri, Sat; 9am-7pm Thur; 10.30am-4.30pm Sun. **Credit** AmEx, MC, V. **For branch see index**.

This store has been supplying London's fun lovers with the tools of their trade for 13 years. The first floor is dedicated to children's party accessories, from quality fancy dress costumes (from £7.99) to novelty hats and wigs, with most items for hire on the ground floor. There's a branch in Sutton.

Food Shops

If you like eating out, you probably like eating in. And London has some fantastic food shops, covering everything from unusual Chinese vegetables and fine French cheeses to organic meat. Here's our pick of the best.

For more on two of the capital's best foodie areas – Marylebone Village in central London and Northcote Road in Battersea – see the feature starting on p8. For more food and drink specialists, see the latest edition of the *Time Out Shopping Guide* (£9.99).

Food halls

Fortnum & Mason
181 Piccadilly, W1A 1ER (7734 8040/ www.fortnumandmason.co.uk). Green Park or Piccadilly Circus tube. **Open** 10am-6.30pm Mon-Sat; noon-6pm Sun. **Credit** AmEx, DC, JCB, MC, V.
This is the kind of venue Londoners tend to overlook, thinking it's only for tourists. More's the pity, as Fortnum's is a useful place to find high-quality food, particularly chocolates and confectionery, jams, condiments, biscuits, cheeses and classy traiteur foods. Then there's the fact that, with its plush carpets, deferential staff and pure Englishness, the store is pleasant in its own right. Traditional luxuries, such as caviar and smoked salmon, are well represented, as are F&M's famous teas and coffees. The hampers, which range from affordable to lavish, are as desirable as ever – put one on your Christmas list now. Wines and spirits round off the selection. Mail order available.

Harrods
87-135 Brompton Road, SW1X 7XL (7730 1234/ www.harrods.com). Knightsbridge tube. **Open** 10am-7pm Mon-Sat. **Credit** AmEx, DC, MC, V.
Certainly the best-looking food halls in London, with magnificent art nouveau tiling and lots of tourists in gawping mode. You can linger for ages deciding between an array of hams, sit down for some fresh sushi or oysters, or get lost in the world's best cheeses. Affordable items can be found in the fabulous selection of chocolates, teas and coffees. Everything else is just as expensive as you'd expect – you can easily spend ten quid putting together a simple lunch of freshly prepared oriental noodles and spring rolls. If money's no object, go the whole hog and indulge in the luxurious foods and well-chosen wines. And be sure to grab some Krispy Kreme doughnuts on your way out. Mail order available.

Harvey Nichols
109-125 Knightsbridge, SW1X 7RJ (7235 5000/ www.harveynichols.com). Knightsbridge tube. **Open** 10am-8pm Mon-Fri; 10am-7pm Sat; noon-6pm Sun. **Credit** AmEx, DC, MC, V.
While as elegantly presented as one would expect, Harvey Nicks has a useful selection of edibles. Some fun and creative dishes are offered, while the fresh fruit and veg encompass everything from gorgeous organic items to sweet Saudi dates. There's a good mix of imports, with homesick Yanks well catered for. The company's own-brand coffees, teas and biscuits are among the most affordable options, and would liven up any kitchen. Mail order available.

Selfridges
400 Oxford Street, W1A 1AB (0870 837 7377/ www.selfridges.com). Bond Street or Marble Arch tube. **Open** 10am-8pm Mon-Fri; 9.30am-8pm Sat; noon-6pm Sun. **Credit** AmEx, DC, MC, V.
A department store food court that merits a visit of its own – and a lengthy one at that. You need at least an hour just to see all that's here, from breads and cakes to cheeses, meat and fish, plus excellent prepared meals and plenty of basics. That's before you've even started on the imports. The bakery items are among the best, with a gorgeous range of loaves to choose from. The meat counter is well stocked, with nice cuts of beef and lamb, while the fish counter is seriously tempting. Nothing is particularly cheap, but it's all so beautiful that you'd be forgiven for blowing your budget. If all that browsing gets a bit overwhelming, take a break at the pretzel counter, lunch at Square Pie, EAT or Yo! Sushi, or make a beeline for the salt beef bar. Mail order available.

Markets

Borough Market
Between Borough High Street, Bedale Street, Stoney Street & Winchester Walk, SE1 1TL (www.boroughmarket.org.uk). London Bridge tube/rail. **Open** noon-6pm Fri; 9am-4pm Sat. **No credit cards**.
Endorsed by many a celebrity chef, Borough Market offers an exciting mix of food from all over the world. Omnivores are well served; there's everything from free-range chicken, geese (in season) and ostrich, to Lake District lamb and mutton, prime beef, rare-breed pork and venison. Add to this fresh fish and seafood, fruit and veg, breads and pastries, organic foodstuffs, exotic teas, flowers, olive oils, dairy produce, beers and wines. Many stalls offer tasters, so you can try before you buy. Quality is high, as are prices. If you want to sample the delights, but can't make it down here, order from the Borough Market selection of delivery company Food Ferry (*see p353*).

Farmers' markets

Shopping at farmers' markets enables you to discover the joys of seasonal produce while supporting the south-east's farmers. All produce at London's accredited farmers' markets comes from within 100 miles of the M25, bringing the industry a welcome £3 million a year. For further information, get in touch with the **National Association of Farmers' Markets** (01225 787914, www.farmersmarkets. net), the umbrella outfit for farmers' markets across the country. **London Farmers' Markets** (7704 9659, www.lfm.org.uk) covers all the true farmers' markets in the capital, except those in Barnes, Richmond and Stoke Newington. Beware a handful of places that call themselves 'farmers' markets', but are nothing of the sort.

Wednesday market
Swiss Cottage O_2 Centre car park, Finchley Road, NW3.

Friday markets
Ilford Ilford High Road (only first and third Friday and Saturday of the month); **Whetstone** Whetstone High Street, opposite Waitrose, N20.

Saturday markets
Barnes Essex House, Station Road, SW13; **Ealing** Leeland Road, W13; **Ilford** Ilford High Road (only first and third Friday and Saturday of the month); **Notting Hill** car park on the corner of

Parties & Shops

Fortnum & Mason

Marylebone
Farmers' Market

Kensington Church Street, W8; **Pimlico** Orange Square, SW1; **Richmond** Heron Square, off Hill Street; **Stoke Newington** 61 Leswin Road, N16; **Twickenham** Holly Road car park, off King Street; **Wimbledon Park** Wimbledon Park First School, Havana Road, SW19.

Sunday markets

Blackheath Blackheath railway station car park, SE3; **Islington** Essex Road, N1; **Marylebone** Cramer Street car park, W1; **Palmers Green** Palmers Green railway station car park, N13; **Peckham** Peckham Square, SE15.

Bakeries & pâtisseries

Many of the places listed in the **Cafés** chapter (starting on p298) specialise in posh pâtisserie, while acclaimed British restaurant **St John** (see p42) has a fabulous bakery, created with the input of master baker Dan Lepard.

& Clarke's

122 Kensington Church Street, W8 4BU (7229 2190/www.sallyclarke.com). Notting Hill Gate tube. **Open** 8am-8pm Mon-Fri; 8am-4pm Sat. **Credit** AmEx, MC, V.
Next door to Sally Clarke's much-praised restaurant (see p215), & Clarke's bakery makes, shapes and bakes over 2,000 loaves a night, using the best ingredients. The range – rosemary and raisin, corn, green olive, black olive, honey wholewheat, fig and fennel, sourdough, 100% rye – are dispatched to some of the finest restaurants in London. Freshly baked almond, cheese and chocolate croissants and brioches are a popular breakfast treat. Not surprisingly given all these goodies, we always find it impossible to leave without a purchase. Mail order available.

Baker & Spice

75 Salusbury Road, NW6 6NH (7604 3636/ www.bakerandspice.com). Queen's Park tube. **Open** 7am-8pm Mon-Fri; 7am-7pm Sat; 8.30am-5pm Sun. **Credit** MC, V.
Baker & Spice's window is crammed full of sweet temptations – vast trays of blueberry muffins and meringues, and dainty stands laden with individual fruit brioches – all lightly dusted with icing sugar. Inside, the treats continue, with cooked fruit tarts, wrapped cakes, own-made jams, a deli counter and around 25 different varieties of bread. Mail order available.
For branches see index.

Lighthouse Bakery

64 Northcote Road, SW11 6QL (7228 4537/ www.lighthousebakery.co.uk). Clapham Junction rail. **Open** 8.30am-5pm Tue-Sat. **Credit** MC, V.
This artisan bakery, where all the bread is handmade and baked freshly on the premises each day, sees itself as a 'champion of the humble British white loaf', offering lovingly made white, wheat and wholemeal loaves. This basic range is supplemented daily by three or four speciality breads, such as rye sourdough, Italian country bread or low-gluten spelt. Savouries include sausage rolls and cornish pasties made at A Dove & Son (see p353), the butcher's just across the street. Fruit and veg used in the bakery comes from Kelly's organic shop or local market stalls.

Poilâne

46 Elizabeth Street, SW1W 9PA (7808 4910/ www.poilane.fr). Sloane Square/Victoria tube/rail. **Open** 7.30am-7.30pm Mon-Fri; 7.30am-6pm Sat. **Credit** MC, V.
Pierre Poilâne started baking in Paris more than 70 years ago, and his son Lionel (until his death in 2002) continued to use his traditional methods in the family's Paris and London bakeries. The best known (and most popular) of his breads is the stone-ground Poilâne sourdough loaf: a beast of a thing, weighing up to 7lb and costing about the same in money; it could feed an army and tastes incredible, especially toasted. There are also raisin and walnut breads, croissants and butter cookies that will last for a month, as well as a special bread bin designed to keep your monster loaf fresh.

Cheese

La Fromagerie

2-4 Moxon Street, W1U 4EW (7935 0341/ www.lafromagerie.co.uk). Baker Street or Bond Street tube/Marylebone tube/rail. **Open** 10.30am-7.30pm Mon; 8am-7.30pm Tue-Fri; 9am-7pm Sat; 10am-6pm Sun. **Credit** AmEx, MC, V.
Patricia Michelson's elegant Marylebone cheese shop comes complete with a café area (see p299), serving a tempting array of freshly prepared food made in the downstairs kitchen. Pride of place goes to the temperature-controlled cheese room, which houses between 100 and 120 artisanal cheeses at any one time, each carefully chosen by Michelson. Highlights include the two-year-old beaufort Chalet d'Alpage (the cheese that inspired Michelson to start her career), fine Spanish manchego and rare raw milk Italian cheeses, including taleggio and gorgonzola. To accompany your cheeses, choose from matchable wines and breads that include Poilâne sourdough and Italian pagnotta. La Fromagerie also offers tutored tastings and special-event dinners.
For branch see index.

Hamish Johnston

48 Northcote Road, SW11 1PA (7738 0741). Clapham Junction rail. **Open** 9am-6pm Mon-Sat. **Credit** MC, V.
This traditional shop sells around 150 types of cheese, with British varieties and goat's and sheep's cheeses featuring heavily. Customers come from far and wide for the Montgomery's cheddar and Hawes blue wensleydale, as well as Welsh llanboidy and soft and creamy stinking bishop. There's also a selection of French, Italian and Spanish cheeses, olive oils, vinegars, smoked salmon, potted shrimps, pâtés, bacon and preserves. Mail order available.

Neal's Yard Dairy

17 Shorts Gardens, WC2H 9UP (7240 5700). Covent Garden tube. **Open** 9am-7pm Mon-Sat. **Credit** MC, V.
The strong whiff of cheese will lead you to Neal's Yard Dairy: one of the city's finest cheese shops, selling artisan cheeses sourced directly from small, independent English, Irish, Scottish and Welsh producers. The quality is impressive, and the knowledgeable staff encourage customers to taste. Classic British farmhouse cheeses, such as Montgomery's cheddar, Appleby's cheshire and Kirkham's lancashire, are well represented, alongside more unusual cheeses such as harbourne blue, a creamy goat's cheese. Other in-store treats include membrillo (quince paste), good olives, delicious yoghurts, farmhouse butter, chutneys, breads (from & Clarke's, Poilâne and St John) and fab oatcakes. At Christmas, the queue for stilton stretches down the street.

Paxton & Whitfield

93 Jermyn Street, SW1Y 6JE (7930 0259/ www.paxtonandwhitfield.co.uk). Green Park or Piccadilly Circus tube. **Open** 9.30am-6pm Mon-Sat. **Credit** AmEx, MC, V.
Established over 200 years ago, Britain's oldest cheesemonger's is a delightful shop on Jermyn Street, where loyal cheese-lovers head for outstanding produce and friendly service. Alongside the classics are unusual delights such as berkswell (an English sheep's milk cheese) and l'ami du chambertin (soft cheese with marc de bourgogne-washed rind). Wines continue to be a strong point, and, in addition to the biscuits, olives and charcuterie, P&W sells an increasingly large range of accessories such as cheese domes and knives. Mail order available.

Rippon Cheese Stores

26 Upper Tachbrook Street, SW1V 1SW (7931 0628). Pimlico tube/Victoria tube/rail. **Open** 8am-5.15pm Mon-Sat. **Credit** MC, V.
Around 550 cheeses are in stock at any one time – mainly from France and the UK, but the rest of Europe gets a look in. Needless to say, all the popular bases are covered, but it's the more unusual cheeses that catch the eye: vacherin (a soft cheese from the French Alps available between September and March) is immensely popular, as is the Portuguese serra da estrela (a soft sheep's milk cheese). Mail order available.

Confectioners

L'Artisan du Chocolat

89 Lower Sloane Street, SW1W 8DA (7824 8365/www.artisanduchocolat.com). Sloane Square tube. **Open** 10am-7pm Mon-Sat. **Credit** MC, V.
Combining artistry and craftsmanship, Gerald Coleman creates London's most innovative chocolates. Unusual flavour combinations and excellent ingredients have won him high renown – Heston Blumenthal is a fan of his tobacco chocs. House classics include delectable sea-salted caramels and intense pavé truffles (£5/100g), but there are also quirkier varieties such as ganaches of green cardamom. There's a stall at Borough Market on most Saturdays. Mail order available.

La Maison du Chocolat

45-46 Piccadilly, W1J 0DS (7287 8500/ www.lamaisonduchocolat.com). Piccadilly Circus tube. **Open** 10am-7pm Mon-Sat. **Credit** AmEx, MC, V.
At this handsome, spacious shop, London's crème de la crème can enjoy legendary Parisian chocolatier Robert Linx's sophisticated handmade chocolates. Black-suited staff help you choose from delights that include Linx's trademark assorted ganache (Spanish lemon or fresh mint), pralines and champagne truffles. No preservatives here; the ganache's shelf-life is just four weeks. Other treats are jewel-like pâtisserie, candied peel and classic French fruit jellies. Elegant packaging and formidable prices (£32 for 400g) round things off.

Best Foodie Websites

www.bbc.co.uk/food
Recipes, news and general info on the Beeb's stable of celeb chefs.

www.egullet.com
American-based food writers' forum.

www.epicurious.com
A US site styling itself 'the world's greatest recipe collection' – use it to create an Eton mess or a drunken chicken.

www.farmshopping.com
Details on farm shops and farmers' markets across Britain.

www.foodcomm.org.uk
The website of the Food Commission, a London-based campaigning organisation at the cutting edge of food politics. Get the lowdown on the giants of the food industry.

www.frencheese.co.uk
Extensive information on almost every French cheese to walk this planet.

www.gfw.co.uk
Run by the UK's Guild of Food Writers, the site includes a recipe of the month, news of campaigns and awards, and links to many UK food sites.

www.globalgourmet.com
Wide-ranging online info sheet, best for its links to a compendium of international recipe sites. Click on NetFood Directory.

www.vegsoc.org
A wealth of meat-free information, run by the UK-based Vegetarian Society.

Parties & Shops

Pierre Marcolini

6 Lancer Square, W8 4EH (7795 6611/www.pierremarcolini.co.uk). High Street Kensington tube. **Open** 10am-7pm Mon-Sat. **Credit** AmEx, MC, V.
The god of Belgian chocolate has finally come to London. This award-winning company is one of the few to develop its chocolate all the way from the selection of the bean to the final product, pralines being the pièce de résistance. The shop showcases 100 different chocs – choose from those moulded into the shape of golf balls (white chocolate encasing a shelled walnut in liquid caramel), delicately flavoured raspberry hearts or champagne truffles. Or go for a mixed box of favourites (£25/250g). Chocoholics can sample treats in the café section, including hot chocolate, gateaux and ice-cream. Mail order available.

Rococo

321 King's Road, SW3 5EP (7352 5857/www.rococochocolates.com). Sloane Square tube then 11, 19, 22 bus. **No credit cards**.
Founded by Chantal Coady two decades ago, Rococo is the capital's wittiest chocolate shop. Quality is high, and favourites include various praline gift ideas, from huge quails' eggs (£6.75/225g) to asparagus spears (£9.50/300g) and gloriously gooey truffles. Bars are made with 60% cocoa solids and delicately infused with original flavours, such as coffee mocha java, orange and geranium, basil and lime, and Earl Grey – all in Rococo's trademark blue and white packaging. Vegan options and mail order are available.
For branch see index.

Delicatessens

For more upmarket deli goods, visit restaurants **Flâneur Food Hall** (*see p292*) and **Villandry** (*see p209*).

East Dulwich Deli

15-17 Lordship Lane, SE22 8EW (8693 2525). East Dulwich rail. **Open** 9am-6pm Mon-Sat; 10am-4pm Sun. **Credit** MC, V.
This posh but friendly deli has a fantastic array of fresh produce and store-cupboard items. There are excellent quiches and salads, own-cooked ham carved off the bone, salamis, sausages and bacon; mozzarella is flown in twice a week from Italy; and olive oil (from Lazio, exclusive to the shop) is sold 'loose' in reusable bottles. Pop in on a Saturday and you can try some of the deli's latest goodies at the tasting table.

Mise-en-Place

21 Battersea Rise, SW11 1HG (7228 4329/www.thefoodstore.co.uk). Clapham Junction rail. **Open** 8.30am-8pm Mon-Fri; 9am-8pm Sat, Sun. **Credit** AmEx, MC, V.
Now in its tenth year, this large deli puts a strong emphasis on customer service. If you can't find exactly what you're after, staff are happy to source it for you. The deli's excellent gourmet lines range from pork pies and quiches to truffle salamis, pata negra ham and confit of duck. There are also lots of fresh salsas and sauces (such as rocket pesto), plus a wide selection of cheeses from the UK and the rest of Europe. Traiteur dishes are another strong point. Mail order available.

Mortimer & Bennett

33 Turnham Green Terrace, W4 1RG (8995 4145/www.mortimerandbennett.com). Turnham Green tube. **Open** 8.30am-6pm Mon-Fri; 8.30am-5.30pm Sat. **Credit** MC, V.
This amenable little shop is packed to the gills with good things. Deli classics, such as cheeses, charcuterie, smoked fish, olive oils, vinegars, olives and coffees, are well represented, plus bread from Clarke's and Poilâne. Sweet-toothed gourmets aren't neglected either, with chocolates, jams and buffalo milk ice-cream for sale. Mail order available.

Mr Christian's

11 Elgin Crescent, W11 2JA (7229 0501/www.mrchristians.co.uk). Ladbroke Grove tube. **Open** 6am-7pm Mon-Fri; 5.30am-6.30pm Sat; 7am-5pm Sun. **Credit** AmEx, MC, V.

Lighthouse Bakery. See p347.

This friendly, unpretentious, well-established deli is always busy, mainly with local customers taking their pick from the huge variety of cheese, meats, breads, fresh pasta, olives, own-made chutneys and preserves, and daily changing traiteur dishes, such as broad bean, pea, mint and lemon risotto. On Saturdays, a stall is set up outside the shop selling more than 40 varieties of bread and freshly made pastries. Mr Christian's has recently been bought by Jeroboams, so the selection of wines is growing. Mail order available.

Panzer's

13-19 Circus Road, NW8 6PB (7722 8596/www.panzers.co.uk). St John's Wood tube. **Open** 8am-7pm Mon-Fri; 8am-6pm Sat; 8am-2pm Sun. **Credit** MC, V.
This huge, family-run deli has been around for over half a century and is still going strong. Fruit and veg, attractively displayed outside, range from seasonal basics to the likes of multi-coloured heritage tomatoes, pink-fleshed baby guavas and persimmons. Inside, the shelves are packed with an impressively eclectic range of foodstuffs from around the world (including Italy, Greece, South Africa, Japan and the USA), as well as a large kosher range. The excellent deli counter does a roaring business in smoked salmon and cream cheese, while breads range from bagels to sourdough. Mail order available.

Rosslyn Delicatessen

56 Rosslyn Hill, NW3 1ND (7794 9210/www.delirosslyn.co.uk). Hampstead tube. **Open** 8.30am-8.30pm Mon-Sat; 8.30am-8pm Sun. **Credit** AmEx, MC, V.
The shelves at this lovely deli are lined with own-made jams, an extensive range of olive oils (including some infused with lemon or garlic and pepper), Ortiz tuna, Taylor's tea, Seggiano honey and lots of American goods such as Libby's pumpkin pie filling and Hershey bars. There's also a superb choice of cheeses from all over Europe and plenty of charcuterie. Ready-made meals line the refrigerator. If you're planning a trip to nearby Hampstead Heath, the deli can also make up a delicious picnic hamper. Mail order available.

International

Arigato Japanese Supermarket

48-50 Brewer Street, W1R 3HN (7287 1722). Piccadilly Circus tube. **Open** 10am-9pm Mon-Sat; 11am-8pm Sun. **Credit** MC, V. Japanese
Arigato is bright, spacious and very accessible to non-Japanese. It's also calmer than the nearby Chinese supermarkets and cheaper than the Japan Centre. The range has been enlarged and now covers all the Japanese staples, from natto to nori and beer to saké. Aspiring sushi chefs can buy a kit, complete with everything except the fish. Alternatively, visit the popular snack bar. Mail order is also available.

Athenian Grocery

16A Moscow Road, W2 4BT (7229 6280). Bayswater tube. **Open** 8.30am-7pm Mon-Sat; 8.30am-1pm Sun. **No credit cards**. Greek
A Bayswater institution, this Greek delicatessen has been in business for 50 years and has a loyal following. Quality fruit and vegetables flown in daily from Cyprus include lemons, fresh vine leaves, figs and prickly pears, plus deli staples of Greek cuisine, including village bread, dried pulses, kalamata olives and olive oil.

Brick Lane, E1

Aldgate East tube. Indian
Sustaining London's curry-pot is an abundance of Bangladeshi and Punjabi food stores. **Taj Stores** (No.112, E1 6RL; 7377 0061) is the daddy, with imported fresh fruit, veg and herbs, rows of pickles and sauces, a halal butcher and a tankful of frozen tropical fish in freezers. **Zaman Bros**, formerly known as Bangla (Nos.17-19, E1 6BU; 7247 1009), continues to sell staples such as

vegetables, ghee, meat and a chaotically racked array of bagged rice and pulses, plus tinned sauces. Round the corner, **Ali Bros** does the same, but in even bigger bags and at wholesale prices. Snack hunters should head for the local **Ambala** (No.55, E1 6DU; 7247 8569), which sells Indian sweets and superb samosas. Across the road, **Alauddin Sweetmeat** (No.72, E1 6RL; 7377 0896) makes melt-in-the-mouth sweets and cakes that are heavy on milk and sugar.

Brindisa
32 Exmouth Market, EC1R 4QE (7713 1666/ www.tapas.co.uk). Farringdon tube/rail. **Open** 10am-6pm Mon-Sat. **Credit** MC, V. Spanish
This bricks-and-mortar sibling of a stall at Borough Market is the sole importer of over 80% of its stock. Homesick Spaniards can stockpile Forum vinegars, Núñez de Prado olive oil, tins of smoked pimentón, Catalan yoghurts, Andalucian chestnuts and seasonal truffles. That aside, there's fresh bread and a deli range, including abundant chorizo, hand-sliced cured ham and Iberian cheeses. Sandwiches, olives and salads make excellent takeaway fodder.

Brixton, SW9
Brixton tube/rail. African & Caribbean
Brixton Village (formerly Granville Arcade) at Brixton Market is superb for traditional Afro-Caribbean foods. **Back Home Foods** (Units 83-84, SW9 8PF; 7738 5655) does exactly what the name says, selling a wide range of yams, plantains and bananas alongside Indian and English staples. Nearby, **First Choice Bakery** (40 Atlantic Road, SW9 8JW; 7737 2766) stocks Caribbean bread, pastries and savouries, while **D-Bess Bakery** (12-14 Brighton Terrace, SW9 8DG; 7738 7394) sells hard-dough breads and also does a buzzing take-out trade in breads and patties filled with saltfish, beef and chicken. There are also plenty of yummy traditional pastries and cakes, such as West Indian ginger cake.

I Camisa & Son
61 Old Compton Street, W1D 6HS (7437 7610). Leicester Square or Piccadilly Circus tube. **Open** 8.30am-6pm Mon-Sat. **Credit** MC, V. Italian
This friendly shop offers an excellent range of alimentari classics. There are hams, salamis, fresh Italian sausages, olives and cheeses, including excellent parmesan. Packets of De Cecco and Barilla dried pasta line one wall, while the fresh pasta is made in-house. Luxuries include fresh truffles (in season), porcini and truffle paste. You can wash down your rarities with a bottle from the exclusively Italian wine rack.

Chinatown, WC2
Leicester Square or Piccadilly Circus tube. Chinese
Just off Leicester Square, London's Chinatown remains the place to buy Chinese and South-east Asian ingredients. You'll find fresh produce such as leafy Chinese greens, herbs and exotic fruit, as well as noodles, myriad condiments and other staples. Bustling **Loon Fung** (42-44 Gerrard Street, W1D 5QG; 7437 7179) is the largest Chinese foodstore, complete with a fresh meat counter dominated by pork parts, while nearby **New Loon Moon Supermarket** (9 Gerrard Street, W1D 5PN; 7734 3887) is strong on fresh fruit, vegetables and herbs. **Newport Kitchen Supermarket** (28-29 Newport Court, WC2H 7PQ; 7437 2536) offers a good range of stock, including fruit and veg, preserved foods, noodles and sauces, and around the corner are **Good Harvest Fish & Meat** (14 Newport Place, WC2H 7PR; 7437 0712), predominantly a fishmonger, and **Golden Gate Grocers** (16 Newport Place, WC2 7PR; 7437 0014), where goods are helpfully labelled in English and clearly priced. On Lisle Street, there's **See Woo** (No.19, WC2 7P; 7439 8325), a large shop that's particularly strong on South-east Asian ingredients, and small, neatly arranged **Golden Gate Hong Supermarket** (No.14, WC2 7PR; 7437 0014).

Comptoir Gascon
61-63 Charterhouse Street, WC1M 6HJ (7608 0851). Farringdon tube/rail. **Open** 8am-8pm Mon-Fri; 9am-6pm Sat. **Credit** MC, V. French
Part of the growing Club Gascon (*see p78*) empire, Comptoir Gascon sells a well-chosen array of delicacies that are highbrow to the English, standard to the French. Well, the south-western French anyway, as that is the region is where the produce and recipes are sourced. Highlights include meat, fish and game confits, fresh meat dishes (beef fillet and diabolo sauce or melting lamb with sweet chilli), terrines and foie gras. The in-store bakery turns out irresistible gateaux, pastries and bread. While you're here, it's also worth examining the Gascon jams and chutneys, cheeses, charcuterie and wines, as well as the interesting selection of artisanal oils, including hard-to-find cashew nut and raisin pip.

Ealing Road, Wembley, Middlesex
Alperton tube. Indian
A host of stores feeds the area's sizeable Hindu and Muslim communities. The sweet-toothed should head to the Wembley branch of the Southall-based **Royal Sweets** franchise (280 Ealing Road, HA0 4LL; 8903 9359), where rasmalai, gulab jamun and numerous barfi are offered. Just along the road, **Prashad Sweets** (No.222, HA0 4QL; 8902 1704) sells more of the same, plus tasty samosas. Abundantly stocked **Wembley Exotics** (Nos.133-135, HA0 4BP; 8900 2607) has a fine range of spices, condiments, pulses, flours and dairy products, plus fruit and veg imported from India, Thailand and the West Indies. Further up the road, you'll find good-quality meat at **Sri Lankan Bismillah Butchers** (Nos.18 & 33, HA0 4YA; 8903 4922), while **VB & Sons** (No.147, HA0 4BU; 8795 0387) sells all of the above, cash-and-carry style.

R García & Sons
248-250 Portobello Road, W11 1LL (7221 6119). Ladbrooke Grove tube. **Open** 9am-6.30pm Mon-Sat; 10am-5pm Sun. **Credit** AmEx, MC, V. Spanish
All the staples of the Spanish kitchen can be found in this small supermarket, founded and run by the Garcia family. Salt cod, paella rice, saffron, smoked pimentón and pulses line the shelves. The long deli counter at the back serves a steady stream of eager customers with the likes of assorted chorizo and anchovy-stuffed olives.

German Wurst & Delicatessen
127 Central Street, EC1V 8AP (7250 1322/ www.german-wurst-deli.co.uk). Barbican tube/ Old Street tube/rail. **Open** 10am-7pm Mon-Fri; 10am-5pm Sat. **No credit cards**. German
London's only German food shop is a shrine to sausages. If you thought sausages were made of rusk and fat, get a taste of the meatier reality here, with 20 types of banger made on site, and more imported from Germany. Top dogs include leberwurst, neurenbergers and bratwurst. The rest of the food continues along carnivorous lines with German meatloaf and pâtés, plus genuine German mustards to season your meat, and pickles, packets of spätzle noodles and knödel mixes. There's also a stall in Borough Market where you can sample the best of the wurst.

A Gold, Traditional Foods of Britain
42 Brushfield Street, E1 6AG (7747 2487/ www.agold.co.uk). Liverpool Street tube/rail. **Open** 11am-8pm Mon-Fri; 11am-6pm Sun. **Credit** AmEx, MC, V. British
Flying in the face of world opinion, this deli by Old Spitalfields Market proves that British food, if properly produced, can be excellent. The counter bursts with a range of cheeses, sausages, game, fish, cold meats, pies and old faves like the humble pickled egg. Those with a sweet tooth will enjoy feasting on Cornish saffron cake, marshmallows and Vimto lollies. Booze-wise, there's a number of British fruit wines, liqueurs and traditional tipples such as mead. Mail order available.

Parties & Shops

La Fromagerie. See p347.

Japan Centre

212 Piccadilly, W1J 9HG (7434 4218/ www.japancentre.com). Piccadilly Circus tube. **Open** 10am-7pm Mon-Fri; 10.30am-8pm Sat; 11am-7pm Sun. **Credit** MC, V. Japanese
With a café just inside the door, as well as a travel agent, noticeboard service, bookshop, internet service, money exchange and food hall downstairs, this place is a lifeline for visiting Japanese. Food-wise, stock ranges from sushi trays to fresh fish to staples such as dried noodles, miso, natto, nori, tofu, pickles and sweets.

Korona

30 Streatham High Road, SW16 1DB (8769 6647). Streatham rail. **Open** 9am-7pm Mon-Fri; 9am-6pm Sat; 9.30am-2.30pm Sun. **Credit** MC, V. Polish
Polish, Russian and Eastern European tastes are all represented at this friendly shop. Sausages are made in-store and top an international line-up that features Jewish specialities, Russian leczo and South African biltong. Wild mushrooms are imported dried from Italy or fresh from Poland in season. Polish beers and vodkas are also sold.

Lina Stores

18 Brewer Street, W1R 3FS (7437 6482). Piccadilly Circus tube. **Open** 9am-6.30pm Mon-Fri; 9am-5.30pm Sat. **Credit** AmEx, MC, V. Italian
For an authentic Italian deli experience, Lina Stores, with its old-fashioned fittings and leisurely atmosphere, is worth a visit. Lina's own-made fresh pasta is famous, with the pumpkin tortelloni a speciality. This spacious store also sells Italian cheeses, salami, fresh sausages, dried pulses and rice (sold loose from great sacks), as well as pasta sauces, olive oils and balsamic vinegars.

Lisboa

54 Golborne Road, W10 5PR (8969 1052). Ladbroke Grove tube. **Open** 9.30am-7.30pm Mon-Sat; 10am-1pm Sun. **Credit** MC, V. Portuguese
This established Portuguese deli, run with knowledgeable friendliness by Mr and Mrs Gomes, is stocked with staples like chouriço sausages, cheeses (such as evora), tinned seafood and pulses, with bacalhau (salt cod) sawed to order in a small back room. *See also p234.*

Luigi's Delicatessen

349 Fulham Road, SW10 9TW (7352 7739). Fulham Broadway or South Kensington tube/ bus 14. **No credit cards.** Italian
Bustling with customers and crammed with stock, this is a good place to pick up freshly made dishes. There is also a great range of cheese and charcuterie, fresh veg and herbs, and dozens of vinegars and oils. Naughties include Italian sweets and amaretti, plus over 600 wines.

Manila Supermarket

11-12 Hogarth Place, SW5 0QT (7373 8305). Earl's Court tube. **Open** 9am-9pm daily. **Credit** AmEx, MC, V. Filipino
The long-established Manila supermarket is a home from home to London's Filipino population. Stock here is South-east Asian with a Filipino bias, ranging from pork sausages, fresh fruit and vegetables and frozen seafood, to jars of purple yam and packets of Filipino cake mix.

Le Maroc

94 Golborne Road, W10 5PS (8968 9783). Ladbroke Grove or Westbourne Park tube. **Open** 9am-7pm Mon-Sat. **No credit cards.** Moroccan
The cuisine of Morocco is packed and stacked at this colourful shop, so the shelves are full of such items as couscous, green tea, rosewater and orange flower water, while the halal butcher turns out tasty merguez sausages.

Oriental City

399 Edgware Road, NW9 0JJ (8200 0009). Colindale tube. **Open** 10am-9pm Mon-Sat; noon-6pm Sun. **Credit** AmEx, MC, V. Oriental
Oriental City is a shopping mall catering to the Japanese, Chinese, Korean, Thai and Indonesian communities. A large supermarket on the ground

Parties & Shops

Green Lanes N4, N8, N16

Manor House or Turnpike Lane tube. Turkish
The stretch halfway between Manor House and Turnpike Lane tube stations is home to many of London's Turks, Turkish-Cypriots, Greek-Cypriots and, latterly, Kurds. Interspersed among numerous kebab emporia are sweet shops, butchers, and fruit and veg shops, many open 24 hours a day. Fans of Greek and Turkish halva, baklava and mamoul, fragrant with flower waters and studded with pistachios, should head straight to **Nasrullah Pâtisserie** (No.483, N4 1AJ; 8342 9794). Exotic-looking fruit and veg, row upon row of tinned pulses and halal meat are to be had at **Turkish Food Market** (Nos.385-387, N4 1EU; 8340 4547). Nearby **Salah Eddine** (51 Grand Parade, N4 1AG; 8800 4333) is a recommended halal butcher's, specialising in good-quality lamb and chicken. But the undisputed champion is **Yasar Halim** (493 Green Lanes, N4 1AL; 8348 1074). Half the shop is a grocery, with fresh fruit, veg and herbs, deli produce (halloumi, Turkish salami, houmous) and a halal butcher's counter; next door you can pick up English and Turkish breads straight out of the oven, plus pies, börek and pastries. There's another enclave of Turkish businesses at the Newington Green end of Green Lanes.

Green Valley

36-37 Upper Berkeley Street, W1H 5QF (7402 7385). Marble Arch tube. **Open** 8am-midnight daily. **Credit** MC, V. Middle Eastern
The truly splendid window display of pastries is a tempting showcase for this spacious Lebanese supermarket in Mayfair. Stock is extensive, ranging from store-cupboard staples, fresh fruit and veg and a halal meat section to Middle Eastern traiteur dishes, a delectable assortment of nuts and an ice-cream counter.

Huong-Nam Supermarket

185-187 Mare Street, E8 3RD (8985 8050). Hackney Central or London Fields rail/48, 55, 106, 253 bus. **Open** 9.30am-8.30pm Mon-Fri; 10am-9pm Sat, Sun. **No credit cards.** Vietnamese
Huong-Nam sells mostly Vietnamese specialities, with a sideline in Chinese and Thai goods. The chiller cabinets hold fresh goods (egg noodles, tofu, fish balls and pigs' trotters), while at the back of the shop a tightly packed freezer stores fish, meat, dim sum and specialist Vietnamese imports. Most imported goods are labelled in French and/or Vietnamese; very little English is spoken so it helps if you know what you're after.

floor has an eye-catching display of fresh fruit and vegetables (including daikon, mangosteen, jackfruit and chillies), while the chiller cabinets carry a range of meat products, from finely sliced Scotch beef sirloin for shabu shabu to duck's feet. Fish and seafood is extensive and decently priced. Head down the aisles to stock up on dried, pickled and preserved goods, miso pastes, condiments, rice, noodles and sweets. Mail order available.

Platters
10 Hallswelle Parade, Finchley Road, NW11 0DL (8455 7345). Golders Green tube then 82, 102, 260 bus. **Open** 8.30am-4.30pm Mon-Fri; 8.30am-4pm Sat; 8.30am-2pm Sun. **Credit** AmEx, MC, V. Jewish
This friendly, family-run Jewish deli does a roaring trade in traditional food, with mainstays including chopped herring, hand-cut smoked salmon, gefilte fish, salt beef, fish balls and potato latke.

St Marcus Fine Foods
1 Rockingham Close, SW15 5RW (8878 1898). Barnes rail/337 bus. **Open** 9am-6pm daily. **Credit** MC, V. South African
You can get a good Aberdeen Angus steak here, but that's about all you'll recognise from a meat counter surrounded by the likes of emu, kangaroo, springbok, ostrich, crocodile and South African biltong made from beef, kudu and springbok. Mail order available.

I Sapori di Stefano Cavallini
146 Northcote Road, SW11 6RD (7228 2017). Clapham South tube/Clapham Junction rail. **Open** 9.30am-7pm Mon-Sat. **Credit** MC, V. Italian
Owned by acclaimed chef Stefano Cavallini, much of the superlative Italian food here is cooked on the premises. Pasta dishes, fresh pasta, pasta sauces and salads all go down well with local foodies. Imports include olive oils, Caffè Sicilia marmalades and Domori chocolates.

Southall, Middlesex
Southall rail. Punjabi
Centred around the Broadway, this is perhaps the capital's most thriving South Asian shopping area. Many locals are of Punjabi origin (from either the Indian or Pakistani side of the border). **Dokal & Sons** (Nos.133-135, UB1 1LW; 8574 1647) is typical of the food shops, crammed with huge bags of rice, several types of pulses and drums of ghee. Down the road, **Kaz's Halal Meat** (No.31, UB1 1JY; 8574 1444) sells plenty of fine cuts, while **Royal Sweets** (14 King Street, UB2 4DA; 8574 8814) is home to sugary Indian treats. **Quality Foods** (47-61 South Road, UB1 1SQ; 8917 9188) offers a wide range of tropical fruit, vegetables and herbs, plus spices, pickles, pulses and flours.

Speck
2 Holland Park Terrace, W11 4ND (7229 7005/ www.speck-deli.co.uk). Holland Park tube.
Open 8am-8.30pm Mon-Fri; 8am-7pm Sat.
Credit AmEx, MC, V. Italian
Speck brings the fun of the Italian kitchen into the English home. 'Pasta for Kids' sees staff turn up at your house with pasta machines and sauces, and help youngsters make pasta shapes. They even clean up afterwards. Back at the store, there's a good sweep of Italian cheese, wine and charcuterie. The prepared meals are great, with cannelloni with spinach and ricotta, and wild mushroom risotto remaining firm favourites.
For branch see index.

Sri Thai
56 Shepherd's Bush Road, W6 7PH (7602 0621). Goldhawk Road tube. **Open** 9am-6.30pm Mon-Sat; 10am-5pm Sun. **Credit** AmEx, MC, V. Thai
Sri Thai's shelves bulge with pretty much everything a budding Thai cook needs, including stone pestle and mortars and the woven baskets traditionally used to keep sticky rice warm. Every Tuesday, fruit, vegetables, herbs, curry pastes and Thai sweets wing their way west from Bangkok, and on Saturday you'll find fresh takeaway meals such as barbecue pork and sticky rice.

Stroud Green, N4
Finsbury Park tube/rail. African & Caribbean
The various constituents of the PAK Trading Co, which includes **KM Butchers** (29 Stroud Green Road, N4 3EF; 7263 6625), sell yams, bananas, breadfruit, mutton, goat and oxtail. A few doors along, **Haseeb Mini-Supermarket** has African and Asian fruit and veg and a well-stocked butcher's. **Stroud Green Food Store** (65 Stroud Green, N4 3ED; 7272 0348) offers racks of herbal bitters and fiery Caribbean sauces and pickles; it also has a great range of veg and saltfish.

Super Bahar
349A Kensington High Street, W8 6NW (7603 5083). High Street Kensington tube. **Open** 9am-9pm daily. **Credit** AmEx, MC, V. Middle Eastern
Importing direct from Iran, this is a good place to find Persian specialities. Super Bahar is proud of its caviar, which features alongside dried fruit, nuts and traditional dried fish. There's also fresh fruit and vegetables, herbs, spices (try the Iranian saffron), plus a tempting selection of pastries.

Tawana Oriental Supermarket
18-20 Chepstow Road, W2 5BD (7221 6316/ www.tawana.co.uk). Notting Hill Gate tube.
Open 9.30am-8pm daily. **Credit** MC, V. Thai
Here you'll find an extensive range of Thai food, supplemented by goods from across South-east Asia. Tawana's freezers offer great bulk buys in squid, shrimps, prawns and scallops, alongside bags of purple yam, jute leaves and grated coconut. There are also trays of frozen dim sum, plus wun tun wrappers. Dried goods, tinned fruit, sauces and curry pastes pack the shelves, and ready-made meals include pad Thai and green and red curries.

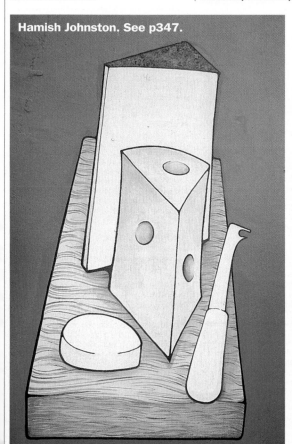

Hamish Johnston. See p347.

Ginger Pig

& Kidney pie
£5.00

Lamb & Apricot
£5.50

Parties & Shops

L Terroni & Sons

*138-140 Clerkenwell Road, EC1R 5DL
(7837 1712). Farringdon tube/rail.* **Open**
9am-5.45pm Tue-Fri; 9am-3pm Sat; 10.30am-2pm
Sun. **Credit** MC, V. Italian

A firm favourite for the most authentic Italian
grocer's award, this well-stocked shop has been in
business since 1878. A heroic range of pasta comes
fresh or dried, and you can take home some revered
own-made pesto to stir through it. The deli counter
offers Italian cheeses, charcuterie and antipasti
dishes. And you can soak the lot in the wide range
of olive oil and vinegar. Or yourself in over 600
Italian red and white wines.

Tooting

Tooting Broadway or Tooting Bec tube.
South Asian

People hailing from all over the Indian
subcontinent – Pakistan, Sri Lanka and both north
and south India – have made their home in Tooting.
Consequently it's a great place to look for South
Asian food. Try **Deepak** (953-959 Garratt Lane,
SW17 0LR; 8767 7810) for general provisions; **Shiv
Darshan** (169 Upper Tooting Road, SW17 7TJ;
8682 5173) or **Pooja** (168 Upper Tooting Road,
SW17 7ER; 8682 5148) for Indian sweets; and
Patel Brothers (187 Upper Tooting Road, SW17
7TG; 8672 2792) for 'Utensils Gifts Novelties'. The
fruit and veg shops – **Nature Fresh** (126-128
Upper Tooting Road, SW17 7EN; 8682 4988) and
Daily Fresh Foods (152 Upper Tooting Road,
SW17 7ER; 8767 7861) – stock an abundance of
fresh Asian ingredients.

Truc Vert

*42 North Audley Street, W1K 6ZR (7491 9988).
Bond Street tube.* **Open** 7.30am-10pm Mon-Fri;
7.30am-5pm Sat; 9.30am-4pm Sun. **Credit** AmEx,
MC, V. French

Though primarily a brasserie (*see p293*), Truc
Vert's deli counter is a select affair. Here you'll find
around 20 charcuterie items, plus 15 British and
European farmhouse cheeses, supplemented by
breads (both bought in and made on the premises),
chutneys, jams and sauces. Dishes from the daily
changing menu can be taken home too. Mail order
is also available.

Health food & organic

Alara Wholefoods

*58-60 Marchmont Street, WC1N 1AB (7837
1172). Russell Square tube.* **Open** 9am-6pm
Mon-Wed, Fri; 9am-7pm Thur; 10am-6pm Sat.
Credit MC, V.

Alara is a centrally located, family-run shop and
café whose friendly, unpretentious service is as
wholesome as its food. Enjoy organic coffee and
a tremendous range of hot specials and salads
in-store, or take them away, along with organic
groceries, grains, pulses, cereals, fruit and
vegetables, and supplements. Prices are among the
most reasonable we've seen.

Bumblebee

*30, 32 & 33 Brecknock Road, N7 0DD (7607
1936/www.bumblebee.co.uk). Kentish Town
tube/rail/29 bus.* **Open** 9am-6.30pm Mon-Wed,
Fri, Sat; 9am-7.30pm Thur. **Credit** AmEx, MC, V.

Bumblebee's three adjacent shops are ideal for
stocking up on your health food needs. Between
them, you'll find freshly baked bread, deli food,
grains, organic booze, loose nuts and pulses, an
impressive range of miso and dried seaweed, and
fresh produce, including seasonal organic fruit and
veg, eggs and an enticing cheese counter. They
also have a delivery service throughout London.

Bushwacker Wholefoods

*132 King Street, W6 0QU (8748 2061).
Hammersmith tube.* **Open** 9.30am-6pm Mon,
Wed-Sat; 10am-6pm Tue. **Credit** MC, V.

The old wooden counter at the front of this health
food shop is packed with herbs and spices, while
vitamins, supplements and homeopathic remedies
are lined up behind the tills. Bushwacker's stock is
GMO-free, and includes its own-label goods along
with familiar brand names on grains, pulses and
cereals. Fridges stock organic milk, non-dairy
alternatives and vegetarian lunchtime treats.

Fresh & Wild

*49 Parkway, NW1 7PN (7428 7575/
www.freshandwild.com). Camden Town tube.*
Open 8am-9pm Mon-Fri; 9.30am-9pm Sat;
11am-8pm Sun. **Credit** AmEx, MC, V.

Its prices may seem slightly higher than elsewhere,
but Fresh & Wild is hard to beat. With more than
5,000 different product lines covering supplements,
organic fruit and veg, frozen and chilled food and
pet care, plus a select library of books, it's a
challenge to find something the store doesn't stock.
Where possible, local suppliers are used. Smooth
design combines an earthy wholefood shop ethic
with a supermarket layout for easy navigation. In
addition to groceries, many branches have cafés
with freshly prepared takeaway foods, organic
coffee, smoothies and juices. Home delivery too.
For branches see index.

Here

*Chelsea Farmers' Market, 125 Sydney Street,
SW3 6NR (7351 4321). Sloane Square or South
Kensington tube.* **Open** 9.30am-8pm Mon-Sat;
10am-6.30pm Sun. **Credit** MC, V.

Leading the way with supermarket-style health
food shops, Here is a slick, award-winning outfit
just off the King's Road, with 100% organic stock.
The fruit and vegetables range is inspiring,
including seasonal and exotic produce in
abundance. Staff are friendly and helpful.

Kelly's Organics

*46 Northcote Road, SW11 1NZ (7207 3967).
Clapham junction rail/319 bus.* **Open** 9am-8pm
Mon-Thur; 9am-6pm Fri, Sat. **Credit** AmEx,
MC, V.

Daniel Kelly's attractive corner shop covers the
bases when it comes to organic produce, from baby
food to bread and bacon, with a very tempting
display of fresh fruit and veg out the front. From
Thursday to Saturday, you can also pick up
spanking-fresh fish courtesy of Copes Seafood,
which sets up in a little annexe next to the shop.
Snacks are available to take away or eat in, with a
clutch of tables on the pavement.

Oliver's Wholefoods Store

*5 Station Approach, Kew, Surrey TW9 3QB
(8948 3990). Kew Gardens tube/rail.* **Open**
9am-7pm Mon-Sat; 10am-7pm Sun. **Credit**
DC, MC, V.

This villagey shop is an inspiration. Attractive
displays feature organic chocolate, organic
cooking oils and alcohol. Stock ranges from tofu to

organic poultry, chicken sausages and meat. Many things make the store stand out, notably regular bakers' deliveries from Cranks and the Authentic Bakery, and the fact that the entire Dr Hauschka range is sold, including the make-up. Education is a key theme – as well as selling books galore, Oliver's runs weekly lectures from health experts such as Dr John Briffa.

Planet Organic
42 Westbourne Grove, W2 5SH (7221 7171/ www.planetorganic.com). Bayswater tube. **Open** 9.30am-8.30pm Mon-Sat; noon-6pm Sun. **Credit** AmEx, MC, V.
Established nearly a decade ago, Planet Organic now has three branches around town. As the name dictates, all produce is 100% organic. As if that wasn't healthy enough, food is also free from artificial preservatives, additives and refined sugars or fats. The meat counter is superb, the choice of lunchtime takeaways excellent, the fruit and veg fresh, and the bakery brims with croissants, pastries and speciality loaves. The health and beauty section is so extensive it could do with its own shop (expect to find Dr Hauschka and REN, to name but two ranges), while the attached clinic offers a variety of treatments. Local deliveries are made on eco-friendly bikes.
For branches see index.

Home delivery

The boom in supermarket online shopping means that the weekly trudge down the aisles is no longer a necessity. Supermarkets offering online shopping include **Sainsbury's** (www. sainsburys.com), **Tesco** (www.tesco.com) and **Waitrose** (www.ocado.com). For organic box schemes and gastronomic treats delivered to your door, try the outfits below.

Abel & Cole
8-15 MGI Estate, Milkwood Road, SE24 0JF (7737 3648/www.abel-cole.co.uk). **Phone enquiries** 9am-7pm Mon-Thur; 9am-6pm Fri. **Credit** MC, V.
Named Organic Retailer of the Year in 2004 by the Soil Association, this well-established enterprise, founded in 1993, offers a weekly home delivery service of organic fruit and vegetables, plus meat, fish and dairy goods. It guarantees that 70% of the fresh produce is British.

The Food Ferry Co
Units B24-27, New Covent Garden Market, 9 Elms Lane, SW8 5HH (7498 0827/ www.foodferry.com). **Phone enquiries** 8am-6pm Mon-Fri. **Credit** AmEx, MC, V.
Good food to your doorstep is what's offered by this award-winning, New Covent Garden-based company. An impressive range of foodstuffs can be delivered, from the everyday through to organic, free-range and luxurious treats. Shrewdly, Food Ferry has teamed up with Borough Market producers (see p345), so you can sample their assorted goodies the easy way.

Forman & Field
30A Marshgate Lane, E15 2NH (8221 3939/ www.formanandfield.com). **Phone enquiries** 9am-5pm Mon-Fri. **Credit** MC, V.
With the emphasis very much on the 'best of British', Forman & Field offers upmarket foodstuffs, ranging from decent sausages and fish cakes to luxuries such as potted lobster. Much is made of such seasonal ingredients as asparagus and wild salmon in the summer months.

Fresh Food Co
The Orchard, 50 Wormholt Road, W12 0LS (8749 8778/www.freshfood.co.uk). **Phone enquiries** 9am-5pm Mon-Fri. **Credit** AmEx, MC, V.
Billed as Britain's first online organic food retailer, the Fresh Food Co has been in the business of supplying fresh organic food to the door since 1989. Boxes contain fruit, veg, herbs and salad, plus organic meat, farmed salmon, wine and bread, and are delivered weekly or fortnightly.

Meat, fish & game

Allen & Co
117 Mount Street, W1K 3LA (7499 5831). Bond Street or Green Park tube. **Open** 4am-4pm Mon-Fri; 5am-noon Sat. **Credit** (over £20) MC, V.
Tuck into a piece of meat at restaurants Le Gavroche (see p113) or Lindsay House (see p45) and chances are it came from this veteran Mayfair outfit, supplier of British meats for more than 175 years. Top-class meat, notably beef and game when in season, plus expert staff.

A Dove & Son
71 Northcote Road, SW11 6PJ (7223 5191/ www.doves.co.uk). Clapham Junction rail. **Open** 8am-4pm Mon; 8am-5.30pm Tue-Sat. **Credit** MC, V.
Gutting and chopping since 1889, Dove's does an excellent line in free-range and organic meats, the highlights of which are Scottish beef and English lamb. There's also free-range pork and poultry, proper sausages and cured bacon, and a hugely popular range of pies. Residents of south-west London can have a hamper delivered to their door.

Ginger Pig
8-10 Moxon Street, W1U 4EW (7935 7788). Baker Street or Bond Street tube/Marylebone tube/rail. **Open** 8.30am-6.30pm Mon-Sat; 9am-3pm Sun. **Credit** MC, V.
Meat-lovers are in for a treat at this butcher's shop, showcasing beef, pork and lamb from owners' Anne and Timothy Wilson's Yorkshire Moors farm, plus game in season and French poultry and veal. The bacon knocks the socks off watery supermarket varieties and comes treacle- or honey-cured. Ginger Pig also offers some of the very best bangers in the land, with a range of 25 sizzlers that include the humble cumberland and fiery jamaican jerk. There's a popular array of dishes made on the premises, featuring pâtés, terrines and pies ranging from steak and kidney to chicken and mushroom. Ginger Pig also has a stall at Borough Market (see p345).
For branch see index.

Frank Godfrey
7 Highbury Park, N5 1QJ (7226 2425). Highbury & Islington tube/rail. **Open** 8am-6pm Mon-Fri; 8am-5pm Sat. **Credit** MC, V.
Though refreshingly friendly and unpretentious, this family-run butcher sells only the best free-range meat and poultry. Orkney Island Gold beef and lamb are a particular speciality, while excellent pork, poultry, Christmas turkeys and award-winning sausages are also offered.

Kingsland, the Edwardian Butchers
140 Portobello Road, W11 2DZ (7727 6067). Notting Hill Gate tube. **Open** 7.30am-6pm Mon-Sat. **Credit** AmEx, MC, V.
Stocking only free-range and organic meats, this picturesque shop has a loyal following. Beef is pure-bred Aberdeen Angus, while pork, sausages and bacon come from Old Spot and Tamworth pigs. There's also a good range of deli-style cooked meats, black puddings, pickles and condiments. Pies are available too; the steak and kidney version is especially recommended.

Lidgate
110 Holland Park Avenue, W11 4UA (7727 8243). Holland Park tube. **Open** 7am-6pm Mon-Fri; 7am-5pm Sat. **Credit** MC, V.
This select butcher justifiably prides itself on the quality of its free-range and organic meat and poultry from farms including Highgrove Estate. Rare-breed meats are well represented and the shop does a roaring Thanksgiving and Christmas trade in free-range bronze and black turkeys and geese. Award-winning, own-made pies and oven-ready dishes, including best-selling steak teriyaki, go down a treat, as do Lidgate's own sausages and hams. It's also a great place for stocking up on barbecue goodies, with kebabs including lemon and coriander chicken, and mint and orange lamb.

Macken Bros
44 Turnham Green Terrace, W4 1QP (8994 2646). Turnham Green tube. **Open** 7am-6pm Mon-Fri; 7am-5.30pm Sat. **Credit** AmEx, MC, V.
A loyal local following testifies to the excellence of this small shop's stock. Customers queue patiently to buy prime beef, pork and lamb, free-range poultry, game and free-range turkeys and geese when in season.

M Moen & Sons
24 The Pavement, SW4 0JA (7622 1624/ www.moen.co.uk). Clapham Common tube. **Open** 8am-6.30pm Mon-Fri; 8am-5pm Sat. **Credit** MC, V.
A well-established shop that stocks only free-range and additive-free or organic meat, including prime Scottish beef, lamb and pork. Game, from snipe to wild venison, is a particular passion, and sold in season. Marinated meats (with marinades made here from scratch) and sausages (including cumberland and toulouse) are also popular.

Randalls Butchers
113 Wandsworth Bridge Road, SW6 2TE (7736 3426). Fulham Broadway tube. **Open** 7am-5.30pm Mon-Fri; 7am-4pm Sat. **Credit** MC, V.
This popular butcher's sells a top-class selection of free-range meat and poultry, and also does a brisk business in prepared meats, such as marinated chicken breasts or spiced moroccan lamb.

Simply Sausages
Harts Corner, 341 Central Markets, EC1A 9NB (7329 3227). Farringdon tube/rail. **Open** 8.30am-6pm Mon-Fri; 9am-2.30pm Sat. **Credit** MC, V.
Simply Sausages does exactly what it says on the cover, with a peerless selection of bangers, both traditional and exotic. Permanent fixtures are the indigenous faves – lincolnshire, cumberland and london rich breakfast – while past specialities have included black treacle and cloves, duck and black cherry, and chicken, asparagus and parmesan.

Fishmongers

Decent displays of fresh fish can be found in many London food halls (see p345); there are also several outstanding stalls at Borough Market (see p345) on Fridays and Saturdays.

B&M Seafoods *258 Kentish Town Road, NW5 2AA (7485 0346). Kentish Town tube/rail.* **Open** 7.30am-9.30pm Mon-Sat. **Credit** MC, V.
John Blagden Fishmongers *66 Paddington Street, W1U 4JQ (7935 8321). Baker Street tube.* **Open** 7.30am-1pm Mon, Sat; 7.30am-5pm Tue-Fri. **No credit cards.**
Cope's Seafood Company *700 Fulham Road, SW6 5SA (7371 7300). Parsons Green tube.* **Open** 10am-8pm Mon-Fri; 9am-6pm Sat. **Credit** AmEx, DC, MC, V. **Branch:** c/o 46 Northcote Road, SW11; open Thur-Sat.
Covent Garden Fishmongers *37 Turnham Green Terrace, W4 1RG (8995 9273). Turnham Green tube.* **Open** 8am-5pm Tue, Sat; 8am-5.30pm Wed-Fri. **Credit** MC, V.
France Fresh Fish *99 Stroud Green Road, N4 3PX (7263 9767). Finsbury Park tube/rail.* **Open** 9am-6.45pm Mon-Sat; 11am-5pm Sun. **No credit cards.**
Golborne Fisheries *75 Golborne Road, W10 5NP (8960 3100). Ladbroke Grove tube.* **Open** 8am-6pm Mon-Sat. **No credit cards.**
Steve Hatt *88-90 Essex Road, N1 8LU (7226 3963). Angel tube.* **Open** 7am-5pm Tue-Sat. **No credit cards.**
Moxon's *Shop E, Westbury Parade, Nightingale Lane, SW4 9DH (8675 2468). Clapham South tube.* **Open** 9am-8pm Tue-Fri; 9-6pm Sat.
Northcote Fisheries *14 Northcote Road, SW11 1NX (7978 4428). Clapham Junction rail.* **Open** 7.30am-5.30pm Tue-Sat.
Walter Purkis & Sons *17 The Broadway, N8 8DU (8340 6281/www.purkis4fish.co.uk). Finsbury Park tube/rail then W7 bus.* **Open** 8am-5pm Tue-Sat. **Credit** AmEx, MC, V.
Sandy's *56 King Street, Twickenham, Middx TW1 3SH (8892 5788). Twickenham rail.* **Open** 8am-5pm Mon-Sat. **Credit** AmEx, MC, V.

CONNOISSEUR

Wine Courses   Tasting   Special Events

10 Wedderburn Road
London NW3 5QG
Tel 020 7328 2448
Fax 020 7681 9905

E-Mail: tastings@connoisseur.org
Web page: www.connoisseur.org

Wine & Spirit Education Trust
www.wset.co.uk

Based in central London the Wine & Spirit Education Trust (WSET®) was founded 35 years ago to provide training in wines, spirits and other alcoholic beverages to those in the wine and spirit trade and for the general public

We run four levels of qualification courses and also one-off seminars for those that just want to understand a bit more about wine, whilst having a fun evening out

Why not purchase some WSET Gift Vouchers which make the perfect present!

Over 11,000 people took WSET® qualifications last year in 24 countries

020 7236 3551
www.wset.co.uk
wset@wset.co.uk

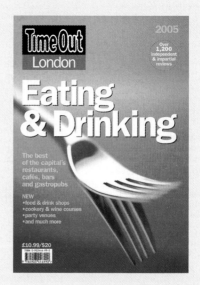

Courses

Cookery courses

Art of Hospitality
St James Schools, Earsby Street, W14 8SH (7348 1755/www.artofhospitality.co.uk). Kensington (Olympia) tube/rail. **Phone enquiries** 8.30am-4pm Mon-Fri. **No credit cards.**
This cookery school puts the emphasis on the joys of sharing good food. For example, there's the 'create-a-dinner-party-invite-a-friend' class, for a maximum of nine cooks and nine friends, resulting in a three-course dinner (from £18.30 per person). Other options include 'survive and thrive' classes for school leavers and students, corporate team-building classes – lunch or dinner is included in both – and lessons for children (two hours for £20).

Books for Cooks
4 Blenheim Crescent, W11 1NN (7221 1992/www.booksforcooks.com). Ladbroke Grove tube. **Open** 10am-6pm Tue-Sat. **Credit** MC, V.
This much-loved cookery bookshop, a Notting Hill institution, offers an imaginative range of cookery workshops (from £25 for three hours), held in an upstairs demonstration kitchen. Teachers include Books for Cooks owner and French chef Eric Treuille, Italian cookbook writer Ursula Ferrigno and Australian cookery teacher Jennifer Donovan-Pyle. Mouth-watering topics such as Italian Easter treats, Keralite cooking and Asian street foods include recipe demonstrations, tasting, a recipe booklet and a glass of wine.

Cookery School
15B Little Portland Street, W1W 8BW (7631 4590/www.cookeryschool.co.uk). Oxford Circus tube. **Phone enquiries** 9am-5pm Mon-Fri. **Credit** MC, V.
Rosalind Rathouse's friendly cookery school offers courses aimed at enthusiastic amateurs, with the emphasis on simple but imaginative cooking. Classes (£40-£60) are very much hands-on and include wine and food pairings and how to make chocolate and sushi.

Le Cordon Bleu
114 Marylebone Lane, W1M 6HH (7935 3503/www.lcblondon.edu). Bond Street tube. **Phone enquiries** 8.30am-7.30pm Mon-Fri. **Credit** MC, V.
This international cookery school offers a range of courses. Professionals can take two-month courses in cuisine or pâtisserie (£3,220 for intensive basic pâtisserie, up to £18,945 for a grande diplome). Keen amateurs can sample short gourmet courses, run in the evenings or daytime over two to eight weeks, with prices from £100 to £1,490, or sit in on a professional demonstration.

La Cuisine de Pierre
29 College Cross, N1 1PT (7700 1349/www.lacuisinedepierre.com). Angel tube/Highbury & Islington tube/rail. **Phone enquiries** 3-10.30pm Mon-Fri. **No credit cards.**
Experienced French chef Pierre Béghin teaches practical, hands-on cookery classes (£70) to small groups in his well-equipped Islington home. Each class teaches beginners how to cook a three-course menu; they take place on weekday mornings and Wednesday evenings. Types of cuisine covered include French, Italian, Thai and Japanese.

Divertimenti
33-34 Marylebone High Street, W1U 4PT (7935 0689/www.divertimenti.co.uk). Baker Street tube. **Open** 9.30am-6pm Mon-Wed, Fri; 9.30am-7pm Thur; 10am-6pm Sat; 11am-5pm Sun. **Credit** AmEx, DC, MC, V.
An appetising selection of classes and courses are run in the well-equipped demonstration basement kitchen at this lovely kitchenware shop. Talented chefs and food writers, including fusion master Peter Gordon and vegetarian specialist Celia Brooks Brown, are among the teachers. Prices range from £20 for a demonstration with food and recipes to £395 for a six-lesson course.

Leiths School of Food & Wine
21 St Alban's Grove, W8 5BP (7729 0177/www.leiths.com). High Street Kensington tube. **Phone enquiries** 9am-5pm Mon-Fri. **Credit** MC, V.
Caroline Waldegrave's respected cookery school offers courses for both professional and amateur cooks. Amateurs can take part in relaxed Saturday morning sessions (£86), where you make your own three-course lunch, or the beginner's cookery skills evening course (ten classes for £530). Professional training for the Leiths diploma in food and wine is a serious three-term affair.

À Table
7 Arlington Road, Richmond, Surrey TW10 7BZ (8940 9910). Richmond tube/rail. **Phone enquiries** 9am-5pm Mon-Fri. **No credit cards.**
Self-taught Austrian chef Martina Lessing teaches small groups in her own kitchen once a week during the day and/or evening. Daytime classes cover themes such as starters, soups, finger food, desserts and vegetarian food. In the evening, she teaches how to cook a seasonal three-course French, Italian, Austrian, Thai or English dinner party menu. Classes cost £25 (£20 if you book for three or more), and are aimed at beginners.

Tasting Places
Unit 108, Buspace Studios, Conlan Street, W10 5AP (7460 0077/www.tastingplaces.com). **Phone enquiries** 9am-5pm Mon-Fri. **Credit** AmEx, DC, JCB, MC, V.
Glimpse behind the scenes at some of London's top restaurants with Tasting Places' exclusive master classes with chefs – held in their own kitchens around the capital. The line-up varies from year to year, but has included the likes of Sam Clarke at Moro, David Thompson at Nahm, Atul Kochhar at Benares, Mark Edwards at Nobu and Jeremy Lee at the Blue Print Café. Prices range from £100 to £175, with recipe packs and lunch or dinner at the restaurant included in the price. A day (£195) at Le Manoir aux Quat' Saisons also figures, and the company's week-long cooking holidays (in Italy, Spain, France, Thailand and elsewhere) are exceedingly popular.

Wine courses

Leiths School of Food & Wine (*see above*) also runs wine-tasting evening classes, at the end of which you decide whether or not to take an exam. Courses include matching food with wine (£55) and a champagne evening (£70).

For tips on choosing the right wine course, see the feature starting on p15.

Christie's
153 Great Titchfield Street, W1P 7FR (7665 4350/www.christies.com). Great Portland Street or Warren Street tube. **Phone enquiries** 9am-5pm Mon-Fri. **Credit** MC, V.
Christie's wine courses for beginners start with an introductory course – one evening a week for five weeks – for £210. Buffs can expand their knowledge at a master class run by a leading wine specialist, such as Anthony Hanson MW.

Connoisseur
7328 2448/www.connoisseur.org. **Phone enquiries** 8am-8pm Mon-Sat. **No credit cards.**
Well established in the wine trade, Eric Sabourin and Margaret Silbermann offer relaxed, informal courses and tastings. The introductory course (five sessions for £169) focuses on topics such as the role of the winemaker, and choosing wine in a restaurant; an intermediate course (six sessions, £95) looks at Old and New World wines, and beginner's day classes are held on Saturdays (£75).

International Wine & Food Society
9 Fitzmaurice Place, Berkeley Square, W1J 5JD (7495 4191/www.iwfs.org). **Phone enquiries** 9am-5pm Mon-Fri. **Credit** MC, V.
This international outfit (founded in 1933) aims to promote 'a greater understanding and pleasure in good food, good wine and good company'. Each of the three branches organises its own events: tastings, dinners, newsletters and the like. You can join the society for a one-off fee of £10; thereafter membership is £30 a year (£39 for joint members), or £14 (£21 joint) for those aged under 36. Life membership is £250 (£375 joint). Renowned wine writer Hugh Johnson is honorary president.

Sotheby's
34-35 New Bond Street, W1A 2AA (7293 5727/www.sothebys.com). Bond Street tube. **Phone enquiries** 9am-5pm Mon-Fri. **Credit** MC, V.
Develop a sound base of oenological knowledge on the varietal and regional courses, run alternately throughout the academic year. Prices are £200 for six sessions or £380 for two consecutive courses.

Tim Atkin's Wine 'Uncorked' Series
7379 5088. **Phone enquiries** 9am-5pm Mon-Fri. **Credit** AmEx, DC, MC, V.
Award-winning wine writer Tim Atkin teaches two courses at Bank restaurant (Aldwych or Westminster). Both cost £270, take place on six evenings over a period of three months, and are sociable affairs. The beginner's course teaches how to taste wines and identify key grape varieties; the intermediate looks at such issues as choosing wines in restaurants, and oaked wines.

Vinopolis, City of Wine
1 Bank End, SE1 9BU (0870 241 4040/www.vinopolis.co.uk). London Bridge tube/rail. **Open** noon-9pm (last tour 7pm) Mon, Fri, Sat; noon-6pm Tue-Thur, Sun. **Credit** MC, V.
Vinopolis is a wine museum, with an impressive wine bar (Wine Wharf). It also runs an educational programme, including an hour-long introductory class (£25), a 'contemporary choice' wine-tasting course (£35), matching food and wine (£50), and a fine wine-tasting class for the more advanced wine lover (£75, minimum 15 people). The price includes a tour of the exhibition, which takes you around the vinous globe by way of themed rooms.

Wine & Spirit Education Trust
Five Kings House, 1 Queen Street Place, EC4R 1QS (7236 3551/www.wset.co.uk). Mansion House tube/Cannon Street tube/rail. **Phone enquiries** 9-5pm Mon-Fri. **Credit** MC, V.
The WSET's intermediate certificate (£283), advanced certificate (£503) and diploma (£1,260 a year for two years, or £2,468 for evening classes over one year) equip both professionals and amateurs with recognised qualifications in the world of wine. The new foundation certificate (£98) is a one-day course for beginners; other options include tutored tastings and a summer school.

WineWise
107 Culford Road, N1 4HL (7254 9734/www.michaelschusterwine.com). Highbury & Islington tube/rail/30, 38, 73, 76, 141 bus. **Phone enquiries** 8.30am-8.30pm Mon-Fri. **No credit cards.**
Winewise's well-regarded classes are run by Michael Schuster. Two six-session courses are held throughout the year: the beginner's one costs £175; the fine wine one is £275.

The world's your oyster

Drink Shops

Beer

Shops

The Beer Shop
*14 Pitfield Street, N1 6EY (7739 3701/
www.pitfieldbeershop.co.uk). Old Street tube/rail.
Open 11am-7pm Tue-Fri; 10am-4pm Sat.
Credit MC, V.*
A beer lover's mecca, packed with a constantly changing range of some 600 unusual bottled beers (and a few cans) from around the globe, with Belgium and Britain making a sizeable contribution. Expect to find gems such as Dragonhead Stout from the Orkney Islands or Lucifer from Belgium. Draught can be ordered, though you'll need to get a barrel (36 pints); if you've really got your beer head on, go for the 72-pint option, costing £100-£120. There's also a range of six historic beers, made using old-style malt recipes. Seven beers are also brewed at Pitfield's organic brewery next door. In addition to home-brewing equipment and brewery collectibles, there's a good range of organic wines and celebration beers.

Mail order & internet

Beers in a Box
01924 489222/www.beersinabox.com.
Bored with the same old supermarket and off-licence beers? Then order something different from Clarke's Organic Group, a small bottling company in Yorkshire run by ale enthusiast Patrick Clarke. He persuades local microbreweries to let him bottle their rare brews, and sells them in myriad permutations to fans. A mixed box of six 500ml bottles starts at around £20.

Wine

Wine merchants

Some retailers also have wine bars; for details, see **Wine Bars**, starting on p320.

Balls Brothers
*313 Cambridge Heath Road, E2 9LQ (7739
1642/www.ballsbrothers.co.uk). Bethnal Green
tube. **Open** 9am-5.30pm Mon-Fri. **Credit** AmEx,
DC, MC, V.*
A quintessentially traditional wine merchant, combining the charm of the old school with the accessibility of the new – witness the easy-to-handle website, the descriptive wine list and the popular events (where you can try and buy), as well as the list of French classics. The company takes pride in the fact that it ships, ages and stores the wines itself, and therefore retains the trappings of a London wine merchant in the old-fashioned sense. But don't call it stuffy: visit one of 18 wine bars/restaurants around London (check the website for details) and you'll sample the most up-to-date of wine selections. The Australian and South African choices are particularly current. Mail order available.

Berry Bros & Rudd
*3 St James's Street, SW1A 1EG (7396 9600/
www.bbr.com). Green Park tube. **Open** 10am-
6pm Mon-Fri; 10am-4pm Sat. **Credit** AmEx, DC,
MC, V.*
Operating in gentlemanly St James's since the mid 17th century, Berry Bros still sells wine from its quaint, antique premises, but has taken on the trappings of the 21st century without flinching. As well as three new rooms in which customers can peruse the shelves, off-licence style (the wines were traditionally brought up from the cellar on demand), the firm now has a strong internet presence. In fact, it's one of the most forward-looking companies around, determined to blend traditional reliability with the need for affordable, recognisable wines, a full range of classics and a characterful range from the New World. There's nothing here that isn't genuinely good. Prices start at £4.50 then ascend to the dizzy heights of thousands of pounds. Frequent special offers and tastings are available, and there's also a wine school. Mail order available.

Corney & Barrow
*194 Kensington Park Road, W11 2ES (7221
5122/head office 7265 2400/www.corneyand
barrow.com). Ladbroke Grove tube. **Open**
10.30am-9pm Mon-Fri; 10.30am-8pm Sat.
Credit AmEx, MC, V.*
A blue-chip wine merchant, with the finest Bordeaux chateaux and Burgundy domains on offer (vintages date back to 1900), plus a one-to-one broking division to guide you through any complexities. C&B was established in 1780, when this kind of service was the norm. The past few years have also seen the addition of extra layers of quality in the form of some fabulous German rieslings and the very expensive Spanish estate Domaine de Pingus. This isn't bargain wine territory, nor is it much of a haven for New World fans, but for glitz and sophistication wine merchants don't come much better. Mail order available; call the head office for details.

Handford Wines
*105 Old Brompton Road, SW7 3LE (7589 6113/
www.handford.net). South Kensington tube. **Open**
10am-8.30pm Mon-Sat. **Credit** AmEx, MC, V.*
Not your run-of-the-mill wine selection, but choice pickings from France. If you feel it's time you got to know your Costières de Nîmes from your Coteaux de Languedoc, this is the place to come to find the best of them. Similarly, if you're tired of the usual supermarket choices, this is an outlet at which individuality shines. Bottles are opened at noon on Saturdays to try for free, and the friendly team can offer advice. For those in a hurry there are more conventional wines from the New World.

Jeroboams
*6 Pont Street, SW1X 9EL (7235 1612/
www.jeroboams.co.uk). Knightsbridge or Sloane
Square tube. **Open** 10am-8pm Mon-Fri; 10am-
7pm Sat. **Credit** AmEx, MC, V.*
This salubriously located shop, one of six in the capital, offers a suitably highbrow selection, focusing on France – the claret choices are better than the Burgundies, and the Languedoc/Mediterranean range is better than the Loire and Rhône. You'll have to dig deep, as many of these exclusive tipples are expensive – though worth it if you want something a bit different. Look out for the Western Australian range and the improving American and South African options.

Lea & Sandeman
*170 Fulham Road, SW10 9PR (7244 0522/
www.londonfinewine.co.uk). Gloucester Road tube.
Open 10am-8pm Mon-Sat. **Credit** AmEx, MC, V.*
Browse this merchant's extensive mail order literature if you wish, but a visit to one of its three shops (in Chelsea, Kensington and Barnes) will allow you to peruse the imaginative selection in the flesh and buy on the spot. The classics are definitely the main event – Chianti, Bordeaux, Burgundy, the Loire and the Rhône – plus reliably chosen vineyard wines from the New World (the buying team try to steer away from bland cross-regional blends). You might not recognise the name of the producer, but Charles Lea and Patrick Sandeman know their wines, so put yourself in their capable hands. Mail order available.

Majestic Wine Warehouse
*63 Chalk Farm Road, NW1 8AN (7485 0478/
www.majestic.co.uk). Chalk Farm tube. **Open**
10am-8pm Mon-Fri; 9am-7pm Sat; 10am-5pm
Sun. **Credit** AmEx, MC, V.*
This cheerful chain is a top choice for a pre-party spree. Wines are sold by the case, but you can mix and match from a wealth of New and Old World options. Much as the feel of the place is upbeat and Aussie-style, it's French wine that's the traditional basis of business – choose, for example, from the finest classic Médoc chateaux, or pick up a case of competitively priced Champagne. There are usually a few open bottles around to try, and good deals can be had. Mail order available. Check the website for the branch nearest you.

Nicolas
*157 Great Portland Street, W1W 6QR (7580
1622/www.nicholas-wines.com). Great Portland
Street or Oxford Circus tube. **Open** 10am-7.30pm
Mon-Fri; 11am-6pm Sat. **Credit** AmEx, MC, V.*
With more than 300 branches in France, and now 20 shops in London (two with wine bars), we're privileged to have this resolutely Gallic outlet on our doorsteps. The wines, unsurprisingly, are mostly French, and quite often from the country's smaller, quirkier regions such as Jura, Savoie and Savennières. These provide a great way of getting to know the *terroir* – and they're decently priced too. Keep an eye out for discounted champers in the May and November sales, and for bargain Bordeaux and Burgundies.

Oddbins
*57 Lombard Road, SW11 3RX (7738 1029/
www.oddbins.com). Clapham Junction rail.
Open 10am-9pm Mon-Thur; 10am-10pm Fri,
Sat; 10am-8pm Sun. **Credit** AmEx, MC, V.*
Oddbins is still streets ahead of the rest of the high-street chains in terms of adventurous wine choices. The slightly wacky interiors still pervade, and the atmosphere is as laid-back as ever. Plus, there's always plenty of knowledgeable help on hand. Australia and Chile are highlights, the South African selection is ever-strengthening, and there's no shortage of interesting labels from France, Spain, Italy, Greece and many others – plus expensive classics and a full range of Champagne. Mail order available. There are some 50 branches within the M25; check the website for your nearest.

Philglas & Swiggot
*21 Northcote Road, SW11 1NG (7924 4494/
www.philglas-swiggot.co.uk). Clapham Junction
rail. **Open** 11am-7pm Mon-Sat; noon-5pm Sun.
Credit AmEx, MC, V.*
Karen and Mike Rogers make it their mission to supply interesting and highly individual wines – the sort that are made in quantities too small for the major chains even to consider stocking. Australia is the speciality: in the form of premium Western Australian wines, top rieslings and verdelhos, with New Zealand and Italy also well represented. Prices for these genuinely exciting wines start at around £10.

La Réserve
*56 Walton Street, SW3 1RB (7589 2020/
www.la-reserve.co.uk). Knightsbridge tube.
Open 10am-8pm Mon-Fri; 10am-6pm Sat.
Credit AmEx, MC, V.*
Mark Reynier is a keen believer in wines with flavour – 'why should everything taste like an Australian fruit bomb?' – and he determinedly seeks out the most individual bottles possible. Burgundy and Italy shine out as specialist areas, with selections from the finest producers. Aged clarets are another forte, and wines from around the world are well represented. The cheapest bottles are between £5 and £10, but rise swiftly

thereafter. Whisky lovers are well looked after too: La Réserve owns the Bruichladdich distillery, producer of fine Islay malt, and Milroy's of Soho (*see right*). There's a tasting programme and other events, and mail order is available. There are also outlets in Hampstead and Fulham.

Wine of Course

216 Archway Road, N6 5AX (8347 9006/ www.wineofcourse.com). Highgate tube. **Open** 10.30am-9pm Mon, Wed-Sun. **Credit** AmEx, MC, V.
It's not often you stroll into an off-licence to find Naomi Klein's *No Logo* displayed on the shelves. But Wine of Course prides itself on avoiding the big, heavily branded wines, and instead stocking bottles from over 150 small producers that are superior to many supermarket wines for the same cost. The staff are unusually well informed and enthusiastic. This bottle stop is particularly recommended if you're en route to a party of wine-lovers, and don't want to make the faux pas of turning up with a bottle of Gallo or Blossom Hill.

Mail order & internet

Many of the wine merchants listed above also sell by mail order or will take orders via their website. Online-only merchants usually sell by the case only (12 bottles) and tend to be specialists, offering wines you'd be hard-pressed to find elsewhere.

Adnams Wines

East Green, Southwold, Suffolk IP18 6JW (01502 727220/www.adnamswines.co.uk). **Phone enquiries** 9am-6.30pm Mon-Fri; 9am-noon Sat. **Credit** MC, V.
The famous East Anglian brewery is also a top-quality wine merchant, now with a burgeoning mail order operation. Chairman Simon Loftus has created a list of wines in which quality rules without compromise; many are made organically or biodynamically. All budgets are catered for, and the team can put together a number of interesting mixed-case options.

Bibendum Wine

113 Regents Park Road, NW1 8UR (7449 4120/ www.bibendum-wine.co.uk). **Phone enquiries** 8.30am-6.30pm Mon-Fri. **Credit** AmEx, MC, V.
Service doesn't get much better than at Bibendum. Those wishing for advice on fine wines will be given all the guidance they need, but there are plenty of everyday names too. Indeed, the wines here are worth the minimum 36-bottle purchase as they cover the likes of Bordeaux and Burgundy with a flourish, but don't stint on trendy southern French or glugging New World options either.

Farr Vintners

220 Queenstown Road, SW8 4LP (7821 2000/ www.farr-vintners.com). **Phone enquiries** 9am-6pm Mon-Fri. **No credit cards.**
No other wine merchant offers quite such a fabulous range of rare Bordeaux chateaux, Burgundy and Rhône wines, nor does any match the array of vintages on offer here. Access to such top tipples is by mail order or the net, and the minimum spend is £500 – and you can't pay by credit card. However, if you're into fine wine, this shouldn't put you off, as the Farr team is one of the friendliest around.

Justerini & Brooks

61 St James's Street, SW1A 1LZ (7493 8721/ www.justerinis.com). **Phone enquiries** 9am-5.30pm Mon-Fri. **Credit** AmEx, MC, V.
The focus of this traditional St James's wine merchant is mostly on mail order these days, as its retail outlet is now restricted to by-the-case sales. Not that this has affected the quality of the wines, which are superb. Germany, Bordeaux and Burgundy are specialities, but it's hard to fault any of the others in the comprehensive range. Quality wines of a more offbeat nature include a wide variety from Alsace, Austria, Madeira and Italy's Piedmont, and a number of older vintages. A broking service is also offered.

Lay & Wheeler

Holton Park, Holton St Mary, Suffolk CO7 6NN (01206 764446/www.laywheeler.com). **Phone enquiries** 9am-6pm Mon-Fri; 9am-1pm Sat. **Credit** MC, V.
Lay & Wheeler continues its class act. This family-owned business might have been established in 1854, but it caters to the modern-day customer, with an efficient mail order service, a full range of organic and biodynamic wines, entertaining twice-yearly wine lists (full of detail about the growers), plenty of choice from around the world and wines of genuine quality. Add to this a solid range of en primeur claret each year, and a succession of bargain mixed-case offers, and you could hardly wish for more.

Vinceremos Wines & Spirits

74 Kirkgate, Leeds LS2 7DJ (0113 244 0002/ www.vinceremos.co.uk). **Phone enquiries** 9am-5.30pm Mon-Fri. **Credit** AmEx, MC, V.
Every bottle on this list has been made using organic or biodynamic vineyard practices, or with holistic vineyard management in mind. Jem Gardener is convinced that, with time, this outlook will result in wines that taste better. Dip into his carefully chosen selection of wines from around the world and you'll probably agree that they taste pretty good already. Average prices are between £4-£8 and, in addition to the wines, Vinceremos offers organic beers, ciders and spirits.

Vintage Roots

Farley Farms, Reading Road, Arborfield, Berkshire RG2 9HT (0118 976 1999/ www.vintageroots.co.uk). **Phone enquiries** 8.30am-5.30pm Mon-Fri. **Credit** MC, V.
Neil Palmer and Lance Pigott believe organic wines should become readily available throughout the UK wine trade, and to this end are an energetic supplier of supermarkets and high-street outlets. You can also buy direct from their wide range, covering Champagne, Bordeaux, biodynamic Loire wines, Australia, Chile, Mediterranean France and the Rhône. Leave your prejudices behind and indulge in a case of the holistic best – you'll rarely have to pay more than £10 a bottle. Organic beers, spirits, liqueurs, ciders and perries are also sold. Vegetarian and vegan wines also feature. The minimum purchase is one case.

The Wine Society

Gunnels Wood Road, Stevenage, Hertfordshire SG1 2BG (01438 740222/www.thewine society.com). **Phone enquiries** 8.30am-9pm Mon-Fri; 9am-5pm Sat. **Credit** MC, V.
The fact that the wines offered here are so good is a spectacular achievement given this co-operative supplies 80,000 members. Life membership costs £40; thereafter you'll receive a copy of the Society's informative wine list, issued quarterly, and be given free rein to dip into a terrific array of wines, including some of the very best (top wines from Bordeaux chateaux, Australia and the Loire), as well as plenty of everyday offerings. All the services of a traditional wine merchant are on hand. If you don't have a cellar, the Society will store your wines in its own temperature-controlled vaults. Other benefits of membership include tastings, dinners and en primeur deals.

Yapp Bros

The Old Brewery, Mere, Wiltshire BA12 6DY (01747 860423/www.yapp.co.uk). **Phone enquiries** 9am-6pm Mon-Sat. **Credit** MC, V.
A family-owned merchant specialising in family-made wines, particularly from France. Browse the website to pick up highly individual labels from the Rhône, Languedoc-Roussillon, Provence and the Loire, many of them exclusive (and very loyal) to Yapp. Despite the quality, the prices aren't astronomical, and bin-end offers are a bonus.

Gerry's

74 Old Compton Street, W1D 4UW (7734 4215). Leicester Square tube. **Open** 9am-6.30pm Mon-Fri; 9am-5.30pm Sat. **No credit cards.**

This Old Compton Street classic is a purveyor of all that's weird and wonderful in the spirit and liqueur world – and then some. The shop's window and shelves are crammed with such curiosities as an Eiffel Tower-shaped bottle of absinthe (£35), while its impressive range of more than 100 different varieties of vodka includes 'vod-ca', which is flavoured with cannabis.

Milroy's of Soho

3 Greek Street, W1V 6NX (7437 9311). Tottenham Court Road tube. **Open** 10am-8pm Mon-Sat. **Credit** AmEx, MC, V.
London's most famous whisky specialist has been in existence for almost 40 years and stocks one of the biggest ranges in the capital, with around 650 different types on offer, plus a decent range of wines (Milroy's is now part of the La Réserve stable; *see above*). Whisky and wine tasting nights (£30-£50 a head including food) offer a chance to sample the stock.

Tea & coffee

Fortnum & Mason (*see p44 and p346*) is renowned for its collection of fine teas from around the world.

Algerian Coffee Stores

52 Old Compton Street, W1V 6PB (7437 2480/ www.algcoffee.co.uk). Leicester Square or Piccadilly Circus tube. **Open** 9am-7pm Mon-Sat. **Credit** AmEx, MC, V.
Founded in 1887, this Soho store is one of the oldest coffee establishments in the UK, and offers around 100 different blends of coffee and 140 teas (herbals, Chinese, Japanese and fruit infusions). Beans have been carefully selected from all corners of the world, and variations include espresso coffees (the Cuban Turquino Lavado is particularly sought after) and estate coffees from Colombia and Hawaii. Special offers change on a monthly basis. Mail order available.

HR Higgins

79 Duke Street, W1K 5AS (7629 3913/ www.hrhiggins.co.uk). Bond Street tube. **Open** 9.30am-5.30pm Mon-Fri; 10am-5pm Sat. **Credit** AmEx, MC, V.
Now into its third generation, this shop is run by friendly staff, who are happy to share their knowledge with customers. The wide range of freshly roasted and ground coffee is prepared daily on the premises. Speciality blends include breakfast and Chagga (from Mount Kilimanjaro) as well as the smooth Mocha and Mysore. Teas from Ceylon, China, Taiwan and India as well as flavoured varieties like lemon or mango can be tasted first. Smart gift boxes are also up for grabs. Mail order available.

Monmouth Coffee House

27 Monmouth Street, WC2H 9EV (7379 3516/ www.monmouthcoffee.co.uk). Covent Garden tube. **Open** 9am-6.30pm Mon-Sat. **Credit** MC, V.
At Monmouth a lot of care goes into choosing the ethically sourced, top-quality beans (mostly Brazilian, South American and African), and coffee-lovers will appreciate the discerning selection. Friendly and informed staff can provide any necessary details and there's a cosy tasting area at the back, so you can sample a brew with a pastry before you buy.

The Tea House

15A Neal Street, WC2H 9PU (7240 7539). Covent Garden tube. **Open** 10am-7pm Mon-Sat; 11am-6pm Sun. **Credit** AmEx, MC, V.
Although it's in the middle of the Covent Garden tourist bubble, the Tea House is more than just a twee trap. Sure, there are plenty of decorative tea strainers and 'Welcome to London' teapots on the shelves, but most of the space in the well-laid out shop is given over to numerous varieties of loose leaf and bagged teas. As well as the classics, there's also plenty of fruit blends, specialist green teas, global teas (such as South African rooibos) and organic teas on offer. The staff are very friendly. Mail order available.

Maps

The following maps highlight London's key restaurant areas – the districts with the highest density of good places to eat and drink. The maps show precisely where each restaurant is located, as well as underground stations and major landmarks. For an overview of every area, see **Key to Maps** below; this shows which areas are covered, and places them in context.

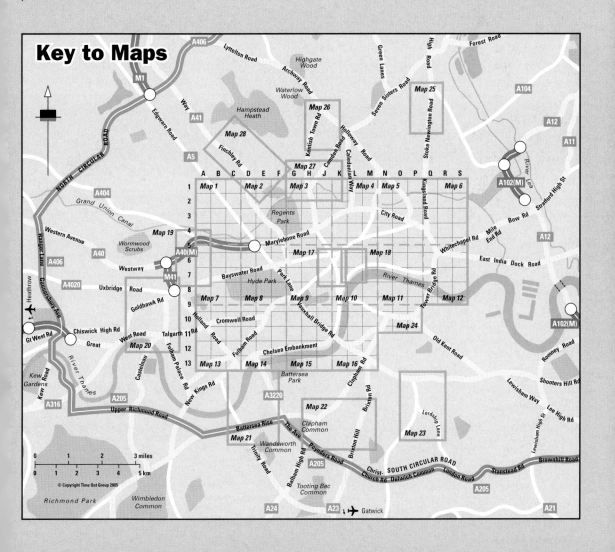

Key to Maps

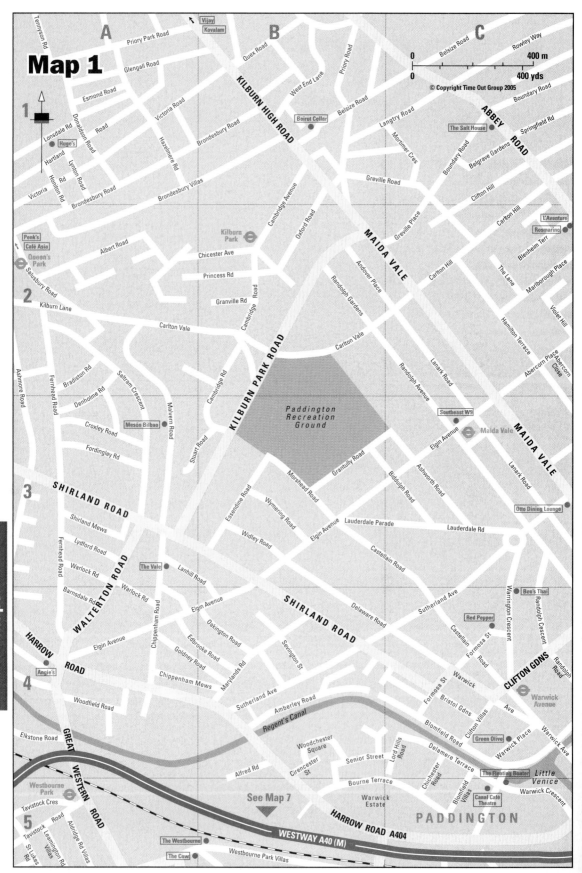

Map 1

A B C

Tennyson Rd
Priory Park Road
Vijay
Kovalam
Quex Road
Priory Road
West End Lane
Belsize Road
Rowley Way
0   400 m
0   400 yds
© Copyright Time Out Group 2005

Glengall Road
Esmond Road
Victoria Road
Brondesbury Road
KILBURN HIGH ROAD
Beirut Cellar
Belsize Road
Langtry Road
Mortimer Cres
The Salt House
ABBEY ROAD
Springfield Rd
Boundary Road

1

Lonsdale Rd
Donaldson Road
Road
Hazelmere Rd
Greville Road
Boundary Road
Belgrave Gardens
Clifton Hill

Hugo's
Hartland
Lynton Road
Brondesbury Villas
Cambridge Avenue
Oxford Road
Greville Place
MAIDA VALE
Carlton Hill
Carlton Hill
L'Aventure
Rosmarino

Victoria
Honiton Rd
Brondesbury Road
Kilburn Park
Blenheim Terr
The Lane
Marlborough Place

Penk's
Café Asia
Queen's Park
Albert Road
Chicester Ave
Princess Rd
Andover Place
Randolph Gardens
Carlton Hill
Violet Hill

2

Salusbury Road
Granville Rd
Cambridge Road
Carlton Vale
Hamilton Terrace
Abercorn Place Abercorn Close

Kilburn Lane
Carlton Vale
Kilburn Park Road
Randolph Avenue
Lanark Road

Ashmore Road
Fernhead Road
Bradiston Rd
Denholme Rd
Saltram Crescent
Malvern Road
Cambridge Rd
Stuart Road
Paddington Recreation Ground
Grantully Road
Southeast W9
Elgin Avenue
Maida Vale
MAIDA VALE
Lanark Road

Croxley Road
Fordingley Rd
Mesón Bilbao
Morshead Road
Biddulph Road
Ashworth Road

3

SHIRLAND ROAD
Shirland Mews
Lydford Road
Essendine Road
Wymering Road
Elgin Avenue
Lauderdale Parade
Lauderdale Rd
Otto Dining Lounge

Fernhead Road
Warlock Rd
Widley Road
Castellain Road

Barnsdale Road
Warlock Rd
The Vale
Lanhill Road
Warrington Crescent
Ben's Thai
Randolph Crescent

WALTERTON ROAD
Chippenham Road
Elgin Avenue
Oakington Road
Edbrooke Road
SHIRLAND ROAD
Delaware Road
Sutherland Ave
Red Pepper
Castellain Road
Formosa St

HARROW ROAD
Angie's
Elgin Avenue
Goldney Road
Maryland Rd
Sevington St
CLIFTON GDNS
Randolph Road

4

Chippenham Mews
Formosa St
Warwick
Bristol Gdns
Clifton Villas
Warwick Avenue
Ave

Woodfield Road
Sutherland Ave
Amberley Road
Blomfield Road
Green Olive
Warwick Place
Warwick Ave

Elkstone Road
GREAT WESTERN ROAD
Regent's Canal
Woodchester Square
Alfred Rd
Cirencester St
Senior Street
Lord Hills Road
Delamere Terrace
Chichester Road
The Floating Boater
Little Venice
Warwick Crescent

Westbourne Park
Tavistock Cres
Bourne Terrace
Blomfield Villas
Canal Café Theatre
Warwick Crescent

5

Tavistock Road
Aldridge Rd Villas
St Lukes Rd
Leamington Rd Villas
See Map 7
Warwick Estate
HARROW ROAD A404
PADDINGTON

The Westbourne
The Cow
WESTWAY A40 (M)
Westbourne Park Villas

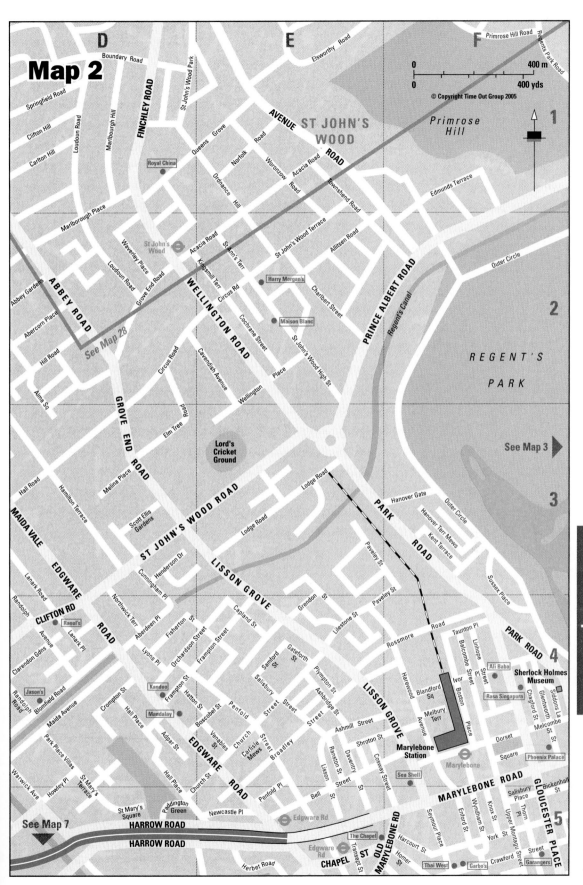

Map 2

D · E · F

Boundary Road
St John's Wood Park
Springfield Road
FINCHLEY ROAD
Elsworthy Road
Primrose Hill Road
Regents Park Road

400 m
400 yds
© Copyright Time Out Group 2005

Clifton Hill
Marlborough Hill
AVENUE
ST JOHN'S WOOD
Primrose Hill
1
Loudoun Road
Queens Grove
Carlton Hill
Ordnance Hill
Norfolk Road
Woronzow Road
Acacia Road
ROAD
Townshend Road
Edmunds Terrace

Royal China
Marlborough Place

Marlborough Place
Waverley Place
WELLINGTON ROAD
Acacia Road
St Ann's Terr
Circus Rd
St John's Wood Terrace
Allitsen Road
PRINCE ALBERT ROAD
Outer Circle
2
Abbey Gardens
ABBEY ROAD
St John's Wood
Kingsmill Terr
Harry Morgan's
Charlbert Street
Regent's Canal
Abercorn Place
Grove End Road
Loudoun Road
Cochrane Street
Maison Blanc
St John's Wood High St
REGENT'S PARK
Hill Road
See Map 28
Circus Road
Cavendish Avenue
Wellington Place
Alma Sq
GROVE END ROAD
Elm Tree Road
Lord's Cricket Ground
Wellington
See Map 3
3
Hall Road
Hamilton Terrace
Melina Place
Lodge Road
Lodge Road
Hanover Gate
Outer Circle
MAIDA VALE
Scott Ellis Gardens
ST JOHN'S WOOD ROAD
Lodge Road
PARK ROAD
Hanover Terr Mews
Kent Terrace
Lanark Road
EDGWARE
Cunningham Pl
Henderson Dr
LISSON GROVE
Paveley St
Sussex Place
Randolph
CLIFTON RD
Raoul's
Northwick Terr
Aberdeen Pl
Fisherton St
Capland St
Grendon St
Paveley St
Road
Taunton Pl
PARK ROAD
4
Avenue
Lanark Pl
Lyons Pl
Orchardson Street
Frampton Street
Samford St
Plympton St
Lilestone St
Rossmore
Ali Baba
Sherlock Holmes Museum
Clarendon Gdns
ROAD
Salisbury
Gateforth St
Ashbridge St
Harewood
Blandford Sq
Linhope Street
Balcombe Street
Boston Place
Rasa Singapura
Jason's
Kandoo
Hatton St
Boscobel St
Penfold
Street
Street
Ashmill Street
Ivor
Melbury Terr
Chagford St
Glentworth St
Melcombe St
Randolph Road
Blomfield Road
Mandalay
Frampton St
Venables
Church
Carlisle Mews
Broadley
Ashmill Street
LISSON GROVE
Siddons La
Maida Avenue
Crompton St
Hall Place
Adgar St
Street
Shroton St
Avenue
Dorset Square
Phoenix Palace
Park Place Villas
Howley Pl
St Mary's Terrace
Church Street
Venables
Ranston St
Daventry St
Cosway Street
Marylebone Station
Marylebone
Bickenhall St
Warwick Ave
EDGWARE ROAD
Penfold Pl
Lisson Street
Bell St
Sea Shell
MARYLEBONE ROAD
GLOUCESTER PLACE
St Mary's Square
Paddington Green
Newcastle Pl
Edgware Rd
Salisbury Place
Knox St
Thorn Pl
Upper Montagu Street
See Map 7
HARROW ROAD
The Chapel
Harcourt St
Enford St
Wyndham St
York St
Garangers
HARROW ROAD
Edgware Rd
Transept St
Homer St
Thai West
Garbo's
Crawford Street
CHAPEL ST
OLD MARYLEBONE RD
Seymour Place
Herbet Road

Maps

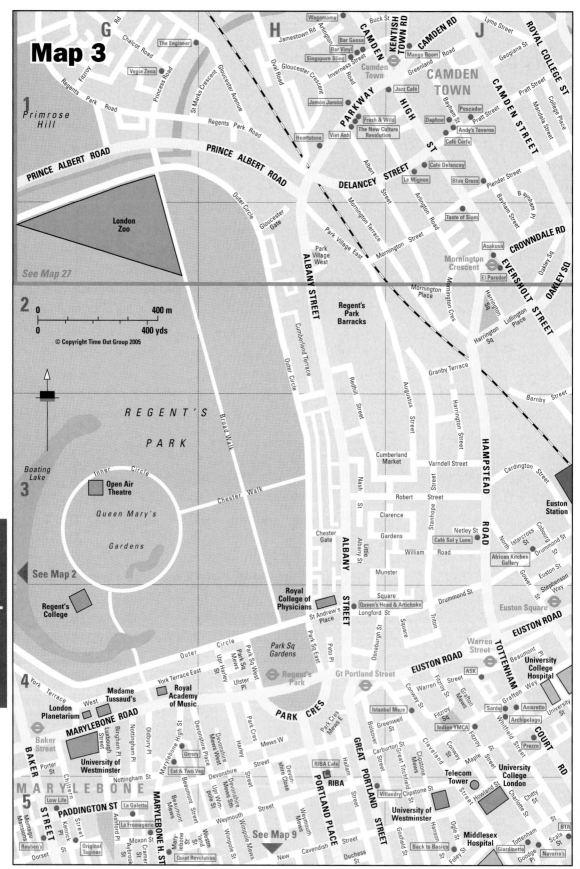

Map 3

G   **H**   **J**

Wagamama · Buck St · KENTISH · CAMDEN RD · ROYAL COLLEGE ST · Lyme Street

The Engineer · Jamestown Rd · Arlington · Bar Gansa · CAMDEN · TOWN RD · Mango Room · Greenland · Road · Geogiana St · Pratt Street · College Place

Chalcot Road · Oval Road · Gloucester Crescent · Bar Vinyl · Camden · Greenland · CAMDEN · Mandela Street

Vegia Zena · Fitzroy Rd · Singapore Sling · Inverness Street · Town · CAMDEN · TOWN · Bayham Street · College Place

Regents · Princess Road · Park · Road · Jamón Jamón · PARKWAY · Jazz Café · Pescador · Pratt Street · CAMDEN STREET

1 *Primrose Hill*

St Marks Crescent · Gloucester Avenue · Regents Park Road · Fresh & Wild · Daphne · Andy's Taverna · Mandela Street

Heartstone · The New Culture Revolution · Viet Anh · Café Corfu · HIGH ST · Bayham Street

PRINCE ALBERT ROAD · PRINCE ALBERT ROAD · Café Delancey · Plender Street · B aynham Pl

DELANCEY · STREET · Le Mignon · Bluu Grass · Plender Street · Bayham Street

Albert Street · Arlington Road · Taste of Siam · CROWNDALE RD

London Zoo · Outer Circle · Gloucester Gate · Park Village East · Mornington Street · Asakusa · EVERSHOLT STREET · Oakley Sq · OAKLEY SQ

Mornington Terrace · Mornington Crescent · El Parador · Harrington Sq · Lidlington Place

See Map 27 · ALBANY STREET · Park Village West · Mornington · Mornington Place · Harrington Sq

2 · 0 — 400 m · 0 — 400 yds · © Copyright Time Out Group 2005 · Cumberland Terrace · Regent's Park Barracks · Mornington Cres · Harrington Place · Lidlington Place

Outer Circle · Granby Terrace · Barnby Street

Redhill Street · Augustus Street · Harrington Street

REGENT'S PARK · Broad Walk · Nash St · Cumberland Market · Varndell Street · Cardington Street

Boating Lake · Inner Circle · Open Air Theatre · Chester Walk · Robert Street · Stanhope Street · Euston Station

3 · Queen Mary's Gardens · Chester Gate · Clarence Gardens · Netley St · Café Sol y Luna · North Istarcross St · Cobourg St · Drummond St

Little Albany St · William Road · African Kitchen Gallery · Euston St · Gower St · Stephenson Way

See Map 2 · Regent's College · Munster Square · ALBANY STREET · Triton Street · Euston Square

Royal College of Physicians · St Andrew's Place · Queen's Head & Artichoke · Longford St · Drummond St

Outer · Circle · Park Sq Mews · Park Sq Gardens · Peto Pl · EUSTON ROAD · Warren Street · University College Hospital

4 · York Terrace · Upr Harley St · Ulster Pl · Regent's Park · Gt Portland Street · ASK · Beaumont Pl · Way

York Terrace East · Madame Tussaud's · Royal Academy of Music · Warren St · Fitzroy St · Grafton Mews · Sardo · Amaretto · University

London Planetarium · MARYLEBONE ROAD · West · Bingham Pl · Nottingham Pl · Oldbury Pl · Marylebone High St · Devonshire Place · PARK CRES · Park Cres Mews · Greenwell St · Conway St · Archipelago · COURT

Baker Street · Luxbough Street · Devonshire Mews West · Park Cres · Mews W · Istanbul Meze · Bolsover St · Fitzroy St · Indian YMCA · Whitfield Street · Prezzo · RD

5 · Porter St · University of Westminster · Orrery · Harley Street · Devonshire Street · RIBA Café · Hallam · Carburton St · Great Titchfield · Cleveland St · Conway · Maple St · University College London

BAKER STREET · Eat & Two Veg · Devonshire St · Devon-shire Close · PORTLAND STREET · RIBA · Telecom Tower · Clipstone St · Howland · Villandry · Chitty St · Charlotte St

MARYLEBONE · Low Life · La Galette · Upr Wim pole St · Weymouth Street · GREAT PORTLAND STREET · PORTLAND PLACE · University of Westminster · Ogle St · BTR

PADDINGTON ST · La Fromagerie · Beaumont Mews · Upr Wimpole St · Wimpole Mews · Weymouth Mews · Middlesex Hospital · Gosfield St · Scala St

Montagu Mansions · Kendrick Pl · Ashford Pl · Moxon St · Cramer · Aybrook · Beaumont St · Wesm · Yand · *See Map 9* · Cavendish · New · Duchess · Back to Basics · Foley St · Goodge · Pl · Navarro's · Giardinetto

Reuben's · Dorset St · Original Tagines · Quiet Revolution · Weymouth · Wimpole · Street · Hanson

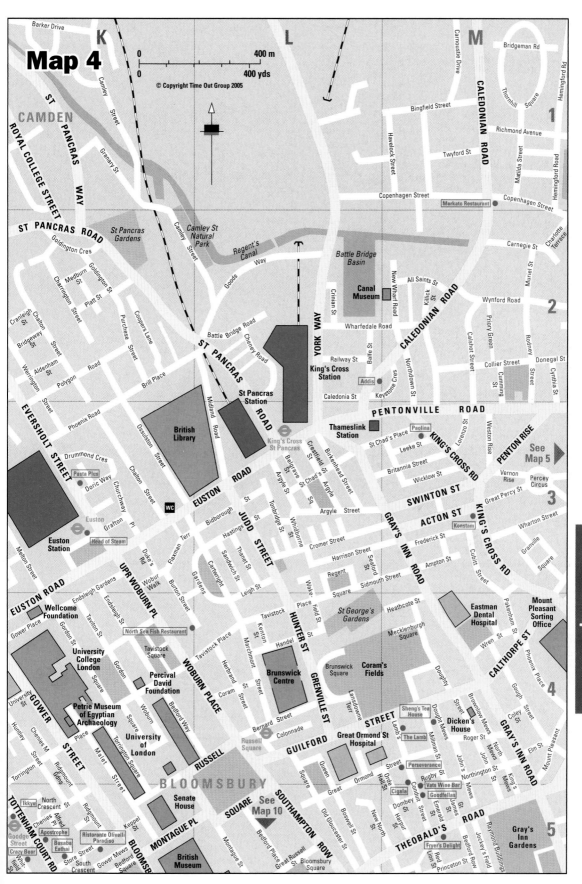

Map 4

0 ——————— 400 m
0 ——————— 400 yds

© Copyright Time Out Group 2005

K   L   M

1

2

3

4

5

CAMDEN

ROYAL COLLEGE STREET

ST PANCRAS WAY

ST PANCRAS ROAD

St Pancras Gardens

Camley Street Natural Park

Regent's Canal

Battle Bridge Basin

Canal Museum

Barker Drive

Camley Street

Granary St

Goldington Cres

Medburn St

Goldington Street

Charrington Street

Platt St

Cranleigh St

Chalton St

Bridgeway

Aldenham Street

Werrington St

Polygon Road

Purchese Street

Coopers Lane

Brill Place

Phoenix Road

Battle Bridge Road

Cheney Road

Crinan St

Goods Way

York Way

Bingfield Street

Havelock Street

Copenhagen Street

Twyford St

Carnegie St

Merkato Restaurant

Copenhagen Street

CALEDONIAN ROAD

Carnoustie Drive

Bridgeman Rd

Hemingford Rd

Thornhill Square

Richmond Avenue

Matilda Street

Hemingford Road

Charlotte Terrace

Muriel St

New Wharf Road

All Saints St

Killick St

Wharfedale Road

Wynford Road

CALEDONIAN ROAD

Priory Green

Calshot Street

Rodney Street

Collier Street

Donegal St

Cumming St

Cynthia St

EVERSHOLT STREET

Drummond Cres

Pasta Plus

Doric Way

Churchway

Chalton Street

Ossulston Street

Midland Road

British Library

St PANCRAS ROAD

EUSTON ROAD

WC

Euston

Grafton Pl

Head of Steam

Euston Station

St Pancras Station

King's Cross St Pancras

King's Cross Station

Railway St

Battle Bridge Road

Caledonia St

Addis

Keystone Cres

Balfe St

Northdown St

Pancras Road

Thameslink Station

St Chad's Place

Paolina

Leeke St

Britannia Street

Wicklow St

PENTONVILLE ROAD

KING'S CROSS RD

Weston Rise

PENTON RISE

See Map 5

Vernon Rise

Percey Circus

Great Percy St

Wharton Street

Granville Square

KING'S CROSS RD

Cubitt Street

SWINTON ST

ACTON ST

Konstam

Frederick St

GRAY'S INN ROAD

Melton Street

Melton Street

EUSTON ROAD

Wellcome Foundation

Gower Place

Endsleigh Gardens

University College London

Gordon St

Taviton St

Endsleigh St

UPR WOBURN PL

Wobur Walk

Duke's Rd

Flaxman Terr

Burton Street

Cartwright Gardens

Bidborough St

Hastings St

Thanet St

Sandwich St

Leigh St

Wakefield St

Regent Square

Tavistock Place

Kenton St

Marchmont Street

Handel Street

HUNTER ST

JUDD STREET

Tonbridge St

Whidborne St

Argyle Square

Argyle St

Belgrave St

St Chad's St

Crestfield St

Birkenhead Street

Argyle Street

Cromer Street

Harrison Street

Regent

Seaford St

Sidmouth St

Ampton St

GRAY'S INN ROAD

St George's Gardens

Heathcote St

Mecklenburgh Square

Eastman Dental Hospital

Mount Pleasant Sorting Office

Pakenham St

Wren St

CALTHORPE ST

Phoenix Place

Gough St

Coley St

GRAY'S INN ROAD

Mount Pleasant

North Sea Fish Restaurant

Tavistock Place

Tavistock Square

Percival David Foundation

Petrie Museum of Egyptian Archaeology

WOBURN PLACE

Bedford Way

Woburn Square

Gordon Square

Coram St

Herbrand Street

Bernard Street

Colonnade

Marchmont Street

Brunswick Centre

GRENVILLE ST

Brunswick Square

Coram's Fields

Lansdowne Terr

Guilford STREET

Great Ormond St Hospital

Doughty Street

Brownlow Mews

Doughty Mews

Millman St

Dickens House

Roger St

John's Mews

North Mews

Northington St

John St

Elm St

Mount Pleasant

University of London

University St

GOWER STREET

Huntley St

Chenies M

Ridgmount Gdns

Malet Street

Torrington Square

Woburn Place

Bedford Way

RUSSELL SQUARE

Montague Place

Russell Square

Great Russell St

Guilford Street

Queen Square

Great Ormond Street

Lamb's Conduit St

Sheng's Tea House

The Lamb

Perseverance

Cigala

Vats Wine Bar

Goodfellas

Rugby St

Conduit St

Dombey St

Emerald St

James St

Gt James St

Harpur St

New North St

Old Gloucester St

Boswell St

Red Lion St

Princeton St

Northington St

King's Mews

Bedford Row

Raymond Buildings

Jockey's Field

Gray's Inn Gardens

BLOOMSBURY

TOTTENHAM COURT RD

Ikkyu

North Crescent

Alfred

Keppel Street

Chenies St

Apostrophe

Goodge Street

Crazy Bear

Wit...

Ristorante Olivelli Paradiso

Busaba Eathai

Gower Mews

Store Street

South Crescent

MONTAGUE PL

Senate House

BLOOMSB...

British Museum

SQUARE

See Map 10

SOUTHAMPTON ROW

Bedford place

Bloomsbury Square

THEOBALD'S ROAD

Fryer's Delight

Bedford Row

Gray's Inn Gardens

Maps

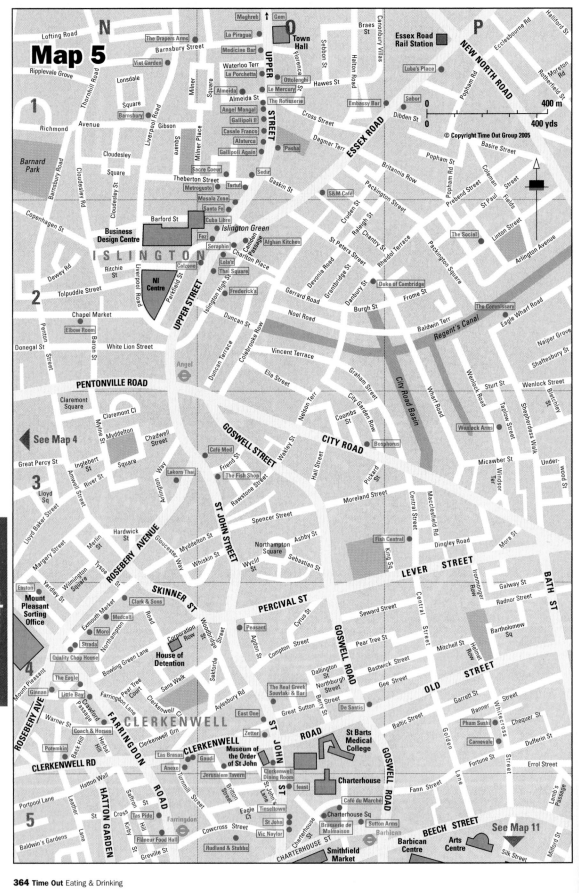

Map 5

N

Lofting Road

The Drapers Arms

Barnsbury Street

Ripplevale Grove

Viet Garden

Lonsdale

Maghreb

Gem

La Piragua

Town Hall

Medicine Bar

Braes St

Essex Road Rail Station

P

Ecclesbourne Rd

Halliford St

NEW NORTH ROAD

Moreton St

Rotherfield St

O

Waterloo Terr

La Porchetta

Ottolenghi

Le Mercury

UPPER STREET

Sebbon St

Florence St

Hawes St

Halton Road

Canonbury Villas

Luba's Place

Popham Rd

Basire Street

Almeida

Almeida St

The Rotisserie

Cross Street

Sabor

Embassy Bar

Dibden St

400 m

400 yds

© Copyright Time Out Group 2005

Richmond

Barnsbury

Milner

Square

Gibson

Square

Angel Mangal

Gallipoli II

Casale Franco

Alaturca

Pasha

Gallipoli Again

Dagmar Terr

Britannia Row

Popham Rd

Prebend Street

St Paul

Street

Coleman

Linton Street

Avenue

Cloudesley

Square

Milner Place

Sacre Coeur

Theberton Street

Sedir

Tartuf

Gaskin St

Packington Street

S&M Café

Cruden St

Raleigh St

Chantry St

Rheidol Terrace

Packington Square

The Social

Arlington Avenue

Barnard Park

Barnsbury Road

Cloudesley Rd

Cloudesley Street

Copenhagen St

Barford St

Business Design Centre

Metrogusto

Masala Zone

Santa Fe

Cuba Libre

Islington Green

Afghan Kitchen

St Peters Street

Devonia Road

Grantbridge St

Danbury St

Duke of Cambridge

Frome St

The Commissary

I S L I N G T O N

Fez

Seraphin

Camden Passage

Charlton Place

Lola's

Calzone

Thai Square

Frederick's

Gerrard Road

Burgh St

Baldwin Terr

Regent's Canal

Eagle Wharf Road

Naiper Grove

Shaftesbury St

Ritchie St

Dewey Rd

Tolpuddle Street

NI Centre

Parkfield St

Liverpool Road

Islington High St

Duncan St

Noel Road

Wharf Road

City Road Basin

Wenlock Road

Sturt St

Wenlock Street

Blackley St

Chapel Market

Elbow Room

Baron St

White Lion Street

Penton Street

Donegal St

Duncan Terrace

Colebrooke Row

Vincent Terrace

Graham Street

Micawber St

Windsor Ter

Under- wood St

Angel

Elia Street

Nelson Terr

City Garden Row

Coombs St

Wenlock Arms

Claremont Square

Claremont Cl

Mylne St

Myddelton

See Map 4

Chadwell Street

Café Med

Friend St

GOSWELL STREET

Wakley St

CITY ROAD

Bosphorus

Great Percy St

Inglebert St

River St

Way

Arlington

Lekorn Thai

The Fish Shop

Rawstone Street

Moreland Street

Central Street

Macclesfield Rd

Dingley Road

Mora St

Lloyd Sq

Lloyd Baker Street

Amwell Street

Hardwick St

Gloucester Way

Myddelton St

Whiskin St

Friend St

ST JOHN STREET

Spencer Street

Northampton Square

Wyclif St

Sebastian St

Ashby St

Fish Central

King Sq

LEVER STREET

Ironmonger Row

Galway St

Radnor Street

BATH ST

Margery Street

Merlin St

Tysoe St

ROSEBERY AVENUE

SKINNER ST

PERCIVAL ST

Seward Street

Central Street

Bartholomew Sq

Wilmington Square

Yardley St

Easton

Mount Pleasant Sorting Office

Clark & Sons

Exmouth Market

Medcalf

Moro

Strada

Quality Chop House

Northampton Road

Woodbridge St

Corporation Row

Sekforde St

Peasant

Agdon St

Compton Street

Cyrus St

GOSWELL ROAD

Pear Tree St

Dallington St

Northburgh Street

Bastwick Street

Gee Street

OLD STREET

Mitchell St

Helmet Row

Mount Pleasant

The Eagle

Ginnan

Little Bay

Bowling Green Lane

House of Detention

Sans Walk

Aylesbury Rd

The Real Greek Souvlaki & Bar

Great Sutton

Berry Street

De Santis

Garrett St

Banner Street

Whitecross

Chequer St

Dufferin St

ROSEBERY AVE

Warner St

Crawford Passage

FARRINGDON

CLERKENWELL

Clerkenwell Grn

Pear Tree Court

Farringdon Lane

Clerkenwell Cl

East One

Zetter

ST JOHN

Baltic Street

Pham Sushi

Carnevale

Golden Lane

Fortune St

Errol Street

Potemkin

Back Hill

Herbal Hill

Coach & Horses

CLERKENWELL RD

Las Brasas

Gaudi

Anexo

Museum of the Order of St John

ROAD

St Barts Medical College

GOSWELL ROAD

Fann Street

Lamb's Passage

Portpool Lane

Hatton Wall

HATTON GARDEN

Saffron Hill

FARRINGDON ROAD

Turnmill Street

Britton Street

Jerusalem Tavern

Clerkenwell Dining Room

St John's Lane

feast

Charterhouse

Café du Marché

BEECH STREET

Silk Street

Milford St

Leather Lane

Baldwin's Gardens

Greville St

Cross St

Kirby St

Hatton

Tas Pide

Flâneur Food Hall

Farringdon

Cowcross Street

Eagle Ct

Tinseltown

St John

Vic Naylor

Rudland & Stubbs

Charterhouse St

Charterhouse Sq

Brasserie de Malmaison

Sutton Arms

Barbican

CHARTERHOUSE ST

Smithfield Market

Barbican Centre

Arts Centre

See Map 11

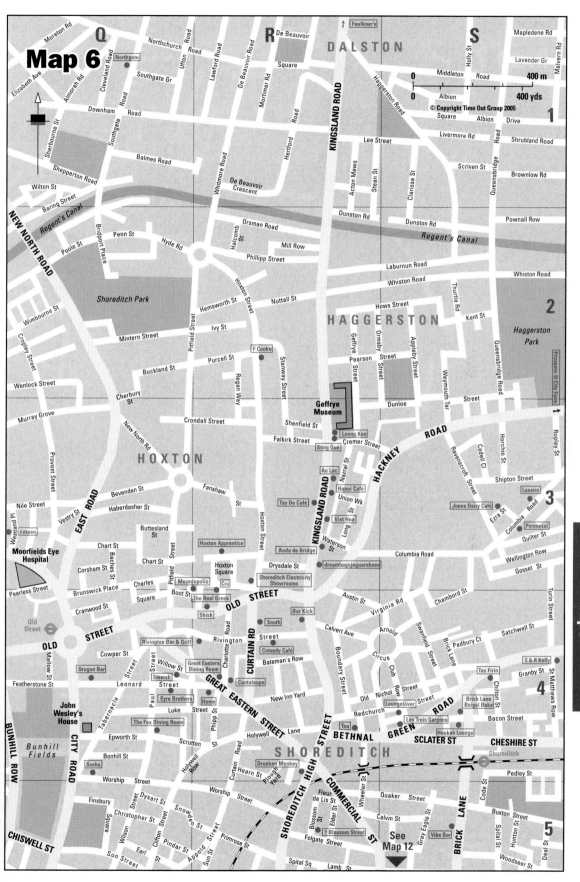

Map 6

Q   **R**   **S**

↑ Faulkner's

De Beauvoir   D A L S T O N

Mapledene Rd

Moreton Rd

Northchurch   Road

Cleveland Road

Northgate

Elizabeth Ave

Almorah Rd

Ufton   Road

Lawford Road

De Beauvoir Road

Mortimer Rd

Square

Holly St

Lavender Gr

Malvern Rd

Southgate Gr

Southgate   Road

Downham   Road

Middleton   Road

0   400 m
0   400 yds

Albion   Square   Albion   Drive

© Copyright Time Out Group 2005

Sherbourne St

Baring Street

Shepperton Road

Balmes Road

Whitmore Road

Hertford   Road

KINGSLAND ROAD

Lee Street

Haggerston Road

Livermore Rd

Shrubland Road

Scriven St

Queensbridge

Brownlow Rd

Wilton St

NEW NORTH ROAD

Regent's Canal

De Beauvoir Crescent

Penn St

Bridport Place

Poole St

Hyde Rd

Halcomb St

Orsman Road

Mill Row

Phillipp Street

Dunston Rd

Dunston Rd

Regent's Canal

Pownall Row

Laburnun Road

Whiston Road

Whiston Road

Road

Thurtle Rd

Kent St

Shoreditch Park

Hemsworth St

Hoxton Street

Nuttall St

H A G G E R S T O N

Hows Street

Queensbridge Road

Haggerston Park

Wimbourne St

Ivy St

Pitfield Street

Mintern Street

Purcell St

Stanway Street

Regan Way

F Cooke

Geffrye Street

Pearson Street

Ormsby Street

Appleby Street

Weymouth Ter

Street

Frizzante @ City Farm

Cropley Street

Wenlock Street

Cherbury St

Buckland St

Crondall Street

Shenfield St

Geffrye Museum

Dunloe

H A C K N E Y   R O A D

Horchio St

Ropley St

Murray Grove

New North Rd

Falkirk Street

Loong Kee

Cremer Street

Shipton Street

Provost Street

H O X T O N

Fanshaw

St

Au Lac

Nazral St

Ravenscroft Street

Cadell Cl

Laxeiro

Columbia Road

Nile Street

Bevenden St

Haberdasher St

Hoxton Street

Hanoi Café

Union Wk

KINGSLAND ROAD

Jones Dairy Café

Ezra St

Perennial

Westland Pl

Vestry St

Tay Do Café

Viet Hoa

Long St

Quilter St

Filteen

Butlesland St

Chart St

Hoxton Apprentice

Waterson St

Columbia Road

Wellington Row

Gosset St

Moorfields Eye Hospital

Corsham St

Chart St

Pitfield

Anda de Bridge

dreambagsjaguarshoes

Peerless Street

Brunswick Place

Charles Square

Boot St

Mezedopolio

Cru

Drysdale St

Shoreditch Electricity Showrooms

Austin St

Virginia Rd

Chambord St

Turin Street

The Real Greek

OLD   STREET

Cranwood St

Shish

Bar Kick

Calvert Ave

Arnold

Swanfield Street

Brick Lane

Satchwell St

Padbury Ct

Old Street

OLD   STREET

Mallow St

Cowper St

Rivington Bar & Grill

Rivington

Street

South

Comedy Café

Bateman's Row

Circus

Club Row

S & R Kelly

Granby St

St Matthews Row

Dragon Bar

Street

Willow St

Great Eastern Dining Room

Charlotte Road

CURTAIN RD

Boundary Street

Tas Firin

Chilton St

Featherstone St

Leonard   Street

Smersh

Cantaloupe

New Inn Yard

Old Nichol

Row

Loungelover

Street

Brick Lane Beigel Bake

Bacon Street

John Wesley's House

Paul

Eyre Brothers

Home

GREAT EASTERN STREET

Redchurch

Les Trois Garçons

Luke   Street

Philpp St

The Fox Dining Room

Holywell   Lane

Tea1

BETHNAL   GREEN   ROAD

SCLATER ST

Hookah Lounge

CHESHIRE ST

Bunhill Fields

CITY ROAD

Epworth St

Scrutton   St

S H O R E D I T C H

Shoreditch

Bonhill St

Sesha

Holywell Row

Curtain Road

Hearn St

Drunken Monkey

SHOREDITCH HIGH STREET

Pedley St

BUNHILL ROW

Worship   Street

Dysart St

Snowden St

Plough Yard

Fleur de Lis St

Elder St

COMMERCIAL ST

Quaker   Street

Calvin St

Grey Eagle St

Code St

BRICK LANE

Buxton Street

Finsbury Square

Christopher St

Clifton St

Pindar St

Appold St

Primrose St

Blossom St

1 Blossom Street

See Map 12

Vibe Bar

Spital St

Hunton St

CHISWELL ST

Wilson   St

Earl   St

Sun   Street

Folgate Street

Spital Sq

Lamb St

Woodseer St

Deal St

Maps

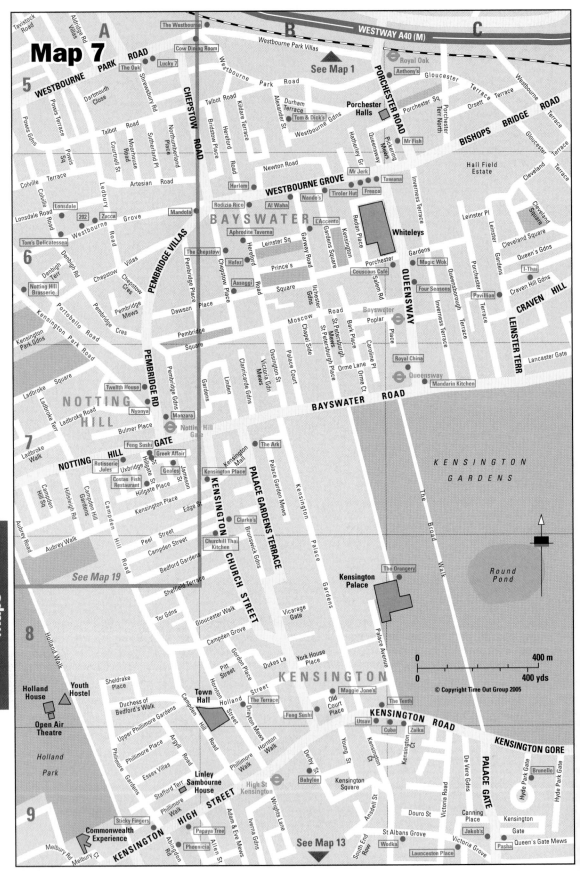

Map 7

WESTWAY A40 (M)

The Westbourne

Cow Dining Room

A

PARK ROAD

The Oak   Lucky 7

5 WESTBOURNE

Dartmouth Close

Powis Terrace

Powis Gdns

Powis Sq

Colville Terrace

Colville Road

Lonsdale

Lonsdale Road

202   Zucca

Tom's Delicatessen

Westbourne   Grove

Denbigh Rd

Denbigh Terr

Notting Hill Brasserie

SHREWSBURY RD

Shrewsbury Rd

Talbot Road

Northumberland Place

Moorhouse Road

Sutherland Pl

Courtnell St

Artesian Road

Ledbury   Grove

Chepstow Cres

Chepstow Road

Portobello   Road

Kensington Park Gdns

B

Westbourne Park Villas

Westbourne   Park   Road

See Map 1

Talbot Road

Kildare Terrace

Bridstow Place

Hereford   Road

Newton Road

Durham Terrace

Alexander St

Westbourne Gdns

Tom & Dick's

Harlem

Rodizio Rico   Al Waha

Mandola

WESTBOURNE GROVE

Nando's   Tiroler Hut

Mr Jerk

Fresco

Tawana

BAYSWATER

Aphrodite Taverna

Hereford

Hafez

Assaggi

PEMBRIDGE VILLAS

Chepstow   Place

Chepstow   Villas

The Chepstow

Pembridge Place

Pembridge Cres

Pembridge Mews

Pembridge   Road

Dawson   Place

Pembridge   Square

Leinster Sq

Prince's   Square

L'Accento

Garway Road

Gardens Square

Ilchester Gdns

Moscow   Road

St Petersburgh Mews

St Petersburgh Place

Chapel Side

Palace Court

Ossington St

Victoria Gdn Mews

Clanricarde Gdns

Linden   Gardens

PEMBRIDGE RD

Twelfth House

Nyonya

Manzara

Ladbroke   Square

Ladbroke Terr

NOTTING HILL

Ladbroke Road

Bulmer Place

Notting Hill Gate

C

Royal Oak

Anthony's   Gloucester   Terrace

Porchester Sq   Porchester Terr North

Orsett   Terrace

Westbourne   Terrace

BISHOPS   BRIDGE   ROAD

Gloucester   Terrace

PORCHESTER ROAD

Porchester   Halls

Queensway

Pickering Mews

Mr Fish

Hatherley Gr

Hall Field Estate

Cleveland Terrace

Redan Place

Kensington   Gardens

Whiteleys

Porchester   Gardens

Magic Wok

Couscous Café   Salem Rd

Four Seasons

Inverness Terrace

Leinster Pl

Leinster   Gardens

Cleveland Square

Cleveland Square

Queen's Gdns

I-Thai

Pavillion

Craven Hill Gdns

Queensborough Terrace

Porchester   Terrace

CRAVEN   HILL

LEINSTER TERR

QUEENSWAY

Bayswater   Poplar

Bayswater

Lancaster Gate

Royal China

Queensway

Mandarin Kitchen

Inverness Terrace

Orme Lane   Orme Ct   Caroline Pl

BAYSWATER   ROAD

The Broad   Walk

KENSINGTON   GARDENS

Round Pond

0   400 m
0   400 yds

© Copyright Time Out Group 2005

Feng Sushi

Greek Affair

Rotisserie Jules   Uxbridge St

Costas Fish Restaurant

Geales   Jameson St

Hillgate St

Hillgate Place

Kensington Place

NOTTING   HILL   GATE

Camden Hill Gardens

Camden Hill Sq

Hillsleigh Rd

Aubrey Road

Aubrey Walk

Campden Hill   Road

Peel   Street

Campden Street

Bedford Gardens

Sheffield Terrace

See Map 19

The Ark

Kensington Mall

Kensington Place

Clarke's

Churchill Thai Kitchen

KENSINGTON   CHURCH   STREET

PALACE GARDENS TERRACE

Palace Garden Mews

Brunswick Gdns

Edge St

Kensington   Church   Street

Palace   Gardens

Vicarage Gate

Kensington   Palace

The Orangery

Palace   Avenue

Tor Gdns

Gloucester Walk

Campden Grove

Pitt Street

Gordon Place

Dukes La

York House Place

KENSINGTON

Maggie Jones'

The Tenth

KENSINGTON   ROAD

KENSINGTON GORE

Holland Walk

Holland House

Youth Hostel

Open Air Theatre

Holland   Park

Sheldrake Place

Duchess of Bedford's Walk

Upper Phillimore Gardens

Phillimore Place

Phillimore Gardens

Essex Villas

Campden Hill   Road

Town Hall

Stafford Terr

Phillimore Gardens

Linley Sambourne House

Holland   Street

The Terrace

Feng Sushi

Horton Walk

Drayton Mews

Phillimore Walk

HIGH   STREET

Old Court Place

Utsav

Cuba   Zaika

Ct

Young St

Kensington   Ct

De Vere Gdns

PALACE GATE

Brunello

Hyde Park Gate   Hyde Park Gate

Sticky Fingers

Commonwealth Experience

KENSINGTON

Melbury Rd   Melbury Ct

Papaya Tree

Phoenicia

HIGH   STREET

Abingdon   Rd

Argyll Road

Adam & Eve Mews

Allen St

Babylon

High St Kensington

Derby St

Kensington Square

Iverna Gdns

Wrights Lane

See Map 13

Young St

Kensington   Ct

Ansdell St

Douro St

St Albans Grove

South End Row

Wodka

Launceston Place

Victoria Road

Canning Place

Jakob's

Victoria Grove

Pasha

Kensington Gate

Queen's Gate Mews

Map 8

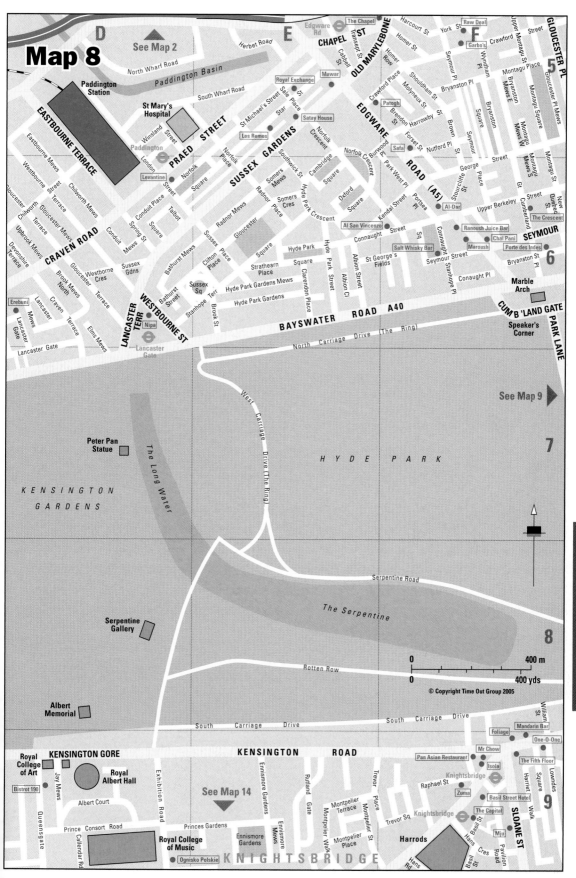

See Map 2

Paddington Station

Paddington Basin

North Wharf Road

Herbet Road

South Wharf Road

St Mary's Hospital

EASTBOURNE TERRACE

Eastbourne Mews

Westbourne Terrace

Chilworth Mews

Gloucester Terrace

Chilworth Terrace

Gloucester Mews

Upbrook Mews

Devonshire Terrace

CRAVEN ROAD

Gloucester Terrace

Westbourne Cres

Brook Mews North

Sussex Gdns

Craven Terrace

Elms Mews

Lancaster Mews

Erebuni

Lancaster Gate

Lancaster Gate

PRAED STREET

Winsland Street

Paddington

London Street

Levantine

Norfolk Square

Talbot Square

Conduit Place

Spring St

Conduit Mews

Bathurst Mews

Bathurst Street

Stanhope Terr

Sussex Sq

Brook St

WESTBOURNE ST

LANCASTER TERR

Nipa

Lancaster Gate

St Michael's Street

Sale Place

Star St

Los Remos

Norfolk Place

Norfolk Square

Southwick St

Somers Mews

Radnor Mews

Radnor Place

Somers Cres

Gloucester Square

Sussex Place

Clifton Place

Sussex Square

Strathearn Place

Hyde Park Gardens Mews

Hyde Park Gardens

SUSSEX GARDENS

Cambridge Square

Oxford Square

Hyde Park Crescent

Hyde Park Square

Hyde Park Street

Clarendon Place

Albion Street

Albion Cl

St George's Fields

Connaught Street

The Chapel

Edgware Rd

CHAPEL ST

Transept St

OLD MARYLEBONE

Cabbell St

Crabbel St

Royal Exchange

Mawar

Satay House

Norfolk Crescent

Burwood Pl

Norfolk Crescent

Connaught Street

Harcourt St

Homer St

Homer Row

Shouldham St

Crawford Place

Molyneux St

Patogh

Brendon St

Harrowby St

Forset St

Safa

Nutford Pl

Al San Vincenzo

Kendal Street

Salt Whisky Bar

Albion Street

EDGWARE ROAD (A5)

York St

Raw Deal

Garbo's

Seymour Pl

Wyndham Pl

Brown St

Bryanston Pl

Bryanston Square

George Street

Stourcliffe St

Portsea Pl

Al-Dar

Connaught St

Seymour Street

Stanhope Pl

Harcourt St

Crawford St

Upper Montagu St

Montagu Place

Montagu Square

Montagu Mansions E

Montagu Mews W

Montagu Mews S

Montagu St

Gr Cumberland

New Quebec St

The Crescent

Ranoush Juice Bar

Chai Pani

Maroush

Porte des Indes

Bryanston Pl

SEYMOUR

Conaught Pl

Marble Arch

Speaker's Corner

GLOUCESTER PL

Gloucester Pl Mews

Upper Berkeley Street

CUMB'LAND GATE

PARK LANE

BAYSWATER ROAD A40

North Carriage Drive (The Ring)

See Map 9

Peter Pan Statue

The Long Water

HYDE PARK

West Carriage Drive (The Ring)

KENSINGTON GARDENS

Serpentine Road

Serpentine Gallery

The Serpentine

Rotten Row

0   400 m

0   400 yds

© Copyright Time Out Group 2005

Albert Memorial

South Carriage Drive

South Carriage Drive

Foliage

Mandarin Bar

William St

One-O-One

Mr Chow

Royal College of Art

KENSINGTON GORE

Jay Mews

Bistrot 190

Albert Court

Royal Albert Hall

Exhibition Road

KENSINGTON ROAD

See Map 14

Ennismore Gardens

Rutland Gate

Pan Asian Restaurant

Isola

Knightsbridge

Raphael St

Zuma

The Fifth Floor

Isola

Basil Street Hotel

Harriet Walk

Lowndes Square

SLOANE ST

Queensgate

Prince Consort Road

Royal College of Music

Ognisko Polskie

Princes Gardens

Ennismore Gardens

Ennismore Mews

KNIGHTSBRIDGE

Montpelier Terrace

Montpelier Walk

Montpelier Place

Montpelier St

Trevor Place

Trevor Sq

Knightsbridge

Harrods

Hans Rd

The Capital

Basil St

Hans Cres

Mju

Pavilion Road

Callendar Rd

Maps

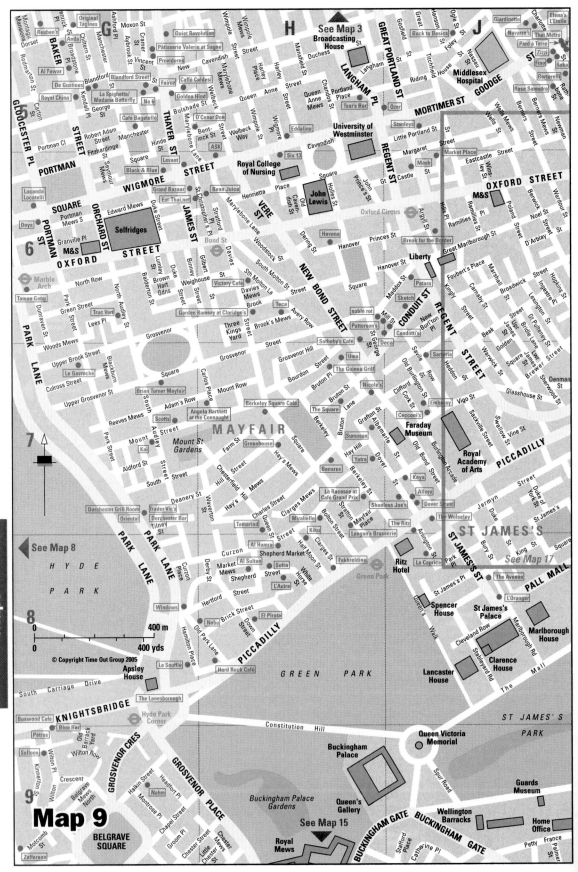

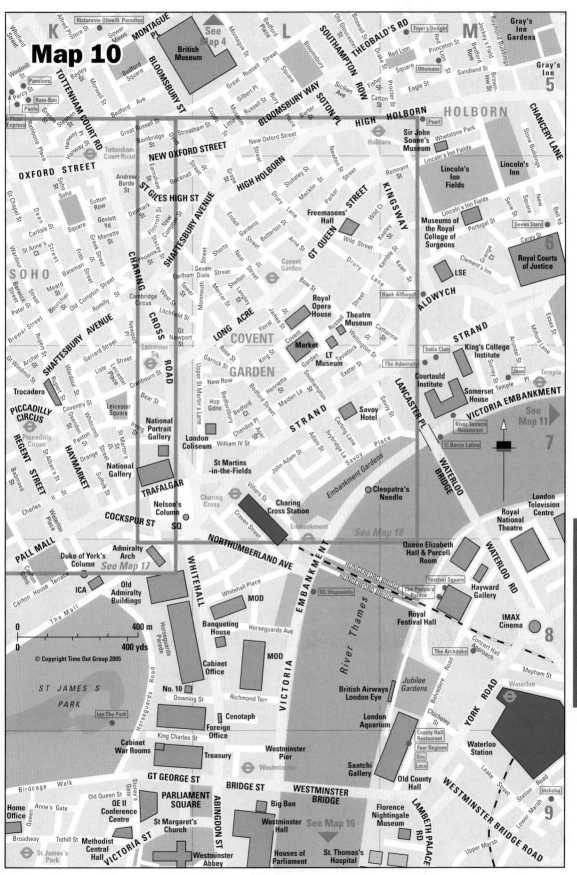

Map 10

Ristorante Olivelli Paradiso

K

Alfred Pl
Windmill St
Whitfield Street
Store St
Gower Mews
MONTAGUE PL
See Map 4
British Museum

Bayley St
Bedford Square
Montague St
Bedford Place
Bedford Square

Percy St
Passione
Bam-Bou
Paolo
Pizza Express
Rathbone Place

Morwell St
Gresse St
Stephen St
Bayley St

BLOOMSBURY ST

Gilbert Pl
Great Russell Street

Russell Square
Bury Place

L

Old Gloucester St
Boswell St
THEOBALD'S RD
Fryer's Delight
Red Lion
Red Lion Square
Princeton St
Ottomans
Sandland St

M

Gray's Inn Gardens
Jockey's Field
Raymond Buildings
Bedford Row
Brown-low St

Gray's Inn

5

SOUTHAMPTON ROW
BLOOMSBURY WAY
SOTON PL
Sicilian Ave

Fisher St
Procter St
Eagle St
Catton St

HIGH HOLBORN
Pearl
HOLBORN
Whetstone Park
Stone Buildings

CHANCERY LANE

TOTTENHAM COURT RD
Great Russell St
Bainbridge St
Streatham St
NEW OXFORD STREET
New Oxford Street
Holborn
Sir John Soane's Museum

Hanway St
Hanway Pl
Dyott St
Bucknall St

Lincoln's Inn Fields

Lincoln's Inn Fields
Lincoln's Inn

6

OXFORD STREET
Soho St
Sutton Row
St GILES HIGH ST
Denmark St
New Compton St
Stukeley St
Macklin St

Newton St
Remnant St
Lincoln's Inn Fields
Portugal St
Serle St
New Square
Bell Yd

Gt Chapel St
Dean St
Carlisle St
Andrew Borde St
Flitcroft St
Stacey St
Drury Lane
Parker St

Freemasons' Hall

Museums of the Royal College of Surgeons
Seven Stars

SOHO
Goslett Yd
Manette St
Greek St
Phoenix St

Endell St
Betterton St
Arne St
GT QUEEN STREET

KINGSWAY

Clement's Inn
Grange Ct

Carey St
Royal Courts of Justice

St Anne's Ct
Bateman St
Old Compton Street
Cambridge Circus
Shorts Gardens

Keeley St
Kemble St
Kean St

LSE

Frith St
Greek St
Romilly St
West St
Neal St
Shelton St
Langley St

Wild Street
Drury Lane

Peter St
Meard St
Bourchier St
Tower St
Earlham St
Seven Dials
Mercer St

Bow St
Russell St

Bank Aldwych
ALDWYCH

STRAND

Berwick Street
Brewer Street
SHAFTESBURY AVENUE
Cambridge Circus
Litchfield St
LONG ACRE

Floral St
James St
Covent Garden

Royal Opera House
Theatre Museum
Catherine St

India Club
King's College Institute

Essex St
Milford Lane

Rupert St
Archer St
Gerrard Street
Newport Pl
Gt Newport St

COVENT GARDEN
Rose St
King St
Market
LT Museum
Wellington St
Exeter St
Tavistock St

The Admiralty

Jaan
Temple Pl
Temple

Gt Windmill St
Lisle St
Leicester Place
Garrick St
Bedford St
Henrietta St
Maiden La
Southampton St

Arundel St

Trocadero
Leicester Square
Cranbourn St
New Row
Hop Gdns
Bedfordbury
Chandos Pl
Adam St

Courtauld Institute
Somerset House
VICTORIA EMBANKMENT

See Map 11

7

PICCADILLY CIRCUS
Coventry St
Whitcomb St
Bear St
Upper St Martin's Lane
William IV St

STRAND
Savoy
Carting Lane
Savoy Pl
Savoy Hotel

River Terrace Restaurant
El Barco Latino

Piccadilly Circus
Panton St
Orange St
Irving St
National Portrait Gallery
London Coliseum

Ivybridge La

REGENT STREET
Babmaes St
St Alban's St
St Martin's St
National Gallery
St Martins -in-the-Fields

John Adam St
Adam St
Embankment Gardens

Cleopatra's Needle

WATERLOO BRIDGE

London Television Centre

HAYMARKET
Suffolk St
TRAFALGAR
Nelson's Column
SQ
Charing Cross
Villiers St

Charing Cross Station

Royal National Theatre

Charles II St
Waterloo Pl
COCKSPUR ST
Craven Street

Embankment

See Map 18

PALL MALL
Admiralty Arch
NORTHUMBERLAND AVE

Duke of York's Column
See Map 17

EMBANKMENT
HUNGERFORD BRIDGE
HUNGERFORD BRIDGE

Queen Elizabeth Hall & Purcell Room

WATERLOO RD

Carlton House Terrace
ICA
Old Admiralty Buildings

WHITEHALL
Whitehall Place
MOD
RS Hispaniola
Festival Square
The People's Palace
Hayward Gallery

The Mall
Banqueting House
Horseguards Ave

Royal Festival Hall
IMAX Cinema

8

Horseguards Parade
Cabinet Office
MOD

River Thames

The Archduke
Concert Hall Approach
Mepham St

ST JAMES'S PARK
Inn The Park
No. 10
Downing St
Richmond Terr

British Airways London Eye
Jubilee Gardens

Belvedere Road
Chichley St

Waterloo

YORK ROAD

Horseguards Road
King Charles St
Cenotaph
Foreign Office

London Aquarium
County Hall Restaurant
Four Regions
Ozu
Loco

Waterloo Station

Cabinet War Rooms
Treasury
Westminster Pier

Saatchi Gallery
Old County Hall

Leake Street
Station Road
Inshoku

9

Birdcage Walk
GT GEORGE ST
BRIDGE ST
WESTMINSTER BRIDGE

WESTMINSTER BRIDGE ROAD
Lower Marsh

Home Office
Anne's Gate
Old Queen St
Storey's Gate
PARLIAMENT SQUARE
ABINGDON ST
Big Ben

Florence Nightingale Museum

LAMBETH PALACE RD

QE II Conference Centre
St Margaret's Church
Westminster Hall
See Map 16

Upper Marsh

Broadway
Tothill St
Methodist Central Hall

VICTORIA ST
Westminster Abbey
Houses of Parliament
St. Thomas's Hospital

St James's Park

0   400 m
0   400 yds
© Copyright Time Out Group 2005

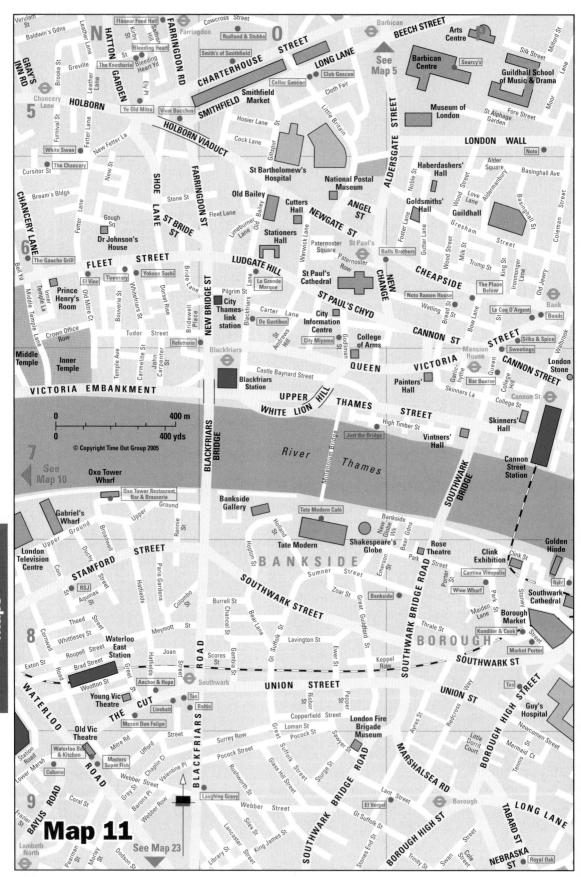

Map 11

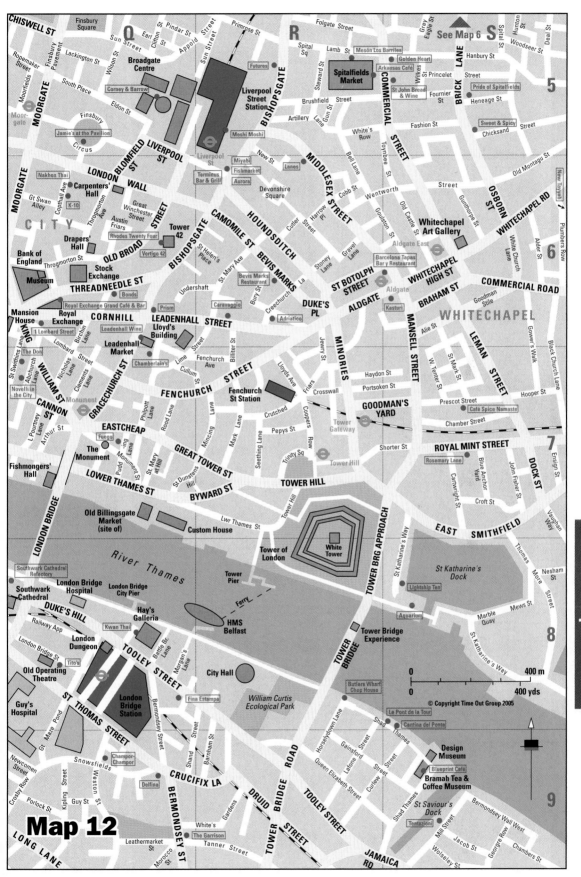

Map 12

Maps

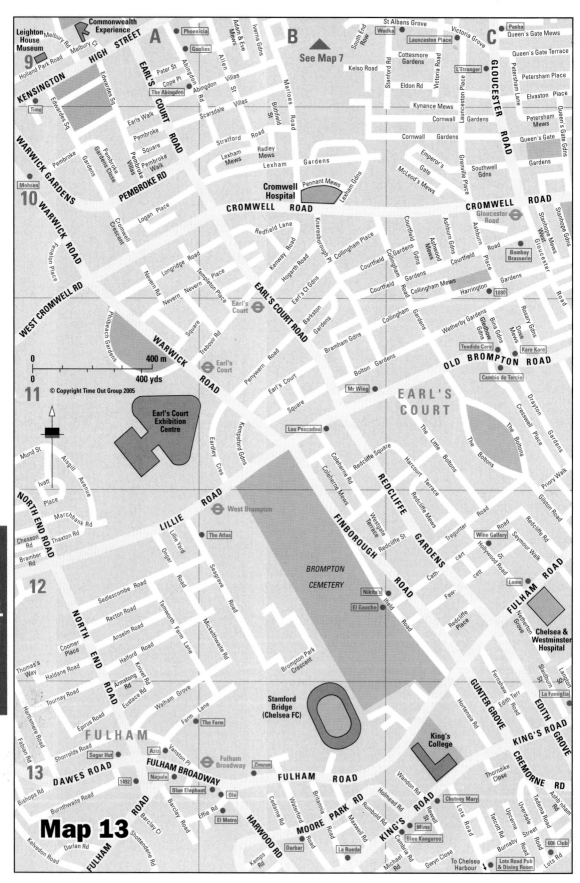

Leighton House Museum
Commonwealth Experience
Melbury Rd
Melbury Ct
HIGH STREET
KENSINGTON
Holland Park Road
Phoenicia
Goolies
Adam & Eve Mews
Iverna Gdns
St Albans Grove
South End Row
Wodka
Victoria Grove
Pasha
Queen's Gate Mews
Launceston Place
See Map 7
Kelso Road
Stanford Rd
Cottesmore Gardens
Eldon Rd
L'Etranger
Queen's Gate Terrace
Petersham Lane
Petersham Place
Elvaston Place
Petersham Mews
Queen's Gate Gdns
Queen's Gate
Gardens
A
B
C
9
Pater St
Cope Pl
The Abingdon
Abingdon Rd
Abingdon Villas
Allen St
Marloes Road
Birthfield St
Kynance Mews
Cornwall
Cornwall Gardens
Emperor's Gate
McLeod's Mews
Grenville Place
Southwell Gdns
GLOUCESTER ROAD
Timo
EARL'S COURT ROAD
Earls Walk
Pembroke Square
Pembroke Villas
Pembroke Walk
Pembroke Gardens Close
Pembroke Gardens
Scarsdale Villas
Stratford Road
Radley Mews
Lexham Mews
Lexham Gardens
Lexham Gdns
Mohsen
PEMBROKE RD
Logan Place
Cromwell Crescent
Cromwell Hospital
Pennant Mews
CROMWELL ROAD
Redfield Lane
Knaresborough Pl
Collingham Place
Courtfield Gdns
Courtfield Gardens
Ashwood Mews
Ashburn Gdns
Ashburn Place
CROMWELL ROAD
Gloucester Road
Stanhope Gdns
West Gloucester
Stanhope Mews
Bombay Brasserie
10
WARWICK GARDENS
WARWICK ROAD
Fenelon Place
Longridge Road
Templeton Place
Nevern Rd
Nevern Place
Kenway Road
Hogarth Road
Earl's Ct Gdns
Collingham
Courtfield Gardens
Collingham Road
Collingham Mews
Harrington Gardens
1880
WEST CROMWELL RD
Philbeach Gardens
Trebovir Rd
Nevern Square
Earl's Court
EARL'S COURT ROAD
Barkston Gardens
Bramham Gardens
Collingham Gardens
Wetherby Gardens
Bina Gdns
Rosary Gdns
Gledhow Gdns
Dove Mews
Tendido Cero
Kare Kare
OLD BROMPTON ROAD
Cambio de Tercio
400 m
400 yds
© Copyright Time Out Group 2005
11
Earl's Court
WARWICK ROAD
Penywern Road
Earl's Court Square
Kempsford Gdns
Bolton Gardens
Mr Wing
EARL'S COURT
Drayton Gardens
Cresswell Place
Priory Walk
Gilston Road
Earl's Court Exhibition Centre
Lou Pescadou
Eardley Cres
Redcliffe Square
Coleherne Rd
Coleherne Mews
The Little Boltons
Harcourt Terrace
The Boltons
Mund St
Aisgill Avenue
Ivatt Place
Marchbank Rd
LILLIE ROAD
Lillie Yard
Ongar Road
West Brompton
BROMPTON CEMETERY
Westgate Terrace
Redcliffe Mews
Redcliffe St
Tregunter Road
Hollywood Road
Wine Gallery
Seymour Walk
Redcliffe Rd
FULHAM ROAD
Chesson Rd
Bramber Rd
The Atlas
FINBOROUGH ROAD
REDCLIFFE GARDENS
cart
Cath-
cett
Faw-
Lomo
12
NORTH END ROAD
Sedlescombe Road
Racton Road
Anselm Road
Tamworth Farm Lane
Micklethwaite Rd
Seagrave Road
Nikita's
Ifield Road
El Gauche
Netherton Grove
Chelsea & Westminster Hospital
Coomer Place
Halford Road
Knivet Rd
Armstrong Rd
Brompton Park Crescent
Slaidburn St
Langton
Fenshaw Rd
La Famiglia
Thomas's Way
Haldane Road
Tournay Road
Eustace Rd
Walham Grove
Stamford Bridge (Chelsea FC)
GUNTER GROVE
Hortensia Rd
Edith Terr
EDITH GROVE
KING'S ROAD
Epirus Road
Farm Lane
The Farm
King's College
Wandon Rd
Thorndike Close
CREMORNE RD
FULHAM
Shorrolds Road
Sugar Hut
Aziz
Vanston Pl
Fulham Broadway
Zimzun
FULHAM ROAD
Holmead Rd
Ashb'ham Rd
Tadema Road
Uverdale Road
DAWES ROAD
Bishops Rd
Burnthwaite Road
1492
Napule
FULHAM BROADWAY
Blue Elephant
Olé
Effie Rd
El Metro
Barclay Road
HARWOOD RD
Cedarne Rd
Waterford Rd
MOORE PARK RD
Britannia Rd
Rumbold Rd
Maxwell Rd
KING'S ROAD
Rewell St
Chutney Mary
Lots Rd
Upcerne Road
Burnaby Street
606 Club
13
Fabian Rd
Hartismere Rd
Kelvedon Road
Darlan Rd
Shottendene Rd
FULHAM ROAD
Barclay Cl
Kemps Rd
Darbar
La Rueda
Cambria Rd
Michael Rd
Gwyn Close
Mims
Blue Kangaroo
To Chelsea Harbour
Lots Road Pub & Dining Room
Lots Rd

Map 13

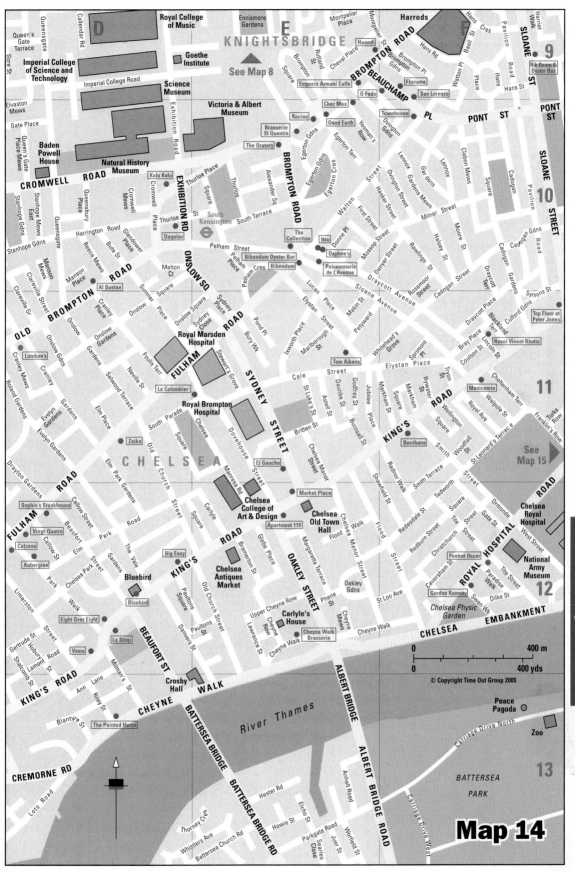

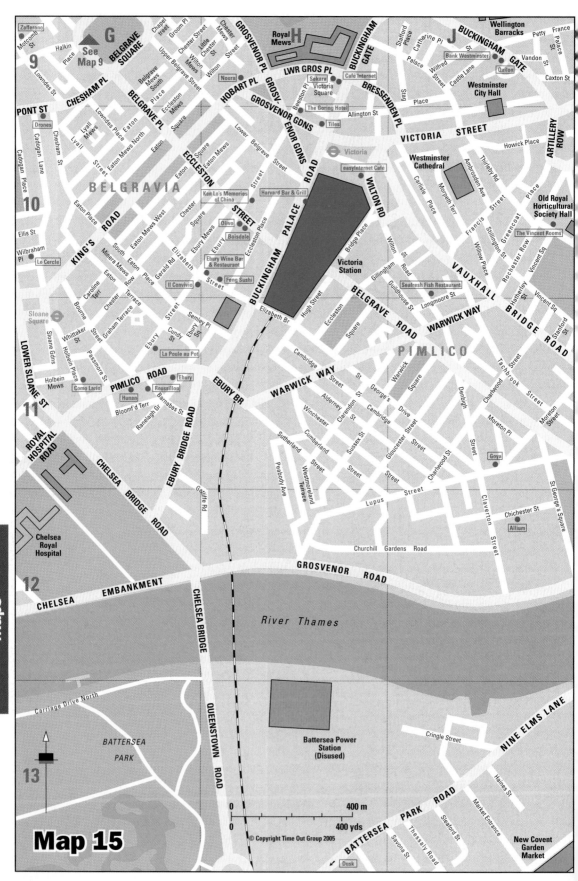

Map 15

© Copyright Time Out Group 2005

| 0 | | | 400 m |
| 0 | | | 400 yds |

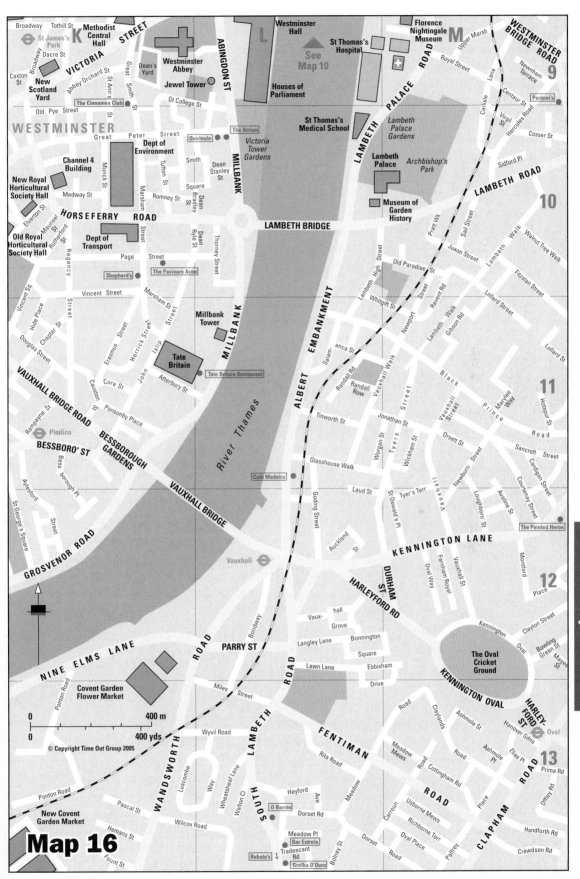

Map 16

Maps

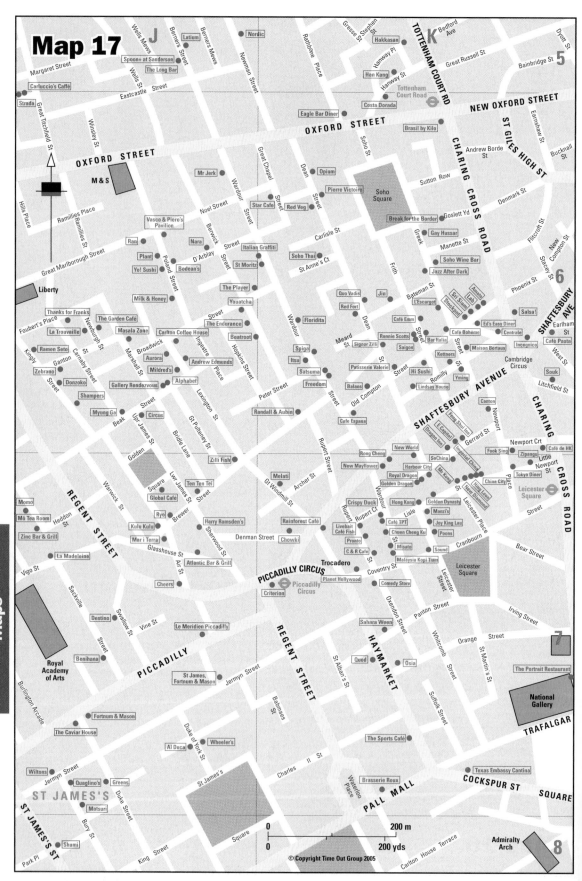

Map 17

J

Nordic
Latium
Berners Mews
Wells Mews
Margaret Street
Spoon+ at Sanderson
The Long Bar
Carluccio's Caffè
Eastcastle Street
Strada
Great Titchfield St
Winsley St

OXFORD STREET
M&S
Ramillies Place
Ramillies St
Great Marlborough Street
Hills Place

Liberty

Thanks for Franks
The Garden Café
La Trouvaille
Foubert's Place
Ramen Seto
Ganton Street
Zebrano
Donzoko
Shampers
Myung Ga
Beak Street
Circus

Momo
Mò Tea Room
Zinc Bar & Grill
La Madeleine
Vigo St
REGENT STREET
Heddon St
Warwick Street
Golden Square
Destino
Swallow St
Vine St
Cheers

Royal Academy of Arts
PICCADILLY
Benihana
Sackville Street
Le Meridien Piccadilly

Fortnum & Mason
The Caviar House
Burlington Arcade
Al Duca
Wheelers
Duke of York St
Wiltons
Jermyn Street
Quaglino's
Greens
ST JAMES'S
Matsuri
Duke Street
Bury St
Shumi
Park Pl
ST JAMES'S ST
King Street

K

Hakkasan
TOTTENHAM COURT RD
Bedford Ave
Gresse St
Stephen St
Rathbone Place
Great Russell St
Hanway Pl
Han Kang
Hanway St
Bainbridge St
5
Dyott St

Tottenham Court Road
Costa Dorada
NEW OXFORD STREET
Andrew Borde St
ST GILES HIGH ST
Earnshaw St
Bucknall St
Eagle Bar Diner
Brasil by Kilo
OXFORD STREET
Soho St
Sutton Row
Denmark St
Fitcroft St
New Compton St
Stacey St

Mr Jerk
Opium
Dean Street
Pierre Victoire
Star Café
Red Veg
Wardour Street
Soho Square
Break for the Border
Goslett Yd
Greek St
Gay Hussar
Manette St
6
Vasco & Piero's Pavilion
Carlisle St
Soho Wine Bar
Phoenix St
Ran
Nara
D'Arblay Street
Italian Graffiti
Soho Thai
Jazz After Dark
SHAFTESBURY AVE
Plant
Poland Street
St Moritz
St Anne's Ct
Frith Street
Earlham St
Yo! Sushi
Bodean's
Quo Vadis
Jin
Sri Siam
Amato
Salsa!
Berwick Street
The Player
Red Fort
Bateman St
L'Escargot
Stockpot
Ed's Easy Diner
Centrale
Milk & Honey
Yauatcha
Café Emm
Café Boheme
Incognico
Café Pasta
The Endurance
Floridita
Dean Street
Ronnie Scotts
Bar Italia
Maison Bertaux
West St
Masala Zone
Carlton Coffee House
Beatroot
Signor Zilli
Saigon
Kettners
Souk
Broadwick Street
Meard St
Yming
Cambridge Circus
Litchfield St
Aurora
Andrew Edmunds
Spiga
Itsu
Patisserie Valerie
Hi Sushi
Romilly St
Mildred's
Alphabet
Lexington St
Satsuma
Balans
Old Compton Street
Lindsay House
Gallery Rendezvous
Freedom
Canton
Randall & Aubin
Newport St
CHARING CROSS ROAD
Bridle Lane
Gt Pulteney St
Peter Street
Cafe Espana
Jeng Shui Inn
E Capital
Gerrard St
Newport Crt
Café de HK
Zilli Fish
Dragons Inn
Imperial China
Fook Sing
Zipangu
Little Newport St
Melati
New World
Rong Cheng
SoChina
Tokyo Diner
Ten Ten Tei
New Mayflower
Harbour City
Chine City
Leicester Square
Global Café
Gt Windmill St
Archer St
Rupert Street
Royal Dragon
Mr Kong
New Diamond
Ryo
Golden Dragon
Hing Loon
Lwr James St
Brewer Street
Harry Ramsden's
Crispy Duck
Hong Kong
Golden Dynasty
Joy King Lau
Kulu Kulu
Denman Street
Rainforest Café
Livebait Café Fish
Café TPT
Lisle St
Manzi's
Poons
Mar i Terra
Chowki
Pronto
Chuen Cheng Ku
Leicester Place
Glasshouse St
Sherwood St
C & R Cafe
Misato
Sound
Atlantic Bar & Grill
Rupert Ct
Malaysia Kopi Tiam
Leicester Square
Bear Street
Air St
Trocadero
Coventry St
PICCADILLY CIRCUS
Planet Hollywood
Comedy Store
Leicester Street
Cranbourn St
Criterion
Piccadilly Circus
Irving Street
7
Ovendon Street
Panton Street
Sahara Ween
Whitcomb Street
St Martin's St
REGENT STREET
HAYMARKET
Quod
Osia
Orange Street
The Portrait Restaurant
St James, Fortnum & Mason
Jermyn Street
St Alban's St
National Gallery
Regent Street
Babmaes St
Suffolk Street
TRAFALGAR
The Sports Café
Charles II St
COCKSPUR ST
SQUARE
St James's Street
Waterloo Place
Brasserie Roux
Texas Embassy Cantina
PALL MALL
Square
Admiralty Arch
8

0   200 m
0   200 yds

© Copyright Time Out Group 2005
Carlton House Terrace

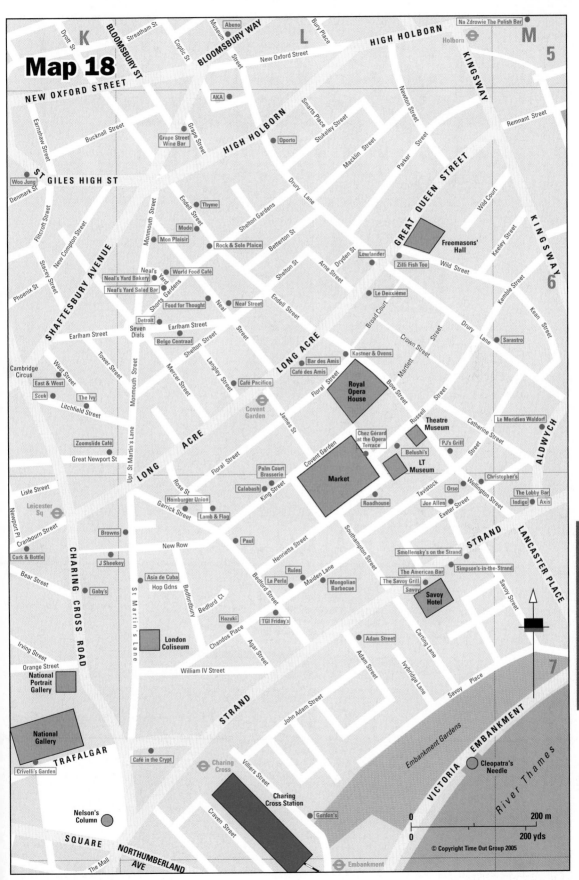

Map 18

New Oxford Street

St Giles High St

Shaftesbury Avenue

High Holborn

High Holborn

Kingsway

Great Queen Street

Aldwych

Long Acre

Long Acre

Strand

Strand

Charing Cross Road

Victoria Embankment

Lancaster Place

River Thames

Trafalgar Square

Northumberland Ave

The Mall

K 5 L M
6
7

Streatham St
Coptic St
Dyott St
Bloomsbury St
Bloomsbury Way
Museum Street
New Oxford Street
Bury Place
High Holborn
Holborn
Kingsway
Remnant Street
Newton Street
Abeno
Na Zdrowie The Polish Bar
AKA
Earnshaw Street
Bucknall Street
Grape Street
Grape Street Wine Bar
Smarts Place
Stukeley Street
Macklin Street
Parker Street
Wild Court
Keeley Street
Oporto
Drury Lane
Denmark St
Woo Jung
New Compton Street
Monmouth Street
Endell Street
Shelton Gardens
Betterton St
Dryden St
Lowlander
Wild Street
Kemble Street
Kean Street
Thyme
Mode
Mon Plaisir
Rock & Sole Plaice
Shelton St
Arne Street
Zilli Fish Too
Freemasons' Hall
Flitcroft Street
Phoenix St
Stacey Street
Neal's Yard
World Food Café
Neal's Yard Bakery
Neal's Yard Salad Bar
Shorts Gardens
Food for Thought
Neal Street
Endell Street
Broad Court
Le Deuxième
Crown Street
Martlett
Drury Lane
Sarastro
Earlham Street
Detroit
Seven Dials
Earlham Street
Belgo Centraal
Shelton Street
Langley Street
Long Acre
Bar des Amis
Café des Amis
Kastner & Ovens
Bow Street
Le Meridien Waldorf
Cambridge Circus
West Street
Tower Street
Mercer Street
Monmouth Street
Floral Street
James St
Royal Opera House
Russell Street
Catherine Street
East & West
Souk
The Ivy
Café Pacifico
Covent Garden
Theatre Museum
PJ's Grill
Litchfield Street
Long Acre
Belushi's
Christopher's
Zoomslide Café
Rose St
Covent Garden
LT Museum
Wellington Street
Orso
The Lobby Bar
Indigo Axis
Great Newport St
Upr St Martin's Lane
Floral Street
Hamburger Union
Garrick Street
King Street
Palm Court Brasserie
Calabash
Market
Tavistock Street
Joe Allen
Exeter Street
Roadhouse
Lisle Street
Leicester Sq
Lamb & Flag
Newport Pl
Cranbourn Street
Browns
Paul
New Row
Henrietta Street
Southampton Street
Smollensky's on the Strand
Strand
Cork & Bottle
Bear Street
J Sheekey
Gaby's
Asia de Cuba
Hop Gdns
Bedfordbury
Rules
La Perla
Maiden Lane
Mongolian Barbecue
The American Bar
Simpson's-in-the-Strand
The Savoy Grill
Savoy
Savoy Street
Irving Street
Orange Street
St Martin's Lane
Bedford Ct
Hazuki
Chandos Place
Agar Street
TGI Friday's
London Coliseum
Savoy Hotel
Carting Lane
Adam Street
National Portrait Gallery
William IV Street
Strand
John Adam Street
Adam Street
Ivybridge Lane
Savoy Place
National Gallery
Trafalgar
Embankment Gardens
Cleopatra's Needle
Nelson's Column
Square
Café in the Crypt
Charing Cross
Villiers Street
Crivelli's Garden
Craven Street
Charing Cross Station
Gordon's
Embankment
Chez Gérard at the Opera Terrace
Bedford Street

0 200 m
0 200 yds
© Copyright Time Out Group 2005

Maps

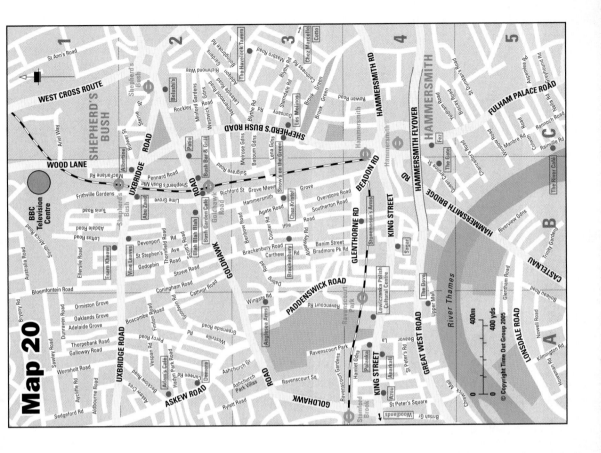

Map 20

WEST CROSS ROUTE

WOOD LANE

BBC Television Centre

SHEPHERD'S BUSH

UXBRIDGE ROAD

ASKEW ROAD

GOLDHAWK ROAD

PADDENSWICK ROAD

SHEPHERD'S BUSH ROAD

HAMMERSMITH RD

HAMMERSMITH

HAMMERSMITH FLYOVER

HAMMERSMITH BRIDGE

FULHAM PALACE ROAD

LONSDALE ROAD

CASTELNAU

GREAT WEST ROAD

KING STREET

GLENTHORNE RD

BEADON RD

River Thames

Belushi's
Patio
Bush Bar & Grill
Snow on the Green
Albertine
Abu Zaad
Lime Grove
Blah Blah Blah
Bush Garden Café
Los Molinos
Chez Kristof
Esarn Kheaw
Vine Leaves
Adam's Café
Demera
Anglesea Arms
Brackenbury
The Havelock Tavern
Chez Marcelle
Cotto
Foz
The Gate
Stonemason's Arms
Sagar
The Dove
Azou
Anarkali
Polanka
The River Café

0   400m
0   400 yds

© Copyright Time Out Group 2005

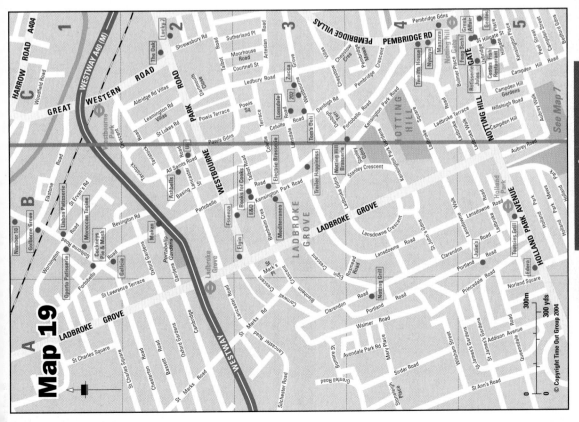

Map 19

HARROW ROAD A404

GREAT WESTERN ROAD

WESTWAY A40 (M)

WESTBOURNE PARK ROAD

LADBROKE GROVE

NOTTING HILL

HOLLAND PARK AVENUE

PEMBRIDGE VILLAS

PEMBRIDGE RD

NOTTING HILL GATE

WESTWAY

See Map 7

Number 10
Lisboa Patisserie
Oporto Patisserie
Moroccan Tagine
Galicia
Makan
Cockneys Pie & Mash
The Oak
Lucky 7
Zucca
202
Lonsdale
Tom's Deli
Books for Cooks
Essenza
E&O
Electric Brasserie
Mediterraneo
Elgin
Trailer Happiness
Notting Grill
Ashbells
Greek Affair
Manzara
Nyonya
Twelfth House
Rotisserie Jules
Costas Fish Restaurant
Feng Sushi
Geales
Julie's
Tootsies Grill
Edera

0   300m
0   300 yds

© Copyright Time Out Group 2004

Maps

Time Out Eating & Drinking 379

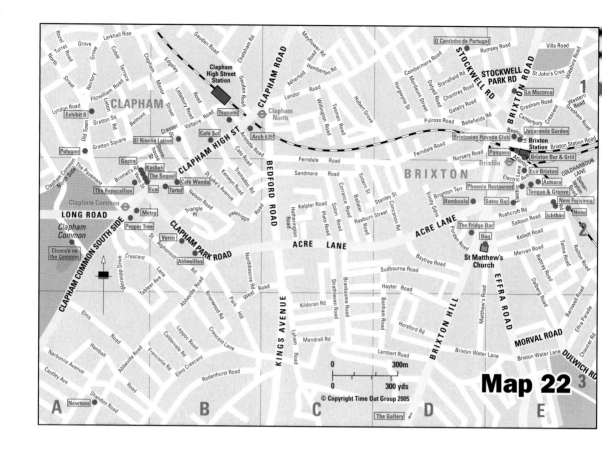

CLAPHAM

BRIXTON

O Cantinho de Portugal

STOCKWELL PARK RD

BRIXTON ROAD

La Mazorca

Jacaranda Garden

Brixtonian Havana Club

Pangaea

Brixton Bar & Grill

Eco Brixton

Asmara

Phoenix Restaurant

Tongue & Groove

Bamboula

Satay Bar

New Fujiyama

Ichiban

Neon

The Fridge Bar

Bug

St Matthew's Church

Exhibit B

Tsunami

Café Sol

El Rincón Latino

Polygon

Gastro

Kasbah

The Sequel

Café Wanda

The Rapscallion

Eco

Tartuf

Metro

Pepper Tree

Verso

Cicero's on the Common

Abbevilles

Map 22

© Copyright Time Out Group 2005

The Gallery

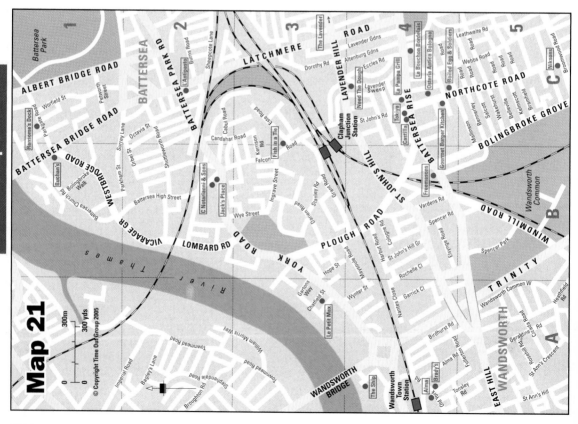

Map 21

BATTERSEA

WANDSWORTH

The Lavender

L'Antipasto

Need The Dough

La Pampa Grill

Le Bouchon Bordelais

Osteria Antica Bologna

Boiled Egg & Soldiers

Niksons

Tokiya

Castilla

Gourmet Burger Kitchen

Freemasons

Ransome's Dock

Buchan's

C Notarianni & Sons

Jack's Place

Fish in a Tie

Le Petit Max

Brady's

The Ship

Alma

© Copyright Time Out Group 2005

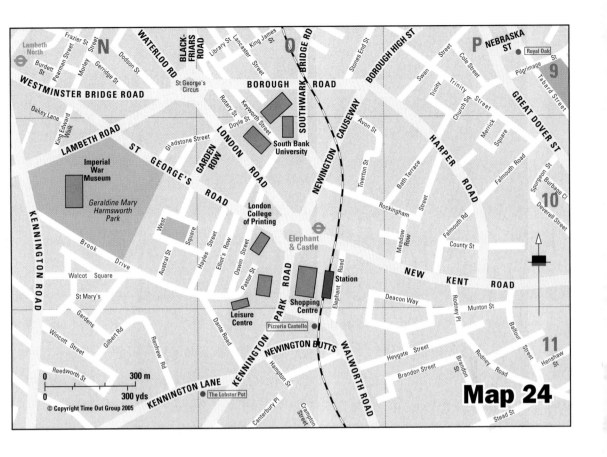

Map 24

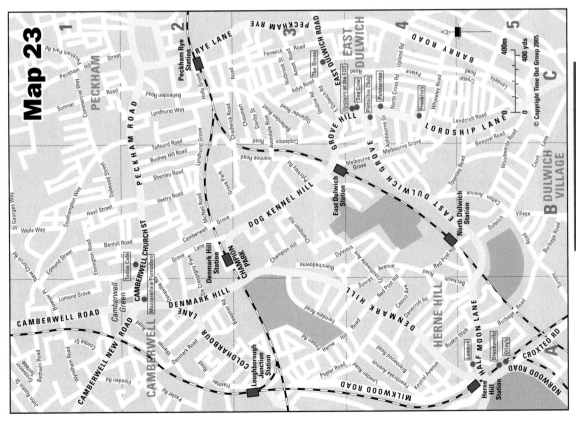

Map 23

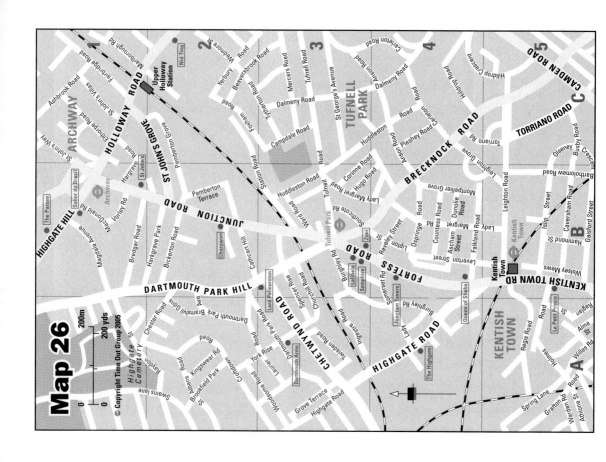

Map 26

200m
200 yds
© Copyright Time Out Group 2005

ARCHWAY
HIGHGATE HILL
HOLLOWAY ROAD
ST JOHN'S GROVE
Upper Holloway Station
Nid Ting
TUFNELL PARK
BRECKNOCK ROAD
TORRIANO ROAD
CAMDEN ROAD
JUNCTION ROAD
DARTMOUTH PARK HILL
CHETWYND ROAD
FORTESS ROAD
HIGHGATE ROAD
KENTISH TOWN
KENTISH TOWN RD
Kentish Town
The Parsee
Sabor de Brasil
Archway
Charuwan
Lord Palmerston
Dartmouth Arms
Zumi
Lalibela
Samphire
Bullet
Junction Tavern
Queen of Sheba
The Highgate
Le Petit Prince
Highgate Cemetery

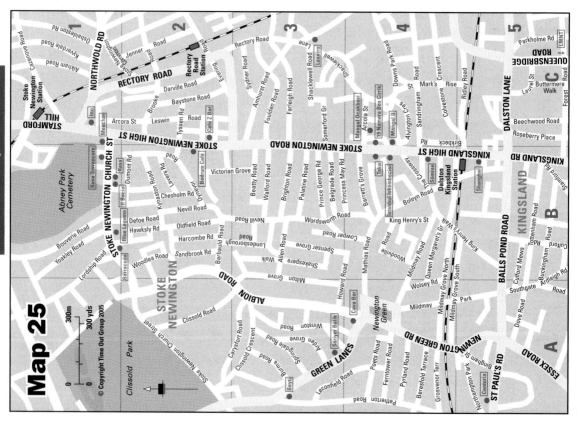

Map 25

300m
300 yds
© Copyright Time Out Group 2005

STAMFORD HILL
NORTHWOLD RD
RECTORY ROAD
Rectory Road Station
Stoke Newington Station
STOKE NEWINGTON CHURCH ST
STOKE NEWINGTON HIGH ST
STOKE NEWINGTON ROAD
KINGSLAND HIGH ST
Dalston Kingsland Station
KINGSLAND RD
DALSTON LANE
QUEENSBRIDGE ROAD
STOKE NEWINGTON
ALBION ROAD
GREEN LANES
NEWINGTON GREEN RD
Newington Green
BALLS POND ROAD
KINGSLAND
ST PAUL'S RD
ESSEX ROAD
Abney Park Cemetery
Clissold Park
Itto
Mesclun
Rasa Travancore
Rasa
Il Bacio
Blue Legume
Barracuda
Café Z Bar
Burdum Cafe
Cava Bar
Sariyer Balik
Beryl
Centuria
Laxeiro
Mangal Ocakbasi
19 Numara Bos Cirrik
Mangal II
Takai
Istanbul Iskembecisi
Somine
Shanghai
Buttermere Walk
LMNT

Maps

Map 28

Brew House
Jack Straw's Castle
HAMPSTEAD HEATH
Vale of Health Pond
Whitestone Pond
Heath
Pryors Field
Keats' House
HAMPSTEAD HIGH STREET
The Wells
Safir
Al Casbah
Jin Kichi
Base
Jim T café
Maison Blanc
Fenton House
HEATH STREET
HAMPSTEAD HEATH
Oriental
Zamoyski Restaurant & Vodka Bar
Zara
Wong Wah House
HAVERSTOCK HILL
The Hill
Chalk Farm
Primrose Hill Station
Chalcot Road
Primrose Hill
Café de Maya
BELSIZE PARK
Haleni
Eriki
Globe
Swiss Cottage
ADELAIDE ROAD
AVENUE RD
FINCHLEY ROAD
Royal China
St John's Wood
ST JOHN'S WOOD
WELLINGTON ROAD
Camden Arts Centre
FINCHLEY
WEST HAMPSTEAD
Finchley Road & Frognal Station
Tobia
Green Cottage
Harben
Hampstead Station
South Hampstead Station
FINCHLEY ROAD
Walnut
La Brocca
West Hampstead Station
Mario's
The Czech Restaurant
BELSIZE ROAD
Singapore Garden
Greek Valley
ABBEY ROAD
No.77 Wine Bar
W Hampstead Thameslink Station
WEST END RD
© Copyright Time Out Group 2005
200m
200 yds

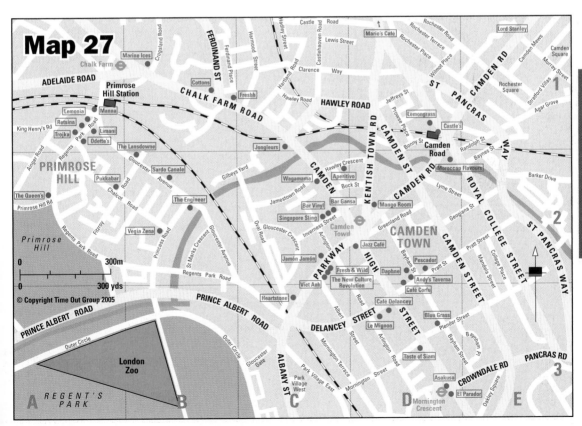

Map 27

ADELAIDE ROAD
Marine Ices
Chalk Farm
Primrose Hill Station
FERDINAND ST
CHALK FARM ROAD
Cottons
Freshh
HAWLEY ROAD
Mario's Café
Lord Stanley
CAMDEN RD
Camden Square
Camden Mews
Murray Street
ST PANCRAS
Rochester Square
Stratford Villas
Agar Grove
Lemonia
Retsina
Trojka
Limani
Odette's
Manna
The Lansdowne
Jongleurs
Lemongrass
Castle's
Camden Road
Moroccan Flavours
WAY
Barker Drive
PRIMROSE HILL
Pukkabar
The Engineer
Sardo Canale
Gilbeys Yard
Wagamama
Aperitivo
Buck St
CAMDEN
Mango Room
Lyme Street
ROYAL COLLEGE STREET
The Queen's
Vegia Zena
Bar Vinyl
Bar Gansa
Singapore Sling
CAMDEN TOWN
ST PANCRAS WAY
Primrose Hill
Jazz Café
Jamón Jamón
Fresh & Wild
Viet Anh
The New Culture Revolution
Heartstone
Daphne
Pescador
Andy's Taverna
Café Corfu
Café Delancey
Blue Grass
CAMDEN STREET
PANCRAS RD
PRINCE ALBERT ROAD
Le Mignon
DELANCEY STREET
HIGH STREET
Taste of Siam
Asakusa
CROWNDALE RD
ALBANY ST
Mornington Crescent
El Parador
Oakley Square
London Zoo
Outer Circle
Gloucester Gate
Park Village East
Mornington Terrace
REGENT'S PARK
300m
300 yds
© Copyright Time Out Group 2005

Maps

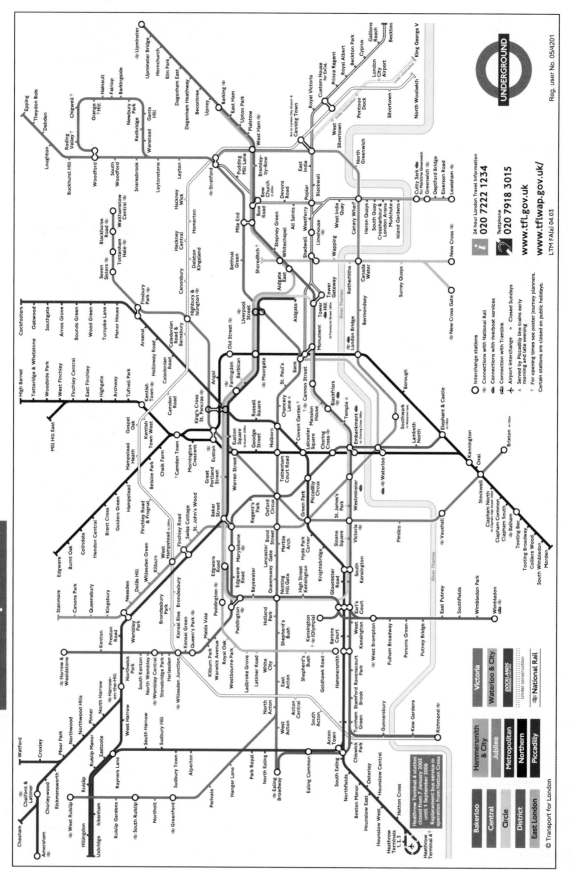

Maps

Street Index

Index

Index

Index

Index

Advertisers' Index

Index

Subject Index

Index

Restaurants Area Index

Index

Index

Index

Index

Index

Pizza Express
316 Kennington Road,
SE11 4LD (7820 3877)

Fish

The Lobster Pot p74
3 Kennington Lane,
SE11 4RG (7582 5556/
www.lobsterpotrestaurant.
co.uk)

Indian

The Painted Heron p129
205-209 Kennington Lane,
SE11 5QS (7793 8313/
www.thepaintedheron.com)

Spanish

The Finca p244
185 Kennington Road,
SE11 4EZ (7735 1061/
www.thefinca.co.uk)

Kensal NW10

Gastropubs

William IV p93
786 Harrow Road,
NW18 1TF (8969 5944/
www.william-iv.co.uk)

Kensington W8, SW7

The Americas

Sticky Fingers p34
1A Phillimore Gardens,
W8 7QG (7938 5338/
www.stickyfingers.co.uk)

Branches

ASK
222 Kensington High Street,
W8 7RG (7937 5540)

Balans
187 Kensington High Street,
W8 6SH (7376 0115)

Black & Blue
215-217 Kensington Church
Street, W8 7LX (7727 0004)

Café Med
184A Kensington Park Road,
W11 2ES (7221 1150)

easyInternetcafé
160-166 Kensington High
Street, W8 7RG (7241 9000)

Feng Sushi
24 Kensington Church Street,
W8 4EP (7937 7927)

Giraffe
7 Kensington High Street,
W8 5NP (7938 1221)

Maison Blanc
7A Kensington Church Street,
W8 4LF (7937 4767/
www.maisonblanc.co.uk)

Koi (branch of Hi Sushi)
1E Palace Gate,
W8 5LS (7581 8778)

Pizza Express
35 Earl's Court Road,
W8 6ED (7937 0761)

Prezzo
35A Kensington Court,
W8 5BA (7937 2800)

Pâtisserie Valerie
27 Kensington Church Street,
W8 4LL (7937 9574)

Ranoush Juice Bar
86 Kensington High Street,
W8 4SG (7938 2234)

The Stratford
(branch of Lou Pescadou)
7 Stratford Road,
W8 6RF (7937 6388)

Wagamama
26 Kensington High Street,
W8 4PF (7376 1717)

British

Maggie Jones's p47
6 Old Court Place,
Kensington Church Street,
W8 4PL (7937 6462)

Cafés

The Orangery p306
Kensington Palace,
Kensington Gardens,
W8 4PX (7376 0239)

East European

Wódka p67
12 St Alban's Grove,
W8 5PN (7937 6513/
www.wodka.co.uk)

Indian

Utsav p125
17 Kensington High Street,
W8 5NP (7368 0022/
www.utsav-restaurant.co.uk)

Zaika p125
1 Kensington High Street,
W8 5NP (7795 6533/
www.zaika-restaurant.co.uk)

International

Abingdon p145
54 Abingdon Road,
W8 6AP (7937 3339)

Italian

Brunello p160
Baglioni Hotel, 60 Hyde Park
Gate, Kensington Road,
SW7 5BB (7368 5700)

Timo p162
343 Kensington High Street,
W8 6NW (7603 3888/
www.atozrestaurants.com)

Middle Eastern

Phoenicia p200
11-13 Abingdon Road,
W8 6AH (7937 0120/
www.phoeniciarestaurant.
co.uk)

Modern European

Babylon p215
The Roof Gardens,
Seventh Floor, 99 Kensington
High Street, W8 5ED
(7368 3993/www.roof
gardens.com)

Clarke's p215
124 Kensington Church
Street, W8 4BH (7221 9225/
www.sallyclarke.com)

Kensington Place p215
201-209 Kensington
Church Street, W8 7LX
(7727 3184)

Launceston Place p215
1A Launceston Place,
W8 5RL (7937 6912/
www.egami.co.uk)

The Terrace p215
33C Holland Street,
W8 4LX (7937 3224/www.
theterracerestaurant.co.uk)

Thai

Papaya Tree p249
209 Kensington High Street,
W8 6BD (7937 2260)

Wine Bars

Whits p323
21 Abingdon Road, W8 6AH
(7938 1122/www.whits.co.uk)

Kentish Town NW1, NW5

African & Caribbean

Lalibela p27
137 Fortess Road,
NW5 2HR (7284 0600)

Queen of Sheba p27
12 Fortress Road,
NW5 2EU (7284 3947)

Branches

Nando's
227-229 Kentish Town Road,
NW5 2JU (7424 9363)

Pizza Express
187 Kentish Town Road,
NW1 8PD (NW18PD)

French

Le Petit Prince p88
5 Holmes Road,
NW5 3AA (7267 3789)

Gastropubs

Highgate p101
79 Highgate Road,
NW5 1TL (7485 8442)

Junction Tavern p101
101 Fortess Road,
NW5 1AG (7485 9400)

Kew, Surrey

Branches

Kew Grill
(branch of Notting Grill)
10B Kew Green, Kew, Surrey
TW9 3BH (8948 4433)

Ma Cuisine
9 Station Approach, Kew,
Surrey TW9 3QB (8332 1923)

Cafés

Kew Greenhouse p306
1 Station Parade, Kew, Surrey
TW9 3PS (8940 0183)

Modern European

The Glasshouse p222
14 Station Parade, Kew,
Surrey TW9 3PZ (8940
6777)

Kilburn NW6

African & Caribbean

Planet Caribbean p29
11 Malvern Road,
NW6 5PS (7372 4980)

Branches

easyInternetcafé
McDonalds, 127-129
Kilburn High Road, NW6 6JJ
(7241 9000)

Little Bay
228 Belsize Road,
NW6 4BT (7372 4699)

Nando's
308 Kilburn High Road,
NW6 2DG (7372 1507)

Budget

Small & Beautiful p279
351-353 Kilburn High Road,
NW6 2QJ (7328 2637)

Indian

Kovalam p136
12 Willesden Lane,
NW6 7SR (7625 4761)

Vijay p137
49 Willesden Lane,
NW6 7RF (7328 1087/
www.vijayindia.com)

Middle Eastern

Beirut Cellar p204
248 Belsize Road,
NW6 4BT (7328 3472)

King's Cross N1, WC1

African & Caribbean

Addis p24
42 Caledonian Road,
N1 9DT (7278 0679)

Merkato Restaurant p24
196 Caledonian Road,
N1 0SL (7713 8952)

Budget

Konstam p279
109 King's Cross Road,
WC1X 9LR (7833 5040/
www.konstam.co.uk)

Thai

Paolina p246
181 King's Cross Road,
WC1X 9BZ (7278 8176)

Kingston, Surrey

Branches

Carluccio's Caffè
Charter Quay, Kingston upon
Thames, Surrey KT1 1HT
(8549 5898)

China Royal
(branch of Cammasan)
110 Canbury Park Road,
Kingston upon Thames,
Surrey KT2 6JZ (8541 1988)

Nando's
37-38 High Street, Kingston
upon Thames, Surrey KT1 1LQ
(8296 9540)

Pizza Express
Kingston Rotunda, Kingston
upon Thames, Surrey KT1 1QJ
(8547 3133)

TGI Friday's
The Bentall Centre, Wood
Street, Kingston upon
Thames, Surrey KT1 1TR
(8547 2900)

Wagamama
16-18 High Street, Kingston
upon Thames, Surrey KT1 1EY
(8546 1117)

Zizzi
43 Market Place, Kingston
upon Thames, Surrey KT1 1JQ
(8546 0717)

Oriental

Cammasan p234
8 Charter Quay, High Street,
Kingston upon Thames,
Surrey KT1 1NB (8549 3510/
www.cammasan.co.uk)

Pizza & Pasta

La La Pizza p289
138 London Road, Kingston
upon Thames, Surrey
KT2 6QJ (8546 4888)

Thai

Ayudhya p256
14 Kingston Hill, Kingston
upon Thames, Surrey
KT2 7NH (8546 5878/
www.ayudhyakingston.com)

**Knightsbridge
SW1, SW3, SW7**

Bars

Blue Bar p309
The Berkeley, Wilton Place,
SW1X 7RL (7235 6000/
www.the-berkeley.co.uk)

Mandarin Bar p309
Mandarin Oriental Hyde Park,
66 Knightsbridge, SW1X 7LA
(7235 2000/www.mandarin
oriental.com)

Branches

Base Deli
67 Beauchamp Place,
SW3 1NZ (7584 2777)

Patara
9 Beauchamp Place,
SW3 1NQ (7581 8820)

Pâtisserie Valerie
17 Mortcomb Street,
SW1X 8LB (7245 6161)

Pâtisserie Valerie
215 Brompton Road,
SW3 2EJ (7823 9971)

Wagamama
Lower Ground Floor, Harvey
Nichols, 109-124
Knightsbridge, SW1X 7RJ
(7201 8000)

Yo! Sushi
Fifth Floor, Harvey Nichols
Food Hall, 109-124
Knightsbridge, SW1X 7RJ
(7235 5000)

British

Rib Room & Oyster Bar p43
Carlton Tower, 2 Cadogan
Place, SW1X 9PY (7858
7053/www.carltontower.com)

Cafés

Basil Street Hotel p305
8 Basil Street,
SW3 1AH (7581 3311/
www.thebasil.com)

Chinese

Mr Chow p56
151 Knightsbridge,
SW1X 7PA (7589 7347)

French

Brasserie St Quentin p79
243 Brompton Road,
SW3 2EP (7589 8005/
www.brasseriestquentin.co.uk)

Drones p79
1 Pont Street, SW1X 9EJ
(7235 9555)

Racine p79
239 Brompton Road,
SW3 2EP (7584 4477)

Global

Lundum's p105
117-119 Old Brompton Road,
SW7 3RN (7373 7774/
www.lundums.com)

Hotels & Haute Cuisine

Allium p114
Dolphin Square, Chichester
Street, SW1V 3LX (7798
6888/www.allium.co.uk)

Boxwood Café p111
The Berkeley Hotel,
Wilton Place, SW1X 7RL
(7235 1010/www.gordon
ramsay.com)

The Capital p111
22-24 Basil Street, SW3 1AT
(7589 5171/7591 1202/
www.capitalhotel.co.uk)

Foliage p111
Mandarin Oriental Hyde Park
Hotel, 66 Knightsbridge,
SW1X 7LA (7201 3723/
www.mandarinoriental.com)

Mju p111
The Millennium Knightsbridge,
16-17 Sloane Street,
SW1X 9NU (7201 6330)

One-O-One p112
101 William Street,
SW1X 7RN (7290 7101)

Pétrus p112
The Berkeley Hotel,
Wilton Place, SW1X 7RL
(7235 1200/www.marcus
wareing.com)

Indian

Haandi p117
7 Cheval Place, SW3 1HY
(7823 7373/www.haandi-
restaurants.com)

Italian

Emporio Armani Caffè p155
191 Brompton Road,
SW3 1NE (7823 8818)

Floriana p155
15 Beauchamp Place,
SW3 1NQ (7838 1500)

Isola p155
145 Knightsbridge, SW1X 7PA
(7838 1044/1099)

San Lorenzo p155
22 Beauchamp Place,
SW3 1NH (7584 1074)

Zafferano p155
15 Lowndes Street,
SW1X 9EY (7235 5800)

Japanese

Zuma p173
5 Raphael Street,
SW7 1DL (7584 1010/
www.zumarestaurant.com)

Modern European

The Fifth Floor p209
Harvey Nichols, Knightsbridge,
SW1X 7RJ (7235 5250/
www.harvey nichols.com)

Oriental

Pan Asian Restaurant p229
The Paxton's Head, 153
Knightsbridge, SW1X 7PA
(7589 6627)

Portuguese

O Fado p235
49-50 Beauchamp Place,
SW3 1NY (7589 3002)

**Ladbroke Grove
W10, W11**

The Americas

Ashbells p35
29 All Saints Road,
W11 1HE (7221 8585/
www.ashbells.co.uk)

Branches

S&M Café
268 Portobello Road,
W10 5TY (8968 8898)

Brasseries

Electric Brasserie p295
191 Portobello Road,
W11 2ED (7908 9696/
www.electricbrasserie.com)

Budget

Cockneys Pie & Mash p280
314 Portobello Road,
W10 5RU (8960 9409)

Gastropubs

Golborne Grove p93
36 Golborne Road,
W10 5PR (8960 6260/
www.groverestaurants.co.uk)

North Pole p93
13-15 North Pole Road,
W10 6QH (8964 9384/
www.massivepub.com)

Italian

Essenza p160
210 Kensington Park Road,
W11 1NR (7792 1066)

Mediterraneo p160
37 Kensington Park Road,
W11 2EU (7792 3131)

**Malaysian, Indonesian
& Singaporean**

Makan p190
270 Portobello Road,
W10 5TY (8960 5169)

Modern European

Number 10 p215
10 Golborne Road,
W10 5PE (8969 8922/
www.number10london.com)

North African

Moroccan Tagine p225
95 Golborne Road,
W10 5NL (8968 8055)

Oriental

E&O p231
14 Blenheim Crescent,
W11 1NN (7229 5454/
www.eando.nu)

Uli p231
16 All Saints Road,
W11 1HH (7727 7511)

Portuguese

Lisboa Patisserie p234
57 Golborne Road,
W10 5NR (8968 5242)

Index

Index

Index

Index

Index

Index

Spanish

Mesón Don Felipe p243
53 The Cut, SE1 8LF
(7928 3237)

Wine Bars

The Archduke p323
Concert Hall Approach,
SE1 8XU (7928 9370)

Wembley, Middx

Branches

Pizza Express
456 High Road, Wembley,
Middx HA9 7AY (8902 4918)

Indian

Cinnamon Gardens p142
42-44 Ealing Road,
Wembley, Middx HA0 4TL
(8902 0660)

Jashan p142
1-2 Coronet Parade,
Ealing Road, Wembley, Middx
HA0 4AY (8900 9800/
www.jashan restaurants.com)

Karahi King p143
213 East Lane, North
Wembley, Middx HA0 3NG
(8904 2760/4994)

Sakonis p143
129 Ealing Road,
Wembley, Middx HA0 4BP
(8903 9601)

West Hampstead NW3, NW6

African & Caribbean

Tobia p27
First Floor, Ethiopian
Community Centre, 2A Lithos
Road, NW3 6EF (7431 4213)

Branches

Good Earth Express
335 West End Lane,
NW6 1RS (7433 3111)

Gourmet Burger Kitchen
331 West End Lane,
NW6 1RS (7794 5455)

Nando's
252-254 West End Lane,
NW6 1LU (7794 1331)

Pizza Express
319 West End Lane,
NW6 1RN (7431 8229)

Fish & Chips

Nautilus p283
27-29 Fortune Green Road,
NW6 1DT (7435 2532)

Greek

Mario's p110
153-155 Broadhurst Gardens,
NW6 3AU (7625 5827)

Modern European

Walnut p222
280 West End Lane,
NW6 1LJ (7794 7772/
www.walnutwalnut.com)

Pizza & Pasta

La Brocca p289
273 West End Lane,
NW6 1QS (7433 1989)

Wine Bars

No.77 Wine Bar p324
77 Mill Lane, NW6 1NB
(7435 7787)

West Kensington W14

Branches

Best Mangal II
66 North End Road,
W14 9ET (7602 0212)

Turkish

Best Mangal p258
104 North End Road,
W14 9EX (7610 1050/
www.londraturk.com)

Westbourne Grove W2, W11

The Americas

Rodizio Rico p37
111 Westbourne Grove,
W2 4UW (7792 4035)

Bars

Tom & Dick's p311
30 Alexander Street,
W2 5NU (7229 7711/
www.tomanddicks.com)

Branches

Fairuz
27 Westbourne Grove,
W2 4UA (7243 8555)

Gourmet Burger Kitchen
50 Westbourne Grove,
W2 5FH (7243 4344)

Cafés

202 p303
Nicole Farhi, 202 Westbourne
Grove, W11 2RH (7727 2722)

Tom's Delicatessen p303
226 Westbourne Grove,
W11 2RH (7221 8818)

Italian

Zucca p162
188 Westbourne Grove,
W11 2RH (7727 0060)

Portuguese

Nando's p235
63 Westbourne Grove,
W2 4UA (7313 9506/
www.nandos.co.uk)

Westbourne Park W2, W9

African & Caribbean

Angie's p25
381 Harrow Road, W9 3NA
(8962 8761/www.angies-
restaurant.co.uk)

The Americas

Lucky 7 p35
127 Westbourne Park Road,
W2 5QL (7727 6771)

Gastropubs

Cow Dining Room p94
89 Westbourne Park Road,
W2 5QH (7221 0021)

Oak p94
137 Westbourne Park Road,
W2 5QL (7221 3599)

Westbourne p94
101 Westbourne Park Villas,
W2 5ED (7221 1332/
www.thewestbourne.com)

Westcombe Park SE3

International

**Thyme Restaurant
& Bar** p148
1A & 3 Station Crescent,
SE3 7EQ (8293 9183/
www.thymerestaurant.co.uk)

Westminster SW1

Brasseries

The Vincent Rooms p294
Westminster Kingsway
College, Vincent Square,
SW1P 2PD (7802 8391/
www.westking.ac.uk)

British

Shepherd's p47
Marsham Court, Marsham
Street, SW1P 4LA (7834
9552/www.langans
restaurants.co.uk)

Indian

The Cinnamon Club p125
The Old Westminster Library,
Great Smith Street,
SW1P 3BU (7222 2555/
www.cinnamonclub.com)

International

The Atrium p145
4 Millbank, SW1P 3JA
(7233 0032/www.simpsons
ofmayfair.com)

Italian

Quirinale p159
North Court, 1 Great
Peter Street, SW1P 3LL
(7222 7080)

Modern European

Bank Westminster p213
45 Buckingham Gate,
SW1E 6BS (7379 9797/
www.bankrestaurants.com)

Whetstone N20

Branches

ASK
1257 High Road,
N20 0EW (8492 0033)

Pizza Express
1264 High Road,
N20 9HH (8446 8800)

Whitechapel E1, EC3

Indian

Café Spice Namaste p135
16 Prescot Street,
E1 8AZ (7488 9242/
www.cafespice.co.uk)

Kasturi p135
57 Aldgate High Street,
EC3N 1AL (7480 7402/
www.kasturi-restaurant.
co.uk)

**New Tayyab/
Tayyab Kebab House** p135
83 Fieldgate Street,
E1 1JU (7247 9543/
www.tayyabs.co.uk)

Jewish

Rinkoff's p181
79 Vallance Road,
E1 5BS (7247 6228)

Willesden NW2, NW10

Branches

Shish
2-6 Station Parade,
NW2 4NH (8208 9290)

Indian

Sabras p137
263 High Road,
NW10 2RX (8459 0340)

Saravanas p137
77-81 Dudden Hill Lane,
NW10 1BD (8459 4900/
2400)

Japanese

Sushi-Say p180
33B Walm Lane,
NW2 5SH (8459 2971)

Turkish

Mezerama p266
76 Walm Lane,
NW2 4RA (8459 3311)

Wimbledon SW19

The Americas

Jo Shmo's p35
33 High Street,
SW19 5BY (8879 3845/
www.joshmos.com)

Branches

**Common Room
(branch of Jamies)**
18 High Street,
SW19 5DX (8944 1909)

Good Earth Express
81 Ridgway, SW19 4FT
(8944 8883)

Nando's
1 Russell Road,
SW19 1QN (8545 0909)

Pizza Express
84 High Street,
SW19 5EG (8946 6027)

San Lorenzo
38 Wimbledon Hill Road,
SW19 7PA (8946 8463)

Strada
91 High Street, SW19 5EG
(8946 4363)

International

Light House p147
75-77 Ridgeway,
SW19 4ST (8944 6338)

Japanese

Makiyaki p179
149 Merton Road,
SW19 1ED (8540 3113/
www.makiyaki.com)

Vegetarian

Service-Heart-Joy p269
191 Hartfield Road,
SW19 3TH (8542 9912)

Windsor, Berkshire

Branches

Thai Square
29 Thames Street,
Windsor, Berks SL4 1TR
(5386 8900)

Wood Green N22

Branches

Mosaica@the factory
The Chocolate Factory,
Wood Green Business
Centre, Clarendon Road,
N22 6XJ (8889 2400/
www.mosaicarestaurants.
com)

Nando's
Hollywood Green, Redvers
Road, N22 6EN (8889 2936)

Greek

Vrisaki p109
73 Myddleton Road,
N22 8LZ (8889 8760)

Restaurants
A-Z Index

Index

Index

Index

Index

Index

Index

Index

Index

Index

Index

Index

Parties & Shops
A-Z Index

Index

Index